R503

G131

v.6

DETROIT PUBLIC LIBRARY

3 S0-BRZ-609

CH

The GALE
ENCYCLOPEDIA
of SCIENCE

The GALE
ENCYCLOPEDIA
of SCIENCE

VOLUME 6
States of matter – Zooplankton

Bridget Travers,

Editor

Gale Research

An ITP Information/Reference Group Company

I(T)P
Changing the Way the World Learns

NEW YORK • LONDON • BONN • BOSTON • DETROIT
MADRID • MELBOURNE • MEXICO CITY • PARIS
SINGAPORE • TOKYO • TORONTO • WASHINGTON
ALBANY NY • BELMONT CA • CINCINNATI OH

The GALE ENCYCLOPEDIA of SCIENCE

Bridget Travers, *Editor*

Sheila M. Dow, *Coordinating Editor (Advisors)*
James Edwards, *Coordinating Editor (Databases)*
Paul Lewon, *Coordinating Editor (Illustrations)*
Jacqueline Longe, *Coordinating Editor (Contributors)*
Donna Olendorf, *Coordinating Editor (Submissions, Indexing)*

Christine B. Jeryan, Kyung-Sun Lim, Kimberley A. McGrath, Robyn V. Young, *Contributing Editors*

Kristine M. Binkley, Zoran Minderovic, *Associate Editors*

Nicole Beatty, Pamela Proffett, Carley Wellman, *Assistant Editors*

Linda R. Andres, Shelly Andrews, Dawn R. Barry, Ned Burels, Melissa Doig, David Oblender, *Contributors*

Marlene S. Hurst, *Permissions Manager*
Margaret A. Chamberlain, *Permissions Specialist*
Susan Brohman, *Permissions Associate*

Victoria B. Cariappa, *Research Manager*
Maureen Richards, *Research Specialist*

Mary Beth Trimper, *Production Director*
Evi Seoud, Assistant *Production Manager*
Shanna Heilveil, *Production Assistant*

Cynthia Baldwin, *Product Design Manager*
Mary Krzewinski, *Art Director*
Barbara Yarrow, *Graphic Services Manager*
Randy Bassett, *Image Database Supervisor*
Robert Duncan, *Digital Imaging Specialist*
Pamela A. Hayes, *Photography Coordinator*

Benita L. Spight, Manager, *Data Entry Services*
Gwendolyn S. Tucker, *Data Entry Supervisor*
Beverly Jendrowski, *Senior Data Entry Associate*
Francis L. Monroe, *Data Entry Associate*

Jeffrey Muhr, Roger M. Valade, III, *Editorial Technical Services Associates*

Indexing provided by the Electronic Scriptorium

Since this page cannot legibly accommodate all copyright notices, the acknowledgments constitute an extension of the copyright notice.

While every effort has been made to ensure the reliability of the information presented in this publication, Gale Research neither guarantees the accuracy of the data contained herein nor assumes any responsibility for errors, omissions or discrepancies. Gale accepts no payment for listing, and inclusion in the publication of any organization, agency, institution, publication, service, or individual does not imply endorsement of the editors or publisher. Errors brought to the attention of the publisher and verified to the satisfaction of the publisher will be corrected in future editions.

 This book is printed on recycled paper that meets Environmental Protection Agency standards.

 The paper used in this publication meets the minimum requirements of American National Standard for Information Sciences—Permanence Paper for Printed Library Materials, ANSI Z39.48-1984.

This publication is a creative work fully protected by all applicable copyright laws, as well as by misappropriation, trade secret, unfair competition, and other applicable laws. The authors and editors of this work have added value to the underlying factual material herein through one or more of the following: unique and original selection, coordination, expression, arrangement, and classification of the information.

All rights to this publication will be vigorously defended.

Copyright © 1996
Gale Research
835 Penobscot Building
Detroit, MI 48226-4094

All rights reserved including the right of reproduction in whole or in part in any form.

ISBN 0-8103-9841-9 (set)
    0-8103-9836-2 (Vol. 1)
    0-8103-9837-0 (Vol. 2)
    0-8103-9838-9 (Vol. 3)
    0-8103-9839-7 (Vol. 4)
    0-8103-9840-0 (Vol. 5)
    0-8103-9892-3 (Vol. 6)

I(T)P™ Gale Research, an International Thomson Company
The ITP logo is a trademark under license.

Printed in the United States of America
10 9 8 7 6 5 4 3 2

Gale encyclopedia of science / Bridget E. Travers, editor.
    p.   cm.
    Includes bibliographical references and index.
    Summary: Contains 2,000 entries ranging from short definitions to major overviews of concepts in all areas of science.
    ISBN 0–08103–9841–9 (alk. paper)
    1. Science--Encyclopedias, Juvenile.   [1. Science--Encyclopedias.]   I. Travers, Bridget.
    Q121.G35 1995
503--dc20   95-25402
                                                             CIP
                                                             AC

CONTENTS

ORGANIZATION OF THE ENCYCLOPEDIA

The Gale Encyclopedia of Science has been designed with ease of use and ready reference in mind.

- Entries are **alphabetically arranged** in a single sequence, rather than by scientific field.

- Length of entries varies from **short definitions** of one or two paragraphs to longer, more **detailed entries** on complex subjects.

- Longer entries are arranged so that an **overview** of the subject appears first, followed by a detailed discussion conveniently arranged under subheadings.

- A list of **key terms** are provided where appropriate to define unfamiliar terms or concepts.

- Longer entries conclude with a **further reading** section, which points readers to other helpful sources.

- The **contributor's name** appears at the end of longer entries. His or her affiliation can be found in the "Contributors" section at the front of each volume.

- **"See-also" references** appear at the end of entries to point readers to related entries.

- **Cross-references** placed throughout the encyclopedia direct readers to where information on subjects without their own entries can be found.

- A comprehensive **general index** guides readers to all topics and persons mentioned in the book.

ADVISORY BOARD

A number of experts in the library and scientific communities provided invaluable assistance in the formulation of this encyclopedia. Our advisory board performed a myriad of duties, from defining the scope of coverage to reviewing individual entries for accuracy and accessibility. We would therefore like to express our appreciation to them:

Academic Advisors

Bryan Bunch
Adjunct Instructor
Department of Mathematics
Pace University

David Campbell
Head
Department of Physics
University of Illinois at Urbana Champaign

Neil Cumberlidge
Professor
Department of Biology
Northern Michigan University

Bill Freedman
Professor
Department of Biology and School for Resource and Environmental Studies
Dalhousie University

Clayton Harris
Assistant Professor
Department of Geography and Geology
Middle Tennessee State University

William S. Pretzer
Curator
Henry Ford Museum and Greenfield Village
Dearborn, Michigan

Theodore Snow
Fellow and Director
Center for Astrophysics and Space Research
University of Colorado at Boulder

Robert Wolke
Professor emeritus
Department of Chemistry
University of Pittsburgh

Richard Addison Wood
Meteorlogical Consultant
Tucson, Arizona

Librarian Advisors

Donna Miller
Director
Craig-Moffet County Library
Craig, Colorado

Judy Williams
Media Center
Greenwich High School
Greenwich, Connecticut

Carol Wishmeyer
Science and Technology Department
Detroit Public Library
Detroit, Michigan

CONTRIBUTORS

Nasrine Adibe
Professor Emeritus
Department of Education
Long Island University
Westbury, New York

Mary D. Albanese
Department of English
University of Alaska
Juneau, Alaska

James L. Anderson
Soil Science Department
University of Minnesota
St. Paul, Minnesota

Susan Andrew
Teaching Assistant
University of Maryland
Washington, D.C.

John Appel
Director
Fundación Museo de Ciencia y
  Tecnología
Popayán, Colombia

David Ball
Assistant Professor
Department of Chemistry
Cleveland State University
Cleveland, Ohio

Dana M. Barry
Editor and Technical Writer

Center for Advanced Materials
  Processing
Clarkston University
Potsdam, New York

Puja Batra
Department of Zoology
Michigan State University
East Lansing, Michigan

Donald Beaty
Professor Emeritus
College of San Mateo
San Mateo, California

Eugene C. Beckham
Department of Mathematics and
  Science
Northwood Institute
Midland, Michigan

Martin Beech
Research Associate
Department of Astronomy
University of Western Ontario
London, Ontario

Massimo D. Bezoari
Associate Professor
Department of Chemistry
Huntingdon College
Montgomery, Alabama

John M. Bishop III
Translator
New York, New York

T. Parker Bishop
Professor
Middle Grades and Secondary
  Education
Georgia Southern University
Statesboro, Georgia

Carolyn Black
Professor
Incarnate Word College
San Antonio, Texas

Larry Blaser
Science Writer
Lebanon, Tennessee

Jean F. Blashfield
Science Writer
Walworth, Wisconsin

Richard L. Branham Jr.
Director
Centro Rigional de
  Investigaciones Científicas y
  Tecnológicas
Mendoza, Argentina

Patricia Braus
Editor
American Demographics
Rochester, New York

David L. Brock
Biology Instructor
St. Louis, Missouri

CONTRIBUTORS

Leona B. Bronstein
Chemistry Teacher (retired)
East Lansing High School
Okemos, Michigan

Brandon R. Brown
Graduate Research Assistant
Oregon State University
Corvallis, Oregon

Lenonard C. Bruno
Senior Science Specialist
Library of Congress
Chevy Chase, Maryland

Scott Christian Cahall
Researcher
World Precision Instruments, Inc.
Bradenton, Florida

G. Lynn Carlson
Senior Lecturer
School of Science and
    Technology
University of Wisconsin—
    Parkside
Kenosha, Wisconsin

James J. Carroll
Center for Quantum Mechanics
The University of Texas at Dallas
Dallas, Texas

Steven B. Carroll
Assistant Professor
Division of Biology
Northeast Missouri State
    University
Kirksville, Missouri

Rosalyn Carson-DeWitt
Physician and Medical Writer
Durham, North Carolina

Yvonne Carts-Powell
Editor
Laser Focus World
Belmont, Massachustts

Chris Cavette
Technical Writer
Fremont, California

Kenneth B. Chiacchia
Medical Editor

University of Pittsburgh Medical
    Center
Pittsburgh, Pennsylvania

M. L. Cohen
Science Writer
Chicago, Illinois

Robert Cohen
Reporter
KPFA Radio News
Berkeley, California

Sally Cole-Misch
Assistant Director
International Joint Commission
Detroit, Michigan

George W. Collins II
Professor Emeritus
Case Western Reserve
Chesterland, Ohio

Jeffrey R. Corney
Science Writer
Thermopolis, Wyoming

Tom Crawford
Assistant Director
Division of Publication and
    Development
University of Pittsburgh Medical
    Center
Pittsburgh, Pennsylvania

Pamela Crowe
Medical and Science Writer
Oxon, England

Clinton Crowley
On-site Geologist
Selman and Associates
Fort Worth, Texas

Edward Cruetz
Physicist
Rancho Santa Fe, California

Frederick Culp
Chairman
Department of Physics
Tenneesse Technical
Cookeville, Tennessee

Neil Cumberlidge
Professor

Department of Biology
Northern Michigan University
Marquette, Michigan

Mary Ann Cunningham
Environmental Writer
St. Paul, Minnesota

Les C. Cwynar
Associate Professor
Department of Biology
University of New Brunswick
Fredericton, New Brunswick

Paul Cypher
Provisional Interpreter
Lake Erie Metropark
Trenton, Michigan

Stanley J. Czyzak
Professor Emeritus
Ohio State University
Columbus, Ohio

Rosi Dagit
Conservation Biologist
Topanga-Las Virgenes Resource
    Conservation District
Topanga, California

David Dalby
President
Bruce Tool Company, Inc.
Taylors, South Carolina

Lou D'Amore
Chemistry Teacher
Father Redmund High School
Toronto, Ontario

Douglas Darnowski
Postdoctoral Fellow
Department of Plant Biology
Cornell University
Ithaca, New York

Sreela Datta
Associate Writer
Aztec Publications
Northville, Michigan

Sarah K. Dean
Science Writer
Philadelphia, Pennsylvania

Sarah de Forest
Research Assistant
Theoretical Physical Chemistry
  Lab
University of Pittsburgh
Pittsburgh, Pennsylvania

Louise Dickerson
Medical and Science Writer
Greenbelt, Maryland

Marie Doorey
Editorial Assistant
Illinois Masonic Medical Center
Chicago, Illinois

Herndon G. Dowling
Professor Emeritus
Department of Biology
New York University
New York, New York

Marion Dresner
Natural Resources Educator
Berkeley, California

John Henry Dreyfuss
Science Writer
Brooklyn, New York

Roy Dubisch
Professor Emeritus
Department of Mathematics
New York University
New York, New York

Russel Dubisch
Department of Physics
Sienna College
Loudonville, New York

Carolyn Duckworth
Science Writer
Missoula, Montana

Peter A. Ensminger
Research Associate
Cornell University
Syracuse, New York

Bernice Essenfeld
Biology Writer
Warren, New Jersey

Mary Eubanks

Instructor of Biology
The North Carolina School of
  Science and Mathematics
Durham, North Carolina

Kathryn M. C. Evans
Science Writer
Madison, Wisconsin

William G. Fastie
Department of Astronomy and
  Physics
Bloomberg Center
Baltimore, Maryland

Barbara Finkelstein
Science Writer
Riverdale, New York

Mary Finley
Supervisor of Science Curriculum
  (retired)
Pittsburgh Secondary Schools
Clairton, Pennsylvania

Gaston Fischer
Institut de Géologie
Université de Neuchâtel
Peseux, Switzerland

Sara G. B. Fishman
Professor
Quinsigamond Community
  College
Worcester, Massachusetts

David Fontes
Senior Instructor
Lloyd Center for Environmental
  Studies
Westport, Maryland

Barry Wayne Fox
Extension Specialist,
  Marine/Aquatic Education
Virginia State University
Petersburg, Virginia

Ed Fox
Charlotte Latin School
Charlotte, North Carolina

Kenneth L. Frazier
Science Teacher (retired)
North Olmstead High School

North Olmstead, Ohio

Bill Freedman
Professor
Department of Biology and
  School For Resource and
  Environmental Studies
Dalhousie University
Halifax, Nova Scotia

T. A. Freeman
Consulting Archaeologist
Quail Valley, California

Elaine Friebele
Science Writer
Cheverly, Maryland

Randall Frost
Documentation Engineering
Pleasanton, California

Robert Gardner
Science Education Consultant
North Eastham, Massachusetts

Gretchen M. Gillis
Senior Geologist
Maxus Exploration
Dallas, Texas

Kathryn Glynn
Audiologist
Portland, Oregon

Natalie Goldstein
Educational Environmental
  Writing
Phoenicia, New York

David Gorish
TARDEC
U.S. Army
Warren, Michigan

Louis Gotlib
South Granville High School
Durham, North Carolina

Hans G. Graetzer
Professor
Department of Physics
South Dakota State University
Brookings, South Dakota

CONTRIBUTORS

Jim Guinn
Assistant Professor
Department of Physics
Berea College
Berea, Kentucky

Steve Gutterman
Psychology Research Assistant
University of Michigan
Ann Arbor, Michigan

Johanna Haaxma-Jurek
Educator
Nataki Tabibah Schoolhouse of
 Detroit
Detroit, Michigan

Monica H. Halka
Research Associate
Department of Physics and
 Astronomy
University of Tennessee
Knoxville, Tennessee

Jeffrey C. Hall
Astronomer
Lowell Observatory
Flagstaff, Arizona

C. S. Hammen
Professor Emeritus
Department of Zoology
University of Rhode Island

Beth Hanson
Editor
The Amicus Journal
Brooklyn, New York

Clay Harris
Associate Professor
Department of Geography and
 Geology
Middle Tennessee State
 University
Murfreesboro, Tennessee

Catherine Hinga Haustein
Associate Professor
Department of Chemistry
Central College
Pella, Iowa

Dean Allen Haycock
Science Writer
Salem, New York

Paul A. Heckert
Professor
Department of Chemistry and
 Physics
Western Carolina University
Cullowhee, North Carolina

Darrel B. Hoff
Department of Physics
Luther College
Calmar, Iowa

Dennis Holley
Science Educator
Shelton, Nebraska

Leonard Darr Holmes
Department of Physical Science
Pembroke State University
Pembroke, North Carolina

Rita Hoots
Instructor of Biology, Anatomy,
 Chemistry
Yuba College
Woodland, California

Selma Hughes
Department of Psychology and
 Special Education
East Texas State University
Mesquite, Texas

Mara W. Cohen Ioannides
Science Writer
Springfield, Missouri

Zafer Iqbal
Allied Signal Inc.
Morristown, New Jersey

Sophie Jakowska
Pathobiologist, Environmental
 Educator
Santo Domingo, Dominican
 Republic

Richard A. Jeryan
Senior Technical Specialist
Ford Motor Company
Dearborn, Michigan

Stephen R. Johnson
Biology Writer
Richmond, Virginia

Kathleen A. Jones
School of Medicine
Southern Illinois University
Carbondale, Illinois

Harold M. Kaplan
Professor
School of Medicine
Southern Illinois University
Carbondale, Illinois

Anthony Kelly
Science Writer
Pittsburgh, Pennsylvania

Amy Kenyon-Campbell
Ecology, Evolution and
 Organismal Biology Program
University of Michigan
Ann Arbor, Michigan

Eileen M. Korenic
Institute of Optics
University of Rochester
Rochester, New York

Jennifer Kramer
Science Writer
Kearny, New Jersey

Pang-Jen Kung
Los Alamos National Laboratory
Los Alamos, New Mexico

Marc Kusinitz
Assistant Director Media
 Relations
John Hopkins Medical Instituition
Towsen, Maryland

Arthur M. Last
Head
Department of Chemistry
University College of the Fraser
 Valley
Abbotsford, British Columbia

Nathan Lavenda
Zoologist
Skokie, Illinios

Jennifer LeBlanc
Environmental Consultant
London, Ontario

Benedict A. Leerburger
Science Writer
Scarsdale, New York

Betsy A. Leonard
Education Facilitator
Reuben H. Fleet Space Theater
 and Science Center
San Diego, California

Scott Lewis
Science Writer
Chicago, Illinois

Frank Lewotsky
Aerospace Engineer (retired)
Nipomo, California

Karen Lewotsky
Cartographer
Portland, Oregon

Kristin Lewotsky
Editor
Laser Focus World
Nashua, New Hamphire

Stephen K. Lewotsky
Architect
Grants Pass, Oregon

Sarah Lee Lippincott
Professor Emeritus
Swarthmore College
Swarthmore, Pennsylvania

David Lunney
Research Scientist
Centre de Spectrométrie
 Nucléaire et de Spectrométrie de
 Masse
Orsay, France

Steven MacKenzie
Ecologist
Spring Lake, Michigan

J. R. Maddocks
Consulting Scientist
DeSoto, Texas

Gail B. C. Marsella
Technical Writer
Allentown, Pennsylvania

Karen Marshall
Research Associate
Council of State Governments
 and Centers for Environment
 and Safety
Lexington, Kentucky

Liz Marshall
Science Writer
Columbus, Ohio

James Marti
Research Scientist
Department of Mechanical
 Engineering
University of Minnesota
Minneapolis, Minnesota

Elaine L. Martin
Science Writer
Pensacola, Florida

Lilyan Mastrolla
Professor Emeritus
San Juan Unified School
Sacramento, California

Iain A. McIntyre
Manager
Electro-optic Department
Energy Compression Research
 Corporation
Vista, California

G. H. Miller
Director
Studies on Smoking
Edinboro, Pennsylvania

J. Gordon Miller
Botanist
Corvallis, Oregon

Christine Miner Minderovic
Nuclear Medicine Technologist
Franklin Medical Consulters
Ann Arbor, Michigan

David Mintzer
Professor Emeritus
Department of Mechanical

Engineering
Northwestern University
Evanston, Illinois

Christine Molinari
Science Editor
University of Chicago Press
Chicago, Illinois

Frank Mooney
Professor Emeritus
Fingerlake Community College
Canandaigua, New York

Partick Moore
Department of English
University of Arkansas at Little
 Rock
Little Rock, Arkansas

Robbin Moran
Department of Systematic Botany
Institute of Biological Sciences
University of Aarhus
Risskou, Denmark

J. Paul Moulton
Department of Mathematics
Episcopal Academy
Glenside, Pennsylvania

Otto H. Muller
Geology Department
Alfred University
Alfred, New York

Angie Mullig
Publication and Development
University of Pittsburgh Medical
 Center
Trafford, Pennsylvania

David R. Murray
Senior Associate
Sydney University
Sydney, New South Wales
Australia

Sutharchana Murugan
Scientist Three Boehringer
 Mannheim Corp.
Indianapolis, Indiana

Muthena Naseri
Moorpark College

Moorpark, California

David Newton
Science Writer and Educator
Ashland, Oregon

F. C. Nicholson
Science Writer
Lynn, Massachusetts

James O'Connell
Department of Physical Sciences
Frederick Community College
Gaithersburg, Maryland

Dónal P. O'Mathúna
Associate Professor
Mount Carmel College of
   Nursing
Columbus, Ohio

Marjorie Pannell
Managing Editor, Scientific
   Publications
Field Museum of Natural History
Chicago, Illinois

Gordon A. Parker
Lecturer
Department of Natural Sciences
University of Michigan—
   Dearborn
Dearborn, Michigan

David Petechuk
Science Writer
Ben Avon, Pennsylvania

John R. Phillips
Department of Chemistry
Purdue University, Calumet
Hammond, Indiana

Kay Marie Porterfield
Science Writer
Englewood, Colorado

Paul Poskozim
Chair
Department of Chemistry, Earth
   Science and Physics
Northeastern Illinois University
Chicago, Illinois

Andrew Poss
Senior Research Chemist
Allied Signal Inc.
Buffalo, New York

Satyam Priyadarshy
Department of Chemistry
University of Pittsburgh
Pittsburgh, Pennsylvania

Patricia V. Racenis
Science Writer
Livonia, Michigan

Cynthia Twohy Ragni
Atmospheric Scientist
National Center for Atmospheric
   Research
Westminster, Colorado

Jordan P. Richman
Science Writer
Phoenix, Arizona

Kitty Richman
Science Writer
Phoenix, Arizona

Vita Richman
Science Writer
Phoenix, Arizona

Michael G. Roepel
Researcher
Department of Chemistry
University of Pittsburgh
Pittsburgh, Pennsylvania

Perry Romanowski
Science Writer
Chicago, Illinois

Nancy Ross-Flanigan
Science Writer
Belleville, Michigan

Gordon Rutter
Royal Botanic Gardens
Edinburgh, Great Britain

Elena V. Ryzhov
Polytechnic Institute
Troy, New York

David Sahnow
Associate Research Scientist

John Hopkins University
Baltimore, Maryland

Peter Salmansohn
Educational Consultant
New York State Parks
Cold Spring, New York

Peter K. Schoch
Instructor
Department of Physics and
   Computer Science
Sussex County Community
   College
Augusta, New Jersey

Patricia G. Schroeder
Instructor
Science, Healthcare, and Math
   Division
Johnson County Community
   College
Overland Park, Kansas

Randy Schueller
Science Writer
Chicago, Illinois

Kathleen Scogna
Science Writer
Baltimore, Maryland

William Shapbell Jr.
Launch and Flight Systems
   Manager
Kennedy Space Center, Florida

Anwar Yuna Shiekh
International Centre for
   Theoretical Physics
Trieste, Italy

Raul A. Simon
Chile Departmento de Física
Universidad de Tarapacá
Arica, Chile

Michael G. Slaughter
Science Specialist
Ingham ISD
East Lansing, Michigan

Billy W. Sloope
Professor Emeritus
Department of Physics

Virginia Commonwealth
 University
Richmond, Virginia

Douglas Smith
Science Writer
Milton, Massachusetts

Lesley L. Smith
Department of Physics and
 Astronomy
University of Kansas
Lawrence, Kansas

Kathryn D. Snavely
U.S. General Accounting Office
Policy Analyst, Air Quality Issues
Raleigh, North Carolina

Charles H. Southwick
Professor
Environmental, Population, and
 Organismic Biology
University of Colorado at
 Boulder
Boulder, Colorado

John Spizzirri
Science Writer
Chicago, Illinois

Frieda A. Stahl
Professor Emeritus
Department of Physics
California State University, Los
 Angeles
Los Angeles, California

Robert L. Stearns
Department of Physics
Vassar College
Poughkeepsie, New York

Ilana Steinhorn
Science Writer
Boalsburg, Pennsylvania

David Stone
Conservation Advisory Services
Gai Soleil
Chemin Des Clyettes
Le Muids, Switzerland

Eric R. Swanson
Associate Professor

Department of Earth and Physical
 Sciences
University of Texas
San Antonio, Texas

Cheryl Taylor
Science Educator
Kailua, Hawaii

Nicholas C. Thomas
Department of Physical Sciences
Auburn University at
 Montgomery
Montgomery, Alabama

W. A. Thomasson
Science and Medical Writer
Oak Park, Illinois

Marie L. Thompson
Science Writer
Ben Avon, Pennsylvania

Melvin Tracy
Science Educator
Appleton, Wisconsin

Karen Trentelman
Research Associate
Archaeometric Laboratory
University of Toronto
Toronto, Ontario

Robert K. Tyson
Senior Scientist
W. J. Schafer Assoc.
Jupiter, Florida

James Van Allen
Professor Emeritus
Department of Physics and
 Astronomy
University of Iowa
Iowa City, Iowa

Julia M. Van Denack
Biology Instructor
Silver Lake College
Manitowoc, Wisconsin

Kurt Vandervoort
Department of Chemistry and
 Physics
West Carolina University
Cullowhee, North Carolina

Chester Vander Zee
Naturalist, Science Educator
Volga, South Dakota

Jeanette Vass
Department of Chemistry
Cuyahoga Community College
Timberlake, Ohio

R. A. Virkar
Chair
Department of Biological
 Sciences
Kean College
Iselin, New Jersey

Kurt C. Wagner
Instructor
South Carolina Governor's
 School for Science and
 Technology
Hartsville, South Carolina

Cynthia Washam
Science Writer
Jensen Beach, Florida

Joseph D. Wassersug
Physician
Boca Raton, Florida

Tom Watson
Environmental Writer
Seattle, Washington

Jeffrey Weld
Instructor, Science Department
 Chair
Pella High School
Pella, Iowa

Frederick R. West
Astronomer
Hanover, Pennsylvania

Glenn Whiteside
Science Writer
Wichita, Kansas

John C. Whitmer
Professor
Department of Chemistry
Western Washington University
Bellingham, Washington

CONTRIBUTORS

Donald H. Williams
Department of Chemistry
Hope College
Holland, Michigan

Robert L. Wolke
Professor Emeritus
Department of Chemistry
University of Pittsburgh
Pittsburgh, Pennsylvania

Jim Zurasky
Optical Physicist
Nichols Research Corporation
Huntsville, Alabama

ACKNOWLEDGEMENTS

Photographs appearing in the *Gale Encyclopedia of Science* were received from the following sources:

© Account Phototake/Phototake: **Genetic disorders**; © James Allem, Stock Market: **Gazelles**; © A. W. Ambler, National Audubon Society Collection/Photo Researchers, Inc.: **Goats, Newts, Sedimentary rock**; © Toni Angermayer, National Audubon Society Collection/Photo Researchers, Inc.: **Hamsters**; © Mark Antman/Phototake: **Textiles**; AP/Wide World Photos: **Elements, formation of**; © Archiv, National Audubon Society Collection/Photo Researchers, Inc.: **Astrolabe**; © Bachman, National Audubon Society Collection/Photo Researchers, Inc.: **Wombats**; © Bill Bachman, National Audubon Society Collection/Photo Researchers, Inc.: **Grasslands**; Baiyer River Sanctuary, New Guinea © Tom McHugh, National Audubon Society Collection/Photo Researchers, Inc.; © M. Baret/RAPHU, National Audubon Society Collection/Photo Researchers, Inc.: **Biotechnology**; Jen and Des Bartlett, National Audubon Society Collection/Photo Researchers, Inc.: **Sea lions**; © Jen and Des Bartlett, National Aububon Society Collection/Photo Researchers, Inc.: **Cicadas, Langurs and leaf monkeys, Aardvark, Bandicoots, Grebes, Lorises, Monitor lizards, Opossums, Pipefish, Sea horses, Secretary bird, Spiny anteaters**; © Bat Conservation Int'l: **Bats**; © John Bavosi, National Audubon Society Collection/ Photo Researchers, Inc.: **Hernia**; Tom Bean: **Archaeology**; © Tom Bean, Stock Market: **Volcano**; © James Bell, National Audubon Society Collection/Photo Researchers, Inc.: **Buds and budding**; © Pierre Berger, National Audubon Society Collection/Photo Researchers, Inc.: **Beech family**; © J. Bernholc et al, North Carolina State University/Science Photo Library, National Audubon Society Collection/Photo Researchers, Inc.: **Buckminsterfullerene**; © The Bettmann Archive: **Chemical warfare, Photography**; © Art Bileten, National Audubon Society Collection/Photo Researchers, Inc.: **North America**; © Biophoto Associates, National Audubon Society Collection/Photo Researchers, Inc.: **Acne, Chromosome, Tropical diseases, Spina bifida**; © Wesley Bocxe, National Audubon Society Collection/Photo Researchers, Inc.: **Oil spills**; © Mark Boulton, National Audubon Society Collection/Photo Researchers, Inc.: **Bustards, Erosion**; © Malcolm Boulton, National Audubon Society Collection/Photo Researchers, Inc.: **Porcupines, Baboons**; © Mark N. Boulton, National Audubon Society Collection/Photo Researchers, Inc.: **Yak**; © Dr. Tony Brain/Science Photo Library, National Audubon Society Collection/Photo Researchers, Inc.: **Aerobic**; © Thomas H. Brakefield, Stock Market: **Cats**; © Tom Brakefield, Stock Market: **Wolverine**; © 1980 Ken Brate, National Audubon Society Collection/Photo Researchers, Inc.: **Citrus trees**; Andrea Brizzi, Stock Market: **Sewage treatment**; © S. Brookens, Stock Market: **Mynah birds**; © John R. Brownlie, National Audubon Society Collection/Photo Researchers, Inc.: **Lyrebirds**; © Dr. Jeremy Brugess/Science Photo Library, National Audubon Society Collection/ Photo Researchers, Inc.: **Leaf, Chloroplast, Aphids, Battery**; © John Buitenkant 1993, National Audubon Society Collection/Photo Researchers, Inc.: **Buttercup**; © 1994, Michele Burgess/Bikderberg, Stock Market: **Elephant**; © Michele Burgess, Stock Market: **Flightless birds**; © Jane Burton, National Audubon Society Collection/Photo Researchers, Inc.: **Pangolins**; © Diana Calder/Bikderberg, Stock Market: **Barometer**; © Scott Camazinr, National Audubon Society Collection/Photo Researchers, Inc.: **AIDS**; © Tardos Camesi/Bikderberg, Stock

Market: **Transformer**; © John Cancalosi: **Numbat**; © Robert Caputo, National Audubon Society Collection/Photo Researchers, Inc.: **Hyena**; © Alan D. Carey, National Audubon Society Collection/Photo Researchers, Inc.: **Captive breeding and reintroduction, Coffee plant**; © Carolina Biological Supply Company/Phototake: **Chemoreception, Microscopy, Plant, Cashew family, Yeast**; © Tom Carrill/Phototake: **Pollution control**; © Tom Carroll/Phototake: **Air pollution, Bridges, Freeway**; © CBC/CBC/Phototake: **Petrels and shearwaters**; © Jean-Loup Charmet, National Audubon Society Collection/Photo Researchers, Inc.: **Anesthesia, Rabies**; © Ann Chawatsky/Phototake: **Burn**; © Ron Church, National Audubon Society Collection/Photo Researchers, Inc.: **Barracuda**; © Geoffrey Clifford,Stock Market: **Fractal**; © CNRI/ Science Photo Library, Nationa Audubon Society Collection/Photo Researchers, Inc.: **Influenza**; © CNRI/Phototake: **Leprosy**; © CNRI/Science Photo Library, National Audubon Society Collection/ Photo Researchers, Inc.: **Enterobacteria**; © Pedro Coll, Stock Market: **Cave, Machine tools**; © Holt Confer/Phototake: **Cranes**; © Judd Cooney/Phototake: **Weasels**; © Tony Craddock, National Audubon Society Collection/Photo Researchers, Inc.: **Microwave communication**; © Allan D. Cruickshank, National Audubon Society Collection/Photo Researchers, Inc.: **Cuckoos, Gila monster**; © Russell D. Curtis, National Audubon Society Collection/ Photo Researchers, Inc.: **Sleep disorders**; © Tim Davis, National Audubon Society Collection/Photo Researchers, Inc.: **Colobus monkeys, Finches**; © John Deeks, National Audubon Society Collection/Photo Researchers, Inc.: **Clouds**; © E.R. Degginger, National Audubon Society Collection/Photo Researchers, Inc.: **Tundra**; © Nigel Dennis, National Audubon Society Collection/Photo Researchers, Inc.: **Flamingos**; © Jack Dermid, National Audubon Society Collection/Photo Researchers, Inc.: **Dune**; © Jack Dermid 1979, National Audubon Society Collection/Photo Researchers, Inc.: **Bromeliad family**; © Jack Dermid, National Audubon Society Collection/Photo Researchers, Inc.: **Puffer fish**; © 1992 Alan L. Detrick, National Audubon Society Collection/Photo Researchers, Inc.: **Amaranth family**; © Mike Devlin, National Audubon Society Collection/Photo Researchers, Inc.: **Prosthetics**; © Richard Dibon-Smith, National Audubon Society Collection/Photo Researchers, Inc.: **Sheep**; © Gregory G. Dimijian 1990, National Audubon Society Collection/Photo Researchers, Inc.: **Coca**; © Thomas Dimock, Stock Market: **Crabs**; © Martin Dohrn, National Audubon Society Collection/Photo Researchers, Inc.: **Interference, Skeletal system**; © Martin Dohrn/Science Photo Library, National Audubon Society Collection/Photo Researchers, Inc.: **Wave motion**; © Dopamine-CNRI, National Audubon Society Collection/Photo Researchers, Inc.: **Ulcers**; © A. B. Dowsett/Science Photo Library, National Audubon Society Collection/ Photo Researchers, Inc.: **Virus**; © John Dudak/Phototake: **Arrowroot, Composite family**; © Richard Duncan,National Audubon Society Collection/Photo Researchers, Inc.: **Geometry**; © Hermann Eisenbeiss, National Audubon Society Collection/Photo Researchers, Inc.: **Surface tension**; © Thomas Ernsting, Stock Market: **Metric system**; © Thomas Ernsting/Bikderberg, Stock Market: **Virtual reality**; © 1992 Robert Essel/Bikderberg, Stock Market: **Electricity**; © Robert Essel, Stock Market: **Moose**; © Kenneth Eward/BioGrafx, National Audubon Society Collection/Photo Researchers, Inc.: **Atom**; © Dr. Brian Eyden, National Audubon Society Collection/Photo Researchers, Inc.: **Cancer**; © Douglas Faulkner, National Audubon Society Collection/Photo Researchers, Inc.: **Manatee, Coral reef**; © Fawcett, National Audubon Society Collection/ Photo Researchers, Inc.: **Cell**; © Fawcett/Phillips, National Audubon Society Collection/Photo Researchers, Inc.: **Flagella**; © Kenneth W. Fink, National Audubon Society Collection/Photo Researchers, Inc.: **Turacos**; © Cecil Fox/Science Source, National Audubon Society Collection/Photo Researchers, Inc.: **Alzheimer's disease**; © Carl Frank, National Audubon Society Collection/Photo Researchers, Inc.: **Rivers**; © Stephen Frink, Stock Market: **Squirrel fish**; © Petit Fromat/Nestle, National Audubon Society Collection/Photo Researchers, Inc.: **Embryo and embryonic development**; © G.R. Gainer, Stock Market: **Spiral**; Gale Research Inc.: **Jet engine**; © Gordon Garrado/Science Photo Library, National Audubon Society Collection/Photo Researchers, Inc.: **Thunderstorm**; © Frederica Georgia, National Audubon Society Collection/Photo Researchers, Inc.: **Hydrothermal vents**; © Ormond Gigli, Stock Market: **Frigate birds**; © 1989 Ned Gillette, Stock Market: **Mass wasting**; © A. Glauberman, National Audubon Society Collection/Photo Researchers, Inc.: **Cigarette smoke**; © F. Gohier 1982, National Audubon Society Collection/Photo Researchers, Inc.: **Amaryllis family**; © Francois Gohier, National Audubon Society Collection/Photo Researchers, Inc.: **Stromatolites**; © Spencer Grant, National Audubon Society Collection/Photo Researchers, Inc.: **Robotics**; © Stephen Green-Armytage, Stock Market:

Boas; © Al Greene and Associates, National Audubon Society Collection/Photo Researchers, Inc.: **Coast and beach**; © Barry Griffiths, National Audubon Society Collection/Photo Researchers, Inc.; © Tommaso Guicciardini/Science Photo Library, National Audubon Society Collection/Photo Researchers, Inc.: **Gravity**; © Dan Guravich 1987, National Audubon Society Collection/Photo Researchers, Inc.: **Atmospheric optical phenomena**; © Dan Guravich, National Audubon Society Collection/Photo Researchers, Inc.: **Alluvial systems**; © A. Gurmankin 1987/Phototake: **Begonia**; © Clem Haagner, National Audubon Society Collection/Photo Researchers, Inc.: **Giraffes and okapi**; © Hugh M. Halliday, National Audubon Society Collection/Photo Researchers, Inc.: **Shrikes**; © David Halpern, National Audubon Society Collection/Photo Researchers, Inc.: **Oil drilling**; © Chris Hamilton, Stock Market: **Waterwheel**; © Craig Hammell/Bikderberg, Stock Market: **Caliper**; © Hammond Incorporated, Maplewood, New Jersey.: **Bar code**; © 1993 Brownie Harris, Stock Market : **Antenna**; © Brownie Harris, Stock Market: **Turbine**; © Adam Hart-Davis/Science Photo Library, National Audubon Society Collection/Photo Researchers, Inc.: **Electrostatic devices**; © Adam Hart-Davis, National Audubon Society Collection/Photo Researchers, Inc.: **Thermometer, Integrated circuit**; © Anne Heimann, Stock Market: **Horseshoe crabs**; © Robert C. Hermes,National Audubon Society Collection/Photo Researchers, Inc.: **Mayflies**; © John Heseltine, National Audubon Society Collection/Photo Researchers, Inc.: **Geodesic dome**; © Andrew Holbrooke, Stock Market: **Landfill, Prosthetics**; © Holt Studios International, National Audubon Society Collection/Photo Researchers, Inc.: **Cashew family**; © Eric Hosking, F.R.P.S., National Audubon Society Collection/Photo Researchers, Inc.: **Auks**; © Eric Hosking, National Audubon Society Collection/Photo Researchers, Inc.: **Kingfishers, Loons, Mice, Stilts and avocets**; © John Howard, National Audubon Society Collection/Photo Researchers, Inc.: **Electromagnetic Field**; Robert J. Huffman/Field Mark Publications.: **Anoles, Anteaters, Armadillos, Bison, Blackbirds, Butterflies, Cactus, Capybaras, Carnivorous plants, Carnivorous plants, Composting, Cormorants, Cranes, Crayfish, Crows and jays, Deer, Ducks, Eagles, Falcons, Fossil and fossilization, Frogs, Fungi, Geese, Goats, Gulls, Hawks, Herons (2 photos), Horsetails, Ibises, Iguanas, Juniper, Koalas, Mockingbirds and thrashers, Moths (2 photos), Nuclear fission, Nuthatches, Oaks, Owls (2 photos), Parrots, Peafowl, Peccaries, Pelican, Pheasants, Pigeons and doves, Prairie dog, Praying mantis, Quail, Recycling, Rhinoceros, Sandpipers, Seals, Sparrows and buntings, Squirrels, Starfish, Swallows and martins, Swans, Terns, Thistle, Thrushes, Turkeys, Turtles, Tyrant flycatchers, Warblers, Waste management, Wetlands, Wrens, Zebras**; IBM Almaden: **Compact disc**; © Institut Pastuer/Phototake: **Immune system**; © Bruce Iverson/Science Photo Library, National Audubon Society Collection/Photo Researchers, Inc.: **Electric motor**; © Jacana, National Audubon Society Collection/Photo Reasearchers, Inc.: **Tuna**; © Y. Lanceau Jacana, National Audubon Society Collection/Photo Researchers, Inc.: **Carp**; JLM Visuals: **Acid rain, Africa, Agricultural machines, Agronomy, Alternative energy sources, Animal breeding, Antarctica, Arachnids, Astroblemes, Australia, Barrier Islands, Bitterns, Blue revolution, Brick, Bridges, Buoyancy, Principle of, Camels, Carnivore, Chameleons, Coal, Cotton, Crop rotation, Cycads, Deposit, Desert, Dinosaur, Disturbance, ecological, Dogwood tree, Dust devil, Earthquake, Endangered species, Europe, Fault, Ferns, Ferrets, Flax, Flooding, Fold, Fossil and fossilization, Freshwater, Gerbils, Ginger, Ginkgo, Glaciers, Goatsuckers, Gourd family, Grasses, Grasshoppers, Groundwater, Heath family, Hornbills, Horse chestnut, Ice ages, Igneous rocks, Introduced species, Iris family, Irrigation, Karst topography, Lagomorphs, Lake, Land use, Legumes, Lice, Lichens, Liverwort, Lobsters, Mangrove tree, Marmots, Mass wasting, Milkweeds, Mint family, Mistletoe, Mulberry family, Muskoxen, Mutation, Myrtle family, Nightshade, Octopus, Olive family, Orchid family, Oviparous, Paleobotany, Palms, Pandas, Penguins, Peninsula, Petroleum, Pigs, Pike, Plate tectonics, Pollination, Poppies, Prairie chicken, Pythons, Radio astronomy, Rushes, Savanna, Saxifrage family, Scavenger, Scorpionfish, Sculpins, Sea anemones, Sea level, Sedges, Sediment and sedimentation, Segmented worms, Sequoia, Shrimp, Silk cotton family, Skinks, Snails, Species, Spiderwort family, Storks, Swamp cypress family, Symbiosis, Tea plant, Terracing, Territoriality, Thermal expansion, Tides (2 photos), Trains and railroads, Turbulence, Vireos, Volcano, Vultures, Walnut family, Waterlilies, Wheat, Woodpeckers**; © Mark A. Johnson, Stock Market: **Jellyfish**; © Verna Johnston 1972, National Audubon Society Collection/Photo Researchers, Inc.: **Amaryllis family**; © Verna R. Johnston, National Audubon Society Collection/Photo

Researchers, Inc.: **Gophers**; © Darrell Jones, Stock Market: **Marlins**; © Chris Jones Photo, Stock Market: **Mining**; © Chris Jones, Stock Market: **Mass Production**; © Joyce Photographics, National Audubon Society Collection /Photo Researchers, Inc.: **Soil**, **Eutrophication**; © Robert Jureit, Stock Market: **Desert**; © John Kaprielian, National Audubon Society Collection/Photo Researchers, Inc.: **Buckwheat**; © Ed Kashi/Phototake: **CAD/CAM/CIM**; © Ted Keane, National Audubon Society Collection/Photo Researchers, Inc.: **Arum family**; © Michael A. Keller 1989, Stock Market: **Nutrition**; © Tom Kelly/Phototake : **Submarine**; © Karl W. Kenyon, National Audubon Society Collection/Photo Researchers, Inc.: **Otters**; © Paolo Koch, National Audubon Society Collection/Photo Researchers, Inc.: **Ore**; © Carl Koford, National Audubon Society Collection/Photo Researchers, Inc.: **Condors**; © Stephen J. Krasemann, National Audubon Society Collection/Photo Researchers, Inc.: **Prescribed burn**; © Charles Krebs, Stock Market: **Dating techniques**, **Walruses**; © J. Kubec A. NR.m, Stock Market: **Glass**; © Dr. Dennis Kunkel/Phototake: **Membrane**, **Natural fibers**; © Dennis Kunkel/Phototake : **Blood**; Dennis Kunkel (2) /Phototake: **Mites**; © Maurice & Sally Landre, National Audubon Society Collection/Photo Researchers, Inc.: **Bromeliad family**; © Lawrence Livermore National Laboratory/Science Photo Library, National Audubon Society Collection/Photo Researchers, Inc.: **States of matter**; © Lawrence Berkeley Laboratory/Science Photo Library, National Audubon Society Collection/Photo Researchers, Inc.: **Cyclotron**, **Particle detectors**; © Francis Leroy, Biocosmos/Science Photo Library, National Audubon Society Collection/Photo Researchers, Inc.: **Hydrothermal vents**; © Tom & Pat Lesson, National Audubon Society Collection/Photo Researchers, Inc.: **Old-growth forests**; © Yoav Levy/Phototake: **Acupuncture**, **Motion**, **Machines, simple**, **Phases of matter**, **Superconductor**, **Viscosity**, **Water pollution**; © Dr. Andrejs Liepins, National Audubon Society Collection/Photo Researchers, Inc.: **Hodgkin's disease**; © Norman Lightfoot, National Audubon Society Collection/Photo Researchers, Inc.: **Albinism**; © Suen-O Linoblad,National Audubon Society Collection/Photo Researchers, Inc.: **Eland**; © R. Ian Lloyd, Stock Market: **Island**; © Paul Logsdon/Phototake: **Contour plowing**; Courtesy of Jacqueline Longe.: **Ultrasonics**; © Dr. Kari Lounatimaa/ Science Photo Library, National Audubon Society Collection/Photo Researchers, Inc.: **Asexual reproduction**; © Alexander Lowry, National Audubon Society Collection/Photo Researchers, Inc.: **Hazardous wastes**; © Renee Lynn, National Audubon Society Collection/Photo Researchers, Inc.: **Capuchins**; © John Madere, Stock Market: **Mass transportation**; © Dr. P. Marazzi, National Audubon Society Collection/Photo Researchers, Inc.: **Edema**; © Andrew J. Martinez, National Audubon Society Collection/Photo Researchers, Inc.: **Flatfish**; © Bob Masini/Phototake: **Radial keratotomy**; © Karl H. Maslowski, National Audubon Society Collection/Photo Researchers, Inc.: **Caribou**, **Weaver finches**; © Don Mason, Stock Market: **Bats**; © Cynthia Matthews, Stock Market: **Birth**; © C. G. Maxwell, National Audubon Society Collection/Photo Researchers, Inc.: **Cattails**; © Henry Mayer, National Audubon Society Collection/Photo Researchers, Inc.: **Beech family**; © Fred McConnaughey, National Audubon Society Collection/Photo Researchers, Inc.: **Boxfish**, **Cuttlefish**, **Mackerel**; © Tom McHugh/Science Source, National Audubon Society Collection/Photo Researchers, Inc.: **Fossil and fossilization**; © Tom McHugh, National Audubon Society Collection/Photo Researchers, Inc.: **Bowerbirds**, **Canines**, **Elapid snakes**, **Elephant shrew**, **Gibbons and siamangs**, **Gorillas**, **Mole-rats**, **Skates**, **Sturgeons**, **Vipers**, **Salamanders**; © Will and Deni McIntyre, National Audubon Society Collection/Photo Researchers, Inc.: **Canal**, **Dyslexia**, **Amniocentesis**, **Lock**; © Eamonn McNulty, National Audubon Society Collection/Photo Researchers, Inc.: **Pacemaker**; © Dilip Mehia/Contact Giza, Stock Market: **Pyramid**; © Anthony Merciece Photo, National Audubon Society Collection/Photo Researchers, Inc.: **Bluebirds**; © Astrid & Hanns-Frieder Michler/Science Photo Library, National Audubon Society Collection/Photo Researchers, Inc.: **Precipitation**; © 1983 Lawrence Midgale, National Audubon Society Collection/Photo Researchers, Inc.: **Composite family**; Courtesy of J. Gordon Miller.: **Horses**; © Mobil Solar Energy Corporation/Phototake: **Photovoltaic cell**; © Viviane Moos, Stock Market: **Perpendicular**, **Smog**; © Moredun Animal Health LTD, National Audubon Society Collection/Photo Researchers, Inc.: **Thrombosis**; © Hank Morgan, National Audubon Society Collection/Photo Researchers, Inc.: **In vitro fertilization**; © Hank Morgan, National Audubon Society Collection/Photo Researchers, Inc.: **Radiation detectors**; © Roy Morsch, Stock Market: **Bioluminescence**, **Seeds**, **Toucans**; © Roy Morsch/Bikderberg, Stock Market: **Dams**; © John Moss, National Audubon Society Collection/Photo Researchers, Inc.: **Aqueduct**; © Prof. P. Motta/Dept. of Anatomy/University La Sapienza,

Rome/Science Photo Library, National Audubon Society Collection/Photo Researchers, Inc.: **Connective tissue, Skeletal system, Osteoporosis**; © Prof. P. Motta/G. Macchiarelli/University La Sapienza, Rome/Science Photo Library, National Audubon Society Collection/ Photo Researchers, Inc.: **Heart**; © Mug Shots, Stock Market: **Electrocardiogram**; © Joe Munroe, National Audubon Society Collection/Photo Researchers, Inc.: **Amaranth family, Starlings**; © Dr. Gopal Murti, National Audubon Society Collection/Photo Researchers, Inc.: **Sickle cell anemia**; © S. Nagendra, National Audubon Society Collection/Photo Researchers, Inc.: **Spider monkeys**; © NASA/Science Photo Library, National Audubon Society Collection/Photo Researchers, Inc.: **Radar**; © NASA, National Audubon Society Collection/Photo Researchers, Inc.: **Satellite**; NASA: **Aircraft (2 photos), Airship, Balloon, Black Hole, Comets, Constellation, Dark Matter, Earth, Jupiter (3 photos), Mars (3 photos), Mercury (2 photos), Meteors and meteorites, Moon (3 photos), Neptune (2 photos), Planetary nebulae, Pluto, Rockets and missiles, Saturn (2 photos), Saturn, Solar flare, Solar system, Space Shuttle, Spacecraft, manned, Sun (2 photos), Sunspots, Telephone, Tropical cyclone, Uranus (2 photos), Venus (2 photos)**; © National Aububon Society Collection/Photo Researchers, Inc.: **Monoculture, Aye-ayes, Bass, Chinchilla, Crocodiles, Fossa, Lemur, Plastics, Pneumonia**; © Tom Nebbia, Stock Market: **Drought**; © Nelson-Bohart & Associates/Phototake: **Metamorphosis**; © Ray Nelson/Phototake: **Amplifier**; © Joseph Nettis, National Audubon Society Collection/Photo Researchers, Inc.: **Computerized axial tomography**; © Mark Newman/Phototake: **Glaciers**; © Newman Laboratory of Nuclear Studies, Cornell University, National Audubon Society Collection/Photo Researchers, Inc.: **Subatomic particles**; © NIH, National Audubon Society Collection/Photo Researchers, Inc.: **Artificial heart and heart valve**; © Novosti Press Agency, National Audubon Society Collection/Photo Researchers, Inc.: **Nuclear fusion, Spacecraft, manned**; © Richard Nowitz/Phototake: **Engraving and etching**; © Gregory Ochocki, National Audubon Society Collection/Photo Researchers, Inc.: **Ocean sunfish**; © John Olson , Stock Market : **Brewing, Metal production**; © Omikron, National Audubon Society Collection/Photo Researchers, Inc.: **Lampreys and hagfishes, Squid**; © Omikron, National Audubon Society Collection/Photo Researchers, Inc.: **Tarsiers**; © Stan Osolinski 1993, Stock Market: **Predator**; © Stan Osolinski 1992, Stock Market: **Evolution**; © 1992 Gabe Palmer/Bikderberg, Stock Market: **Sextant**; © David Parker, ESA/National Audubon Society Collection/Photo Researchers, Inc.: **Rockets and missiles**; © David Parker/Science Photo Library, National Audubon Society Collection/Photo Researchers, Inc.: **Oscilloscope**; © David Parker, National Audubon Society Collection/Photo Researchers, Inc.: **Computer, digital**; © Claudia Parks, Stock Market: **Coast and beach**; © David Parler, National Audubon Society Collection/Photo Researchers Inc.: **Particle detector**; © Pekka Parviatnen, National Audubon Society Collection/Photo Researchers, Inc.: **Auroras**; © Alfred Pasieka/Science Photo Library, National Audubon Society Collection/Photo Researchers, Inc.: **Magnetism**; © Bryan F. Peterson, Stock Market: **Natural Gas**; © David M. Phillips/The Population Council/Science Source, National Audubon Society Collection/Photo Researchers, Inc.: **Fertilization**; © Mark D. Phillips, National Audubon Society Collection/Photo Researchers, Inc.: **Monkeys**; © Phototake: **Oryx**; Phototake (CN) /Phototake: **Abscess**; © Photri, Stock Market: **Explosives**; © 1973 Photri/Bikderberg, Stock Market: **Tornado**; © Roy Pinney, National Audubon Society Collection/Photo Researchers, Inc.: **Arum family**; © Philippe Plailly, National Audubon Society Collection/Photo Researchers, Inc.: **Hologram and holography, Microscopy, Gene therapy**; © Philippe Plailly/Eurelious/Science Photo Library, National Audubon Society Collection/Photo Researchers, Inc.: **Microscopy**; © Philippe Plailly/Eurelios, National Audubon Society Collection/Photo Researchers, Inc.: **Electrostatic devices**; © Rod Planck, National Audubon Society Collection/Photo Researchers, Inc.: **Mosquitoes**; © Planet Earth: **Coelacanth, Crocodiles, Orang-utan, Tapirs**; © 1986 David Pollack/Bikderberg, Stock Market: **Concrete**; © J. Polleross, Stock Market: **Emission**; © Marco Polo/Phototake: **Slash-and-burn agriculture**; © Cecilia Posada/Phototake: **Assembly line**; © Masud Quraishy, National Audubon Society Collection/Photo Researchers, Inc.: **Cats**; © E. Hanumantha Rao, National Audubon Society Collection/Photo Researchers, Inc.: **Bee-eaters**; © Rapho, National Audubon Society Collection/Photo Researchers, Inc.: **Dik-diks**; © G. Carleton Ray, National Audubon Society Collection/Photo Researchers, Inc.: **Sharks**; © Hans Reinhard/Okapia 1990, National Audubon Society Collection/Photo Researchers, Inc.: **Carrot family**; © H. Reinhard/Okapia, National Audubon Society Collection/Photo Researchers, Inc.: **Buzzards**; © Roger Ressmeyer/Starlight/for the W. M. Keck Observatory, cour-

ACKNOWLEDGEMENTS

tesy of California Associate for Research and Astronomy.: **Telescope**; © Chris Rogers/Bikderberg, Stock Market: **Laser**; © Otto Rogge, Stock Market: **Precious metals**; © Frank Rossotto, Stock Market: **Temperature regulation**; © Martin M. Rotker/Phototake: **Adrenals, Aneurism**; Neasaphus Rowalewkii: **Fossil and fossilization**; © Royal Greenwhich Observatory, National Audubon Society Collection/Photo Researchers, Inc.: **Atomic clocks**; © Royal Observatory, Edinburgh/AATB/Science Photo Library, National Audubon Society Collection/Photo Researchers, Inc.: **Star cluster**; © Royal Observatory, Edinburgh/National Audubon Society Collection/Photo Researchers, Inc.: **Telescope**; © Ronald Royer/Science Photo Library, National Audubon Society Collection/Photo Researchers, Inc.: **Star**; © Leonard Lee Rue III, National Audubon Society Collection/Photo Researchers, Inc.: **Groundhog, Kangaroos and wallabies, Mongooses, Muskrat, Coatis, Rats, Rusts and smuts, Seals**; © Leonard Lee Rue, National Audubon Society Collection/Photo Researchers, Inc.: **Camels**; © Leonard Lee Rue, National Audubon Society Collection/Photo Researchers, Inc.: **Shrews**; © Len Rue Jr., National Audubon Society Collection/Photo Researchers, Inc.: **Badgers**; © S.I.U.,National Audubon Society Collection/Photo Researchers, Inc.: **Lithotripsy**; © 1994 Ron Sanford, Stock Market: **Behavior**; © Nancy Sanford, Stock Market: **Mink**; © Ron Sanford, Stock Market: **Beavers, Raccoons**; © Science Photo Library, National Audubon Society Collection/Photo Researchers, Inc.: **Arthritis, Gangrene, Artificial fibers**; Science Photo Library: **Binary star, Galaxy, Halley's comet, Milky Way, Paleontology, Star formation**; Science Source: **Eclipses, Quasar**; © Secchi-Lecague/Roussel-UCLAF/CNRI/Science Photo Library, National Audubon Society Collection/Photo Researchers, Inc.: **Neuron**; © Nancy Sefton, National Audubon Society Collection/Photo Researchers, Inc.: **Sponges**; © Dr. Gary Settles/Science Source, National Audubon Society Collection/Photo Researchers, Inc.: **Aerodynamics**; James Lee Sikkema: **Elm , Gesnerias, Grapes, Holly family, Lilac, Lily family, Lily family, Maples, Mustard family, Nightshade, Pines, Rose family, Spruce, Spurge family, Swamp cypress family, Willow family**; © Lee D. Simon, National Audubon Society Collection/Photo Researchers, Inc.: **Bacteriophage**; © James R. Simon, National Audubon Society Collection/Photo Researchers, Inc.: **Sloths**; © Ben Simon, Stock Market: **Elephant;** © SIU, National Audubon Society Collection/Photo Researchers, Inc.: **Frostbite**; © SIU, National Audubon Society Collection/ Photo Researchers, Inc.: **Birth**; © Prof. D. Skobeltzn, National Audubon Society Collection/Photo Researchers, Inc.: **Cosmic rays**; © Howard Sochurek, Stock Market: **Gene**; © Dr. M.F. Soper, National Audubon Society Collection/Photo Researchers, Inc.: **Plovers**; Courtesy of Charles H. Southwick: **Macaques, Rhesus monkeys**; © James T. Spencer, National Audubon Society Collection/Photo Researchers, Inc.: **True eels**; © Hugh Spencer, National Audubon Society Collection/Photo Researchers, Inc.: **Spore**; © Spielman/CNRI/Phototake: **Lyme disease**; © St Bartholomew's Hospital, National Audubon Society Collection/Photo Researchers, Inc.: **Bubonic Plague**; © Alvin E. Staffan, National Audubon Society Collection/Photo Researchers, Inc.: **Walkingsticks**; © S. Stammers, National Audubon Society Collection/Photo Researchers, Inc.: **Interferons**; © Peter Steiner, Stock Market: **LED**; © Tom Stewart, Stock Market: **Icebergs**; © David Stoeklein, Stock Market: **Partridges**; © Streinhart Aquarium, National Audubon Society Collection/Photo Researchers, Inc.: **Geckos**; © Mary M. Thacher, National Audubon Society Collection/Photo Researchers, Inc.: **Genets**; © Mary M. Thatcher, National Audubon Society Collection/Photo Researchers, Inc.: **Carrot family**; © Asa C. Thoresen, National Audubon Society Collection/Photo Researchers, Inc.: **Slash-and-burn agriculture**; Geoff Tompkincon, National Audubon Society Collection/Photo Researchers, Inc.: **Surgery**; © Geoff Tompkinson, National Audubon Society Collection/Photo Researchers, Inc.: **Cryogenics**; © Tom Tracy, National Audubon Society Collection/Photo Researchers, Inc.: **Refrigeration**; © Alexander Tsiaras, National Audubon Society Collection/Photo Researchers, Inc.: **Cauterization, Transplant, surgical**; © George Turner, National Audubon Society Collection/Photo Researchers, Inc.: **Cattle family;** © U.S. Fish & Wildlife Service: **Canines, Kangaroo rats, Toads, Turtles**; © Akira Uchiyama, National Audubon Society Collection/Photo Researchers, Inc.: **Saiga antelope**; © Howard Earl Uible, National Audubon Society Collection/Photo Researchers, Inc.: **Marmosets and tamarins**; © Howard E. Uible, National Audubon Society Collection/Photo Researchers, Inc.: **Tenrecs**; © R. Van Nosstrand, National Audubon Society Collection/Photo Researchers, Inc.: **Gibbons and siamang**; © G. Van Heijst and J. Flor, National Audubon Society Collection/Photo Researchers, Inc.: **Chaos**; © Irene Vandermolen, National Audubon Society Collection/Photo Researchers, Inc.: **Banana**; © K. G. Vock/Okapia, National Audubon Society Collection/Photo

Researchers, Inc.: **Birch family**; © Ken Wagner/Phototake: **Herbicides, Agrochemicals**; © Susan Woog Wagner, National Audubon Society Collection/Photo Researchers, Inc.: **Down's syndrome**; © M. I. Walker/Science Photo Library, National Audubon Society Collection/Photo Researchers, Inc.: **Copepods**; © Kennan Ward, Stock Market: **Chimpanzees, Salmon**; Bill Wassman: **Dinosaur**; © C. James Webb/Phototake: **Smallpox**; C. James Webb/Phototake: **Elephantiasis**; © Ulrike Welsch, National Audubon Society Collection/Photo Researchers, Inc.: **Deforestation**; © Jerome Wexler 1981, National Audubon Society Collection/Photo Researchers, Inc.: **Carnivorous plants**; © Herbert Wexler, National Audubon Society Collection/Photo Researchers, Inc.: **Livestock;** © Jeanne White, National Audubon Society Collection/Photo Researchers, Inc.: **Hippopotamuses, Dragonflies**; © George Whiteley, National Audubon Society Collection/Photo Researchers, Inc.: **Horticulture**; © Mark Wilson, National Audubon Society Collection/Photo Researchers, Inc.: **Falcons**; © Charles D. Winters, National Audubon Society Collection/Photo Researchers, Inc.: **Centrifuge**; © Anthony Wolff/Phototake: **Boobies and Gannets**; Illustrations reprinted by permission of Robert L. Wolke.: **Air pollution (2 illustrations), Aluminum, Amino acid, Atom, Barbiturates, Calorimetry, Carbon (3 illustrations), Chemical bond (3 illustrations), Chemical compound (2 illustrations), Crystal, Deoxyribonucleic Acid (DNA), Earth's interior, Electrolysis, Electrolyte, Electromagnetic spectrum, Ester, Fatty acids, Gases, properties of (4 illustrations), Hydrocarbon (3 illustrations), Metric system, Metabolism, Molecule, Nuclear fission (2 illustrations), Plastics, Radiation, Soap, Solution, States of matter (2 illustrations), Water, X rays**; © David Woods, Stock Market: **Cockatoos**; © Norbert Wu, Stock Market: **Courtship, Rays**; © Zefa Germany, Stock Market: **Codfishes, Forests, Hummingbirds, Mole, Rain forest**; © 1994 Zefa Germany, Stock Market: **Bears, Mimicry, Pollination**.

Line art illustrations provided by Hans and Cassady of Westerville, Ohio.

States of matter

Matter includes all the material that makes up the universe. It has mass and it takes up space. It includes everything around us: the food we eat, the water we drink, the air we breathe, the ores deep within the earth as well as the atmosphere above it, the substances that make up the moon and the stars as well as the dust in the tail of a comet. It is fairly easy to observe that matter exists in different forms or states: solids, liquids, gases, and the less familiar plasma state.

Nature of matter

All matter is composed of very small, discrete particles, either atoms, ions, or molecules. The nature of a particular substance depends on the type and arrangement of the atoms within the molecule.

It is possible for these particles to assume different arrangements in space. For example, they can be arranged close together or far apart. They can be neat and orderly or random and disordered. Since two particles cannot occupy the same place at the same time, they can be pushed closer together only if there is empty space between particles. Sometimes they slip and slide past each other and sometimes they are locked rigidly into a specific position. The state in which any particular piece of matter exists depends on these properties. Under the right conditions, any substance can exist in all of the states of matter: solid, liquid, gas, or plasma.

The atoms, molecules, and ions that make up all matter are in constant motion, which can range from vibrating within a fairly rigid position to moving randomly at very high speeds. Movement is always in a straight line until some other force interferes with the motion. Like billiard balls, the moving particles can hit other particles or objects such as the walls of their container. These collisions cause the particles to change direction and, although no energy can be lost, it can be transferred to other particles.

Various forces exist between the particles of matter. The degree of attraction or repulsion depends on such factors as whether the particles are electrically neutral or carry a charge, whether the charges are localized or balanced out, how big or small the particles are, and how far apart the particles are from each other.

Solids

Matter is said to be in the solid state when it is rigid, that is, when it retains a definite shape and vol-

A piece of SEAgel sitting on soap bubbles. SEAgel (Safe Emulsion Agar gel) is a material claimed to be the first lighter-than-air solid. It is made from agar, a seaweed derivative used as a thickening agent in the food industry, and is biodegradable. SEAgel could be used as a thermal insulator instead of plastic foam or balsa wood. High density SEAgel could be used instead of plastic packaging. The substance is soluble in water above 122°F (50°C).

ume against the pull of gravity. Strong attractive forces exist among the particles that make up solids, causing them to position themselves close together in an orderly and definite arrangement in space. Their motion consists mainly of vibrating in a fixed position so the shape and the volume (amount of space they occupy) are maintained. The atoms, ions, or molecules cannot be pushed closer together; therefore, solids cannot be compressed.

Many solids exist in the form of crystals, which have simple geometric shapes, reflecting the regular spatial arrangement forms and shapes depending on the arrangement of the atoms, ions, or molecules of which they are made. This arrangement is called a lattice. Other solids, such as lumps of clay, seem to have no preferred shapes at all. They are said to be amorphous (without form). This is true because the individual crystals may be very tiny or because the substance consists of several kinds of crystals, randomly mixed together. Other solids, such as glass, contain no crystals at all.

When solids are cooled to lower temperatures, the orderly arrangement of their particles stays basically the same. The vibrations become slightly slower and weaker, however, causing the particles to move closer together, and the solid contracts slightly. But when solids are heated, the vibrations become faster and broader. This causes the particles to move slightly farther apart, and the solid expands a little. If heated enough, the particles will vibrate so vigorously that the rigid structure can no longer be maintained. The lattice begins to fall apart, first into clumps, and eventually

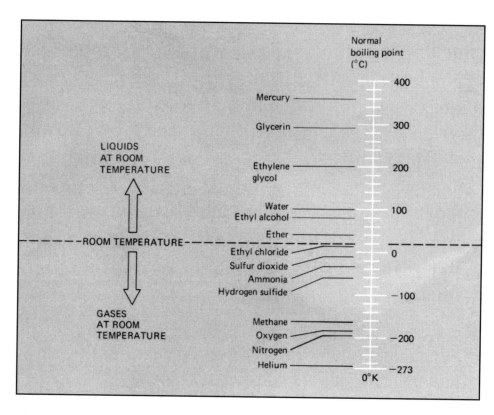

The normal boiling points of some substances.

into individual particles which can slip and slide past each other as they move about freely. At this point, the solid has become a liquid.

The temperature at which a solids loses its rigid form and turns into a liquid is called the melting point. Different substances have different melting points that are dependent on the sizes of the particles and the strength of the attractions between the particles. In general, heavier particles require more energy (higher temperatures) in order to vibrate vigorously enough to come apart. Also, the stronger the attractions between the particles, the more energy is required to break them apart and change the solid into a liquid. In both cases—heavier particles and stronger attractions—the melting point will be higher. Water serves as a good example. Liquid water freezes at the same temperature that ice melts, and the melting and freezing points are therefore identical. This is true for all substances. Ice melts at 32°F (0°C) which is uncharacteristically high for particles the weight of water molecules. This unusually high melting/freezing point is caused by the very strong attractive forces that exist between the molecules, making it very difficult for particles to move away from their neighbors and for the crystalline structure to collapse. Metals melt at much higher temperatures than ice. For example, copper is made into various shapes by

melting it at 1,985° F (1,083°C), pouring it into molds and cooling it. It is then usually purified further by electrolysis before it is commercially useful. Since pure substances have unique melting points which are usually quite easy to determine, chemists often use them as the first step in identifying unknown substances.

The amount of energy required to change a solid to a liquid varies from substance to substance. This energy is called the heat of fusion. Ice, for example, must absorb 80 calories per gram in order to melt into liquid water. Similarly, water releases 80 calories per gram of water to freeze into ice. Each of these changes occurs at the melting/freezing point of water, 32°F (0°C). In melting, since all the heat energy is used up in breaking the crystalline lattice, there is no change in temperature. However, once all the ice has melted, the absorbed energy causes the temperature of the liquid water to rise. This is generally true of the melting of all solids.

Liquids

The change from solid to liquid is a physical rather than chemical change because no chemical bonds have been broken. The individual particles—atoms, ions, or molecules—that made up the solid are the same individual particles that make up the liquid. What does

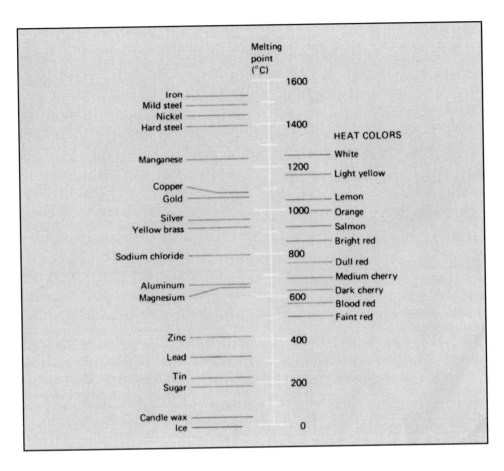

The melting points of some substances.

change is the arrangement of the particles. In the liquid, the particles are at a higher temperature, having more energy than in the solid, and this allows them to move away from their nearest neighbors. The attractions between liquid particles, though less than those of solids, is still fairly strong. This keeps the particles close to each other and touching, even though they can around past one another. They cannot be pushed closer together, and so, like solids, liquids maintain their volume and cannot be compressed. Because their particles move freely around, liquids can flow, and they will assume the shape of any container.

Like solids, the particles of liquids are close to each other; therefore, and the amount of space occupied by liquids is quite close to that of their corresponding solids. However because of the disorderly arrangement, the empty space between the liquid particles molecules is usually slightly greater than that between the particles of the solid. Therefore, liquids usually have a slightly larger volume—that is, they are less dense—than solids. A very unusual exception to this is the case of ice melting to form water, when the volume actually decreases. The crystalline lattice of ice has a cage-like structure of

H_2O molecules with big, open spaces in the middle of the cages. When the ice melts and the crystal breaks down, the cages collapse and the molecules move closer together, taking up less space. Consequently, a given weight of water occupies more volume as ice than as liquid. In other words, ice is less dense than water. Therefore, ice floats on liquid water. Also, a full, closed container of water will break as it freezes because the ice must expand. A water pipe may break if it freezes in winter because of this unusual property of water.

Boiling

As the temperature of a liquid is increased, the particles gain more energy and move faster and faster. Jostling about and colliding increases until eventually the particles at the surface gain enough energy to overcome the attractive forces from their neighbors and break away into the surrounding space. At this point, the liquid is becoming a gas (also called a vapor). The temperature at which this happens depends on what the substance is. This temperature, known as the boiling point, remains constant during the entire process of boiling because the added heat is being used up to break the attraction between the particles. The reverse process, condensation, occurs at the same temperature as boiling. Like the melting point, the boiling point is unique for each pure substance, and can be used as an analytical tool for determining the identities of unknown substances.

The amount of energy required for a given amount of a liquid to vaporize or become a gas is called the heat of vaporization (or condensation). It varies from substance to substance because the particle of different substances may be heavier or lighter and may exert different attractive forces. The amount of energy absorbed when 1 gram of water completely changes to a vapor is 540 calories. Conversely, 540 calories are released when 1 gram of water vapor changes back to liquid.

When a liquid reaches the boiling point, particles on the surface actually gain enough energy to break away from the surface. But as heating continues, particles throughout the liquid are also increasing in energy and moving faster. In a body of the liquid, however, the particles cannot escape into the air, as those on the surface can. That is not only because they happen to be buried deep down below the surface. It is also because the atmosphere is pushing down on the entire liquid and all the particles within it, and, in order to break away, these particles deep within the liquid must acquire enough energy to overcome this additional pressure. (The surface particles can just fly off into the spaces between the air molecules.) When a group of interior particles finally do get enough energy—get hot enough—to overcome the atmospheric pressure, they can push each other away, leaving a hollow space within the liquid. This is a bubble. It is not entirely empty, however, because it contains many trapped particles, flying around inside. The light-weight bubble then rises through the liquid and breaks at the surface, releasing its trapped particles as vapor. We then say the liquid is boiling.

Since the pressure inside the bubbles must overcome atmospheric pressure in order for the bubbles to form, the boiling point of a substance depends on atmospheric pressure. Liquids will boil at lower temperatures if the atmospheric pressure is lower, as it is on a mountain. At the top of Mount Everest, 29,000 ft (8,839 m) above sea level, where the pressure is only about one-third that at sea level, water boils at 158°F (70°C). At 10,000 ft (3,048 m) above sea level, water boils at 192° F (89°C). It would take longer to cook an egg where the boiling point is 192° F (89°C) than at sea level where the boiling point is 212°F (100°C). The normal boiling point of a liquid is defined as its boiling point when the atmospheric pressure is exactly 760 mm Hg, or 1 atmosphere.

With the diminishing supplies of fresh water today, it is increasingly important to find ways of desalinating—removing the salt from—sea water in order to make it useful for human consumption, agriculture and industry. Changes in state, both boiling and freezing, are useful for this purpose. When salt water is heated to boiling and the vapors cooled, they condense to form water again, but the salt stays behind in a very salty residue called brine. By this process, called distillation, fresh water has been recovered from salt water. Similarly, when salt water freezes, much of the salt stays behind as a very salty slush. The ice is removed from the brine and melted to produce relatively fresh water.

Gases

When a substance has reached the gaseous state, the particles are moving at relatively high speeds, and in straight lines, until they encounter other particles or some other barrier. The spaces between the particles are many times the size of the particles themselves. Generally, gas particles travel large distances through space before colliding with another particle or object. When colliding, although energy can be lost by one particle, it is gained by another and there is no net gain or loss of energy.

Because the particles are flying freely in the gaseous state, gases will fill whatever space is available to them. Thus, 100, 1000, or ten million particles of gas in a container spread out and fill the entire container.

Plasma

Plasmas are considered by some to be the fourth phase of matter. They are closely related to gases. In a plasma, the particles are neither atoms nor molecules, but electrons and positive ions. Plasmas can be formed at very high temperatures—high enough to ionize (remove electrons from) the atoms. The resulting electrons and positive ions can then move freely, like the particles in a gas. Although not found on earth except in the outermost atmosphere, plasmas are probably more prevalent in the universe than all of the other three states of matter. The stars, comets' tails, and the aurora borealis are all plasmas. Because their particles are electrically charged, plasmas are greatly influenced by electric and magnetic fields.

Much research today involves the study of plasmas and the ability to control them. One possible method for producing enormous amounts of energy through nuclear fusion involves the production and control of plasmas.

See also Atom; Crystal; Density; Desalination; Distillation; Desalination; Electrolysis; Evaporation; Gases, properties of; Ionization; Molecule.

Further Reading:

Burgess, David. "Stronger than Atoms." *New Scientist* 140, (November 1993): 28-33.

Caro, Paul. *Water*. New York: McGraw Hill, 1993.

Close, Frank. *Too Hot to Handle: The Race for Cold Fusion*. Princeton: Princeton University Press, 1991.

Fortman, John J. "States of Matter." *Journal of Chemical Education* 70, (January 1993): 56-57.

David Burgess, "Stronger than Atoms." *New Scientist* 140, (November 1993): 28-33.

Leona B. Bronstein

Static electricity see **Electrostatic devices**

Statistical mechanics

Statistical mechanics is a sub-branch of physics that attempts to explain the behavior of a macroscopic system based on the behavior and properties of that system's microscopic elements.

The number of these microscopic elements is usually very large, and it is impossible to accurately predict the behavior of each of these elements as they interact. However, the large number of interactions makes it theoretically possible for statistical mechanics to predict the behavior of the system as a whole.

Statistics

Statistics is that branch of mathematics devoted to the collection, compilation, display, and interpretation of numerical data. In general, the field can be divided into two major subgroups, *descriptive statistics* and *inferential statistics*. The former subject deals primarily with the accumulation and presentation of numerical data, while the latter focuses on predictions that can be made based on those data.

Some fundamental concepts

Two fundamental concepts used in statistical analysis are population and sample. The term *population*

refers to a complete set of individuals, objects, or events that belong to some category. For example, all of the players who are employed by Major League Baseball teams make up the population of professional major league baseball players. The term *sample* refers to some subset of a population that is representative of the total population. For example, one might go down the complete list of all major league baseball players and select every tenth name. That subset of every tenth name would then make up a sample of all professional major league baseball players.

Another concept of importance in statistics is the distinction between discrete and continuous data. Discrete variables are numbers that can have only certain specific numerical value that can be clearly separated from each other. For example, the number of professional major league baseball players is a discrete variable. There may be 400 or 410 or 475 or 615 professional baseball players, but never 400.5, 410.75, or 615.895.

Continuous variables may take any value whatsoever. The readings on a thermometer are an example of a continuous variable. The temperature can range from 10°C to 10.1°C to 10.2°C to 10.3°C (about 50°F) and so on upward or downward. Also, if a thermometer accurate enough is available, even finer divisions, such as 10.11°C, 10.12°C, and 10.13°C, can be made. Methods for dealing with discrete and continuous variables are somewhat different from each other in statistics.

In some cases, it is useful to treat continuous variable as discrete variables, and vice versa. For example, it might be helpful in some kind of statistical analysis to assume that temperatures can assume only discrete values, such as 41°F, 50°F, 59°F, (5°C, 10°C, 15°C), and so on. It is important in making use of that statistical analysis, then, to recognize that this kind of assumption has been made.

Collecting data

The first step in doing a statistical study is usually to obtain raw data. As an example, suppose that a researcher wants to know the number of female African-Americans in each of six age groups (1-19; 20-29; 30-39; 40-49; 50-59; and 60+) there are in the United States. One way to answer that question would be to do a population survey, that is, to interview every single female African-American in the United States and ask what their age is. Quite obviously, such a study would be very difficult and very expensive to complete. In fact, it would probably be impossible to do.

TABLE 1. STATISTICS

Number of Female African-Americans in Various Age Groups

Age	Number
0 - 19	5,382,025
20 - 29	2,982,305
30 - 39	2,587,550
40 - 49	1,567,735
50 - 59	1,335,235
60 +	1,606,335

A more reasonable approach is to select a sample of female African-Americans that is smaller than the total population and to interview this sample. Then, if the sample is drawn so as to be truly representative of the total population, the researcher can draw some conclusions about the total population based on the findings obtained from the smaller sample.

Descriptive statistics

Perhaps the simplest way to report the results of the study described above is to make a table. The advantage of constructing a table of data is that a reader can get a general idea about the findings of the study in a brief glance. An example of the kind of table that might result from the study described above would be Table 1.

Graphical representation

The table shown above is one way of representing the frequency distribution of a sample or population. A *frequency distribution* is any method for summarizing data that shows the number of individuals or individual cases present in each given interval of measurement. In the table above, there are 5,382,025 female African-Americans in the age group 0-19; 2,982,305 in the age group 20-29; 2,587,550 in the age group 30-39; and so on.

A common method for expressing frequency distributions in an easy-to-read form is a graph. Among the kinds of graphs used for the display of data are histograms, bar graphs, and line graphs. A histogram is a graph that consists of solid bars without any space between them. The width of the bars corresponds to one of the variables being presented and the height of the bars, to a second variable. If we constructed a histogram based on the table shown above, the graph would have six bars, one for each of the six age groups included in the study. The height of the six bars would correspond to the frequency found for each group. The first bar (ages 0-19) would be nearly twice as high as the second (20-29) and third (30-39) bars since there are nearly twice as many individuals in the first group as in the second or third. The fourth, fifth, and six bars would be nearly the same height since there are about the same numbers of individuals in each of these three groups.

Another kind of graph that can be constructed from a histogram is a frequency polygon. A frequency polygon can be made by joining the midpoints of the top lines of each bar in a histogram to each other.

Distribution curves

Finally, think of a histogram in which the vertical bars are very narrow . . . and then very, very narrow. As one connects the midpoints of these bars, the frequency polygon begins to look like a smooth curve, perhaps like a high, smoothly shaped hill. A curve of this kind is known as a *distribution curve*.

Probably the most familiar kind of distribution curve is one with a peak in the middle of the graph that falls off equally on both sides of the peak. This kind of distribution curve is known as a "normal" curve. Normal curves result from a number of random events that occur in the world. For example, suppose you were to flip a penny a thousand times and count how many times heads and how many times tails came up. What you would find would be a normal distribution curve, with a peak at equal heads and tails. That means that, if you were to flip a penny many times, you would most commonly expect equal numbers of heads and tails. But the likelihood of some other distribution of heads and tails—such as 10% heads and 90% tails—would occur much less often.

Frequency distributions that are not normal are said to be skewed. In a skewed distribution curve, the number of cases on one side of the maximum is much smaller than the number of cases on the other side of the maximum. The graph might start out at zero and rise very sharply to its maximum point and then drop down again on a very gradual slope to zero on the other side. Depending on where the gradual slope is, the graph is said to be skewed to the left or to the right.

Other kinds of frequency distributions

Bar graphs look very much like histograms except that gaps are left between adjacent bars. This difference is based on the fact that bar graphs are usually used to represent discrete data and the space between bars is a reminder of the discrete character of the data represented.

Line graphs can also be used to represent continuous data. If one were to record the temperature once an hour all day long, a line graph could be constructed with the hours of day along the horizontal axis of the graph and the various temperatures along the vertical axis. The temperature found for each hour could then be plotted on the graph as a point and the points then connected with each other. The assumption of such a graph is that the temperature varied continuously between the observed readings and that those temperatures would fall along the continuous line drawn on the graph.

A circle graph, or "pie chart," can also be used to graph data. A circle graph shows how the total number of individuals, cases or events is divided up into various categories. For example, a circle graph showing the population of female African-Americans in the United States would be divided into pie-shaped segments, one (0-19) twice as large as the next two (20-20 and 30-39), and three about equal in size and smaller than the other three.

Measures of central tendency

Both statisticians and non-statisticians talk about "averages" all the time. But the term average can have a number of different meanings. In the field of statistics, therefore, workers prefer to use the term measure of central tendency for the concept of an "average."

One way to understand how various measures of central tendency (different kinds of "average") differ from each other is to consider a classroom consisting of only six students. A study of the six students shows that their family incomes are as follows: $20,000; $25,000; $20,000; $30,000; $27,500; $150,000. What is the "average" income for the students in this classroom?

The measure of central tendency that most students learn in school is the *mean*. The mean for any set of numbers is found by adding all the numbers and dividing by the number of numbers. In this example, the mean would be equal to $20,000 + $25,000 + $20,000 + $30,000 + $27,500 + $150,000 ÷ 6 = $45,417. But how much useful information does this answer give about the six students in the classroom? The mean that has been calculated ($45,417) is greater than the household income of five of the six students.

Another way of calculating central tendency is known as the *median*. The median value of a set of measurements is the middle value when the measurements are arranged in order from least to greatest. When there are an even number of measurements, the median is half way between the middle two measurements. In the above example, the measurements can be rearranged from least to greatest: $20,000; $20,000; $25,000; $27,500; $30,000; $150,000. In this case, the middle two measurements are $25,000 and $27,500, and half way between them is $26,250, the median in this case. You can see that the median in this example gives a better view of the household incomes for the classroom than does the mean.

A third measure of central tendency is the *mode*. The mode is the value most frequently observed in a study. In the household income study, the mode is $20,000 since it is the value found most often in the study. Each measure of central tendency has certain advantages and disadvantages and is used, therefore, under certain special circumstances.

Measures of variability

Suppose that a teacher gave the same test to two different classes and obtained the following results: Class 1: 80%, 80%, 80%, 80%, 80% Class 2: 60%, 70%, 80%, 90%, 100% If you calculate the mean for both sets of scores, you get the same answer: 80%. But the collection of scores from which this mean was obtained was very different in the two cases. The way that statisticians have of distinguishing cases such as this is known as measuring the *variability* of the sample. As with measures of central tendency, there are a number of ways of measuring the variability of a sample.

Probably the simplest method is to find the range of the sample, that is, the difference between the largest and smallest observation. The range of measurements in Class 1 is 0, and the range in class 2 is 40%. Simply knowing that fact gives a much better understanding of the data obtained from the two classes. In class 1, the

TABLE 2. STATISTICS

	Improved	*Not Improved*	*Total*
Experimental Group	62	38	100
Control Group	45	55	100
Total	107	93	200

mean was 80%, and the range was 0, but in class 2, the mean was 80%, and the range was 40%.

Other measures of variability are based on the difference between any one measurement and the mean of the set of scores. This measure is known as the *deviation*. As you can imagine, the greater the difference among measurements, the greater the variability. In the case of Class 2 above, the deviation for the first measurement is 20% (80%-60%), and the deviation for the second measurement is 10% (80%-70%).

Probably the most common measures of variability used by statisticians are the variance and standard deviation. Variance is defined as the mean of the squared deviations of a set of measurements. Calculating the variance is a somewhat complicated task. One has to find each of the deviations in the set of measurements, square each one, add all the squares and divide by the number of measurements. In the example above, the variance would be equal to $[(20)^2 + (10)^2 + (0)^2 + (10)^2 + (20)^2] \div 5 = 200$.

For a number of reasons, the variance is used less often in statistics than is the standard deviation. The standard deviation is the square root of the variance, in this case, $\sqrt{200} = 14.1$. The standard deviation is useful because in any normal distribution, a large fraction of the measurements (about 68%) are located within one standard deviation of the mean. Another 27 percent (for a total of 95 percent of all measurements) lie within two standard deviations of the mean.

Inferential statistics

Expressing a collection of data in some useful form, as described above, is often only the first step in a statistician's work. The next step will be to decide what conclusions, predictions, and other statements, if any, can be made based on those data. A number of sophisticated mathematical techniques have now been developed to make these judgments.

An important fundamental concept used in inferential statistics is that of the null hypothesis. A null hypothesis is a statement made by a researcher at the beginning of an experiment that says, essentially, that nothing is happening in the experiment. That is, nothing other than natural events are going on during the experiment. At the conclusion of the experiment, the researcher submits his or her data to some kind of statistical analysis to see if the null hypothesis is true, that is, if nothing other than normal statistical variability has taken place in the experiment. If the null hypothesis is shown to be true, than the experiment truly did not have any effect on the subjects. If the null hypothesis is shown to be false, then the researcher is justified in putting forth some alternative hypothesis that will explain the effects that were observed. The role of statistics in this process is to provide mathematical tests to find out whether or not the null hypothesis is true or false.

A simple example of this process is deciding about the effectiveness of a new medication. In testing such medications, researchers usually select two groups, one the control group and one the experimental group. The control group does not receive the new medication; it receives a neutral substance instead. The experimental group receives the medication. The null hypothesis in an experiment of this kind is that the medication will have no effect and that both groups will respond in exactly the same way, whether they have been given the medication or not.

Suppose that the results of one experiment of this kind was as follows, with the numbers shown being the number of individuals who improved or did not improve after taking part in the experiment.

At first glance, it would appear that the new medication was at least partially successful since the number of those who took it and improved (62) was greater than the number who took it and did not improve (38). But a statistical test is available that will give a more precise answer, one that will express the probability (90%, 75%, 50%, etc.) that the null hypothesis is true. This test, called the *chi square test*, involves comparing the observed frequencies in the table above with a set of expected frequencies that can be calculated from the

KEY TERMS

Continuous variables—A variable that may take any value whatsoever.

Deviation—The difference between any one measurement and the mean of the set of scores.

Discrete variable—A number that can have only certain specific numerical value that can be clearly separated from each other.

Frequency polygon—A type of frequency distribution graph that is made by joining the midpoints of the top lines of each bar in a histogram to each other.

Histogram—A bar graph that shows the frequency distribution of a variable by means of solid bars without any space between them.

Mean—A measure of central tendency found by adding all the numbers in a set and dividing by the number of numbers.

Measure of central tendency—Average.

Measure of variability—A general term for any method of measuring the spread of measurements around some measure of central tendency.

Median—The middle value in a set of measurements when those measurements are arranged in sequence from least to greatest.

Mode—The value that occurs most frequently in any set of measurements.

Normal curve—A frequency distribution curve with a symmetrical, bell-shaped appearance.

Null hypothesis—A statistical statement that nothing unusual is taking place in an experiment.

Population—A complete set of individuals, objects, or events that belong to some category.

Range—The difference between the largest and smallest numbers in a set of observations.

Standard deviation—The square root of the variance.

lated, with each other. For example, many medical studies have attempted to determine the connection between smoking and lung cancer. One way to do such studies is to measure the amount of smoking a person has done in her or his lifetime and compare the rate of lung cancer among those individuals. A mathematical formula allows the researcher to calculate the Pearson correlation coefficient between these two sets of data—rate of smoking and risk for lung cancer. That coefficient can range between 1.0, meaning the two are perfectly correlated, and -1.0, meaning the two have an inverse relationship (when one is high, the other is low).

The correlation test is a good example of the limitations of statistical analysis. Suppose that the Pearson correlation coefficient in the example above turned out to be 1.0. That number would mean that people who smoke the most are always the most likely to develop lung cancer. But what the correlation coefficient does not say is what the cause and effect relationship, if any, might be. It does not say that smoking causes cancer.

Chi square and correlation coefficient are only two of dozens of statistical tests now available for use by researchers. The specific kinds of data collected and the kinds of information a researcher wants to obtain from these data determine the specific test to be used.

See also Accuracy; Mean; Median; Mode; Sample.

Further Reading:

Downie, N. M., and R. W. Heath. *Basic Statistical Methods*, 4th edition. New York: Harper & Row, 1977.
Glass, G. V., and J. C. Stanley. *Statistical Methods in Education and Psychology*. Englewood Cliffs, NJ: Prentice-Hall,, 1970.
Jaeger, Richard M. *Statistics: A Spectator Sport*. Beverly Hills, CA: Sage Publications, 1983.
Reidel, Manfred. *Winning with Numbers: A Kids' Guide to Statistics*. Englewood Cliffs, NJ: Prentice-Hall, Inc., 1978.
Witte, Robert S. *Statistics*, 3rd ed. New York: Holt, Rinehart and Winston, Inc., 1989.

David E. Newton

number of individuals taking the tests. The value of chi square calculated can then be compared to values in a table to see how likely the results were due to chance and how likely to some real affect of the medication.

Another example of a statistical test is called the *Pearson correlation coefficient*. The Pearson correlation coefficient is a way of determining the extent to which two variables are somehow associated, or corre-

Steady-state theory

Was there a moment of creation for the universe, or has the universe always existed? The steady-state theory is a cosmological theory for the origin of the universe that suggests the universe has always existed and did not have a moment of creation. This theory was popular during the 1950s and 1960s, but because of observations made during the 1960s, few, if any, astronomers now think that the steady-state theory is correct. The basic tenet of the steady-state theory is that the universe on a large scale does not change with time (evolve). It has always existed and will always continue to exist looking much as it does now. The universe is, however, known to be expanding. To allow for this expansion in an unchanging universe, the authors of the steady-state theory postulated that hydrogen atoms appeared out of empty space. These newly created hydrogen atoms were just enough to fill in the gaps caused by the expansion. Because hydrogen is continuously being created, the steady-state theory is sometimes called the continuous creation theory. This theory achieved great popularity for a couple of decades, but mounting observational evidence caused its demise in the late 1960s. The discovery in 1965 of the cosmic background radiation provided one of the most serious blows to the steady-state theory.

Cosmological assumptions

The steady-state model is based on a set of four assumptions collectively known as the *perfect cosmological principle*. The first assumption is that physical laws are universal. Any science experiment if performed under identical conditions will have the same result anywhere in the universe because physical laws are the same everywhere in the universe. Second, on a sufficiently large scale the universe is homogeneous. We know there is large scale structure in the universe, such as clusters of galaxies; so, we assume that the universe is homogenous only on scales large enough for even the largest structures to average out. Third, we assume that the universe is *isotropic*, meaning that there is no preferred direction in the universe. Fourth, we assume that over sufficiently long times the universe looks essentially the same at all times.

Collectively the first three of the above assumptions are the *cosmological principle* (not to be confused with the perfect cosmological principle). In a nutshell, the cosmological principle states that the universe looks essentially the same at any location in the universe. This principle remains a largely untested assumption because we cannot travel to every location in the universe to perform experiments to test the assumption.

Adding the fourth assumption, that the universe does not change on the large scale with time, gives us the perfect cosmological principle. Essentially, the uni-verse looks the same at all times as well as at all locations within the universe. The perfect cosmological principle forms the philosophical foundation for the steady-state theory. With the addition of the fourth assumption, the universe does not evolve in the steady-state theory, so observational evidence that the universe evolves would be evidence against the steady-state theory.

Cosmological observations

There are a number of observations that astronomers have made to test cosmological theories, including both the steady-state and the big bang theory. Some of these cosmological observations are described below.

Evolution of the universe

When we look at the most distant objects in the universe, we are looking back in time. For example if we observe a quasar that is 3 billion light years away, it has taken the light 3 billion years to get here, because a light year is the distance light travels in one year. We are therefore seeing the quasar as it looked 3 billion years ago. Quasars, the most distant objects known in the universe, are thought to be very active nuclei of distant galaxies. The nearest quasar is about a billion light years away. The fact that we do not see any quasars closer than a billion light years away suggests that quasars disappeared at least a billion years ago. The universe has changed with time. Several billion years ago quasars existed; they no longer do. This observation provides evidence that the perfect cosmological principle is untrue, and therefore that the steady-state theory is incorrect. Note however that when the steady-state theory and the perfect cosmological principle were first suggested, we had not yet discovered quasars.

Expansion of the universe

In his work measuring distances to galaxies, Edwin Hubble, after whom the Hubble space telescope was named, noticed an interesting correlation. The more distant a galaxy is, the faster it is moving away from us. This relationship is called the Hubble law. This relationship can be used to find the distances to additional galaxies, by measuring the speed of recession. More importantly, Hubble deduced the cause of this correlation. The universe is expanding. To visualize this expansion, draw some galaxies on an ordinary balloon and blow it up. Notice how the "galaxies" move farther apart as the balloon expands. Measuring distances between the drawn in galaxies at the rates at which they move apart, would give a relationship similar to Hubble's law.

The expanding universe can be consistent with either the big bang or the steady state theory. However in the steady state theory, new matter must appear to fill in the gaps left by the expansion. Normally as the universe expands, the average distance between galaxies would increase as the density of the universe decreases. These evolutionary changes with time would violate the fundamental assumption behind the steady-state theory. Therefore in the steady-state theory hydrogen atoms appear out of empty space and collect to form new galaxies. With these new galaxies, the average distance between galaxies remains the same even in an expanding universe.

The Hubble plot also provides evidence that the universe changes with time. The slope of the Hubble plot gives us the rate at which the universe is expanding. If the universe is not evolving, this slope should remain the same even for very distant galaxies. The measurements are difficult, but the Hubble plot seems to curve upward for the most distant galaxies. The universe was expanding faster in the distant past, contrary to the prediction of the steady-state theory that the universe is not evolving.

Cosmic background radiation

In the mid 1960s, Arno Penzias and Robert Wilson were working on a low noise (static) microwave antenna when they made an accidental discovery of cosmic significance. After doing everything possible to eliminate sources of noise, including cleaning out nesting pigeons and their waste, there was still a small noise component left. This weak noise did not vary with direction or with the time of day or year, because it was cosmic in origin. It also corresponded to a temperature of 3K (three degrees above absolute zero, -270°C). This 3K cosmic background radiation turned out to be the leftover heat from the initial big bang that had been predicted by proponents of the big bang theory as early as the 1940s.

Because this cosmic background radiation was a prior prediction of the big bang theory it provided strong evidence to support the big bang theory. Proponents of the steady-state theory have been unable to explain in detail how this background radiation could arise in a steady-state universe. The cosmic background radiation therefore gave the steady-state theory its most serious setback. Penzias and Wilson received the 1978 Nobel Prize in physics for their work.

Steady-state theory

The steady-state theory was inspired at least in part by a 1940s movie entitled *Dead of Night*. The movie had four parts and a circular structure such that at the end the movie was the same as at the beginning. After seeing this movie in 1946, Thomas Gold, Hermann Bondi, and Fred Hoyle wondered if the universe might not be constructed the same way. The discussion that followed led ultimately to the steady-state theory.

In 1948, Hermann Bondi and Thomas Gold proposed extending the cosmological principle to the perfect cosmological principle, so that the universe looks the same at all times as well as at all locations. They then proposed the steady-state theory based on the new perfect cosmological principle. Because Hubble had already observed that the universe is expanding, Bondi and Gold proposed the continuous creation of matter. Hydrogen atoms created from nothing combine to form galaxies. In this manner the average density of the universe remains the same as the universe expands. In the steady-state, the rate at which new matter is created must exactly balance the rate at which the universe is expanding. Otherwise the average density of the universe will change and the universe will evolve, violating the perfect cosmological principle. To maintain the steady-state, in a cubic meter of space one hydrogen atom must appear out of nothing every 5 billion years. In a volume of space the size of the Earth the amount of new matter created would amount to roughly a grain of dust in a million years. In the entire observable universe, roughly one new galaxy per year will form from these atoms. Bondi and Gold recognized that a new theory must be developed to explain how the hydrogen atoms formed out of nothing, but did not suggest a new theory.

In the same year, Fred Hoyle proposed a modification of Einstein's general theory of relativity. Hoyle worked independently of Bondi and Gold, but they did discuss the new theories. Hoyle's modification used a mathematical device to allow the creation of matter from nothing in general relativity. No experiments or observations have been made to justify or contradict this modification of general relativity.

Arguments for and against the steady-state theory

There are a number of problems with the steady-state theory, but at the time the theory was proposed, there were also points in its favor.

The steady-state theory rests on the foundation of the perfect cosmological principle. Hence, any evidence that the universe evolves is evidence against the steady state theory. The existence of quasars and the change in the expansion rate of the universe a few billion years in the past discussed earlier are evidence against the steady-state. This evidence for the evolution of the universe did not exist in 1948, when the steady-state theory originated. It became part of the cumulative weight of evidence that had built up against the steady-state theory by the mid 1960s. In gallant attempts to save the steady-state theory, its proponents, chiefly Hoyle and Jayant Narlikar, have argued that the universe can change over time periods of a few billion years without violating the perfect cosmological principle. We must look at even longer time spans to see that these changes with time average out.

The cosmic background radiation is widely considered the final blow to the steady-state theory. Again proponents of the steady-state theory have made gallant efforts to save their theory in the face of what most astronomers consider overwhelming evidence. They argue that the background radiation could be the cumulative radiation of a large number of radio sources that are to faint to detect individually. This scheme requires the existence of roughly 100 trillion (about 10,000 times the number of observable galaxies) such sources that about are one millionth as bright as the radio sources we do detect. Few astronomers are willing to go to such great lengths to rescue the steady-state theory.

Another objection raised against the steady-state theory is that it violates one of the fundamental laws of physics as that law is currently understood. The law of conservation of matter and energy states that matter and energy are interchangeable and can change between forms, but the total amount of matter and energy in the universe must remain constant. It can be neither created nor destroyed. The steady-state theory requires continuous creation of matter in violation of this law. However laws of science result from our experimental evidence and are subject to change, not at our whim, but as experimental results dictate. The rate at which matter is created in the steady-state theory is small enough that we would not have noticed. Hence we would not have discovered experimentally any conditions under which matter could be created or any modifications required in this law.

Were there ever any points in favor of the steady-state theory? When the steady-state model was first suggested, our best estimate of the age of the universe in the context of the big bang model was about 2 billion years. However the Earth and solar system are about 5 billion years old. The oldest stars in our galaxy are at least 10 to 12 billion years old. These age estimates present the obvious problem of a universe younger than the

KEY TERMS

Cosmic background radiation—The left over heat radiation from the big bang.

Cosmological principle—The set of fundamental assumptions behind the big bang theory that state the universe is essentially the same at all locations.

Hubble's law—The observation that tells us the universe is expanding: distant galaxies are receding at a speed proportional to their distance.

Perfect cosmological principle—The set of fundamental assumptions behind the steady-state theory that state the universe is essentially the same at all locations and times.

objects it contains. This problem is no longer so severe. Modern estimates for the age of the universe range from about 10 billion years to about 20 billion years. The lower end of this range still has the problem, but the upper end of the range gives a universe old enough to contain the oldest objects we have found so far. In the steady-state theory the universe has always existed, so there are no problems presented by the ages of objects in the universe.

For some people there are philosophical or esthetic grounds for preferring the steady-state theory over the big bang theory. The big bang theory has a moment of creation, which some people prefer for personal or theological reasons. Those who do not share this preference often favor the steady-state theory. They prefer the grand sweep of a universe that has always existed to a universe that had a moment of creation and may, by inference, also have an end in some far distant future time.

The weight of evidence against the steady-state theory has convinced most modern astronomers that it is incorrect. The steady-state theory does however still stand as a major intellectual achievement and as an important part of the history of the development of cosmology in the twentieth century.

See also Big bang theory; Cosmology; Doppler effect.

Further Reading:
Harrison, Edward R. *Cosmology The Science of the Universe.* Cambridge: Cambridge University Press, 1981.
Hoyle, Fred. *Astronomy.* London: Rathbone Books, 1962.
Hoyle, Fred. *The Nature of the Universe.* New York: Harper & Row, 1960.

Hoyle, Fred, and Jayant Narlikar. *The Physics-Astronomy Frontier.* San Francisco: Freeman. 1980.

Narlikar, Jayant V. *The Primeval Universe.* Oxford: Oxford University Press, 1988.

Paul A. Heckert

Steam engine

A steam engine is a machine that converts the heat energy of steam into mechanical energy by means of a piston moving in a cylinder. As an external combustion engine—since it burns its fuel outside of the engine—a steam engine passes its steam into a cylinder where it then pushes a piston back and forth. It is with this piston movement that the engine can do mechanical work. The steam engine was the major power source of the Industrial Revolution and dominated industry and transportation for 150 years. Today it is still useful in certain situations.

History

The earliest known steam engines were the novelties created by the Greek engineer and mathematician named Hero who lived during the first century A.D. His most famous invention was called the aeliopile. This was a small, hollow sphere to which two bent tubes were attached. The sphere was attached to a boiler which produced steam. As the steam escaped from the sphere's hollow tubes, the sphere itself would begin to whirl and rotate. Hero of Alexandria and several other Greeks designed many other steam-powered devises, such as a steam organ and automatic doors, but always in the context of playfulness and seemingly without any interest in using steam in a practical way. Nonetheless, their work established the principle of steam power and their playful devices were a real demonstration of converting steam power into some kind of motion.

Although the Greeks established the principle of steam power, it lay ignored for over 1,500 years until the late 1600s in Europe. During this long period, the main sources of power were first, human muscle power or draft animals, and later, wind and water power. Windmills and waterwheels were adequate for slow, repetitive jobs like grinding corn in which an interruption of power was of little consequence. But for certain jobs, like pumping water from a mine shaft, a power source that could cease at any time was not always sat-

isfactory. In fact, it was the very deepness of the English mines that spurred engineers to search for pumps that were quicker than the old water pumps. By the mid-sixteenth century, work on air pumps had established the notion of a piston working in a cylinder, and around 1680, the French physicist Denis Papin (1647-1712), put some water at the bottom of a tube, heated it and converted it to steam, and saw that the expanded steam pushed forcibly and moved a piston just ahead of it. When the tube cooled, the piston returned to its previous position. Although Papin was well aware he had created an engine that could eventually do work, he was deterred by the very real mechanical difficulties of his time and chose to work on a smaller scale—creating the world's first pressure cooker.

Following Papin, an English military engineer, Thomas Savery (c.1650-1715), built what most regard as the first practical steam engine. Unlike Papin's system, this had no piston since Savery wanted only to draw water from the coal mines deep below the earth. Knowing that he could use steam to produce a vacuum in a vessel, he connected such a vessel to a tube leading into the water below. The vacuum then drew water up the tube and it would be blown out by steam pressure. Savery's system was called the "Miner's Friend" as it raised water from the mines using the suction produced by condensing steam. A few years later, an English engineer and partner of Savery named Thomas Newcomen (1663-1729) improved the steam pump by reintroducing the piston. By 1712 he had built an engine that used steam at atmospheric pressure (ordinary boiling water) and which was fairly easy to build. His piston engine was very reliable and came into general use in England around 1725. His machine was called a beam engine because it had a huge rocking-arm or seesaw beam at its top whose motion transferred power from the engine's single cylinder to the water pump.

Understanding how the Newcomen engine worked provides insight into all later steam engines. First, the entire machine was contained in an engine house, about three stories high, out of whose top wall poked out a long oak beam which could rock up and down. The house was constructed off to the side of the mine shaft. At the bottom of the shaft was the water pump which was connected to the engine by a long pump-rod. Below the beam inside the house was a long brass cylinder which sat atop a brick boiler. The boiler was fed by coal and supplied the steam. Inside the cylinder was the piston which could slide up and down and which was connected to the beam above. The engine always started with the piston in the up position. Then steam filled the cylinder from an open valve. When filled, the cylinder was sprayed with water which caused the steam inside to condense into water and create a partial vacuum. With this, the pressure of the outside air would force the piston down which rocked the beam and pulled up the pump rods and sucking up about 12 gallons (45 liters) of water. The piston then returned to its starting position (up) in the cylinder and the process was repeated. Besides being called a beam engine, Newcomen's engine was also called an atmospheric engine since it used air pressure to move the piston (down).

The most important improvement in steam engine design was brought about by the Scottish engineer James Watt (1736-1819). In 1763, Watt was asked to repair a Newcomen engine and was struck by what he considered its inefficiency. He set out to improve its performance and by 1769 had arrived at the conclusion that if the steam were condensed separately from the cylinder, the latter could always be kept hot. That year he introduced a steam engine with a separate condenser. Since this kept the heating and cooling processes separate, his machine could work constantly without any long pause at each cycle to reheat the cylinder. Watt continued to improve his engine and made three additions that were highly significant. First, he made it double-acting by allowing steam to enter alternately on either side of the piston. This allowed the engine to work rapidly and deliver power on the downward as well as on the upward piston stroke. Second, he devised his sun-and-planet gearing which was able to translate the reciprocal or to-and-fro motion of the beam into rotary motion. Third, he added a centrifugal governor which maintained a constant engine speed despite varying loads. This highly innovative device marks the early beginnings of automation since Watt had created a system that was essentially self-regulating. Watt also devised a pressure gauge which he added to his engine. By 1790, Watt's improved steam engines offered a powerful, reliable power source that could be located almost anywhere. This meant that factories no longer had to be sited next to water sources but could be built closer to both their raw materials and transport systems. More than anything, it was Watt's steam engine that speeded up the Industrial Revolution both in England and the rest of the world.

Watt's steam engine was not perfect however, and did have one major limitation. It used steam at low pressure. High pressure steam meant greater power from smaller engines, but it also meant extreme danger since explosions of poorly-made boilers were common. The first to show any real success with it was the English inventor Richard Trevithick (1771-1833). By the end of the 18th century, metallurgical techniques were improving and Trevithick believed he could build a sys-

tem that would handle steam under high pressure. By 1803 Trevithick had built a powerful, high-pressure engine that he used to power a train. His technical innovations were truly remarkable, but high-pressure engines had earned such a bad reputation in England that twenty years would pass before English inventor George Stephenson (1781-1848) would prove their worth with his own locomotives. In the United States however, there was little bias against or hardly any knowledge of steam power. Toward the end of the 18th century, Evans began work on a high-pressure steam engine that he could use as a stationary engine for industrial purposes and for land and water transport. By 1801 he had built a stationary engine that he used to crush limestone. His major high-pressure innovation was placing both the cylinder and the crankshaft at the same end of the beam instead of at opposite ends. This allowed him to use a much lighter beam. Over the years, Evans built some 50 steam engines which were not only used in factories but also to power an amphibious digger. High-pressure steam ran this odd-looking scow which was a dredge that could move on land as well as in water. It was the first powered road vehicle to operate in the United States. Despite Evans' hard work and real genius, his innovative efforts with steam met with little real success during his lifetime. He was often met with indifference or simple reluctance on the part of manufacturers to change their old ways and convert to steam. His use of steam for land propulsion was set back by poor roads, vested interest in horses, and woefully inadequate materials. After Evans, high-pressure steam became widely used in America, unlike England where Watt's low-pressure engines took a long time to be replaced. But improvements were made nonetheless, and iron would eventually replace timber in engine construction, and horizontal engines came to be even more efficient than the old, vertical ones.

The workings of a steam engine

Throughout all of this development and improvement of the steam engine, no one really knew the science behind it. Basically, all of this work had been accomplished on an empirical basis without reference to any theory. It was not until 1824 that this situation changed with the publication of *Reflexions sur La Puissance Motrice du Feu* by the French physicist, Nicolas Leonard Sadi Carnot (1796-1832). In his book *On the Motive Power of Fire*, Carnot founded the science of thermodynamics (or heat movement) and was the first to consider quantitatively the manner in which heat and work are related. Defining work as "weight lifted through a height," he attempted to determine how efficient or how much "work" a Watt engine could pro-

KEY TERMS
. . . .

Condenser—An instrument for compressing air or gases.

Cylinder—The chamber of an engine in which the piston moves.

Governor—A mechanical regulating device that functions automatically and allows for self-regulation of an engine's speed.

Piston—A sliding piece that is moved by or moves against fluid pressure within a cylindrical vessel or chamber.

duce. Carnot was able to prove that there was a maximum theoretical limit to the efficiency of any engine, and that this depended upon the temperature difference in the engine. He showed that for high efficiency, steam must pass through a wide temperature range as it expands within the engine. Highest efficiency is achieved by using a low condenser temperature and a high boiler pressure. Steam was successfully adapted to power boats in 1802 and railways in 1829. Later, some of the first automobiles were powered by steam, and in the 1880s, the English engineer Charles A. Parsons (1854-1931) produced the first steam turbine. This high-powered, highly efficient turbine could produce not only mechanical energy but electrical energy as well. By 1900, the steam engine had evolved into a highly sophisticated and powerful engine that propelled huge ships the oceans and ran turbogenerators that supplied electricity.

Once the dominant power source, steam engines eventually declined in popularity as other power sources became available. Although there were more than 60,000 steam cars made in the U. S. between 1897 and 1927, the steam engine eventually gave way to the internal combustion engine for vehicle propulsion. Today, interest in steam has revived somewhat as improvements make it increasingly efficient and its low-pollution factors make it more attractive.

See also Diesel engine; Internal combustion engine; Jet engine.

Further Reading:

Hindle, Brooke and Steven Lubar. *Engines of Change.* Washington: Smithsonian Institution Press, 1986.

Rutland, Jonathan. *The Age of Steam.* New York: Random House, 1987.

Leonard C. Bruno

Steam pressure sterilizer

Steam pressure sterilization requires a combination of pressure, high temperatures and moisture, and serves as one of the most widely used methods for sterilization where these functions will not effect a load. The simplest example of a steam pressure sterilizer is a home pressure cooker, though it is not recommended for accurate sterilization. Its main component is a chamber or vessel in which items for sterilization are sealed and subjected to high temperatures for a specified length of time, known as a cycle.

Steam pressure sterilizer has replaced the term autoclave for all practical purposes, though autoclaving is still used to describe the process of sterilization by steam. The function of the sterilizer is to kill unwanted microorganisms on instruments, in cultures, and even in liquids, because the presence of foreign microbes might negatively effect the outcome of a test, or the purity of a sample. A sterilizer also acts as a test vehicle for industrial products such as plastics that must withstand certain pressures and temperatures.

Larger chambers are typically lined with a metal jacket, creating a pocket to trap pressurized steam. This method preheats the chamber to reduce condensation and cycle time. Surrounding the unit with steam-heated tubes produces the same effect. Steam is then introduced by external piping or, in smaller units, by internal means, and begins to circulate within the chamber. While steam is lighter than air it quickly builds enough mass to displace it, forcing interior air and any air-steam mixtures out of a trap or drain.

Most sterilization processes require temperatures higher than that of boiling water (212°F) which it is not sufficient to kill microorganisms, so pressure is increased within the chamber to increase temperature. For example, at 15 psi the temperature rises to 250°F. Many clinical applications require a cycle of 20 minutes at this temperature for effective sterilization. Cycle variables can be adjusted to meet the requirements of a given application. The introduction of a vacuum can further increase temperature and reduce cycle time by quickly removing air from the chamber. The process of steam sterilization is kept in check by pressure and temperature gauges, as well as a safety valve that automatically vents the chamber should the internal pressure build beyond the unit's capacity.

Further Reading:

Gardner, Joan F. and Peel Margaret M. *Introduction to Sterilization and Disinfection.* Melbourne: Churchill Livingstone, 1986

The structure of a steam pressure sterilizer.

Reichert, Marimargaret and Young, Jack H., eds. *Sterilization Technology for the Health Care Facility.* Maryland: Aspen Publishers, 1993.

Webster, John G., ed. *Encyclopedia of Medical Devices and Instrumentation.* New York: John Wiley & Sons, 1988.

Stearic acid

Stearic acid is a saturated fatty acid and a major ingredient in mammalian fats. Stearic acid is also known as octadecanoic acid, a name derived from the Latin word *octadeca*, meaning eighteen, indicating the number of carbon atoms in the molecule. Stearic acid occurs abundantly in natural fats and oils, and has the highest molecular weight among the saturated fatty acids. It is a waxy solid that melts at 93.3°F (69.6°C) to form an oily liquid. It is water insoluble but will dissolve in many organic solvents (e.g., chloroform, ether, hexane, etc.).

As a fatty acid, stearic acid belongs to the broad family of lipids and serves several vital functions in the human body. Stearic acid is not an essential fatty acid. Humans and animals can synthesize this saturated fatty acid through anabolism—a process by which simple substances are assimilated into bio-polymers, the more complex materials of living systems. Once it is synthesized, stearic acid becomes the building blocks of phospholipids and glycolipids.

The major physiological importance of stearic acid is its caloric content, stored in the form of glycolipids. This amounts to a complex physiological reservoir which is an energy source for the body's vital needs. When the body needs energy, a message is sent by the physiological control system and the process of catabolism (the opposite of anabolism) is initiated. The glycolipids are hydrolyzed, then they are broken down into smaller and smaller fractions all the way down to two carbon fragments.

Another important function of stearic acid is its contribution to the complex role of the cell membrane. Phospholipids, which are built from stearic acid molecules, are the major constituent of the cell membrane. Stearic acid and other fatty acids provide suitable solvents for fat-soluble vitamins, such as vitamins A, D, and E. They are also protective insulators against heat loss.

See also Fatty acids; Lipid.

Steel

Steel is the most widely used of all metals with uses ranging from concrete reinforcement in highways and in high-rise buildings to automobiles, aircraft, and vehicles in space. Steel is iron combined or alloyed with other metals or nonmetals such as carbon. Steel is more ductile (able to deform without breakage) and durable than cast iron and is generally forged, rolled, or drawn into various shapes.

Since the beginning of the Iron Age, about 1000 B.C., mankind's progress has been greatly dependent on tools and equipment made with iron. The iron tools were then used to fashion many other much needed goods. Eventually this was followed by the Industrial Revolution, a period of change beginning in the middle of the eighteenth century in England where extensive mechanization of production systems resulted in a shift from home manufacturing and farms to large-scale factory production. Machine tools and other equipment made of iron and steel significantly changed the economy of both farm and city.

The history of iron and steel began at least 6,000 years ago. It is speculated that early mankind first learned to use iron from fallen meteorites. Many meteorites are composed of iron and nickel which forms a much harder metal than pure iron. The ancients could make crude tools and weapons by hammering and chipping this metal. Because this useful metal came from the heavens, early human beings probably did not associate it with the iron found in the ground. It is likely that metallic iron was found in the ashes of fires that had been built on outcroppings of red iron ore, also called iron oxide. The red ore was called paint rock, and fires were built against banks of ore that had been exposed to wind and weather. Iron ore is found worldwide on each of the seven continents.

Smelting iron, a primitive direct reduction method of separating iron from its ore using a charcoal forge or furnace, probably began in China and India and then spread westward to the area around the Black Sea. Unlike copper ores, which yielded molten copper in these furnaces, iron would not melt at temperatures below 2,799°F (1,537°C) and the highest temperature that could be reached in these primitive smelters appears to have been about 2,192°F (1,200°C). Iron ore subjected to that temperature does not melt but instead results in a spongy mass (called "sponge" iron) mixed with impurities called slag. The iron worker removed this spongy mass from the furnace and then squeezed the slag out of it by hammering. This "wrought" iron had less tendency to corrode and had a fibrous quality from the stringers of slag which gave it a certain toughness.

The Hittites, an ancient tribe living in Asia Minor and northern Syria, produced iron starting about 2500 B.C.. The Chalybes, a subject tribe of the Hittites, invented a cementation process about 1400 B.C. to make the iron stronger. The iron was hammered and heated in contact with charcoal. The carbon absorbed from the charcoal produced a much harder iron. With the fall of the Hittite empire, the various tribes scattered carrying the knowledge of smelting and the cementation process with them to Syria, Egypt, and Macedonia. Widespread use of iron for weapons and tools began about 1000 B.C. marking the beginning of the Iron Age.

The ancient Egyptians learned to increase smelting temperature in the furnace by blowing a stream of air into the fire using blowpipes and bellows. The Greek soldiers around 500 B.C. used iron weapons which had been hardened by quenching the hot metal in cold water. The Romans learned to reheat the iron after quenching in a process called tempering which made the iron less brittle.

During the Middle Ages, from about 500 A.D. to 1500 A.D., the old methods of smelting and cementation continued. Early blacksmiths made chain mail, weapons, nails, horseshoes, and tools such as iron plows. The *Stückofen*, a furnace first developed by the Romans, was made larger and higher for better air draft. This was a forerunner of the modern blast furnace. Waterwheels came into use for ironmaking between

1200 A.D. and 1350 A.D. The waterwheels converted the energy of swift stream currents into work which moved air bellows that forced blasts of air into the furnace. The resulting higher temperature melted the iron, which was then formed into "pigs" (so named because as the pig iron was cast, the runners and series of ingots resembled pigs suckling their mother) of cast iron. As time progressed, these early blast furnaces were built larger and better, reaching 30 ft (9 m) in height and able to operate continuously for weeks at a time.

Ironmakers about 1500 A.D. faced wood shortages which affected their source of charcoal. Increased warfare and the resulting demand for more iron weapons forced ironmakers to use coal as an alternate source of fuel. A major problem with coal was that it contained impurities such as sulfur and phosphorus which tended to make the iron brittle. In 1709 Abraham Darby, of England, used "coke," the residue left after soft coal was heated to remove impurities, to successfully smelt pig iron. Crucible cast steel was invented around 1740 by Benjamin Huntsman of England. A clay crucible, or cup, of iron ore was placed in a furnace and when molten, was cast. The resulting cast steel was of very high purity since the molten steel did not come into contact with the fuel. In 1784 another improvement was made by Henry Cort, an English ironmaker, who invented the puddling of molten pig iron. Puddling involved stirring air into the liquid iron by a worker who stood near the furnace door. A reverberatory furnace was used in which the coal was separated from the iron to prevent contamination. After the pig iron had been converted into wrought iron, it was run through a rolling mill which used grooved rollers to press out the remaining slag. Cort's rolling mill was patented in 1783 and could make iron bars about 15 times faster than the old hammer method.

From 1850 to 1865 great advances were made in iron and steel processing. Steel was gaining more popularity than iron beginning around 1860 as less expensive manufacturing methods were discovered and greater quantity and quality were being produced.

William Kelly of the United States, and Henry Bessemer of England, both working independently, discovered the same method for converting iron into steel. They subjected molten pig iron to a blast of air which burned out most of the impurities and the carbon contained in the molten iron acted as its own fuel. Kelly built his first converter in 1851 and received an American patent in 1857. He also went bankrupt the same year and the method finally became known as the Bessemer process. In 1856 Bessemer completed his vertical converter, and in 1860 he patented a tilting converter which could be tilted to receive molten iron from the furnace and also to pour out its load of liquid steel. The Bessemer converter made possible the high tonnage production of steel for ships, railroads, bridges, and large buildings in the mid-nineteenth century. However, the steel was brittle from the many impurities which remained, especially phosphorus and sulfur, and by the oxygen from the air blast. An English metallurgist, Robert F. Mushet, discovered in 1856 that adding an iron alloy (spiegeleisen) containing manganese would remove the oxygen. Around 1875 Sidney G. Thomas and Percy Gilchrist, two English chemists, discovered that by adding limestone to the converter they could remove the phosphorus and most of the sulfur.

In England another new furnace was introduced in 1861 by two brothers, William and Frederick Siemans. This was the open-hearth furnace, also known as the regenerative open-hearth because the outgoing hot gases were used to preheat the incoming air. Pierre Émile Martin of France improved the process in 1864 by adding scrap steel to the molten iron to speed purification. During this period hardened alloy steels came into commercial use; Mushet made a high carbon steel in 1868 which gave tools longer life, in France a chromium steel alloy was produced in 1877 and a nickel steel alloy in 1888. An Englishman, Sir Robert Hadfield, discovered in 1882 how to harden manganese tool steel by heating it to a high temperature and then quenching it in water.

Around 1879 the electric furnace was developed by William Siemans. This furnace was used very little prior to 1910 because of the high electrical costs and the poor quality of electrodes used to produce the arc for melting.

The open-hearth furnace was the most popular method of steel production until the early 1950s. Pure oxygen became more economical to produce in large quantities and in 1954 the first basic oxygen process facility opened for production in the United States. Today most of the world's steel is made by either a basic oxygen furnace or an electric furnace.

Raw materials

The ores used in making iron and steel are iron oxides, which are compounds of iron and oxygen. The major iron oxide ores are hematite, which is the most plentiful, limonite, also called brown ore, taconite, and magnetite, a black ore. Magnetite is named for its magnetic property and has the highest iron content. Taconite, named for the Taconic Mountains in the northeastern United States, is a low-grade, but important ore, which contains both magnetite and hematite.

Ironmaking furnaces require at least a 50% iron content ore for efficient operation. Also, the cost of shipping iron ores from the mine to the smelter can be greatly reduced if the unwanted rock and other impurities can be removed prior to shipment. This requires that the ores undergo several processes called "beneficiation." These processes include crushing, screening, tumbling, floatation, and magnetic separation. The refined ore is enriched to over 60% iron by these processes and is often formed into pellets before shipping. Taconite ore powder, after beneficiation, is mixed with coal dust and a binder and rolled into small balls in a drum pelletizer where it is then baked to hardness. About two tons of unwanted material is removed for each ton of taconite pellets shipped.

The three raw materials used in making pig iron (which is the raw material needed to make steel) are the processed iron ore, coke (residue left after heating coal in the absence of air, generally contains up to 90% carbon) and limestone ($CaCO_3$) or burnt lime (CaO) which are added to the blast furnace at intervals, making the process continuous. The limestone or burnt lime is used as a fluxing material which forms a slag on top of the liquid metal. This has an oxidizing effect on the liquid metal underneath which helps to remove impurities. Approximately two tons of ore, one ton of coke, and a half ton of limestone are required to produce one ton of iron.

There are several basic elements which can be found in all commercial steels. Carbon is a very important element in steel since it allows the steel to be hardened by heat treatment. Only a small amount of carbon is needed to produce steel: up to .25% for low carbon steel, .25-.50% for medium carbon steel, and .50-1.25% for high carbon steel. Steel can contain up to 2% carbon, but over that amount it is considered to be cast iron, in which the excess carbon forms graphite. The metal manganese is used in small amounts (.03-1.0%) to remove unwanted oxygen and to control sulfur. Sulfur is difficult to remove from steel and the form it takes in steel (iron sulfide, FeS) allows the steel to become brittle, or *hot-short*, when forged or rolled at elevated temperatures. Sulfur content in commercial steels is usually kept below .05%. A small quantity of phosphorus (usually below .04%) is present which tends to dissolve in the iron slightly increasing the strength and hardness. Phosphorus in larger quantities reduces the ductility or formability of steel and can cause the material to crack when cold worked in a rolling mill, making it *cold-short*. Silicon is another element present in steel, usually between .05-.3%. The silicon dissolves in the iron and increases the strength and toughness of the steel without greatly reducing ductility. The silicon also deoxidizes the molten steel through the formation of silicon dioxide (SiO_2) which makes for stronger, less porous castings. Another element which plays an important part in the processing of steel is oxygen. Some large steel mills have installed their own oxygen plants, which are located near basic oxygen furnaces. Oxygen injected into the mix or furnace "charge" improves and speeds up steel production.

Steel can be given many different and useful properties by alloying the iron with other metals such as chromium, molybdenum, nickel, aluminum, cobalt, tungsten, vanadium, and titanium, and with nonmetals such as boron and silicon.

Manufacturing processes

Most steel is produced using one of four methods: Bessemer converters, open-hearth furnaces, basic oxygen furnaces, and electric furnaces. The basic oxygen process is the most efficient while the Bessemer and open-hearth methods have become obsolete. Electric furnaces are used to produce high quality steels from selected steel scrap, lime, and mill scale (an iron oxide that forms on the surface of hot steel and falls off as black scale).

Until 1909, most steel made in the United States came from Bessemer converters. A Bessemer converter looks like a huge pear-shaped pot and can hold anywhere from 5-25 tons. It is balanced on axles so that its open top can be tilted one way to take a charge and the other way to pour out steel. After the converter is charged with hot metal, it is swung to the upright position. Air is then blown through holes in its bottom at a typical rate of 30,000 cubic feet per minute. Sparks and thick, brown smoke pour from the converter's mouth as the oxygen in the blow combines with the iron, silicon, and manganese to form slag. Then 30-ft (9-m) flames replace the smoke as the oxygen combines with the carbon fuel and burns. The whole process took less than 15 minutes. Unfortunately, the blowing air contained contaminants (such as nitrogen) and also removed some desirable elements such as carbon and manganese. This was solved by adding the necessary elements back into the converter after the blow. Because of stricter air pollution regulations and more efficient processes, the Bessemer converter is no longer used.

From 1909 until the 1960s, the open-hearth process was the most popular method of steel production. Open-hearth furnaces got their name from a shallow area called a hearth that is exposed to a blast of flames that alternately sweeps across the hearth from one side for a period of time and then from the other side of the furnace. To make a "heat," or one batch of steel, pig iron, limestone, and scrap steel, are initially "charged" or loaded into the hearth. These materials are heated for about two hours at temperatures 2,700-3,000°F (1,482-1,649°C) until they begin to fuse. Then the furnace is charged with many tons of molten pig iron. Scrap is placed in the furnace with a charging machine which usually serves a series of open hearth furnaces in a single building. Other elements, such as fluxing agents, carbon (usually in the form of anthracite coal pellets), and alloying materials, are then added to improve the steel. These elements can be added either in the furnace charge, the melt or "bath," ladle, or the ingot molds to meet the desired chemical composition of the finished steel or to eliminate or counteract the effect of oxides or other impurities. Fluxing agents (primarily lime, added in the form of either limestone or burnt lime and supplemented by magnesia, MgO, and lime from the furnace bottom and sides) melt and combine with the impurities to form slag at the top of the melt which is poured off into a separate slag pot. Mill scale, a form of iron oxide (Fe_3O_4), is used to reduce carbon content. Aluminum ferrosilicon is added if the steel is to be "killed." A killed steel is one that has been deoxidized to prevent gas evolution in the ingot mold, making a more uniform steel. "Rimmed" steel is steel that has not been deoxidized and gas pockets and holes from free oxygen form in the center of the ingot while the rim near the surface of the ingot is free of defects. Rolling processes are used in later operations to remove these defects. Semikilled steels are a compromise between rimmed and killed steels and is mainly limited to steels to be rolled into sheet bar, plate, and structural sections. The quantity of deoxidizers used must be closely controlled to allow a limited evolution of gas from the carbon-oxygen reaction.

When the contents of the heat are acceptable and the temperature is right, the furnace is tapped and the molten metal is poured into a ladle. An open-hearth furnace is tapped through a hole in the furnace's bottom. A heat is refined into steel during an 8-12 hour time period. Oxygen released from the ore and additional injected oxygen combine with carbon in the molten pig iron to form carbon gases. These, along with any additional gases from the burned fuel, are used to heat incoming air and this is why the open-hearth process is sometimes called the regenerative open-hearth.

The basic oxygen converter resembles a Bessemer converter. It receives materials from the top and tips to pour off the finished steel into ladles. The main element is a water-cooled oxygen lance, which is placed into the top of the converter after it is charged with scrap steel, molten pig iron, and fluxing agents. The lance, lowered to within a few feet of the charge, directs high-purity oxygen at supersonic speeds into the molten metal. This burns out the impurities and also enables the making of steel with a minimum amount of nitrogen, which can make steel brittle. The oxidation of the carbon and impurities causes a violent rolling agitation which brings all the metal into contact with the oxygen stream. The furnace ladle is first tipped to remove slag and then rotated to pour molten steel into a ladle. The speed and efficiency of the oxygen process has had a significant impact on the steel industry. An oxygen converter can produce a heat of quality steel in 30-45 minutes. An open-hearth furnace without an oxygen lance requires as much as eight hours to produce steel of a similar quality. Recent advances in refractory "brick," the insulating ceramics that protect vessels from the hot steel, have allowed injection of oxygen from the bottom of a vessel without a large complicated lance. This allows for a much more efficient use of the oxygen and can lower the capital costs in constructing a basic oxygen facility, especially if the building and cranes of a retired open-hearth facility is used.

High-quality carbon and alloy steels, such as tool and stainless steels, are produced in electric arc furnaces. These furnaces can make 150-200 tons in a single heat in as little as 90 minutes. The charge is melted by the arcing between carbon electrodes and high quality scrap steel. Some of the electrodes can be 2 ft (0.6 m) in diameter and 24 ft (7.2 m) long. The entire electric furnace is tilted during a tapping operation in which molten steel flows into a waiting ladle. Electric furnaces are the most competitive where low-cost electricity is available and where very little coal or iron ore is found.

After the steel in the ladle has cooled to the desired temperature, the ladle is moved by a traveling crane to either a pouring platform for ingot production or to a continuous caster. Ingots may be square, rectangular, or round and weigh anywhere from a few hundred pounds to 40 tons. A small amount of steel is cast directly into the desired shape in molds of fine sand and fireclay. Small rail cars carrying a series of heavy cast iron ingot molds wait alongside the pouring platform. The steel is "teemed" or poured into the molds through a fire-clay nozzle in the bottom of the ladle. After the steel in the molds has solidified, the cars are pulled under a stripping crane. The crane's plunger holds down the ingot top as its jaws lift the mold from the glowing hot ingot. The ingots are then taken to soaking pits for further processing.

An underground soaking pit is used to heat the steel ingots to a uniform temperature throughout. The ingots must be the same temperature throughout so that they can be easily plastically deformed and to prevent damage to the heavy machinery of the mills. The jaws of the crane clamp onto the ingots and lower them into the open soaking pits. The roof of the pits is then closed and burning oil or gas heats the ingots to about 2,200°F (1,200°C). After "soaking" in the pits for several hours, the ingots are then lifted out by crane and transported by rail to the blooming and slabbing mills.

The mechanical working of steel, such as rolling, forging, hammering, or squeezing, improves it in several ways. Cavities and voids are closed, harmful concentrations of nonmetallic impurities are broken up and more evenly disbursed, and the grain structure is refined to produce a more homogeneous or uniform product. Some ingots are sent directly to a universal plate mill for immediate rolling of steel plates. Most ingots, however, are sent to semifinishing mills (also known as slabbing or blooming mills) for reduction and shaping into slabs, blooms, or billets. A slab is generally a large flat length of steel wider than a bloom, a bloom is a length of steel either square or rectangular with a cross-sectional area larger than 36 inches (90 cm), and a billet is generally two to five inches square, although some billets can be round or rectangular. The exact sizes of slabs, blooms, and billets depend on the requirements of further processing.

In slabbing and blooming mills, the steel ingot is gradually squeezed between heavy rolls. To make billets, the steel is first shaped into blooms, then further reduced in a billet mill. Each time the ingot is forced through the rolls, it is further reduced in one dimension. Blooming mills can be classified as either two-high or three-high, depending on the number of rolls used. The two rolls of the two-high mill can be reversed so that the ingot is flattened and lengthened as it passes back and forth between the rolls. The top and bottom rolls of the three-high mill turn in one direction while the middle roll turns in the opposite direction. The ingot is flattened first between the bottom and middle rolls and ends up on a runout table. The table rises and the steel is then fed through the top and middle rolls. The continuous, or cross-country, mill is a third type of blooming mill. This mill has a series of two-high rolls. As many as 15 passes may be required to reduce an ingot 21 in^2 (135 cm^2) in cross section to a bloom 8 in^2 (52 cm^2) in cross section. The two and three-high blooming mills roll the top and bottom of the steel in every pass. After one or two passes, mechanical manipulators on the runout table turn the steel to bring the side surfaces under the rolls for a more uniform material. After the steel is rolled, the uneven ends are sheared off, and the single long piece is cut into shorter lengths. The sheared off ends are reused as scrap. Most of the rolls used in these mills are horizontal, but there are also vertical

rolls which squeeze the blooms or slabs from the sides. High-pressure water jets are used to remove mill scale which forms on the surface. Surface defects on the finished blooms and slabs are burned off, or scarfed, with an oxygen flame. The hot lengths of steel are moved from one station to another on a series of roller conveyors. The mill operations are automatically controlled by workers in an overhead glass-enclosed room called a "pulpit."

The slabs, blooms, and billets are then taken to finishing mills where they are formed into special shapes and forms such as bars, beams, plates, and sheets. The steel is still not completely "finished" but it is closer to the form in which it will eventually be used in manufactured goods. Blooms and billets are finished into rails, wire rods, wires, bars, tubes, seamless pipe, and structural shapes such as I and H beams. Slabs are converted into plates, sheets, strips, and welded pipe.

After they are hot rolled, steel plates or shapes undergo further processing such as cleaning and pickling by chemicals to remove surface oxides, cold rolling to improve strength and surface finish, annealing (also known as stress relieving), and coating (galvanizing or aluminizing) for corrosion resistance.

Continuous or "strand" casting of steel eliminates the need to produce ingots and the use of soaking pits. In addition to costing less, continuously cast steels have more uniform compositions and properties than ingot cast steels. Continuous casting of steel produces an endless length of steel which is cut into long slabs or blooms that are ready for shaping in rolling mills. Molten steel is poured into the top of a continuous casting machine and is cooled by passing through a water-cooled mold. Pinch rolls draw the steel downward as it solidifies. Additional cooling is provided by water sprays along the travel path of the solidifying metal. The thickness of the steel "strand" is typically 10 in (25 cm) but new developments have reduced this thickness to 1 in (2.5 cm) or less. The thinner strand reduces the number of rolling operations required and improves the economy of the overall process. Some continuous cast machines bend the steel while it is still hot and flexible so that it comes out of the bottom in a horizontal position. Other machines cut the steel into sections while it is still in a vertical position. The continuous cast process has become the most economical method to produce large quantities of conventional steels. Small heats of alloy and specialty steels are still cast in ingots because the small size makes the continuous cast process impractical.

Some steel shapes are produced from powder. There are several chemical, electrochemical, and

STEEL

mechanical ways to make steel powder. One method involves improving the ore by magnetically separating the iron. A ball mill is then used to grind the ore into a powder which is then purified with hot hydrogen. This powder, under heat and pressure, is pressed into molds to form irregularly shaped objects, objects that would be hard to form any other way.

Quality control

To specify the various physical and mechanical properties of the finished product, various tests, both destructive and nondestructive, are performed. Metallurgical, hardness, hardenability, tension, ductility, compression, fatigue, impact, wear, corrosion, creep, machinability, radiography, magnetic particle, ultrasonic, and eddy current are some of the major tests that are performed by quality control personnel.

Metallurgical testing is used to determine the quality of steel by analyzing the microstructure of a sample under a microscope. A cross section of a sample is first highly polished and then examined at a magnification from 100-500 diameters. The microstructure of steel consists of grains of different compositions and sizes. Generally a sample of steel with fine grains is tougher than one with large grains. Different characteristics are produced through alloying the steel with other substances. It is possible to determine grain size and the size, shape, and distribution of various phases and inclusions (nonmetallic material) which have a great effect on the mechanical properties of the metal. Some grains are made of ferrite, or pure metallic iron; graphite, a crystal form of carbon; pearlite, an alloy of iron of carbon; cementite, also called iron carbide, a hard compound of iron and carbon and other carbide-forming elements; austenite, a solid solution of carbon in gamma iron, a nonmagnetic form of iron; and martensite, an extremely hard constituent of steel produced by heat-treating. The sample can also be etched to make visible many structural characteristics of the metal or alloy by a preferential attack on the different constituents. The microstructure will reveal the mechanical and thermal treatment of the metal, and it may be possible to predict its expected behavior under a given set of conditions.

Hardness is not a fundamental property of a material but is related to elastic and plastic properties. The hardness value obtained in a particular test serves only as a comparison between materials or treatments. The test procedure and sample preparation are fairly simple and the results may be used in estimating other mechanical properties. Rockwell and Brinell are two popular hardness tests that are widely used for inspection and control. These tests are usually performed by impressing into the test specimen, which is resting on a rigid platform, an indenter of fixed and known geometry, under a known static load.

Hardenability is a property that determines the depth and distribution of hardness induced by quenching. The standardized test used is called the end-quench hardenability test, also known as the Jominy test. A 1-in (2.54 cm) round 4-in (10 cm) long sample is heated uniformly to the austenitizing temperature (this temperature depends on the material composition, ranging from 1,500-1,900°F/816-1,038°C). The sample is removed from the furnace and placed on a fixture where a jet of water contacts the bottom face of the sample. After 10 minutes on the fixture, the sample is removed and two flat parallel surfaces are ground on the sample. Rockwell hardness readings are taken along the ground surfaces at certain intervals from the quenched end. The results are expressed as a curve of hardness values versus distance from the quenched end. Plain carbon steels tend to be hard on the surface, near the quenched end, but remain relatively soft at the core, or further away from the quenched end. Alloyed steels, in general, have an increased depth of hardenability which is one of the main advantages of using alloyed steels.

Next to the hardness test, the tensile test is the most frequently performed test to determine certain mechanical properties. A specifically prepared tensile sample is placed in the heads of a testing machine and an axial load is placed on the sample through a hydraulic loading system. The tensile test is used to determine several important material properties such as yield strength, where the material starts to exhibit plastic or permanent deformation, and the ultimate tensile or breaking strength.

Ductility of a material is indicated by the amount of deformation that is possible until fracture and can be determined by measuring elongation and reduction in area of a tensile sample that has been tested to failure.

Compression tests are performed on small cylinders, blocks, or strips to determine the ability of a material to undergo large plastic deformations (a mechanical property also known as malleability) and its limits. Stress-strain relations determined from this testing are used to predict the pressures and forces arising in industrial forming operations such as rolling, forging, or extrusion. Samples are placed between anvils or pressure plates and are compressed (friction is also a factor to consider as the material slides sidewise over the anvils).

The fatigue test is used to determine the behavior of materials when subjected to repeated or fluctuating loads. It is used to simulate stress conditions developed in materials under service conditions. The fatigue potential, or endurance limit, is determined by counting the number of cycles of stress, applied first in one direction and then another, to which the metal can be subjected before it breaks. Fatigue tests can be used to study the material behavior under various types and ranges of fluctuating loads and also the effect of corrosion, surface conditions, temperature, size, and stress concentrations.

Impact tests are used to determine the behavior of materials when subjected to high rates of loading, usually in bending, tension, or torsion. The quantity measured is the energy absorbed in breaking the specimen in one blow, two such tests are called the Charpy and the Izod, which use notched bar specimens. A swinging pendulum of fixed weight raised to a standard height is used to strike the specimen. Some of the energy of the pendulum is used to rupture the specimen so that the pendulum rises to a lower height than the standard height. The weight of the pendulum times the difference in heights indicates the energy absorbed by the specimen, usually measured in foot-pounds.

Wear resistance is represented by few standardized tests because of its complex nature. One test is the "pin on disk" method where a pin is moved against a disk of the test material. Usually wear testing is application specific and the equipment is designed to simulate actual service conditions.

Corrosion involves the destruction of a material by chemical, electrochemical, or metallurgical interaction between the environment and the material. Various types of environmental exposure testing is done to simulate actual use conditions, such as salt bath immersion testing. Zinc coating, or *galvanizing*, is commonly applied to sheet and structural steel used for outdoor applications to protect against corrosion.

Creep tests are used to determine the continuing change in the deformation of a material at elevated temperatures when stressed below the yield strength. This is important in the design of parts exposed to elevated temperatures. Creep may be defined as a continuing slow plastic flow under constant load conditions. A creep test is a tension test run at a constant load and temperature. The percent elongation of the sample is measured over time.

Machinability is the ease with which a metal may be machined. Many factors are considered in arriving at machinability ratings. Some of the more important factors are the rate of metal removal, quality of the finished surface, and tool life. Machinability ratings are expressed as a percentage, in comparison with AISI 1112 steel, which is rated at 100%. Metals which are more difficult to machine have a rating of less than 100% while metals which machine easily have a rating more than 100%.

Radiography of metals involves the use of x rays or gamma rays. The short-wavelength electromagnetic rays are capable of going through large thicknesses of metal and are typically used to nondestructively test castings and welded joints for shrinkage voids and porosity.

Magnetic particle inspection (also called "Magnaflux") is a method of detecting cracks, tears, seams, inclusions, and similar discontinuities in iron and steel. This method will detect surface defects too fine to be seen by the naked eye and will also detect discontinuities just below the surface. The sample is magnetized and then covered with a fine iron powder. The presence of an imperfection is indicated by a pattern that assumes the approximate shape of the defect.

Ultrasonic testing utilizes sound waves above the audible range with a frequency of 1-5 million Hz (cycles per second). Ultrasonics allow for fast, reliable nondestructive testing which employs electronically produced high-frequency sound waves to penetrate metals and other materials at speeds of several thousand feet per second. If there is a flaw in the path of the ultrasonic wave, part of the energy will be reflected and the signal received by a receiving transducer will be reduced. Ultrasonic inspection is used to detect and locate such defects as shrinkage voids, internal cracks, porosity, and large nonmetallic inclusions.

Eddy current inspection is used to inspect electrically conducting materials for defects and variations in composition. Eddy current testing involves placing a varying magnetic field (which is produced by connecting alternating current to a coil) near an electrically conducting sample. Eddy currents are induced in the sample which then produces a magnetic field of its own. A detection unit measures this new magnetic field and converts the signal into a voltage which can be read on a meter for comparison. Properties such as hardness, alloy composition, chemical purity, and heat treat condition influence the magnetic field and may be measured through the use of eddy current testing.

Byproducts/waste

There are a number of waste byproducts from the steel making process. Mine tailings from the ore beneficiation process are returned to the mining site. Growing vetches (a species of plant valuable for fodder), grasses, and trees on some of these barren landscapes has been a project of biologists and foresters. Gases that are given off from the coke ovens, blast furnaces, and steel furnaces are largely recovered for reuse. After use in iron and steelmaking, most slags are used for other purposes such as railroad ballast and road fill, an ingredient in cement or blocks, insulating material, or fertilizer.

The future

In the future there will be many new developments involving computer controls and automation that will improve economy and quality and lower energy consumption and pollution. More automation will also lead to more robots replacing humans in hazardous areas. Computers can be used to control several rolling mills operating as a continuous unit. The decreasing material thickness can be maintained automatically as it passes through the various mills to produce a more uniform final sheet. Continued research and development is ongoing to connect continuous casting machines with rolling mills to provide a single continuous process from molten metal to the final product. This will produce energy and cost savings because the material would not have to be reheated for processing and result in a higher quality end product.

The use of 100% scrap in charging electric furnaces has cut the dependence on pig iron and ores and has resulted in the development of more small steel mills, also called mini-mills, which can be located far from natural resources to serve wider geographical areas.

More net steel shapes will be formed using powder metallurgy as direct reduction processes produce steel powders directly from iron ore, bypassing the blast furnace and making difficult shapes easier to form.

See also Alloy; Iron; Metal production; Metallurgy.

Further Reading:

ASM Publication. *ASM Metals Handbook Vol. 1: Properties and Selection: Irons, Steels, and High Performance Alloys.*

Hudson, Ray and Sadler, David. *The International Steel Industry.* Routledge, 1989.

Kalpakjian, Serope. *Manufacturing Processes for Engineering Materials, 2nd Ed.* Addison-Wesley Publishing, 1991.

Walsh, Ronald A. *McGraw-Hill Machining and Metalworking Handbook.* McGraw-Hill, Inc., 1994.

Steenbok see **Dwarf antelopes**

Stellar evolution

Since stars shine, they must change. The energy they lose by shining must come from the stuff of which the star is made. This will lead to a change in its composition. Thus stars are formed from the material between stars, shine until they exhaust their fuel, and then must end their existence. The changes that occur during a star's life are called stellar evolution. The material between stars occurs in clouds of varying mass. By processes that are still not completely clear, but involve cooling of the cloud-center with the formation of molecules, and the squeezing of the cloud by outside star light or perhaps a stellar explosion, the cloud begins to collapse under its own self gravity. The collapse of the cloud results in the material becoming hotter simply from the squeezing of the collapse. At this point, the interior of the star churns like a pot of boiling water. This churning process we call convection. Its rate of collapse is determined by the rate at which it can lose energy from its surface. Atomic processes keep the surface near a constant temperature so that a rapid collapse is slowed by the radiating surface area shrinking during the collapse. The star simply gets fainter while the interior gets progressively hotter.

Finally, the internal temperature rises to the point where atoms located at the center of the star, where the temperature is the hottest, are moving so fast from the heat that they begin to stick together. We call this process nuclear fusion, and it results in an additional production of energy. Thus the star has a new source of heat. The subsequent evolution of the star will be largely determined by its mass.

If the mass of the star is about like that of the sun or less the nuclear "fires" which now provide the energy for the star to shine will determine its internal structure. A central radiative core is surrounded by a convective envelope. In the radiative core the material remains quiescent while energy generated by nuclear fusion of hydrogen to helium simply diffuses through it like the light from auto headlights shines through a fog. It is at the very center of this radiative core that the helium "ash" of the nuclear "fires" accumulates as the star ages. Beyond the radiative core lies the churning convective envelope through which the energy is carried by blobs of hot matter rising past returning cooler blobs. At the atmospheric surface the energy again flows as it did in the core until it physically leaves the star as starlight.

The structure of stars more than twice the mass of the sun is essentially the reverse of the low mass stars. The cores of these stars are fully convective so that the energy produced by nuclear fusion is carried outward by the churning motion of the material in the core. The surrounding radiative envelope behaves much like the cores of lower mass stars except no new energy is produced there. The churning motion of the material in the convective core causes the nuclear ash of helium to be well mixed with the surrounding hydrogen fuel. This motion ensures that virtually all the hydrogen will be available to nuclear fires which heat the star.

Both high and low mass stars respond to the depletion of hydrogen fuel in a similar manner. In order to supply the heat to oppose its own self gravity, the star's core again responds by shrinking. In sort of a reflex reaction, the outer regions of the star expand causing a great increase of its radiating surface area. Although the total energy output of the star increases during this phase, the greatly enhanced surface area results in a cooling of the surface and star takes on a redder appearance. The size and color change lead to the name of red giant for these stars. Indeed, if the star is very massive, it may become what is called a red supergiant.

For the low mass stars the expansion to the red giant phase will begin when about 90% of its hydrogen has been converted to helium. During the contraction of its core a complicated sequence of events occurs. The shrinkage required to produce the energy radiated by the large giant causes the core to shrink to the dimensions of a white dwarf while hydrogen continues to burn by nuclear fusion in a thin shell surrounding the core. It is this shell that provides most of the energy that is radiated away by the star. However, the core material having attained the dimensions of a white dwarf behaves very differently than the high density gas that it was earlier in its life. No longer must it be heated to generate the pressure required to oppose the weight of the overlying material. When matter reaches this state we call it degenerate matter. The degenerate core just sits there, becoming hotter from the energy released by the surrounding hydrogen-burning shell, and growing slowly from the helium ash generated by the shell. The hydrogen burning shell is required to produce increasing amounts of energy from decreasing amounts of hydrogen fuel to sustain the brightening red giant. This continuing increase in the energy output from the shell heats the core, which finally reaches a temperature where the helium begins to undergo nuclear reactions producing carbon. In this fusion process three helium nuclei collide yielding one carbon nucleus and additional energy for the support of the star. The star now has a new energy source. However, the degenerate nature of the core doesn't allow it to expand and cool as would a core made of ordinary gas. Thus the onset of helium burning leads to a rapid rise in core temperature which is not balanced by a cooling expansion. The increased core temperature leads to a dramatic increase in helium burning. This sequence is known as the helium flash which continues until the degeneracy of the material making up the core is removed by the intense heat. The return of the material to its ordinary gaseous state leads to a rapid expansion which cools the core and reduces the helium burning. An equilibrium is established with the star generating progressively more energy from helium fusion while the energy from the hydrogen burning shell is reduced and it ultimately goes out from lack of fuel. The star continues to shine through the red giant phase by converting helium into carbon through nuclear fusion. As the helium becomes depleted, the outer layers of the star become unstable and rather gently lift off the star to be slowly blown away by the light from the star. We see such shells of expanding gas as greenish disks which eventually become greenish rings and the material becomes less dense. These greenish clouds are called planetary nebulae even though they have nothing whatever to do with planets. Astronomers of two centuries ago gave them that name for their telescopic appearance was like that of the outer planets Uranus and Neptune. The remaining core of the red giant, now exposed, cools rapidly, again becomes degenerate and is known as a white dwarf. A white dwarf has reached a stalemate between its own self gravity and the nature of the degenerate stuff of which it is now composed. It may now simply cool off to become a dark stellar cinder about the size of the earth.

The evolution of a massive stars follows a somewhat different course. The churning of the convective core makes most of the hydrogen fuel available for consumption in the nuclear fires. Thus these stars will not suffer the effects of core contraction until more than 99.9% of their hydrogen has been consumed. Even though they can consume more of their hydrogen, on a percentage basis, and they have more fuel to burn, they also shine much brighter than the low mass stars. Thus their over all lifetimes will be far less than the low mass stars. While the lifetime of a star like the sun may approach 10 billion years, a star with ten times the mass of the sun may last less than 10 million years.

The exhaustion of the hydrogen convective core leads to its contraction and the expansion of the outer layers as was the case with the low mass stars. However, the fate of the core is rather different from that of the low mass stars. The core is far too massive to reach equilibrium as a degenerate structure like a white dwarf so that contraction continues heating the core until the ignition of helium fusion is achieved. Unlike the lower mass stars where the onset of helium burning occurs with a flash, the helium fusion in massive stars begins

KEY TERMS

Convective core—The central, or surrounding regions of a star where the energy is carried by envelope convection. Convective transport of energy is the same as that found in a pan of boiling water where hot material physically rises, carrying energy and having deposited that energy at the top of the region descends as cooler material.

Deflagration—The explosive onset of nuclear fusion leading to the disruption of the reaction structure.

Degenerate gas—A gas whose constituents are packed to such high densities that further packing would violate the Pauli Exclusion Principle. The pressure of such a gas exhibits almost no dependence on temperature.

Ideal gas—Gas which obeys the Ideal Gas Law where the pressure is proportional to the product of the local temperature and density.

Neutrino—A small nuclear particle resulting from nuclear reactions. Neutrinos interact poorly with ordinary matter and can easily traverse a normal star without colliding with any of the stellar material.

Neutron—Together with protons, neutrons comprise the basic building blocks of the nuclei of the elements. They have a mass close to that of a proton, but lack its electric charge.

Neutron star—This is a star with a mass similar to the sun, but composed almost entirely of neutrons. The neutrons are packed so tightly that they are degenerate like the electrons of a white dwarf, but the resulting density is far greater. The typical size of such a star is about 6.2 mi (10 km).

Nuclear fusion—The combining of the nuclei of two elements so as to produce an new more massive element. The process is accompanied by the release of energy as long as the end product of the reaction is less massive than iron.

Planetary nebula—An expanding shell of gas ejected by a low mass red giant which may take on the appearance of one of the outer planets of the solar system when seen in a small telescope.

Radiative core—The central, or surrounding regions of a star where the energy is carried by envelope radiative diffusion. Radiative diffusion describes the flow of particles of light (photons) through a medium where there is little mechanical change to the medium.

Supernova—The term describes the cataclysmic destruction of a star at the end of its nuclear evolution.

White dwarf—This star is comprised of electrons packed so tightly as to be effected by the Pauli Exclusion Principle so as to be called degenerate.

slowly and systematically takes over from the hydrogen burning shell surrounding the core. Throughout the red giant or supergiant phase the role of energy production steadily shifts from hydrogen burning to helium burning. Eventually helium becomes exhausted around a growing carbon core. While helium continues to undergo fusion in a shell surrounding the core, carbon fusion is ignited. Just as a degenerate helium core gives rise to the unstable ignition of helium, called the helium flash in low mass stars, so the degenerate carbon core of moderate mass stars can result in an unstable ignition of carbon. However, whereas the helium flash is quickly quelled in low mass stars, the carbon ignites explosively in the cores of these moderate mass stars. The process is called carbon deflagration and may result in the destruction of the star.

In even more massive stars, the onset of carbon burning is a controlled process and the star develops multiple shells of energy sources involving carbon fusion, helium fusion, and even some hydrogen fusion in the outer regions of the star. The ignition by nuclear fusion of each new element yields less energy than the one before it. In addition, the increased temperature required for the nuclear fusion of these additional sources leads to an increase in the stellar luminosity. The result is an ever increasing rate of the formation of less efficient energy sources. When nuclear fusion in the core of the star yields iron, further nuclear fusion will no longer yield energy. Instead, nuclear fusion of iron will use up energy robbing thermal energy from the surrounding material. This sudden cooling of the core will bring about its collapse. However, as the density increases in the collapsing core there is less and less room for the free electrons that have been stripped from the atomic nuclei by the extreme temperature. These electrons must go somewhere so they will begin to be "absorbed" in the protons of the atomic nuclei, turning them into neutrons. The process is called neutronization. This reaction generates particles called neutrinos which interact very weakly with ordinary matter and so normally escape directly from the star. The energy robbed from the core by the neutrinos also adds to the energy crises in the core and contributes to the core collapse.

The production of elements with masses greater than iron also produces large quantities of neutrinos so that whichever process dominates, a great deal of energy is lost directly from the star resulting in a catastrophic gravitational collapse of the core. This is followed promptly by the collapse of the entire star. The rapid increase in the density of the collapsing core finally reaches the point where the material becomes opaque to the energy-robbing neutrinos and their continued escape is stopped. The sudden deposition of the neutrino energy in the collapsing core reverses the collapse, bringing about an explosion of unprecedented magnitude. The infalling matter and trapped photons are hurled into space, liberating as much energy in a few minutes as the star has radiated in its lifetime of millions of years.

The remains of this titanic explosion depend on the initial mass of the collapsing star. Very massive stars may leave a black hole of completely collapsed matter behind. Should the collapse involve a star of less mass, the remainder may be something called a neutron star similar to that formed by the collapse of a white dwarf. It some instances, the entire star may be involved in the explosion and there will be no remains at all. While there have been recent attempts to refine the classification of these explosions, astronomers still refer to the explosion of a massive star as a supernova of type II. Supernovae of type I are thought to result from the collapse of a white dwarf which has exceeded its critical mass. Unlike the evolution of low mass stars in which an accommodation between the forces of gravity and degenerate structure of the star is achieved through the formation of a white dwarf, the evolution of a massive star must end in a violent stellar explosion. Gravity appears to win its struggle with nuclear physics, but at the last moment, the energy of collapse is turned to an explosion leaving either a collapsed corpse or perhaps nothing at all.

See also Gravity and gravitation; Nuclear reactions; Red giant star; Star; Star formation; Supernova; White dwarf.

Further Reading:

Abell, G.O., *Exploration of the Universe*. New York, Philadelphia: Saunders College Publishing, 1982.

Arny, T.T., *Explorations—an Introduction to Astronomy*. St. Louis, Boston Mosby, 1994.

Collins, G.W., II, *Fundamentals of Stellar Astrophysics*. New York: W.H. Freeman, 1989.

Seeds, M.A., Horizons—Exploring the Universe, 1995, Wadsworth Pub. Co. Belmont Cal., pp. 180-234.

Wolsey, S. *Supernovae*, New York, Berlin: Springer-Verlage, 1994.

George W. Collins, II

Stellar magnitudes

Magnitude is the unit used in astronomy to describe a star's brightness in a particular portion of the electromagnetic spectrum. Stars emit different amounts of radiation in different regions of the spectrum, so a star's brightness will differ from one part of the spectrum to the next. An important field of research in modern astronomy is the accurate measurement of stellar brightness in magnitudes in different parts of the spectrum.

How bright it looks: apparent magnitude

The Greek astronomer Hipparchus devised the first magnitudes in the second century B.C. He classified stars according to how bright they looked to the eye: the brightest stars he called "1st class" stars, the next brightest "2nd class," and so on down to "6th class." In this way all the stars visible to the ancient Greeks were neatly classified into six categories.

Modern astronomers still use Hipparchus' categories, though in considerably refined form. With modern instruments astronomers measure a quantity called V, the star's brightness in the visual portion of the spectrum. Since visual light is what our eyes most readily detect, V is analogous to Hipparchus' classes. For example, Hipparchus listed Aldebaran, the brightest star in the constellation Taurus (the Bull), as a 1st class star, while today we know that for Aldebaran $V = 0.85$. Astronomers often refer to a star's visual brightness as its apparent magnitude, which makes sense since this describes how bright the star appears to the eye (or the telescope). You will hear an astronomer say that Aldebaran has an apparent magnitude of 0.85.

Hipparchus' scheme defined from the outset one of the quirks of magnitudes: they run backwards. The fainter the star, the larger the number describing its magnitude. Therefore, the Sun, the brightest object in the sky, has an apparent brightness of -26.75 magnitudes, while Sirius, the brightest star in the sky other than the Sun and visible on cold winter nights in the constellation Canis Major (the Big Dog), has an apparent magnitude of -1.45. The faintest star you can see without optical aid is about +5 (or +6 if your eyes are very sharp), and the faintest objects visible to the most powerful telescope on Earth have an apparent magnitude of about +30.

How bright it really is: absolute magnitude

More revealing than apparent magnitude is absolute magnitude, which is the apparent magnitude a star would have if it were ten parsecs from the Earth (a parsec is a unit of distance equal to 12 trillion mi [19 trillion 308 billion km]). This is important because apparent magnitude can be deceiving. You know that a lit match is not as bright as a streetlight, but if you hold the match next to your eye, it will appear brighter than a streetlight six blocks away. That's why V is called apparent magnitude: it is only how bright the star appears to be. For example, the Sun is a fainter star than Sirius! Sirius emits far more energy than the Sun does, yet the Sun appears brighter to us because it is so much closer. Absolute magnitude, however, reveals the truth: the Sun has an absolute magnitude of +4.8, while Sirius is +1.4 (remember, smaller numbers mean brighter, not fainter).

The nature of the magnitude scale

In 1856, the British scientist N. R. Pogson noticed that Hipparchus' 6th class stars were roughly 100 times fainter than his 1st class stars. Pogson did the sensible thing: he redefined the stars' V brightness so that a difference of five magnitudes was exactly a factor of 100 in brightness. This meant that a star with V = 1.00 appeared to be precisely 100 times brighter than a star with V = 6.00. One magnitude is then a factor of about 2.512 in brightness. Try it: enter 1 on a calculator and multiply it by 2.512 five times—you've just gone from first magnitude to sixth (or eight to thirteenth, or minus seventh to minus second, or any other combination).

Looking back to the numbers above, we see that the Sun (V = -26.75) has an apparent visual brightness 25 magnitudes greater than Sirius. That's five factors of five magnitudes, or 100 x 100 x 100 x 100 x 100: ten billion! And the difference in apparent brightness between the Sun and the faintest object humans have ever seen is more than 55 magnitudes, or a factor of ten billion trillion.

Magnitudes in modern astronomy

In the 140 years since Pogson created the modern magnitudes, astronomers have developed many different brightness systems, and the most popular are less

---

KEY TERMS

· ·

Absolute magnitude—The brightness of a star, measured in units of magnitudes, at a fixed distance of 10 parsecs.

Apparent magnitude—The brightness of a star, measured in units of magnitudes, in the visual part of the electromagnetic spectrum, the region to which our eyes are most sensitive.

Brightness—The amount of energy a star radiates in a certain portion of the electromagnetic spectrum in a given amount of time, often measured in units of magnitudes.

Magnitude—The unit used in astronomy to measure the brightness of a star. One magnitude corresponds to a factor of 2.512 in brightness, so that five magnitudes equals a factor of 100.

---

than 50 years old.

For example, in 1953, H. L. Johnson created the *UBV system* of brightness measurements. We've already met V, which is measured over that portion of the electromagnetic spectrum to which our eyes are most sensitive. B is the star's brightness in magnitudes measured in the blue part of the spectrum, while U is the brightness in the ultraviolet—a spectral region our eyes cannot detect. There are many other brightness measurement systems in use, so many that astronomers often disagree on how measurements in one system should be converted to another.

Accurate measurement of stellar brightness is important because subtracting the brightness in one part of the spectrum from the brightness in another part reveals important information about the star. For many stars the quantity B-V gives a good approximation to the star's temperature. And it was established in 1978 that the quantity V-R, where R is the brightness in the red part of the spectrum, can be used to estimate a star's radius. Advances in our understanding of the stars require knowledge of basic parameters like temperature and radius, and careful measurements of brightness can provide some of that information.

See also Constellation; Spectral classification of stars; Star.

Further Reading:

Kaufmann, William. *Discovering the Universe*. New York: W. H. Freeman, 1990.
Sherrod, P. Clay. *A Complete Manual of Amateur Astronomy*. New York: Prentice-Hall, 1981.

Mitton, Simon P., ed. *The Cambridge Encyclopedia of Astronomy.* Cambridge: Cambridge University Press, 1977.

Jeffrey C. Hall

Stellar populations

Stars fall into distinct groups or populations. The basic stellar populations are Population I stars and Population II stars. The Sun and most stars near the Sun are Population I stars. They are young second to third generation stars with compositions that include 2% of elements heavier than hydrogen and helium. Population II stars, on the other hand, are older stars whose compositions are just hydrogen and helium. The brightest stars in a group of Population I stars are blue and in a group of Population II stars are red. There are also additional sub classifications within this basic classification.

History

Walter Baade discovered the stellar populations during World War II, which contributed to his discovery. During the war, most scientists worked on war-related projects, such as the Manhattan Project. Baade, who was on the staff of Mount Wilson Observatory near Los Angeles, was not allowed to work on war projects because he was German-born. He did however conduct research at Mount Wilson Observatory, which at the time had the world's largest telescope. The wartime blackouts in Los Angeles contributed to darker skies on Mount Wilson. There were also few astronomers wanting to use the telescope because they were working on war related projects. So Baade had lots of time to use the world's largest telescope under better than normal sky conditions.

During this time Baade was able to resolve, for the first time, the stars in the Andromeda Galaxy. He noticed that there were two distinct populations composed of predominantly red and blue stars. He labeled them Population I and Population II. Further study since that time has produced the additional subclassifications.

Properties of populations

Population I

Population I stars have properties similar to those of the sun. They are less than 10 billion years old and include newly formed and still forming stars. Because they are younger second to third generation stars they contain heavy elements that were manufactured in previous generations of stars. To astronomers a heavy element is anything heavier than hydrogen or helium. These two lightest elements make up roughly 98% of the matter in the universe. Population I stars contain roughly 2% heavy elements and 98% hydrogen and helium.

In a group of Population I stars, the brightest stars will be hot blue giants and supergiants. These stars, much more massive than the Sun, are in the main part of their life cycles, burning Hydrogen in their cores. The dominance of hot blue stars does not mean that cooler less massive red and yellow stars such as the Sun can not be Population I stars. Rather, the cooler stars like the Sun are not as bright, so in a group of Population I stars viewed from a distance they will be less noticeable.

It turns out that the stellar populations also have dynamic properties in common. Population I stars are concentrated in the disk of the galaxy. They have circular orbits around the center of the galaxy with very little motion in a direction perpendicular to the galactic plane. They tend to have a patchy distribution within the disk and spiral arms of the galaxy. They also tend to be located in regions that have significant amounts of interstellar gas and dust, the raw materials for forming new stars.

Population II

The older Population II stars are usually over 10 billion years old. Because they are first generation stars, that formed early in the history of the universe, they are devoid of heavy elements. Their composition is similar to that of the early universe. The brightest stars in a group of Population II stars are red giants. Red giants are stars in the process of dying. They have run out of hydrogen fuel in the core and swollen into cool red giants typically the size of the Earth's orbit around the Sun. Because they are so large they are very bright and stand out in a group of Population II stars. Groups of Population I stars do not contain red giants simply because they are younger; they have not had enough time to exhaust the hydrogen fuel in their cores.

The Population II stars also have different dynamical properties. They are not confined to the plane of the galaxy. They have highly eccentric noncircular orbits that often go far above or below the plane of the galaxy to form a smoothly distributed spherical halo around the galaxy. They therefore must have significant components of their motions that are perpendicular to the plane of the galaxy. They also have much higher orbital velocities than Population I stars. Population I stars have orbital velocities that are typically about 5-6 mi (8-10 km) per second. Population II stars zip along at velocities ranging up to 45 mi (75 km) per second for the extreme case.

Other populations

Like most initial classifications, the division of stars into Population I and Population II stars is a bit of an oversimplification. Astronomers now classify stars into five distinct populations based on how strongly they exhibit the Population I or II characteristics. These populations are: Extreme Population I, Older Population I, Disk Population II, Intermediate Population II, and Halo Population II. Astronomers are currently arguing over whether these groups represent distinct populations, or a gradual blending from Population I properties to Population II properties.

There are also some exceptions to the rule that young Population I stars have heavy elements while older Population II stars do not. For example, the Magellanic Clouds, irregular companion galaxies to the Milky Way, are Population I stars with few heavy elements. The core of the Milky Way also contains Population II stars that do contain heavy elements. Why? Most likely in the core of the galaxy there was a very rapid generation of very massive stars. They are gone now, but they enriched the core with heavy elements very quickly. The high concentration of stars near the core contributed to this process. The opposite occurred in the Magellanic Clouds. Star formation proceeded so slowly, that there was not an early generation of massive stars to produce heavy elements.

Reasons for different populations

These different populations can be understood in the context of stellar evolution. When the universe formed in the big bang, only hydrogen and helium were made. The heavy elements were made later in the cores of stars. Therefore the older Population II stars are deficient in heavy elements, while the younger Population I stars contain heavy elements that were made by the massive first generation stars. Massive stars manufacture and recycle heavy elements. These stars are blue giants and supergiants most of their lives, which are very short by stellar standards. These stars are the brightest blue stars in a group of Population I stars. In a group of older Population II stars, these stars have finished their life cycles, so the brightest stars are the red giants formed near the end of stellar life cycles. The distribution of these different populations is then related to the evolution of the galaxy.

KEY TERMS

. . . .

Blue giant, supergiant—The most massive stars in the hydrogen burning stage.

Heavy elements—To astronomers, anything that is not hydrogen or helium.

Population I—The younger second to third generation stars.

Population II—The younger first generation stars.

Stellar population studies help us understand stellar evolution, evolution of the galaxy, and the history of the universe.

See also Star; Stellar evolution.

Further Reading:

Morrison, David, Wolff, Sidney, and Fraknoi, Andrew. *Abell's Exploration of the Universe* 7th ed. Philadelphia: Saunders College Publishing, 1995.

Zeilik, Michael. *Astronomy: The Evolving Universe.* 7th ed. New York: Wiley, 1994.

Zeilik, Michael, Gregory, Stephen, and Smith, Elske. *Introductory Astronomy and Astrophysics.* Philadelphia: Saunders, 1992.

Paul A. Heckert

Stellar structure

It is said that Fred Hoyle once described the evolution of a star as a continual war between nuclear physics and gravity. The structure of a star can be characterized as a polarized battle in that war. The gravity of the stellar material pulls on all the other stellar material striving to bring about a collapse. However, the gravity is opposed by the internal pressure of the stellar gas which normally results from heat produced by nuclear reactions. This balance between the forces of gravity and the pressure forces is called hydrostatic equilibrium and the balance must be exact or the star will quickly respond by expanding or contracting in size. So powerful are the separate forces of gravity and pressure that should such an imbalance occur in the sun, it would be resolved within half an hour. That fact that the sun is about 5 billion years old emphasizes just how exactly and continuously that balance is maintained.

In addition to its reliance on balance between gravity and pressure, the internal structure depends on the behavior of the stellar material itself. Most stars are made primarily of hydrogen since it is the dominant form of matter in the universe. However, the behavior of hydrogen will depend on the temperature, pressure and density of the gas. Indeed, the quantities temperature, pressure, and density, are known as state variables' since they describe the state of the material. Any equation or expression that provides a relationship between these variables is called an equation of state. The relevant equation of state and hydrostatic equilibrium go a long way toward specifying the structure of the star. However, there is one more ingredient necessary in order to determine the structure of the star.

Most of the energy which flows from a star originates at its center. The way in which this energy travels to the surface will influence the internal structure of the star.

There are basically three ways by which energy flows outward through a star. They are conduction, convection, and radiation. The flow of energy up an iron poker, which has one end in a fire, is energy transfer by conduction. This mode of energy flow is too inefficient to be of any interest in most stars. Most people have watched the energy flow from the bottom of a heated pot of water to the top. One sees large motion of heated material rising which is balanced by cooler material falling to the bottom where it, in turn, becomes heated and rises. This organized churning is called convection. In the interior of stars, when convection takes place it dominates the transport of energy over radiation. When the conditions are such that no convective churning takes place, no energy is carried by convection and the only remaining alternative is radiative transport.

The heat produced by an infrared heat lamp or the warmth of the sun on a clear day are good examples of energy transport by radiation. Radiative transport simply means the direct flow of radiant energy from one place to another. If the material through which the energy flows is relatively transparent, the flow takes place at virtually the speed of light. However, the more opaque the material is the slower the flow of energy will be. In the sun where light flowing out from in the core will travel less than a centimeter before it is absorbed, it may take a million years for the light energy to make its way to the surface.

The mode of energy transport, equation of state, and hydrostatic equilibrium can be quantified and self-consistent solutions found numerically on a computer for a star of given mass, composition and age. Such solutions are called model stellar interiors and supply the detailed internal structure of a particular star. For the vast majority of stars which derive their energy

from the nuclear fusion of hydrogen into helium the internal structure is quite similar. We call such stars main sequence stars.

The sun is such a star and has a central region where the material is quiescent and the energy flows through by radiative diffusion. The radiative core is surrounded by a churning convective envelope which carries the energy to within a few thousand kilometers of the surface. This outer percent or so of the sun is called the atmosphere and here the energy again flows primarily by radiation as it escapes into space. This structure is common to all main sequence stars with mass less than about one and a half time the mass of the sun. The structure of more massive stars is nearly reversed. They consist of a convective core surrounded by a radiative envelope which in turn gives way to an atmosphere where the energy also leaves the star by radiation.

There is a class of very dense stars known as white dwarfs. These stars originate as main sequence stars, but have changed dramatically over time. As a result their internal structure has changed drastically. The matter of a white dwarf no longer behaves like a normal gas, and it has a different equation of state, and the structure of such a star is vastly different from main sequence star. For example, while a white dwarf has a comparable mass to that of the sun, it is not much larger than the earth. This means that their average density is huge. A cubic inch of white dwarf material might weigh forty tons and exerts a tremendous pressure to balance the fierce gravity resulting from as much material as one finds in the sun in a sphere no larger than the earth. Material in such a state is said to be degenerate. In these weird stars, conduction by free moving electrons becomes extremely efficient so that any internal energy is transported almost instantly within the star. The entire interior is at the same temperature and only a thin outer blanket of more normal non-degenerate material keeps the energy from leaking quickly into interstellar space.

More than 90% of all stars fall into the categories described above. The remaining stars are called red giants or red supergiants. These names are derived from the external appearance for they are relatively cool and therefore red, but are extremely distended. If one were to replace the sun with the typical red giant, it would occupy most of the inner solar system. Should the replacement involve a red supergiant even the planet Mars would find itself within the supergiant's atmosphere and Jupiter itself would be heated to the point where much of its substance would evaporate away. However, so huge is the volume occupied by these stars that their average density would be considered a pretty good vacuum by most physicists. The situation is made even worse since the inner cores of these stars are about

Hydrostatic equilibrium—Expresses a static balance between the forces of gravity and the forces due to the internal pressure.

Ideal gas—A term used to describe the behavior of a gas composed of simple atoms under standard conditions. An ideal gas obeys the following relation for the state variables of temperature T, number density n , and pressure P. The constant k is known as the Boltzmann constant. $P = nkT$.

Main sequence—A sequence of stars of differing mass, but all deriving their energy from the nuclear fusion of hydrogen into helium.

Nuclear fusion—The combining of the nuclei of two elements so as to produce an new more massive element. The process is accompanied by the release of energy as long as the end product of the reaction is less massive than iron.

the size of the earth and contain about ninety percent of the mass of the giant. Most red giants have an object much like a white dwarf located at their center. Therefore, their structure would best be described as a white dwarf surrounded by an extensive fog. The energy for most of these stars is supplied by the nuclear fusion of helium into carbon which is a much less energy efficient source than the fusion of hydrogen to helium. This is the basic reason why there are so many more main sequence stars than red giants and super giants. Another reason is that a star uses up its helium much more quickly and spends relatively little time in the red gaint phase. By determining how the structure of a star changes with time we can construct the evolutionary history and fate of that star. This is called the theory of stellar evolution.

See also Red giant star; Star; Stellar evolution; White dwarf.

Further Reading:

Abell, G.O. *Exploration of the Universe,* Philadelphia, New York: Saunders College Publishing, 1982

Arny, T.T. *Explorations—an Introduction to Astronomy.* St. Louis, Boston: Mosby, 1994.

Collins, G.W. II, *Fundamentals of Stellar Astrophysics.* New York: W.H. Freeman, 1989.

Seeds, M.A. *Horizons—Exploring the Universe,* Belmont California: Wadsworth Pub. Co. 1995.

George W. Collins, II

Stellar wind

The Sun emits a constant stream of particles, mostly protons and electrons, that are known as the solar wind. Many stars also have a similar phenomenon, known as stellar wind. The solar wind is fairly gentle. Stellar winds as gentle as the solar wind are difficult to detect from the Earth because other stars are so distant. However many stars at certain stages in their evolution have very strong stellar winds. These strong winds produce effects that we can observe from Earth. They also can cause the star to lose significant amounts of mass.

Solar wind

The outermost layer of the Sun is the corona, which is a very hot tenuous gas visible only during a solar eclipse. Because the coronal temperatures are typically one or two million degrees Kelvin the individual atoms are ionized and moving very rapidly. The fastest ions are moving faster than the Sun's escape velocity. So they escape, forming the solar wind.

Near the Earth's orbit the solar wind particles rush by at speeds of roughly 248-310 mi per second (400-500 km per second). There is considerable variation in the speed because the solar wind is gusty. The solar wind density is also variable but typically runs to a few particles per cubic centimeter. The solar wind extends well beyond the orbit of Pluto to roughly 100 astronomical units (100 times the Earth to Sun distance). At this point, called the heliopause, the solar wind merges into the interstellar gas and dust.

Stellar winds

Analogous to the solar wind many stars have stellar winds. Because stars are so distant, stellar winds that are as gentle as the solar wind do not produce dramatic effects as seen from Earth. The stellar winds that we observe are therefore much stronger than the solar wind. A variety of different types of stars display interesting stellar winds.

Massive hot stars

The hottest, most massive stars are O spectral class stars, which have at least 15 times the mass of the Sun. Wolf-Rayet stars have many characteristics in common with the O stars, but their nature is still not completely understood. Both O stars and Wolf-Rayet stars often have very strong stellar winds.

The surface temperatures of O stars are above 30,000 degrees Kelvin. Their stellar winds can blow as much as the Sun's mass into space in 100,000 to one million years, the mass of the Earth every year or so. The winds travel outward at speeds as high as 2,175 mi per second (3,500 km per second), almost ten times as fast as the solar wind. The Wolf-Rayet stars are hotter, 50,000K, and their winds are more powerful than the O stars.

These powerful winds from hot stars create huge bubbles around the stars that can be as big as a few hundred light years across. These bubbles form when the stellar wind interacts with the surrounding interstellar medium, the gas and dust between the stars. The stellar wind slows down as it pushes into the interstellar medium. Dragging the interstellar medium along, it creates a region of higher density that is moving more slowly than the stellar wind. But the stellar wind keeps coming and slams into this region, creating a shock wave. The shock wave heats up the gas in this region and makes it glow, so that we see a bubble around the star. The bubbles are produced from the powerful stellar winds described above. There are also O stars with weaker stellar winds that have less dramatic effects.

Baby stars

The Sun and similar stars form from collapsing clouds of gas and dust. After the star forms, the leftover material still surrounds it in a cocoon of gas and dust. How do stars like the Sun shed their cocoons? One way is stellar winds. Astronomers think that shortly after the Sun formed it went through a period when it had a very strong solar wind, which helped blow away the cocoon. It is difficult to know how accurate this scenario is because no one was around to witness the birth of the solar system.

We can however watch the birth of other stars similar to the Sun. T Tauri stars are stars in the process of forming that astronomers think will eventually have properties similar to the Sun's. Among other properties T Tauri stars show evidence of strong stellar winds. They also show a range of thick and thin circumstellar cocoons. Studying the stellar winds from T Tauri stars will help us understand how the Sun and similar stars shed their initial cocoons.

Many young stars show bipolar outflows, which are two streams of material blowing away from the star in opposite directions. They usually occur in the birth of stars more massive than the Sun. The bipolar outflow stage only lasts about 10,000 years or so, but during that time we see a strong stellar wind from the newly forming star. Why is the outflow bipolar? One theory suggests that the outflow is bipolar because an equatorial disk of material surrounding the star constrains the wind to flow out from the two polar regions. This disk

may be the material that will eventually form planets around the star. Another possibility is that the star's magnetic field forces the outflow into a direction perpendicular to the equatorial disk. The study of stellar winds from newly forming stars will eventually provide us with clues to help us understand how the sun and solar system formed.

Dying stars

Old stars in the process of dying can also have very strong stellar winds. When stars like the Sun exhaust the hydrogen fueling their nuclear fires, they expand into red giants. A typical red giant is about the size of the Earth's orbit around the Sun. Because red giants are so large and the gravitational force decreases with distance from the center, the gravitational force at the surface of a red giant is much less than at the surface of the sun. Hence only a gentle push is needed to allow matter to escape and form a stellar wind. This push might come from the light leaving the star. Light or other radiation striking an object will produce a very small but non zero force that is called radiation pressure. The radiation pressure on dust grains might provide the needed push. Similarly, this radiation pressure might also play a role in causing the stellar winds from the hot O stars mentioned in a previous paragraph. In addition, many red giants pulsate. They expand and contract in periods of a few years. These pulsations can also provide the needed push to cause significant stellar winds and to cause the loss of quite a bit of mass.

In some cases red giants form planetary nebulae, glowing shells of gas around the star. According to one model, the pulsations create a gentle wind moving at about 6 mi per second (10 km per second). This wind is gentle but can carry away the mass of the Sun in as little as 10,000 years. Removing this much mass from the shell of the star exposes the more violent core and unleashes a wind blowing out thousands of kilometers per second. The fast wind slams into the slow wind and creates a shock wave that heats up the shell of gas until it glows as a planetary nebula. The remaining core of the star collapses into a white dwarf star about the size of the Earth.

Mass loss

The single most important property affecting the evolution of a star is its mass. Therefore when the stellar wind causes a star to lose mass, its evolution is affected. In some cases these effects are still poorly understood. One reasonably well understood effect occurs for red giants collapsing into white dwarfs as described above. A star having more than 1.4 times the mass of the Sun can not collapse into a stable white

Stem cells see **Blood**

KEY TERMS

Interstellar medium—Gas and dust between the stars.

O stars—The hottest most massive stars when classified on the basis of the star's spectrum..

Planetary nebula—A shell of hot gas surrounding a star in the late stages of its evolution.

Red giant—A large cool star, which is a stage in its evolution after it runs out of hydrogen fuel.

Solar wind—A stream of particles blowing out from the Sun.

Stellar wind—A stream of particles blowing out from a star.

T Tauri star—An early stage in the evolution of stars like the Sun.

White dwarf—A hot very small star, which is the final corpse for stars like the Sun.

Wolf-Rayet star—A very hot energetic star that ejects a shell of gas.

dwarf. Stars that exceed this mass limit collapse into neutron stars or black holes. Stellar winds can cause red giants with masses up to about 8 times the mass of the Sun to lose enough mass to collapse into a white dwarf having less than 1.4 times the mass of the Sun.

Roughly half of all stars occur in binary systems. When a star in a binary system has a stellar wind it loses mass. Some of this mass is transferred to the other star in the system, so it gains mass. Hence the mass of both stars in the system changes when one of the stars has a stellar wind. The evolution of both stars in the system is affected.

See also Binary star; Red giant star; Solar wind; Stellar evolution; White dwarf.

Further Reading:

Frank, Adam. "Winds of Change." *Discover* (June 1994): 100-104.

Morrison, David, Sidney Wolff, and Andrew Fraknoi. *Abell's Exploration of the Universe* 7th ed. Philadelphia: Saunders College Publishing, 1995.

Van Buren, David. "Bubbles in the Sky." *Astronomy* (January, 1993): 46-49.

Zeilik, Michael. *Astronomy: The Evolving Universe.* 7th ed. New York: Wiley, 1994.

Paul Heckert

Stereochemistry

Stereochemistry is the area of chemistry that is associated with the three-dimensional arrangement of the atoms that make up molecules. The term stereochemistry is derived from the Greek word *stereos*, which means solid. Solids are composed of molecules which have three dimensions: length, width, and depth. The chemical formula of a molecule is only a simple representation of which atoms are connected to which and how they are connected. The chemical formula does not show the three-dimensional structure of the molecule. It is usually left up to the reader to translate the chemical formula into its geometric arrangement. For example the chemical formula for methane is CH_4. This formula indicates that a central carbon atom is bonded to four hydrogen atoms (C-H). In order to convert this formula into the three dimensional molecular array for methane, one must know that when a carbon atom has four single bonds to four atoms, each of the bonds points towards a different corner of a tetrahedron. In the figure, the solid wedge shaped bonds are coming out of the paper and the dotted wedges are going into the paper, as shown in Figure 1.

Another way to visualize a carbon atom with four single bonds is to consider yourself the central carbon atom and you are standing in the center of an Egyptian pyramid. At each point in the pyramid is located a hydrogen atom that is bonded to you. One hydrogen or pyramid point is directly above your head. One is in front of you, one point is behind you to your right, and another behind you to your left. These three hydrogen atoms or points are all on a level below the one you are on. The three dimensional arrangement of each carbon

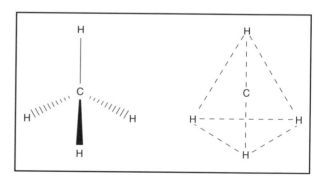

Figure 1.

atom with four single bonds is always the same and the angle between any two bonds is 109.5°.

If the molecule has a double bond in its chemical formula—for example, formaldehyde, $O=CH_2$—then the three-dimensional structure of the molecule is somewhat different. To translate formaldehyde into its geometric structure, one must know its chemical formula indicates a central carbon atom that has a double bond to an oxygen atom (C=O) and two single bonds to hydrogen atoms (C-H). In the geometric arrangement of a carbon atom that has a double bond to another atom, there is a 120° angle between any two bonds, and each bond points away from the central carbon atom. (Figure 2.)

If the bonded atoms are connected, they represent the corners of an equilateral triangle. In molecules that contain two carbon atoms connected by a double bond and each of which is bonded to a hydrogen atom and another atom, then the geometric isomer that has both hydrogen atoms on the same side is called *cis*. The molecule with the hydrogen atoms on opposite sides of the double bond is designated as *trans*. For example, *cis*-1,2-dichloroethene has the hydrogen atoms on the same side of the double bond, where as *trans*-1,2-dichloroethene has them on opposite sides. Both of these compounds have the same chemical formula (ClHC=CHCl), but their geometric representations are different, as shown in Figure 3.

The only other type of bond a carbon atom can have is a triple bond—that is, three bonds to the same atom. Acetylene (HCCH) is a molecule that contains a triple bond between the two carbon atoms, and each carbon atom is bonded to a hydrogen atom (C-H). A carbon atom with a triple bond to another atom is geometrically straight or linear.

$$H — C \equiv C — H$$

The three-dimensional structure of a molecule determines its physical properties, such as the temperature at which it turns from a liquid to a gas (boiling point) and the temperature at which it changes from a solid to a liquid (melting point). The geometric structure of a molecule is also responsible for its chemical properties, such as its strength as an acid or base. The compound *trans*-1,2-dichloroethene becomes a gas at a much higher temperature than the structurally similar *cis*-1,2-dichloroethene. The compound *cis*-3-phenylpropenoic acid is a stronger acid than *trans*-3-phenylpropenoic acid only because the hydrogen atoms are connected to the doubly bonded carbon atoms differently.

The geometric structure of a molecule can also have a dramatic effect on how that molecule tastes or

Formaldehyde (O=CH₂)

Figure 2.

Cis-1,2-dichloroethene   Trans-1,2-dichloroethene

Figure 3.

S-Carvone   R-Carvone

Figure 4.

Antibacterial   Inactive

Figure 5.

how it functions as a drug. The compound carvone has two three-dimensional structures, one called S and the other R (Figure 4).

The compounds differ in their three-dimensional structure by the position of the indicated hydrogen atom. In S-Carvone, only the hydrogen atom is pointed

KEY TERMS

Cis—The geometric isomer of a molecule that contains a double bond between two carbon atoms and has both hydrogen atoms on the same side of the double bond.

Trans—The geometric isomer of a molecule that contains a double bond between two carbon atoms and has both hydrogen atoms on opposite sides of the double bond.

into the paper, while in the R compound, the hydrogen atom is coming out of the paper. S-Carvone has a caraway flavor when tasted, whereas the R compound has the flavor of spearmint.

The antibacterial drug chloramphenicol is commercially produced as a mixture of the two compounds shown in Figure 5. One three-dimensional arrangement of atoms is an active drug, the other geometric structure is ineffective as an antibacterial agent.

See also Chemical bond; Formula, chemical; Formula, structural; Molecule.

Further Reading:

J. McMurry. *Organic Chemistry*. Pacific Grove, California: Brooks/Cole Publishing Company, 1992.
Eliel, E. L., and S. H. Wilen. *Stereochemistry of Organic Compounds*. New York: Wiley & Sons, 1994.
K. Mislow. *Introduction to Stereochemistry*. New York: W. A. Benjamin, 1966.

Andrew J. Poss

Sterilization, surgical see **Contraception**

Sticklebacks

Sticklebacks are small bony fish in the family Gasterosteidae that rarely exceed 3 in (8 cm) in length. These fishes are found in the Northern Hemisphere in North America, and Northern Europe. The name stickleback is derived from the thick spines arising in the first dorsal fin. The number of these spines forms the basis for the identification of the different species.

Sticklebacks lack scales; instead they have bony plates on their sides. Sticklebacks provide a good example of male dominance in the mating ritual and nesting behavior. At the beginning of the breeding season the male stickleback selects a suitable spot in quiet waters, where he builds a nest of stems, pieces of sea plants, and roots, stuck together by a sticky liquid produced from his kidneys. The nest is shaped by the fish's body movements. A normally blue-green male three spined stickleback then changes color, turning a red color for the breeding season. The male ten-spined stickleback becomes brown, and the 15-spined male stickleback changes to a blue color. Breeding male sticklebacks are aggressive and will fight with other breeding males when seeking females. The male performs a courtship dance to entice a suitable female into the nest, but if this is not successful he will attempt to chase the female into his nest, where she deposits her eggs. The male will then expel sperm (milt) over the eggs. The male searches for another female, repeating the process until he fills his nest with eggs. The male protects the eggs for over a month and repairs the nest if it is damaged. The eggs are aerated by swimming movements of the male around the nest, when he sets up a water current with his pectoral fins. He continues to guard the brood after they hatch, maintaining them in the nest until they are able to obtain their own food.

The brook stickleback, *Culaea inconstans,* is common in brooks in the United States from Pennsylvania to Kansas. It is a small fish less than 3 in (8 cm) in length, with five to six spines on its back.

The fifteen-spine stickleback, *Spinachia spinachia,* is found in saltwater in the British Isles and around the North Sea. The nine-spine stickleback, *Pungitius pungitius,* is found on both sides of the Atlantic in the northern latitudes. Its coloring is dark brown, but the male turns black during courtship and spawning.

See also Bony fishes.

Stigma see **Flower**

Stilts and avocets

Stilts and avocets are long-legged, long-beaked wading birds of the muddy shores of shallow lakes and lagoons, including both fresh and saline waters.

There are fewer than 10 species of stilts and avocets all of which are included in the family Recurvirostridae. These birds occur in the temperate and tropical zones of all of the continents except

A black-winged stilt.

Antarctica. The bill of stilts is rather straight, while that of avocets curves upwards, and that of the ibisbill curves downwards.

The habitat of the ibisbill (*Ibidorhyncha struthersii*) is the shores of cold, glacial streams of the mountains of the Himalayas. The Andean avocet (*R. andina*) utilizes similarly cold, but shallow-lake habitat in the Andes of South America.

Stilts and avocets feed on small invertebrates on the water surface or at the mud-water interface. The ibisbill feeds by probing among the cobble and pebbles of the cold streams that it inhabits.

Stilts and avocets commonly construct nests as mounds of vegetation, on the boggy edges of lakes or on islands. The chicks of these species are *precocial*, meaning that they can leave the nest within a short time of being born. Remarkably, stilt and avocet chicks feed themselves, and are not fed by their parents.

Some stilts and avocets breed in semi-arid climates, where the rainfall is unpredictable. Under such conditions, these birds nest opportunistically, whenever recent rains have been sufficient to develop wetlands containing enough water to support the breeding effort of these birds. Stilts and avocets tend to be gregarious, forming small breeding colonies numbering as many as tens of pairs. After breeding has been accomplished, birds from various colonies congregate in flocks that can number hundreds of birds.

Species of stilts and avocets

The American avocet (*Recurvirostra americana*) is a chestnut-headed bird with a white body and black wings. This species is relatively abundant, and breeds on the shores of shallow lakes and marshes in the western United States and adjacent parts of Canada. The black-necked stilt (*Himantopus mexicanus*) is more southwestern in its distribution in the United States. Both of these species are migratory, mostly spending the winter months in Central America.

The Hawaiian stilt or ae'o (*Himantopus mexicanus knudseni*) is a distinct subspecies of the black-necked stilt that breeds in wetlands in the Hawaiian Islands. Fewer than 1,000 pairs of this bird remain. The subspecies is considered to be endangered, mostly by the loss of its wetland habitat through conversion to agricultural uses or for residential or tourism development.

The pied or black-winged stilt (*Himantopus himantopus*) is a very wide-ranging species, occurring in suitable habitat in Eurasia, Africa, Southeast Asia, and Australia. The black-winged stilt (*Himantopus melanurus*) of South America is closely related to the previous species. The banded stilt (*Cladorhynchus leucocephalus*) occurs in Australia.

The avocet (*Recurvirostra avosetta*) occurs in parts of Eurasia and Africa. Australia has a red-necked avocet (*R. novaehollandiae*), while the Andean avocet (*R. andina*) occurs in montane habitats of South America.

The ibisbill (*Ibidorhyncha struthersii*) occurs in the mountain zone of the Himalayan Mountains of south Asia.

Most ornithologists believe that the family Recurvirostridae is not a very natural grouping of birds. The several species of avocets are obviously closely related to each other, as are the various stilts. However, the ibisbill does not seem to be closely related to the stilts and avocets, and may eventually be assigned to a separate family.

See also Endangered species; Migration.

Further Reading:

Harrison, C.J.O., ed. *Bird Families of the World*. New York: H.N. Abrams Pubs., 1978.

Bill Freedman

Stimulants see **Amphetamines**

Stimulus

The term stimulus has many meanings; very generally, it is any occurrence (be it an external event, or anything perceived or thought) that causes a detectible response. Stimulus is often used with qualifying terms to further specify its meaning, for example, conditioned stimulus and neutral stimulus.

Various fields of study use the term stimulus in different ways. In psychology, it is most often used to describe energy forms that reach sense organs and cause a response. For example, the visual sense using the eyes responds to photic radiation or light. Because human sense organs respond to a limited number of energy forms, and even then to only limited amounts of that energy, some energy reaching the sense organs is not detected and does not cause a response. The energy reaching the sense organs but not causing a response may be deemed a stimulus to a physiologist, but for psychologists it would not be considered a stimulus unless it had been responded to or detected by the organism. A stimulus may also be an internal mental event that causes a response.

Stimulus is the primary term in stimulus-response theory, which refers to a number of learning theories that are theoretically based on conditioned bonds or associations between a stimulus and response. The associative bonds are formed through the repeated pairing of certain stimuli and certain responses. Most of these theories are also behavioristic in that they focus on behaviors and do not look at mental processes, and they see the environment as the most important determinant of human behavior. Indeed, these theories view the bond between stimulus and response as the basis of behavior and believe that psychology's primary goal should be to discover rules governing how stimuli and responses interact. The two dominant stimulus-response theories are classical and operant conditioning theories.

See also Conditioning; Perception; Psychology.

Further Reading:

Atkinson, R.L. , R.C. Atkinson, E.E. Smith, and D.J. Bem. *Introduction to Psychology.* 10th ed. New York: Harcourt Brace Jovanovich, 1990.
Masin, S.C., ed. *Foundations of Perceptual Theory.* New York: Elvesier Science, 1993.
Rachlin, H. *Introduction to Behaviorism.* New York: W.H. Freeman, 1990.
Schiffman, H.R. *Sensation and Perception: An Integrated Approach.* 3rd ed. New York: Wiley, 1990.

Stink bugs see **True bugs**

Stoats see **Weasels**

Stomach see **Digestive system**

Stone and masonry

It is possible that ever since people first came to be, stone was used in constructing something: a fence, an oven in a hole or trench, or a shelf in a cave. And it is possible that sometime during this era, someone coined the statement: "Leave no stone unturned."

The many cairns and stone hedges erected for religious or astronomical uses were the initial attempts at masonry. However, true masonry did not begin until the Egyptians built the pyramids. Previous to this, most stone structures were constructed by placing one stone upon, or next to, another, regardless of size or shape.

In constructing the pyramids, the stone was first hewn or carved into a certain shape and then placed into a preplanned position. Other great stone undertakings were the walls, the wall of China being the largest. The Roman wall in England was 10 ft (3 m) thick at the base and up to 15 ft (4.6 m) in height in some places. Although it was filled with mud and pebbles, both faces were constructed with squared stones. It ran for over 70 mi (113 km). Surviving portions are about 6 ft (1.8 m) high.

It was during the Norman period that most old stone structures were erected in England. And many of the craftsmen were of Norman descent. Therefore many of the architectural terms used in the English language are of French origin. Some of these are vault, buttress, niche, oriel, trefoil, fillet, and chamfer. French influence is also evident in the standardization of various building units, such as the course heights and in various moldings and carvings. Many of these were designed to fit the individual blocks of stone rather than create a regular repetitive pattern. The majority of the original stone buildings were cathedrals, churches, and castles. But as time went on, especially where stone was quite abundant, manor houses, farmhouses, and even barns began to be built of stone.

In America, especially in northern America, when settlers first came, many were tillers of the soil, or became such. The last glacier brought many stones from Canada and northern America and deposited them on the land. The settlers then used them for fences and for barns and house foundations. Today stones are used to face many buildings.

Stone types

In working with stone one should know the various types of stone. There are three main types, given their name from the manner whereby they were formed. Igneous stone is formed when magma from below the earth's crust comes to the surface and solidifies. The liquified material from beneath the crust of the earth spews forth from a volcano as lava. Basalt is the most common stone to be formed volcanically. It is composed mainly of silica, as is diabase and other primordial stone. Feldspar, which contains aluminum and calcium compounds, is the other common mineral spewed from a volcano.

Metamorphic stones are made from existing materials that have undergone change. As an example, when weathered on the surface, feldspar becomes clay, which can undergo tremendous pressure and become metamorphic slate. Granite is often taken for granted, but comes from quartz and feldspar, sometimes at molten temperatures. It can be either igneous or metamorphic. Most metamorphic rocks have been crushed into their present state by a parent stone upon it. Thus limestone under pressure becomes marble. Quartzite is metamorphic quartz. Gneiss and schist are two other metamorphic rocks.

Sedimentary stones are formed from sediments on the earth's surface. Such stones cover three fourths of the earth's crust, but account for less than five percent of the earth's volume. Shale, sandstone, and limestone make up ninety-nine percent of the sedimentary stone. Shale comes from clay deposits which were formed from feldspar. Sandstone comes from river carried erosion of other stones and minerals that build up at continents' edges. It can also be formed by erosion of igneous stone. Limestone is formed mainly from the buildup of exoskeletons of tiny sea animals drifting to shore. The shell material is mainly calcium carbonate. Limestone is often quarried for building stone, gravel, cement or agricultural lime. Weathered stone supplies the minerals that plants and animals need for their existence.

Chemical composition

The builder of a stone structure is more concerned with its chemical composition than its geological classification. There are three main categories for stone chemical content. Siliceous stone has as its main element, silica, or silicon dioxide (SiO2). Most stone from volcanoes is siliceous. This type of stone also includes compressed sediments of siliceous stone, like sandstone. Quartz is a very pure pressurized sandstone.

Argillaceous stone has as its main element alumina (AlO_2). It, along with its compounds, comes from feldspar in the crust. When these meet up with the atmosphere, they change into claylike compounds. Slate, a sort of petrified clay, is the most common to the mason. When clay combines with other stone in varying degrees, it can overlap into other types. If clay and sand mix, brownstone is formed. Brick is artificial argillaceous stone.

Calcareous stone is made up mostly of calcium carbonate ($CaCO_3$), or lime. Lime comes from the bodies of sea creatures, whose skeletons have accumulated at the bottom of the seas. When lime is pressurized for millennia, it becomes marble. Marble is mainly a metamorphic rock. But because it is still mainly lime after metamorphosis, it is calcareous in classification.

Certainly, there are many combinations of the above three classifications, but rocks are distinguished by the abundance of glassy (siliceous), clayey (argillaceous) or limy (calcareous) stuff in them. It is the quantity of each basic compound found in rocks, along with the way they were formed and the presence of other minerals in smaller amounts found in them, that give rocks their particular desirability by masons.

Construction rocks

The strongest rock is trap, a very old igneous and siliceous primeval stone that can withstand over 67,000 lbs/sq.in (3,900 kg/sq. cm) pressure. Gabbro and basalt are similar. But these rocks are very difficult to work, or quarry. They are not formed in layers and hence are very difficult to layer. Granite is somewhat manageable, and is used where great strength or resistance to weather are needed. But it is difficult to work with and therefore quite expensive. Other qualities of rock that make it more desirable for use in constructions are ease of quarrying, nearness to quarry, durability, resistance to absorbing water, and strength. However, stone masons look mainly for shape (they desire stones more or less square), their proximity, and the price. The stone most often used by masons is sandstone or limestone.

Stone masonry always has stood for permanence. Anything properly made of stone outlasts the same thing made of any other material, even concrete with steel mesh imbedded. But one must be certain of one's work. It can take weeks to repair a mistake. Stone masonry differs entirely from brick or block masonry, where every layer must lie in a straight line, where there must be square and level units and mortar joints that are uniform. The main reasons for building with stone are its beauty, endurance, strength, and mass.

KEY TERMS

. . . .

Arch—Curved path or span across an opening, constructed of voussoirs (curved arch stones).

Bed—A stratified layer of stone in sedimentary rock, laid down by nature. A bed is also the term used to describe the horizontal layer of mortar, cement, sand, etc. on which the blocks or stone are laid. It is the base for the first layer.

Bevel—An instrument to determine that a layer of stone or brick does not change height over a distance. It also is the name for a splayed angle on a worked stone.

Block stone—A large stone block, roughly squared at the quarry.

Bonder—Any stone or brick which is so laid that it increases the strength of a wall, either in thickness or in length.

Brought to course—Where random walling is brought up to a level line, such as at the top of a wall or the bottom of a window.

Buttress—A strong stone pier built against a wall to give additional strength. (Flying buttresses extend quite far out from the wall.) A buttress must be bonded to the wall.

Capital—The top stone of a column or pilaster. Often they are richly carved.

Carborundum saw—A circular saw whose rim has carborundum abrasive.

Chamfer—A flat splayed edge between two flat plain surfaces.

Chisel—A generic term for a certain type of cutting tool.

Cladding—Non-load bearing thin stone slabs or bricks used for facing a building.

Cock's comb—A thin shaped steel plate with a serrated edge. It is used for finishing moldings and other shapes.

Corbel—A bracket of stone that projects from the face of a wall. It usually is used to give support to some feature above.

Course—A continuous layer of stone or brick of uniform height in a wall.

Diamond saw—A saw whose cutting edge has industrial diamonds inserted.

Dormer—A window that projects vertically from a sloping roof.

Dowel—A sort piece of metal (not iron) or slate fixed into a mortise or adjoining stones or tile to prevent movement.

Dressings—A generic term used to wart, chimneys, etc. made of freestone, on the elevation of a building.

Drum—A separate circular stone in a shaft or column.

Stone construction

To build a wall with stones, it depends on whether one wishes to construct a dry stone wall or what is termed a wet wall, one using mortar. Dry walls are used mainly for fences or retaining walls. Dry walls are usually 2-3 ft (0.6-0.9 m) thick. The base is usually a bed of sand around 5 in (12.1 cm) thick. At the beginning of the first layer of stones usually one lays a stone, the bonding stone, which is faced relatively even. This helps keep the wall together. The bottom course should consist of alternating larger and smaller stones, all with the longest side along the outside surface. Such stones are placed on either side of the wall. Then stones are put between the sides, filling in the center. The layers that are above the base layer are constructed such that stones connect two lower stones, and, if possible, are kept reasonably level. If spaces result, and stones do not seat firmly, gaps are filled by chinking, by driving narrow stones or chips in

the spaces so that the wall is locked tight and weight is pressed inward to prevent collapsing.

A wet wall, one that is mortared, begins with a mortared bed. A trench is dug and filled with sand or gravel. This then is allowed to settle for a few days. An inch of mortar is then laid on the top of the slab. As above, a bonding stone is placed at the end. Other stones are added along the sides, leaving spaces for the mortar which is poured as one moves along. The inside is filled with small stones, and mortar added. After laying but not filling in the next course, insert a broomstick in between stones on the first tier to make weep holes, which should pass entirely through the wall. When the wall is finished, it should be raked with a piece of wood to compact the mortar.

Most modern stone houses have stone faces only; the entire wall is usually not completely stone. The main reason is that stone is very expensive and the

KEY TERMS

Eave—The part of a roof or other structure which oversails the wall face.

Entablature—In classical architecture, the upper part of an order. It comprises architrave, frieze and cornice.

Fault—A natural fissure in a bed or stratum of stone at a quarry. Usual faults are somewhat vertical.

Fillet—A small member between moldings. It also is called a quirk.

Flagstone—Stone that is naturally stratified in slabs about two to three inches thick, used mainly for pavings, copings, etc.

Float—A rectangular wooden hand trowel, used for smoothing surfaces.

Fluted stone—Stone worked with regular concave grooves, as found in columns.

Gauge—A tool used for marking parallel lines when setting out a piece of work.

Grain—A word used at times to describe the natural visible bedding planes in stone.

Grout—Mortar used for filling vertical joints (perpends).

Header—A stone which has its longest dimension built into the thickness of the wall to improve bonding and strength.

Hip—The inclined angle at which two sloping roofs meet. The converse of valley.

Hod—A device used for carrying mortar or other materials when climbing. It is placed on the shoulder

Hydrated lime— Quicklime processed into an inert powdered lime ready for use.

In Situ—Done in position, on the spot.

Jack hammer—A hand-held pneumatic dressing hammer.

Jamb—Vertical side of an archway, doorway or window.

Keystone—The central stone in an arch

Ledger—A large flat stone covering an altar tomb or grave. Often forms part of a church floor.

Level—A tool for telling if horizontal surfaces are true and level.

Lintel—The block or stone that spans the top of an opening, such as a doorway or window. Sometimes called a head.

Mortar board—A board placed near the work. It holds the mortar, allowing the mason to pick it up with a trowel.

Mortise—A recess in a block cut to receive a dowel or tenon.

Mould—A shaped pattern used to set out the work. Called a template in carpentry.

Molding—A projecting or recessed part, used to give shadows to a wall, arch, or other surfaces.

---

inner part of the wall usually is blocked by furniture, pictures or other view blocking items. So only an outer facade of stone is added to the house. This is between 3-4 inches (7.6-10 cm) thick, and can be either field or quarried stone. One of the hardest stones that is relatively easy to work with is limestone. One of the hardest limestones is quarried in Valders, Wisconsin, which is about 30 mi (48 km) south of Green Bay. Here the Valders glacier covered the area. But when one digs beneath the glaciated land, an extra dense level of the Niagara ledge is found. Valders dolomite limestone ranges in color from a silvery white to a buff texture. It is one of the most enduring limestones in the U.S.

Marble is another stone used by masons, and is found in almost every state. Depending on color, porosity, and strength, various marbles are used in various buildings, such as churches, museums, art galleries and the like. Again, due to expense, today the most common stone used in construction (for facing mainly) is limestone, although some marble can be found.

Bricks

Bricks are manmade argillaceous rock. Brick and cement or cinder block masonry are not quite as artistic as stone masonry, but are usually quicker and cheaper. Like stone masonry, a footing is laid, and tiers of block or brick are placed upon the footing. The way a brick is positioned in a wall is given a name. The long part of the brick is termed the stretcher, the short end, the header, and the flat face of the brick is the bed. A tier or layer of brick can be a stretcher course (if all faces showing are stretchers), a headed course (ends showing are heads), a sailor course (where bricks are upright,

KEY TERMS

Niche—A recess in a wall, usually prepared to receive a carved figure.

Oriel window—A window that projects from an upper story.

Pilaster—A flat pier attached to a wall, with a base and a capital.

Plinth—The projecting base of a wall or column, generally molded at the top.

Plumb rule—A straightedge about four or six feet long with a spirit level recessed in it. It is used to ensure vertical with when building a wall. (Along with the level, it is one of a mason's most important tools.)

Pointing—Filling of mortar joints in masonry.

Quarry—Usually an open-cast pit (but sometimes a mine) from which stone is extracted.

Rendering—A coating, usually of cement and sand, that covers rough stone.

Sill—Either the threshold stone under a doorway, if flush, that is not a step; or the stone across the base of a window opening.

Soffit—The underside of an arch, vault, cornice, lintel, or the like.

Square—A tool having a fixed right angle. It is used to set out work and keep angles truly square.

Straightedge—A perfectly straight rule of any length, used to set out and keep the work straight.

Throat—A name sometimes given to the small grove under a window sill or dripstone. Its purpose is to deflect water from the wall.

Transom—A structural part dividing a window horizontally.

Valley—The line at which two sloping roofs meet.

Vein—A colored marking in limestone, marble, etc.

Weathered—Stones that have been exteriorly exposed in a building for many years to the elements can be weathered, well or badly.

with beds showing) or soldier course (where bricks are upright, with stretchers showing). Bricks laid in stretcher position with headers abutting are termed rowlock stretchers,and with headers upright are termed rowlock headers. There are various patterns that are used in brick laying. Strictly, in bricklaying, pattern refers to changes in arrangement or varied brick texture or color used in the face. But the different methods of joining bricks with the mortar can also be termed patterns. There are five various types of bonding. They are:

Running bond—Consists of all stretchers, but each tier is moved over one half brick.

Block or stack bond—Each tier is placed over the previous in exactly the same position.

American bond—A variation of running bond, with a full course of headers every fifth, sixth or seventh course.

English bond—Alternates block bond tiers with header tiers.

Flemish bond—Similar to English bond, but differs in that instead of alternating tiers, it alternates stretcher and header in the same tier.

Modern building codes require that masonry-bonded walls have no less that 4 percent headers in the wall surface. Headers bond the wall across its thickness. Metal ties are usually recommended for bonding an exterior wall. This allows for stretching and resistance to cracking.

The surface of the brick wall can vary, depending on how the joints are finished. There are about seven types of finished joints.

Concave is the most common. It keeps moisture out and the mortar is forced tightly between the brick and thus makes an excellent bond.

The V-joint is formed with a special jointer, a piece of wood or a trowel, and it stands out as a sharp line. V-joints direct water off.

The raked forms a deep recess, does not keep water out, but produces a shading that accentuates the brick courses.

The weathered sheds the water better than any other. It is recessed at the top, and is level with the brick surface at the bottom of the joint.

The struck is the opposite of weathered—it is recessed at the bottom and slants towards the top.

The flush is the easiest of all to make. One simply uses the trowel to smooth the face. It is water resistant but not very strong since the mortar is not compacted.

The extruded, also called the "weeping" joint, is water resistant and is used mainly for garden walls or where a rustic appearance is desired. It is made by using an excess of mortar between tiers of brick. When a brick is put into place the excess mortar is then squeezed out, and left where it hangs over.

As to when a certain type of stone or brick, or what type of bonding is to be used, it depends on purpose and desire of the one building. But whatever type is chosen, stone and brick last the longest, besides being pleasant to the eye.

See also Brick; Concrete; Igneous rocks; Metamorphic rock; Sedimentary rock.

Melvin Tracy

Stoneflies

Stoneflies or salmonflies are a group of insects with aquatic nymphal stages in the order Plecoptera. Stoneflies have a simple metamorphosis, with three life-history stages: egg, nymph or naiad, and adult.

Adult stoneflies have two pairs of membranous wings, that are folded back over the abdomen when not in use. Stoneflies are rather weak fliers, and are not usually found very far from the aquatic habitat of their nymphs. Adult stoneflies do not feed, their short life being devoted to procreation.

The nymphs of stoneflies are soft-bodied, rather flattened, and usually occur in well-aerated, running waters of streams and rivers, or sometimes along rocky lake shores, where they hide in gravel and organic debris. Stonefly nymphs have an abdomen with ten segments, and with two extended appendages known as cerci sticking out from the back end. Stonefly nymphs are most easily differentiated from superficially-similar mayfly nymphs (order Ephemeroptera) on the basis of their two cerci (mayflies almost always have three abdominal "tails"). The nymphal stage of stoneflies is long-lived, commonly lasting for a year or more. There can be more than 20 nymphal stages, each separated by a molt.

Stoneflies are an abundant component of the bottom fauna of many aquatic communities, especially in streams. Although their biomass and productivity are not usually as large as that of mayflies, stoneflies are an important food of sportfish such as trout and salmon, and for this reason these insects are economically important. Some of the best designs for fish-catching "flies" are based on the shape and color of stoneflies, especially the adult insects.

Stoneroller see **Minnows**

Storks

Storks are large wading birds of the tropics and subtropics. They belong to order Ciconiiformes, which also includes the ibises and spoonbills, and are in family Ciconiidae. Unlike most tall wading birds, storks perch in trees. They also look for high places to nest, and they often return to the same place to nest year after year. These tendencies have long made the white stork (Ciconia ciconia) a favorite among the villagers of Europe, to which this bird has annually returned after wintering in Africa. Tales of the storks, as well as the folklore that children are delivered by storks, were brought to America by European settlers.

Storks look somewhat like cranes, but their bills are considerably longer and heavier. Most species have perfectly straight bills. Cranes have three front toes like most birds, but they have an additional toe at the back of the foot that lets them cling to branches. Herons and egrets also have this special toe.

During flight, all 17 species of storks except the adjutant storks (Leptoptilos), fly with their necks outstretched. They have broad, strong wings that allow them to soar for long periods on rising warm air currents. The different species are often distinguished by the color of their bills and the bare skin on their heads and legs.

The most amazing part of a stork is its bill. It can be 9 inches (23 cm) long and about 7 inches (18 cm) around at the thick base. The bird is adept at using it almost like hands, to build nests, find food, care for the young, and even fighting. The saddle-bill stork (Ephippiorhynchus senegalensis) of Africa has a vivid orange bill with a wide black band around it. It also has orange anklets at the bend in its legs (which are actually its ankles). The Asian open-bill (Anastomas lamelligerus) of India has a bill in which the two mandibles

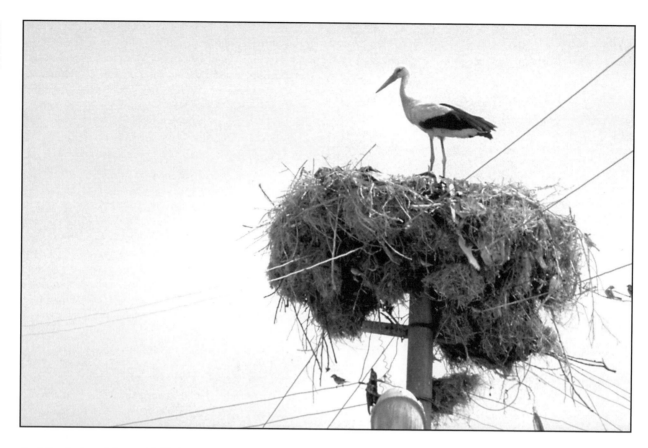

A white stork and its nest in Turkey.

do not close together. This doesn't stop it from maintaining itself on a diet of mussels.

The most amazing bill is found in the whale-headed stork *(Balaeniceps rex)* of freshwater swamps in Africa from Sudan down through Zaire. Instead of being narrow and pointed, its bill is thick, rounded, spotted, and hooked on the end. Although called a stork, this large gray bird does not actually belong to the stork family. It is in a family of its own, Balaenicipitidae.

All storks except the wood storks study the ground or water intently when looking for food. Their keen eyesight and quick reaction time lets them grab moving animals almost as quickly as they see them. The two adjutant storks of India don't have this problem because they eat carrion. The greater adjutant *(L. dubius)* and the lesser adjutant *(L. javanicus)* can be found along with vultures feeding at the leftovers from a predator's kill. However, they don't tear meat off the carcass. Instead, they steal bits from the vultures. The marabou stork *(L. crumeniferus)* of African savanna is also a carrion thief. Not an attractive bird, the marabou stork has a splotchy head, very short neck, and a huge pink pouch hanging from its neck area. The soft feathers on its tail have been used for hat decorations for many decades,

although these feathers also came from adjutant storks.

The American storks

The only true American stork is the wood stork *(Mycteria americana),* sometimes erroneously called the wood ibis. The wood stork has white feathers with black flight feathers, and gray legs and a blue-gray featherless head. Its 9-inch (23-cm) bill is also gray, but unlike most storks' bills, it curves downward slightly at the end.

The wood stork lives primarily in the swamps of southern Florida, where for generations it regarded the giant bald cypress trees as its rightful home. However, these trees have been cut down and the birds' habitat has been destroyed as the Everglades and other areas like it have been harmed by fertilizers and water control. In the 1950s, these birds were seriously threatened, until Corkscrew Swamp Sanctuary was developed to protect a large nesting population.

Wood storks feed primarily on fish, plus assorted small frogs and reptiles with a topping of crustaceans and mollusks. They use both their feet and their bills to feel the presence of food. They rarely depend on sight to spot it, a fact that lets them feed at night as well as in the daytime. Some storks feed in open fields instead of water. These birds are often seen in farm fields, where they hunt for insects in newly turned soil.

These birds do not mate according to the season but to the level of water in their swampy homes. Storks raise their young during the dry season, because the water—and the life it contains—concentrates into pools. These concentrated food supplies makes feeding hungry young storks easier. At the proper time, the male selects a nesting site, preferably a bald cypress. At first, any female approaching him is driven away, but soon they agree to mate. The female holds the chosen nesting site while the male collects sticks as nesting material. The female lays between two and five eggs, although incubation starts as soon as the first one is laid. After about 30 days of incubation by both birds, the eggs hatch. The fluffy white young remain in the nest until they are fully feathered, about 55 days.

However, being in the nest does not make the young birds safe. Adolescent storks are prone to an activity that has been likened to juvenile gang activity. Gangs of immature storks—probably below the age of 3—will attack nests, trying to drive the parents away. Then they tear apart the nest and kill the young. If this happens, the parents will build another nest and lay more eggs.

The only other American stork is also among the largest storks. The jabiru (*Jabiru mycteria*) can stand as tall as a man. It resides primarily in South America, making only infrequent visits to the southern United States. Except for its head and neck which are black, its plumage is white. The wings may span 7 feet (2.2 m) or even more. Its 12-inch (30-cm)-long bill is also black. The name *jabiru* is also sometimes given to the saddle-billed stork of Africa.

All large flying birds are in danger from hunters, but storks have the added problem of losing wetland areas to development. The presence of white storks on the rooftops of Europe has long been considered good luck. However, the numbers of these famous storks have dropped by about 90% in the last hundred years. No one reason explains this loss. Among its causes are pesticides, loss of nesting habitat, changing weather conditions, deforestation, hunting, even the way farm fields are plowed.

Further Reading:

Kerrod, Robin. *Birds: The Waterbirds.* Encyclopedia of the Animal World series. New York: Facts on File, 1989.

Jean F. Blashfield

Storm

A storm is any disturbance in the atmosphere that has noticeable effects on the Earth's surface. The term suggests disagreeable weather conditions that may bring discomfort, inconvenience, economic disaster and loss of human lives. In spite of that fact, storms have a generally positive effect on the environment and on human societies because they are the source of most of the rain and snow on which the planet depends.

Among the many kinds of storms that exist are thunderstorms, hurricanes, tornadoes, blizzards, and ice and hail storms. As different as these types of storms may be, they possess a few common characteristics. They all result from significant atmospheric instabilities, and they all involve dramatic convection currents in which air masses travel upwards at high rates of speed.

The formation of a thunderstorm is typical of the way many storms develop. Imagine that a large mass of air encounters conditions that force it to move upwards. An approaching front or some kind of geographical barrier might produce such an effect. The air mass will continue to rise as long as it is warmer than the atmosphere around it. The upward movement of such an air mass constitutes a convection current.

At some point, moisture within the air mass may begin to condense, releasing heat as it does so. When this happens the convection current may begin to move even more rapidly. The upward movement of air in a thunder cloud has been measured at more than 50 miles per hour (80 kph). As the upward movement of air continues, more moisture condenses out of the air mass and a large cloud begins to form. Depending on atmospheric conditions, a thundercloud of this type may rise to a height of anywhere from 6-9 miles (10-15 km). Eventually, ice crystals within the thundercloud will begin to condense as rain, snow, or some other form of precipitation and a thunderstorm will occur.

Some of the most severe types of storms (tornadoes and hurricanes, for example) occur when the upward convention current receives a rotational push. This push converts a purely vertical air movement into a spiralling motion characteristic of these great tropical and midlatitude storms.

See also Air masses and fronts; Cyclone and anticyclone; Precipitation; Thunderstorm; Tornado.

St. Peter's fish see **Dories**

Strabismus see **Vision disorders**

Strata

Strata (singular: stratum) are the horizontal layers, or beds, present in most sedimentary rocks. During or immediately after the accumulation of sediments, physical, biological, and chemical processes produce sedimentary structures. Strata are probably the most common sedimentary structures, as almost all sedimentary rocks display some type of bedding. A rock that contains beds is stratified or displays stratification.

Strata form during sediment deposition, that is, the laying down of sediment. Meanwhile, if a change in current speed or sediment grain size occurs or perhaps the sediment supply is cut off, a bedding plane forms. Bedding planes are surfaces that separate one stratum from another. Bedding planes can also form when the upper part of a sediment layer is eroded away before the next episode of deposition. Strata separated by a bedding plane may have different grain sizes, grain compositions, or colors. Sometimes these other traits are better indicators of stratification as bedding planes may be very subtle.

The strata in an exposure or outcropping of sedimentary rock can range from layers as thin as paper, known as lamina (plural: laminae or laminations) to beds tens of feet thick. Generally, the more stable and consistent the environmental conditions during deposition, the thicker the strata. For example, in a river with very consistent current speeds, thick sediment layers with widely spaced bedding planes form. In a different river, where current speeds vary often, thin sediment layers and closely spaced bedding planes form instead.

The area covered by a bed, that is its areal extent, is also highly variable. Some beds can be traced for hundreds of square miles. Others may cover an area of only a few hundred square feet. Many factors influence the areal extent of beds. Among the more important factors is the setting in which the bed formed. Rivers, for obvious reasons, deposit beds shaped like a shoe string (long and thin); deposits in the open ocean often extend for great distances in all directions. Erosion of strata after deposition also affects their areal extent.

Bedding planes indicate variable environmental conditions during sediment deposition, but they may also be evidence of a gap in the geologic record. Many times a bedding plane develops because no sediment accumulates for at least a brief period of time or it is later eroded away. This represents an interval of time for which there is no sediment record. If we think of strata as a record of geologic time preserved in sediment (or sedimentary rock), this break or gap between sedimentation events actually is a gap in the geologic record. In other words, think of an outcrop of rock as being like a book; strata are pages and bedding planes are pages that have been torn from the book.

The time gap represented by a bedding plane may be very short, a fraction of a second, or perhaps a few minutes. After that interval passes, recording continues in the form of sediment deposition. However, sometimes the amount of time that is unrepresented (the gap) can be quite long, perhaps hundreds or thousands of years. These longer gaps are called unconformities. In some rock outcrops, more geologic time may be represented by the bedding planes (the gaps) than by the strata that lie between them.

See also Sediment and sedimentation; Sedimentary rock; Unconformity.

Strawberry see **Rose family**

Strepsiptera

Also known as twisted-winged parasites, strepsipterans are small insects which are internal parasites of other insects. Measuring between 0.02-0.16 inch (0.5 and 4 mm) long, the males and females lead totally different lives. Males are free, winged insects—resembling some forms of beetles—and females are wingless, shapeless insects living as parasites. Strepsipterans live all over the world, except Antarctica.

Belonging to the largest class of animals in the world—the class Insecta—the superclass Hexapoda contains over 750,000 species. There are two subclasses within Hexapoda: (1) Apterygota (insects without wings) which contains two orders, and (2) Pterygota (insects with wings, accounting for 99.9% of all insect species) which contains twenty-eight orders. Further classification of strepsipterans is continuously being revised. Sometimes, they are considered to be a suborder of the Order Coleoptera, an order containing beetles; however, often they are given their own order—the Order Strepsiptera. Currently, there are seven families within the Order Strepsiptera, containing about 300 species of insects, 60 of which live in North America.

As mentioned before, the appearance and behavior of the male and female strepsipterans differ markedly. The female resembles a grub, having no wings, legs, eyes, or mouth. Also, her nervous system is very diminished. She generally attaches herself to another insect as a host. For instance, the female of the Stylopidae species attaches herself to the stomach of a wasp or bee. She burrows almost her entire body into her host, sticking out slightly. While she does not usually kill her host, her presence sterilizes it, causing it to have both male and female sexual organs, and alters its appearance otherwise.

The male strepsipteran is independent of any host, having antennae, wings, and large eyes. He darts about during his ten hour lifetime, continuously looking for a female to mate. She lures him with a special odor, since she is almost invisible within her host. He injects his sperm through a small hole located between her thorax and abdomen. The male dies soon after mating; when he dies, his forewings dry out and twist up like a corkscrew, giving these insects their common name.

After a few days, the female hatches about 1,500 tiny larvae that are born with eyes, mouths, and three pair of legs ending in suckers. Leaving their mother through an opening in her back, they continue to exist on the host bee (or other insect) until it lands on a flower. At this point, the offspring climb onto the flower and await another bee. Being consumed by a new bee, the young strepsipterans ride back to the hive. The bee regurgitates them when it stocks its nest with nectar, and the young strepsipterans are free to bore into the bee larvae and molt to their legless, inactive forms. Thus, the cycle begins again.

Stress

Stress is mental or physical tension brought about by internal or external pressures. Stress may be a factor in causing disease. Researchers have found that there are significant biochemical changes that take place in the body when a person experiences stress. Hormones like adrenalin and noradrenalin play an important role in producing the condition of stress.

People experience stress from many different sources and the experience can be mild or severe, acute—when responding to an immediate danger—or chronic—when a person is involved in a long-term stressful situation. Stress can come from having to take a test or dealing with an difficult person, or it can come from traumatic experiences such as the death of a loved one or a serious illness.

The response to stress has been implicated in many serious illnesses such as heart disease, cancer, and immunological disorders. It is believed that reactions to stress contribute to a weakening of vulnerable systems in the body and to subsequent illness. Researchers believe that stress disrupts the body's homeostasis, which helps maintain a biological balance among the systems that operate within the body.

People who experience severe traumas, such as soldiers experience during combat, may develop a condition called post-traumatic stress disorder (PTSD). During World War I it was called shell shock and during World War II it was called battle fatigue. Since 1980, PTSD has been listed as a diagnostic category by the American Psychiatric Association. Sufferers of PTSD experience depression, feelings of guilt for having survived, nightmares, and flashbacks to the traumatic events. They may be excessively sensitive to noise and may even become violent.

Hans Selye

Dr. Hans Selye, an endocrinologist, developed a three-stage model of the body's response to stress. He called his theory the General Adaptation Syndrome (GAS). The first phase is an alarm reaction, the second stage is one of resistance or adaptation, and the final stage is one of exhaustion.

In the alarm stage the body responds to a stressor, which could be physical or psychological. Perhaps you are crossing the street and a car suddenly speeds toward you. Your heart begins to beat fast and the release of adrenaline makes you move quickly from the path of the oncoming car. Other responses in the alarm stage might include butterflies in your stomach, a rise in your blood pressure, heavy breathing, dilation of your eyes, dry mouth, and the hair on your arms might even stand on end. To help you meet the sudden danger, your blood flows away from the organs you don't need to confront the danger, your muscles tense up, and you will not be able to concentrate on any kind of problem solving outside the danger confronting you.

During the resistance stage of a stress reaction, your body remains on alert for danger. When this part of the GAS is prolonged, your immune system may become compromised and you may become susceptible to illness. Even within days of becoming stressed and maintaining a stress alertness, changes take place that weaken your body's ability to fight off disease. The final stage of Selye's GAS is the exhaustion stage. As your body readjusts during this period, hormones are released to help bring your body back to normal, to the state of balance called homeostasis. Until balance is reached, though, the body is still releasing hormones and suppressing your immune system.

Stress and illness

There have been numerous studies that try to determine the relationship of illness and the state of mind of the patient. Physicians at the University of California Medical Center in Los Angeles, during the 1980s, determined that emotional stress affected the immune system. They found that the reduction of stress boosted the immune system in patients. Other studies have demonstrated elevated cholesterol levels caused by stress and the exacerbation of heart disease, ulcers, and cancer from stress.

In heart disease, chronic stress has the effect of wearing out the branch points of arteries that run throughout the body and causing the accumulation of fat, starch, calcium, and other substances in the linings of the blood vessels. This can ultimately lead to atherosclerosis, a thickening of the walls of the arteries that impedes the flow of blood.

Other diseases associated with stress are the onset of adult diabetes (type 2 non-insulin-dependent), ulcers, respiratory infections, and depression. The stress can be psychological or it can come from stressful situations such as accidents or illness. It is believed that stress can worsen an illness during its course. With stomach conditions that lead to ulcers there are a number of ways that stress can worsen the condition. It is thought that stress can affect acid production in the stomach, decrease normal blood flow, by suppressing the immune system and allowing bacteria to increase, by decreasing the amount of prostaglandins (a fatty acid in the stomach that protects it from ulceration), and by causing stomach contractions that add to the risk of ulcers.

Treatments for stress reduction

A form of psychotherapy called medical psychotherapy is one of the methods used to deal with stress. It is primarily a talking therapy based on the principle that when people can talk about what is troubling them, they can lessen the amount of stress they feel, perhaps even relieve it. Medications may also be used, such as antianxiety or antidepressant drugs. This type of therapy is usually administered by a psychiatrist, but sometimes it is given by a nurse, social worker, or other medical therapist. It is important for the therapist to understand the nature of the illness around which the stress is involved. In this kind of supportive therapy the goal is to help patients deal with the feelings stimulated by traumatic events, illness, or conflicts that produce stress in the patient.

While it may come as a surprise, it has been reported by the American Academy of Family Physi-

---

KEY TERMS

Adrenalin—A chemical released from the adrenal gland in response to stress, exercise, or strong emotions.

Atherosclerosis—A disease of the arteries in which the linings thicken and impede the flow of blood.

General Adaptation Syndrome (GAS)—The three-phase model of stress reaction.

Homeostasis—The state of being in balance.

Post-traumatic stress disorder (PTSD)—A response to traumatic events such as those experience in combat.

Prostaglandin—A fatty acid in the stomach that protects it from ulcerating.

Noradrenalin—A chemical produced by the adrenal glands to maintain constant blood pressure.

---

cians that two-thirds of their patients come for treatment of a stress-related condition. Selye believed that the stress of life contributed a great deal to aging. A method of treatment for stress that was developed after his theories became popular was called progressive relaxation. Relaxation training has been found to reduce stress and boost immunity as well.

Other therapists help patients develop coping strategies to reduce or eliminate stress from their lives. Some life-style changes are often recommended by therapists to help people reduce stress. Among them are changes in diet, development of stress-management techniques, smoking cessation, aerobic exercise, and group discussions. Knowing the causes of stress and being able to talk about them are considered important for reducing or eliminating stress. Denial of stress is considered a contributing factor to intensifying the stress.

Recognition of stress

Some of the physical signs of stress are a dry mouth and throat, tight muscles in the neck, shoulders, and back, chronic neck and back problems, headaches, indigestion, tremors, muscle tics, insomnia, and fatigue. Emotional signs of stress could include difficulty in concentrating, feeling tense, negative thinking, brooding, worrying, feeling depressed, anxious, or worthless.

Irritability, restlessness, impulsive behavior, difficulty in making a decision, poor judgment, difficulty relating to people and mistrusting them, and the use of tobacco, alcohol, or drugs could all be indications of stress. Of course there could be other causes of these symptoms, but they all carry an element of stress. Illness itself will cause stress and a cycle of feeling stressed and becoming ill and increasing the feeling of stress can become difficult to overcome.

Further Reading:

Cotton, Dorothy H.G. *Stress Management*. New York: Bruner/Mazel, 1990.

Friedman, Howard S., ed. *Hostility, Coping and Health*. Washington, DC: American Psychological Association, 1992.

Green, Stephen A. *Feel Good Again*. Mount Vernon, New York: Consumers Union, 1990.

Moyers, Bill. *Healing and the Mind*. New York: Doubleday, 1993.

Sapolsky, Robert M. *Why Zebras Don't Get Ulcers*. New York: W.H. Freeman and Company, 1994.

Schafer, Walter E. *Stress Management for Wellness*. New York: Holt, Rinehart & Winston, 1992.

Vita Richman

Stress, ecological

Environmental stress refers to physical, chemical, and biological constraints on the productivity of species and ecological development. When the exposure to environmental stressors increases or decreases in intensity, ecological responses result. Stressors can be natural environmental factors, or they may result from the activities of humans. Some environmental stressors exert a relatively local influence, while others are regional or global in their scope. Stressors are challenges to the integrity of ecosystems and to the quality of the environment.

Species and ecosystems have some capacity to tolerate changes in the intensity of environmental stressors. This is known as resistance, but there are limits to this attribute which represent thresholds of tolerance. When these thresholds are exceeded by further increases in the intensity of environmental stress, substantial ecological changes are caused.

Environmental stressors can be grouped into the following categories: (1) Physical stress refers to brief but intense exposures to kinetic energy. This is a type of ecological disturbance because of its acute, episodic nature. Examples include volcanic eruptions, wind-

storms, and explosions. (2) Wildfire is also a disturbance during which much of the biomass of an ecosystem is combusted, and the dominant species may be killed. (3) Pollution occurs when chemicals are present in concentrations large enough to affect organisms and thereby cause ecological changes. Toxic pollution can be caused by gases such as sulfur dioxide and ozone, by elements such as arsenic, lead, and mercury, and by pesticides such as DDT. Inputs of nutrients such as phosphate and nitrate can influence productivity and other ecological processes, causing a type of pollution known as eutrophication. (4) Thermal stress occurs when releases of heat influence ecosystems as happens in the vicinity of natural hot-water vents in the ocean and with industrial discharges of heated water. (5) Radiation stress is associated with excessive loads of ionizing energy. This can occur on mountain tops where there are intense exposures to ultraviolet radiation and in places where there are exposures to radioactive materials. (6) Climatic stress is associated with excessive or insufficient regimes of temperature, moisture, solar radiation, and combinations of these. Tundra and deserts are examples of climatically stressed ecosystems, while tropical rainforests occur under a relatively benign climatic regime. (7) Biological stresses are associated with the diverse interactions that occur among organisms of the same or different species. Biological stresses can result from competition, herbivory, predation, parasitism, and disease. The harvesting and management of species and ecosystems by humans is a type of biological stress.

Various types of ecological responses occur when the intensity of environmental stress causes significant changes. For example, disruption of an ecosystem by an intense disturbance causes mortality of organisms and other ecological damages followed by recovery through succession.

More permanent ecological adjustments occur in response to longer-term increases in the intensity of environmental stress, associated perhaps with chronic pollution or climate change. The resulting effects can include reductions in the abundance of vulnerable species, their elimination from sites stressed over the longer term, and replacement by species that are more tolerant of the changed environmental conditions. Other commonly observed responses to longer-term increases in stress include a simplification of species richness and decreased rates of productivity, decomposition, and nutrient cycling. In total, these changes represent a longer-term change in the character of the ecosystem or an ecological conversion.

See also Ecological integrity; Pollution; Wildfire.

Striper see **Bass**

Stroke

A stroke, also called a cerebral vascular accident or CVA, is a sudden, often crippling disturbance in blood circulation in the brain. Interruption in blood circulation may be the result of a burst artery or of an artery that has become closed off because a blood clot has lodged in it. Blood circulation to the area of the brain served by that artery stops at the point of disturbance, and the brain tissue beyond that is damaged or dies.

Stroke is the third leading cause of death in the U.S. Heart attack is the leading cause of death, and all forms of cancer are second. Approximately 500,000 strokes, new and recurrent, are reported each year. Of these, about 150,000 will be fatal. Today approximately 3 million Americans who have had a stroke are alive.

The death rate from stroke has been steadily declining since the early 1970s. A great part of this success has been the efforts of various agencies to make physicians and the general population aware of the danger of high blood pressure. The importance of regular blood pressure checks has begun to infiltrate the general public's knowledge. High blood pressure, or hypertension, is the most important risk factor for stroke.

The brain requires a constant and steady infusion of blood to carry out its functions. Blood delivers the oxygen and nutrients needed by the brain cells, so the circulation to the brain is copious. The carotid arteries on each side of the throat and the vertebral arteries in the back of the neck carry blood to the brain. As the arteries enter the brain they begin to divide into smaller and smaller vessels until they reach the microscopic size of capillaries. The venous system to drain blood from the brain is equally large.

A burst blood vessel, which may occur in a weak area in the artery, or a blood vessel that becomes plugged by a floating blood clot no longer supplies blood to the brain tissue beyond the point of the occurrence. The effect of the interruption in circulation to the brain depends upon the area of the brain that is involved. Interruption of a small blood vessel may result in a speech impediment or difficulty in hearing or an unsteady gait. If a larger blood vessel is involved the result may be the total paralysis of one side of the body. Damage to the right hemisphere of the brain will result in injury to the left side of the body, and vice versa. The onset of the stroke may be so sudden and severe that the

KEY TERMS

Cerebral—Refers to the brain. Cerebral vascular is reference to the blood supply to the brain.

Death rate—The number of deaths from a given cause per specified number of people. The death rate from a disease may be given as 30 per 10,000 population.

Pathologist—A physician who studies the disease process. He learns by conducting autopsies on people who have died.

patient is literally struck down in his tracks. Some patients have early warnings that a stroke may be developing, however.

These people have what is called transient ischemic attacks, or TIAs. These usually result when a cerebral artery is closing because of the build-up of fatty deposits inside the vessel, a condition called atherosclerosis. Slight disturbances in circulation occur at intervals in such a case and the patient will experience momentary symptoms such as unexplained dizziness, blurring of vision, loss of hearing, or other event. It is important in this case to consult a physician so that proper testing can be carried out to determine the cause of the TIAs and steps taken to prevent development of a full stroke.

A stroke that results from a burst blood vessel is called a hemorrhagic stroke. In addition to the damage to brain tissue caused by lack of blood, additional damage may be brought about by the blood clot formed from the bleeding. The doctor may need to surgically remove the clot to relieve pressure on the brain.

A stroke caused by a clot sealing a blood vessel is called a thrombotic stroke, for the technical name of the clot, a thrombus. The clot can be formed elsewhere in the body and be carried in the circulating blood until it reaches a vessel too small for it to pass through. At that point it will lodge and dam up the flow of blood, inflicting damage on the tissue beyond the blockage. A thrombotic stroke, if attended quickly, sometimes can be minimized in terms of damage.

People who are known to form blood clots in their circulatory system can be given medications to prevent it. Also, current therapy includes medications that can be given to dissolve clots (a process called thrombolysis) and remove the barrier to blood flow. Some brain function may be preserved in this way that would otherwise be lost if the clot is allowed to remain in place.

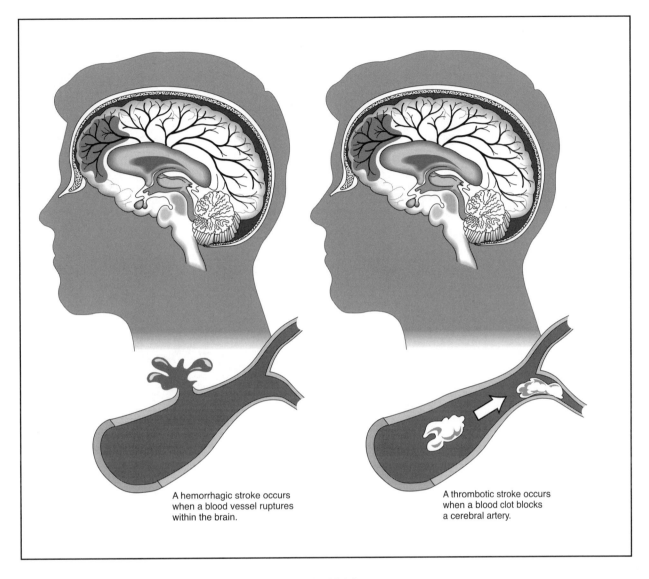

A hemorrhagic stroke occurs when a blood vessel ruptures within the brain.

A thrombotic stroke occurs when a blood clot blocks a cerebral artery.

A hemorrhagic stroke (left) compared to a thrombotic stroke (right).

Not all vascular events bring on a stroke. Pathologists often find areas in the brain in which a small blood vessel has ruptured but the patient was not reported to have suffered a stroke. Blood vessels that form what is called collateral circulation often make up for the blood circulation lost by a plugged or ruptured vessel. Collateral circulation is carried by other vessels that help to supply blood to a given area of the brain.

Strokes can be prevented by effective treatment of high blood pressure and by taking an aspirin tablet every day, for those who can tolerate such medication. The aspirin helps to prevent clot formation and a number of clinical trials have shown it to be effective in stroke reduction.

Recovery from a stroke varies from one person to the next. Swift treatment followed by effective physical therapy may restore nearly full function of an affected area of the body. Some individuals have experienced severe enough damage that their recovery is minimal and they may be confined to a wheelchair or bed for the remainder of their lives.

See also Brain; Thrombosis.

Further Reading:

Aldhous, P. "A hearty endorsement for aspirin." *Science*, 263 (January 7, 1994):24.

National Heart, Lung, and Blood Institute, *Report of the Joint National Committee on Detection, Evaluation, and Treatment of High Blood Pressure*, Bethesda MD, 1993, available upon request.

Larry Blaser

Stromatolites at Hamelin Pool in western Australia.

Stromatolite

A stromatolite is a preserved structure in sedimentary rock that is a series of thin layers of sediment. These layers formed when a colony of algae trapped loose sediment particles.

Stromatolites occur in rocks that range in age from very recent to more than 3.5 billion years old. Ancient stromatolites are the oldest evidence of life that is visible without a microscope. They are also the most common evidence of life found in rocks dating from about 3.5 billion years ago to 1.5 billion years ago. The algae that form them are of the blue-green variety. Also called cyanobacteria due to their primitive nature, blue-green algae carry on photosynthesis to produce their own food. Thin algal mats (colonies) grow today in almost any moist environment—rocky stream beds, boat piers, shower stalls, etc.

Stromatolites are not true fossils. They contain no preserved body parts (bones, for example) or impressions (for example, footprints). Stromatolites consist of only layered sediment. They form when algal mats trap sediment on a sticky "carpet" of thin, thread-like fila-ments. Currents or waves move sediment over algal mats located in shallow water. Fine sediment—especially particles less than 0.0025 inches (1/16 mm)—sticks to the filaments. Sediment collects on the algal filaments like dirt sticking to a rug where you spilled a soft drink. Eventually the sediment limits the amount of light available to the algae for photosynthesis. In response, the algae send new filaments up through the accumulated sediment layer, creating a "clean carpet," that is, a new algal mat. Another sediment layer then begins to accumulate. In this way, many thin layers of sediment form. Later, the algal filaments usually decay so that only the sediment layers remain.

Most stromatolites occur in limestones, rather than in sandstones or shales. The sediments that form limestones are usually bound together (cemented) soon after the particles accumulate. Cementation occurs much later in most sandstones and shales. Thanks to this early cementation, stromatolites in limestones are more likely to avoid destruction by burrowing animals and other disruptive processes. Stromatolites also are less common in rocks younger than about 500 million years old. Plant-eating animals (herbivores) probably began to evolve about 850-900 million years ago. For the next few hundred million years, herbivores became increasingly common, and their grazing activities began to destroy more and more stromatolites. By 500 million years ago, preservation of stromatolites became much less likely.

Ancient stromatolites probably populated the sea bottom in much the same way as modern coral reefs, preferring shallow, well-lit areas. However, modern stromatolites are common only in very salty, shallow ocean waters or in highly mineralized lake water. These high salinity (salty) environments are hostile to many organisms, but stromatolites thrive there because of the absence of grazing herbivores. In this setting, algal mats build dome- and column-shaped stromatolites that reach as much as 3 ft (1 m) in height.

See also Algae; Sedimentary rock.

Strong acid see **Acids and bases**

Strong base see **Acids and bases**

Strong electrolyte see **Electrolyte**

Strong interactive force see **Subatomic particles**

Strontium 90 see **Radioactive pollution**

Strontium see **Alkaline earth metals**

Structural formula see **Formula, chemical**

Strychnine see **Nux vomica tree**

Sturgeons

Sturgeon are large sharklike fish, with a heterocercal tail like that of a shark and a small ventral mouth behind an extended snout. The mouth has long barbels used for feeding on small animals on the bottom. Sturgeons feed on aquatic insects, snails, crayfish, small clams, and small fish.

Sturgeons have a cartilaginous skeleton with bony plates instead of scales in their skin which cover the sides of the body, and which completely cover the head.

Sturgeons are distributed throughout North America, Asia and northern Europe. A few species are species are anadromous, living in the oceans but swimming up rivers to spawn, and other species live only in fresh water. Of the anadromous sturgeons, one of the two species on the Pacific coast, *Acipenser transmontanus*,

A lake sturgeon (*Acipenser fulvesceus*).

may weigh over 1000 pounds (450 kg). The two anadromous species on the Atlantic coast have been recently greatly reduced in population.

Sturgeons are found both in the rivers and the eastern coasts of North America. The most common species in North America is the lake sturgeon, *Acipeuser folvesceus*. In Europe they are found in the rivers and the coast line from Scandinavia to the Black Sea. From time to time trawlers fishing along the coasts of Britain and Ireland may catch sturgeons. Pollution and the presence of weirs have been instrumental in reducing the populations to the point of extinction in rivers where they were once plentiful.

Spawning occurs from May to July when the sturgeons enter the rivers of the United States and continental Europe. A female sturgeon may lay up to 3 million eggs, each about 0.08 inch (2 mm) in diameter, and covered with gelatin. Eggs remain on the bottom of the river, hatch within 3 to 7 days, and release larvae which measure about 0.4 inch (9 mm). At one month the young fish may measure 4-5.5 inches (10-14 cm) long. The young may not start the seaward journey until they reach two or three years of age and are 3 feet (1 m) long.

The flesh of the sturgeon is edible but is not prized; it is the sturgeons eggs which are used to make caviar meat are in great demand. The swim bladders of sturgeons are used to make isinglass, a semi-transparent whitish gelatin used in jellies, glues and as a clarifying agent.

Since the population of sturgeons has been greatly diminished, commercial fishing of these fish is now limited. Some sturgeons may provide considerable excitement because of the battle they provide when hooked on light tackle.

The sturgeon family has the distinction of providing the largest freshwater fish in North America. In the last century three fish were reported to exceed 1,500 lbs (675 kg). At present some specimens may weigh over 1,000 lbs (450 kg), and one fish caught by gill net weighed 1,285 lbs (578 kg). Although the species extends from Alaska to the middle of California, the largest fish are found mainly in the Columbia and Fraser rivers in British Columbia, Washington, and Oregon.

The white sturgeon is actually grayish brown with a white belly. When at 9 feet (3 m) long, it may be about 50 years of age. The 3,000,000 eggs laid by a 10 foot female may weigh almost 250 lbs (113 kg). Laws that protect the large sturgeons, that tend to be females with eggs, are now in effect.

The green sturgeon, *A. medirostris*, grows up to 7 feet (2.5 m) and weighs about 350 lbs (158 kg). It has a greenish color and its barbels are located nearer to the end of the snout, and has fewer bony plates along the back.

The largest fish caught in the fresh water along the Atlantic coast is the Atlantic coast is the Atlantic sturgeon, *A. oxyrhynchus*. It has been verified that 14 foot (4.2 m) fish weighing 611 lbs (275 kg) has been caught. As is the case with the Pacific sturgeon, the Atlantic sturgeon populations are being depleted because of pollution and dams, which prevent them from reaching their breeding grounds.

Nathan Lavenda

Style see **Flower**

Subatomic particles

Subatomic particles are particles that are smaller than an atom. Historically subatomic particles were considered to be electrons, protons, and neutrons. However, the definition of subatomic particles has now been expanded to include elementary particles and all the particles they can be combined to make.

Elementary particles are particles which cannot be divided up into smaller particles. There are two kinds of elementary particles. One kind of elementary particles make up matter. Examples of these particles include electrons and quarks (which make up protons and neutrons). Baryons and mesons are combinations of quarks and are considered subatomic particles. The most famous baryons are protons and neutrons. The other elementary particles are mediators of the fundamental forces. These mediator particles enable the matter particles to interact with each other. To illustrate this idea, let's say two boys want to play catch. The boys represent the matter particles, and playing catch represents the fundamental force. In this case, the ball would represent the mediator particle.

Discovery of particles

Electrons

The first particle to be discovered is thought to be the electron. In 1897 Joseph John Thomson measured the velocity and charge-to-mass ratio of what he called cathode rays. He found their mass was much smaller than their charge. This indicated to him that he had found a particle, which he gave the name "corpuscle" and was later changed to electron. The charges of all particles are traditionally measured in terms of the size of the charge of the electron. The electron has a charge, e, of 1.6×10^{-19} Coulombs.

Photons

The first mediator particle to be discovered was the photon. In 1900, Max Planck reported that light came in little packages of energy, which he called quanta. Albert Einstein, in 1905, figured out that radiation is quantized by its nature. Thus a photon is one of these quanta, the smallest possible piece of energy. Einstein called this the photoelectric effect and won a Nobel Prize in physics for it. The name photon was coined later, by chemist Gilbert Lewis in 1926.

Protons

The proton was one of the earliest particles known. The word proton is Greek for "the first one." In 1906 the first clues to the nature of the proton were seen. Joseph John Thomson reported detecting positively charged hydrogen "atoms." These were in fact, hydrogen nuclei, or protons, but atomic structure was not understood at the time. Conversely, Thomson thought that protons and electrons were randomly scattered throughout the atom, the so-called "plum-pudding model." In 1909-1911 Ernest Rutherford and his colleagues Hans Wilhelm Geiger and Ernest Marsden, did the famous scattering experiments of alpha particles (two protons and two neutrons) onto gold foil. They found that atoms had relatively hard and small centers, thus discovering the atomic nucleus and disproving the plum-pudding model.

In 1913, the Bohr model of the atom was introduced. In this model, the hydrogen atom consists of an electron orbiting the nucleus (a proton), as the earth

An electronic display of the decay of an upsilon, a particle made of a bottom quark and an antiquark, in the CLEO detector at the CESR collider at Cornell University. An electron and a positron have met and annihilated (center); their energy produces an excited upsilon, which lives too briefly to show. It decays into a lower energy state by emitting a photon which converts into a positron (which curves away tightly to the left) and an electron (which curves to the right). The lower-energy upsilon then decays to its ground state by emitting another photon (detected in the bottom right sector of the grid). The ground-state upsilon finally decays into a high energy electron-positron pair (seen as the two long paths that cut diagonally across the grid in opposite directions from the center).

orbits the sun. The Bohr model also requires that the angular momentum (mass times velocity times distance) of the electron be limited to certain values (be "quantized"), so that the electron doesn't fall into the nucleus. Rutherford gave the proton its name in 1920.

When the principles of quantum mechanics were developed, the Heisenberg uncertainty principle meant the Bohr atom had to be modified. The Heisenberg uncertainty principle tells us that it is impossible to determine both the position and the momentum (mass times velocity) of a subatomic particle. This means that the electrons in an atom still orbit the nucleus, but in clouds of unknown position instead of in well-defined orbits.

Neutrinos

In 1930, scientists started to suspect the existence of another subatomic particle which came to be known as the neutrino. Neutrinos are considered matter parti-

cles, but they do not make up earth matter by themselves. Neutrinos are very common, but we don't observe them because they don't interact very much with other particles. In 1930 a problem with a process called nuclear beta decay had developed. Nuclear beta decay is when an unstable, or radioactive, nucleus decays into a lighter nucleus and an electron. Scientists observed that the energy before the beta decay was greater than the energy after the beta decay. This was puzzling because one of the main laws of physics, the law of conservation of energy, states that the amount of energy in any process must remain the same. To keep the idea of energy conservation intact, Wolfgang Pauli proposed that another particle which carried off the missing energy was given off in the decay. In 1933 Enrico Fermi named this hard-to-detect particle the neutrino and successfully explained the theory of beta decay. At this time, the mass of the neutrino was assumed to be zero.

TABLE 1. ELEMENTARY MATTER PARTICLES

1st family			2nd family			3rd family		
particle	*charge*	*mass*	*particle*	*charge*	*mass*	*particle*	*charge*	*mass*
leptons								
ν_e	0 e	0	ν_μ	0 e	0	ν_τ	0 e	0
e-	-1 e	.511	μ-	-1 e	106	τ^-	-1 e	1777
quarks								
u	2/3 e	2-8	c	2/3 e	1000-1600	t	2/3 e	176000
d	-1/3 e	5-15	s	-1/3 e	100-300	b	-1/3 e	4100-4500

Positrons

In 1931-1932 Carl Anderson experimentally observed the anti-electron, which he called the positron, after its positive charge. The positron is an antiparticle which had been predicted by Paul Adrain Maurice Dirac in 1927-1930. It turns out every particle has an antiparticle partner which has the same properties except for an opposite electric charge. Antiparticles make up antimatter.

Neutrons

In 1932 James Chadwick discovered another matter particle, the neutron. The neutron is very similar to the proton except that it is electrically neutral. Chadwick found it by hitting a chemical called beryllium with alpha particles. When this occurred, highly penetrating radiation was emitted. This "radiation" turned out to be a stream of neutrons. After Chadwick's experiment Werner Heisenberg claimed that the nucleus is made of protons and neutrons.

Pion, muons, kaons

The second mediator particle discovered was thought to be the pion. In 1935 Hideki Yukawa formulated the idea that protons and neutrons were held together by a nuclear force, which was mediated by a particle called a pion. Yukawa described it in detail. In 1937 the first evidence for it was observed by studying cosmic rays (rays from space). By 1947 it became clear that cosmic rays did contain Yukawa's pions, but also contained another particle, a heavy electron. This was given the name muon. In 1947 another particle was detected from cosmic rays, the kaon. The kaon is like a heavy pion, and decays into two pions. The kaons are considered strange particles because they can be made fairly quickly, but it takes a long time for them to decay. Usually we would expect the time to make a particle and the time for it to decay to be about the same, but this wasn't true for the kaon. The kaon ended up being the first of many new particles to be detected.

Quarks

In 1980 Maurice Jacob and Peter Lanshoff detected small, hard, solid objects inside the proton by firing high energy electrons and protons at it. Most of the high energy particles seemed to pass through the proton. A few of the high energy particles were reflected back, as if they had hit something. These experiments indicate that the proton contains three small, hard, solid objects. Thus protons are not elementary, but the objects inside them may be. These objects are now called quarks.

Quark model

Quarks had been postulated much earlier, in 1964, by Murray Gell-Mann and independently by George Zweig. The theory describing quarks can be called the quark model. In 1964 there were believed to be three different quarks. These different quarks each have a unique property called flavor. These first three quarks had flavors up, down, and strange. Up flavored quarks have an electric charge of 2/3 e, where e is the electric charge of the electron. Down and strange flavored quarks have an electric charge of -1/3 e. The quark model also says that quarks must remain bound inside particles. In nature, quarks cannot exist by themselves.

TABLE 2. ELEMENTARY MEDIATOR PARTICLES

particle	charge	mass	force
γ	0 e	0	Electromagnetic
g	0 e	0	Strong
$W^{\pm}$	± 1 e	80200	Weak
Z^0	0 e	91200	Weak

This idea is called quark confinement, and is based on experiment. Since we cannot isolate quarks, it is very difficult to determine their masses.

In 1964 Oscar W. Greenberg suggested each quark has a quality called color. The label "color" for this quark property does not refer to the usual definition of color. It is just a way to keep track of quarks. Using this idea of color, the improved quark model says only colorless particles can exist in nature. There are only three different kinds of color in the quark model, usually designated red, blue, and green. Color had to be introduced when a particle called the Δ++ (Delta-plus-plus) baryon was discovered to avoid violating the Pauli exclusion principle. The Pauli exclusion principle says that each particle must have unique properties like electric charge, and mass, and spin. The Δ++ baryon is made of three up quarks. Without color, each of its three up quarks cannot have its own properties. Color has been proven experimentally. A theory called the standard model of elementary particles has updated the quark model.

Subatomic particle classifications

Elementary matter particles

There are two kind of elementary (indivisible) matter particles, the quarks and the leptons. The two lowest mass leptons are the electron (e$^-$) and its partner neutrino, usually called the electron-neutrino (ν_e). For unknown reasons, this lepton pairing is repeated two more times, each time with increasing mass. These leptons are called the muon (μ^-), and mu-neutrino (ν_μ), and the tau (τ^-), and tau-neutrino (ν_τ). We say there are three families or generations of leptons.

As in the lepton sector, the quark sector has three families or generations. The first family quarks have flavors called up (u), and down (d). The second family quarks are referred to by flavor as charm (c) and strange

(s). The third generation quarks are called top (t) and bottom (b).

Another way of classifying elementary particles is by a property called spin. Spin is the rotation of a particle on its axis, as the earth spins on its axis to give us day and night. The spin of elementary particles is so small it is measured in special units called "h-bar" related to Planck's constant which is defined as 4.1×10^{-21} MeV seconds. Using the property called spin, all matter particles are fermions which have spin one-half h-bar or three-halves h-bar. All quarks and leptons have spins of one-half h-bar. The matter particles and some of their properties are summarized in Table 1. Masses are given in units of MeV/c^2, where c is the speed of light (three-hundred-million meters per second). The quark masses are approximate.

Elementary mediator particles

Bosons are particles defined to have spin of zero h-bar, one h-bar, or two h-bar. The elementary mediator particles are bosons with spins of one h-bar. The force we are most familiar with is the electromagnetic force. The electromagnetic force is responsible for keeping electrons and nuclei together to form atoms. The electromagnetic force is mediated by photons (γ). The mediators of the strong force are called gluons (g), because they glue quarks together to form mesons and baryons. Like the quarks, the gluons carry the property described by color. The weak force is more uncommon. It is responsible for radioactive decays like nuclear beta decay. The mediators of the weak force are the electrically charged W-bosons (W$\pm$), and the electrically neutral Z-bosons (Z^0). Some properties of the mediator particles are given in Table 2. Masses are given in MeV/c^2.

Baryons

One of the main rules of the standard quark model is that combinations of three quarks are called baryons. Protons (p) and neutrons (n) are the most important

TABLE 3. BARYONS

baryon	quark content	spin	charge	mass
p	u u d	1/2	+1 e	938
n	u d d	1/2	0 e	939
Λ	u d s	1/2	0 e	1116
Σ⁺	u u s	1/2	1 e	1189
Σ⁰	u d s	1/2	0 e	1192
Σ⁻	d d s	1/2	-1 e	1197
Ξ⁰	u s s	1/2	0 e	1315
Ξ⁻	d s s	1/2	-1 e	1321
Λ_c^+	u d c	1/2	1 e	2281
Δ⁺⁺	u u u	3/2	2 e	1232
Δ⁺	u u d	3/2	1 e	1232
Δ⁰	u d d	3/2	0 e	1232
Δ⁻	d d d	3/2	-1 e	1232
Σ*⁺	u u s	3/2	1 e	1383
Σ*⁰	u d s	3/2	0 e	1384
Σ*⁻	d d s	3/2	-1 e	1387
Ξ*⁰	u s s	3/2	0 e	1532
Ξ*⁻	d s s	3/2	-1 e	1535
Ω⁻	s s s	3/2	-1 e	1672

baryons. Protons are made of two up quarks and one down quark. Neutrons are made of two down quarks and one up quark. Since the quark model requires that naturally-occurring particles be colorless, a baryon must be made of a red, a blue, and a green quark. These combine to make a white, or colorless particle. Spin is important in classifying baryons. Baryons are fermions and so have spins of one-half h-bar or three-halves h-bar. Table 3 summarizes several kinds of baryons, with masses in MeV/c² and spin in terms of h-bar.

Mesons

The second main idea of the standard quark model is that combinations of one quark and one antiquark are called mesons. Pions (π) and kaons (K) are examples of mesons. Thus now we see Yukawa's nuclear force mediator particle, the pion, is really a matter particle made of a quark and an antiquark. This means the nuclear force is not a basic or fundamental force. There are several kinds of pions. For example, the positively charged pion, π^+, is made of an up quark and a down antiquark. Similarly there are several kinds of kaons. One kind of kaon, K^+, is made of an up quark and a strange antiquark. The colorless rule requires that mesons must be made of quarks with opposite color, red and anti-red for example. All mesons are bosons and so have spins of zero h-bar or one h-bar.

Current and future research

Subatomic particles are very important in many technologies. Television sets use beams of electrons to create their pictures. A television set picks up the television signal which is then sent to electron guns. Electron guns shoot off beams of electrons which hit the face of the picture tube. When electrons hit the tube, it lights up, creating the picture. A common type of smoke detector that uses subatomic particles is an ionization smoke detector. In an ionization smoke detector alpha particles take away or add electrons ("ionize") to groups of air atoms called air molecules. These ionized air molecules cause electric current to flow in the detector. If there is a fire, other particles enter the detector and interfere with the flow of the electric current, which makes the alarm go off.

In the 1990s, particle physics is particularly exciting. There have been several recent experimental developments. At Los Alamos National Laboratory in New Mexico physicists announced in 1995 that they observed neutrinos and that they have mass. If true, this would be an important breakthrough. Traditionally the neutrino has been very difficult to detect because it reacts rarely with other matter particles. If the neutrinos are observed to have mass, they may play an important part in the fate of the universe.

The matter that astronomers can observe is called visible matter. There is not enough mass from visible matter in the universe for it to collapse due to its own gravity someday into another Big Bang (the explosion that started our universe). If it does not collapse, the universe will continue to expand forever, and everything, including stars, will die. Since neutrinos are not visible matter (to astronomers), they may be considered dark or "missing" matter. If the mass of neutrinos is enough, this neutrino missing matter may be great enough to "close" the universe, allowing it to collapse and be reborn someday.

KEY TERMS

. . . .

Coulomb—The standard unit of electric charge, defined as the amount of charge flowing past a point in a wire in one second, when the current in the wire is one Ampere.

Fundamental force—A basic force, which has its own elementary mediator particle(s). There are four fundamental forces: the strong force, the electromagnetic force, the weak force, and gravity.

Quark—An elementary particle which feels the Strong Force, and which makes up subatomic particles like protons and neutrons.

Mega electron volt (MeV)—A unit of energy. One MeV is one million Electron Volts. An Electron Volt is the amount of energy an electron gains as it passes through one Volt of potential difference.

See also Antiparticle; Atom; Electron; Neutron; Photon; Proton; Quantum mechanics; Spin of subatomic particles.

Further Reading:
"Building Blocks of Matter." *Nature* 372 (November 1994): 20.
Griffiths, David. *Introduction to Elementary Particles.* New York: Harper and Row, 1987.
Freedman, David H. "Over the Top." *Discover* 16 (February 1995): 74.
"The Weight of the Evidence: The Neutrino Seems to Pose New Problems as Quickly as It Solves Old Ones." *The Economist* 334 (11 February 1995): 71.

Lesley L. Smith

Subduction zone see **Plate tectonics**

Submarine

The first known treatise on submarines was written in 1578. Published by William Bourne in his *Inventions or Devices*, the document describes a ship with two hulls, the outer made of wood. While no record exists concerning its manufacture, the ship, according to Bourne, could be submerged or raised by taking in or

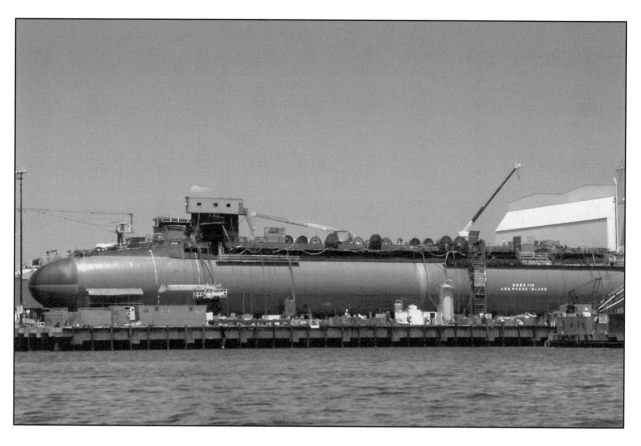

A Trident submarine under construction in Groton, Connecticut.

expelling water from between the double hulls. The first known submarine to be built was that of Dutch inventor Cornelius Drebbel, which consisted of greased leather over a wooden framework. It was propelled either on or beneath the surface by eight oars sealed through the sides with leather flaps. During a demonstration for James I in 1620, this vessel was successfully piloted just under the surface of the Thames River. It was unable, however, to make deep descents.

During the American Revolution David Bushnell built a one-man submarine called the Turtle. It resembled an egg squashed thin with a height of 6 ft (2 m), and had two hand-cranked screw propellers, a hand-operated control lever connected to the rudder, foot-operated pumps to let water in or send it out (to submerge or surface), and a crudely-lit control panel. As if it was not dangerous enough simply to get in the water sealed inside this device, the Turtle also had a large explosive attached to it in the hopes the operator could maneuver under an enemy ship, screw the explosive into the ship's hull, and depart before the explosive's timing device discharged it. Unfortunately, the Turtle failed to sink any ship. On its only test mission, the Turtle was assigned the task of bombing the British HMS

Eagle in New York, but its pilot was unable to screw the explosive into the Eagle's copper hull.

Others, such as English carpenters Symons and Day, included ballast systems on their submarines to permit descents. Day's submarine resembled a sloop, and had two large bags of stones hanging from its bottom to serve as ballast. Day would sink, then jettison the rocks to return to the surface. After two successful tests, Day confidently decided he would test his vessel off Plymouth Sound, a site with a depth of 900 ft (274 m). Apparently his ship was crushed by high water pressure, for when he and his crew descended, a crowd of onlookers waited in vain for his return. Day and his crew had become the first victims of a submarine mishap.

Perhaps the most successful early submarine was designed by Robert Fulton. In an age of naval battles, Fulton, who detested war, felt that a device capable of neutralizing the effectiveness of warshipswould end war altogether. While living in France in 1767, he outlined plans to build a sub called the Nautilus and unsuccessfully attempted to interest the French government in his idea. By 1801, however, he had managed to complete a submarine on his own. A 21 ft (6 m) vessel with a two-bladed propeller, the Nautilus performed well in tests, even sinking a ship with an explosive charge. But he was once again rejected by the French government, so he moved to England, hoping for a better reception there.

It soon became clear that the English did not want his submarine either. In fact, Fulton had failed not because his vessel did not work, but because major naval powers feared his vessel and did not want to participate in developing a weapon that could negate their military strength. Fulton went on to produce his famous steamboats in the United States.

After the American Civil War, designers, spurred on by the invention of the self-propelled torpedo in 1866, increasingly sought alternatives to human-powered propulsion for submarines. Several systems proved unsuitable— steam engines made the craft unbearably hot and an electric battery could not be recharged at sea. In the late 1890s, however, Irish-born American John Holland solved the problem with the use of a new power source, the gasoline engine. Because it needed oxygen, the gasoline engine could not be used while a submarine was underwater, but on the surface it could not only provide propulsion but also charge the batteries used while submerged. Holland's vessels incorporated many of the features we associate with modern subs: a powerful engine, advanced control and balancing systems, and a circular-shaped hull to withstand pressure. The United States Navy accepted his submarine, the Holland, in 1900.

Around this time, two other improvements were introduced. Simon Lake (1866-1945), who also built an early gasoline-powered submarine, created the first periscope specifically for submarines: it provided a magnified view and a wide angle of vision. In the 1890s Rudolf Diesel invented an engine that was fired by compression rather than an electric spark. The diesel engine was more economical than the gasoline engine and its fumes were much less toxic and volatile. This new engine became the mainstay of all submarines until nuclear power was introduced as a means of propulsion in the 1950s.

Germany made good use of diesel propulsion. Unlike Britain's small, coastal subs, Germany's vessels, displacing up to 3,200 tons, were capable of crossing the Atlantic. Their U-boat (short for unterseeboot) sent more than 11 million tons of Allied shipping to the bottom and, in the process, created a new, terrifying type of warfare.

In World War II submarines played an even larger role in Germany's repeated attacks on Allied shipping, eventually destroying 14 million tons of shipping. meanwhile, American submarines crippled the Japanese by sinking nearly 1,400 merchant and naval ships. The greatest improvement came through the development of the snorkel, a set of two fixed air pipes that projected from the sub's topside. One tube brought fresh air into the vessel, and the other vented engine exhaust fumes. Now a sub could stay hidden below the surface when running on its diesel engine and recharging its batteries.

The greatest advance in submarine technology was the advent of nuclear power. With the encouragement of United States Navy Captain Hyman Rickover, American inventors Ross Gunn and Phillip Abelson designed the U.S.S. Nautilus, the first nuclear-powered submarine. Launched in 1955, the Nautilus carried a reactor in which controlled nuclear fission provided the heat that converted water into steam for turbines. With this new power source, the submarine could remain under water indefinitely and cruise at top speed for any length of time required.

For a submarine able to remain under water for longer distances at higher speeds, a needle-like shape proved inefficient. The Davis Taylor Model Basin in the United States developed a new teardrop design, first tested on its Albacore submarine. Vessels with this improved shape easily drove through the water at speeds of 35-40 knots per hour. The United States Navy later adopted the Albacore's shape for its submarines.

Submarines have also benefited from advances in navigation equipment. Inertial navigation systems, relying on gyroscopes now fix their position with extreme accuracy. The U.S.S. Skate used this system to navigate under the polar ice cap at the North Pole in 1959.

See also Diesel engine; Internal combustion engine; Nuclear power.

Submarine canyon see **Continental margin**

Subsidence

The term subsidence is used in both atmospheric and geological sciences. Atmospheric subsidence refers to the sinking of air that is denser (heavier) than the air below. As it subsides, increasing air pressure compresses the air parcel, causing it to warm. Geologic subsidence is a form of mass wasting that refers to the sinking of geologic materials (rocks or sediments) as underlying materials are removed or change their position.

Atmospheric subsidence

Atmospheric subsidence occurs when the normal upward flow of air in the atmosphere, known as atmospheric convection, is disturbed. To understand what happens during convection, imagine a parcel of air located immediately above the ground during sunrise. As solar energy warms the earth, heat is transferred to that parcel of air. Warm air is less dense than cold air, so the heated parcel has a tendency to rise upward, or convect, into the atmosphere. As the parcel rises, it expands, causing cooling. Cooling causes water vapor (gas) in the air to change state to a liquid; water droplets form, producing clouds. An air parcel will continue to rise upward until its density is equal to the surrounding atmosphere, that is, until it is stable.

Convection, which creates a large area of low pressure and converging winds at the Earth's surface, known as a cyclone, is not always present. Subsidence, or sinking of air, may happen instead, forming an area of high pressure, an anticyclone. Large scale subsidence occurs when air several thousands of feet overhead is denser than the surrounding air. This denser air is produced when winds aloft converge or air aloft is very cold, or warm, but unusually dry. The dense air sinks due to the pull of gravity, compressing the air, creating high pressure at the surface and diverging winds just above the surface. Warming of the air as it subsides increases evaporation, causing clear skies. That is why high pressure systems are usually associated with fair weather.

The subsiding air may settle onto a cooler air layer, creating what is known as a temperature inversion, or subsidence inversion. In a temperature inversion, a warm air layer, several hundred or thousand feet above the surface, is trapped between cooler layers above and below. This inversion resists convection of surface air, since the surface air is stable, and causes air pollution to be trapped at the surface. Subsidence inversions commonly occur at high latitudes during the winter and over the eastern United States during the late summer months. During an inversion, an urban area's air pollution may become a serious health hazard.

Geologic subsidence

Geological subsidence involves the settling or sinking of a body of rock or sediment. Subsidence is a type of mass wasting, or mass movement—transport of large volumes of earth material primarily by gravity. Subsidence may occur as the result of either natural or human-caused events.

Earthquakes are commonly associated with subsidence. When two blocks of the Earth's crust slide against each other, causing an earthquake, ground movement may occur, raising or lowering the ground surface. During Alaska's 1964 Good Friday earthquake, an area of at least 70,000 square miles (180,000 sq km), much of it coastline, subsided 3 ft (1 m) or more—some areas now flood at high tide.

Another way that earthquakes can cause subsidence is by rapidly decreasing the load-bearing capacity, or strength, of loose earth materials, or sediments, due to liquefaction. Liquefaction occurs when vibrations from an earthquake, or other disturbance, cause water-saturated sediments to temporarily lose their grain-to-grain contact, which is what gives them their load-bearing capacity. For just an instant, the weight of the overlying materials is supported only by the water between the grains. An instant later, when the grains begin to settle, the weight of the overlying sediment (or buildings) causes the grains to be forced closer together and the land to subside.

During the 1989 earthquake along the San Andreas Fault in California, some of the most serious damage occurred in San Francisco's Marina District. Buildings were constructed on old bay deposits, unconsolidated water-saturated sediments, which when shaken by the earthquake temporarily lost their strength due to liquefaction. In the Marina district, sediment that had previously supported large buildings quickly turned into a mud-like material that could no longer support a building's weight.

Another example of natural subsidence can be found in regions where caves are common. Caves form when underground water dissolves limestone and carries it away. The resulting void spaces grow larger and larger over time until they become the features we call caves.

If limestone dissolves for a long enough time, the hole (cave) that forms becomes too large to support the weight of its walls. In such a case, the ceiling of the cave will subside, either slowly or in a catastrophic collapse, forming a large depression at the surface, known as a sinkhole. If conditions are right, the sinkhole may eventually fill with water, forming a lake. A landscape containing many dry or water-filled sinkholes formed by limestone dissolution is called karst topography.

Yet another cause of subsidence is volcanic eruption. Whether molten rock, or magma, is lost suddenly and dramatically, as in the Mt. St. Helens eruption of 18 May 1980, or the slow flow of lava (magma flowing on the surface), as happens in the Hawaiian Islands, land subsidence is likely to follow. The material ejected from the Earth's interior leaves an empty space that must be filled in one way or another. In many cases, a large section of the overlying crust—along with the geologic and human features attached to it—collapses into the Earth's interior, forming what is called a caldera.

Subsidence may also result from the accumulation of large volumes of sediment at the Earth's surface in what is known as a sediment basin. An obvious setting in which this occurs is at river deltas. Each day, the Mississippi River deposits up to 1.8 million metric tons of sediment at its mouth near New Orleans. The weight of this sediment contributes to a gradual subsidence of the land on which New Orleans resides. Basins between mountains also can subside due to the weight of accumulating sediments.

Human causes of subsidence

Many forms of human activities can result in subsidence. One of the most widespread of these problems involves the removal of ground water for agricultural, municipal, and other purposes. In large parts of the United States, for example, farmers and ranchers depend heavily on water removed from underground aquifers to irrigate their crops and water their livestock. Such activities have now been going on with increasing intensity for at least a century.

This practice will not lead to subsidence as long as enough rainfall filters downward to replace, or recharge, the groundwater removed by humans. However, when the rate of removal exceeds the rate of recharge, significant decreases in the volume of the aquifer begin to occur. The pore spaces between the grains of the aquifer, previously occupied by water, are emptied. The grains then begin to compact more tightly, and the collapse. Eventually, the aquifer begins to subside.

A dramatic example of subsidence as a result of ground water removal has taken place in a region southeast of Phoenix, Arizona. There a section of land covering 120 sq mi (310 sq km) has sunk more than 7 ft (2 m). This phenomenon has occurred at many locations above the Ogallala Aquifer, which lies beneath the High Plains region, stretching from Kansas and Nebraska to Wyoming and from Texas and New Mexico to Colorado.

The removal of fossil fuels is also a major human cause of subsidence. A traditional method of removing coal, for example, is known as room-and-pillar because vertical columns of the coal (the "pillar") are left in position while the coal around it is removed. When such mines are abandoned, however, the pillars of coal left behind are often not strong enough to hold up the over-

lying ground. When the pillars break, the ceilings of the mined room collapse and the overlying ground does so also. With more than 90,000 abandoned mines in the United States, this source of subsidence is likely to be a problem into the foreseeable future.

The pumping of oil and natural gas from underground sources can have similar effects. Similar to removal of water from an aquifer, when these materials are removed from the reservoir, the reservoir's grains compact and the reservoir occupies a smaller volume than it did before the oil or gas was removed. As a result, overlying ground subsides as the reservoir slowly collapses.

One of the most famous of these instances occurred as far back as the late 1920s in Southern California. Oil removed from the Wilmington and Signal Hill oil fields caused unstable ground to subside by as much as 29 ft (9 m). Since this region lies along the coastline of the Pacific Ocean, drastic efforts were required to prevent ocean water from flowing into lands that were now lower in some places than sea level. By 1968, subsidence in the area had been stopped, but only after huge quantities of seawater had been injected into the empty oil wells in order to prop open the pores in the reservoir. This success in restoring stability to the area came at a high price, however, as docks, highways, sewer systems, and other municipal structures had, by that time, been completely rebuilt.

Effects of subsidence

Whether caused by natural or human activities, subsidence often has a number of serious consequences for human societies. Probably the most dramatic, of course, is the disappearance of whole sections of land, as occurred in Alaska's Good Friday earthquake. Today, the sudden appearance of sinkholes in Florida is no longer unusual news. In many cases, these sinkholes appear because the removal of ground water has left limestone caves that are unable to support the land overlying them.

Even relatively modest subsidence can also damage a variety of human structures. Buildings are weakened and collapse, railway lines and roads are twisted and broken, and underground sewer, power, and water lines are torn apart. Due to its ability to destroy property on a large scale, subsidence is a very expensive type of mass wasting that also poses some risk to human lives.

See also Atmospheric circulation; Earthquake; Karst topography; Mass wasting; Volcano.

KEY TERMS

. . . .

Aquifer—An underground layer of rock from which water can be extracted.

Karst topography—A region in which numerous caves, sinkholes, and other formations resulting from the dissolving of underground limestone rock are apparent.

Liquefaction (of rocks)—The process by which changes in pressure cause a rocky material that was originally strong and stable to change into a liquid-like material.

Temperature inversion—A situation in which a layer of cool air is trapped beneath a layer of warmer, less dense air.

Further Reading:

Erickson, Jon. *Quakes, Eruptions, and Other Geologic Cataclysms.* New York: Facts on File, 1994.

David E. Newton

Substance abuse see **Addiction**

Subsurface detection

Making inferences about the nature and structure of buried rock bodies, without access to them, is called subsurface detection. Using geophysical techniques, we obtain data at the surface which characterizes the feature buried below. Then we construct models of the feature, trying to invent combinations of reasonable rock bodies which are consistent with all of the observations. Finally, using intuition, logic, and guesswork, we may select one or a few of the models as representing the most likely subsurface situation.

Seismic techniques

An earthquake generates seismic waves which can travel through the entire earth. If you stamp on the ground you make the same kinds of waves, although obviously they are much weaker and do not travel as far. We know a great deal about how these waves travel through rock. By generating waves and then carefully timing how long it takes them to travel different distances we can learn a lot about the structures of rock units at depth.

Seismic reflection

The next time you go to a shopping mall on a bright afternoon, notice your reflection in the two sets of double doors at the entrance. You'll probably see yourself reflected twice, once from the outer set, and once from the inner set. Unlike opaque mirrors, glass doors permit some light to go through them, while at the same time they reflect some light back. Rock layers behave in a similar manner with respect to seismic waves. An explosion detonated at the surface will reflect off of many layers at depth. Detectors set up in an array can time the arrival of each of these reflected waves. Just as bats and dolphins can use the echoes of sound waves to locate food, geophysicists can use the echoes of seismic waves to locate reflecting boundaries at depth. These reflecting boundaries occur where there is an abrupt contrast in some seismic wave transmission properties (usually velocities) of the material. Most often this is a result of the sedimentary layering. A seismic reflection profile, which actually shows reflection horizons, is usually interpreted as revealing the structure of the underlaying layers. The oil bearing structure in many productive oil and gas fields were located using reflection seismic surveys, so this technique has been very important to the petroleum industry.

At first seismic reflection profiling was used only by oil companies. Because it is economical to recover oil only if it is relatively near the surface, such surveys did not seek out much information at great depths. Over the last fifteen years or so, however, scientists have adapted the technique to probe the very deepest parts of the crust. One remarkable discovery is a nearly horizontal fault underlying much of Georgia and the adjacent continental shelf.

Explosives are still used to generate seismic waves in some areas, particularly at sea, but in many places they have been supplanted by special trucks which vibrate the ground beneath them with hydraulic jacks. The signals generated by these vibrations reflect just like any other seismic waves, but because the energy is put into the ground over a period of time, instead of instantly, there is less damage to structures in the area.

Seismic refraction

If you live in a good sized city and want to travel a few blocks, you would probably take the direct route and put up with the stoplights and traffic. If you want to go further, though, you might find it takes less time to go out of your way to use an expressway. Although you have to travel a greater distance, you save time because the expressway is so much faster.

Similarly, seismic waves may go further, but reach faster layers at depth and arrive at a sensor before those taking the direct route do. When this occurs the path of the waves bends as it crosses boundaries between layers of different velocities, a phenomenon called "refraction."

This technique can be used to determine how thick the soil is above bedrock. (This might be an important consideration in siting a landfill, for example.) Solid rock has faster seismic velocities than soil. If the depths of interest are small, the source of the seismic waves does not need to be very energetic. A sledgehammer, a dropped weight, or a blasting cap might be used. A detector located near this source will pick up the waves traveling through the soil. By plotting up how long it takes them to travel different distances, their velocity through the soil can be determined. As the detector is moved further from the source, however, a point will be reached where the waves traveling through the bedrock start arriving first. This is equivalent to the distance you would need to go (in the city example) before it was quicker to use the expressway. Continuing to measure travel times for more distant stations permits the seismic velocity in the bedrock to be found. Knowing the physics of refraction, the two velocities, and the location where the bedrock path became faster yields the thickness of the soil layer.

The same principles can be applied to problems where the depths of interest are much greater, but the source of the seismic waves must be more energetic. When Andrija Mohorovicic observed a similar set of two lines for the arrival times of earthquake generated seismic waves, he realized that the Earth must have a layered structure. In this case the upper layer was the crust, and it was about 18.5 mi (30 km) thick. The transition zone between the core and mantle now bears his name, the Mohorovicic discontinuity.

Potential field methods

Some properties of a material can be sensed at a distance because they generate *potential fields*. Gravitational fields are produced by any object with mass, and magnetic fields can be produced or distorted by objects with appropriate magnetic properties. Techniques to measure and interpret such fields are extremely useful in subsurface detection.

Gravity

Every object with mass produces a gravitational field. In theory it should be possible to detect objects which are denser than average or less dense than average lying beneath the surface. A large body of lead ore, for example, should cause the gravitational field above it to be somewhat greater than normal. A deep trough of loose sediments should result in a weaker gravitational field. The problem is that the gravitational attraction of the planet is huge, so that it is difficult to separate and measure that little modification produced by an anomalous mass.

Halite is a rock made of salt, NaCl. Therefore, rock salt, which is composed of halite, is much lighter than most other rocks, and deforms very easily. Big blobs of it sometimes develop at depth and rise toward the surface in bubble-like structures called diapirs or salt domes. As they move up, they can warp the sedimentary rock units they move through, producing rich, but localized, accumulations of oil. Much of the oil found in the Gulf Coast states occurs in association with these salt domes, and so the petroleum industry had considerable incentive to develop techniques to detect them. As a result, the gravity meter, or gravimeter, was invented.

Essentially a very delicate bathroom scale, the gravimeter measures how much a spring is extended by the gravitational force acting on a mass at the end of the spring. What makes it work, and also makes it expensive, is that this extension can be measured with great precision, generally one part per million or better. That precision is equivalent to measuring a mile to within a sixteenth of an inch.

Such instruments immediately proved their worth, successfully detecting scores of salt domes beneath the nearly flat Gulf Coast states. Extending this technique to regional surveys, involving larger areas extending over greater elevation ranges, required refinements in our models for the gravitational field of the planet. This work has continued in conjunction with ever more refined gravity surveys. In the process a major rift running down the center of North America has been discovered, subsurface continuations of rock units cropping out at the surface have been delimited, and even precursors for earthquakes have been detected.

Magnetism

Few phenomena seem so magical as the invisible attraction and repulsion we can feel when we play with magnets. When we stick a paper clip on one end of a magnet, it becomes a magnet, too, capable of holding up another paper clip. Some rock types exhibit their own magnetic fields, much like the magnets on a refrigerator door. Others distort the Earth's magnetic field, similar to the way a paper clip temporarily becomes a magnet if it is in contact with a kitchen magnet. Sedimentary rocks rarely exhibit either magnetic behavior, and so they are effectively transparent to the magnetic signal.

Using a magnetometer we can measure the strength of the magnetic field anywhere on Earth. Often this is done with airborne surveys, which cover tremendous areas in little time. The results are mapped up and the maps are used in several different ways.

The thickness of the sedimentary cover over igneous and metamorphic rocks (often called the "depth to basement") can often be inferred qualitatively from the magnetic maps. Just as a newspaper picture looks like a gray block when seen from a distance, a photograph when seen from arm's length, and a collection of printed dots when seen under a magnifying lens, so to the magnetic signal from the basement looks considerably different when seen from different distances. Little detail and subdued images suggest a thick blanket of sedimentary rocks, often miles. Sweeping patterns or textures, caused by the combination of many outcrops involve in the same tectonic deformation, suggest a sedimentary cover of moderate thickness. If we can see distinct outlines, produced by the basement rock's outcrop patterns, we can safely infer that there is little or no sedimentary cover.

Magnetic maps are also utilized to map the continuation of units from places where they crop out into areas where they are buried. Much of the recent increase in our knowledge of the geology of the Adirondack Mountains in New York stems from this use of magnetic maps.

A third technique uses the strength and form of the magnetic signals to put limits on the geometry of buried units. This is similar to the situation with gravity, where models are developed and tested for consistency with the data. Often magnetic data can be used to constrain gravity models, and vice versa.

Electric techniques

The various responses of earth materials to electric fields of different types permits additional characterization of the subsurface. Natural and artificial signals at a variety of different frequencies can be observed to travel through different parts of the earth. Measurements are made of how they are modified in their paths, and then models are constructed which try to emulate this behavior. Often these techniques are most useful where the extension of a geological body with distinctive electrical properties is sought in the subsurface. Metallic ore deposits or ion-rich pollutant plumes are

good examples. Measurements of electrical resistivity, the resistance of a material to passing a current of electricity, have been used for decades in the oil industry to help locate oil- or gas-bearing rock units.

Nuclear survey methods

Nuclear survey methods are of two basic types. The more common of the two involves measurement of natural radioactivity in rocks or soils. This method might be used, for example, to identify potential uranium ores for mining. In this case a hand-held geiger counter could be employed. Another use is to measure the natural gamma ray emissions from rock formations in a drill hole when searching for oil. A gamma ray counter is lowered down the hole on a wire, and the natural gamma ray emissions of the rocks in the borehole wall are measured. Different rocks exhibit various levels of radioactivity, making remote identification of rock type possible. Geophysical surveys of boreholes that are done in this manner are called wireline surveys or wireline bogs.

The second type of nuclear survey method is stimulated radioactivity. In this method, a radioactive source is used to bombard a rock and induce radioactive decay in the rock. The level of induced radioactive decay is measured and the rock type is interpreted from the measurements. Wireline surveys employing this method are often used when exploring for oil.

Satellite altimeter data

Satellites can measure the elevation of the sea level surface with astonishing precision. Because their path crosses the same place on earth over and over again, the effects of waves and tides can be accounted for, and the actual variations in the elevation of sea level can be determined. These variations are most often the result of relief on the ocean floor. Where there is a mountain on the ocean floor, its additional mass draws extra water toward it, which will elevate the level of the sea above it. Where a trench exists on the ocean floor, the absence of mass attracts less water and a depression in the elevation of sea level will occur above it. Many of the detailed maps of the sea floor were obtained indirectly in this way.

The inverse problem

Subsurface detection relies on solutions to what is often called the "inverse problem." A particular set of data are observed, and then models are developed which attempt to fit all the data. Sometimes, when a very nice match is made, it is tempting to assume that a particular model is the only model which can fit the data, although this is rarely true.

An example may illustrate this: Imagine that I am trying to figure out the value of the change you have in your pocket. Suppose I have a device which will detect how many coins you have, and it says you have seven. Then I would know that you have at least $0.07 and at most $1.75. Suppose I have another device which tells me that the coins are of two different sizes, with four of them larger than the other three. The big ones might be quarters, leaving a range from $1.03 to $1.30, or they could be nickels, leaving a range from $0.23 to $0.50. Finally, if I were to think about this more carefully, I would see that not all of the values in these ranges are possible. So you could have $1.03, $1.12, $1.15, $1.21, $1.30 if the larger coins are quarters, or $0.23, $0.32, $0.41, $0.50, if the larger coins are nickels. We have reduced the number of possibilities to nine, but there is no way we can use these "subsurface detection" techniques to constrain things further. Because each of these nine possibilities fits the data perfectly, we might find one and erroneously conclude that because it fit the data so well it must be true. Assumptions were built into our conclusions, also; we assumed it is United States currency, and no half dollars or dollar coins. Such assumptions make sense for most pockets we are likely to run into in this country, but are obviously not valid in other countries.

This example illustrates the nature of subsurface detection. Results are usually somewhat ambiguous, depend on assumptions, and do not directly give the answers we seek. Yet they can provide important constraints. I may be able to make some additional assumptions from other data, hunches, or guesses. For instance, I may know you well enough to figure that you would not keep pennies, which would reduce the number of options to three.

Usefulness of subsurface detection

The techniques described here are very often used together to improve our understanding of what exists below the surface. By adjusting the sensitivity of the instruments and the spacing of the measurements, the scale and the depth of interest may be varied. The same theory and principles used with magnetic techniques which delineate the rift running through the crust of North America, at a depth of 18 miles (30 km), can be used to locate buried pipes and cables at a depth of less than 10 ft (3 m).

Often, subsurface detection is the only way to study the area of interest, because it lies too deep to be reached directly. Other times it is used because it is less

---

KEY TERMS

. . . .

Reflection—When some of the energy of a seismic wave bounces off a boundary between two media, instead of traveling through it.

Refraction—Change in the direction of propagation of a seismic wave at the boundary between two media, such as soil and bedrock, caused by the change in the velocity of the wave as it crosses between the media.

Seismic wave—A disturbance produced by compression or distortion on or within the earth, which propagates through earth materials; a seismic wave may be produced by natural (e.g. earthquakes) or artificial (e.g. explosions) means.

---

expensive than digging or drilling, or because it disrupts the environment less.

See also Oil drilling; Seismograph.

Further Reading:

Press, Frank, and Raymond Siever. *Understanding Earth.* New York: W.H. Freeman and Co., 1994.

Telford, William Murray, L.P. Geldart, and R.E. Sheriff. *Applied Geophysics.* Cambridge ; New York : Cambridge University Press, 1990.

Otto H. Muller

Subtraction

Subtraction is the operation which is the inverse of addition. Subtracting a number has the effect of nullifying the addition of that same number. For example, if one adds 11 to 41 then subtracts 11, the result is 41 again.

Symbolically, for any numbers a and b, $(a + b) - b = a$

Or one can subtract first, then add: $(a - b) + b = a$

Thus, one can say that subtraction and addition are "inverse operations."

The definitions of subtraction

The second of the two rules above can be taken as a definition of subtraction. That is "the difference of two numbers, a – b, is the number which must be added to the second number, b, to equal the first, a."

Before the widespread use of electronic cash registers, grocery clerks and others, making change, would use this definition directly. If, for example, a customer bought groceries worth $3.70 and gave the clerk $5.00 to pay for them, the clerk would not subtract in order to compute the change. Instead he (or she) would count it out. Starting with "three seventy," he would give the customer a nickel, and say, "three seventy-five." He would give the customer a quarter and say, "four." Then he would give the customer a dollar and say, "five." This method is still in use when no calculator is available.

A second definition of subtraction is often given in algebra books after the introduction of negative numbers. There a – b is defined as a + (-b), i.e. "To subtract a number, add its opposite." This definition is mathematically efficient, but it hides a lot of the ways in which subtraction is used, as in the change-making example above.

Terminology

In a subtraction problem it is useful to have names for the various parts. In a – b the entire expression is called a "difference," and the "answer" to a – b is *the* difference, or occasionally the "remainder." These two terms arise from two ways is which subtraction is used in practical problems. The first number, a, is called the "minuend." This is the part which is diminished or made smaller when something is subtracted from it (provided that that something is positive). The second number, b, is the "subtrahend" or the part subtracted.

Properties

It matters very much which of the two parts of a difference are named first. Taking $500 from an account with $300 in it is very different from taking $300 from $500. For this reason, subtraction is *not* commutative: $a - b \neq b - a$

Subtraction is not associative either: $(a - b) - c \neq a - (b - c)$

An example will demonstrate this: $(20 - 10) - 3$ is 7, but $20 - (10 - 3)$ is 13.

Often one encounters expressions such as $5x^2 - 2 - 3x^2$, with no indication of which subtraction is to be done first. Since subtraction is non-associative, it matters. To avoid this ambiguity one can agree that subtractions, unless otherwise indicated, are to be done left-to-right. This is a rather limiting agreement, however. It might be more convenient to use some other order, and

in this example, would be. Another agreement, which is the common agreement of algebra, is to treat the minus sign as a plus-the-opposite-of sign. Thus one would interpret the example above as $5x^2 + (-2) + (-3x^2)$. In this interpretation it becomes a sum, whose terms can be combined in any order one pleases.

In certain sets subtraction is not a closed operation. The set of natural numbers, for instance, is not closed with respect to subtraction. If a merchant will not extend credit, one cannot buy an article whose price is greater than the amount of money one has.

Uses of subtraction

The most familiar meaning for subtraction is called "take away." To find the answer if you take 5 eggs from a dozen, you subtract: $12 - 5 = 7$.

Subtraction is also used to compare two numbers. When one wants to know how much colder -7.3° is than 13.8°, one computes the difference -7.3 - 13.8 to get -21.1°.

A third use of subtraction is to figure out a missing addend. If one has a certain sum of money, say $45.20 and wants to buy an article costing $85.50, subtraction is used to compute that needed amount: $85.50 – 45.20$.

See also Addition.

J. Paul Moulton

Succession

Succession is a process of ecological change, involving the progressive replacement of earlier biotic communities with others over time. Succession usually begins with the disturbance of a pre-existing ecosystem, followed by recovery. In the absence of further stand-level disturbance, succession culminates in a stable climax community, the nature of which is determined by climate, soil, and the nature of the local biota. Primary succession occurs on bare substrates that have not been previously modified by biological processes. Secondary succession occurs on substrates that have been modified biologically, and it follows disturbances that have not been so intense as to eliminate the regenerative capacity of the vegetation.

Disturbance, stress, and succession

Disturbance is an episodic stress that causes substantial changes in the structure and function of ecosystems. Depending on its severity and extent, disturbance can influence individual organisms or entire stands, disrupting relationships among individuals within the community, and affecting ecological processes such as productivity, nutrient cycling, and decomposition.

Natural disturbances can be caused by intense events of physical disruption associated with, for example, a hurricane, tornado, oceanic tidal wave, earthquake, the blast of a volcanic eruption, or over geological timespans, the advance and retreat of glaciers. Natural disturbances are also associated with wildfire, and with biological events, such as an irruption of defoliating insects that can kill a mature forest. Human activities are also important sources of ecological disturbances, as is the case of agricultural practices such as plowing, the harvesting of trees from forests, construction activities, and explosions associated with military activities. There are numerous other examples of disturbances caused by human activities.

Note that all of these disturbances can operate at various spatial scales. In some cases, they can result in extensive disturbances over very large areas, for example, when a very severe wildfire consumes millions of hectares of forest. In other cases a disturbance may not cause a stand-level mortality, as when a lightning strike kills a single mature tree in a forest, creating a gap in the overstory, and initiating a microsuccession that culminates in occupation of the gap by another mature tree. Scale is a very important aspect of succession.

Once the intense physical, chemical, or biological stress associated with an event of disturbance is relaxed, succession begins, and this process may eventually restore an ecosystem similar to that present prior to the disturbance. However, depending on environmental circumstances, a rather different ecosystem may develop through post-disturbance succession. For example, if climate change has resulted in conditions that are no longer suitable for the establishment and growth of the same species of trees that dominated a particular stand of old-growth forest prior to its disturbance by a wildfire, then succession will result in the development of a forest of a different character.

Succession can also follow the alleviation of a condition of longer-term, chronic environmental stress. For example, if a local source of pollution by poisonous chemicals is cleaned up, succession will occur in response to the decreased exposure to toxic chemicals. This might occur, for example, if emissions of toxic sulfur dioxide and metals from a smelter are reduced or stopped. This abatement of longer-term environmental stress allows pollution-sensitive species to invade the vicinity of the source, so that succession could proceed. Similarly, removal of some or all of a population of cattle that are chronically overgrazing a pasture would allow the plant community to develop to a more advanced successional stage, characterized by greater biomass and possible more biodiversity.

Succession can also be viewed as a process of much longer-term ecological change occurring, for example, as a lake basin gradually in-fills with sediment and organic debris, eventually developing into a terrestrial habitat such as a forest. This particular succession, which occurs through the development and replacement of a long series of community types, can take thousands of years to achieve its progression through the aquatic to terrestrial stages. The series of ecological changes is still, however, properly viewed as a successional sequence (or sere).

Primary succession

Primary successions occur after disturbances that have been intense enough to obliterate any living organisms from the site, and even to have wiped out all traces of previous biological influences, such as soil development. Natural disturbances of this intensity are associated with glaciation, lava flows, and very severe wildfires, while human-caused examples might include the abandonment of a paved parking lot, or an aboveground explosion of a nuclear weapon. In all of these cases, organisms must successfully invade the disturbed site for succession to begin.

A well-known study of primary succession after deglaciation has been conducted in Alaska. This research examined a time series of substrates and plant communities of known age (this is called a chronosequence) at various places along a fiord called Glacier Bay. In this study, historical positions of the glacial front could be dated by various means, including written records and old photographs. The primary succession begins as the first plants colonize newly deglaciated sites and, in combination with climatic influences, begin to modify the post-glacial substrate. These initial plants include mosses, lichens, herbaceous dicotyledonous species such as the river-beauty (*Epilobium latifolium*), and a nitrogen-fixing cushion plant known as mountain avens (*Dryas octopetala*). These pioneers are progressively replaced as succession continues, first by short statured species of willow (*Salix* spp.), then by taller shrubs such as alder (*Alnus crispa*, another nitrogen-fixing plant), which dominates the community for about 50 years. The alder is progressively replaced by sitka spruce (*Picea sitchensis*), which in turn is succeeded by a forest of western hemlock (*Tsuga heterophylla*) and mountain hemlock (*T. mertensiana*). The primary succession at Glacier Bay culminates in the hemlock forest—this is the climax stage, dominated by species that are most tolerant of stresses associated with competition, in a mature habitat in which access to resources is almost fully allocated among the dominant biota.

The plant succession at Glacier Bay is accompanied by other ecological changes, such as soil development. The mineral substrate that is initially available for plant colonization after the meltback of glacial ice is a fine till, with a slightly alkaline pH of about 8, and as much as 7-10% carbonate minerals. As this primary substrate is progressively leached by percolating water and modified by developing vegetation, its acidity increases, reaching pH 5 after about 70 years under a spruce forest, and eventually stabilizing at about pH 4.7 under a mature hemlock forest. The acidification is accompanied by large reductions of calcium concentration, from initial values as large as 10%, to less than 1%, because of leaching and uptake by vegetation. Other important soil changes include large accumulations of organic matter and nitrogen, due to biological fixations of atmospheric carbon dioxide (CO_2) and dinitrogen (N_2).

Other studies of primary succession have examined chronosequences on sand dunes of known age. At certain places on the Great Lakes, sandy beach ridges are being slowly uplifted from beneath the lakewaters by a ponderous rebounding of the land. The process of uplifting is called isostasy, and it is still occurring in response to meltback of the enormously heavy glaciers that were present only 10,000 years ago. The initial plant colonists of newly exposed dunes that were studied on Lakes Michigan and Huron are short-lived species, such as sea rocket (*Cakile edentula*) and beach spurge (*Euphorbia polygonifolia*). These ephemeral plants are quickly replaced by a perennial dunegrass community, dominated by several grasses (*Ammophila breviligulata* and *Calamovilfa longifolia*). With time, a tall-grass prairie develops, dominated by other species of tall grasses and by perennial, dicotyledonous herbs. The prairie is invaded by shade-intolerant species of shrubs and trees, which form nuclei of forest. Eventually a climax forest develops, dominated by several species of oaks (*Quercus* spp.) and tulip-tree (*Liriodendron tulipifera*). This series of successional plant communities is accompanied by soil development, with broad characteristics similar to those observed at Glacier Bay (although, of course, the rates of change are different).

Secondary succession

Secondary succession occurs after disturbances that are not intense enough to kill all plants, so that regeneration can occur by re-sprouting and growth of surviving individuals, and by the germination of pre-existing seeds to establish new plants. This regeneration by surviving plants and seeds is supplemented by an aggressive invasion of plant seeds from elsewhere. Another characteristic of secondary succession, is that the soil still retains much of its former character, including previous biological and climatic influences on its development.

Secondary successions are much more common than primary successions, because disturbances are rarely intense enough to obliterate previous ecological influences. Most natural disturbances, such as windstorms, wildfires, and insect defoliations, are followed by ecological recovery through secondary succession. The same is true of most disturbances associated with human activities, such as the abandonment of agricultural lands, and the harvesting of forests.

Secondary succession can be illustrated by an example involving natural regeneration after the clear-cutting of a mature, mixed-species forest in northeastern North America. In this case, the original forest was dominated by a mixture of angiosperm and coniferous tree species, plus various plants that are tolerant of the stressful, shaded conditions beneath a closed forest canopy. Some of the plants of the original community survive the disturbance of clear-cutting, and they immediately begin to regenerate. For example, each cut stump of red maple (*Acer rubrum*) rapidly issues hundreds of new sprouts, which grow rapidly, and eventually self-thin to only 1-3 mature stems after about 50 years. Other species regenerate from a long-lived seed bank, buried in the forest floor and stimulated to germinate by the environmental conditions occurring after disturbance of the forest. Pin cherry (*Prunus pensylvanica*) and red raspberry (*Rubus strigosus*) are especially effective at this type of regeneration, and these species are prominent during the first several decades of the secondary succession. Some of the original species do not survive the clear-cutting in large numbers, and they must re-invade the developing habitat. This is often the case of coniferous trees, such as red spruce (*Picea rubens*). Another group of species is not even present in the community prior to its disturbance, but they quickly invade the site to take advantage of the temporary conditions of resource availability and little competition immediately after disturbance. Examples of these so-called ruderal species are woody plants such as alders (in this case, *Alnus rugosa*) and white birch (*Betula* _papyrifera_), and a great richness of herbaceous perennial plants, especially species in the aster family (Asteraceae), such as goldenrod (_Solidago canadensis_) and aster (_Aster umbellatus_), along with various species of grasses, sedges, and other monocotyledonous plants.

This secondary succession of plant communities is accompanied by a succession of animal communities. For example, the mature forest is dominated by various species of warblers, vireos, thrushes, woodpeckers, flycatchers, and others. After clear-cutting, this avian community is replaced by a community made up of other native species of birds, which specialize in utilizing the young habitats that are available after disturbance. Eventually, as the regenerating forest matures, the bird species of mature forest re-invade the stand, and their community re-assembles after about 30-40 years has passed.

Mechanisms of succession

As noted previously, succession generally begins after disturbance creates a situation of great resource availability that can be exploited by organisms, but under conditions of little competition. The classical explanation of the ecological mechanism of community change during succession is the so-called _facilitation_ model. This theory suggests that the recently disturbed situation is first exploited by certain pioneer species that are most capable of reaching and establishing on the site. These initial species modify the site, making it more suitable for invasion by other species, for example, by carrying out the earliest stages of soil development. Once established, the later-successional species eliminate the pioneers through competition. This ecological dynamic proceeds through a progression of stages in which earlier species are eliminated by later species, until the climax stage is reached, and there is no longer any net change in the community.

Another proposed mechanism of succession is the _tolerance_ model. This concept suggests that all species in the succession are capable of establishing on a newly disturbed site, although with varying successes in terms of the rapid attainment of a large population size and biomass. In contrast with predictions of the facilitation model, the early occupants of the site do not change environmental conditions in ways that favor the subsequent invasion of later-successional species. Rather, with increasing time, the various species sort themselves out through their differing tolerances of the successionally increasing intensity of biological stresses associated with competition. In the tolerance model, competition-intolerant species are relatively successful early in succession when site conditions are characterized by a free availability of resources. However, these species are eliminated later on because they are not as competitive as later species, which eventually develop a climax community.

A third suggested mechanism of succession is the _inhibition_ model. As with the tolerance model, both early- and later-successional species can establish populations soon after disturbance. However, some early species make the site less suitable for the development of other species. For example, some plants are known to secrete toxic biochemicals into soil (these are called allelochemicals), which inhibit the establishment and growth of other species. Eventually, however, the inhibitory species die, and this creates opportunities that later-successional species can exploit. These gradual changes eventually culminate in development of the climax community.

All three of these models, facilitation, tolerance, and inhibition, can be supported by selected evidence from the many ecological studies that have been made of succession (especially plant succession). Although these models differ significantly in their predictions about the organizing principles of successional dynamics, it appears that none of them are correct all of the time. Facilitation seems to be most appropriate in explaining changes in many primary successions, but less so for secondary successions, when early post-disturbance site conditions are suitable for the vigorous growth of most species. The relatively vigorous development of ecological communities during secondary succession means that competition rapidly becomes an organizing force in the community, so there is an intensification of interactions by which organisms interfere with and inhibit each other. Aspects of these interactions are more readily explained by the tolerance and inhibition models. Overall, it appears that successions are idiosyncratic—the importance of the several, potential mechanisms of succession varies depending on environmental conditions, the particular species that are interacting, and the influence of haphazard events, such as which species arrived first, and in what numbers.

Climax—The end point of succession

The climax of succession is a relatively stable community that is in equilibrium with environmental conditions. The climax condition is characterized by slow rates of change in an old-growth community, compared with more dynamic, earlier stages of succession. The climax stage is dominated by species that are highly tolerant of the biological stresses associated with competition, because access to resources is almost completely allocated among the dominant organisms of the climax

KEY TERMS

Canopy closure—A point in succession where the sky is obscured by tree foliage, when viewed upward from the ground surface.

Chronosequence—A successional series of stands or soils of different age, originating from a similar type of disturbance.

Competition—An interaction among organisms of the same or different species, associated with their need for a common resource that is present in an insufficient supply relative to the biological demand.

Cyclic succession—A succession that occurs repeatedly on the landscape, as a result of a disturbance that occurs at regular intervals.

Ruderal—Refers to plants that occur on recently disturbed sites, but only until the intensification of competition-related stresses associated with succession eliminates them from the community.

Sere—A successional sequence of communities, occurring under a particular circumstance of types of disturbance, vegetation, and site conditions.

Successional trajectory—The likely sequence of plant and animal communities that is predicted to occur on a site at various times after a particular type of disturbance.

community. However, it is important to understand that the climax community is not static, because of the dynamics of within-community microsuccession, associated, for example, with gaps in a forest canopy caused by the death of individual trees. Moreover, if events of stand-level disturbance occur relatively frequently, the climax or old-growth condition will not be achieved.

See also Climax (ecological); Competition; Stress, ecological.

Further Reading:

Begon, M., J. L. Harper, and C. R. Townsend. *Ecology. Individuals, Populations and Communities.* 2nd ed. London: Blackwell Sci. Pub., 1990.

Freedman, B. *Environmental Ecology.* 2nd ed. San Diego: Academic Press, 1994.

Bill Freedman

Suckers

Suckers are cylindrical fish with a downward-pointing suckering mouth in the family Catostomidae, which is in the large suborder Cyprinoidea, which also includes minnows, carps, and loaches.

Most species in the sucker family occur in the Americas, over a range that extends from the boreal forest of North America through much of Central America. A few other species occur in eastern Siberia, and there is one isolated species in eastern China.

Suckers are distinguished from other members of the Cyprinoidea by aspects of their jaw structure, the presence of a single row of teeth in their pharynx, a lack of barbels, and their round, downward-pointing, fleshy-lipped, sucking mouth. Suckers generally have a cylindrical or slightly compressed body.

Most species of suckers occur in flowing waters, such as rivers and streams. Some species also occur in still waters such as lakes and large ponds, but suckers living in these habitats spawn in nearby rivers.

The largest species of suckers can attain a length of 6.6 ft (2 m), but most are much smaller than this. Male suckers are smaller than the females. Both sexes become relatively brightly colored during the breeding season.

The primary food of suckers are aquatic invertebrates, which are mostly hunted in the sediment. Suckers that live in lakes may also eat some aquatic vegetation. The larger species of suckers are of some economic importance as food-fishes for humans, although their flesh is rather bony. Other, smaller species are important as forage species for larger, more valuable species of fishes.

Species of suckers

There are over one hundred species of suckers. The common or white sucker (*Catostomus commersoni*) is a widespread species throughout much of northern and central North America. This species has a round mouth, useful for feeding on its usual prey of bottom-dwelling insects, crustaceans, molluscs, and other invertebrates. The common sucker is a relatively large species, attaining a length of up to 10 inches (45 cm), and a weight of 2.2 lbs (1 kg). The common sucker is often found in lakes and ponds. These fish generally run up nearby streams to spawn in gravel beds in the springtime, but they sometimes lay their eggs in gravel along shallow lakeshores. Individuals of this species can live as long as 12 years.

The longnose or northern sucker (*Catostomus catostomus*) is also widely distributed in northern North

KEY TERMS

Bait fish—Small fish that are used as live bait to catch larger fish.

Forage fish—This refers to small fish that are eaten by larger, economically important fish.

America, and it also occurs in eastern Siberia. The long-nose sucker generally inhabits cooler waters and occurs in deeper lakes and larger rivers and streams than the common sucker. This species is exploited commercially on the Great Lakes and elsewhere, although it is not considered to be a high-value species of fish. Other species of suckers are more local in distribution, for example, the Sacramento sucker (*C. occidentalis*) of northern California.

Both the bigmouth buffalo (*Ictiobus cyprinellus*) and the smallmouth buffalo (*I. bubalus*) are widely distributed in the eastern United States. These species have also been transplanted farther to the west to establish some sportfishing populations. These fish can attain a large size, exceeding 22 lbs (10 kg) in some cases, and are commonly fished as food.

The northern redhorse or redfin sucker (*Moxostoma macrolepidotum*) occurs widely in central North America. The lake or northern chub (*Couesius plumbeus*) is a small minnow-sized fish that occurs widely across northern North America. This is an important forage and bait fish. The lake chubsucker (*Erimyzon sucetta*) occurs in the eastern United States, including Lake Saint Clair and Lake Erie.

Further Reading:
Page, L. and Burr, B. *Field Guide to Freshwater Fishes of North America*. Boston, MA: Houghton Mifflin, 1991.

Bill Freedman

Sucrose see **Carbohydrate**

Sudden infant death syndrome (SIDS)

Sudden infant death syndrome (SIDS), (also called crib death), is the death without apparent cause of an infant under the age of one year. A diagnosis of SIDS can only be made after experts have investigated the death scene, autopsied the dead infant, reviewed the baby's medical history, and ruled out all other possible explanations. About 7000 babies die of SIDS each year in the United States. This baffling disorder is the leading cause of death in infants ages 1-12 months. Although SIDS cannot be prevented completely parents can reduce the risk by putting their baby to sleep on its back or side rather than on its stomach.

The mysterious malady

The SIDS definition is purposefully vague and reflects how little actually is known about what causes the syndrome. SIDS victims seem to stop breathing in their sleep. They typically are found lifeless, limp, and blue. Often they have blood-tinged mucus coming from their mouth or nose. Ninety percent of SIDS victims die before six months. Most appear perfectly healthy beforehand or at most have a slight cold. Although they are usually found in their cribs babies have died of SIDS in car seats, strollers, and their mother's arms.

Although SIDS researchers have investigated hundreds of possible theories regarding the causes of SIDS no clear answers have been found. Autopsies fail to show any abnormalities in SIDS victims; they seem to be healthy, normal babies. Scientists aren't even sure whether death is caused by cardiac arrest or respiratory failure.

Some experts estimate that 1-20% of all diagnosed SIDS deaths are actually the result of other causes including child abuse and murder. For this reason an autopsy and a thorough examination of the scene of death must be done. This suspicion adds to the parents' grief and guilt. It also confuses the public's understanding of SIDS. But until a more definitive diagnosis of SIDS exists such steps must be taken to rule out the possibility of murder.

SIDS research

The age of its victims offers an important clue towards better understanding SIDS. Almost all sudden deaths occur between one week and six months of age a time of rapid growth and change in a baby. Neurological control of the baby's circulatory and respiratory systems is still evolving. Some scientists theorize that very subtle flaws in the baby's physical development are responsible for SIDS. Instead of breathing evenly young babies tend to stop breathing for a few seconds and then begin again with a gasp. According to one theory babies who die of SIDS have difficulty in restarting their breathing. Much more needs to be known about the normal respiratory processes and sleep patterns of babies in order to detect abnormalities.

Another clue may lie in the observation that many SIDS victims have a cold in the weeks before death. SIDS deaths are more common in the winter, a season when colds are frequent. This suggests that an upper respiratory infection might somehow trigger a series of events that leads to sudden death. Some researchers believe that no one factor is responsible for SIDS but that a number of events must come together to cause the syndrome.

Risk factors

By studying large groups of young infants a few of whom eventually go on to die of SIDS, scientists have found certain factors that occur more frequently in sudden death victims. Babies born prematurely are at greater risk for SIDS. So are twins and triplets. Boys are more susceptible than girls. Formula-fed infants are more susceptible than breast-fed babies. The syndrome is more common in the babies of mothers who are poor, under 20 years old, have other children, and receive little medical care during pregnancy. Mothers who smoke during pregnancy and the presence of cigarette smoke in the home after birth also increases the likelihood of SIDS. Other proposed risk factors including childhood vaccines and allergies to cow's milk have failed to show any link to SIDS.

It is important to remember that more than two-thirds of SIDS cases occur in babies without risk factors. Some scientists believe that all infants are potential victims if certain factors in their bodies and their environment interact in a particular unknown way. By studying risk factors researchers hope to gain important insights into the causes of the syndrome.

SIDS is not believed to be hereditary. Siblings of SIDS victims have only a slightly higher risk of sudden death compared to the average population. Yet some parents who have a subsequent baby after suffering the loss of a baby to SIDS find it very reassuring to use a home monitor. Attached to the baby, this machine sounds an alarm if the baby's respiration or heart rate drops below normal. The National Institutes of Health has stated that home monitors have not been shown to prevent SIDS.

"Back to sleep" campaign

SIDS occurs more frequently in New Zealand and the United States than in Japan and China. Within the United States it is more common in African-American babies than Hispanic babies. These differences suggest that certain cultural factors of baby care particularly

how he or she is put to bed may affect the incidence of SIDS. Scientists do not understand exactly why these differences matter—just that they do.

The single most important thing a parent or caregiver can do to lower the risk of SIDS is to put the baby to sleep on its back or side rather than on its stomach. In 1992 the American Academy of Pediatrics recommended placing healthy infants to sleep on their backs or sides. The group made the recommendation after reviewing several large studies done in New Zealand, England, and Australia. The studies demonstrated that SIDS declined as much as 50% in communities that had adopted this sleeping position for infants.

In the past the supine (or back-sleeping) position has been discouraged for fear that a sleeping infant might spit up and then suffocate on its own vomit. A careful examination of studies of infants placed prone (or on their stomachs) has shown that this does not happen. Some infants with certain health problems might best be placed prone. Parents who suspect this should check with their doctor.

SIDS in history

The phenomenon of sudden death in babies has been recorded for centuries. SIDS, has been described as a distinct disorder for nearly a century. In 1979 it was officially accepted as a cause of death. The current definition of the condition was developed by the National Institutes of Health in 1989.

As sleeping habits for families and babies changed over time so have the explanations offered for sudden death. Until a century ago infants and small children slept in the same beds as their mother. When babies were found dead their mothers were often blamed for rolling on top of them. In the 1700s and 1800s mothers were accused of rolling on their babies while drunk. After noting that SIDS is very rare in Asian countries where parents and babies typically sleep together, some recent researchers have theorized that sleeping with a parent might help regulate an infant's respiration and thus prevent SIDS.

In the early 1900s in the United States when co-sleeping became rare sudden death was blamed on dressing a baby too warmly at night. Before physicians realized that all babies have large thymus glands enlargements of the thymus gland were also blamed for SIDS.

Support groups for parents

Parents who suffer the loss of a child to SIDS typically feel immense sorrow and grief over the unex-

KEY TERMS

Co-sleeping—Two people sleeping in the same bed such as a baby and its mother.

Cot death—Another name for Sudden Infant Death Syndrome.

Prone—Lying face-down on the stomach.

Supine—Lying on the back.

pected and mysterious death. They also may feel guilty and blame themselves for not being more vigilant although there was nothing they could have done. Parents and other relatives of SIDS victims may find it helpful to attend support groups designed to offer them a safe place to express their emotions.

Everyone affected by the death of a baby to SIDS may need special support. This includes doctors, nurses, paramedics, other health care providers, police officers, and the babysitter or friend who may have been caring for the baby when it died. Ideally counseling should be made available to these people. Health care professionals and law enforcement officers often have special training to help comfort the grieving survivors of a SIDS death.

Further Reading:

Bower, Bruce. "Co-sleeping Gives Babies a Boost." *Science News*. 144 (4 December 1993): 380.

Dempsey, Susan Carey. "SIDS: Every New Parent's Nightmare." *Women's Day*. (7 January 1992).

Horchler, Joani Nelson and Robin Rice Morris. *The SIDS Survival Guide*. Hyattsville: SIDS Educational Services, 1994.

Sunshine-Genova, Amy. "Sleep Position and SIDS." *Parents* magazine (January 1994).

Toufexis, Anastasia. "When is Crib Death a Cover for Murder?" *Time*. (11 April 1994): 63.

Winthrop, Anne. "What is SIDS?" *American Baby*. (December 1992).

Liz Marshall

Sugar see **Carbohydrate**

Sugar cane see **Grasses**

Sulfur

Sulfur is the non-metallic chemical element of atomic number 16. It has a symbol of S, an atomic weight of 32.07, and a specific gravity of 2.07 (rhombic form) or 1.96 (monoclimic form). Sulfur boils at 832.5° F (444.7° C) and consists of four stable isotopes of mass numbers 32 (95.0%), 33 (0.75%), 34 (4.2%) and 36 (0.015%). Sulfur atoms found in different locations have slightly different percentages of the four isotopes, however.

Sulfur is a bright yellow solid that can exist in many allotropic forms with slightly different melting points, all around 239° F (115° C). The two main forms are called rhombic sulfur and monoclinic sulfur. There is also a rubbery, non-crystalline form, called plastic or amorphous—without shape—sulfur. An ancient name for sulfur is brimstone, meaning "burning stone." It does indeed burn in air with a blue flame, producing sulfur dioxide:

$$S \quad + \quad O_2 \quad \rightarrow \quad SO_2$$

| sulfur | oxygen gas | sulfur dioxide gas |

Sulfur itself has no odor at all, but it has a bad reputation because it makes many smelly compounds. Sulfur dioxide is one of them; it has a sharp, choking, suffocating effect on the unfortunate breather. The "fire and brimstone" of the Bible was one of the worst punishments that its authors could think of. The fact that sulfur comes from deep under the ground and that sulfur dioxide can be smelled in the fumes of volcanoes further fueled people's imaginations of what Hell must be like.

Where sulfur is found

Sulfur makes up only 0.05% of the Earth's crust, but it is easy to get because it occurs uncombined as the element, S_8. That's eight sulfur atoms tied together into each molecule of the element and joined around in a ring.

Sulfur occurs in huge, deep underground deposits of almost-pure element, notably along the Gulf coast of the U.S. and in Poland and Sicily. However, miners do not have to go underground to get it. They make the sulfur come to them by a clever arrangement of three pipes within pipes, drilled down into the sulfur bed. This arrangement is called the Frasch Process. Superheated steam is shot down through the outermost pipe to melt the sulfur. (The steam has to be superheated because sulfur doesn't melt until 239° F [115° C], which is hotter than "regular" steam.) Then, compressed air is shot down the innermost pipe, which forces the liquid sulfur up and out the middle pipe.

Sulfur is also widely distributed in the form of minerals and ores. Many of these are in the form of sulfates, including gypsum (calcium sulfate, $CaSO_4 \cdot 2H_2O$), barite (barium sulfate, $BaSO_4$) and Epsom salts (magnesium sulfate, $MgSO_4 \cdot 7H_2O$). Others are metal sulfides, including iron pyrites (iron sulfide, FeS_2), galena (lead sulfide, PbS), cinnabar (mercuric sulfide, HgS), stibnite (antimony sulfide, Sb_2S_3) and zinc blende (zinc sulfide, ZnS). The sulfur is recovered from these metal ores by roasting them—heating them strongly in air, which converts the sulfur to sulfur dioxide. For example,

$$2PbS + 3O_2 \rightarrow 2PbO + 2SO_2$$
lead   oxygen   lead   sulfur
sulfide   oxide   dioxide

Then the sulfur dioxide can go directly into the manufacture sulfuric acid, which is where more than 90% of the world's mined sulfur winds up.

Compounds of sulfur

Some sulfur is used directly as a fungicide and insecticide, in matches, fireworks, and gunpowder, and in the vulcanization of natural rubber. Most, however, is converted into a multitude of useful compounds.

Sulfur is in group 16 of the periodic table, directly below oxygen. It can form compounds in any one of its three major oxidation states: -2, +4 or +6.

Sulfuric acid is the parent acid of all sulfate compounds. Among the most important sulfates is calcium sulfate ($CaSO_4$), which occurs naturally as gypsum, alabaster and selenite. Copper sulfate is used as an agricultural insecticide and to kill algae in water supplies. Alums are double sulfates of aluminum and another metal such as potassium, chromium or iron. The most common alum is potassium aluminum sulfate, $KAl(SO_4)_2 \cdot 12H_2O$. In water, it makes a gelatinous, goopy precipitate of aluminum hydroxide, $Al(OH)_3$, which, when it sinks to the bottom, carries along with it all sorts of suspended dirt, leaving behind clear water. Alum is therefore used in water purification.

Hydrogen sulfide is the parent acid of the sulfides, a family of compounds that contain nothing but sulfur and a metal. This family includes many metal ores, including iron pyrites, galena, cinnabar, stibnite and zinc blende, as mentioned above, plus sulfides of copper and silver. Other sulfides are used in leather tanning, as pesticides, and in depilatories—creams that remove "unwanted hair" from the hides of cattle and from people.

Hydrogen sulfide itself is one of the worst-smelling gases anywhere. When eggs and certain other animal matter go rotten and putrefy, the stench is mostly hydrogen sulfide. It is often present in flatus—expelled intestinal gas. Hydrogen sulfide is extremely poisonous, but fortunately, it smells so bad that people don't hang around long enough to be overcome by it. Other very bad-smelling compounds of sulfur are the mercaptans, a family of organic sulfur-containing compounds. A mercaptan is the major ingredient in the aroma of skunks. A tiny amount of a gaseous mercaptan is deliberately added to the natural gas that is used for home heating and cooking, so that dangerous gas leaks can be detected by smell. Natural gas itself is odorless.

See also Sulfur dioxide; Sulfuric acid.

Further Reading:

Emsley, J., *The Elements*, Clarendon Press, 1991.
Greenwood, N. N., *Chemistry of the Elements*, Pergamon Press, 1985.
Kirk-Othmer Encyclopedia of Chemical Technology, Wiley.
Lide, David R., Ed., *Handbook of Chemistry and Physics*, 73rd ed., pp 4-28.

Robert L. Wolke

Sulfur cycle

Sulfur is an important nutrient for organisms, being an key constituent of certain amino acids, proteins, and other biochemicals. Plants satisfy their nutritional needs for sulfur by assimilating simple mineral compounds from the environment. This mostly occurs as sulfate dissolved in soil water that is taken up by roots, or as gaseous sulfur dioxide that is absorbed by foliage in environments where the atmosphere is somewhat polluted with this gas. Animals obtain the sulfur they need by eating plants or other animals, and digesting and assimilating their organic forms of sulfur, which are then used to synthesize necessary sulfur-containing biochemicals.

In certain situations, particularly in intensively managed agriculture, the availability of biologically useful forms of sulfur can be a limiting factor to the productivity of plants, and application of a sulfate-containing fertilizer may prove to be beneficial. Sulfur compounds may also be associated with important environmental damages, as when sulfur dioxide damages vegetation, or when acidic drainages associated with sulfide minerals degrade ecosystems.

Chemical forms and transformations of sulfur

Sulfur (S) can occur in many chemical forms in the environment. These include organic and mineral forms,

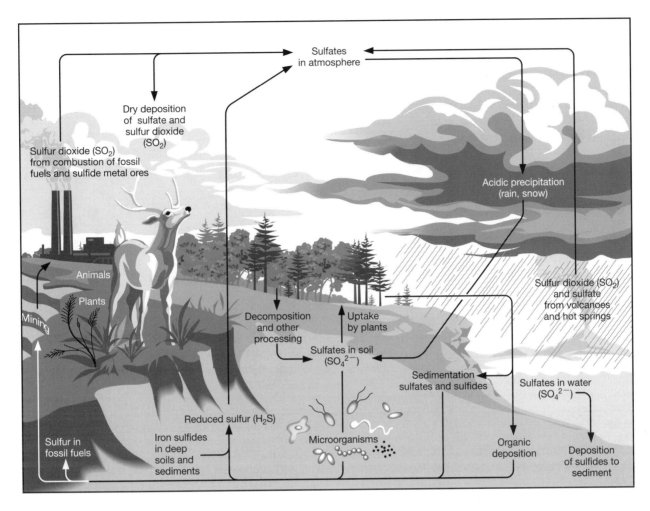

Sulfates
in atmosphere

Dry deposition
of sulfate and
sulfur dioxide
(SO_2)

Sulfur dioxide (SO_2)
from combustion of fossil
fuels and sulfide metal ores

Acidic precipitation
(rain, snow)

Sulfur dioxide (SO_2)
and sulfate
from volcanoes
and hot springs

Animals

Plants

Mining

Decomposition
and other
processing

Uptake
by plants

Sulfates in soil
(SO_4^{2-})

Sedimentation
sulfates and sulfides

Sulfates in water
(SO_4^{2-})

Reduced sulfur (H_2S)

Sulfur in
fossil fuels

Iron sulfides
in deep
soils and
sediments

Microorganisms

Organic
deposition

Deposition
of sulfides to
sediment

The sulfur cycle.

which can be chemically transformed by both biological and inorganic processes.

Sulfur dioxide (SO_2) and sulfate (SO_4^{-2})

Sulfur dioxide is a gas that can be toxic to plants at concentrations much smaller than one part per million in the atmosphere, and to animals at larger concentrations. There are many natural sources of emission of SO_2 to the atmosphere, such as volcanic eruptions and forest fires. Large emissions of SO_2 are also associated with human activities, especially the burning of coal and the processing of certain metal ores. In the atmosphere, SO_2 is oxidized to sulfate, an anion that occurs as a tiny particulate in which the negative charges are electrochemically balanced by the positive charges of cations, such as ammonium (NH_4^+), calcium (Ca^{2+}), or hydrogen ion (H^+). These fine particulates can serve as condensation nuclei for the formation of ice crystals, which may settle from the atmosphere as rain or snow, delivering the sulfate to terrestrial and aquatic ecosys-

tems. If the sulfate is mostly balanced by hydrogen ion, the precipitation will be acidic, and can damage some types of freshwater ecosystems.

Hydrogen sulfide (H_2S)

Hydrogen sulfide is another gas, with a strong smell of rotten eggs. Hydrogen sulfide is emitted from situations in which organic sulfur compounds are being decomposed in the absence of oxygen. Once H_2S is emitted to the atmosphere, it is slowly oxidized to sulfate, which behaves as described above.

Metal sulfides

Sulfur can occur in many chemically reduced mineral forms, or sulfides, in association with many metals. The most common metal sulfides in the environment are iron sulfides (such as FeS_2; these are called pyrites when they occur as cubic crystals), but all heavy metals can occur in this mineral form. Whenever metal sulfides are exposed to an oxygen-rich environment, certain bacteria begin to oxidize the sulfide, generating sulfate as a product, and tapping energy from the process which is used to sustain their own growth and reproduction. This autotrophic process is called chemosynthesis, and the bacteria involved are named *Thiobacillus thiooxidans*. When a large quantity of sulfide is oxidized in this way, an enormous amount of acidity is associated with the sulfate product.

Organic sulfur

Organic sulfur refers to an extremely diverse array of sulfur-containing organic molecules. These can range in weight and complexity from amino acids, proteins, and nucleic acids, to large molecules such as humic substances in soil or water. Organic sulfur is a chemically reduced form of sulfur. When it is exposed to an oxygen-rich atmosphere, bacteria oxidize the organic sulfur to derive energy, while liberating sulfate, usually in association with hydrogen ions and acidity.

Humans and the sulfur cycle

Human activities influence the rates and character of certain aspects of the sulfur cycle in important ways, sometimes causing substantial environmental damages.

Acid rain is a well known environmental problem. Acid rain is ultimately associated with large emissions of sulfur dioxide to the atmosphere by human sources, such as oil- and coal-fired power plants, metal smelters, and the burning of fuel oil to heat homes. The SO_2 is eventually oxidized in the atmosphere to sulfate, much of which is balanced by hydrogen ions, so the precipitation chemistry is acidic. In addition, the vicinity of large point-sources of SO_2 emission is generally polluted by relatively large concentrations of this gas. If its concentration is large enough, the SO_2 can cause toxicity to plants, which may be killed, resulting in severe ecological damages. In addition, atmospheric SO_2 can be directly deposited to surfaces, especially moist soil, plant, or aquatic surfaces, since SO_2 can readily dissolve in water. When this happens, the SO_2 becomes oxidized to sulfate, generating acidity. This means of direct input of sulfur dioxide is called dry deposition, and is a fundamentally different process from the so-called wet deposition of sulfate and acidity with precipitation.

Acid mine drainage is another severe environmental problem that is commonly associated with coal and metal mining, and sometimes with construction activities such as road building. In all of these cases, physical disturbance results in the exposure of large quantities of mineral sulfides to atmospheric oxygen. This causes the sulfides to be oxidized to sulfate, a process accompanied by the generation of large amounts of acidity. Surface

KEY TERMS

Acid mine drainage—This refers to surface or ground water that has been acidified through the oxidation of reduced-sulfur minerals, such as pyrite.

Electrochemical balance—In an aqueous solution, the number of positive charges associated with cations must equal the number of negative charges of anions, so the solution does not develop an electrical charge.

waters exposed to acid mine drainage can become severely acidified, to a pH less than 3, resulting in severe biological damages and environmental degradation.

Sulfur is also an important mineral commodity, with many industrial uses in manufacturing. Sulfur for these purposes is largely obtained by cleaning sour natural gas of its content of H_2S, and from pollution control at some metal smelters.

In a few types of intensively managed agriculture, crops may be well fertilized with nitrogen, phosphorus, and other nutrients, and in such cases there may be a deficiency of sulfate availability. Because sulfate is an important plant nutrient, it may have to be applied in the form of a sulfate-containing fertilizer. In North America, sulfate fertilization is most common in prairie agriculture.

See also Nutrients; Sulfur; Sulfur dioxide.

Further Reading:
Freedman, B. *Environmental Ecology*, 2nd ed. San Diego: Academic Press, 1994.
Atlas, R. M. and R. Bartha. *Microbial Ecology.* Menlo Park: Benjamin/Cummings, 1994.

Bill Freedman

Sulfur dioxide

Sulfur dioxide, SO_2, is a colorless gas with an irritating, choking odor. It is produced naturally in volcanoes and in geysers, and is produced in ever-increasing amounts by the burning of sulfur-containing coal. Sulfur dioxide is a key contributor to acid rain. It is used in the manufacturing of sulfuric acid, in preserving many foods, as a disinfectant, and in the wine industry.

Sulfur dioxide is produced naturally inside the earth by the reaction of sulfur with oxygen gas. This accounts for the "sulfur" smell around active volcanoes and geysers. Sulfur is a natural component of most coal, and it is the burning of sulfur-containing coal that has contributed the most to the acid rain problem in the world. When burned, the sulfur in coal reacts with oxygen and makes sulfur dioxide gas. This gas may react with water to make sulfurous acid (H_2SO_3, a moderately strong acid), or it may react with addition oxygen to form sulfur trioxide, SO_3, which then reacts with water in the atmosphere to produce sulfuric acid, H_2SO_4, the major contributor to acid rain. This same series of reactions is used to make sulfuric acid, the most widely produced chemical in the world. Efforts to reduce the amounts of sulfur dioxide in the atmosphere use two approaches. Low sulfur coal can be used, and this reduced the emissions, although, as we use up more and more of the low sulfur coal, we are forced to use what remains, higher sulfur content coal. Many factories now use *scrubbers*, which put sulfur dioxide gas into contact with calcium oxide (CaO) to produce solid calcium sulfite, thus preventing the sulfur dioxide from reaching the atmosphere. The reaction is shown below:

$$CaO + SO_2(g) \longrightarrow CaSO_3$$

One drawback to this approach is that for every ton of sulfur dioxide that reacts, two tons of solid calcium sulfite are produced, and they must be disposed of.

Sulfur dioxide is used widely to prevent dried fruits (especially apricots and peaches) from becoming discolored. Sulfur dioxide is a strong reducing agent, and prevents the formation of discolored oxidation products in the fruits. It is also used to bleach vegetables and in the wine industry is used to prevent wines from discoloring and turning brown. In the food industry, sulfur dioxide is used as a disinfectant during the manufacturing process.

See also Acid rain; Sulfur; Volcano.

Sulfuric acid

Sulfuric acid, H_2SO_4, is a viscous (thick and syrupy), oily liquid which has for years been the most widely used chemical in the world. Over 100 billion lbs (45 billion kg) of sulfuric acid are produced each year. It is also one of the least expensive acids, which makes it a favorite of industries around the world. It is used in

the production of fertilizers and as an industrial catalyst (a substance which speeds up chemical reactions).

One of the major uses of sulfuric acid is in the production of fertilizers. Phosphate rock is treated with sulfuric acid to produce water soluble phosphates, which are essential for plant growth and survival. It is also the acid used in car batteries. Automobile batteries contain lead, lead oxide, and sulfuric acid. These lead storage batteries are used because they can not only provide the electric current needed to start a car, but can be recharged by the car's electrical system while the car is running.

Sulfuric acid is one of the major components of acid rain. Coal contains sulfur as a natural impurity and when coal is burned sulfur dioxide (SO_2) and sulfur trioxide (SO_3) gases are produced. Sulfur trioxide then reacts with water in the air, creating sulfuric acid. This acid rain can damage buildings, corrode metal, and destroy plant and animal life. Acid rain is an increasing problem not only in major industrialized nations, but also in neighboring countries that are downwind, since pollutants produced by a country do not stay in the air above that country.

One of the major industrial uses of sulfuric acid is as a dehydrating agent (a substance that removes water from other substances). Sulfuric acid is an extremely effective dehydrating agent. Upon contact with living tissue it kills cells by removing water from them.

See also Acid rain; Fertilizers; Sulfur.

Sumac see **Cashew family**

Sun

The Sun is the star at the center of our solar system. It has a diameter of about 420,000 miles (700,000 km) and a surface temperature of 5,800 Kelvin (5,627°C). Its visible "surface" is actually a thin gas, as is the rest of its atmosphere and interior.

The Sun shines as a result of thermonuclear fusion reactions in its core, and the energy produced by these reactions heats the gas in the Sun's interior sufficiently to prevent the weight of its own matter from crushing it. This energy also is the source of heat and life on Earth, and small variations in the Sun's energy output, or even in the features present in its atmosphere, may be sufficient to profoundly affect terrestrial climate. Although the Sun is by far the nearest star, the processes causing solar variability are still poorly understood and continue to challenge astronomers.

A brief history of solar observations

The Sun is about 90 million miles (150 million km) away from Earth. It is modest by stellar standards, although it is over 100 times larger than the Earth and over 300,000 times more massive. Although it consumes more than half a billion tons of its nuclear fuel each second, it has been shining continuously for five billion years, and it will continue to shine for another five billion. We call this star the Sun, and it is a central element of human existence.

We find the Sun on the first page of the Bible, created by God and set in the heavens. To the ancient Egyptians it *was* a god, for anyone who felt its warmth and watched the renewal of crops it brought in the spring realized it was a bringer of life. Greek mythology recounts the tale of Icarus, who died in a brazen attempt to fly too close to the Sun. Even today a skin tan, a sign of frequent exposure to the Sun's rays, is sometimes regarded as a sign of health.

Ancient dogma held that the Sun orbited the Earth. It was not until 1543 that Nikolaus Copernicus (1473-1543) published the heliocentric theory of the Universe, in which the Sun lay at the center and Earth was relegated to a circular orbit around it. Copernicus refused to have this magnificent work published until after his death. This was a wise decision, since earlier publication would have resulted in his equally earlier death at the hand of Church authorities who regarded his work as heresy.

Around 1610, the newly invented telescope was trained on the Sun. The early solar observers, including Galileo (1564-1642), noticed that the surface of the Sun had dark spots on it. Not only that, the spots moved across the solar surface, leading Galileo to conclude that the Sun rotated. This sent further shock waves through the religious world. The poor cardinals had hardly recovered from Copernicus's heresy, and now along came Galileo telling them that the backup embodiment of celestial perfection, the Sun, had ugly blemishes on its surface. Galileo got into serious trouble with the Church for this and other statements he made, and it would be 380 years before Pope John Paul II exonerated him.

In the nineteenth century an amateur German astronomer named Heinrich Schwabe (1789-1875) did some of the first scientific analysis of solar data. Observers had kept records over the years of the number of sunspots visible, and Schwabe noticed that the sunspot number rose and fell in a cyclic fashion, with a period of about 11 years. Later workers confirmed this *activity cycle*, and the sunspot number remains today an important piece of information about our star.

The nature of sunspots was first investigated by George Ellery Hale (1868-1938), who devoted his life to studying the Sun from the observatory he founded on Mt. Wilson near Los Angeles. Hale discovered that sunspots were cooler than the surrounding solar surface—which is why they appear dark—and that sunspots are associated with strong magnetic fields. Hale also discovered that the Sun's magnetic field reverses itself with each 11-year cycle, so that there is a more fundamental 22-year *magnetic activity cycle* behind the sunspot cycle.

Since Hale's time, solar research has developed along two great lines of investigation. First, a huge observational database has been created. The national solar observing facilities of the United States are located at Sacramento Peak just east of Alamogordo, New Mexico, and at Kitt Peak, 30 miles (48 km) west of Tucson, Arizona. In addition to sunspots, these observatories have monitored prominences and flares, which are spectacular, eruptive events in the solar atmosphere, the solar magnetic field itself, the solar granulation, which is a result of the turbulent movement of the gas beneath the solar surface, and the total energy output of the Sun. Space-based satellites have studied the Sun in wavelength regimes, such as the ultraviolet and the x ray, not accessible from the ground. The result of these investigations is a detailed set of observations about the phenomena that occur on our star.

The other line of investigation is the theoretical analysis of processes within the Sun and in its atmosphere. Scientists have developed models to explain what is observed; if a model fails to fit the observations, it must be discarded. The goal of this work is to explain *why* the various features seen on the Sun appear. Why is there an 11-year-long solar activity cycle? What do the forces producing granulation have to do with the nature of the solar magnetic field? Where does the magnetic field originate? These questions, and many others, are only partially answered.

A fruitful line of research toward answering these questions involves observing not just the Sun, but many other stars like the Sun. You would have a difficult time understanding what the human race was like by oberving only one person; similarly, it is hopeless to try to understand the complex nature of the stars by observing only one of them. Long-term observations of solarlike stars have been carried out at the Mount Wilson Observatory near Los Angeles and at Lowell Observatory in Flagstaff, Arizona. Understanding the so-called "solar-stellar connection," derived from observations of other

A photograph of the Sun taken with a coronagraph, a telescope that creates an artificial eclipse, so that the solar corona is visible. The shape of the corona varies with time and in some areas is nearly absent. Much of its radiation is in the x-ray and extreme UV range, and the corona is many times hotter than the surface of the Sun itself.

stars, may yield important clues about the processes at work in our own star.

Two million years after our earliest ancestors looked up and shielded their eyes from the brilliant, life-giving object in the sky, we still have only a rudimentary understanding of it. Copernicus and Galileo may not have imagined just how complex an object the Sun is. But were they alive today, they probably would appreciate it.

A journey through the Sun

Let us now take a trip through the Sun. We will start at the very center, and work our way out to empty space.

The solar furnace

Here we are, then, in the Sun's core. We'd better have a really good air conditioner with us, because it is unthinkably hot: 15,000,000 Kelvin (15,000,000°C). The matter here has a density of roughly 1 kilogram (2.2 lbs) per cubic centimeter—about 1000 times the density of water. It is compressed to this degree by the crushing weight of all the matter between it and the sur-

face—and it is a *very* long way, about 210,000 miles (350,000 km)—to the surface.

There are no atoms here. No atom—a nucleus of protons and neutrons, orbited by electrons, could exist in this inferno. There is nothing but a swirling sea of particles. We know from physics that the hotter a medium is, the faster its particles move. In the Sun's core the protons race around at blinding speeds, and because they are so tightly packed, they are constantly crashing into one another.

What is a proton? It is a hydrogen ion—a hydrogen atom that has had its sole electron stripped away. The Sun is made mostly of hydrogen. In the cool regions of its atmosphere the hydrogen exists as atoms, with a single electron bound to the proton; here in the core there are only the ions.

Suddenly, right in front of our (super-powerful) eyes, something happens: four hydrogen nuclei smash together in a quick series of collisions, with catastrophic force. So violent are these collisions that the protons' natural tendency to repel one another—they all have the same positive charge—is overcome. When the various interactions are over, a new particle has emerged: a *helium* nucleus containing two protons and two neutrons. The helium nucleus gets its share of battering by the other particles, but it is larger and tightly bound together, and even the maelstrom around us cannot disrupt it.

There is one more product of this fusion reaction. In the series of collisions leading to the formation of the helium nucleus, two particles called *photons* are produced. A photon is a bundle of electromagnetic radiation, also known as a ray of light. The photons race away from the Sun's core at the incredible speed of 180,000 miles (300,000 km) per second, the speed of light.

Toward the surface

Let us ride along with one of these photons. Like the hydrogen nuclei, it doesn't go in a straight line. It constantly hits other particles, bouncing off them in a random direction. Sometimes an atom absorbs its energy, only to re-emit it a fraction of a second later in a different direction. This is the so-called random walk, and it describes how our photon works its way out from the Sun's core.

As we head toward the surface, being buffeted in all directions, we notice that the temperature, pressure and density of the gas are all dropping. This is because there is now less material between us and the surface. There is not as much weight pressing down on the gas, so it doesn't need to be at as high a pressure to support the material above it. Lower pressure means lower temperature and density.

Here, halfway from the Sun's core to its surface, we are in the zone of *radiative* energy transport, where uncountable trillions of photons flow away from the Sun's core where they were produced. As they flow past, new photons, freshly created in the core, flow into it from below.

Into the convection zone

But then, a little more than two-thirds of the way out, something happens. The gas is getting quite cool now, less than 100,000 Kelvin (99,700°C). Instead of individual particles, we now encounter atoms, which are capable of absorbing the photons rather than simply scattering them in a different direction. Photons have difficulty flowing through this cool gas. As they get absorbed, new photons flow into the gas from below, heating it even more. The gas begins to overheat. As a result, energy transport is now more efficient if a huge bubble of hot gas forms and begins to rise toward the surface. This is called *convection*, and we are now in the Sun's zone of convective energy transport.

Let's jump off our photon and ride along with the bubble. Like the surging top of a cumulus cloud, we rise buoyantly. Our hot gas bubble rises into progressively cooler gas, releasing its heat into smaller bubbles. Following them along, we finally reach the very cool region just below the Sun's surface. The bubbles release their pent-up heat. With their heat gone, they are now cooler than their surroundings, so they sink back into the Sun's interior, to pick up more heat and begin the convective cycle anew.

In the atmosphere

We are now at the Sun's surface. It is about thirty thousand years since our photon was created in the Sun's core. Had the photon gone in a straight line, it would have reached the surface in just over one second, but ten billion trillion interactions with matter in the Sun's interior slowed it considerably.

We are in a thin (300 mile/500 km) layer of matter called the *photosphere*. The temperature here is 5,800 Kelvin (5,527°C), and for the first time, a photon of visual light—that is, with a wavelength that places it in the visual portion of the spectrum—has a chance of escaping directly to outer space. The density of the gas is now so low that it is nearly a vacuum, thousands of times less dense than air, and so little matter is left between us and space that photons all around us are escaping with no further interactions.

The photosphere is a seething region of hot, rising granules and cooler, sinking ones. In places there are great, dark spots, perhaps 6,200 miles (10,000 km) across, where the temperature is only 4,000 Kelvin (3,700°C) and where matter is constrained to flow along the intense and tangled lines of the strong magnetic fields that permeate the spots. (One phenomenon thought to contribute to the tangling of the solar magnetic field is the Sun's rotation. The Sun's equator rotates once every 26 days, its poles once every 36 days. This *differential rotation* contributes to twisting the magnetic fields and producing active features like sunspots.)

The magnetic fields are invisible, but observations have revealed that they can arch high into the Sun's atmosphere, forming loops. Hot gas becomes confined in these loops, forming spectacular prominences. Violent rearrangements or eruptions in twisted magnetic fields result in flares, which spew matter and intense radiation into space. Some of this radiation may interrupt radio communications on Earth, while the particles will soon stream into Earth's atmosphere, causing aurorae.

Leaving our convective bubble, we jump on a photon of visual light. It races outward. We are confident now that the temperature will continue to decrease, as it has since we left the Sun's core so long ago. But just above the photosphere, we get a surprise. The temperature starts to climb, reaching 10,000 Kelvin (9,700°C) a few thousand miles above the photosphere. This is the *chromosphere*, one of the most baffling regions in the Sun. Most of it is ten million times less dense than air. The causes for the temperature rise are still not fully understood. One possibility is that mechanical energy from the convection zone—the energy associated with the motion of the gas—is deposited into the Sun's upper atmosphere, heating it. Because it is so thin and tenuous, the chromosphere is very faint, and under normal circumstances is invisible with the brilliant photosphere behind it. We can see the chromosphere by photographing the Sun with special filters sensitive to light that originates in the chromosphere, or during an eclipse, when the Moon blocks the photosphere and the chromosphere appears as a glowing ring girdling the solar limb.

Now we are 1,800 miles (3,000 km) above the photosphere, and suddenly the temperature rises sharply—20,000 Kelvin, then 100,000, then half a million! We pass quickly through this narrow *transition region* and enter the *corona*, an incredibly tenuous and hot (2,000,000 Kelvin/2,000,000°C) region extending 3,000,000 miles (5,000,000 km) above the photosphere. The corona is also very faint, and can only be observed in visible light with the photosphere blocked, as it is during an eclipse. Because the corona is so hot, it is also spectacular in x ray photographs, which can be obtained only from space-based observatories.

The solar wind

Finally we reach the end of the corona, leaving behind the last of the Sun's strong magnetic field regions. Our photon races into empty space.

But we are not alone. All around is a swarm of particles. There are only a few per cubic centimeter—an almost perfect vacuum. They are all part of the solar wind, a continuous stream of matter flowing away from the Sun. Slowly, the Sun is losing material to space. The rate of this loss is very small, so it will not seriously affect the Sun's evolution. (Some stars, however, have powerful winds that can carry off a substantial fraction of their mass.) The solar wind permeates the entire solar system, and beyond.

A small blue planet

Eight minutes after our photon leaves the Sun's photosphere, it reaches Earth. Along with countless billions of other photons, it streams through Earth's

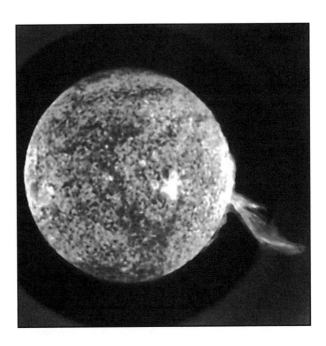

An ultraviolet image of the Sun showing a massive prominence.

atmosphere, and finally reaches your eye. You no longer need make an imaginary trip to the center of the Sun. The photon, a product of a hydrogen fusion reaction 30,000 years ago, has finished its trip. Obviously the Sun has a profound impact on doings here on Earth, but recent research suggests the connections may run deeper than initially thought.

The link may lie in the solar activity cycle, which is the periodic variation in active features such as sunspots, prominences, and flares, in the Sun's atmosphere and on its visible surface. The cause of the activity cycle is not well understood, but astronomers generally agree that the Sun's differential rotation, combined with the turbulent motions in its convection zone, create a magnetic dynamo that results in a perpetual tangling and rearrangement of the Sun's magnetic field. When magnetic field lines, which normally lie below the photosphere, become tangled and burst into the Sun's atmosphere, active features such as sunspots and prominences invariably form. When the magnetic field becomes tangled to a critical level, it rearranges and simplifies its configuration, and the amount of solar activity decreases correspondingly. The sunspot cycle typically has a length of about 11 years, but there is compelling circumstantial evidence that variations in the length of the solar activity cycle are closely related to changes in the global temperature, with shorter solar cycles corresponding to warmer temperatures on Earth.

And in the end, the Sun will have its final and greatest impact on our small blue planet. What of the

KEY TERMS

. . . .

Chromosphere—The narrow middle layer of the Sun's atmosphere. It is about 10,000 Kelvin and is very faint relative to the photosphere.

Convection zone—The outermost third of the solar interior. Here heat is transported to the surface in giant convective bubbles of gas, which rise to the surface, release their heat, and then sink back into the interior to pick up more heat.

Core—The central region of the Sun, where thermonuclear fusion reactions take place.

Corona—The highest and hottest layer of the solar atmosphere. Matter in the corona may have a temperature of 2,000,000 Kelvin and may be several million miles above the photosphere.

Photosphere—The lowest layer of the solar atmosphere, where most of the visible light is emitted. Because this is the layer we see in white-light photographs, it is often called the solar "surface," even though it is a very thin gas.

Prominence—A large region of glowing gas suspended in magnetic fields, often arching far above the photosphere. Some prominences are *quiescent*, remaining for days, while others are *eruptive*, and dissipate violently.

Radiative zone—The central two-thirds of the solar interior. Here energy is transported by the flow of photons, or light waves, through the matter.

Further Reading:

Giampapa, Mark S. "The Solar-Stellar Connection." *Sky & Telescope* (August 1987): 142.

Pasachoff, J. "The Sun: A Star Close Up," *Mercury* (May/June 1991): 66.

Seeds, M. A., *Horizons, Discovering the Universe.* New York. Wiley, 1991.

Jeffrey C. Hall

Sunbirds

Sunbirds are 105 species of small, lovely birds that make up the family Nectariniidae. Sunbirds occur in Africa, South and Southeast Asia, New Guinea, and Australia. They occupy a wide range of habitats, from forests and savannahs to shrubby grasslands, and some agricultural habitats.

Sunbirds range in body length from 4-9 inches (9-22 cm). The wings are short and rounded, and the tail is quite long in some species. They have a long, pointed, down-curved beak, which in some species exceeds the length of the head. The tongue is long, tubular for about 2/3 of its length, and its tip is split. The unusual bill and tongue of sunbirds are adaptations to feeding on the nectar of flowers. There are fine serrations near the tip of the beak, which are thought to be an adaptation to gripping insects.

Male sunbirds are brightly and garishly colored in bold patterns of green, blue, purple, red, black, or white. Many of these superb hues are due to a iridescence of the feathers, which is a prism-like, physical phenomenon, rather than the color of pigments. Female sunbirds are more subdued in their coloration, and are not iridescent. The sunbirds and hummingbirds (family Trochilidae) are not related, but they are similar in aspects of their iridescent coloration, and their feeding.

Sunbirds are active, strongly flying birds. They mostly feed on nectar, and also on insects. Sunbirds sometimes hover while feeding.

Sunbird nests are hanging, purselike structures, with a side entrance. The nest is constructed by the female of fibrous plant materials, partly held together using spider webs. The 1-3 eggs are incubated mostly by the female, but she is fed by the male while on the nest. Both parents care for the babies, which have a straight bill when born.

core, which our photon left a million years ago? Five billion years from now, the seemingly countless hydrogen nuclei will all have been converted into helium "ash"—the Sun's fuel will be gone. To stave off destruction by the inexorable force of gravity, the Sun's core will contract and heat to the point that the helium will ignite. In the process, the Sun will expand into a red giant star, swallowing the innermost planet, Mercury, and turning Earth into a charred wasteland. But the helium is the last fuel reserve the Sun will be able to use, and it will eject its outer layers, leaving behind only its collapsed core, a small, dying *white dwarf*. For the purposes of any one of us, the Sun will always be there, but there are timescales and events greater than we, and the Sun is part of them.

See *also* Heliocentric theory; Nuclear reactions; Seasons; Solar activity cycle; Solar flare; Solar system; Solar wind; Star; Star formation; Stellar evolution; Sunspots.

There are 78 species of sunbirds in the genus *Nectarinia*. Males of the superb sunbird (*Nectarinia superba*) of central Africa have a metallic-green back, a purple throat, and a burgundy breast, with black wings and tail. Clearly, this bird is appropriately named. Males of Gould's sunbird (*Aethopyga gouldiae*) of Southeast Asia have a blue head and tail, a crimson back, scarlet breast, and a lemon-yellow belly.

The spiderhunters (*Arachnothera* spp.) are greenish, less-garishly colored birds, and they have very long bills. The long-billed spiderhunter (*Arachnothera robusta*) of Indochina and Southeast Asia is a spider- and insect-eating bird that inhabits montane forests.

Sundew see **Carnivorous plants**

Sundog see **Atmospheric optical phenomena**

Sunfish see **Bass**

Sunflower see **Composite family**

Sun pillar see **Atmospheric optical phenomena**

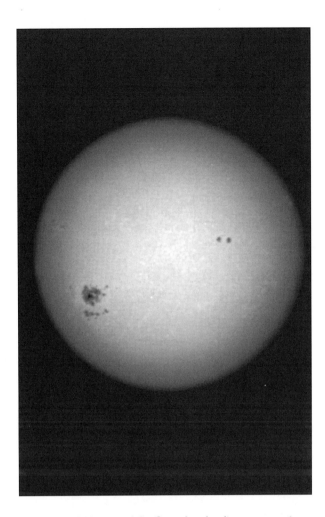

A visible light image of the Sun, showing large sunspots.

Sunspots

As the word implies, sunspots are dark areas that appear on the Sun from time to time. Although large spots, visible to the naked eye, have been noted by the Chinese since antiquity, the first mention of them in the western literature is by Galileo in the "Starry Messenger" published in 1610. Their occurrence has been carefully noted by astronomers ever since. Astronomers have found that the frequency of sunspots varies with a period of between 11 and 13 years. This corresponds to the period of solar activity cycle involving solar flares, prominences and other phenomena associated with the outer layers of the Sun.

At the beginning of the solar cycle a few sunspots appear at the higher latitudes on the Sun near the poles. The sunspots then appear to move across the face of the sun due to its rotation. Large spots may last for several rotation periods of about a month in length. As the cycle progresses the number of spots increases and they tend to be formed at lower latitudes toward the equator. The end of the cycle is marked by a marked drop in the number of low-latitude sunspots which is followed immedi-

ately by the beginning of the next cycle, as small numbers of spots begin to appear at high latitudes.

We now know that sunspots are essentially 'magnetic storms' on the surface of the Sun. The spots usually occur in pairs. Just as a bar-magnet placed under a sheet of paper will show a characteristic looping magnetic field when iron filings are scattered over the paper, so the sunspots making up the pair appear to be connected by a similar field. We characterize the ends of the bar magnet as being north or south magnetic poles depending on how a magnetic compass is affected by the poles. Similarly each of the members of a sunspot pair will have the characteristics of either a north or south magnetic pole. During a particular cycle, the leading spot of the pair will always have the same polarity for spots formed in a particular hemisphere. The order of polarity is reversed for sunspot-pairs formed in the opposite hemisphere. Thus, if spots-pairs formed in the northern hemisphere of the Sun have the lead spot behaving as a south magnetic pole, the leading spot of a pair formed in the southern hemisphere will have north magnetic pole. This order of polar progression for the leading and trailing spots is preserved throughout the entire 11-13 year cycle. However, during the following sunspot cycle the order will be reversed in both hemispheres. This has led most astronomers to feel that the proper sunspot cycle should be reckoned as consisting of two 11-13 year cycles, since two cycles must pass before conditions are duplicated and the full pattern can repeat.

While there have been attempts to link the solar cycle to affairs on earth most of the correlations appear to result from chance. An exception to that may lie in the Earth's weather. There have been some strongly suggestive correlations between solar activity and global temperature as well as rainfall variations. Analysis of tree-ring data spanning many centuries clearly shows the presence of 11-13 year cycle. There is even compelling evidence from ancient rock layers that the solar cycle has been present since Precambrian times. Those involved in the launching and maintenance of earth satellites are acutely aware that the upper layers of the Earth's atmosphere respond to solar activity by expanding thereby increasing the atmospheric drag on satellites in low Earth orbit. Finally, there is a curious period of about 75 years shortly after Galileo's discovery when few sunspots were observed. This era is called the Maunder Minimum after the astronomer who first noted its existence. Other phenomena such as the aurora borealis (northern lights) that are associated with solar activity are also missing from European records during this period. The interval is also associated with a time of unusually severe winters in both Europe and the North America and is often called the "little ice age." In this century, Jack Eddy has found evidence that there may have been similar periods of cold associated with earlier interruptions of the solar cycle. Unfortunately our understanding of the solar cycle is sufficiently crude that we have no explanation of what might cause these interruptions. Indeed, our understanding of the basis for the cycle itself is still largely in a phenomenological phase.

The very strong magnetic fields (i.e. several thousand times the general field of the Earth) in a sunspot account for the dark appearance of the spot. The hot atmosphere of the Sun contains a significant number of atoms having a net positive charge resulting from collisions between them (i.e., they are ionized, having lost one or more electrons). Charged particles may move along magnetic field lines, but not across them. Thus, a magnetic field exerts a kind of pressure on the gas and helps to support it against the gravitational force of the

KEY TERMS

Maunder minimum—A period of time from about 1650-1725 when the Sun did not appear to have sunspots. This interval is associated with a time of unusually severe winters in Europe and North America known as the "little ice age."

Penumbra—The lighter, outer region of a sunspot.

Umbra—The dark, central region of a sunspot.

Sun itself. This force is usually balanced only by the pressure of the hot gas surrounding a sunspot. With part of the pressure being supplied by the magnetic field, the gas will cool to a lower temperature. Since it is not as hot, it appears dark compared to the bright surrounding region called the photosphere. While they appear dark by comparison, sunspots are still hotter than any blast furnace on the Earth and are only dark by contrast with the brilliant solar surface. A close inspection of a sunspot shows it to have a dark central region called an umbra surrounded by a lighter radial structured region called a penumbra. These regions can be understood in terms of the spreading and weakening magnetic field emanating from the core of the sunspot.

In the second half of this century Eugene Parker suggested a mechanism which accounts for much of the descriptive behavior of sunspots. To understand how it works we need to know that the Sun does not rotate as a rigid body. The polar regions rotate somewhat more slowly than the equator. Because of the charged nature of the solar material, the Sun's general magnetic field is dragged along with the solar rotation. However, it will be dragged faster and further at the equator than at the rotational poles. Although the general field of the Sun is quite weak (i.e., similar to that of the Earth), the differential rotation strengthens and distorts the field over time. One can imagine the faster-rotating regions of the equator dragging the local magnetic field so that the field lines are drawn out into long thin tubes. The more these tubes are stretched, the stronger the field becomes. The magnetic pressure exerted on the surrounding gas causes the material within the tube to become "buoyant" compared to the surrounding material and rise toward the surface. As the magnetic tube breaks the surface of the Sun it forms two spot-like cross sections where it clears the lower solar atmosphere. A the field direction is out of the solar surface at one spot and into it at the other, one of these spots will appear to have one kind of magnetic pole and the other spot will appear to have the other. The global nature of the general solar field will guarantee that the stretched magnetic tubes will yield leading spots with opposite polarities in opposite hemispheres. A reversal of the Sun's general field between 11-13 year cycles would account for the reversal of this order. However, there is no compelling explanation of why the general field should reverse after each 11-13 year solar cycle. Nevertheless, this relatively simple conceptual picture based on observed large scale features of the Sun does provide a basis for understanding the apparently complicated nature of sunspots.

See also Solar activity cycle; Sun.

Further Reading:

Abell, G.O., *Exploration of the Universe*, Philadelphia, New York: Saunders College Publishing, 1982, pp. 509-518.

Arny, T.T., *Explorations—an Introduction to Astronomy*, St. Louis, Boston: Mosby, 1994, pp. 299-301 .

Seeds, M.A., *Horizons—Exploring the Universe*, Belmont Cal: Wadsworth Pub. Co., 1995, pp. 139-141.

Williams, G.E. "The Solar Cycle in Precambrian Time," *Scientific American,* 255, No. 2, 1986, pp. 88-96.

Zirin, H. *Astrophysics of the Sun*, Cambridge University Press, 1988, pp. 303-333.

George W. Collins II

Superclusters

Superclusters are currently the largest structures known in the universe. Stars and clusters of stars group together into galaxies which can contain anywhere from a few million to a few trillion stars. Galaxies collect into groups known as clusters of galaxies. On a larger scale superclusters are clusters of clusters of galaxies. As clusters of galaxies group into superclusters they leave empty spaces called voids between the superclusters. Superclusters and voids typically extend for hundreds of millions of light years.

History

In 1924 Edwin Hubble (after whom the Hubble Space Telescope was named) proved that galaxies were indeed structures outside the Milky Way galaxy. The groupings of galaxies in the sky were so obvious that the existence of clusters of galaxies was accepted

immediately. The existence of superclusters is less obvious. Finding the distances to galaxies, to get their three dimensional distribution in space, is hard. Most astronomers accepted Hubble's word that superclusters did not exist. Clyde Tombaugh, who discovered Pluto, once showed Hubble his first map of a supercluster. Hubble refused to believe it so the idea was ignored.

Gerard deVaucouleurs was not so easily discouraged. In the early 1950s he suggested that our galaxy and its cluster, the Local Group, are at the edge of a much larger group. This larger group is now known as the Local Supercluster. DeVaucouleurs' suggestion was initially "received with resounding silence" (his words) but after 25 years his view became widely accepted.

By the 1970s, improvements in instrumentation, allowed astronomers to measure distances to a large number of galaxies and work out the three dimensional structure of the universe. The first definite supercluster was mapped out by Stephen Gregory, Laird Thompson, and William Tifft in the 1970s. They found the Coma Supercluster extending about 100 million light years. Two clusters, the Coma cluster and A1367 (the 1367th cluster in a catalog by Abell), were bridged together by galaxies and small clusters. The trio also unintentionally found the first void in front of the Coma supercluster. Astronomers quibble about the details of superclusters but most accept the fact that the large scale structure of the universe includes superclusters and relatively empty voids.

Large scale structures

Since the 1970s large scale structure surveys have provided a picture of the superclusters and voids in the universe. All major known clusters of galaxies and at least 95% of all galaxies are found in superclusters. The voids between superclusters may contain faint galaxies but no bright galaxies. The voids tend to be spherical but superclusters are not. Superclusters have long filamentary or sheet-like structures that provide the boundaries for the voids.

Our galaxy is located at one end of the Local Group: a small cluster of galaxies with the Andromeda galaxy at the other end. The Local Group is near the outskirts of the Local Supercluster which has a diameter of 100 million light years. This somewhat flattened supercluster consists of two major hot dog-shaped groups of galaxies. It contains a total of 10^{15} times the mass of the Sun, most of which is concentrated into 5% of the volume of the supercluster.

KEY TERMS

. . . .

Cluster of Galaxies—A group of galaxies that are gravitationally bound.

Galactic (open) cluster—A cluster of roughly a few hundred young stars in a loose distribution. This is not the same thing as a cluster of galaxies.

Galaxy—A large collection of stars and clusters of stars containing anywhere from a few million to a few trillion stars.

Light year—The distance light travels in one year roughly 6 trillion mi (9.5 trillion km).

Supercluster—A connected group of clusters of galaxies that may extend for hundreds of millions of light years.

Void—A region of space extending for hundreds of millions of light years that contains few if any galaxies.

The biggest supercluster is the Perseus-Pegasus Filament discovered by David Batuski and Jack Burns of New Mexico State University. This filament contains the Perseus supercluster and stretches for roughly a billion light years. It is currently the largest known structure in the universe.

Margaret Geller and John Huchra have mapped a region that is 500 million light years long but only 15 million light years thick, but this area, the Great Wall, has not been completely mapped. They may find it extends longer than 500 million light years when the mapping is complete.

A number of other superclusters and voids are known but astronomers have only mapped the large scale structure of a small part of the universe. They need to do much more work before we completely understand the structure of superclusters and voids. There may even be larger scale structures.

One of the pressing issues related to superclusters is how such structures formed in the early universe. This question remains unanswered but observations of the cosmic background radiation indicate that its beginnings developed even before galaxy formation.

See also Galaxy.

Further Reading:

Bartusiak, Marcia. *Thursday's Universe*. Redmond, WA: Tempus Books, 1988.
Hodge, Paul. *Galaxies*. Cambridge, MA: Harvard University Press, 1986.
Morrison, David, Sidney Wolff and Andrew Fraknoi. *Abell's Exploration of the Universe*. 7th ed. Philadelphia: Saunders College Publishing, 1995.
Zeilik, Michael. *Astronomy: The Evolving Universe*. 7th ed. New York: Wiley, 1994.
Zeilik, Michael, Stephen Gregory and Elske Smith. *Introductory Astronomy and Astrophysics*. Philadelphia: Saunders, 1992.

Paul A. Heckert

Superconductivity see **Superconductor**

Superconductor

Superconductors are the materials that exhibit zero electrical resistivity and become diamagnetic when they are cooled to a sufficiently low temperature. In the superconducting state, persistent electrical currents will flow without attenuation in superconducting rings for many years, and permanent magnets can be levitated by a superconductor. Because of these unique electrical and magnetic properties, superconductors have found wide applications in power transmission, magnetic energy storage, magnetometry, magnetic shielding, high-speed digital signal and data processing.

Superconductivity history and theory

Superconductivity was first discovered by Dutch physicist H. Kamerlingh Onnes at the University of Leiden in 1911. After success in the liquification of helium (He), Onnes observed that the electrical resistance of a mercury filament drops abruptly to an experimentally undetectable value at a temperatures near 4.2 K, the boiling point of liquid He (see Figure 1).

As he wrote, "Mercury has passed into a new state, which because of its extraordinary electrical properties may be called the *superconductive state*". The temperature below which the resistance of the material reaches zero is referred to as the *superconducting transition temperature* or the *critical temperature*, T_c. Another unique characteristic of superconductors is their diamagnetic susceptibility that was discovered by W. Meissner and R. Ochsenfeld in 1933. In a weak magnetic field H and below T_c, a persistent supercurrent (or screening current) is set up on the superconductor's surface. This persistent current induces a magnetic field which exactly cancels the external field. The interior of the superconductor remains field-free, i.e., the magnetic induction B = 0. This phenomenon is called *Meissner effect*.

A small cube magnet hovering over a nitrogen-cooled specimen of a superconducting ceramic demonstrates the Meissner effect. Walther Meissner observed in 1933 that a magnetic field does not penetrate a superconductor. Magnetic lines of force loop around them, so the magnet is neither attracted nor repelled but instead floats above. Because the effect is so distinctive it is used as a test for identifying superconducting materials.

In general, superconductors are categorized as *type-I* and *type-II*. For type-I (soft) superconductors (e.g., most pure superconducting elements such as lead or tin), superconductivity is completely destroyed when subjected to a magnetic field greater than a critical field, Hc, called the *thermodynamic critical field*. In the case of type-II (hard) superconductors (e.g., some superconducting alloys and compounds such as Nb_3Sn), the superconductivity can persist beyond the Meissner state until a much higher magnetic field $H > H_{c2}$ is reached where the cores of these flux bundles completely overlap and hence the superconductivity of the sample is lost. The field at which individual vortices are first nucleated is called the lower critical field, H_{c1}. In the field regime $H_{c1} < H < H_{c2}$, which is usually called the *mixed* or *vortex state*, the superconducting state coexists with tiny filaments of magnetic flux that penetrate the bulk of the material (see Figure 2).

This is manifest in the core of quantized units of magnetic flux, called *vortices*, which enter the sample, and in equilibrium form a two-dimensional lattice called the *Abrikosov lattice*, with the vortex lattice parameter given by

$$ao = 1.072 \left(\frac{\phi_o}{B} \right)$$

0.5, where ϕ_o (= 2.0678 x 10-15 Weber) is the flux quantum.

The underlying microscopic mechanism for superconductivity has been suggested to be an electron-lattice interaction. John Bardeen, Leon Cooper, and Robert Schrieffer (BCS) derived a theory at the University of Illinois in 1957 and proposed that such an interaction, leading to a pairing of electrons, occurs between electrons with opposite momentum and spin. These electron pairs are called *Cooper pairs*, and as described by Schrieffer, they condense into a single state and flow as a totally frictionless fluid. BCS theory also predicted that an energy gap—energy levels with a discrete amount below those of normal electrons—exists in superconductors. This was verified by the experiment of electron tunneling which further led Brian Josephson, in 1962, to propose that Cooper pairs would also

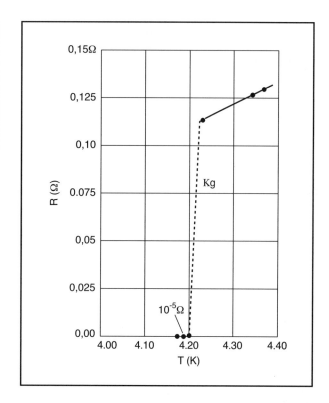

Figure 1. The curve of resistance R(Ω versus temperature T (K) of a mercury filament [after H. Kamerlingh Onnes, 1911]).

tunnel from one superconductor to another through a thin insulating layer. Such a structure called *Josephson junctions* for years has been fabricated widely for superconductive electronic devices and hybrid circuits.

High temperature superconductors

Before 1987, although a variety of superconductors had been discovered and synthesized, they all had to be operated in liquid He (e.g., Pb at 7.19 K and Nb_3Sn at 18.05 K, see Figure 3), which is an expensive cryogen.

The first superconductor with Tc > 77 K (the boiling point of the cheaper cryogen, liquid N_2) is $YBa_2Cu_3O_7$ (T_c ~ 92 K). The Y-Ba-Cu-O compound was discovered by M. K. Wu and C. W. Chu in 1987 following the central idea of the work performed by G. Bednorz and K. A. Müller who discovered La-Ba-Cu-O oxide superconductor (T_c ~ 36 K) in January 1986. One year later, in 1988, Bi-based (e.g., $(Bi, Pb)_2Sr_2Ca_2Cu_3O_{10}$, T_c ~ 110 K) and Tl-based (e.g., $Tl_2Ba_2Ca_2Cu_3O_{10}$, T_c ~ 125 K) superconductors were successfully synthesized with their T_c's 20 K higher than that in Y-Ba-Cu-O. Very recently, mercury-based cuprates $HgBa_2Ca_{n-1}Cu_nO2_{n+2+\delta}$ have been demonstrated to reach T_c values higher than 130 K in which T_c = 153 K was reported for n = 3 under quasi-hydrostatic pressure. These oxide superconductors, exhibiting the superconductivity at T > 77 K, are now classified as the high-temperature (or high-T_c) superconductors (HTSCs). They have the unit cell with a multi-layer perovskite crystal structure with oxygen atoms missing from some specific layers, and are highly anisotropic in the electrical, magnetic, and mechanical properties measured between parallel and perpendicular to the CuO_2 planes.

In HTSCs, the *critical current density*, Jc, which is the largest current density that a superconductor can carry non-resistively, flowing along the CuO_2 plane is orders of magnitude higher than that in the direction normal to the CuO_2 plane. For HTSCs to carry a large

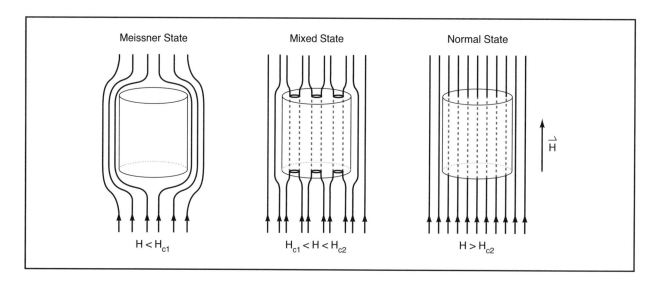

Figure 2. A type-II superconductor in various states under the application of magnetic field.

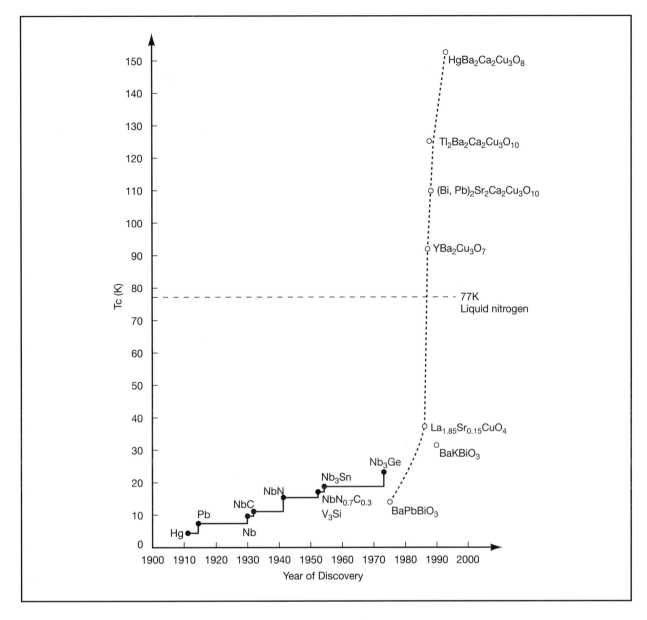

Figure 3. Increase in T$_c$ with time since superconductivity was discovered.

amount of current, this implies that individual crystalline grains in conductors (e.g., wires or tapes) of HTSC material should be well aligned with the current transport direction. Significant grain misorientation and chemistry inhomogeneity at grain boundaries can form weak links between neighboring grains and lower local Jc values. In addition, as a type-II superconductor in HTSC, for practical applications free motion of flux bundles through the superconductor causing energy dissipation has to be inhibited. This can be achieved by pinning vortices at microstructural defects in the material which then induces a magnetic field gradient and gives rise to a net current carried by the superconductor.

Therefore, several bulk material manufacture technologies such as the melt-powder-melt-growth (MPMG) method for Y-Ba-Cu-O and the oxide-powder-in-tube (OPIT) process for Bi- and Tl-based superconductors have been demonstrated to introduce flux-pinning centers and to develop textured structures. Jc values of 10^6 - 10^8 Amp/cm^2 at 77 K are currently achieved. For thin-film growth, dual ion beam sputtering (DIBS), molecular beam epitaxy (MBE), pulsed laser deposition (PLD), and metal-organic chemical vapor deposition (MOCVD) have been shown as successful methods. By optimizing processing temperature and pressure and using proper buffer layers, epitaxial HTSC films can be deposited on templates of other crystalline materials such as Si and MgO. With the integration of Si-based microelectronics processes, HTSC thin-film devices can be fabricated for a variety of applications.

Superconductivity applications

Superconductivity applications fall into two main areas—magnets and electronics. Due to their power consumption much lower than that in conventional copper-wound magnets, superconductors are particularly attractive for high-field applications in terms of system stability and operating costs. Superconducting magnets can be used in magnetic resonance imaging, magnetic separation, magnetic levitation trains, and magnetic shielding. For power utility applications, superconductors are promising for magnetic energy storage, electrical power transmission, motors and generators. They are also useful as the coatings for radio-frequency cavities. In electronic applications, thin-film interconnections and Josephson junctions are two key elements. Superconductors offer fast switching speeds and reduced wiring delays so that they are applicable for logic devices and memory cells. Superconducting field-effect transistors and Josephson-junction integrated circuits have been demonstrated. At the liquid nitrogen temperature, 77 K, superconductors can be further integrated with semiconductors to form hybrid devices. For sensor operation, superconducting quantum interference devices (SQUIDs), again, based on the Josephson junction technology, are the most sensitive detector for measuring changes in magnetic field. They can detect very faint signals produced by the human brain (in the order of 10^{-15} Tesla) and heart. SQUID-based gradiometry is a very powerful instrument for non-destructive evaluation of materials. The increased energy gap in HTSCs allows the fabrication of superconducting electromagnetic radiation detectors used for over the spectrum from x ray to the far infrared.

As time goes by, superconductors will find more and more applications in multidisciplinary technical fields when many conceptual ideas are exploited for device and system realization. Recently, Y-Ba-Cu-O has been shown to be a good material for the top and bottom electrodes of oxide ferroelectric thin-film capacitors that exhibit superior fatigue resistance than those conventionally with Pt electrodes for dynamic random access memories (DRAMs). This suggests that when the microstructures and the properties of material can be well controlled and tailored, oxide superconductors are promising for many hybrid designs. We can also expect upcoming hybrid fabrication technologies. Processes for thin films, thick films, wires and tapes

KEY TERMS

Critical current density, J_c—The largest current density that a superconductor can carry non-resistively.

Diamagnetic—The material with a magnetization vector opposite to the applied magnetic field which gives rise to a negative magnetic susceptibility.

Flux pinning—The term used to describe interactions between flux vortices and various types of structural and compositional inhomogeneities in the superconducting material.

Josephson junction—A structure with two superconductors separated by a thin insulating barrier.

Meissner effect—The expulsion of magnetic flux lines from a superconductor when the superconductor is cooled to a temperature below T_c.

Superconducting transition temperature, T_c—The highest temperature at which a material becomes superconducting.

Thermodynamic critical field, H_c—The phase boundary between normal and superconducting phases in H-T phase diagram for type-I superconductors.

Vortex state—A situation where a type-II superconductor is threaded partially by flux lines in a certain range of magnetic field.

may all be needed for the integration of a single superconductor-based instrument. With no doubt in mind, future growth in superconductors applied to electronic components as well as health, geology, military, transportation, and utility facilities is very promising, especially when superconducting transition temperature and critical current density both can be further increased.

See also Electric circuit; Electrical resistance; Electromagnetism; Nanotechnology.

Further Reading:

Burns, G. *High-Temperature Superconductivity*. Boston: Academic Press, 1992.

Fossheim, K., ed. *Superconductivity Technology: Ten Case Studies*. Teaneck, NJ: World Scientific, 1991.

Kittel, C. *Introduction to Solid State Physics*. New York: John Wiley & Sons, 1986.

Orlando, T. P., and K. A. Delin. *Foundations of Applied Superconductivity*. Reading, MA: Addison-Wesley, 1991.

Rose-Innes, A. C., and E. H. Rhoderick. *Introduction to Superconductivity*. New York: Pergamon Press, 1978.

Pang-Jen Kung

Superheavy element, see **Element, transuranium**

Supernova

A *supernova* is the massive explosion of a star, and is one of the most violent events in the Universe. There are two types of supernovae. A Type I supernova happens when a dead star called a white dwarf accretes so much matter from a companion star that it becomes unstable and explodes. A Type II supernova occurs when a high-mass star runs out of thermonuclear fuel. In this case, the star's core collapses and becomes tremendously hard and rigid. The collapsing outer layers of the star bounce off the core and are flung outward with a burst of energy that can rival the output of an entire galaxy.

Guest stars

In 1054 A.D., a brilliant new star blazed into view into the constellation of Taurus, the Bull. The Chinese astronomers who observed it called it a "guest star," and at its peak brightness they could see it even during the day. Over the following months it gradually faded and disappeared. When we train our telescopes on the location of the former guest star, we see an angry-looking cloud of gas called the Crab Nebula. Several other "guest stars" appear in the historical record, usually separated by intervals of a few hundred years. They are therefore quite uncommon. Two appeared in 1572 A.D. and 1604 A.D., but after then astronomers would have to wait more than 380 years before the next one.

Studies of the Crab Nebula show that it is expanding, as if the enormous cloud of gas had been flung outward from a central point. Modern stellar evolution theory has provided a reason for this: the "guest stars" were the final acts in the lives of a massive star. These stars end their lives as supernovae, massive explosions that blast the stars' outer layers into space. For a short time they can rival the brightness of a small galaxy; later, like a dying coal in a fire, they fade away.

Types of supernovae

A *supernova* is the explosion of a star. In a single cataclysm, a massive star may blow itself to bits, releasing as much energy, for a brief time, as an entire galaxy. There are two types of supernovae.

A Type I supernova is the explosion and complete destruction of a dead star called a white dwarf. (The Sun, after it dies, will become a white dwarf.) If the white dwarf is made of carbon (the end product of the thermonuclear reactions that took place during the star's life), and if it is a member of a binary system, a Type I supernova can potentially occur. Two important effects contribute to a Type I supernova. First, a white dwarf cannot be more massive than about 1.4 solar masses and remain stable. Second, if the white dwarf's companion star expands to become a red giant, some of its matter may be drawn away and sucked onto the surface of the white dwarf. If you could hover in a spacecraft at a safe distance from such a system, you would see a giant stream of matter flowing from the large, bloated star to its tiny companion, swirling into an accretion disk which then trickles onto its surface. A white dwarf that is almost 1.4 solar masses may be pushed over the critical mass limit by the constant influx of material. If this happens, the white dwarf will explode in an instantaneous nuclear reaction that involves all the mass of the star.

The popular image of a massive, supergiant star ending its life in one final, dazzling, swan song is what astronomers classify as a Type II supernova. In a Type II supernova, a massive star runs out of thermonuclear fuel and can no longer sustain itself against the inward pull of its own gravity. In a matter of seconds, the star collapses. The core is crushed into a tiny object called a nuetron star, which may be no more than 6 miles (10 km) across. The outer layers collapse as well, but when they encounter the extremely hard, rigid, collapsed core, they bounce off it. An immense cloud of glowing gas rushes outward, and some of the nebulae visible in small telescopes are these dispersed outer layers of stars.

Astronomers can tell the type of a supernova by observing its total brightness as well as its spectrum. Type I supernovae release more energy and therefore have a lower absolute magnitude (about -19 at peak brightness, which is as bright as a small galaxy). Since a Type I supernova is the explosion of a dead star made largely of carbon, there is little evidence in its spectrum for the element hydrogen. Type II supernovae, however, have prominent hydrogen lines in their spectra, for hydrogen is the primary element in the exploding star.

Type I supernovae are useful to astronomers trying to determine the distances to other galaxies, which is a very difficult task. Since all Type I supernovae have about the same aboslute brightness, astronomers can calculate how far away a Type I supernova is by measuring its apparent brightness and then calculating how far away it must be to appear that bright. Type I supernovae therefore serve as one of several kinds of *distance indicators* that help us determine the size of the Universe.

Why a supernova explodes

If a Type II supernova is the collapse of a massive star, why does a huge explosion result? We do not have the answer, partly because the physical conditions that exist in the extreme temperatures (about a trillion degrees) and pressures in a collapsing stellar core, and partly because everything happens very rapidly. The more rapidly the situation is changing, the more difficult it is to simulate it on a computer.

The usual explanation is that the outer layers "bounce" off the collapsed core. Try this experiment: hold two superballs, one larger than the other, about five feet off the floor. Hold the smaller superball so that it is on top of and touching the larger one. Drop them simultaneously, so they fall with the little ball just above the big one (this takes some practice). If you do it right, the large ball (the "core") will stop dead on the floor, and the little ball (the "outer layers") will be flung high in the air. Something akin to this is thought to happen in a supernova. As the core collapses, a shock wave develops as the material gets jammed together. The incredible energy involved blasts the star's outer layers far into space.

Supernova 1987A

Supernovae ought to happen in our Galaxy about once every 30 years. Until 1987, however, no bright supernova had been seen since 1604. By no means were we "due for one"—that is an all-too-frequent abuse of statistics—but nevertheless a supernova did explode on February 23, 1987. It was not in our galaxy, but in one of the small satellite galaxies orbiting it, the Large Magellanic Cloud, visible in the southern hemisphere. The star that exploded was a blue supergiant, probably 20 times more massive than the Sun, and when it exploded it was visible to the naked eye. Supernova 1987A became one of the most studied events in astronomical history, as observations of the expanding blast revealed numerous exciting results.

As a star's core collapses, the protons and neutrons in it are smashed together to form a neutron, and every time such a reaction happens, an evanescent particle called a *neutrino* is created. The neutrinos travel outward from the core at the speed of light, and they are created in such vast numbers that they carry off most of the energy produced during the supernova. Just before the SN 1987A became visible, surges of neutrinos were indeed detected here on Earth. Since the neutrinos escape from

KEY TERMS

Core collapse—The sudden collapse of a star's central region when the star's last fuel reserves are exhausted. With no energy being produced to sustain it against its own gravity, the core collapses in a fraction of a second, triggering a supernova explosion.

Type I Supernova—The explosion of a white dwarf in a binary system. Often the white dwarf, which is the dead remnant of a star originally about as massive as the Sun, has a stream of matter being dumped onto its surface by its companion. The white dwarf may be pushed past the limit of 1.4 solar masses, after which it will become unstable and explode.

Type II Supernova—The explosion of a massive star that has run out of thermonuclear fuel.

the star before the visible explosion, the timing of the event provided important observational supprt for the idea that core collapse and the subsequent bounce of infalling outer layers drives some supernova explosions.

There are several stars in our celestial neighborhood that are prime supernova candidates. Betelgeuse, the red supergiant that marks Orion's right shoulder, and Antares, the brightest star in Scorpio, are two notable ones. They might explode in 10 years, or in 10,000, but they are unquestionably doomed, and astronomers are keeping an eye on them.

See also Star; Stellar evolution; White dwarf.

Further Reading:

Filippenko, A. "A Supernova with an Identity Crisis," *Sky & Telescope*, (December 1993): 30.

Naeye, R., "Supernova 1987A Revisited," *Sky & Telescope*, (February 1993): 39.

Seeds, M. A., *Horizons: Discovering the Universe*, Chap. 10. Wiley, 1991.

Thorpe, A., "Giving Birth to Supernovae," *Astronomy*, (December 1992): 47.

Jeffrey C. Hall

Surface tension

Surface tension is the result of the cohesive forces that attract water molecules to one another. This surface

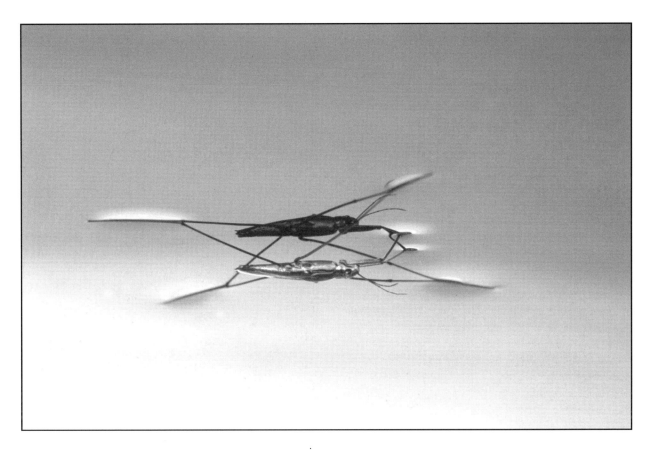

The long legs of a waterstrider (*Gerris paludum*) allow it to distribute its weight across the water and be supported by surface tension.

force keeps objects which are more dense than water (meaning they should not float) from sinking into it. The surface tension of water makes it puddle on the ground and keeps it in a droplet shape when it falls.

If you use a table fork to carefully place a paper clip on the surface of some clean water, you will find that the paper clip, although more dense than water, will remain on the water's surface. If you look closely, you will see that the surface is bent by the weight of the paper clip much as your skin bends when you push on it with your finger.

A molecule inside a volume of water is pulled equally in all directions by the other molecules of water that surround it. A molecule on the water's surface, on the other hand, is pulled by the molecules below it and to its sides. The net force on this surface molecule, is inward. The result is a surface that behaves as if it were under tension. If a glob of water with an irregular shape is created, the inward forces acting on the molecules at its surface quickly pull it into the smallest possible volume it can have, which is a sphere.

A simple apparatus can be used to measure the forces on a liquid's surface. A force is applied to a wire of known length which forms a circle parallel to the surface of the water. The force balances the surface forces acting on each side of the wire. The surface tension of the liquid, γ, is defined as the ratio of the surface force to the length of the wire (the length along which the force acts). For this kind of measurement, $\gamma = F/2L$. The force, F, applied to the wire is that required to balance the surface forces; L is the length of the wire. The 2 appears in the denominator because there is a surface film on each side of the wire. Thus, surface tension has units of force per length—dynes/cm, newtons/m, ounces/inch, etc.

Water has a relatively high surface tension that, not surprisingly, decreases with increasing temperature. The increased kinetic energy of the molecules at higher temperature would oppose the forces of cohesion. In fact, at the boiling temperature, the kinetic energy of molecules is sufficient to overcome their cohesive forces of attraction and the molecules separate to form a gas.

Surfbird see **Sandpipers**

Surgery

Surgery is the part of medicine which employs operative or manual treatment of disease or injury. Although surgery was practiced in ancient times, modern anesthesia was not developed until the 19th century. For centuries, most types of operative surgery involved high risk to patients due to infection. With the development of antiseptic surgical methods in the 19th century, the risks linked to surgery diminished. Some types of surgery remain risky, but many have high rates of success. Advances in technological knowledge offer new horizons in surgery.

Ancient surgeons

Traditionally, wars have been the proving ground of surgeons and new types of surgery. Early surgeons developed methods to anesthetize their patients and tools to operate effectively. Because there was no global communication, many surgical advances remained geographically isolated. The Western tradition of medicine developed independently of traditions in India, South America, and elsewhere, although traders and others reported some medical advances.

One of the earliest operative practices was *trepanation*, or the making of a hole in the head. Evidence of trepanation is present in skulls of individuals who lived as long ago as 10,000 B.C. in areas ranging from Northern Africa to Tahiti, France, and Peru. Ancient surgeons appear to have performed trepanation for reasons ranging from the relief of pressure on the brain due to head injury to the release of demons. The practice is still used in some cases to relieve pressure on the brain.

Ancient Egyptians also practiced surgery. According to the Smith Papyrus, a document written about 1600 B.C., Egyptians were well acquainted with a variety of surgical problems. They set broken collarbones using splints, treated medical problems ranging from tumors to fractures, and treated wounds with an adhesive plaster.

Surgery was also mentioned in the Code of Hammurabi, the code of law developed in 1760 B.C. during the reign of the Mesopotamian King Hammurabi. The code called for strict discipline of surgeons. Surgeons who caused the death of a free man in surgery were to have their right hand amputated as punishment, while surgeons who damaged a slave had to repay the owner for the value of the slave.

Greeks and Romans used surgery as a last resort. The Greeks used herbs mixed in wine or water to dress and clean wounds, and performed surgical procedures

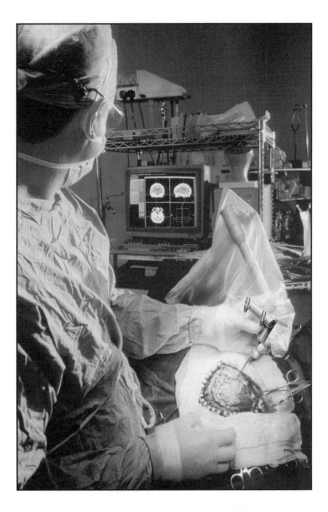

A neurosurgeon using a computer-controlled robot arm (called a "magic-wand") during an operation to remove a brain tumor. In the background, a screen shows a number of computer tomography (CT) scans of the patient's head. With the CT scan data being fed into the robot's computer, even a small tumor can be found and removed with minimal damage to surrounding tissue.

ranging from trepanation to the cauterization of blood vessels.

The Greeks used a number of natural anesthetics, including opium and the mandrake, a plant which can have a narcotic affect. A first century Greek physician in Nero's army wrote that after using mandrake, patients receiving surgery "do not apprehend the pain, because they are overborn with dead sleep." The Greeks also developed anatomical studies based on the dissection of human bodies. Dissection for the advance of medical knowledge was forbidden during the Roman Era and during the Middle Ages, and was not revived until the 15th century.

The Romans developed many new surgical procedures. Roman surgeons used dilators to take barbed arrows out of wounds, amputated limbs, performed plastic surgery, and developed techniques for removing bladder stones, hernias, and cataracts.

Surgery also flourished in the 1st century A.D. in India. Medical texts document the practice of operations ranging from tonsillectomy to plastic surgery. Certain practices sound familiar, such as the use of an operating room, the use of various types of forceps, and the use of anesthesia to reduce pain. One anesthetic used was burning hemp, the plant used today in the drug marijuana. Indians also fumigated the area where surgery was to take place to reduce infection.

Other practices suggest a far different place and time, including the use of large black ants as clips for tears in the intestines. As India continued to develop its medical tradition, the Middle Ages descended on Western Europe, casting a cloud of religious fervor over surgery, science, and the development of medicine as a whole.

The sponge of sleep

The Roman Catholic Church was the overwhelming authority in Medieval life, dictating everything from worship to medical care. Medical teaching was seen as less important than theology. While the Greeks had idealized good health, Christian doctrine in the Middle Ages considered suffering a potentially valuable entity, which could test one's faith. As a result, the idea of healing the sick was controversial, particularly in the early Middle Ages. Some religious authorities suggested that medical treatment could be sinful. This climate was not conducive to an expansion of knowledge about surgery.

During the early Middle Ages, traveling surgeons often wandered the countryside, operating on individuals for hernias, stones, and cataracts, then frequently leaving town before complications developed. By this time, surgery was separate from medicine, and surgeons, whose work was often of low quality, had little prestige.

As the Middle Ages progressed in Europe, medical training changed. Medical doctors moved from an education based on apprenticeship to an education which included formal instruction at a university. With the founding of universities in Europe in the 13th and 14th centuries, the idea of a central well of medical knowledge expanded. Surgeons were left out of this formal educational world, with most learning their trade as apprentices. Eventually, colleges specifically for surgeons were developed. Those with the least education were called barber-surgeons.

By the 13th century, technical guides to surgery started to emerge, complete with records of innovative techniques. These techniques included the use of the soporific sponge, a sponge soaked in a mixture of ingredients to promote sleep. The sponge could include opium, mandrake, and other ingredients. Such ingredients were difficult to regulate, and could cause drug dependence, death, or other less serious side effects.

During the Middle Ages in Europe, the golden era of Islamic medicine transformed surgery. An Arab text from the 11th century documented the use of cauterization to stop hemorrhaging and as therapy for chronic migraine headaches and epilepsy.

Beyond boiling oil

The Scientific Revolution in the 16th and 17th centuries revolutionized medicine. William Harvey (1578-1657) advanced all branches of medicine with his discoveries about circulation of the blood. A fascination with the human body, and the renewed study of anatomy helped forge dramatic advances in the understanding of how the body worked. The era also saw the innovations of great surgeons such as Ambroise Pare (1510-1590).

Trained as a barber-surgeon, Pare's writings on surgery influenced the profession for centuries. His books were translated into Japanese, Latin, German, English and Dutch. Pare, a military surgeon for four kings of France, made his first great innovation at the Siege of Turin in 1537. At the time, conventional treatment of gunshot wounds called for treatment that today would be considered sadistic torture: the cleansing of wounds by boiling oil.

Stationed at the battle field where many soldiers were wounded, Pare used up the supply of boiling oil before all the men's wounds could be treated. To treat the others, he developed a milder mixture consisting of egg yolk, turpentine, and oil of roses. The soldiers who had received Pare's mixture looked better the next morning, while the other soldiers' wounds remained unchanged. The success of the milder treatment lead to abandonment of the boiling oil dressing.

Pare's books on surgery related everything from effective treatment of gunpowder wounds to methods for removing arrows and treatment of urinary-tract infections. He also discussed the use of ligature to repair damaged blood vessels. Pare and other surgeons enhanced the reputation of the profession. But until the 19th century, surgeons and their patients were limited by their inability to fend off infection or control pain. Their failure to do so meant that surgery was generally painful and life-threatening.

The limits of anesthesia in the pre-modern era shaped the way doctors operated on patients. One measure of the need to limit pain was the value placed on speed in surgery. Reportedly, Scottish surgeon Robert Liston could amputate a limb in 29 seconds. Long operations were impossible, because patients died on the operating table due to shock, pain, and heart failure.

Surgeons from ancient times developed anesthetics drawn from plants or plant products, such as opium from the poppy plant and wine drawn from grapes. But all of these substances had flaws, such as dangerous side effects. All were difficult to control for dosage, and none provided surgeons with what they most needed—a patient who would lie still and not feel pain during surgery, then awaken after the procedure was over.

This changed with the development of effective anesthesia in the 18th century. There was no single inventor of anesthesia. Indeed, controversy marked the early use of anesthesia, with many different individuals claiming credit. Ether, the first gas to be used widely, was described as early as 1540 as a solvent which could also be used to aid patients with pleurisy and pneumonia. The gas gained new life in the early 1800s, when American and British pleasure-seekers marveled at the changes in behavior and perception induced by inhaling ether or nitrous oxide.

The story of the first public display of anesthesia by dentist William Thomas Green Morton is a story of claims, counterclaims, and frustration. The first to have his claims of innovation overlooked was Crawford Williamson Long, a physician in Jefferson, Georgia. Long reported the safe removal of a tumor in the neck of a patient anesthetized with ether in 1842. His failure to promptly report his use of the substance to medical journals resulted in the eclipse of his achievement by Morton in 1846.

Another dentist, Horace Wells, also was frustrated in his claim to be the first to successfully use a gas anesthetic. Wells used nitrous oxide in 1844 to anesthetize patients while their teeth were being pulled. Wells attempted to perform a dental procedure under anesthesia before a class of Harvard Medical students. The 1845 demonstration was a failure. The patient cried out in pain, and Wells was ridiculed. Eventually he committed suicide, after a bitter campaign to gain credit for his discovery.

Morton did not know about the use of nitrous oxide as an anesthetic until after Wells, a former teacher, traveled to Boston to display the new technology in 1845. Taking a more careful and politic route than Wells, Morton conducted a series of experiments using ether with dogs, goldfish, and other animals. He applied for a patent, and in 1846 performed a successful tooth extraction on a patient who had inhaled ether. He also associated himself with a number of prestigious physicians, then scheduled a public display of ether anesthetic. The 1846 display, during which a prominent surgeon operated on a vascular tumor, was a success.

Though Morton received credit for the first successful use of ether anesthesia, his credit was challenged a second time after the procedure was deemed successful. This time, he was accused by a chemist who had advised him, Charles T. Jackson, who said he was the true inventor.

A sanitary leap forward

The development of anesthesia cleared the way for more ambitious types of surgery and more careful surgical endeavors. Without the need to operate so quickly, surgeons could focus on operating more carefully. Yet surgery still had not entered the modern era, for infection continued to make recovery treacherous.

Patients who survived surgery in the middle 19th century continued to face frightening odds of dying from infection. An 1867 report noted that 60% of patients who received a major amputation in a Paris hospital died. Physicians routinely plunged their unwashed hands inside the body and often wore the same outfit for repeated surgical operating, unknowingly passing one patient's germs on to the next.

Ignorance about the nature of germs lead to drastic surgical measures. For example, individuals with compound fractures, in which the bone protruded through the skin, faced serious risk of infection and death in the early 19th century. To avoid infection, surgeons often amputated the limb.

Joseph Lister (1827-1912), the British surgeon who is credited with bringing antiseptic surgery to medicine, drew upon the work of his French contemporary, Louis Pasteur (1822-1895). Pasteur observed that germs could be present in the air and on certain surfaces. Lister was the first to apply Pasteur's observation to surgery.

Lister shook the medical world with his use of carbolic acid on compound fracture wounds after surgery. Because surgery for such fractures had a high rate of infection, Lister's report of success with nine out of eleven patients in 1867 was a dramatic finding. Cheered by the success of this effort, Lister continued his drive to remove germs from surgery. His efforts included immersing surgical instruments in a carbolic acid solution, requiring surgical assistants to wash their hands in soap and water, and careful washing of the area to be operated upon.

The success of the sterile surgical technique transformed surgery, over time, from a risky endeavor to one which carried a low risk for most procedures. The new safety of surgery made the practice more familiar, less risky, and far more open to innovation.

A third discovery helped clear the way for the dramatic surgical developments of the 20th century. This was the finding by immunologist Karl Landsteiner (1868-1943) that blood varied by blood group types. Landsteiner, who received the Nobel Prize in 1930 for his work, described four different blood groups. Knowledge about the compatibility of certain blood types and the incompatibility of others, enabled the development of safe blood transfusions during surgery.

The modern era

By the late 19th century, surgery was still performed rarely. For example, in 1867, only 3.2% of the hospital admissions involved surgery at the Charity hospital in New Orleans. By 1939, surgery was involved in about 40% of admissions.

But surgeons of the 19th century broke many barriers. As recently as the 1880s, most surgeons would not intentionally operate on the head, the chest, or the abdomen unless an injury already existed. Over the next few years, surgeons mastered numerous abdominal operations, including surgery for appendicitis, new types of hernia operations, and surgery for ovarian disorders.

During the 20th century, surgeons created successful techniques to operate on the brain and the heart and even techniques for organ transplantation. Surgeons became elite members of the medical establishment, earning more money than general practitioners and gaining celebrity as medical trailblazers.

Once a last resort, surgery is now performed frequently. Each year, a total of 25 million surgical operations calling for anesthesia are conducted in the United States. These operations cost a total of about $125 billion annually.

Heart of hearts

The emergence of heart surgery in the 20th century defied earlier beliefs that the heart was inviolate and untouchable. Contemporary surgeons replace hearts in heart transplant operations, create new pathways for the blood using tissue from other parts of the body in coronary bypass operations, and clear out the blood vessels of the heart using special tools in coronary angioplasty. But the story of the development of heart surgery makes

clear the high cost in human lives of medical advancement in this area.

As early as 1882, the German physician M.H. Block wrote of his successful suturing of rabbit hearts and suggested that human hearts could also be sutured. Surgeons in the early 20th century who attempted surgery on heart valves found limited success. A 1928 survey of the 12 known cases of surgery on heart valves reported that 83% of those who received the procedure had died.

Due to overwhelming death rates, heart valve surgery waned until the 1940s and 1950s, when the procedure was reintroduced and surgeons could take advantage of several research advances. These included procedures which enabled surgeons to maintain circulation during surgery and to slow the beating of the heart. In 1950, the first electric pacemaker was developed. The race to add new ways to preserve the precious heart intensified.

In 1967, the first successful human heart transplant was performed by South African surgeon Christian Barnard. Although the patient died in 18 days, Barnard was celebrated internationally for his surgical skill. The thrill of transplanting hearts, and the great potential for saving lives, encouraged surgeons around the world to try the operation. The results were disappointing, as patient after patient died in a number of days or, sometimes, months. Most died after their bodies rejected the donated organ. Enthusiasm for the operation faded. While 99 transplants had been conducted in 1968, nine were performed in 1971.

As a small number of surgeons continued performing transplants, success rates for the operation improved. In addition, effective drugs to fight organ rejection were developed. By the early 1980s, heart transplants had regained popularity and in 1984, about 300 heart transplants were performed in the U.S. In 1994, a total of 83% of individuals receiving heart transplants were expected to survive one or more years, making the surgery far safer than life with a failing heart.

A more common, and safer, procedure for individuals whose hearts are weak but not in need of complete replacement is the coronary artery bypass, a procedure developed in the late 1960s. The procedure takes tissue from elsewhere in the body to form new, clear pathways for blood to flow through the heart. A total of 309,000 coronary artery bypass grafts were performed in the United States in 1992. The procedure is not without risk, and the death rate linked to bypass surgery is from one to two individuals out of 100. Yet the prospect of a limited life without the surgery makes coronary bypass a common procedure.

One vivid measure of the extent to which surgery has become routine is the high number of babies born using caesarean section, the surgical delivery of a baby. In 1992, a total of 921,000 cesarian sections were performed, making the procedure the most common type of major inpatient surgery. The procedure is used when labor fails to progress, when a child being born is in distress and in other situations where normal birth is considered unwise or dangerous. The frequency of the procedure is controversial, with many critics saying that caesareans are used too frequently, placing mothers at risk and adding to the high cost of health care.

Many contemporary experts challenge the long-told story that caesarean birth was named after the birth of Roman statesman Julius Caesar. They say that had Caesar been delivered using caesarian section, his mother probably would have died, due to the high risk of infection. Historical evidence suggests that she survived the birth of her son. Caesarean sections were mentioned in ancient Indian medical texts, although the outcomes are unclear. In the modern era, the first caesarean births in which mother and child were expected to survive were performed in the early 1800s. Death due to infection still occurred frequently following the surgery. Caesarean births did not become popular until the late 1920s and they did not approach their current popularity until recently.

A prettier face

Another type of surgery which has recently flourished is plastic surgery. Evidence of the reconstruction of noses, ears, and lips can be found as early as the 1st century A.D., in ancient Indian medical texts. In the contemporary era, surgery to repair injuries or to treat disease, particularly cancer, continues to be the most common type of plastic surgery.

But cosmetic plastic surgery has also become popular, and procedures to make breasts larger, noses smaller, and buttocks less saggy have gained in popularity. For example, in 1992, a total of 50,175 procedures for nose reshaping were performed, and 32,607 procedures to increase the size of the breast were performed. Nearly nine out of 10 individuals who received plastic surgery in 1992 were women, but men were also recipients of facelifts, buttock lifts and so-called "tummy tucks." The popularity of cosmetic plastic surgery testifies to the public perception of surgery as a safe, predictable activity.

Fetal surgery

Contemporary surgeons have taken the concept of surgery well beyond what their counterparts as little as

KEY TERMS

. . . .

Cauterization—The use of heat, electricity or other substance to destroy tissue.

Ligature—Material used to tie a blood vessel or body part.

Prosthesis—An artificial body part.

Sutures—Substance used to stitch closed a surgical wound.

Trepanation—The operation in which a circular area is removed, usually in the skull.

Uterus—Organ in female mammals in which embryo and fetus grow to maturity.

100 years ago believed to be their domain. One of the most dramatic types of surgery is fetal therapy on the unborn. The first successful effort to address fetal problems in the womb took place in the early 1960s, with the first prenatal blood transfusion. Effective techniques for human fetal surgical therapy were first performed in the 1980s and are still being developed. Because such surgery presents a risk to the fetus and the mother, surgery on the fetus is performed rarely. Such procedures are only performed if the potential benefit to the fetus is deemed to be great. Successful surgery has been performed on fetuses suffering from certain types of life-threatening hernias and urinary-tract obstructions.

The procedure involves placing the mother under anesthesia and opening the uterus to expose the fetus. Following the surgery, amniotic fluid is replaced with a liquid solution containing antibiotics. The uterus is then stitched closed.

Surgery of the future

Technological advances in robotics and imaging devices suggest dramatic changes in the operating room of the future. Robots have already performed certain procedures in clinical trials. One such trial involves using a robot in surgery to help replace non-functioning hips with a prosthesis. Hip-replacement procedures are commonly performed and have a high rate of success. But surgeons have long been concerned about the procedures that do not succeed due, in part, to the difficulty of creating an exact fit for the prosthesis.

Developers of the robot used in the clinical trials hope the robot will be able to do a better job. The robot is linked to a CT scanner which measures the exact dimensions of the thigh bone. These measurements are used to help the robot hollow out a cavity in the thigh bone which will be an exact fit for the prosthesis. Successful use of such robots could change the role of the surgeon, whose tasks may include robot supervision in the future.

New imaging devices should also help surgeons operate more safely and efficiently in the future. Researchers are currently working on imaging devices that combine powerful computer technology with existing imaging technology to produce images of the body during surgery. Such images could be used for surgeons in training, to see how the body changes during surgery. They may also be used during surgery to limit the amount of potentially harmful cutting that is done. As technology enables surgeons to be more precise about where they cut, surgery could become more effective and less invasive.

One possible result of this could be what has been dubbed "trackless" surgery, procedures performed without cutting the patient. If images of harmful tissue, such as a breast tumor, could be sharpened, surgeons may be able to operate by simply focusing ultrasound waves on the tissue. Mastery of such techniques could make scalpels, sutures, and other conventional surgical tools obsolete.

Surgery of the future may bear little resemblance to the bloody, messy surgery of the present. But certain elements of surgery are unlikely to change. Surgical innovation will continue to require patients willing to take a risk and surgeons willing to challenge convention. Surgical skill will continue to require the traits Hippocrates urged surgeons to honor in ancient Greece: "ability, grace, speed, painlessness, elegance, and readiness." Finally, surgical progress will continue to depend on the ability of skilled surgeons to use their physical ability and their medical knowledge to heal patients.

See also Cauterization; Laser surgery; Neurosurgery; Plastic surgery; Prenatal surgery; Psychosurgery; Thoracic surgery; Transplant, surgical.

Further Reading:

Bollinger, Randal R. and Stickel, Delford L. "Transplantation." *Textbook of Surgery*, 14th ed., David C. Sabiston, Jr., ed. Philadelphia: W.B. Saunders Co, 1991.

Brieger, Gert H. "The Development of Surgery." *Textbook of Surgery,* 14th ed. David C. Sabiston, Jr., ed., Philadelphia: W.B. Saunders Co, 1991.

Kobus, Nancy. *1992 Plastic Surgery Statistics*. The American Society for Aesthetic Plastic Surgery, Inc., 1992.

Magner, Lois N. *A History of Medicine*. New York: Marcel Dekker, Inc., 1992.

Nuland, Sherwin B. *Doctors: The Biography of Medicine.* New York: Alfred A. Knopf, 1988.

Patricia Braus

Surveying instruments

Surveying is the apportionment of land by measuring and mapping. It is employed to determine boundaries and property lines, and to plan construction projects.

Any civilization that had any degree of sophistication in construction methods required surveys to ensure that work came out according to plan. Surveying is thought to have originated in ancient Egypt as early as 2700 B.C., with the construction of the Great Pyramid of Khufu at Giza, though the first recorded evidence of boundary surveying dates from 1400 B.C. in the Nile River valley.

The classic surveyors were the Romans. In order to forge an Empire that stretched from the Scottish border to the Persian Gulf, a large system of roads, bridges, aqueducts, and canals was built, binding the country economically and militarily.

Surveying was a major part of Roman public works projects. It also was used to divide the land among the citizens. Roman land surveying was referred to as centuriation after the century, which was a common rectangular unit of land area. These land parcels can still be seen in aerial photographs taken over France and other parts of Europe, the work of the Roman agrimensores, or measurers of land. The property lines were usually marked by stone walls and boundary markers. With the advent of new methods of trigonometry and calculus, new surveying instruments emerged. The theodolite was invented in the sixteenth century. Its precise origin is unclear, but one version was invented by English mathematician Leonard Digges in 1571, who gave it its name. A great theodolite was invented by Jesse Ramsden more than 200 years later in 1787. Its use led to the establishment of the British Ordnance Survey.

Made up of a telescope mounted on a compass or of a quadrant plus a circle and a compass, the theodolite is used to measure horizontal and vertical angles. The modern theodolite is usually equipped with a micrometer, which gives magnified readings up to $1/3600°$, or one second of arc. The micrometer is derived from the vernier scale, which was invented by French engineer and soldier Pierre Vernier (1584-1638) in 1631 to measure in fractions.

The transit is a theodolite capable of measuring horizontal and vertical angles, as well as prolonging a straight line or determining a level sight line. A telescope atop a tripod assembly is clamped in position to measure either horizontal or vertical angles. The transit employs a plumb bob hanging from the center of the tripod to mark the exact location of the surveyor.

The practice of triangulation was introduced by Gemma Frisius in 1533. By measuring the distance of two sides of a triangle in a ground survey, the third side and the triangle's area can be calculated. Triangulation was aided by the inventions of the prismatic astrolabe and the heliotrope. The latter was invented by German mathematician Johann Gauss (1777-1855), who is considered the father of geodesy, the science of earth measurement. Both instruments used a beam of sunlight to signal the positions of distant participants in a land survey.

Other survey instruments include the surveyor's compass, which is used for less precise surveying. The surveyor's level is used to measure heights of points above sea level or above local base points. Metal tapes, first introduced by English mathematician Edmund Gunter in 1620, are used for shorter measurements.

In the late twentieth century, surveying has been aided greatly by remote sensing: Photogrammetry employs aerial photography to survey large areas for topographic mapping and land assessment purposes, satellite imagery has increased the aerial coverage of surveys, and laser technology has increased the precision of survey sightings.

See also Photography; Satellite.

Survey techniques see **Archaeology**

Sustainable development

Sustainable development refers to managing the economy and renewable resources for the common good of the entire human community and also for a healthy environment. The goals of sustainable development are to provide resources for the use of present generations of humans without compromising the availability of those resources for future generations and without causing environmental damages that challenge the survival of other species and natural ecosystems.

The notion of sustainable development recognizes that individual humans and their larger economic systems can only be sustained through the exploitation of natural resources. By definition, the stocks of non-renewable resources such as metals, coal, and petroleum can only be diminished by use, which is referred to as mining. Consequently, sustainable economies cannot be based on the exploitation of non-renewable resources. Ultimately, sustainable economies must be supported by the use of renewable resources such as biological productivity, and solar, wind, and geothermal energy sources.

However, it is also possible to mine potentially renewable resources through overexploitation and other types of environmental degradation. In fact, this is commonly done. Central to the notion of sustainable development is the requirement that renewable resources be utilized in ways that do not diminish their capacity for renewal so that they will always be present to sustain future generation of humans.

It is also critical that sustainable systems of resource use do not degrade aspects of environmental quality that do not represent resources that are directly required by humans. Such resources are not usually assigned value in the marketplace. Biodiversity is one example of a so-called non-valuated resource as are many ecological services such as the cleansing of air, water, and land of pollutants by ecosystems, the provision of oxygen by vegetation, and the maintenance of agricultural soil capability. These are all important values, but their importance is rarely measured in terms of dollars.

In summary, sustainable development refers to the use by society of a sustainable economic system. Such a system must be capable of yielding a flow of resources for use by humans, but that flow must be maintainable over the longer term. In addition, an ecologically sustainable economy must also be capable of supporting viable populations of native species, viable areas of natural ecosystems, and acceptable levels of other aspects of environmental quality that are not conventionally valued as resources for direct use by humans.

Natural resources

In economic terms, resources (or capital) are regarded as actual or potential wealth that can be applied towards the creation of additional wealth. There are three broad types of capital: (1) Manufactured capital is industrial infrastructure that can be applied to the production of goods and services. Examples include factories, mines, harvesting equipment, buildings, tools and machinery, computers, and information networks. (2) Human capital is the cultural means of production, encompassing a workforce with particular types of knowledge and skills. (3) Natural capital refers to quantities of raw, natural resources that can be harvested, processed, used in manufacturing, and otherwise utilized to produce goods and services for an economy.

There are two types of natural resources: non-renewable and renewable. Non-renewable resources are present in a finite quantity on Earth. Therefore, their stock diminishes as they are mined from the environment. Non-renewable resources can only be used in an unsustainable manner. The lifetime of a non-renewable resource is determined by the size of the recoverable stock and the rate of mining. However, some non-renewable resources can be reused and recycled to some degree, and this can extend the effective lifetime of the resource. Common examples of non-renewable resource include metal ores, coal, and petroleum. Potentially, renewable resources can sustain harvesting indefinitely. However, sustainable use requires that the rate of harvesting does not exceed the rate of renewal of the resource. Most renewable resources are biological and include trees, hunted animals such as fish, waterfowl, and deer, and agricultural productivity. Flowing surface water is an example of a non-biological resource that can potentially be sustainably used for irrigation, to generate hydroelectricity, and as a means of transportation. All of the above are examples of renewable resources that can be harvested and managed to indefinitely sustain human economic systems.

However, it is important to recognize that potentially renewable resources can easily be "over-harvesting" or exploited at a rate exceeding that of renewal, resulting in degradation of the resource. During over-harvesting, the resource is essentially being mined, that is, it is managed as a non-renewable resource. Regrettably, mining is by far the most common way in which humans have used potentially renewable resources. Examples of unsustainable use of potentially renewable resources are legion and include collapses of stocks of hunted fish, mammals, and birds, deforestation, declines of agricultural soil capability, and diminished river flows due to excessive withdrawals for use by humans.

Another important characteristic of renewable resources is that they can provide meaningful, ecological services even when they are in their natural, unharvested state. For example, intact, natural forests provide biological productivity, cycling of nutrients and water, a sink for atmospheric carbon, control of erosion, cleansing of pollutants emitted into the environment by humans, habitat for diverse elements of biodiversity, pleasing esthetics, and other important ecological services. Some of these goods and services are of potential value as resources that humans require; for example, the biomass and productivity of trees and hunted animals. However, most of the services listed above are not recognized by the conventional marketplace, although they are certainly important to ecological integrity and environmental health.

The undeniable ecological reality is that humans have an absolute dependence on a continuous flow of natural resources to sustain their societies and economies. Over the longer term, this is particularly true of renewable resources because sustainable economies cannot be supported by non-renewable resources. Therefore, the only way to achieve a condition of sustainable development is to build an economy that is supported by the wise harvesting and management of renewable resources.

Economics

A goal of economic systems is to maximize the utility of goods and services to society. Usually, these products are assigned value in units of currency, for example, in dollars. Examples of valuated goods and services include the following: (1) manufactured products, such as automobiles, computers, highways, and buildings, (2) harvested natural resources, such as wood, hunted animals, and agricultural production, and (3) the services provided by farmers, industrial workers, doctors, politicians, and other workers.

Conventional economics does not seriously consider non-valuated resources, that is, goods and services that are not assigned value in the marketplace. Examples of non-valuated, ecological resources include the aesthetics of natural landscapes, services such as nutrient and water cycling, and rare species and natural ecosystems. Although conventional economics could, potentially, assign value to these resources, this is rarely done. Consequently, the merits of non-valuated, ecological resources cannot be easily compared with those of valuated goods and services. As a result, degradations of non-valuated resources are not usually considered to be true "costs" by conventional economists, and they do not have a strong influence in cost-benefit calculations.

This means that in conventional accountings, large profits can often be made by undertaking activities that cause substantial environmental damages, including the exhaustion of potentially renewable resources. Clearly, this is an ecologically false accounting, but it has been rationalized by considering degradations of environmental quality to be externalities, or costs that are not directly paid by the individuals or companies that are causing the damages. However, the costs of resource and environmental degradation are very real, and they are borne by society at large. The great failure of conventional economics is that its marketplace has not recognized the value of important but non-valuated services, especially common-property or public-good, ecological services.

Ecological economics is a new, actively developing sub-discipline within economics. The principal distinction of ecological economics is that it attempts to find a non-anthropocentric system of valuation. This is different from conventional economics in which valuations are based almost entirely in terms of the importance of good and services to humans as determined in the marketplace.

Accountings in ecological economics include the important social and environmental costs that may be associated with the depletion of resources and the degradation of environmental quality. These costs are critical to achieving and measuring sustainable development, but they are not seriously considered during accountings in conventional economics.

Sustainable development and sustained growth

The notion of sustainable development refers to an economic system that is ultimately based on the wise utilization of renewable natural resources, that is, in a manner that does not threaten the availability of resources for use by future generations of people. As is discussed later, it is also important that damages to non-valuated resources also be kept within acceptable limits.

Clearly, the existing human economy is grossly unsustainable in these respects. Modern economies are characterized by resolute economic growth and achieved by the vigorous mining of non-renewable resources, potentially renewable resources, and, more broadly, environmental quality.

Since the mid-1980s when the notion was first introduced, "sustainable development" has been enthusiastically advocated by many politicians, economists, and resource managers. However, many of these people have confused sustainable development with "sustained economic growth" which by definition is impossible because resources eventually become limiting. The first popularization of the phrase "sustainable development" was in the widely applauded report of the *World Commission of Environment and Development* (also known as the "Brundtland Report" after the chairperson of the commission, Gro Harlem Brundtland of Norway). However, this report appears to confuse some of the fundamental differences between economic growth and sustainable development.

Although the Brundtland Report supports the need for sustainable development, it also calls for a large increase in the size of the global economy. The Brundtland Report suggests that a period of strong economic growth is needed in concert with a redistribution of some of the existing wealth if the living standards of peoples in poorer countries are to be improved. It is

believed that once this has been accomplished, social and economic conditions will favor an end to population growth and the over-exploitation of natural resources, so an equilibrium condition of a non-growing economy can be achieved.

However, the sorts of economic growth rates recommended in the Brundtland Report are equivalent to an increase of per-capita, global income of 3% per year, sufficient to double per-capita income every 23 years. In addition, the economic growth must compensate for growth of the human population which amounts to about 2% per year. Therefore, the adjusted rate of economic growth would have to be about 5% per year (that is, 3% + 2%), which would result in a doubling of the global economy every 14 years. Of course, in poorer countries with even larger rates of population growth, including most of Africa, Asia, and Latin America, the rate of economic growth would have to compensate and be correspondingly larger. In total, the Brundtland Report suggested that an expansion of the global economy by a factor of 5-10 times was needed to create conditions appropriate to subsequently achieving a condition of sustainable development.

Of course, the Brundtland Report does not only recommend a great deal of economic growth. It also recommends the development of technologies that would allow a more efficient economic growth which would consume fewer resources of material and energy per unit of growth achieved. The Brundtland Report also advocates a redistribution of wealth from richer to poorer people and countries as well as greater efforts towards the elimination of population growth.

Unfortunately, the Brundtland Report and many other champions of "sustainable development" are actually staunch proponents of economic growth as a cure for the present ills of human economies. However, there are profound doubts that a 5-10 times increase in the size of the human economy could be sustained by the environment and its ecosystems. Economic growth may, in fact, be more of a cause of the environmental crisis than a cure.

Resolution of the environmental crisis and achievement of sustainable economies may require the immediate, aggressive pursuit of more difficult and unpopular solutions than those recommended by the Brundtland Report. These would include much less use of resources by richer peoples of the world, immediate redistributions of some of the existing wealth to poorer peoples, vigorous population control, and an overall focus on preventing further deteriorations of ecological integrity and environmental quality more generally.

Sustainable development

A truly sustainable economic system recognizes that the human economy must be limited within the carrying capacity of Earth's remaining natural resources. In fact, many resource economists, environmental scientists, and ecologists believe that the human economy may already be too large to be sustained by Earth's resources and ecosystems. If these specialists are correct, then not only is further economic growth undesirable, it may have to be reversed.

Non-sustainable economic growth occurs through a crude maximization of the flow of resources through an economy. In large part, economic growth is achieved by mining resources and environmental quality.

In contrast, sustainable development is ultimately based on the efficient use of renewable resources which are not degraded over time. Moreover, this use occurs under conditions in which environmental quality is also protected. A sustainable economic system would have the following characteristics: (1) Renewable resources must be exploited at or below their capability for renewal. Present economies are greatly dependent on the use of non-renewable resources, but these are being rapidly diminished by use. As non-renewable resources become exhausted, renewable resources will become increasingly more important in the economic system. Ultimately, sustainable economic systems must be based on the wise use of renewable resources. (2) Non-renewable resources can also be utilized in a sustainable economy. However, the rates at which non-renewable resources are utilized must be balanced by the rate at which renewable substitutes are created, that is, by growth of a renewable resource. For example, fossil fuels can only be used in a truly sustainable economy if their utilization is compensated by net growth of a renewable energy substitute, for example, by an increase in forest biomass. To discourage the use of non-renewable resources and the unsustainable mining of potentially renewable resources, it might be possible to implement a system of natural-resource depletion taxes. (3) There must be a markedly increased efficiency of the use and recycling of non-renewable resources, aimed at extending their useful lifetime in the economic system. Information systems and new technologies will be important in achieving this increased efficiency. There must also be well-designed systems of use and management of renewable resources to ensure that these are sustainably utilized over the longer term. (4) It is critical that ecological resources that are not conventionally valuated also be sustained. The use and management of natural resources for human benefits will inevitably cause declines of some

KEY TERMS

Anthropocentric—Consideration of utility and value on the basis of the usefulness to humans.

Natural resource—Any naturally occurring commodity that can be used by people. Non-renewable resources are of a finite quantity, and they can only be mined. Renewable resources can potentially by exploited indefinitely but only if they are not degraded by overexploitation or used at a rate that exceeds renewal.

Valuation—The assignment of economic worth, for example, in dollars.

species and natural ecosystems as well as other environmental damages. However, viable populations of native species, viable areas of natural ecosystems, and other aspects of environmental quality must be preserved in an ecologically sustainable economic system. Some of these ecological values cannot be accommodated on landscapes that are primarily managed for the harvesting and management of economic resources, and they will therefore have to be preserved in ecological reserves. These ecological values must be accommodated if an economic system is to be considered truly sustainable.

Sustainable economic systems represent a very different way of doing business in comparison with the manner in which economies are now conducted. Sustainable development requires the implementation of a sustainable economy. This would be difficult on the short term, although the longer-term benefits to society and ecosystems would be enormous. The longer-term benefit would be achievement of an economic system that could sustain humans, other species, and natural ecosystems for a long time. However, there would be short-term pains, largely associated with substantially less use of natural resources, abandonment of the ambition of economic growth, and rapid stabilization of the human population.

As a result of these short-term inconveniences, truly sustainable development would not be initially popular among much of the public, politicians, government bureaucrats, and industry. This is because individual humans and their societies are self interested, and they think on the shorter-term. However, for the sake of future generations of humans and for other species and natural ecosystems, it remains absolutely necessary that sustainable economic systems be designed and implemented.

See also Carrying capacity; Ecological economics; Population, human; Recycling.

Further Reading:

Costanza, R. *Ecological Economics: The Science and Management of Sustainability.* New York: Columbia University Press, 1991.

Costanza, R., and H. E. Daly. "Natural Capital and Sustainable Development." *Conservation Biology* 6 (1992): 37-46.

Freedman, B. *Environmental Ecology.* 2nd. ed. San Diego: Academic Press, 1994.

Bill Freedman

Barn swallows (*Hirundo rustica*) at Point Pelee National Park, Ontario.

Swallows and martins

Swallows and martins are small fast-flying agile birds in the family Hirundinidae. There are 74 species in this family worldwide, mostly found in open habitats, where they forage aerially for their prey of flying insects.

There is no particular biological difference between swallows and martins. Sometimes these names are used interchangeably, as in the case of *Riparia riparia*, known as the sand martin in Western Europe, and as the bank swallow in North America.

Biology of swallows and martins

Swallows and martins have relatively long, pointed wings, and they are swift and agile fliers. The feet of these birds tend to be small and weak, and are used for little more than perching. These birds often rest on wires and exposed branches of trees. During migration, large numbers of swallows and martins may roost together on these sorts of perches, often in mixed-species flocks. Swallows may also forage in large, mixed-species flocks during migration.

Many species of swallows and martins are rather plainly marked with dark brown or black backs and wings and a white breast. Other species are more boldly patterned, and may be brightly colored with red, yellow, and iridescent green and purple. Most species have a notched tail, and some have a deeply forked tail.

Swallows have a short but broad mouth, which can open with a very wide gape, an adaptation for catching insects on the wing. This food of flying insects is sometimes referred to as *aeroplankton*.

Many species of swallows and martins nest in colonies of various size, and most species are gregarious during the non-breeding season. Some swallows nest in natural or artificial cavities. Other species nest in tunnels that they dig in earthen banks. Many species construct an urn-like cavity of hardened mud or clay, or they make cup-shaped nests of these materials. The natural substrate for attachment of the constructed nests is cliffs and other sheer surfaces. However, some species use bridges and buildings as substrata upon which to build their clay nests.

All species of swallows and martins migrate between their breeding and non-breeding habitats. Species that breed at high latitudes can migrate great distances, for example, about 6,831 m (11,000 km) in the case of the European swallow (*Hirundo rustica*), some of which breed in northern Europe and winter in South Africa.

North American swallows and martins

The most familiar swallow in North America is the barn swallow (*Hirundo rustica*). This is a cosmopolitan species that also occurs under other common names in Eurasia, Africa, Southeast Asia, and Australia. The barn swallow is an attractive bird, with a deeply forked tail, an iridescent purple back, and a brick-red breast. Barn swallows often nest in small colonies. The natural nesting habitat is cliffs and caves, where these birds build their cup-nests of mud bonded with grass. Barn swallows also commonly build their nests on the sides of buildings and bridges. The barn swallow breeds south of the tundra over most of North America and Mexico, and winters in South America.

The cliff swallow (*Petrochelidon pyrrhonota*) looks rather similar to the barn swallow, but it does not have a forked tail, and it has a white patch on its forehead, a buff rump, and a white breast. The cliff swallow is a colonial nester, building its roofed, mud nests on cliffs, and also on structures made by humans, such as bridges, dams, and buildings. The cliff swallow breeds locally over a wide range, from the subarctic tundra to southern Mexico, and winters in South America.

The bank swallow (*Riparia riparia*) also breeds over much of North America south of the tundra, as well as in Eurasia. North American populations of bank swallows winter in South America. The bank swallow is a brown-backed species, with a brown band across the chest. The bank swallow nests in colonies, typically excavating tunnels for its nests in the earthen banks of rivers. This species also uses the sides of gravel pits as a place to nest.

The rough-winged swallow (*Stelgidopteryx ruficollis*) is similarly marked to the bank swallow, but it lacks the brown breast-band, and has a darker breast. This is a non-colonial nester, which digs burrows in riverbanks, or sometimes nests in holes in cement bridges and other built structures. This species breeds widely south of the boreal forest of North America and into northern South America. The rough-winged swallow winters from the southern United States to South America.

The tree swallow (*Tachycineta bicolor*) has an iridescent, dark-blue or green back, and a white breast. This species breeds south of the low-arctic tundra to the northern states, and winters from the southern United States to Central America. The tree swallow nests in natural cavities in trees, or in cavities previously excavated and used by woodpeckers. This species will also take readily to nest boxes.

The violet-green swallow (*Tachycineta thalassina*) has a superficial resemblance to the tree swallow, with an iridescent violet-green back. This species breeds in the western United States, and winters in northern Central America and Mexico. The violet-green swallow generally nests in cavities in trees or in crevices of cliffs.

The purple martin (*Progne subis*) is the largest swallow in North America. Male purple martins are a uniformly iridescent purple, while females are brown. The natural nesting sites of this colonial species are hollow cavities in trees, but purple martins also utilize multi-celled nesting boxes provided by humans. This species breeds in an area from southern Canada to Mexico, and winters in South America.

Interactions with humans

Swallows are boisterous and active birds, which maintain a stream of cheerful twitterings that many people find pleasing. The fact that some species nest in the vicinity of human habitations means that people can easily watch the comings and goings of these small, charismatic birds. Observers can gain an impression of the daily life of the swallow, from the building of nests, through the rearing of nestlings, to the trials and tribulations by which fledglings learn to fly and to hunt their own food of insects.

Swallows of all species eat enormous numbers of flying insects. Some of the prey insects (such as mosquitos and blackflies) are regarded as pests by humans. As a result, swallows nesting near homes are often considered to be beneficial. Barn and cliff swallows construct their mud nests on buildings. These species do not need encouragement, only tolerance of the small annoyances that some people might perceive about the defecations of these birds. The nesting of tree swallows can be assisted by providing simple nest boxes, while purple martins can be attracted by providing multiple-unit apartment boxes. Because of the relatively large number of birds that can be supported, a colony of purple martins can have a significant effect on the abundance of biting flies in its vicinity.

See also Insectivore; Migration.

Further Reading:

Harrison, C.J.O., ed. *Bird Families of the World.* New York: H.N. Abrams Pubs., 1978.
Turner, A. *The Swallow.* U.K.: Hamlyn, 1994.

Bill Freedman

Swamp see **Wetlands**

Swamp cypress family

The swamp cypress family is more formally called the Taxodiaceae. This is a family of coniferous trees within the Gymnosperms, that is, plants which produce naked seeds (not in a fruit) borne on scales. These scales are usually arranged to form a cone.

Within the Taxodiaceae some species are evergreen, and some deciduous. There are nine genera which contain 16 species. These can be found in temperate and subtropical regions, in both the Old and New Worlds. Only one genus is represented in the Southern Hemisphere. Most of these are fast growing trees which can achieve a large size and an impressive age. Some members of this group have been known to be 3,000 years old.

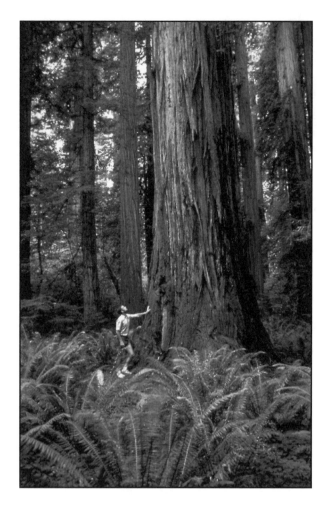

Redwoods in Jediah Smith State Park, California.

Characteristics

All of the trees in this family produce resin when their branches are damaged. They all have one main trunk with a fibrous bark, usually of a reddish color. As the tree grows older the basal branches are lost, leaving a clear trunk. The leaves are usually dark green, needle like structures.

All of the Taxodiaceae are wind pollinated, with male and female reproductive structures on the same individual plant, but physically separate in different canes. The male part is a cluster of catkin-like cones which release pollen, which is then blown by the wind. The female cones are larger and occur singly or in groups, a drop of fluid is exuded from them on which pollen grains land. Once the pollen has been captured in this manner, the fluid is taken back in, bringing the pollen and ovule into close association so that pollination may occur. Some species are capable of reproducing very early in their life (e.g., *Taxodium*) while others must first achieve a few centuries of age (e.g., *Taiwania*).

The seeds are produced in mature cones, and when they are released from their high branches they can disperse over long distances due to the presence of wing-like, aerodynamic structures. Some, such as *Sequoiadendron,* only release their seeds after a forest fire, allowing a relatively competition-free start in life. The adult is little affected by the fire due to a protective layer of fibrous bark that is burnt off. However, the living wood underneath is not damaged, except by exceptionally severe fires.

Recognizable fossils of some of these species have been found from the Cretaceous and Tertiary eras.

The modern Taxodiaceae are found in warm temperate regions of the world, mostly in eastern Asia, east and west North America, and with a single genus in Tasmania. These plants, favor areas of high rainfall with rich soil, tending to occur in local groves. One species, the swamp cypress (Taxodium distichum), is tolerant of wet conditions and will grow in swampy places.

Members of the Taxodiaceae

Athrotaxis comprises three species found only on the islands of Taiwan in east Asia. It is possible that one species is a hybrid between the other two, due to its intermediate characteristics. These are moderately tall, pine-like trees.

Cunninghamia is a tall tree of great commercial importance in its native China and Taiwan. Two, rather similar species are known.

Another genus, with two or three species, is *Taiwania*, from China, Taiwan and north Burma. These are felled for their timber, but they are rather scarce in their native habitats, provoking much concern among conservationists.

Cryptomeria is similar to the above groups, but the several species are more-widely spread in their native Japan and China. Due to the fast growing nature and height of this group, they have been widely introduced to other areas where they are important timber producers.

The big-tree or giant redwood (*Sequoiadendron giganteum*) produces the world's most massive trees, with the tallest measured example being 344.5 ft (105 m) tall with a trunk diameter of 39 ft (12 m). These massive trees are native to California; they will not survive an intense frost and are intolerant of pollution. They are, however, remarkably fire tolerant due to their fibrous bark. In fact, disposal of their seeds is aided by fire, which makes the cones open, and also reduces competition for the new seedlings.

A closely related, and physically slightly taller genus is the coast redwood (*Sequoia sempivirens*),

Cypress knees are extensions of the root system of the cypress. Their function is to carry out gas exchange between the air and the waterlogged roots.

found naturally from southwest Oregon to California in small numbered groups.

All of the above genera are evergreens, that is, they do not lose all of their leaves in the autumn. The remaining members of the Taxodiaceae are all seasonally deciduous.

Perhaps the most endangered member of the whole group is the dawn redwood (*Metasequoia glyptostroboides*), which was found for the first time in 1941, in a small valley in Central China. No other wild populations have ever been discovered. The specific name is due to the initial physical similarity to the previous genus. While endangered in the wild, the dawn redwood can be cultivated and is widely grown.

Another endangered species endemic to China is *Glyptostrobus pensilis.*

The swamp or bold cypress (*Taxodium distichum*) is a moderately hardy tree native to the southeastern United States. This species is not as massive as some of its relatives, but it is more hardy, and is a cultivated species. Two other *Taxodium* species are known.

See also Conifer; Gymnosperm; Sequoia.

Further Reading:

Kubitzki , K., Kramer , K. U., Green, P. S. and Page, C. N. "Pteridophytes and Gymnosperms," *The Families and Genera of Vascular Plants*, vol. 1. Springer, 1990.

Vidakovic, M. *Conifers: Morphology and Variation*. Groficki Zavod Hrvatske , 1991.

Welch, H. and Haddow, G. *The World Checklist of Conifers.* Landsmons Bookshop, 1993.

Gordon Rutter

Swamp eels

Belonging to the order Synbranchiformes, swamp eels are very slim fish with elongated bodies and reduced fins. Their gill system, which is very small, is linked to other organs to help them breath air. Swamp eels live in tropical and subtropical habitats. They usually are found in stagnant fresh or brackish water; only one species lives in the sea. These fish are found in Central and South America, Asia, and Africa.

According to some publications, the order Synbranchiformes is made up of only one family, Synbrachidae, which contains four genera of swamp eels: the *Macrotrema*, the *Ophisternon*, the *Synbranchus*, and the *Monopterus*. Other sources report that there are three separate families within the Synbranchiform Order: the swamp eels, the singleslit eels, and the cuchias. Whichever way these fish are categorized, in total, there are about 15 distinct species.

Fish that look like snakes and live in dark, murky water are commonly called eels. Swamp eels are a great example of this type of fish. Indeed, they lack pectoral and pelvic fins, and their dorsal and anal fins are very small. Furthermore, while all species have small eyes, some are functionally blind with their eyes sunken below the skin. Some species live in caves, and many others burrow in mud. The maximum length these fish can attain is almost 3 feet (1 meter). While swamp eels look a lot like eels, they are in no way related to them. Swamp eels are significantly different from eels internally and can breath air. Furthermore, some of them estivate, which means that they sleep through the hot, summer months.

All 15 species of swamp eels have one or two gill openings at their throats which are designed to absorb oxygen from water. However, several species that live in water with small amounts of oxygen—like stagnant pools—are able to breath air from the surface through their open mouths. One such species is the rice eel. Fish of this species live in rivers, ditches, and swamps of Southeast Asia, Indonesia, and the Philippines. During the extensive dry season, these fish burrow into the mud and can remain alive until the rainy season starts, as long as their skin remains damp. Interestingly, when Rice Eels reproduce, which is during the summer months, the males form the nests using air bubbles and mucus. As the female rice eels lay the eggs, the males pick them up, one by one, and spit them into the floating nests. The males guard their nests and eggs as they float freely in the water and stay with their young until they are independent. Rice eels have successfully adapted to living in rice patties and are an important source of food for people in some regions.

Swans

Swans are large birds in the waterfowl family, *Anatidae*, which also includes ducks and geese. There are seven species of swans, occurring on all continents except Antarctica. Three species of swan, the mute swan (*Cygnus olor*), the tundra swan (*C. colombianus*),

A tundra swan (*Cygnus columbianus*) at the Kellogg Bird Sanctuary, Michigan.

and the trumpeter swan (*C. buccinator*) breed regularly in North America.

Swans have a very long neck, and all North American species have a white body. Swans are well adapted to the aquatic environment, having fully webbed feet for swimming. However, these birds are not capable of submerging; instead they feed by tipping up and using their long neck to reach for their food of aquatic plants and occasional invertebrates. The plumage and external morphology of the sexes is similar. Swans are big birds, the largest species being the mute swan weighing as much as 33 lbs (15 kg). Swans are flightless during the moult of late summer. They generally spend this time on large lakes, where they are relatively safe from terrestrial predators.

Most species of swans undertake substantial migrations between their breeding grounds (large ponds and lakes) and wintering grounds (lakes or estuaries), sometimes travelling thousand of miles, back and forth each year. Swans are highly territorial on the breeding grounds, trumpeting loudly and often engaging in fights with other swans, and sometimes driving other species of water fowl from their lake. Swans typically mate for life, the pair staying together until one of the spouses dies.

Swans of North America

Three species of swan are regular breeders in North America. Mute swans breed in ponds and rivers in urban parks and other disturbed places, as well as more natural and wild habitats. The graceful and charismatic mute swan is familiar to most people. This species is native to Eurasia and was introduced to North America, where it has become the commonest of our swans.

The most abundant of the truly native species is the tundra or whistling swan (*Cygnus columbianus*), closely related to the Bewick's swan (*C. c. bewickii*) of Eurasia. The tundra swan breeds widely on the low-arctic tundra of mainland Canada and southern Baffin Island, and mostly winters on estuaries of the Pacific and Atlantic coasts. During migration the tundra swan occurs on lakes and rivers, and sometimes in agricultural fields near water. This species usually nests beside marsh-fringed ponds or lakes. Soon after hatching the brood of 3-5 young swans (cygnets) accompany the parents, feeding on invertebrates during their first month or so, as well as on terrestrial grasses and sedges and aquatic vegetation.

The trumpeter swan (*C. buccinator*) is a somewhat larger than the whistling swan breeding in isolated populations in Alaska, Yukon, British Columbia, and as far south as Oregon and Wyoming. This species once had a much more widespread breeding range, probably extending east to Ontario and Quebec. Unfortunately, because of agricultural conversions of its habitat and over hunting this species was perilously close to extinction. However, the population of trumpeter swans has recently increased to more than five thousand individuals, and appears to be slowly expanding. Nevertheless, the trumpeter swan remains vulnerable to population decline. The trumpeter swan winters on Pacific estuaries and offshore islands, and on a few inland lakes.

Conservation of swans

Although swans are not abundant birds, during migration and winter these birds congregate in large numbers. Moreover, swans are large animals, and are relatively easy to approach on land when they are husbanding their young, or on water when they are in moult. Because of these factors, wild swans have long been hunted for subsistence or sport. However, because of their low reproductive potential, populations of swans are easily depleted and extirpated by overhunting. This occurred during the heyday of sport and market hunting of the nineteenth century, a population decline that was exacerbated by the widespread loss of breeding, migrating, and wintering habitats. Some species of swans, including the trumpeter swan of North America, became endangered species, and almost extinct. However, the populations of most species of swans have generally been stable or have increased due to conservation efforts by government, especially during the latter half of the twentieth century. Today, there is no legal hunt of swans in North America, although there is some poaching of these birds, and a small aboriginal harvest of tundra swans occurs on their breeding grounds.

Swans are also at risk from other environmental stresses. The occurrence of lead pellets from shotgun ammunition in the surface sediment of their wintering habitat poses a toxic risk for wild swans. Water fowl are poisoned when they retain the lead shot in their gizzard for use in grinding their food of seeds, resulting in the abrasion and dissolving of the lead, which enters into the bloodstream, causing a range of symptoms, leading to death (see entry on ducks). During recent years, it is likely that hundreds or thousands of swans have died each year in North America from poisoning by lead shot, and probably more than a million ducks and geese. Fortunately, the use of lead shot has been, or soon will be banned over most of North America, so this will be less of a problem in the future.

Swans are also vulnerable to certain types of infectious diseases, especially avian cholera. This disease is caused by a food and water borne pathogen, and it can occur as a local epidemic that kills tens of thousands of water fowl. Potentially, the trumpeter swan is especially at risk from the effects of this sort of epidemic disease, because large numbers congregate on wintering grounds in a few lakes in Montana, Idaho, and Wyoming. Birds wintering on coastal estuaries are at less risk.

Because of their positive aesthetics, of swans have been widely cultivated in waterfowl collections and in public parks. The most commonly kept species is the mute swan, but other species are also bred, including the unusual black swan (*Cygnus atratus*) of Australia. Viewings of wild swans are also widely sought after by birders and other naturalists. Both the cultivation of swans and their non-consumptive use in ecotourism have positive economic effects, and do not endanger populations of these birds.

Further Reading:

Bellrose, F. C. *Ducks, Geese, and Swans of North America.* Harrisburg: Stackpole Books, 1976.
Godfrey, W. E. *The Birds of Canada.* Toronto: University of Toronto Press, 1986.
Johnsgard, P. A. *Ducks in the Wild: Conserving Waterfowl and Their Habitats.* Swan Hill Press, 1992.
Owen, M., and J. M. Black. *Waterfowl Ecology.* London: Blackie Pub., 1990.

Bill Freedman

Sweat glands see **Integumentary system**

Sweet gale family (Myricaceae)

The sweet gale or bayberry family (Myricaceae) is

made up of about 50 species of shrubs and trees. Minor economic uses of some species involve the extraction of a fragrant wax from their fruits and cultivation as ornamental shrubs.

The foliage of plants in the Myricaceae can be deciduous or evergreen, and the leaves are commonly fragrant when crushed. The flowers are small and occur in catkin-like inflorescences, which are made up of either male (staminate) or female (pistillate) flowers. The fruits are a one-seeded berry or drupe, often with a thick, waxy coating.

One of the most interesting characteristics of species in the sweet gale family is their ability to fix atmospheric nitrogen gas (N_2-sometimes known as dinitrogen) into ammonia (NH_3), an inorganic form of nitrogen that can be utilized by plants as a nutrient. The nitrogen fixation is carried out inside of specialized nodules on the roots and rhizomes of these plants. This is done by the enzyme nitrogenase, which is synthesized by bacteria that live in a mutualism with the vascular plant. The ability to fix atmospheric dinitrogen into ammonium is an extremely useful trait, because it allows species in the sweet gale family to be relatively successful in nutrient deficient habitats.

The most diverse genus in the Myricaceae is *Myrica*, of which several species occur widely in North America. The sweet gale (*Myrica gale*) is a common shrub along lakeshores and in other moist places over much of the temperate and boreal zones of North America and Eurasia. The sweet fern or fern-gale (*M. asplenifolia*) is widespread in eastern North America. Both the wax-myrtle (*M. cerifera*) and the bayberry or waxberry (*M. carolinensis*) of eastern North America produce fruits with thick, whitish, waxy coats. These fruits can be collected, the wax extracted using boiling water and then used to fragrantly scent candles.

See also Mutualism; Nitrogen fixation; Symbiosis

Bill Freedman

Sweet potato

The sweet potato (*Ipomoea batatas*) is a creeping, vine-like plant that is cultivated in tropical climates for its starchy, nutritious tubers. The sweet potato is in the morning glory family (Convolvulaceae). The sweet potato is sometimes referred to as a yam, but it is quite different from the true yam (*Dioscorea batatas*), which is another species of tropical root-crop.

The sweet potato is a perennial, trailing vine that develops tubers at the ends of adventitious roots. Sweet potatoes are easily propagated vegetatively, by planting small pieces of roots or vine cuttings.

Although sweet potatoes are not consumed in large quantities in North America or Europe, they are a very important crop in the tropics. The global production of sweet potatoes ranks this plant with the eight most important foods grown by people in terms of the annual production of edible biomass (about 127,000,000 tons [140,000,000 mt] per year).

Sweet potatoes have an ancient history of cultivation as a food crop. Archaeological evidence suggests that sweet potatoes may have been grown in Peru for as long as 5,000 years. This crop is known to have been cultivated in the tropical Americas, Southeast Asia, and Polynesia at the time of the first visits to these regions by Europeans. Many botanists believe that the sweet potato originated in Central America or northern South America, and was then somehow transported to Asia during pre-historic times. This dispersal may have happened by now-forgotten, trans-Pacific trade or migration voyages, or possibly by seed capsules floating across the ocean.

There are many varieties of sweet potatoes, but these can be categorized into two broad groups. One group has moist, sweet tubers with an orange-colored interior—this is the type most commonly found in markets in North America. The other, more diverse group of sweet potatoes has a drier and mealier tuber, with a yellow, white, or red-colored interior, and is most extensively grown and eaten throughout the tropics.

Sweet potatoes are a valuable source of carbohydrate, beta-carotene, and fiber, containing as much as 5% protein. However, a diet rich in sweet potatoes must be balanced with other foods, mostly to ensure an adequate intake of proteins, and a balance of essential amino acids. Sweet potatoes can be eaten after boiling or roasting, or they can be manufactured into a flour, or used to make a product known as Brazilian arrowroot, and sometimes fermented into alcohol. Sweet potatoes are also fed to livestock, as are the vines and foliage of the plant. Because the tubers are rather moist, sweet potatoes spoil relatively easily, and crops do not always store well.

See also **Tuber**; **Yam**.

Swifts

Swifts are the fastest fliers of all of the small birds, reaching speeds of 172-218 mph (275-349 kph), although 35-80 mph (56-128 kph) is more common. They belong to the family Apodidae, a name meaning "without feet" and a reference to the fact that a swift in flight appears to have no legs or feet. Indeed, the legs of swifts are small and weak so that a swift that lands on the ground may have difficulty taking off again.

Swifts gather food, drink, bathe, court, and mate all while on the wing. They are more closely related to the hummingbirds than to the swallows, which they resemble. There are about 80 species of swifts, and they are found throughout the world except in the Arctic and Antarctic. Swifts are generally small birds, ranging from the size of a sparrow to the size of a small hawk. They are generally gray or brown, although some species are marked with white.

The wings of swifts are slender and pointed, the ideal shape for a rapid flier. The tail contains 10 feathers, and may be forked or short and stiff. Although their legs are weak, swifts' claws are strong and ideally suited to clinging to chimneys or rock walls on which they roost. The bill of swifts is tiny, but the gape is large, and well-suited for catching insects while in flight. Among the insects eaten by swifts are spiders, aphids, ants, bees, wasps, midges, mayflies, beetles, and termites. One Alpine swift was found to have a ball (called a bolus) of 600 insects in its throat, which it was taking back to feed its young.

Swifts can be distinguished from the superficially-similar swallows by their style of flight. Swifts alternate a short glide with a series of shallow, rapid wingbeats, and in flight can be mistaken for bats. Swallows, on the other hand, are more fluid fliers. It was thought that swifts alternated their wing beats in flight—using first the left then the right, but stroboscopic studies have confirmed that the wings in fact beat in unison (if jerkily) because of the swifts' short, massive wing bones.

Not only are swifts rapid flyers, but they also have great endurance. One bird was estimated to have flown more than million miles in its nine-year life span. Since swifts are long-lived birds (some have been known to live for nearly 20 years), it is not unreasonable to assume that some individuals may have flown far more miles than that. Swifts migrate seasonally with species from North America generally wintering in South America. However, one North American species, the white-throated swift, becomes torpid during periods of cold weather, much like its relative the hummingbird.

Swifts are gregarious. A large colony of chimney swifts nested in an air shaft at Kent State University in Ohio. When chimney swifts prepare to roost for the night, a flock will circle about a chimney for as long as an hour. The bird closest to the chimney will be the first to enter, and the rest follow, looking like a puff of smoke going down the chimney.

Nesting is usually a solitary affair. Swifts are loyal to both their traditional nesting site and to their mate. The male and female gather twigs for the nest by grabbing the twig while in flight; if it breaks off, the bird adds it to the nest. Nests are cup-shaped agglomerations of twigs, mud, moss, and saliva (building materials vary by species), usually in a spot secluded and inaccessible to predators, such as a crevice in a high cliff face. Because the birds need so much saliva during breeding season, their salivary glands increase in size accordingly, swelling to as much as 12 times the normal size.

The glutaneous saliva is considered by some people a delicacy. In Southeast Asia, swift nests are harvested for use in bird's-nest soup, which some believe keeps people young. The nests of these Asian species are constructed entirely of fast-drying saliva. Some swift species have become rare because of the harvesting of the nests. And, predictably, as the nests have become more rare, they have become more expensive, commanding as much as $1,000 per pound. The escalating price has not reduced demand, and nest collectors are traveling farther afield in China, Thailand, Vietnam, and other Asian countries in search of nests.

Depending on her species, the female lays between one and six white eggs. Both the male and female incubate the eggs, which hatch 17-28 days after being laid. The young swifts fledge at about 30 days old.

The chimney swift (*Chaetura pelagica*) is the only North American species generally found east of the Mississippi River. Other species include Vaux's swift (*Chaetura vauxi*), the smallest North American species, which weights just 0.66 oz (18.9 g), and the black swift (*Cypseloides niger*), the largest North American swift, which is rarely seen because of its high mountain habitat. The swift is not a songbird, and its voice consists of high, piercing screams.

See also Hummingbirds; Swallows and martins.

Further Reading:

Perrins, Christopher M., and A. L. A. Middleton, eds. *Encyclopedia of Birds*. New York: Facts on File, 1985.
Terres, John K. *The Audubon Society Encyclopedia of North American Birds*. New York: Wing Books, 1991.

F. C. Nicholson

Swine see **Pigs**

KEY TERMS

. . . .

Dorsal fin—The fin on the back of the fish.

Serrated—The sword is notched resembling the teeth of a saw.

Swordfish

The swordfish (*Xiphias gladius*), also known as the broadbill, or the forktail, is the only species in the bony fish family Xiphiidae. The swordfish is highly prized as a food fish, and as a game fish. Its distinguishing characteristic is the elongation of the upper jaw which resembles a long, flattened, serrated sword, which may extend up to one-third of the body length. The sword is used by the fish as an offensive weapon, and to spear prey, which may be other fish or large mollusks. Swordfish often attack schools of mackerel gashing several fish with its sword before devouring them. The swordfish are dark in color, most often brownish black or black with a lighter brown below. Adult swordfish are devoid of scales and of teeth. Commercially swordfish are caught by harpooning, and fish in excess of 1,200 pounds (600 kg) have been caught by this method. Swordfish are spotted by their curved dorsal fins exposed above the water surface. Swordfish are baited by trolling squid or mackerel, and caught on heavy tackle. When hooked, swordfish make extreme efforts to free themselves by leaping out of the water several times before eventually tiring. The angler may patiently play the fish for three or four hours before it is subdued. The record catch for a swordfish by rod and reel is 1,182 pounds (532 kg).

When injured or hooked swordfish may thrust itself out of the water, squirm violently and attack anyone or anything in its path. When approached by a boat the fish may pretend to be exhausted and then suddenly ram its sword into the side of the boat. The force of the thrust may be sufficient to pierce solid wood of the boat side 2 inches (5 cm) thick. If the ship is wooden the sword may have gone in too deep to be removed and may be broken off in order to escape.

The sail fish (*Istiophorus*), the spearfish (*Tetrapturus*) and the Marlin (*Makaira*) are relatives of the swordfish in the family Istiophoridae.

See also Bony fishes.

Sycamore see **Plane family**

Symbiosis

Symbiosis is a word used to refer to intimate relationships among species. Symbioses can involve interactions of individuals of different species, or associations of populations of one or more species. Symbiosis can involve obligate relationships, in which the symbionts cannot live apart in nature, but usually the association is more flexible than this.

Various types of symbiosis

Mutualism is a symbiosis between species in which both partners benefit. Mutualism is considered by some biologists to be the archetypal form of symbiosis. The examples of symbiosis that are discussed in the next section are all mutualisms.

Parasitism is another type of symbiotic association, in which one organism obtains nourishment from a host, usually without killing it. In most parasitisms, the parasite has a close and sometimes obligate relationship with the host. However, to be healthy, the host by no means needs the parasite, and in fact usually suffers a detriment from the symbiosis. Commensalism is a relationship in which one symbiont benefits from the interaction, while the host species is neither positively or negatively affected. For example, small epiphytic plants derive a substantial ecological benefit from living on larger plants, but the latter are not usually affected to a meaningful degree.

Examples of natural symbioses

Most biologists, when confronted by the need to illustrate the concept of symbiotic mutualism, describe the case of lichens. Lichens are an obligate association between a fungus (the mycobiont) and an alga or blue-green bacterium (the phycobiont). Lichen mutualisms are very distinctive, and they can be identified on the basis of the size, shape, color, and biochemistry of their biomass. Lichenologists have developed systematic and taxonomic treatments of lichens, even though these mutualisms are not true "organisms" in the conven-

A cape buffalo with an oxpecker on its back in Kenya. The relationship between the oxpecker and the buffalo is a type of symbiosis called mutualism; the oxpecker feeds from the supply of ticks on the buffalo, which in turn benefits from tick removal.

tional meaning of the word. The fungus benefits from the lichen mutualism through access to photosynthetic products of the alga or blue-green bacterium, while the phycobiont benefits from provision of a relatively moist habitat and enhanced access to inorganic nutrients.

Certain species of fungi also occur in intimate associations with the roots of vascular plants, in a mutualism referred to as mycorrhizae. The plant benefits from the mycorrhiza through increased access to inorganic nutrients, especially phosphate, while the fungus gains an advantage through access to nutritious exudates from the roots of the plant. This is a very widespread mutualism—most vascular plants have mycorrhizae.

Some vascular plants live in a mutualism with particular microorganisms that have the ability to fix atmospheric dinitrogen into ammonia, a form of inorganic nitrogen that the plant can utilize in its nutrition (see entry on nitrogen cycle). The best known examples of this mutualism involve various species of plants in the legume family (Fabaceae) and a bacterium known as *Rhizobium japonicum*. In this mutualism, the plant benefits from increased access to an important nutrient, while

the bacterium gains an advantage through the provision of an appropriate habitat in the form of root nodules, as well as fixed energy provided by the host plant.

Another common mutualism occurs in the guts of animals that eat plant matter. Many animals consume plant biomass, but most are not very effective at digesting polymeric biochemicals such as cellulose and lignin. Often, these animals live in a symbiosis with microorganisms, which inhabit part of the gut and secrete specialized enzymes, such as cellulases, which digest cellulose. The herbivorous animal benefits from access to a large source of fixed energy, while the microorganisms benefit from access to a safe and appropriate habitat, and to nutritious chemicals available in the animal gut. This sort of mutualism occurs, for example, between termites and symbiotic bacteria and protozoans. In the case of the termite *Eutermes*, protozoans in the gut may account for 60% of the insect's weight. Many herbivorous mammals also live in a cellulose-digesting symbiosis with bacteria and protozoans, as is the case of ruminants such as the domestic sheep (*Ovis aries*) and cow (*Bos taurus*).

Symbioses between humans and other species

Humans live in symbioses of various intensities with a number of domesticated animals and plants. To varying degrees, these cultural symbioses are mutualistic, with both humans and the other species benefitting.

For example, all important agricultural plants exist in tight mutualisms with humans. Agricultural varieties of corn or maize (*Zea mays*), for example, are no longer capable of reproducing independently of human management. This is because over time the fruiting structure of maize has been selected to be enclosed in a leafy sheath that does not open, and to have seeds that do not easily separate (or shatter) from the supporting tissue (the cob). If humans did not plant the seeds of maize, the species would rapidly become extinct, because it no longer occurs as wild populations. The same is substantially true for most agricultural plants that have become extensively modified through cultural selection by humans. Humans, of course, benefit greatly from their mutualisms with agricultural plants, through the provision of crops of food, fiber, and other products.

Similarly, agricultural animals live in a symbiotic mutualism with humans. Cows (*Bos taurus*), for example, benefit from their human-managed access to fodder, veterinary services, and protection from predators, while humans benefit from access to milk and meat.

Even the keeping of animals as pets represents a type of mutualism. Pet dogs (*Canis familiaris*) and cats (*Felis catus*) are fed and kept safe in domestication, while humans benefit from the companionship of these animals, and sometimes from other services, as when cats kill pest rodents.

Symbiosis and evolution

Ideas about symbiosis have made some important contributions to theories that help explain the evolution of complex life forms on Earth. The first organisms on Earth were prokaryotic viruses and blue-green bacteria, which do not have an organized nucleus. Eukaryotic cells are more complex, having their nuclear material bounded within a nucleus, as well as other cellular organelles such as ribosomes, chloroplasts, cilia, flagellae, and other important structures. An exciting theory of the origin of eukaryotic cellular organization postulates the occurrence of a series of symbioses, in which prokaryotic cells became intimately associated with each other, with certain cellular functions being mutualistically divided amongst the symbionts. For example, certain tiny symbionts might have become responsible for the most of the respiratory function of the mutualism, and could then

---

KEY TERMS

Mutualism—A mutually beneficial relationship between species.

Symbiosis—An intimate biological relationship, in which different species interact in some meaningful way.

---

have evolved into mitochondria. Other symbionts, such as blue-green bacteria, could have been responsible for photosynthesis by the cell, and may have evolved into chloroplasts. To a degree these ideas are supported by the observation that both ribosomes and chloroplasts contain small amounts of genetic material (DNA, or deoxyribonucleic acid), which may be relict from an earlier, independent existence.

Another recent and highly controversial theory, called the Gaia hypothesis, suggests that Earth may represent an enormous, quasi-organismic entity, in which all species comprise a global, symbiotic, physiological system that maintains environmental conditions within a range that life can tolerate. Supporting evidence for this hypothesis includes the suggestion that the oxygen in Earth's atmosphere is ultimately of biological origin, having been emitted by photosynthetic organisms. Without oxygen, of course, most species could not survive. In addition, some ecologists suggest that the concentration of carbon dioxide in Earth's atmosphere is to a large degree regulated by a complex of integrated biological and physical processes by which CO_2 is emitted and absorbed. This gas is well known to be important in the planet's greenhouse effect, which is critical in maintaining the average surface temperature within a range that organisms can tolerate.

See also Gaia hypothesis; Lichens; Mutualism; Parasites.

Further Reading:

Begon, M., Harper, J. L., and Townsend, C. R. *Ecology: Individuals, Populations and Communities,* 2nd ed. London: Blackwell Sci. Pub., 1990.

Brewer, R. *The Science of Ecology,* 2nd ed. Fort Worth: Saunders, 1994.

Margulis, L. and L. Olendzenski, eds. *Environmental Evolution: Effects of the Origin and Evolution of Life on Planet Earth.* Cambridge: MIT Press, 1992.

Bill Freedman

Symbol, chemical

Chemical symbols are shorthand abbreviations of the names of the 109 known elements. Each element has its own unique symbol. Since science is an international enterprise, chemical symbols are determined by international agreement.

The use symbols for the chemical elements existed long before a systematic method was developed. The alchemists associated the symbols of the planets not only with the days of the week, but also with the seven metals known at the time: gold, silver, iron, mercury, tin, copper and lead. By the beginning of the nineteenth century, there were about 26 known elements, but by the beginning of the twentieth century, there were more than 81. As more elements were discovered, the need for symbolic representations for these elements became more evident.

During the first half of the nineteenth century, an outstanding Swedish chemist, Jöns Jacob Berzelius, systematically assigned letters as symbols for the elements. This method soon became accepted by chemists everywhere. Today, the International Union of Pure and Applied Chemistry (IUPAC) is the organization that makes the final decision on the names and symbols of the element.

Chemical symbols are composed of one or two letters. The first letter is always capitalized and the second, if there is one, is always lowercase. Often these are the first two letters of the element's, name but this is not always possible, because it would sometimes cause duplication. For example, the symbol C represents carbon, Ca represents calcium, Cd represents cadium, and Cf represents californium.

Most of the elements have symbols derived from their English name, but a few symbols stem from other languages. Notable among these are ten common elements whose names and symbols are derived from the Latin. These are: antimony, Sb, from stibium; copper, Cu, from cuprum; gold, Au, from aurum; iron, Fe, from ferrum; potassium, K, from kalium; lead, Pb, from plumbum; mercury, Hg, from hydrargyrum; silver, Ag, from argentum; sodium, Na, from natrium; and tin, Sn, from stannum.

Chemical symbols are used by chemists everywhere in writing chemical formulas, in which the symbols represent the atoms of the elements present in a compound.

Some strange-looking element names with even stranger-looking three-letter symbols have been in general use recently for the heaviest chemical elements. Because they may still be seen in periodic tables published between 1980 and 1994, it is important to know what they mean. For example the element of atomic number 104 was referred to as unnilquadium, with the symbol Unq, and element 108 was referred to as unniloctium, with the symbol Uno. These names and symbols are based entirely on the atomic numbers themselves: un means 1, nil means 0, and quad means 4; therefore unnilquad means 104. These names and symbols were recommended by the International Union of Pure and Applied Chemistry to be used temporarily, until certain disputes about who discovered these elements could be resolved.

The discoverers of a new element have historically been given the right to suggest a name. But three groups of nuclear chemists all claim to have been the first to discover some of the transuranium elements: an American group at the Lawrence Berkeley Laboratory in California, a Russian group at the Joint Institute for Nuclear Research in Dubna, and a German group at the Gesellschaft für Schwerionenforschung in Darmstadt. In 1994, the International Union of Pure and Applied Chemistry attempted to settle the issues by recommending "official" names and symbols for elements 101 through 109, but they are still being hotly debated.

See also Element, chemical; Periodic table.

Symbolic logic

Logic is the study of the rules which underlie plausible reasoning in mathematics, science, law, and other discliplines.

Symbolic logic is a system for expressing logical rules in an abstract, easily manipulated form.

Symbols

In algebra, a letter such as x represents a number. Although the symbol gives no clue as to the value of the number, it can be used nevertheless in the formation of sums, products, etc. Similarly P, in geometry, stands for a point and can be used in describing segments, intersections, and the like.

In symbolic logic, a letter such as p stands for an entire statement. It may, for example, represent the statement, "A triangle has three sides."

In algebra, the plus sign joins two numbers to form a third number. In symbolic logic, a sign such as V connects two statements to form a third statement. For example, V replaces the word "or" and replaces the word "and."

The following is a list of the symbols commonly encountered:

p, q, r,…	statements
v	"or"
∧	"and"
~	"it is not the case that"
=>	"implies" or "If…, then…"
⟷	"implies and is implied by" or "…. if and only if…"

Statements

Logic deals with statements, and statements vary extensively in the precision with which they may be made. If someone says, "That is a good book," that is a statement. It is far less precise, however, than a statement such as "Albany is the capital of New York." A good book could be good because it is well printed and bound. It could be good because it is written in good style. It could tell a good story. It could be good in the opinion of one person but mediocre in the opinion of another.

The statements which logic handles with the greatest certainty are those which obey the law of the excluded middle, i.e., which are unambiguously true or false, not somewhere in between. It doesn't offer much help in areas such as literary criticism or history where statements simple enough to be unequivocally true or false tend also to be of little significance. As an antidote to illogical thinking, however, logic can be of value in any discipline.

By a "statement" in logic one means an assertion which is true or false. One may not know whether the statement is true or false, but it must be one or the other. For example, the Goldbach conjecture, "Every even number greater than two is the sum of two primes," is either true or false, but no one knows which. It is a suitable statement for logical analysis.

Other words that are synonyms for "statement" are "sentence," "premise," and "proposition."

Conjunctions

If p stands for the statement, "All right angles are equal," and q the statement, "Parallel lines never meet," one can make a single statement by joining them with "and": "All right angles are equal and parallel lines never meet." This can be symbolized p ∧ q, using the inverted V-shaped symbol to stand for the conjunction "and." Both the combined statement and the word "and" itself are called "conjunctions."

In ordinary English, there are several words in addition to "and" which can used for joining two statements conjunctively, for example, "but." "But" is the preferred conjunction when one wants to alert the reader to a relationship which otherwise might seem contradictory. For example, "He is 6 ft (1.8 m) tall, but he weighs 120 lbs (54 kg)." In logic the only conjunctive term is "and."

Negation

Negation is another logical "operation." Unlike conjunction and disjunction, however, it is applied to a single statement. If one were to say, "She is friendly," the negation of that statement would be, "She is not friendly."

The symbol for negation is "~." It is placed in front of the statement to be negated, as in ~(p∧q) or ~ p. If p were the statement, "She is friendly," ~ p means "She is not friendly," or more formally, "It is not the case that she is friendly." Prefacing the statement with, "It is not the case that…," avoids embedding the negation in the middle of the statement to be negated. The symbol lips is read "not p."

The statement ~ p Is true when p is false, and false when p is true. For example, if p is the statement "x < 4," ~ p is the statement "x ≥ 4." Replacing x with S makes p false but ~ p true. If a boy, snubbed by the girl in "She is friendly," were to hear the statement, he would say that it was false. He would say, "She is not friendly," and mean it.

Truth tables

The fact that someone says something doesn't make it true.

Statements can be false as well as true. In logic, they must be one or the other, but not both and not neither. They must have a "truth value," true or false, abbreviated T or F.

A very useful aid in symbolic logic is a truth table:

p	q	~p	p∧q	p∨q
T	T	F	T	T
T	F	F	F	T
F	T	T	F	T
F	F	T	F	F

Whether a conjunction is true depends on the statements which make it up. If both of them are true, then the conjunction is true. If either one or both of them are false, the conjunction is false. For example, the familiar expression 3 < x < 7, which means "x > 3 and x < 7" is true only when both conditions are satisfied simultaneously, that is for numbers between 3 and 7.

Disjunctions

Another word used in both ordinary English and in logic is "or." Someone who says, "Either he didn't hear me, or he is being rude," is saying that at least one of those two possibilities is true. By connecting the two possibilities about which he or she is unsure, the speaker can make a statement of which he or she is sure.

There is one imp7

In logic, "or" means "and/or." If p and q are statements, p V q is the statement, called a "disjunction," formed by connecting p and q with "or," symbolized by "V."

For example if p is the statement, "Mary Doe may draw money from this account," and q is the statement, "John Doe may draw money from this account," then p V q is the statement, "Mary Doe may draw money from this account, or John Doe may draw money from this account."

The disjunction p V q is true when p, q, or both are true. In the example above, for instance, an account set up in the name of Mary or John Doe may be drawn on by both while they are alive and by the survivor if one of them should die. Had their account been set up in the name Mary and John Doe, both of them would have to sign the withdrawal slip, and the death of either one would freeze the account. Bankers, who tend to be careful about money, use "and" and "or" as one does in logic.

One use of truth tables is to test the equivalence of two symbolic expressions. Two expressions such as p and q are equivalent if whenever one is true the other is true, and whenevet one is false the other is false. One can test the equivalence of ~(p V q) and ~p Λ A ~ q (as with the minus sign in algebra, "~" applies only to the statement which immediately follows it. If it is to apply to more than a single statement, parentheses must be used to indicate it):

p	q	~p	~q	pVq	~(pVq)	~pΛ~q
T	T	F	F	T	F	F
T	F	F	T	T	F	F
F	T	T	F	T	F	F
F	F	T	T	F	T	T

The expressions have the same truth values for all the possible values of p and q, and are therefore equivalent.

For instance, if p is the statement "x > 2" and q the statement "x < 2," p V q is true when x is any number except 2. Then (p V q) is true only when x = 2. The negations p and q are "x 2" and "x 2" respectively. The only number for which ~ p Λ ~ q is true is also 2.

Algebra of statements

Equivalent propositions or statements can be symbolized with the two-headed arrow "←→." In the preceeding section we showed the first of De Morgan's rules:

1. ~(p V q) ←→ ~p Λ ~q

2. ~(p Λ q) ←→ ~p V ~q

Rules such as these ore useful for simplifying and clarifying complicated expressions. Other useful rules are

3. p ←→ ~(~p)

4. p Λ(q V r) ←→ (p Λ q) V (p Λ r) (a distributive law for "and" applied to a disjunction)

5. p Λ q ←→ q Λ p p V q ←→ q V p

6. (p Λ q) V r ←→ p V (q V r) (p V q) V r ←→ p V (q V r)

Each of these rules can be verified by writing out its truth table.

A truth table traces each of the various possibilities. To check rule 4 with its three different statements, p, q, and r, would require a truth table with eight lines. On occasion one may want to know the truth value of an expression such as ((T V F) Λ A (F V T)) V ~ F where the truth values of particular statements have been entered in place of p1 q, etc. The steps in evaluating such an expression are as follows:

((T V F) Λ (F V T)) V ~ F Given

(T Λ T) v T Truth tables for V,~

T V T Truth table for Λ

T Truth table for V

Such a compound expression might come from the run-on sentence, "Roses are red or daisies are blue, and February has thirty days or March has 31 days; or it is not the case that May is in the fall." Admittedly, one is not likely to encounter such a sentence in ordinary conversation, but it illustrates how the rules of symbolic logic can be used to determine the ultimate truth of a complex statement. It also illustrates the process of replacing statements with known truth values instead of filling out a truth table for all the possible truth values. Since this example incorporates five different statements, a truth table of thirty-two lines would have been needed to run down every possibility.

Implication

In any discipline one seeks to establish facts and to draw conclusions based on observations and theories. One can do so deductively or inductively. In inductive reasoning, one starts with many observations and formulates an explanation that seems to fit. In deductive reasoning, one starts with premises and, using the rules of logical inference, draws conclusions from them. In disciplines such as mathematics, deductive reasoning is the predominant means of drawing conclusions. In fields such as psychology, inductive reasoning predominates, but once a theory has been formulated, it is both tested and applied through the processes of deductive thinking. It is in this that logic plays a role.

Basic to deductive thinking is the word "implies," symbolized by "=>." A statement p => q means that whenever p is true, q is true also. For example, if p is the statement, "x is in Illinois," and q is the statement "x is in the United States," then p => q is the statement, "If x is in Illinois, then x is in the United States."

In logic as well as in ordinary English, there are many ways of translating p => q into words: "If p is true, then q is true"; "q is implied by p"; "p is true only if q is true"; "q is a necessary condition for p"; "p is a sufficient condition for q."

The implication p => q has a truth table some find a little perplexing:

p	q	p=>q
T	T	T
T	F	F
F	T	T
F	F	T

The perplexing part occurs in the next to last line where a false value of p seems to imply a true value of q. The fact that p is false doesn't imply anything at all. The imolication says only that q is true whenever p is. It doesn't say what happens when p is false. In the example given earlier, replacing x with Montreal makes both p and q false, but the implication itself is still true.

Implication has two properties which resemble the reflexive and transitive properties of equality. One, p p, is called a "tautology." Tautologies, although widely used, don't add much to understanding. "Why is the water salty?" asks the little boy.

"Because ocean water is salty," says his father.

The other property, "If p=> q and q=> r, then p=>r,"

is also widely used. In connecting two implications to form a third, it characterizes a lot of reasoning, formal and informal. "If we take our vacation in January, there will be snow. If there is snow, we can go skiing. Let's take it in January." This property is called a "syllogism."

A third property of equality1 "If a = b, then b = a,5 called symmetry may or may not be shared by the implication p=>q. When it is, it is symbolized by the two-headed arrow used earlier, "p $\longleftrightarrow$ q." p $\longleftrightarrow$ q means (p=> q) $\wedge$ (q=> p). It can be read "p and q are equivalent'; "p is true if and only if q is true"; "p implies and is implied by q"; "p is a necessary and sufficient condition for q"; and "p implies q, and conversely."

In p=> q, p is called the "antecedent" and q the "consequent." If the antecedent and consequent are interchanged, the resulting implication, q=> p, is called the "converse." If one is talking about triangles, for example, there is a theorem, "If two sides are equal, then the angles opposite the sides are equal." The converse is, "If two angles are equal, then the sides opposite the angles are equal."

If an implication is true, it is never safe to assume that the converse is true as well. For example, "If x lives in Illinois, then x lives in the United States," is a true implication, but its converse is obviously false. In fact, assuming that the converse of an implication is true is a significant source of fallacious reasoning. If the battery is shot, then the car won't start." True enough, but it is a good idea to check the battery itself instead of assuming the coverse and buying a new one.

Implications are involved in three powerful lines of reasoning. One, known as the Rule of Detachment or by the Latin *modus ponendo ponens,* states simply "If p=> q and p are both true, then q is true." This rule shows up in all sorts of areas. "If x dies, then y is to receive $100,000. " When x dies and proof is submitted to the insurance, y gets a check for the money. The statements p=> q and p are called the "premises" and q the "conclusion."

A second rule, known as *modus tollendo tollens,* says if p=>q is true and q is false, then p is false. "If x ate the cake, then x was home." If x was not at home, then someone else ate the cake.

A third rule, *modus tollerdo ponens,* says that if p V q and p are true, then q is true. Mary or Ann broke the pitcher.

Ann did not; so Mary did. Of course, the validity of the argument depends upon establishing that both premises are true.

KEY TERMS
. . . .

Logic—The study of the rules which underlie deductive reasoning.

Statement—A sentence which can be classified as either true or false, but not both.

It may have been the cat.

Another type of argument is known as *reductio ad absurdum*, again from the Latin. Here, if one can show that ~p=> (q ∧ ~q), then p must be true. That is, if assuming the negation of p leads to the absurdity of a statement which is both true and false at the same time," then p itself must be true.

Further Reading:

Carroll, Lewis. *Symbolic Logic* New York: Dover Publications Inc. 1958.
Christian, Robert R. *Logic and Sets* Waltham, Massachusetts: Blaisdell Publishing Co., 1965.
Suppes, Patrick, and Hill, Shirley. *First Course in Mathematical Logic*, Waltham, Massachusetts: Blaisdell Publishing Co., 1964.

J. Paul Moulton

Sympathetic system see **Nervous system**

Syndrome

A syndrome is a collection of signs, symptoms, and other indications which, taken together, characterize a particular disease or abnormal medical condition. Medical workers place a heavy reliance on the collection of such indicators in the diagnosis of health problems and disorders.

The usual approach is to question patients about the nature of their complaints and then to conduct examinations and tests suggested by these reports. The collection of data resulting from the verbal report and clinical examination may then fall into a pattern — a syndrome — that makes it possible for the physician to predict the disorder responsible for the patient's problems. That diagnosis, in turn, may lead to a course of therapy designed to deal with the problem.

As an example, a patient may complain to a physician of headaches, visual problems, and difficulty in breathing when lying down. Clinical examination may then indicate a dilation of veins in the upper part of the chest and neck with collection of fluid in the region around the eyes. An experienced physician may recognize this collection of symptoms as an indication of superior vena cava (SVC) syndrome, an obstruction of venous drainage.

Hundreds of syndromes are now recognized by medical authorities. Indeed, a specific dictionary (*Dictionary of Medical Syndromes*, by Sergio I. Magalini, J. B. Lippincott Company) has been published to summarize and describe the named syndromes.

See also Disease.

Synthesis, chemical

Chemical synthesis is the preparation of compound, usually an organic compound, from easily available or inexpensive commercial chemicals. Compounds are prepared or synthesized by performing various chemical reactions using an inexpensive starting material and changing its molecular structure, by reactions with other chemicals. The best chemical syntheses are those that use cheap starting materials, require only a few steps, and have a good output of product based on the amounts of starting chemicals. The starting materials for organic synthesis can be simple compounds removed from oil and natural gas or more complex chemicals isolated in large amounts from plant and animal sources. The goal of chemical synthesis is to make a particular product that can be used commercially for example as a drug, a fragrance, a polymer coating, a food or cloth dye, a herbicide, or some other commercial or industrial use. Compounds are also synthesized to test a chemical theory, to make a new or better chemical, or to confirm the structure of a material isolated from a natural source. Chemical synthesis can also be used to supplement the supply of a drug that is commonly isolated in small amounts from natural sources.

Chemical synthesis has played an important role in eradicating one of the major infectious diseases associated with the tropical regions of the world. Malaria is a disease that affects millions of people and is spread by mosquito bites. It causes a person to experience chills followed by sweating and intense fever, and in some cases can cause death. In about 1633, the Inca Indians told the Jesuit priests that the bark from the cinchona or quina-quina tree could be used to cure malaria. The cinchona tree is an evergreen tree that grows in the mountains of Peru. The healing properties of the bark were quickly introduced in Europe and used by physicians to treat the disease. The chemical responsible for the healing properties of the cinchona bark was isolated in 1820 and named quinine, after the quina-quina tree. By 1850, the demand for cinchona bark was so great that the trees in Peru were near extinction. To supplement the supply of quinine, plantations of cinchona trees were started in India, Java, and Ceylon, but by 1932, they were only able to supply 13% of the world's demand for the antimalarial drug. Chemical synthesis was used by German scientists from 1928 to 1933 to make thousands of new compounds that could be used to treat malaria and make up for the deficiency of natural quinine. They were able to identify two new antimalarial drugs and one of them, quinacrine, was used as a substitute for quinine until 1945. During World War II, the supply of cinchona bark to the Allied Forces was constantly interrupted and a new drug had to be found. British and American scientists began to use chemical synthesis to make compounds to be tested against the disease. Over 150 different laboratories cooperated in synthesizing 12,400 new substances by various and often long, involved chemical sequences. In just four years, they were able to identify the new antimalarial chloroquine and large quantities were quickly prepared by chemical synthesis for use by the Allied Forces in malarial regions. Today, there are more than half a dozen different drugs available to treat malaria and they are all prepared in large quantities by chemical synthesis from easily available chemicals.

Taxol is an anticancer drug that was isolated in the 1960s from the Pacific yew tree. In 1993, taxol was approved by the Food and Drug Administration (FDA) for treatment of ovarian cancer and is also active against various other cancers. The demand for this compound is expected to be very large, but only small amounts of the drug can be obtained from the yew bark, so rather than destroy all the Pacific yew trees in the world, chemists set out to use chemical synthesis to make the compound from more accessible substances. One chemical company found that they could convert 10-deacetylbaccatin III, a compound isolated from yew twigs and needles, into taxol by a series of chemical reactions. Furthermore, in 1994, two research groups at different universities devised a chemical synthesis to synthesize taxol from inexpensive starting materials.

Chemical synthesis can also be used to prove the chemical structure of a compound. In the early nineteenth century, the structure of a compound isolated from natural sources was deduced by chemical reactions that converted the original compound into substances of known, smaller molecular arrangements.

In 1979, chemical synthesis was used as a tool to determine the molecular structure of periplanone B, the sex excitant of the female American cockroach. In the Netherlands in 1974, C. J. Persons isolated 200 micrograms of periplanone B from the droppings of 75,000 virgin female cockroaches. He was able to deduce the gross chemical structure of the compound by modern analytical methods, but not its exact three dimensional structure. Without knowing the stereochemistry or three dimensional arrangement of the carbon atoms, larger quantities of the excitant could not be prepared and tested. In 1979, W. Clark Still at Columbia University in New York, set out to determine the structure of periplanone B. He noted that four compounds had to be made by chemical synthesis in order to determine the structure of the cockroach excitant. He chose an easily prepared starting material and by a series of chemical reactions was able to make three of the four compounds he needed to determine the chemical structure. One of the new substances matched all the analytical data from the natural material. When it was sent to the Netherlands for testing against the natural product isolated from cockroaches, it was found to be the active periplanone B.

Further Reading:

Borman, S. *Chemical and Engineering News*, February 21, 1994, pg 32.

McMurry, J. *Organic Chemistry*. Pacific Grove, CA: Brooks/Cole Publishing Company, 1992.

Mundy, B.P. *Concepts of Organic Synthesis*. New York: Marcel Dekker Inc, 1980.

Stinson, S.C. *Chemical and Engineering News*, April 30, 1979, pg 24.

Warren, S. *Organic Synthesis: The Disconnection Approach*. New York: John Wiley & Sons, 1983.

Andrew Poss

Synthesizer, music

The virtuoso demands that composers placed on musicians at the end of the 1800s were but a foretaste of things to come in the twentieth century. Members of the orchestra were complaining that the music of contemporary composers was unplayable because of the enormous difficulty of complex orchestral writing styles. With the Paris premiere of Igor Stravinsky's "Le Sacre Du Printemps" in 1913, it seemed that the limits of per-formability had been reached and that the music world was about to go over the brink.

After a break in compositional flow during World War I, composers explored new, uncharted musical domains. In the 1920s and 1930s, some composers created intricate and complex avant garde music, demonstrating the ultimate limitations of human musicians. They did not know it at the time, but these pioneers were attempting to write electronic music before the needed technology had been invented.

After World War II, European composers began to experiment with a new invention, the tape recorder. Here was a medium in which an artist could actually hold sounds in her own hands. Chopping up a tape recording and reassembling the pieces in a different order opened up a new world of sounds for composers to explore. It also required artists to come to grips with the phenomenon of sound itself, and questions like what it was made of and how sounds differed from each other. These problems were eventually solved on paper but a real tool was required to give composers the ability to actually manipulate the building blocks of sound. In the 1950s, electronics technology had been developed to the point where it was finally able to meet this demand, leading ultimately to the development of the first music synthesizer by Harry Olson and Herbert Belar in the laboratories and studios of RCA.

The synthesizer is a device that creates sounds electronically and allows the user to change and manipulate the sounds. All sounds in nature consist of waves of varying air pressure. A synthesizer creates sounds by generating an electrical signal in the form of a waveform, usually either a sine wave or other simple mathematical wave, which is amplified and used to drive an acoustic speaker. Unfortunately, the sound quality of a simple waveform is somewhat raw and unmusical, at least to most people. The waveform is usually altered in numerous ways, using filters to create the interesting timbres, or colors, of sound that are usually associated with certain acoustical instruments. Changing the frequency of the waveform raises or lowers the pitch of the sound. A synthesizer can control and change the beginning attack of a sound, its duration, and its decay, in addition to controlling the waveform itself.

Synthesizers can receive information from numerous sources about how to set the different parameters of its output sound. Any electronic device, such as a computer program, or person can control the synthesizer. An obvious way to accomplish this is to build the synthesizer in such a manner that it resembles an already-existing musical instrument, such as a piano. A piano-like keyboard is often used to generate signals that control the pitch of the synthesizer, although a keyboard is not required, or even necessarily desirable, to do the job. One of the first commercially available keyboard-based synthesizers marketed to the general public was built by Robert Moog in the 1960s. Other early competitors of the Moog Synthesizer were built by Don Buchla and Al Perlemon.

All of the early synthesizers were built using analog computer technology. Since the late 1970s, however, digital synthesis has developed as the premiere technology in synthesizer design. In the process of digitally recording a sound, called sampling, any sound recording can be converted into a series of numbers that a computer can analyze. The computer takes snapshots of the sampled sound in very short increments, about forty thousand times a second. Mathematical techniques, such as Fourier analysis, are then used to calculate the complex waveform of the original sound. The sound can then be easily reproduced in real-time from a synthesizer keyboard. This technique for creating sounds, and others, form the design basis of most digital synthesizers such as the New England Digital Synclavier and the Kurzweil music synthesizer. The same technique can be applied to synthesize drums, voices or any other kind of sound. Digital instruments can also receive input not just from a keyboard, but from the actual breath of the performer, for instance. Digital flutes and other wind-instrument synthesizers convert the force of the musicians breath into a signal that can modify any desired parameter of the output sound.

Synthesizers have shown themselves capable of creating a wide variety of new and interesting sounds. Their one limitation, of course, is that they sound only as good as the speaker that amplifies their signal. Most humans can hear sounds far beyond the range that even the best speakers can reproduce, sounds that acoustical instruments have always been capable of generating. Because of this limitation, and others, synthesizers are not viewed as replacements of traditional instruments, but rather as a creative tool that enhances the musician's already rich palette of musical possibilities.

See also Computer, digital; Electronics; Synthesizer, voice.

Synthesizer, voice

The earliest known talking machine was developed in 1778 by Wolfgang von Kempelen. Eyewitnesses reported that it could speak several words in a timid, childlike voice. While the talking machine's success appears genuine, Baron von Kempelen's accomplishments are not above suspicion. Nine years earlier, he had built a chess-playing machine, which defeated many players, including Napoleon (who, incidentally, made several unsuccessful attempts to cheat). Eventually, it was discovered that the machine was a fraud—its cabinet concealed a hidden, human chess player, who controlled the game.

In 1830, Professor Joseph Faber of Vienna, Austria, produced his own speaking automaton. Faber's machine, dubbed Euphonia, had taken 25 years to construct. Designed to look like a bearded Turk, the creation could recite the alphabet, whisper, laugh, and ask "How do you do?" Speech was produced by its inner workings—double bellows, levers, gears, and keys located inside the mannequin. Strangely enough, Euphonia spoke English with a German accent.

The first talking machines employing electronic technology were developed in the 1930s. The Voice Operation Demonstrator, or Voder, invented by Dudley in 1933, could imitate human speech and even utter complete sentences as its operator pressed keys on a board. Speech-synthesis technology evolved further with the rapid development of computer technology in the 1950s. During the late 1960s, the MITalk System was developed at the Massachusetts Institute of Technology. Although originally designed as a reading machine for the blind, once completed, the system could convert virtually any type of text into speech-synthesized output.

Raymond Kurzweil also developed speech-synthesis technology to aid the blind. In 1976, he produced the Kurzweil reading machine which could read everything from a phone bill to a full-length novel and provided unlimited-vocabulary synthesized output. Sometimes called a set of eyes for the blind, the reading machine has proved very popular.

Today, speech synthesis is a useful way to convey information in public places. Cars, appliances, and even games are being equipped with voice-synthesizer chips. A recently developed talking chessboard plays an amateurish game of chess and announces each move it makes.

Syphilis see **Sexually transmitted diseases**

Syrphids see **True flies**

Systematics see **Taxonomy**

Systems of equations

Systems of equations are a group of relationships between various unknown variables which can be expressed in terms of algebraic expressions. The solutions for a simple system of equation can be obtained by graphing, substitution, and elimination addition. These methods became too cumbersome to be used for more complex systems however, and a method involving matrices is used to find solutions. Systems of equations have played an important part in the development of business and quicker methods for solutions continue to be explored.

Unknowns and linear equations

Many times, mathematical problems involve relationships between two variables. For example, the distance that a car moving 55 mph travels in a unit of time can be described by the equation $y = 55x$. In this case, y is the distance traveled, x is the time and the equation is known as a linear equation in two variables. Note that for every value of x, there is a value of y which makes the equation true. For instance, when x is 1, y is 55. Similarly, when x is 4, y is 220. Any pair of values, or ordered pair, which make the equation true are known as the solution of the equation. The set of all ordered pairs which make the equation true are called the solution set. Linear equations are more generally written as $ax + by = c$ where a, b and c represent constants and x and y represent unknowns.

Often, two unknowns can be related to each other by more than one equation. A system of equations includes all of the linear equations which relate the unknowns. An example of a system of equations can be described by the following problem involving the ages of two people. Suppose Lynn is twice as old as Ruthie, but two years ago, Lynn was three times as old as Ruthie. Two equations can be written for this problem. If we let x = Lynn's age and y = Ruthie's age, then the two equations relating the unknown ages would be $x = 2y$ and $x - 2 = 3(y - 2)$. The relationships can be rewritten in the general format for linear equations to obtain,

(Eq. 1) $x - 2y = 0$

(Eq. 2) $2x - 3y = -4$

The solution of this system of equations will be any ordered pair which makes both equations true. This system has only solution, the ordered pair of $x = 8$ and $y = 4$, and is thus called consistent.

Solutions of linear equations

Since the previous age problem represents a system with two equations and two unknowns, it is called a system in two variables. Typically, three methods are used for determining the solutions for a system in two variables, including graphical, substitution and elimination.

By graphing the lines formed by each of the linear equations in the system, the solution to the age problem could have been obtained. The coordinates of any point in which the graphs intersect, or meet, represent a solution to the system because they must satisfy both equations. From a graph of these equations, it is obvious that there is only one solution to the system. In general, straight lines on a coordinate system are related in only three ways. First, they can be parallel lines which never cross and thus represent an inconsistent system without a solution. Second, they can intersect at one point, as in the previous example, representing a consistent system with one solution. And third, they can coincide, or intersect at on all points indicating a dependent system which has an infinite number of solutions. Although it can provide some useful information, the graphical method is often difficult to use because it usually provides us with only approximate values for the solution of a system of equations.

The methods of substitution and elimination by addition give results with a good degree of accuracy. The substitution method involves using one of the equations in the system to solve for one variable in terms of the other. This value is then substituted into the first equation and a solution is obtained. Applying this method to the system of equations in the age problem, we would first rearrange the equation 1 in terms of x so it would become x = 2y. This value for x could then be substituted into equation 2 which would become 2y - 3y = -4, or simply y = 4. The value for x is then obtained by substituting y = 4 into either equation.

Probably the most important method of solution of a system of equations is the elimination method because it can be used for higher order systems. The method of elimination by addition involves replacing systems of equations with simpler equations, called equivalent systems. Consider the system with the following equations equation 1x - y = 1 equation 2 x + y = 5 By the method of elimination, one of the variable is eliminated by adding together both equations and obtaining a simpler form. Thus equation 1 + equation 2 results in the simpler equation 2x = 6 or x =3. This value is then put back into the first equation to get y = 2.

Often, it is necessary to multiply equations by other variables or numbers to use the method of elimination.

KEY TERMS

Consistent system—A set of equations whose solution set is represented by only one ordered pair.

Dependent system—A set of equations whose solution set has an infinite amount of ordered pairs.

Elimination—A method for solving systems of equations which involves combining equations and reducing them to a simpler form.

Graphical solution—A method for finding the solution to a system of equations which involves graphing the equations and determining the points of intersection.

Inconsistent system—A set of equations which does not have a solution.

Linear equation—An algebraic expression which relates two variables and whose graph is a line.

Matrix—A rectangular array of numbers written in brackets and used to find solutions for complex systems of equations.

Ordered pair—A pair of values which can represent variables in a system of equations.

Solution set—The set of all ordered pairs which make a system of equations true.

Substitution—A method of determining the solutions to a system of equation which involves defining one variable in terms of another and substituting it into one of the equations.

This can be illustrated by the system represented by the following equations:

equation 1 2x - y = 2

equation 2 x + 2y = 10

In this case, addition of the equations will not result in a single equation with a single variable. However, by multiplying both sides of equation 2 by -2, it is transformed into -2x - 4y = -20. Now, this equivalent equation can be added to the first equation to obtain the simple equation, -3y = - 18 or y = 6.

Systems in three or more variables

Systems of equations with more than two variables are possible. A linear equation in three variables could be represented by the equation ax + by + cz = k, where a, b, c, and k are constants and x, y, and z are variables.

For these systems, the solution set would contain all the number triplets which make the equation true. To obtain the solution to any system of equations, the number of unknowns must be equal to the number of equations available. Thus, to solve a system in three variables, there must exist three different equations which relate the unknowns.

The methods for solving a system of equations in three variables is analogous to the methods used to solve a two variable system and include graphical, substitution, and elimination. It should be noted that the graphs of these systems are represented by geometric planes instead of lines. The solutions by substitution and elimination, though more complex, are similar to the two variable system counterparts.

For systems of equations with more than three equations and three unknowns, the methods of graphing and substitution are not practical for determining a solution. Solutions for these types of systems are determined by using a mathematical invention known as a matrix. A matrix is represented by a rectangle array of numbers written in brackets. Each number in a matrix is known as an element. Matrices are categorized by their number of rows and columns.

By letting the elements in a matrix represent the constants in a system of equation, values for the variables which solve the equations can be obtained.

Systems of equations have played an important part in the development of business, industry and the military since the time of World War II. In these fields, solutions for systems of equations are obtained using computers and a method of maximizing parameters of the system called linear programming.

See also Graphs and graphing; Solution of equation; Variable.

Further Reading:

Barnett, Raymond & Michael Ziegler. *College Mathematics.* San Francisco: Dellen Publishing Co, 1984.
Marcucci, Robert & Harold Schoen. *Beginning Algebra.* Boston: Houghton Mifflin Company, 1990.
Paulos, John Allen. *Beyond Numeracy.* New York: Alfred A. Knopf Inc., 1991.

Perry Romanowski

Tanagers

Tanagers are 239 species of very colorful, perching birds that make up the family Thraupidae. The evolutionary history and phylogenetic relationships of the tanagers and related birds are not well known. Recent taxonomic treatments have included the tanagers as a subfamily (Thraupinae) of a large family of New World birds, the Emberizidae, which also includes the wood warblers, cardinals, sparrows, buntings, blackbirds, and orioles. Whether the tanagers are treated as a family or as a sub-family, they nevertheless constitute a distinct group of birds.

Tanagers are birds of forests, forest edges, and shrublands. Species of tanagers occur from temperate southern Alaska and Canada south to Brazil and northern Argentina. Almost all species, however, breed in the tropics. Tanagers that breed in temperate habitats are all migratory, spending their nonbreeding season in tropical forests. In the ecological sense, these migratory tanagers should be viewed as tropical birds that venture to the temperate zone for a few months each year for the purpose of breeding.

Tanagers are small birds, ranging in body length from 3-12 in (8-30 cm), and are generally smaller than 8 in (20 cm). This bird's body shape is not particularly distinctive, but its brilliant colors are. Tanagers' plumage can be quite spectacularly and extravagantly colored in rich hues of red, crimson, yellow, blue, or black, making these among the most beautiful of all the birds. In most species, the female has a more subdued coloration than the male.

Tanagers feed in trees and shrubs on fruit, seeds, and nectar; their diet also includes insects and other invertebrates.

Tanagers defend a territory during the breeding season. An important element of the defense is song, and some species are accomplished vocalists, although tanagers are not renowned in this respect. The cup-

shaped or domed nest is built by the female, who also incubates the 1-5 eggs. In general, tropical tanagers lay fewer eggs than the species that breed in the temperate zone. The female tanager is fed by the male during her egg-incubating seclusion. Both parents tend and feed their young.

North American tanagers

Four species of tanagers are native breeders in North America, and a fifth species has been introduced. Mature males of all of the native species are brightly colored, while the females and immature males are a more subdued olive-green or yellow color.

The western tanager (*Piranga ludovicianus*) breeds in conifer and aspen forests of western North America, as far north as southern Alaska. The male has a red head, and a yellow body, with black wings and tail.

The scarlet tanager (*P. olivacea*) breeds in mature hardwood and mixed-wood forests, and in well-treed suburbs of the eastern United States and southeastern Canada. The male has a brilliantly scarlet body with black wings and tail. The scarlet tanager winters in tropical forests in northwestern South America. This species is sometimes kept as a cagebird.

The summer tanager (*P. rubra*) occurs in oak and oak-pine forests and riparian woodlands of the eastern and southwestern United States. Male summer tanagers have an bright red body with slightly darker wings.

The hepatic tanager (*P. flava*) is a bird of oak-pine, oak, and related montane forests in the southwestern United States, as well as suitable habitats in Central and South America. The male of this species is a bright brick red color, rather similar to the summer tanager. However, the hepatic tanager has a heavier dark bill and a dark patch on the cheeks.

The blue-grey tanager (*Thraupis virens*) is a native species from Mexico to Brazil, but it has been introduced to the vicinity of Miami, Florida. This species has a brightly hued, all blue body, with the wings and tail a darker hue. The male and the female are similarly colored in the blue-grey tanager.

Tanagers elsewhere

There are hundreds of species of tanagers in the American tropics. All of these are brilliantly and boldly colored, and are very attractive birds. Because of their habitat—usually areas with thick vegetation, their beauty is not always easily seen.

One of the showiest species is the paradise tanager (*Tangara chilensis*) of southern South America, a brilliant bird with a crimson rump, a purple throat, bright blue belly, and black back.

Tanagers are not known for their singing abilities. One of the more prominent singers, however, is the blue-hooded euphonia (*Euphonia musica*), a wide-ranging species that occurs from Mexico to Argentina. This attractive bird has a bright yellow belly and rump, a sky blue cap, and a black throat, wings, back, and tail.

Some species of tanagers of deep, old-growth tropical forests are still being discovered. *Hemispingus parodii* was only discovered in a Peruvian jungle in 1974.

Further Reading:

Harrison, C. J. O., ed. *Bird Families of the World.* New York: H. N. Abrams, 1978.

Farrand, J., ed. *The Audubon Society Master Guide to Birding.* New York: Knopf, 1983.

Bill Freedman

Tantalum see **Element, chemical**

Tapeworm see **Flatworms**

Taphonomy

Taphonomy is the study of how organisms are preserved in the fossil record (the term is derived from the Greek word *taphos*, which means *grave*). Taphonomists seek to understand how an organism died and what happened to its body before and during burial. They also try to determine what factors may have contributed to unequal representation of certain groups in the fossil record due to differences in their rates of preservation.

One of the challenges taphonomists are often presented with is the interpretation of fossilized broken bones. The scientists must determine if the damage occurred while the animal was alive, after it died, or even after the bone was buried. If the bone broke while the animal was alive, there may be new growth showing that the injury was healing. Bones broken after the animal died will not show any signs of healing. Unfortunately, it is sometimes difficult to determine whether the damage occurred before burial, perhaps by gnawing or trampling, or afterwards.

The study of preservation processes is central to taphonomy. There is much to be learned from the nature of a fossil's preservation, but if a fossil is not well preserved, then there will be little evidence to study.

Rapid burial is crucial to good preservation. One reason why is that buried remains are much less likely to be disturbed by scavengers or swept away by rivers. Scavengers pull skeletons apart, scatter bones, and eat some parts preferentially to others. Rivers transport animal and plant remains far from the site of death. Indeed, most organisms are not buried where they die, but are first shuffled around either in part or in whole. This movement may be small, as in the sinking of a fish to the bottom of a lake, or extensive, as when an animal's body floats hundreds of miles in ocean currents. A second reason is that burial, especially in fine-grained muds, may slow down bacterial decay so tissues are better preserved.

Of the organisms that eventually become fossilized, few are preserved intact. This is due to differences in the ability of various parts to resist decay. On the one hand, teeth and bones are very hard, and fossilized specimens are relatively common. On the other, it is quite a find indeed to recover a fossilized heart or other soft part. Since soft parts nearly always decay, even if deeply buried, their pattern can only be preserved if minerals such as carbonate, pyrite, or phosphate replace the soft tissues. Such tissues will not decay if the organism happens to be buried in a sterile environment such as amber or a peat bog.

The hard parts of an organism are held together by soft parts, and when these decay, the organism's anatomy often becomes jumbled and scattered. This may make it difficult to determine what type of organism a part came from, and sometimes different parts of the same organism are accidentally classified as different species. A case in point is *Anomalocaris canadensis.* Until intact specimens of this prehistoric animal were found, the body was thought to be a sea cucumber, the mouth a jellyfish, and the feeding appendages shrimp-like creatures. By helping to solve puzzles like this, taphonomists increase our understanding of the fossil record.

See also Fossil and fossilization.

Tapirs

Tapirs, of the family Tapiridae, are large, forest-dwelling mammals with long flexible snouts found in tropical South and Central America, as well as in southeast Asia. There are four species of tapirs in the single genus, *Tapirus*. Tapirs are grouped with horses and rhinoceroses, in the order Perissodactyla, which are the odd-toed, hoofed mammals. Tapirs have a fourth toe on their front feet. Each toe is covered by a small hoof.

These rounded forest animals with flexible snouts have been called living fossils because they have existed, basically unchanged, for perhaps 40 million years. The fact that they are found in two widely separated locations (the Neo-Tropics and tropical Asia) is explained as an example of what happened when the ancient landmass called Gondwana split into continents that drifted apart.

The muscular snout of tapirs is developed from the fusion of the upper lip and the nose, and has nostrils at the tip. The end of the snout often dangles down and over the mouth, and is flexible enough to grasp vegetation and pull it toward the mouth. Solitary tapirs browse on leaves and forest plant shoots. Tapirs frequent river banks and sometimes are found in farm fields, where they can damage crops. Male tapirs mark their territories with sprays of urine.

The largest of the fair species is the Malayan or Asian tapir, *(T. indicus)* which is found in the rain forest regrass of Burma, Thailand, and Malasia. This species stands 40 in (1 m) tall at the shoulder and may be more than 8 ft (2.4 m) long, weighing up to 1,200 lbs (550 kg). The Malayan tapir has very distinctive coloring with a solid black body and a vivid white saddle around the middle. This cryptic coloring conceals this animal in the patches of bright sun and dark shade in its rain forest habitat.

Baird's tapir *(T. bairdi)* is found in swampy land in the rain forest regions of central America from Mexico to as far south as Ecuador in South America. The Brazilian tapir *(T. terrestris)* is the most common of the tapirs and is found in South America as far south as Brazil. Both Bairds and the Brazilian tapirs have bristly manes that may deflect the attacks of jaguars, which seize the necks of their prey. The fourth species is the mountain tapir *(T. pinchaqua)* found in the high-altitude forests of the northern Andes Mountains. It is reddish-brown in color, and has thick hair to insulate it against the cold temperatures found at such high altitudes. The mountain tapir is the smallest of the four species, measuring less than 6 ft (2 m) long and weighing not more than 500 lbs (227 kg); it is also the rarest of the tapirs.

The mountain tapir (*Tapirus pinchaque*) is the only tapir adapted to a cold climate.

Tapirs spend a lot of time in streams or lakes, which both cools them and may dislodge ectoparasites. The Malayan tapir walks on the bottom of rivers rather like the hippoptamus. Female tapirs protect their young from the attacks of caymans and other predators when in the water. On land the main defense of tapirs is to run away, but a cornered tapir will also turn and bite.

Tapirs breed at any time of the year, and the courtship and mating behavior is often accompanied by much noise and squealing, after which the male resumes a solitary life. Female tapirs usually produce a single offspring about every 18 months. The young tapirs, are born after a long gestation period of between 390 to 400 days, and have light-colored stripes and spots on a dark reddish-brown background. This protective coloration conceals the young tapirs while they lie motionless on the forest floor as their mothers feed elsewhere. The coloring of the young begins to disappear at about two months and is gone by six months. Young tapirs reach maturity at about two or three years, and can live for up to 30 years.

Tapirs are often hunted for their meat and hide, but the greatest danger they face today is from loss of habitat. The rain forest habitat of all four species is rapidly under attack and the populations of all the species are becoming fragmented. The endangered mountain tapir is now officially protected; its remote mountain forests are rarely supervised.

Further Reading:

Knight, Linsay. *The Sierra Club Book of Small Mammals.* San Francisco: Sierra Club Books for Children, 1993.
Patent, Dorothy Hinshaw. *Horses and Their Wild Relatives.* New York: Holiday House, 1981.

Stidworthy, John. "Mammals: The Large Plant-Eaters." *Encyclopedia of the Animal World.* New York: Facts On File, 1988.

Jean F. Blashfield

Taro see **Arum family**

Tarpons

Tarpons are large silvery fish, measuring 4-8 ft (1.25-2.5 m) in length, with large scales, a compressed body, a forked caudal fin, and a long ray extending from its dorsal fin. The tarpon's mouth is large, containing rows of sharp, fine teeth, and its lower jaw protrudes. The large-eyed tarpon is one of the best known and most impressive of the sport fish. It can live equally well in fresh and salt water.

Taxonomy

Tarpons are the most primitive fish classified among the 30 orders of spiny-rayed fish designated as true bony fish (superorder Teleosti). Tarpons belong to the Order Elopiformes, which is subdivided into two suborders: the Elopoidei and the Albuloidei, which include three families. These are Elopidae (tenpounders, or ladyfish), the Megalopidae (the tarpons), and the Albulidae (bonefishes). The larva (leptocephalus) of fish in the order Elopiformes resembles the larva of eels.

The family Megalopidae include one genus (*Megalops*) and two species of tarpon: the *Megalops cyprinoides* and *Megalops atlanticus*. The *Megalops cyprinoides* lives in the Indo-West Pacific Ocean—from Africa to the Society Islands, while the *Megalops atlanticus* lives in the western Atlantic Ocean—from North Carolina to Brazil, and off the tropical West African shores.

Physical characteristics and distribution

Tarpons are large fish, measuring up to 8 ft (2.5 m) in length and weighing up to 350 lb (159 kg), with dorsal and anal fins having an elongated ray, forming a threadlike projection that trails behind the fish. Tarpons are recognized by their silvery color, forked caudal fin, and underbite caused by an extended jawbone that juts out in front of the upper jaw, giving the fish a turned-down, frowning mouth. Both the upper and lower jaw bones extend well behind the large eyes, and the large

mouth, jaws, the roof of the mouth, and the tongue all have rows of sharp, needlelike teeth.

Tarpons are widely distributed in oceans throughout the world, and are also found in fresh and brackish water. The swim bladder of tarpons has an open connection with the gullet, and is an adaptation for taking in air. Tarpons are often seen swimming in rivers, canals, and mangrove estuaries. In warm months, tarpons swim north, only to return to warmer waters when the weather gets cold.

Megalops atlanticus is found in the Atlantic, from Massachusetts to Brazil, although it is more common in tropical regions. It also lives in the Caribbean, in the Gulf of Mexico, and off the coast of Florida, especially in the Keys. *Megalops cyprinoides* inhabits the Indian and Pacific Oceans.

Development

Tarpons do not mature sexually until they are six or seven years old. A large female tarpon weighing about 140 lb (63.5 kg) may contain over 12 million eggs. Tarpon spawning sites have not been located, and fresh tarpon eggs have not been found. Females probably lay their eggs in shallow seas, or on the ocean floor, starting in the end of June, and continuing throughout July and August.

Tarpon larvae (leptocephali) are transparent and shaped like leaves or ribbons, closely resembling eel larvae. Other than having a forked caudal fin, the larvae do not resemble adult tarpons. The larvae of tarpons can be differentiated from eel larvae because the leptocephali of eels have a rounded tail. Ocean currents carry the tarpon larvae close to shore, to areas such as shallow marshes, swamps, estuaries, and ponds, where they begin their metamorphosis into young tarpons, eating young fish, small crustaceans, and insects.

When tarpons grow large enough to survive without the protection of these habitats, they move out of the lagoons into the open sea. Adult tarpons eat fish and crustaceans; their favorite fish is the grunion-like silverside. Tarpons do not form schools, but they are often found together in bays and canals, since these are the areas where they primarily feed, usually at night. Additionally, groups of tarpons have been seen swimming into schools of small fish and attacking them side by side. The natural enemies of tarpons are sharks and dolphins, and young tarpons have been found in the stomachs of other fish.

Tarpons as game fish

Tarpons are the original big game fish and are well known to fishermen throughout the world. Long before

KEY TERMS

. . . .

Brackish water—Fresh water containing some salt; not as salty as sea water.

Caudal fin—The tarpon's tail fin.

Dorsal fin—The fin located on the tarpon's back.

Dorsal ray—A stout filament extending closely above the tarpon's back, behind its dorsal fin.

Gullet—The throat and esophagus.

Leptocephalus—Mature larva (plural form is *leptocephali*).

Metamorphosis—A marked change in anatomy and behavior resulting from maturing.

fishermen began to catch sailfish, marlin, or tuna for sport, they angled for tarpon. To catch this fish, the angler must be strong, skilled, and have a great deal of endurance.

Fishermen who specialize in catching game fish look for tarpon as far north as Long Island, but they concentrate their efforts in those locations where tarpons are known to live. The best places to catch *Megalops atlanticus* is in the waters surrounding the Florida Keys, off of Florida's west coast, in the Rio Encantado in Cuba, and in the Rio Panuca in Mexico. *Megalops cyprinoides* is also coveted by sports fishermen off the east coast of Africa.

Tarpons are exciting fish to catch because of their fighting tenacity. The instant that the fish is hooked, it hurls itself upward into the air and goes through an astounding series of leaps in an effort to free itself. In fact, this fish can jump as high as 9.75 ft (3 m) and as long as 19.5 ft (6 m). These leaps are so violent that, after a while, the tarpon exhausts itself; at this point, it is brought to the boat.

Tarpons are not often prized as a food fish in North America, because the adults are said to be tough and full of bones. There are exceptions, however. In Mexico, and in South America, the inhabitants eat tarpon salted and smoked. Smaller tarpon are also eaten in Africa. Silver scales of the tarpon are sometimes used to make jewelry.

Further Reading:

Grzimek, H. C. Bernard, ed. *Grzimek's Animal Life Encyclopedia*. New York: Van Nostrand Reinhold, 1993.
La Gorce, John Oliver, ed. *The Book of Fishes*. Washington, DC: National Geographic Society, 1952.
Lythgoe, John, and Gillian Lythgoe. *Fishes of the Sea*. Cambridge, MA: Blandford Press, 1991.
Nelson, Joseph S. *Fishes of the World*. 3rd ed. New York: Wiley, 1994.
Robins, C. Richard, and G. Carlton Ray. *Atlantic Coast Fishes*. Boston: Houghton Mifflin, 1986.
Webb, J. E. *Guide to Living Fishes*. Macmillan, 1991.

Kathryn Snavely

Tarsiers

Tarsiers are prosimians, or primitive primates, in family Tarsiidae, found the islands of Southeast Asia. Tarsiers have only 34 teeth, unlike their closest prosimian relatives, the lemurs and lorises, which have 36 teeth,. Also, the upper lip of tarsiers is not fastened to the gum underneath, so that the face can be mobile, rather like the more advanced primates, monkeys and apes. Tarsiers are the only prosimians with a nose that does not stay moist. A moist nose usually indicates that a mammal depends heavily on its sense of smell.

Tarsiers are often called "living fossils" because they most resemble fossil primates from about 40 million years ago. Thus, instead of being grouped with other prosimians, tarsiers are placed in a separate order, the Tarsioidea.

The head and body of the tarsier measure about 5 in (12.5 cm) in length, and its long, thin, naked tail is an additional 8 or 9 in (20-22 cm). Their average weight is only slightly over 4 oz (114 g). Tarsiers have soft, brown, olive, or buff fur on their head and back, which is a lighter buff or gray below. The tail may have a small puff of fur on the end. Both the second and third toes of the hind feet have toilet claws, which are long claws used for grooming and digging for insects. When grooming, tarsiers make a foot fist, from which these claws protrude.

Locomotion

Moving somewhat like a small, furry frog, a tarsier can leap from small branch to small branch. In order to do this efficiently, the tibia and the fibula (the two lower leg bones) are fused about half-way down their length, giving the leg more strength. Tarsiers also have elongated ankle bones, which helps them leap, and which gives them their name, *tarsier,* a reference to the

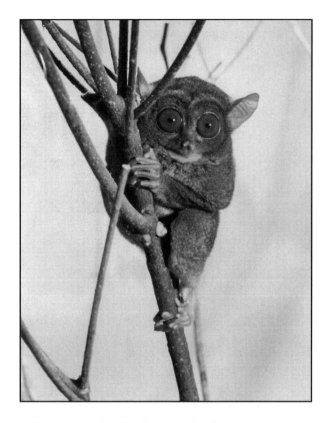

A Mindanao tarsier (*Tarsius syrichta carbonarius*).

KEY TERMS

. . . .

Binocular—Using two eyes set so that their fields of vision overlap, giving the ability to perceive depth.

Dental comb—A formation of lower incisor teeth that have moved close together and horizontally to make a grooming tool.

Diurnal—Active in or related to daytime.

Nocturnal—Active in or related to nighttime.

tarsal, or ankle, region. The legs are much longer than their arms.

These curious little nocturnal creatures dart around the undergrowth and low trees, keeping out the realm of the larger animals until they want to leap across the ground to gather up prey. Tarsiers are carnivorous, eating insects and small lizards. They have fat pads on the tips of their thin fingers and toes that help them cling to trees. These primates probably do not build nests.

Tarsiers have large bulging eyes, which close quickly for protection if large insect prey comes near. The eyes also face forward, providing binocular vision, an aid in catching insects at night. The animals' large ears can also be folded for protection. Their eyes do not move in their head, but they can turn their heads in a full half circle, like an owl. This fact accounts for the belief, recorded in Borneo, that tarsiers have detachable heads. The brain of some tarsier species weighs less than a single eye. Their big ears constantly move, listening for sounds of danger.

Tarsiers form family groups consisting of the male, the female, and their young. Each family stays in its own territory, and fusses loudly if another tarsier enters it. After a 180-day gestation, the female produces a single, fairly mature infant. The offspring rides either under its mother's abdomen or in her mouth. When she is off hunting, she may leave it in a safe place. The young can hunt on its own by the age of one month old, when it is also ready to leap.

There are only three species of tarsier in a single genus, *Tarsius*. All are endangered to some degree, and their ranges do not overlap.

The Mindanao or Philippine tarsier *(T. syrichta)* lives on several Philippine islands, where its forest habitat is being destroyed. The Western, or Horsfield's tarsier, *T. bancanus,* lives on Sumatra, Borneo, Java, and the nearby islands, and has been protected in Indonesia since 1931. The middle finger of its hand is amazingly long, almost as long as its upper arm.

The spectral, eastern, or Sulawesi tarsier *(T. spectrum)*, lives in three areas of Sulawesi (formerly Celebes) and nearby islands. Unlike the other species, the spectral tarsier has scales on a skinny tail, rather like a mouse. There is the possibility that another species, *T. pumilus,* still exists in the mountains of central Celebes.

Over the years, many attempts have been made to domesticate tarsiers. However, without a continuous source of live food, these primates quickly die.

See also Primates.

Further Reading:

Knight, Linsay. *The Sierra Club Book of Small Mammals.* San Francisco: Sierra Club Books for Children, 1993.

Napier, J. R., and P. H. Napier. *The Natural History of the Primates.* Cambridge: MIT Press, 1985.

Napier, Prue. *Monkeys and Apes.* New York: Grosset & Dunlap, 1972.

Peterson, Dale. *The Deluge and the Ark: A Journey into Primate Worlds.* Boston: Houghton-Mifflin, 1989.

Preston-Mafham, Rod, and Ken Preston-Mafham. *Primates of the World.* New York: Facts on File, 1992.

Jean F. Blashfield

Tartaric acid

Tartaric acid is an organic (carbon based) compound of the chemical formula $C_4H_6O_6$, and has the official name 2,3-dihydroxybutanedioic acid. In this name, the *2,3-dihydroxy* refers to the 2 OH groups on the second and third carbon atoms, and the butane portion of the name refers to a four-carbon molecule. The *dioic acid* portion communicates the existence of 2 organic acid (COOH) groups on the molecule. Tartaric acid is found throughout nature, especially in many fruits and in wine. In addition to existing freely, it is also found as a salt (salts are the products of acids and bases), the most common of which are calcium tartrate, potassium tartrate, and sodium tartrate.

Tartaric acid is used making silver mirrors, in the manufacturing of soft drinks, to provide tartness to foods, in tanning leather and in making blueprints. Tartaric acid is used in cream of tartar (for cooking) and as an emetic (a substance used to induce vomiting). It readily dissolves in water and is used in making blueprints. Tartaric acid is a molecule that demonstrates properties of optical activity, where a molecule can cause the rotation of plane-polarized light. Tartaric acid exists in four forms (isomers are molecular rearrangements of the same atoms), each of which affects plane-polarized light differently.

The chemistry of tartaric acid

Tartaric acid is a white solid, possessing two alcohol groups and two acid groups. The second and third carbons of the molecule are asymmetrical (these are called chiral centers). The naturally occurring form of tartaric acid is the L-isomer, which rotates light to the left. The D-form of the acid, which rotates plane-polarized light to the right (the *D* refers to dextro, or right hand direction) is far less common in nature and has almost no practical uses. In general, where biological molecules have optical isomers, only one of the isomers or forms will be active biologically. The other will be unaffected by the enzymes in living cells. The *meso* form of the molecule does not affect polarized light. The figures below show the D, L, and meso forms of tartaric acid. The fourth form—the DL mixture—is not a single molecule, but a mixture of equal amounts of D and L isomers. It does not rotate polarized light either (like the meso form) because the rotation of light by the D and L forms is equal in amount but opposite in direction. It is possible to separate the DL mixture into the two isomers, each of which does rotate light. In the 1840s Louis Pasteur determined that each of the two isomers of tartaric acid rotated light in opposite direc-

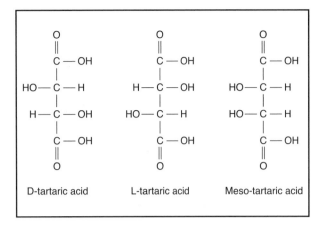

Figure 1. The D, L, and meso forms of tartaric acid.

tions, and the meso form was inactive in this respect. He also separated by hand crystals of the racemic mixture to show that it was made of equal amounts of the D and L forms, making it different than the meso form of tartaric acid.

Uses of tartaric acid

Tartaric acid is found in cream of tartar, which is used in cooking candies and frostings for cakes. Tartaric acid is also found in baking powder, where it serves as the source of acid that reacts with sodium bicarbonate (baking soda). This reaction produces carbon dioxide

---

KEY TERMS

Chiral center—A carbon atom with four different atoms or groups of atoms attached to it (sometimes called an asymmetrical carbon). Chiral centers can cause the rotation of polarized light.

Emetic—A substance used to induce vomiting, usually to remove a poison from the body.

Isomers—Molecules that have the same atoms, but in different arrangements. Isomers based on chiral centers (such as tartaric acid) are sometimes called stereoisomers.

Polarized light—Light in which the waves vibrate in only one plane, as opposed to the normal vibration of light in all planes.

Salts—Compounds that are the products of the reaction of acids and bases. Sodium tartrate is the product of the reaction between sodium hydroxide and tartaric acid.

---

gas, and lets products "rise," but does so without any "yeasty" taste, that can result from using active yeast cultures as a source of the carbon dioxide gas. Tartaric acid is used in silvering mirrors, tanning leather, and in Rochelle Salt, which is sometimes used as a laxative. Blue prints are made with ferric tartarte as the source of the blue ink. In medical analysis, tartaric acid is used to make solutions for the determination of glucose. Common esters of tartaric acid are diethyl tartrate and dibutyl tartrate, which are made by reacting tartaric acid with ethanol and butanol. In this reaction, the H of the COOH acid group is replaced with a CH_3CH_2 (ethyl) group or a butyl group ($CH_3CH_2CH_2CH_2^-$). These esters are used in manufacturing lacquer and in dyeing textiles.

Further Reading:

Hunter, Beatrice. "Technological vs. Biological Needs." *Consumer Research Magazine* (August 1988): 8.

Louis Gotlib

Tartigrades see **Water bears**

Tasmanian devil

The Tasmanian devil (*Sarcophilus harrisii*) is the largest surviving marsupial predator, occurring only on the island of Tasmania in dense thickets and forests. The Tasmanian devil is one of about 45 species of marsupial predators that make up the family Dasyuridae.

The Tasmanian devil once occurred widely in Australia and Tasmania. However, the Tasmanian devil became extirpated from Australia following the prehistoric introduction of the dingo (*Canis dingo*; this is a placental, wild dog) by aboriginal people, and the species is now confined to the island of Tasmania.

Male Tasmanian devils can attain a body length of 32 in (80 cm) and a tail of 12 in (30 cm), and can weigh more than 20 lbs (9 kg). Their pelage is colored dark brown or black, with several white spots on the rump and sides and a pinkish snout. The body is stout and badgerlike, and the jaws and teeth are strong.

As is the case with all marsupials, young Tasmanian devils are born in an early stage of embryonic development. The tiny babies crawl slowly to a belly pouch (or marsupium) on their mother, where they suckle until they are almost fully grown and ready for an independent life.

Tasmanian devils sleep in a den during the day, located in a hollow log, cave, or another cavity. This species is a fierce, nocturnal predator of smaller animals, and a scavenger of dead bodies, filling a niche similar to those of placental carnivores such as foxes, cats, badgers, and wild dogs. Tasmanian devils feed on a wide range of species, including domestic chickens and sheep.

Sometimes, individual Tasmanian devils will invade a chicken coop and create havoc there. Unfortunately, this and sheep-killing often turn out badly for the Tasmanian devil in the end. Because many people consider the Tasmanian devil a pest, this extraordinary and uncommon animal is still persecuted over much of its remaining native range. This is highly unfortunate, because the Tasmanian devil is the last of the large marsupial predators, and it is essential that this species survives the human onslaught on its habitat.

See also Marsupials.

Bill Freedman

Taste

Taste is one of the five senses (the others being smell, touch, vision, and hearing) through which all animals interpret the world around them. Specifically, taste is the sense for determining the flavor of food and other substances. One of the two chemical senses (the other being smell), taste is stimulated through the contact of certain chemicals in substances with clusters of taste bud cells found primarily on the tongue. However, taste is a complex sensing mechanism that is also influenced by the smell and texture of substances. An individual's unique sense of taste is partially inherited, but factors such as culture and familiarity can help determine why one person's favorite food made be hot and spicy while another just can't get enough chocolate.

The biology of taste

The primary organ for tasting is the mouth. Clusters of cells called taste buds (because under the microscope they look similar to plant buds) cover the tongue and are also found to a lesser extent on the cheek, throat, and the roof of the mouth. First discovered in the 19th century by German scientists Georg Meissner and Rudolf Wagner, taste buds lie on the elevated or ridged surface of the

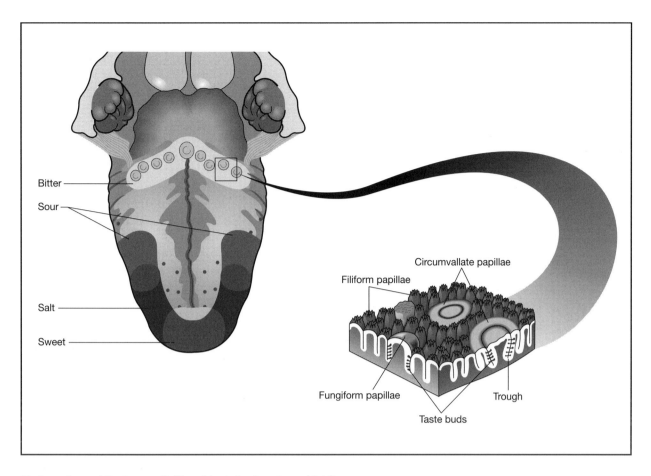

Taste regions of the tongue (left) and taste bud anatomy (right).

tongue (called the papillae) and have hairlike extensions (microvilli) to increase the receptor surface of the cells. For most foods and substances, saliva breaks down the chemical components which travel through the pores in the papillae to reach the taste buds which specialize primarily in processing one of the four major taste groups: sweet, sour, salty, and bitter.

Taste occurs when specific proteins in the food bind to receptors on the taste buds. These receptors, in turn, send messages to the brain's cerebral cortex, which interprets the flavor. The actual chemical processes involved for each major taste group vary. For example, salty and sour flavors occur when saliva breaks down sodium or acids, respectively. The chemical constituents of foods that give bitter and sweet tastes, however, are much harder to specify because many chemical components are involved.

Although certain taste buds seemed to have an affinity for one of the four major flavors, continued research into this intricate biological process has revealed a complex neural and chemical network that precludes simple black and white explanations. For

example, each taste bud actually has receptors for sweet, sour, salty, and bitter sensations, indicating that taste buds are sensitive to a complex flavor spectrum just like vision is sensitive to a broad color spectrum grouped into the four major colors of red, orange, yellow, and green. Particular proteins of taste are also under study, like gustducin, which may set off the plethora of chemical reactions that causes something to taste bitter.

Taste buds for all four taste groups can be found throughout the mouth, but specific kinds of buds are clustered together in certain areas. Think about licking an ice cream cone; taste buds for sweetness are grouped on the tip of our tongue. The buds for sour tastes are on the sides of the tongue and salty on the front. Bitter taste buds on the back of the tongue can make people gag, a natural defense mechanism to help prevent poisoning.

People constantly regenerate new taste buds every 3-10 days to replace the ones worn out by scalding soup, frozen yogurt and the like. Unfortunately, as people grow older, their taste buds lose their fine tuning because they are replaced at a slower rate. As a result, middle-aged and older people require more of a substance to produce the same sensations of sweetness or spiciness, for example, than would be needed by a child eating the same food.

Scientists have also discovered that genetic makeup partially accounts for individual tasting abilities and preferences for specific foods. According to researchers at Yale University, some people are genetically programmed to have more taste buds and, as a result, taste more flavors in a particular food. (The number of taste buds varies in different animal species. For example cows have 25,000 taste buds, rabbits 17,000, and adult people approximately 10,000.)

In general, a person's ability to taste can lie anywhere in a spectrum from poor to exceptional, with the ability to sense tastes increasing in proportion to the number of taste buds present. The difference in the number of taste buds can be extreme. Researchers have found anywhere from 11 to 1,100 taste buds per square inch in various young people tested. They have also found that women tend to have more taste buds than men and, as a result, are often better tasters. How well people taste greatly affects what they like. Studies at Yale, for example, revealed that children with fewer taste buds who are classified as poor tasters liked cheese more often than exceptional tasters, who experienced a more bitter sensation, probably because of increased sensitivity to the combination of calcium and the milk protein casein found in cheese.

Despite the important role that taste buds play in recognizing flavors, they do not work alone in providing the experience of taste. For example, the amount of naturally occurring salt in saliva varies; the result being that those with less saliva can better taste the saltiness of certain foods than others, who may end up adding salt to get a similar flavor. The smell and texture of foods are also important contributing factors to how people perceive a food to taste and whether or not they like it. Food in the mouth produces an odor that reaches the nose through the nasopharynx (the opening that links the mouth and the nose). Since smell is much more sensitive to odors than taste is to flavors, people often first experience the flavor of a food by its odor. A cold or flu is probably the most common example of how important smell is to taste. People with congestion often experience a diminished ability to taste. The taste buds, however, are working fine; it's the lack of smell that hinders the brain's ability to process flavor. The texture and temperature of food also influences how it tastes. For example, many people would not think of drinking cold coffee, while others will not eat pears because of a dislike for the fruit's gritty texture.

The predilection for certain foods and tastes is not determined merely by biology. Culture and familiarity with foods greatly influence taste preferences. The Japanese have long considered raw fish, or sushi, to be a savory delicacy. But only a decade or so ago, few Americans would have enjoyed such a repast. But as the number of Japanese restaurants with sushi bars grew, so did American's familiarity with this delicacy and, as a result, their taste for it.

Taste disorders

The inability to taste is so intricately linked with smell that it is often difficult to tell whether the problem lies in tasting or smelling. An estimated two to four million people in the United States suffer from some sort of taste or smell disorder. The inability to taste or smell not only robs an individual of certain sensory pleasures, it can also be dangerous. Without smell or taste, for example, people cannot determine whether food is spoiled, making them vulnerable to food poisoning. Also, some psychiatrists believe that the lack of taste and smell can have a profoundly negative affect on a person's quality of life, leading to depression or other psychological problems.

There are a variety of causes for taste and smell disorders, from a biological breakdown to the effects of environmental toxins. In addition to cold or flu, common physical ailments that can assault the sense of taste and smell include allergies and various viral or bacterial infections that produce swollen mucous membranes. Fortunately, most of these problems are temporary and treatable. However, neurological disorders due to brain injury or diseases like Parkinson's or Alzheimer's can cause more permanent damage to the intricate neural network that processes the sense of taste and smell. Some drugs can also cause these disorders by inhibiting certain enzymes, affecting the body's metabolism, and interfering with the neural network and receptors needed to taste and smell. Exposure to environmental toxins like lead, mercury, insecticides, and solvents can also wreak havoc on the ability to smell and taste by causing damage to taste buds & sensory cells in the nose or brain.

See also Perception.

Further Reading:

Ackerman, Diane. *A Natural History of the Senses*. New York: Vintage Books, 1991.

Lewis, Ricki. "When Smell and Taste Go Awry." *FDA Consumer*, (November 1991): 29-33.

Rivlin, Robert and Gravelle, Karen. *Deciphering the Senses. The Expanding World of Human Perception*. New York: Simon and Schuster, 1984.

KEY TERMS

. . . .

Casein—The primary protein found in cow's milk and a major component of cheese.

Cerebral Cortex—The external gray matter surrounding the brain and made up of layers of nerve cells and fibers. Thought to process sensory information and impulses.

Microvilli—Hair- or fingerlike projections found on cell membranes which increase surface area to better receive outside stimuli.

Papillae—Nipple-like projections found on tissue which constitute the ridge-like surfaces on the tongue.

Protein—Macromolecules that constitute three-fourths of cell matter's dry weight and which play an important role in a number of life functions, such as sensory interpretation, muscle contraction, and immunological response.

Taste buds—Cells found primarily on the tongue that are the primary biological components for interpreting the flavor of foods and other substances.

Tyler, Aubin. "Disorders That Rob You of Taste & Smell." *Good Housekeeping*, (October 1992): 257-258.
Willoughby, John. "Taste? Bud to Bud, Tongues May Differ." *New York Times* (December 7, 1994): C1, C11.

David Petechuk

Taxonomy

Taxonomy is the field of biology which deals with the nomenclature, identification, and classification of organisms. There are over one million known species on the Earth and probably several million more which have not yet been identified. Taxonomists are responsible for identifying, naming, and classifying all these different species. Systematics is a discipline of biology which explicitly examines the natural variation and relationships of organisms, and which includes the field of taxonomy. Systematics also deals with the relationships of different groups of organisms, as most systematicists strive to construct natural classification systems which reflect evolutionary relationships. Many biologists use the terms taxonomy and systematics interchangeably.

Definition of species

Clearly, taxonomists need to agree on a definition of the concept of *species* before they can identify, name, and classify organisms.

The definition of *species* is not as simple as it may seem, and has been debated by biologists and philosophers alike for many years.

Most modern biologists agree that species, unlike higher taxa (genus, family, order, and so on), are authentic taxonomic units. In other words, species really do exist in nature, and are not merely artificial human constructs. Some of the most persuasive evidence in support of this is the close correspondence between the species identified by western taxonomists and those identified in the "folk taxonomy" of relatively isolated non-western societies. For example, Ernst Mayr, a noted bird taxonomist, identified 137 species of birds in his field work in the mountains of New Guinea; the folk taxonomy of the native New Guineans identifies 136 species. Similar correlations occur with plants. For example, an extensive interdisciplinary study of the native people and plants of the Chiapas highlands of Mexico showed a very close correspondence between species identified by western botanists and those identified by Chiapas natives.

Many modern biologists, particularly zoologists, define species according to the "biological species concept," a definition which has been forcibly advocated by Ernst Mayr. According to this definition, a species is a group of organisms which are reproductively isolated from other organisms. In other words, a species is a group of organisms which interbreed and produce fertile offspring only with one another.

Some microbiologists and botanists are dissatisfied with the biological species concept. Microbiologists have noted that single-celled organisms do not reproduce sexually in nature (although they may undergo genetic recombination), yet they can still be segregated into discrete natural groups which can be considered species. Botanists have noted that many species of related plants can hybridize with one another in nature. For example, the different species in the sub-genus *Leucobalanus* (white oak) can hybridize and produce fertile offspring. Thus, rigorous application of the biological species concept would require that all of these separate species of oak be considered a single species, even though they have very different morphologies.

Most biologists basically accept the biological species concept, but argue that it is really an idealized concept, since only rarely is an actual test for reproductive compatibility performed. Thus, in practice, nearly all biologists think of species as morphologically distinct groups of organisms.

Nomenclature

Nomenclature (from the Latin term *nomenclatura*, indicating the procedure of assigning names) is the naming of organisms. For many centuries, naturalists used Latinized names to refer to different species of plants and animals in their scientific writings. Following the lead of the Swedish naturalist Carl von Linné (1707-1778) (Linneaus) in the mid-1700s, scientists began using a binomial (two word) Latinized name for all species. The first word is the genus name and the second word is the specific epithet, also called the trivial name.

Modern taxonomists have devised formal rules of nomenclature so that scientists throughout the world can more easily communicate with one another. For example, biologists use the term *acer* to refer to a genus of trees commonly called *maple* in England and America, *érable* in France, *acre* in Spain, and *Ahorn* in Germany. The rules of nomenclature in botany and zoology were established by different governing bodies, and are very similar, though not identical. In both systems the genus, species, and subspecies are italicized.

In the modern scientific literature, the complete name for a species has three parts: the genus, a name which is usually Latinized, is written in italics, and begins with a capital letter; the specific epithet, a name which is usually Latinized, is written in italics, but begins with a small letter; and the author, the name of the person who gave the organism its Latinized name, which is capitalized and written in normal typeface. For example, the sugar maple is named *Acer saccharinum* L., where *Acer* is the genus, *saccharinum* is the specific epithet, and *L.* stands for Linneaus, who first named the species.

If subsequent studies indicate that a plant species should be transferred to a new genus, the original author's name is given in parenthesis and this is followed by the name of the botanist who changed the name. For example, a shrub known as *inkberry* is named *Ilex glabra* (L.) Gray, indicating that Linneaus first named this plant, but Gray gave it its current name. For animals, the convention is different, in that a renamed species only lists the first author's name, but places it in parentheses. For example, the red squirrel is named *Tamiasciurus hudsonicus* (Banks), indicating that a biologist named Banks was the original author, but someone else gave it its current name. The year of publication of the original description of the species is often included with the name of the original describer.

In addition to being given a genus name, specific epithet, and author and year of publication, all species are assigned broader taxonomic categories. Thus, related genera are placed in the same family; related families are placed in the same order; related orders are placed in the same class; related classes are placed in the same phylum (botanists prefer the term *division* over *phylum*); and related phyla are placed in the same kingdom. Occasionally, additional groups are added to this classification scheme, such as subphylum, subclass, or suborder.

For example, human beings (*Homo sapiens* L.) are placed into the following taxonomic categories:

Kingdom—Animalia Phylum—Chordata Subphylum—Vertebrata Class—Mammalia Order—Primata Family—Hominoidea Genus—*Homo* Species—*Homo sapiens* L.

Identification

Taxonomic identification is the recognition of the identity or essential character of an organism. Taxonomists often present organized written descriptions of the characteristics of similar species so that other biologists can identify unknown organisms. These organized descriptions are referred to as taxonomic keys. A taxonomic key is often published with pictures of the species it describes. However, written descriptions are usually preferred over pictures, since pictures cannot convey the natural variation in the morphology of a species, nor the small, yet characteristic, morphological features of a species. In addition, matching an unidentified organism to one picture in a book of hundreds or thousands of pictures can be very time-consuming.

The dichotomous key is the best and most-used format for taxonomic keys. A dichotomous key sequentially presents pairs of alternative morphological features (dichotomies) and requires the user to decide which alternative best describes the unknown organism. A very simple hypothetical key for identifying four species of flowering plants illustrates the dichotomous key:

a. Flowers white; stem woody b. Sepals present; bark deep-furrowed—species A bb. Sepals absent; bark not deep-furrowed—species B aa.Flowers not white; stem herbaceous c. Flowers blue; flowers with five petals—species C cc. Flowers red; flowers with three petals—species D

The first dichotomy asks the user to choose between *a* and *aa*. If alternative *a* is chosen, the user must choose between *b* and *bb*. If alternative *aa* is chosen, the user must choose between *c* and *cc*.

Taxonomic keys often require knowledge of the morphology of the taxa in question and consequently rely upon technical terminology. In the above example, it is assumed the user knows that sepals constitute the leaf-like, outermost whorl of a flower.

Interestingly, taxonomic keys often use the sexual organs of animals (genitalia), plants (flowers, fruits, and cones), and fungi (sporebearing structures), because these differ significantly among closely related species. This indicates that sexual organs of animals, plants, and fungi tend to evolve rapidly and divergently, presumably because they are subjected to great evolutionary selection pressures. Differences in reproductive structures also indicate that mating may not be successful, and that two organisms may be reproductively isolated—that is, different species.

Classification

Taxonomic classification is the grouping together of different organisms into different taxa (taxonomic categories), such as family, genus, and species. In the time of Linneaus (mid-1700s), taxonomists and naturalists did not generally acknowledge that all species have evolutionary affinities to other species. Thus, early classification systems were artificial, in that they did not represent the lines of evolutionary descent. Most early taxonomists classified species according to their overall similarity because they thought this revealed the divine origin of nature.

Evolution and classification

The theory of organic evolution, developed by Charles Darwin in the mid-1800s, revolutionized taxonomy. In the *Origin of Species*, Darwin proposed that "community of descent—the one known cause of close similarity in organic beings" be used as the basis for taxonomic classification systems. Ever since Darwin, taxonomists have tried to represent phylogeny (lines of evolutionary descent) in their classification systems. Thus, modern taxonomists who study plants or animals do not merely name and catalog species, they also try to construct evolutionary trees showing the relationships of different species.

The early evolutionary taxonomists relied on morphological features to classify organisms. Many early animal taxonomists found similarities in the embryos of related organisms and proposed that these similarities indicate evolutionary affinities. For example, early in development, all animals exist as a ball of cells, referred to as a blastula. The blastula of higher animals, called the coelomates, forms an invagination, called a blastopore, which later develops into the digestive cav-

ity. Early taxonomists further divided coelomate animals into two large taxonomic groups, the proterostomes, in which the blastopore opening develops into the mouth, and the deuterostomes, in which the blastopore opening develops into the anus. In contrast to the coelomates, the blastula of lower animals does not form a blastopore and these animals are called the acoelomates. When acoelomate animals are fully grown, they lack true digestive systems.

Thus, the early evolutionary taxonomists concluded that humans are more closely related to segmented worms than to flatworms, since humans and segmented worms both have coelomate embryos, whereas flat worms have an acoelomate embryo. In addition, humans are more closely related to sea urchins than to segmented worms, since humans and sea urchins are both coelomate deuterostomes whereas round worms are coelomate proterostomes.

Modern trends

Modern biologists accept many of the conclusions of the early evolutionary taxonomists, such as the relationships of the major animal phyla, as determined by the comparative morphology of their embryos. However, these early classification systems all had a weakness in that they were based, at least in part, on the intuition of taxonomists. Thus, all early classification systems had a strong element of subjectivity.

In the 1950s, R. R. Sokal and P. H. A. Sneath advocated the use of *numerical taxonomy* to remove the subjectivity of classification. In their method, all relevant characters (morphological features) of a group of organisms are numerically coded and the overall similarity is calculated by use of a mathematical algorithm. Initially, many traditional taxonomists rejected numerical taxonomy, since its results sometimes contradicted their own decade-long studies of comparative morphology. However, nearly all modern taxonomists currently use numerical methods in taxonomy, although there is often very contentious debate about which particular algorithms should be used.

In recent years, advances in molecular biology have had a profound impact on the field of taxonomy. In particular, biologists can now clone and sequence the DNA (deoxyribonucleic acid) in the genes of many different organisms and compare these DNA sequences to estimate relationships and construct classification systems. The use of such molecular data in taxonomy has several advantages. First, classification schemes for groups such as the fungi, whose phylogeny has long confounded the many taxonomists who rely upon more traditional morphological characters, can now be determined more easily. Second, organisms typically have many thousands of different genes, so there is a potential data base of characters which is virtually unlimited in size. Third, since changes in DNA form the basis for all other evolutionary changes, such as changes in morphology, comparison of gene sequences allows study of evolution at its most basal level. Comparative studies of morphology will continue to play an important role in taxonomy, but gene sequences are becoming more widely used as gene sequencing becomes easier.

Methods of classification

Most modern taxonomists agree that classification systems should reflect evolutionary relationships. Thus, they agree that one should distinguish between homologous features and analogous features in constructing a classification system.

Homologous features have a common evolutionary origin, although they may differ in superficial morphology. For example, the arms of a human, fins of a whale, and front legs of a dog are all homologous. The underlying skeletal system of these appendages is similar and these three species had a common mammalian ancestor which had appendages with similar skeletal structure.

Analogous features are superficially similar, but the similarity is not a result of common evolutionary origin. For example, the wings of a bird, bat, and butterfly are all analogous. Although they all have a similar superficial morphology and function, their underlying structure is very different. In other words, birds, bats, and butterflies did not share a common ancestor which had wings with a common design. The wings of birds, bats, and butterflies are similar merely because the laws of physics places certain restrictions on the shape of an appendage which can support flight.

Although taxonomists agree on the distinction between analogous and homologous features, they sometimes disagree about which specific method should be used to classify species. The three most commonly used methods are phenetics, cladistics, and evolutionary taxonomy. Some taxonomists use a combination of several of these different methods.

Phenetics

Phenetics, also known as numerical taxonomy, was proposed by Sokal and Sneath in the 1950s. Although very few modern taxonomists currently use phenetics, Sokal and Sneath's methods clearly revolutionized taxonomy by introducing computer-based numerical algorithms, now an essential tool of all modern taxonomists.

Phenetics classifies organisms based on their overall similarity. First, many different characteristics of a group of organisms are measured. These measurements are then used to calculate similarity coefficients between all pairs of organisms. The similarity coefficient is a number between 0 and 1, where 1 indicates absolute identity, and 0 indicates absolute dissimilarity. Finally, the similarity coefficients are used to develop a classification system.

Critics of phenetic classification have argued that it tends to classify unrelated organisms together, because it is based on an overall morphological similarity, and does not distinguish between analogous and homologous features. Pheneticists have responded that they ignore the distinction between analogous and homologous features because analogous features are usually numerically overwhelmed by the larger number of homologous features. Most evolutionary biologists would consider this response questionable, at best.

Cladistics

Cladistics is a method which classifies organisms based on the order in which different evolutionary lines branch off from one another. It was first proposed in the 1950s by Willi Hennig, a German entomologist. Subsequently, many other scientists have made Hennig's original method more practicable by developing various cladistic numerical algorithms, some of which are very sophisticated. Cladistics is currently the most widely used method of classification.

One might reasonably ask: how can cladistics possibly determine the branching points of different evolutionary lines, given that we never have a complete fossil record and often have only living species for constructing a classification system? The answer is that cladistics relies upon the fact that all new species evolve by descent with modification. In other words, cladistics determines the evolutionary branching order on the basis of shared derived characteristics. It does not use shared primitive characteristics as a basis for classification, since these may be lost or modified through the course of evolution. To establish which characters are primitive and which are derived, cladistic classification generally relies upon one or more outgroups, species hypothesized to be primitive ancestors of all the organisms under study.

An example illustrates the distinction between shared derived and shared primitive characteristics in cladistic classification. The common mammalian ancestor of humans, cats, and seals had five digits on each hand and foot. Thus, the presence of five digits is a shared primitive characteristic and cladistics does not segregate humans and cats, which have five digits on their hands and feet, from seals, which have flippers instead of distinct digits. Instead, cladistics classifies seals and cats in the order Carnivora, based on certain shared derived characteristics of the Carnivora, and humans in the order Primata, based on other derived characteristics of the Primates.

It is important to note that a cladistic classification is not based on the amount of evolutionary change after the branching off of an evolutionary line. For example, although chimps and orangutans appear more similar to one another then either does to humans, cladistic classification places humans and chimps together since they share a more recent common ancestor than chimps and orangutans. Such a classification may seem counterintuitive; however, cladistic taxonomists would argue that such classifications should be considered the starting point for subsequent comparative studies. Such comparative studies might seek to discover why human morphology evolved so rapidly, relative to that of chimps and orangutans.

Some botanists have noted a limitation of cladistics, in that it does not recognize the role of interspecific hybridization in the evolution of new species. In interspecific hybridization, two different species mate and produce offspring which constitute a new species. Certain derived features of the parent species revert to primitive features in the new hybrid species. Hybrid species appear to be more common among plants than animals, but taxonomists who study any group of organisms clearly need to account for the possibility of interspecific hybridization in the evolution of new species.

W. H. Wagner, a noted plant taxonomist, has shown that interspecific hybridization has had a particularly important role in the evolution of ferns. He has advocated the development of a new methodology, which he calls *reticulistics*, to account for the evolution of hybrid species. In reticulate phylogeny, one evolutionary line can split to form two new species or two evolutionary lines can join together to form one new species. Unfortunately, there are not yet any numerical algorithms which can be used to reconstruct a reticulate phylogeny.

Evolutionary taxonomy

Evolutionary taxonomy can be considered to be a mixture of phenetics and cladistics. It classifies organisms partly according to their evolutionary branching pattern and partly according to the overall morphological similarity. Evolutionary taxonomy is basically the method used by the early evolutionary taxonomists and is also called classical taxonomy.

The major limitation of evolutionary taxonomy is that it requires a highly arbitrary judgment about how much information about overall similarity to use and

how much information about branching pattern to use. This judgment is always highly subjective, and makes evolutionary taxonomy a very poor method of classification, albeit one which survives in the hands of certain older taxonomists.

The kingdoms of organisms

In the past, biologists classified all organisms into the plant kingdom or animal kingdom. Fungi were placed into the plant kingdom and single-celled organisms were rather arbitrarily placed into one kingdom or the other. Very few biologists currently use this simple two kingdom system. In recent years, biologists have proposed a great variety of classification systems, based on as many as 13 separate kingdoms of organisms. The five kingdom system, based on proposals by ecologist Robert Whittaker in 1959 and 1969, is currently used as a framework for discussing the diversity of life in most modern biology textbooks.

Five kingdom system

According to a recent modification of the five kingdom system by L. Margulis and K. V. Schwartz, all organisms are classified into one of five kingdoms: Monera, single-celled prokaryotes (bacteria); Protoctista, single-celled eukaryotes (algae, water molds and various other protozoans); Fungi, multicellular eukaryotic organisms which decompose organic matter (molds, lichens, and mushrooms); Plantae, multicellular eukaryotic photosynthetic organisms (seed plants, mosses, ferns, and fern allies); and Animalia, multicellular eukaryotic organisms which eat other organisms (animals).

Clearly, the five kingdom system does not segregate organisms according to their evolutionary ancestry. The Monera and Protoctista are single-celled organisms only distinguished by their intracellular organization. The Animalia, Fungi, and Plantae are distinguished by their mode of nutrition, an ecological, not a phylogenetic, characteristic. Plants are considered producers, in that they use photosynthesis to make complex organic molecules from simple precursors and sunlight. Fungi are considered decomposers, in that they break down the dead cells of other organisms. Animals are considered consumers, in that they primarily eat other organisms, such as plants, fungi, or other animals.

Alternative systems

Many cladistic taxonomists have criticized Whittaker s five kingdom classification system because it is not based on the branching pattern of evolutionary lineages. Cladistic classification systems seek to place organisms into monophyletic taxa. A monophyletic taxon is one which includes all species descended from a single common ancestor. For example, since biologists believe that different groups of multicellular animals evolved from different single-celled eukaryotic ancestors, the kingdom Animalia is clearly not a monophyletic group.

Several cladistic taxonomists advocate a classification system which groups all organisms into three apparently monophyletic kingdoms, the Eukaryota, Eubacteria, and Archaebacteria (alternatively called Eukarya, Bacteria, and Archaea). The Eukaryota kingdom include eukaryotic organisms, and all organisms in the Plantae, Animalia, Fungi, and Protoctista kingdoms. The kingdoms Eubacteria and Archaebacteria both consist of single-celled prokaryotes, all of which Whittaker placed into the Monera kingdom. The Archaebacteria (*ancient bacteria*) were originally considered more primitive than the Eubacteria. The Archaebacteria includes the methanogens (methane-producing bacteria), halophiles (salt-loving bacteria), and thermophiles (heat-loving bacteria), all rather unusual prokaryotes which live in very unusual habitats.

Many cladistic taxonomists are currently studying the relationships of the Eubacteria, Archaebacteria, and Eukaryota, and have proposed different classification schemes based on comparisons of different gene sequences of these organisms. Ironically, although Archaebacteria acquired their name because they were considered primitive to Eubacteria, many taxonomists now believe that Archaebacteria are in fact more modern and more closely related to the Eukaryota than are the Eubacteria. Some taxonomists have proposed a fourth kingdom called the Eocytes, a group of hyperthermophilic bacteria which other biologists include within the Archaebacteria. One of the most intriguing recent studies found that Eukaryota have some genes which are most like those in Archaebacteria and other genes which are most like those in Eubacteria. This suggests that the Eukaryota may have evolved as a chimera of some primitive Eubacterium and Archaebacterium.

Taxonomists who are intrigued by this controversy are encouraged in knowing that there are many undiscovered species of bacteria, perhaps millions, and that only a very small portion of Eubacterial, Archaebacterial, and Eukaryotal DNA sequences have been studied to date.

See also Adaptation; Evolution; Phylogeny; Species.

Further Reading:

Gould, S. J. *The Pandas Thumb*. New York, W.W. Norton, 1980.

Lewis, R. "A New Place for Fungi?" *Bioscience* 44 (1994): 389-391.

KEY TERMS

Algorithm—Method for solving a numerical problem which consists of a series of mathematical steps.

Analogous features—Characteristics of organisms which are superficially similar, but have different evolutionary origins.

Chimera—Organism or part of an organism which consists of two or more genetically distinct types of cells.

Eukaryote—Cell whose DNA occurs within a nucleus, considered more advanced than a prokaryote.

Homologous Features—Characteristics of organisms which have a common evolutionary origin, but are not necessarily similar in form.

Monophyletic—Group which includes all species or other taxa which have descended from a single common ancestor.

Outgroup—Primitive ancestor of all organisms being classified by cladistics, used so that primitive and derived characteristics can be identified.

Phylogeny—Evolutionary history or lineage of an organism or group of related organisms.

Prokaryote—Cell without a nucleus, considered more primitive than a eukaryote.

Taxon (plural, *taxa*)—Taxonomic group, such as species, genus, or family.

Taxonomic Key—Descriptions of the characteristics of species or other taxa organized in a manner to assist in identification of unknown organisms.

Luria, S. E., S. J. Gould, and S. Singer. *A View of Life*. Redwood City, CA: Benjamin-Cummings, 1989.

Margulis, L., and K. V. Schwartz. *Five Kingdoms*. New York: W.H. Freeman, 1988.

Mayr, E. *Principles of Animal Taxonomy*. New York: Columbia University Press.

Peter A. Ensminger

Tay-Sachs disease

Tay-Sachs disease is a genetic disorder that causes progressive neurological degeneration. Although the disease primarily affects infants, juvenile and adult forms of Tay-Sachs disease also exist. Tay-Sachs disease is incurable, and infants with the disease usually die by age 4. The defective genes responsible for Tay-Sachs disease are especially prevalent in Jews of Eastern European descent, but non-Jewish cases of Tay-Sachs have also been identified. Genetic screening can be performed on persons whose ethnic descent or family history place them at high risk for carrying the defective genes.

Tay-Sachs disease is named for two researcher who first noticed the characteristic symptoms in the 1880s. Tay, an opthamologist, noted the typical eye disorders that occur late in the disease in several infants of Jewish descent. Sachs, a neurologist, identified the neurological disturbances in infants with the disease. By the 1940s, researchers noted that the disease occurred primarily in Jews, and also uncovered the physiological basis of the disease: a deadly accumulation of fatty acids in the brain that destroys nerve cells. In the 1960s, researchers discovered that decreased levels of an important enzyme caused the ganglioside accumulation in the brain. By the 1970s, screenings were conducted for carriers of the defective gene, and in 1989, the actual genes responsible for Tay-Sachs were discovered.

Genetic basis and physiological cause of Tay-Sachs disease

Tay-Sachs disease has been traced to a defect in the HEXA gene, the gene that encodes an enzyme called hexosaminidase A. Enzymes are proteins that break down substances in the body. Hexosaminidase A breaks down a group of fatty acids called the GM_1 gangliosides. In Tay-Sachs disease, however, the defective HEXA genes do not function correctly, leading to low levels of hexosaminidase A. Without proper amounts of this enzyme, gangliosides accumulate in the brain and destroy nerve cells.

Tay-Sachs is a homozygous recessive genetic disorder. In homozygous recessive genetic disorders, two defective alleles, or copies, of the gene, one from each parent, must combine to produce the defective gene. If two people who each carry a defective allele have a child, chances are one in four that the child will have Tay-Sachs disease.

The defective Tay-Sachs allele is prevalent in Jews of Eastern European descent. About 1 in 27 people of this descent are thought to be carriers, and about 1 in 3600 Jewish infants are born with this disease, accounting for approximately 90% of all Tay-Sachs cases world-wide. Among non-Jews, about one in 300 people are carriers of the defective allele. Carriers do not have

symptoms of Tay-Sachs, although their levels of the hexosaminidase A enzyme may be reduced as much as 50%. This reduction, however, is not sufficient to produce symptoms.

Symptoms of Tay-Sachs disease

Infants born with Tay-Sachs disease typically have pink, translucent skin and doll-like features. Starting at age 3 to 6 months, feeding difficulties and listlessness develop. Infants have an exaggerated startle reflex, flexing the legs sharply upward at the sound of a muffled noise. As the disease progresses, movements weaken, a hallmark of the destruction of the nerve cells in the brain. In addition, red spots develop on the retina, the portion of the eye that contains the light-sensitive cells necessary for vision. Late stages of the disease are characterized by deafness, blindness, convulsions, and seizures. The head may also enlarge. Death by pneumonia usually occurs between the ages of 2 to 4 years.

In the adult form of Tay-Sachs, the symptoms do not appear until age 30 or 40. Like the infantile form, the adult form of Tay-Sachs is characterized by progressive neurological degeneration, including seizures and psychosis. Also like the infantile form, no cure for this form of Tay-Sachs exists.

Prevention

Since no cure exists for Tay-Sachs disease, efforts to identify genetic carriers are essential in controlling the disease. Carriers are at risk for having children with Tay-Sachs if they have children with another carrier. In 1969, a nationwide screening program was initiated in the United States. With the help of religious and community leaders, screenings for low levels of the hexosaminidase A enzyme (a sign of carrier status) were conducted in synagogues, community centers, and on college campuses. Carriers were told their status and informed of their options. The results of this screening and educational program were extraordinarily successful. In 1970, the number of children born in the United States with Tay-Sachs disease dropped from 100 to 50; in 1980, the number dropped even further, to 13. Many carriers identified in this screening program opted not to have children. However, carriers could also reduce their risk of having children with the disease if they made sure their potential partners were also tested for carrier status.

A newer, better screening test is now available. Instead of testing for hexosaminidase A enzyme deficiency, the accuracy of which is sometimes affected by pregnancy and other factors, researchers now use a

KEY TERMS
. . . .

Allele—One of two or more copies of a gene.

Enzyme—Proteins that perform various functions in the body, including the break-down of certain substances.

Fatty acid—A component of lipids, or fats.

Ganglioside—A fatty acid that accumulates in the brains of people with Tay-Sachs disease, destroying nerve cells.

Hexoaminidase A—Enzyme that breaks down gangliosides.

Homozygous recessive genetic disorder—Genetic disorder caused by the presence of two defective alleles.

Mutation—A change in a gene.

Retina—The portion of the eye that contains light sensitive cells necessary for vision.

Further Reading:

Kabak, Michael, et. al. "Tay-Sachs disease: carrier screening, prenatal diagnosis, and the molecular era: an international perspective, 1970-1993." *Journal of the American Medical Association* 270 (19): 2307-16, November 17, 1993.

Navon, Ruth and Proia, Richard L. "The mutations in Ashkenazi Jews with adult GM2 gangliosidosis, the adult form of Tay-Sachs disease." *Science* 243 (4897): 1471-5, March 17, 1989.

Roberts, Leslie. "One worked; the other didn't." *Science* 247: (4938): 18, January 5, 1990.

Triggs-Raine, Barbara L., et. al. "Screening for carriers of Tay-Sachs disease among Ashkenazi Jews: a comparison of DNA-based and enzyme-based tests." *New England Journal of Medicine* 323 (1): 6-13, July 5, 1990.

Kathleen Scogna

T cells see **Immune system; Lymphatic system**

Teak see **Verbena family**

Teals see **Ducks**

genetic test that searches for evidence of the defective gene in a blood sample. In 1989, researchers identified three genetic changes, or mutations, responsible for Tay-Sachs disease. Two of these mutations cause the infantile form of the disease. By testing for the existence of these mutations in a person's blood, carriers are more accurately identified. The test is more specific than the enzyme test and is also easier to perform.

Some researchers have attempted novel treatments for Tay-Sachs disease, but these attempts have not proven successful in most cases (although some isolated attempts have been successful). In one treatment, the missing enzymes, encased in a protective bubble of lipid (fat-like) material are infused into the brain. This technique is only temporarily successful, however. In addition, usually the neurological damage has progressed to such a degree that treatment is not useful.

In the future, researchers hope that gene therapy may cure Tay-Sachs disease. In gene therapy, cells that have been infected with viruses carrying normal genes are injected into the body. The healthy genes would then encode enough hexosaminidase A to break down the accumulating gangliosides. Because the defective genes responsible for Tay-Sachs are known, this therapy is a possibility. Researchers, however, must solve many technical difficulties before gene therapy for Tay-Sachs is a reality.

See also Childhood diseases.

Tea plant

The tea plant *Camellia sinensis*, which is a member of the plant family Theaceae, is a small evergreen tree that is related to the camellias commonly grown in gardens. Although there are more than 3,000 different types, or grades, of true tea that are produced, nearly all are derived from this single species. Other plants such as peppermint and jasmine, which are also often steeped to yield a hot drink, are not true teas. Next to water, tea is said to be the most common drink in the world, with production exceeding two million tons per year worldwide.

Tea is thought to be native to China and/or Tibet, but not to India or Sri Lanka, where most commercial tea is grown today. The practice of drinking hot tea likely originated in China, and was later taken up in Japan, where elaborate tea drinking ceremonies developed. It was only much later, during the 1600s, that the export of tea to Europe began. Today, tea is consumed worldwide, and a great variety of practices has evolved regarding how and when tea is served and consumed. For example, Americans often drink tea with or after meals, adding milk, sugar, or lemon, while in Great Britain, it has long been the practice to serve tea in the late afternoon, often accompanied by cakes or biscuits.

A tea plantation in east central China.

KEY TERMS

Caffeine—A bitter alkaloid present in tea, coffee, and other drinks, that acts as both a stimulant and a diuretic.

Tannin—An organic constituent of tea that influences the taste, color, and pungency.

Theaceae—A tropical and subtropical family of trees and shrubs that includes the tea plant and a variety of cultivated species, including *Camellias*.

The tea plant is grown almost exclusively for the drink that is made by brewing the flower buds and leaves. Before reaching the consumer, either as loose tea, tea bags, or bricks, a rather complex series of steps takes place. Dried tea is prepared by harvesting steps that usually include drying, rolling, crushing, fermenting, and heating. The result is the drink that is consumed, both hot and cold, primarily because of the stimulatory effect of the caffeine and the astringent effect of the tannins that the plant contains. Depending on where and how the tea is grown, when and how much of the plant is harvested, and the details of the processing, the resulting tea can take on an astounding range of tastes and colors. Commercial teas are generally of two forms—black or green—with black by far the more common. Black tea differs from green primarily because of an additional fermentation step caused by microorganisms on the dried, crushed leaves. In addition to black and green teas, other major classes of tea are produced as a result of alterations of the basic production process.

Tea was originally steeped from the loose leaves, which could be added to boiling water, or through which boiling water could be poured. In North America, and increasingly elsewhere, most tea is now brewed from tea bags rather than from loose tea. By steeping tea bags for shorter or longer periods of time, the color and the strength of the tea can be controlled—yet one more example of how the final drink can be manipulated. Regardless of the type of tea, virtually all commercial teas are blends of several to many different types that have been combined in such a way—and often based on secret recipes—to achieve a particular taste and color. In addition, dried leaves or oils from other plants are sometimes added to achieve a particular taste, as in the case of Earl Grey tea. Although purists sometimes scoff at such practices, there are many teas in which interesting flavors have been achieved in this way.

In thinking about tea, students of U.S. history recall the Boston Tea Party of 1773. In this uprising, the tea cargo on three British ships was thrown into Boston Harbor by small group of colonists disguised as Native Americans, this to protest a tax levied by Britain's King George III. The resulting closing of Boston Harbor by the British can be interpreted as but one of the many events of history leading to the writing of the Declaration of Independence. Thus, tea can be seen as having played a significant role in world history. Today, tea plays a considerably less dramatic role in world history. In everyday life, however, tea is still important. Consumed hot, tea often represents a time during the day in which to sit back and relax; and served over ice, perhaps with a wedge of lemon, tea serves, along with the backyard grill and the ice cream cone, as a symbol of the days of summer.

See also Caffeine.

Further Reading:

Harrison, S. G., G. B. Masefield, and M. Wallis. *The Oxford Book of Food Plants.* Oxford: Oxford University Press, 1969.

Hobhouse, H. *Seeds of Change.* New York: Harper and Row, 1986.

Klein, R. M. *The Green World: An Introduction to Plants and People.* New York: HarperCollins, 1987.

Lewington, A. *Plants for People.* Oxford: Oxford University Press, 1990.

Simpson, B. B., and M. C. Ogorzaly. *Economic Botany: Plants in Our World.* New York: McGraw-Hill, 1986.

Steven B. Carroll

Technetium see **Element, chemical**

Tectonics

Tectonics is the study of the deformation of the Earth's lithosphere—both the causes of deformation and its effects. Tectonics focuses primarily on mountain-building, but involves other unrelated activities as well. Since the development of the theory of plate tectonics, tectonics has become an especially active area of research in geology.

Deformation of rocks, known as tectonism or diastrophism, is a product of the release and redistribution of energy from the Earth's interior. This energy is provided by a combination of heat, produced by radioactive decay within the Earth and by gravity. Uneven heating (or unequal distribution of mass) within the Earth's interior creates pressure differences, or gradients. These pressure gradients cause rocks to experience compression, extension, uplift, or subsidence. As a result, rocks deform and shift about on the Earth's surface. When deformed, rocks may break, bend, warp, slide, flow (as solids), or even melt. Structures that indicate past episodes of tectonism include faults, folds, and volcanoes. Among activities that suggest active tectonism are earthquakes and volcanic eruptions.

Tectonism is generally divided into two categories of deformation—orogenesis and epeirogenesis. Orogenesis (derived from the Greek words *oros*, meaning mountain, and *genesis*, meaning origin), or mountain-building, involves the formation of mountain ranges by folding, faulting, and volcanism. Most mountain ranges form where lithospheric plates converge (that is, along plate margins) and are a product of plate tectonics. Epeirogenesis (*epeiros* means *mainland* in Greek) involves vertical displacement (uplift or subsidence) of large regions of the Earth's lithosphere, as opposed to the elongated belts of lithosphere involved in orogenesis. There are a number of other important differences between epeirogenesis and orogenesis as well. Folding and faulting is less significant in epeirogenesis and volcanism is not often involved. Epeirogenesis is also not as closely related to plate tectonics and is common throughout all areas of plates, not just at plate margins.

The products of orogenesis are obvious—mountains. Epeirogenesis is usually more subtle. Erosion of material from a region could cause uplift (epeirogenesis) in response to the decrease in crustal mass. Conversely, sediments eroded from one area of the Earth's crust may accumulate elsewhere. The weight of these accumulated sediments could cause subsidence (epeirogenesis) of the crust. The vertical movements in these examples are driven by gravity and result from changes in crustal mass within an area. Such movements are known as isostatic adjustments—among the most common, but subtle, epeirogenic activities.

Prior to the development of the plate tectonic theory in the 1960s, many theories had been proposed which attempted to explain regional tectonic activity, especially mountain building. None of these theories could adequately account for the range of activities and structures observed. One of the main reasons plate tectonic theory was so quickly and widely accepted is that it provides a workable explanation for a wide variety of tectonic processes and products.

In fact, plate tectonics has been called the "unifying theory of geology" because it explains and relates so many different aspects of the Earth's geology. Many Earth processes, which previously were not even believed to be connected, are now known to be closely interrelated. As a result, tectonic research is now highly interdisciplinary. Thorough interpretation of the causes and effects of a single episode of deformation often requires input from a large number of geologic subdisciplines (structural geology, sedimentology, geomorphology, geochemistry, etc.) And to further complicate matters, most areas of the Earth have been involved in multiple tectonic episodes.

See also Earthquake; Lithosphere; Mountain; Plate tectonics; Volcano.

Teeth see **Digestive system**

Telegraph

A telegraph is any system that transmits encoded information by signal across a distance. Although it is associated with sending messages via an electric current, the word telegraph was coined to describe an optical system of sending coded messages. From its invention until the telephone became a viable system, the telegraph was the standard means of communicating both between and within metropolitan areas in both Europe and the United States. Telephones did not make the telegraph obsolete but rather complemented it for many decades. Telegrams and telexes used telegraphy but are rapidly being replaced by facsimile (fax) transmissions through telephone lines. Satellite transmission and high-frequency radio bands are used for international telegraphy.

History

The earliest forms of sending messages over distances were probably both visual and acoustic. Smoke signals by day and beacon fires by night were used by the ancient people of China, Egypt, and Greece. Drum beats extended the range of the human voice and are known to have sent messages as have reed pipes and the ram's horn. The Greek poet Aeschylus (c.525-c.455 B.C.) described nine beacon fires used on natural hills that could communicate over 500 mi (805 km), and the Greek historian, Polybius (c.200-c.118 B.C.), recounted a visual code that was used to signal the 24-letter Greek alphabet. It is also known that Native Americans used signal fires before colonial times and later. Visual systems had a greater range than ones that depended on being heard, and they were greatly stimulated by the seventeenth century invention of the telescope.

In 1791, the French engineer Claude Chappe (1763-1805) and his brother Ignace (1760-1829) invented the semaphore, an optical telegraph system that relayed messages from hilltop to hilltop using telescopes. The Chappes built a series of two-arm towers between cities. Each tower was equipped with telescopes pointing in either direction and a cross at its top whose extended arms could each assume seven easily-seen angular positions. Together, they could signal all the letters of the French alphabet as well as some numbers. Their system was successful and soon was duplicated elsewhere in Europe. It was Chappe who coined the word telegraph. He combined the Greek words *tele* meaning distance and *graphien* meaning to write, to define it as "writing at a distance." Its shortcomings however were its dependence on good weather and its need for a large operating staff. Advances in electricity would soon put this system out of business.

It was the invention of the battery and the resultant availability of electric charges moving at 186,000 mi (299,274 km) a second that accomplished this. Prior to this invention by the Italian physicist Alessandro Giuseppe A. A. Volta (1745-1827) in 1800, attempts to use electricity to communicate had failed because a dependable source of electricity was not available and the long, iron wires needed did not conduct electricity well and could not be properly insulated. Volta's new battery meant that experimenters had for the first time a reliable current of sufficient strength to transmit signals. The next major development was in 1819 when the Danish physicist Hans Christian Oersted (1777-1851) demonstrated that he could use an electric current to deflect a magnetic needle. Further, he showed that the direction of the movement depended on the direction of the flow of the current. This pointed the way to the true telegraph. While several researchers in different countries were attempting to exploit the communications aspects of this discovery, two Englishmen, William Fothergill Cooke (1806-1879) and Charles Wheatstone (1802-1875), formed a partnership and designed a five-needle telegraph system in 1837. Their system used needles to point to letters of the alphabet and numbers that were arranged on a panel. Their electric telegraph was immediately put to use on the British railway system. This system was used primarily for railroad signalling until 1845 when an event raised the public's awareness of the potential of the telegraph. On New Year's Day, 1845, the telegraph was used to catch a murderer who had been seen boarding a train bound for London. The information was telegraphed ahead and the murderer was arrested, tried, and hanged.

Although Cooke and Wheatstone built the first successful telegraph based on electricity, it was an American artist and inventor, Samuel Finley Breese Morse (1791-1872), who would devise a telegraph method that would eventually become universally adopted. Morse had begun investigating telegraphy at about the same time as his English rivals, but he had no scientific background and was getting nowhere until he was informed about the 1825 invention of the electromagnet that had been made by the English physicist William Sturgeon (1783-1850). Fortunately for Morse, he took his inquiries to the American physicist Joseph Henry (1797-1878), who had built in 1831 an extremely powerful electromagnet (it could lift 750 lbs (341 kg) compared to Sturgeon's 9 lbs (4.1 kg)). More importantly, Henry had successfully experimented with using the electromagnet to transmit signals and clearly understood what would become the fundamental principle of the telegraph—the opening and closing of an electric circuit supplied by a battery. Henry gladly enlightened Morse on the mysteries of electromagnetism, and the determined Morse took it from there. He enlisted the aid of a young mechanic, Alfred Vail, and together they improved on the work Morse had already started. These early attempts using an electromagnet resulted in a pen touching a moving piece of paper to record a series of dots and dashes. This system presumes a coded message, and Morse had created his own system which, when he collaborated with Vail, resulted in the now-famous Morse code. Vail contributed significantly to the code, having visited a printer to determine which letters were most and least often used. Their code was then based on the most common letters having the simplest, shortest of symbols (dots and dashes). By 1837, they had put together a system which used a single, simple operator key which, when depressed, completed an electric circuit and sent a signal to a distant receiver over a wire. Their first public demonstration was made at Vail's shop in Morristown, New Jersey, and in 1843, the U. S. Government appropriated funds to build a pole line spanning the 37 mi (595 km) between Baltimore, Maryland and Washington, D. C. On May 24, 1844, the historic message, "What hath God wrought?" was sent and received. Once the system became practiced, it was found that skilled operators could "read" a message without looking at the dots and dashes on the paper by simply listening to the sound of the electromagnet's clicking. This led to the elimination of the paper and an even simpler electric telegraph system that used only a key, battery, pole line, and a new sounder to make the dot or dash clicking sound clear. Using such simple equipment and a single, insulated copper wire, Morse's telegraph system spread quickly across the United States and eventually replaced the older, English versions in Europe.

As the telegraph system grew and spread across the world, improvements followed fairly quickly. One of the first was Morse's development of a relay system to cover longer distances. His relay used a series of electromagnet receivers working on low current, each of which opened and shut the switch of a successive electric circuit supplied by its own battery. Telegraph use increased with the invention in Germany of the duplex circuit, allowing messages to travel simultaneously in opposite directions on the same line. In 1874, American inventor Thomas Alva Edison (1847-1931) designed a double duplex called a quadruplex. This higher-capacity system needed eight operators who handled four messages at one time, two in each direction. A high-speed automatic Morse system also had been invented by Wheatstone in 1858, whose punched-paper tape idea offered a means by which a message could be stored and sent by a high speed transmitter that could read the holes in the tape. This system could transmit up to 600 words per minute. The most revolutionary and innovative improvement however was a time-division, multiplex-printing telegraph system devised in 1872 by the French engineer, Jean Maurice Emile Baudot (1845-1903). His system was based on his new code which replaced the Morse code. It employed a five-unit code whose every character contained five symbol elements. The heart of his system was a distributor consisting of a stationary faceplate of concentric copper rings that were swept by brushes mounted on a rotating assembly. This logical system greatly increased the traffic capacity of each line and was so far ahead of its time that it contained many elements from which modern systems have evolved.

By the end of the nineteenth century, most of the world was connected by telegraph lines, including several cables that crossed the Atlantic Ocean. The first underwater conductor was laid by Morse in New York Harbor in 1842. Insulated with India rubber, it did not last long. After the German-English inventor, William Siemans (1823-1883) devised a machine to apply guttapercha as insulation in 1847, submarine cables were laid across the English Channel from Dover, England to Calais, France in 1850-51. Unsuccessful attempts to span the Atlantic were made in 1857, 1858, and 1865, all under the guidance of American entrepreneur, Cyrus West Field (1819-1892). On July 27, 1866, Field was successful in his fourth attempt, and having connected the United States to Europe, he immediately returned to sea, recovered the lost 1865 cable, and had a second transatlantic telegraph cable working that same year. By 1940 there were 40 transatlantic cables in operation. Ten years later, some of these began to fail and were not repaired for economic reasons. In 1956, transatlantic telephone cables were first laid, and in 1966, the last of the exclusively telegraph cables were abandoned.

Throughout its history, the telegraph proved especially useful to the military. It was first used for these purposes in 1854 by the Allied Army in Bulgaria during the Crimean War. A transcontinental telegraph line had been completed in the U. S. just as the Civil War began, and the telegraph proved enormously useful to both sides. During the Spanish-American War in 1898, undersea telegraph cables were cut as an act of belligerency for the first time, and in World War I, teleprinters with secret codes were heavily used by all combatants.

The earliest teleprinter was invented by an American, Royal E. House, in 1846, only two years after Morse's first success. The transmitter had 28 character keys and employed a fairly crude system that even had a hand crank. Although it was used for only a few years, it was the forerunner of both the teleprinter and the stock ticker. At the turn of the century, a Nova Scotia inventor, Frederick G. Creed (1871-1957), experimented in Scotland with using a typewriter to send printed messages without using the Morse Code. His teleprinter system did not catch on in England, and in 1907, Charles L. Krumm of the United States designed the prototype version of the modern teleprinter. This system was subsequently improved, and during the 1920s became known by the American telephone and Telegraph trade name, Teletype. Commercial teleprinter exchange services called TRX and Telex were developed during the next decade that were capable of printing up to 500 characters per minute. By 1964, this was up to 900 characters per minute. By then, technical improvements in the tele-

KEY TERMS

Code — A system of symbols arbitrarily used to represent words.

Electromagnet—A temporary magnet whose effect is caused by an electric current.

Gutta-percha — A yellowish-to-brownish, somewhat leathery solid that is prepared from the latex of a South Sea Island tree. On heating, it becomes plastic and very resistant to water.

Semaphore — A signalling device that uses moving arms, human or mechanical, whose position indicates letters or numbers.

Sounder — The receiving device used in the aural type of telegraph reception that consists of an electromagnet constructed to give slightly different sounds to dots or dashes.

Teleprinter — A device also called a teletypewriter that sends and receives written messages along lines or via satellites.

phone had made an entire new range of technology available to telegraphy, and today, the telegraph has evolved into a modern digital data-transmission system. Today's modern systems use television coaxial cables, microwave, optical fiber, and satellite links to achieve an extremely high transmission rate.

The invention of the telegraph could in some ways be seen as the real beginning of our modern age, given the way in which it so interconnected the entire world. Almost coincidental with its birth there was the emergence of a new kind of journalism that made currency its stock in trade. Reporting events that had only just occurred took precedence over a newspaper's traditional editorial role, and news was reported almost as soon as it happened. Corporations also could become larger and more far-flung, and nations became necessarily more interdependent. With the telegraph, information—in all its aspects and forms—began to assume the critical role it plays today.

Further Reading:

Coe, Lewis. *The Telegraph: A History of Morse's Invention and Its Predecessors in the United States.* Jefferson, North Carolina: McFarland, 1993.

Holzmann, Gerald J. and Bjorn Pehrson. *The Early History of Data Networks.* Los Alamitos, CA: IEEE Computer Society Press, 1995.

Israel, Paul. *From Machine Shop to Industrial Laboratory: Telegraphy and the Changing Context of American Invention.* Baltimore: Johns Hopkins University Press, 1992.

Leonard C. Bruno

Telemetry

Telemetry is the science of obtaining quantities or making measurements from a distant location and transmitting them to receiving equipment where they are recorded, monitored, or displayed. A basic telemetry system consists of a measuring instrument or detector, a medium of transmission (sending), a receiver, and an output device that records and displays data. Today, telemetric systems are mainly used for monitoring manned and unmanned space flights, obtaining meteorological, oceanographic, and medical data, and for monitoring power-generating stations.

History

The word telemetry did not come into use until some medium of transmission had been invented. Since it is defined as the communication of measurements that were taken from some distant point, the earliest telemetry system was one based on a electrical wire. Following the invention of the telegraph and later the telephone, one of the earliest known United States patents for a telemetry system was granted in 1885. These first telemetry systems were used by electric power companies to monitor the distribution and use of electricity throughout their systems. They were called supervisory systems because of their monitoring abilities. One of these original telemetry systems was installed in Chicago, Illinois, in 1912. This network used the city's telephone lines to transmit data on its several electric power generating plants to a central control station. Following World War I, this data was transmitted by the electric power lines themselves. Although electrical telemetry systems are still in use, most modern telemetry systems use radio transmissions to span substantial distances.

System components

Most of today's telemetry systems consist of an input device known as a transducer, the radio wave medium of transmission, an instrument to receive and process the signal, and some type of recording or display instrumentation. The transducer obtains whatever it is that is being measured or monitored, like temperature or pressure, and converts that value into an electrical impulse. Transducers can have their own power source or they can be externally powered. Some examples of today's transducers are those used in weather balloons to obtain and convert measurements of temperature, barometric pressure, and humidity. Transducers are also used in manned space flights to measure an astronaut's heartbeat, blood pressure, and temperature as well as other biomedical indices. Transducers can also be employed for such mundane tasks as measuring the flow rate in a pipe.

Once something is measured and converted into an electrical signal by the transducer, this data must then be transmitted. Simple forms of telemetry, like a remote metering system, use wire links to a central control room. While radio is the preferred medium for use over long distances, other more specialized alternates are available, such as beams of light or sonic signals. Manned and unmanned space systems use radio communications, and we have become more familiar with the notion of telemetry as it applies to a distant, unmanned spacecraft taking measurements as it approaches another planet and sending them back to earth. These radio telemetry systems use what is called a modulated signal since the data is varied by a radio link. This means that the data is varied or modulated by a subcarrier signal that actually carries it. This radio signal may be either a single data channel or it may be carry several types of information. Called multiplexing, this system combines several types of information into a single signal and is used for reasons of cost and efficiency. To be effective, various forms of separating out the data from the single signal are employed. One method is called the time division multiplexing system in which data is sent and received in a certain, set order or pattern. Time division multiplexing that involves a sequential action are common and very efficient. An alternative to time division in multiplexing is a system called frequency division. Where time division combines channels sequentially, frequency division system assign each channel its own frequency band. Although the frequency bands are individually allocated, they are still combined for simultaneous transmission.

Another communication link is called the address-replay system. This special program sends data only after receiving a command signal. Modulation by a subcarrier has already been noted, and there are mainly two different methods available. The first is an AM or FM system similar to commercial radio. The other is one of several types of pulse-based methods in which data is coded digitally into pulse groups and then transmitted.

User needs and preferences usually depend which system is chosen. At the receiving end of the entire telemetry system, signals are separated and can be displayed in real time and/or stored by computers. Telemetry technology is being extended to the point where we can obtain astronomical information from the farthest planet, or biological data from within a person's body via microminiature transmitters.

See also Transducer.

Leonard C. Bruno

Teleost fish see **Bony fishes**

Telephone

The term telephone (from Greek *tele*, afar, and *phone*, sound) in a broad sense means a specific type of telecommunications which permits people to carry direct conversations over almost any distance. The articulate speech is transmitted in a form of either modulated electric current propagating along conductors or radio waves. The apparatus used for converting the verbal sounds into electromagnetic signals and vice versa is called a telephone set and is also commonly referred to as a telephone. Telephone communication is one of the most widespread and expeditious forms of communication. It has proved to be invaluable for an exchange of information in all areas of human life, whether it is business, government, science, public health, personal services or social contacts. There were about 200,000 telephones in the world in 1887, approximately 30 million in 1928, 118 million in 1958, and more than 330 million in 1975.

The general concept of the telephone as a system involves a number of elements. First comes a telephone apparatus itself. Next, there is a variety of means for conveying the electromagnetic signals over distances (transmission paths). Third, the transmission paths are arranged in multi-leveled structures (networks) in a way that permits to interconnect (switch) any desired telephone sets upon request. And finally, there are signalling facilities for directing the switching operations, alerting the person called, and clearing the circuits upon the completion of the call.

A scientific and technological discipline which studies and develops all of the telephone-system's constituents is called telephony. Many problems in telephony draw on the principles and techniques of the electromagnetic theory, the theory of linear and nonlinear circuits, the probability theory, and the queuing theory.

Invention and historical development of the telephone

Electrical telecommunication originated in the nineteenth century, with the invention of the telegraph—a method of transferring intelligence between distant places through metallic wires in a form of spaced bursts of electricity. A sender, using a special letter code, produced regulated electrical pulses in a circuit. These signals were converted at the receiving end into a pattern of sound clicks, that was decoded by an operator or an automatic device. The next logical step beyond sending of non-articulate messages was the instantaneous transmission of conversation over wires. The intricate and very individual nature of sounds produced by the human vocal cords with the participation of the lips, as well as of the oral and nasal cavities, made this task difficult to accomplish. Articulate (spoken) speech involves not only the elementary sounds and their assembly into syllables, words, and sentences, but also infinite variations in accent, emphasis, intonation, and voice timbre—characteristics of no importance for other types communication.

By no chance, the invention of a way to transmit the human voice electrically was made by a man deeply involved in the study of vocal physiology and the mechanics of speech. A native of Scotland, Alexander Graham Bell (1847-1922) inherited from his father, who was a famous professor of elocution and an author of several textbooks on speech correction, a profound interest in speech and hearing theory, and put his knowledge primarily for the teaching of the deaf. Being interested in electricity, Bell set up a little laboratory and experimented on transmission of sound tones over an electric circuit in an attempt to make a "harmonic telegraph"—a device capable of sending multiple telegraph messages simultaneously over the same wire. On the basis of his experimental observations, Bell gradually came to the conclusion that oscillations of air pressure (sound waves) could be used to modulate the intensity of electric current in a circuit. Using his knowledge ear anatomy, Bell attached one end of a metallic organ reed to a thin diaphragm intended to simulate the eardrum. In presence of even weak air-pressure variations caused by the human voice, the diaphragm forced the metallic reed to oscillate in front of the electromagnet and, therefore, to undulate the electric current in the circuit.

Telephones successfully served to the public for almost 23 years before scientists could explain theoreti-

Alexander Graham Bell on the telephone at the formal opening of telephone service between New York and Chicago in 1892.

cally why the telephone worked. Bell's perception of an "analog" relationship between sound pressure and electromotive force was one of the most fascinating examples of the ingenious intuition in the history of technological discoveries.

Bell first started testing his device for voice transmission in June, 1875, and patented it nine months later. The demonstration of the working apparatus at the Philadelphia Centennial Exposition attracted substantial public interest, which helped to raise some additional monetary funds. On 1 August 1877, with Bell's four patents as a tangible basis for a wide manufacturing of a speaking telephone, the Bell Telephone Company was formed. Bell outlined a general concept of a telephone system as a universal means of voice communication between individuals, at any time, from any location, and without any special skill requirements. This concept might seem obvious today, but it was far in advance of any existing techniques of its time. Giant technological and organizational efforts were required to make Bell's vision of a telephone communication a reality.

The number of existing telephones at that time counted 778, but rapidly growing demand presented the challenge of operating the existing telephone while pro-

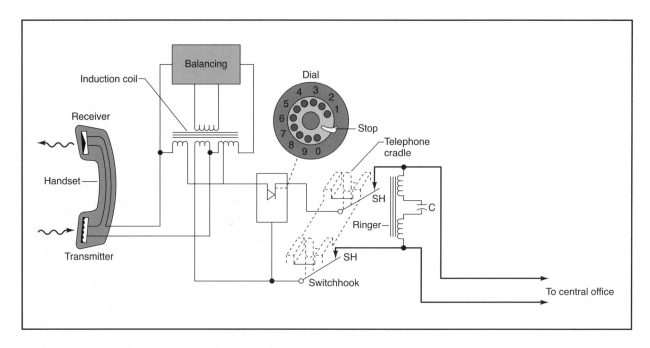

Figure 1. Telephone set simplified circuit.

ducing new ones. The first telephone subscribers were directly connected to each other. Under such arrangement, a community of 100 subscribers used 9,900 separate wire connections. For 1,000 subscribers the number of needed wire connections was more than 100 times bigger. The evident impracticality of full-time point-to-point connections stimulated the idea of a central office, or exchange. All the telephone sets in a particular area, instead of being wired permanently to each other, were connected to the same central office, which could establish a temporary link between any two of them on demand. The process of line connecting and disconnecting (switching) was initially performed by trained operators on a switchboard. However, with more and more telephones coming into use the manual switching was becoming increasingly complex. In 1891, the first automatic switching system was introduced.

As local telephone lines emerged and expanded, the idea of the creation and commercial operation of long-distance telephone communication became a necessity. Unfortunately, the already existing telegraph lines were of little use for this purpose. Feeble electric currents used in telephony were rapidly dissipated (attenuated) on their way through iron wires. Compensating for attenuation was one of the main problems of telephony during its first 50 years. Considerable success in reducing the attenuation was achieved by using copper in place of iron wire. The innovation extended the limits of the voice transmission through bare wires to a distance between Boston and Chicago—1180 mi

(1,900 km)—in 1893. Later, the effectiveness of wire lines was crucially increased by inserting inductances, or "loading coils," at regular distances in a circuit. For crossing small bodies of water telephone lines were laid in a form of insulated cables instead of bare wires. The invention of radio transmission at the beginning of the twentieth century led to the development of wireless telephone links and accelerated creation of the worldwide telephone system.

Long-haul facilities grew swiftly. In 1900, toll lines totalled 621,000 mi (1 million km) of wire. It took only 25 years to increase this number by a factor of ten. In 1925, almost one-half of the long-distance circuits was cable. The first transatlantic telephone cable (TAT-1) became operational in 1956. Nine years later, the first transatlantic telephone satellite "Earlybird" went into service.

Telephone technology

Telephone set

A typical telephone instrument includes a number of main blocks (a switchhook, a ringer, a dial, a receiver, a transmitter, and a balancing network), which make it capable of numerous operations. 1) It requests the use of the telephone system when the handset is lifted, and signals the system that a call is finished when a caller returns the handset to the cradle. 2) It announces the incoming call by sending audible signals. 3) It sends to the system the telephone number

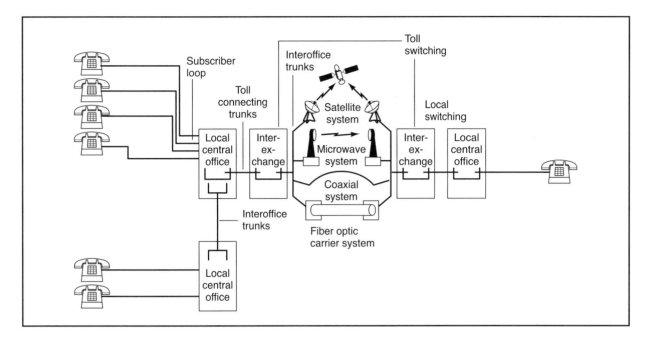

Figure 2. Telephone network.

which is specified by the caller, who rotates a dial or presses number keys. 4) It converts the speech of the caller to electrical signals for transmission through the system and changes received electrical signals to speech. 5) It controls the level of unwanted sounds.

The switchhook interrupts the connection with the central office when the telephone set is idle (the handset is on the cradle) and completes the circuit whenever the handset is lifted off. The ringer is initiated by the system each time when an incoming call is waiting. Alternating current passing through a coil and drives a permanent magnet which makes the attached clapper periodically strike the bell.

The rotary dial is an electric contact that interrupts the circuit periodically sending to the central office a series of current pulses, corresponding to the identification number of the telephone called. When the tone dialling is used, as in Touch-Tone service, pressing of a number key results in sending a signal of two frequencies to the central office circuit, which identifies it and accordingly sets up the switching for the communication path. The use of tones speeds up the dialing operation and allows to send commands and control information directly to the called location.

The telephone transmitter responds to the acoustic frequencies from 250 to 1,000 Hz. It consists of an electrical capacitor adjacent to a diaphragm, so that air-pressure vibrations caused by sound make the membrane produce changes in the value of capacitance of the circuit and, therefore, the variable electric voltage. As a result, a pulsating direct current occurs.

The typical receiver consists of a lightweight diaphragm attached to a permanent magnet associated with a coil of wire. When the alternating current of the telephone signal passes through the winding of the coil, changes are produced in the magnetic forces acting on a permanent magnet. The diaphragm moves in response to these variations, creating an acoustic pressure, more or less exactly reproducing the original sound wave from the distant telephone transmitter.

Sidetone is the sound of the speaker's voice heard in his own receiver. To keep the level of this unwanted sound in acceptable range, the balancing network is used.

Special signals informing users on the status of their calls originate from the central office. When a caller lifts off the handset from the cradle the direct current flows through a complete circuit to the central office, which immediately registers the line initiating a call and places a dial tone on it. This tone signals to the subscriber that he may proceed with dialing the number of the called party. If the connection cannot be established, the tone generator in the central office produces one of three possible busy signals. A signal interrupted 60 times per minute means that the called party is busy. A signal interrupted only 30 times per minute indicates that the toll line between the central offices is busy, while a signal with 120 interruptions per minute means that all the intra-office paths are busy.

Telephone network

The telephone-network's structure may be defined as an entire plant of existing connections between telephone exchanges. It consists of three broad categories: local, exchange area, and long-haul networks.

The local network links telephones in residences and businesses to a central office serving a particular geographical area. The size of the area may vary from 11.5 sq mi (30 km^2) in cities to 123.5 sq mi (320 km^2) in the country. The telephone lines connecting a subscriber to the central office are called local lines or loops. Central offices are interconnected through the exchange area network, and all of the above are interconnected with toll (long-distance) exchanges. The telephone lines connecting one telephone exchange with another are called trunks in North America and junctions in Europe.

Each telephone is assigned a number indicating its location in the system. The switching network recognizes which telephone initiates the call and which telephone is to receive the call. From this information, it sets up the circuit connection for a signal path. Modern transmission facilities for conveying the electric analog of speech between telephone stations use diverse transmission paths, such as wire or cable circuits and microwave-radio or infrared-optical channels.

Quality of telephone communication

The intelligibility, naturalness, and audibility of transmitted speech are the main requirements for high quality telephone transmission. In technical terms, these requirements mean that: all the harmonic components of the human voice in the frequency range from 300 to 3,400 Hz pass through the communication channel; the loss of a signal during passing the channel does not exceed 30 dB; and the level of noise arising from all types of interference be at least 35 dB lower than the level of the main signals.

The quality of the telephone service is greatly dependent upon the structure of the networks by which subscribers are connected. The number of subscribers making telephone calls at one time is always substantially less than the total amount of subscribers. That is why the number of channels in the commercial telephone system is considerably less than the number of subscribers served by a central office (usually by a factor of 7-10 in a local office and 200-250 in toll exchanges). Because of such a design, a connection may be blocked when the telephone traffic is high. The quality of the automatic telephone service can be defined as the percentage of blocked (refused) calls during the hours of the heaviest telephone traffic. To reduce the incidence of channel overload, good planning based on statistical analysis is used.

Another way to improve network quality is to increase the amount of channels that can be carried by a single underlying medium. For example, in 1940, a coaxial cable could carry 600 voice channels. By the early 1950s, this amount increased to 1,860 voice channels and reached the number 13,200 in the 1980s. The microwave radio system experienced similar bandwidth growth, with 2,400 channels in the 1950s increased to 42,000 channels in the 1980s. The potential of the fiber optic technology promises even faster progress in this direction.

Wireless telephone systems

In wireless communication the information is superimposed on a carrier radio signal, which is sent through the air to a receiving location, where the original information is detected and isolated. Cordless, mobile, and cellular telephones perform all functions of the conventional telephone but partially use a radio link instead of wires.

The cordless telephone uses low-power radio transmissions only between the portable handset and its base. The telephone base is wired in a regular way to the telephone line completing the local loop to the central office. An internal antenna in the handset receives the transmission from the base unit over a range from 49 to 948.5 ft (15-300 m). The handset is powered by a battery which is automatically recharged when placed in a receptacle in the base unit. When the user dials the number for the outgoing calls, the dial tones are transmitted to the base unit which sends the tones to the regular telephone line.

The mobile telephone has no direct hardware connection with the conventional telephone line. It uses a high-power transmitter and an elevated antenna to establish a wireless link with the base station antenna serving a circular area of up to 31 mi (50 km) in radius. The base station receives and transmits on several different frequencies simultaneously, providing clear reliable communications. The control terminal of the base station directs telephone calls to and from the conventional telephone system, just like calls that are carried out entirely over wires. When the user in his moving vehicle lifts the handset of the mobile telephone to place a call, the control terminal automatically selects an available channel. If a channel is found, the user hears the normal dial tone and proceeds as usual.

The cellular telephone concept, first developed and implemented in the United States in the late 1970s, is a

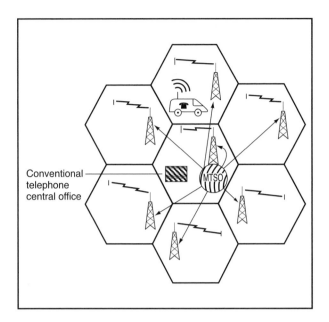

Conventional telephone central office

Figure 3. Cellular network.

method of providing high quality telephone service to subscribers when they move beyond the boundaries of the home area. This concept suggests dividing a service area into a number of small cells. Each cell is served by a control terminal, which, like a local central office, can switch, transmit, and receive calls to/from any mobile telephone located in the cell. Each cell transmitter and receiver operates on a designated channel.

There are two essential features of the cellular concept: frequency reuse and cell splitting. Frequency reuse means that the same channel may be used for conversations in cells located far apart enough to keep interference low. This is possible, because each cell uses relatively low-power transmitter covering only limited area, so cells located sufficiently far from each other may use the same frequency. Cell splitting is based on the notion that cell sizes do not have to be fixed. A system with a relatively small number of subscribers uses large cells, which can be divided into smaller ones as demand grows.

The cells are interconnected and controlled by a central Mobile Telecommunications Switching Office (MTSO), which connects the system to the conventional telephone network and keeps track of all call information for billing purposes. During the call, the terminal at the serving cell site examines the signal strength once every few seconds. If the signal level becomes too low, the MTSO looks for a closest to the active user cell site to handle the call. The actual "hand-off" from one cell to the next occurs without getting noticed by a user. Decision to hand off is made by the

computer, based on the location analysis, the quality of the signal and potential interference.

The convenience and efficiency of wireless telephone communication is the reason for the impressive growth of this service. Recent market data indicate that there are currently about 13 million cellular subscribers in the United States, comparing with approximately 4.4 million in 1990, and 90,000 subscribers in 1984. Currently, cellular telephone service is available mainly in urban areas. The future expansion of cellular network on a global scale will be based on employing low altitude low weight satellites.

Modern developments in telephony

Along with the television and the telegraph, the telephone is only a part of a large family of complex telecommunication systems. The past few years have seen the digitalization of the networks. Digital technology uses a simple binary code to represent any signal as a sequence of ones and zeros, somewhat similar to the Morse code, which assigns dot-dash combinations to the letters of the alphabet. The smallest unit of information for the digital transmission system is a bit, which is either 1 or 0. Binary codes are very stable against different distortions, and are therefore extremely effective for long-distance transmissions. Conversion to digital form allows for the integration of various modes of information management, opening new possibilities for information display, transmission, processing, and storage.

The introduction of the new transmission media— optic fibers—has extended the capabilities and quality of telecommunication services as a whole and telephone service in particular. The fiber optic cable has an almost infinite bandwidth, and is suited especially well for digital transmission. Current tendencies in optical fiber transmission technology include the development of new fiber materials producing a signal loss of no more than 0.001 dB per km as compared to 0.15 dB per km in existing silica-based fibers; the development of effective amplifiers; and the use of the fiber's special transmission modes, called solitons, which are so stable that they preserve their shape even after having traveled thousands of miles.

For short distances a cable-free, easily deployed, and cost-effective communication for voice, data, and video is offered by an infrared optical communication system, employing air as the transmission medium. Infrared signal is another type of electromagnetic emission which is characterized by a considerably higher frequency than microwave. Due to higher frequency, an infrared signal is considerably more directional than a microwave one. The current commercial infrared sys-

KEY TERMS

. . . .

Attenuation—Loss of energy in a signal as it passes through the transmission medium.

Bandwidth—The total range of frequencies that can be transmitted through a transmission path; the bigger bandwidth means bigger information-carrying capacity of the path. As a rule, transmission path carries multiple channels.

Bel—Unit of measurement associated with a tenfold increase in sound energy. Decibel (dB) is one-tenth of a bel, and represents the smallest difference in sound intensity that the trained ear can normally perceive at a frequency of 1,000 Hz. In telephony, 0 dB level is prescribed to a reference point, which is usually the sending end of the transmission line.

Hertz (Hz)—Unit of frequency indicating number of cycles per second.

Optical fiber—Glass strands which act as "light pipes" for light beams created by lasers.

Switching—Process whereby the temporary point-to-point connection between telephone sets is established.

Transmission channel—The range of frequencies needed for a transmission of a particular type of signals (for example, voice channel has the frequency range of 4,000 Hz).

tems are capable of providing reliable telephone links over a range of a half-mile and are ideal for local inter-building communications.

Both voice communications and data communications today exist separately. As technologies become more advanced, the best of both worlds will be integrated into a multimedia telecommunication network. Multimedia conferences or one-to-one multimedia calls will be set up as easily as voice calls from a desktop device. The same device will be used to access FAX and e-mail messaging. Multimedia will enable people to combine any media they need to send, receive, or share information in the form of speech, music, messages, text, data, images, video, animation, or even varieties of virtual reality.

Conventional networks can already accommodate some of the multimedia communication services, such as the direct participation of about 20 conferees in an audio/video/data/image work session. Technology, economics, and even environmental factors stimulate people's readiness to rely on networked contacts. Meeting

somebody no longer implies being in the same place together. People separated geographically can still communicate face to face and collaborate productively. The emerging capabilities offered by the unified, intelligent telecommunication network gradually transform the way people interact, work, and learn.

Further Reading:

Brooks J. *Telephone: The First Hundred Years*. Harper & Row, 1976.

Chang, J. J. C., R. A. Miska, and R. A. Shober. "Wireless Systems and Technologies: An Overview." *A&T Technical Journal* 72 (July-August 1993).

Freeman, R. L. *Telecommunication System Engineering*. New York: Wiley, 1989.

Udell, J. "Computer Telephony." *Byte* 19 (July 1994).

Elena V. Ryzhov

Telescope

The telescope is an instrument which collects and analyzes the radiation emitted by distant sources. The most common type is the optical telescope, a collection of lenses and/or mirrors which is used to allow the viewer to see distant objects more clearly by magnifying them or to increase the effective brightness of a faint object. In a broader sense, telescopes can operate at most frequencies of the electromagnetic spectrum, from radio waves to gamma rays. The one characteristic all telescopes have in common is the ability to make distant objects appear to be closer (from the Greek *tele* meaning far, and *skopein* meaning to view).

The first optical telescope was probably constructed by a Dutch lens-grinder, Hans Lippershey, in 1608. The following year Galileo Galilei built the first astronomical telescope, from a tube containing two lenses of different focal lengths aligned on a single axis (the elements of this telescope are still on display in Florence, Italy). With this telescope and several following versions, Galileo made the first telescopic observations of the sky and discovered lunar mountains, four of Jupiter's moons, sunspots, and the starry nature of the Milky way. Since then, telescopes have increased in size and improved in image quality. Computers are now used to aid in the design of large, complex telescope systems.

Operation of a telescope

Light gathering

The primary function of a telescope is that of light

gathering. As will be seen below, resolution limits on telescopes would not call for an aperture much larger than about 30 in (76 cm). However, there are many telescopes around the world with diameters several times this. The reason for this is that larger telescopes can see further because they can collect more light. The 200 in (508 cm) diameter reflecting telescope at Mt. Palomar, California, for instance can gather 25 times more light than the 40 in (102 cm) Yerkes telescope at Williams Bay, Wisconsin, the largest refracting telescope in the world. The light gathering power grows as the area of the objective increases, or the square of its diameter if it is circular. The more light a telescope can gather, the more distant the objects it can detect, and therefore larger telescopes increase the size of the observable universe.

Resolution

The resolution, or resolving power, of a telescope is defined as being the minimum angular separation between two different objects which can be detected. The angular resolution limit, θ, of a telescope operating under ideal conditions is given by the simple formula:

$$\theta = 2.5 \times 10^{5} \frac{\lambda}{D}$$

where λ is the wavelength of radiation being detected and D is the limiting aperture of the telescope, usually the diameter of the objective, or primary optic. Unfortunately, we are not able to increase the resolution of a telescope simply by increasing the size of the light gathering aperture to as large a size as we need. Disturbances and nonuniformities in the atmosphere limit the resolution of telescopes to somewhere in the range 0.5-2 arc seconds, depending on the location of the telescope. Telescope sights on top of mountains are popular since the light reaching the instrument has to travel through less air, and consequently the image has a higher resolution. However, a limit of 0.5 arc seconds corresponds to an aperture of only 12 in (30 cm) for visible light: larger telescopes do not provide increased resolution but only gather more light.

Magnification

Magnification is not the most important characteristic of telescopes as is commonly thought. The magnifying power of a telescope is dependent on the type and quality of eyepiece being used. The magnification is given simply by the ratio of the focal lengths of the objective and eyepiece. Thus a 0.8 in (2 cm) focal length eyepiece used in conjunction with a 39 in (100 cm) focal length objective will give a magnification of 50. If the field of view of the eyepiece is 20°, the true field of view will be 0.4°.

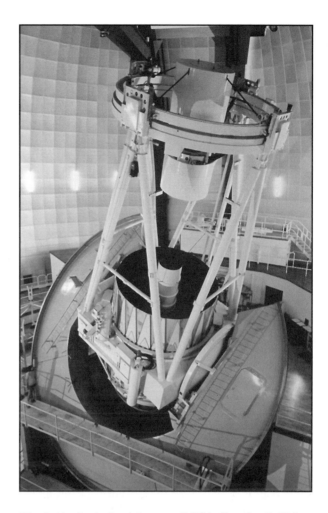

The Anglo-Australian telescope (AAT) in New South Wales, Australia. The principal mirror of this optical telescope has a diameter of 12.8 ft (3.9 m) and lies at the bottom of the white frame. During the day it is protected by an array of steel petals that are seen here in open position. The larger horseshoe shaped frame is part of the supporting structure. AAT was one of the first electronically controlled telescopes.

Types of telescope

Most large telescopes built before the twentieth century were refracting telescopes because techniques were readily available to polish lenses. Not until the latter part of the nineteenth century were techniques developed to coat large mirrors which allowed the construction of large reflecting telescopes.

Refracting telescopes

A simple, uncorrected refracting telescope is shown in Figure 1.

The parallel light from a distant object enters the objective, of focal length f1, from the left. The light then comes to a focus at a distance f1 from the objec-

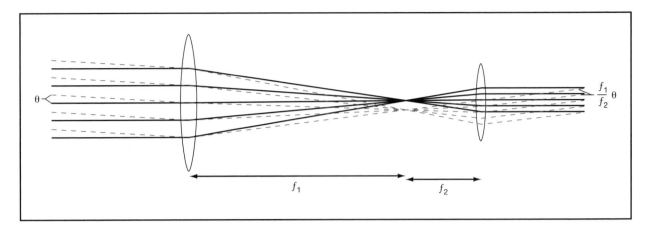

Figure 1.

tive. The eyepiece, with focal length f2, is situated a distance f1+f2 from the objective such that the light exiting the eyepiece is parallel. Light coming from a second object (dashed lines) exits the eyepiece at an angle equal to f1/f2 times the angle of the light entering.

Refracting telescopes, i.e. telescopes which use lenses, can suffer from problems of chromatic and other aberrations, which reduce the quality of the image. In order to correct for these, multiple lenses are required, much like the multiple lens systems in a camera lens unit. The advantages of the refracting telescope include having no central "stop" or other diffracting element in the path of light as it enters the telescope, and the alignment and transmission characteristics are stable over long periods of time. However the refracting telescope can have low overall transmission due to reflection at the surface of all the optical elements and the largest refractor ever built has a diameter of only 40 in (102 cm): lenses of a larger diameter will tend to distort under their own weight and give a poor image. Additionally, each lens needs to have both sides polished perfectly and be made from material which is of highly uniform optical quality throughout its entire volume.

Reflecting telescopes

All large telescopes, both existing and planned, are of the reflecting variety. Reflecting telescopes have several advantages over refracting designs. First, the reflecting material (usually aluminum), deposited on a polished surface, has no chromatic aberration. Second, the whole system can be kept relatively short by folding the light path, as shown in the Newtonian and Cassegrain designs below. Third, the objectives can be made very large, since there is only one optical surface to be polished to high tolerance, the optical quality of the mirror substrate is unimportant and the mirror can be supported from the back to prevent bending. The dis-

advantages of reflecting systems are 1) alignment is more critical than in refracting systems, resulting in the use of complex adjustments for aligning the mirrors and the use of temperature insensitive mirror substrates and 2) the secondary or other auxiliary mirrors are mounted on a support structure which occludes part of the primary mirror and causes diffraction.

Figure 2 shows four different focusing systems for reflecting telescopes.

These are a) the prime focus, where the detector is simply placed at the prime focus of the mirror; b) the Newtonian, where a small, flat mirror reflects the light out to the side of the telescope; c) the Cassegrain, where the focus is located behind the plane of the primary mirror through a hole in its center and d) the Coudé, where the two flat mirrors provide a long focal length path as shown.

Catadioptric telescopes

Catadioptric telescopes use a combination of lenses and mirrors in order to obtain some of the advantages of both. The best known type of catadioptric is the Schmidt telescope or camera, which is usually used to image a wide field of view for large area searches. The lens in this system is very weak and is commonly referred to as a corrector-plate.

Overcoming resolution limitations

The limits to the resolution of a telescope are, as described above, a result of the passage of the light from the distant body through the atmosphere which is optically nonuniform. Stars appear to twinkle because of constantly fluctuating optical paths through the atmosphere, which results in a variation in both brightness and apparent position. Consequently, much information is

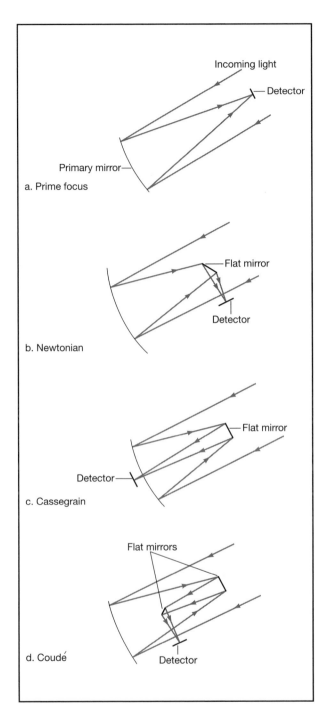

Incoming light

Detector

Primary mirror

a. Prime focus

Flat mirror

Detector

b. Newtonian

Flat mirror

Detector

c. Cassegrain

Flat mirrors

d. Coudé

Detector

Figure 2.

lost to astronomers simply because they do not have sufficient resolution from their measurements. There are three ways of overcoming this limitation, namely setting the telescope out in space in order to avoid the atmosphere altogether, compensating for the distortion on a ground-based telescope and/or stellar interferometry. The first two methods are innovations of the 1990s and are expected to lead to a new era in observational astronomy.

Space telescopes

The best known and biggest orbiting optical telescope is the Hubble Space Telescope (HST), which has an 8 ft (2.4 m) primary mirror and five major instruments for examining various characteristics of distant bodies. After a much publicized problem with the focusing of the telescope and the installation of a package of corrective optics in 1993, the HST has proved to be the finest of all telescopes ever produced. The data collected from HST is of such a high quality that researchers can solve problems that have been in question for years, often with a single photograph. The resolution of the HST is 0.02 arc seconds, close to the theoretical limit since there is no atmospheric distortion, and a factor of around twenty times better than was previously possible. An example of the significant improvement in imaging that space-based systems have given is the Doradus 30 nebula, which prior to the HST was thought to have consisted of a small number of very bright stars. In a photograph taken by the HST it now appears that the central region has over 3,000 stars.

Another advantage of using a telescope in orbit is that the telescope can detect wavelengths such as the ultra-violet and various portions of the infra-red which are absorbed by the atmosphere and not detectable by ground-based telescopes.

Adaptive optics

In 1991, the United States government declassified adaptive optics systems—systems which remove atmospheric effects—which had been developed under the Strategic Defense Initiative for ensuring that a laser beam could penetrate the atmosphere without significant distortion. The principle behind adaptive optical telescope systems is as illustrated in Figure 3.

A laser beam is transmitted from the telescope into a layer of mesospheric sodium at 56-62 miles (90-100 km) altitude. The laser beam is resonantly backscattered from the volume of excited sodium atoms and acts as a guide-star whose position and shape are well defined except for the atmospheric distortion. The light from the guide-star is collected by the telescope and a wavefront sensor determines the distortion caused by the atmosphere. This information is then fed back to a deformable mirror, or an array of many small mirrors, which compensates for the distortion. As a result, stars which are located close to the guide-star come into a focus which is many times better than can be achieved without compensation. Telescopes have operated at the theoretical resolution limit for infra-red wavelengths and have shown an improvement in the visible region of more than ten times. Atmospheric distortions are con-

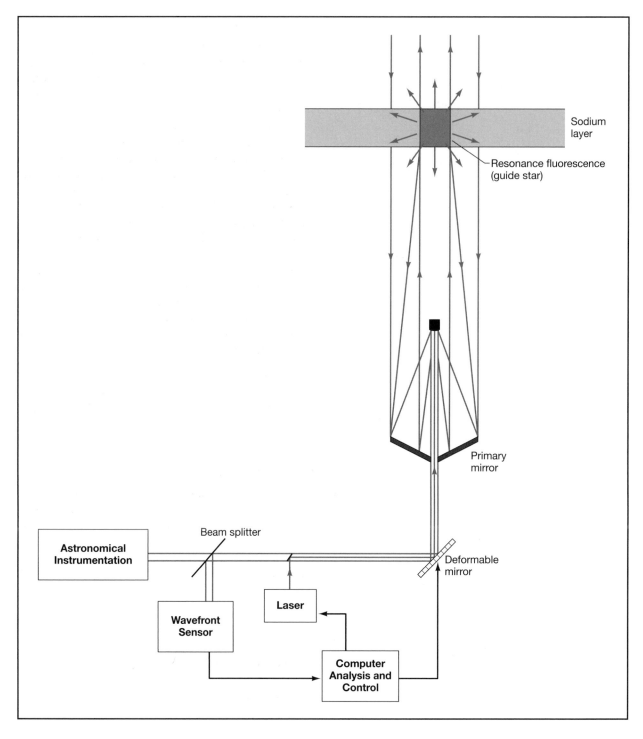

Sodium layer

Resonance fluorescence (guide star)

Primary mirror

Beam splitter

Astronomical Instrumentation

Deformable mirror

Wavefront Sensor

Laser

Computer Analysis and Control

Figure 3.

stantly changing, so the deformable mirror has to be updated every 5 milliseconds, which is easily achieved with modern computer technology.

Recording telescope data

Telescopes collect light largely for two types of analysis, imaging and spectrometry. The better known is imaging, the goal of which is simply to produce an accurate picture of the objects which are being examined. In past years, the only means of recording an image was to take a photograph. For long exposure times, the telescope had to track the sky by rotating at the same speed as the Earth, but in the opposite direction. This is still the case today, but the modern telescope no longer uses photographic film but a charged coupled device (CCD) array. The CCD is a semiconductor light detector which is fifty times more sensitive than photographic film, and is able to detect single photons. Being fabricated using semiconductor techniques, the CCD can be made to be very small, and an array typically has a spacing of 15 microns between CCD pixels. A typical array for imaging in telescopes will have a few million pixels. There are many advantages of using the CCD over photographic film or plates, including the lack of a developing stage and the output from the CCD can be read directly into a computer and the data analyzed and manipulated with relative ease.

The second type of analysis is spectrometry, which means that the researcher wants to know what wavelengths of light are being emitted by a particular object. The reason behind this is that different atoms and molecules emit different wavelengths of light; measuring the spectrum of light emitted by an object can yield information as to its constituents. When performing spectrometry, the output of the telescope is directed to a spectrometer, which is usually an instrument containing a diffraction grating for separating the wavelengths of light. The diffracted light at the output is commonly detected by a CCD array and the data read into a computer.

Modern optical telescopes

For almost 40 years the Hale telescope at Mt. Palomar was the world's largest with a primary mirror diameter of 200 in (5.1 m). During that time improvements were made primarily in detection techniques, which reached fundamental limits of sensitivity in the late 1980s. In order to observe fainter objects, it became imperative to build larger telescopes, and so a new generation of telescopes is being developed for the 1990s and beyond. These telescopes use revolutionary designs in order to increase the collecting area; 2,260 ft² (210 m²) is planned for the European Southern Observatory. This new generation of telescopes will not use the solid, heavy primary mirror of previous designs, whose thickness was between 1/6 and 1/8 of the mirror diameter, but will use a variety of approaches to reduce the mirror weight and improve its thermal and mechanical stability, including using 1) many hexagonal mirror elements forming a coherent array, 2) a single large meniscus mirror (with a thickness 1/40 of the diameter), with many active support points which bend the mirror into the correct shape and 3) a single large mirror formed from a honeycomb sandwich (see Table 1 for a listing of some new large telescopes). These new telescopes,

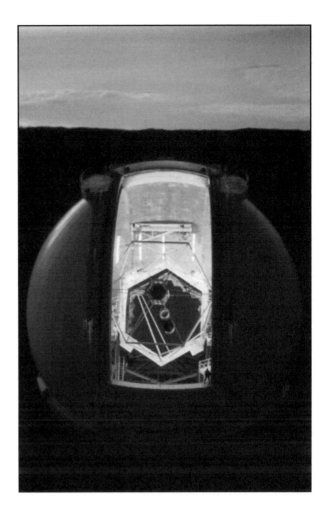

Figure 4.

combined with quantum-limited detectors, distortion reduction techniques, and coherent array operation will allow astronomers to see objects more distant than have been observed before.

One of this new generation, the Keck telescope located on Mauna Loa in Hawaii, is currently the largest operating telescope, using a 32 ft (10 m) effective diameter hyperbolic primary mirror constructed from 36 6 ft (1.8 m) hexagonal mirrors. The mirrors are held to relative positions of less than 50 nm using active sensors and actuators in order to maintain a clear image at the detector. Figure 4 shows a view looking in the dome of the Keck at the hexagonal array mirror.

Because of its location at over 14,000 ft (4,270 m), the Keck is useful for collecting light over the range 300 nm-30 μm. In the late 1990s, this telescope will be joined by an identical twin, Keck II, which will result in an effective mirror diameter of 279 ft (85 m) through the use of interferometry.

TABLE 1. MAJOR GROUND-BASED OPTICAL TELESCOPES FOR THE 1990s

Name	Collector Area	Design Type
Multi-mirror Telescope Conversion Kitt Peak, Arizona	33 m²	6.5 m honeycomb glass
Magellan Las Campanas, Chile	50 m²	8 m honeycomb glass
Keck Telescope Mauna Kea, Hawaii	76 m²	36 x 1.8 m hexagonal array
Keck I and II Mauna Key, Hawaii mirror	152 m²	two 36 x 1.8 m hexagonal arrays, spaced by ~ 75 m
Columbus, Arizona	110 m²	2 x 8.4 m honeycomb glass
Very Large Telescope Cerro Paranal, Chile	210 m²	4 x 8.2 m diameter meniscus

Alternative wavelengths

Most of the discussion so far has been concerned with optical telescopes operating in the range 300 nm-1100 nm. However, valuable information is contained in the radiation reaching us at different wavelengths and telescopes have been built to cover wide ranges of operation, including radio and millimeter waves, infrared, ultra-violet, x rays and gamma rays.

Infra-red telescopes

Infra-red telescopes (operating from 1-1000 µm) are particularly useful for examining the emissions from gas clouds. Since water vapor in the atmosphere can absorb some of this radiation, it is especially important to locate infrared telescopes in high altitudes or in space. In 1983, NASA launched the highly successful Infra-red Astronomical Satellite which performed an all-sky survey, revealing a wide variety of sources and opening up new avenues of astrophysical discovery. With the improvement in infrared detection technology in the 1980s, the 1990s will see several new infra-red telescopes, including the Infrared Optimized Telescope, an 8 m diameter facility, on Mauna Kea, Hawaii.

Several methods are used to reduce the large thermal background which makes viewing infrared difficult, including the use of cooled detectors and dithering the secondary mirror. This latter technique involves pointing the secondary mirror alternatively at the object in question and then at a patch of empty sky. Subtracting the second signal from the first results in the removal of most of the background thermal (infrared) noise received from the sky and the telescope itself, thus allowing the construction of a clear signal.

Radio telescopes

Radioastronomy was born on the heels of World War II, using the recently developed radio technology to look at radio emissions from the sky. The first radio telescopes were very simple, using an array of wires as the antenna. In the 1950s, the now familiar collecting dish was introduced and has been widely used ever since.

Radio waves are not susceptible to atmospheric disturbances like optical waves are, and so the development of radio telescopes over the past forty years has seen a continued improvement in both the detection of faint sources as well as in resolution. Despite the fact that radio waves can have wavelengths which are meters long, the resolution achieved has been to the sub-arc second level through the use of many radio telescopes working together in an interferometer array, the largest of which stretches from Hawaii to the United States Virgin Islands (known as the Very Long Baseline Array).

See also Astrometry; Interferometry; Radio astronomy; Spectroscopy.

Further Reading:

Consolmagno, Guy and Davis, Dun M. *Turn Left at Orion*, Cambridge, U.K.: Cambridge University Press, 1989.

KEY TERMS

. . . .

Chromatic aberration—The reduction in image quality arising from the fact that the refractive index in varies across the spectrum.

Objective—The large light collecting lens used in a refracting telescope.

Reflecting telescope—A telescope which uses only reflecting elements, i.e. mirrors.

Refracting telescope—A telescope which uses only refracting elements, i.e. lenses.

Spectrometry—The measurement of the relative strengths of different wavelength components which make up a light signal.

Field, George and Goldsmith, Donald. *The Space Telescope*, Chicago: Contemporary Books, 1989.

Malin, David. *A View of the Universe*, Cambridge: Sky Publishing, 1993.

Martin, Buddy, Hill, John M., and Angel, Robert. "The New Ground-Based Optical Telescopes," *Physics Today*, March 1991.

Parker, Barry. *Stairway to the Stars*, New York: Plenum, 1994.

Tucker, Wallace and Tucker, Karen. *The Cosmic Inquirers*, Cambridge: Harvard University Press, 1986.

Iain A. McIntyre

Television

The name television means distance seeing. Television, or TV, is the technology used to transmit pictures with sound using radio-frequency and microwave signals or closed-circuit connections.

In principle, a picture as large as a billboard could be passed through a keyhole by cutting the image into narrow horizontal strips. After passing the strips through the keyhole, end to end, the picture could then be reassembled on the other side. Television transmits pictures similarly, sending the details of the picture one dot at a time.

The basic decisions about the principal television process used in North America and Japan were made in the 1940s by the U.S.'s National Television Standards Committee, known as the NTSC since that time. This committee made technical choices that set the engineering characteristics of TV for 50 years. There are differently-defined systems called PAL and SECAM used in the rest of the world.

The NTSC standards are based on 525 horizontal lines to make up each complete picture. Some of these lines are hidden so don't expect to count them all on a TV screen. More lines per picture would have resulted in sharper images, but at the cost of a larger allocation of scarce frequencies. It was decided that a new complete frame should display 30 times each second. The 525 lines per picture 30 times per second results in horizontal lines 15,750 times per second, the original horizontal-line rate for NTSC television.

When the NTSC standards were written, it was thought to be necessary to choose the horizontal and vertical scan rates to have a simple numerical relationship compared to the powerline frequency. In the United States at the time most electrical power had a frequency of 60 Hz.

Synchronization

To control the reassembly of the scan lines so that a TV picture is presented without rolling vertically or tearing horizontally, sync pulses are inserted in the NTSC video signal to tell the TV set when it's time to start the trace of each horizontal line and when it's time to begin each new field. These pulses are transmitted when the dot is not visible so the sync pulses are invisible.

Television achieves the illusion of motion by presenting a series of pictures. The eye sees change from one frame to the next as an approximation of continuous motion. Early tests suggested that a 30-Hz frame rate tended to create a jumpy image when the picture displayed fast action. The committee divided each frame into two fields. The first field presented half the frame from top to bottom, skipping every other line. The next field filled in the lines missing from the first field. This caused at least part of the image to display 60 times each second. This process was called interlaced scanning.

Bandwidth and television pictures

There is a basic principle of communications called the Hartley Bandwidth Rule, that states that required bandwidth is directly proportional to the information transmission rate. So much information is required for television that each signal requires a wide channel of frequencies. The NTSC traded off the width of a single-station's channel against sharpness of the pictures. Each channel was given a width of 6 MHz. They filled this spectrum space with information as complete as the technology of the 1940s permitted. The NTSC standards have been modified over the years, with the addition of color to pictures and stereo to sound, but each NTSC TV signal still squeezes into the original channel allotment.

Television and vision

If you photograph a television picture with a fast shutter speed the results are disappointing. The photograph shows only part of the picture even though the eye sees a full image. The human eye exhibits a characteristic called persistence of vision. Images are seen for a brief instant after the source disappears. A TV picture is constructed by a single spot of light tracing over the screen. The eye will see the entire picture because of the persistence of vision. As the spot traces over the screen, it becomes brighter where the picture is brighter, dim where the picture is dim and the bright and dark image remains after the spot has moved on.

Black and white television

As the dot traces out a TV picture the dot's brightness varies. The part of the video signal that controls the brightness of the dot creating the picture is called the luminance signal. The luminance signal is a voltage that varies rapidly when the picture contains a lot of fine detail and changes slowly when a large area without detail is displayed.

Color television

As soon as it became evident that black and white (monochrome) television was increasingly popular, the industry began planning the addition of color to broadcast TV. Initially a mechanical system was selected that would mechanically rotate a succession of colored filters before the screen in synchronization with a similar wheel in the TV cameras. This system was actually used for the color-tv cameras used from space during the Apollo moon flights.

The color-wheel system was abandoned before it was adopted so that an entirely-electronic color system could be developed that was compatible with NTSC monochrome transmissions. Any color-tv system had to make it possible for TV receivers already in use to see color transmissions, if only in black and white. This goal was met, and by the middle 1950s color-television programming was on the air.

Color TV is possible because of another peculiarity of human vision. The eye cannot distinguish individual

color components of two or more differently colored light sources if they are mixed or are very close together. Mix red and green, the eye sees yellow. Mix red, green, and blue in the right proportions and the result seems white. Almost any color the eye can see can be produced by mixing the right proportions of red, green, and blue, the additive primary colors. Look closely at the screen of a color TV set using a magnifying lens, you'll see red, green, and blue dots or stripes flickering on and off as the picture changes. Back away and you'll see the hues of the original picture.

Color-tv video must include information that balances the instantaneous brightness of red, green, and blue as needed. Another signal, called a chrominance signal is squeezed into the 6-MHz wide channel occupied by every on-air TV station. This chrominance signal is stronger when colors are saturated, is weaker when the colors are pastel, and disappears when the picture is black and white. Only certain chrominance frequencies minimize interference effects. Several frequencies were evaluated, and 3.579,545 MHz was chosen. The horizontal and vertical scan frequencies were adjusted slightly to match this choice.

There are three separate pictures superimposed on a color-tv screen, one picture for each of the three additive-primary colors. Three sets of different chemical phosphors glow red, green, or blue when illuminated with an electron beam. A metal shadow mask, made from a special alloy that is dimensionally stable with temperature changes, has cutouts to match the pattern of phosphor dots or stripes on the face of the picture tube. Parallax permits the separate control of each color. To show green grass, only the green phosphor is illuminated. To show a yellow rose petal, the red and green phosphors are both made to glow. To show a white cloud, all three phosphors are turned on. Pink is produced by turning on red with just a touch of green and blue to add a little white. To show black, all phosphors remain dark.

Many compromises were made to squeeze color into the bandwidth defined for monochrome. The eye sees the most detail when color is blue-green, so this color was given the largest share of the chrominance signal's bandwidth. The eye cannot see details well when the color is orange-red, so the color bandwidth for orange red is reduced. You may have noticed that when orange-red lettering appears in a TV-movie title the letters appear smeared and fuzzy. No color information is transmitted for the small details, because the eye cannot see color well in small areas. NTSC color television is very much like the comic section of a Sunday newspaper, black and white outlines with large areas filled in with colors. The system works quite well, considering the compromises, and it has improved over the years as a result of better equipment even though the original standards have been preserved.

TV stereo sound

In the 1980s a system similar to FM stereo was authorized to enhance television transmissions. The technical standards for TV stereo are based on different subcarrier frequencies, compared to FM-broadcast stereo, but the basic concept is very similar. The main difference was the addition of DBX noise reduction to the TV stereo system to minimize the effect of noise from the picture-signal components.

Video-cassette recorders

Video is to television as audio is to radio. A video signal is the electrical waveform obtained from a television camera that contains all of the information needed to reconstruct the image on a television monitor. Just as an audio signal can be recorded on magnetic tape, a video signal can be recorded on magnetic tape. Audio recording existed long before it was possible to record pictures from television because of the much-wider frequency response required for television.

A natural-sounding audio recording needs to reproduce only the range from 20 Hz through 15,000 Hz. A typical television picture, however, contains frequency components throughout a range that is more than 200 times as broad as a full-spectrum audio recording. If the higher-frequency parts of the video signal are not preserved the reproduced picture will lack fine detail. It won't be sharp.

An audio-cassette tape moves at a standard speed of 1-7/8 inch each second. That is much too slow to record the high frequencies of a video signal. It would be difficult to move tape through a recorder at the more than 200 times the speed of an audio cassette. The home VCR was made possible by a process called helical scanning.

In a VCR, the magnetic video heads are located on a rotating cylinder. The cylinder rotates at 1800 rpm. The video heads move at a very-high speed relative to the tape even though the tape moves more slowly than the tape in an audio-cassette recorder. The video tape wraps partly around the head wheel skewed at a slight angle. The video heads write or read along a path that angles from one edge of the videocassette's one-half inch tape to the other edge. Each of these angled stripes contains information covering many horizontal scan lines.

The tape's speed through a VCR is stabilized by a magnetic control track recorded along one edge of the tape. The control track consists of a series of regular-spaced recorded pulses that the VCR uses to determine playback speed. When a videocassette is played back it is not necessary, not even possible, to select different playback speeds. The VCR automatically moves the tape at a speed that plays back the control-track pulses at the standard rate. If a single tape includes two sequential programs recorded at different speeds the playback speed will automatically adjust as one program ends and the other begins.

Newer VHS VCRs can record programs at two speeds, sometimes called SP, the standard-play speed, and EP, the extended-play speed. (Older VHS recorders offered an intermediate speed, but licensees of the VHS format have been required to abandon this option as a condition of their agreement. The intermediate, or LP speed compromises performance and will be phased out when older VCRs are retired.

There are two sound-tracks recorded on a VHS videotape. There is a so-called linear sound track recorded along one edge of the tape, using a process that is virtually identical to that used for audio recordings. This track has a limited frequency range because even at the SP speed the tape crawls past the sound head more slowly than is the case for an audio cassette.

The Hi-Fi track is recorded as a wide-band FM signal by special heads on the revolving head wheel. Because of the resulting very-high head-to-tape speed, the Hi-Fi audio signal has a very-wide frequency range. Because it is an FM signal that is recorded, the signal-to-noise ratio is excellent. The Hi Fi track records a signal in full stereo or it can be used to record one track in mono and the other track can save the second audio program transmitted by some TV stations. Because the head wheel rotates at a high rate, storing a great deal of rotational-kinetic energy, the speed is very constant. Frequency flutter discernible on the linear track sound recording is rendered all but inaudible in the Hi-Fi alternative. The sound quality from a Hi-Fi VCR track can rival the quality of sound from a compact disk.

Cable television

Television signals are transmitted on frequencies that are limited in range. Only persons residing within the a few-dozen miles of a TV transmitter can usually receive clear and interference-free reception. Community Antenna Television systems, often referred to as CATV, or simply cable, developed to provide a few television signals for subscribers far beyond the service area of big-city transmitters. As time passed cable moved to the big cities. Cable's appeal, even to subscribers able to receive local TV signals without an outdoor antenna, is based on the tremendous variety of programs offered. Some systems provide subscribers with a choice of hundreds of channels.

Cable systems prevent viewers from watching programs they have not contracted to buy by scrambling or by placing special traps in the subscriber's service drop that remove selected channels. The special tuner box that descrambles the signals can often be programmed by a digital code sent from the cable-system office to, adding or subtracting channels as desired by the subscriber.

Wired cable systems generally send their programming from a central site called a head end. All TV signals are combined at the head end, then sent down one or more coaxial-cable trunk lines. Signals for various neighborhoods along the trunk split away to serve individual neighborhoods from shorter branches called spurs.

Coaxial cable, even the special type used for CATV trunk lines, is made of lossy material which dissapates electrochemicals passing through. Signals must be boosted in power periodically along the trunk line, usually every time the signal level has fallen by approximately 20 decibels, the equivalent of the signal having fallen to 1/100 of its original power. The line amplifiers used must be very sophisticated to handle the wide bandwidth required for many programs without degrading the pictures or adding noise. The amplifiers must adjust for changes in the lossiness of the coaxial cable due primarily to temperature changes. The amplifiers used are very much improved over those used by the first primitive community antenna systems, but even today trunk lines are limited in length to about a dozen miles. Not much more than about one hundred line amplifiers can be used along a trunk line before problems become unmanageable.

Cable's program offerings are entirely confined within the shielded system. The signals provided to subscribers must not interfere with over-the-air radio and television transmissions using the same frequencies. Because the cable system's offerings are confined within the shielded system, pay-per-view programs can be offered on cable.

Cable is potentially able to import TV signals from a great distance using satellite or terrestrial-microwave relays. Cable systems are required to comply with a rule called Syndex, for syndication exclusivity, where an over-the-air broadcaster can require that imported signals be blocked when the imported stations carry programs they've paid to broadcast.

The next step in CATV technology is the replacement of wire-based coaxial systems with fiberoptic service. Fiberoptics is the technology where electrical signals are converted to light signals by solid-state laser diodes. The light waves are transmitted through very-fine glass fibers so transparent that a beam of light will travel through this glass fiber for miles.

Cable's conversion to fiberoptics results in an enormous increase in system bandwidth. Virtually the entire radio and TV spectrum is duplicated in a fiberoptic system. Every radio and TV station transmitting "over the air" can be carried in a single thread of fiberglass; 500 separate television channels on a single cable system is a not beyond reach.

A fiberoptic CATV system can be used for two-way communication more easily than can a wire-cable plant with electronic amplifiers. Fiberoptic cable service has great potential to support interactive television services.

ATV—Advanced TV for the future

ATV stands for Advanced Television, the television system expected to replace the NTSC system in the U.S. Television technology is moving resolutely toward the ATV digital system planned to replace the aging analog NTSC process. ATV is a digital-television system, where luminance and chrominance are processed as computer-like data. Digitally-processed TV offers several tremendous advantages over analog TV methods. In addition to sharper pictures with less noise, a digital system can be much more frugal in the use of spectrum space.

Most TV frames are filled with information that has not changed from the previous frame. A digital TV system can update only the information that has changed since the last frame. The resulting picture looks to be as normal as the pictures seen for years, but many more images can be transmitted within the same band of frequencies.

TV audiences have been viewing images processed digitally in this way for years, but the final product has been converted to a wasteful analog signal before it leaves the television transmitter. Satellite relays have relayed TV as digitally-compressed signals to maximize the utilization of the expensive transponder equipment in orbit. The small satellite "dishes" offered for home reception receive digitally-encoded television signals.

ATV will not be compatible with current analog receivers, but it will be phased in gradually in a carefully-considered plan that will allow older analog receivers to retire gracefully over time.

KEY TERMS

. . . .

Chrominance—Color information added to a video signal

Coaxial Cable—Concentric cable, shielded, for wide-bandwidth signals

Compact Disk—Digital recording with extraordinary fidelity

DBX—Proprietary audio-noise reduction system

Digital—Data processed as a succession of binary numbers

Field—Half a TV frame, a top to bottom sweep of alternate lines

Frame—Full TV frame composed of two interlaced fields

Helical—Spiral

Hz—SI abbreviation for Hertz, one cycle per second

Luminance—TV video component that controls instantaneous brightness

MHz—SI abbreviation for MegaHertz, one-million cycles per second

Monochrome—Black and white

Parallax—Shift in apparent alignment of objects at different distances

Phosphor—Chemical that gives off colored light when struck by electron

Rolling—When successive TV frames strobe down or up on screen

Spectrum—Set of frequencies having similar properties

Sync—Synchronization, a pulse used to stabilize TV pictures

Syndication—Licensing practice for TV programs

Tearing—Horizontal-line instability, TV-sweep synchronization error

Transponder—Microwave repeater that receives then retransmits signals

---

Further Reading:

Gray, Laurence, Graham, Richard. *Radio Transmitters,* McGraw-Hill Book Company, Inc., 1961.

Shrader, Robert L. *Electronic Communications*, McGraw-Hill Book Company.

Donald Beaty

Tellurium see **Element, chemical**

Teludu see **Badgers**

Temperature

Temperature is intuitively associated with the sense of hot and cold. Put your finger in a pan of hot water and energy flows as heat from the water to your finger; you say that the water is at a higher temperature than your finger. Now put your finger in a glass of ice water and energy flows as heat in the other direction. The direction of energy flow as heat is the basis of our definition of temperature. Temperature is the property of objects—or more generally systems—that determines the direction of energy flow as heat when the objects are put in direct contact with each other. Energy flows as heat from objects at higher temperature to ones at lower temperature. When energy as heat ceases to flow, the objects are at the same temperature and are said to be in thermal equilibrium.

Molecular interpretation

At the molecular level, temperature is related to the random motions of the particles (atoms and molecules) in matter. Because there are different types of motion, the particles' kinetic energy (energy of motion) can take different forms, and each form contributes to the total kinetic energy of the particles.

For example, when water squirts from a hose, part of the kinetic energy of the water is due to the movement of the molecules as a collection in a single direction out the nozzle. But the individual water molecules are also moving about with random, constantly changing speeds and directions relative to each other. This kind of kinetic energy is called molecular translational energy. This energy remains even after the squirted water becomes a quiet puddle. The temperature of the puddle, or of any object, is a measure of the average of the individual translational energies of all of its atoms or molecules.

If a swimming pool were filled from this same hose, the total molecular translational energy of the molecules in the pool would be much greater than those in the puddle because there are many more molecules in the pool. The temperatures of the puddle and the pool, however, would be the same because temperature is a measure of the average molecular translational energies.

The molecules in a kettle of boiling water have a higher average molecular translational energy—a higher temperature—than those in the swimming pool. Place the kettle on the surface of the pool and the direction of energy flow is obvious: from hotter to cooler, from higher temperature to lower, from greater average molecular translational energy to lesser. These are three ways of saying the same thing.

The reason that heat flows from an object of higher temperature to one of lower temperature is that once they are in contact, the molecular agitation is contagious. Fast-moving molecules will collide with slower-moving ones, kicking them up to higher speed and thereby raising their translational energy.

Thermometers and temperature scales

There is no easy way to measure directly the average molecular translational energies in an object. Therefore, temperature is determined indirectly by measuring a temperature-dependent property of a device that is in thermal equilibrium with the object to be measured. We call such a device a thermometer. One of the earliest kinds of thermometers, still in use today, has a liquid in a glass bulb attached to a glass capillary tube—a tube with a very narrow bore. The tube is sealed to make the thermometer independent of atmospheric pressure. The expansion and contraction of the liquid volume as the temperature goes up and down results in a rise and fall of the thin column of liquid in the tube, which can be calibrated in terms of temperature.

Early thermometry used water or water-alcohol mixtures as the liquid. Water turned out to be an especially poor choice, however, because the volume of water does not change uniformly with changes in temperature. When cooled down from room temperature, liquid water at first contracts. Then, as the water approaches its freezing point, it expands. This unusual property of expansion upon cooling means that a water thermometer not only goes down as the temperature falls, but it sometimes goes up. This is certainly not a desirable characteristic of a thermometer liquid.

The Fahrenheit scale of temperature

In 1714, the German physicist Gabriel Daniel Fahrenheit (1686-1736) made a better choice by selecting liquid mercury. Mercury has a uniform volume change with temperature, a lower freezing point and higher boiling point than water, and does not wet glass. Mercury thermometers made possible the development of reproducible temperature scales and quantitative temperature measurement. Fahrenheit first chose the name "degree" (Grad, in German) for his unit of tem-

perature. Then, to fix the size of a degree, he decided that it should be of such size that there are exactly 180 degrees between the temperature at which water freezes and the temperature at which water boils. (180 is a "good" number because it is divisible by one and by 16 other whole numbers. That is why 360, or 2 X 180, which is even better, was originally chosen as the number of "degrees" into which to divide a circle.)

Fahrenheit now had a size for his degree of temperature, but no standard reference values. Should the freezing and boiling points of water be called zero and 180? Or 180 and 360, or something else? In other words, where shall zero degrees fall on the scale? He eventually decided to fix zero at the coldest temperature that he could make in his laboratory by mixing ice with various salts that make it colder. (Salts, when mixed with cold ice, lower the melting point of ice, so that when it is melting it is at a lower temperature than usual.) When he set his zero at that point, the normal freezing point of water turned out to be 32 degrees higher. Adding 180 to 32 gave 212 degrees for the normal boiling point of water. Thus, freezing water falls at 32 degrees and boiling water falls at 212 degrees on the Fahrenheit scale. And the normal temperature of a human being turns out to be about 99 degrees.

The Celsius scale

In 1742, the noted Swedish astronomer Anders Celsius (1701-1744), professor of astronomy at the University of Uppsala, proposed the temperature scale which now bears his name, although for many years it was called the centigrade scale. As with the Fahrenheit scale, the reference points were the normal freezing and normal boiling points of water, but he set them to be 100 degrees apart instead of 180. Because the boiling point and, to a lesser extent, freezing point of a liquid depend on the atmospheric pressure, the pressure must be specified: "normal" means the freezing and boiling points when the atmospheric pressure is exactly one atmosphere. These points are convenient because they are easily attained and highly reproducible. Interestingly, Celsius at first set boiling as zero and freezing as 100, but this was reversed in 1750 by the physicist Martin Strömer, Celsius's successor at Uppsala.

Defined in this way, a Celsius degree (°C) is 1/100 of the temperature difference between the normal boiling and freezing points of water. Because the difference between these two points on the Fahrenheit scale is 180° F, a Celsius degree is 1.8 times (or 9/5) larger than a Fahrenheit degree. You cannot convert between Fahrenheit and Celsius temperatures simply by multiplying by 1.8, however, because their zeroes are at different places. That would be like trying to measure a table in both yards and meters, when the left-hand ends (the zero marks) of the yardstick and meter stick are not starting at the same place.

To convert a temperature from Fahrenheit to Celsius or vice versa, you first have to account for the differences in their zero points. This can be done very simply by adding 40 to the temperature you want to convert. That is because -40 degrees (40 below zero) happens to come out at the same temperature on both scales, so adding 40 gets them both up to a comparable point: zero. Then you can multiply or divide by 9/5 to account for the difference in degree size, and finally remove the 40 degrees that you added.

Thus, to convert from Celsius to Fahrenheit, (1) Add 32 (2) Multiply by 9/5

And to convert from Fahrenheit to Celsius, (1) Subtract 32 (2) Multiply by 5/9.

The Kelvin scale

About 1787 the French physicist, Jacques Charles (1746-1823) noted that a sample of gas at constant pressure regularly contracted by about 1/273 of its volume at 0° C for each Celsius degree drop in temperature. This suggests an interesting question: If a gas were cooled to 273° below zero, would its volume drop to zero? Would it just disappear? The answer is no, because most gases will condense to liquids long before such a low temperature is reached, and liquids behave quite differently from gases.

In 1848 William Thomson (1824-1907), later Lord Kelvin, suggested that it was not the volume, but the molecular translational energy that would become zero at about -273° C, and that this temperature was therefore the lowest possible temperature. Thomson suggested a new and more sensible temperature scale that would have the lowest possible temperature—absolute zero—set as zero on this scale. He set the temperature units as identical in size to the Celsius degrees. Temperature units on Kelvin's scale are now known as Kelvins (abbreviation, K); the term, degree, and its symbol, °, are not used anymore. Lord Kelvin's scale is called either the Kelvin scale or the absolute temperature scale. The normal freezing and boiling points of water on the Kelvin scale, then, are 273 K and 373 K, respectively, or, more accurately, 273.16 K and 273.16 K. To convert a Celsius temperature to Kelvin, just add 273.16.

The Kelvin scale is not the only absolute temperature scale. The Rankine scale, named for the Scottish engineer William Rankine (1820-1872), also has the lowest possible temperature set at zero. The size of the Rankine degree, however, is the same as that of the Fahrenheit degree. The Rankin temperature scale is rarely used today.

Absolute temperature scales have the advantage that the temperature on such a scale is directly proportional to the actual average molecular translational energy, the property that is measured by temperature. For example, if one object has twice the Kelvin temperature of another object, the molecules, or atoms, of the first object actually have twice the average molecular translational energy of the second. This is not true for the Celsius or Fahrenheit scales, because their zeroes do not represent zero energy. For this reason, the Kelvin scale is the only one that is used in scientific calculations.

Temperature extremes

The highest recorded weather temperature on Earth was 57.8° C (136° F; 184 K), observed in North Africa in 1922. The record low temperature is -89.2° C (-129° F), observed in the Antarctic in 1983. Elsewhere in the universe, temperature extremes are much greater. The average surface temperatures of the most distant planets in our solar system (Uranus, Neptune, Pluto) are about -220° C (-364° F; 53 K). Although temperatures on and within the sun vary, the core is about 15 million° C (27 million° F). (At very high temperatures Celsius and Kelvin temperatures are virtually identical; the 273 is negligible).

Temperatures produced in laboratories can be even more extreme. The study of very low temperatures, called cryogenics, is an active field of scientific research because of the unusual properties of many substances when they are close to absolute zero. Using magnetic techniques, temperatures below one microkelvin have been achieved. (A microkelvin, μK, is 0.000001 K.) Absolute zero itself, however, has not yet been reached.

Less extreme low temperatures can be obtained relatively easily with dry ice or liquid nitrogen. Dry ice, solid carbon dioxide, vaporizes (sublimes) under normal pressures rather than melting to a liquid. The sublimation temperature of dry ice is -78.5° C (195 K). Liquid nitrogen can be used to obtain even lower temperatures. It is used at its normal boiling point, which is of liquid nitrogen is -196° C (77 K).

Scientific interest in very high temperatures is largely due to the hope of achieving controlled nuclear fusion—the energy producing process in the sun and stars. By the use of powerful lasers, temperatures over 400 million Kelvins have been achieved for short periods of time.

See also Gases, properties of; Heat; States of matter.

KEY TERMS

Absolute temperature scale—A temperature scale that has the lowest possible temperature set at zero.

Absolute zero—The lowest possible temperature.

Kinetic energy—Energy of an object or system due to its motion.

Molecular translational energy—Kinetic energy of an object or system due to the random constantly changing motion of individual molecules (or atoms) relative to each other.

Thermal equilibrium—A condition between two or more objects in direct thermal contact in which no energy as heat flows from one to the other. The temperatures of such objects are identical.

Thermometer—A device for obtaining temperature by measuring a temperature-dependent property (such as the height of a liquid in a sealed tube) and relating this to temperature.

Triple point—The unique temperature at which three phases of a single substance can coexist in equilibrium. The triple point for ice-liquid water-water vapor is about 0.01°C above the normal freezing point of water.

Further Reading:

Atkins, Peter W. *The Second Law*. New York: Freeman, 1984.

Kikoyin, A. "Temperature, Heat, and Thermometers." *Quantum* (May 1990): 16-21.

Klein, Herbert A. *The Science of Measurement*. New York: Dover, 1974.

John C. Whitmer

Temperature regulation

An organism maintains homeostasis, a steady internal state, only if its body temperature stays within prescribed limits. Cellular activities require an optimum amount of heat. They depend on enzyme action, and enzymes function within a narrow range of temperature. For this reason, living things can only tolerate a limited rise or drop in temperature from the optimum. Mecha-

Canines, like this North American timber wolf, use panting as a means of temperature regulation.

nisms exist that regulate body temperature to stay within its survival limits.

Cells require a source of heat for their activities. The heat source can be external or internal. The Sun is an external source of heat for living things. Cellular metabolism is an internal heat source. During cellular respiration, the chemical energy in food is converted to high-energy phosphate groups in adenosine triphosphate, ATP. In the process, cells lose about 60% of the released energy as heat. Plants and most animals give up this heat to the environment. Birds and mammals, however, make use of some of the heat that metabolism yields.

Organisms exchange heat with the environment by four major physical processes. First, there is conduction, the direct transfer of heat from a warmer to a cooler object. We cool off during a swim because the heat of the body is conducted to the cool water. During another process called convection, a breeze passes over a surface and brings about heat loss. This is why a fan cools us on a hot day. Radiation, the emission of electromagnetic waves, transfers heat between objects that are not in direct contact. Animals absorb heat that the sun radiates. Finally, evaporation, the physical change of liquid to gas removes heat from a surface. Sweating and panting are cooling processes. Perspiration evaporates from the skin, and panting increases evaporation from the respiratory system. Both procedures take heat away from the body.

Externally heated animals

Ectotherms are animals that warm their bodies by absorbing heat from their surroundings. In most ectotherms, the body temperature fluctuates with changes in the surrounding temperature. The body temperature of snakes, for example, cools in cold weather and warms up in hot weather. Marine fish and invertebrates, however, live in water that stays the same temperature. Their body temperature, therefore, does not change. In everyday language, we say that these animals are cold–blooded. Amphibians, reptiles, fish and invertebrates are considered cold-blooded. This term is misleading, however, because many lizards have high body temperatures. External temperature plays a major role in the activity rate of ectothermic animals. When the weather is warm, they become active. They slow down when the temperature drops.

Certain ectotherm behaviors help regulate body temperature. To warm up, reptiles find sunny places, and stretch out for maximum exposure. If it gets too warm, lizards alternate between sun and shade. Amphibians warm up by moving into the sun or diving into warm water. They cool off by entering the shade. In cold weather, honeybees huddle together to retain heat. Bees and large moths build up heat before takeoff by contracting their flight muscles without moving their wings.

In addition to behaviors, physiological adaptations help ectotherms regulate temperature. Diving reptiles conserve heat because their blood circulates inward toward the body core during a dive. The skin of bullfrogs secretes more mucus when it is hot, allowing more cooling by evaporation. The blood of large active fish, such as the bluefin tuna, absorbs heat from swimming muscles. The heated blood makes the animal's interior warmer, allowing the muscles to be more vigorous. Many ectotherms exist at a lower temperature during torpor, a state of slowed metabolism. This helps them survive a food shortage. If the food supply increases, they come out of torpor in a few hours.

Internally heated animals

Endotherms are animals that warm their bodies mainly from their own metabolism. Mostly birds and mammals, they maintain a constant body temperature regardless of changes in the surrounding temperature. We commonly call them warm-blooded, because the internal temperature they generate is usually higher than the environmental temperature. Endotherms have certain advantages. Their consistent higher temperature allows them to be active at all times. It also gives them the freedom to live in varied habitats. It helps them survive on land where air temperature changes more drastically than water temperature.

Certain adaptations accompany the maintenance of a constant body temperature. A high metabolic rate helps supply heat. An efficient circulatory system conducts and distributes heat around the body. Fat layers,

---

KEY TERMS

Cooling center—Thermoregulating area of the hypothalamus whose impulses result in temperature-lowering activities of various parts of the body.

Ectotherm—Animal that warms its body mainly by absorbing heat from the environment.

Endotherm—Animal that warms its body mainly from its own metabolism.

Heating center—Thermoregulating area of the hypothalamus whose impulses result in temperature-raising activities of various parts of the body.

Hibernation—A type of torpor in which an animal's body temperature drops, thereby enabling it to withstand prolonged cold and little food.

---

fur, and feathers insulate the body and retain heat. Shivering muscles contract to increase body heat, and hormones such as epinephrine and thyroxin increase the rate of metabolism. Under unfavorable conditions some endotherms experience torpor, for example, hibernation, in which the body temperature drops. Hibernation enables animals to survive long periods of cold and lack of food.

Receptors in various parts of the body, such as the skin, deliver information to the hypothalamus of the brain about the body's temperature. The hypothalamus acts as a thermostat. It contains two thermoregulating areas that stimulate nerve impulses. One area, the heating center, sends out impulses that raise the body temperature. It causes blood vessels near the surface of the body to contract, thus preventing heat loss. It also causes fur to stand erect and become more insulating. It causes shivering by muscles that produce heat when they contract, and it stimulates hormonal production. The other area, the cooling center, sends out impulses that bring about a temperature drop. It causes surface blood vessels to expand thereby releasing heat. It brings about sweating or panting.

See also Endothermic; Metabolism.

Further Reading:

Abass, Mageed, and C. B. Rajashekar. "Abscisic Acid Accumulation in Leaves and Cultured Cells During Heat Acclimation in Grapes." *HortScience* (January 1993).

Bookspan, Jolie. "Exposing the Myths of Heat Loss and Gain for Divers." *Underwater USA* (July 1993).

Comis, Don. "Resetting a Plant's Thermostat." *Agricultural Research* (July 1992).

Coping with Change. Films for the Humanities and Sciences, Princeton, 1994-95.

Heinrich, Bernd. "Kinglets' Realm of Cold." *Natural History* (February 1993).

Luck-Baker. "Taking the Temperature of T. Rex." *New Scientist* (23 July 1994).

Monastersky, Richard. "The Pulse of T. Rex." *Science News* (14 May 1994).

Tortora, Gerard J., and Sandra Reynolds Grabowski. *Principles of Anatomy and Physiology*. New York: Harper-Collins, 1993.

Bernice Essenfeld

Tench see **Carp**

Tenrecs

Tenrecs are four-legged nocturnal mammals belonging to the Order Insectivora. Tenrecs have evolved into more distinct forms than any other family of animals within the order. Tenrecs can resemble hedgehogs, moles, shrews, or muskrats, depending on the species. Some species of tenrecs have a long tail and long hind legs, while others have a stumpy tail and short hind legs. Furthermore, some species of tenrec have a spiny coat, similar to that of hedgehog, while others have velvety fur.

Within the Order Insectivora, there are five superfamilies, eight families, and around 370 species. In total, there six general types of insectivores: shrew type, rat type, hedgehog type, mole type, jeroba type, and otter type. Tenrecs are grouped together with the shrews, and are characterized by an elongated body, and long, pointed snout. Tenrecs belong to the superfamily Tenrecoidea superfamily and the family Tenrecidae.

Evolution of insectivores

Insectivores are the most primitive of all higher mammals, and insectivore-like animals predated all of the orders of today's mammals. The fossil remains of Insectivores indicated that they lived during the Cretaceous period. Rat-sized ancestors of today's insectivores date even back further—to the Jurassic and Lower Cretaceous periods. These fossils also indicate that tenrec-like animals and golden moles are related to each other.

Family Tenrecidae

The family Tenrecidae includes between 30-34 species, all but three of which live on the island of Madagascar. The remaining three species (all otter shrews) live in Central and West equatorial Africa.

In general, tenrecs have poor vision, but their senses of smell, hearing, and touch are acute. Like other insectivores, they have an elongated snout, a small, primitive brain, and their skull is relatively small, long, and narrow. Their fur can be soft, coarse, or even spiny. Tenrecs have retained some reptilian characteristics, such as a cloaca-like common chamber into which their digestive, reproductive, and urinary systems empty, and from which these substances leave their body.

The family Tenrecidae family includes three subfamilies: the Tenrecinae (tenrecs), the Oryzorictinae (rice tenrecs), and the Potamogalinae (otter shrews). The best known tenrecs are similar in appearance to hedgehogs, and belong to the Tenrecinae subfamily. This subfamily includes three genera and three species. The rice tenrecs have a long tails, and are closely related to the spiny hedgehogs; this subfamily includes three genera and 24 species. There are two genera and three species of otter shrews.

Tailless or common tenrecs (*Tenrec ecaudatus*)

Tailless tenrecs are, perhaps, the best known species of tenrec. Vaguely resembling hedgehogs, they measure about 12.5 in (32 cm) long, with a stubby tail measuring 0.4-0.6 in (1-1.6 cm) in length. They have a long snout and coarse, bristly fur interspersed with spines. These tenrecs prefer sandier environments, such as highland plateaus and cliffs along riverbanks. During the day, these animals rest in crevices or burrows; at night, they forage for food by digging with their claws and snout. Tailless tenrecs mainly eat insects, lizards, eggs, roots, and fruit. In the dry season, these tenrecs hibernate in deep underground burrows. At the beginning of October, after a long hibernation, they mate. Female tailless tenrecs commonly have as many as 16 surviving offspring.

If threatened, tailless tenrecs stand on their hind legs and bristle their coats, and try to push the bristles into the intruder, while snorting, grunting, and hissing. Although tailless tenrecs are protected by law, the people of Madagascar hunt these animals for their fatty meat.

Rice tenrecs (*Oryzorictes hova*)

Rice tenrecs are spinier than tailless tenrecs and, are more closely related to hedgehogs. Rice tenrecs are classified with the shrews because of similarities in their skeletons. The body of rice tenrecs measures

A tenrec (*Tenrec ecaudatus*).

between 1.5-5 in (4-13 cm), and their tail measures between 1-6.5 in (3-16 cm). These tenrecs acquired their name because they live on and within the banks of rice paddies, as well as in warm, moist forests, swamps, and meadows. Their front limbs are well adapted for digging and these tenrecs spend a great deal of time underground. Rice tenrecs are only seen above ground at night, but it is assumed that they are very active during the day underground, eating invertebrates and crustaceans. Rice growers in Madagascar consider rice tenrecs to be pests.

Reproduction

Some species of tenrec are prolific. Tenrecs produce the most young per litter (averaging between 12-15) of all the world's mammals. The number of offspring can be even higher; for example, common tenrecs have been known to have as may as 32 young in one litter. Because female tenrecs almost always have multiple births, they have numerous nipples to feed their young. In fact, common tenrec females have 29 nipples.

Female tenrecs must sometimes forage for food in daylight, when the danger presented by predators is the highest, to adequately nourish themselves, so that they are able to meet the huge demand for milk. In some tenrec species, the young have extra camouflage to protect themselves from predators, which they lose as they mature. Young tenrecs are fairly independent creatures; they are able to run soon after they are born. By the time they are four weeks old, they are completely independent.

Temperature regulation

The body temperature of tenrecs is maintained between 78.8-86°F (26-30°C). The activity levels of streaked tenrecs vary with the surrounding temperature. Increases in physical activity generate the extra body heat that they need to survive in colder conditions. On a normal day, with a daytime temperature of about 68°F (20°C), streaked tenrecs rest inside their burrows; by early evening, their activity level increases. At midnight, they start taking more frequent rests and, by dawn, they crawl back inside their shelters. However, when the outside temperature goes down to 60.8-64.4°F (16-18°C), tenrecs become much more active, both day and night. If the temperature gets colder than 60.8°F (16°C), even increased activity is insufficient to keep them warm, and they perish. Because the streaked tenrec inhabits moist areas with little temperature change, these animals rarely die of cold.

The habitat of tailless tenrecs, however, is much more variable than that of streaked tenrecs. On Madagascar, there is little rain in the winter, the land becomes very dry, and temperatures fall to as 50°F (10°C). At this point, tailless tenrecs, which have been accumulating fat all summer, roll into a ball and hibernate in their deep underground burrows for about six months. During hibernation, they are cold to the touch and breath about once every three minutes. During this time, they neither eat nor defecate.

Further Reading:

Grzimek, H. C. Bernard, ed. *Grzimek's Animal Life Encyclopedia.* New York: Van Nostrand Reinhold, 1993.
Gunderson, Harvey L. *Mammalogy.* New York: McGraw-Hill, 1976.
Lawlor, Timothy E., *Handbook to the Orders and Families of Living Mammals.* Eureka, CA: Mad River Press, 1979.

Kathryn Snavely

Teratogen

A teratogen is an environmental agent that can cause abnormalities in a developing organism resulting in either fetal death or congenital abnormality. The human fetus is separated from the mother by the placental barrier, but the barrier is imperfect and permits a number of chemical and infectious agents to pass to the fetus. Well known teratogens include (but are not limited to) alcohol, excess vitamin A and retinoic acid, the rubella virus and high levels of ionizing radiation. Perhaps the best known teratogenic agent is the drug thalidomide, which induced severe limb abnormalities known as phocomelia in children whose mothers took the drug.

See also Birth defects; Embryo and embryonic development; Fetal alcohol syndrome.

Terbium see **Lanthanides**

Term

A term is an algebraic expression which can form a separable part of another expression such as an algebraic equation or a sequence. Terms are a specific part of the symbolic language of algebra. The symbols of this language were primarily developed during the sixteenth and seventeenth centuries and are used to represent otherwise lengthy expressions. They can be as simple as using the single character, +, to mean addition, or as complicated as $y = 4x^2 + 2x - 3$ to represent an algebraic polynomial equation.

In general, there are three types of algebraic expressions which can be classified as terms. These include expressions made up of a single variable or constant, ones that are the product or quotient of two or more variables and/or constants, and those that are the product or quotient of other expressions. For example, the number 4 and the variable x are both terms because they consist of a single symbol. The expression 2z is also a term because it represents the product of two symbols. It should be noted that terms like 2z, in which a number and a variable are written together, are indicated products because multiplication is implied. Therefore, the symbol 2z means 2 * z. Finally, an expression like $2pq(a + 5)n$ is a term because it represents a quotient (the result of division) of two expressions.

The symbols that make up a term are known as coefficients. In the term 4x, the number 4 is known as a numerical coefficient and the letter x is known as the literal coefficient. For this expression, we could say that 4 is the coefficient of x or x is the coefficient of 4.

Terms should be thought of as a single unit that represents the value of a particular number. This is particularly useful when discussing the terms of a larger expression such as an equation. In the expression $5x^3 + 2x^2 + 4x - 7$, there are four terms. Numbering them from left to right, the first term is $5x^3$, the second is $2x^2$, the third is 4x, and the fourth is -7. Notice that the sign in front of a term is actually part of it.

Some expressions contain terms which can be combined to form a single term. These "like terms" contain the same variable raised to the same power. For example, the like terms in the expression 3x + 2x can be added and the equation simplifies to 5x. Similarly, the expression $7y^2 - 3y^2$ can be simplified to $4y^2$. Expressions containing unlike terms can not be simplified. Therefore, $4x^2 - 2x$ is in its simplest form because the differences in the power of x prevents these terms from being combined.

See also Algebra.

Termites

Termites are slender, social insects, ranging in size from .007-.072 in (2-22 mm) long. The reproductive members of the species have wing spans of .03-.3 in (10-90 mm). Inhabiting nests of their own construction, they live in permanent and often highly developed communities. While termites thrive in warm, humid environments, some species have also adapted to open savannas and temperate zones. They are most commonly found in the tropical parts of Africa, Southeast Asia, Australia, and the Americas.

Termites belong to the order Isoptera, which includes seven families of termites, containing about 200 genera and about 2300 species. The families are: (1) the Mastotermitidae, (2) the Kalotermitidae, (3) the Termopsidae, (4) the Hodotermitidae, (5) the Rhinotermitidae, (6) the Serritermitidae, and (7) the Termitidae. The first five families are referred to as the lower termites, while the last two are known as the higher termites.

The classification into lower and higher termites refers to the termites' level of evolution, both in terms of behavior and anatomy. The higher termites have a more complex and developed social structure and build a more complex and varied nest. The most advanced nests start below the ground and form a mound above. A termite nest in Australia measured almost 20 feet (6.66 m) high and 98 feet (33 m) around. Three-quarters of all species of termites belong to the higher termite groups.

Caste system

The individuals making up a termite community are anatomically and functionally distinct from each other, depending upon their role within the community. The particular duty that each termite performs determines the specific caste to which each termite belongs. Each caste can perform only a certain task, and individual termites cannot stay alive without the rest of the colony. In total, there are four basic kinds of adult termite castes: the king and queen (primary reproductives), the supplementary reproductives, the soldiers, and the workers.

Reproductives

There are two reproductive castes providing for the continuation of the species. The primary reproductive caste—known as alates—consists of potential kings and queens. At a specific time each year, depending on the species and environment, a swarm of these alates leaves the original nest to start a new colony. The vast majority of swarming alates fall prey to birds, bats, lizards, snakes, and ants. When the male and female alates land, they shed their wings and look for mates. Once the pairing occurs, they run on the ground in tandem, the female ahead of the male, looking for the site on which to build their new nest.

The supplementary reproductives develop functional reproductive organs but never leave the parent colony. Their purpose is to act as substitutes for the king or queen if either or both dies. Further, female reproductives can supplement the queen's egg-laying volume, should her egg-laying capacity prove insufficient to maintain the colony.

The nesting location chosen by the alates is highly dependent upon the particular species of termite. Some species prefer to nest in the ground, while others prefer to nest in wood. Regardless of the nest, the pair digs a chamber, closes it off from the outside world, and never leaves it again. The pair mates in the chamber, and the female lays the eggs. Her first laying contains relatively few eggs. The young king and queen care for their larvae for four to six months. During this period, wood termites get the sustenance they need from the wood in their nests, while soil termites feed their young with the excess fat stored in their own bodies and by digesting their now-useless wing muscles.

Newly hatched termite larvae are tiny, measuring about .08 inches (2 mm) in length. Their coats are colorless and their bodies are soft. Furthermore, they are blind; their main sensory organs are their antennae, but they also have a series of small receptors situated on their heads.

After hatching, the young termites—or nymphs—have the general appearance of adult termites. They continue to grow and molt at intervals. After several stages of development, some finally become sexually mature individuals with wings. Others either become workers or soldiers. Both the workers and the soldiers—which are usually blind, and always infertile and wingless—are the result of specialized, incomplete development.

Workers

The workers form by far the largest caste and live exclusively underground; they are pale, have large toughened heads, and lack eyes. When the first workers are old enough to leave the nest, they begin to undertake their multiple duties. First, they search for food, leaving the queen free to devote all of her time to egg-laying. Eventually, the workers provide food for the king, queen, larvae, and soldiers. Dead wood is the main part of a worker termite's diet. Often, workers eat wood before returning to the colony with it. In such cases, they partially digest it and transform it into a milky liquid. When they reach the colony, the workers feed the other termites through regurgitation; this form of food is called stomodeal food.

Most species of termite eat wood, but their digestive enzymes are not able to break down the nutritious part of the wood, called cellulose. To do this, termites have the help of microorganisms residing in their bodies that break down the cellulose into a substance that they can digest.

The workers also take part in building the colony. In the majority of species, the workers dig underground systems of tunnels. They create complex structures, which protect the inhabitants from their enemies. Because some nests contain as many as three million termites, the nests need the right level of oxygen and carbon dioxide for the members to survive. Therefore, workers build nests with ventilation systems regulating the colony's environment. It is thought that intestinal gases, including methane, rise to the top of the nest and diffuse through the walls and out of venting shafts.

Another task that the workers must carry out is caring for the colony's young. When the queen lays her second series of eggs—about one month after her initial laying—the workers take the larvae into the brooding chamber where they care for them. As part of their care, the workers turn over the eggs periodically and check them for signs of parasite damage.

Soldiers

The soldier termites' main responsibility is defending the colony. Unlike other termites, soldiers have large armor-plated heads, a tough outer skeleton, and sometimes have glands for squirting poison at their enemies. Furthermore, the soldiers are equipped with biting

KEY TERMS

Alates—Primary reproductive termites; winged, sexually mature adults taking part in the colony's swarming activities.

Microorganisms—One celled creatures that enable the workers to break down and digest cellulose found in wood.

Molting—The process that nymphs undergo during their development. They shed their outer layers to make room for new growth.

Nymphs—Juvenile termites.

Proctodeal food—A liquid excreted from the rectal pouches in response to the tactile stimuli of other termites. Only produced among lower termites.

Reproductives—Termites with mature sexual organs; kings and queens.

Stomodeal food—A clear liquid, presumably saliva, regurgitated by the workers to the dependent castes.

Supplementary reproductives—Part of the reproductive caste; these termites never leave their parent colony; their functions are (1) to replace the king or queen should either one die and (2) to supplement the queen's egg-laying capacity if she is not producing enough eggs to support the colony.

Thorax—The area just below the head and neck; the chest.

mandibles, which include cutting edge teeth and even hooks.

Although termites are often preyed upon by aardvarks, reptiles, and other amphibians, their main predators are army and chirping ants. Even though the soldiers are blind, they can sense intruders with their antennae. To warn the colony, the soldiers beat their heads against the ground. Soldiers are never able to feed themselves.

The mature colony

Deep within the nest, protected by soldiers and cared for by workers, the queen begins to grow. While her head and thorax do not change, her abdomen increases in size as her ovaries enlarge and her egg-laying capacity increases. In some highly evolved species with extraordinarily large colonies, the queen can swell

to more than 5.5 inches (77 cm) in length and 1.5 inches (3.81 cm) in diameter; thus, her abdomen swells to about 200 to 300 times it original size. In such a state, the queen is incapacitated and cannot feed herself.

By her third year, the queen reaches the peak of her egg production, when she typically lays over 30,000 eggs per day. The most fertile queens belong to the species *Odontotermes obesus*, which can lay about one egg per second or about 86,400 eggs each day. In all species, the king, her constant companion, changes very little throughout his life.

See also Protozoa.

Further Reading:

Grzimek, H.C. Bernard, Dr., ed. *Grzimek's Animal Life Encyclopedia*. New York: Van Nostrand Reinhold Company, 1993.

Harris, W. Victor. *Termites: Their Recognition and Control*. London: Longmans, Green and Co. Ltd., 1964.

Lee, K.E. and T.G. Wood. *Termites and Soils*. New York: Academic Press, 1971.

Pearl, Mary Corliss, Ph.D. Consultant. *The Illustrated Encyclopedia of Wildlife*. London: Grey Castle Press, 1991.

The New Larousse Encyclopedia of Animal Life. New York: Bonanza Books, 1987.

Kathryn Snavely

Terns

Terns are fast-flying coastal seabirds, birds in the family Sternidae, which includes some 42 species. Although the nest species terns are found in the tropics and subtropics, these birds occur on all continents, ranging from the limits of land in the highest Arctic, to the fringes of Antarctica. Most terns breed and occur in coastal marine environments, or in the vicinity of inland lakes, rivers, and marshes.

Biology of terns

Terns are slender birds with long, pointed wings, and are adept fliers. Their tails are usually forked to some degree and their bills are sharply pointed. The usual coloration is some combination of white, grey, and/or black.

The smallest species of tern is the little tern (*Sterna albifrons*), which is only 9.1 in (23 cm) in body length and 1.75 oz (50 g) in weight. The largest species is the

Royal terns (*Sterna maxima*) on Estero Island, Florida.

Caspian tern (*Hydroprogne caspia*), which is 19.7 in (50 cm) long, and weighs 24.6 oz (700 g).

Most terns feed on fish, small squid, or large invertebrates. Species occurring in freshwater habitats may also eat amphibians and large insects. Terns typically hunt their aquatic prey by plunging head-first into water, often after having located their quarry by hovering.

Terns typically nest in colonies, some of which are large. The usual nesting locale is a gravel shore, on an island or relatively isolated peninsula, or on inland lakes and ponds. The typical nest built by terns is a simple scrap, but tropical terns known as noddies (Anons spp.) build a more substantial nest, and nest in trees and on cliff ledges. Some fairy terns do not build a nest at all—they lay a single egg, wedged into the fork between two branches of a tree.

Terns of North America

Fourteen species of terns breed regularly in North America. The most abundant species is the common tern (*S. hirundo*), which also breeds widely in Eurasia. The breeding range of this species is from the subarctic, the Great Lakes, to the temperate regions of the Atlantic coast. The common tern winters from southern parts of coastal North America through to southern South America. This tern has a black cap, a grey mantle (the back of the wings), a white breast, and a red beak with a blackish tip.

The arctic tern (*Sterna paradisaea*) is an abundant species that breeds from subarctic regions to the very limits of land in the Arctic of North America and Eurasia, and winters in the waters of the Southern Ocean. The arctic tern undertakes extraordinarily long migrations between its breeding and wintering habitats, with some populations traversing a distance of 22,356 mi (36,000 km) each year. Because it spends so much time

in high latitudes of both hemispheres, where day length is long during the summer, the arctic tern is thought to see more hours of daylight each year than any other creature. The arctic tern has similar coloration to the common tern, but the arctic tern has an all-red beak and shorter, red legs.

Forster's tern (*S. forsteri*) breeds in salt and freshwater marshes of the northern prairies, and to a lesser degree along the southern coasts of the Pacific and Atlantic Oceans. The roseate tern (*S. dougallii*) is locally common along the Atlantic coast of the eastern United States. The roseate tern also breeds in coastal places in western Europe, the West Indies, Venezuela, Africa, the Indian Ocean, south and southeast Asia, Australia, and many south Pacific islands.

The royal tern (*Thalasseus maximus*) is a relatively large, crested species that breeds on the Atlantic and Pacific coasts of North America, and also in Eurasia. This species winters on the coasts of south Florida, the Gulf of Mexico, and parts of the Caribbean.

The Caspian tern is the largest species of tern. This species breeds on large lakes and rivers and at a few places along the subarctic seacoast of North America. The Caspian tern is a wide-ranging species, also breeding in Eurasia, Africa, Australia, and New Zealand. This species winters along the coasts of southern California, Baha California, the Gulf of Mexico, and Caribbean islands.

The black tern (*Chlidonias niger*) is a dark-grey locally abundant species breeding on lakes and freshwater marshes in both North America and Eurasia. North American birds winter in Central America and northern South America. The sooty tern (*S. fuscata*) and noddy tern (*Anous stolidas*) only breed in the Dry Tortugas, small U.S. islands south of West Florida.

Conservation of terns

During the 19th century, many species of terns were rapaciously hunted for their plumage, which was valuable at the time for decorating the clothing of fashionable ladies. Sometimes, an artistic statement was made by mounting entire, stuffed terns onto broad-brimmed, ladies hats. Fortunately, the plumage of terms or other birds is not much used for these purposes any more.

In many places, terns have been deprived of important nesting habitats, as beaches and other coastal habitats have been appropriated and developed for human use. Frequent disturbances by pedestrians, all-terrain vehicles, boats, and other sources also disrupt the breeding of terns, usually by causing brooding adults to fly, which exposes their eggs or young to predation by other birds.

In many parts of their breeding range, terns eggs and chicks are taken by a number of the larger species of gulls (*Larus* spp.). The populations of gulls have increased enormously in most of the world, because these birds have benefited greatly from the availability of fish wastes discarded by fishing boats and processing plants, and from other foods available at garbage dumps. Gulls are highly opportunistic feeders, and will predate tern chicks, and sometimes adults, whenever it is easy to do so. The negative effects of gulls on terns are an important, indirect consequence of the fact that gulls have benefitted so tremendously from the activities of humans.

See also Gulls; Migration.

Further Reading:

Harrison, C.J.O., ed. *Bird Families of the World.* New York: H.N. Abrams Pubs., 1978.

Hay, J. *The Bird of Light.* New York: Norton, 1991.

Bill Freedman

Terracing

The word terrace is applied to geological formations, architecture such as a housing complex built on a slope, or an island between two paved roads. However, the act of terracing specifies an agricultural method of cultivating on steeply graded land. This form of conservation tillage breaks a hill into a series of steplike benches. These individual flat structures prevent rainwater from taking arable topsoil downhill with it. The spacing of terraces is figured mathematically by comparing the gradient of the land, the average rainfall, and the amount of topsoil which must be preserved.

Different forms of terracing are required, depending upon how steep the ground is that is intended for cultivation. The bench is the oldest type, used on very steep territory. A little dam called a riser marks off each bench, and can slow down rainwater runoff on slopes as extreme as 30 percent. Just the way a steplike or "switchback" layout of railroad tracks prevent trains from having to go up one steep grade, the effect of gravity is lessened by bench terracing. Climate as well as soil condition and farming methods must be taken into account, so the Zingg conservation bench is a type of flat-channel terrace constructed in semiarid climates. Slopes between each bench store runoff water after each rain.

KEY TERMS

Agroecosystem—This compound term refers to a man-made environment of cultivated land. Even if an agroecosystem is abandoned, it is still affected by the farming methods once used.

Arable—An agricultural term describing fertile ground or topsoil, which can be cultivated as cropland.

Contour farming—The modern term for horizontal plowing or contour plowing, often used in conjunction with terracing to further prevent erosion.

Erosion—Damage caused to topsoil by rainwater runoff. There are various special terms for patterns of erosion caused in the soil, like sheet, rill or gully erosion.

Point rows—These crop areas are "dead-ends" in a field, which cannot be cultivated with modern heavy farm equipment without requiring the machines to turn and pass over them a second time, in order to reach the rest of the crops. These areas are prevented during terracing by moving arable turf to a more easily farmed area and smoothing.

Topographic map—A map of the surface height and contour of a piece of land designated for terracing; used to plan the optimum terracing layout and techniques for the particular area.

Newer formats were developed to accommodate for mechanized farm equipment, so now variations such as the narrow-base ridge terrace and the broadbase terrace are used for less extreme gradients. Two approaches to broadbase terracing are used, depending upon the conditions of the topsoil and its vulnerability. The Nichols or channel variation is a graded broadbase terrace for which the soil is cultivated from above. Water is channeled off by this construction at a steady rate. The Mangum or ridge type is a level broadbase terrace used in permeable soil. This type shores up the topsoil from above and below. A less ambitious form than the broadbase is the steep-backslope terrace, which takes soil from the downhill side of a ridge, but this backslope cannot be used as cropland.

Modern practices

Parallel terraces are a recent innovation in conservation farming. This method incorporates land forming

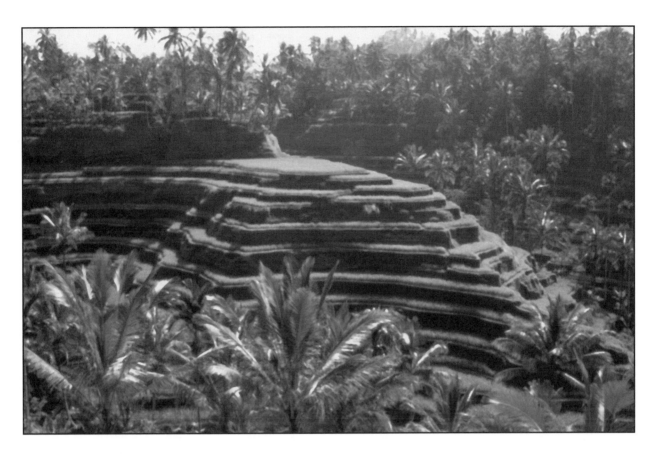

Rice terraces in Bali, Indonesia.

or landscaping by moving earth to make the terraces more uniform. The resulting formation allows room for the use of heavy machinery, and prevents "point rows," which are areas that cannot be efficiently cultivated without doubling back over the same area. Modern terrace planning incorporates the use of topological maps, known more simply as contour maps, which take into account the surface variations of an area slated for cultivation. Otherwise, there is no need for special equipment for terracing, which can be done with an old-fashioned moldboard plow or with mechanized rigs like the bulldozer.

Worldwide methods

In Africa a certain method called "fanya juu" comes from the Swahili phrase meaning "make it up." It began in Kenya during the 1950s, when standard Western practices could not control the fierce erosion in the area and also took too much arable land out of circulation. Fanya juu produces embankments by carving out ditches and depositing the soil uphill to form embankments. The ditches can be used to grow banana plants while another crop is planted on the embankments. A variation involving Western channel terracing

is called "fanya chini," but this is less popular because the ditches must be desilted of churned-up topsoil on a regular basis. Additionally, in very steep areas only bench terracing can be truly effective.

Yemeni mountain land was once cultivated widely by farmers, but it made for a difficult living. So when oil became a bigger economy than agriculture in the surrounding countries, the farmers slowly migrated to places like Saudi Arabia in order to seek greater fortunes in a new business. The agroecosystem left behind began to slowly contribute to soil erosion, because the arrangement of bench terraces, small dams and irrigation or runoff conduits was decaying. By 1987, one researcher found that thin or shoestring rills were deepening into gullies on the mountainsides.

The benches of Lebanon, some of which have existed for over two and a half thousand years after being instituted by the Phoenicians, were threatened by the battles of civil conflict in the area. Farmers were driven away to safer and more convenient living conditions in cities or in other countries. An investigation in 1994 warned of long-term damage to untended terraced lands including an increased possibility of landslides, and the chance that the land may be rendered eventually unfarmable.

Further Reading:

Moldenhauer et al., eds. *Development of Conservation Farming on Hillslopes.* The Soil and Water Conservation Society, 1991.

"Rehabilitating the Ancient Terraced Lands of Lebanon." *Journal of Soil & Water Conservation.* March/April 1994.

"Bench Terracing in the Kerinci Uplands of Sumatra." *Journal of Soil & Water Conservation.* September/October 1990.

"Terrace Channel Design and Evaluation." *Transactions of the ASAE.* September/October 1992.

Turner, B. L. *Once Beneath the Forest.* Boulder, CO: Westview Press, 1983.

Jennifer Kramer

Terrapins see **Turtles**

Territoriality

Territoriality is the behavior by which an animal lays claim to and defends an area against others of its species, and occasionally members of other species as well. The territory defended could be hundreds of square miles in size, or only slightly larger than the animal itself. It may be occupied by a single animal, a pair, family, or entire herd or swarm of animals. Some animals hold and defend a territory year-round, and use the territory as a source of food and shelter. Other animals establish a territory only at certain times of the year, when it is needed for attracting a mate, breeding, and/or raising a family.

The advantages of territoriality

Many different species exhibit territorial behavior, because it offers several advantages to the territorial animal. An animal which has a "home ground" can develop reflexes based on its surroundings. Thus it can react quickly to dangerous situations without having to actively seek hiding places or defensible ground. By spacing out potential competitors, territoriality also prevents the depletion of an area's natural resources. This regulation of population density may also slow down the spread of disease. In addition, territorial behavior exposes weaker animals (which are unable to defend their territory) to predation, thereby promoting a healthy population.

Types of territories

Some animals will establish a territory solely for the purpose of having a place to rest. Such a territory is known as a roost, and may be established in a different area every night. Roosts are often occupied and defended by large groups of animals, for the protection offered in numbers. Individual personal spaces within the roost may be fought over as well. Roosting spots nearer the interior of a group of animals are often the safest, and therefore the most highly prized.

Several species of birds and a few mammals are known to establish specialized territories during the breeding season, which are used only to attract mates through breeding displays. This type of territory is known as a lek, and the associated behavior is called lekking. Leks are among the most strongly defended of all territories, since holding a good lek increases the chances of attracting a mate. Leks are generally of little use for feeding or for bringing up young, and the animals will abandon its lek once it attracts a mate or mates, or if it becomes too weak to defend it.

Defending a territory

Some animals will defend their territory by fighting with those who try to invade it. Fighting, however, is not often the best option, since it uses up a large amount of energy, and can result in injury or even death. Most animals rely on various threats, either through vocalizations, smells, or visual displays. The songs of birds, the drumming of woodpeckers, and the loud calls of monkeys are all warnings that carry for long distances, advertising to potential intruders that someone else's territory is being approached. Many animals rely on smells to mark their territories, spraying urine, leaving droppings or rubbing scent glands around the territories' borders. Approaching animals will be warned off the territory without ever encountering the territory's defender.

On occasion, these warnings may be ignored, and an intruder may stray into a neighboring territory, or two animals may meet near the border of their adjacent territories. When two individuals of a territorial species meet, they will generally threaten each other with visual displays. These displays often will often exaggerate an animal's size by the fluffing up of feathers or fur, or will show off the animals weapons. The animals may go through all the motions of fighting without ever actually touching each other, a behavior known as ritual fighting. The displays are generally performed best near the center of an animal's territory, where it is more likely to attack an intruder, and become more fragmented closer

Walrus battling over a hauling-out spot, Bristol Bay, Alaska.

KEY TERMS

. . . .

Lek—An area defended by animals of one sex (usually males) because ownership increases the chance of attracting members of the other sex.

Territory—An area defended by an animal against others, usually of the same species.

to the edges, where retreating becomes more of an option. This spectrum of performances results in territorial boundaries, where displays of neighbors are about equal in intensity, or where the tendency to attack and the tendency to retreat are balanced.

Actual fighting usually only happens in overcrowded conditions, when resources are scarce. Serious injury can result, and old or sick animals may die, leading to a more balanced population size. Under most natural conditions, territoriality is an effective way of maintaining a healthy population. The study of social behaviors such as territoriality in animals may help us also to understand human society, and to learn how individual behavior affects human populations.

See also Competition; Natural selection.

Further Reading:

Parker, Steve, Jane Parker, and Terry Jennings. *Territories.* New York: Gloucester Press, 1991.

David Fontes

Testes see **Reproductive system**

Tetanus

Tetanus, also known as lockjaw, is a disease caused by a type of bacteria that lives in the soil and the intestines of people and animals. When these bacteria get into the body, the poisons they produce affect the nervous system, causing muscle spasms and, in many cases, death. Tetanus is not contagious and can be prevented with a vaccine.

Tetanus is caused by the bacteria *Clostridium tetani.* Tetanus bacteria can enter the body through an open wound, such as a puncture or a cut; the disease can also be transmitted via improperly sterilized hypodermic needles and practices such as tattooing. Since the bacteria live in the intestines of animals, animal bites can also cause tetanus.

Once the bacteria enter the body, it generally takes anywhere from three days to three weeks for symptoms to develop. The poison, or toxin, produced by the tetanus bacteria enters the central nervous system, affecting the body's nerve cells and causing muscle spasms. When these spasms occur in the muscles involved in chewing, the condition is commonly known as lockjaw. If the muscles of the throat and chest go into spasms, tetanus can be fatal. It is estimated that 40% of the incidences are fatal. Tetanus can be treated with antibiotics and antitoxin medication.

Tetanus is preventable through immunization. In the United States, infants are vaccinated against the disease at 2 months, 4 months and 6 months. This vaccination is known as the DTP shot; it protects against diphtheria, tetanus, and pertussis (whooping cough). In order to insure immunity, it is necessary to get a booster shot every ten years.

Tetanus can also be prevented through the proper cleaning and disinfection of wounds. If the nature of the wound indicates the possibility of tetanus infection (for example, puncture wounds), treatment may include a booster shot.

In the United States, tetanus often occurs among senior citizens, who may not be up to date on their immunizations. In countries where immunization against tetanus is not routine, however, the disease is common among infants. Generally, babies are infected during childbirth or through the newly cut umbilical cord. In infants, the disease is often fatal. However, due to improving immunization programs, the incidence of tetanus worldwide has been declining in recent decades.

See also Childhood diseases; Vaccine.

Tetrahedron

A tetrahedron is a polyhedron with four triangular faces. It is determined by four points (the *vertices*) that are not all in the same plane. A *regular* tetrahedron is one where all of the faces are congruent equilateral triangles.

A tetrahedron is the same as a pyramid with a triangular base.

See also Polygons; Pyramid.

Textiles

Textiles are generally considered to be woven fabrics. They may be woven from any natural or synthetic fibers, filaments, or yarns that are suitable for being spun and woven into cloth.

History of textiles

The earliest known textiles were recovered from a neolithic village in southern Turkey. Rope, netting, matting, and cloth have been found in the Judean desert (dating from 7160 to 6150 B.C.).

Flax was the most common plant fiber used in antiquity. Hemp, rush, palm, and papyrus were also employed as textile fibers in ancient times. Early evidence of the use of flax has been found in north Syria (c. 6000 B.C.), Iraq (c. 5000 B.C.), and Egypt (c. 6000 B.C.). Evidence that fibers from sheep, goats, and dogs were used in textiles as early as the eighth century B.C.has been found in northwest Iran; early use of these fibers has also been traced to Palestine and southern Turkey. Cotton, native to India, was used in Assyria around 700 B.C. The use of silk, originally exclusive to China, appears to have spread to Germany by around 500 B.C.

The ancient Egyptians and later the Israelites preferred garments of white linen and wool. But Kushites, Nubians, and Libyans apparently preferred dyed fabrics. The principal dyes and mordants such as alum were probably known since earliest times. Royal purple was produced by the Phoenicians, who had become major traders in dyes and wools by around 1700 B.C., from murex. Evidence exists of trade in textiles as early as 6000 B.C., in which wool and cloth were important trade goods.

Textile techniques

Spinning

Spinning is the process of making yarn or thread by the twisting of vegetable fibers, animal hairs, or man-made fibers, i.e., filament-like elements only a few inches in length. In the spinning mill, the raw material is first disentangled and cleaned. Various grades or types of fibers may then be blended together to produce yarn having the desired properties. The fibers are next spread out parallel to one another in a thin web, from which a yarn-like material is formed.

A computer controlled textile mill.

Weaving

In its simplest form, i.e., basketry, weaving probably pre-dated spinning, as in early cultures individuals presumably interlaced long fibrous stems with their fingers before they learned to convert short fibers into continuous yarn. Woven structures consist of two sets of threads, the warp and the weft, which are interlaced to form cloth. Warp threads are held parallel to each other under tension; the weft is worked over and under them, row by row. Looms have been used since the time of ancient Egyptians to keep the warp threads evenly spaced and under tension.

The following techniques are used to prepare the warp and the weft prior to weaving: 1) In doubling, two or more yarns are wound on a bobbin without undergoing any twisting (as distinct from spinning, in which fibers are twisted together to give them the requisite strength). In twisting doubling, two or more yarns are twisted around each other; 2) Sizing is done to make the warp threads smooth, to reduce the friction of the threads. The threads are coated or saturated with an adhesive paste (size); 3) Twisting joins the ends of a new warp with those of the one already in the loom. It is done by twisting the ends together, either by hand or with the aid of a special device.

Simple weaves are of three types: tabby, twill, and satin. Tabby weave, or plain weave, is produced by passing the weft across the warp twice. Twill weaves are characterized by a diagonal movement caused by starting the weave sequence one place to the right or left on each successive passage of the weft. Satin weave is distinguished by the spacing of the binding points, the normal sequence being over one warp, and under four or more. Compound weaves are based on the three basic weaves with the addition of extra warp, weft, or both. Velvet is a compound weave that starts as a basic weave.

Finger weaving techniques include twining and braiding. Twining uses two sets of yarns. In weft twining, the warp is stretched between two bars and the weft worked across in pairs. One thread passes over a warp and the other under, with the two yarns making a half turn around each other between each warp.

Finishing

Most fabrics produced by weaving or knitting have to undergo further processing before they are ready for sale. In finishing, the fabric is subjected to mechanical and chemical treatment in which its quality and appearance are improved and its commercial value enhanced. Each type of fabric has its own particular finishing operations. Textiles produced from vegetable fibers require different treatment than textiles produced from animal fibers or synthetic fibers.

Woven cloth is usually boiled with dilute caustic soda to remove natural oils and other impurities. It is then rinsed, scoured in an acid bath, further processed, and bleached with sodium chlorite. Singeing may be done to remove any fibers on cotton or rayon materials, especially if they have to be printed.

In the course of spinning, weaving, and finishing, the fabric is subjected to much pull and stretch. When the material gets wet, the material reverts to its original shape. Sanforizing mechanically shortens the fibers, so that they will not shrink in the wash.

Raising (or napping) is a process in which small steel hooks tear some of the fibers or ends of fibers out of the weft yarn, so the fibers acquire a wooly surface (called the "nap"). This improves heat retention and absorptive properties (as in flannel fabrics), making them softer to the touch. Raising is chiefly used for cotton, rayon, or woolen fabrics. It can be applied to one or both sides.

Types of textiles

Tapestries

Although the term tapestry usually conjures up images of large pictorial wall-hangings of the sort used in medieval and post-medieval Europe, tapestries are in fact distinctive woven structures consisting specifically of a weft-faced plain weave with discontinuous wefts. This means that the weft crosses the warp only where its particular color is need for the fabric design. The technique has been used in many cultures to produce fabrics ranging from heavy, durable floor coverings to delicate Chinese silk. Compared to other weaving techniques, tapestry allows the weaver much more freedom of expression.

Woven rugs

Rugs can be made by a number of techniques, including tapestry, brocade (in which a plain weave foundation is supplemented with supplementary wefts), and pile weaving. Pile rugs are most commonly associated with rug weaving, however. These rugs are made of row after row of tiny knots tied on the warps of a foundation weave which together form a thick pile.

Embroidery

Embroidery is a method of decorating an already existing structure, usually a woven foundation fabric, with a needle. Embroideries have also been done on other media such as parchment or bark. For the past 100 years, it has been possible to produce embroidery by machine as well as by hand. Embroidery yarns are woven into a fabric after it has come off the loom, unlike brocade, which in which yarns are placed in the fabric during the weaving process.

Lace

Lace is essentially an openwork fabric constructed by the looping, plaiting, or twisting of threads using either a needle or a set of bobbins. It is not woven. Needle lace is made with one thread at a time. Bobbin lace is constructed with many different threads, each wound on its own bobbin. These are manipulated in a manner similar to that used in braiding. Machine-made lace was first produced around 1840.

Printed and dyed textiles

Aside from exploiting the effects achieved by using natural fibers, the only ways to introduce color into textiles are by printing or dyeing.

In textile printing, the dyes are dissolved in water. Thickening agents (e.g., starch) are added to the solutions to increase viscosity. The oldest method is block printing, usually from wooden blocks in which a design is carved. Stencil printing is done with the aid of paper or thin metal stencils. In silk screen printing, the design is formed on a silk screen, which then serves as a stencil. Most cloth is printed by roller printing. The printing area is engraved on a copper roller to form a recessed pattern (intaglio), which is coated with a color paste. The roller transfers the paste to the cloth.

Pattern dyeing uses two principal procedures: resist dyeing and mordant dyeing. In resist dyeing, a resist substance such as hot wax, rice paste, or clay is applied to those areas chosen to resist the dye and remain white. The cloth is then dyed and the resist is later removed. The technique is widely known in China, Japan, and West Africa, but is most often identified with Javanese batik. Tie dyeing is a resist technique in which parts of the cloth are tied with bast or waxed cord before dyeing. The dyeing is done quickly so the wrappings are not penetrated, and a negative pattern emerges. Many dyestuffs are not directly absorbed by fibers, so mordants or fixing agents are used that combine with the dye and fibers to make the color insoluble.

There are two main types of textile dyeing machines: in one type the dye solution is circulated through the fabric, which remains at rest; in the other, the fabric is passed through a stationary bath of the dye solution.

Knits

Knitting is a looped fabric made from a continuous supply of yarn. The yarn need not be continuous throughout the piece, however. Different colors or qualities or yarn may be introduced into a single knitted piece.

Knitting is used for the production of underwear and outer garments, curtain fabrics, etc. The materials used are yarn and threads of cotton, wool, and man-made fibers; as well as blended yarns and paper yarns. The products are either flat fabrics (later made into garments) or ready-fashioned garments. In weft fabric, the threads extend crosswise across the fabric; in warp fabric, the threads extend lengthwise. Warp fabric has less elasticity than weft fabric and is not used as much for socks and stockings.

Netting, knotting, and crochet

Netted fabrics have been known since antiquity when they were probably used for fishing nets. In knotting, knots are first made with a small shuttle at intervals in lengths of string, linen, silk, or wool. The knotted thread is then applied to a suitable ground fabric, forming patterns or covering it completely. Twentieth century macrame is a form of knotting. Crochet is a looped fabric made with a continuous thread that forms horizontal rows, with loops locked laterally as well as vertically.

Felt and bark cloth

Felt is a fabric formed by applying pressure to hot, wet fibers (usually wool). The fibers become interlocked, and the process cannot be reversed. In Polynesia, bark cloth was traditionally obtained from bark stripped from trees of the mulberry family. The bark was first soaked for several days to make it soft and flexible, then the rough outer bark was scraped from the inner bark. The inner bark was next beaten with mallets to form sheets of cloth, which were treated in a variety of ways before use.

Significance of textiles

Textiles serve the everyday needs of people, but they may also serve to distinguish individuals and groups of individuals in terms of social class, gender,

KEY TERMS
. . . .

Bobbin—A small cylinder or similar article round which thread or yarn is wound, in order to be wound off again and as required, for use in weaving, sewing, etc.; a spool.

Fiber—A complex morphological unit with an extremely high ratio of length to diameter (typically several hundred to one) and a relatively high tenacity.

Loom—A machine in which yarn or thread is woven into fabrics by the crossing of vertical and horizontal threads (called respectively the warp and the weft).

Mordant—A substance enabling a dye to become fixed in the fabric on which it is used, usually applied beforehand.

Shuttle—A bobbin with two pointed ends used in weaving for carrying the thread of the weft across between the threads of the warp.

Warp—The threads stretched lengthwise in a loom.

Weft—The threads woven at right angles across a warp in making a fabric.

occupation, and status with the group. Traditional societies associated special meaning with textile designs. These meanings tended to have specific meanings for particular ethnic groups alone. It was assumed that everyone in the group knew them. However, once the meanings have become lost, it is almost impossible to reconstruct them. The patterns in Javanese batiks, for example, originally had meaning to the wearer, but these meanings are now largely lost. Textiles also have real as well as symbolic value. Under Byzantine emperors, silk was a powerful political tool: foreign governments out of favor were denied trading privileges; those in favor were rewarded with silks.

Textiles have played major roles in the social, economic, and religious lives of communities. In many parts of Europe and Asia, young girls spent many months preparing clothing and furnishing textiles for their wedding trousseaus as a demonstration of their skills and wealth. Traditionally, women have played a far larger role than men in producing textiles. In many parts of Africa, however, men produce both woven and dyed textiles, and in many urban or courtly textile traditions, men were the main producers (e.g., Asian rug weaving, European tapestry).

Textiles are thus a major component of material culture. They may be viewed as the products of technology, as cultural symbols, as works of art, or as items of trade. The textile arts are a fundamental human activity, expressing symbolically much of what is valuable in any culture.

See also Cotton; Flax; Dyes and pigments.

Further Reading:

Harris, Jennifer. *Textiles-5000 Years.* New York: H. N. Abrams, 1993.

Simmons, Paula. *Spinning and Weaving Wool.* Seattle: Pacific Search Press, 1987.

Randall Frost

Thalidomide

Thalidomide is a drug that was marketed in the late 1950s and early 1960s in Great Britain and Europe. It was used both as a sleeping pill and as an antidote to morning sickness in pregnant women.

In 1962, a host of usually rare limb abnormalities suddenly became much more common. About ten thousand babies were born displaying, in particular, a shortening of the arms and/or legs called phocomelia. In phocomelia, for example, the baby may be born with the upper arm and forearm completely absent, and the hand attached to the trunk of the body by a short little bone. This same situation can occur with the legs, so that the majority of the leg is totally absent, and the foot is attached to the trunk of the body. Other babies were born with amelia, the complete absence of one or more limbs. Other birth defects involving the eyes, teeth, heart, intestine, and anus were similarly noted to be significantly more common.

These birth defects were soon traced to the drug thalidomide, which was proven to be a potent teratogen (substance which interferes with normal development in the embryo). In fact, studies showed that fully 20% of all babies exposed to thalidomide during their first eight weeks in the uterus were born with the characteristic abnormalities described above. Because the skeletal system begins to be formed as early as the third week of development, and small buds which will become the limbs appear around week five, anything which interferes with development at this very early stage has devastating effects. Once the marketing of thalidomide was halted, these birth defects again became rare occurrences.

Currently, thalidomide has been shown to have some use in the treatment of two different illnesses. In leprosy, a bacterial disease causing both skin and nervous system problems, thalidomide has some effect against inflammation and pain. Studies are also underway to explore using thalidomide to help guard against immune system rejection of bone marrow transplants.

See also Birth defects; Embryo and embryonic development.

Further Reading:

Behrman, Richard E., et al. *Nelson Textbook of Pediatrics.* Philadelphia: W.B. Saunders Company, 1992.

Berkow, Robert and Andrew J. Fletcher. *The Merck Manual of Diagnosis and Therapy.* Rahway, NJ: Merck Research Laboratories, 1992.

Fanaroff, Avroy A. and Richard J. Martin. *Neonatal-Perinatal Medicine.* St Louis: Mosby Year Book, Inc., 1992.

Sadler, T.W. *Langman's Medical Embryology.* Baltimore: Williams & Wilkins, 1985.

Sanford, Louis and Alfred Gilman. *Goodman and Gilman's Pharmacological Basis of Therapeutics.* New York: Pergamon Press, Inc., 1990.

Taeusch, H. William, et al. *Schaffer and Avery's Diseases of the Newborn. 6th ed.* Philadelphia:W.B. Saunders Company, 1991.

Thallium see **Element, chemical**

Theorem

A theorem (the term is derived from the Greek *theoreo*, which means *I look at*) denotes either a proposition yet to be proven, or a proposition proven correct on the basis of accepted results from some area of mathematics. Since the time of the ancient Greeks, proven theorems have represented the foundation of mathematics. Perhaps the most famous of all theorems is the Pythagorean theorem.

Mathematicians develop new theorems by suggesting a proposition based on experience and observation which seems to be true. These original statements are only given the status of a theorem when they are proven correct by logical deduction. Consequently, many propositions exist which are believed to be correct, but are not theorems because they can not be proven using deductive reasoning alone.

Historical background

The concept of a theorem was first used by the ancient Greeks. To derive new theorems, Greek mathematicians used logical deduction from premises they believed to be self-evident truths. Since theorems were a direct result of deductive reasoning, which yields unquestionably true conclusions, they believed their theorems were undoubtedly true. The early mathematician and philosopher Thales (640-546 B.C.) suggested many early theorems, and is typically credited with beginning the tradition of a rigorous, logical proof before the general acceptance of a theorem. The first major collection of mathematical theorems was developed by Euclid around 300 B.C. in a book called *The Elements*.

The absolute truth of theorems was readily accepted up until the eighteenth century. At this time mathematicians, such as Karl Friedrich Gauss (1777-1855), began to realize that all of the theorems suggested by Euclid could be derived by using a set of different premises, and that a consistent non-Euclidean structure of theorems could be derived from Euclidean premises. It then became obvious that the starting premises used to develop theorems were not self-evident truths. They were in fact, conclusions based on experience and observation, and not necessarily true. In light of this evidence, theorems are no longer thought of as absolutely true. They are only described as correct or incorrect based on the initial assumptions.

Characteristics of a theorem

The initial premises on which all theorems are based are called axioms. An axiom, or postulate, is a basic fact which is not subject to formal proof. For example, the statement that there is an infinite number of even integers is a simple axiom. Another is that two points can be joined to form a line. When developing a theorem, mathematicians choose axioms which seem most reliable based on their experience. In this way, they can be certain that the theorems which are proved are as near to the truth as possible. However, absolute truth is not possible because axioms are not absolutely true.

To develop theorems, mathematicians also use definitions. Definitions state the meaning of lengthy concepts in a single word or phrase. In this way, when we talk about a figure made by the set of all points which are a certain distance from a central point, we can just use the word *circle*.

See also Postulate; Proof; Symbolic logic.

KEY TERMS

Axiom—A basic fact which is not subject to a formal proof.

Deductive reasoning—A type of logical reasoning which leads to conclusions which are undeniably true if the beginning assumptions are true.

Definition—A single word or phrase which states a lengthy concept.

Pythagorean theorem—A famous theorem which states that the sum of the squares of the sides is equal to the square of the hypotenuse.

Further Reading:
Dunham, William. *Journey Through Genius*. New York: Wiley, 1990.
Kline, Morris. *Mathematics for the Nonmathematician*. New York: Dover, 1967.
Lloyd, G. E. R. *Early Greek Science: Thales to Aristotle*. New York: W. W. Norton, 1970.
Newman, James R., ed. *The World of Mathematics*. New York: Simon and Schuster, 1956.
Paulos, John Allen. *Beyond Numeracy*. New York: Knopf, 1991.

Perry Romanowski

Thermal expansion

The most easily observed examples of thermal expansion are size changes of materials as they are heated or cooled. Almost all materials (solids, liquids and gases) expand when they are heated, and contract when they are cooled. Increased temperature increases the frequency and magnitude of the molecular motion of the material and produces more energetic collisions. Increasing the energy of the collisions forces the molecules further apart and causes the material to expand.

Common observations

Different materials expand or contract at different rates. In general, gases expand more than liquids, and liquids expand more than solids. Observation of thermal expansion in a solid object requires careful scrutiny. Several everyday examples are: 1) The sag in outdoor electrical lines is much larger on hot summer

| (a) Warm | (b) Cold | (c) Hot |
| Iron | Aluminum | Iron | Aluminum | Iron | Aluminum |

Figure 1. Representation of thermally induced change in a bimetallic strip made of iron and aluminum. The strip bends because the two materials do not expand or contract equally.

days than it is on cold winter days. 2) The rails for trains are installed during warm weather and have small gaps between the ends to allow for further expansion during very hot summer days. 3) Because the metal expands more than glass a stuck metal lid on a glass container can be loosened by running hot water over the joint between the lid and the container.

Liquids generally expand by larger amounts than solids. This difference in expansion rate is sometimes observed when the gas tank of a car is filled on a hot day. Gasoline pumped from the underground container is cold and it gradually heats to the temperature of the car as it sits in the gas tank. The gasoline expands in volume faster than the gas tank and overflows onto the ground.

Gases expand even more than liquids when heated. The expansion difference between a gas and a solid can

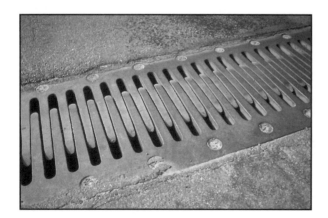

Joints like this one are used in bridges to accomodate thermal expansion.

be observed by filling a plastic air mattress in a cool room and then using it on a hot beach. The difference in thermal expansion between the container and the gas could unexpectedly over inflate the mattress and blow a hole in the plastic.

Practical applications and problems associated with thermal expansion

Sometimes man's ingenuity has led him to find practical applications for these differences in thermal expansion between different materials. In other cases, he has developed technologies or applications that overcome the problems caused by the difference in thermal expansion between different materials.

The thermally induced change in the length of a thin strip of metal differs for each material. For example, when heated, a strip of steel would expand by half as much as an equal length piece of aluminum. Welding together a thin piece of each of these materials produces a bimetallic strip.

The difference in expansion causes the bimetallic strip to bend when the temperature is changed. This movement has many common uses including: thermostats to control temperature, oven thermometers to measure temperature, and switches to regulate toasters. Some practical solutions to everyday thermal expansion problems in solids are: 1) The material developed for filling teeth has the same expansion as the natural enamel of the tooth. 2) The steel developed to reinforce concrete has the same expansion as the concrete. 3) Concrete roads are poured with expansion joints between the slabs to allow for thermal expansion (these

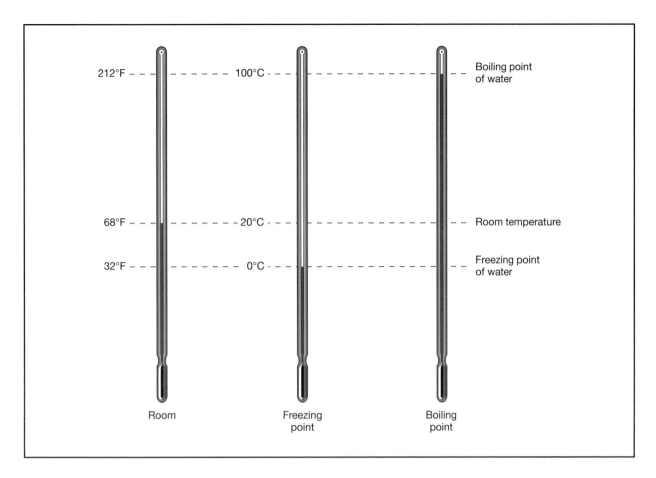

212°F — — — — — — — 100°C — — — — — — — — — — — — — — Boiling point
of water

68°F — — — — — — — 20°C — — — — — — — — — — — — — Room temperature

32°F — — — — — — — 0°C — — — — — — — — — — — — — Freezing point
of water

Room   Freezing
point   Boiling
point

Figure 2. Mercury and alcohol thermometers function because of the expansion difference between liquids and solids. Because the liquid expands at a different rate than the tube, it rises as the temperature increases and drops as the temperature decreases.

joints are the cause of the thumping noise commonly experienced when traveling on a concrete highway).

The manufacture of mercury and alcohol thermometers is based upon the expansion difference between solids and liquids. Thermometer fabrication consists of capturing a small amount of liquid (mercury or alcohol) inside an empty tube made of glass or clear plastic.

Because the liquid expands at a faster rate than the tube, it rises as the temperature increases and drops as the temperature decreases. The first step in producing a thermometer scale is to record the height of the liquid at two known temperatures (i.e. the boiling point and freezing point of water). The difference in fluid height between these point is divided into equal increments to indicate the temperature at heights between these extremes.

Automobile engine coolant systems provide a practical example of a liquid-thermal expansion problem. If the radiator is filled with coolant when the engine is cold, it will overflow when the engine heats during operation. In older car models, the excess fluid pro-

duced by the hot temperatures was released onto the ground. Periodic replacement was required to avoid overheating. Newer cars have an overflow container that collects the released fluid during thermal expansion and returns it to the radiator as the engine cools after operation. This improvement in the coolant system reduces the number of times the coolant fluid level must be checked and avoids the expense of replacing costly antifreeze material mixed with the radiator fluid.

Hot-air balloons are an obvious example of the practical use of the thermal expansion difference between a gas and a solid. Because the hot air inside the balloon bag increases in size faster than the container it stretches the bag so that it expands and displaces the colder (heavier) air outside the bag. The difference between the lower density of the air inside the bag compared to the lower density of the air outside the bag causes the balloon to rise. Cooling the air inside the bag causes the balloon to descend.

Water, like most other liquids, expands when heated and contracts when cooled, except in the temper-

Figure 3.

ature region between 32°F (0°C) and 39.2°F (4°C). A given mass of fresh water decreases in volume until the temperature is decreased to 39.2 °F (4° C). Below this temperature, the volume per unit mass increases until the water freezes (see Figure 3.) This unusual behavior is important to fresh water plants and animals that exist in climates where water freezes in the colder seasons of the year. As the water surface cools to 39.2°F (4° C), it

becomes more dense and sinks to the bottom, pushing the warmer water to the surface.

This mixing action continues until all of the water has reached this temperature. The upper layer of water then becomes colder and less compact and stays near the surface where it freezes. When an ice layer forms, it provides an insulation barrier that retards cooling of the remaining water. Without this process, fresh water animal and plant life could not survive the winter.

See also Balloon; Gases, properties of; States of matter; Temperature; Thermometer; Thermostat.

KEY TERMS

. . . .

Bimetallic strip—A thin strip of metal composed of two different materials whose heat sensitive characteristics can be used to control pointer positions and to open and close electrical circuits.

Thermostat—A device which responds to temperature changes and can be used to activate switches controlling heating and cooling equipment.

Further Reading:

Davis, Kenneth S. and Day, John Arthur. *Water, the Mirror of Science*. Doubleday, 1961.
Halliday and Resnick. *Physics*. John Wiley & Sons, Inc, 1965.
Hewitt, Paul G. *Conceptual Physics*. Little Brown & Company, 1977.
Merkin, Melvin. *Physical Science*. W. B. Sanders Company, 1976.

Jim Zurasky

Thermocouple

Accurately measuring temperatures over a wide range is a challenge to engineers, physicists, and other scientists. Many techniques have been devised to deal with a wide range of conditions and temperatures. One such technique is a thermocouple. A thermocouple makes use of one aspect of the thermoelectric effect to measure temperatures, the voltage produced between two different wires with junctions at different temperatures. Depending on the types of wires chosen, a thermocouple can be used for temperatures ranging from -454° F to 4,172° F (-270° C to 2300° C).

A thermocouple must consist of two wires of different compositions. A popular combination is copper and constantan. Constantan is an alloy of copper and nickel. The different wires are joined at the ends to make two junctions. One of the wires is then cut so that a voltmeter can be placed in the circuit to measure the voltage between the two junctions. This voltage will depend on the temperature difference between the two junctions. A scientist wanting to use a thermocouple will then place one of the junctions in the object whose temperature is to be measured. Because the voltage depends on the temperature difference between the two junctions, the other junction must be maintained at an accurately known temperature. One way to maintain a known temperature is to place the junction in an ice water bath that will be at the freezing point of water. To find the unknown temperature the scientist must know what temperature difference corresponds to the measured voltage. These figures are determined by careful experiments and then tabulated, so the scientist uses the table to find the unknown temperature.

What causes this voltage difference? The two different types of metal, having different compositions, will have different densities of electrons. The electrons will tend to diffuse from the higher to the lower densities. These electron densities both depend on the temperature, so if the two junctions are at different temperatures the diffusion of electrons will proceed at different rates at each junction. The net result is a motion of the electrons, so there is a voltage between the two junctions.

Thermocouples have the advantage of being accurate over a wide temperature range and of being able to accurately follow rapid temperature changes. They can however be cumbersome to use. The need to keep one junction at an accurately known temperature limits their portability.

Thermodynamics

Thermodynamics is the science that deals with work and heat, and the transformation of one into the other. It is a macroscopic theory, dealing with matter in bulk, disregarding the molecular nature of materials. The corresponding microscopic theory, based on the fact that materials are made up of a vast number of molecules, is called statistical mechanics.

Historical background

Benjamin Thompson, Count von Rumford (1753-1814) recognized from observing the boring of cannon that the work (or mechanical energy) involved in the boring process was being converted to heat by friction, causing the temperature of the cannon to rise. With the experiments of James Joule (1818-1889), it was recognized that heat is a form of energy that is transferred from one object to another, and that work can be converted to heat without limit. However, the opposite is found not to be true: that is, there are limiting factors in the conversion of heat to work. The research of Sadi Carnot (1796-1832), of Lord Kelvin (1824-1907), and of Rudolph Clausius (1822-1888), among others, has led to an understanding of these limitations.

Temperature

The idea of temperature is well known to everyone, but the need to define it so that it can be used for measurements is far more complex than the simple concepts of "hot" and "cold." If a rod of metal is placed in an ice-water bath and the length is measured, and then placed in a steam bath and the length again measured, it will be found that the rod has lengthened. This is an illustration of the fact that, in general, materials expand when heated, and contract when cooled (however, under some conditions rubber can do the opposite, while water is a very special case and is treated below). One could therefore use the length of a rod as a measure of temperature, but that would not be useful, since different materials expand different amounts for the same increase in temperature, so that everyone would need to have exactly the same type of rod to make certain that they obtained the same value of temperature under the same conditions.

However, it turns out that practically all gases, at sufficiently low pressures, expand in volume exactly the same amount with a given increase in temperature. This has given rise to the constant volume gas thermometer, which consists of a flask to hold the gas, attached to a system of glass and rubber tubes containing mercury. A small amount of any gas is introduced into the (otherwise empty) flask, and the top of the mercury in the glass column on the left is placed at some mark on the glass (by moving the right hand glass column up or down). The difference between the heights of the two mercury columns gives the difference between atmospheric pressure and the pressure of the gas in the flask. The gas pressure changes with a change in temperature of the flask, and can be used as a definition of the temperature by taking the temperature to be proportional to the pressure; the proportionality factor can be found in the following manner. If the temperature at the freezing point of water is assigned the value 0° and that at the boiling point is called 100°, the temperature scale is called the Celsius scale (formerly called Centigrade); if those points are taken at 32° and 212°, it is known as the Fahrenheit scale. The relationship between them can be found as follows. If the temperature in the Celsius scale is $T(°C)$, and that in the Fahrenheit scale is $T(°F)$, they are related by $T(°F)=(9/5)T(°C)+32°$. The importance of using the constant volume gas thermometer to define the temperature is that it gives the same value for the temperature no matter what gas is used (as long as the gas is used at a very low pressure), so that anyone at any laboratory would be able to find the same temperature under the same conditions. Of course, a variety of other types of thermometers are used in practice (mercury-in-glass, or the change in the electrical resistance of a wire, for example), but they all must be calibrated against a constant volume gas thermometer as the standard.

Expansion coefficients

An important characteristic of a material is how much it expands for a given increase in temperature. The amount that a rod of material lengthens is given by $L=L_0 [1+ \alpha (T-T_0)]$, where L_0 is the length of the rod at some temperature T_0, and L is the length at some other temperature T; α (Greek alpha) is called the coefficient of linear expansion. Some typical values for α x 10^6 (per °C) are: aluminum, 24.0; copper, 16.8; glass, 8.5; steel, 29.0 (this notation means that, for example, aluminum expands at a rate of 24.0/1,000,000 for each degree Celsius change in temperature). Volumes, of course, also expand with a rise in temperature, obeying a law similar to that for linear expansion; coefficients of volume expansion are approximately three times as large as that for linear expansion for the same material. It is interesting to note that, if a hole is cut in a piece of material, the hole expands just as if there were the same material filling it!

Thermostats

Since various metals expand at different rates, a thermostat can be made to measure changes in tempera-

ture by securely fastening together two strips of metal with different expansion coefficients. If they are straight at one temperature, they will be bent at any other temperature, since one will have expanded or contracted more than the other. These are used in many homes to regulate the temperature by causing an electrical contact to be made or broken as temperature changes cause the end of the strips to move.

Water

Water has the usual property of contracting when the temperature decreases, but only down to 39.2°F (4°C); below that temperature it expands until it reaches 32°F (0°C). It then forms ice at 0°C, expanding considerably in the process; the ice then behaves "normally," contracting as the temperature decreases. Since the density of a substance varies inversely to the volume (as a given mass of a substance expands, its density decreases), this means that the density of water increases as the temperature decreases until 4°C, when it reaches its maximum density. The density of the water then decreases from 4°C to 0°C; the formation of the ice also involves a decrease in density. The ice then increases its density as its temperature falls below 0°C. Thus, as a lake gets colder, the water at the top cools off and, since its density is increasing, this colder water sinks to the bottom. However, when the temperature of the water at the top becomes lower than 4°C, it remains at the top since its density is lower than that of the water below it. The pond then ices over, with the ice remaining at the top, while the water below remains at 4°C (until, if ever, the entire lake freezes). Fish are thus able to live in lakes even when ice forms at the top, since they have the 4°C water below it to live in.

The First Law of Thermodynamics

The conservation of energy is well known from mechanics, where energy does not disappear but only changes its form. For example, the potential energy of an object at some height is converted to the kinetic energy of its motion as it falls. Thermodynamics is concerned with the internal energy of an object and those things that affect it; conservation of energy applies in this case, as well.

Heat

As noted in the introduction, doing work on an object (for example, by drilling a hole in a piece of metal, or by repeatedly bending it) causes its temperature to rise. If this object is placed in contact with a cooler object it is found that they eventually come to the same temperature, and remain that way as long as there are no outside influences (this is known as thermal equilibrium). This series of events is viewed as follows. Consistent with the concept of the conservation of energy, the energy due to the work done on the object is considered to be "stored" in the object as (what may be called) internal energy. In the particular example above, the increase in the internal energy of the object is recognized by the increase in temperature, but there are processes where the internal energy increases without a change in temperature. By then placing it in contact with an object of lower temperature, energy flows from the hotter to the colder one in the form of heat, until the temperatures become the same. Thus heat should be viewed as a type of energy which can flow from one object to another by virtue of a temperature difference. It makes no sense to talk of an object having a certain amount of heat in it; whenever it is placed in contact with a lower-temperature object, heat will flow from the hotter to the cooler one.

The First Law of Thermodynamics

These considerations may be summarized in the First Law of Thermodynamics: the internal energy of an object is increased by the amount of work done on it, and by the amount of heat added to it. Mathematically, if U_f is the internal energy of an object at the end of some process, and U_i is the internal energy at the beginning of the process, then $U_f - U_i = W + Q$, where W is the amount of work done on the object, and Q is the amount of heat added to the object (negative values are used if work is done by the object, or heat is transferred from the object). As is usual for an equation, all quantities must be expressed in the same units; the usual mechanical unit for energy (in the International System of Units-formerly the MKS system) is the joule, where 1 joule equals 1 kg-m^2/s^2.

Specific heats; the calorie

An important characteristic of materials is how much energy in the form of heat it takes to raise the temperature of some material by one degree. It depends upon the type of material being heated as well as its amount. The traditional basic unit, the calorie, is defined as the amount of heat that is needed to raise one gram of water by one degree Celsius. In terms of mechanical energy units, one calorie equals 4.186 joules (J).

The corresponding amount of heat necessary to raise the temperature of other materials is given by the specific heat capacity of a material, usually denoted by c. It is the number of kilojoules (kJ) needed to raise 1 kg of the material by 1°C. By definition, the value for water is 4.186 kilojoules. Typical values for c in kilojoules per kg (kJ/kg), at 0°C, are: ice, 2.11; aluminum,

0.88; copper, 0.38; iron, 0.45. It should be noted that water needs more heat to bring about a given rise in temperature than most other common substances.

Change of phase

The process of water changing to ice or to steam is a familiar one, and each is an example of a change in phase. Suppose a piece of ice were placed in a container and heated at a uniform rate, that is, a constant amount of heat per second is transferred to the material in the container. The ice (the solid phase of water) first rises in temperature at a uniform rate until its temperature reaches 0°C, when it begins to melt, that is, some of the ice changes to water (in its liquid phase); this temperature is called the melting point. It is important to note that the temperature of the ice-water mixture remains at 0°C until all the ice has turned to water. The water temperature then rises until it reaches 100°C, when it begins to vaporize, that is, turns to steam (the gaseous phase of water); this temperature is called the boiling point. Again, the water-steam mixture remains at 100°C until all the liquid water turns into steam. Thereafter, the temperature of the steam rises as more heat is transferred to the container. It is important to recognize that during a change in phase the temperature of the mixture remains constant. (The energy being transferred to the mixture goes into breaking molecular bonds rather than in increasing the temperature.) Many substances undergo similar changes in phase as heat is applied, going from solid to liquid to gas, with the temperature remaining constant during each phase change. (Some substances, such as glass, do not have such a well-defined melting point.) The amount of heat needed to melt a gram of a material is known as the heat of fusion; that to vaporize it is the heat of vaporization. On the other hand, if steam is cooled at a uniform rate, it would turn to liquid water at the condensation temperature (equal to the boiling point, 100°C), and then turn to ice at the solidification temperature (equal to the melting point, 0°C). The heat of condensation is the amount of heat needed to be taken from a gram of a gas to change it to its liquid phase; it is equal to the heat of vaporization. Similarly, there is a heat of solidification which is equal to the heat of fusion. Some typical values are shown in Table 1.

It is interesting to note that water has much larger heats of fusion and of vaporization than many other usual substances. The melting and boiling points depend upon the pressure (the values given in the table are for atmospheric pressure). It is for this reason that water boils at a lower temperature in high-altitude Denver than at sea level.

TABLE 1. THERMODYNAMICS

Material	Melting Point °C	Heat of Fusion cal/gm	Boiling Point °C	Heat of Vaporization cal/gm
Water	0	79.7	100	539
Ethyl alcohol	-114	24.9	78	204
Oxygen	-219	3.3	-183	51
Nitrogen	-210	6.1	-196	48
Mercury	-39	2.8	357	65

Finally, below certain pressures it is possible for a substance to change directly from the solid phase to the gaseous one; this case of sublimation is best illustrated by the "disappearance" of dry ice when it is exposed to the atmosphere.

Equations of state; work

When an object of interest (usually called the system) is left alone for a sufficiently long time, and is subject to no outside influences from the surroundings, measurements of the properties of the object do not change with time; it is in a state of thermal equilibrium. It is found experimentally that there are certain measurable quantities which give complete information about the state of the system in thermal equilibrium (this is similar to the idea that measurements of the velocity and acceleration of an object give complete information about the mechanical state of a system). For each such state relationships can be found which hold true over a wide range of values of the quantities. These relationships are known as equations of state.

Equations of state

Thermodynamics applies to many different types of systems; gases, elastic solids (solids which can be stretched and which return to their original form when the stretching force is removed), and mixtures of chemicals are all examples of such systems. Each system has its own equation of state which depends upon the variables that need to be measured in order to describe its internal state. The relevant variables for a system can only be determined by experiment, but one of those variables will always be the temperature.

The system usually given as an example is a gas, where the relevant thermodynamic variables are the pressure of the gas (P), its volume (V), and, of course, the temperature. (These variables are the relevant ones for any simple chemical system, e.g., water, in any of its phases.) The amount of gas may be specified in grams or kilograms, but the usual way of measuring mass in thermodynamics (as well as in some other fields) is in terms of the number of moles. One kilomole (kmol) is defined as equal to M kilograms, where M is the molecular weight of the substance, with carbon-12 being taken as M=12. (One mole of any substance contains 6.02×10^{23} molecules, known as Avogadro's number.) Thus one kilomole of oxygen has a mass of 70.56 lb (32 kg); of nitrogen, 61.76 lb (28.01 kg); the molar mass of air (which is, of course, actually a mixture of gases) is commonly taken as 63.87 lb (28.97 kg). It is found, by experiment, that most gases at sufficiently low pressures have an equation of state of the form: PV=NRT, where P is in Newtons/m^2, V is in m^3, N is the number of kilomoles of the gas, T is the temperature in K, and R=8.31 kJ/kmol-K is known as the universal gas constant. The temperature is in degrees Kelvin (K), which is given in terms of the Celsius temperature as T(°K)=T(°C)+273.15°C. It should be noted that real gases obey this ideal gas equation of state to within a few percent accuracy at atmospheric pressure and below.

The equation of state of substances other than gases is more complicated than the above ideal gas law. For example, an elastic solid has an equation of state which involves the length of the stretched material, the stretching force, and the temperature, in a relationship somewhat more complex than the ideal gas law.

Work

Work is defined in mechanics in terms of force acting over a distance; that definition is exactly the same in thermodynamics. This is best illustrated by calculating the work done by a force F in compressing a volume of gas. If a volume of gas V is contained in a cylinder at pressure P, the force needed on the piston is (by the definition of pressure) equal to PA, where A is the area of the piston. Let the gas now be compressed in a manner which keeps the pressure constant (by letting heat flow out, so that the temperature also decreases); suppose the piston moves a distance d. Then the work done is W=Fd=PAd. But Ad is the amount that the volume has decreased, V_i - V_f, where V_i is the initial volume and V_f is the final volume. (Note that this volume difference gives a positive value for the distance, in keeping with the fact that work done on a gas is taken as positive.) Therefore, the work done on a gas during a compression at constant pressure is P(V_i - V_f).

The First Law thus gives a straightforward means to determine changes in the internal energy of an object (and it is only changes in the internal energy that can be measured), since the change in internal energy is just equal to the work done on the object in the absence of any heat flow. Heat flow to or from the object can be minimized by using insulating materials, such as fiberglass or, even better, styrofoam. The idealized process where there is zero heat flow is called an adiabatic process.

The Second Law of Thermodynamics

One of the most remarkable facts of nature is that certain processes take place in only one direction. For example, if a high temperature object is placed in contact with one of lower temperature, heat flows from the hotter to the cooler until the temperatures become equal. In this case (where there is no work done), the First Law simply requires that the energy lost by one object should be equal to that gained by the other object (through the mechanism of heat flow), but does not prescribe the direction of the energy flow. Yet, in a situation like this, heat never flows from the cooler to the hotter object. Similarly, when a drop of ink is placed in a glass of water which is then stirred, the ink distributes itself throughout the water. Yet no amount of stirring will make the uniformly-distributed ink go back into a single drop. An open bottle of perfume placed in the corner of a room will soon fill the room with its scent, yet a room filled with perfume scent will never become scent-free with the perfume having gone back into the bottle. These are all examples of the Second Law of Thermodynamics, which is usually stated in two different ways. Although the two statements appear quite different, it can be shown that they are equivalent and that each one implies the other.

Clausius statement of the Second Law

The Clausius statement of the Second Law is: No process is possible whose only result is the transfer of heat from a cooler to a hotter object. The most common example of the transfer of heat from a cooler object to a hotter one is the refrigerator (air conditioners and heat pumps work the same way). When, for example, a bottle of milk is placed in a refrigerator, the refrigerator takes the heat from the bottle of milk and transfers it to the warmer kitchen. (Similarly, a heat pump takes heat from the cool ground and transfers it to the warmer interior of a house.) An idealized view of the refrigerator is as follows. The heat transfer is accomplished by having a motor, driven by an electrical current, run a compressor. A gas is compressed to a liquid, a phase change which generates heat (heat is taken from the gas to turn it into its liquid state). This heat is dissipated to the kitchen by passing through tubes (the condenser) in the back of (or underneath) the refrigerator. The liquid passes through a valve into a low pressure region, where it expands and becomes a gas, and flows through tubes inside the refrigerator. This change in phase from a liquid to a gas is a process which absorbs heat, thus cooling whatever is in the refrigerator. The gas then returns to the compressor where it is again turned into a liquid. The Clausius statement of the Second Law asserts that the process can only take place by doing work on the system; this work is provided by the motor which drives the compressor. However, the process can be quite efficient, and considerably more energy in the form of heat can be taken from the cold object than the work required to do it.

Kelvin-Planck statement of the Second Law

Another statement of the Second Law is due to Lord Kelvin and Max Planck (1858-1947): No process is possible whose only result is the conversion of heat into an equivalent amount of work. Suppose that a cylinder of gas fitted with a piston had heat added, which caused the gas to expand. Such an expansion could, for example, raise a weight, resulting in work being done. However, at the end of that process the gas would be in a different state (expanded) than the one in which it started, so that this conversion of all the heat into work had the additional result of expanding the "working fluid" (in this case, the gas). If the gas were, on the other hand, then made to return to its original volume, it could do so in three possible ways: (a) the same amount of work could be used to compress the

KEY TERMS

. . . .

Adiabatic process—A process in which there is no transfer of heat from the system.

Avogadro's number—The number of molecules in one mole (one-thousandth of a kilomole) of a substance (equal to 6.02×10^{23} molecules).

Boiling point—The temperature at which a liquid changes into a gas.

Calorie—The amount of heat necessary to increase the temperature of water by one degree Celsius.

Celsius temperature(°C)—The temperature scale on which the freezing point of water is 0° and the boiling point is 100°.

Change in phase—Change in the form and characteristics of a substance, e.g., changes from gas to liquid, or liquid to solid.

Coefficient of linear expansion(α)—The fractional rate of change in length of an object with a change in temperature.

Condensation temperature—The temperature at which a gas changes into a liquid (equal to the boiling point).

Equation of state—Relationship among the (experimentally determined) variables which give complete information about the state of a system.

Fahrenheit temperature(°F)—The temperature scale on which the freezing point of water is 32° and the boiling point is 212°.

First Law of Thermodynamics—The internal energy of a system is increased by the amount of work done on the system and the heat flow to the system (Conservation of Energy).

Heat of condensation—The amount of heat needed to be removed from a gas to change it to its liquid phase (equal to the heat of vaporization).

Heat of fusion—The amount of heat needed to be added to a solid to change it to its liquid phase.

Heat of solidification—The amount of heat needed to be removed from a liquid to change it to its solid phase (equal to the heat of fusion).

Heat of vaporization—The amount of heat needed to be added to a liquid to change it to its gaseous phase.

Ideal gas—A gas obeying the ideal gas equation of state, PV=NRT, where, e.g., P is in Newtons/meter², V is in m³, N is the number of kilomoles of the gas, T is the temperature in K, and R=8.31 kJ/kmol-K.

Internal energy—The change in the internal energy of a system is equal to the amount of adiabatic work done on the system.

Kelvin temperature(K)—The Celsius temperature plus 273.15°C.

Kilomole(kmol)—A quantity of matter equal to M kilograms, where M is the molecular weight of the substance, with carbon-12 being taken as M=12 (one kilomole equals 1000 moles).

Macroscopic theory—A theory which ignores the molecular nature of matter.

Melting point—The temperature at which a solid changes into a liquid.

Microscopic theory—A theory which is based on the molecular nature of matter.

Second Law of Thermodynamics—No process is possible whose only result is the transfer of heat from a cooler to a hotter object (Clausius statement). No process is possible whose only result is the conversion of heat into an equivalent amount of work (Kelvin-Planck statement).

Solidification temperature—The temperature at which a liquid changes into a solid(equal to the melting point).

Specific heat capacity (c)—The amount of heat needed to increase the temperature of a mass of material by one degree.

Statistical mechanics—The microscopic theory of matter for which the macroscopic theory is thermodynamics, or the molecular basis of thermodynamics.

Sublimation—The change of a material from its solid phase directly to its gaseous phase.

Temperature (T)—The (experimentally determined) variable which determines the direction of heat flow; the variable which is common to all equations of state.

Thermal equilibrium—The state of a system in which there are no changes with time in any of its properties.

Universal gas constant (R)—The constant in the ideal gas equation of state (as well as elsewhere); equal to 8.31 kJ/kmol-K.

gas, and the same amount of heat as was originally added would then be released from the cylinder; (b) if the cylinder were insulated so that no heat could escape, then the end result would be that the gas is at a higher temperature than originally; (c) something in-between. In the first case, there is no net work output or heat input. In the second, all the work was used to increase the internal energy of the gas, so that there is no net work and the gas is in a different state from which it started. Finally, in the third case, the gas could be returned to its original state by allowing some heat to be transferred from the cylinder. In this case the amount of heat originally added to the gas would equal the work done by the gas plus the heat removed (the First Law requires this). Thus, the only way in which heat could be (partially) turned into work and the working fluid returned to its original state is if some heat were rejected to an object having a temperature lower than the heating object (so that the change of heat into work is not the only result). This is the principle of the heat engine (an internal combustion engine or a steam engine are examples).

Heat engines

The working fluid (say, water for a steam engine) of the heat engine receives heat Q_h from the burning fuel (diesel oil, for example) which converts it to steam. The steam expands, pushing on the piston so that it does work W; as it expands, it cools and the pressure decreases. It then traverses a condenser, where it loses an amount of heat Q_c to the coolant (cooling water or the atmosphere, for example), which returns it to the liquid state. The Second Law says that, if the working fluid (in this case the water) is to be returned to its original state so that the heat-work process could begin all over again, then some heat must be rejected to the coolant. Since the working fluid is returned to its original state, there is no change in its internal energy, so that the First Law demands that $Q_h - Q_c = W$. The efficiency of the process is the amount of work obtained for a given cost in heat input: $E = W/Q_h$. Thus, combining the two laws, $E = (Q_h - Q_c)/Q_h$. It can be seen therefore that a heat engine can never run at 100% efficiency.

It is important to note that the laws of thermodynamics are of very great generality, and are of importance in understanding such diverse subjects as chemical reactions, very low temperature phenomena, and the changes in the internal structure of solids with changes in temperature, as well as engines of various kinds.

See also Avogadro's number; Gases, properties of; Heat; Refrigeration; Temperature; Thermometer; Thermostat.

Further Reading:

DiLavore, Philip, *Energy: Insights from Physics.* New York: Wiley, 1984.)

Goldstein, Martin, and Inge F. Goldstein. *The Refrigerator and the Universe.* Cambridge: Harvard University Press, Cambridge, 1993.

David Mintzer

Thermoluminescence dating see **Dating techniques**

Thermometer

A thermometer is a device that registers the temperature of a substance relative to some agreed upon standard. Thermometers use changes in the physical or electronic properties of the device to detect temperature variations. For example, the most common thermometer consists of some sort of liquid sealed into a narrow tube, or capillary, with a calibrated scale attached. The liquid, typically mercury or alcohol, has a high coefficient of thermal expansion, that is to say the volume changes significantly with changes in temperature. Combined with the narrowness of the tube, this means that the height of the column of liquid changes significantly with small temperature variations.

The oldest thermometers were not sealed, which means that air pressure caused inaccurate readings. The first sealed thermometers were manufactured in the seventeenth century. A further improvement took place in 1714, when the German physicist Daniel Fahrenheit (1686-1736) started using mercury instead of alcohol as the measuring liquid. Fahrenheit thermometer set a standard for accuracy that was accepted by scientists.

All material exhibits a certain resistance to electric current that changes as a function of temperature; this is the basis of both the resistance thermometer and the thermistor. The resistance thermometer consists of fine wire wrapped around an insulator. With a change in temperature, the resistance of the wire changes. This can be detected electronically and used to calculate temperature change from some reference resistance/temperature. Thermistors are semiconductor devices that operate on the same principle.

A thermocouple is another temperature sensor based on electrical properties. When two wires of different materials are connected, a small voltage is estab-

A digital thermometer measuring the temperature of boiling water. Pure water boils at 100 Celsius in standard atmospheric conditions, but the boiling point may be elevated by increased atmospheric pressure and the presence of impurities in the water.

lished that varies as a function of temperature. Two junctions are used in a typical thermocouple.

One junction is the measurement junction, the other is the reference junction kept at some constant temperature. The voltage generated by the temperature difference is detected by a meter connected to the system, and as with the thermistor, this information is converted to temperature.

A pyrometer is a temperature sensor that detects visible and infrared radiation and converts it to temperature. There is a direct relation between the color of light emitted by a hot body and its temperature; it's no accident that we speak of things as "red hot" or "white hot." All surfaces (including animals) emit or reflect radiation whose wavelength is proportional to their temperature. Pyrometers essentially compare the brightness and color of a reference filament to the radiation being emitted or reflected by the surface under test. They are excellent devices for non-contact measurements.

A wide variety of devices exist for measuring temperature; it is up to the user to choose the best thermometer for the job. For contact measurements requiring only moderate accuracy, a capillary thermometer is appropriate. Thermocouples measure temperature over a very wide range with good precision. A more accurate thermal sensor is a thermistor, which boasts the added advantages of being easy to use and inexpensive. Extremely precise contact measurements can be made with a resistance thermometer, but the devices are costly, and pyrometers are useful for non-contact measurements.

See also Temperature; Thermocouple.

Thermostat

A thermostat is a device for controlling heating and cooling systems. It consists of a circuit controlled by a temperature sensitive device and connected to the environmental system. The most common thermostat, such as the one seen in homes and offices, is based on a bimetallic strip. As its name suggests, a bimetallic strip consists of thin strips of two different metals bonded together. One metal of the strip expands significantly with changes in temperature, the other metal changes very little with temperature increase or decrease. When the temperature increases, for example, one side of the strip will expand more than the other side, causing the strip to bend to one side. When it bends far enough, it closes the circuit that directs the air conditioner to turn on. The thermostat adjustment knob varies the distance that the bimetallic strip must bend to close the circuit, allowing selection of temperature level. As the air in the room gets cooler, the metal that expanded with heat will now contract, causing the bimetallic strip to straighten out until it no longer completes the circuit that allows the air conditioner to operate. The air conditioner will turn off until the air becomes warm enough to cause the strip to deform and close the circuit once again.

A number of thermostats that are variations on this theme have been developed. Some are based on a brass bellows filled with a thermally sensitive vapor. When the vapor is heated, it expands, pushing out the bellows until it closes the circuit and triggers the heater/air conditioner. Another thermostat design is the bulb type, which includes a bulb and capillary, similar to a thermometer, and a diaphragm. When the bulb is heated, the material expands and travels down the capillary to the diaphragm. The diaphragm in turn moves, moving a lever or spring post and eventually controlling the heating and cooling system.

Electronic thermostats have become increasingly popular in the past few years, offering the dual benefits of low cost and minimal moving parts. The active element is a thermistor, a semiconductor device whose resistance to electrical current changes with temperature. Temperature change is signified by a change in measured voltage, which can be used to pass information to the control systems of the heating/cooling units.

See also Temperature.

Thistle

Thistle is the common name given to some plants in several genera of the Cynareae tribe, family Asteraceae. These genera include *Cirsium, Carduus, Echinops, Onopordum, Silybum, Centaurea,* and *Cnicus*. The name thistle most often refers to the weedy, prickly plants belonging to the genera *Cirsium* and *Carduus*. Thistles are composite flowers, which means their flower is actually a group of small flowers that give the appearance of one, larger flower. The flowers, which are of the disc type, are surrounded by bracts. Many people group Carduus and Cirsium together, but a closer look at these two genera would reveal a distinct difference. While both genera have hairs or bristles mixed with the flowers and a hairy pappus, the hairs on *Cirsium* species are plumose (they are feathery—the hairs have branch hairs) and the *Carduus* hairs are not.

The most notable characteristic of thistles are the prickly stems, leaves, and the bracts around the flower head. Among the thistle genera, there are various leaf shapes and colors. The flowers are most often purple, but some species have pink, white, or yellow flowers. Thistles can be found in temperate regions, can grow in many climates and soils, and their height can range from 1 foot (0.3 m) to 12 ft (3.5 m). Some well known *Cirsium* thistles are *C. vulgare* or bull thistle, C. *arvense* or Canada thistle, and *C. eriophorum* or woolly thistle. *C. nutans* or nodding thistle is the best known of the *Carduus* species. Globe thistles of the *Echinops* genus are often grown for ornamental purposes. *Onopordum acanthium* or Scottish thistle is well known for its large purple flower. *Silybum marianum* or milk thistle, *Centaurea calcitrapa* or star thistle, and *Cnicus benedictus* or holy thistle, have been used and cultivated for medicinal purposes.

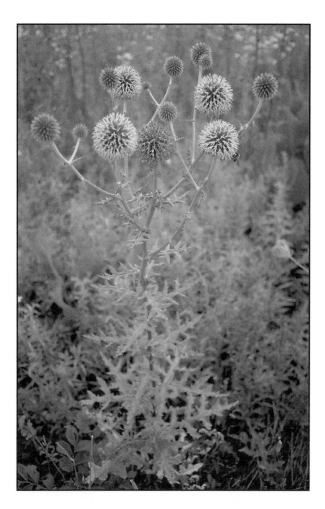

A great globe thistle (*Echinops sphaerocephalus*) at Seven Ponds Nature Preserve, Michigan. This massive, bushy plant can grow to 6 ft (1.8 m) in height.

Cynara scolymus or globe artichoke is closely related to thistle. What is eaten of the artichoke that shows up on our dinner plate is the unopened flower head and bracts of the plant. Some plants such as sow thistle (genus Sonchus of the Chicory tribe-Lactuceaea) and Russian thistle (Salsola kali of the Goosefoot family), are called thistle because of their prickliness but are not true thistles.

Thoracic surgery

Thoracic surgery refers to surgery performed in the thorax or chest. The anatomy and physiology of the thorax require special procedures to be carried out for the surgery to be done.

The thorax is the bony cage consisting of the ribs, the spine, and the breastbone or sternum. The floor of the thorax is formed by the diaphragm.

Within the thorax lie the two lungs and the heart, the organs whose function it is to oxygenate and pump blood. The lungs are large, relatively cone-shaped, spongy organs that lie with their narrow ends at the top and the broad ends at the bottom of the thorax. Between the paired lungs in an area called the mediastinum lies the heart. The inside of the chest cavity is lined with a sheet of elastic tissue, the pleura, which also covers each lung. The pleura on each side of the chest is independent from the other side; that is, the lining on the right covers the right lung and the right half of the thorax. A fluid called the pleural fluid fills the area between the two layers of pleura so that the membrane slides easily as the lungs work.

A constant negative pressure or vacuum is maintained in the chest to keep the lungs inflated. The diaphragm controls respiration. In its relaxed state it is dome shaped and projects into the chest. When it is tensed the diaphragm flattens and pulls air into the lungs. Carbon dioxide and oxygen are exchanged in the blood circulating through the lungs, the diaphragm relaxes and forces the air out of the thorax, and the oxygenated blood is returned to the heart for circulation.

Thoracic surgery may be needed as a result of a heart or lung disease, or to correct an abnormality of one of the large blood vessels. The heart may have a faulty valve that needs replacing, or a partially occluded coronary artery for which a bypass graft is needed. A hole in the wall separating the right and left sides of the heart may require patching. A lung tumor or a foreign object may need to be removed. A more serious procedure such as a heart transplant or heart-lung transplant may be needed. Any lung surgery will disrupt the negative pressure in the chest and render the lungs inoperable.

Thoracic surgery did not advance as rapidly as did surgery on other areas of the body because the means could not be found to maintain lung function during surgery and restore it after the surgery is completed. Not until early in the 20th century did Samuel Meltzer and John Auer describe successful lung surgery carried out under positive-pressure air forced into the lungs. With this method the lungs remained inflated and the surgery could be completed without the lungs collapsing. Ironically, Andreas Vesalius (1514-1564) had described this methodology centuries earlier.

Heart surgery is carried out by placing the patient's heart and lung functions on a heart-lung machine, or cardiopulmonary bypass machine. First, the thorax is opened by cutting through the superficial tissue and

KEY TERMS

Coronary arteries—The arteries that supply blood to the heart muscle.

Donor organs—Organs, such as a heart, kidney, or lung, removed from a person who has died to be implanted in a living person to replace a diseased organ.

Negative pressure—A pressure maintained inside the chest that is lower than the air pressure outside the body. This allows the lungs to remain inflated. Loss of negative pressure may result in a collapsed lung.

Valve—A device that controls the flow of blood between the chambers of the heart and blood entering and leaving the heart. All the valves are one-way, allowing blood to pass in one direction and not in the reverse direction.

using a saw to cut the sternum. A device called a retractor spreads the cut sternum to allow the surgeon to have full view of the heart.

The patient is connected to the bypass machine by tubes, or cannulas, attached to the large veins returning blood to the right side of the heart, the superior and inferior vena cavae. The cannula to return blood to the patient is implanted in the aorta, the large blood vessel leading from the heart to the body, or to a major artery such as the femoral artery in the thigh. When the machine is turned on blood is drawn from the vena cavae into the machine where it is cooled, oxygenated, and filtered to remove any unwanted particles and bubbles. The newly oxygenated blood is returned to the aorta which takes it to the body. Cooling the blood in turn cools the body temperature of the patient which reduces the amount of oxygen the tissues need. A third tube gathers blood at the point of surgery and shunts it into the machine to reduce blood loss.

With the patient safely on the heart-lung machine, the surgeon can stop the heart and lungs and carry out whatever procedure is needed. Attempting surgery on the beating heart or surgery while the lungs inflate and deflate would be difficult. Stopping the heart by cooling it and stopping lung action by giving a muscle relaxant that quiets the diaphragm provides an immobile field for the procedure. A vein taken from the leg, usually, can be grafted in place to bypass one or more blocked areas in the coronary arteries. A diseased heart valve can be removed from the heart and an artificial valve made from plastic and steel, pig valve, or monkey valve can be implanted. The entire heart or the heart and both lungs can be removed, emptying the chest cavity, and replaced with donor organs.

At the conclusion of the operation the chest is closed, the heart-lung machine warms the blood to restore normal body temperature, and the cannulae are removed from the vena cavae and aorta.

See also Heart; Heart diseases; Heart-lung machine; Surgery.

Further Reading:

Larson, David E. (Ed.). *Mayo Clinic Family Health Book.* New York: William Morrow & Company, Inc. 1990.

Larry Blaser

Thorium see **Actinides**

Thrashers see **Mockingbirds and thrashers**

Thrips

Thrips are minute (less than 0.20 in or 5 mm) slender-bodied insects of the order Thysanoptera, characterized by two pairs of veinless, bristle-fringed wings, which are narrow and held over the back when at rest. Although thrips have wings, they do not fly. There are 4,500 species of thrips worldwide. In North America, there are 694 species of thrips in a number of families in two suborders, the Terebrantia and the Tubulifia. Greenhouse thrips (*Heliothrips haemorrhoidalis*) in the suborder Terebrantia deposit their eggs into slits made on plant tissues. Black hunter thrips (*Haplothrips mali*) in the suborder Tubulifera lay their eggs on protected plant surfaces. Red-banded thrips (*Heliothrips rubrocinctus*) are widespread in North America, sucking plant juices and possibly spreading plant viruses.

Several species of predatory thrips feed on mites, aphids, and other thrips. The majority of thrips are fond of trees and shrubs, roses, onions, and many other herbaceous plants. Pale or white flowers are most attractive to thrips. Their rough mouthparts break open plant tissues, allowing them to suck up plant juices. The most obvious signs of thrip damage are tiny black specks of feces, silvering foliage, distorted flowers and leaves, or buds that fail to open. The insects themselves are rarely seen without a hand lens.

In warm weather, thrips eggs hatch in days, although cold weather may delay hatching for weeks to months. Thrips undergo incomplete metamorphosis, with eggs hatching into a series of nymphs (which resemble adults), which finally metamorphose into adult thrips. The wingless thrip nymphs eat their way through two larval stages, then find a protected crevice (either on the plant or in soil) to complete the transition to a winged adult. Female thrips can reproduce parthenogenetically—that is, without mating with males. This strategy allows rapid population explosions when conditions are optimal. The complete life cycle can occur in as little as two weeks. Adults are relatively long-lived.

Adult thrips are attracted to yellow and blue sticky traps hung a few feet above plants. Conventional pesticides (such as Malathion) used to control aphids and whiteflies also kill thrips. Less toxic control can be accomplished by maintaining plant health, for water-stressed plants and weedy areas are especially attractive to thrips. Treatment of infested plants involves removing infested plant tissues and mulching with plastic or newspaper to prevent successful development, followed by surrounding the plant stems with aluminum foil to prevent reinfestation. Predatory mites (*Neoseiulus mackenziei*, *Amblyseius cucumeris*) eat thrip eggs and larvae. Larval lacewings (*Chrysoperta carnea*) will also control greenhouse thrips as long as aphids, the preferred prey of lacewings, are not abundant. Predatory nematodes also consume larval thrips found in soils. Other control measures such as tobacco water spray, garlic/hot pepper spray, pyrethrin, and insecticidal soap sprays can be effective in controlling thrips.

Rosi Dagit

Thrombosis

Thrombosis is the formation of a blood clot, or thrombus, in a blood vessel. The process is an exaggeration of a normal and useful event by which the body prevents the loss of blood from veins and arteries as a result of an injury. During thrombosis, the blood clotting process goes beyond the construction of a blockage for a damaged blood vessel and actually produces a solid clump (the clot) that reduces or even interrupts the flow of blood in the blood vessel.

Thrombosis most commonly occurs for one of three reasons. First, the blood's normal clothing system

A scanning electron micrograph (SEM) of a thrombus (clot) completely occluding a major pulmonary blood vessel in a human lung. At center is the blood clot. The thick wall of the pulmonary vessel surrounds it. On the outside is the fibrous tissue and alveoli of the lung.

may become more active with the result that clots within a vein or artery are more likely to form. After childbirth, for example, a woman's clotting mechanism becomes more active to reduce her loss of blood. If the system becomes too efficient, however, clots may form within a blood vessel.

A reduction in blood circulation can also result in the production of a clot. Primitive clots that might otherwise be swept away by the normal flow of blood may be left undisturbed on a vessel wall, allowing them to develop in size.

Finally, the normal aging of blood vessels may contribute to the formation of clots. The first signs of atheroma, or degeneration of blood vessels, can be observed as early as childhood. The more advanced stage—"hardening of the arteries"—usually does not become a medical problem until old age, however. At this state, scarring of the interior walls of veins and arteries provides sites on which clots can begin to form.

A variety of medical problems can result from thrombosis depending on the location of the thrombus. When thrombosis occurs in a coronary artery of the heart, the result is a myocardial infarction, otherwise known as a heart attack. If a thrombus forms in the brain, a stroke occurs. Thrombosis in a leg vein, especially the long saphenous vein, causes the condition known as venous thrombosis or phlebitis.

A secondary consideration in thrombosis is the possibility that a piece of the thrombus may become detached and carried away by the blood. The embolus thus formed may lodge in another part of the body, such as the lungs, where it may cause further medical problems.

Researchers have identified a number of conditions that may lead to thrombosis. These include one's genetic make-up, bodily injury, surgery, pregnancy, smoking, stress, hypertension, and arteriosclerosis.

The most suitable form of treatment depends on the form of thrombosis that occurs. With phlebitis, for example, bed rest and elevation of the limb is recommended. In some instances, by-pass surgery may be required. For many cases of thrombosis, anticoagulant drugs — drugs that reduce the rate of blood clotting — can also be effective.

See also Blood; Circulatory system.

Thrushes

Thrushes are a diverse group of about 305 species of common, medium-sized, perching, song birds ranging from 4.5-13 in (11-33 cm) in body length in the family Turdidae. Thrushes occur world-wide in a wide range of habitats, but mostly in forests.

Some species of thrushes are common in parks and gardens that contain shrubs and trees and are not intensively treated with insecticides. Examples of these familiar species of thrushes include robins, bluebirds, and the European song thrush and blackbird.

Biology of thrushes

The generalized body plan of thrushes includes relatively short wings with rounded tips, a longish, weakly forked or rounded tail, stout legs and feet, and a slender beak. Coloration ranges from all-black, through various combinations of brown, blue, red, and white. The juveniles of most species have spotted breasts, as do the adults of some species.

Many thrushes are accomplished singers, with relatively loud, melodious songs that carry over a rather long distance. The rich songs of thrushes provide a pleasing component of the ambience of spring and early summer in the temperate zones of the world, when these migratory birds are actively establishing and defending their breeding territories.

Most species of thrushes occur in forested or shrubby habitats; others occur in grasslands, tundra, and semi-desert. A wide range of food is eaten by thrushes. Most species feed upon small invertebrates (insects, caterpillars, and earthworms) of diverse types, especially when these birds are raising young, which require

An American robin (*Turdus migratorius*) on Oakland University campus, Michigan.

a high-protein food. Some species feed on berries during at least part of the year.

Most thrushes, usually the female, build mud-lined, cup-shaped nests of twigs, herbaceous stems, or leaves. The nests are usually located in relatively protected places in trees or shrubs, or on the ground. The young birds are naked and helpless for the first weeks of their life and are fed and tended by both adults. Most species of thrushes raise several broods each year, using the same or different nests each time.

Species of thrushes

Robins are among the world's better known thrushes. The American robin (*Turdus migratorius*) is probably the native bird with which North Americans are most commonly familiar. The American robin has a brick-red breast and slate-grey back and is very widespread, breeding from the northern limit of trees and tall shrubs, through to southern Mexico. The American robin utilizes a wide range of natural habitats, and it also breeds in parks and gardens. As is implied by the scientific name of the species, the American robin is migratory, spending the non-breeding season in the more southern regions of its breeding range, as far south as Guatemala. The varied thrush (*Ixoreus naevius*) is a robin-like bird of mature and old-growth conifer forests of western North America.

The European robin (*Erithacus rubecula*) is the original "robin red-breast," after which were named other, superficially similar species of thrushes, such as the American robin. The European robin is common in much of Europe and western Russia, breeding in open forests, shrubby habitats, hedgerows, and parks and gardens.

Another common thrush of Europe and North Africa is the European blackbird (*Turdus merula*). This species occurs in a wide range of forest types, and also in parks and gardens.

Bluebirds are a familiar group of thrushes in North America. The eastern bluebird (*Sialia sialis*) occurs in open, shrubby habitats of various types in eastern and central North America and south to Nicaragua. Male eastern bluebirds have a blue back and a red breast, while the color of the female is more subdued. The western bluebird (*S. mexicana*) and mountain bluebird (*S. currucoides*) are found in western North America.

Five species of thrushes occur in the forests of North America. These thrushes have a basic coloration of grey-brown to brown-red backs, with a white, spotted breast. All of these birds have pleasing, flute-like songs. These species include the wood thrush (*Hylocichla mustelina*), hermit thrush (*H. guttata*), olive-backed thrush (*H. ustulata*), gray-cheeked thrush (*H. minima*), and veery (*H. fuscescens*). Numbers of some of the more southern populations of these forest thrushes appear to be declining substantially, in part because of excessive nest parasitism by the brown-headed cowbird (*Molothrus ater*). The breeding range of the cowbird has expanded tremendously because of fragmentation of forests by human activities, especially the conversion of forests to agricultural and residential land-use. The cowbird poses a risk for many species of birds, in addition to forest thrushes.

The wheatear (*Oenanthe oenanthe*) is an arctic species of thrush, breeding as far north as the limits of land in both North America and Eurasia.

Thrushes and people

Because species of thrushes are among the more familiar and well-appreciated native birds, they are an important component of the aesthetic environment. This is true of both natural habitats and managed habitats, such as gardens and parks. As such, the activities and songs of a number of species of thrushes provide people with a meaningful link to the more natural aspects of the human experience.

The European blackbird and European song thrush (*Turdus philomelos*) were introduced to New Zealand and Australia by British colonists. This was done as part of a larger attempt to make their new, foreign surroundings more familiar in the context of west European culture.

In some places, populations of thrushes have suffered badly as a result of poisoning caused by their exposure to insecticides used in agriculture or for other purposes. For example, during the 1950s and 1960s, populations of American robins declined greatly in places where the insecticide DDT was used to kill the beetle vectors that were spreading Dutch elm disease. The latter is an introduced pathogen that is still killing native elm trees over large areas, including large and valuable trees in cities and suburbs. The disappearance of robins and their prominent, melodious songs was an important component of the so-called "silent spring" that became a metaphor for the ecological damage associated with some types of pesticide uses. As such, the health of robin populations became a very important indicator of the broader health of the urban and suburban environment.

See also Blackbirds; Bluebirds; Robins.

Further Reading:

Brooke, M., and T. Birkhead, eds. *The Cambridge Encyclopedia of Ornithology.* Cambridge: Cambridge University Press, 1991.

Harrison, C. J. O., ed. *Bird Families of the World.* New York: Abrams, 1978.

Bill Freedman

Thulium see **Lanthanides**

Thunderstorm

A thunderstorm is a strong disturbance in the atmosphere bringing heavy rain, lightning, and thunder to areas from one to hundreds of kilometers across. Thunderstorms are formed when humid air near the surface begins rising and cooling. The rising air forms clouds. Storms develop when the clouds cool enough to bring about the growth of rain droplets or ice crystals. Eventually the growing drops or crystals fall out of the cloud as precipitation. Strong updrafts and downdrafts are inside a thunderstorm which cause static charges to build up in the cloud. Charges of opposite sign accumulate in different parts of the cloud until a spark occurs between them, resulting in the jagged bolts of lightning associated with thunderstorms. Severe thunderstorms may include hail, tornadoes, and damaging straight line winds, making these storms among nature's most destructive.

Thunderstorm development

Thunderstorms develop in the same process that forms the puffy clouds of summer skies cumulus clouds. These clouds form when humid air (that is, air with an abundance of water vapor) near the surface is pushed up by being forced over a mountain range, a front, strong solar heating of the surface, or some other means. As the air rises through the atmosphere, it expands and cools. Eventually the rising air cools to the point where its water vapor condenses to form droplets of liquid water. A huge collection of these tiny suspended droplets forms a cloud. At this stage the rising air is visible as a cumulus cloud, called a convective cloud since it forms by convection (vertical air movement). During fair weather the convective clouds stop their vertical growth at this point and do not bring rain.

To form a thunderstorm from a convective cloud several conditions are necessary. Most importantly the atmosphere must be unstable. In an unstable atmosphere the air temperature drops rapidly with height, meaning any bubble of air that begins rising and cooling will remain warmer than its surroundings. At every point in its ascent the rising air acts like a hot air balloon: since it is warmer and less dense than the surrounding air it continues to rise.

A second requirement for a strong thunderstorm is plenty of humid air. This condition supports the growth of cloud droplets and actually fuels the rising air through latent heat. The water vapor in the air comes from the evaporation of liquid water somewhere most likely the oceans. To evaporate the water into vapor, energy is required just as heat must be added to a kettle to make its water boil. This energy carried with the water vapor wherever it goes is latent or hidden heat. If and when the vapor condenses to form liquid water, the latent heat will be released back into the environment. Thus when the water vapor in rising air condenses to form water droplets a significant amount of heat is released to the surrounding air. Heating the air makes it less dense and increases the tendency of the air bubble, now a cloud, to rise.

As the air continues to rise and cool, droplets within the cloud begin to grow by coalescence (sticking together). In the clouds of colder climates droplets may freeze to form ice crystals which grow as more and more water vapor condenses on them. The droplets or ice crystals, known as precipitation particles, only grow as long as they can be supported by the updrafts. When they grow too large, they begin to fall out of the cloud as drizzle or raindrops. If the updrafts in the cloud are vigorous enough, much larger precipitation will be formed. In a thunderstorm the uplift process is so strong that the cloud grows to the height of the entire lower atmosphere (about 40,000 ft [12 km] above the surface) allowing large raindrops and hailstones to form.

Lightning over Tamworth, New South Wales, Australia.

At least two distinct types of thunderstorms can be observed. Over warm humid areas such as the Gulf of Mexico the air-mass thunderstorm is the most common. These thunderstorms grow from converging cumulus clouds that rise and cool as described above. As the storm matures, rain begins to fall from the upper part of the cloud. The falling precipitation causes downdrafts. This downward moving air eventually overwhelms the rising air. The downdrafts effectively shut off the uplift necessary for the storm to grow, so the storm dissipates as the air sinks and no more rain is formed. These types of thunderstorms are common over the Florida peninsula bringing showers and lightning strikes but rarely any hail or damaging winds unless frontal action is nearby.

Potentially more severe thunderstorms form in temperate regions such as the central and eastern United States. Called frontal thunderstorms these storms often form ahead of the advancing edge of a cold air mass (a cold front). In the summer months the air ahead of the cold front is usually warm humid air that is highly unstable. The denser cold air forces the warmer lighter air ahead of it to rise forming convective clouds which eventually rain. As in an air mass thunderstorm, the falling rain causes downdrafts in the cloud. Unlike the air mass storm, a frontal thunderstorm is arranged so that it is intensified by the downdrafts. The downdrafts become strong gusts of down–flowing air. When they reach the ground the downdrafts spread out and force more warm humid air to begin rising into the thunderstorm. This provides the storm with more latent heat, strengthening the cloud's updrafts, increasing its wind speeds, and improving the chances of heavy rain and hail. The storm advances into the warm air, vacuuming up humid air, and transforming it into a very organized system of powerful updrafts and downdrafts. After the

THUNDERSTORM

storm and the front passes, the affected area is often affected by the cold air behind the front where temperatures and humidities are usually much lower.

Hail, lightning, and tornadoes

Strong updrafts in a thunderstorm support the growth of large rain drops and ice crystals. In a severe storm some of the ice crystals may be dragged down by the downdrafts then swept up again by updrafts. Ice particles may be circulated several times through the storm cloud in this manner picking up water with each cycle. In a process called riming, rain water freezes onto the ice particles and eventually grows to be large hailstones. Hailstones continue to be recirculated through the cloud until they grow large enough to fall out under their own weight falling against the strong updrafts. If located in the right part of the storm, hailstones can grow to impressive sizes. Hail as large as 5.5 in (14 cm) in diameter has been recorded.

Another product of the vigorous up and down drafts in the storm cloud is lightning. Lightning is a giant spark caused by a buildup of static electrical charges, a larger version of the spark one gets by touching a metal doorknob after walking across a cloth carpet. By processes that still are not understood fully, thunderstorm clouds build up a large separation of electric charge with positive charges located near the top of the cloud and negative charges concentrated near the middle. Usually the cloud base has a smaller pocket of positive charge. Separating charges results in huge voltage differences within the cloud and between the cloud base and the ground. The voltage difference is equalized suddenly by a bolt of lightning between these areas. The spark heats the air in the lightning channel to over 54,000°F (30,000°C) causing a rapid expansion. The resulting sound is heard as thunder.

Severe thunderstorms also may form tornadoes, columns of air spinning at extremely high wind speeds. Tornadoes pack wind speeds of 100 m/second (over 220 mph) in a small area making them capable of great destruction.

See also Air masses and fronts; Atmospheric circulation; Clouds; Precipitation; Storm; Tornado.

Further Reading:
Battan, Louis J. *Weather*. Engelwood Cliffs: Prentice-Hall Inc., 1985.
Battan, Louis J. *Weather in Your Life*. New York: W.H. Freeman & Co., 1983.

KEY TERMS

Air-mass thunderstorm—A thunderstorm typical of tropical areas which may produce heavy rain but rarely any hail or tornadoes.

Convective cloud—A cloud formed from the vertical uplift (convection) of surface air.

Frontal thunderstorm—Thunderstorms associated with cold fronts moving through warm humid air.

Latent heat—The heat given off when water vapor condenses to form liquid water.

Precipitation particles—Rain drops or ice crystals that have grown heavy enough to fall out, or precipitate, out of a storm cloud.

Riming—The freezing on contact of raindrops as they are collected by an ice pellet growing to a hailstone.

Unstable atmosphere—The atmosphere is said to be unstable when a bubble of air initially pushed upward continues to move upward due to the temperature difference between it and the surrounding air. If the atmosphere lacks this tendency as it usually does it is called stable.

Hardy, Ralph, Peter Wright, John Kington, and John Gribben. *The Weather Book*. Boston: Little, Brown and Co., 1982.
McNeill, Robert. *Understanding the Weather*. Las Vegas: Arbor Publishers, 1991.
Miller, Albert, Jack C. Thompson, Richard E. Peterson, and Donald R. Haragan. *Elements of Meteorology*. Columbus, MO: Charles E. Merrill Publishing, 1983.
Mogil, H. Michael and Barbara G. Levine. *The Amateur Meteorologist*. New York: Franklin Watts, 1993.
Wallace, John M., and Peter V. Hobbs. *Atmospheric Science: An Introductory Survey*. New York: Academic Press, 1977.

James Marti

Thymus gland see **Endocrine system**
Thyroid gland see **Endocrine system**
Ticks see **Arachnids**
Tidal energy see **Alternative energy sources**
Tidal wave see **Earthquake; Tsunami**

Tides

Tides are deformations in the shape of a body caused by the gravitational force of one or more other bodies. At least in theory, any two bodies in the universe exert such a force on each other, although obvious tidal effects are generally too small to observe. By far the most important examples of tidal forces as far as humans are concerned are ocean tides that occur on Earth as a result of the Moon and Sun's gravitational attraction.

History

Perhaps the first careful observer of ocean tides was the Greek geographer Pytheas of Massalia. In about the third century B.C., Pytheas traveled outside the Straits of Gibraltar and observed tidal action in the Atlantic Ocean, action that was essentially absent from the Mediterranean Sea, which was far more familiar to his contemporaries. Pytheas also proposed an explanation for tidal action. He suggested that the pull of the Moon on the Earth's oceans caused the tides, an explanation that is now known to be largely correct, although it was not widely accepted by scientists until the 18th century. Sir Isaac Newton first succeeded in mathematically describing the tides and what cause them in what is known as the equilibrium tidal theory.

The tides have long been studied by mariners because of their importance in ocean travel. Over the centuries during which scientists have argued about the precise causes of the tides, sailors accumulated huge volumes of data about tidal actions and developed a very practical and useful system for predicting the occurrence of tides for most parts of the world.

Theories of tidal action

First we will consider lunar tides. The side of the Earth facing the Moon, due to the Moon's proximity, experiences a larger gravitational pull, or force, than other areas. This force causes ocean water, since it is able to flow, to form a slight bulge, making the water in that area slightly deeper.

At the same time, another bulge forms on the opposing side of the Earth. This second bulge, which is perhaps a bit harder to understand, forms due to centrifugal force. Contrary to popular belief, the Moon does not revolve around the Earth, but rather the Earth and Moon revolve about a common point that is within the Earth, but no where near its center (2880 miles or 4640 km away). As you probably already know, when you twirl a ball above your head at the end of a piece of string, the ball pulls against the string. This pull is known as centrifugal force.

When the Earth-Moon system revolves around its common axis, the side of the Earth that is farthest from the Moon experiences a centrifugal force, like a ball spinning at the end of a string. This force causes a second tidal bulge to form, which is the same size as the first. The result is that two lunar tidal bulges exist on the Earth at all times—one on the side of the Earth facing the Moon and another directly opposite to it. These bulges account for the phenomenon known as high tide.

The formation of these two high tide bulges causes a belt of low water to form at 90° to the high tide bulges. This belt, which completely encircles the Earth, produces the phenomenon known as low tide.

As the Earth rotates on its axis, land areas slide underneath the bulges, forcing the oceans up over some coastlines and beneath the low tide belt, forcing water out away from other coastlines. In a sense, as the Earth rotates on its axis, the high tide bulges and the low tide belt remain stationary and the continents and ocean basins move beneath them. As a result, most coastal areas experience two high tides and two low tides each day.

In addition to the lunar bulges, the Sun forms its own tidal bulges, one due to gravitational force and the other due to centrifugal force. However, due to the Sun's much greater distance from the Earth, its tidal effect is approximately one half that of the Moon.

When the Moon and Sun are in line with each other (new Moon and full Moon), their gravitational, or tidal forces, combine to produce a maximum pull. The tides produced in such cases are known as spring tides. The spring high tide produces the highest high tide and the spring low tide produces the lowest low tide of the fortnight. This is the same as saying the spring tides have the greatest tidal range, which is the vertical difference between high tide and low tide.

When the Moon and Sun are at right angles to each other (first and third quarter Moon), the two forces act in opposition to each other to produce a minimum pull on the oceans. The tides in this case are known as neap tides. The neap high tide produces the lowest high tide and the neap low tide produces the highest low tide, or the smallest tidal range, of the fortnight.

Variables affecting tidal forces

It is now possible to write very precise mathematical equations that describe the gravitational effects of the Moon and the Sun. So, in theory, it should be possible to make very precise predictions of the time, size,

High tide and low tide at Big Pine Key, Florida.

and occurrence of tides. In fact, such predictions are not possible because a large number of factors contribute to the height of the oceans at high and low tide at a particular location. Primary among these is that the shape of ocean basins is so irregular that water does not behave in the "ideal" way that mathematical equations would predict. However, a number of other variables also complicate the situation. These include variations in the Earth's axial rotation, and variations in Earth-Moon-Sun positioning, including variations in orbital distance and inclination.

Scientists continue to improve their predictions of tidal variations using mathematical models based on the equilibrium theory of tides. However, for the present, estimates of tidal behavior are still based previous tidal observations, continuous monitoring of coastal water levels, and astronomical tables. This more practical approach is referred to as the dynamical theory of tides, which is based on observation rather than mathematical equations.

Tide tables

The accumulated information about tidal patterns in various parts of the world is used to produce tide tables. Tide tables are constructed by looking back over past records to find out for any given location the times at which tides have occurred for many years in the past and the height to which those tides have reached at maximum and minimum levels. These past records are then used to predict the most likely times and heights to be expected for tides at various times in the future for the same locations. Because of differences in ocean bottoms, coastline, and other factors, unique tide tables must be constructed for each specific coastline every place in the world. They can then be used by fishermen, those on ocean liners, and others who need to know about tidal actions.

The nature of tides

In most places, tides are semidiurnal, that is, there are two tidal cycles (high and low tides) each day. In other words, during a typical day, the tides reach their highest point along the shore and their lowest point twice each day. The high water level reached during one of the high tide stages is usually greater than the other high point, and the low water level reached during one of the low tide stages is usually less than the other low tide point. This consistent difference is called the diurnal inequality of the tides.

In a few locations, tides occur only once a day, with a single high tide stage and a single low tide stage. These are known as diurnal tides. In both diurnal and semidiurnal settings, when the tide is rising, this is called the flood tide. When the tide is falling, this is the ebb tide. The point when the water reaches its highest point at high tide, or its lowest point at low tide is called the slack tide, since the water level is static, neither rising nor falling, at least for a short time.

As the Moon revolves around the Earth, the Earth also rotates on its axis. Consequently, the Earth must rotate on its axis for 24 hours, 50 minutes, known as a lunar day, to return to the same position relative to the Moon above. The additional 50 minutes allows the Earth to "catch up" to the Moon, so to speak. In other words, if the Moon was directly overhead at Boston, Massachusetts, at noon yesterday, it will again be above Boston at 12:50 PM today. As a result, on a coast with diurnal tides, each day the high tide (or low tide) will occur 50 minutes later than the day before. Whereas, on a semidiurnal coast, each high tide (or low tide) will occur 12 hours, 25 minutes later than the previous high tide.

The movement of ocean water as a result of tidal action is known as a tidal current. In open water, tidal currents are relatively weak and tend to change direction slowly and regularly throughout the day. They form, therefore, a kind of rotary current that sweeps around the ocean like the minute hand on a clock. Closer to land, however, tidal currents tend to change direction rather quickly, flowing toward land during high tide and away from land during low tide. In many cases, this onshore and offshore tidal current flows up the mouth of a river or some other narrow opening. The tidal current may then attain velocities as great as 9 miles (15 km) an hour with crests as high as 10 feet (3 m) or more.

Most tides attain less than 10 feet in size; 3-10 ft (1-3 m) is common. In some locations, however, the tides may be much greater. These locations are characterized by ocean bottoms that act as funnels through which ocean waters rush upward towards or downward away from the shore at very rapid speeds. In the Bay of Fundy, between Nova Scotia and New Brunswick, for example, the difference between high and low tides, the tidal range, may be as great as 46 feet (14 m). In comparison, some large bodies of water, such as the Mediterranean, Baltic, and Caribbean Seas, have areas with tides of less than a foot (0.3 m). All coastal locations (as well as very large lakes) experience some variation in tidal range during a fortnight, due to the affects of neap versus spring tides.

Tidal power plants

Engineers have long recognized that the movement of tidal currents might be an inexpensive, efficient, and environmentally safe source of power for human use. In general, the plan would be to construct a dam across the entrance of an estuary through which tidal currents flow with significant speed. Then, as tidal currents flow into and out of the estuary twice each day, they could be used to drive turbines which, in turn, could be used to operate electrical generators.

One of the few commercial tidal power stations in operation is located at the mouth of the La Rance River in France. Tides at this location reach a maximum of 44 feet (13.5 m). Each time the tide comes in, a dam at the La Rance station holds water back until it reaches its maximum depth. At that point, gates in the dam are opened and water is forced to flow into the La Rance River, driving a turbine and generator in the process. Gates in the dam are then closed, trapping the water inside the dam. At low tide, the gates open once again, allowing water to flow out of the river, back into the ocean. Again the power of moving water is used to drive a turbine and generator.

KEY TERMS

Diurnal—Occurring once every day.

Ebb tide—The period when the water level is falling; the period after high tide and before low tide.

Flood tide—The period when the water level is rising; the period after low tide and before high tide.

High tide—The event corresponding to the largest increase in water level in an area that is induced by tidal forces.

Low tide—The event corresponding to the largest decrease in water level in an area that is induced by tidal forces.

Neap tides—Period of minimum tidal range that occurs about every two weeks when the Moon and Sun are at 90° to each other, that is, at the first and third quarter moons.

Period—The interval of time between two recurring events, such as the high tides in an area.

Semidiurnal—Occurring twice every day.

Slack tide—Period during which the water level is neither rising nor falling.

Spring tides—Period of maximum tidal range that occurs about every two weeks when the Moon and Sun are in line with each other, this is, at the new and full moons.

Tidal current—Horizontal movements of water due to tidal action.

Tidal range—Vertical distance between high tide and low tide during a single tidal cycle.

The plant is able to produce electricity only four times each day, during each of two high tides and each of two low tides. It generates a modest 250 megawatts in this way with an efficiency about equal to that of a fossil-fuel plant, 25%. With present technology, few other sites exist where tidal power generation is currently considered economically feasible.

See also Alternative energy sources; Gravity and gravitation; Moon; Ocean.

Further Reading:
McGraw-Hill Encyclopedia of Science & Technology, 7th edition. New York: McGraw-Hill Book Company, 1992, volume 18, pp. 370-77.

David E. Newton

Tiger see **Cats**

Tiger cat see **Marsupial cats**

Time

Time is a measurement to determine the duration of an event; or, to determine when an event occurred. Time has different incremental scales (year, day, second, etc.); and, it has different ways by which it is reported (Greenwich Mean Time, Universal Time, Ephemeris Time, etc.). There is also the popular notion of time reversal; or, whether or not we can tell if a process is proceeding forward in time or backward in time.

Time measurement systems

Our time scale is based upon the movement of the sun. Since the sun appears to move from east to west in the sky, when it is twelve noon in New Jersey, the people in Seattle, Washington, say that the sun has not yet reached its apex, or noontime position. In fact, if you say that the sun has attained its noontime position, someone who is west of you by one degree of longitude will say it takes approximately four minutes before the sun reaches its noontime position.

In October of 1884, an international agreement divided the planet into 24 time zones (longitudinally into 15° segments); allowing us to standardize time keeping. The starting point, or zero meridian, was the longitude that ran through the Royal Observatory in Greenwich, England. This is the common position from which we measure our time and is generally referred to as Greenwich Mean Time (GMT).

As you move westward from Greenwich, you add one hour for every 15° meridian you cross. As you move eastward from Greenwich, you subtract one hour for every 15° meridian you cross. (On land the time zones are not always straight lines, this is sometimes done to keep countries, states, cities, etc. all within the same time zone.) It should also be noted that these time zones are also listed by letters of the alphabet as well as 15° increments. Greenwich is designated Z for this purpose, the zones to the East are designated A through M, omitting the letter J, and the zones to the West are N through Y.

In North America, most people measure time based upon two 12 hour intervals. To distinguish the first 12 hours from the second, we label the time. The first twelve hours are denoted by the letters A.M. (for the Latin *ante meridiem*, meaning *before noon*—before the sun has reached its highest point in the sky). The second twelve hours is denoted by P.M. (for *post meridiem*, which means *after noon*—the time after the sun has reached its highest point in the sky).

The International Date Line is near the 180° longitude in the Pacific Ocean. When you cross it going west you add 24 hours (one day), and when you cross it going east you subtract 24 hours (one day). This fact is what allowed Jules Verne's character Phileas Fogg to win his bet in the novel *Around the World in Eighty Days*.

If you ask someone from Europe, or someone in the armed services, what time it is, he or she will answer you using a 24 hour system. Their time starts at midnight of every day, which they call 0000 hours (or 2400 hours of the previous day). Their time then proceeds forward for 24 hours, at which point it starts again. If someone tells you it is 0255 Zulu time, it means that it is 2:55 A.M. in Greenwich, England. This type of time reckoning is extremely important to synchronizing clocks for navigation, etc.

Astronomers found GMT to be awkward to work with in their calculations, because its measurements were based upon the sun's actual motion and period between successive occurrences at its noontime position. Therefore, in 1972 they defined a Universal Time which starts at midnight. They also realized that the solar day, the time from noon to noon, is not necessarily constant because of the irregular motion of the Earth. To compensate for this, they have adopted a mean (average) solar day, time from noon to noon, upon which to base their measurements.

Both GMT and Universal Time are solar based time systems; which means that they are based upon the apparent movement of the Sun. Since the Earth's orbit around the Sun is not circular (it is an ellipse), our rotation rate (how fast we spin on our axis) is not constant, and our rotation axis is nutating (wobbling), this is not an accurate enough standard for all scientific measurements.

Astronomers have thus compensated for the Earth's "imperfections"; by using a Sidereal Time measurement, or a measurement system based upon the repetitive motion of the stars. This motion is, in fact, due to the Earth's motion. Ephemeris time is a Sidereal Time based on the apparent repetitious motion of the Moon and the planets.

During World War II a "war time" was instituted to save on electricity. Later, this became daylight saving Time. However, some states and cities no longer use daylight saving time, because they see it as a needless complication.

Einstein's Theory of Relativity prompted scientists to revise the idea of time as an absolute; for example the German mathematician Hermann Minkowski (1864-1909) described time as the fourth dimension of space, postulating a space-time continuum, which scientists, including Einstein, accepted. Essentially, time cannot the basis for measurement. Because we are all in motion, in one form or another, our time measurements are dependent upon how we are moving. Relativistic time measurements depend upon who is measuring it, how fast the person is moving, and whether or not they are undergoing an acceleration.

Time measuring devices

We measure time, in general, with a clock. However, not all clocks are based on the same time scale. Measurement systems, and types of time differ widely. We have just seen that clocks in different places are calibrated to different schemes; and so, are likely to tell different times.

The first clock was natural, the motion of the Sun through the sky. This led to the invention of the sundial to measure time; as well as, the evening version using the Moon's position. Later came the hourglass, candles and clocks which burned wax, or oil, at a specified rate, and water clocks, which allowed water to flow at a specified rate. Early clocks of greater accuracy, used a pendulum arrangement invented in the 1656 by the Dutch astronomer Christiaan Huygens (1629-1695). Balance wheels then replaced pendulums in some clocks, which allowed clocks to become portable. In recent times, coupled pendulum clocks were used to keep extremely accurate times.

Most of today's clocks and watches use a quartz crystal to keep the time. The specially manufactured quartz crystal, with a specific frequency voltage passing through it, will in turn vibrate at a constant (characteristic) frequency. This frequency, when amplified, drives an electric motor which makes the hands of the clock turn, or makes the digital display change accordingly.

Atomic clocks are the most accurate clocks, and are used by the United States Naval Observatory. They vibrate at a constant sustainable frequency. The process is analogous to setting a pendulum in motion, or a quartz crystal vibrating; except, the atoms "vibrate" between two different energies. This "vibration" between energy levels is associated with a specific frequency, just like the oscillating quartz crystal. This atomic frequency is what drives the clock. The current standard for atomic clocks is one that uses an isotope of Cesium, ^{133}Cs. In 1967, the second was redefined to allow for this accuracy. The second is now defined as 9,192,631,770 times one period, the time for one complete oscillation, of ^{133}Cs.

Research continues into ion clocks such as the hydrogen maser clock. This type of clock is more accurate than a ^{133}Cs clock; however, after several days its accuracy drops to, or below, that of a ^{133}Cs clock.

Time reversal

We perceive time as always proceeding forward into the future; there is no way we know of to travel into the past (except through memories). Time reversal refers the attempt to understand whether a process is moving forward or backward in time. For example, if you watch a movie of two isolated billiard balls colliding on a billiard table, can you tell if the movie is being shown forward or backward? If the two balls are exactly the same, and you do not see one of them being hit to start the process, probably not. If we were to film the process of an egg being dropped and hitting the ground, and then show the film, you could definitely determine in which direction the process continued. The ability to distinguish between forward and backward processes, between past and future on all scales, is crucial for scientific research.

To see if there really is an "arrow of time," or preferred direction in which time flows, experimentalists have been conducting many different types of experiments for more than 40 years. According to theory, we should be able to tell forward time processes from backward time processes. Experimental verifications of this theory delineate how difficult some experiments are to design and perform. The latest are designed to observe atomic particles as they undergo different processes. If the processes are then "run backward," any differences that show up mean that we can tell a forward process from a backward running process. At this time, the experiments are continuing to search for the "arrow of time."

See also Atomic clocks; Relativity, special; Orbit.

Further Reading:

Tudge, Colin. "How long is a piece of time?" *New Scientist,* Vol. 129, January 1991.

Feynman, Leighton, and Sands. *The Feynman Lectures on Physics.* New York: Addison-Wesley, 1989.

Cleere, Gail S. "Got a Second?" *Natural History*, June 1992.

Michelson, Neil F. (compiler). *The American Ephemeris 1931 to 1980 & Book of Tables.* San Diego: Astro Computing Services, 1982.

KEY TERMS

Ephemeris Time — This time scale is based on the apparent repetitious motion of the Moon and planets due to the motion of the Earth. It is corrected for, and based on, the mean solar motion.

Greenwich Mean Time — The location of the Royal Observatory in Greenwich, England where the zero time scales corresponding to time zones have their origin. To synchronize clocks worldwide, all comparisons are made to this scale. It is the period between successive noontime transits of the Sun.

Time reversal — The attempts to discover if we can tell if a process is moving forward or backward in time.

Universal Time — On January 1, 1972 this time scale replaced Greenwich Mean Time as the reference for scientific work. It is based upon an atomic clock, which keeps time from midnight to midnight.

Lineman, Rose and Popelka, Jan. *Compendium of Astrology.* West Chester, PA: Schiffer, 1984.

Itano, Wayne A. and Ramsey, Norman F. "Accurate Measurement of Time." *Scientific American*, Vol. 269, July 1993.

Westerhout, Gart and Winkler, Gernout M.R. "Astrometry and Precise Time." *Oceanus,* Vol. 33, Winter 90/91.

Zee, A. "Time Reversal." *Discover,* Vol. 13, October 1992.

Hunter, L.R. "Tests of Time-Reversal Invariance in Atoms, Molecules, and the Neutron." *Science,* Vol. 252, April 1991.

Peter K. Schoch

Timothy see **Grasses**

Tin see **Element, chemical**

Tinamous

Tinamous are about 45-50 species of ground-dwelling birds that comprise the family Tinamidae, the only member of the order Tinamiformes. Tinamous have a plump, partridge-like body, but they are not related to the partridge, which is in the same family as the pheasants (Phasianidae). The evolutionary relationships of tinamous are not well understood, but their closest living relatives may be the rheas, which are large, flightless birds of South America that make up the order Rheiformes.

Tinamous occur from Mexico in Central America, to Patagonia in South America. Species of tinamous breed in a highly variable range of habitats, from lush tropical rain-forests, to savannahs, grasslands, and alpine tundra. Tinamous are resident in their habitats — they do not migrate.

Tinamous range in body length from 7.8-20 in (20 to 53 cm). These birds have a stout body, short, rounded wings, and a short tail. The legs of tinamous are short but robust, and the strong feet have three or four toes. The sternum, or breastbone, is strongly keeled for the attachment of the large flight muscles. The small head is placed at the end of a rather long neck, and the beak is downward-curved, hooked at the end, and generally fowl-like in appearance.

Tinamous are brown colored, with streaky, barred, or mottled patterns. This coloration is highly cryptic, and helps tinamous to blend in well with their surroundings, and thereby avoid predators to some degree. The sexes are colored alike, but females of some species are slightly larger than males.

Tinamous are running, terrestrial birds. They have sonorous, whistling calls, which may function in the defence or proclamation of their territories. Tinamous can fly rapidly, but they tire quickly, and can only fly over a short distance. Tinamous sometimes prostrate themselves in thick vegetation to hide from predators. Tinamous eat roots, seeds, fruits, buds, and other plant materials, and insects when available.

The eggs of tinamous are brightly colored in glossy, solid hues, and are considered to be among the most beautiful of all birds' eggs. Depending on the species, the egg color can be brown, purple, black, grey, olive, or green. The clutch size is highly variable among species, ranging from one to twelve, although the large numbers may represent the output of several females.

Tinamous nest on the ground. Only the male tinamou incubates the eggs, and only he cares for the brood of young birds. This is, of course, a reversal of the usual role of the sexes in most groups of birds, in which females play a more prominent role. Newly hatched tinamous are highly precocious, and can leave the nest and run well within a few days of hatching. Soon after birth, the chicks follow their male parent about, feeding themselves.

Species of tinamous

Tinamous are obviously different from all other living birds, and this is the reason why they are assigned to their own order, the Tinamiformes. Although some avian systematists believe that the Tinamiformes is most closely related to the order Rheiformes, there are important differences between these groups, especially the presence of a keeled sternum in tinamous. Rheas and other ratites, such as ostriches, emus, and cassowaries, are characterized by a nonkeeled sternum, and are incapable of flight.

While they may be different from all other birds, the various species of tinamous are all rather similar to each other in their color, size, and shape. The entire group is believed to be composed of rather closely related taxa, and consequently, the taxonomy of tinamous is not well established. Although 45-50 species are named, further study may result in some of these taxa being joined together as subspecies of the same bird, while other species may be split into several.

Two of the more common species are the variegated tinamou (*Crypturellus variegatus*) and the Martineta or crested tinamou (*Eudromia elegans*). Both of these are birds of open grasslands of South America, known as pampas. The Martineta tinamou is one of the few social tinamous, occurring in flocks with as many as one-hundred individuals.

The rufescent tinamou (*Nothocercus julius*) occurs in Venezuela, Ecuador, and Columbia. The thicket or rufescent tinamou (*Crypturellus cinnamomeus*) breeds in brushy habitats from Mexico to Columbia and Venezuela.

The Chilean tinamou (*Nothoprocta perdicaria*) is native to tundra-like habitats of southern South America. This species was introduced to Easter Island in the South Pacific in the late nineteenth century, and it still breeds there.

Wherever they are abundant, tinamous are hunted as a source of wild meat, or for sport.

See also Flightless birds.

Further Reading:

Harrison, C.J.O. (ed.). *Bird Families of the World.* New York: H.N. Abrams Pubs., 1978.
Sick, H. *Birds in Brazil: A Natural History.* Princeton, N.J: Princeton University Press, 1993.

Bill Freedman

Tissue

A tissue is a collection of similar cells grouped to perform a common function. Different tissues are made of their own specialized cells that are adapted for a given function.

All animal cells are basically similar. Each cell has a cell wall or plasma membrane that surrounds the cell and contains various receptors that interact with the outside area, a nucleus, Golgi apparatus, mitochondria, and other structures are contained in each cell. Beyond that, cells are specialized in structure for a given function.

The study of tissues is called histology. Studying the structure of tissue is done by staining a thin specimen of the tissue and placing it under a microscope. An experienced histologist can look at a specimen and immediately determine from which organ it was taken. A histologist can also see and diagnose a disease if it is present in the tissue. The study of disease processes is called pathology.

Tissues are divided by function into a number of categories. Muscle tissue, for example, makes up the muscles of the body. A muscle belongs to one of three categories—voluntary muscle which can be controlled for movement or lifting, involuntary muscle which is not under conscious control (such as the muscle tissue in the digestive organs), and cardiac muscle which forms the heart.

Connective tissues compose the bones, tendons, and ligaments that make up the support of the body. The body also consists of adipose tissue or fat.

Nervous tissue forms the brain, spinal cord, and the nerves that extend through the body. Digestive tissue is found in the digestive system including the stomach, intestines, liver, pancreas, and other organs involved in digestion. Vascular tissue comprises the blood-forming portion of the bone marrow and the blood cells themselves. Epithelial tissue forms sheets that cover or line other tissues. The skin and the lining of the stomach are both examples of epithelial tissue. Various reproductive tissues form the ovaries, testes and the resulting gametes (ova and sperm).

Combined, these tissues form the human body and carry out its functions.

See also Cell.

Titanium see **Element, chemical**

Tit family

The tit family, Paridae, consists of 46 species of small birds, variously known as tits, titmice, and chickadees. These are all song birds, in the order Passeriformes. All are rather small birds, ranging in body length from about 4 to 8 in (11 to 20 cm), and mostly occurring in forests, shrubby woodlands, and in urban and suburban habitats. This family of birds is widespread, and its representatives are found in North America, Africa, and Eurasia.

Tits are all active feeders, constantly searching foliage and gleaning bark and branches for insects, spiders, and other arthropods. These birds are highly acrobatic when feeding, often hanging upside down from small twigs to gain access to their prey. During winter, when arthropods are scarce, these birds will eat seeds, and they may be among the most common species at bird feeders.

Tits actively defend territories, proclaiming their ownership by a series of loud whistles and songs. Tits nest in cavities in trees, either naturally occurring or a hole excavated by the tits in soft, rotted wood. Sometimes, tits will utilize a cavity that has previously been excavated and used by smaller species of woodpeckers, and some species of tits will use nest boxes. The clutch size is large, with sometimes more than ten eggs laid at one time. Once the young are fledged, the family of tits stays together during autumn and winter, and often joins with other families to form large foraging flocks, sometimes mixed with other species of similar sized birds.

There are seven species of chickadees in North America. These are rather tame and familiar birds, with a dark cap, and a bib on the throat, a whitish breast, and a brownish or grey back. The most widespread species is the black-capped chickadee (*Parus atricapillus*), occurring throughout the southern boreal and northern temperate forests. The territorial song of this species is a loudly whistled teea-deee, but more familiar to most people is the alarm call, chicka-dee-dee-dee, given when potentially dangerous intruders are near. The Carolina chickadee (*P. carolinensis*) occurs in southeastern North America. The boreal chickadee (*P. hudsonicus*) is common in northern coniferous forests. The mountain chickadee (*P. gambeli*) occurs in montane coniferous forests of western North America. The chestnut-backed chickadee (*P. rufescens*) is abundant in forests of the Pacific coast.

There are four species of titmice in North America. These birds have small crests on the top of their head, and are slightly larger than chickadees, with which they often flock during the non-breeding season. The most widespread species is the tufted titmouse (*P. bicolor*) of southeastern North America. The most common species in the southwest is the plain titmouse (*P. inornatus*).

Tits, titmice, and chickadees are all familiar and friendly birds, and many species can be successfully attracted to the vicinity of homes using a well-maintained feeder. Some species will quickly learn to feed directly at a steadily held hand, lured by crushed peanuts or sunflower seeds.

Bill Freedman

T lymphocytes see **Immune system; Lymphatic system**

Titmice see **Tit family**

Titration see **Quantitative analysis**

Toadfish

Toadfish are a poorly known group of marine fishes, the vast majority of which live close to the shoreline but remain close to the sea bed. Unlike most fish, these animals are extremely vocal, with some authorities even reporting that their loud calls can be heard out of water. One North American genus, *Porichthys*, is more commonly known as the singing midshipman. The calls are produced by muscular contractions of the swimming bladder; the intensity of the sound is related to the degree of stimulation by the muscles. Toadfish are renowned for their territorial behavior, and it is likely that these loud calls have developed to warn off potential rivals through a series of grunts and postures. As an additional deterrent to potential attackers, toadfish have a number of venomous spines which can inflict an irritating, if not lethal, injection of toxins to a would-be predator.

Another peculiar adaptation of toadfish is the large number of light-emitting cells, or photophores, that are scattered around the body. A toadfish can have as many as 700 of these specialized glands. They are thought to contain large numbers of luminescent bacteria, but their purpose is not yet fully understood. In some species these lights, which may flash on and off, serve to attract prey or mates. However, these features are most often found in deep sea fishes and often those that inhabit the deepest and darkest reaches of the oceans.

See also Fish.

Toads

The true toads are amphibians in the order Anura, family Bufonidae. There are 355 species of toads in 25 genera. The largest group is the genus *Bufo*, which includes 205 species.

Toads are characterized by thick, dry, warty skin, with large poison glands on the side of the head and a relatively terrestrial habit as adults. In contrast, adult frogs have a smooth, slimy skin, and a more aquatic habitat.

Toads have a wide natural distribution, occurring on all major land masses except Australasia, Madagascar and Antarctica. In some regions toads range as far north as the boreal forest, but most species occur in temperate or tropical climatic regimes.

The largest toads are from Central and South America, and include *Bufo marinus*, which can reach a body length (excluding the outstretched legs) of 11 in (29 cm), and *B. blombergi* at 10 in (25 cm). The smallest species of toad is a species of *Opeophrynella*, with a body length of only 0.75 in (20 mm).

Biology of toads

Toads are amphibious animals, breeding in water, but able to use terrestrial habitats as adults. As adults, toads potentially can live a long time—one of the longest-lived toad was a European common toad (*Bufo bufo*), which survived for 36 years in captivity.

Toads have a complex life cycle, similar to that of frogs. Toads lay their eggs in water, typically inside of long, intertwined strings of a gelatinous material (toad spawn). The eggs hatch into small, dark-colored aquatic larvae (called tadpoles) which have a large head that is not distinctly separated from the rest of the body, internal gills, and a large, flattened tail which undulates sideways to achieve locomotion. Toad larvae are herbivores that feed on algae, bacteria, and other materials occurring on the surface of vegetation, stones, and sediment.

The larval stage ends with a metamorphosis into the adult life form. Adult toads are characterized by internal lungs used for the exchange of respiratory gases, a tailless body, a pelvis that is fused with many of the vertebra to form a bulky structure known as the urostyle, large hind legs adapted for hopping and walking, and small forelegs used to achieve stability, and to help with eating by feeding certain types of prey, such as long earthworms, into the mouth. Adult toads also have a relatively thick, dry skin that is heavily cornified

The endangered Houston toad (*Bufo houstonensis*).

with the protein keratin, and provides these terrestrial animals with some degree of protection against dehydration and abrasion. Adult toads are exclusively carnivorous, feeding on a wide range of invertebrates and other small animals.

During the breeding season, toads congregate in their breeding ponds, sometimes in large numbers. The males have species-specific songs that are used to attract females. The vocalizations range from long, trilling songs, to shorter, barking sounds. Singing is enhanced by the inflatable vocal sac of male toads, which amplifies their sounds by serving as a resonance chamber. Mating involves the male sitting atop the female in amplexus, gripping tightly using his forelegs, and fertilizing the ova as they are laid by the female. Once laid, the eggs are abandoned to develop by themselves.

Toads are very fertile. As many as 30,000 eggs may be laid by the cane toad (*Bufo marinus*), and even the much smaller American toad (*B. americanus*) may lay as many as 25,000 eggs.

The skin of all amphibians contains glands that secrete toxic chemicals, used to deter predators. These glands are quite large and well developed in the warty skin of adult toads, especially in the paired structures at the sides of the head, known as the parotoid glands. In large toads, such as the cane toad, the quantity and toxicity of the contained poison is sufficient to kill a naive, large predator that foolishly takes a toad into its mouth.

Although toads are relatively resistant to dehydration, they are by no means immune to this stress. Adult toads tend to stay in a cool, moist, secluded place during the day, emerging to feed at night when the risk of dehydration is less. When the opportunity arises, toads will sit in a pool of water to rehydrate their body.

Adult toads use their tongues when feeding. The tongue is attached near the front of the mouth, and can be flipped forward to use its sticky surface to catch a prey animal, which is then retrieved into the mouth. This method of feeding is known as the "lingual flip," a maneuver that can be executed in less than 0.2 seconds, and is especially useful for capturing relative small, flying prey, such as insects.

Toads will attempt to eat any moving object of the right size. However, some prey are considered distasteful by toads, and are spat out.

Toads of North America

The only genus of true toads in North America is *Bufo*, of which 17 species occur north of Mexico. One of the most widespread species is the American toad (*Bufo americanus*), an abundant animal in eastern North America. The common or Woodhouse toad (*B. woodhousei*) is most abundant in the eastern and central United States, but occurs as far west as California. The great plains toad (*B. cognatus*) occurs in moist places throughout the prairie region. The western toad (*B. boreas*) is a widespread, western species.

Some other toad-like animals also bear mentioning, even though they are not "true" toads, that is, they are not in the family Bufonidae.

There are three species of narrow-mouthed toads (family Microhylidae) in southern North America. These are burrowing, nocturnal amphibians that specialize in eating ants, and are rarely seen outside of their breeding season. The eastern narrow-mouthed toad (*Gastrophryne carolinensis*) occurs in the southeastern states, while the western narrow-mouthed toad (*G. olivacea*) has a southwestern distribution.

The narrow-toed toads (family Leptodactylidae) lack webbing between their toes. These animals lay their eggs on land, with the tadpole developing within the egg, and a small toad hatching directly from the egg. The only exception is the white-lipped toad (*Leptodactylus labialis*) of Mexico, which lays its eggs near water, into which the tadpoles wriggle as soon as they hatch. All of the seven North American species of narrow-toed toads have restricted distributions. The greenhouse toad (*Eleutherodactylus planirostris*) occurs over much of peninsular Florida, while the barking toad (*Hylactophryne augusti*) occurs locally in Texas.

There is one species of bell toad (family Leiopelmatidae), the tailed toad (*Ascaphus truei*) of the northwestern states and adjacent Canada. The "tail" of the males is actually a copulatory organ, used to achieve the unusual, internal fertilization of this species.

There are five species of spadefoot toads (family Pelobatidae) in North America. These are nocturnal animals of relatively dry habitats, which breed opportunistically in the springtime if recent rains have provided them with appropriate, temporary ponds. The eastern spadefoot (*Scaphiopus holbrooki*) occurs in the southeast of the continent, while the plains spadefoot (*Spea bombifrons*) is widespread in the shortgrass prairie of the interior, and the western spadefoot (*Spea hammondi*) occurs in the southwest.

Toads and humans

Like most creatures of wetlands and other relatively specialized habitats, some species of toads have suffered large population declines through losses of their natural habitats. This has been an especially important problem for species whose original distribution was quite restricted, for example, the rare and endangered Houston toad (*Bufo houstonensis*).

One species of toad has become an important pest in some parts of the world. The cane or marine toad (*Bufo marinus*) is a large species, reaching a body length of 11.5 in (29 cm) and weighing as much as 2 lb (1 kg). The cane toad is native to parts of Central America, but it has been introduced to many other subtropical and tropical regions in misguided attempts to achieve a measure of biological control over some insects that are agricultural pests.

The cane toad now occurs in Australia, New Guinea, Florida, and many other places, especially tropical islands. Cane toads have become serious pests in many of their introduced habitats, in part because of great damages that are caused to the breeding populations of large species of birds, lizards, and other predators, including domestic cats and dogs. These animals are often naive to the dangers of attempting to eat the poisonous cane toad, and they can therefore be killed in large numbers. The parotoid glands of the cane toad can emit a large quantity of a frothy substance containing noxious chemicals that block neurotransmission, and can lead to death by paralysis.

In small doses, the cane toad secretions can cause a hallucinogenic effect in humans, and people are known to lick the parotoid glands of cane toads in order to achieve this effect. However, it is easy to receive too large a dose of this chemical, and people have been made significantly sick, and have even died, while trying to get high in this manner.

See also Amphibians; Metamorphosis.

KEY TERMS

· ·

Complex life cycle—A life marked by several radical transformations in anatomy, physiology, and ecology.

Metamorphosis—A marked anatomical and physiological transformation occurring during the life of an individual organism. This term is used to describe the changes occurring when a larval amphibian transforms into the adult form.

Further Reading:

Duellman, W.E. and L. Trueb. *Biology of Amphibians.* New York: McGraw-Hill, 1986.
Harris, C.L. *Concepts in Zoology.* New York: HarperCollins, 1992.
Smith, H. M. *Amphibians of North America.* New York: Golden Press, 1978.

Bill Freedman

Tobacco plant see **Nightshade**

Tomato see **Nightshade**

Tonguefish see **Flatfish**

Tongue worms

Tongue worms are bloodsucking endoparasites with a flattened, tongue-like body, and are in the phylum Linguatulida. The final host of these parasites is a predaceous vertebrate, usually a reptile, but sometimes a mammal or a bird. The intermediate host (in which the parasite lives as a larva) can be any of a number of animals, including insects, fish, amphibians, reptiles, and mammals. The 70 species of tongue worms are primarily tropical and subtropical in distribution.

Adult tongue worms live in the lungs or nasal passages of the host. Mature females reach a length of up to 15 cm (6 in) and a width of 0.4 in (1 cm), while males are 0.8-1.6 in (2-4 cm) long and 3-4 mm wide. The mouth is sited at the anterior end of the worm, and has a set of hooks for attachment to the tissues of the host. In most species of the tongue worm, the body has superficial ringlike markings, giving it the appearance of segmentation. The only internal body structures are the digestive and reproductive organs, and certain

glands. Respiratory, circulatory, and excretory organs are absent.

An typical life cycle of a tongue worm is that of *Porocephalus crotali*, whose adult stage lives and reproduces in the lungs of the rattlesnake, and whose larval stage is found in the muskrat and other hosts which constitute the rattlesnake's food. Following copulation, the female tongue worm releases her eggs into the host's lungs. The eggs leave the host's body in its respiratory secretions, and might be accidentally ingested by the intermediate host. In the digestive tract of the intermediate host, the eggs hatch to produce four-legged larvae which superficially resemble the immature stage of a mite. The larva penetrates the wall of the host's digestive tract, migrates to another tissue such as the liver, and encysts. If the intermediate host is now eaten by a rattlesnake, the parasite is transferred to the snake's digestive tract. Here it emerges from the cyst and migrates up the host's esophagus and into its lungs, where it eventually matures. *Armillifer* and *Linguatula* are two other well known genera of tongue worms, each with different final and intermediate hosts, but with an essentially similar life cycle.

Zoologists consider linguatulids to be closely related to the arthropoda, and in some classifications the tongue worms are included in that phylum.

See also Parasites.

Tonsillitis

Tonsillitis is an inflammation or infection of the tonsils, caused by either bacteria or viruses. The tonsils usually become swollen and very painful, making swallowing difficult. Sometimes the tonsils have spots of exudates (usually leukocytes) or pus on the surface. The surface of the tonsils is covered by recesses or crypts (*cryptae tonsillares*) that may branch and extend deep into the tonsil. The crypts often hold a variety of bacteria, some of which can cause tonsillitis.

The tonsils are conglomerations of lymphoid nodules, covered by a mucous membrane. They help to provide immune responses by, for example, providing lymphocytes and antibodies. There are three types of tonsils that form an irregular, circular band (Waldeyer's ring) around the throat, at the very back of the mouth. Tonsils are strategically located, guarding the opening to the digestive and respiratory tracts. The pharyngeal tonsils (adenoids) are embedded in the posterior wall of the pharynx. The lingual tonsils are located at the base of

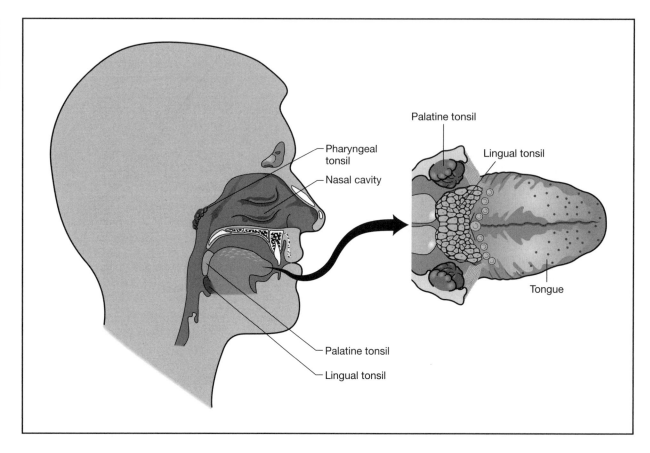

The palatine, lingual and pharyngeal tonsils.

the tongue, and the palatine tonsils are the oval shaped masses situated on both sides of the throat.

It is usually the prominent, palatine tonsils that become infected or inflamed, and these are the tonsils that are removed surgically (tonsillectomy) when medically indicated, to treat chronic tonsillitis or repeated episodes of acute tonsillitis. Occasionally the pharyngeal tonsils or adenoids are also removed surgically (adenotonsillectomy) if they cause ear infections, or block the Eustachian tubes or nasal passages. Adenoviruses (upper respiratory infection or "common cold") are the most common cause of viral tonsillitis. The Epstein-Barr virus (infectious mononucleosis) can also cause tonsillitis. The most common bacteria to cause tonsillitis are any of the group A streptococcus bacteria (*Streptococcus pyogenes*). Bacterial tonsillitis is treated with antibiotics. However, antibiotics are ineffective with viral tonsillitis. Symptoms can be relieved with aspirin (or other anti-inflammatories), gargling with saltwater, and rest.

Tonsils see **Lymphatic system**

Toothed herring see **Mooneyes**

Topi see **Antelopes and gazelles; Hartebeestes**

Topology

Topology, which is often described as "rubber-sheet geometry," is a branch of geometry that focuses on distortion. Topology describes mathematically the features of a geometric shape that do not change when the shape is twisted, stretched, or squeezed. Tearing, cutting, and combining shapes do not apply to topology. Topology helps to solve problems about determining the number of colors necessary to illustrate maps, about distinguishing the characteristics of knots, and about understanding the structure and behavior of DNA molecules.

Topological equivalency

The crucial problem in topology is deciding when two shapes are equivalent. Unlike Euclidean geometry,

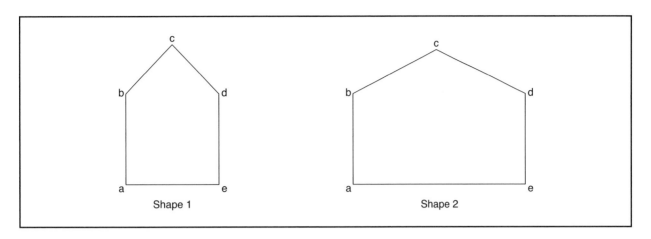

Figure 1.

which focuses on the measurement of distances between points on a shape, topology focuses on the similarity and continuity of certain features of geometrical shapes. For example, in Figure 1 above, each of the two shapes has five points: a through e. The sequence of the points does not change from shape 1 to shape 2, even though the distance between the points, for example, between points b and d, changes significantly because shape 2 has been stretched. Thus the two shapes in Figure 1 are topologically equivalent, even if their measurements are different.

Similarly, in Figure 2, each of the closed shapes is curved, but shape 3 is more circular, and shape 4 is a flattened circle, or ellipse. However, every point on shape 3 can be mapped or transposed onto shape 4.

Shapes 1 and 2 are both topologically equivalent to each other, as are shapes 3 and 4. That is, if each were a rubber band, it could be stretched or twisted into the same shape as the other without connecting or disconnecting any of its points. However, if either of the shapes in each pair is torn or cut, or if any of the points

in each pair join together, then the shapes are not topologically equivalent. In Figure 3, neither of the shapes is topologically equivalent to any of the shapes in Figures 1 or 2, nor are shapes 5 and 6 equivalent to each other. The circles in shape 5 are fused; and the triangle in shape 6 has a broken line hanging from its apex.

Famous topologists

Topological ideas can be traced back to Gottfried Wilhelm Leibniz (1646-1716), but three of the most famous figures in the development of topology are Möbius, Riemann, and Klein.

Augustus Ferdinand Möbius (1790-1868) is best known for his invention of the Möbius strip, which is a simple strip of paper that is twisted and connected so that it has only one side. Normally, cutting a strip of paper into a long, narrow rectangle and connecting the ends will result in a belt-like loop with two sides. A person cannot draw a single line with a pencil on both sides of the belt-like loop without crossing an edge. In constructing the Möbius strip, however, the strip of paper is twisted as it is looped, as illustrated in Figure 4, and the result is a one-sided object.

Figure 2.

Figure 3.

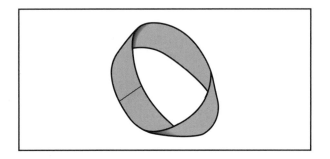

Figure 4. A Möbius strip.

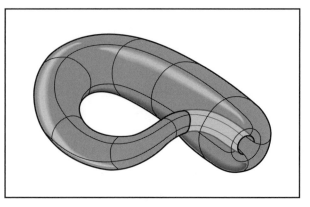

Figure 5. A Klein bottle.

At first, this one-sided construction seems impossible, but if a person draws a straight, continuous line on the Möbius strip, the line will cover the entire length of both sides of the strip without ever crossing an edge, and it will return to its starting point in one long stroke.

Georg Friedrich Bernhard Riemann (1826-1866) developed some of the most important topological ideas about the stretching, bending, and twisting of surfaces, but he died prematurely at the age of 39 before he could expand significantly upon his ideas.

Felix Klein (1849-1925) is best known for the paradoxical figure illustrated in Figure 5 which was named after him: the Klein bottle.

The Klein bottle is a one-sided object that has no edge. It is a tapered tube whose neck is bent around to enter the side of the bottle. The neck continues into the base of the bottle where it flares out and rounds off to form the outer surface of the bottle. Like the Möbius strip, any two points on the bottle can be joined by a continuous line without crossing an edge, which gives the impression that the inside and outside of the Klein bottle are continuous.

Classifications

Topological shapes are classified according to how many holes they have. Shapes with no holes at all-spheres, eggs, and convex or concave shapes like bowls-are regarded as genus (or type) 0 shapes.

Genus 1 shapes have one hole in them: a donut (or torus), a wedding band, a pipe, or anything with a looped handle (a teacup). Genus 2 shapes have two holes in them, for example, a figure eight. Genus 3 shapes (most pretzels) have three holes in them. And so on.

The determining feature in classifying the topological genus of a shape is deciding if every point in one shape can be transposed or mapped onto a point in the other. Sometimes this process is easy, as in the case of a wedding ring and a donut, which are genus 1 topological shapes. But with complex genus shapes of 4 and above, the determination can be difficult.

Current research

Topology has a number of interesting applications, including molecular biology and synthesizing new chemical compounds to help in gene therapy. For example, strands of DNA (deoxyribonucleic acid, which contains the genetic code that defines life) often become knotted. Researchers need to know if the knotted mass of DNA is just one strand of DNA that has wound back upon itself, or if it is several strands of DNA which have become entangled. Topology, especially knot theory, helps molecular biologists solve such problems of equivalency.

Topology also has applications in synthesizing new molecules, called dendrimers, which may be used in gene therapy. Dendrimers are branching, tree-like polymers (strings of smaller molecules) synthesized in laboratories by chemically attaching the polymers to a core molecule. Dendrimers are approximately the same size as many naturally occurring molecules, including DNA and proteins. In gene therapy, new genetic material needs to be transported to the nucleus of a cell to replace damaged or defective genes in human cells. Then the repaired cells can reproduce more healthy cells. However, there must be a way to transport the healthy DNA into cells, which is where dendrimers come in. Normally, DNA wraps itself around clusters of proteins called histones. Gene therapists can fool the immune system of the human body by substituting dendrimers for naturally occurring clusters of histones and thus transport healthy DNA into damaged cells. Topology is useful in this process, because its purpose is to decide mathematically which shapes are equivalent. The closer that synthetic dendrimers mimic the naturally-occurring histones, then the greater are the chances that the DNA will be transported to create healthy cells.

See also Geometry; Polymer; Torus.

KEY TERMS

Dendrimer molecules—Branching, tree-like polymers synthesized in laboratories by attaching the polymers to a core molecule.

DNA—Deoxyribonucleic acid, a thin, ladder-like molecular structure which contains the genetic code that defines life.

Euclidean geometry—Geometry based upon the postulates of the Greek educator, Euclid who lived roughly 300 B.C. Euclid's parallel postulate—that only one line may be drawn through a given point such that it is parallel to another line—was overthrown in the nineteenth century and gave way to the non-Euclidean geometries created by Gauss and Riemann.

Geometry—The area of mathematics that deals with deductions concerning the measurements and relationships between points, lines, angles, and figures in physical space.

Polymers—Strings of smaller molecules.

Further Reading:

Boyer, Carl B. *A History of Mathematics.* Princeton: Princeton University Press, 1985.

Jacobs, Harold R. *Mathematics: A Human Endeavor.* San Francisco: W.H. Freeman,1970.

Kline, Morris. *Mathematical Thought: From Ancient to Modern Times.* 3 Vols. New York: Oxford University Press, 1972.

Peterson, Ivars. *The Mathematical Tourist: Snapshots of Modern Mathematics.* New York: W. H. Freeman,1988.

Tomalia, Donald A. "Dendrimer Molecules." *Scientific American* 272 (May 1995): 62-66.

Patrick Moore

Tornado

A tornado is a rapidly spinning column of air formed in severe thunderstorms. The rotating column, or vortex, forms inside the storm cloud then grows downward until it touches the ground. Although a tornado is not as large as its parent thunderstorm, it is capable of extreme damage because it packs very high wind speeds into a compact area. Tornadoes have been known to shatter buildings, drive straws through solid wood, lift locomotives from their tracks, and pull the water out of small streams. Due to a combination of geography and meteorology, the United States experiences most of the world's tornadoes. An average of 800 tornadoes strike the United States each year. Based on statistics kept since 1953, Texas, Oklahoma, and Kansas are the top three tornado states. Tornadoes are responsible for about 80 deaths, 1500 injuries, and many millions of dollars in property damage annually. While it is still impossible to predict exactly when and where tornadoes will strike, progress has been made in predicting tornado development and detecting tornadoes with Doppler radar.

Tornado formation

Most tornadoes form during the months of March through June. These are months when conditions are right for the development of severe thunderstorms. To understand why tornadoes form consider the formation and growth of a thunderstorm. Thunderstorms are most likely to develop when the atmosphere is unstable; that is when atmospheric temperature drops rapidly with height. Under unstable conditions air near the surface that begins rising will expand and cool, but remains warmer (and less dense) than its surroundings. The rising air acts like a hot air balloon; since it is less dense than the surrounding air it continues to rise. At some point the rising air cools to the dew point where the water vapor in the air condenses to form liquid water droplets. The rising column of air is now a visible cloud. If the rising air, or updraft, is sustained long enough water droplets will begin to fall out of the rising air column making it a rain cloud.

For this cloud to become a severe storm capable of producing tornadoes requires several conditions. Severe storms are often associated with a very unstable atmosphere and moving low pressure systems that bring cold air into contact with warmer more humid air masses. Such a weather situation commonly occurs in the eastern and midwestern United States during the spring and summer months. Large scale weather systems often sweep moist warm air from the Gulf of Mexico over these regions in a layer 2-3 km (1.2-1.9 mi) deep. At the same time winds aloft (above about 4 km (2.5 mi) in altitude) from the southwest bring cool dry air over the region. Cool air overlying humid air forms a very unstable atmosphere and sets the stage for the growth of strong thunderstorms.

The warm surface air is separated from colder air lying farther north by a fairly sharp temperature boundary called a front. A low pressure center at the surface causes the cold air to advance into the warmer air. The

A tornado that formed during a storm in Union City, Oklahoma, on May 24, 1973.

edge of the advancing cold air, called a cold front, forces the warmer air ahead of the front to rise and cool. Since the atmosphere is so unstable the displaced air keeps rising and a cloud quickly forms. Rain that begins to fall from the cloud causes downdrafts (sinking air) in the rear of the cloud. Meanwhile the advancing edge of the storm has strong updrafts and humid air is pulled into the storm. The water vapor in this air condenses to form more water droplets as it rises and cools. When water vapor condenses it releases latent heat. This warms the air and forces it to rise more vigorously strengthening the storm.

The exact mechanism of tornado formation inside severe thunderstorms is still a matter of dispute but it appears that tornadoes grow in a similar fashion to the small vortices that form in draining bathtubs. When the plug is pulled in a bathtub water from other parts of the tub rushes in to replace that going down the drain. If the water has any swirl in it the drain soon has a little vor-

tex. Tornadoes appear to be upside down versions of this phenomenon. As updrafts in a severe thunderstorm cloud get stronger more air is pulled into the base of the cloud to replace the rising air. Some of this air may be rotating slightly since the air around the base of a thunderstorm usually contains some rotation, or vorticity. As the air converges into a smaller area it begins to rotate faster due to a law of physics known as the conservation of angular momentum. This effect can be seen when an ice skater begins spinning with arms outstretched. As the skater brings his or her arms inward his or her rotational speed increases. In the same way air moving into a severe storm begins in a tighter column and increases its rotational speed. A wide vortex is created called the mesocyclone. The mesocyclone begins to build vertically extending itself upward throughout the entire height of the cloud. The rapid air movement causes the surrounding air pressure to drop pulling more air into growing vortex. The lowered pressure causes the incoming air to cool quickly and form cloud droplets before they rise to the cloud base. This forms the wall cloud, a curtain-shaped cloud that is often seen before a tornado forms. The mesocyclone continues to contract while growing from the base of the storm cloud all the way up to 10 km (6.2 mi) above the surface. When the mesocyclone dips below the wall cloud it is called a funnel cloud because of its distinctive funnel shape. This storm is on its way to producing a tornado.

Tornado characteristics

A funnel cloud may form in a severe storm and never reach the ground. If and when it does the funnel officially becomes a tornado. The central vortex of a tornado is typically about 100 m (328.1 ft) in diameter. Wind speeds in the vortex have been measured at greater than 100 m/sec (220 mph). These high winds make incredible feats of destruction possible. They also cause the air pressure in the tornado to drop below normal atmospheric pressure by over 100 millibars (the normal day-to-day pressure variations we experience are about 15 millibars). The air around the vortex is pulled into this low pressure zone where it expands and cools rapidly. This causes water droplets to condense from the air making the outlines of the vortex visible as the characteristic funnel shaped cloud. The low pressure inside the vortex picks up debris such as soil particles which may give the tornado an ominous dark color. A tornado can act as a giant vacuum cleaner sweeping over anything unlucky enough to be in its path. The damage path of a tornado may range from 300 m (328.2 yards) to over a kilometer (.62 mi) wide.

Tornadoes move with the thunderstorm that they are attached to traveling at speeds of about 15-45 kph

(10-30 mph). Since a typical tornado has a lifetime of about 5-10 minutes it may stay on the ground for 5-10 miles although occasionally a severe tornado may cut a path of destruction over 200 mi (321.8 km) long. Witnesses to an approaching tornado often describe a loud roaring noise made by the storm similar to jet engines at takeoff. There is no generally accepted explanation for this phenomenon although it has been suggested that supersonic winds inside the vortex cause it.

The destructive path of tornadoes appears random. One house may be flattened while its neighbor remains untouched. This has been explained by the tornado "skipping," lifting up off the surface briefly then descending again to resume its destructive path. Studies made of these destructive paths after the storm suggest another possible explanation: tornadoes may have two to three smaller tornado-like vortices circling around the main vortex like horses on a merry-go-round. According to this theory these "suction vortices" may be responsible for much of the actual damage associated with tornadoes. As they rotate around the main tornado core they may hit or miss objects directly in the tornado's path depending on their position. Thus if two houses were in the tornado path one may be destroyed by a suction vortex but the vortex had moved into a different position (and the next vortex had not yet taken its place) by the time it reached the next house. The tornado's "skipping" behavior is still not completely understood.

When houses or other structures are destroyed by a tornado they are not simply blown down by the high winds: they appear to explode. For many years it was believed that the low pressure of the tornado vortex caused such explosions. If the pressure outside a building drops very quickly the air inside may not escape fast enough (through cracks, holes, and the like) to equalize the pressure difference. The higher pressure inside the building then pushes out windows or whole walls, and the structure looks like it had exploded. Studies of tornado damage have shown that buildings do not actually explode in this manner. Instead high wind passing over a house roof acts like the air moving over an airplane wing: it gives the roof an upward force or lift which tends to raise the roof vertically off the house. Winds also enter the building through broken windows or doors pressurizing the house as one would blow up a balloon. The combination of these forces tends to blow the walls and roof off the structure from the inside out giving the appearance of an explosion.

Tornado strength is classified by the Fujita scale using a scale of one to six to denote tornado wind speed. Since direct measurements of the vortex are not possible the observed destruction of the storm is used to estimate its "F scale" rating.

Tornado history

The single most violent tornado in United States history was the Tri-State tornado on March 18, 1925. Beginning in Missouri the tornado stayed on the ground for over 350 km (217.4 mi) crossing Illinois, moving into Indiana, and leaving a trail of damage over 1.5 km (.9 mi) wide in places. Tornado damage often is limited since they usually strike unpopulated areas but the Tri-State tornado plowed through nine towns and destroyed thousands of homes. When the storm was over 689 people had lost their lives and over 2,000 were injured making the Tri-State the deadliest tornado on record.

Another historic storm was the severe tornado outbreak of April 3-4, 1974. As a strong low pressure system moved over the midwest an advancing cold front ran into warm Gulf air over the southern states. The resulting storm triggered 148 tornadoes over 13 states in the next 24 hours some reaching F4 and F5 in strength. As severe as this outbreak was the death toll was less than half of that from the Tri-State tornado because of advances in tornado forecasting and warnings.

Prediction and tracking of tornadoes

The precise tracking and prediction of tornadoes is not yet a reality. Meteorologists can identify conditions that are likely to lead to severe storms. They can issue warnings when atmospheric conditions are right for the development of tornadoes. They can use radar to track the path of thunderstorms that might produce tornadoes. It is still not possible to detect a funnel cloud by radar and predict its path, touchdown point, and other important details. Much progress has recently been made in the detection of tornadoes using Doppler radar.

Doppler radar can measure not just the distance to an object, but also its velocity by using the Doppler effect: if an object is moving toward an observer radar waves bounced off the object will have a higher frequency than if the object were moving away. This effect can be demonstrated with sound waves. If a car is approaching with its horn sounding the pitch of the horn (that is, the frequency of the sound waves) seems to rise. It reaches a peak just as the car passes then falls as the car speeds away from the listener. Doppler radar is used to detect the motion of raindrops and hail in a thunderstorm which give an indication of the motion of the winds. With present technology it is possible to detect the overall storm circulation and even a developing mesocyclone. The relatively small size of a tornado makes direct detection very difficult with the current generation of Doppler radar. In addition any radar is limited by the curvature of Earth. Radar waves go in straight lines which means that distant storms which are "below the horizon" from the radar cannot be probed with this technique.

Tornadoes which have long fascinated people with their sudden appearance and awesome destructive power are still subjects of intense scientific study. Research continues on the formation life history and detection of these most impressive storms.

See also Atmospheric pressure; Cyclone and anticyclone; Thunderstorm; Tropical cyclone.

Further Reading:
Battan, Louis J. *Weather*. Engelwood Cliffs: Prentice-Hall Inc., 1985.
Battan, Louis J. *Weather in Your Life*. New York: W.H. Freeman & Co., 1983.
Hardy, Ralph, Peter Wright, John Kington, and John Gribben. *The Weather Book*. Boston: Little, Brown and Co., 1982.
Lewellen, W.S. "Tornado Vortex Theory," in *The Tornado: Its Structure, Dynamics and Hazards*. Washington, D.C.: American Geophysical Union, 1993.
McNeill, Robert. *Understanding the Weather*. Las Vegas: Arbor Publishers, 1991.
Miller et al. *Elements of Meteorology*. Columbus: Merril Publishing Co., 1983.
Mogil, H. Michael and Barbara G. Levine. *The Amateur Meteorologist*. New York: Franklin Watts, 1993.

James Marti

KEY TERMS

Dew point—The temperature at which water vapor in the air condenses to form liquid water droplets.

Doppler radar—A type of radar that measures both the position and the velocity of an object.

Front—A fairly sharp temperature boundary in the lower atmosphere.

Fujita scale—A scale of one to six which rates tornado wind speed based upon the observed destruction of the storm.

Funnel cloud—A fully developed tornado vortex before it has touched the ground.

Latent heat—The heat released when water vapor condenses to form liquid water.

Skipping—The tendency of tornado damage to be random as if the tornado skips along in its path.

Suction vortices—Secondary vortices that are theorized to be part of a tornado vortex. They may be responsible for the "skipping" behavior of tornadoes.

Unstable atmosphere—The condition of the atmosphere when air temperature drops rapidly with height. Such conditions support rising air and contribute to strong thunderstorms.

Vortex—A rotating column of a fluid such as air or water.

Vorticity—The tendency of an air mass to rotate.

Wall cloud—The characteristic cloud that forms at the base of a thunderstorm before a funnel cloud appears.

Torque

According to Isaac Newton, an object at rest will remain at rest, and an object will remain in motion unless acted upon by an outside force. A force, therefore, is what causes any object to move. Any force which causes an object to rotate, turn, or twist is called a torque. Torque is equal to the amount of force being exerted on the object times the object's rotation point to the location where the force is being applied on the object.

Seesaws are a good example of torque. Many people have had the experience of a large person sitting on one end of the seesaw, and a small person on the other end. If the larger person is sitting closer to the pivot point of the seesaw, the smaller person can lift them

with little or no problem. The reason this is possible comes from the difference in torque experienced by each person. Even though the smaller person exerts a smaller force, their distance from the pivot point (lever arm) is longer, hence a large torque. The larger person exerts a larger force; however, because he/she is closer to the pivot point their lever arm is shorter, hence a smaller torque.

Wrenches also work by torque. (Some wrenches are even calibrated to display the amount of torque you are applying to a nut; they are called torque wrenches.) The nut (or bolt) is the point of rotation because we either want to tighten or loosen it by having it turn. The force is being exerted by your hand and arm. Since we try to pull or push (exert a force) at right angles on the wrench's handle, the lever arm is then the length of the wrench's handle. To increase the torque on the nut, we must either increase how hard we pull or push on the lever arm; or, increase the length of the lever arm by placing a pipe over the end of the wrench.

Tortoises see **Turtles**

Torus

A torus is a doughnut-shaped, three-dimensional figure formed when a circle is rotated through 360° about a line in its plane, but not passing through the circle itself. Imagine, for example, that the circle lies in space such that its diameter is parallel to a straight line. The figure that is formed is a hollow, circular tube, a torus. A torus is sometimes referred to as an anchor ring.

The surface area and volume of a torus can be calculated if one knows the radius of the circle and the radius of the torus itself, that is, the distance from the furthest part of the circle from the line about which it is rotated. If the former dimension is represented by the letter r, and the latter dimension by R, then the surface area of the torus is given by $4\pi^2Rr$, and the volume is given by $2\pi^2Rr_2$.

Problems involving the torus were well known to and studied by the ancient Greeks. For example, the formula for determining the surface area and volume of the torus came about as the result of the work of the Greek mathematician Pappus of Alexandria, who lived around the third century A.D. Today, problems involving the torus are of special interest to topologists.

See also Topology.

Toucans

Toucans are 42 species of familiar, brilliantly colored arboreal birds that make up the family Ramphastidae. Toucans are in the order Piciformes, which also includes the woodpeckers.

Toucans range from southern Mexico to northern Argentina and Paraguay. Their usual habitat is tropical and subtropical forests and woodlands, and sometimes

> **KEY TERMS**
>
> **Zygodactyl**—This refers to a pattern of arrangement of the toes of certain birds, in which two toes point forward, and two backward. This is the characteristic arrangement in the Piciformes, including the toucans.

more open savannahs with clumps of trees. Most species occur in lowlands, but some live in higher elevation montain forests. Toucans are not migratory, although some species may undertake local movements in search of food.

Toucans are relatively large birds, with a body length of 12-24 in (30-61 cm). Their wings are short and rounded, the tail is long and wide, the legs and feet are stout and strong, with the toes arranged in a zygodactyl pattern.

The most distinctive feature of toucans is their tremendous, seemingly oversized, laterally compressed bill, which in some species is as long as the body. The bill is stout but well-chambered with air-containing cavities, and therefore surprisingly light in weight. The bill curves lightly downwards, and often has a serrated inner margin. There is a small hook at the tip of the upper mandible, and the nostrils are placed at the base of the beak, near the head.

The function of the unusually enormous bill of toucans has not been conclusively determined. It may be helpful in plucking fruits that are far away from branches that are large enough for a toucan to perch on. Alternatively, the large bill may be used to frighten away potential predators, or to intimidate the parents of nestlings or eggs that toucans are predating upon. The bill may also have important social functions, for example, in courtship displays.

The body plumage of toucans is soft, and usually black or dark green, with conspicuous patches of white, yellow, orange, red, or blue. Toucans have bare, brightly colored skin around the eye. The large bill of toucans is brightly colored in most species, and is likely important in species recognition. The sexes of most species do not differ in size or coloration.

Toucans live in small, harshly noisy, often family related groups. They feed together, with an attentive sentry posted to warn against intrusions by predators. Toucans mostly eat fruits, insects, and sometimes the eggs or nestlings of other species of birds. Toucans can

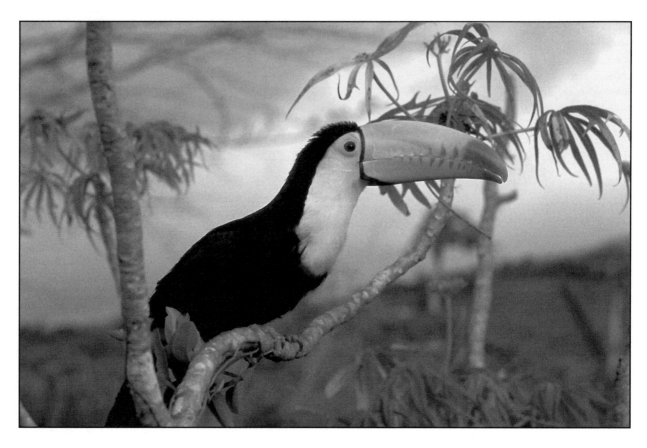

A toucan at Lake Arenal, Costa Rica.

manipulate their foods quite dexterously, in spite of their huge bills.

Toucans have a repertoire of harsh croaks, yelps, mews, rattles, and other sounds. Some of the larger species give a series of almost musical renditions at dawn, which may function as territorial songs.

Toucans roost and nest in cavities in trees, commonly using abandoned holes excavated by woodpeckers, although these may be further enlarged by the toucans. During roosting, several birds may crowd into the same cavity, and when doing this they commonly fold their tail up over the back to save space. Toucans lay 2-4 eggs in an unlined nesting cavity as high up a tree as possible. The eggs are incubated by both parents, who also share the chick-rearing duties, which takes about 40-50 days until fledging occurs.

Species of toucans

The largest toucans are those in the genus *Ramphastos*, which live in lowland, tropical forests. The toco toucan (*R. toco*) occurs in tropical Amazonian forests, while the chestnut-mandibled toucan (*R. swainsonii*) occurs from Honduras to Venezuela.

Species of aracari toucans (*Pteroglossus* spp.) are smaller and are relatively gregarious. The green aracari (*Pteroglossus viridis*) occurs in tropical forests from Venezuela through Brazil.

The toucanets are even smaller. The spot-billed toucanet (*Selenidera maculirostris*) occurs in forests from Venezuela and Guyana to northern Argentina.

Further Reading:

Harrison, C.J.O. (ed.). *Bird Families of the World*. New York: H.N. Abrams Pubs., 1978.

Sick, H. *Birds in Brazil: A Natural History*. Princeton, N.J: Princeton University Press, 1993.

Bill Freedman

Touch

Touch is one of the five senses (the others being smell, taste, vision, and hearing) through which animals and people interpret the world around them. While the other senses are localized primarily in a single area (such as vision in the eyes or taste in the tongue), the sensation of touch (or contact with the outside world) can be experienced anywhere on the body, from the top of the head to the tip of the toe. Touch is based on nerve receptors in the skin which send electrical messages through the central nervous system to the cerebral cortex in the brain, which interprets these electrical codes. For the most part, the touch receptors specialize in experiencing either hot, cold, pain, or pressure. Arguably, touch is the most important of all the senses; without it animals would not be able to recognize pain (such as scalding water), which would greatly decrease their chances for survival. Research has also shown that touch has tremendous psychological ramifications in areas like child development, persuasion, healing, and reducing anxiety and tension.

How we feel the outside world

Our sense of touch is based primarily in the outer layer of skin called the epidermis. Nerve endings that lie in or just below the epidermis cells respond to various outside stimuli, which are categorized into four basic stimuli: pressure, pain, hot, and cold. Animals experience one or a combination of these sensations through a complex neural network that sends electrical impulses through the spinal cord to the cerebral cortex in the brain. The cerebral cortex, in turn, contains brain cells (neurons) arranged in columns that specialize in interpreting specific types of stimuli on certain parts of the body.

The sensation of touch begins with various receptors in the skin. Although these receptors appear to specialize in reacting to certain sensations, there is some debate concerning this specificity since most touch stimuli are a combination of some or all of the four major categories.

Scientists have identified several types of touch receptors. Free nerve ending receptors, located throughout the body at the bases of hair, are associated primarily with light pressure (such as wind) and pain. Meissner corpuscles are nerve endings contained in tiny capsules and are found primarily in the fingertips and areas especially sensitive to touch (in the form of low-frequency vibrations), like the soles of the feet and the tongue. The Pacinian corpuscles look like the cross section of an onion and are found in deep tissues in the joints, the genitals, and the mammary glands. They are extremely sensitive to pressure and are also stimulated by rapid movement of the tissues and vibrating sensations. Ruffini endings, which are also located in the

deeper layers of the skin, respond to continuous stimulation, like steady pressure or tension within the skin. Merkel disks, are found near the base of the epidermis and also respond to continuous stimulation or pressure. The skin also contains specific thermoreceptors for sensing hot and cold and nociceptors that identify high intensity stimulation in the form of pain.

Most, if not all of these receptors, are designed to adapt or become accustomed to the specific stimulation they interpret. In other words, the receptor does not continue to register a constant "feeling" with the same intensity as when it first begins and may even shut off the tactile experience. Imagine, for example, putting on a wool sweater over bare skin. The initial prickly sensation eventually abates, allowing the wearer to become accustomed to the feeling. Other examples include wearing jewelry such as rings, necklaces, and watches.

These receptors are also found in greater numbers on different parts of the body. For example, peoples' backs are the least sensitive to touch, while their lips, tongue, and fingertips are most sensitive to tactile activity. Most receptors for cold are found on the surface of the face while thermoreceptors for warmth usually lie deeper in the skin and are fewer in number. A light breeze on the arm or head is felt because there tend to be more sense receptors at the base of the hairs than anywhere else.

Touch and health

Touch has a tremendous impact on most animals' physical and psychological well being. Numerous studies of humans and other animals have shown that touch greatly impacts how we develop physically and respond to the world mentally. For example, premature babies that receive regular massages will gain weight more rapidly and develop faster mentally than those who do not receive the same attention. When baby rats are separated from their mothers for only 45 minutes, they undergo physiological or biochemical changes, specifically a reduction in a growth hormone. Touching of premature babies can also stimulate growth hormones (such as the hormone needed to absorb food) that occur naturally in healthy babies.

A baby does not have to be premature or sickly to benefit from touch. Even healthy babies show benefits from touch in terms of emotional stability. Difficult children often have a history of abuse and neglect. The reason is that touch serves as a type of reassurance to infants that they are loved and safe, which translates into emotional well being. In general, babies who are held and touched more tend to develop better alertness and cognitive abilities over the long run.

KEY TERMS

Biochemical—The biological or physiological chemicals of living organisms.

Central nervous system—The brain and spinal cord components of the nervous system, which controls activities of internal organs, movements, perceptions, thoughts, and emotions.

Cerebral cortex—The external gray matter surrounding the brain and made up of layers of nerve cells and fibers, thought to process sensory information and impulses.

Epidermis—The outer layer of skin on vertebrates that covers the nest layers of skin called the dermis.

Free nerve endings—Touch receptors in the skin that detect light pressure.

Glucocorticoids—A steroid- or hormone-like compound that affects metabolism and can have an anti-inflammatory effect.

Meissner corpuscles—Touch receptors in the skin that are sensitive to touch. Named after German histologist Georg Meissner.

Neurons—Nervous system unit that includes the nerve cell, dendrites, and axons.

Pacinian corpuscles—Touch receptors in the skin that sense pressure and rapid or vibrating movement of the tissues, named after Italian anatomist Filippo Pacini.

Touch continues to have a great psychological impact throughout peoples' lives. Even adults who are hospitalized or sick at home seem to have less anxiety and tension headaches when they are regularly touched or caressed by caretakers or loved ones. Numerous studies have shown that touch also has a healing power. Researchers have found that touch reduces rapid heart beats and irregular heart beats (arrhythmias). Another study showed that baby rats who are touched often during infancy develop more receptors to control the production of biochemicals called glucocorticoids, which are known as stress chemicals because of their ability to cause muscle shrinkage, high blood pressure, elevated cholesterol, and more.

Touch's psychological impact goes beyond physical and mental health. Researchers have shown that touch is a powerful persuasive force. For example, studies have shown that touch can have a big impact in marketing and sales. Salespeople often use touch to estab-lish a camaraderie and friendship that can result in better sales. In general, people are more likely to respond positively to a request if it is accompanied by a slight touch on the arm or hand. In a study of waiters and waitresses, for example, those that lightly touched a patron often received better tips.

See also Perception.

Further Reading:

Ackerman, Diane. *A Natural History of the Senses*. New York: Vintage Books, 1991.
Barlow, H.B. and Mollon, J.D. *The Senses*. Cambridge: Cambridge University Press, 1982.
Bennet, Thomas L. *The Sensory World. An Introduction to Sensation and Perception*. Monterey, California: Brooks/Cole Publishing Company, 1978.
Ponte, Lowell. "The Sense That Shapes Our Future." *Readers Digest*, (January, 1992): 21-26.
Weider, Betty. "Therapeutic Touch." *Shape* (May, 1992): 32.

David Petechuk

Towers of Hanoi

The towers of Hanoi is an ancient mathematical puzzle likely to have originated in India. It consists of three poles, in which one is surrounded by a certain number of discs with a decreasing diameter. The object of the puzzle is to move all of the discs from one pole onto another pole. The movement of any disc is restricted by two rules. First, discs can only be moved one at a time. Second, a larger disc can not be placed on top of a smaller disc.

Toxicology

Toxicology is the science of the study of poisons (or toxins). Major topics in toxicology include the detection and chemical analysis of poisons, the study of the metabolic effects of these substances on organisms, and the investigation of methods of treatment of poisoning.

All chemicals are potentially toxic, as long as the dose is large enough. This fact was recognized by the Swiss physician and alchemist Philippus Aureolus, also known as Paracelsus (1493-1541), who is commonly said to be the father of the modern science of toxicology, and who wrote that "Dosage alone determines poisoning." In other words, if poisoning is to be caused, an exposure to a potentially toxic chemical must result in a dose that exceeds a physiologically determined threshold of tolerance. Smaller exposures do not cause poisoning.

Physiology is the study of the functioning of organisms, and the disruption of biochemical pathways by poisons is a key aspect of toxicology. Poisons affect normal physiology in many ways, but some of the more common mechanisms involve the disabling of enzyme systems, the induction of cancers, the interference with the regulation of blood chemistry, and the disruption of genetic processes.

Organisms vary greatly in their tolerance of exposure to chemicals, and even within populations of the same species there can be great variations in sensitivity. In extreme cases, some individuals may be extremely sensitive to particular chemicals or groups of similar chemicals, a phenomenon known as hypersensitivity.

Organisms are often exposed to a wide variety of potentially toxic chemicals through medicine, food, water, and the atmosphere. Humans are exposed to complex mixtures of chemicals, many of which are synthetic and have been either deliberately or accidentally released into the environment.

In some cases, people actively expose themselves to chemicals that are known to be toxic, such as when smoking cigarettes, drinking alcohol, or taking recreational drugs. Voluntary exposure to chemicals also occurs when people take medicines to deal with illness, or when they choose to work in an occupation that involves routinely dealing with dangerous chemicals. However, most exposures to potentially toxic chemicals are inadvertent, and involve living in an environment that is contaminated with small concentrations of pollutants, for example, those associated with pesticide residues in food, lead from gasoline combustion, or sulfur dioxide and ozone in the urban atmosphere.

Traditionally, the discipline of toxicology has only dealt with the direct effects of poisonous chemicals on organisms, and particularly on humans. Recently, however, ecologists have broadened the scope of toxicological investigations to include the indirect effects of chemicals in the environment, a field known as ecotoxicology. Ecotoxicology could be defined as the study of the ecological effects of toxic chemicals, including the direct effects, but also the indirect consequences caused by changes in the structure of habitats, or in the abundance of food. A herbicide used in forestry may not cause direct, toxic effects to animals at the doses given during the pesticide application, but the pesticide may change the vegetation, so changing the ecological conditions upon which animals depend.

See also Contamination; Poisons and toxins.

Bill Freedman

Toxic shock syndrome

Toxic shock syndrome (TSS) is a serious, life-threatening disease caused by bacteria called *Staphylococcus aureus* and less typically, *Streptococcus pyrogenes*. Common causes of skin and mucous membrane infections, some strains of *Staph. aureus* and *Strep. pyrogenes* secrete toxins that initiate a cascade of immune reactions. These immune reactions lead to overproduction of immune proteins, and the abnormally high production of these proteins leads to TSS. As its name implies, the most prominent symptom of TSS is shock. During shock, the blood pressure drops to dangerously low levels. If TSS is not quickly diagnosed and treated with antibiotics, it can be fatal.

Toxic shock syndrome toxins

A toxin is a chemical that acts as a poison within the body. TSS is caused by toxins released from certain strains of *Staph. aureus* and *Strep. pyrogenes.* Not all strains of these bacteria release these toxins. About 30% of *Staph aureus* strains and less than 10% of *Strep pyrogenes* strains are TSS-toxin-producing.

Toxins that cause TSS are called "superantigens" because of their effects on the immune system. An antigen is the protein on a bacterial cell or viral coat that certain immune cells, called helper T cells, identify as "foreign." Helper T cells recognize antigens by binding to them. When this recognition occurs, the immune system swings into action against the invader and makes specific proteins, called antibodies, that tag the invader for destruction by other immune cells. The TSS toxins are superantigens because the immune reaction they incite is nonspecific and aggressive. Helper T cells binds to the toxins, but instead of activating one small part of the immune system—the antibody production mechanism—the helper T cells-toxin binding "turns on" *all* of the immune system.

This nonspecific activation of the immune system has devastating effects on the body. As a result of TSS-toxins binding to helper T cells, several immune proteins are overproduced. Monokines and lymphokines, proteins that promote the further proliferation of helper T cells, are produced in large quantities. Histamine, a protein that functions in allergic reactions and the inflammatory response, is released from immune cells. These proteins, in turn, exert several physiological effects. Histamine causes blood vessels to dilate, increasing blood circulation. Monokines and lymphokines contribute to the body's fever response, in which the internal temperature of the body increases in response to an immune signal. The combination of all these effects leads to TSS.

Symptoms of toxic shock syndrome

A "syndrome" is a group of different symptoms and conditions that are traced to one specific cause. Acquired Immune Deficiency Syndrome (AIDS), for example, is a cluster of different diseases that stem from infection of helper T cells with Human Immunodeficiency Virus (HIV). Similarly, TSS is a spectrum of symptoms caused by infection with toxin-producing strains of *S. aureus* and *S. pyrogenes*.

The early stage of TSS is characterized by flu-like symptoms such as sudden fever, fatigue, diarrhea, and dizziness. In a matter of a few hours or days, the blood pressure drops dangerously and a sunburn-like rash forms on the body. The drastic drop in blood pressure is potentially fatal. Circulatory problems develop as a result of low blood pressure, and some extremities—such as the fingers and toes—are deprived of blood as the body tries to shunt blood to vital organs. If the syndrome is severe enough, fingers and toes may become gangrenous due to lack of circulation. TSS can be treated with antibiotics, but these drugs kill only the bacteria that release the toxins: they do not neutralize the toxin that is already in the bloodstream. For treatment to be effective, antibiotics must be given early in the illness, before a large amount of toxin has built up in the bloodstream.

Risk factors for Toxic Shock Syndrome

In 1980, several women in the United States were diagnosed with TSS; a few of these women died. When researchers investigated these cases, they found that all the women had been menstruating and using high-absorbency tampons. Since that time, toxic shock has been associated with the use of tampons in menstruating women, who comprise about 50% of the cases of TSS per year. Researchers speculate that tampons provide a suitable environment for bacteria such as *S. aureus* to grow.

To reduce the risk of TSS, experts recommend that women who use tampons change them frequently

---

KEY TERMS

Antigen—The set of proteins on a bacterium or viral coat that identifies an organism as foreign.

Helper T cell—An immune cell that binds to antigens, initiating the immune response.

Syndrome—a set of diseases or symptoms that are traced to one specific cause; examples include Acquired Immune Deficiency Syndrome (AIDS) and toxic shock syndrome (TSS).

Toxin—A chemical produced by an organism as a result of metabolism that acts as a poison within the host.

(about every 2-4 hours) and use the lowest-absorbency tampon that's practical. To avoid all tampon-associated risk of TSS, avoid using tampons altogether. Since instituting these guidelines, the incidence of toxic shock has fallen significantly over the past ten years. Currently, the incidence of toxic shock syndrome in menstruating women is between 1 and 17 cases per 100,000. However, some cases of TSS in women have been associated with the use of contraceptive sponges and diaphragms. Like tampons, these devices should be worn for the shortest time recommended on the package directions, and for no longer than 8 hours.

Cases of TSS are also found in people with pre-existing skin infections, such as boils and wound infections. Prompt treatment of these conditions can usually prevent TSS.

See also Immune system.

Further Reading:
Berkley, Seth F., *et. al.* "The Relationship of Tampon Characteristics to Menstrual Toxic Shock Syndrome." *Journal of the American Medical Association* 258: 917-20, August 21, 1987.
Bryner, Charles L. Jr. "Recurrent Toxic Shock Syndrome." *American Family Physician* 39: 157-64, March 1989.
Kleinman, Leanne. "Toxic Shock Revisited." *Health* 20: 8, April 1988.
Toxic Shock Syndrome: Assessment of Current Information and Future Research Needs: Report of a Study. Institute of Medicine (United States), Division of Health Sciences Policy. Washington, D.C.: National Academy Press, 1982.
Toxic Shock Syndrome and Tampons. Rockville, MD: United States Department of Health and Human Services, Food and Drug Administration, 1990.

Kathleen Scogna

Toxic wastes see **Hazardous wastes**

Toxins see **Poisons and toxins**

Trace elements

Trace elements are chemicals that are required by organisms in very small quantities for proper physiological and biochemical functioning. Trace elements commonly occur in organisms in concentrations smaller than about 0.001% of the dry weight (less than 10 parts per million, or ppm). Listed in alphabetical order, the most commonly required trace elements for healthy animal or plant nutrition are: boron (B), chlorine (Cl), chromium (Cr), cobalt (Co), copper (Cu), fluorine (F), iodine (I), iron (Fe), manganese (Mn), molybdenum (Mo), selenium (Se), silicon (Si), tin (Sn), vanadium (V), and zinc (Zn). Some organisms also appear to require aluminum (Al) and nickel (Ni).

All of the 92 naturally occurring elements occur ubiquitously in the environment, in at least trace concentrations. In other words, there is a universal contamination of soil, water, air, and biota with all of the natural elements. As long as the methodology of analytical chemistry has detection limits that are small enough, this contamination will always be demonstrable. However, the mere presence of an element in organisms does not mean that it is indispensable for healthy biological functioning. To be considered an essential element, three criteria must be satisfied: (1) the element must be demonstrated as essential to normal development and physiology in several species, (2) the element must not be replaceable in this role by another element, and (3) the beneficial function of the element must be through a direct physiological role, and not related to correction of a deficiency of some other element or indirect correction of a toxic condition.

Research into the physiological roles of trace elements is very difficult, because it involves growing plants or animals under conditions in which the chemical concentrations of food and water are regulated within extremely strict standards, particularly for the trace element in question. In such research, even the slightest contamination of food with the trace element being examined could invalidate the studies. Because of the difficulties of this sort of research, the specific physiological functions of some trace elements are not known. However, it has been demonstrated that most trace elements are required for the synthesis of particular enzymes, or as co-factors that allow the proper functioning of specific enzyme systems.

A principle of toxicology is that all chemicals are potentially toxic. All that is required to cause toxicity is that organisms are exposed to a sufficiently large dose. The physiological effect of any particular dose of a chemical is related to the specific susceptibility of an organism or species, as well as to environmental conditions that influence toxicity. This principle suggests that, although trace elements are essential micronutrients, which benefit organisms that are exposed within certain therapeutic ranges, at larger doses they may cause biological damages. There are many cases of biological and ecological damages being caused by both naturally occurring and human caused pollutions with trace elements. Such occurrences may involve the natural, surface occurrences or metal-rich minerals such as ore bodies, or emissions associated with certain industries, such as metal smelting or refining.

See also Element, chemical; Nutrients; Toxicology.

Trachea see **Respiratory system**

Tragopans

Tragopans are members of the attractive bird family Phasianidae, originating in the Orient and India, without any native to the Americas.

There are various species of Tragopans in Afghanistan, eastward as far as Tibet, and in the Himalayas, in the same area as *Ithaginus cruentus*, a related short-tailed species. Tragopans, however, are more colorful.

Satyr Tragopan, *Tragopan satyra*, of the Himalayas, is a deep cherry red, varied with white and brown. The male bird has large areas of bare blue skin on its cheeks and two finger-like wattles of the same color behind the eyes. During courting these areas become very noticeable as they swell up with blood.

Sophie Jakowska

Train-bearer see **Trogons**

Trains and railroads

Trains were developed during the Industrial Revolution and were arguably that period's most important product. In many ways railroads made the Industrial Revolution possible. Factories could not run without a constant supply of raw materials, or without a method of moving goods to market. More than anything, the progress of the railroads depended on the development of motive power, which was, in turn, being driven by technology. If the story of the Industrial Revolution is the story of the railroads, then, the story of the railroads is the story of technology.

Like so much else in western culture, railroads had their roots in ancient Greece. Farmers and merchants transporting goods realized that their wagons could travel more quickly on a smooth, hard surface with its reduced friction than on soft dirt roads. Where possible, they cut ruts into the rock to guide the wagon wheels. These rutways were limited to areas where the rock was near the surface, but the efficiency of the approach was demonstrated.

The rutway technology was submerged in the full-width Roman roads and lost in the eventual fall of the empire. In the late middle ages, however, a variation of the idea surfaced. In sixteenth and seventeenth century Germany and England, primitive railway systems were developed in which wood-wheeled carts ran on wooden rails. These early lines were developed primarily for heavy industry such as coal mining, to make large volume transport viable. The ascents were made using horse power and the descents were made with the benefit of gravity, brakes, and a few prayers. The reduced friction of the wagonways allowed horses to haul several times the load they could manage on a normal road, and the rails guided the wagons along.

These wooden rail systems had a number of disadvantages. When wet they were extremely slippery, causing the carts to slide out of control on grades. They were not particularly strong or durable. In particular, carts with iron wheels quickly wore out the soft wooden tracks. In 1767, Richard Reynolds of Coalbrookdale, England, fabricated the first iron rails. The metal rails reduced the rolling friction of the wheels while lasting longer than the wooden alternatives. The way was clear for motive power.

The steam locomotive

In its simplest form, a steam locomotive consists of a firebox, a boiler, a cylinder or cylinders, and wheels, all of which are mounted on a rigid frame. The flames in the firebox heat water in the boiler to create steam. The steam is directed into a cylinder where its force is used to push a plunger attached by a connector rod or gears to the driving wheel of the engine. These connecting elements force the wheels to turn, which moves the

A steam locomotive.

engine along the track.

Wheels are classified as drive wheels, which provide motive power, and carrying wheels, which distribute the weight of the engine and add stability. Carrying wheels are further divided into leading wheels, i.e. those ahead of the drivers, and trailing wheels, or those behind the drivers. A common classification scheme for steam locomotives gives the number of leading wheels, the number of driving wheels, and the number of trailing wheels. The "choo-choo" style engine of the American West, for instance, would be classified as a 4-4-0: four leading wheels, four drivers, and no trailing wheels.

The first locomotives

The first self-propelled steam vehicle was built by Frenchman Nicolas Cugnot in 1769, followed by William Murdoch's model experimental locomotive in 1784. In 1802, Richard Trevithick built the first full-size locomotive to run on rails, thus winning a wager for his employer. A horizontal cylinder sat in the boiler and drove a piston, which drove a connecting rod that connected to a crank/flywheel. A set of gears transferred energy from the crankshaft to the drive wheels that moved the engine. To meet the terms of the bet, the locomotive successfully pulled a series of cars loaded with ten tons of iron and 70 people.

Trevithick used an artificial draft through the firebox to fan the flames of the coals, an important innovation. This increased the heat of the fire, generating larger amounts of high pressure steam. He dispensed with any additional traction mechanism to keep the engine from slipping, convinced that the friction between the iron rails and the wheels was enough to drive the vehicle forward. His invention worked admirably. At several tons in weight, however, it was far too heavy for the brittle iron plateway and left a string of broken rails in its wake.

Traction, or wheel to rail adhesion, is fundamental to the operation of a locomotive. In order to move a string of cars, the locomotive drive wheels must grip the track. If traction is insufficient, the wheels simply spin without pulling the train forward, just as car wheels can spin uselessly in mud or on ice. This was an especial concern for early locomotive designers who, unlike Trevithick, were not convinced that wheel-to-rail adhesion was sufficient to move the train down the track. Because frictional force between wheels and rail is proportional to the downward force or weight on the driving wheels, lighter engines were more likely to encounter adhesion problems. Heavier engines had better adhesion but their weight tended to break or split the brittle cast iron tracks, and locomotive builders were under continual pressure to reduce engine weight.

A variety of solutions that balanced the issues were proposed and built. In 1812, John Blenkinsop built a substantially lighter engine than Trevithick's, compensating for any loss of adhesion by using a rack and pinion drive. The drive wheels were cogged and rails were toothed on the outside face. The teeth on the drive wheels meshed with the teeth on the rails, driving the locomotive forward with no chance for slippage. Costly and complicated, the rack and pinion drive soon proved to be unnecessary for conventional railroads and never became popular. Other high traction methods such as chain drive or external pushing legs were simply impractical, and most of the locomotives that followed reverted to adhesion drive.

A second Blenkinsop innovation became a standard feature of almost all subsequent steam locomotives. Blenkinsop designed a two cylinder engine, with a cylinder to power the drive wheel on each side. This eliminated the use of an overhead flywheel to transfer mechanical energy from the cylinder to the drive wheels. Unlike Trevithick's design, however, the cylinders on Blenkinsop's engine were vertical. At high speeds, the rapid bounce of the pistons added a great deal of chop to the engine movement, exacerbated by the fact that the engine had no springs to absorb the motion. Given the weight of the engines, the chop placed a significant amount of stress on the rails, resulting in more splits and fractures.

The next groundbreaking design was an adhesion drive, two cylinder locomotive called the *Puffing Billy*. It was the first steam locomotive to feature cylinders outside of the boiler where they were easily accessible. Designed by William Hedley, the *Puffing Billy* distrib-

uted its weight over eight drive wheels, putting less concentrated load on the track and causing less wear.

One of the major locomotive companies during the nineteenth centuries was run by the father-son team of George and Robert Stephenson. The Stephensons were responsible for some of the most important technical innovations in locomotive operation. George Stephenson replaced the cylinder-to-wheel gear interface by coupling and connecting rods, streamlining the design and bringing it closer to the style of locomotive that we know. He also introduced the locomotive steam spring, which cushioned the action of the engine. The spring consisted of a vertical cylinder with a piston that carried the engine weight. Steam forced the piston to the upper end of the cylinder, applying upward force to counter the downward force of the weight of the engine. As a result of the shock-absorbing effect of the spring, the heavy engine rode more easily on its wheels and caused fewer cracks in the iron rails.

Locomotive wheels also cracked frequently, requiring costly replacements and engine down-time. Robert Stephenson and Timothy Hackworth replaced the solid cast-iron wheels of early engines with a combination design that featured durable, replaceable wrought-iron tires mounted on cast-iron hubs. In his 1827 locomotive the *Rocket*, Robert Stephenson also introduced the multitube boiler. Frenchman Marc Seguin developed a similar design at around the same time. In the multitube boiler, hot gases from the firebox move through tubes that run the length of the boiler. Heat is exchanged over a much greater surface area, making the design far more efficient than the single chamber type. Around this same time, locomotive designers abandoned the vertical cylinder for the smoother horizontally mounted type, though the cylinders on the *Rocket* compromised with a slanted orientation.

The American standard

Steam locomotives were introduced in the United States in 1829. They were initially supplied by British builders, but the development of American locomotives moved in a different direction from British and European locomotives almost immediately. Britain was a prosperous, settled country and British tracks were sturdy and well-built, with flat roadbeds and low grades. The Americans, on the other hand, were still pushing the frontier west across a vast landscape. Railroad companies were were minimally financed, while striving to web the country with rails. Consequently, American tracks were built hastily, with minimal roadbed preparation. Often they consisted of just flat-topped rails spiked onto roughcut ties. Curves were tighter, grades were steeper, and because the roadbeds were poorly graded if at all, the tracks were uneven. The high performance British locomotives with their fixed, four-wheel suspension did not fare well on U.S. tracks, derailing and breaking axels on the twisting, uneven rails.

The *Experiment*, a 4-2-0 engine built by John B. Jervis in 1831, was the first locomotive designed specifically for use on the American railroads. To modify the British fixed-wheel suspension, Jervis added a four-wheeled truck mounted on a center pivot to the front of the *Experiment*. Like the front wheels of a car, this truck could shift and turn with the track, compensating for sharp curves and unevenness. The two drive wheels were at the back of the engine, and the *Experiment* also boasted the novelty of an enclosed cab.

The design was a success and notion of a leading four-wheel truck was widely adopted in the United States. In 1836, Henry R. Campbell patented the 4-4-0 locomotive. Robust and economical, locomotives of this design could soon be ordered from a number of manufacturers. Add a cowcatcher to sweep away livestock from tracks running through open prairie, and the spark supressing smokestack that kept glowing cinders from flying out to start fires, and you have the "American Standard," a rugged, powerful locomotive that was ubiquitous in the nineteenth century United States.

Additional accoutrements were added to these engines. Matthias Baldwin was the first to equip a locomotive with warning bells, and George Whistler added the first steam whistle. Night travel was at first accomplished by maintaining a fire on a small car hooked to the front of the engine, but was soon superceded by a headlamp.

Meanwhile, the focus in Britain was on speed. Whereas the average speed of the American Standard was around 25 mph, British engines were routinely clocking speeds of 60 mph as early as 1860. The tracks were flat and smooth with few curves and low grades, and the swift engines were designed with compact, rigid frames and enormous driving wheels. In 1832, Robert Stephenson built the *Patentee*, a 2-2-0 engine whose design was to dominate in Britain and Europe for many years to come.

Further improvements in steam locomotive technology led to increases in speed and power. To maximize efficiency, double cylinders were constructed in which the steam from the first cylinder was let into a second cylinder to completely exhaust its pushing capabilities. More complete combustion was achieved by installing a firebrick arch in the firebox that routed air around prior to introducing it to the boiler. To improve power, multiwheel behemoths were built. Locomotives

with six and eight wheels were commissioned, as well as the less common ten to twelve wheelers.

Superheated steam was another method of increasing efficiency. In most early locomotives, steam included a significant portion of what was merely hot water. It was unable to do useful work and took up space in the cylinder where steam could normally expand to do useful work. To address this issue, engineers in Germany and Belgium developed the method of superheated steam. Steam headed toward the cylinders was heated a second time to dry it out, minimizing liquid water content. In tandem with improved cylinder valve gearing, the use of superheated steam increased engine efficiency so much that compound cylinders were eventually phased out as unnecessary.

Steam locomotives reached their peak in the middle of the twentieth century. 4-8-4s and 4-6-4s capable of speeds as high as 95 mph were built in the mid-40s, when rail travel dominated overland passenger travel. Even as these streamliners were capturing the imagination of the public, however, diesel and electric locomotives were beginning to take over rail transportation. By the mid-50s, the numbers of steam locomotives were dwindling rapidly, and today they exist only as sentimental reminders of a bygone era.

Diesel and electric locomotives

Diesel engines are internal combustion engines in which fuel oil is injected directly into the cylinder head and ignited by pressure. They power the wheels by direct gearing rather than the connecting rods of the steam locomotive, providing continual power. Railway diesels have been designed with electric, hydraulic, mechanical, and pneumatic transmissions; today the diesel-electric engine is most common.

When they were introduced early in the twentieth century, diesels offered unprecedented efficiency and performance over steam locomotives. Diesel engines could be operated round the clock, without timeouts to take on water for the boiler or clean out ashes from the firebox. They could carry enough fuel for a day or two of continuous operation, and running them was almost absurdly simple. Crewmen for the first diesel locomotive in the US, for example, were trained to operate it in just 15 minutes. Initial capital outlay was high, but operating costs were only a fraction of the cost of steam locomotives.

Electric trains are the other major type of motive rail power. Particularly in Europe, passenger traffic is dominated by electric power.

Electric trains run on both direct and alternating current, with voltage in the 50 to 100 kV range. The choice of current type is driven as much by economics as by performance, involving as it does a tradeoff of cost and efficiency. Alternating current (ac) offers an economical current supply at the expense of motor complexity. Motors for the more expensive direct current (dc) supplies are very simple. Current is fed to the motors from overhead wires, as with trolleys, or from an electrified "third rail" along the ground, commonly seen in subways.

Track

From the beginning of railroad development, British and European line surveyors were extremely careful to lay flat, even track, minimizing curves and grades. A track set down by George Stephenson, for instance, was laid on stone blocks with very compact foundations. By contrast, most early American tracks were laid hastily on wooden ties. The flimsy rails were easily deformed by the repeated weight of trains, sagging where not supported by the ties. Eventually the ends of the rails would rise up due to this sagging action. When they rose high enough, these 'snake heads' would be pushed up in front of the wheels and either derail the train or punch through the floorboards, impaling those unlucky enough to be sitting above them. To avoid this, American railroads began placing the ties very close to one another, a practice still followed today.

The early wood rails were followed by brittle cast-iron rails. It was only later that more ductile wrought iron was used. Steel rail came into play in the 1870s, as a byproduct of the Bessemer process, a method for economical mass production of steel. The steel rail was more durable, capable of supporting harder wheels and heavier loads. In recent years, rails have become heavier, weighing as much as 100 lbs (45 kg) per yard. Much of it is continuously welded rail. To simplify maintenance over miles of rail, special machines have been built that detect flaws in track, raise and align track, or clean and resettle track ballast.

Track gauge, or the width between the rails, varied tremendously in the early years of railroading. Gauges ranged from 3 ft (0.9 m) called "narrow gauge" lines to 6 ft (1.8 m) called "wide gauge" lines. Wide gauges were first believed to be more stable than narrow gauges, able to support broader cars without tipping over on curves. In mountainous areas or the highly populated urban regions of Britain, however, there was not sufficient room for wide gauge tracks, and rails were laid closer together. When it came time for the tracks of different railroads to merge into one enormous net, gauge discrepancies were a major problem.

The "standard" gauge was a 4 ft 8.5 in (1.7 m) spacing. Common in Britain, it was quickly passed along to other countries. In the United States, standard gauge became the official gauge of the American Railway Association toward the end of the nineteenth century. This led to changes in the rail spacing of narrow and wide gauge railroads, necessitating massively coordinated efforts in which the gauge of entire railway lines, as much as 500 or 600 miles, would be changed in a single day.

Brakes and couplers

Early cars were coupled together using a link and pin system. Given that the pins had to be put into place and removed manually while the cars were moved by a distant engine, coupling cars was a dangerous job that all too often led to the loss of fingers and hands. Alternate coupler designs were proposed, and in 1887 a coupler designed by Eli H. Janney was approved by the Master Car Builders' Association. Resembling the curled fingers of two hands, Janney's coupler allowed cars to hook together without the use of pins.

Brakes, too, were a problem with early trains. They had to be applied on each car by hand, a time-consuming process. Brakemen on freight trains had the added difficulty of applying the brakes from a precarious perch on the top of the car while hoping that the train didn't go under any low bridges. In 1869, George Westinghouse patented an air brake that used compressed air to force the brakeshoes against the wheels. Each car had a reservoir of high pressure air [70-100 lbs (32-45 kg)/sq in]. A control pipe filled with compressed air ran the length of the train. If the pressure in the control pipe dropped, the compressed air in the reservoir applied the brakes. This could occur when the brakes were applied or when a car became detached from the train—an added safety measure.

When diesel and electric locomotives came into use, a different approach to braking was possible. Both types of motors can be reversed such that the motor is working against the motion of the train. This dynamic braking system allows minimal use of air brakes, with longer wear on the brake shoes. Some high speed trains have computerized braking systems. If the engineer exceeds permitted speed on a section of line, the brakes are automatically applied.

Locomotive brakes took much longer to catch on than railcar brakes. Robert Stephenson's 1833 *Patentee* design included specifications for a steam brake, but the earliest recorded use of a brake on the driving wheels of an American locomotive was in 1848. Development and implementation was sporadic throughout the 1860s and 1870s, but by 1889 about half of all American locomotives were equipped with driving wheel brakes. By the end of the century, locomotives were routinely equipped with brakes, a necessity given the increased power and speeds of the twentieth century engines.

Switches and signals

In the early days of railroading, switches were set by hand and signal systems consisted of flags during the day and lamps at night. In 1856, an interlocking signal was designed to prevent signalmen from setting signals and switches in conflict with one another. In 1865, Ashbel Welch of the Camden and Amboy RR developed a new type of signal known as the manual block-signal. Trains were spaced apart by a prescribed distance or "block," and new trains couldn't enter this block until the first train left. The electric telegraph was used to pass the word that track was clear and the train ahead had reached the station.

Switch and train location information was conveyed to engineers by stationary signals such as flags, patterned disks that rotated between full view and edge view, or fixtures with semaphore arms. In 1871, electrical control of block-signals was introduced. In 1890, a compressed air switch with electronic control was installed on the Pennsylvania—Baltimore & Ohio railroad crossing. Fully automated switches soon followed in which the train wheels and axels made a complete conducting circuit, operating relays that ran the signals. The colored electronic lights used today are modern versions of these early signals.

Modern switching yards are largely automated. Car speeds are computer controlled and switching is automatic. Meanwhile, sensors and detectors check for loose wheels, damaged flanges, or other faulty equipment.

Ultrafast trains, the modern travel alternative

In 1964, the Japanese inaugurated the Shinkansen train, initially capable of going an unprecedented 100 mph (161 km/h). They have since built a net of high speed railroads across Japan. These trains run on special tracks and have had no serious accidents since the opening of the system. Europe has a number of high speed trains, from the Swedish X2000, capable of running at 136 mph (219 km/h) average speed, to the German Intercity Express. The French, however, are the kings of

KEY TERMS

Adhesion—frictional contact that makes the wheels of an engine grip the rails

Boiler—a single tube or multitube vessel in which water is heated to steam

Cylinder—a cylindrical tank into which steam is introduced to push a piston head back and forth, creating mechanical motion to drive the locomotive wheels

Maglev—a non-contact (frictionless) method of train suspension in which strong magnetic forces are used to levitate the train above the track

Rolling stock—railroad cars. Rolling stock can contain such specialized cars as tank cars, refrigerator cars, and piggyback cars.

high speed rail transport. The TGV trains run regularly over the countryside at nearly 200 mph (322 km/h). A special TGV train running over new track has reached an astounding 319 mph (514 km/h).

At such speeds, the technology of railroads must be rethought. Locomotive and passenger car suspension must be redesigned, and most trains must run on specially graded and built track. Engineers require in-cab signalling, as with average speeds ranging between 150 and 200 mph (241 and 322 km/h), there is not enough time to read the external signals. Brakes must be reconsidered. A train running at 155 mph capable of braking at 1.6 ft/s2 requires about 3 mi (4.8 km) to stop fully after the brakes are first applied.

A high speed option that is the topic of hot research is a non-contact, magnetically levitated (maglev) train. Strong magnetic forces would hold the train above the track. Such a train would have virtually no rolling resistance or friction because there would be no wheels and nothing rolling. The only impedance would be that of air, making it extremely efficient. Maglev trains are still in the research phase, and more development is required before this possibility can be realized.

Railroads were a significant factor in the development of industry and are still a significant mode of transportation for goods and passengers. In terms of efficiency, they cannot be rivaled. While a diesel truck can haul a single or tandem tractor-trailer, a diesel locomotive can haul a string of loaded boxcars. As we become more concerned about the environment and internal combustion engines are phased out, railroads are poised to assume an even larger role in transportation, and a new Age of the Iron Horse may well be upon us.

See also Industrial Revolution; MAGLEV; Mass transportation.

Further Reading:

J.B. Snell, *Early Railways*, London, England: Octopus Books, 1964.

J.F. Stover, *The Life and Decline of the American Railroad*, New York, NY: Oxford University Press, 1970.

G. D. Hiscox, *Mechanical Movements, Powers, and Devices*, Norman W. Henley Publishing Co., New York, NY, 1927.

G.H. Drury, *The Historical Guide to North American Railroads*, Waukesha, WI: Kalmbach Books, 1988.

O.S. Nock, *Locomotion*, Charles Scribner's Sons, New York, NY, 1975.

P. Lorie and C. Garratt, *Iron Horse: Steam Trains of the World*, Doubleday & Company Inc., Garden City, NY, 1987.

Kristin Lewotsky

Tranquilizers

The medical use of drugs to reduce or relieve anxiety has given rise to a group of medications called antianxiety agents. These agents include anxiolytics, tranquilizers, and sedatives.

Tranquilizers were formerly grouped as either "minor" tranquilizers or "major" tranquilizers. The word major stands for "major psychiatric illness," not heavily sedating or tranquilizing. Today, major tranquilizers are more often referred to as neuroleptics or antipsychotic agents and they are used in the treatment of schizophrenia, depression, and bipolar illness. Examples of antipsychotic agents are chlorpromazine (Thorazine), synthesized in France in 1950 and the phenothiazines.

Presently, the common use of the term tranquilizer refers to the "minor" tranquilizers mainly of the benzodiazepine family. This newer group of antianxiety agents has tended to replace the use of barbiturates and meprobamate and certain antihistamines which were used as sedatives and antianxiety agents. It is these drugs that are prescribed as tranquilizers in the non-psychiatric setting of general medicine which treats anxiety brought on by stress rather than some disorder in the central nervous system.

Anxiety

While anxiety is usually an accompanying state of mind of most psychiatric disorders, it is also a special disorder of its own. Anxiety disorder or reaction is characterized by a chronic state of anxiety that does not have an immediate or visible basis. That is, the individual feels alarmed or uneasy but cannot point to any outside or realistic basis for the fear. There is a general state of unease that may become expressed by acute attacks of anxiety or panic, called panic disorder.

The emotional stress of anxiety may be triggered by impulses and mental images that in turn lead to a number of complex physiological responses. The autonomic nervous system may react to signals from the emotional side of the mind which call forth defense reactions of either fight or flight. An excess of adrenalin may be released which cannot be adequately discharged, thus leading to the symptoms of anxiety.

The psychology of anxiety often entails the repression of certain drives and needs. Sexual feelings, aggression at work, in school, in the family, and dependency on a spouse or other social relationship that is being threatened, or that the anxious person feels apprehensive toward are all examples of the circumstances that can unleash a chronic state of anxiety. The loss of a job or the sudden onslaught of an illness may, likewise, be responsible for anxiety states as the individual attempts to cope with these new conditions.

Acute anxiety

Acute anxiety panic attacks have been described as one of the most painful of life experiences. The condition can last for a few minutes to one or two hours. The individual is cast into a state of terror by some nameless imminent catastrophe. All rational thought processes cease during this time.

There are a number of cardiovascular responses to this state such as palpitations, tachycardia (elevated heart rate), arrhythmias of the heart, and sharp chest pain. Breathing becomes very difficult, almost impossible. The term given for this condition is hyperventilation. The extremities (hands and feet) feel cold, numb, and tingle with a feeling of pins and needles being present in the skin which may turn blue in places.

Other symptoms include fine trembling of the hands when they are stretched out, a feeling of "butterflies" in the stomach, sweating, a general sense of weakness, dizziness, nausea, and sometimes diarrhea.

People and the environment and surrounding objects seem remote and unreal. All these symptoms reinforce the anxious patient's belief that either loss of consciousness or death are nearby.

Chronic anxiety

Many of the symptoms of chronic anxiety are similar to acute anxiety, but they are less intense and more prolonged. They can last for days, weeks, or months. There is a considerable amount of tension and expectation of conflict. There is fear about the future and an inability to deal effectively with other people, especially at home, school, and work. The condition is also characterized by chronic fatigue, insomnia, and headaches along with difficulty in concentration. With chronic anxiety the individual is still able to function on some level, but the ability to deal with life situations is substantially compromised.

Treatment for anxiety

Treatment for anxiety can include psychotherapy for those who are responsive for unearthing unconscious conflicts. Supportive psychotherapy is given by physicians, social workers, and therapists to reassure the individual. Relaxation techniques, meditation, and hypnosis also help to alleviate the condition.

Tranquilizers play a role in the pharmacologic treatment of anxiety. Medications, however, are usually not sufficient to deal with the root causes of anxiety, and it is not certain to what extent they play a placebo role in alleviating feelings of anxiety. The attitude of the taker of the medication along with the belief in the medical authority figure administering the drug are further factors in determining the effectiveness of pharmacologic intervention.

Benzodiazepines

There are about 20 tranquilizers in the benzodiazepine family of tranquilizers. Some of the popular ones are diazepam (Valium), Fluorazepam (Dalmane), oxazepam (Serax), and chlordiazepoxide (Librium). In addition to being prescribed for anxiety, they are also used as muscle relaxants, sedatives, anesthetics, and as supportive medication for withdrawal from alcohol. These drugs were introduced in the 1960s, and they quickly replaced other drugs that were then being used as tranquilizers. Their popularity seems to be now in decline, partly due to the more cautious attitude physicians have in prescribing them.

The amount of adverse effects is low. There is only a slight depression in respiratory rate and the amount needed for an overdose is very high, at a ratio of 200 (excess) to 1. Used in suicide attempts the results lead more to confusion and drowsiness without damage of a permanent nature. Librium (chlordiazepoxide) has some record of causing coma when taken in high dosages. Some people may react to benzodiazepines by losing inhibitions and expressing hostile or aggressive behavior that is not characteristic of their personalities, especially if they have been experiencing a high rate of frustration.

Since benzodiazepines produce less euphoria than other types of tranquilizers there is less chance of a dependency reaction that leads to abuse. Minor tranquilizers are generally not sought after by the illegal drug abuse market, nor are any of the other neuroleptic medications used to treat such mental illnesses as schizophrenia, manic depression, or depression. Some withdrawal symptoms can develop with benzodiazepines if they are used for an extended period of time, such as a month or more. While there may be such symptoms as increased anxiety, sensitivity to bright lights, twitching of the muscles, nausea, and even convulsions, there is not a craving for the drug itself. Symptoms can be reduced by withdrawing from the drug gradually and Dilantin can be used for convulsions.

Action

Tranquilizers act as antianxiety agents by depressing the central nervous system without leading to sedation. Barbiturates are seldom used now for managing anxiety or dysphoria because of their addictive potential. The molecules of barbiturate drugs pass through the membranes of the cells in the brain. They are then able to block nerve signals that pass from cell to cell, thus inhibiting the stimulation and conduction of chemical neurotransmitters between the cells. In addition, barbiturates are able to reduce the effect of abnormal electrical activity in the brain which cause seizures, such as in the case of epilepsy. Phenobarbital is a barbiturate that performs this function exceptionally well, therefore it is still useful as an anticonvulsant drug.

Depressant drugs, like alcohol and barbiturates, just as stimulant drugs, like cocaine and amphetamines, all appear to have the ability to stimulate the brain's reward circuit. The behavioral effect of this action is to increase the need for more of the drug, usually to get the same effect (drug tolerance). If it is being taken for its effect as a euphoric, more of the drug is needed each time it is taken to produce a high or for sleep if it is being used as a sedative. Drugs that stimulate the brain reward centers also have the effect of excluding other types of reward sensations like those from food or sex.

Drugs that stimulate the brain reward centers seem to enhance the presence of a chemical found in the brain called gamma aminobutyric acid (GABA). GABA has the effect of quieting the neurons where the GABA receptors are found.

The newer benzodiazepine tranquilizers reduce neuron sensitivity only for cells that do have the GABA receptor sites, but the barbiturates are able to work the sedating effect elsewhere as well, wherever there are chloride channels. That difference in action may account for the higher degree of sedation afforded by the barbiturates over the benzodiazepines. Both types of drugs are able to affect the brain's reward center by increasing the amount of dopamine released into the limbic system, the part of the brain that regulates certain biological functions such as sleep and the emotions.

Choice of tranquilizers

Tranquilizers are the most commonly used prescription drugs in the United States. The three major groups of tranquilizers are the benzodiazepines with the brand names of Valium, Librium, and Alprazolam. The second major group are the dephenylmethanes prescribed under the brand names of Vistaril and Atarax. The third group are the older alcohol-like propanediols that came out in the 1950s, such as tybamate and meprobamate under the brand names of Equanil and Miltown.

The physician chooses among the various tranquilizers the one that will best serve the patient's need. Stress is a normal part of daily living for most people and it will produce in each individual a certain range of anxiety. Tranquilizers are prescribed on a non-psychiatric basis by the physician in general practice when the level of anxiety experienced by the individual interferes with the ability to cope with everyday stressful events or when anxiety symptoms have reached clinical proportions.

Panic attacks respond well with the treatment of alprazolam. Certain antidepressant drugs have also been found useful in treating panic disorder. Other symptoms, such as rapid heart rate, palpitations, involuntary motor reactions, insomnia or other sleep disorders, diarrhea, bandlike headaches, increased urination rate, and gastric discomfort can be temporarily relieved by the use of other tranquilizers.

It is, however, necessary for the physician to point out to the patient that the tranquilizers are covering up the symptoms rather than curing them. The hazard in such palliative treatment is that the underlying condi-

KEY TERMS

Arrhythmia—Irregular heart beats; one of the symptoms of anxiety disorder.

Autonomic nervous system—The part of the nervous system that controls involuntary processes, such as heart beat, digestion, and breathing.

Chronic anxiety—A prolonged period of an abnormal level of anxiety symptoms.

Euphoria—A feeling of intense well being; the opposite of dysphoria.

Gamma aminobutyric acid (GABA)—A chemical in the brain that quiets neuronal activity.

Hyperventilation—An autonomic reaction to anxiety which increases the breathing rate, thereby altering the ratio of the exchange of gases in the lung. That change makes the act of breathing difficult to perform.

"Minor" tranquilizers—As opposed to "major" tranquilizers, the ones used for ordinary, non-psychiatric conditions of anxiety attacks.

Panic disorder—An acute anxiety attack that can last for several minutes to several hours.

Psychotherapy—Consultations with a trained therapist under controlled conditions to relieve emotional tensions.

Tachycardia—An elevated heart rate due to exercise or some other physiological response to a particular condition such as an anxiety attack.

tion may get worse without the conflict resolution necessary for the nervous system to readjust itself to the demands of reality.

Tranquilizers are not suited for long term use and over a period of time higher dosages may be needed, especially for the mild euphoria that some of them produce. While they do not pose the degree of dependency of other psychoactive drugs, some have been limited for general use because of the potential of overdependence. Valium is an example of a benzodiazepine that now is prescribed more cautiously.

Buspirone (BuSpar) appears to avoid the problem of possible dependency as well as that of drowsiness. This drug appeared in the mid-1980s. It is reported to be a "true" tranquilizer in that it does not produce either the slight euphoria of other tranquilizers or the drowsiness which is also characteristic of the sedative effect of other tranquilizers.

See also Anxiety.

Further Reading:

Longenecker, Gesina L. *How Drugs Work.* Emeryville, CA: Ziff-Davis Press, 1994.

Morgan, Robert. *The Emotional Pharmacy.* Los Angeles, CA: The Body Press, 1988.

Nicholi, Armand M. Jr. *The New Harvard Guide to Psychiatry.* Cambridge, MA: Harvard University Press, 1988.

Oppenheim, Mike. *100 Drugs That Work.* Los Angeles: Lowell House, 1994.

Jordan P. Richman

Transcendental numbers

Transcendental numbers, named after the Latin expression meaning *to climb beyond,* are numbers which exist beyond the realm of algebraic numbers. Mathematicians have defined algebraic numbers as those which can function as a solution to polynomial equations consisting of x and powers of x. In 1744, the Swiss mathematician Leonhard Euler (1707-1783) established that a large variety of numbers (for example, whole numbers, fractions, imaginary numbers, irrational numbers, negative numbers, etc.) can function as a solution to a polynomial equation, thereby earning the attribute *algebraic.* However, Euler pointed to the existence of certain irrational numbers which cannot be defined as algebraic. Thus, $\sqrt{2}$, π, and e are all irrationals, but they are nevertheless divided into two fundamentally different classes. The first number is algebraic, which means that it can be a solution to a polynomial equation. For example, $\sqrt{2}$ is the solution of $x^2 - 2 = 0$. But π and e cannot solve a polynomial equation, and are therefore defined as transcendental. While π, which represents the ratio of the circumference of a circle to its diameter, had been known since antiquity, its transcendence took many centuries to prove: in 1882, Ferdinand Lindemann (1852-1939) finally solved the problem of "squaring the circle" by establishing that there was no solution. There are infinitely many transcendental numbers, as there are infinitely many algebraic numbers. However, in 1874, Georg Cantor (1845-1919) showed that the former are more numerous than the latter, suggesting that there is more than one kind of infinity.

See also e (number); Irrational number; Pi; Polynomials.

Transducer

A transducer is a device which converts one form of energy to another. Typically, one of these forms is electrical while the other is either mechanical, optical, or thermal. Transducers are usually classified as either input or output devices, depending on the direction in which they transfer energy or information. Input transducers convert some property or effect into an electrical signal, while output transducers start with electricity and generate a mechanical or other effect.

Transducers play such fundamental roles in modern technology that examples of them abound. In virtually every electronic device or instrument, transducers act as translators between electron flow and the physical world. Loudspeakers are perhaps the most well-known transducers, as they are used in nearly every audio system to convert electrical signals into acoustic ones. Like loudspeakers, audio microphones are transducers. Both devices have a small diaphragm which is free to move in either a magnetic or electric field. In speakers, electricity pushes this diaphragm to generate a sound. In microphones, the opposite happens, and sound pushes the diaphragm to generate an electric signal. Another common transducer in audio systems is the photodetector; in a compact disc player this input device combines with a photoemitter to optically sense encoded information on the disc and convert it to music.

A tremendous collection of transducers can be found in the human body. The senses convert complex sights, sounds, smells, and other experiences to electrical signals, which are then sent to the brain for interpretation.

See also Amplifier; Compact disk; Electronics.

Transexuality see **Sex change**

Transformer

A transformer is an electrical device which changes or transforms an alternating current (AC) signal from one level to another. The device typically consists of two sets of insulated wire, coiled around a common iron core. Electrical power is applied to one of these coils, called the primary coil, and is then magnetically transferred to the other coil, called the secondary. This magnetic coupling of electrical power occurs without any direct electrical contact, and allows transformers to

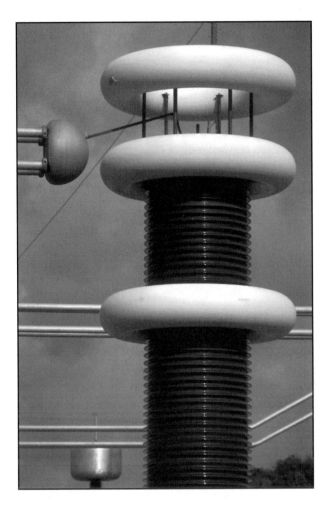

A high voltage transformer.

teams-up with the secondary coil to form a type of generator. (Recall that a generator produces electrical power by moving coils of wire through a stationary magnetic field, the converse of the transformer situation.) At any rate, electrical power in the primary coil is converted into a magnetic field which then generates electrical power in the secondary coil. The beauty of a transformer is that, although the power is neither increased nor decreased in this transfer (except for minor losses), the voltage level can be changed through the conversion. The ratio of the voltages between the two coils is equal to the ratio of number of loops in the two coils. Changing the number of windings allows a transformer to step-up or step-down voltages easily. This is extremely useful as the voltage level is converted many times between a power station, through transmission lines, into a home, and then into a household appliance.

Transistor

A transistor is a solid-state active device capable of amplifying and switching electrical signals. Transistors are made possible by utilizing the special electrical properties of crystals made from semiconductor elements such as silicon or germanium. The name of the transistor is derived by combining parts of TRANSfer and ResISTOR. Transistors are normally used in circuits that contain passive electrical devices, resistors, capacitors, and/or inductors.

A transistor can perform many useful electronic functions because its resistance can be adjusted dynamically by a low-power input signal. The resulting changes in resistance control the current delivered by a power supply, distributing energy to a variety of devices that can be used as loads for the transistors. Resistors are frequently used to convert a changing current into a changing voltage. The changes in voltage across the load resistor can represent many times as much power as available from the signal source at the input to the transistor. The increase in power made possible by the transistor is called amplification, one of the most basic processes in applied electronics.

When a transistor acts as an amplifier it does not create the additional energy appearing in its output signal, just as a faucet doesn't create water it dispenses. A transistor modulates the energy flowing from a battery or power supply in a way that is similar to a faucet adjusting the water flow rate as desired.

change AC voltage level and to completely isolate two electrical circuits from one another.

When a voltage is applied to a coil of wire, an electrical current flows (just as water flows through a pipe when pressure is applied.) The flowing electrical current, however, creates a magnetic field about the coil. This principle can be demonstrated by simply wrapping insulated wire around a nail, and attaching a battery to the ends of that wire. A sufficient number of loops and ample electrical power will enable this electromagnet to lift small metal objects, just as an ordinary magnet can. If, however, the battery is replaced by a varying power source such as AC, the magnetic field also varies. This changing magnetic field is essential for the operation of a transformer.

Because the two coils of a transformer are very close to each other, an electric current through the primary coil generates a magnetic field which is also around the secondary coil. When this magnetic field varies with time (as it does when AC is applied), it

The history of the transistor

The transistor was publicly announced in 1948. Before this date electronics depended almost exclusively upon electron tubes for signal amplification and electronic switching actions. Electron tubes are bulky, comparatively short lived, relatively inefficient, and their performance often degrades gradually with time. In contrast, transistors are small, electrically efficient, and much more resistant to mechanical shocks than are fragile tubes. Transistors and related solid-state devices have now all but completely replaced electron tubes except for specialized applications that involve high power or radio-frequency applications. Transistors themselves are rapidly being replaced by integrated circuits in most applications.

Silicon and germanium

The first transistors were made from an element called germanium, but now most ordinary transistors are made from silicon. Silicon is usually preferred over germanium because of silicon's superior thermal characteristics. Transistors are manufactured by altering the surfaces of very thin slices of a single very-pure crystal of one of these elements.

Silicon and germanium form similar crystal arrangements with similar physical properties. These crystals are not particularly good electrical insulators but neither are they good electrical conductors. Silicon and germanium conduct electricity on a scale midway between metallic conductors and non-metallic insulators. Transistor action is possible because of the unique electrical-conduction properties found in these semiconducting crystals.

Each of the atoms in a silicon or germanium crystal lattice takes up a position so that it has four atoms as close neighbors. Each atom is held in its row, column, and layer in the crystal's orderly structure because each atom shares its four outermost electrons with the outermost electrons of nearby atoms. This sharing holds the atoms together in a process called covalent bonding. Covalent bonding also prevents these outermost electrons from moving through the crystal as easily as do conduction electrons in ordinary metal where the bonding process is called metallic bonding.

The semiconductor atom's outermost electrons are not bound so tightly that they cannot break loose if given a small amount of extra energy but they cannot wander easily through the crystal. Heat, light, or ionizing radiation increase the semiconductor's electrical conductivity by liberating electrons that then support current. Usually these effects are unwanted. It is impor-tant to control the temperature of semiconductors. Ionizing radiation, also, may cause transistors to fail. The first active communication satellite placed in orbit by the United States, Telstar, failed repeatedly when its transistors were exposed to unexpected levels of ionizing radiation.

Types of transistors

The first general-purpose transistors were called bipolar-junction transistors or BJTs. BJTs may be pictured as sandwich-like layers of P-type and N-type semiconductors, created during manufacturing.

A bipolar-junction transistor is the result of careful modifications of a very-pure silicon crystal called intrinsic semiconductor. An intrinsic silicon crystal contains about 1 non-silicon impurity atom for every 100-million silicon atoms in the crystal. A process called doping places a few impurity atoms into the pure crystal. A non-silicon atom takes the place of one out of approximately every 10-million silicon atoms. The impurities locate in the crystal's structure as if they were themselves silicon atoms.

When the doping process deliberately adds impurity atoms with five electrons in their outermost orbit (the outermost orbit is called the valence orbit) the result is called N-type semiconductor. Arsenic, for example, has five electrons is its valence orbit. Arsenic is often used as a pentavalent dopant to produce N-type semiconductor. Pentavalent impurity atoms can share only four of their five valance electrons with their four closest silicon neighbors. The fifth valence electron from the arsenic atom is free to move through the crystal in response to an electric field within the crystal. The fifth electron can move about almost as does a conduction electron in an ordinary metal. N-type semiconductor conducts electricity easily, with much better conductivity than an intrinsic semiconductor crystal.

P-Type semiconductor

If an impurity with only three valence electrons, a trivalent element, is used as the dopant instead of a pentavalent impurity P-type semiconductor results. Trivalent atoms, such as boron, aluminum, gallium, or indium have just three valence electrons in their outer shell. These impurity atoms are short one electron needed to establish a covalent bond with each of its silicon neighbors. The trivalent impurity introduces a defect into the symmetry of the crystal lattice, a location where an electron would be found if a silicon atom had not been displaced by the trivalent impurity. The impurity atom hasn't changed the electrical balance of the crystal, but it has changed the symmetry of the crystal lattice. The defect behaves as would an excess positive electric charge. The defect, called a hole, can move from place to place even though insufficient energy is present that would enable electrons to escape from their covalent bond.

An electron from a neighboring silicon atom in the crystal can fill the hole created by the trivalent impurity without having been given enough energy to become a conduction electron. The hole will have moved from one location to another within the crystal and there will have been a net drift of an electron when a hole moves in this way. The hole can continue to move until it is far from the defect that created it.

Although only the negatively-charged electrons actually move, it is easier to visualize holes moving as movable positive charges, traveling along electric-field lines. Holes travel somewhat more slowly than electrons within an electrical field with same strength, but this difference is speed is usually not important in practice. As with N-type semiconductor, P-type semiconductor is a good electrical conductor but for a different reason.

PN junction diodes

A surprising electrical property results at boundary where P-type semiconductor material becomes N-type material in the same crystal. The result is a combination called a PN junction diode. a junction diode may be thought of as a one-way valve for electricity. A junction diode will carry current in one direction more easily than it carries current in the opposite direction. Understanding the transistor begins with knowledge of the PN-junction diode. A bipolar junction transistor is, in effect, an opposed pair of PN diodes within a single crystal.

In either P-type or N-type semiconductors there are two types of charge carriers that carry current, majority carriers and minority carriers. Electrons are the majority carriers in N-type material and holes are the majority carriers in P-type semiconductors. The minority carriers are the relatively-few unwanted oppositely charged carriers, electrons in P type and holes in N-type, that cannot be eliminated entirely. Heat, ionizing radiation, and unintended impurities in the original intrinsic crystal wafer cause minority carriers. Practical diodes do not behave in an ideal way because minority carriers allow a small reverse current, a trickle of charges leaking backward through a diode, when an ideal diode would present an open circuit. Leakage current occurs in transistors as well as diodes, caused by minority carriers, and these currents can have important consequences.

If voltage is applied across a PN junction diode with polarity that causes the P region of the diode to be more positive than the N region, the majority carriers in both P and N regions will pushed toward each other, meeting at the boundary. A diode polarized in this way is said to be forward biased. A forward-biased diode conducts quite well. If the voltage polarity is reversed causing the N-type material to be more positive than the P-type material, the two types of majority carriers will be pulled away from each other. This condition is called reverse bias, or back bias. The small current does leak through a back-biased diode is the result of minority carriers moving in the opposite direction compared to majority carriers.

There is a very thin volume at the boundary where N-type semiconductor materials interfaces with P-type material, called the depletion region. In the depletion region electrons tend to fill adjacent holes, depleting the crystal of carriers. When majority carriers from each region are pushed toward each other, hole-electron pairs continually annihilate each other. As each hole is filled by an electron, a new hole and a new electron will be injected into the crystal at the ohmic connections to the crystal. In this way current can continue to flow through the diode as long as the circuit is energized.

If the reverse-biasing voltage across a diode increases above a critical threshold the diode will suddenly break into heavy conduction when the electric field in the depletion region between the N and P materials is so strong that electrons are torn from their bonding roles. This condition is called Zener breakdown. Usually transistors are operated at voltages low enough so that this type of breakdown doesn't take place. Unless the breakdown current is limited by the external circuitry the transistor or diode may dissipate so much power that it is destroyed. Transistors are unforgiving when excess voltages or voltages with the wrong polarity are applied.

Bipolar junction transistors

If the same crystal is doped so that each end is N-type and the very thin slice in the center is P-type, the resulting "sandwich" forms a junction transistor. This arrangement is an NPN transistor. In an NPN transistor one of the N-type regions is the collector, the other N-type region is the emitter. The very-thin slice of P-type material in the center is called the base of the transistor. In a PNP transistor the collector and emitter regions are made from P-type semiconductor and the base has the characteristics of N-type material. Both NPN and PNP transistors are in common use but these two transistor types are not directly interchangeable since they require different power-supply polarities. Many circuits employ both NPN and PNP transistors, but the circuitry must supply the correct voltages. It is common to connect the two types of transistors together in an arrangement that is called complementary symmetry.

Transistor action

Transistors are able to amplify signals because their design permits the supply of charge carriers to be adjusted electrically. A transistor will have a high electrical resistance when it is starved for charge carriers but it will conduct quite well when a control signal injects extra carriers that can be used to support increased current.

Common base, common emitter, and common-collector configurations

There are three ways to connect a bipolar junction transistor into a working circuit, depending upon which of the three transistor elements is chosen as the common reference for the other two elements. These variations, called common base, common emitter, and common collector, produce different circuit actions each with unique characteristics. An NPN transistor configured as a common-emitter amplifier, where both the base and the collector circuits are referenced to the emitter, is normally connected with a positive voltage on the collector, as referenced to the emitter. The collector-base diode and the base-emitter diode appear to be in series, connected back-to-back. The collector-base diode is reverse biased so that almost no current will flow unless the base-emitter diode is forward biased. The very-small current in the collector circuit under these conditions is because the P-type material in the base is starved for the N-type majority carriers that the collector circuit requires if it is to conduct a significant current. When the base-emitter junction is forward biased, the carriers needer for current in the collector circuit find their way into the collector.

The base-emitter diode in the transistor offers a very-low resistance to current flow when it is forward biased. It is therefore very easy to cause current in the transistor's input circuit. since the base region is made very thin, most of the majority carriers that flow from the emitter will be caught by the strong electric field in the collector base junction before they can exit through the base connection. It takes only a small amount of power to cause current in the transistor's forward-biased base-emitter input circuit yet almost all this easily forced input current appears in the collector circuit. A low-powered signal becomes a higher-powered signal

when the input current caused by a low voltage appears almost undiminished in the collector circuit, but at a higher voltage.

Field effect transistors (FETs)

Field-effect transistors (FETs) are solid-state active devices based on a different principle than bipolar transistors. FETs are three terminal devices just as are BJTs. The input terminal of an FET is called its gate, one of the electrodes of a reverse-biased diode. FETs achieve current control by channeling current through a narrow N-type or P-type pathway whose conductivity is adjusted by the input signal. The output current controlled by an FET passes between the two remaining terminals called a source and a drain. The current through an FET must find its way through a narrow channel formed by the input-diode junction. Since this input diode is reverse biased, this channel tends to have few charge carriers. The input signal to the FET can deplete or enhance the number of available charge carriers in this channel, regulating the current in the drain circuit. Because the input diode is reverse biased, the FET demands almost no current from the signal source, therefore almost no power must be supplied. The power gain commonly achieved in FET amplifier is very high.

A special type of FET called a MOSFET (Metal Oxide Semiconductor Field Effect Transistor) can have an input resistance as high as one million-trillion Ohms. Because of their very-high input resistance, FETs are instantly destroyed if they receive even a small static-electric charge from careless handling. Sliding across a plastic chair may impart enough charge to a technician's body to destroy a field-effect transistor's input diode at the first touch. FETs must be handled only by persons who ground themselves before touching these devices to first dissipate static charges.

FETs are particularly useful as amplifiers of very-weak signals such as those produced by high-quality microphones. FETs have more desirable overload characteristics than BJTs, so that FETs are able to handle many signals simultaneously, some strong and some weak, without producing troublesome distortion product as a result of signal interactions. Before FETs were used in automobile receivers these radios were easily overloaded by strong signals The introduction of FETs made a tremendous improvement in automobile-radio receiver performance.

Integrated circuits

One of technology's most significant breakthroughs happened when it was discovered that many interconnected transistors could be created simultaneously on a single small chip of semiconductor material. The techniques used to create individual transistors could also connect these devices to form microscopically-small working circuits. The first integrated circuits were primitive arrangements utilizing just a few transistors or diodes in an uncomplicated circuit. Now it is not unheard of for single chips to contain many millions of transistors. ICs, as integrated circuits are called, may implement extremely complex circuitry.

Application-specificintegrated circuits

Special integrated circuits are developed as Application Specific Integrated Circuits, or ASICs, which are single chips targeting a specific set of tasks, useful for only one job. Almost every part of the circuitry needed for an AM-FM radio receiver is routinely produced on a single ASIC chip that replaces the hundreds of individual components required to build a radio from discrete parts. TV receivers have become increasingly dependent upon ASICs. ICs may also take the form of generalized modules intended to be used in a broad range of applications. Many of the first generalized ICs were designed as operational amplifiers, a general-purpose amplifier made from many transistors.

Complementary metal oxide semiconductors

Complementary metal oxide semiconductors or CMOS devices are coupled complementary MOSFETS in series, configured so that either MOSFET will conduct when the other is turned off. CMOS devices are frequently used as on-off switches in computer logic and memory circuits. CMOS devices use so little power that they made it possible for electronic watches to operate for 5 years without battery replacement. CMOS devices only require a significant current when the two complementary FETs in series change their conduction state, i.e. a quick pulse of current flows only during each switching action.

The microprocessors where computer programs process data use CMOS transistor technology. CMOS chips are commonly used in computer and calculator circuits, and CMOS is equally as common in consumer-type entertainment equipment. All CMOS devices must be protected from static electricity, particularly during handling of these sensitive devices when they are not installed on a circuit board.

KEY TERMS

. . . .

Capacitor—Passive circuit component used to introduce capacitance.

Covalent bond—Atoms attached to other atoms by sharing electrons.

Crystal—Ordered three-dimensional array atoms.

Dopant—Impurity added to an intrinsic semiconductor.

Doping—Adding impurities to change semiconductor properties.

Inductor—A component designed to introduce inductance.

Intrinsic—Semiconductor material containing very few impurities.

Pentavalent—An element with five valence electrons.

Photoconducive—A better conductor of electricity when illuminated.

Resistor—Component used to introduce resistance.

Tetravalent—Element with four valence electrons.

Trivalent—Element with four valence electrons.

Valence Electrons—Outermost electrons of an atom that bond with other atom.

The significance of the transistor

Perhaps the principal contribution of the transistor has been that its development created the possibility for microscopically sized sophisticated electronic equipment that could be powered economically. The transistor made it possible to hold more electronics in one's hand than could be installed in a building when only electron tubes were available as active devices.

See also Amplifier; Diode; Electrical conductivity; Integrated circuit; Silicon.

Further Reading:
Stix, Gary. "Toward Point One." *Scientific American* (February 1995).

Malvino, Albert Paul. *Transistor Circuit Approximations*, 2nd ed. McGraw-Hill, 1973.

Cannon, Don L. *Understanding Solid-State Electronics*, 5th ed. Prentice Hall, 1991.

Donald Beaty

Transition metal see **Periodic table**

Transitive

The concept of transitivity goes back at least 2,300 years. In the *Elements*, Euclid includes it as one of his "common notions." He says, "Things which are equal to the same thing are also equal to one another." As Euclid puts it, if a = b and c = b, then a = c, which is equivalent to the modern version, which has "b = c" rather than "c = b."

Transitivity is a property of any relation between numbers, geometric figures, or other mathematical elements. A relation R is said to be transitive if a R b and b R c imply that a R c. For example, 6/4 = 3/2 and 3/2 = 1.5, therefore 6/4 = 1.5.

Of course, one would not be likely to make use of the transitive property to establish such an obvious fact, but there are cases where the transitive property is very useful. If one were given the two equations

$$y = x^2$$
$$x = z + 1$$

one could use transitivity (after squaring both sides of the second equation) to eliminate x.

$$y = z^2 + 2z + 1$$

Transitivity is one of three properties which together make up an "equivalence relation."

Transitive law	If a R b and b R c, then a R c
Reflexive law	a R a
Symmetric law	If a R b, then b R a

To be an equivalence relation R must obey all three laws.

A particularly interesting relation is "wins over" in the game scissors-paper-rock. If a player chooses "paper," he or she wins over "rock'; and if the player chooses "rock," that wins over "scissors'; but "paper" doesn't win over "scissors." In fact, it loses. Although the various choices are placed in a winning-losing order, it is a non-transitive game. If it were transitive, of course, no one would play it.

In *Wheels, Life, and Other Mathematical Amusements*, Gardner describes a set of non-transitive dice. Die A has its faces marked 0, 0, 4, 4, 4, and 4. Each face of die B is marked with a 3. Die C is marked 2, 2, 2, 2, 6, 6. Die D is marked 1, 1, 1, 5, 5, 5. Each player chooses a die and rolls it. The player with the higher

KEY TERMS

Reflexive—A relation R is reflexive if for all elements a, a R a.

Symmetric—A relation R is symmetric if for all elements a and b, a R b implies that b R a.

Transitive—A relation R is transitive if for all elements a, b, and c, a R b and b R c implies that a R c.

number wins. The probability that A will win over B is 2/3. The probability that B will win over C or that C will win over D is also 2/3. And, paradoxically, the probability that D will win over A is also 2/3. Regardless of the die which the first player chooses, the second player can choose one which gives him a better chance of winning. He need only pick the next die in the unending sequence ... < A < B < C < D < A < B < ...

There are many relations in life which are theoretically transitive, but which in practice are not. One such is the relation "like better than." One can like apples better than bananas because they are juicier, pomegranates better than apples because they have more flavor, and still like bananas better than pomegranates. They are, after all, a lot easier to eat. Transitivity, reflexivity, and symmetry are properties of very simple, one-dimensional relations such as one finds in mathematics but not in much of ordinary life.

Further Reading:

Birkhoff, Garrett, and MacLane, Saunders. *A Survey of Modern Algebra.* New York: The Macmillan Co. 1947.
Dantzig, Tobias. *Number, the Language of Science.* Garden City, N. Y.: Doubleday and Co., 1954.
Gardner, Martin. *Wheels, Life, and Other Mathematical Amusements.* New York: W. H. Freeman and Co., 1983.

J. Paul Moulton

Translations

A translation is one of the three transformations that move a figure in the plane without changing its size or shape. (The other two are rotations and reflections.) In a translation, the figure is moved in a single direction without turning it or flipping it over. (Figures 1 and 2.)

A translation can, of course, be combined with the two other rigid motions (as transformations which pre-

Figure 1.

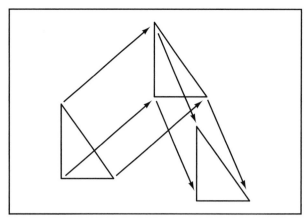

Figure 2.

serve a figure's size and shape are called), and it can in particular be combined with another translation. The "product" of two translations is also a translation, as illustrated in Figure 2.

If a set of points is drawn on a coordinate plane, it is a simple matter to write equations which will connect a point (x,y) with its translated "image" $(x^1 y^1)$. If a point has been moved a units to the right or left and b units up or down, a will be added to its x-cordinate and b to its y-coordinate, as shown in Figure 3. (If a < 0, the motion will be to the left; and if b <0, down.) Therefore

$$x^1 = x + a \quad \text{or} \quad x = x^1 - a$$
$$y^1 = y + b \qquad y = y^1 - b$$

In these equations, the axes are fixed and the points are moved. If one wishes, the points can be kept fixed and the axes moved. This is called a translation of axes. If the axes are moved so that the new origin is at the former point (a,b), then the new coordinates, (x^1, y^1) of a point (x, y) will be $(x - a, y - b)$.

If one has two translations:

$$x^1 = x + 3 \qquad y^1 = y - 6$$
$$x^{11} = x' - 2 \qquad y^{11} = y^1 + 1$$

they can be combined into a single transformation. By substitution one has

$$x^{11} = x + 1 \qquad y^{11} = y - 5,$$

which is another translation. This illustrates that the "product" of two translations is itself a translation, as claimed earlier.

If one has two translations

The idea of a translation is a very common one in the practical world. Many machines are translational in their operation. The machinist who cranks the cutting-tool holder up and down the bed of the lathe, is "translating" it. The piston of an automobile engine is trans-

lated up and down in its cylinder. The chain of a bicycle is translated from one sprocket wheel to another as the cyclist pedals, and so on.

The bicycle chain is not only translated, it works because it has translational symmetry. After a translation of one link, it looks exactly as it did before. Because of this symmetry, it continues to fit over the teeth of the sprocket wheel (which itself has rotational symmetry) and to turn it.

One important use of translations is to simplify an equation which represents a set of points. The equation $xy - 2x + 3y - 13 = 0$ can be written in factored form $(x + 3)(y - 2) = 7$. Then, letting $x^1 = x + 3$ and $y^1 = y - 2$, the equation is simply $x^1 y^1 = 7$, which is a much simpler and more easily recognized form.

Such transformations are useful in drawing graphs where many points have to be plotted. The graph of $x^1 y^1 = 7$ is a hyperbola whose branches lie entirely in the first and third quadrants with the axes as asymptotes. It is readily sketched. The graph of the original equation is also a hyperbola, but that fact may not be immedi-

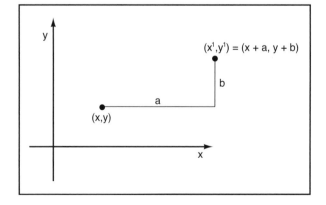

Figure 3.

KEY TERMS

. . . .

Rigid motion—A transformation of a plane figure which does not alter the size or shape of the figure.

ately apparent, and it will have points in all four quadrants. Many points may have to be plotted before the shape takes form.

If one has an equation of the form $ax^2 + by^2 + cx + dy + e = 0$ it is always possible to find a translation which will simplify it to an equation of the form $ax^2 + by^2 + E = 0$.

For example, the transformation $x = x^1 - 2$ and $y = y^1 + 1$ will transform $x^2 + 3y^2 + 4x - 6y - 2 = 0$

into $x^2 + 3y^2 - 9 = 0$ which is recognizable as an ellipse with its center at the origin.

Transformations are particularly helpful in integrating functions such as $\int (x + 5)^4 \, dx$ because $\int x^4 \, dx$ is very easy to integrate, while the original is not. After the translated integral has been figured out, the result can be translated back, substituting $x + 5$ for x.

Translational symmetry is sometimes the result of the way in which things are made; it is sometimes the goal. Newspapers, coming off a web press, have translational symmetry because the press prints the same page over and over again. Picket fences have translational symmetry because they are made from pickets all cut in the same shape. Ornamental borders, however, have translational symmetry because such symmetry adds to their attractiveness. The gardener could as easily space the plants irregularly, or use random varieties, as to make the border symmetric, but a symmetric border is often viewed as esthetically pleasing.

See also Rotation.

Further Reading:

Coxeter, H. S. M.,and S. L. Greitzer. *Geometry Revisited.* Washington, D.C.: The Mathematical Association of America, 1967.

Hilbert, D., and S. Cohn-Vossen. *Geometry and the Imagination.* New York: Chelsea, 1952.

Newman, James, ed. *The World of Mathematics.* New York: Simon and Schuster, 1956.

Pettofrezzo, Anthony. *Matrices and Transformations.* New York: Dover, 1966.

Yaglom, I. M. *Geometric Transformations.* Washington, D.C.: The Mathematical Association of America, 1962.

J. Paul Moulton

Transpiration

Transpiration refers to the evaporation of water from a biological surface, such as leaves, skin, or lungs. In its most common usage, however, transpiration refers to the loss of water from plant foliage, occurring through microscopic pores known as stomata. Transpiration is a component of a larger process known as evapotranspiration, which is the evaporation of water from a landscape, including both inorganic surfaces such as soil and bodies of water, and biological surface such as foliage.

Why do organisms transpire water?

Most transpiration by plants involves water that evaporates from the moist membranes of a tissue known as spongy mesophyll, which occur in the minute cavities beneath the tiny leaf pores called stomata. Stomata can be closed tightly using bordering cells known as guard cells. However, in most plants stomata are kept open much of the time. This is done so that carbon dioxide, which is needed for photosynthesis, can diffuse into the leaf, and oxygen, a waste product, can diffuse out. Therefore, transpiration by plants can be viewed as an unavoidable consequence of having moist mesophyll membranes exposed to the atmosphere. It is important to understand that, in general, any area of vegetation with a multilayered canopy of foliage will evaporate much larger quantities of water than can an equivalent non-foliated area, such as the surface of a lake or moist soil.

A similar explanation can be developed for animals, who must also maintain moist respiratory surfaces open to the atmosphere, for example in the lungs, from which water can freely evaporate. Transpiration can be an important problem for both plants and animals, because it may be difficult to replenish their water losses in relatively dry environments, so that dehydration can occur. If severe, dehydration can kill plants and animals. In some respects, then, transpiration can be regarded as a necessary evil that organisms must endure in order to exchange oxygen and carbon dioxide with the atmosphere.

However, there can sometimes be important benefits of transpiration. It takes about 540 calories of thermal energy to evaporate 1 g of water—at an ambient temperature of 68°F (20°C). This is a rather large amount of energy, and as a result transpiration can be an important way by which some animals and plants cool themselves. For example, when humans are hot, they sweat to distribute water onto their exposed skin, which is then cooled by the subsequent evaporation.

Transpiration as an ecological process

Transpiration is an ecologically important process. In areas where forests are common, evapotranspiration almost entirely occurs as transpiration, and this process can account for a substantial part of the manner by which the landscape deals with water inputs through rain and snow. For example, in typical forested landscapes of northeastern North America, evapotranspiration accounts for about 15-40% of the annual inputs of water with precipitation, the remainder draining to groundwater, or flushing from the system as streamflow.

In any regions with a seasonal climate, rates of evapotranspiration vary greatly during the year. Consider, for example, the case of a landscape in a temperate climate, covered with a seasonally deciduous, angiosperm forest. During winter, very little transpiration occurs because plant tissues are frozen. However, there can still be some physical evaporation of water from the surface of snow and ice, occurring by the direct vaporization of solid water, a process known as sublimation. During the springtime, unfrozen water is abundant, but the trees do not yet have foliage and this greatly reduces the rates of transpiration. During the growing season, air temperatures are warm and the trees are fully foliated, so transpiration occurs in large rates. During this time of the year, so much water is pumped into the atmosphere through foliage that the rate of evapotranspiration typically exceeds water inputs by rainfall. As a result, the soil is dried by the demands of plant roots for water, to the extent that streams may cease to flow by late summer. Once the trees drop their leaves in the autumn, transpiration rates decrease greatly, the water-depleted soil becomes recharged by rainfall, and streams again flow.

Effects of human activities on transpiration

The influence of an intact forest on evapotranspiration is affected by ecological disturbances, such as clearcutting and wildfire. In general, these sorts of stand-level disturbances greatly reduce the transpiration component of evapotranspiration for several years, a change that influences other hydrological processes, such as the timing and amounts of stream flow, which may then have effects on flooding and erosion. In addition, on sites that do not drain well, substantial decreases in transpiration can increase the height of the water table.

An ecological study done at Hubbard Brook, New Hampshire, involved the clear-felling of all trees on a 39.5-acre (16-hectare) watershed, which was then kept clear of regenerating plants for two additional years. The subsequent disruption of transpiration increased the amount of streamwater flow by an average of 31% over

---

KEY TERMS

Evapotranspiration—The evaporation of water from both inorganic and biological surfaces on a landscape.

Stomata—These are microscopic pores in the leaf cuticle, bordered by guard cells. Stomata The singular form is *stoma*) occur very densely, and water vapor, carbon dioxide, and oxygen diffuse through these tiny pores.

Watershed—The total expanse of landscape from which water flows into a lake or stream.

the three-year period. Many other studies of forestry have come to similar conclusions—clear-cutting increases streamflow by decreasing transpiration. However, because disturbed forests regenerate quickly through ecological succession, the amount of foliage on the site quickly recovers, and the effect of disturbance on streamflow tends to be rather short lived. In general, the pre-cutting stream flow volumes are substantially re-attained after 3-5 years of revegetation has occurred, because of the recovery of the transpirational surface area of plant foliage. (Of course, the regenerated foliage occurs on relatively short grasses, herbs, and shrubs, rather than on taller trees as in the initial forest.) The largest increases in stream flow usually occur in the first year after the forest is harvested, with progressively smaller effects afterwards.

See also Evaporation; Evapotranspiration.

Further Reading:
Freedman, B. *Environmental Ecology*. 2nd ed. San Diego: Academic Press, 1994.
Kimmins, J. P. *Forest Ecology*. New York: Macmillan, 1987.

Bill Freedman

Transplant, surgical

A surgical transplant involves the removal of body parts, organs, or tissues from one person and implanting them into the body of another person. Although the idea of transplantation to cure disease dates back several centuries, transplantation has been considered a viable therapy for only a few decades. The relatively recent growth in transplantation stems primarily from expanding knowledge about the body's immune system and the ability to suppress its natural response to attack foreign tissue. Another advance has been the ability to preserve organs out of the body for longer periods of time until they can be transplanted. Although most transplants involve the transference of tissues or organs between two humans, research is rapidly advancing toward using animal organs for transplantation into humans. Unfortunately donor organs are scarce, which has led to ethical questions concerning what patients would most benefit from receiving a transplant. For example, some believe that alcoholics suffering from cirrhosis of the liver should not receive a liver transplant that they may eventually destroy again because of alcohol abuse.

The history of transplants

The idea of transplanting animal or human parts dates back for many centuries. The mythical Chimera, animals made up of different animal parts, was believed to be the work of the gods. Perhaps the most famous chimera is the Sphinx in Egypt, which has the head of a man and the body of a lion.

The first viable transplantation occurred in the 16th century when a technique was developed for replacing noses lost during battle or due to syphilis. The technique involved using skin from the upper inner arm and then grafting and shaping it onto the nose area. In the 18th century, Scottish surgeon John Hunter, successfully transplanted a cock's claw to the animal's comb. Corneal transplants between two gazelles were also successfully performed in the latter part of the century.

During the 19th century, advances in surgery (like the development of antiseptic surgery to prevent infection and anesthetics to the lessen the pain) increased the success rates of most surgical procedures. However, transplantation of organs languished as surgeons had no knowledge of how to "reconnect" the organ to the new body. It wasn't until techniques for vascular anastomosis, or the ability to reconnect blood vessels, was developed near the 20th century that transplant surgery began to move ahead. The first long-lasting renal transplant was performed in Germany in 1902 when a dog kidney was transplanted into another dog by using tube stents (a slender tube used to support the structural integrity of the artery during an operation) and ligatures (wires used to tie off the blood vessels) to make the vascular connections.

The next major advance in transplantation would not occur for more than forty years. Although renal and kidney transplants were attempted, the transplant recipient's body always rejected the organ. In 1944, Peter Medawar showed that the rejection was due to the immune system, which attacked the foreign tissues or organs as foreign invaders, much the same way it works to ward of viruses and other disease. Although short-term successful renal transplants from donor to recipient were achieved in the early 1950s, these transplants usually were rejected by the patient's immune system. As a result, scientists began to focus on manipulating the immune system so it would accept the transplant.

By the early 1960s radiation and drugs were being used to suppress the immune system, in effect, shutting it down to prevent rejection. As a result, that decade saw the first bone marrow transplant, kidney transplant, and kidney/pancreas transplant. In 1967, Christiaan Barnard, a South African surgeon, received world wide notoriety for achieving the first successful heart transplant.

The next major advance came in 1978 with the development of the extremely effective antirejection (also called *immunosuppressant*) drug cyclosporin. Continued research on how to selectively control the immune system has grown to the point that transplantation is now a relatively common operation with more than 35,000 surgical transplants performed in medical centers throughout the world each year.

Transplantation and the immune system

Once surgeons acquired the ability to sever and reconnect arteries, the ability to control the immune system has been the primary concern in transplant surgery. The immune system is a complex biological network intricately linked to cells found in the blood. Many individuals share similar *antigens*, (small molecular proteins found on the surface of tissues that can stimulate an immune response,) and one of the first goals is to match antigens between organ donors and the recipients. The idea is to increase the likelihood that the patient's immune system will not attack because it recognizes a foreign antigen in the donor tissue.

Scientists have identified six primary types of antigens, called histocompatibility-locus antigens. Transplantation between people whose tissues and organs share all of these antigens generally is successful. For example, family members, particularly identical twins, usually have the same antigens. (In fact, the first successful kidney transplant was performed in 1955 when a young man received one of the kidneys of his twin brother.) As a result, relatives are often the source of donor tissues for patients who need kidneys and bone marrow transplants because one kidney or some bone marrow can be donated without causing harm to the donor.

A comparison of the old and new hearts of Dylan Stork, the smallest heart transplant recipient in the world. Dylan weighed 5.5 lbs (2.5 kg) at the time of the operation.

As the number of matching antigens between donor and recipient decreases, the need to suppress the immune system with drugs becomes increasingly important. Unfortunately, many of these drugs have side effects and can suppress the immune system to the point that the patient becomes susceptible to other infections and diseases, which can cause the transplant to be rejected and lead to the patient's death. The advantage of cyclosporin is that it can be targeted somewhat to work in specific tissues and organs of the body, thus keeping the patient from becoming entirely immunocompromised, which can lead to death from any number of diseases and infections not directly related to the transplanted organ's functioning.

The immune responses

Although there are probably many types of immune responses, scientists have only identified a few associated with organ rejection. Hyperacute rejection occurs when the patient's body has already produced a large number of antibodies (proteins manufactured by the immune system to battle disease and infection) that immediately recognize the antigens from the donor organ. This type of rejection, which usually occurs because of incompatible blood types, is often instantaneous, sometimes causing the patient to die even before the surgery is completed.

Acute rejection usually takes several days to occur because the immune system's white blood cells called *lymphocytes*, which are integral to its functioning because they initiate the production of antibodies, are lying dormant until the patient receives the organ. As the immune system initiates a response to the antigens in the donor organ, specific immune cells in the blood begin to attack. Acute rejection is combated by the use of immunosuppressive drugs. The longer the patient survives without a immune response attacking the organ, the greater the chances for keeping the immune system under control and for long-term survival.

However, chronic rejection can occur several months or years later. Although this type of rejection is rare, when it occurs, the donor organ slowly deteriorates despite all efforts at immunosuppression. Scientists do not fully understand why the immune response may kick in months or years after an organ has been successfully transplanted.

Types of transplants

There are many types of transplant surgeries, from specific cell and tissue transplants to entire organs. Cornea tissue transplants for the eye were one of the first successful transplants routinely performed. A thin transparent membrane found in front of the eye, the cornea can cause blindness or clouded fission if it is scarred or clouded by injury or infection. The transplant procedure involves cutting out part of the damaged cornea and replacing it with cornea from a donated eye. Cornea transplants are relatively simple procedures because they require no reconnection of blood supplying arteries, thus removing the danger of an adverse immune response. These procedures are successful 90% of the time.

The transplantation of bone tissue was first performed in the 1890s and involved replacing diseased or injured bone with pieces of bone from donors. The modern procedure involves using donor bone as a type of scaffolding built over metal nails that immobilizes and connects the patient's remaining bone sections.

Unlike bones and the cornea, most other transplants are more difficult to achieve because they involve circulating blood and the immune system. Skin grafts for burn patients, for example, are often achieved using autografts (meaning from the self), in this case, segments of skin from other areas of the patient's own body. A flap graft begins with the partial separation of skin from its original site until adequate blood circulation is achieved, then it is completely severed and grafted onto the transplant site. This technique has a high success rate for curing scars or deformities. A full thickness autograft entails removing small pieces of all the layers of skin for transplantation; these types of skin grafts are particularly suitable for the face to achieve the least amount of scarring. A split-thickness autograft removes tissue-thin layers of skin which heal easily when transplanted. The one drawback to this type of skin graft is that the transplanted tissue usually appears reddish, which makes them more noticeable. Some skin grafts come from the skin of human donors or other animals, like pigs, and are used when large areas must be covered. Unlike the cosmetic goals of other grafts, these grafts are used primarily to stop the patient from losing fluids through the burned area and to prevent infection. Research is also underway to grow skin for grafting from a few donated skin cells.

Bone marrow transplants are often used to treat patients with blood diseases, like leukemia. The transplant procedure involves taking the tissue from the center of bones through a needle, a technique called bone marrow aspiration. The marrow may be an autograft taken from a patient while the diseases is in remission and stored until they need the healthy blood cells. Bone marrow taken from other donors of the same species are called allografts. Unlike most immune responses in transplantation in which the donor's body rejects the transplant, in bone marrow allografts it is often the transplanted marrow that reacts against the host. This is known as graft-versus-host disease.

Organ transplants

By far, organ transplantation has received the most attention in the popular press. People who would be severely debilitated or die because of failing organs are the recipients of organ transplants. The primary organ transplants are heart, liver, pancreas, lung, and kidney transplants. Under certain circumstances, a patient may receive more than one transplant, the most common multiple transplant procedure is the dual heart/lung transplant.

Kidney transplants are designed to treat patients whose kidneys are failing, making them unable to process body waste products. These transplants have approached a 90% success rate. If the transplant fails, the patient may be put on dialysis until a new donor kidney can be found. Dialysis uses a machine to artificially remove blood from the body, clean the waste products by filtering the blood, and then return the blood to the body.

Other transplantable organs include the liver, the heart, and the lungs. With the development of immuno-suppressive drugs, liver transplants have been growing in their success rates, although many patients still die because of organ rejection or from infections. Heart and lung transplants are often performed simultaneously since they share an interrelated vascular system and survival rates are higher for lung transplant patients when they also receive a new heart.

Organ transplants are delicate and complex procedures that require a well trained staff and usually take several hours or much longer to perform. As the surgeon removes the organ, sutures (wire or some other material) are used to close or tie off arteries and other connections to the organ. The new organ is then placed in position and the painstaking task of reconnecting the organ begins. Although the techniques, like vascular anastomosis, for making these connections are well established, they can be difficult procedures. For example, many of the connections to the liver lie underneath the liver and out of the surgeons' immediate view.

Organ preservation

Unlike tissues or cells, which can be maintained in functioning condition by placing them in life sustaining cultures (specially prepared nourishing fluids places in a dish or a bowl), organs that have been donated for transplantation require a more complex approach for their preservation. *Perfusion* is the process of using a pump or other mechanical device to circulate specific electrolyte solutions through the organ's vascular system.

These solutions may support the organ's metabolic (or chemical and physical) functioning. Some solutions are used, in effect, to freeze the organ. For instance, in cornea, skin, kidney, liver, heart, and pancreas transplants, some solutions are designed to cause hypothermia (subnormal body temperatures) in the organ. Organ tissues maintain their ability to function ten or more times longer when kept at a temperature of 32-39°F (0-4°C), and kidneys have been preserved for more than 50 hours using this approach.

Donor organ and tissue networks

Most organs and tissues used for transplantation come from nationwide networks designed to provide quick access to organs when they become available. For example, the United Network for Organ Sharing (UNOS) provides access to organs and tissues throughout North America. The more than 70 organ procurement agencies in the United States are crucial to the success of transplants since they facilitate access to and transportation of organs and tissues that remain viable for transplanting for only a limited amount of time after they are removed from the donor's body.

The procurement begins when a hospital notifies a local organ bank that a seriously ill or dying patient (who is willing to donate his or her organ or whose family has given permission) is under their care. Organ bank staff will go to the hospital to assess the patient to determine whether their organs are healthy enough for transplantation. For example, most donor organs are harvested from people under age 65, and organs from someone who was an intravenous drug user may also be precluded from use since the organs may be infected with the AIDS disease or hepatitis. Once the patient is pronounced dead, a team of surgeons begin to remove the eyes, heart, liver, and kidneys. The next step is to determine who receives the organ. This is usually done on a geographic basis with those patients in the same general geographic area as the donor receiving first consideration to receive the organ.

However, since these organs are a precious commodity, a nationwide computer list of potential transplant recipients is also maintained. The National Organ Procurement and Transplantation Network was established by the National Organ Transplant Act of 1984.

Potential donor recipients are prioritized to receive organs according to the length of time they have been on the UNOS list and on the compatibility to the donor organ in terms of blood types, body sizes, and genetic similarities.

The future of transplantation

Although many transplants, especially organ transplants, would not be needed if people took better care of their bodies by exercising and not smoking or drinking alcohol, the number of organ transplants performed each year is likely to continue to grow as long as donor organs can be obtained. In addition, new kinds of transplants are being pioneered.

One of the more exciting advances is the transplantation of tissues and cells from the central nervous system (CNS). These cells have been transplanted into the brains of people suffering from neurological (or nervous system) diseases, like Parkinson's disease. CNS cells and tissues have the unique ability to regenerate, or grow back. In the case of Parkinson's patients, the substantia nigra area of the brain, can no longer produce the neurotransmitter (chemical messenger) *dopamine*, which usually results in the progressive loss of many motor skills to the point where patients can no longer walk or feed themselves. One of the surgical treatments under investigation is to transplant adrenal medullary tissue in hopes that the transplanted tissue will permanently regenerate new cells in the brain.

Artificial organs and xenografts

Due to the lack of available organs for transplantation, researchers are constantly experimenting with developing new sources of organs and tissues for transplantation. Artificial organs, for example, are being developed. These include electronic devices to make the heart beat and pumps implanted into the body that can supply necessary substances like insulin. Many of these devices are used as "bridges" to transplantation. In other words, they are temporary therapies to keep the patient alive while a suitable donor organ can be found. Artificial skin is also under development as are mechanical implants to help cure deafness.

Although current transplantation deals primarily in allografts, or transplantation within the same species, transplantation between species, called xenografts, is a also rapidly advancing area of study. The first partially successful xenografts were performed over a quarter of a century ago when surgeons transplanted organs from chimpanzees to humans.

But since the use of primates, which are closer to humans in nature, raises certain ethical questions, recent research has focused on non-primate animals. Pigs, for example, are relatively easy to breed and have large litters. They also share with humans many similar anatomical structures, like the heart, that function in similar ways in the body. Although pig organ transplants have, to date, been unsuccessful, advances in the development of immunosuppressive drugs have led some transplant scientists to think that success in this area can be achieved. Another advance in medical science, the ability to manipulate genes (hereditary components found in cells), has led to genetic engineering. This process involves manipulating and combining specific genetic components to achieve desirable traits or effects. In the case of pig organs, the goal is to make them more compatible to humans. However, the primary obstacle to xenografts remains rejection by the host's immune system. Even using immunosuppressant drugs does not guarantee that the immune system will not eventually recognize and destroy the non-human organ.

Ethical issues surrounding transplantation

The primary ethical issue associated with transplanted is the extreme shortage of available donors. Nearly 20,000 people die in the United States each year who would have been suitable organ donors. But only about 3,000 of these organs are ever donated and harvested. Questions surrounding the limited supply of donor organs include who should get the donor. For example, should the organ go to someone who is poor and on welfare or someone who can afford to pay for the operation. There is also concern over buying organs from people before they have died or from their families after the person has died. Some organs, like kidneys, corneas, bones, and bone marrow could even be bought and removed before death since they would not fatally harm the donor if removed.

Another ethical issue surrounding transplantation is the high costs associated with obtaining and transplanting an organ. Some transplant procedures can cost more than $200,000. Since most people cannot afford such operations, the burden falls on society in the form of higher insurance premiums and government subsidies. Even after the surgery is over, it can cost tens of thousands of dollars each year to keep the person alive because of the high cost of antirejection drugs.

Despite the difficulty of obtaining organs, the high costs, and the many ethical concerns, transplantation will continue to thrive since it is the only hope for many terminally ill patients. Society's mandate is to develop ethical regulations to ensure that growing demands are met fairly and humanely.

KEY TERMS

Allografts—Tissues and organs used for transplantation that come other donors of the same species.

Autografts—Tissues and organs used for transplantation that come from the patients themselves.

Bone marrow—Tissue inside bone that produces red blood cells and certain white blood cells.

Graft—Bone, skin, or other tissue that is taken from one place on the body (or, in some cases, from another body), and then transplanted to another place where it begins to grow again.

Immunocompromised—The state of having the immune system suppressed so that it is not functioning completely.

Immunosuppressant—Something used to reduce the immune system's ability to function, like certain drugs or radiation.

Lymphocytes—White blood cells that play a role in the functioning of the immune system.

Vascular anastomosis—A technique for reconnect blood vessels.

Xenografts—Tissues and organs used for transplantation that come from different animal species, like pigs or baboons.

See also Antibody and antigen; Cyclosporine; Immune system; Surgery.

Further Reading:

Fox, Mark D. "The Transplantation Success Story." *Journal of the American Medical Association* (December 7, 1994): 1704.

Gutkind, L. *Many Sleepless Nights*. Pittsburgh: The University of Pittsburgh Press, 1990.

Keyes, C.D. *New Harvest: Transplanting Body Parts and Reaping the Benefits*. Clifton, New Jersey: Humana Press, 1991.

Kittredge, Mary. *Organ Transplants*. New York: Chelsea House Publishers, 1989.

Pizer, H.F. Organ Transplants: A Patient's Guide. Cambridge: Harvard University Press, 1991.

Starzl, T.E. "The Early Days of Transplantation." *Journal of the American Medical Association* (December 7, 1994): 1705.

White, D. and Wallork, J. "Xenografting: Probability, Possibility, or Pipe Dream?" *The Lancet* (October 9, 1993): 879-880.

David Petechuk

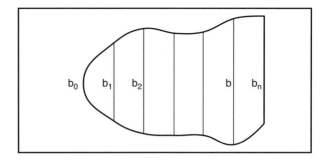

Figure 2.

Trapezoid

A trapezoid is a quadrilateral (four-sided figure) with one pair of parallel sides. The two parallel sides are designated as the bases, with the longer of the bases being described as the lower base and the shorter of the bases, the upper base. The two non-parallel sides of the trapezoid are called the legs. A trapezoid in which the two legs are of equal length is called an isosceles trapezoid. The parallelogram, which consists of two pairs of parallel sides, is sometimes regarded as a special form of the trapezoid.

Two important measurements within a trapezoid are the altitude and the median. The altitude of a trapezoid is the perpendicular distance between the two bases, while the median is the line segment joining the midpoint of the two legs of the trapezoid. The median is parallel to the two bases and has a length equal to half the sum of the two base lengths, or $m = 1/2(b_1 + b_2)$.

The area of a trapezoid can be found by taking one half the product of its altitude multiplied by the sum of its bases, or: $A = 1/2(b_1 + b_2)h$. One of the important practical applications of the trapezoid is in estimating the area under a curve when that area can not be calculated precisely by other mathematical formulas. The first step in using the so-called trapezoidal rule is to divide up the area to be estimated into a number of small trapezoidal segments by drawing a series of parallel lines at equal distances from each other across the area. Then each of the small trapezoids has the same altitude (h). The legs of the small trapezoids consist of the lines of which the curve itself is constructed. For an irregular curve drawn on conventional cartesian coordi-

nates, for example, one leg of the individual trapezoids is the x-axis itself, while the other leg is the curve.

In such a case, the area under the curve can be estimated as the sum of the areas of the individual trapezoids, or: $A = h(1/2b_0 + b_1 + b_2 + b_3 + \ldots + 1/2b_n)$ where h is the common altitude for all trapezoids and b_0, b_1, b_2, b_3, and so forth are the lengths of the bases of the trapezoids, as shown in Figure 2.

See also Quadrilateral.

Tree

A tree is a woody plant which has three principle characteristics: (a) the potential to grow to 20 ft (6.1 m) or more in height; (b) the formation of one or more trunks arising from the ground; and (c) the ability to stand on its own without support. Trees provide many products which are important to humans, such as timber, fruits, and nuts. They are also the dominant plants in the world's forests, and thus provide critical habitats for the other species which live there.

Tree taxonomy

Taxonomy is the identification and classification of organisms. Dendrology is the identification and classification of trees, shrubs, and vines, and is a subdiscipline of taxonomy. Shrubs and vines are also woody plants. Shrubs are shorter than trees and have multiple stems arising from the ground. Vines generally rely upon another plant or other structure for physical support.

Some plant families consist entirely of trees and other types of woody plants. Other plant families have some species which are woody, and some which are herbaceous. This indicates that arborescence, the character of being tree-like, is not a reliable character for distinguishing families and higher taxonomic groups of plants.

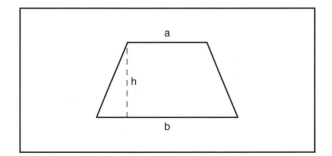

Figure 1. An isosceles trapezoid.

History of taxonomy

Carl von Linné of Sweden began the modern study of taxonomy in the mid-1700s. He classified trees and other plants according to the morphology of their reproductive structures, such as the flowers and fruits of Angiosperms, and the cones of Gymnosperms. Many religious leaders of his time considered it immoral to study the reproductive structures of plants. However, modern taxonomists still rely upon plants' reproductive structures for conclusive identification of species.

Carl Von Linné also advocated that all scientists refer to trees and other organisms by a Latinized name. He even Latinized his own name to Carolus Linneaus. Modern biologists continue to follow this convention. Thus, the tree which Americans call the white pine is known to biologists throughout the world as *pinus strobus*, where "Pinus" is the pine genus and "strobus" is the specific epithet. There are about 90 other species of pine in the world, including red pine (*Pinus resinosa*), sugar pine (*P. lambertiana*), and pitch pine (*P. rigida*).

Charles Darwin's studies of evolution in the mid-1800s led taxonomists to group organisms hierarchically, according to their evolutionary relationships. For example, the pines (genus, *Pinus*), spruces (genus, *Picea*) and about seven other genera are grouped together in the family Pinaceae, because they are evolutionarily related. In turn, the Pineaceae and about six other families are grouped together in the order Coniferales (the conifers, or cone-bearing plants) because they are evolutionarily related.

Modern taxonomy

Traditionally, plant taxonomists have relied upon the morphology of plants' reproductive structures to determine their evolutionary relationships. More recently, they have also used biochemical characteristics, DNA sequences, and additional features. Occasionally, there are disagreements about the relationships of different plant species. These disagreements are important in stimulating further research.

In identifying a tree in nature, dendrologists do not always rely upon its reproductive structures, because these are often only available for a brief time of the year. In practice, they typically rely upon features of a tree's leaves, twigs, bark, wood, habit (general shape and appearance), and habitat as clues for identification.

Secondary growth

Most trees increase in thickness due to cell division in two special layers of undifferentiated tissues near the outside of their stem. This is known as secondary growth. The two tissues are referred to as the vascular cambium and the cork cambium. In contrast, herbs do not have secondary growth, and they stop growing once their primary tissues have matured.

Cell layers in a tree trunk

In a typical, sawed-off sector of a tree trunk, one encounters layers of different cells and a series of concentric, annual growth rings in going from the outside toward the inside.

The cork of bark is on the external surface of the trunk, and consists of dead cells which are impregnated with suberin, a waxy substance which inhibits evaporation of water through the bark. The cork cambium lies just inside the cork. It produces cork cells on its outside face and secondary cortex on its inside face. Growth and division of the cork cambium is different among tree species, and this gives the bark of each species its own characteristic appearance.

Phloem cells lie just inside the secondary cortex. Phloem cells are elongated cells specialized for the transport of plant nutrients, such as the carbohydrates made during photosynthesis. The vascular cambium lies just inside the phloem cells. It produces phloem cells on its outside face, and xylem cells on its inside surface. Xylem cells are elongated cells specialized for transport of water and dissolved ions throughout the tree. Trees growing in places with a strongly seasonal climate typically contain thick layers of xylem cells with readily apparent, concentric growth rings. This thick layer of functional xylem cells is referred to as the sapwood.

Finally, the heartwood is in the center of the tree. This layer is typically darker than the sapwood and consists of dead cells which are very stiff and serve to strengthen the tree. The heartwood may also have readily apparent growth rings.

Growth rings

In most trees growing in a strongly seasonal climate, the vascular cambium produces wide, thin-walled cells in the spring, narrow thick-walled cells in the summer, and few or no cells in the autumn and winter. This seasonal regularity of cell production results in the formation of annual growth rings. The bristle-cone pine (*Pinus aristata*) is the world's longest-lived tree species, and one specimen of this species has about 5,000 growth rings, indicating it is at least 5,000 years old.

Within a given growth ring, the large cells of springwood and the small cells of summerwood are often readily discernible with the naked eye. Light, temperature, soil moisture and other environmental factors affect the growth of trees, and therefore the width of their growth rings.

Evolution

Most botanists believe that the first land plants were herbaceous. The first woody plants were probably Lycopsides, free-sporing plants which had narrow, tubular grass-like leaves. Numerous Lycopsid fossils have been dated to the middle of the Upper Devonian period, more than 370 million years ago. The first known plant with a vascular cambium which exhibited true secondary growth was a species of Protopteridium, a free-sporing plant dated to about 370 million years ago.

Very few modern, free-sporing plants are arborescent. The only living relatives of the Lycopsids are the club mosses (Lycopodophyta), a group of simple, herbaceous, free-sporing plants.

Forests

Trees are the dominant organisms of forests. Climate and other factors determine which tree species grow in a forest. Forest ecologists have classified the forests of the world according to the species of trees which grow there. One classification scheme is described below.

Coniferous forests are characteristic of the boreal forests of cold regions of the northern hemisphere. The boreal forest is found in Canada, southern Alaska, northwestern America, northern Europe, and northern Russia. The dominant trees are conifers (cone-bearing plants) such as pines, spruces, firs, and larches. Many of these trees are important sources of wood used in construction, and of pulp for paper.

Broad-leaf forests are characteristic of temperate zones of central and eastern North America, central and southern Europe, and central Asia. Its dominant trees have broad leaves and are deciduous, in that they shed their leaves once a year. Oaks, hickories, maples, and sycamores are some of the trees commonly found in this forest type. Many broad-leaf trees are hardwoods, and are used for making some of our finest furniture.

Mediterranean forests are characteristic of regions with hot, dry summers and warm, humid winters. This forest type is found in southern California, northwestern Mexico, southern Europe, northern Africa, and southern Australia. The trees which grown in Mediterranean forests are adapted to minimizing water loss. Evergreen oaks and pines are well-known trees of this forest type. In Australia, about 600 different species of Eucalyptus grow in the Mediterranean forest type along the southern coast.

Savannas are characteristic of tropical regions with a very seasonal rainfall. The trees in a savanna are sparsely distributed and are specially adapted to minimize water loss. Savannas are found in northern Mexico, equatorial Asia, central Africa, and northern Australia. Acacias, Dracaenas, and the Talioin Asia Baobab are well known savanna trees.

Tropical rainforests are characteristic of regions with a relatively warm climate and a great deal of rainfall. This forest type is found in Central America, northern and central South America, central and western Africa, and the south Pacific region. Tropical rainforests have a great diversity of plant and animal species. The tropical rainforests of the world are currently threatened by people who are cutting down their trees at an increasing rate. At the same time, conservationists and tropical ecologists devote much effort to the preservation of tropical rainforests with their rich diversity of species.

Ascent of sap

It is vitally important for a tree to transport water from the soil to its upper-most leaves. This process has long fascinated plant physiologists, and has been studied for centuries. How does water move from the roots to the uppermost leaves of tall trees? The significance of this problem is best appreciated by considering the height of some of the world's tallest trees. The world's tallest tree was a *Eucalyptus regnans* of Australia, which was measured at 470 ft (143 m) in 1880. The tallest living tree is a coastal redwood (*Sequoia sempervirens*) of California, which is about 365 ft (111.3 m) in height. Its relative, the giant sequoia (*Sequoidendron giganteum*) is not quite as tall, but is the world's most massive tree species.

Cohesion-tension theory

Most plant physiologists now accept the 'cohesion-tension theory' as an explanation for the ascent of sap. According to this theory, water moves up the trunk of a tree in narrow, elongated cells near the periphery of the trunk, referred to as the xylem, and does not require the expenditure of metabolic energy. The movement of water only depends upon three important physical-chemical properties of water.

The first important property of water is that it always moves from a region with a more positive water potential, to a region with a more negative potential. Water potential is a measure of the energy available in a solution of water. Thus, water moves out of the leaves and into the air because the water potential of the air is more negative; water moves out of the tree trunk and into the leaves because the water potential of the leaves is more negative; water moves out of the roots and into the trunk because the water potential of the trunk is more negative; and water moves out of the soil and into the roots because the water potential of the roots is more negative.

The second important physical-chemical property of water is that it is a cohesive molecule. In other words, water molecules tend to bind to one another through the formation of hydrogen bonds. The cohesiveness of water molecules gives the thin water columns in a tree trunk a very great tensile strength. This prevents breakage of the water column when great longitudinal stresses are placed upon it as it is pulled out of the leaves and into the air.

The third important property of water is that it adheres very tightly to the walls of xylem cells in the tree's transport pathway. Adhesion of water to these cell walls maintains the full hydration of the pathway for water transport. This prevents breakage of the water column, and allows water transport even when a tree is water-stressed in a dry environment.

Economic significance

Trees have great economic significance to humans as a source of food, building materials and paper. Almond, coconut, cherry, prune, peach, pear, and many other tree species are grown in orchards for their fruits and nuts. The apple tree is the orchard tree of greatest economic significance, and there are several hundred different varieties of apples. (Many of North America's best apples grow in New York state and Washington state.)

Many trees are also useful for the wood they produce. Wood is used as a construction material and to make furniture. Wood is a valuable construction material because it is relatively inexpensive, easy to cut, and very strong relative to its weight. Many species of pines and other conifers are important sources of softwoods, and many broadleaf trees are important sources of hardwoods.

There are frequent conflicts between conservationists and loggers. In the United States, the coniferous rainforest of the Pacific northwest has been the site of one such conflict. In this region, loggers want to harvest coniferous trees from the forest just as they have done for many years, whereas conservationists seek to preserve the forest because it provides a habitat for the northern spotted owl, an endangered species.

See also Basswood; Birch family; Cashew family; Citrus trees; Conifer; Cork; Deforestation; Dogwood tree; Ebony; Firs; Forests; Forestry; Horse chestnut; Magnolia; Mahogany; Mangrove tree; Maples; Nux vomica tree; Oaks; Old-growth forest; Palms; Paper; Pines; Rain forest; Rose family; Sapodilla tree; Screwpines; Silk cotton family; Spruce; Swamp cypress family; Walnut family; Willow family; Wood; Yew.

KEY TERMS

· ·

Adhesion—Physical attraction between different types of molecules.

Cohesion—Physical attraction between molecules of the same type.

Cork Cambium—Undifferentiated plant tissue which gives rise to cork cells and secondary cortex.

Dendrology—Identification and classification of woody plants.

Phloem—Plant tissue consisting of elongated cells which function in the transport of carbohydrates and other nutrients.

Vascular Cambium—Undifferentiated plant tissue which gives rise to phloem and xylem.

Xylem—Plant tissue consisting of elongated cells which function in transport of water and dissolved ions.

Further Reading:

Audubon Society and Staff. *Familiar Trees of North America: Eastern Region.* Knopf Inc., 1987.

Audubon Society and Staff. *Familiar Trees of North America: Western Region.* Knopf Inc., 1987.

Johnson, H. *Encyclopedia of Trees.* Random House, 1990.

Platt, R. *One thousand-and-one questions answered about trees.* Dover Inc., 1992.

Peter A. Ensminger

Tree-ring dating see **Dating techniques**

Tree shrews

The tree shrews (order Scandentia, family Tupaiidae) comprise a small number of species that are only found in South and Southeast Asia. Five genera (19 species) are recognized. All occur in forested areas,

ranging from India and Southwest China eastward
through Malaysia, Indonesia (west of Wallace's Line),
and the Philippines. Three genera and 10 species occur
on the island of Borneo alone.

In appearance, tree shrews resemble long-snouted
squirrels (the Malay word *tupai* means squirrel). All
tree shrews are of a slender build; adults generally
weigh 2.5-3.5 oz (70-100 g.) The length of the head and
body ranges from 3.9-8.6 in (100-220 mm), while tail
length varies from 3.5-8.8 in (90-225 mm). Generally a
russet-brown color, they have a long, pointed muzzle
with 38 sharp teeth. One unusual species, the pen-tailed
tree shrew (*Ptilocercus lowi*), can be identified by its
tail, which is naked except for a whitish feather-shaped
arrangement of the hairs near the end. In all species, the
fur consists of long, straight guard hairs and shorter,
softer underfur. Some forms have pale shoulder stripes
and others have facial markings. The ears are squirrel-
like; that is, they are comparatively small and cartilaginous, except in the pen-tailed tree shrew in which they
are larger and more membranous. The feet of tree
shrews are naked beneath; the soles are adorned with
tubercle-like pads which assist with climbing. The long
and supple digits bear sharp, moderately curved claws.
Tree shrews have well developed senses of vision, hearing, and smell.

In addition to their external resemblance to squirrels, tree shrews, like squirrels, are mostly diurnal, and
some of their actions and movements are similar. *Ptilocercus* differs in being mainly nocturnal and, when on
the ground, progresses in a series of hops. Other tree
shrews are swift runners. All tupaiids are capable
climbers, seeking their food in trees as well as on the
ground. Their diet consists mainly of insects and fruit
but occasionally includes other animal food and various
types of plant matter. They are generally fond of water
for both drinking and bathing. Most species nest in
holes in tree trunks or branches 65.7-98.4 ft (20-30 m)
high, the nest consisting of a simple structure of dried
leaves, twigs, and fibers of soft wood.

Few other mammalian families have proved as difficult to classify as the tree shrews. Historically, the
Tupaiidae have been grouped with the Macroscelididae
(elephant shrews), Insectivora (insectivores), and even
the primates. More recent studies of their behavior and
reproduction, however, has led to them being placed in
a distinct order, Scandentia.

Tree shrews display a wide range of social behaviors. The common tree shrew *Tupaia glis*, for example,
lives in permanent pairs, with males occupying an average home range of 12,168 sq yd (10,174 sq m) and
females a smaller area of about 1,052 sq yd (880 sq m).

Although they basically share the same range, they
remain largely solitary and defend the area from possible intruders. In contrast, the pen-tailed tree shrew generally moves about in pairs, but as many as four animals
have been found together in a single nest. Field observations also suggest that many species exist at relatively
low densities: data for *T. glis* show a varied pattern of 1-
2 per acre (2-5 per hectare) in Malaysia or 2-5 per acre
(5-13 per hectare) in Thailand, while *T. palawanensis*
occurs at a local density of 0.5-1 per acre (1.5-2.5 per
hectare).

Scent marking plays an important role in communications among tree shrews, all of which have specialized glands that secrete a wide array of chemical compounds, many of which are unique to the individual
animal. The different compounds in these secretions
covey a range of messages about the animal, particularly information on its sex, age, and breeding status.
Such information is thought to play an important role in
defending individual territories. Tree shrews seem to be
creatures of habit and regularly use the same paths
along the ground or on branches to reach their favorite
feeding or resting areas. As they move around their
ranges, their scent is liberally deposited, usually at
strategic places where other animals have a chance of
finding it. In this way, an intruding animal will be able
to determine that the area is already occupied and
defended by a resident tree shrew and should be able to
withdraw without further conflict. If the intruder is a
male, hoping to mate or take over the territory of a
neighboring animal, it may move further into the territory, but on doing so risks attack and possible injury
from the resident animals.

The reproductive behavior of most species is still
poorly known. Most species apparently breed throughout the year. Following a gestation period of about 45-
50 days, females give birth to one to four young. Some
species, such as *Urogale everetti*, are receptive to
breeding again shortly after giving birth.

Surprisingly, in view of their large size and diurnal
habits, tree shrews have attracted relatively little biological attention. As a result there has been little study
of their ecology or behavior in the wild. All tree shrews
are forest-dwelling species, occupying a wide range of
niches within different forest habitats. Many species
seem capable of adapting to living in secondary forest
and some even occur in rural gardens and well-established plantations.

Tropical forests are, however, their preferred
domain, and because of their dependence on forest
habitat, many of these species are susceptible to excessive levels of clearance and disturbance. Some species,

particularly *Tupaia nicobarica* and *T. longipes*, are thought to be endangered, but other species with restricted ranges, particularly those on islands or where agricultural encroachment and/or logging is a major activity, are also seriously threatened. The most urgent among these are the golden-bellied (*Tupaia chrysogaster*), Palawan (*T. palawensis*), Philippine (*Urogale everetti*), and Madras (*Anathana elliotti*) tree shrews. Although loss of habitat is the main threat to these species, additional pressures such as hunting for food and sport can add to the pressure on these and other native endemic species. Habitat conservation is therefore vital to preserving tree shrews.

The forests that are important to tree shrews are also known to be of great importance to a wide range of plants, mammals, birds, and invertebrates, many of which are endemic. By developing and implementing conservation strategies which include tree shrew conservation requirements in these forests, the overall biological diversity of these unique ecosystems could be far better protected. These same forests also fulfill many other essential roles that benefit humans, particularly through watershed protection and as an important source of fruit, medicinal and herbal plants, and a wide range of timber products of economic importance.

In view of the many uncertainties surrounding the ecological status, distribution, and ability of these species to adapt to secondary habitats, there is an urgent need to promote further action for a large number of these species. Particular aspects which need attention include details of the basic ecology, home range size, feeding priorities, habitat preferences, breeding behavior, and population density of most species.

See also Shrews.

Trevallys see **Jacks**

Triangle see **Trigonometry**

Tricarboxylic acid cycle see **Krebs cycle**

Trichinosis

Trichinosis is a disease caused by the roundworm (nematode) called *Trichinella spiralis* (*T. spiralis*). It is readily avoided by proper handling and cooking of certain meats, particularly pork products.

Life cycle of *Trichinella spiralis*

The life cycle of *Trichinella spiralis* includes sev-

eral different stages. The adult worm lives in the intestinal lining of such carnivorous animals as swine, bears, walrus, and rodents. After mating, the male worm dies, while the female worm goes on to develop the offspring.

The embryonic stage, a stage often occurring after birth in many nematode species, occurs within the uterus of the female *T. spiralis,* so that the offspring which are ultimately discharged from the female are in the larval second stage of life. These larvae (about 1500 from each female worm) travel through the circulatory system, to the heart, then through the blood vessels leading to striated muscle (the muscle of the skeletal system and the heart). Any larvae not arriving in striated muscle will die.

Those larvae that reach striated muscle will grow to a length of about one millimeter, coil, and enclose themselves within a protective wall called a cyst. These cysts continue to live for up to ten years in this form.

Trichinella spiralis in humans

A pig which has been infected with *T. spiralis* may have thousands of cysts waiting dormant within its muscles; the very muscles that humans look forward to dining on in the form of pork chops, ham, barbecued ribs, etc. When humans sit down to a meal of undercooked, *T. spiralis*-infected pig dinner, they are ingesting viable *T. spiralis* cysts. The cyst walls are broken down by the usual process of food digestion in the stomach, allowing the larvae to continue on to the new host's intestine, where the larvae mature to become adult worms, capable of reproducing a new crop of larvae. When these new larvae are born, they begin their migration throughout the human host's bloodstream to the human host's muscles, where they live for a short while before encysting.

Symptoms of trichinosis

A human host who eats *T. spiralis* infected meat may experience symptoms to a varying degree. If the meat ingested has only a few cysts, then the human host's "worm burden" is said to be relatively small, so that symptomatology will be relatively moderate. In fact, many infections are subclinical (exhibiting such mild symptoms as to remain undiagnosed).

In a host with a greater worm burden, the initial symptoms will be caused by the presence of the adult worms in the intestine, and usually include fever, diarrhea, abdominal pain, and perhaps vomiting. These symptoms begin about one to two days after eating the offending meat, and may last for a week or so.

When larvae begin their migration through the blood vessels, the host will begin to experience systemic symptoms (affecting the whole body), such as fever, swelling of the face and the area around the eyes, rash, bleeding into the nail beds, retina, and whites of the eyes, and cough. In very severe cases, inflammation of the heart muscle (myocarditis), lungs (pneumonitis), or brain (encephalitis) may occur, which can lead to the few deaths attributable to trichinosis.

The larvae begin to burrow into the host's muscles and form cysts within about two to three weeks of the initial infection. This produces signs of muscle inflammation (myositis), including swelling of the affected muscle groups, pain, and weakness.

The most frequently affected muscles are the muscles outside of the eye, which control eye movements (extraocular muscles), as well as the muscles of the jaw, neck, upper arm (biceps muscle), lower back (lumbar region), and diaphragm (the muscle which separates the abdominal and chest cavities and aids in inspiration).

Symptoms are at their most severe at about three weeks after infection and decrease very slowly in their severity. Recovery is extremely gradual, and symptoms may be present for as long as three months. Fatigue and myalgia (muscle pain) may take several more months to subside.

Diagnosis

An initial diagnosis of trichinosis relies heavily on the presence of the most classic symptoms of trichinosis (including swelling around the eyes, muscle inflammation, fever, and high levels of the blood cells called eosinophils), coupled with the patient's report of having eaten undercooked meat of a species known to potentially carry trichinosis.

The most common food culprit in the United States has been pork sausage, while outbreaks in Europe have been attributed to wild boar and horse meat, outbreaks in Asia and Africa have been due to dog meat, and outbreaks in Northern Canada have occurred due to consumption of walrus and bear meat.

Treatment

Treatment of trichinosis is primarily aimed at decreasing the severity of the symptomatology— bed rest and medications to relieve fever and muscle pain (aspirin, acetaminophen, or ibuprofen). Steroids (such as prednisone) are reserved for the most severe cases of muscle inflammation, or for complicated cases which include myocarditis.

KEY TERMS

Cyst—In the life cycle of the round worm, a protective, walled-off capsule in which the larvae lie dormant.

Embryonic—In the life cycle of the round worm, a very early life stage occurring within the uterus of the female round worm.

Inflammation—A reaction within the body to an invader (virus, bacteria, fungus, worm, etc.) or to tissue injury. The classic signs include redness, heat, pain, and loss of function.

Larva—In the life cycle of the round worm, the second stage of life, sometimes considered the "adolescent" stage.

Nematode—Roundworms belonging to the class Nematoda.

Striated muscle—Also known as striped muscle; includes muscles of the skeletal system and the heart.

Two related anti-worm medications (mebendazole and thiabendazole) have been reported to work against intestinal larvae, but not against larvae encysted in the muscles. In particular, thiabendazole has been effective when given to patients who knew within 24 hours that they had eaten infected meat.

Prevention

Prevention of trichinosis is relatively simple. Swine should be fed only grain or cooked garbage; uncooked garbage may contain contaminated pork scraps. Meats of animals prone to trichinosis infection should be cooked thoroughly, so that no pink is present. Freezing at an adequately low temperature (5° F /-15° C for one week or 0° F /-18° C for three weeks) can kill most encysted larvae, except those species which infect arctic mammals such as walrus or bear.

See also Roundworms.

Further Reading:

Andreoli, Thomas E. et al. *Cecil Essentials of Medicine.* Philadelphia: W.B. Saunders Company, 1993.
Berkow, Robert and Andrew J. Fletcher. *The Merck Manual of Diagnosis and Therapy.* Rahway, NJ: Merck Research Laboratories, 1992.
Isselbacher, Kurt J. et al. *Harrison's Principles of Internal Medicine.* New York: McGraw Hill, 1994.

Mandell, Douglas et al. *Principles and Practice of Infectious Diseases*. New York: Churchill Livingstone Inc., 1995.
Sherris, John C. et al. *Medical Microbiology*. Norwalk, CT: Appleton & Lange, 1994.

Rosalyn Carson-DeWitt

Triggerfish

Triggerfishes are members of the family Balistidae of the order Tetradontiformes. They derive their name from a unique feature of their dorsal fin. The triggerfish can lock the large dorsal spine in an upright position by supporting it with its smaller secondary spine. This protects the fish from predation by larger fish because the erect spine makes the fish hard to swallow or extract from small crevices. The locked dorsal spine can be "unlocked" by depressing the third spine or "trigger" which is connected to the second spine.

A distinctive characteristic of triggerfish is similarity in size and shape of the second dorsal (back) and anal fins. The belly in front of the anal fin is the widest circumference of the fish. The body of the triggerfish is protected by bony plates.

Triggerfishes are moderately large fish generally found on coral reefs widely distributed throughout the world, in all about 36 species. The gray triggerfish, *Balistes capriscus*, averages under 1 ft (0.3 m) in length but may grow to 2 ft (0.6 m) with a weight of 3 lb (1.4 kg). It is found in the warm waters of the Gulf of Mexico and the Mediterranean. These grayish fish often appear spotted or splotchy when swimming in among seaweeds.

Among the largest in the family is the ocean triggerfish, *Canthidermis sufflamen*, which grows to 2 ft (0.6 m) and weighs about 10 lb (4.5 kg). It ranges in distribution from the coast of Florida to the Caribbean. The ocean triggerfish is capable of making sounds like some of its relatives. One of ways it makes sound is by vibrating some muscles that are attached to its swim bladder.

Several species, such as the redtail triggerfish, are found in the western Pacific. The redtail, *Xanthichthys mento* is a 10 in (25 cm) fish with a purplish-blue color and a red tail. In contrast to the redtail triggerfish, the *Abalistes stellaris* may grow to 24 in (60 cm) in length.

Trigonometry

Trigonometry is a branch of applied mathematics concerned with the relationship between angles and their sides and the calculations based on them. First developed as a branch of geometry focusing on triangles during the third century B.C., trigonometry was used extensively for astronomical measurements. The major trigonometric functions, including sine, cosine, and tangent, were first defined as ratios of sides in a right triangle. Since trigonometric functions are intrinsically related, they can be used to determine the dimensions of any triangle given limited information. In the eighteenth century, the definitions of trigonometric functions were broadened by being defined as points on a unit circle. This allowed the development of graphs of functions related to the angles they represent which were periodic. Today, using the periodic nature of trigonometric functions, mathematicians and scientists have developed mathematical models to predict many natural periodic phenomena.

Historic development of trigonometry

The word trigonometry stems from the Greek words *trigonon*, which means *triangle*, and *metrein*, which means *to measure*. It began as a branch of geometry and was utilized extensively by early Greek mathematicians to determine unknown distances. The most notable examples are the use by Aristarchus (310-250 B.C.) to determine the distance to the Moon and Sun, and by Eratosthenes (c. 276-195 B.C.) to calculate the Earth's circumference. The general principles of trigonometry were formulated by the Greek astronomer, Hipparchus of Nicaea (active 162-127 B.C.), who is generally credited as the founder of trigonometry. His ideas were worked out by Ptolemy of Alexandria (c. 90-168 A.D.), who used them to develop the influential Ptolemaic theory of astronomy. Much of the information we know about the work of Hipparchus and Ptolemy comes from Ptolemy's compendium *The Almagest* written around 150.

Trigonometry was initially considered a field of the science of astronomy. It was later established as a separate branch of mathematics—largely through the work of the mathematicians Johann Bernoulli (1667-1748) and Leonhard Euler (1707-1783).

Angles

Central to the study of trigonometry is the concept of an angle. An angle is defined as a geometric figure created by two lines drawn from the same point, known as the vertex. The lines are called the sides of an angle and their length is one defining characteristic of an angle. Another characteristic of an angle is its measurement or magnitude, which is determined by the amount of rotation, around the vertex, required to transpose one side on top of the other. If one side is rotated completely around the point, the distance travelled is known as a revolution and the path it traces is a circle.

Angle measurements are typically given in units of degrees or radians. The unit of degrees, invented by the ancient Babylonians, divides one revolution into 360° (degrees). Angles which are greater than 360° represent a magnitude greater than one revolution. Radian units, which relate angle size to the radius of the circle formed by one revolution, divide a revolution into 2π units. For most theoretical trigonometric work, the radian is the primary unit of angle measurement.

Triangles and their properties

The principles of trigonometry were originally developed around the relationship between the sides of a triangle and its angles. The idea was that the unknown length of a side or size of an angle could be determined if the length or magnitude of some of the other sides or angles were known. Recall that a triangle is a geometric figure made up of three sides and three angles, whose sum is equal to 180°. The three points of a triangle, known as its vertices, are usually denoted by capital letters.

Triangles can be classified by the lengths of their sides or magnitude of their angles. Isosceles triangles have two equal sides and two congruent (equal) angles. Equilateral, or equiangular, triangles have three equal sides and angles. If no sides are equal, the triangle is a scalene triangle. All of the angles in an acute triangle are less than 90° and at least one of the angles in an obtuse triangle is greater than 90°. Triangles, such as these, which do not contain a 90° angle, are generally known as oblique triangles. Right triangles, the most important ones to trigonometry, are those which contain one 90° angle.

Triangles which have proportional sides and congruent angles are called similar triangles. The concept of similar triangles, one of the basic insights in trigonometry, allows us to determine the length of a side of one triangle if we know the length of certain sides of the other triangle. For example, if we wanted to know the height of a tree, we could use the idea of similar triangles to find it without actually having to measure it. Suppose a person is 6 ft (183 cm) tall and casts an 8 ft (2.44 m) long shadow. The tree, whose height is unknown, casts a shadow that is 20 ft (6.1 m) long. The

triangles that could be drawn using the shadows and objects as sides are similar. Since the sides of a similar triangles are proportional, the height of the tree is determined by setting up the mathematical equality

$$\frac{\text{height of tree}}{\text{length of tree shadow}} = \frac{\text{height of person}}{\text{length of person shadow}} = \frac{x}{20} = \frac{6}{8}$$

By solving this equation, the height of the tree is found to be 15 ft (4.57 m).

Right triangles and trigonometric functions

The triangles used in the previous example were right triangles. During the development of trigonometry, the parts of a right triangle were given certain names. The longest side of the triangle, which is directly across from the right angle, is known as the hypotenuse. The sides which form the right angle, denoted by a box in the diagram, are the legs of the triangle. For either acute angle in the triangle, the leg that forms the angle with the hypotenuse is known as the adjacent side. The side across from this angle is known as the opposite side. Typically, the length of each side is denoted by a lower case letter. In the diagram of triangle ABC, the length of the hypotenuse is indicated by c, the adjacent side is represented by b, and the opposite side by a. The angle of interest is usually represented by θ.

The ratios of the sides of a right triangle to each other are dependent on the magnitude of its acute angles. In mathematics, whenever one value depends on some other value, the relationship is known as a function. Therefore, the ratios in a right triangle are trigonometric functions of its acute angles. Since these relationships are of most importance in trigonometry, they are given special names. The ratio or number obtained by dividing the length of the opposite side by the hypotenuse is known as the sine of the angle θ (abbreviated sin θ). The ratio of the adjacent side to the hypotenuse is called the cosine of the angle θ (abbreviated cos θ). Finally, the ratio of the opposite side to the adjacent side is called the tangent of θ, or tan θ. In the triangle ABC , the trigonometric functions are represented by the following equations.

$$\sin\theta = \frac{a}{c} \quad \cos\theta = \frac{b}{c} \quad \tan\theta = \frac{a}{b} \quad \frac{\sin\theta}{\cos\theta}$$

These ratios represent the fundamental functions of trigonometry and should be committed to memory. Many mnemonic devices have been developed to help people remember the names of the functions and the ratios they represent. One of the easiest is the phrase

"SOH, CAH, TOA." This means: sine is the opposite over the hypotenuse, cosine is adjacent over hypotenuse, and tangent is opposite over adjacent.

In addition to the three fundamental functions, three reciprocal functions are also defined. The inverse of $\sin \theta$, or $1/\sin \theta$, is known as the secant of the angle or $\sec \theta$. The inverse of the $\cos \theta$ is the cosecant or $\csc \theta$. Finally, the inverse of the tangent is called the cotangent of $\cot \theta$. These functions are typically used in special instances.

The values of the trigonometric functions can be found in various ways. They can often be looked up in tables which have been compiled over the years. They can also be determined by using infinite series formulas. Conveniently, most calculators and computers have the values of trigonometric functions preprogrammed in.

Application of the trigonometric functions

One immediate application for trigonometric functions is the simple determination of the dimensions of a right triangle, also known as the solution of a triangle, when only a few are known. For example, if the sides of a right triangle are known, then the magnitude of both acute angles can be found. Suppose we have a right triangle whose sides are 2 in (5 cm) and 4.7 in (12 cm), and whose hypotenuse is 5.1 in (13 cm). The unknown angles could be found by using any trigonometric function. Since the sine of one of the angles is equal to the length of the opposite side divided by the hypotenuse, this angle can be determined. The sine of one angle is 5/13, or 0.385. With the help of a trigonometric function table or calculator, it will be found that the angle which has a sine of 0.385 is 22.6°. Using the fact that the sum of the angles in a triangle is 180°, we can establish that the other angle is 180° - 90° - 22.6° = 67.4°.

In addition to solving a right triangle, trigonometric functions can also be used in the determination of the area when given only limited information. The standard method of finding the area of a triangle is by using the formula, area = 1/2b (base) $\times$ h(altitude). Often, the altitude of a triangle is not known, but the sides and an angle are known. Using the side-angle-side (SAS) theorem, the formula for the area of a triangle then becomes, area = 1/2 (one side) $\times$ (another side) $\times$ (sine of the included angle). For a triangle with sides of 5 cm and 3 cm respectively and an included angle of 60°, the area of the triangle would be equal to $1/2 \times 5 \times 3 \times \sin 60°$ = 13 cm^2.

The formula for the area of a triangle leads to an important concept in trigonometry known as the Law of Sines which says that for any triangle, the sine of each angle is proportional to the opposite its opposite side, symbolically written,

in triangle ABC, $\dfrac{\sin A}{a} = \dfrac{\sin B}{b} = \dfrac{\sin C}{c}$

Using the Law of Sines, we can solve any triangle if we know the length of one side and magnitude of two angles, or two sides and one angle. Suppose we have a triangle with angles of 45° and 70°, and an included side of 15.7 in (40 cm). The third angle is found to be 180° - 45° - 70° = 65°. The unknown sides, x and y, are found with the Law of Sines because

$$\frac{\sin 45}{x} = \frac{\sin 70}{y} = \frac{\sin 65}{40}$$

The lengths of the unknown sides are then x = 12.29 in (31.2 cm) and y = 16.35 in (41.5 cm).

The Law of Sines can not be used to solve a triangle unless at least one angle is known. However, a triangle can be solved if only the sides are known by using the Law of Cosines which is stated in triangle ABC, $c^2 = a^2 + b^2 - 2ab \cos C$, or can be written

$$\cos C = \frac{a^2 + b^2 - c^2}{2ab}$$

which is more convenient when using only the sides to solve a triangle. As an example, consider a triangle with sides equal to 2 in, 3.5 in, and 3.9 in (5 cm, 9 cm, and 10 cm). The cosine of one angle would be equal to $(5^2 + 9^2 - 10^2)/(2 \times 5 \times 9)$ = 0.067, which corresponds to the angle 86.2°. Similarly, the other two angles are found to be 29.9° and 63.9°.

Relationships between trigonometric functions

In addition to the reciprocal relationships of certain trigonometric functions, two other types of relationships exist. These relationships, known as trigonometric identities, include cofunctional relationships and Pythagorean relationships. Cofunctional relationships relate functions by their complementary angles. Pythagorean relationships relate functions by application of the Pythagorean theorem.

The sine and cosine of an angle are considered cofunctions, as are the secant and cosecant, and the tangent and cotangent.

The Pythagorean Theorem states that the sum of the squares of the sides of a right triangle is equal to the square of the hypotenuse. For a triangle with sides of x and y and a hypotenuse of z, the equation for the Pythagorean Theorem is $x^2 + y^2 = z^2$. Applying this theorem to the trigonometric functions of an angle, we find that $\sin^2 \theta + \cos^2 \theta = 1$. Similarly, $1 + \tan^2 \theta = \sec^2 \theta$ and $1 + \cot^2 \theta = \csc^2 \theta$. The terms such as $\sin^2\theta$ or $\tan^2\theta$ traditionally have meant $(\sin\theta)\times(\sin\theta)$ or $(\tan\theta)\times(\tan\theta)$.

In some instances, it is desirable to know the trigonometric function of the sum or difference of two angles. If we have two unknown angles, θ and ϕ, then $\sin (\theta + \phi)$ is equal to $\sin\theta\cos\phi + \cos\theta\sin\phi$. In a similar manner, their difference, $\sin(\theta-\phi)$ is $\sin\theta\cos\phi - \cos\theta\sin\phi$. Equations for determining the sum or differences of the cosine and tangent also exist and can be stated as follows.

$\cos(\theta \pm \phi) = \cos\theta\cos\phi \pm \sin\theta\sin\phi$ $\tan (\theta \pm \phi) = (\tan \theta \pm \tan \phi)/(1 \pm \tan\theta\tan\phi)$

These relationships can be used to develop formulas for double angles and half angles. Therefore, the $\sin 2\theta = 2\sin\theta\cos\theta$ and $\cos 2\theta = 2\cos^2\theta - 1$ which could also be written $\cos 2\theta = 1 - 2\sin^2\theta$.

Trigonometry using circles

For hundreds of years, trigonometry was only considered useful for determining sides and angles of a triangle. However, when mathematicians developed more general definitions for sine, cosine and tangent, trigonometry became much more important in mathematics and science alike. The general definitions for the trigonometric functions were developed by considering these values as points on a unit circle.

A unit circle is one which has a radius of one unit which means $x^2 + y^2 = 1$. If we consider the circle to represent the rotation of a side of an angle, then the trigonometric functions can be defined by the x and y coordinates of the point of rotation. For example, coordinates of point $P(x,y)$ can be used to define a right triangle with a hypotenuse of length r. The trigonometric functions could then be represented by the following equations.

$$\sin \theta = \frac{y}{r}; \quad \cos \theta = \frac{x}{r}; \quad \tan \theta = \frac{y}{x}$$

With the trigonometric functions defined as such, a graph of each can be developed by plotting its value versus the magnitude of the angle it represents.

Since the value for x and y can never be greater than one on a unit circle, the range for the sine and cosine graphs is between 1 and -1. The magnitude of an angle can be any real number, so the domain of the graphs is all real numbers. (Angles which are greater than 360° or 2π radians represent an angle with more than one revolution of rotation). The sine and cosine graphs are periodic because they repeat their values, or have a period,

KEY TERMS
. . . .

Adjacent side—The side of a right triangle which forms one side of the angle in question.

Amplitude—A characteristic of a periodic graph represented by half the distance between its maximum and minimum.

Angle—A geometric figure created by two lines drawn from the same point.

Cosine—A trigonometric function which relates the ratio of the adjacent side of a right triangle to its hypotenuse, or the x coordinate of a point on a unit circle.

Degree—A unit of measurement of an angle which divides one revolution into 360 parts.

Hypotenuse—The longest side of a right triangle which is opposite the right angle.

Law of cosines—A relationship between the cosine of an angle of a triangle and its sides which can be used to determine the dimensions of a triangle.

Law of sines—A relationship between the sine of an angle of a triangle and its side which can be used to determine the dimensions of a triangle.

Opposite side—The side of a right triangle which is opposite the angle in question.

Period—A value at which a periodic function begins to repeat.

Pythagorean Theorem—A mathematical relationship which states that the sum of the squares of the sides in a right triangle is equal to the square of the hypotenuse.

Radian—A unit of angular measurement which relates the radius of a circle to the amount of rotation of the angle. One complete revolution is equal to 2π radians.

Right triangle—A triangle which contains a 90° or right angle

Similar triangles—Triangles which have congruent angles and proportional sides.

Sine—A trigonometric function which represents the ratio of the opposite side of a right triangle to its hypotenuse, or the y coordinate of a point on a unit circle.

Tangent—A trigonometric function which represents the ratio of the opposite side of right triangle to its adjacent side.

Trigonometric functions—Angular functions which can be described as ratios of the sides of a right triangle to each other.

every 360° or 2π radians. They also have an amplitude of one which is defined as half the difference between the maximum (1) and minimum (-1) values.

Graphs of the other trigonometric functions are possible. Of these, the most important is the graph of the tangent function. Like the sine and cosine graphs, the tangent function is periodic, but it has a period of 180° or π radians. Since the tangent is equal to y/x, its range is -∞ to ∞ and its amplitude is ∞.

The periodicity of trigonometric functions is more important to modern trigonometry than the ratios they represent. Mathematicians and scientists are now able to describe many types of natural phenomena which reoccur periodically with trigonometric functions. For example, the times of sunsets, sunrises, and comets can all be calculated thanks to trigonometric functions. Also, they can be used to describe seasonal temperature changes, the movement of waves in the ocean, and even the quality of a musical sound.

See also Function; Pythagorean theorem.

Further Reading:

Paulos, John Allen. *Beyond Numeracy*. New York: Knopf, 1991.
Brown, Richard, and David Robbins. *Advanced Mathematics*. Boston: Houghton Mifflin, 1981.
Hostetler, Robert, and Roland Larson. *Calculus with Analytic Geometry*. Lexington: D. C. Heath, 1986.
Thompson, J. E. *Trigonometry for the Practical Worker*. New York: Van Nostrand Reinhold, 1982.

Perry Romanowski

Trillium see **Lily family**

Triple bond see **Chemical bond**

Tritium

Tritium is an isotope of the chemical element hydrogen. It has not only a single proton but also two neutrons in the nucleus of its atoms. Although technically it is still the element hydrogen, it has its own chemical symbol, T. Chemically, tritium reacts in exactly the same manner as hydrogen, although slightly slower because of its greater atomic weight. A tritium atom has almost three times the mass of a regular hydrogen atom: the atomic weight of tritium is 3.016 whereas the atomic weight of hydrogen is 1.008. Tritium is radioactive, with a half-life of 12.26 years. Its

nucleus emits a low-energy beta particle, leaving behind an isotope of helium, helium-3, that has a single neutron in its atomic nucleus. (The common isotope of helium, helium-4, contains two neutrons in its atomic nucleus.) No gamma rays, which are high-energy electromagnetic radiation, are emitted in the decay of tritium, so the radioactive decay of tritium is of little hazard to humans.

The heavier atomic weight of tritium has an effect on the physical properties of this hydrogen isotope. For example, tritium has a boiling point of -414.6°F (-248.1°C, 25 K), compared with ordinary hydrogen's boiling point of -423°F (-252.8°C, 20.4 K). Molecules containing tritium show similar variances. For example, water made with tritium and having the formula T_2O has a melting point of 40°F (4.5°C), compared with 32°F (0°C) for normal water.

Tritium was present in nature at very low levels, about 1 atom every 10^{18} atoms of hydrogen, before atmospheric nuclear bomb testing. It is produced in the upper atmosphere, as highly-energetic neutrons in cosmic rays bombard nitrogen atoms, making a tritium atom and an atom of carbon-12.

$$N + neutron \rightarrow T + C$$

Industrially, tritium is prepared by bombarding deuterium with other deuterium atoms to make a tritium atom and a regular hydrogen atom:

$$D + D \rightarrow T + H$$

The resulting two types of hydrogen can be separated by distillation. Another way to make tritium is to bombard lithium-6 atoms (the less-abundant isotope of lithium) with neutrons, which produces a helium atom and a tritium atom:

$$Li + neutron \rightarrow T + He$$

Due to the testing of nuclear weapons in the atmosphere (before such testing was banned), the tritium content of the atmosphere rose to ~500 atoms per 10^{18}, declining steadily even since the ban due to radioactive decay.

Tritium is used in nuclear fusion processes because it is easier to fuse tritium nuclei than either of the other isotopes of hydrogen. However, because of its scarcity, it is commonly used with deuterium in fusion reactions:

$$T + D \rightarrow He + neutron + energy$$

This is the nuclear reaction that occurs in fusion bombs, or hydrogen bombs. Such weapons must be recharged periodically due to the radioactive decay of the tritium. Fusion reactions are also being used in experimental fusion reactors as scientists and engineers

KEY TERMS

. . . .

Beta particle—One type of radioactive decay particle emitted from radioactive atomic nuclei. A beta particle is the same thing as an electron.

try to develop controllable nuclear fusion for peaceful power.

Tritium is used as a tracer because it is relatively easy to detect due to its radioactivity. In groundwater studies, tritium-labeled water can be released into the ground at one point, and the amount of tritium-labeled water that appears at other points can be monitored. In this way, the flow of water through the ground can be mapped. Such information is important when drilling oil fields, for example. Tritium can also be substituted for ordinary hydrogen in organic compounds and used to study biological reactions. Because of its radioactivity, it is easy to follow the tritium as it participates in biochemical reactions. In this way, specific metabolic processes at the cellular level can be monitored. Tritium is also used to make "glow-in-the-dark" objects by mixing tritium-containing compounds with compounds like zinc sulfide, which emit light when struck by alpha or beta particles from nuclear decay.

See also Hydrogen; Isotope; Nuclear fusion; Radioactive tracers.

Further Reading:

Evans, E.A. *Tritium and its compounds*. New York: Wiley, Inc., 1974.

Herman, R. *Fusion: The Search for Endless Energy*. Oxford: Cambridge University Press, 1990.

Ihde, A.J. *The Development of Modern Chemistry*. New York: Dover Publications, Inc., 1984.

Romer, A. *Radioactivity and the Discovery of Isotopes*. New York: Dover Publications, Inc., 1970.

David W. Ball

Trogons

Trogons are about 35 species of beautiful arboreal birds that constitute the family Trogonidae. Trogons have a number of peculiar features in their morphology, and are thought to not be closely related to any other groups of living birds. This is why their family is the only one in the order Trogoniformes.

Species of trogons occur throughout the tropical and subtropical parts of the world, a biogeographic distribution that is known as pan-tropical. Most species of trogons occur in Central and especially South America, with three species in Africa, and 11 species in Asia. Most trogons live in dense forests and woodlands, and are unobtrusive birds that tend to sit and fly quietly and are not often seen. Trogons do not undertake long-distance migrations, although some species may make local, seasonal movements.

Trogons range in body length from 9-13.5 in (23-34 cm). The bill of trogons is short and wide, and the upper mandible is hooked at the tip. These birds have short, rounded wings, and a long, broad, square-ended tail. Their legs and feet are small and weak, and are only used for perching. The toe arrangement of trogons is of an unusual and distinctive pattern known as heterodactylous, in which the first and second digits point backwards, and the third and fourth forwards. This arrangement of the toes occurs in no other group of birds.

Trogons are colorful birds, with bold patterns of bright red, green, blue, yellow, black, or white. There is bare, brightly colored skin around the eye. The tail has two rows of large white spots underneath. The sexes are dimorphic, having differing plumages in most species. Female trogons are beautiful birds, but somewhat less so than the males.

Trogons feed largely on insects and spiders, although species of the Americas also eat large quantities of fruits. Some species also eat snails, small lizards, and frogs. Trogons spend much of their time perched in a stiffly erect stance on mid-canopy branches, making occasional sallies to catch insects or pluck fruits, often using a hovering flight.

Trogons are solitary birds. They defend a breeding territory, which is proclaimed by simple calls. Their nests are located in a cavity excavated in rotten wood in a tree, or dug into a termite nest or paper-wasp nest. Trogons lay 2-4 pale-colored, unspotted eggs, which are incubated by both parents. The nestlings are born naked and almost helpless, and are fed by insects regurgitated by the parents. Both sexes share in the care and feeding of the young.

Species of trogons

Most species of trogons are tropical in their distribution. One species, however, breeds as far north as the United States. This is the coppery-tailed or elegant trogon (*Trogon elegans*), which breeds in mountain forests of southern Arizona, and south into Central America

KEY TERMS
. . . .

Dimorphic—This refers to species in which the sexes differ in size, shape, or coloration.

Heterodactyly—An arrangement of the toes, in which the first two point backwards, and the third and fourth forwards. This only occurs in the trogons.

One of the best known of the Central American trogons is the resplendent quetzal (*Pharomachrus mocino*), which ranges from Mexico to Nicaragua. This species is brilliantly colored, with the male having greenish hues on the back, breast, tail, and crested head, a vivid red belly, black around the eyes and wings, and yellow bill and feet. The tail of the resplendent quetzal is extended by 24 in (60 cm) long plumes, several times longer than the body. This impressive tail is the origin of an alternative common name, the train-bearer.

The resplendent quetzal was sacred to the Maya and Aztecs, and represented the god Quetzalcoatl. This bird is still a culturally important symbol within its range. Stylized renditions of quetzals are prominent in much of the folk art in Central America, particularly in Guatemala, where it is the national bird. Unfortunately, the quetzal has become extremely rare over much of its range, because of deforestation and hunting.

The red-headed trogon (*Harpactes erythrocephalus*) is a relatively widespread Asian species, occurring from Nepal and south China through Indochina to Sumatra in Indonesia. The male has a bright red head and breast, a cinnamon back and tail, and black wings, while the female lacks the red head. The Narina trogon (*Apaloderma narina*) occurs over much of sub-Saharan Africa. The blue-crowned trogon (*Trogon curucui*) is a widespread species of American tropical forests, breeding from Columbia to northern Argentina.

The Cuban trogon (*Priotelus temnurus*) only occurs on that island, while the Hispaniolan trogon (*Temnotrogon roseigaster*) only occurs on Hispaniola (Haiti and the Dominican Republic). These are both monotypic genera, each containing one species, both of which are rare and endangered, mostly because of habitat loss.

Further Reading:
Harrison, C. J. O., ed. *Bird Families of the World.* New York: H. N. Abrams, 1978.

Bill Freedman

Trophic levels

Trophic levels describe the various stages within ecological food chains or webs. Examples of trophic levels, all of which will be described below, are primary producers, primary consumers or herbivore, and secondary and higher-level consumers, or predators.

Food webs are based on the productivity of photosynthetic organisms, such as blue-green bacteria, algae, and plants. These are autotrophic organisms, which are capable of fixing some of the diffuse energy of solar radiation into simple organic compounds. This fixed energy can then be utilized by the primary producers to metabolically synthesize a diverse array of biochemicals and to support the growth of these organisms.

The solar energy fixed by photosynthesis is the energetic base that all heterotrophic organisms utilize to achieve their own productivity. Heterotrophic organisms include any animals and microorganisms that feed on the living or dead biomass of plants, or that of other heterotrophs. Heterotrophs include herbivores that feed directly on autotrophs, carnivores that feed on other animals, detritivores that feed on dead biomass, and omnivores that feed on any or all of the above.

Therefore, the food web is a diverse assembly of organisms that are ecologically linked through their feeding relationships, and is ultimately based on the fixation of solar radiation through photosynthesis.

Primary producers

Primary producers are autotrophic organisms that are capable of fixing solar radiation into biochemical energy, through the process of photosynthesis. Photosynthesis is comprised of a series of enzyme-mediated chemical reactions which result in the combination of carbon dioxide and water into glucose, a simple sugar. This chemical reaction requires an input of energy to proceed, and this energy is provided by red and blue wavelengths of solar radiation, which are captured by the photosynthetic pigment chlorophyll. The fixed-energy content of the glucose can then be utilized to drive a great diversity of other metabolic reactions, which are used to synthesize the myriad other biochemicals that are found in the tissues of primary producers.

Primary producers include green plants, algae, and blue-green bacteria. If the rate of photosynthesis by these organisms exceeds their metabolic requirements, then they are able to grow, and their biomass increases.

Primary consumers

The accumulating biomass of primary producers is

a source of fixed energy that can be utilized by heterotrophic organisms by directly feeding on the autotrophic biomass. The primary consumers of autotrophic biomass are also known as herbivores and include the tiny crustacean zooplankton that filter microscopic algal cells out of the surface waters of lakes, ponds, and oceans, as well as much larger, mammalian herbivores, such as mice, deer, cows, and elephants. Herbivores utilize the fixed energy and nutrients in their food of autotrophic biomass to drive their own metabolic processes and to achieve their own growth.

Secondary and higher-order consumers

Herbivores may be fed upon by other heterotrophs, which are known as secondary consumers. If the herbivore must be killed before it is eaten, the secondary consumer is known as a predator. However, if the herbivore does not have to be killed to be eaten, the secondary consumer is known as a parasite. Predators of the tiny zooplankton described in the previous section include somewhat larger, carnivorous zooplankton, as well as small fish. In terrestrial ecosystems, herbivorous mice may be fed upon by predatory weasels and hawks, while deer are killed and eaten by coyotes and cougars.

If the resource base of the ecosystem is large enough, the secondary consumers may be killed and eaten by higher-order consumers, which will generally be the top predators in the system. For example, mature lake trout may be at the top of the food web of a temperate-lake ecosystem, in which the trophic structure is organized as: algae ... herbivorous zooplankton ... predatory zooplankton and small fish ... and the largest predatory fish, such as lake trout. If bald eagles or humans subsequently predate on the lake trout, they would be considered the top predators in the system as well as a trophic linkage to the terrestrial part of the larger ecosystem.

Detritivores

All organisms eventually die, and detritivores are a class of organisms that feed on their dead bodies. Actually, detritivores can themselves be divided into a food web, based on the feeding relationships among the species. In this sense, primary detritivores feed directly on the dead biomass, while secondary detritivores feed on these direct consumers of detritus.

Omnivores

Omnivores are animals that feed at various places within the food web and are therefore difficult to classify in terms of trophic level. For example, grizzly bears are highly opportunistic animals that feed quite widely,

KEY TERMS

Autotroph—This refers to organisms that can synthesize their biochemical constituents using inorganic precursors and an external source of energy.

Heterotrophic—This refers to organisms that require a source of organic matter as food. Compare with: autotroph.

Trophic—Pertaining to the means of nutrition.

on sedges and berries, small mammals, fish, and dead animals (or carrion). Of course, humans are the most omnivorous of all species—we eat just about anything that is not acutely poisonous, and in turn are not eaten by many other creatures, except, eventually, by detritivores.

See also Autotroph; Carnivore; Food chain/web; Herbivore; Omnivore.

Further Reading:

Odum, E.P. *Ecology and Our Endangered Life Support Systems.* New York: Sinauer, 1993.
Ricklefs, R.E. *Ecology.* New York: W.H. Freeman and Co., 1990.

Bill Freedman

Tropic birds

Tropic birds are three species of pan-tropical seabirds that make up the family Phaethontidae, in the order Pelecaniformes, which also includes the pelicans, anhingas, cormorants, gannets, and boobies.

Tropic birds are medium-sized seabirds, weighing about 0.9 lbs (0.4 kg), and having a body length of 16-18.9 in (41-48 cm). This length does not include their greatly elongated tail feathers, which are shaped as streamers that themselves can be 21 in (51-cm) long. The wings of tropic birds are short, stout, and pointed, and their legs are short and the feet small, and the toes completely webbed. Their beak is stout, pointed, and slightly down-curved, with serrated edges to help hold on to their slippery prey of fish or squid.

The usual coloration of the body is white, with black markings on the head and wings. The bill is colored either bright-red or yellow, and the tail-streamer is prized in many species. These streamers are either white or red, depending on the ornaments in Polynesian cultures. The sexes are alike in size and coloration.

Tropic birds have a loud, shrill, piercing scream, which is the origin of one of the common names of these birds, the bosun bird. (Bosuns or boatswains are petty ship's-officers, responsible for maintenance of the ship and its gear, and equipped with a loud, shrill whistle, used to catch the attention of sailors.)

Tropic birds are strong and graceful fliers, typically exhibiting bouts of fluttering, pigeon-like wing-strokes, punctuated by short, straight glides and soaring flights. Tropic birds do not swim well, and they float with their tail held in a cocked, erect position. These birds are extremely awkward on land, and can barely walk.

Tropic birds feed using partially closed-winged, aerial plunge-dives to catch their food of small fish or squid near the surface. They can even catch flying fish, while the fish are in the air. Tropic birds generally occur as solitary birds in off-shore, pelagic waters outside of their breeding season. They may, however, mix with large, feeding flocks of other species, such as shearwaters and terns.

The courtship of tropic birds involves the potential pair engaging in graceful, aerial wheelings and glides, with loud cries. Occasionally one bird will hover over the other, touching it with the tip of its tail-streamer. Tropic birds lay their single egg in a simple scrape in a hidden cavity on a rocky, near-shore cliff, or sometimes under a bush. Both sexes incubate the egg, and they share in guarding and feeding their white-downy, young chick. Juvenile birds leave their birth island as soon as they can fly, and return when they reach sexual maturity. Tropic birds may breed throughout the year.

Species of tropic birds

The red-billed tropic bird (*P. aethereus*) occurs in the tropical Caribbean, Atlantic, eastern Pacific, and Indian Oceans.

The tail-streamer of this species is white, and the upper parts of its body are barred with white and brown.

The red-tailed tropic bird (*P. rubricauda*) occurs in the tropical Indian and Pacific Oceans, but in different regions of those oceans than the red-billed tropic bird. The red-tailed tropic bird has a bright-white body, and a red streamer.

The white-tailed or yellow-billed tropic bird (*P. sepeurus*) occurs in all of the tropical oceans. This smallest tropic bird has a white body, with black patches on its wings and back, a relatively small, yellow beak, and a white streamer.

None of the tropic birds breed in North America. However, all species are rare visitors to coastal waters of the southern United States, especially after a heavy wind-storm. The red-billed tropic bird is a regular but rare bird off southern California, while the white-tailed tropic bird occurs off the southeastern states in the warm Atlantic, Gulf of Mexico, and Caribbean. The red-tailed tropic bird is a very rare visitor to southern California.

Further Reading:

Harrison, C.J.O. *Bird Families of the World*. New York: H.N. Abrams Pubs., 1978.
Harrison, P. *Seabirds. An Identification Guide*. Beckenham. U.K. Croom Helm, 1983.

Bill Freedman

Tropical cyclone

Tropical cyclones are large circulating storm systems consisting of multiple bands of intense showers and thunderstorms and extremely high winds. These storm systems develop over warm ocean waters in the tropical regions that lie within 23.5° latitude of the equator. Tropical cyclones may begin as isolated thunderstorms. If conditions are right they grow and intensify to form the storm systems known as hurricanes in the Americas, typhoons in East Asia, willy-willy in Australia, cyclones in Australia and India, and baguios in the Philippines. A fully developed tropical cyclone is a circular complex of thunderstorms about 403 mi (650 km) in diameter and over 7.5 mi (12 km) high. Winds near the core of the cyclone can exceed 110 mph (50 meters/second). At the center of the storm is a region about 9-12.5 mi (15-20 km) across called the eye where the winds are light and skies are often clear. After forming and reaching peak strength over tropical seas tropical cyclones may blow inshore, causing significant damage and loss of life. The storm destruction occurs by very high winds and forcing rapid rises in sea level which flood low lying coastal areas. Better forecasting and emergency planning has lowered the death tolls in recent years from these extremely powerful storms.

Tropical cyclone geography and season

Several portions of the seas ringing the equator possess all the necessary conditions for forming tropical cyclones. These spots are: the West Indies/Caribbean

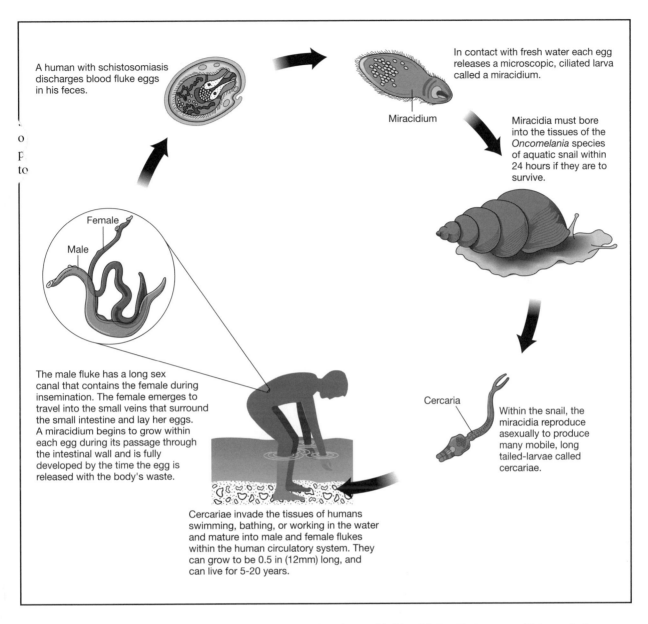

A human with schistosomiasis discharges blood fluke eggs in his feces.

In contact with fresh water each egg releases a microscopic, ciliated larva called a miracidium.

Miracidium

Miracidia must bore into the tissues of the *Oncomelania* species of aquatic snail within 24 hours if they are to survive.

Female

Male

The male fluke has a long sex canal that contains the female during insemination. The female emerges to travel into the small veins that surround the small intestine and lay her eggs. A miracidium begins to grow within each egg during its passage through the intestinal wall and is fully developed by the time the egg is released with the body's waste.

Cercaria

Within the snail, the miracidia reproduce asexually to produce many mobile, long tailed-larvae called cercariae.

Cercariae invade the tissues of humans swimming, bathing, or working in the water and mature into male and female flukes within the human circulatory system. They can grow to be 0.5 in (12mm) long, and can live for 5-20 years.

The life cycle of *Schistosoma japonicum*, one of three species of parasitic blood flukes that cause schistosomiasis.

as measles and diarrhea, are well known in developed areas such as the United States but are rarely fatal.

Young people are highly susceptible to death from disease in these areas. Children under five account for 40 to 60% of all deaths in Africa, Asia, and South America, although they make up only about 15% of the population. Such high death rates reflect the fact that tropical diseases are most prevalent in poor areas where health care is limited. Efforts to improve community health in areas where tropical diseases thrive include the establishment of health clinics and the development of new vaccines.

Battles against malaria

Malaria, a parasitic disease spread by mosquitoes, is the best-known tropical disease and infects the largest number of people internationally. It has been called the "most devastating disease in history" based on the number of people it has attacked or killed. Currently, malaria has been identified in about 100 countries, although 80% of the clinical cases are reported in Africa.

The history of malaria is different than the history of other tropical diseases, due to its immense reach and the concerted effort over time to defeat the disease. But in as much as it has been eliminated or controlled in developed countries and remains a major killer in those that are poor and less developed, its history is also similar to that of other tropical diseases.

The ancient Chinese wrote about malaria as early as 2,700 B.C., describing the symptomatic fever and characteristic enlargement of the spleen. Ancient Greeks and Romans also suffered from malaria. Hippocrates (460-375 B.C.), offered an accurate account of malarial symptoms and theorized that the disease was caused by a miasma, or poisonous cloud, rising up from marshy land.

The first effective treatment for malaria was developed in the seventeenth century and utilized a traditional Peruvian treatment for fever, the cinchona tree bark. In 1630, Jesuit missionaries in Peru introduced the bark of the cinchona tree to Europeans. The active substance in the bark, quinine, was isolated in 1820. Though there were common, serious side effects to the drug, such as ringing of the ears and hearing loss, the substance was effective in treating malaria, which was common in Europe at that time.

Development of a treatment for malaria cleared the way for large scale exploration of tropical areas by Europeans. Development of a synthetic quinine, called chloroquine, in the 1940s, offered effective treatment with fewer common side effects. In the 1960s, malarial parasites became resistant to chloroquine, and the substance no longer worked in many areas.

The most recent effort to control malaria has been effective in many areas, including the southern United States. The pesticide DDT was used, successfully, in the Tennessee River Valley, Greece, Puerto Rico and other locations to kill the mosquitoes carrying malaria and eliminate the disease. A world campaign to eliminate malaria internationally used DDT from 1956-1969. However, mosquitoes became resistant to DDT and the effort failed.

There are four different types of malaria protozoa. One of the four, *P. falciparum,* is responsible for almost all deaths from the disease. Symptoms of the disease do not occur for one to two weeks. They often include chills, muscle aches, fatigue and abdominal discomfort. They may include tremors and high fever which comes and goes at regularly spaced intervals. Complications from severe malaria include renal failure, pulmonary edema, coma and hypoglycemia.

The delayed appearance of malaria's symptoms reflects the measured course the disease takes in the body. The activity of the malaria parasite in the body is aggressive and thorough. The disease is spread by female anopheline mosquitos that inject malaria parasites into the bloodstream with their bite. The parasites,

called sporozoites, travel to the liver, where they enter cells of the liver tissue. Once in the liver, the sporozoite changes to a spore, which replicates itself until there are thousands of spores in a cyst-like structure which has replaced the cell. Malaria manifests no symptoms while this process occurs.

Symptoms develop when the cyst bursts and the spores, called merozoites, are released into the blood stream. At this point, sweating and high fever can occur as the spores enter the host's red blood cells. The parasite consumes hemoglobin from within the red blood cells.

As the parasite grows from consuming the hemoglobin, its nucleus divides into from 6 to 32 parts, each of which becomes a spore of its own. The red cell bursts, and the spore moves to another cell.

After the merozoites have launched their process of reproducing in the red blood cells of the host, some of the merozoites are transformed to male or female gametocytes. These sexual cells form the base for more parasites if the host is bitten again by the female anopheles mosquito. When this occurs, the gametocytes develop into a number of differentiated cells, called gametes, zygotes, ookinetes and oocysts, within the gut of the mosquito. Eventually the parasite reproduces, and sporozoites which travel in the mosquito are formed. These sporozoites move up to the mosquito's salivary gland, where they are ready to infect another host.

Treatment of malaria is usually effective. Because many malaria parasites are resistant to chloroquine, physicians have returned to using quinine in many instances. Travelers and others at risk of malaria receive chloroquine or other drugs, including mefloquine, if journeying to areas where the drugs still work. However, there is no totally effective preventive measure against malaria.

The deadly sandfly and leishmaniasis

Another disease spread by insects is leishmaniasis, a sickness caused by several types of protozoa carried by sand flies. In the mid 1990s, the disease was infecting about 12 million people worldwide, killing about 1,000 annually. It is spread when sand flies draw blood from individuals who already are infected. Hosts can be humans, dogs, or other mammals.

Each of the four major clinical syndromes of the disease have a long incubation period that ranges from three months to 24 months. The disease is marked by one or more skin lesions and varies in severity depending on the type. Kala Azar, one of the types, is commonly found in East Africa and the Sahara. Kala Azar

A skin lesion from cutaneous leishmaniasis.

causes fever, diarrhea, enlarged liver and anemia. Another type, Old World leishmaniasis, usually heals on its own and is marked by multiple lesions.

Treatment depends on the type of leishmaniasis and may include the use of drug therapy and transfusions for several weeks. The need for extended medical care makes treatment of leishmaniasis impossible for many poor individuals in developing countries, raising the mortality rate of the disease.

Dangerous worms

Ascariasis and hookworm

A common disease in tropical countries is ascariasis. The annual death rate due to ascariasis is about 20,000, most due to complications within the intestine, where the worms settle as adults. An estimated 700 million individuals are affected at any given time by the disease.

Ascariasis is spread through dirt. The worm which grows in the intestine, the roundworm *Ascaris lumbricoides,* is the largest such parasite, growing to a length of 19.3 in (49 cm). It can live about a year in the human body.

The disease can cause difficulties, such as bronchial asthma, in the lungs, when the parasite settles in that part of the body. The greatest threat to the human host is the loss of food nutrients which go to the worm instead of the host. Individuals whose diet is already sparse may suffer from malnutrition after infection with ascariasis.

The life cycle of the creature is similar to the life cycle of the blood fluke, though there are some differences. The disease is spread when Ascaris eggs leave the human host in feces. The new host ingests the eggs through soil or by soil-contaminated hands or food. The

eggs then travel through the liver, lungs and throat, before ending up in the intestine. Once they are in the intestine, more eggs are laid, clearing the way for further spread of the disease.

Another parasite that is spread through dirt and grows in the human body is hookworm, which affects approximately 800 million individuals in the developing world and kills about 50,000 annually. Hookworm was at one point common in the American South, but is now seldom reported in the area.

The hookworm, which grows up to 0.5 in (13 mm) in size, sucks blood and normally lives in the small intestine. Establishment of the worm in the host generally results in iron-deficiency anemia because of blood loss, and may cause bronchitis, peptic ulcers, or even heart problems.

Hookworms enter the body as larvae through the skin, taking advantage of hair follicles or other openings to help the creature pierce through the skin with its boring movement. The parasite enters the circulatory system, moving first to the lungs then to the pharynx, where it is swallowed. The final larvae stage typically occurs in the small intestine, where adult worms emerge and ultimately lay eggs. Adult worms normally live from one to 5 years if the host is not treated. They cannot multiply in the body.

Successful control of the hookworm depends on improvements in plumbing and the use of footwear, a challenge in countries where shoes are a luxury. Medication is available to destroy hookworm, but providing it in areas where hookworm infestation is severe does little to alter the problem, as those who are medicated can easily be reinfected.

Schistosomiasis

One of the most common tropical diseases is schistosomiasis, a disease caused by a worm called a blood fluke. The worm, which can be about 0.47 in (12 mm) long, can live in the human body from five to 20 years. About 200 million people are infected by the worm in developing countries, with as many as 500,000 deaths due to the disease each year.

Symptoms include abdominal pain, diarrhea, and weight loss. If untreated, the disease can cause enlargement of the liver, bleeding from blood vessels in the esophagus, and problems to the central nervous system.

The worm, which is usually hosted by Biomphalaria snails, depends on fresh water to survive. The disease is common in areas where bathing occurs in fresh water contaminated by human feces and where many individuals have the disease.

The life cycle of the blood fluke entails travel throughout the human body and through the body of its other host, the snail. The worm enters the human body in a larval stage in fresh water through contact with human skin. The larva enter a blood or lymph vessel and move to the heart and lungs, where they grow for several days. Then they move to the liver and the portal circulation, where they grow for several weeks.

Ultimately, the worms move to the intestinal wall, where they settle. The creatures lay eggs which are released in feces and become new larva after contact with fresh water. These larva enter the host snail, where they eventually produce cercariae, the final larval stage. These are the creatures that enter the human body after contact with skin.

Drug therapy is an effective treatment for the disease. Prevention efforts depend on controlling infection through drug therapy and on convincing individuals to steer clear of fresh water which may be infected.

Microscopic hazard

Amebiasis, a disease caused by a microscopic protozoa spread through dirty water, infects as many as 500 million individuals in the developing world. The disease kills about 70,000 people annually.

The protozoa can live in the large intestine and not cause damage to the host. But it is also capable of causing ulceration of the colonic wall and damage to the liver and other organs, including the brain.

The disease is spread through water contaminated by fecal matter, by contaminated flies, or by other contaminated substances. Hosts swallow cysts, which divide in the small intestine and again in the large intestine to form amoebae. These amoebae divide and form trophozoites, which feed on fecal bacteria. These trophozoites form cysts and are passed out in the feces of the host. This entire cycle takes from 48 hours to four months.

Diarrhea and cholera

Best known in the United States as a benign but unpleasant condition, diarrhea is one of the leading causes of death in developing countries. Indeed, diarrhea causes about 4.3 million deaths each year, more than malaria or many of the other serious tropical illnesses. Though most of the approximately 28 billion individuals who develop diarrhea survive, the health consequences of diarrhea are great in tropical areas.

Infants and small children are most likely to die of diarrhea. This is because loss of even a small amount of

water can be life-threatening to small children. Death due to diarrhea stems from loss of fluid, loss of plasma, and the collapse of the cardiovascular system. Infants being weaned from the mother's breast are particularly susceptible to malnutrition and dehydration. Diarrhea can be caused by bacteria or viruses.

Residents of tropical disease areas are less likely than residents of developed areas to have access to emergency treatment for extreme diarrhea. They are also more likely to be exposed to pathogens that cause intense diarrhea in contaminated food or water. Cholera, a life-threatening condition whose major symptom is watery diarrhea, is spread through dirty water.

Oral rehydration therapy, an approach which uses a solution of glucose or sucrose and salt to hydrate the body, is an effective treatment for life-threatening diarrhea. One problem with the approach is that it must be made available immediately after a child gets sick, as diarrhea can cause enough fluid loss within the first 12 to 24 hours to cause death. Many individuals in tropical disease areas live many hours by foot from medical care. Therefore, health experts are working to make oral rehydration therapy, along with education about the therapy, available at home to residents of tropical-disease areas.

The most infamous type of diarrheal disease is cholera, which is also marked by vomiting, intense thirst and abdominal cramping. Cholera is so common it is endemic in some parts of the world, such as India. In other parts of the world, it occurs as an epidemic or a pandemic.

The disease is caused by the *Vibrio cholerae* bacteria, which typically spreads through dirty water, food, or seafood from areas with contamination. The bacteria that causes cholera multiplies in the human intestinal tract, but has also been known to multiply in water.

Symptoms of cholera are a direct result of the cholera enterotoxin, the toxic substance elaborated by cholera bacteria that affects the cells of the small intestine. The substance forces the mucosal cells to secrete large quantities of fluid, resulting in diarrhea.

Control of cholera calls for good sanitation measures, specifically clean water and good food hygiene. Boiling water eliminates the bacteria. A vaccine that offers limited effectiveness—30 to 80% protection for up to six months—is available.

While treatment is effective, involving antibiotics, nutritional support and treatment for dehydration, the death rate in epidemics may reach 30%.

Malnutrition

Malnutrition is the underlying cause of death for about two million people annually, and the disease most commonly affects children under five and the elderly. As many as 40% of all children under five in developing areas have suffered from malnutrition.

The disease stems for eating inadequate amounts of food or eating foods without enough protein. Different syndromes reflect different types of food deficits. Kwashiorkor reflects a protein deficiency, and marasmus is caused by an energy deficiency linked to failure to consume enough carbohydrates and fats.

Signs of malnutrition are loss of energy, wasting of muscle, and loss of fat. The condition can result in severe anemia, coma, or heart failure. Treatment requires efforts to rehydrate the individual and to replace deficient eating patterns with adequate consumption of healthy food. Education of some families may help improve future eating patterns. Yet, because the condition most often occurs among impoverished families in areas with inadequate food availability, changing eating habits can be difficult or impossible.

Infectious disease killers

The most common killers in tropical areas are not exotic diseases. They are infectious diseases, many of which are not considered life-threatening in developed countries such as the United States. In the least industrialized countries, 40% or more of all deaths are caused by infectious disease. In the United States, about 1% of all deaths are caused by such illnesses. The huge difference in death rates stems from the fact that most infectious diseases are the easiest diseases to treat using modern medical care.

Approximately 10 million people die every year from respiratory diseases in the developing world. Such diseases are caused by the influenza virus or bacteria such as *pneumococcus* and *Hemophilus influenza B*.

Measles, which can be prevented by immunization of infants, kills 2 million people in the developing world annually. The course of the disease in developing countries often includes complications such as diarrhea, ear infection, pneumonia, and weight loss. For some, weight loss leads to malnutrition. Aggressive efforts to curb measles deaths through immunization have reduced the number of potential deaths in recent years.

Whooping cough is another early childhood disease which is seen rarely in the U.S. but is common in developing countries. About 600,000 people die of whooping cough annually in the developing world, with

many of these deaths occurring among small children. About 55 million people develop the disease. Whooping cough is also prevented by immunization.

Another infectious disease which is a common killer in developing countries is tuberculosis, which kills about 900,000 people every year and infects about 7 million people annually. Tuberculosis can be treated through immunization and drug therapy, although drug resistant strains are becoming increasingly prevalent. Though deaths have been reduced internationally over the last 30 years, the disease is still very common in tropical areas.

Tropical-disease areas have also been hit hard by AIDS and HIV infection. An estimated 15 million people internationally are infected by the HIV virus, the World Health Organization estimated in 1994. Of those about one-fifth have developed AIDS, a disease which is fatal in most instances.

A key emphasis of prevention programs in Africa has been promoting the use of condoms during sexual intercourse, a practice which reduces the risk of AIDS. In Africa, condom use increased from 2 million per year in 1986 to about 70 million in 1993. But problems remain, particularly in places where poverty limits the safety of the blood supply, where condoms are in short supply, where access to accurate information about the disease is limited, and where health providers are far away.

Future trends

A hopeful new development in tropical medicine is the vaccine for malaria, which was in field trials in the middle 1990s. The vaccine, developed by Colombian Manuel Patarroyo, is made up of three peptides synthesized chemically and connected using a fourth peptide from the malaria parasite.

The vaccine is designed to protect against falciparum, the most deadly strain of malaria. Results of clinical tests in Colombia, Ecuador, Venezuela and Tanzania reported in 1994 show some success against the disease. The Tanzania trial of about 600 children reduced the incidence of malaria by 31%. This shows that the vaccine has some promise. Experts note that while the vaccine did not provide 100% protection, it still would be valuable to cut sickness and death from malaria by 31%. The next step is to see if the vaccine can be improved and to conduct larger field trials.

Other experimental vaccines are also being tested. A therapeutic vaccine for tuberculosis is currently being tested which reduces the time it takes to treat the disease, which currently is about six months. Shortening

KEY TERMS

Cyst—Refers to either a closed cavity or sac or the stage of life of some parasites during which they live inside a walled-in area.

Dehydration—The condition of having too much fluid lost from the body.

Larva—Immature developmental stage of various species.

Lesion—An injury or wound.

Parasite—Species which depends on another species to survive.

Peptide—A class of chemical compounds that form proteins.

Protozoa—One-celled creatures and the simplest forms of animal life.

Spore—A body created within bacteria; it is a resting stage for the cell.

Further Reading:

Aldhous, Peter. "Vaccine Shows Promise in Tanzania Test." *Science*, Vol. 266, November 4, 1994: 724.

Desowitz, Robert S. *The Malaria Capers*. New York: W.W. Norton and Company, 1991.

Goldsmith, Robert, and Donald Hayneman, eds. *Tropical Medicine and Parasitology*. Norwalk, CT, 1989.

Najera, Jose A., Bernhard H. Liese, and Jeffrey Hammer. *Malaria: New Patterns and Perspectives*. World Bank Technical Paper Number 183, 1992.

"No Shortcuts on International Commitment to Combat AIDS. "*AIDS Weekly*, May 16, 1994: 7.

Warren, Kenneth S., and Adel A.F. Mahmoud. *Tropical and Geographical Medicine*, 2nd ed. New York: McGraw-Hill Information Services Co., 1990.

Patricia Braus

the treatment time would improve the odds that treatment is completed by the diseased.

Another vaccine which could reduce the sickness linked to tropical diseases is a new vaccine for leishmaniasis. The vaccine, which is in clinical trials, has fewer side affects and costs about one-tenth less than drugs currently used to treat the disease. However, because the drug is not in production for distribution yet, the ultimate cost of the medicine is not clear.

Other strategies are also essential to stem the tremendous cost in illness and death from tropical diseases. While World Health Organization efforts have boosted the rate of immunization for many diseases, there are still millions of children who do not receive adequate immunization for common early childhood diseases such as measles and whooping cough. Efforts to provide such proven preventive measures to more children will yield great benefits in health and longer life.

Efforts to boost access to health providers and educational information also stand to benefit residents of tropical disease areas. Knowing how to care for children with diarrhea, adults with hookworm, or many other diseases could make a vast difference. Finally, the prevalence of diseases linked to dirty water and dirty soil drive home the importance of better sewage systems and basic public health measures which western countries generally adopted years ago.

See also Childhood diseases; Cholera; Malaria; Malnutrition; Parasites; Tuberculosis.

Trout-perch

The trout-perch belongs to the family Percopsidae, which includes only one genus—*Percopsis*—with only two species. The fish is found only in the fresh waters of North America. One species (*Percopsis omiscomaycus*) is found mainly on the eastern side; the other species, the sandroller (*P. Transmontana*), is native to the west in the regions around the Columbia River Basin.

Both species are small, with the eastern species averaging 3-5 in (7.6-12.7 cm) in length, with a few reaching 8 in (20.3 cm). The sandroller is a bit smaller.

As the name implies, the trout-perch has characteristics of both the trout and the perch. Like the trout, it has an adipose fin—a fatty fin which projects between the dorsal and caudal fins. It also has a lateral line—or row of sensory pores on its sides—and ctenoid scales—fish scales that have a comblike projection at their margin.

The trout-perch appears to prefer deep water but may enter shallow water in spring to spawn. It may spawn on sandbars in lakes or up rivers, selecting bottoms of sand or gravel. It appears to be sensitive to rises in temperature, and, in some lakes, a considerable number of these fish die off in the summer as the water temperature rises.

Trout-perches are an important source of food for larger fishes.

True bugs

The true bugs are a large and diverse group of about 35,000 species of insects in the order Hemiptera. About 44 families of bugs occur in North America. Bugs typically have a flattened body, and their folded wings cross over their thorax and abdomen, giving a distinctive, cross-like pattern.

Some species of true bugs are of great economic importance as pests of agricultural plants. A few species of bugs are vectors of important diseases of humans.

In popular usage, the word "bug" is often used to refer to non-hemipteran insects, and not only to "true bugs." When used to refer to a species in the Hemiptera, the "bug" part of the name should be written separately, as in: stink bug, or milkweed bug. When used to refer to non-hemipteran insects, the "bug" part of the name should be used to form a single word, as in: ladybug (a family of beetles, order Coleoptera), or mealybug (scale insects, order Homoptera), or sowbug (Crustaceans in the order Isopoda — these are not even insects!).

Biology of true bugs

The true bugs have an incomplete metamorphosis, characterized by three life-history stages: egg, nymph, and adult. The nymphs resemble the adults somewhat in form, but they are not capable of reproduction. Most North American bugs overwinter as the adult stage.

Bugs have two sets of wings. The forewings of most species of true bugs are rather tough and leathery towards their base, and membranous farther away. This unusual forewing structure is the origin of the Latin roots of the name for the order: Hemiptera, or "half wing." The diagnostic, crossed-wing appearance of bugs at rest is also due to this unusual structure of the forewings, which form a well-defined "X" when held flat over the back of the abdomen with the membranous tips overlapping. The hind wings are fully membranous, and are used for flying. Some types of true bugs have greatly reduced wings, and cannot fly.

The mouthparts of bugs are adapted for piercing and sucking. The mouthparts comprise a pointed, elongate structure known as a beak or rostrum that arises at the front of the head, and folds backwards, quite far underneath the body in some species. The beak is itself made up of specialized stylets used for piercing, and others the develop channels used for actual feeding. Most species of bugs feed on plant juices, but a few are parasites of vertebrates, living on the animal's surface and feeding on blood.

Most bugs have long, segmented antennae. Bugs have well developed, compound eyes, and adult bugs may have several simple eyes (or ocelli) as well. Many species of bugs have glands that give off a strongly scented, distasteful odor when the insect is disturbed.

Some species are quite brightly and boldly colored. Usually these bugs feed on plants that contain poisonous chemicals, which also occur in the bugs and render them distasteful or even toxic to potential predators. This type of boldly warning color scheme is known as aposematic coloration.

Most species of bugs are terrestrial, living on vegetation or in organic debris on the surface. Some species of bugs are specialized for living in aquatic habitats, occurring in the water column, or on the surface.

Common families of terrestrial bugs in North America

The most diverse family of bugs is the plant or leaf bugs (family Miridae), species of which can be found in terrestrial habitats world-wide. Almost all plant bugs feed on the juices of plants, some species causing important damages to agricultural crops. Important agricultural pests include the tarnished plant bug (*Lygus lineolaris*), which feeds on a wide range of crop plants, the apple red bug (*Lygidea mendax*), the cotton fleahopper (*Psallus seriatus*), and the four-lined plant bug (*Poecilocapsus lineatus*), a pest of currants and gooseberries. The garden fleahopper (*Halticus bractatus*) is a common, jumping species in gardens and fields, which sometimes causes significant damages.

The assassin bugs (family Reduviidae) are mostly predators of other insects, although many will also give humans a painful bite if they are not handled with care, and a few are blood-sucking parasites. The blood-sucking conenose (*Triatoma sanduisuga*) sometimes occurs in houses in North America, and can inflict a particularly painful bite. In South America, other species in the genus *Triatoma* are the vectors of Chagas' disease, a deadly disease of humans.

The ambush bugs (family Phymatidae) are also predators of other insects. Yellow species of ambush bugs are common hide-and-wait predators on species of goldenrod (*Solidago* spp.) throughout North America.

Seed bugs (family Lygaeidae) are a diverse group of mostly herbivorous bugs. Two common, attractive, red-and-black marked species are the small milkweed bug (*Lygaeus kalmii*) and the large milkweed bug (*Oncopeltus fasciatus*). The bright, aposematic coloration of these milkweed bugs is meant to deter potential predators, because these insects are distasteful due to alkaloid chemicals accumulated from their food of milkweed (*Asclepias* spp.). The chinch bug (*Blissus leucopterus*) is a serious agricultural pest, especially of wheat, corn, and other grains in the grass family, as well as urban lawn-grasses.

The lace bugs (family Tingidae) are herbivorous insects with distinctive, very attractive, finely reticulated patterns on their head, thorax, and wings. The chrysanthemum lace bug (*Corythucha marmorata*) is common in much of North America, feeding on various species in the aster family, and sometimes occurring in greenhouses.

The leaf-footed or coreid bugs (family Coreidae) are common, herbivorous insects. The squash bug (*Anasa tristis*) is a pest of pumpkin and squash crops, feeding on the leaves of these plants and causing them to droop and turn black. The box-elder bug (*Leptocoris trivittatus*) is an attractive, red-and-black colored insect that feeds on species of maples, but does not cause important damages.

The stink bugs (family Pentatomidae) are relatively large and common bugs that produce malodorous smells as a defensive response when they are roughly handled. Many of the stink bugs are brightly colored, for example, the harlequin bug (*Murgantia histrionica*), an important pest of crops in the mustard family, such as cabbages, turnip, and radish.

Common families of aquatic bugs in North America

The water boatmen (family Corixidae) are common aquatic bugs that swim in the water column of lakes and ponds. The hind legs of water boatmen are oar-like in appearance, being long and flattened, and are used for underwater locomotion. Water boatmen do not have gills for the exchange of respiratory gases—they must breath head-first at the surface, although most species can carry a small bubble of air as they swim underwater. Most species of water boatmen are herbivorous, but some others are predators of other aquatic invertebrates. Water boatmen are an important food for some species of wildlife, such as ducks. The water boatman (*Arctocorixa alternata*) is a common and widespread species in North America.

The backswimmers (family Notonectidae) are also aquatic bugs. The especially elongate hind legs of these insects are used for swimming, which the backswimmers accomplish while in an upside-down position—hence, their common name. Backswimmers must breath at the surface, but unlike the water boatmen these insects must break the surface abdomen-first in order to obtain air. Backswimmers are predators of other aquatic

invertebrates, and are themselves an important food for larger species. The backswimmer (*Notonecta undulata*) is a common and widespread species.

The giant water bugs (family Belostomatidae) include the world's largest bugs, one species of which can attain a most-impressive length of 3.9 in (10 cm). Giant water bugs are oval in shape, with a rather flattened body, and are often a shiny brown color. The front legs are large and strong and are used to grasp their prey, which can include other aquatic insects, as well as small fish, tadpoles, and even frogs and salamanders. Giant water bugs sometimes leave their aquatic habitat and fly about, possibly for the purposes of dispersal. At such times these insects are attracted to lights, where they are sometimes known as electric light bugs. Giant water bugs can inflict a painful bite, and should be handled with care—these insects are sometimes known as toe-biters. The giant water bug (*Lethocerus americanus*) is a widespread species in North America, and can reach a body length of more than 2.4 in (6 cm).

Water scorpions (family Nepidae) are another group of predacious aquatic bugs, with long, scissor-like front legs adapted for fiercely grasping their prey of insects and other creatures. Water scorpions can inflict a painful bite.

Water striders (family Gerridae) are semi-aquatic insects, living on the water surface. The long-legged body of water striders is suspended aloft by surface tension, made possible by the structure of their "feet," which are covered with fine hairs that are not easily wetted. In parts of the southern United States, these insects are known as "Jesus bugs" because of their ability to walk on water. Water striders run and skate over the surface of ponds and lakeshores, hunting terrestrial arthropods that fall onto their two-dimensional habitat, and aquatic insects as they come to the surface to breathe. Water striders have odoriferous scent glands, which may be a deterrent against predation by fish. The water strider (*Gerris remigis*) occurs commonly throughout much of North America.

Bugs as a health hazard

Bed bugs (family Cimicidae) are wingless bugs with a body length of about 0.2 in (6 mm). Bed bugs feed by sucking the blood of birds or mammals. Various species will bite humans, and they can be serious pests in homes, hotels, and other places, most usually the common bed bug (*Cimex lectularius*). Bed bugs come out at night, hiding during the day in cracks and crevices in walls and furniture. The bites of these insects are very irritating, but bed bugs are not known to be a vector of human diseases.

KEY TERMS

Aposematic—This refers to distasteful or poisonous animals that are brightly colored, to warn their potential predators that food might best be obtained elsewhere.

Incomplete metamorphosis—This is characterized by three life-history stages: egg, nymph, and adult. The nymphs of true bugs resemble the adults in form, but they are not capable of reproduction.

Vector—A mobile animal that transports a pathogen among hosts. For example, bugs in the genus *Triatoma* are vectors between a Chagas'-disease causing trypanosome, and humans.

Chagas' disease is common in parts of Central and South America, and is spread by blood-sucking bugs in the genus *Triatoma*, especially *T. infestans*. These are sometimes known as kissing bugs because of their tendency to bite near the mouth of their victims. Chagas' disease is a debilitating malady of humans, and is caused by a pathogenic trypanosome, *Trypanosoma cruzi*, a type of parasitic protozoan that lives in the blood. Chagas' disease is characterized by a recurring fever, and often a enfeebling inflammation of the heart muscles.

Further Reading:

Arnett, R. H. *American Insects. A Handbook of the Insects of America North of Mexico.* Gainesville, FL: Sandhill Crane Pub., 1993.

Borror, D. J., C. J. Triplehorn, and N. Johnson. *An Introduction to the Study of Insects.* New York: Saunders, 1989.

Lane, R., and R. Crosskey. *Medical Insects and Arachnids.* New York: Chapman and Hall, 1993.

Lehane, M. *Biology of Blood-sucking Insects.* London: Unwin-Hyman, 1991.

Metcalf, R. L., and R. A. Metcalf. *Destructive and Useful Insects.* New York: McGraw-Hill, 1992.

Swan, L. A., and C. S. Papp. *The Common Insects of North America.* New York: Harper & Row, 1975.

Bill Freedman

True eels

The true eels are elongate bony fish with a snake-like slimy body in the order Anguilliformes. There is one family of freshwater eels (the Anguillidae), and 25 families of exclusively marine eels. The freshwater eels must return to the oceans to spawn.

The general characteristics of eels include soft-rayed fins and elongate dorsal and anal fins which merge with the caudal fin. Eels lack pelvic fins and have small pectoral fins commonly situated immediately behind the head. The jaws of eels are relatively small, but are strong, with numerous small teeth. Most ocean-living eels do not have scales, although the freshwater eels have small, oval-shaped scales embedded in their skin.

All eels are predators, feeding on a wide range of prey, including small fish, crustaceans, mollusks, and worms.

Freshwater eels

The freshwater eels, comprising about 16 species, are the most familiar family of eels to most people. These fish have an unusual characteristic in their life history, known as catadromy, in which the fish spend most of their lives in fresh waters, but run to the ocean to spawn.

The common freshwater eel of North America is the American eel (*Anguilla rostrata*). The European eel (*A. anguilla*) of western Europe and the Japanese eel (*Anguilla japonica*) of the north Pacific coast are closely related to the American eel. Relatively large numbers of eel species, about 12, occur in the Indo-Pacific region.

The American eel can reach a length of about 4 ft (1.2 m). This species is abundant in fresh waters that link directly to the ocean. This range includes coastal rivers, and the larger drainage of the Saint Lawrence River, extending inland to Lake Ontario and to a lesser degree, the upper Great Lakes. There are no freshwater eels on the west coast of the America, or on the east coast of South America.

American eels spends almost all of their life in fresh waters. However, to breed, this species of eel runs to the sea and migrates to a warm-water region between the West Indies and Bermuda that is known as the Sargasso Sea. European eels also commonly spawn in the Sargasso Sea, following a migration of 4,000 or more miles (6,500 km). After spawning, the adult eels die. The baby eels, or elvers, are leaf-shaped and transparent, and migrate to fresh waters, where they transform into miniature but transparent replicas of the adult body form, sometimes known as "glass eels." These small fish then run up rivers, and take up residence in still

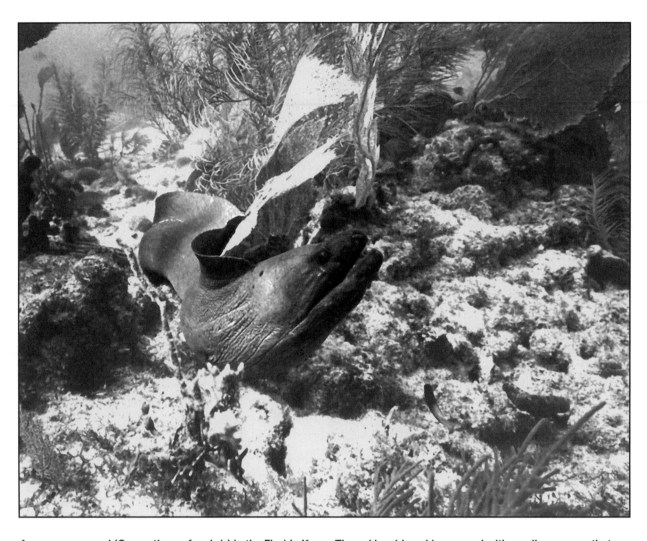

A green moray eel (*Gymnothorax funebris*) in the Florida Keys. The eel has blue skin covered with a yellow mucus that renders its apparent color green. It can reach a maximum size of 6 ft (1.8 m).

waters of large rivers and lakes, where they live as adults for as long as 15 years.

This unusual breeding strategy was discovered only relatively recently. For many centuries, naturalists pondered the fact that they could never find spawning or larval eels, and the breeding habits of these fish were a mystery. It was not until 1922 that newly hatched eel larvae were observed, in the Sargasso Sea.

Freshwater eels are an economically important species of fish, and are particularly appreciated as a food in France, Belgium, The Netherlands, and Great Britain.

Other families of eels

The Moringuidae is a family of 20 species of marine eels found in tropical waters, which includes the genera *Moringua* and *Stilbiscus*. These fish typically occur in shallow, soft-bottomed or gravelly habitats, where they burrow in the substratum during the day. The eel *Stilbiscus edwardsi* is a common species of the western Atlantic, while *Moringua macrochir* occurs in coastal waters of the Hawaiian Islands.

The moray eels (*Muraenidae*) include about 120 species that live in shallow, tropical and subtropical waters. These impressive, snake-like fish have a large mouth, well-armed with teeth and poison fangs. Morays are often brilliantly colored and marked, and are very attractive fish. Morays generally occur in rocky or coral habitats, where they hide during the day in crevices or in burrows in sediment. Many unsuspecting divers have received a nasty surprise in the form of a painful moray bite, when reaching into a rocky crevice after marine animals or other interesting things.

while others eat nectar, some scavenge dead bodies of animals, or are predators of smaller arthropods, or are blood-sucking parasites. These various species have mouth parts and behavioral adaptations to their specific modes of feeding and living. Mosquitoes, for example, have piercing and sucking feeding structures, while flies that feed on soft organic materials have sponging or lapping mouth parts.

Some species of flies that feed on plants inject a growth-regulating chemical into the stem, which causes an abnormal tissue, called a gall, to develop. The gall provides habitat for the feeding and development of the larvae of the fly. Gall-inducing species occur in the families Agromyzidae, Cecidomyiidae, and Tephritidae, as well as in other orders of insects.

There is a great diversity of species of flies, with more than 100,000 species being identified so far, and more than 100 families. The families are mostly distinguished using characters related to the morphology of the antennae, legs, wing venation, body bristles, and other anatomical features. Habitat and other ecological information may also be useful. Aspects of body chemistry may also be used in the identification of closely related species, particularly the chemistry of enzymes and nucleic acids. The diversity of flies is too enormous to discuss in much detail in this entry—only a few prominent examples will be described in the following sections.

Common families of terrestrial flies in North America

The muscid flies (family Muscidae) include more than 700 species in North America, including some important pests. The house fly (*Musca domestica*) is one of the most familiar flies to most people, because it breeds readily in garbage and other organic debris, and can be very abundant in dirty places around homes, villages, and cities. The house fly does not bite, but it can be a vector of some diseases of humans, spreading the pathogens by contact, for example, by walking on food that is later eaten by people. The face fly (*Musca autumnalis*) tends to cluster around the face of cows, where it feeds on mucous secretions around the nostrils and eyes, causing great irritation to the livestock. The stable fly (*Stomoxys calcitrans*) and horn fly (*Haematobia irritans*) are biting flies that greatly irritate livestock. Species of tsetse flies (*Glossina* spp.) occur in Africa, and are the vectors of sleeping sickness and related diseases of people, livestock, and wild large mammals.

Blow flies (family Calliphoridae) are scavengers, whose larvae feed on dead animals, excrement, and similar, rotting debris. Although a carcass teeming with writhing maggots is a rather disgusting spectacle, it must be remembered that blow flies provide a very useful ecological service by helping to safely dispose of unsanitary animal carcasses. A few species of blowflies lay their eggs in wounds on living animals, and the larvae may then attack living tissues, causing considerable damage. The screw-worm (*Cochliomyia hominivorax*) is an important pest in this regard, causing severe damages to cattle populations in some areas.

Flower flies or syrphids (family Syrphidae) include about 1,000 species in North America. Adult syrphids can be quite common in some habitats, where they are typically seen hovering in the vicinity of flowers. Many species of syrphids are brightly colored, sometimes with a black and yellow banding that is an obvious mimicry of bees and wasps.

The fruit fly family (Tephritidae) is made up of several hundred North American species, some of which are important pests in agriculture. The apple maggot (*Rhagoletis pomonella*) burrows in the fruits of apples and other fruits, while the Mediterranean fruit fly or medfly (*Ceratitis capitata*) is a serious pest of citrus fruits.

The small fruit flies (family Drosophilidae) are common in the vicinity of decaying vegetation and fruit. The species *Drosophila melanogaster* has been commonly used in biological laboratories for studies of genetics, because it is easily and quickly bred, and has giant chromosomes that can be readily studied using a microscope.

The warble and bot flies (family Oestridae) are large, stout, fast-flying flies that have a superficial resemblance to bees. The larvae of these flies are parasitic on large mammals, living in the flesh just beneath the skin. Some species are serious pests of agricultural animals, for example, the sheep bot fly (*Oestrus ovis*) and the ox warble fly (*Hypoderma bovis*). Warble flies are extremely irritating to cattle and to wild ungulates — there are reports of caribou being driven to distraction by warble flies, and jumping off cliffs in desperate attempts to escape these nasty pests.

Tachinid flies (family Tachinidae) include more than 1300 species in North America. The larvae of tachinids are parasitic on other species of insects, including some economically important pests, which are essentially eaten alive by the tachinid. As such, some species of tachinids provide a useful service to humans.

The robber flies (family Asilidae) are a diverse group, with more than 800 species in North America.

Robber flies are predators of other insects, which are captured in flight.

Seaweed or wrack flies (family Coelopidae) are dark-colored flies that can be very abundant along marine shores, where they breed in natural piles of seaweed compost, with the adults swarming abundantly above, often attracting large numbers of shorebirds and swallows.

Common families of aquatic flies in North America

There are many families of flies that have aquatic larval and pupal stages, but are terrestrial as adults. Some of the more prominent of these flies are described briefly in the following paragraphs.

The mosquitoes (family Culicidae) are a diverse, well known, and important group of biting flies. Larval mosquitoes, also known as "wrigglers," are aquatic and feed on algae and organic debris, and the adult males feed on flower nectar. Female mosquitoes, however, require a blood meal from a bird or mammal before they can develop eggs. Many species of mosquitoes bite humans, and they can be an enormous cause of annoyance, as well as the means of spreading some important, even deadly diseases. About 150 species of mosquitoes occur in North America, and in some habitats, for example, in northern forests during the summer, these blood-suckers can be enormously abundant and bothersome.

The black flies or buffalo gnats (family Simulidae) are small, dark-colored, hunch-backed flies. Female black flies require a blood meal to develop their eggs, and they obtain this food by biting the skin of a victim, and then sucking the blood that emerges from the wound. Black flies breed in cool streams, and they can be very abundant in some northern habitats. Unprotected animals have actually been killed as a result of the enormous numbers of bites that can be delivered during periods when black flies are abundant.

The horse flies and deer flies (family Tabanidae) are another group of fierce, biting flies with aquatic larvae and pupae, and terrestrial adults. Only the females require a blood meal—the males feed on nectar and plant juices. The eyes of deer flies are often extremely bright-colored, even iridescent.

The biting midges or no-see-ums (family Ceratopogonidae) are very small, blood-sucking flies with aquatic larval and pupal stages, but terrestrial adults. These diminutive pests can be quite abundant along the shores of lakes and oceans. These tiny flies can easily penetrate through fly screens and many types of clothing, and deliver bites that are much more painful than might be expected on the basis of the diminutive, less-than one millimeter size of these insects.

The crane flies (family Tipulidae) have a superficial resemblance to gigantic mosquitoes with extremely long and delicate legs. The larvae of crane flies occur in aquatic or moist terrestrial habitats and mostly feed on decaying organic matter, while the adults are terrestrial and feed on nectar.

The phantom midges (family Chaoboridae) are mosquito-like insects, but they do not bite. Larval phantom midges are predators of other bottom-dwelling arthropods, and have almost transparent bodies—hence their common name.

Flies as a health hazard

Some of the biting and blood-sucking flies are the vectors of important diseases of humans, domestic animals, and wild animals. The microorganisms that cause malaria, yellow fever, encephalitis, filariasis, dengue fever, sleeping sickness, typhoid fever, dysentery, and some other important diseases are all spread to humans by species of Diptera.

Malaria is one of the best-known cases of a disease that is spread by biting flies. Malaria is caused by the protozoan *Plasmodium falciparum*, and is spread to humans by a mosquito vector, especially species of *Anopheles*, which infect people when they bite them to obtain a blood meal. Malaria is an important disease in the tropics and subtropics. During the 1950s, about 5% of the world's population was infected with malaria, and during the early 1960s 2-5 million children died of malaria each year in Africa alone. The incidence of malaria has been greatly reduced by the use of insecticides to decrease the abundance of the *Anopheles* vectors, and by the use of prophylactic drugs that help to prevent infections in people exposed to the *Plasmodium* parasite. However, some of the pesticide-based control programs are becoming less effective, because many populations of *Anopheles* mosquitoes have developed a tolerance of the toxic effects of some insecticides.

The house fly (*Musca domestica*) is a non-biting fly, but it can carry some pathogens on its feet and body, and when it walks over food intended for consumption by humans, contamination can result. The house fly is known to be a contact vector of some deadly diseases, including typhoid fever, dysentery, yaws, anthrax, and conjunctivitis. House flies can be controlled using insecticides, although some populations of this insect have developed resistance to insecticides, rendering

KEY TERMS

· ·

Complete metamorphosis—This is an insect life history characterized by four stages: egg, larva, pupa, and adult.

Parasite—An animal that derives its livelihood by feeding on another, usually much larger animal, but generally without causing the death of the host. For example, many blood-sucking species of flies are parasites of mammals or birds.

Vector—A freely moving animal that transports a pathogen among hosts. For example, mosquitoes in the genus *Anopheles* are vectors between a malaria-causing plasmodium parasite and humans.

these chemicals increasing less effective as agents of control.

See also Flies; Mosquitoes.

Further Reading:

Arnett, R. H. *American Insects. A Handbook of the Insects of America North of Mexico.* Gainesville, FL: Sandhill Crane Pub., 1993.

Borror, D. J., C. J. Triplehorn, and N. Johnson. *An Introduction to the Study of Insects.* New York: Saunders, 1989.

Lane, R., and R. Crosskey. *Medical Insects and Arachnids.* New York: Chapman and Hall, 1993.

Lehane, M. *Biology of Blood-sucking Insects.* London: Unwin-Hyman, 1991.

Metcalf, R. L., and R. A. Metcalf. *Destructive and Useful Insects.* New York: McGraw-Hill, 1992.

Swan, L. A., and C. S. Papp. *The Common Insects of North America.* New York: Harper & Row, 1975.

Bill Freedman

Trumpetfish

Trumpetfish (*Aulostomus maculatus*) are bony fish in the family Aulostomidae, found from the Caribbean Sea to as far north as Bermuda. They are named for the trumpet like shape they exhibit when their mouths are open. Trumpetfish measure up to 2 ft (0.6 m) in length, and have dorsal spines which support separate fins or finlets. They are brownish in color with widespread streaks and spots.

Trumpetfish are poor swimmers, but are well camouflaged, which provides protection from predators and affords a means of obtaining food. They lie motionless, practically unseen, aligned with gorgonian corals (whip corals). They appear to drift about in the water, since they make no visible effort to swim and the rapid movement of their fins cannot be readily detected.

The American trumpetfish has close relatives in the Pacific—*A. valentini* in the Indo-Pacific region and *A. chinesis* along the Asian coast.

Further Reading:

Migdalski, E. C., and G. S. Fichter. *The Fresh and Salt Water Fishes of the World.* New York: Greenwich House, 1983.

Trumpet manucode see **Birds of paradise**

Trunkfish see **Boxfish**

Tsunami

Tsunami, or seismic sea waves, are a series of very long wavelength ocean waves generated by the sudden displacement of large volumes of water. The generation of tsunami waves is similar to the effect of dropping a solid object, such as a stone, into a pool of water. Waves ripple out from where the stone entered, and thus displaced, the water. In a tsunami, the "stone" comes from underneath the ocean or very close to shore, and the waves, usually only three or four, are spaced about 15 minutes apart.

Tsunami can be caused by underwater (submarine) earthquakes, submarine volcano eruptions, falling (slumping) of large volumes of ocean sediment, coastal landslides or even by meteor impacts. All of these events cause some sort of land mass to enter the ocean and the ocean adjusts itself to accommodate this new mass. This adjustment creates the tsunami, which can circle around the world. Tsunami is a Japanese word meaning "large waves in harbors." It can be used in the singular or plural sense. Tsunami are sometimes mistakenly called tidal waves but scientists avoid using that term since they are not at all related to tides.

Tsunami are classified by oceanographers as shallow water surface waves. Surface waves exist only on the surface of liquids. Shallow water waves are defined as surface waves occurring in water depths that are less than one half their wavelength. Wavelength is the distance between two adjacent crests (tops) or troughs (bottoms) of the wave. Wave height is the vertical distance from the top of a crest to the bottom of the adjacent trough. Tsunami have wave heights that are very small as compared to their wavelengths. In fact, no matter how deep the water, a tsunami will always be a shallow water wave because its wavelength (up to 150 mi [240 km]) is so much greater than its wave height (usually no more than 65 ft [20 m]).

Shallow water waves are different than deep water waves because their speed is controlled only by water depth. In the open ocean, tsunami travel quickly (up to 470 mph [760 kph]), but because of their low height (typically less than 3 ft [1 m]) and long wavelength, ships rarely notice them as they pass underneath. However, when a tsunami moves into shore, its speed and wavelength decrease due to the increasing friction caused by the shallow sea floor.

Wave energy must be redistributed, however, so wave height increases, just as the height of small waves increases as they approach the beach and eventually break. The increasing tsunami wave height produces a "wall" of water that, if high enough, can be incredibly destructive. Some tsunami are reportedly up to 200 feet (65 m) tall. The impact of such a tsunami can range miles inland if the land is relatively flat.

Tsunami may occur along any shoreline and are affected by local conditions such as the coastline shape, ocean floor characteristics, and the nature of the waves and tides already in the area. These local conditions can create substantial differences in the size and impact of the tsunami waves even in areas that are very close geographically.

Types of tsunami

Tsunami researchers classify tsunami according to their area of effect. They can be local, regional or ocean-wide. Local tsunami are often caused by submarine volcanoes, submarine sediment slumping, or coastal landslides. These can often be the most dangerous because there is often little warning between the triggering event and the arrival of the tsunami.

Seventy-five percent of tsunami are considered to be regional events. Japan, Hawaii, and Alaska are commonly hit by regional tsunami. Hawaii, for example has been hit repeatedly during this century, about every 5-10 years. One of the worst was the April 1, 1946, tsunami that destroyed the city of Hilo.

Pacific-wide tsunami are the least common as only 3.5% of tsunami are this large, but they can cause tremendous destruction due to the massive size of the waves. In 1940 and 1960, destructive Pacific-wide

tsunami occurred. More recently, there was a Pacific-wide tsunami on October 4, 1994, which caused substantial damage in Japan with 11.5 ft (3.5 m) waves. North America was lucky that time. Waves of only 6 in (15 cm) over the normal height were recorded in British Columbia.

Tsunami in history

Tsunami are not only a modern phenomenon. The decline of the Minoan civilization is believed to have been triggered by a powerful tsunami that hit the area in 1480 B.C. and destroyed its coastal settlements. Japan has had 65 destructive tsunami between 684 A.D. and 1960. Chile was hit in 1562 and Hawaii has a written history of tsunami since 1821. The Indian and Atlantic Oceans also have long tsunami histories. Researchers are concerned that the impact of future tsunami, as well as hurricanes, will be worse because of intensive development of coastal areas in the last 30 years.

The destructive 1946 tsunami at Hilo, Hawaii caused researchers to think about the problem of tsunami prediction. It became clear that if we could predict when the waves are going to hit, we could take steps to minimize the impact of the great waves.

Predicting tsunami—The International Tsunami Warning System

In 1965, the Intergovernmental Oceanographic Commission of the United Nations Educational, Scientific, and Cultural Organization agreed to expand the United States' existing tsunami warning center at Ewa Beach, Hawaii. This marked the formation of the Pacific Tsunami Warning Center (PTWC) which is now operated under the U.S. Weather Service. The objectives of the PTWC are to "detect and locate major earthquakes in the Pacific basin; determine whether or not tsunami have been generated; and to provide timely and effective information and warnings to minimize tsunami effects."

The PTWC is the administrative center for all the associated centers, committees and commissions of the International Tsunami Warning System (ITWS). Japan, the Russian Federation, and Canada also have tsunami warning systems and centers and they coordinate with the PTWC. In total, 27 countries now belong to the ITWS.

The ITWS is based on a world-wide network of seismic and tidal data and information dissemination stations, and specially trained people. Seismic stations measure movement of the earth's crust and are the foundation of the system. These stations indicate that some disturbance has occurred that may be powerful enough to generate tsunami. To confirm the tsunami following a seismic event, there are specially trained people, called tide observers, with monitoring equipment that enables them to detect differences in the wave patterns of the ocean. Pressure gauges deployed on the ocean can detect changes of less than 0.4 in (1 cm) in the height of the ocean, which indicates wave height. Also, there are accelerometers set inside moored buoys that measure the rise and fall of the ocean, which will indicate the wave speed. These data are used together to help researchers confirm that a tsunami has been generated. Tsunami can also be detected by satellite monitoring methods such as radar and photographic images.

The warning system in action

The ITWS is activated when earthquakes greater than 6.75 on the Richter scale are detected. The PTWC then collects all the data, determines the magnitude of the quake and its epicenter. Then they wait for the reports from the nearest tide stations and their tide observers. If a tsunami wave is reported, warnings are sent to the information dissemination centers.

The information dissemination centers then coordinate the emergency response plan to minimize the impact of the tsunami. In areas where tsunami frequency is high, such as Japan, the Russian Federation, Alaska and Hawaii, there are also Regional Warning Systems to coordinate the flow of information. These information dissemination centers then decide whether to issue a "Tsunami Watch," which indicates that a tsunami may occur in the area, or a more serious "Tsunami Warning," which indicates that a tsunami will occur. The entire coastline of a region is broken down into smaller sections at predetermined locations known as "breakpoints" to allow the emergency personnel to customize the warnings to account for local changes in the behavior of the tsunami. The public is kept informed through local radio broadcasts. If the waves have not hit within two hours of the estimated time of arrival, or, the waves arrived but were not damaging, the tsunami threat is assumed to be over and all Watches and Warnings are canceled.

Current and future research

One of the more recent changes in the ITWS is that the Regional Centers will be taking on greater responsibility for tsunami detection and warning procedures. This is being done because there have been occasions when the warning from Hawaii came after the tsunami hit the area. This can occur with local and regional tsunami that tend to be smaller in their area of effect. Some seismically active areas need to have the warning

KEY TERMS

· ·

Breakpoints—Points at which the Regional Tsunami Warning Centers arbitrarily split their coastline to create smaller sections that receive customized information in the event of a tsunami.

Return rates—The predicted frequency at which a tsunami will hit a certain area.

Seismic activity/event—An earthquake or disruption of the earth's crust.

Shallow surface wave—A wave that exists only on the surface of a liquid and has a wavelength that is greater than the water depth.

Slumping—A sudden falling of unstable sediments, usually used to refer to underwater environments.

Submarine—Below the surface of the ocean.

Wave height—The vertical change in height between the top, or "crest," of the wave and the bottom, or "trough," of the wave.

Wavelength—The distance between two crests or troughs in a wave.

system and equipment closer than Hawaii if they are to protect their citizens. For example, the Aleutian Islands near Alaska have 2-3 moderate earthquakes/week. As of May 1995, centers such as the Alaska Tsunami Warning Center located in Palmer, Alaska have assumed a larger role in the management of tsunami warnings.

In terms of basic research, one of the biggest areas of investigation is the calculation of return rates. Return rates, or recurrence intervals, are the predicted frequency with which tsunami will occur in a given area and are useful information, especially for highly sensitive buildings such as nuclear power stations, offshore oil drilling platforms and hospitals. The 1929 tsunami in Newfoundland has been extensively studied by North American researchers as a model for return rates and there has been some dispute. Columbia University researchers predict a reoccurrence in Newfoundland in 1,000-35,000 years. However, a marine geologist in Halifax, believes that it may reoccur as soon as 100-1,000 years. His calculations are based on evidence from mild earthquakes and tsunami in the area. He also suggests that the 1929 tsunami left a sedimentary record that is evident in the soil profile, and that such records can be dated and used to calculate return rates. He is currently working with an American scientist to test this theory.

See also Earthquake.

Further Reading:
Whelan, M. "The Night the Sea Smashed Lord's Cove." In: *Canadian Geographic* (November/December 1994): 70-73.

Jennifer LeBlanc

Tuatara lizard

Tuataras are unusual, lizard-like animals that are the only living representatives of the order Sphenodonta of the vertebrate class Reptilia. The lineage of the sphenodonts is an ancient one, with a fossil record extending back 200 million years, prior even to the evolution of dinosaurs and the lizards. Until the discovery of tuataras in New Zealand, biologists had believed that this reptilian lineage had been extinct for 100 million years. Hence, the tuatara became celebrated as a "living fossil."

Tuataras have a number of unusual anatomical features. The arrangement of bones and cavities in the skull of Tuataras is considered to be a primitive character. Tuataras also have a relatively well developed, light sensitive organ on the top of their head, called the *pineal organ* or *median eye*, capable of sensing light and darkness. This primitive structure has similarities to a true eye, and even has a lens and retinal tissue. The function of the pineal eye is not understood by physiologists, but it appears to regulate activity of the pineal gland. This organ occurs in the forebrain of vertebrates, and secretes the hormone melatonin into the blood, which changes skin coloration in some animals, regulates diurnal or 24-hour biological rhythms, and possibly influences seasonal reproductive cycles. A unique characteristic of tuataras, not shared with other reptiles, is the fusion of teeth into the jawbones, rather than being set in sockets in the bone.

Tuataras are rather long-lived animals, which can exceed 75 years in age, and reach about 27.6 in (70 cm) in body length. Tuataras are slow moving, sluggish animals, which mostly eat large insects. These reptiles live in burrows, dug by themselves, which they often share with nesting petrels (seabirds).

The two surviving species of tuatara, *Sphenodon punctatus* and *S. guntheri*, are very rare animals, living only on a few isolated small islands off New Zealand. These species used to have much broader ranges, but they were widely extirpated from the mainland and many islands of New Zealand after European colonization. The catastrophic decline of tuataras was mainly due to predation of adults and eggs by introduced mammals, such as cats, foxes, rats, and others. It is significant that these predators do not occur on the few, closely protected islands where the world's last tuataras live.

The initial survival of tuataras was due to the early isolation of New Zealand from other continents, where ecologically more capable types of reptiles, birds, and mammals evolved and came to dominate animal communities. In other parts of Gondwanaland (the southern continent which New Zealand was originally a part of) tuataras and their relatives were incapable of competing with the better adapted creatures, and so became extinct. Tuataras are truly extraordinary survivors, relics from a bygone era of the evolution of animal forms on Earth. However, tuataras are now critically endangered as a result of recent influences by humans. The continued, though precarious, survival of tuataras now depends on their strict and perpetual protection on a few small islands.

See also Reptiles.

Bill Freedman

Tubal ligation see **Contraception**

Tuber

A tuber is a swollen, underground storage organ that develops on the roots of certain species of plants. Some types of tubers are highly nutritious, mostly because of their energy content in the form of starch.

Agricultural species of plants that develop edible tubers include the white potato (*Solanum tuberosum*), sweet potato (*Ipomoea batatas*), tapioca or cassava (*Manihot esculenta*), and yam (*Dioscorea batatas*).

The white potato is the most important and best-known of the agricultural tubers. The potato is a native of the Andean plateau of South America. In this species, tubers develop at the end of roots that emerge from underground stems, known as stolons. Potato tubers have stem buds known as "eyes" which can sprout and grow new, aboveground stems. It appears that potatoes have been cultivated by indigenous peoples of the Andean plateau for at least 6,500 years.

The varieties of potatoes that are most commonly cultivated in modern, industrial agriculture typically develop rather large tubers with white centers. However, there is a great diversity of other varieties of potatoes, especially in their native Andean range. These varieties commonly form relatively small tubers with brown, red, yellow, or purple skin, and white or darker-colored interiors.

Potato tubers are very nutritious, especially as a source of starch. However, they also contain about 2% protein and valuable minerals and vitamins, especially vitamins B and C. Interestingly, potato foliage is poisonous because of its content of a toxic alkaloid known as solanin. This chemical also occurs in green sprouts of the eyes of the tubers, which is why these should be excised and not eaten.

The potato was first discovered by Europeans in the mid-1530s when Spanish conquistadors observed its cultivation in Peru. The potato subsequently became a commonly cultivated food in Europe, initially as a food for livestock. Around the beginning of the seventeenth century, people also began to commonly eat the potato. Its high productivity and favorable nutritional qualities are believed to have been important in allowing population growth in Europe during the next several centuries. However, at the beginning of the nineteenth century a new disease of potatoes occurred. The potato blight, caused by the fungus *Phytophthora infestans*, became a recurrent disaster, and widespread famine resulted. In some regions such as Ireland, poor people ate little else but potatoes, and the blight caused mass starvation which to some degree was alleviated by massive immigration to North America. The potato blight is still an important disease. However, this disease is now controlled by growing resistant varieties of potatoes by managing the environment to make it less favorable to the fungus and by the use of fungicides.

See also Nightshade; Sweet potato; Yam.

Bill Freedman

Tuberculosis

Tuberculosis (TB), is an infectious disease of the lungs caused by bacteria called tubercle bacilli, or more precisely, *mycobacterium tuberculosis*. In the mid-nineteenth century, about one-fourth of the mortality rate was attributable to tuberculosis. It was particularly ram-

pant in early childhood and young adulthood. Its presence was felt throughout the world, but by the 1940s, with the introduction of antibiotics, there was a sharp decline of cases in developed countries. For poorer countries it is still a major problem. Since 1989, however, there has been an increase in reported cases in economically advanced countries due mainly to the AIDS epidemic and the emergence of antibiotic-resistant strains of TB.

The bacillus infects the lungs of uninfected people who inhale the infected droplets formed during coughing by an individual who has an advanced case of the disease. It also is transmitted by unpasteurized milk since animals can be infected with the bacteria. The disease is dormant in different parts of the body until it becomes active and attacks the lungs, leading to a chronic infection. Symptoms include fatigue, loss of weight, night fevers and chills, and persistent coughing with sputum-streaked blood. The virulent form of the infection can then spread to other parts of the body. Without treatment the condition is usually fatal.

Chest X-rays can show the presence of tuberculosis along with sputum examinations and skin tests. The test is usually administered to the arm. Tuberculin, a purified protein taken from the tuberculosis bacilli, is placed under the skin with the use of a small needle. In two or three days if there is a red swelling at the site of the needle prick, the test is positive, that is, it indicates the presence of TB infection. Early detection of the disease facilitates effective treatment to avoid the possibility of it becoming active later on.

Populations at risk of contracting TB are people with certain medical conditions or those using drugs for medical conditions that weaken the immune system. Others at risk are low-income groups, people from poorer countries with high TB rates; people who work in or are residents of long-term care facilities (nursing homes, prisons, hospitals), those who are very underweight, alcoholics and intravenous drug users.

History

Evidence suggests tuberculosis goes back to the last Ice Age and longer. Traces of lesions from tuberculosis have been found in the lungs of ancient Egyptian mummies. The recent discovery of a Pre-Columbian mummy has resolved the debate on whether or not European explorers introduced the disease to the New World. Lung samples from a Peruvian woman who lived 500 years before Columbus discovered America show a lump that was identified as tuberculosis by DNA testing. Hippocrates, the Greek physician who lived from 460 to 370 BC, described the disease.

The Greek name for the disease was phthisis, derived from the verb phthinein, meaning to waste away. Tuberculosis was also called consumption because of the "wasting away effects" (notably, significant losses of weight over a period of time) of the disease.

In 1839 Johann Schonlein is credited with first calling the disease tuberculosis. In 1882 the tubercle bacillus was discovered by Robert Koch, the German physician who pioneered the science of bacteriology. This landmark discovery was followed eight years later by his extraction of a protein from dead bacilli called tuberculin. This protein is still used to test for the presence of TB infection in a dormant or early stage. Another important diagnostic breakthrough came in 1895 with the discovery of Wilhelm Conrad Roentgen's x rays. The presence of TB lesions was detected on x rays.

Two twentieth century French scientists, Albert Calmette and Camille Guerin, developed a vaccine against tuberculosis from a weakened strain of bovine bacillus. Called BCG for Bacillus-Calmette-Guerin this vaccine is the only one still in use though its effectiveness tends to be questioned. Despite doubts about the vaccine, it is still widely used.

Throughout the nineteenth century and up until the 1960s, physicians sent their TB patients to sanitoriums which were rest homes located in mountains or semi-arid regions like the American southwest. These locations were supposed to help the breathing process by providing clean and dry air. Physicians believed that deeper, easier breathing in a work-free environment would help overcome the disease. Prior to the advent of antibiotics, these retreats were the only hope for chronically ill tubercular patients. Although treatment in sanitoriums did help many, they were phased out by the 1960s. They were replaced by antibiotic drug chemotherapy which can be administered in either a hospital or home environment. Over 90% of TB patients can be cured by several inexpensive antibiotics, but it is necessary they be used for a period of at least six months.

TB and the arts

The impact of tuberculosis was evident in the nineteenth and early twentieth centuries in literature, art, and music. Puccini's opera, L'Boheme, was created around the tragic death of the tubercular heroine, Mimi. Since it attacked the young, many poets, artists and musicians fell prey to the disease before they had a chance to fulfill their creative work. Among them, Amedeo Modigliani, John Keats, Frederic Chopin, and

Anton Chekov were claimed by the disease, along with millions of other young people during the period.

In the United States, American playwright, Eugene O'Neil, was one of the fortunate few who did recover in a sanitorium and went on to write his plays. His early play, The Straw, written in 1919, dramatically shows what life was like in a sanitorium. Patients were weighed daily. Those who maintained weight could stay at the facility or be discharged if there was significant improvement. Those who could not pass the test were sent to another facility where they were expected to die. In this play, the anguish of the two lovers, afraid to kiss, then eventually separated, is poignantly shown. The Straw must have come from a part of O'Neil's own experience with the disease.

Vaccination versus skin testing

The BCG vaccine was first formulated in 1908 and then given to people in 1921. Over 3 billion people throughout the world have since then received the vaccine. Even though no other vaccine is used as much as BCG, there are still conflicting reports and studies concerning its effectiveness. Figures range from an 80 percent degree of effectiveness to none at all. Many explanations have been offered for these discrepant figures. Some researchers maintain there are enough slight differences in the composition of the vaccine from place to place to account for the potency of the vaccine. Despite the questions raised, the World Health Organization (WHO) still recommends its worldwide use.

The U.S. Public Health Service's policy, on the other hand, recommends testing and drug therapy for those infected instead of vaccination. The two factors responsible for this policy are the low incidence of TB in the United States and the doubts raised about BCG, which is the only vaccine. The Centers for Disease Control and Prevention, (CDC), however, in its concern over the rising incidence of TB in the United States and the appearance of multidrug-resistant tuberculosis (MDR TB) which is difficult to treat, is now reexamining the question of TB vaccination.

Of 8 million cases, the world death rate from TB is 2.9 million. Tuberculosis has the highest infectious disease mortality rate. In the United States the infection rate for 1993 was 26,673 new cases, 20% higher than that recorded for 1985.

The CDC has been reluctant to advise vaccination because it has relied on the use of the skin test to find the infected cases. Drug therapy is 90 percent effective in stopping the infection. Since those vaccinated test positive with the skin test, a vaccination program would interfere with skin testing. Those not receiving immunity from the vaccine risk giving up a test that provides an early warning. Relying on the drug treatment program to stop TB epidemics, however, has one major drawback. The drug therapy takes 6 months to a year before stopping the infection. People infected are often among the homeless, poor, drug addicted, or criminal societies. Unless these people are carefully supervised to make sure they complete a complicated regimen of drug therapy, it is difficult to maintain a cure for the disease.

Physicians have taken a second look at vaccinations because MDR TB has become more prevalent. It is easier to transmit through saliva, and makes the skin test, followed by a one-drug therapy program less viable. The issue is not yet resolved. In the past, city and state governments were actively involved in regulations that controlled infected people from spreading the infection. At present, federal, state, and local agencies must again take a leading role in formulating a public policy on this complicated health problem.

Directly observed therapy (DOT)

New York City and State; Ft. Worth, Texas; Baltimore, Maryland; Mississippi; South Carolina; and other sites are using a program called Directly Observed Therapy (DOT) to combat the rising incidence of TB. This program has met with considerable success in lowering reported cases of TB as much as 15% in New York City.

DOT is offered at soup kitchens, clinics, hospitals, neighborhood health centers, and drug rehabilitation centers. Outreach workers enable those with TB to get help with the least amount of red tape. The wide array of medicines needed to treat the disease is made available, and ample funding has been provided from federal, state, and local agencies. Apartments are located for homeless patients and special provisions are made to help released prison inmates and those on parole. Guidelines for compassionate, supervised medical services are periodically reviewed for the successful implementation of the DOT program.

Tuberculosis forecast

The U.S. Department of Health and Human Services predicts tuberculosis, the "forgotten plague," will spread further by the year 2005. In 1990 there were 7,537,000 TB cases worldwide. That number is expected to rise to 11,875,000 in 2005, a 58% increase. Most of the rise in rate is attributed to demographic factors (77%) while 23% accounts for the epidemiological factors, i.e., the rise in HIV infection. Approximately 30 million people around the world will die of TB from

1990 to 1999. These predictions are considered conservative because many cases of TB are never reported.

See also Respiratory diseases; Respiratory system; Vaccine.

KEY TERMS

BCG vaccine—Antituberculosis vaccine developed by two French scientists in 1908 and tested for the first time in 1921.

CDC—The Center for Disease Control—the federal agency that collects data and issues guidelines for monitoring and controlling the spread of contagious diseases.

Consumption—An older name for tuberculosis; the disease "consumes" the patient. The name TB for the disease remains in active use.

Demographics—Studies of population distributions and tendencies especially in relation to different types of medical conditions.

DOT—Directly observed therapy, a state and local approach to control the spread of TB.

Epidemiology—The study of disease spread and its control.

HIV—Human immunodeficiency virus, the retrovirus responsible for acquired immunodeficiency disorder (AIDS).

Mycobacterium tuberculosis—The bacteria responsible for tuberculosis.

Sanitoriums—Rest homes for people with TB in the past to help them recover from the disease under presumably favorable climatic conditions.

Tuberculin skin test—Pin prick needle test under the skin using the protein derivative from the tuberculosis bacteria to test for TB infection at an early stage.

WHO—World Health Organization; monitors and supervises world health.

Further Reading:

Bellin, Eran, et al. "Efficacy of BCG Vaccine." *The Journal of the American Medical Association.* v. 272, Sept 14, 1994, 765.

Christensen, Damaris. "Another Look at TB Vaccine: Should the United States Use BCG Widely?" *Science News.* v. 145, June 18, 1994, 393.

Ryan, Frank. *The Forgotten Plague: How the Battle Against Tuberculosis Was Won—and Lost.* Boston: Little Brown, 1993.

Tynes, Lee. "Tuberculosis: The Continuing Story." *The Journal of the American Medical Association.* v. 270, Dec. 1. 1993, 2616.

Tube-worms see **Acorn worm**

Tulip see **Lily family**

Tulu see **Camels**

Tumbleweed

The true tumbleweeds are various species of herbaceous plants in the amaranth family (Amaranthaceae). These are usually annual plants that develop a spherical, bush-shaped biomass. At the end of the growing season when their small seeds are ripe, the tumbleweeds wither and detach from their base and are blown about by winds, scattering their seeds widely over the surface of the ground. Therefore, the tumbling habit of these plants is an adaptation to extensive dispersal of their ripe seeds.

One common species of tumbleweed is *Amaranthus graecizans*. This annual plant is native to semi-deserts but is now a common weed of recently disturbed land in agricultural and urban areas. This plant has a whitish stem, green leaves, and numerous small, greenish flowers. *Amaranthus albus*, also known as tumble pigweed, is a closely related tumbleweed.

Other unrelated species of plants also tend to tumble to disperse their seeds. Two examples in the goosefoot family (Chenopodiaceae) are the Russian-thistle or Russian tumbleweed (*Salsola kali*) and the Russian pigweed (*Axyris amaranthoides*). These are both introduced species and can be important weeds. The winged pigweed or tumbleweed (*Cycloloma atriplicifolium*) is a related native species of arid habitats of the West which has also become weedy in open, disturbed habitats. Another species with a tumbling habit is the tumble mustard (*Sisymbrium altissimum*), in the mustard family (Brassicaceae). Tumble panic-grass (*Panicum capillare*, family Poaceae) produces a large, bushy inflorescence that often detaches and blows about at the end of the growing season.

The "tumbling tumbleweeds" have become a romanticized element of the landscape of the American West through the pervasive influence of their images in songs and movies. However, many of these very capable and opportunistic tumbleweeds are also extremely widespread as weeds. As such, the tumbleweeds are taking advantage of many types of disturbed habitats that are created on the landscape by humans and their activities.

See also Amaranth family.

Tumor

A tumor (also known as a neoplasm) is an abnormal tissue growth. Neoplasm means "new formation." Tumors can be either malignant (cancerous) or nonmalignant (benign) but either type may require therapy to remove it or reduce its size. In either case the tumor's growth is unregulated by normal body control mechanisms. Usually the growth is not beneficial to the organ in which it is developing and may be harmful.

It is not known what triggers this abnormal growth. Normally cells are generated at a rate needed to replace those that die or are needed for an individual's growth and development. Muscle cells are added as one grows as are bone cells and others. Genetic controls modulate the formation of any given cells. The process of some cells becoming muscle cells, some becoming nerve cells, and so on is called cell differentiation. Tumor formation is an abnormality in cell differentiation.

A benign tumor is a well-defined growth with smooth boundaries. This type of tumor simply grows in diameter. A benign growth compresses adjacent tissues as it grows. A malignant tumor usually has irregular boundaries and invades the surrounding tissue. This cancer also sheds cells that travel through the bloodstream implanting themselves elsewhere in the body and starting new tumor growth. This process is called metastasis.

It is important that the physician determine which kind of tumor is present when one is discovered. In some cases this is not a simple matter. It is difficult to determine whether the growth is benign without taking a sample of it and studying the tissue under the microscope. This sampling is called a biopsy. Biopsy tissue can be frozen quickly, sliced thinly, and observed without staining (this is called a frozen section); or it can be sliced, stained with dyes, and observed under the microscope. Cancer tissue is distinctly different from benign.

A benign tumor can be lethal if it compresses the surrounding tissue against an immovable obstacle. A benign brain tumor compresses brain tissue against the skull or the bony floor of the cranium and results in paralysis, loss of hearing or sight, dizziness, and/or loss

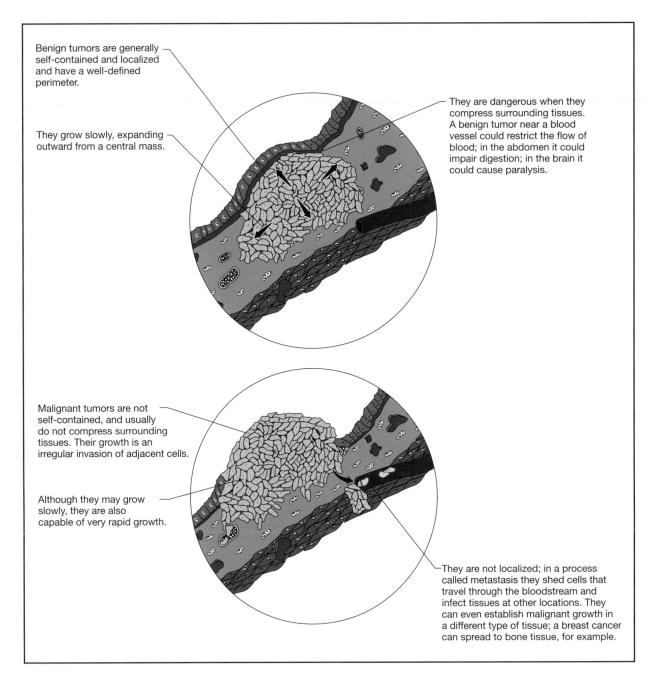

Benign tumors are generally self-contained and localized and have a well-defined perimeter.

They grow slowly, expanding outward from a central mass.

They are dangerous when they compress surrounding tissues. A benign tumor near a blood vessel could restrict the flow of blood; in the abdomen it could impair digestion; in the brain it could cause paralysis.

Malignant tumors are not self-contained, and usually do not compress surrounding tissues. Their growth is an irregular invasion of adjacent cells.

Although they may grow slowly, they are also capable of very rapid growth.

They are not localized; in a process called metastasis they shed cells that travel through the bloodstream and infect tissues at other locations. They can even establish malignant growth in a different type of tissue; a breast cancer can spread to bone tissue, for example.

A comparison of benign and malignant tumor characteristics.

of control of the extremities. A tumor growing in the abdomen can compress the intestine and interfere with digestion. It also can prevent proper liver or pancreatic function. The benign tumor usually grows at a relatively slow pace and may stop growing for a time when it reaches a certain size.

A cancer may grow quite rapidly or slowly, but usually is irregular in shape. It invades the neighboring tissue instead of pressing it aside. Most importantly, a cancer sheds cells, that is, metastasizes, so that new

cancer growths can spring up in areas distant from the original cancer. The cancerous cells also can establish a cancer in tissue that is different from the original cancer. A breast cancer could spread to bone tissue or to liver.

A benign tumor can be removed surgically if it is in a location that a surgeon can reach. A tumor growing in an unreachable area of the brain can be treated using radiation. It can also be treated by inserting thin probes through the brain tissue into the tumor and circulating

KEY TERMS

. . . .

Biopsy—The surgical removal of a small part of a tumor. The excised tissue is studied under the microscope to determine whether it is benign or malignant.

Chemotherapy—Use of powerful drugs to kill cancer cells in the human body.

Differentiation—The process by which cells take the form of a given type of tissue. That is basic cells become muscle cells, neurons, stomach lining, kidney, or other cell types.

Metastasis—Spreading of a cancerous growth by shedding cells that grow in other locales.

liquid nitrogen through the probe to freeze the tumor. This operation is called cryosurgery.

A malignancy requires steps to remove it but consideration must be given to the possibility that the tumor has begun to metastasize. The main or primary tumor may be removed surgically but if the tumor has been growing for some time the patient also may require treatment with powerful drugs to kill any stray cells. This treatment is called chemotherapy. Chemotherapy allows the antitumor drug to be circulated throughout the body to counter any small tumor growths.

See also Cancer; Tissue.

Further Reading:
Carpi, J. "Progress Against Cancer." *American Health* 13 (October 1994): 15-16+.
DeVita, E. "Conquering Cancer." *American Health* 13 (November 1994): 66-73.

Larry Blaser

Tuna

Tuna are fast-swimming large bony fish (teleosts of the family Scombridae) found in waters of the world's oceans. All species of tuna are economically important, usually supporting a large commercial fishery, and sometimes a local sport fishery. The largest species is the bluefin tuna (*Thunnus thynnus*), which can achieve a length of 16 ft (4 m) and a weight of up to 1,765 lb (800 kg). Populations of bluefin tuna occur in temperate and warm waters throughout the world. Smaller species of tunas include the albacore tuna (*T. alalunga*), yellowfin tuna (*T. albacares*), skipjack tuna (*Euthynnus pelamis*), bonitos (*Sarda* spp.), frigate mackerels (*Auxis* spp.), Spanish mackerels (*Scomberomorus* spp.), and the wahoo (*Acanthocybium* spp.).

Biology of tuna

A remarkable aspect of the physiology of tunas in the genus *Thunnus*, is their ability to maintain their body temperature significantly warmer than that of the ambient seawater. For example, the bluefin tuna can maintain a core body temperature of 78-98°F (24-35°C), even in water as cold as 46°F (6°C). However, unlike typical endothermic creatures such as mammals and birds, the body temperatures of tuna are not held constant within a relatively narrow range.

The endothermy of tunas is achieved by conserving the heat that is generated through normal body metabolism. This is accomplished through the action of an intertwined meshwork of veins and arteries, known as the rete mirable (meaning "wonderful net"), located in the periphery of the body. The rete mirable reclaims much of the heat in the venous blood, and transfers it to arterial blood through the action of a counter-current exchange system. This heat transfer slows down the rate of cooling of the tuna at the body surface, and thereby allows the animal to maintain a warmer core temperature. Higher body temperatures allow tuna to use their muscles more efficiently, and therefore swim more quickly with relatively little expenditure of energy. Higher temperatures of the body core may also contribute to the rapid and efficient digestion and absorption of food.

Tuna are fast swimmers, reaching speeds of up to 56 mph (90 kph) in the case of the large bluefin tuna. Moreover, tuna are well adapted for cruising over great distances at a relatively brisk speed. However, tuna can also accelerate quickly while predating on other fish, or to avoid their own predators. A tuna's body is relatively elongated and fusiform, that is, tapering at both ends. Their fins are of a size and position that are designed to minimize drag, so that maximum speeds can be achieved and maintained with relatively small expenditures of energy. The major source of forward thrust while swimming is side-to-side movements of the caudal, or tail fin. Tunas also have relatively large median fins (especially the dorsal, or top fin), which is an adaptation to minimizing the drag associated with sideways slippage of the body during swimming.

A tuna.

Tuna fisheries

Tuna support large commercial fisheries wherever they are abundant, and are thus economically important fish. However, as with any fishery, stocks of tuna can be easily exhausted through excessive harvesting. Indeed, many stocks of tuna have been significantly degraded by overharvesting. This problem can be illustrated by the case of the fishery for bluefin tuna in the western Atlantic Ocean.

The bluefin tuna is a very large, fast-swimming fish which undertakes regular trans-oceanic migrations. Bluefin tuna are extremely valuable since they are eagerly sought for sale as a delicacy in Japanese sushi restaurants. During the early 1990s, a prime bluefin tuna caught in North America could be sold for $30,000 (U.S. currency) at the wharf, and then for at least $60,000 at an auction in Tokyo. The tuna meat might then be sold for about $350 per lb ($770 per kg), as prepared sushi in restaurants. This is equivalent to about $230,000 to $385,000 per fish, depending on its weight.

Because bluefin tuna are so enormously valuable, they have been exploited intensively, and their populations are declining rapidly. For example, in 1975 there were an estimated 150-thousand bluefin tuna in the western Atlantic Ocean, but by the early 1990s this number had decreased by 90% through excessive harvesting, to only 22,000 animals. This resource collapse occurred even though the fishery was regulated by an international agency, the Atlantic Commission for the Conservation of Atlantic Tunas. The problem was that the managers of the commission consistently ignored the advice of their resource scientists, and set the allowable catches higher than was recommended, or was prudent. In addition, there was a substantial unregulated pirate fishing by ships flying the flags of nations that are not members of the commission.

The regulated and non-regulated overfishing were both ultimately caused by greed, and a desire to reap large, short-term profits. This was done without significant regard for the sustainability of the enterprise, or of the natural resource of bluefin tuna.

Some of the smaller species of tuna are caught using a type of net called a purse seine, set around a school of fish. The net initially floats vertically, with one side buoyed at the surface. Once the purse seine is set around a group of fish, the deeper side of the net is closed using a drawstring-like apparatus, trapping the

Harris, C. L. *Concepts in Zoology.* New York: Harper-Collins, 1992.

Nelson, J. S. *Fishes of the World.* 2nd ed. New York: Wiley, 1984.

Safina, C. "Bluefin Tuna in the West Atlantic: Negligent Management and the Making of an Endangered Species." *Conservation Biology.* 7: (229-34).

Scott, W. B., and M. G. Scott. *Atlantic Fishes of Canada.* Toronto: University of Toronto Press, 1988.

Bill Freedman

KEY TERMS

Counter-current exchange—An exchange of heat or respiratory gases between two fluids that are moving across each other in different directions. In the rete mirable of tunas, the fluids are contained in veins and arteries, and the transfer of heat occurs across the walls of these vessels.

Endothermy—Refers to animals that maintain their body temperatures within a range that is substantially warmer than that of their ambient environment. The source of heat is from internal metabolism.

Overharvesting—The unsustainable exploitation of a potentially renewable, biological resource. In such a case, the harvesting rate exceeds the rate of regeneration, so the quantity of the resource diminishes over time, sometimes to commercial or even biological extinction.

fish inside the "purse." Unfortunately, purse seines also trap other species, including dolphins and porpoises that often associate with schools of tuna in some regions. In fact, in some fishing sectors boat captains deliberately set their nets around groups of these marine mammals, because they know that schools of tuna are generally found beneath them. From the 1960s to the late 1980s, huge numbers of some species of dolphins and porpoises were killed in purse seines set for tuna, perhaps 200,000 of these marine mammals each year. More recently, the dolphin kill rate has declined to about 100,000 per year. This non-target fishing mortality has significantly depleted the populations of dolphins and porpoises in some regions.

Large tuna often have a significant contamination of their flesh with mercury. This commonly occurs to a degree that exceeds the maximum acceptable concentration of mercury in fish that is intended for human consumption, that is, 0.5 ppm (parts per million, on a fresh weight basis). The contamination of tuna and other large, oceanic fish by mercury is apparently a natural phenomenon. One study found no difference in the mercury concentrations of modern tuna, and animals collected between 1878 and 1909 and stored in a museum.

See also Drift net; Mackerel.

Further Reading:

Freedman, B. *Environmental Ecology.* San Diego: Academic Press, 1994.

Tundra

Tundra is a generic name for a low-growing ecosystem found in climatically stressed environments with short and cool growing seasons. Latitudinal tundra occurs in the Arctic and to a much lesser extent in the Antarctic, where the environments are characterized by cool, short growing seasons. Altitudinal tundra occurs under a similar climatic regime, but at the tops of mountains.

After temperature, the second most-important environmental factor affecting most tundra communities is moisture. Under wet conditions, sedge and grass-dominated meadow communities develop, while moist conditions favor a vegetation dominated by dwarf shrubs and herbaceous species, and dry sites have cushion plants and lichens. The vegetation of arctic and alpine tundras share many structural characteristics, most genera, and some species. However, there are important environmental differences between these two tundras, with the alpine type being subject to much larger variations of daily temperature during the growing season, as well as more intense inputs of solar radiation during the day. In contrast, arctic tundra can experience continuous exposure to the sun's rays, with 24-hour days for an extended period during the growing season.

Arctic tundra

Arctic tundra occurs in the northern most parts of the Northern Hemisphere, intergrading across the latitudinal tree-line with the boreal forest to the south. In North America, arctic tundra occurs on all non-glaciated regions of the islands of northern Canada and on Greenland, as a northern fringe of Alaska and continental Canada, and penetrating to relatively southern latitudes in the vicinity of Hudson Bay, which acts as a climate-influencing extension of the cold Arctic Ocean.

(An ecological analogue of arctic tundra occurs on the southernmost islands of the Southern Ocean and as a narrow fringe of parts of Antarctica. However, compared with arctic tundra, antarctic tundras are less well developed and have few species of plants.)

The distribution of arctic tundra is determined by climate, generally occurring where the annual precipitation is less than about 2 in (50 cm) each year, and the average annual temperature is colder than 23° F (-5° C). Much of the arctic tundra covers permanently frozen ground, or permafrost, above which only the active layer—comprised of the surface 1.6 ft (0.5 m) or so—thaws during the growing season. Arctic tundra experiences continuous inputs of solar radiation during much of the growing season, a condition that can last for more than two months, depending on latitude. The incessant insolation during this time allows the vegetation to be relatively productive, as long as the availabilies of moisture and nutrients are not excessively constrained. During the arctic winter, when plants are dormant but some animals remain active, there is continuous night for several months, and extremely cold conditions.

There are several categories of arctic tundra vegetation. The low-arctic tundra occurs in southern areas. On wet sites, the low-arctic tundra of North America develops as relatively productive wet meadows dominated by a tussock-forming cottongrass (*Eriophorum vaginatum*), while better-drained sites are dominated by shrubs such as willow (e.g, *Salix glauca*) and birch (e.g., *Betula glandulosa*), growing to about 1.6 ft (0.5 m) in height. These sites also support herbaceous plants, such as arctic lupin (*Lupinus arcticus*).

The high-arctic tundra is less productive and the plants are of lower stature. In North America, poorly drained wet meadows are dominated by graminoid plants, especially sedges (e.g., *Carex membranacea* and *C. stans*) and cottongrass (*Eriophorum angustifolium*). Drier sites are typically dominated by dwarf shrubs such as arctic willow (*Salix arctica*), arctic heather (*Cassiope tetragona*), mountain cranberry (*Vaccinium vitis-idaea*), and arctic bilberry (*V. uliginosum*), along with herbaceous plants such as lousewort (*Pedicularis* spp.), grasses (such as *Arctagrostis latifolia*), mosses, and lichens.

The polar desert is a very sparse tundra that occurs where climatic extremes of temperature and moisture availability allow only an incomplete cover of vegetation to develop. Such sites typically have a sparse cover of lichens and a few species of vascular plants, including cushion plants such as arctic avens (*Dryas integrifolia*) and purple saxifrage (*Saxifraga oppositifolia*), along with a few grasses and herbs. However, within

Rocky tundra on Bear Island in the Barents Sea.

the polar desert landscape there are occasional places that, because of their topography and drainage patterns, are relatively warm and moist throughout the growing season. These more moderate places are called high-arctic oases. They sustain a relatively lush growth of vegetation and, if the oasis is large enough, relatively large populations of animals.

The arctic tundra sustains only a few species of resident animals that remain active throughout the year. In the high-arctic tundra of North America, resident birds include the raven (*Corvus corax*) and rock ptarmigan (*Lagopus mutus*). Resident mammals include Peary caribou (*Rangifer tarandus pearyi*), muskox (*Ovibos moschatus*), arctic fox (*Alopex lagopus*), collared lemming (*Dicrostonyx torquatus groenlandicus*), and arctic hare (*Lepus arcticus*). However, there is a much larger number of seasonally abundant animals. These include insects, some of which can be very abundant during the growing season, including dense populations of mosquitoes. Migratory species of birds include finches such as snow bunting (*Plectrophenax nivalis*), Lapland longspur (*Calcarius lapponicus*), and hoary redpoll (*Acanthis hornemanni*); shorebirds such as Baird's sandpiper (*Calidris bairdii*) and red knot (*Calidris canutus*); waterfowl such as oldsquaw duck (*Clangula hyemalis*) and greater snow goose (*Chen caerulescens atlantica*); and larids such as arctic tern (*Sterna paradisaea*), glaucous gull (*Larus hyperboreus*), and parasitic jaeger (*Stercorarius parasiticus*).

Alpine tundra

Alpine tundra occurs in climatically stressed environments at high mountainous altitudes. Alpine tundra can even occur on mountaintops at tropical latitudes, although this vegetation type is much more common in temperate regions. Compared with the arctic tundra, alpine environments have much larger daily variations of temperature and solar radiation during the growing season. Because of the thinness of the atmosphere at high altitude, alpine tundra is also subject to large inputs of ultraviolet radiation, which can be an important biological stressor. Because the skies are often clear at high altitude, the surface cools very quickly at night, so that frost can be a daily occurrence during the growing season.

In general, alpine tundra is considerably richer in plant species than arctic tundra. At temperate latitudes, this occurs because alpine environments were not regionally obliterated by glacial ice during the most recent glaciations, so the component species were able to endure this period of intense climatic stress. This survival was made possible by the occurrence of non-glaciated refugia where plants could survive on some mountaintops (these are called nunataks). In addition, as the climate deteriorated, alpine tundra could migrate to lower-altitude, non-glaciated parts of mountainous regions, as the tree-line moved downwards. In contrast, almost all of the arctic tundra was destroyed by the extensive continental glaciers that covered northern regions during the most recent ice ages. It is believed that after deglaciation the arctic tundra was re-established by a northward migration of some of the plant species of alpine tundra. However, because only some species were capable of undertaking the extensive migrations that were necessary, the arctic tundra is relatively poor in species, compared with temperate alpine tundras.

There are relatively few animals that only occur in alpine tundra and not in other types of ecosystems. In North America some of the characteristic mammals of alpine tundra include a small relative of rabbits called the pika (*Ochotona princeps*), and the hoary marmot (*Marmota caligata*). The gray-crowned rosy finch (*Leucostichte tephrocotis*), horned lark (*Eremophila alpestris*) and water pipit (*Anthus spinoletta*) all breed in alpine tundra of North America, but also in arctic tundra (the lark also breeds in other open habitats, such as prairie and fields).

See also Ecosystem.

Further Reading:

Barbour, M.G. and W.D. Billings. *North American Terrestrial Vegetation.* Cambridge: Cambridge University Press, 1988.
Barbour, M.G., J.H. Burk, and W.D. Pitts. *Terrestrial Plant Ecology, 2nd ed.* Don Mills, Ontario: Benjamin/Cummings Pub. Co., 1987.

Bill Freedman

Tungsten see **Element, chemical**

Tunicates see **Sea squirts and salps**

Tunneling

Tunneling, also known as the tunnel effect, is a quantum mechanical phenomenon by which a tiny particle can penetrate a barrier that it could not, by any classical or obvious means, pass. Though seemingly miraculous, the effect does have some intuitive characteristics. For instance, thin barriers allow more particles to tunnel than do thick ones, and low barriers permit more tunneling than do high ones.

Tunneling does not generally show itself in the macroscopic world. It only starts to become a factor for microscopic items. Atoms can tunnel, as can electrons, but things such as tennis balls and grapes, easily seen with the naked eye, will not. For microscopic particles, the barrier heights are described in terms of energy instead of distance, (see Figure 1), but for conceptual purposes there is little difference.

It is important to note that the effect can only be understood with the aid of quantum mechanics. Classical mechanics, the system pioneered by Isaac Newton that stood unchallenged until the early twentieth century, has no way of explaining tunneling. In the Newtonian philosophy, all particles, even the tiniest of microscopic particles, can be located precisely. Any uncertainty is seen as the result of an imperfect measuring device or a sloppy scientist. In addition, each microscopic particle is considered to be like a tiny pebble and there can be nothing wave-like about it.

The quantum view of the universe is fundamentally different from the Newtonian view. Each particle is said to have both corpuscular (pebble-like) *and* wave-like properties. Furthermore, a quantum particle cannot, in general, be located precisely. It has a built-in uncertainty that cannot be taken away by the best of measuring instruments. For these reasons, a particle in quantum mechanics is often treated as a wave function. This is another way of saying that the particle is akin to a small bundle of waves.

Representing a quantum particle as such a bundle has two advantages. For one, it reveals that the particle is, in some sense, blurry and can never be exactly pinned down. It exists over a range of space, not a specific point. For another, the wave function format allows particles to exhibit wave-like properties (see

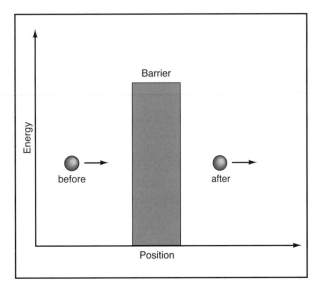

Figure 1. A particle before and after tunneling. It approaches from the left with far less energy than it would need to pass over the energy barrier.

interference and diffraction). Tunneling is a one of these wave-like properties. By the more general name of "barrier penetration," it is a well-established characteristic of waves. Light waves, for instance, have long been observed to overcome daunting optical barriers.

In a fundamental sense, the quantum mechanical explanation of tunneling can be illustrated by an analogy. If we roll a ball very slowly toward, say, a cement speed bump, we confidently say that it will not surpass the barrier and predict that it will roll back toward us. However, if a very modest ocean swell approaches an offshore sandbar, we are not as sure of the results and rightly so. The character of the wave, even if diminished in size, often makes its way past the sandbar. Similarly, treating a microscopic particle with the mathematical model of a ball clearly tells us tunneling is impossible, while using the mathematical model of a wave just as clearly states that particles will always have a chance to tunnel.

History

Some scattering experiments of the early twentieth century paved the way for tunneling. Ernest Rutherford, the pioneer of the scattering method, came across a paradox in a series of uranium experiments in 1910. Scattering involves the probing of a microscopic object by bombarding it with other particles and then keenly observing how the particles are, literally, scattered by the object in question. Specifically, Rutherford tried to pinpoint where the bombarding particles were scattered and how fast they were moving.

An example using tennis balls gives one a simple and accurate picture of a scattering experiment. Say a statue exists in a dark courtyard and we want information about the statue without being able to see it. Mainly, we want to know what it's shape is (e.g. a horse or a person) and from what materials it is made (e.g. granite or clay). To learn more about the statue, we stand at the edge of the courtyard and toss tennis balls into the dark area, hoping to hit the statue. After many thousands of tennis balls, we've learned a lot. If only a few of the tennis balls have hit anything, we know the statue is probably quite small. Also, the directions that tennis balls were scattered are important. If most of them come straight back to us, we can ascertain that the statue has a large, flat front like a wall. Moreover, by observing the speed of the scattered tennis balls, we can get an idea of how hard the statue is. Atomic scattering set a similar scene for Rutherford, but he was interested in the nuclei of atoms and he preferred alpha particles to tennis balls.

Through a series of remarkable scattering experiments, Rutherford, working in conjunction with his students Hans Geiger and Ernest Marsden, had accurately mapped the insides, or nucleus, of the uranium atom. Uranium was of great interest at the time because of its radioactive properties. The summation of Rutherford's results for Uranium came in the form of a potential diagram. Potential refers to electric potential energy, so his diagram, (see Figure 2), mapped out an energy barrier. Any particle that escaped the nucleus (i.e. any particle of nuclear radiation) would have to overcome this energy obstacle before it left. Rutherford estimated the top of this barrier to be at least about nine units of energy high. However, when observing the occasional radiated alpha particle (see radiation), he found that it had only four units of energy. The paradox was born. How could a particle with so little energy overcome a barrier of such height? Such a problem can be compared to a man walking next to a huge baseball stadium and suddenly seeing a baseball floating toward him, as if gently tossed. Surely any ball hit out of the stadium would have been moving fast enough to at least sting his palm.

The question lingered for eighteen years until George Gamow, assisted by his colleagues Edward Uhler Condon and Ronald Gurney, proposed a solution. In 1928, quantum mechanics was gaining credibility, and the three physicists performed a relatively simple calculation, treating the alpha particle as a quantum mechanical wave function. In essence, they analyzed the problem from the viewpoint that an alpha particle was not located precisely at any given spot, but rather that its existence was spread out, like a wave. Their explanation proposed that the alpha particles tunneled

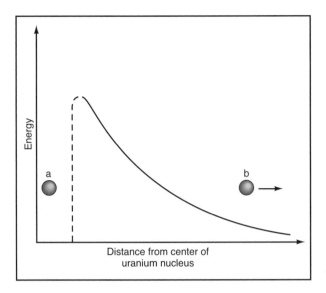

Energy

a

b →

Distance from center of
uranium nucleus

Figure 2. Rutherford's potential energy map (dark curve) and the theoretical other side of the barrier(dashed curve) which serves to contain the pieces of the nucleus; (a) shows an alpha particle as part of the nucleus and (b) shows its troublesome appearance outside the uranium atom.

KEY TERMS

· ·

Electron—One of the fundamental particles of the universe; carries a negative charge and has very little mass.

Energy barrier—An obstacle analogous to a physical wall, where any object that passes must either possess an energy greater than the barrier's or tunnel through the barrier.

Macroscopic—Not needing a microscope to be seen, readily observed by the human eye.

Potential—Closely related to potential energy, which is known as the "energy of position" or the energy that a body possesses due to its circumstances as opposed to its motion.

Quantum mechanics—A system of physical principles that arose in the early twentieth century to improve upon those of Isaac Newton, specifically with respect to microscopic phenomena.

Scattering—An experimental technique by which an item of interest is studied by inducing other particles to collide with it.

Wave function—A useful mathematical construct commonly employed in quantum mechanics to represent both a particle's wave-like characteristics and its uncertainty in location.

out of uranium's energy barrier, and it fit Rutherford's observations perfectly. The acceptance and practical application of tunneling theory had begun.

Applications

One of the first applications of tunneling was an atomic clock based on the tunneling frequency of the nitrogen atom in an ammonia (chemical formula NH_3) molecule. The rate at which the nitrogen atom tunnels back and forth across the energy barrier presented by the hydrogen atoms is so reliable and so easily measured that it was used as the timing mechanism in one of the earliest atomic clocks.

A current and quickly advancing application of tunneling is Scanning Tunneling Microscopy (abbreviated STM). This technique can render high-resolution images, including individual atoms, that accurately map the surface of a material. As with many high-tech tools, its operation is fairly simple in principle, while its actual construction is quite challenging.

The working part of a tunneling microscope is an incredibly sharp metal tip. This tip is electrically charged and held near the surface of an object (known as the sample) that is to be imaged. The energy barrier in this case is the gap between the tip and the sample. When the tip gets sufficiently close to the sample surface, the energy barrier becomes thin enough that a

noticeable number of electrons begin to tunnel from the tip to the object. Classically, the technique could never work because the electrons would not pass from the tip to the sample until the two actually touched. The number of tunneling electrons, measured by incredibly sensitive equipment, can eventually yield enough information to create a picture of the sample surface.

Another application of tunneling has resulted in the tunnel diode. The tunnel diode is a small electronic switch and, by incorporating electron tunneling, it can process electronic signals much faster than any ordinary physical switch. At peak performance, it can switch on and then off again ten billion times in a single second.

See also Quantum mechanics.

Further Reading:
Eisberg, Robert and Robert Resnick. *Quantum Physics of Atoms, Molecules, Solids, Nuclei and Particles.* New York: John Wiley and Sons, 1974.
Liboff, Richard L. *Introductory Quantum Mechanics.* Menlo Park, CA: Addison-Wesley, 1988.

Tipler, Paul A. *Modern Physics*. New York: Worth Publishers, 1987.
Wiesendanger, Roland and Hans-Joachim Gœntherodt (Eds.). *Scanning Tunneling Microscopy I.* New York: Springer-Verlag 1993.

Brandon Brown

Tur see **Goats**

Turacos

Turacos, or touracos, are 18 species of sub-Saharan birds that make up the family Musophagidae, in the order Cuculiformes, which also includes the cuckoos, anis, coucals, and roadrunner. The usual habitat of turacos is dense tropical forests or forest edges. Turacos do not migrate, although they may move locally.

Turacos are medium- to large-sized birds, with a body length of 1.2 - 2.5 ft (38 - 76 cm). They have short, rounded wings, long, broad tails, and small, crested heads. Their bills are short, stout, and slightly hooked at the tip of the upper mandible. The outer toe is highly dexterous, and can be turned and used in a forward or backward position.

Turacos have a soft, thick plumage, colored in hues of green, brown, blue, or grey, with patches of white and red. The feather pigments of turacos are rather unusual. Most birds achieve a green coloration using a combination of yellow and melano-blue pigments, but in turacos an actual, green pigment known as turacoverdin is present in the feathers. Turacos also produce a unique red copper-containing pigment known as turacin.

Turacos are arboreal birds. They are weak, undulating fliers, and they commonly run along branches through tree foliage, suggesting the movements of a small mammal, such as a squirrel. These birds eat fruits, seeds, buds, and invertebrates. The family name, Musophagidae, translates from the Greek as banana eater, although this is a misnomer, because these birds are not actually known to feed on bananas or plantains.

Turacos are somewhat gregarious, congregating in small, noisy groups. Courtship includes fluttering displays to reveal bright patches of coloration, along with raising of the conspicuous crest on the head, and energetic bobbing of the tail. These displays are accompanied by loud calls, and feeding of the female with fruit offered by the male.

A Hartlaub's turaco (*Tauraco hartlaubi*).

Turacos lay two to three eggs in a frail, arboreal nest made of twigs. These are incubated by the female, but both parents share in the feeding and care of the downy young.

The giant blue plantain-eater (*Corythaeola cristata*) is the biggest turaco, achieving a length of 2.5 ft (76 cm).

See also Cuckoos.

Bill Freedman

Turbine

A turbine is any of various rotary machines that convert the kinetic energy in a stream of fluid (gas or liquid) into mechanical energy by passing the stream through a system of fixed and moving fans or blades. Turbines are simple but powerful machines that embody Newton's third law of motion which states that for every action there is an equal and opposite reaction. They are classified according to the driving fluid they use: steam, gas, water, and wind. Today, different types of turbines generate electricity, power ships and submarines, and propel jet aircraft.

History

The idea of using naturally moving water or air to help do work is an ancient one. Waterwheels and windmills are the best examples of ancient mankind's ability to capture some of nature's energy and put it to work. The Romans were grinding corn with a waterwheel as early as 70 B.C., and modern-type windmills were being used in Persia around 700 A.D. Both are ancestors of the turbine. Both have large surfaces (paddles, buckets, or a sail) at their wheel edges that are struck by moving wind or water which forces the wheel to turn. It was through the turning of this large central wheel, which could turn other smaller wheels, that mechanical energy was obtained and work, like grinding corn or operating a pump, could be accomplished.

The most ancient of these methods was the undershot wheel or paddle wheel. On these old waterwheels, only the very lowest part of the wheel was submerged beneath a moving body of water, and the entire wheel was turned as the river flowed past it, pushing against its paddles. This was a prototype for what came to be called an impulse turbine, which is one that is driven by the force of a fluid directly striking it. The undershot waterwheel was followed during medieval times by the overshot wheel. This first made its appearance in Germany around the middle of the 12th century and became the prototype for the modern reaction turbine. Contrasted to the impulse turbine whose energy source is kinetic energy (something striking something else and giving it some of its energy), the energy source for an overshot wheel (or reaction turbine) is known as potential energy. This is because it is the weight of the water acting under gravity that is used to turn the wheel. Renaissance engineers studied the waterwheel and realized that the action of water on a wheel with blades would be much more effective if the entire wheel were somehow enclosed in a kind of chamber. They knew very well that only a small amount of the water pushing or falling on a wheel blade or paddle actually strikes it, and that much of the energy contained in the onrushing water is lost or never actually captured. Enclosing the wheel and channeling the water through this chamber

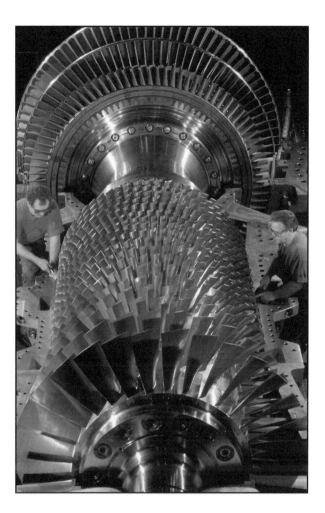

Gas turbine manufacturing in South Carolina.

would result in a machine of greater efficiency and power. They were hampered however by a lack of any theoretical understanding of hydraulics as well as by a lack of precision machine tools with which they could carefully build things. Both of these problems were resolved to some degree in the eighteenth century, and one of the earliest examples of a reaction turbine was built in 1750 by the German mathematician and naturalist, Johann Andres von Segner (1704-1777). In his system, the moving water entered a cylindrical box containing the shaft of a runner or rotor and flowed out through tangential openings, acting with its weight on the inclined vanes of the wheel. A really efficient water turbine was now within reach it appeared, and a prize was offered in France by the Societe d'Encouragement pour l'Industrie Nationale. The prize was won by the French mining engineer, Claude Burdin (1778-1873), who published his results in 1828. It was in this publication that Burdin coined the word "turbine" which he took from the Latin "turbo" meaning a whirling or spinning top. It was Burdin's student, Benoit Fourneyron

(1801-1867), who improved and developed his master's work and who is considered to be the inventor of the modern hydraulic turbine. Fourneyron built a six-horsepower turbine and later went on to build larger machines that worked under higher pressures and delivered more horsepower. His main contribution was his addition of a distributor which guided the water flow so that it acted with the greatest efficiency on the blades of the wheel. His was a reaction type turbine, since water entering through the vanes of the distributor (that was fitted inside the blades) then acted on the blades of the wheel. Following Fourneyron's first turbine, which happened to be a hydraulic or water turbine, other turbines were developed that used the energy of a different material like gas or steam. Although these different types of turbines have different means of operation and certainly different histories, they still embody the basic characteristics of a turbine. They all spin, or receive their energy from some form of a moving fluid, and they all convert it into mechanical energy.

Types of turbines

While turbines can be classed as either impulse or reaction according to the way they function, there are four broad types of turbines categorized according to the fluid that supplies the driving force: steam, gas, water, or wind. Steam, water, and wind turbines are all used to generate electricity, and gas turbines are most often used by jet aircraft for propulsion. The steam turbine is mainly used by power plants that burn either fossil fuels or use nuclear energy to drive generators for consumer electricity. Steam turbines also power submarines and ships. The water or hydraulic turbine is used almost exclusively in hydroelectric plants to power an electric generator which then produces electric power for homes, offices, and factories. Wind turbines are the least common, but Scotland now uses the vertical machines called Darrieus turbines whose giant, bow-shaped blades look like huge egg beaters to generate electricity via the wind. The gas turbine is primarily used by jet aircraft.

Steam turbines transform the thermal energy stored in steam into mechanical work. The earliest steam turbine was also the earliest known steam engine. During the first century A.D., the Greek mathematician and engineer, Hero of Alexandria, built what was basically a novelty and produced no useful work, but was nonetheless the first steam turbine. It consisted of a small, hollow sphere with two nozzles or bent tubes sticking out of it. The sphere was attached to a boiler which produced steam. As the steam escaped from the sphere's hollow tubes, the sphere itself would rotate on its axis

and continue to whirl. This was in principle a reaction steam turbine because the force of the escaping steam itself provided the thrust to make it spin. Steam was not considered in any type of turbine context again until the Italian, Giovanni Branca, published a work in 1629 in which he suggested the principle of the impulse steam turbine. In his book he details that it would be simple to convert the linear motion of a cylinder into the rotary motion needed for work by directing a jet of steam onto the vanes of a wheel, like water against a waterwheel. It is not known if he ever built such an engine. Despite the advances made in understanding and managing steam that were gained in the eighteenth century, the steam turbine could not be built until the precision and strength of machining and materials had reached a certain level. In 1884, English engineer Charles Algernon Parsons (1854-1931) produced the first practical steam turbine engine. Although designed for the production of electric power, it was soon applied to marine propulsion and drove a ship named *Turbinia* in 1887. The spectacular speed and performance of this great ship opened a new era of steam propulsion at sea. Parsons overcame several major engineering difficulties involving stress, vibration, and balancing and truly deserves the title of father of the modern steam turbine. Besides their use at sea, steam turbines went on to generate an overwhelming proportion of the electricity used in the twentieth century. Today, the bulk of our electricity is generated by power stations using steam turbines. The steam is produced by the burning of fossil fuels (coal or gas) or by the use of nuclear energy. Most agree that steam turbines are still evolving and will play a considerable role in the generation of electrical power for some time to come.

Water or hydraulic turbines are identified with dams and the generation of hydroelectric power. When a turbine is operated by rapidly flowing or falling water, it is called an impulse turbine. The huge hydro-electric plant at Niagara Falls that was built at the end of the 19th century is this type of turbine. Water conditions usually determine what type of turbine is needed, and impulse water turbines require a constant flow of water to operate efficiently. Two aspects of this water flow is critical, its volume and its head. Water head is the distance water must fall before it strikes the turbine's wheel. With a sufficient volume and head like Niagara, the impulse turbine can have its wheel or rotor mounted on either a vertical or a horizontal shaft. The ends of the turbine's blades act like cup-shaped buckets, and as the water is directed at them at very high speeds by jets, the blades turn. As might be expected, most hydraulic turbines are of the reaction type since they are best suited to low-head situations. Here, the turbine is underwater and is turned by both the weight and speed of its flow.

Its shaft is vertical and has either spirally-curved blades or ones that resemble a ship's propeller. Unlike impulse turbines which achieve rotation by the acceleration of water from the supply nozzles, reaction turbines work because of the acceleration of water in the rotor or runner. Both then transform the energy from the rushing water into mechanical energy.

Wind turbines are the least common or significant of all turbine types, and many technical texts do not even mention them. Unlike waterwheels which directly led to the hydraulic turbine, the windmill has for the most part not evolved as a significant source of modern energy. As with the noted Darrieus turbines in Scotland however, wind turbines do exist and have proved useful in areas of high, continuous winds. Wind turbine clusters generate electricity in the Tehachapi Mountains near Barstow, California as well as in certain areas of Hawaii and New Hampshire.

The best-known use for gas turbines is for jet engines. Gas turbines utilize hot gases as their names implies, and they are the newest type of turbine engine. Their gases are produced by the burning of some type of fuel, like kerosene. Air is then drawn into the front of the turbine and passed through a compressor where the compressed air is mixed with fuel in a combustion chamber and is burned. This produces hot gases that expand and therefore rush through the turbine rotors, causing them to spin. This spinning can be used to power an electric generator or a pump, but in the case of a jet aircraft, the hot expanding gases are sent out at very high speed from the rear nozzle of the engine, producing thrust which then pushes the engine and the aircraft forward. Gas turbines attain temperatures higher than those of a steam turbine (the hotter a gas turbine is, the more efficiently it runs) and consequently cannot be built with ordinary metals.

Turbine engines are an example of an idea that could not be put into practice until technology had accomplished certain advances. Probably the most important technical advance was the widespread introduction of steel and its alloys that occurred during the second half of the nineteenth century. The popularity and use of certain types of turbine engines rises and falls as needs, priorities, and situations change. A good example is the use of steam turbines for ship propulsion. After dominating sea travel for many years, steam turbines for declined after the 1973 oil embargo because the fuel to make steam became prohibitively expensive. Diesels moved in to take their place since they required less fuel. Diesels can only use liquid fuel however, and as oil becomes scarcer in the next century, steam turbines for ships may again be the choice, since they can be driven by coal-burning boilers.

> ## KEY TERMS
>
> **Hydroelectric power**—Electric power derived from generators that are driven by hydraulic or water turbine engines.
>
> **Impulse turbine**—The force of a fast-moving fluid striking the blades that makes the rotor spin.
>
> **Kinetic energy**—That part of the energy of a body that it possesses as a result of its motion.
>
> **Mechanical energy**—Energy in the form of mechanical power.
>
> **Reaction turbine**—The rotor turns primarily as a result of the weight or pressure of a fluid on the blades.

See also Alternative energy sources; Jet engine; Waterwheel.

Further Reading:
Balje, O. E. *Turbo-Mechanics,* 1981.
IEEE Guide for the Operation and Maintenance of Turbine Generators. Institute of Electrical and Electronics Engineers, 1990.
Vennard, J. K. and R. L. Street. *Elementary Fluid Mechanics.* Wiley, 1976.

Leonard C. Bruno

Turbot see **Flatfish**

Turbulence

Turbulence is the formation of eddies in a fluid (liquid or gas). It is produced whenever a fluid—under certain conditions—is in contact with a solid and there is relative motion between them; for example: when wind flows past a building or past a mountain; when the ocean flows past an island; when a baseball flies by; when a jet plane moves in the stratosphere; or when a river flows past a bridge pier. In all these cases, eddies form behind the obstacle (i.e., "downstream"), and eventually are carried away by the main body of fluid.

Historical overview

Turbulence has long been observed, but its scientific study began with the work of William John Mac-

Turbulence in the water below Niagara Falls.

quorn Rankine (1820-1872); later, Osborne Reynolds (1842-1912) defined the number bearing his name, and Ludwig Prandtl (1875-1953) put forth the limiting-layer hypothesis.

Today, the study of turbulence, experimental and theoretical, continues; but an agreement between both approaches is still in the future.

The Reynolds number

There is a number—called Reynolds number—whose values indicate clearly whether the motion of a fluid in a certain region is turbulent or not. It is defined as:

$$R = \frac{\text{Inertial force}}{\text{frictional force}} = \frac{vd}{\eta}$$

Whether an obstacle carries any eddies, and whether these are released into the flow downstream depends upon the speed of the incoming fluid, the size of the obstacle and the internal friction (viscosity) of the fluid, according to Karen J. Heywood writing in *Physics Education*. Just like a solid body, a parcel of liquid or

gas has mass, and therefore inertia. Inertial force is the amount of force required to stop a body that is moving along steadily with its own inertia (for example, the force to stop a charging rhino moving towards you would be greater than that needed to stop a humming-bird at the same speed). The inertial force necessary to stop a parcel of water that occupies a unit volume (1 m^3, say) is proportional to the square of its speed (v^2) divided by a length typical of the obstacle (d)—say, the diameter of a stone in a river. All fluids, as they flow, present friction between their different parts. This property is called viscosity. Liquids are more viscous than gases, and, among liquids, corn syrup is much more viscous than water. The viscous force (internal friction) working on an object of diameter d moving through a fluid at speed v is proportional to $\eta.d/d^2$, where η is the viscosity coefficient of the fluid. Dividing the expression for the inertial force by that for the frictional force, we obtain R as given by the above equation.

Formation of eddies

If we place an obstacle—e. g., a sphere—at rest in the midst of a fluid stream, our physical intuition sug-

KEY TERMS

Fluid—A piece of matter that flows; i.e., is deformed under the action of even the weakest forces.

Inertia—The resistance of a piece of matter to acceleration i. e., to change its state of motion or rest.

Viscosity—Internal friction between parts of a fluid. The effect of viscosity is to slow fluid motion and to dissipate energy.

gests that the part of the fluid which is really in contact with the obstacle must be at rest. However, photographs taken in different laboratories appeared not to support this idea. In order to explain what was happening, Ludwig Prandtl (1875-1953) introduced the hypothesis of the "limiting layer," according to which in the immediate neighborhood of the obstacle there is a very thin layer of fluid whose velocity parallel to the surface of the object brows very rapidly, from zero at the surface itself to the velocity of the main body of fluid far from the object. This limiting layer is very thin upstream, but broadens downstream, i. e., behind the obstacle.

Inside the downstream limit layer the fluid begins to move backwards and in circles, until the eddies form when the Reynolds number is $R=5$. As the fluid velocity grows, bringing R to a value of 70, the limit layer broadens still more downstream, forming what is called a "von Karman vortex street" after Theodor von Karman (born 1881). These eddies finally leave the vicinity of the obstacle and float away with the main fluid current. If R keeps increasing to values of 1000 or 2500, eddies become more frequent and the vortex street broadens still more, finally breaking up and forming a "turbulent wake." At this stage the motion of fluid particles is chaotic and varies in time.

See also Fluid dynamics.

Further Reading:

Heywood, Karen J. "Fluid flows in the environment: an introduction." *Physics Education.* 28: 43 (1993).
Simon, R.A. "La Hidrodinamica." *Charlas de Fisica.* 9: 43 (1992).

Raul A. Simon

Turkeys

Turkeys are relatively large, powerful, ground-feeding, North American birds with colorful, featherless heads, classified in the family Meleagridae. The original range of the common turkey (*Meleagris gallopavo*) was from extreme southern Ontario to Mexico, but it now occupies a much smaller area. The second species in this family is the ocellated turkey (*Agriocharis ocellata*), which occurs in southern Mexico, Guatemala, and Belize.

Turkeys are economically important birds. They are widely hunted in the wild, and are intensively reared on farms. The populations of wild turkeys are now greatly reduced, and much of their natural habitat has been destroyed, but many millions of these birds occur in captivity.

Biology of turkeys

Wild turkeys have a rather dark plumage, with some degree of iridescence. Turkeys have an featherless head, with brightly colored naked skin which is blue and red in the common turkey, and blue and orange in the ocellated turkey.

Turkeys are sexually dimorphic. Male turkeys (called "toms") are relatively colorful and large, with a body length in the common turkey of up to 4 ft (1.2 m), and a weight of up to 20 lb (9 kg). Turkeys have powerful legs, and male birds have a sharp spur on the back of the foot that can inflict serious wounds during combat with other males or possibly when fending off a predator.

The beak of male common turkeys is adorned by a wattle, which is a long, red, pendulous appendage that develops from tissues over the base of the upper mandible. During courtship displays the wattle is extended to a droopy length that is several times that of the beak. Male common turkeys also develop a fat-rich growth on their breast prior to the breeding season. This tissue helps to sustain the male turkeys during this intensive period of the year, when their frequent, time-consuming, aggressive encounters with other males do not allow them to feed regularly. The constant preoccupation with displaying, mating, and fighting during the breeding period is hard on the toms, and they can be quite emaciated by the time this season has passed.

Wild turkeys mostly occur in forested and shrubby habitats, often with open glades. Turkeys forage on the ground in small groups, and spend the night roosting in trees. Turkeys are mostly herbivorous birds, eating a wide range of plant foods, although they also eat insects

Wild turkeys (*Meleagris gallopavo*) at the Arizona Sonora Desert Museum, Arizona.

as they are encountered. Hard tree fruits such as acorns and other nuts, known collectively as "mast," is an important food that is gleaned from the forest floor. These hard seeds are ground with small stones and other grit in the powerful gizzard of turkeys, so that the nutritious matter can be digested and assimilated.

Turkeys are polygamous, meaning that a male bird will mate with as many females as possible. Male turkeys court females by elaborately spreading their fan-like tail feathers, and by other visual displays, in which the wattle figures prominently. These displays are given while the tom struts proudly about, making loud "gobbling" noises. Male turkeys are extremely aggressive amongst themselves during the breeding season, and well-matched toms may fight to the death over access to females.

Female turkeys are alone responsible for building the ground nest, brooding the 8-15 eggs, and raising the young. Turkey chicks are precocious, leaving the nest within a day of being born, and following the female about and feeding themselves. Turkeys are gregarious after the breeding season, forming flocks that forage and roost together.

Turkeys and humans

Because of their large size and mild-tasting flesh, turkeys have long been hunted by humans as food and for sport. Until recently, wild common turkeys were badly overhunted in North America. This caused the wild populations of turkeys to decline over large areas, a resource collapse that was especially intense during the nineteenth century. Turkey populations were also badly damaged wherever there were extensive conversions of their forest habitat into agriculture, a change that has occurred over widespread regions.

Today, common turkeys do not occupy much of their former range, and they generally occur as isolated populations in fragmented habitats. However, turkeys have been re-introduced to many areas from which they were eliminated, and also to some regions to which they were not native. These introductions, coupled with controls over hunting pressures, have allowed substantial increases in the populations of wild turkeys over much of their North American range.

It is not known when the common turkey was first domesticated, but this had already been accomplished by indigenous peoples of Mexico long before the Spanish conquest. The first turkeys viewed by Europeans were apparently those domestic birds, some of which were taken to Europe for display and cultivation as a novel and tasty food from the New World. The turkeys that are raised intensively today are derived from Mexican wild turkeys. Most domestic turkeys are white, although some varieties are black. Domestic turkeys have been artificially selected to have large amounts of meat, especially on the breast.

If the turkey came from the Americas, how did this bird receive its common name, which implies a Turkish origin? During the sixteenth century, when the domestic turkey was first introduced to England, the bird was thought to resemble the helmeted guinea fowl (*Numida meleagris*). This species had been kept domestically since the fourth century B.C., but had disappeared from Europe after the collapse of the Roman Empire. During the fifteenth and sixteenth centuries, Portuguese traders re-introduced domestic guinea fowl to Europe, using birds that had been obtained in the region of Turkey. The common name in England of these re-introduced guinea fowl was "turkey," and this name was transferred to the superficially similar domestic turkey of the Americas when it was introduced somewhat later on.

Further Reading:

Harrison, C. J. O., ed. *Bird Families of the World.* New York: H. N. Abrams, 1978.

Bill Freedman

Turnstone see **Sandpipers**

Turtles

Turtles are easily recognized as those four-legged animals whose bodies are enclosed between two bony shells. They constitute the reptilian order Testudines. The 257 living species inhabit all continents except Antarctica, many isolated islands, and the tropical and temperate oceans.

History and fossil record

These are the oldest of living four-legged animals, having first appeared in the Triassic period about 215 million years ago. They were observers of the first dinosaur clans and dodged the footsteps of their ancestors for 150 million years. They shared the seas with icthyosaurs, watched pterosaurs soar overhead, and saw

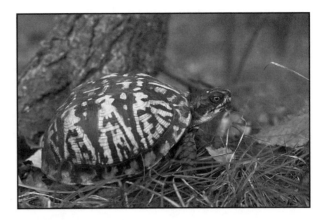

An eastern box turtle (*Terrapene carolina*) at Baker Sanctuary, Michigan.

the first small furry animals that became mammals. They remained the same pragmatic four-footed, shelled creatures while some dinosaurs grew feathers and wings, becoming birds, and some of the furry animals became elephants and whales, and bats—and human beings. With their early-determined plodding style, they have been the ultimate survivors among terrestrial vertebrates.

Turtles suddenly appeared in the fossil record in the Triassic period and their ancestors are unknown. The earliest known fossil turtles (*Proganochelys*) are from the late Triassic (Norian) deposits of Germany. They are rather large (3ft [1m], shell length) and appear to be terrestrial, perhaps marsh-dwelling animals. The shell is already present, similar to that in all living turtles. It is made up of a rounded upper carapace and a flattened lower plastron. The carapace incorporates 10 vertebrae and their associated ribs, together with additional bone between the ribs. The skull is very solidly made, without temporal openings, and the jaws are toothless (and presumably beaked as in modern turtles), although there are some small teeth in the palate, which are not found among living members of this group. The eight cervical (neck) vertebrae are primitive, in that they are not modified to allow the head to withdraw into the shell.

Since turtles are fairly large, have a great deal of bone, and often occupy aquatic or marshy habitats where they are likely to be buried and preserved, their fossils are found in many ancient sediments from the Jurassic to the present. Many are found in the Cretaceous deposits of North America.

Morphology

The appearance of a turtle is unmistakable. With its head, tail, and four legs projecting from a broad bony

The endangered Kemp's ridley sea turtle (*Lepidochelys kempii*).

shell, it looks like no other animal. The domed upper shell (carapace) and flattened lower shell (plastron) serve to protect the main body organs and in most land-dwelling species the head, limbs, and tail that project from the shell can be withdrawn inside this box if danger threatens. A horny beak (like that of a bird) covers the jaws. The head, legs, and tail are covered by horny scales, and the feet have typical horny nails. The bony shell is covered with an epidermal layer of scutes in most turtles, with the scutes occurring in a regular pattern that is typical for the various species. Only the Leatherback sea turtle and the Softshell freshwater turtles lack these horny plates.

Inside, a turtle is a typical vertebrate animal, with two lungs, a typical reptilian three-chambered heart and associated circulatory system, and the usual digestive system with an esophagus, stomach, small and large intestines, and the associated liver. As in other reptiles, the digestive, urinary, and reproductive systems end in

an expanded chamber, the cloaca, which also encloses the penis of the male animals. The nervous system comprises a well-developed brain, a spinal cord that is enclosed in a vertebral column, and peripheral nerves. Both vision (including color vision) and hearing are acute.

The size range of turtles is extreme. Some adults, such as the American mud turtle (*Kinosternon subrubum*), are less than five inches (12.5 cm) long, whereas giant tortoises may attain lengths of 4.6 ft (140 cm) with a weight of 575 pounds (260 kg). The giant leatherback sea turtle attains a length of at least 6.1 ft (183 cm) with weights up to 1,500 pounds (680 kg).

Ecology

Most modern turtles are semiaquatic pond- or swamp-dwelling types, as were, apparently, their early ancestors. Nevertheless, in spite of their slow pace, both behaviorly and evolutionarily, they have diversified into a number of distinct kinds that have become specialized in different ways. Some, such as the sea turtles, have become ocean-dwelling animals, literally flying through the water with their paddle-like forelimbs, and returning to land only to lay their eggs. Others, such as the softshells, have become river-dwellers, flattened like a pancake to merge with the sandy or muddy stream bottoms. Still others, such as the tortoises, have become strictly land-dwellers with elephantlike feet, and range into the grasslands and semi-desert regions of the world.

Many turtles are omnivores, eating both plants and animals, but others are highly specialized in their food requirements. Both the giant tortoises and some of the sea turtles are vegetarians as adults, although the young may eat insects or small vertebrates. Some river turtles, such as the map turtles (*Graptemys*), are specialists, feeding on snails and clams. Softshell turtles are mainly fish-eaters, and snapping turtles (*Chelydra serpentina*) will eat almost any animal that they can subdue; they are a major predator of baby ducks.

Behavior and life history

Turtles generally mate in the spring, when the males actively search for receptive females. Courtship includes many striking activities, including those of the American red-eared turtle (*Trachemys scripta*) which swims backward in front of the female, while stroking her head and neck with his greatly-elongate fingernails. The males of some tortoises call, either during courtship or during mating. The smaller species, such as Mediterranean tortoises (*Testudo*), cluck like chickens (perhaps the Bible's "voice of the turtle" in the spring), whereas the giant Galapagos tortoises (*Geochelone*) bellow like bulls.

All turtles lay eggs, which vary in shape from that of elongate sausages to that of ping-pong balls. The smaller species may lay only two or three eggs in a clutch, whereas sea turtles may lay three or more clutches of 100-150 eggs in a single year. Most turtles dig a hole (with their hind feet), lay their eggs inside and cover the entrance, leaving them to be incubated by the heat of the sun. Some take a long time to hatch; 60-90 days is typical.

Given the opportunity, most turtles are very long-lived. Even the small eastern box turtle (*Terrapene carolina*) may live 100 years, and some of the giant tortoises have been reported to live for at least 150 years. Thus, the populations of these old turtles may give a false impression of the vigor of the species. It took several decades before it was realized that the giant tor-

toises on some of the islands in the Galapagos were producing no young at all.

Classification

Morphologically and evolutionarily, the living turtles are separated into two major groups (subclasses) that can be identified by the way they retract their head into their shell.

Side-neck turtles

The "side-neck" turtles (Pleurodira) fold their neck into a lateral S-shape so that one side of the head can be seen tucked between the shells when it is retracted. This is a relatively small group of mainly pond turtle-like animals that are found only on the southern continents: South America, Africa (and Madagascar), and Australia. Although both families (Pelomedusidae and Chelidae) occur in South America, they differ in their distributions in other continents. The pelomedusids are found in Africa, Madagascar, and some of the other islands of the Indian Ocean, whereas the chelids occur otherwise only in Australia and New Guinea.

Perhaps the best-known side-neck is the bizarre-looking South American matamata (*Chelus fimbriatus*), which lies quietly on the bottom of ponds or streams and until a small fish comes near, then suddenly opens its mouth and expands its throat to "suck in" the fish.

Hidden-neck turtles

The "hidden-neck" turtles (Cryptodira), on the other hand, retract their head with the neck in a vertical S-shape, and appear to pull the head directly back into the shell with nothing showing except the snout. This is a larger and much more diversified group, including the common pond turtles, the land-dwelling tortoises, and the large sea turtles. They are found throughout the temperate and tropical regions of the world.

Three of the more primitive families are found mainly in North America, with some ranging into South America. The snapping turtles comprise two genera, each with a single species. The common snapper (*Chelydra serpentina*) is best known, ranging from Canada to Ecuador. Its large size (shell length of up to 18 in (47 cm) and long, alligator-like tail make it a conspicuous animal when it comes out of the streams or ponds that it inhabits. (Its duck-eating habits were mentioned above.) The even larger alligator snapper (*Macrochelys temminckii*) is (24 in [66 cm or more], but is much less aggressive. It feeds mainly on small fishes that it attracts with a worm-like "bait" on its tongue.

and seldom leaves the water. Both species lay 20-80 round eggs, which they place in a flask-shaped hole.

The mud and musk turtles include about 25 small to medium sized species that are found from Canada to Brazil. Most of these are carnivorous, feeding on insects, worms, and other small animals. They lay only a few (2-10) elongate, brittle-shelled eggs.

There is a single living species of the highly aquatic Central American river turtles (*Dermatemys mawii*). It is a rather large turtle (to 25 in [65 cm] that is seldom found more than a few feet from the water. The adults are entirely herbivorous and are highly prized as food by the people who live in their range.

The pond turtles (Emydidae) and tortoises (Testudinidae) comprise the largest number of turtles, and occur throughout the tropical and temperate regions of the world, other than the Australian region. The American pond turtles are closely related to the pond turtles of southern Asia, as are the European turtles. The tortoises (*Gopherus*) appear to have been in North America for a very long time.

The pelagic sea-turtles are among the best-known of all animals. Although they comprise only a few genera, they are large and conspicuous, and used to occur in huge numbers. Although sea turtles spend most of their lives in the open sea, they must come to land to lay their eggs. They have established certain tropical and subtropical beaches as laying areas, and they return year-after-year to these same locations. Although formerly these were in remote locations, most of these are no longer remote. Miami Beach was once such a laying location.

The largest of the sea-turtles (in fact, the largest of all living turtles) is the giant leatherback. As its name suggests, it lacks the horny plates that cover the shells of most turtles, and instead has a rather smooth leathery covering. It feeds on jellyfishes to a large extent and is probably the fastest swimmer of all turtles. It has a thick fatty layer under the skin that helps it to retain body heat as well as a heat-exchanging mechanism that conserves the heat from muscular effort, thus allowing this species to range into colder waters.

Turtles and humans

Turtles as food

The observation that no large tortoises live near large human populations, and that all giant tortoises live on isolated islands, suggest that they have always been looked upon by humans as a ready source of meat. The sight of a 250 pound (114 kg) slow-moving, harmless animal was sufficient to bring great glee to a hungry hunter and those giants (many much larger than any living species) on the mainlands disappeared before humans began writing history. Those on islands in the Caribbean and in the Indian Ocean, except for those on Aldabra, disappeared early in human history.

The giant tortoises of the Galapagos Islands, west of Ecuador, were taken by whalers from New England and elsewhere because if dumped into the hold of a whaling ship, they would survive for months in the cold Antarctic climate, providing a source of fresh meat during the long hunting season. Because the smaller female tortoises were preferred (the males being too heavy to carry), several of the islands were left with none but large male tortoises. The competition of the goats and the rats that escaped from these ships contributed to the continuing decline in the remaining populations.

According to the sailors of the 16th and 17th centuries, the sea turtles used to occur in great flotillas that "covered the sea" in regions such as the Caribbean. However, the various species, especially the green turtle (*Chelonia mydas*), were (and are) killed for their meat (turtle soup, served in fine restaurants, is made from the meat and cartilage of this species), while others such as the hawksbill (*Eretmochelys imbricata*) were killed for their beautiful "tortoise shell," which is used for combs and ornaments (although these are now illegal in the United States). The sea turtles are most vulnerable on their nesting beaches where people and their associated dogs and rats take both the eggs and the female turtles. In spite of the conservation measures initiated by many countries, however, the sea turtle populations are continuing to decline.

More recently the American salt-water terrapins (*Malaclemmys terrapin*) were eaten in such numbers that (in spite of "turtle farms") by the early 1900s a single individual cost $10—the price of a silk shirt! Fortunately, the few survivors have increased to some extent under legal protection.

Even more recently the snapping turtles (*Chelydra sepentina*), which were one of the most common turtles in North America, have shown signs of over-exploitation. Turtle soup from these animals was especially appreciated in Philadelphia, and for several decades a major soup company used thousands of turtles per year to supply this demand, and many more were prepared as turtle soup by restaurant chefs in other East Coast cities.

Captive turtles

The various zoological parks have salvaged a number of turtle species from almost certain extinction.

Many of these species are large or brightly colored tortoises that provide good exhibits, but zoos have attempted also to preserve small populations of less conspicuous species.

In addition, there is a huge commercial trade in turtles. For many years, turtle-farmers in Louisiana and elsewhere provided millions of baby turtles (mainly red-eared turtles, *Trachemys scripta*) to the pet trade each year. Ultimately, the turtle farms became contaminated with disease organisms such as *Salmonella* and the sale of baby turtles was made illegal in the United States. However, baby turtles are still being produced by these farms, and unknown millions are still sold overseas.

In recent years a number of rare species of turtles and tortoises are being bred and reared commercially, with the rarest bringing prices of more than $2,000 each. Europeans, who have always kept captive animals of many kinds, are now major consumers for both captive-bred and wild-caught turtles, and recently have been accused of badly depleting eastern populations of American box turtles (*Terrapene carolina*) by their purchases.

The future of turtles

In addition to the hazards mentioned above, all turtles suffer from the destruction of their habitats by the rapidly expanding human population. The sandy hills of the Florida gopher tortoise (*Gopherus polyphemus*) habitat are prime land for homes and shopping malls. The arid fields of California and Arizona desert tortoises (*Gopherus agassizii*) are ideal for motorcycle and off-road vehicle races, and all over the world the marshes and swamps, that are home to so many other species, are being dredged and drained for boat basins and still more home sites.

In the United States, the automobile is also a major killer of turtles. Many thousands die on the highways each year by being run over throughout the nation. There is little question that most species are badly depleted, and most populations are continuing to decline.

See also Reptiles.

Further Reading:
Ernst, C.H., and R. W. Barbour. *Turtles of the United States.* Lexington: University Press of Kentucky, 1972.
Ernst, C.H., and R. W. Barbour. *Turtles of the World.* Washington DC: Smithsonian Institution Press, 1989.
Minton, S.A., Jr. and M. R. Minton. *Giant Reptiles.* New York: Scribner's Sons, 1973.

KEY TERMS

Carapace—The upper part of a turtle's shell.

Cryptodires—Hidden-necked turtles, found throughout most of the temperate and tropical regions of the earth; they fold their neck vertically.

Pelagic—Swimming in the open ocean.

Plastron—The bottom part of a turtle's shell.

Pleurodires—Side-necked turtles, found only on the southern continents; they fold their neck laterally.

Obst, F.J. Turtles, *Tortoises and Terrapins.* New York: St. Martin's Press, 1988.
Pritchard, P.C.H. *Living Turtles of the World.* Jersey City: T.F.H. Publications, 1967.

Herndon G. Dowling

Twisted-winged parasites see **Strepsiptera**

Typhoid fever

Typhoid fever is a severe infection causing a sustained high fever, and caused by the bacteria *Salmonella typhi*. *S. typhi* is in the same tribe of bacteria as the type spread by chicken and eggs, commonly known as "Salmonella poisoning," or food poisoning. *S. typhi* bacteria, however, do not multiply directly in food, as do the *Salmonella* responsible for food poisoning, nor does it have vomiting and diarrhea as the most prominent symptoms. Instead, persistently high fever is the hallmark of infection with *Salmonella typhi*.

How *Salmonella typhi* is spread

S. typhi bacteria are passed into the stool and urine of infected patients, and may continue to be present in the stool of asymptomatic carriers (individuals who have recovered from the symptoms of the disease, but continue to carry the bacteria). This carrier state occurs in about 3% of all individuals recovered from typhoid fever.

The disease is passed between humans, then, through poor hygiene, such as deficient hand washing after toileting. Individuals who are carriers of the disease and who handle food can be the source of epidemic spread of typhoid. One such individual is the source for the expression "Typhoid Mary," a name given to someone with whom others wish to avoid all contact. The real "Typhoid Mary" was a cook named Mary Mallon (1855-1938) who lived in New York City around 1900. She was a carrier of typhoid and was the cause of at least 53 outbreaks of typhoid fever.

Typhoid fever is a particularly difficult problem in parts of the world with less-than-adequate sanitation practices. In the United States, many patients who become afflicted with typhoid fever have recently returned from travel to another country, where typhoid is much more prevalent, such as Mexico, Peru, Chile, India, and Pakistan.

Progression and symptomatology

To cause disease, the *S. typhi* bacteria must be ingested. This often occurs when a carrier does not wash hands sufficiently well after defecation, and then serves food to others. In countries where open sewage is accessible to flies, the insects land on the sewage, pick up the bacteria, and then land on food to be eaten by humans.

Ingested bacteria head down the gastrointestinal tract, where they are taken in by cells called mononuclear phagocytes. These phagocytes usually serve to engulf and kill invading bacteria and viruses. However, in the case of *S. typhi*, the bacteria survive ingestion by the phagocytes, and multiply within these cells. This period of time, during which the bacteria are multiplying within the phagocytes, is the 10-14 day incubation period. When huge numbers of bacteria fill an individual phagocyte, the bacteria are discharged out of the cell and into the bloodstream, where their presence begins to cause symptoms.

The presence of increasingly large numbers of bacteria in the bloodstream (called bacteremia) is responsible for an increasingly high fever, which lasts throughout the four to eight weeks of the disease, in untreated individuals. Other symptoms include constipation (initially), extreme fatigue, headache, a rash across the abdomen known as "rose spots," and joint pain.

The bacteria move from the bloodstream into certain tissues of the body, including the gallbladder and lymph tissue of the intestine (called Peyer's patches). The tissue's inflammatory response to this invasion causes symptoms ranging from inflammation of the gallbladder (cholecystitis) to intestinal bleeding and actual perforation of the intestine. Perforation of the

intestine refers to an actual hole occurring in the wall of the intestine, with leakage of intestinal contents into the abdominal cavity. This causes severe irritation and inflammation of the lining of the abdominal cavity, called peritonitis, which is frequently a fatal outcome of typhoid fever.

Other complications of typhoid fever include liver and spleen enlargement (sometimes so extreme that the spleen ruptures), anemia (low red blood cell count due to blood loss from the intestinal bleeding), joint infections (especially frequent in patients with sickle cell anemia and immune system disorders), pneumonia (due to a superimposed infection, usually by *Streptococcus pneumoniae*), heart infections, meningitis and infections of the brain (causing confusion and even coma). Untreated typhoid fever may take several months to resolve fully.

Diagnosis

Samples of a patient's stool, urine, blood, and bone marrow can all be used to culture (grow) the *S. typhi* bacteria in a laboratory for identification under a microscope. These types of cultures are the most accurate methods of diagnosis.

Treatment

Chloramphenicol is the most effective drug treatment for *S. typhi*, and symptoms begin to improve slightly after only 24-48 hours of receiving the medication. Another drug, ceftriaxone, has been used recently, and is also extremely effective, lowering fever fairly quickly.

Carriers of *S. typhi* must be treated even when asymptomatic, as they are responsible for the majority of new cases of typhoid fever. Eliminating the carrier state is actually a fairly difficult task, and requires treatment with one or even two different medications for four to six weeks. In the case of a carrier with gall stones, surgery may need to be performed to remove the gall bladder, because the *S. typhi* bacteria are often housed in the gall bladder, where they may survive despite antibiotic treatment.

Prevention

Hygienic sewage disposal systems in a community, as well as hygienic personal practices, are the most important factors in preventing typhoid fever. For travelers who expect to go to countries where *S. typhi* is a known public health problem, immunizations are available. Some of these immunizations provide only short

KEY TERMS

. . . .

Asymptomatic—A state in which an individual experiences no symptoms of a disease.

Bacteremia—Bacteria in the blood.

Carrier—An individual who has a particular bacteria present within his/her body, and can pass this bacteria on to others, but who displays no symptoms of infection.

Epidemic—A large number of cases of the same disease or infection all occurring within a short time period in a specific location.

Mononuclear phagocytes—A type of cell of the human immune system which is responsible for ingesting bacteria, viruses, and other foreign matter, thus removing potentially harmful substances from the bloodstream.

term protection (for a few months), while others may be protective for several years. Immunizations which provide a longer period of protection, with fewer side effects from the vaccine itself, are being developed.

See also Food poisoning.

Further Reading:

Berkow, Robert, and Andrew J. Fletcher. *The Merck Manual of Diagnosis and Therapy.* Rahway, NJ: Merck Research Laboratories, 1992.

Isselbacher, Kurt J., et al. *Harrison's Principles of Internal Medicine.* New York: McGraw Hill, 1994.

Sherric, John C., et al. *Medical Microbiology.* Norwalk, CT: Appleton & Lange, 1994.

Rosalyn Carson-DeWitt

Tympanic membrane see **Ear**

Typhus

Typhus is a disease caused by a group of bacteria called *Rickettsia*. Three forms of typhus are recognized: epidemic typhus, a serious disease that is fatal if not treated promptly; rat-flea or endemic typhus, a milder form of the disease; and scrub typhus, another fatal form. The *Rickettsia* species of bacteria that cause all three forms of typhus are transmitted by insects. The

bacteria that cause epidemic typhus, for instance, are transmitted by the human body louse; the bacteria that cause endemic typhus are transmitted by the Oriental rat flea; and bacteria causing scrub typhus are transmitted by chiggers.

Characteristics of typhus

Typhus takes its name from the Greek word "typhos," meaning smoke, which accurately describes the mental state of infected persons. Typhus is marked by a severe stupor and delirium, as well as headache, chills, and fever. A rash appears within four to seven days after the onset of the disease. The rash starts on the trunk and spreads to the extremities. In milder forms of typhus, such as endemic typhus, the disease symptoms are not severe. In epidemic and scrub typhus, however, the symptoms are extreme, and death can result from complications such as stroke, renal failure, and circulatory disturbances. Fatality can be avoided in these forms of typhus with the prompt administration of antibiotics.

Epidemic typhus

Epidemic typhus is a disease that has played an important role in history. Because typhus is transmitted by the human body louse, epidemics of this disease break out when humans are in close contact with each other under conditions in which the same clothing is worn for long periods of time. Cold climates also favor typhus epidemics, as people will be more likely to wear heavy clothing in colder conditions. Typhus seems to be a disease of war, poverty, and famine. In fact, according to one researcher, Napoleon's retreat from Moscow in the early 19th century was caused by a louse. During World War I, more than three million Russians died of typhus, and during the Vietnam war, sporadic epidemics killed many American soldiers.

Epidemic typhus is caused by *Rickettsia prowazekii*. Humans play a role in the life cycle of the bacteria. Lice become infected with the bacteria by biting an infected human; these infected lice then bite other humans. A distinguishing feature of typhus disease transmission is that the louse bite itself does not transmit the bacteria. The feces of the lice are infected with bacteria; when a person scratches a louse bite, the lice feces that have been deposited on the skin are introduced into the bloodstream.

If not treated promptly, typhus is fatal. Interestingly, a person who has had epidemic typhus can experience a relapse of the disease years after they have been cured of their infection. Called Brill-Zinsser dis-

TYPHUS

ease after the researchers who discovered it, the relapse is usually a milder form of typhus which is treated with antibiotics. However, a person with Brill-Zinsser disease can infect lice, which can in turn infect other humans. Controlling Brill-Zinsser relapses is important in stopping epidemics of typhus before they start, especially in areas where lice infestation is prominent.

Endemic typhus

Endemic typhus is caused by *R. typhi*. These bacteria are transmitted by the Oriental rat flea, an insect that lives on small rodents. Endemic typhus (sometimes called murine typhus or rat-flea typhus) is found worldwide. The symptoms of endemic typhus are mild compared to those of epidemic typhus. In fact, many people do not seek treatment for their symptoms, as the rash that accompanies the disease may be short-lived. Deaths from endemic typhus have been documented, however; these deaths usually occur in the elderly and in people who are already sick with other diseases.

Scrub typhus

Scrub typhus is caused by *R. tsutsugamushi*, which is transmitted by chiggers. The term "scrub typhus" comes from the observation that the disease is found in habitats with scrub vegetation, but the name is somewhat of a misnomer. Scrub typhus is found in beach areas, savannas, tropical rains forests, and deserts—in short, anywhere chiggers live. Scientists studying scrub typhus label a habitat that contains all the elements that might prompt an outbreak of the disease a "scrub typhus island." A scrub typhus island contains chiggers, rats, vegetation that will sustain the chiggers, and, of course, a reservoir of *R. tsutsugamushi*. Scrub typhus islands are common in the geographic area that includes Australia, Japan, Korea, India, and Vietnam.

The rash that occurs in scrub typhus sometimes includes a lesion called an eschar. An eschar is a sore that develops around the chigger bite. Scrub typhus symptoms of fever, rash, and chills may evolve into stupor, pneumonia, and circulatory failure if antibiotic treatment is not administered. Scrub typhus, like epidemic typhus, is fatal if not treated.

Prevention of typhus

Prevention of typhus outbreaks takes a two-pronged approach. Eliminating the carriers and reservoirs of *Rickettsia* is an important step in prevention. Spraying with insecticides, rodent control measures, and treating soil with insect-repellent chemicals have all been used successfully to prevent typhus outbreaks.

KEY TERMS

Brill-Zinsser Disease—A relapse of typhus symptoms experienced by persons who have had epidemic typhus. Symptoms are usually milder than those experienced with the first bout of typhus.

Endemic typhus—A relatively mild form of typhus that is transmitted by the Oriental rat flea.

Epidemic typhus—A form of typhus that is transmitted by the human body louse and can be fatal if not promptly treated.

Scrub typhus—A form of typhus that is transmitted by chiggers and can be fatal if not promptly treated.

In scrub typhus islands, cutting down vegetation has been shown to lessen the incidence of scrub typhus. The second preventative prong is protecting the body from insect bites. Wearing heavy clothing when venturing into potentially insect-laden areas is one way to protect against insect bites; applying insect repellent to the skin is another. Proper personal hygiene, such as frequent bathing and changing of clothes, will eliminate human body lice and thus prevent epidemic typhus. A typhus vaccine is also available; however, this vaccine only lessens the severity and shortens the course of the disease, and does not protect against infection.

See also Lice; *Rickettsia*.

Further Reading:
Dumler, Stephen J., et al. "Clinical and Laboratory Features of Murine Typhus in South Texas, 1980 through 1987." *The Journal of the American Medical Association* 266 (11 September 1991): 1365-70.
Green, Cornelia R., and Ira Gleiberman. "Brill-Zinsser: Still With Us." *The Journal of the American Medical Association* 264 (10 October 1990): 1811-12.
Hardy, Anne. *The Epidemic Streets: Infectious Diseases and the Rise of Preventive Medicine, 1956-1900*. New York: Oxford University Press, 1993.
Joklik, Wolfgang, et al. *Zinsser Microbiology*. 20th edition. Norwalk, Conn.: Appleton and Lange, 1992.

Kathleen Scogna

Tyndall effect see **Colloid**

Typhoon see **Tropical cyclone**

Tyrant flycatchers

The tyrant flycatchers are a large family of perching birds, containing 367 species, and making up the family Tyrannidae in the order Passeriformes. Tyrant flycatchers only breed in the Americas, from the northern boreal forest of Canada, through the rest of North America, Central America, and to South America as far south as Patagonia. Rarely, individual tyrant flycatchers may occur in coastal Europe, but they would have been blown there by a windstorm.

Species of tyrant flycatchers occur in a great diversity of habitats, ranging from sparsely treed prairies to savannahs, and forests and woodlands of all types. Species that occur in strongly seasonal, temperate climates are migratory, spending their non-breeding season in the tropics or subtropics.

The species in the Tyrannidae are a highly variable group. The range of body lengths is from 3-9 in (8-23 cm)—not including the long tail of some species. Their wings are relatively long and pointed in species that pursue their prey in the air, or short and rounded in species that glean arthropods from foliage. The tail is usually square-backed or forked, but is very long in some species.

The head of tyrant flycatchers is relatively large, and the beak is stout, somewhat flattened, and has a hook at the tip of the upper mandible. However, fly-catching species have a relatively large bill, while gleaners have a small, more-pointed beak. The fly-catching species also have stiff bristles, known as rictal bristles, around the base of their mouth. The feet are small and weak, and only used for perching.

The plumage of tyrant flycatchers is typically a rather plain, olive-green brown, or grey, with a lighter belly. Some species, however, can be quite brightly colored, and may have bright hues of yellow or red. Except for the brighter-colored species, the plumage of male and female birds does not differ.

Tyrant flycatchers typically feed by sitting upright at a well-vantaged, prominent perch, from which they can scan the local environment for flying insects, or for insects or spiders on the ground or on foliage. When likely prey items are observed, they are caught in the beak after a brief sally. Often the bird returns to the same perch. This foraging strategy is known, quite appropriately, as "fly-catching." Almost all of the North American flycatchers fly-catch for their living, but many species of tropical forests glean their prey from foliage and other surfaces. Some species add fruit to

A least flycatcher (*Empidonax minimus*).

their diet, and some of the larger species will prey on mice and small lizards, which are caught on the ground.

Tyrant flycatchers are solitary, and do not form flocks. Tyrant flycatchers are strongly territorial during their breeding season, and some hyper-aggressive species, such as kingbirds, even drive other species away from the proximity of their territory. Tyrant flycatchers have distinctive calls, but the song is not very well developed in most species.

Most species of tyrant flycatchers build cup-shaped nests in trees or shrubs. The clutch size ranges from two to six eggs, with northern species having larger clutches than tropical ones. The eggs are usually incubated by the female. However, the male flycatcher assists with the care and feeding of the young, downy birds.

North American species of tyrant flycatchers

A total of thirty-one species of tyrant flycatchers breed regularly in the United States or Canada. All of these are migratory, spending their non-breeding season in Central and South America. Many of the species of tyrant flycatchers are remarkably similar in appearance, and they can be extremely difficult to identify to species, even for experienced birders. This problem is especially acute during the spring and autumn migrations, when the birds are not necessarily in their typical, breeding habitat, and are not singing.

Some of the North American species, and also species elsewhere, are virtually impossible to tell apart by color or morphology. However, the species occupy different sorts of habitats and niches, have different songs, do not interbreed, and are reproductively isolated. These sorts of difficult-to-distinguish species are known to evolutionary biologists as sibling species.

In North America, the best examples of sibling species are two types in the so-called Traill's flycatcher (*Empidonax traillii*) group, which was shown by detailed field studies to be composed of two, morphologically identical, species. The alder flycatcher (*E. alnorum*) has a relatively northern distribution, breeding from central Alaska and northern Canada south of the tundra, to southern British Columbia, Michigan, New York, New England, and Appalachia as far south as Maryland. This species breeds in wet alder and willow thickets, bogs, and regenerating burns and cutovers, and its song sounds like: "*fee-bee-ow*." The willow flycatcher (*E. traillii*) breeds further to the south through most of the continental United States, in shrubbery along grassy lake edges and streams, and its song sounds like: "*fitz-bew*."

Actually, the difficulties do not end with these two sibling species. The alder and willow flycatchers and the Acadian flycatcher (*Empidonax virescens*) of the eastern United States are the same size, and they have a very similar coloration, as does the almost imperceptibly smaller least flycatcher (*E. minimus*). As in true sibling species, these four types breed in distinctively different habitats, they have different songs, and they do not interbreed. Biologically, therefore, they are different species, even if frustrated bird-watchers cannot always tell who is what during the migrations of the birds, when they do not occur in typical habitat, and do not usually sing.

Other tyrant flycatchers are considerably easier to deal with. One of the more familiar species over much of the continent is the eastern kingbird (*Tyrannus tyrannus*), a slaty-backed, white breasted species of open country. The western kingbird (*T. verticalis*) has a more southwestern distribution.

The great-crested flycatcher (*Myiarchus crinitus*) occurs in southeastern North America, and is a relatively large, olive-backed bird, with a rufous tail and a yellow belly. The ash-throated flycatcher (*M. cinerascens*) occurs in the western United States.

The eastern phoebe (*Sayornis phoebe*) is a small, grey-backed species that ranges widely in eastern North America south of the tundra. This species was named

KEY TERMS

Sibling species—Pairs or groups of very-closely related species that cannot be distinguished morphologically, and may even occur in the same region. However, they do not hybridize, they utilize different habitats, and may be different in other respects.

after is call, which sounds like: "*fee-bee*." Say's phoebe (*S. saya*) has a more-western distribution. Another species that says its name is the eastern wood peewee (*Contopus virens*) of southeastern North America, whose call sounds like: "*pee-awee*."

The olive-sided flycatcher (*Nuttallornis borealis*) is another widespread species, whose call sounds like: "*whip-three-wheers*," although most birders actually learn it as: "*quick-three-beers*."

All of the above species are lively and interesting birds, but they are not strikingly colored or patterned. However, some of the more southern species of tyrant flycatchers are quite gaudy. The scissor-tailed flycatcher (*Muscivora forficata*) has a light-grey back, with a pink-orange wash on the flanks, and a spectacular, forked tail that is about two-times as long as the bird's body. The kiskadee flycatcher (*Pitangus sulphuratus*) has a bold, black-and-white pattern on its face, and a bright-yellow belly. However, the most spectacular of the North American species is the vermilion flycatcher (*Pyrocephalus rubinus*), in which the male is garbed in a dark-charcoal black and tail, but has a fiery, vermilion breast and head.

Further Reading:

Ehrlich, P., D. Dobkin, and D. Wheye. *The Birders Handbook*. New York: Simon and Schuster, 1989.
Farrand, J., ed. *The Audubon Society Master Guide to Birding*. New York: Knopf, 1983.
Harrison, C. J. O., ed. 1978. *Bird Families of the World*. New York: H. N. Abrams, 1978.

Bill Freedman

U

Ulcers

An ulcer is a sore that develops in the lining of the stomach or the duodenum, the short section of small intestine that leads away from the stomach, or on the surface of the skin as a result of infection with bacteria. An ulcer in the stomach is called a gastric ulcer; an ulcer in the duodenum is called a duodenal ulcer; and an ulcer on the skin is called a decubitus ulcer.

Gastric and duodenal ulcers

Until recently, the sole cause of gastric and duodenal ulcers was thought to be overproduction of stomach acid due to prolonged stress, smoking, or poor eating habits. However, in 1992, researchers confirmed that many ulcers are caused by infection with bacteria capable of living in the highly acidic environment of the stomach. This revolution in ulcer research has radically changed the way ulcers are diagnosed and treated. For instance, instead of treating ulcer patients with acid-reducing drugs for months or even years, patients with the bacterially–caused ulcers take a week-long course of antibiotics. And in contrast to the 50% to 95% relapse rate with conventional treatment, the new antibiotic treatment has reduced the recurrence rate to 20%.

Cause of gastric and duodenal ulcers

Until recently, excess stomach acid was believed to be the cause of ulcers. Hydrochloric acid (HCL) is normally produced in the stomach to help break down food. HCL is secreted from special cells in the stomach lining, is mixed with the stomach contents, and initiates the preliminary digestion of proteins in the stomach. From the stomach, the partially digested food moves into the duodenum, where more digestion takes place. But before the partially broken down food moves from the stomach to duodenum, the acid must be neutralized. If it is not, the acidic food will irritate the sensitive duodenum. Sodium bicarbonate—the active ingredient in

A clinical photograph of a large duodenal ulcer after surgical resection (removal). The ulcer is the prominent triangular crater at center.

baking soda—is released from other cells in the stomach lining and neutralizes the acid in the partially digested food before it moves into the duodenum.

Sometimes, however, the acid is not neutralized effectively, and the duodenum is irritated by the acidic food. In this case, a duodenal ulcer may develop. Sometimes the lining of the stomach itself cannot tolerate the high levels of acid that are released within the stomach. In this case, a gastric ulcer lining may result. In either of these cases, the ulcers can be traced to a sensitivity to acid or to its overproduction.

But acid overproduction or sensitivity are not the only causes of ulcers. A bacterium called *Heliobacter pylori*, discovered and named in 1982, has been shown to cause ulcers by colonizing the lining of the stomach. These bacteria can survive in the stomach's highly acidic environment because they have an enzyme that neutralizes acid. Scientists now believe that most—60%—of all ulcers diagnosed throughout the world can be traced to the *H. pylori* bacterium.

Symptoms of gastric and duodenal ulcers

The classic symptom of an ulcer is stomach pain. Usually the pain is sharp or burning. Patients commonly note that the pain is more intense when the stomach is empty. Eating can sometimes relieve the pain of an ulcer because excess acid is neutralized by food being introduced into the stomach and duodenum.

If the ulcer is severe enough, it may perforate, or "punch through," the lining of the stomach. If this perforation occurs, stomach contents may leak into the body cavity, causing infection. The patient may also bleed internally, which may lead to shock. A perforated ulcer is extremely serious. Blood in the stool or vomiting blood are signs that require immediate medical attention.

Treatment of gastric and duodenal ulcers

Before 1992, most ulcers were treated with a regimen of diet and medication. Patients were advised to take over–the–counter antacids and to control their intake of irritating foods and substances, such as alcohol, caffeine, and fried foods. In the 1980s, drug researchers developed sophisticated medications that target the stomach's acid production mechanism. The patient must take these medications for at least a month, and sometimes years, to suppress the stomach's acid secretion. These drugs only treat the symptoms of ulcers; they do not cure them. Unfortunately, most ulcers recurred despite these state–of–the–art drugs.

Since the discovery of *Heliobacter pylori*, new treatments for ulcers that target the bacteria have been implemented in ulcer patients, with good results. Tests can confirm whether or not a patient has *Heliobacter pylori*. In one of these tests, a tube with a tiny camera on the end is snaked through the patient's esophagus into the stomach and duodenum. An instrument can be passed through the tube to pinch a bit of the intestinal lining. If *Heliobacter pylori* bacteria are found in the sample, the patient is put on a course of antibiotic drugs that kill the bacteria, effectively curing the ulcer. In addition, researchers have found that bismuth subsalicylate—the active ingredient in the over the counter medication Pepto Bismol—is also effective against these bacteria. Some evidence suggests that a medication regiment combining antibiotics and bismuth subsalicylate may be the best treatment for bacterial ulcers.

Prevention of gastric and duodenal ulcers

Since the discovery of *H. pylori*, some researchers have suggested that bacterial ulcers may be prevented with a vaccine given early in childhood. Research has already begun into this kind of vaccine; however, it is unlikely that an *H. pylori* vaccine will be available within the next few years.

Evidence also suggests that *H. pylori* infection is highest in areas with poor sanitation facilities, suggesting that the bacteria may be transmitted—like many other human pathogens—by drinking fecally contaminated water. Researchers are currently working on this question, as well as studying transmission routes in the United States. Interestingly, *H. pylori* has been found in dental plaque, which may explain why the United States, with its excellent sanitation facilities, has large numbers of people with *H. pylori* infection: it may be transmitted by kissing or other oral contact.

Despite the revolution brought about by *H. pylori*, ulcers caused by acid overproduction still represent about 40% of all diagnosed ulcers. But instead of tracing the acid overproduction to nerves, physicians are now digging deeper for the actual cause of the excess acid. Cigarette smoking has long been linked to ulcers. Smoking causes acid to be secreted into the stomach, and if the stomach does not have adequate defenses, the acid secretion, over time, can lead to an ulcer. Aspirin intake is also another culprit. Aspirin irritates the lining of the stomach and may set the stage for an ulcer.

Prevention of both kinds of ulcers is a matter of maintaining a healthy lifestyle. Good hygiene habits and the avoidance of cigarettes and excess aspirin may keep the stomach lining free of ulcers. In the future, a vaccine may entirely eliminate the cause of most ulcers, but until that time, lifestyle still plays the major role in avoiding the pain of ulcers.

Decubitus ulcers

Ulcers on the skin are caused by an infection with certain kinds of bacteria called the Enterocci and the Streptococci. These bacteria invade the skin tissues and multiply, causing the ulcer, or sore, to erupt on the skin surface. Experts believe that many people with bacteria–related ulcers acquired these infections during a stay in a hospital. When bacteria are transmitted within hospital settings, the infection is described as nosocomial. Skin ulcers caused by bacteria are treated with antibiotics.

Others skin ulcers are caused by constant pressure against the skin that does not allow air circulation. For instance, people who are bedridden for long periods of time frequently develop ulcers on the back, buttocks, and backs of the legs. If these ulcers are not treated

KEY TERMS

....

Acute gastritis—Irritation of the stomach that lasts for a short period of time

Antibiotic—A drug that targets and kills bacteria

Chronic gastritis—Irritation of the stomach that is long-lasting

Duodenum—The short segment of the small intestine that leads away from the stomach.

Esophagus—The tube that extends from the mouth to the stomach in which food travels

promptly, they can quickly become infected with bacteria, and deep wounds can result. Pressure ulcers can be avoided in the bedridden if patients are turned periodically throughout the day so that all the surfaces of the body are exposed to air.

Still another type of skin ulcer primarily affects people with diabetes. One of the complications of diabetes is neuropathy, a condition in which nerve endings become irritated. The nerves may eventually die and the area in which the nerves are located becomes anesthetized. Diabetic patients typically experience neuropathy in the feet. If they injure their feet, the neuropathy may prevent them from feeling any pain from the injury. The injury worsens until a full-blown ulcer develops. People with diabetes are encouraged to examine their feet daily for signs of injury and to seek prompt care for any foot injury, even minor injuries.

Kathleen Scogna

Ultracentrifuge

An ultracentrifuge is a mechanical device that separates substances of different densities by spinning them very fast. It greatly reduces the time it would take to separate substances that would eventually separate if left alone. The first successful centrifuge was invented in 1883 by Swedish engineer Carl de Laval. It was used to separate cream from milk. Forty years later, another Swede, chemist Theodor Svedberg, invented the ultracentrifuge.

Centrifuges use centrifugal force, the force directed outward from a something spinning in a circle, to separate particles. You can feel the effects of centrifugal force when you swing a rope with a weight tied to one end above your head. The faster you swing the rope, the more centrifugal force you create on the weight. A washing machine is a type of centrifuge during its spin cycle. It spins water out of wet clothes using centrifugal forces far less powerful than those created by an ultracentrifuge.

In an ultracentrifuge, samples are placed in a container holding closed, narrow tubes like test tubes. It spins them so fast that the centrifugal forces created can be more than one-half million times greater than the force of gravity. The tubes are suspended horizontally while they are spinning and heavier, denser particles, or those with high specific gravity, travel farther in the outstretched tubes than lighter, less dense particles or those with lower specific gravity. (Specific gravity is the mass of a substance divided by the mass of an equal volume of distilled water at 4° F (15° C). It is a way to compare objects based on how much mass they have packed into the space they occupy.)

One common use of ultracentrifuges is to separate mixtures of different sized molecules. They are also used to separate and determine the relative sizes and densities of microscopic particles such as parts of cells. Ultracentrifuges are so powerful, for example, that they can separate two groups of molecules that differ only by having different types of nitrogen in their structures, nitrogen-14 versus nitrogen-15. Nitrogen-15 differs from nitrogen-14 by having one more neutron in its atomic nucleus.

See also Centrifuge; Gravity and Gravitation; Mass.

Ultrasonics

Ultrasonics or ultrasound, derived from the Latin words "ultra," meaning beyond, and "sonic," meaning sound, is a term used to describe sound waves that vibrate more rapidly than the human ear can detect.

Sound waves travel as concentric hollow spheres. The surfaces of the spheres are compressed air molecules, and the spaces between the spheres are expansions of the air molecules through which the sound waves travel. Sound waves are thus a series of compressions and expansions in the medium surrounding them.

An ultrasound image of Anabelle Ashlyn Longe at 20 weeks.

Although we are used to thinking of sound waves as traveling through air, they may also propagate through other media.

The technical name for one expansion and one compression is a cycle. Thus, a vibration rate of 50 cycles per second produces 50 expansions and 50 compressions each second. The term *frequency* designates the number of cycles per unit of time that a sound wave vibrates. One cycle per second is called a hertz and is abbreviated Hz. Other useful units of scale in ultrasonics are kilohertz (kHz), which represents 1,000 Hz; and megahertz (MHZ), representing 1,000,000 Hz or 1,000 kHz.

Most people can only detect frequencies of sound that fall between 16 and 16,000 Hz. Ultrasonics has come to describe sound waves with frequencies greater than 16,000 Hz, or 16 kHz. Some insects can produce ultrasound with frequencies as high as 40 kHz. Small animals such as cats and dogs hear frequencies of up to 30 kHz; and bats are known to detect frequencies of up to 100 kHz.

A sound wave that causes compressions and expansions of the molecules in the medium surrounding it as it propagates is called a *longitudinal wave*. The distance from one compression to the next is known as the *wavelength* of the sound wave. Sound waves with long wavelengths pass over small objects in much the same way that ocean waves pass over small objects. Sound waves with short wavelengths, on the other hand, tend to be diffracted or scattered by objects comparable to them in size.

The propagation *velocity* of a sound wave is obtained by multiplying the frequency of the sound

wave by its wavelength. Thus, if the wavelength and frequency of the sound wave in a given medium are known, its velocity can also be calculated. The sound velocities in a variety of materials are shown in Table 1.

As ultrasonic waves tend to have very high frequencies, it follows that they also have very short wavelengths. As a result, ultrasonic waves can be focused in narrow, straight beams.

How ultrasonic waves are generated

In order to duplicate ultrasonic frequencies, humans have harnessed the electrical properties of materials. When a specially cut piezoelectric quartz crystal is compressed, the crystal becomes electrically charged and an electric current is generated: the greater the pressure, the greater the electric current. If the crystal is suddenly stretched rather than being compressed, the direction of the current will reverse itself. Alternately compressing and stretching the crystal has the effect of producing an alternating current. It follows that by applying an alternating current that matches the natural frequency of the crystal, the crystal can be made to expand and contract with the alternating current. When such a current is applied to the crystal, ultrasonic waves are produced.

Depending on which way the crystal is cut, the waves can be focused along the direction of ultrasound propagation or at right angles to the direction of propagation. Waves that travel along the direction of propagation are called *longitudinal waves*; as noted above, these waves travel in the direction in which molecules in the surrounding medium move back and forth. Waves that travel at right angles to the propagation direction are called *transverse waves*; the molecules in the surrounding medium move up and down with respect to the direction that the waves propagate. Ultrasound waves can also propagate as surface waves; in this case, molecules in the surrounding medium experience up-and-down motion as well as expanding and contracting motion.

In most applications, ultrasonic waves are generated by a transducer that includes a piezoelectric crystal that converts electrical energy (electric current) to mechanical energy (sound waves). These sound waves are reflected and return to the transducer as echoes and are converted back to electrical signals by the same transducer or by a separate one. Alternately, one can generate ultrasonic waves by means of magnetostriction (from *magneto,* meaning magnetic, and *strictio,* meaning drawing together.) In this case an iron or nickel ele-

TABLE 1. VELOCITY OF SOUND IN VARIOUS MEDIA[a]

Material	Velocity (ft/sec)
Sea water	5023
Distilled water	4908
Chloroform	3237
Dry air at 0°C	1086
Hydrogen at 0°C	4212
Brick	11,972
Clay rock	11,414
Cork	1640
Paraffin	4264
Tallow	1279
Polystyrene	3018
Fused silica	18,893
Aluminum	16,400
Gold	6658
Silver	8790
Concrete	12,000
Stainless steel	16,400

[a] All measurements at 25°C (room temperature) unless otherwise indicated.

ment is magnetized to change its dimensions, thereby producing ultrasonic waves. Ultrasound may also be produced by a whistle or siren–type generator. In this method, gas or liquid streams are passed through a resonant cavity or reflector with the result that ultrasonic vibrations characteristic of the particular gas or liquid are produced.

Applications

The number of applications for ultrasound seems to be limited only by the human imagination. There are literally dozens of ways that people have already found to make use of ultrasound.

Coagulation

Ultrasound has been used to bind, or coagulate, solid or liquid particles that are present in dust, mist, or smoke into larger clumps. The technique is used in a process called ultrasonic scrubbing, by which particulate matter is coagulated in smokestacks before it pollutes the atmosphere. Coagulation has also been used at airports to disperse fog and mist.

Humidification

In ultrasonic humidification, water is reduced to a fine spray by means of ultrasonic vibrations. The water droplets are propelled into a chamber where they are mixed with air, and a mist of air and water leaves the humidifier and enters the room to be humidified.

Ultrasonic dispersion

Two liquids that do not ordinarily mix, i.e., oil and water, can be combined as a liquid by exposing a solution of the two to very high frequency sound waves. Such mixtures are called *dispersions*. With this technique, alloys of aluminum and lead, iron and lead, and aluminum and cadmium can be mixed as liquids—and kept mixed—until they solidify. This technique is known as ultrasonic dispersion. It is also used to produce stable and consistent photographic emulsions.

Milk homogenization and pasteurization

Ultrasonic waves can be used to break up fat globules in milk, so that the fat mixes with the milk (homogenization). In addition, pasteurization, the removal of harmful bacteria and microorganisms, is sometimes done ultrasonically.

Ultrasonic cleaning

Ultrasound is routinely used to clean, process, and degrease metal parts, precision machinery, and fabrics. The technique has found heavy use in the automotive, aircraft, and electronics industries, as well as for cleaning optical, dental, surgical, and other precision instruments. Fabrics can be laundered using ultrasound because the ultrasonic vibrations break down the attraction between dirt particles and fabrics, literally shaking the dirt loose. The principle by which ultrasonic cleaning is accomplished is known as *cavitation*. In cavitation, ultrasonic waves produce microscopic bubbles that collapse, sending out many tiny shock waves. These shock waves loosen the dirt and other contaminants on metals, plastics, or ceramics. The frequencies used in ultrasonic cleaning range from 15 kHz to 2 MHZ.

Welding

Intense ultrasonic vibrations can be used to locally heat and weld two materials together. This technique works well with both plastics and metals. Thus, metal wire leads can be connected to semiconductor devices, or thermoplastic films sealed using ultrasound to locally heat, melt, and fuse the materials' surfaces. When used to bond metals to plastics, ultrasonic waves create an even flow of molten plastic at the point of contact. When the liquid plastic solidifies, cohesive bonding takes place.

Drilling

By attaching an ultrasonic impact grinder to a magnetostrictive transducer and using an abrasive liquid, holes of practically any shape can be drilled in hard, brittle materials such as tungsten carbide or precious stones. The actual cutting or drilling is done by feeding an abrasive material, frequently silicon carbide or aluminum oxide, to the cutting area.

Soldering

In ultrasonic soldering, high frequency vibrations are used to produce microscopic bubbles in molten solder. This process removes the metal oxides from the joint or surface to be soldered, and eliminates the need for flux.

Nondestructive testing

When used as flaw detectors, ultrasonic devices locate defects in materials and bounce back images of the defects, thus revealing their shapes and locations. Nondestructive testing neither damages the object being tested, nor harms the person performing the test. Metals, glasses, ceramics, liquids, plastics, and rubbers can be evaluated by this technique. Nondestructive testing of forged parts is now a standard manufacturing practice. The technique is used to detect corrosion in metal parts. It is also used to measure the thicknesses of many materials (with accuracies of up to 0.0001 in [0.00025 cm] for metals, and 0.001 in [0.0025 cm] for plastics), including concrete structures. Farmers have even used ultrasound to measure the fat layers on their cattle prior to sending them to market.

Scientific research

Ultrasound has been used to investigate the physical properties of materials, to determine the molecular weights of liquid polymers, to investigate the associated states of water, and to induce and speed up chemical reactions. Ultrasound has also been used to break up high molecular weight polymers, thereby making possible the creation of new plastic materials. Agricultural research indicates that seeds have been found to germinate more rapidly and to give higher yields after they have been subjected to ultrasound.

Medicine

Perhaps in no other field has there been such an explosion of ultrasound applications as in medicine. Ultrasound has been used in the following applications:

(1) to photograph body organs and bones. Body parts as small as 0.004 in (0.1 mm) may be imaged using ultrasound. Heart examinations may be performed to locate tumors, valve diseases, and accumulation of fluids. Pregnancies may be detected as early as five weeks after conception, and fetal size and development is monitored throughout pregnancy and delivery using ultrasonic imaging.

(2) to measure the rate and direction of blood flow using the principle that the frequency of sound changes as it travels toward an observer, but decreases as it moves away. This phenomenon, known as the *Doppler effect*, accounts for why the pitch of a train whistle, for example, becomes higher as a train first approaches, then becomes lower as it passes people standing on a station platform. Doctors can determine the direction of blood flow in the body by observing increases or decreases in the frequency of the ultrasonic measurements.

(3) to detect tumors in the body and to distinguish between malignant tumors and healthy tissue. Ultrasound is also employed by oncologists to destroy malignant tumors and inclusions, eliminating the need for surgery. Cancer cells are destroyed using ultrasound to produce microscopic bubbles that collapse and send out intense shock waves (cavitation effect). The same technique is used to destroy gallstones and kidney stones.

(4) to view living cells without damaging them. Ultrasonic microscopes can be used to image cellular structures to within 0.2 microns (two–thousandths of a millimeter). Ultrasonic methods are also used to locate foreign objects in the eye during surgery and in routine eye examinations, and to measure the depth of burns in burn patients. This technique affords an accuracy of 0.05–0.1 in (0.1–0.2 mm).

KEY TERMS

· ·

Cycle—One wave expansion and compression.

Hertz (Hz)—One cycle per second.

Kilohertz (kHz)—One thousand hertz.

Megahertz (MHZ)—One thousand kilohertz.

Piezoelectric—A material that becomes electrically charged when compressed, generating an electric current.

Transducer—An electronic device used to generate ultrasound.

Ultrasound—Another term for ultrasonic waves; sometimes reserved for medical applications.

Wavelength—The distance from one compression to the next in a sound wave.

Radio

Radio talk shows routinely use ultrasonic delay lines to monitor and cut off abusive callers before their comments are aired during radio talk shows. The ultrasonic delay line bounces the voice signal back and forth between two transducers until it is has been monitored, then releases it for broadcast.

See also Acoustics; Doppler effect; Electric current; Frequency; Sonar; Solder and soldering iron.

Further Reading:

Knight, David C. *Silent Sound: The World of Ultrasonics.* New York: Morrow, 1980.

Randall Frost

(5) to relieve muscle strain. Ultrasonic heat has been used to treat arthritis, bursitis, myelitis, neuralgia, malignancy, lumbago, rheumatism, arthritis, sciatica, sinitis, and post–operative pain.

(6) to clean teeth by means of ultrasonic prophylaxis units operating at 25 kHz.

Electronic eavesdropping

Conversations can be overheard without using microphones by directing ultrasonic waves at the window of the room being monitored. Sounds in the room cause the window to vibrate; the speech vibrations produce characteristic changes in the ultrasonic waves that are reflected back into the monitor. A transducer can be used to convert the reflected vibrations to electrical signals that can be reconstructed as audible sounds.

Detection devices

Ultrasound has been used to detect undersea naval vessels, to measure the depth of the ocean floor, and to locate schools of fish. When used in these ways, ultrasound is usually referred to as sonar, an acronym for SOund NAvigation and Ranging. The frequencies used in most sonar systems range from 5 to 50 kHz. Ultrasonic detectors also measure chemical fluid levels automatically in tanks and containers, as well as in the fuel tanks of aircraft. In addition, ultrasonic devices are used in burglar alarms. When an intruder trips an ultrasonic alarm, a signal can be relayed to the local police station, and the burglar apprehended.

Ultraviolet astronomy

Ultraviolet astronomy is the study of astronomical objects in the ultraviolet portion of the electromagnetic spectrum. Because Earth's atmosphere prevents ultraviolet radiation from reaching its surface, ground–based observatories cannot observe in the ultraviolet. Only with the advent of space–based telescopes has this area of astronomy become available for research. Ultraviolet radiation has a shorter wavelength and more energy than visual radiation, and much of ultraviolet astronomy therefore centers on energetic processes in stars and galaxies. Hot regions of stellar atmospheres, for example, invisible to optical telescopes, reveal a wealth of information to the ultraviolet telescope. The crowded, violent regions at the centers of some galaxies are also prime targets for ultraviolet telescopes.

Ultraviolet radiation

We often refer to electromagnetic radiation in terms of its wavelength, the distance from one peak of a light wave to the next peak. A convenient unit of wavelength is the Angstrom Å. One Angstrom equals one 10 billionth of a meter.

Visual light, the light our eyes are sensitive to, has wavelengths from 4,000 to about 7,000 Angstroms. Beyond the visual is infrared light—we cannot see it, but we can feel it as heat. On the short wavelength side of the visual part of the spectrum is the ultraviolet. Ultraviolet (often just called UV) light has wavelengths from 100 to 4,000 Angstroms.

Earth's atmosphere is opaque to UV light, meaning UV radiation cannot penetrate it. This is fortunate for us, since UV light is what causes sunburn and in sufficiently large doses, skin cancer. Optical telescopes cannot see wavelengths much shorter than 3,600 Angstroms, and to observe UV radiation from astronomical objects it is therefore necessary to go above the atmosphere. Orbiting, space–based telescopes are needed, and only in the past few decades have they been available.

Ultraviolet observatories

Astronomers have developed many different kinds of telescopes besides the familiar optical instruments. Radio, infrared, ultraviolet, x ray, and gamma–ray telescopes all have unique design requirements to maximize their efficiency in the part of the spectrum they are intended to study.

Like gamma–ray and x ray telescopes, UV telescopes have only been possible in the era of spaceflight, and the longest lived and most important of these so far has been the *International Ultraviolet Explorer*. Launched in 1978, IUE was designed to observe the UV sky for five years. As of 1995, the telescope was still functioning and had taken tens of thousands of spectra of stars, nebulae, and galaxies.

IUE was a joint project of United States and European space agencies, and was operated for 16 hours each day at the Goddard Space Flight Center in Greenbelt, MD, and for eight hours each day at the Villafranca Satellite Tracking Station in Spain. Astronomers around the world have used IUE for their research, and it has been one of the most productive missions in the history of spaceflight.

Despite its glowing track record, IUE had some important limitations. Its primary mirror was only 17 in (45 cm) in diameter, and IUE therefore could not observe very faint objects. Also, its instrumentation was developed in the 1970s and was not as technologically advanced as that available in the 1980s and 1990s. For this reason, a new generation of UV observatories was designed and built.

On June 7, 1992, the Extreme Ultraviolet Explorer (EUVE) was launched. This satellite was designed to extend the spectral coverage of IUE, which only went down to 1,100 Å. The EUVE telescope observed at wavelengths as short as 70 Å, and extended the observing capability of space–based observatories throughout the UV.

These observatories — IUE and EUVE — are what NASA calls "Explorer–class" missions. These are

---

KEY TERMS
....

EUVE — The Extreme Ultraviolet Explorer, launched in 1992. The EUVE telescope observes the short–wavelength end of the UV, from 70 to 760 Angstroms.

GHRS — The Goddard High Resolution Spectrograph. An ultraviolet instrument that is part of the Hubble Space Telescope, GHRS extends the capabilities of IUE owing to its more modern instrumentation and the HST's large mirror.

IUE — The International Ultraviolet Explorer. Launched in 1978, IUE has operated for nearly two decades despite its original five–year design lifetime. IUE has been one of the most successful and productive of space–based observatories, and has been used to observe nearly every kind of astronomical object, from planets and comets to stars, nebulae, and galaxies.

UV radiation — Radiation with wavelengths between 100 and 4,000 Angstroms. UV radiation causes sunburn and, in sufficient doses, skin cancer. Fortunately for us, Earth's atmosphere prevents most UV radiation from reaching the ground, but this also means that the ultraviolet radiation from astronomical objects can only be studied by telescopes orbiting above the atmosphere.

---

smaller, less ambitious and expensive projects, designed to perform a specific task. This is in contrast to the "Great Observatories" such as the Hubble Space Telescope (HST), which includes a UV instrument called the Goddard High Resolution Spectrograph (GHRS). The GHRS can observe the same part of the spectrum as IUE, but the 8.5 ft (2.6 m) mirror of the HST is much larger than the 16 in (45 cm) mirror of IUE, and GHRS can observe much fainter objects than IUE.

Research with UV telescopes

UV telescopes reveal a wealth of information about hot and energetic processes in astronomical objects. This is because the hotter an object is, the more energy it radiates at short wavelengths. UV radiation has shorter wavelengths than visual light, so hot objects are brighter in the UV than in the visual. For example, a hot star like Rigel (the blue–white star that forms Orion's left foot) emits much more UV radiation than the Sun.

UV telescopes have greatly enhanced our understanding of the stars. It is well known that the temperature rises in the outer atmospheres of stars like the Sun, but the causes of this temperature rise are poorly understood. Because the atmospheres get very hot, they emit much of their radiation in the UV, and until the launch of IUE in 1978, the nature of these hot atmospheres was largely unknown. UV telescopes have also been used to study winds from hot stars, stars that are still in the process of forming, and hot, dead stars that orbit other stars, drawing matter off them and heating it until it emits large amounts of UV and x ray radiation.

Another place where hot, high–energy conditions prevail is at the center of galaxies. The so–called active galaxies have intense high–energy sources at their centers. These galaxies often have huge jets of hot, high–energy material streaming out of them. A hypothesized source of the intense energy generation is an enormous black hole at the galactic center. IUE and other UV telescopes have been used to study galactic centers in an effort to understand the processes occurring in the crowded, violent environments thought to prevail there.

See also Electromagnetic spectrum; Galaxy; Telescope.

Further Reading:

Hamle, P. A., and V. Chamberlain. *Space Science Comes of Age.* Washington: Smithsonian, 1981.

Kaufmann, W., *Discovering the Universe.* 2nd ed. Freeman, 1991.

Jeffrey C. Hall

Ultraviolet radiation see **Radiation**

Uncertainty principle, Heisenberg's see **Quantum mechanics**

Unconformity

An unconformity is a widespread surface separating rocks above and below, which represents a gap in the rock record. Unconformities occur when either erosion wears away rocks, or rock deposits never formed. Therefore, a time gap exists between when the rocks below the unconformity formed and when those above it formed.

Unconformities are classified as three types. The most easily recognized are angular unconformities, which show horizontal layers of sedimentary rock lying on tilted layers of sedimentary rock. The upper layers may not be perfectly horizontal, but they do not lie parallel to the lower layers. The second type of unconformities are disconformities, which lie between parallel layers of sedimentary rock. The third type are nonconformities, which divide sedimentary layers from metamorphic and intrusive (cooled inside the Earth) igneous rocks. Common to all three, erosion forms them and younger rocks sit on older rocks.

Angular unconformities

Four basic steps create angular unconformities. In step one, sediment weathered from land and carried to the sea accumulates on the sea floor and over millions of years turns to rock layers. Then the collision of plates, giant sections of the Earth's crust that constantly shift, lift and tilt the layers until the layers rise above sea level and then weather and erode. They erode for millions of years until the edges of the tilted layers become a flattened plane (a "peneplain" is a broad land surface flattened by erosion). Finally, in step four, sea level rises or land sinks. Sediments wash down, forming new horizontal layers that cover the submerged, tilted, layers. These four steps could take hundreds of millions of years to complete.

The Colorado River at the Grand Canyon exposed one of the best angular unconformities in the world. From even miles away on the rim of the canyon, observers can see tilted layers of rock truncated roughly 550 million years ago by a horizontal sedimentary layer called the Tapeats Sandstone. The inner gorge of the Grand Canyon provides a great example of angular unconformity formation. Except, instead of four steps, the rocks tell of seven: (1) Over 2 billion years ago, layers of sediment accumulated and turned to rock. (2) Around 2 billion years ago, plate collisions lifted mountains and turned the sedimentary rocks into the Vishnu Schist, a metamorphic rock. (3) A half a billion years later, the mountains eroded into a peneplain. (4) The land subsided or sea level rose to deposit new layers (known as the Grand Canyon Series) on the old Vishnu Schist. (5) New plate collisions tilted and uplifted the Grand Canyon Series. (6) Erosion truncated the tilted Series and created another peneplain. The erosional episode lasted almost a billion years. (7) The land subsided eventually and the Tapeats Sandstone accumulated on the tilted Grand Canyon Series. In some places in the canyon, the Tapeats lies not on the angled Series but directly on the metamorphic Vishnu Schist—making this a nonconformity.

Another famous angular nonconformity is Scotland's Siccar Point, a site which played a part in the development of modern geology. In the 18th century, most people believed the Earth to be only 6,000 years old, a figure arrived at earlier by Bishop Ussher, a prominent theologian who added the ages of Biblical characters and thus concluded the world was created in 4004 B.C. Scottish scientist James Hutton, however, realized that thousand–year–old Roman ruins in Great Britain were barely touched by weathering and erosion. He therefore wondered how long it takes for whole mountains, like those in Scotland, to wear down.

The angular unconformity he discovered at Siccar Point in Scotland provided dramatic evidence for his time "expansion." He saw nearly horizontal sandstone resting on nearly vertical graywacke (a sedimentary rock similar to sandstone) and marveled at how long it took to deposit the graywacke, tilt it, erode it, and then lay sandstone across it. As his friend, John Playfair, wrote "The mind seemed to grow giddy by looking so far into the abyss of time."

Disconformity

From a mile away, or perhaps from a few hundred feet away, disconformities can hide. The layers appear regular, all parallel. However, between the layers, a disconformity can lie. Not until a geologist closely examines the fossils in the layers for the presence or absence of certain organisms, can he or she recognize the gap in time—an erosional period when sediment accumulation or deposition halted or perhaps when anything laid down washed away.

As with an angular unconformity, disconformities form in steps. In step one, sediments collect on an ocean floor (or perhaps on the bed of a large lake). They compact and become rock layers. In the second phase, sea level falls or the sea floor rises to expose the layers to weathering and erosion. The main difference in the formation of disconformities and angular unconformities lies in this second step. As the layers of the future disconformity rise above sea level, they remain horizontal—no tilting occurs. If they tilt in this step, they later form an angular unconformity. Then, in step three, the land subsides or sea level rises, and new sediments collect on the older, still horizontal, layers.

Back in the Grand Canyon, where our story paused roughly 550 million years ago, the Tapeats Sandstone draped across the Grand Canyon Series and the Vishnu Schist to form the Great Unconformity. At least two more layers of sediments—the Bright Angel Shale and the Muav Limestone—collected on the Tapeats over the next 50 million years. Other layers may have been

---

KEY TERMS

Angular unconformity—An unconformity, or gap in the rock record, where horizontal rock layers overlie tilted layers.

Disconformity—An unconformity, or gap in the rock record, situated between parallel rock layers.

Nonconformity—An unconformity or gap in the rock record, where sedimentary rocks overlie metamorphic or igneous rocks.

---

formed, too, but disappeared when the land rose and eroded for the next 80 million years. When the area again sank beneath the sea, the Temple Butte Formation, 80 million years younger than the Mauv, accumulated on the disconformity. The cycle of deposition, uplift, erosion, subsidence, and more deposition repeated at least four times from 550 to 250 million years ago.

Nonconformities

Nonconformities separate sedimentary rock layers from metamorphic rock layers and from intrusive igneous rock (like granite). In a step–by–step process similar to the other two unconformities, sediment accumulates and becomes rock. Then plate collisions deform these layers and change them into metamorphic rocks. Associated with this mountain–building, molten rock often squeezes upward in to the metamorphic rock fractured by the deformities and solidifies, forming igneous rock (usually granite). In phase three, the mountains erode to a peneplain. Then, finally, new layers collect over the flattened metamorphic and igneous rocks. As described earlier, the Tapeats Sandstone layer in the Grand Canyon forms an angular unconformity where it overlies the tilted Grand Canyon Series and a nonconformity where it rests on the Vishnu Schist.

An ongoing process

As rocks continue to wear away, more unconformities appear. As road crews cut through mountains, they expose unconformities for the speeding motorist as well as the geologist to enjoy. However, these new exposures and the mountains that contain them will erode flat. The Appalachians, the Himalayas, the Alps, the Rockies, even the Grand Canyon, will die their slow erosional deaths as nature levels the continents, which may then subside beneath the seas. However, more sediment will

---

soon accumulate, which will uplift and erode, and so on into eternity—an unbroken cycle of geologic processes.

See also Erosion; Geologic time; Uplift.

Further Reading:

Baars, Donald L. *The Colorado Plateau: A Geologic History.* Albuquerque, NM: University of New Mexico Press, 1983.

Chronic, Halka. *Pages of Stone: Geology of Western National Parks and Monuments.* Vol. 4. *Grand Canyon and the Plateau Country.* Seattle: The Mountaineers, 1988.

Chronic, Halka. *Roadside Geology of Arizona.* Missoula, MT: Mountain Press, 1984.

Dixon, Dougal, and Raymond L. Bernor, ed. *The Practical Geologist.* New York: Simon and Schuster, 1992.

Harris, Ann G., Esther Tuttle, and S. D. Tuttle. *Geology of National Parks*, 4th ed. Dubuque, IA: Kendall/Hunt Publishing Co., 1990.

McPhee, John. *Basin and Range.* New York: Farrar, Strauss & Giroux, 1982.

Ungulates

Ungulates are large grazing animals whose toenails have become enlarged into hooves. There are two orders of ungulates—Perissodactyla and Artiodactyla.

Animals in the order Artiodactyla have an even number of toes (usually two) that form a cloven hoof. This order is relatively diverse, containing 82 genera and several hundred species. There are nine families in this order, the most familiar of which are the pigs (Suidae), peccaries (Tayasuidae), hippopotamuses (Hippopotamidae), camels (Camelidae), deer (Cervidae), giraffes (Giraffidae), sheep, cattle, antelopes (Bovidae), and pronghorn antelopes (Antilocapridae).

Animals in the order Perissodactyla have an odd number of toes (usually one) that forms a single large hoof. Examples of this order include horses (family Equidae), tapirs (Tapiridae), and rhinos (Rhinocerotidae), together comprising six extant genera and 16 species.

At the time of the European discovery of North America, the native fauna of ungulates included bison (*Bison bison*), pronghorn antelope (*Antilocapra americana*), collared peccary (*Tayassu tayacu*), muskox (*Ovibos moschatus*), mountain goat (*Oreanmnos americanus*), and mountain and Dall sheep (*Ovis canadensis* and *O. dalli*). The North American Cervidae includes white–tailed deer and mule deer (*Odocoileus virginianus* and *O. hemionus*), wapiti or elk (*Cervus elaphus*), moose (*Alces alces*), and caribou (*Rangifer tarandus*).

About 8,000–10,000 years before Europeans first came to America, North America supported a substantially larger number of ungulate species, including 10 species of horses, four species of camels, a species of cow, two additional species of bison, and the saiga antelope (*Saiga tatarica*). There were also other large, now–extinct mammals, including four species of elephants, such as the mastodon (*Mammut americanum*) and mammoth (*Mammuthus primigenius*), a giant ground sloth (*Gryptotherium listai*), and large predators such as the sabertooth cat (*Smilodon fatalis*) and the American lion (*Panthera leo atrox*). These large mammals disappeared during a great wave of extinctions that occurred at the end of the last ice age (about eight to 12 thousand years ago), which may have been caused by overhunting by the first human inhabitants of North America, migrants from Asia who colonized the continent about that time.

Some species of ungulates which have been domesticated are important to agriculture and sometimes as draft animals. The most abundant domesticated ungulates are sheep (*Ovis aries*), goats (*Capra hircus*), cows (*Bos taurus*), zebu cows (*B. indica*), pigs (*Sus scrofa*), horses (*Equus caballus*), camels (*Camelus dromedarius* and *C. bactrianus*), and water buffalo (*Bubalus bubalis*).

Many of the wild species of ungulates have recently become endangered and some have become extinct as a result of human influence. The most important of the human activities that endanger wildlife are the habitat loss associated with extensive conversions of natural ecosystems into agricultural or urban lands, and overhunting for the meat, hide, horns, or antlers of these large animals. It is critical that these human influences be rigorously controlled, if there is to be room on Earth to sustain all living species of ungulates. Natural ecosystems would be severely impoverished if there remain only those few species of ungulates that are used in agriculture, or that are adapted to other ecosystems dominated by humans.

Bill Freedman

Uniformitarianism

Uniformitarianism is the belief that current Earth processes—mountain building, eroding, depositing sediments—have occurred since the beginning of the Earth, for roughly 4.5 billion years. Mountains rise, valleys deepen, and sand grains collect now the same way they uplifted, eroded, and deposited over these millions of years. Therefore, based on processes operating today, they interpret the history of the Earth.

For example, modern glaciers erode, mix, and drop multi–sized sediments in a unique way, as if the materials had been processed through a blender. Geologists find these jumbled sediments at the bases of mountains like the Rockies and the Alps, in places where no glaciers exist today, and assume that these places were glacially active in the past. Glacial deposits even occur in rocks hundreds of millions of years old, leading geologists to conclude that those parts of the world experienced glaciation at the time the rocks formed.

Although this belief may sound logical today, the ideas of uniformitarianism were initially dismissed because of the amount of time required for these processes. In the mid–sixteenth century, Bishop Ussher of Ireland, by counting the ages of Biblical characters, calculated the Earth to be merely 6,000 years old. Because he based his calculations on the Bible, scientists were bound by tradition (and even by law) to work within this short time frame. Contradictions of the Bible were considered heresy, sometimes punishable by death. Scientists of the time, therefore, explained the placement and composition of rocks with more acceptable theories like catastrophism, the belief that the Earth changes suddenly during cataclysmic earthquakes, floods, or eruptions.

Before scientists could accept uniformitarianism, they needed to increase the predicted age of the earth to accommodate the slowness of its processes. Generally credited with this expansion, two Scots, James Hutton (1726–1797) and Charles Lyell (1797–1875), observed sedimentary rocks and concluded that the time required for thousands of feet of sediment to collect, solidify, and become land was much greater than Ussher's 6,000 years. After all, the Romans constructed walls and buildings in Great Britain that remained relatively unchanged for 2,000 years. How long must it have taken for whole mountains to erode nearly flat and leave behind the sediments that became the observed rocks? Eventually, the scientific community embraced uniformitarianism because it explained a majority of geological mysteries, and it did not rely on any kind of divine intervention to enact change.

Modern uniformitarianism differs slightly from its original version. It agrees that the laws of nature operate the same way today as they did millions of years ago, with this exception: the way the Earth's processes work today is the same as throughout time, but the speed and intensity of the processes may vary. Volcanoes erupt as they have all along (as shown in rocks),

but there were times of greater volcanism than today. Land erodes now as it did millions of year ago, but land eroded faster when there were no plants to hinder the rocks and soil from washing into seas.

Geologists also recognize that mountains gradually rise thousands of feet in episodes of small uplifts of a few feet at a time, followed by long periods of relative inactivity—not in one catastrophic upheaval.

Uniformitarianism allows us to interpret the events of the past in rocks; it allows us to write the history of the earth.

In addition to allowing the interpretation of the past, uniformitarianism allows us to predict the future. Understanding how and when rivers flood, what causes earthquakes and where they are likely to shake, or how and when a volcano will erupt can limit damage from these events. Although short–term prediction still eludes geologists, long range forecasting of disasters leads to better building codes, levees, emergency preparation, and erosion controls, which ultimately save lives and property.

See also Catastrophism.

Units and standards

A unit of measurement is some specific quantity that has been chosen as the standard against which other measurements of the same kind are made. For example, the meter is the unit of measurement for length in the metric system. When an object is said to be four meters long, that means that the object is four times as long as the unit standard (one meter).

The term "standard" refers to the physical object on which the unit of measurement is based. For example, for many years the standard used in measuring length in the metric system was the distance between two scratches on a platinum–iridium bar kept at the Bureau of Standards in Sèvres, France. A standard serves as a model against which other measuring devices of the same kind are made. The meter stick in your classroom or home is thought to be exactly one meter long because it was made from a permanent model kept at the manufacturing plant that was originally copied from the standard meter in France.

All measurements consist of two parts: a scalar (numerical) quantity and the unit designation. In the measurement 8.5 meters, the scalar quantity is 8.5 and the unit designation is meters.

History

The need for units and standards developed at a point in human history when people needed to know how much of something they were buying, selling, or exchanging. A farmer might want to sell a bushel of wheat, for example, for 10 dollars, but he or she could do so only if the unit "bushel" was known to potential buyers. Furthermore, the unit "bushel" had to have the same meaning for everyone who used the term.

The measuring system that most Americans know best is the British system, with units including the foot, yard, second, pound, and gallon. The British system grew up informally and in a disorganized way over many centuries. The first units of measurement probably came into use shortly after 1215. These units were tied to easily obtained or produced standards. The yard, for example, was defined as the distance from King Henry II's nose to the thumb of his outstretched hand.

The British system of measurement consists of a complex, irrational collection of units whose only advantage is its familiarity. As an example of the problems it poses, the British system has three different units known as the quart. These are the British quart, the United States dry quart, and the United States liquid quart. The exact size of each of these quarts differs.

In addition, a number of different units are in use for specific purposes. Among the units of volume in use in the British system, (in addition to those mentioned above) are the bag, barrel (of which there are three types—British and United States dry, United States liquid, and United States petroleum), bushel, butt, cord, drachm, firkin, gill, hogshead, kilderkin, last, noggin, peck, perch, pint, and quarter.

The metric system

In an effort to bring some rationality to systems of measurement, the French National Assembly established a committee in 1790 to propose a new system of measurement, with new units and new standards. That system has come to be known as the metric system and is now the only system of measurement used by all scientists and in every country of the world except the United States and the Myanmar Republic. The units of measurement chosen for the metric system were the gram (abbreviated g) for mass, the liter (l) for volume, the meter (m) for length, and the second (s) for time.

A specific standard was chosen for each of these basic units. The meter was originally defined as one ten–millionth the distance from the north pole to the equator along the prime meridian. As a definition, this standard is perfectly acceptable, but it has one major disadvantage: a person who wants to make a meter stick would have difficulty using that standard to construct a meter stick of his or her own.

As a result, new and more suitable standards were selected over time. One improvement was to construct the platinum–iridium bar standard mentioned above. Manufacturers of measuring devices could ask for copies of the fundamental standard kept in France and then make their own copies from those. As you can imagine, the more copies of copies that had to be made, the less accurate the final measuring device would be.

The most recent standard adopted for the meter solves this problem. In 1983, the international Conference on Weights and Measures defined the meter as the distance that light travels in $1/299,792,458$ second. The standard is useful because it depends on the most accurate physical measurement known—the second—and because anyone in the world is able, given the proper equipment, to determine the true length of a meter.

Le Système International d'Unités (the SI system)

In 1960, the metric system was modified somewhat with the adoption of new units of measurement. The modification was given the name of Le Système International d'Unités, or the International System of Units—more commonly known as the SI system.

Nine fundamental units make up the SI system. These are the meter (abbreviated m) for length, the kilogram (kg) for mass, the second (s) for time, the ampere (A) for electric current, the kelvin (K) for temperature, the candela (cd) for light intensity, the mole (mol) for quantity of a substance, the radian (rad) for plane angles, and the steradian (sr) for solid angles.

Derived Units

Many physical phenomena are measured in units that are derived from SI units. As an example, frequency is measured in a unit known as the hertz (Hz). The hertz is the number of vibrations made by a wave in a second. It can be expressed in terms of the basic SI unit as s^{-1}. Pressure is another derived unit. Pressure is defined as the force per unit area. In the metric system, the unit of pressure is the Pascal (Pa) and can be expressed as kilograms per meter per second squared, or $kg/m\ x^2$. Even units that appear to have little or no relationship to the nine fundamental units can, nonetheless, be expressed in these terms. The absorbed dose, for example, indicates that amount of radiation received by a person or object. In the metric system, the unit for this measurement is the gray. One gray can be defined in terms of the fundamental units as meters squared per second squared, or $m^2 \times s^2$.

Many other commonly used units can also be expressed in terms of the nine fundamental units. Some of the most familiar are the units for area (square meter: m^2), volume (cubic meter: m^3), velocity (meters per second: m/s), concentration (moles per cubic meter: mol/m^3), density (kilogram per cubic meter: kg/m^3), luminance (candela per square meter: cd/m^2), and magnetic field strength (amperes per meter: A/m).

A set of prefixes is available that makes it possible to use the fundamental SI units to express larger or smaller amounts of the same quantity. Among the most commonly used prefixes are milli– (m) for one–thousandth, centi– (c) for one–hundredth, micro– (μ) for one–millionth, kilo– (k) for one thousand times, and mega– (M) for one million times. Thus, any volume can be expressed by using some combination of the fundamental unit (liter) and the appropriate prefix. One million liters, using this system, would be a megaliter (ML) and one millionth of a liter, a microliter (μL).

Natural Units

One characteristic of all of the above units is that they have been selected arbitrarily. The committee that established the metric system could, for example, have defined the meter as one one–hundredth the distance between Paris and Sèvres. It was completely free to choose any standard it wished.

Some measurements, however, suggested "natural" units. In the field of electricity, for example, the charge carried by a single electron would appear to be a natural unit of measurement. That quantity is known as the elementary charge (e) and has the value of $1.6021892 \times 10^{-19}$ coulomb. Other natural units of measurement include the speed of light (c: 2.99792458×10^8 m/s), the Planck constant ($\hbar$: 6.626176×10^{-34} joule per hertz), the mass of an electron (m_e: $0.9109534 \times 10^{-30}$ kg), and the mass of a proton (m_p: $1.6726485 \times 10^{-27}$ kg). As you can see, each of these natural units can be expressed in terms of SI units, but they are often used as basic units in specialized fields of science.

Unit conversions between systems

For many years, an effort has been made to have the metric system, including SI units, adopted worldwide. As early as 1866, the United States Congress legalized the use of the metric system. More than a hundred years later, in 1976, the Congress adopted the Metric Conversion Act declaring it the policy of the nation

KEY TERMS

British system—A collection of measuring units that has developed haphazardly over many centuries and is now used almost exclusively in the United States and for certain specialized types of measurements.

Derived units—Units of measurements that can be obtained by multiplying or dividing various combinations of the nine basic SI units.

Metric system—A system of measurement developed in France in the 1790s.

Natural units—Units of measurement that are based on some obvious natural standard, such as the mass of an electron.

SI system—An abbreviation for Le Système International d'Unités, a system of weights and measures adopted in 1960 by the General Conference on Weights and Measures.

to increase the use of the metric system in the United States.

In fact, little progress has been made in that direction. Indeed, elements of the British system of measurement continue in use for specialized purposes throughout the world. All flight navigation, for example, is expressed in terms of feet, not meters. As a consequence, it is still necessary for an educated person to be able to convert from one system of measurement to the other.

In 1959, English–speaking countries around the world met to adopt standard conversion factors between British and metric systems. To convert from the pound to the kilogram, for example, it is necessary to multiply the given quantity (in pounds) by the factor 0.45359237. A conversion in the reverse direction, from kilograms to pounds, involves multiplying the given quantity (in kilograms) by the factor 2.2046226. Other relevant conversion factors are 1 inch = 2.54 centimeters and 1 yard = 0.9144 meter.

See also Metric system.

Further Reading:

Adams, Herbert F. R. *SI Metric Units: An Introduction.* Toronto: McGraw–Hill Ryerson, 1974.
Jerrard, H. G., and D. B. McNeil. *A Dictionary of Scientific Units: Including Dimensionless Numbers and Scales.* London: Chapman and Hall, 1980.

Nelson, Robert A. *SI: The International System of Units.* Stony Brook, N.Y.: American Association of Physics Teachers, 1982.

David E. Newton

Universal product code see **Bar code**
Universe see **Big bang theory; Cosmology**

Uplift

Uplift is the process by which the Earth's surface slowly rises either due to increasing upward force applied from below or decreasing downward force (weight) from above.

During uplift, land, as well as the sea floor, rises. The outer shell of the Earth, the crust, divides into moving sections called plates. Uplift, forming mountains and plateaus, usually results as these plates crash into each other over millions of years. Although the plates move at roughly the speed fingernails grow, their motion still has a tremendous impact on the earth, since plates can be as big as a continent or the Pacific Ocean. Sometimes mountains rise from crust separating rather than colliding. The study of these moving plates is plate tectonics.

Collision between two pieces of continents lifts the tallest mountains. When India, formerly a large island, slammed into the south side of Asia around 55 million years ago, the Himalayas uplifted. When Africa and Europe smashed into North America 300 million years ago, the Appalachians uplifted. As the western edge of the westward–moving North America smacked into various islands over the past 200 million years, the Rockies uplifted. In these uplifts, pieces of ocean floor trapped between the approaching continents rise as well. Limestone, a rock formed on the sea floor, composes the summit of Mt. Everest, over 26,000 ft (8,000 m) above sea level.

Uplift also results when sea floor crust collides with continental crust or with other pieces of sea floor crust. Volcanic mountains (Andes, Cascades) or volcanic islands (Indonesia, Japan, Aleutians) result from sea floor colliding with and diving beneath a continent or another sea floor. As the sea floor crust descends, some of the sediment on the floor scrapes off the plunging crust and piles up to form a ridge called an accretionary wedge. For example, as the Indo–Australian plate dove beneath the Eurasian plate at Indonesia, the scraped and folded sediments form the Java Ridge off the west coast of the volcanic island of Java.

Sea floor also uplifts along mid–ocean ridges where crust separated as magma (melted rock) from inside the Earth tries to reach the surface. The magma that rises from below these ridges lifts the ocean floor. Mid–ocean ridges circle the Earth like the seams on a giant baseball. If the magma rises similarly beneath a continent, the land will bulge and eventually crack, potentially tearing the continent in half and creating a new ocean, as at the Red Sea.

Although compression creates most uplift, the Basin and Range region of western North America resulted from a combination of collision and then extension. A map of North America illustrates a series of parallel north–south oriented mountain ranges separated by north–south trending valleys (basins) extending from Nevada and Utah down into Mexico. These mountains formed when first the crust arched from the collision of North America with a piece of ocean floor, and then later the crust began to separate. As the top of the arches cracked (similar to how the top of a bent piece of clay cracks along its upper surface when bent), pieces of the crust dropped down to form the valleys, and other pieces formed the mountain ranges.

Finally, when a huge weight is removed from the crust, the crust will slowly rise up in a process called isostatic rebound. During an ice age, when glaciers up to 1.9 mi (3 km) thick cover continents, the weight of that ice pushes down on the crust causing it to sink or subside. When the ice melts, the crust uplifts just as a raft in a pool rises when the swimmer gets off it. Scandinavia still responds to glaciers melting 10,000 years ago by uplifting by as much as a centimeter per year.

See also Glaciers; Mountain; Plate tectonics; Volcano.

Upwelling

Upwellings are a flow to the surface of deep, cold, nutrient–rich waters from greater depths in the ocean. The most extensive upwellings are associated with persistent coastal currents that draw surface water away from or along the coast to be replaced by a surface-ward flow of deeper waters. The most famous of these sorts of regional upwellings are found off the west coast of southern South America and in parts of the Antarctic Ocean.

Extensive upwellings can also develop where large currents are moving in opposite directions. This occurs in parts of the Pacific Ocean where the equatorial current in the Southern Hemisphere tends to move in a southerly direction, while that in the Northern Hemisphere moves to the north. Where these divergent equatorial currents flow beside each other, they develop extensive upwellings of deep waters.

More local upwellings can be caused when currents encounter surface or subsurface obstructions to their flow which can also force deeper water to the surface. Upwellings also develop on the leeward (down–flow) side of islands that obstruct the passage of a prevalent current.

Upwellings are most common in high–latitude regions of the Arctic and Antarctic Oceans, along the equator, and in certain coastal locations on the eastern sides of oceans. The most important of the latter types of upwellings are associated with the California current, the Peru current off South America, and the Benguala current off west Africa.

Upwelling waters are relatively rich in inorganic nutrients such as nitrate and phosphate. As a result, upwelling waters can sustain a large productivity of phytoplankton when they reach the surface of the ocean where there is ample sunlight to support photosynthesis. The relatively great primary productivity of phytoplankton can in turn support a large productivity of zooplankton which can sustain a great abundance of fish, seabirds, and marine mammals. Because of their intrinsic fertility, upwelling waters are much more ecologically productive than the open ocean, which is generally highly deficient in nutrients.

Some of the world's largest fisheries are associated with extensive upwellings. These include the cold–water fisheries of certain regions of the Antarctic and Arctic Oceans and the temperate fisheries off Peru, Chile, California, and west Africa. The world's largest and most productive populations of seabirds and marine mammals also occur in those upwelling–driven marine ecosystems.

See also Ocean; Plankton; Zooplankton.

Uranium

Uranium is the metallic chemical element with an atomic number of 92. Its symbol is U, atomic weight is 238.0, and specific gravity is 18.95. It melts at 2,075° F (1,135° C) and boils at 7,473.2° F (4,134° C). Natural uranium consists of three isotopes of mass numbers 234 (0.005%), 235 (0.711%) and 238 (99.283%). All are radioactive.

History and applications

With the exception of tiny amounts of neptunium, uranium is the heaviest element found on Earth—that is, the element with the highest atomic number and atomic weight. It has held that distinction ever since it was first recognized as an element by the German chemist Martin H. Klaproth in 1789, who named it uranium in honor of the new planet that had recently been discovered: Uranus. Until 1896, when Henri Becquerel discovered radioactivity, uranium remained a dull, uninteresting metal that found occasional use in making pretty yellow glass. But then it acquired the distinction of being one of only two known elements that possessed the mysterious property of being radioactive. (The other element was thorium.)

When nuclear fission was discovered in 1938, uranium suddenly became the most fateful element in the Periodic table. Because of its ability to undergo nuclear fission with the release of huge amounts of energy, it became a brand–new source of power, which people would use for both peaceful and destructive purposes.

Aside from its nuclear properties of radioactivity and fission, uranium is still a rather dull element. In fact, it is literally dull; freshly–cut uranium metal is silvery white, but it soon develops a dull gray color in air because of a thin coating of black uranium oxide. That pretty yellow glass is not made anymore, because we now know that uranium is dangerous—both from its radioactivity and because, like most heavy metals, it is chemically very poisonous. If you ever see some uranium glass in an antique shop—it has a hazy, fluorescent, greenish yellow color—do not buy it. It is not radioactive enough to do any real harm, but who needs more radioactivity around the house?

In spite of its radioactivity, uranium has a few useful applications because it is so heavy. Having a density of 19.0 grams per cubic centimeter, it is almost as dense as gold (19.3) and platinum (21.5). But it is much cheaper for two reasons: it is much more plentiful on Earth (40 or 50 times as abundant as silver) and it is a byproduct of the nuclear power industry after the very valuable uranium–235 isotope has been removed. It therefore finds some military uses in which a lot of weight is needed in a small space, such as for counterweights in aircraft control systems, ballast for missile reentry vehicles, and shielding against radiation.

Chemically, uranium is a member of the actinide series of elements, which runs from atomic number 89 (actinium) to atomic number 102 (nobelium). Those with atomic numbers higher than uranium's 92 are the transuranium elements. Uranium's most important features lie not in its chemistry, but in its radioactivity and its ability to undergo nuclear fission.

Uranium's radioactivity

Although uranium is indeed radioactive—the discovery of radioactivity occurred during a study of uranium's properties—it has a very long half–life, which means that it emits its radiations at a rather leisurely pace. Also, it emits mostly alpha particles, which do not travel very far through the air and will not even penetrate the skin. Its radiations are therefore not very harmful, and uranium and its compounds can be handled with a reasonable amount of care, like any other highly poisonous chemicals.

The half–life of the most abundant uranium isotope, uranium–238, is 4.47×10^9 years, or about 4.5 billion years, which happens to be equal to the age of the Earth as a planet. This fact allows scientists to use the disintegration of uranium as a sort of clock to determine the ages of rocks and other geological features of the Earth.

Uranium–238 is the "parent" atom of a series of radioactive isotopes that we find associated with it in uranium ores. Through radioactive disintegrations, the uranium has been producing these "daughter" isotopes ever since the ore was laid down where we find it today. Uranium–235, which has a half–life of 7.04×10^8 (700 million) years, is the parent of another radioactive series. Among the daughters in these two series are various radioactive isotopes of radium, radon, and other elements. Both series of disintegrations proceed by producing consecutive radioactive isotopes until they wind up as stable isotopes of lead. Thus, the uranium isotopes are slowly turning into lead at a steady rate that is well known from their half–lives. By measuring the relative amounts of uranium and lead isotopes in a uranium–containing rock, scientists can calculate how old it is.

One of the disintegration products of uranium is radium, the element of atomic number 88. Radium was discovered by Marie Curie (1867–1934), who isolated it from a uranium ore. Another important disintegration product of uranium–238 is radon–222, which has a half–life of 3.8 days. Radon is a gas (a rare gas) that can diffuse out of uranium in the ground and seep into people's houses. Radon can cause lung cancer because when breathed in, it can emit its alpha particles directly in the lung, where they can do the most damage. Testing houses for radon gas has become an important precaution ever since this hazard was uncovered only 10 or 15 years ago.

The fission of uranium

By far the most important characteristic of uranium is that it undergoes the nuclear reaction called fission. Uranium–235, which is only about 0.7% of all uranium atoms, is the isotope that fissions most readily. For use in nuclear reactors, natural uranium is enriched in the 235 isotope (that is, the percentage of the 235 isotope is increased) by gaseous diffusion. In this process the uranium is converted into the gaseous compound uranium hexafluoride, UF_6, and allowed to diffuse through a series of porous barriers. Those molecules which contain atoms of the slightly lighter uranium–235 isotope diffuse slightly faster and therefore separate themselves from the heavier, more slowly moving molecules that contain uranium–238.

See also Element, chemical; Isotope; Nuclear fission; Radioactivity; Periodic table.

Further Reading:

Emsley, J. *The Elements*, Clarendon Press, 1991.
Greenwood, N. N. *Chemistry of the Elements*, Pergamon Press, 1985.
Kirk–Othmer Encyclopedia of Chemical Technology, Wiley.
Parker, Sybil P., ed. *McGraw–Hill Encyclopedia of Chemistry,* 2nd ed. 1993.

Robert L. Wolke

Uranium-series dating see **Dating techniques**

Uranus

Uranus is the seventh planet from the Sun. It has a large size (its diameter is almost four times that of the Earth) and mass, low mean density, fairly rapid rotation, and well–developed ring (11 components) and satellite (15 members) systems. The planet has a strong magnetic field with a large tilt (58.6°) to its rotation axis and offset (0.3 Uranus radius) from its center. Analysis of the observations made by *Voyager 2* during its flyby of Neptune in August 1989 shows that Uranus and Neptune are similar in most of these properties and form a subgroup of the Jovian planets; Jupiter and Saturn, much larger and more massive, form the other subgroup.

Discovery

William Herschel (1738–1822) fortuitously discovered Uranus in 1781; it was the first planet discovered telescopically. It was found to orbit the Sun at a mean distance of about 19.2 astronomical units (a.u.) (2,870,000,000 km), about twice as far from the Sun as Saturn (9.54 a.u), the most distant planet known before 1781.

Observations from Earth

Knowledge about Uranus came slowly because of its distance. Even when it is closest, Uranus shows a disk of only 4 in (10 cm) in apparent diameter through a telescope and is 5.7^m apparent magnitude (barely visible to the unaided eye even in the best observing conditions). Herschel discovered Oberon and Titania, the outermost and largest, respectively, satellites of Uranus in 1787. Determination of their orbits around Uranus from observations gave their periods of revolution P and mean distances A from Uranus. This allowed one to determine Uranus' mass from the general form of Kepler's Third Law; it turned out to be 14.5 Earth masses. Using its radius of 15,873 mi (25,560 km), one calculated Uranus' mean density (its mass divided by its volume), which is 1.27 grams/cm³. This indicated that Uranus is a smaller type of Jovian planet similar to Jupiter and Saturn; they are characterized by large masses and sizes and low mean densities (compared to the Earth), and are inferred to consist largely of gases.

The planes of the orbits of Oberon and Titania were expected to lie in or near the plane of Uranus' equator, since most other planetary satellites have orbital planes that are in or near the equatorial planes of their planets. When the orbital planes of Oberon and Titania were determined, however, they indicated that the plane of Uranus' equator is almost perpendicular to the plane of its orbit around the Sun (and also to the ecliptic). This is unlike the other planets, whose equatorial planes are tilted by at most 30° to the planes of their orbits around the Sun. This implied that Uranus' axis (and poles) of rotation lie almost in its orbital plane. This conclusion has been confirmed by observations of Uranus' rotation from the *Voyager 2* spacecraft in 1986. This is the first of several interesting characteristics we have discovered for Uranus, and gives Uranus interesting seasons during its year (period of revolution around the Sun), which is 84.1 Earth years long. The Uranian seasons will be discussed in more detail below. The cause of this unusual orientation of Uranus' rotation axis is still unknown and is now the subject of considerable speculation and theoretical research. One theory is that the orientation of its rotation axis was produced by the collision of an Earth–sized body with Uranus near the end of its formation.

Unexplained perturbations of Uranus' orbit in the early nineteenth century led to the prediction of the existence of a still more distant large planet, resulting in the discovery of Neptune in 1846. Neptune is the most distant (30.06 a.u. mean distance from the Sun) Jovian planet, and it has several properties (mass, size, rotation period, rings, and magnetic field) like those of Uranus.

Three more satellites of Uranus, closer to it than Titania, were discovered during the 105 years after Neptune's discovery. They are, in order of closeness to Uranus, Umbriel and Ariel, discovered in 1851 by Lassell (1799–1880), and Miranda, discovered in 1948 by G. P. Kuiper (1905–1973). These discoveries showed that Uranus has a satellite system comparable to those of Jupiter and Saturn, although Titania, its largest (980 mi [1,580 km] diameter) and most massive satellite, and the slightly smaller Oberon are comparable in size and mass to Saturn's satellites Iapetus and Rhea rather than to its much larger satellite Titan and Jupiter's four Galilean satellites. All other satellites of Uranus are smaller and less massive.

The best telescopic observations of Uranus from the Earth's surface show a small, featureless, bluish-green disk. Spectroscopic observations show that this color is produced by the absorption of sunlight by methane gas in its atmosphere; this gas is also present in the atmospheres of Jupiter and Saturn. Observations of occultations (similar to eclipses) or stars by Uranus indicated that Uranus' atmosphere is mostly composed of molecular hydrogen and helium, which are also the main components of the atmospheres of Jupiter and Saturn.

Observations at infrared wavelengths (that are longer than those of red light), where planets radiate away most of their heat energy, show that Uranus radiates at most only slightly more infrared radiative energy than its atmosphere absorbs from sunlight. Any excess energy originating from Uranus' interior can be attributed to the decay of radioactive elements, which also produces much of the heating in the Earth's interior. This is not true for the other Jovian planets, which all emit as much as twice as much infrared energy as their atmospheres absorb from sunlight; this requires another internal energy source for them, which is possibly continuing gravitational contraction.

One of the last major discoveries about the Uranus system from Earth–based observations was made on March 10, 1977, during observations of Uranus' occultation of the star SAO 158657, when J. L. Elliot's (1943–) group and other observers noticed unexpected dimmings of the star's light before the occultation and again after it. These dimmings were correctly identified

The surface of Titania, the largest of the Uranian satellites at 980 miles (1580 km) in diameter, is marked by both impact craters and past geologic activity. The deep fault valley visible in this image near the terminator (day-night boundry) is the result of at least one episode of tectonic activity, and the basin-like feature near the top of the image appears to be the result of a heavy impact on Titania's surface.

with the existence of several faint, thin rings orbiting Uranus well inside Miranda's orbit which were hitherto undetected; unlike Saturn's rings, they are too faint to be directly observed from the Earth's surface by ordinary methods. Uranus' rings have been observed several times since then during stellar occultations and by the *Voyager 2* spacecraft. The rings are very dark; their albedos (the fraction of the light that falls on them which they reflect) are only about 0.05.

A second major discovery made by Earth–based infrared observations was the detection of water ice on the surfaces of some of Uranus' satellites.

Let us now return to the seasons of Uranus. The fact that Uranus' rotation axis lies almost in the plane of its orbit around the Sun means that at some season its south pole will be pointed nearly at the Sun, and nearly all of its southern hemisphere will be in continuous sunlight (early southern hemisphere summer), while nearly all of its northern hemisphere will be in continuous night (early northern hemisphere winter). These seasons occurred in 1901 and in late 1985, and will occur next in 2069. The Sun was last above Uranus' equator in December 1965, when it rose at Uranus' south pole and set at the north pole; the Sun will then shine continuously on Uranus' south pole for the next 41.6 years until mid–2007, when it will again be above Uranus' equator and will set at the south pole and rise at the north pole, which will be in continuous sunlight for the next 42.5 years while the south pole will be in continuous night. The north pole will point closest to the Sun in early 2030 (early northern hemisphere summer), and the Sun will set there and rise at the south pole in 2050. Calculations show that a horizontal unit surface area, say a square meter, at either pole will receive over a Uranian year about 1.5 times the sunlight that the same surface would receive at Uranus' equator over a Uranian year (84.1 Earth years).

Results from the flyby of the *Voyager 2* spacecraft

The *Voyager 2* spacecraft was launched from Earth on August 20, 1977. As it flew by Jupiter in July 1979,

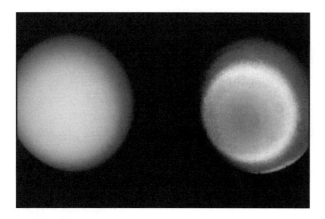

Unlike the other gas giants, Uranus reveals few atmospheric features in visible light. However, latitudinal atmospheric bands do exist, as can be seen in the enhanced image on the right; because Uranus has such an inclined axis of rotation (which is pointing almost directly down into this image), atmospheric bands that cross the surface of the planet (in the same way that atmospheric bands cross Jupiter's surface) appear as concentric circles in the photo.

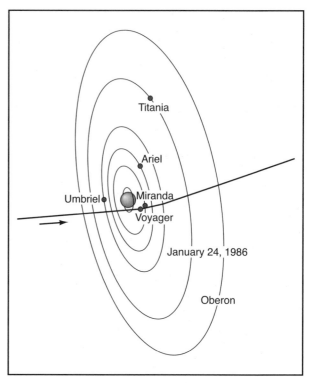

Figure 1. Trajectory of *Voyager 2* through the Uranus system in January 1986.

it was accelerated toward Saturn which, in turn, accelerated *Voyager 2* toward Uranus during the August 1981 flyby. *Voyager 2* flew by Uranus on a hyperbolic orbit, passing it at a minimum distance of 66,447 mi (107,000 km) from the center of Uranus on January 24, 1986. The observations that *Voyager 2* made of the Uranus system from November 4, 1985 to February 26, 1986 added immensely to our knowledge about it. Because Uranus' rotation axis was pointed less than 8° from the Sun then, and because *Voyager 2* was approaching Uranus along a path that made about a 35° angle with the line from the Sun, *Voyager 2* passed through Uranus' ring and satellite system much like a bullet passing through a "bull's eye target" (see Fig. 1) and could not pass fairly close to any more than two of Uranus's satellites at most.

The satellites closely approached by *Voyager 2* were Miranda and Ariel; the spacecraft passed by these two at distances of 16,146 mi (26,000 km) and 17,388 mi (28,000 km), respectively.

The main discoveries made by *Voyager 2* during its encounter with Uranus are the following:

Uranus's magnetic field

Like the Earth and the other Jovian planets, Uranus has a strong magnetic field which arises in its interior. Evidence for Uranus' magnetic field and magnetosphere (the region of space where the planet's magnetic field is dominant over the interplanetary field) was not

found until January 22, 1986, two days before closest approach to Uranus, when radio noise from charged particles trapped in its magnetosphere was detected. *Voyager 2* crossed into Uranus' magnetosphere on January 24 and remained inside it for 45 hours. Uranus' magnetic field was found to be quite strong but very unusual. First, Uranus' magnetic poles were found to be 58.6° from its poles of rotation, which is much greater than the tilts of the magnetic fields to the poles of rotation found for the Earth (11°), Jupiter (9.6°), and Saturn (0°). Second, the center of Uranus' magnetic field was found to be offset from its center of mass by 0.3 of Uranus' radius, a much greater offset than those found for the above–named planets. One effect of this magnetic field offset is that the magnetic field strength at the cloud level in Uranus' atmosphere is expected to vary by factors of five to 10 depending on Uranian latitude and longitude.

Radiation belts of charged particles trapped in Uranus' magnetosphere were detected. They consist mainly of low energy protons and electrons; very few heavy ions are detected. The particle densities in these radiation belts are low compared with those densities in the radiation belts of the Earth and Jupiter, possibly because the large tilt of Uranus' magnetic field to the interplanetary magnetic field allows the solar wind to make convective sweeps of particles out of Uranus' radiation belts fairly frequently.

Uranus' rotation

2. The fact that Uranus' magnetic field is tilted to its rotation axis and is offset from its center causes fluctuations of its magnetic field that are associated with the rotation of Uranus' interior. From measurements of these fluctuations by *Voyager 2*, the rotation period of Uranus' interior was found to be 17 hours 14 minutes. This is the first accurate rotation period for Uranus; earlier attempts in the last 100 years to determine its rotation period from spectroscopic and photometric observations gave very diverse, conflicting, and, as we now know, incorrect results. Other somewhat different rotation periods found from *Voyager 2* observations of cloud features in Uranus' atmosphere, which range from 16 to 17.5 hours, are caused by winds in Uranus' atmosphere.

Atmospheric temperature

In the earlier discussion of Uranus' seasons, it was mentioned that a unit surface at the poles will receive about 1.5 times as much sunlight as the same surface would on Uranus equator over a Uranian year. Based on this, one might expect Uranus' south polar region, which at the time of the *Voyager 2* flyby had been in continuous sunlight for the order of 20 years, to be warmer than its equatorial region, which would be warmer than the north polar region, which had been in prolonged night. *Voyager 2's* infrared instruments did not observe this; at the level of clouds in Uranus' atmosphere, the temperature seemed to be the same, about –346° F (–210° C), from the south pole across the equator to the north pole. The most evident temperature change at this level was a 34° F (1° C) decrease centered at about 30° south latitude. This surprising observation shows the great capacity of the enormously thick atmosphere of Uranus (and those of the other Jovian planets) to absorb and transport away almost all the sunlight energy from a region sunlit continuously for decades.

Uranus' atmosphere

By solar and stellar occultations and visual, infrared, and radio observations from *Voyager 2,* the structure and circulation of Uranus' atmosphere has been mapped from just below the cloud layers to its exosphere. The main components of the atmosphere are hydrogen and helium, the most abundant elements in the universe. Methane comprises 1% to 2% of the observable troposphere. Water vapor and ammonia are inferred to be important components of the atmosphere below the clouds, but they have not been detected in the

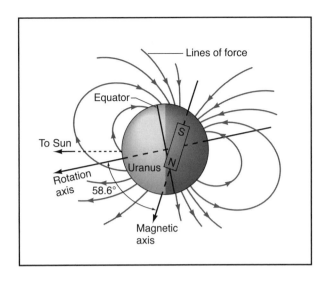

Figure 2. Diagram of offset and tilted magnetic field of Uranus.

observable part of the troposphere because it is too cold and freezes them out.

Uranus' upper atmosphere is dominated by hydrogen, mainly molecular. Methane and other hydrocarbons are nearly all frozen out by the underlying cold atmosphere, especially the lower stratosphere (at 428° F [220° C] temperature). Molecular hydrogen is broken down into atomic hydrogen mainly by the absorption of ultraviolet radiation from the Sun, and some atomic hydrogen is ionized into free protons and electrons, forming an ionosphere. The temperature of the upper atmosphere increases to 482° F (250° C) at 497 mi (800 km) above the cloud layers, and continues to increase to over 932° F (500° C) at 3,105 mi (5,000 km) above the clouds. Atomic hydrogen becomes the main component of Uranus' upper atmosphere above 4,658 mi (7,500 km) above the clouds, forming a hydrogen thermal corona in its exosphere that extends at least 15,525 mi (25,000 km) above the clouds (extending through the zone of the rings from 9,936 mi [16,000 km] to 16,146 mi [26,000 km] above the clouds). The source of most of the heating of Uranus' upper atmosphere is still unknown as is also true for the heating of the upper atmospheres of the Earth, Jupiter, and of Saturn.

Uranus's rings

Voyager observations of the rings during the flyby discovered two more rings (the Lamda ring and a broad dust band closer to Uranus than Ring 6), and stellar occultation observations added greatly to our knowledge about the detailed structures, shapes, and orientations of the nine rings discovered earlier by Earth–based observations. The *Voyager 2* observations also indicate that the rings contain a large fraction of large particles; the average particle size in the rings was calculated to be between 8 and 28 in (20–70 cm). An appreciable amount of micron–sized dust seems to be distributed throughout the ring system. However, this dust is probably transitory; atmospheric drag on the dust particles from Uranus' hydrogen corona that was mentioned above is expected to decelerate them and cause them to spiral into the denser layers of Uranus' atmosphere after, at most, a few thousand years. Uranus has 10 known rings that are nearly circular and lie in or nearly in the plane of Uranus' equator. The Epsilon ring is not only the most distant ring from Uranus, but it is also the most elliptical and the widest one.

Additional sattelites

Voyager 2 discovered 10 more small satellites which all orbit Uranus closer to it than Miranda and are all smaller than Miranda. Surface albedo could be found for only Puck and Cordelia, which are 0.08 and 0.07, respectively, indicating that they are somewhat brighter than the ring particles. The other eight newly found satellites seem to be dark like Puck, Cordelia, and the rings. Cordelia and Ophelia, the two satellites closest to Uranus, seem to serve as "shepherd satellites" for the Epsilon ring, keeping its particles in the ring by their gravitational perturbations on them, thereby increasing this ring's orbital stability. Gravitational perturbations produced by several other satellites near the rings may make the rings more stable. Ophelia is slightly more and Cordelia slightly less than two Uranus radii from Uranus' center; this raises the possibility that the rings were formed by satellites inside Uranus' Roche limit that were torn to pieces by collisions or by tidal forces produced in them by Uranus.

Observations of Miranda and other satellites

Since *Voyager 2* passed fairly close to Miranda, it was possible to determine Miranda's mass from its perturbation of *Voyager 2's* hyperbolic orbit past Uranus found from an analysis of the *Voyager 2* radio data. Ariel's mass was then determined from its perturbations of the orbits of Miranda and *Voyager 2*. *Voyager 2* did not approach Umbriel, Titania, and Oberon closely enough for reliable determination of their masses from perturbations of its flyby orbit. Instead their masses are determined from their perturbations of Ariel's orbit and each other's orbits using both *Voyager 2* observations and Earth–based observations made over many years. Accurate radii were found for all five satellites from *Voyager 2* images; this allowed the calculation of mean densities for these satellites. Their mean densities, which range from 1.20 grams/cm³ for Miranda to 1.69

grams/cm³ for Titania, are compatible with their interiors being largely composed of water ice, which was detected earlier on their surfaces. All five satellites were found to be tidally locked to Uranus, as predicted by theory, so their rotation periods are the same as their orbital periods of revolution. Their rotation axes have become aligned nearly parallel to Uranus' rotation axis, so that only their southern hemispheres could be imaged. *Voyager 2* infrared measurements near the south poles of Miranda and Ariel gave temperatures of –304.6° F (–187° C) and –308.2° F (–189° C), respectively, considerably warmer than the cloud layer of Uranus' atmosphere, but understandable for a surface that has been in continuous sunlight for about 20 years. None of the satellites show an appreciable atmosphere.

Voyager 2 obtained detailed images of parts of the sunlit surface of all five previously known satellites and also of Puck. Bright and dark (albedo) regions, craters with or without bright ray systems around them, mountains, cliffs, scarps, valleys, canyons, graben, faults and other geological features are clearly seen on these images. Maps of the parts of the satellite surfaces that have been imaged have been made, and names have been assigned to many surface features. Summaries of the surface features of the six satellites with imaged surface features are given below. The images with the best resolution obtained were Ariel and Miranda because *Voyager 2* flew closest to them.

Oberon

Oberon, Uranus' most distant and second largest satellite, has extensive, heavily cratered terrain interrupted by canyons and scarps. Some craters are surrounded by bright ray systems; others show dark matter on their floors. A prominent feature on Oberon's limb is a large mountain 7 mi (11 km) high and 28 mi (45 km) wide. Oberon shows the least evidence from modification of its cratered terrain by geologic activity of any Uranian satellite. Image resolution is poor due to Oberon's distance.

Titania

Titania, Uranus' largest and most massive satellite, shows similar geological features to those found on Oberon. Heavily cratered plains are the most extensive surfaces found here. Image resolution is somewhat better for Titania than Oberon, since *Voyager 2* was closer to Titania. A prominent system of canyons and scarps is the most noticeable class of features on Titania's surface; shadows indicate some of them may be as deep as 3.7 mi (6 km). Moderately cratered and smooth plains are also observed, which indicate resurfacing. These features indicate that more geologic activity occurred on Titania than on Oberon after the end of the heavy bombardment (crater formation) phase of their histories. Here the resurfacing material should be liquid or icy water, ammonia, or methane, perhaps mixed with rocky material, rather than terrestrial type volcanic lava. Impact and/or internal heating may have melted or softened these ices, which then erupted and flowed over the satellite surfaces, resurfacing them. This phenomenon is called cryovolcanism (sometimes "water volcanism"), and it may have been important in the geological histories of many of the satellites of the Jovian planets.

Umbriel

With an average albedo of 0.21, Umbriel is the darkest of Uranus' five largest satellites. It also has a more uniform albedo than Titania and Oberon, showing only a few striking albedo features on the part of its surface imaged by *Voyager 2*. Umbriel also has extensive, heavily cratered terrain and several groups of canyons, scarps, and lineaments which seem to be of more recent origin than the craters which they cut. Evidence is also seen of resurfacing in and near several craters, indicating cryovolcanism. Much of its surface may have been resurfaced with dark material of uncertain origin (cryovolcanic, dark ejecta from a crater, or from an external source).

Ariel

Ariel is similar in size and mass to Umbriel, but whereas Umbriel is the darkest of Uranus' five largest satellites, Ariel is the brightest, with a 0.40 average albedo. Ariel's surface seems to have evolved more like Titania's surface than that of Umbriel; it shows global–scale faulting (canyons, scarps, and lineaments) and resurfacing by cryovolcanism, but on a more extensive scale than occurred on Titania. Ariel's most heavily cratered plains show less cratering than the most cratered units on Titania and Oberon. Evidence has been found for the extrusion of ice into Ariel's surface, filling part of a valley and partially burying a crater.

Miranda

Miranda shows the most interesting evidence for geologic activity and surface modification among Uranus' satellites. In addition to old cratered plains, canyons, scarps, lineaments, and valleys, the three coronae Arden, Elsinore, and Inverness exist on its surface; they are its most prominent surface features. They are large, lightly cratered regions of up to 186 mi (300 km) or more extent; Arden shows banded regions, while Elsinore and Inverness show numerous grooves and ridges. A cliff near Miranda's south pole may be as high as 12 mi (20 km). One plausible model for Miranda's evolution hypothesizes the following sequence of

events. First, Miranda accreted from several smaller bodies near Uranus and nearly in its equatorial plane; impacts during accretion formed the old cratered plains. Some of the canyon systems were formed near the end of accretion. Next, a large body impacted Miranda, forming the Arden basin. Debris was scattered over and ejected from Miranda, and cryovolcanism flooded the basin, forming Arden Corona. Then the Inverness basin was flooded, forming Inverness Corona. The last main cryovolcanic activity formed Elsinore Corona. This left Miranda's surface early in its present state, with only a few more recent craters added since then.

Puck

Puck's surface was also imaged by *Voyager 2*, revealing a cratered surface that is considerably darker (0.08 average albedo) than that for any of the five larger satellites. The *Voyager 2* images also show that Puck is almost spherical.

The interior of Uranus, like the interiors of the other planets, is largely unknown. Its mean density indicates that it is probably mainly a mixture of water, ammonia, carbon compounds, and rocky materials, with the latter having sunk into its central regions. Gravitational effects of the non–spherical components of Uranus, the largest of which should be its equatorial bulge, which is closely related to its oblateness (polar flattening) on the orbits of Uranus' rings, and nearer satellites can give information about the distribution of mass in its interior. The information on ring and satellite orbits obtained from Earth–based observations and the *Voyager 2* flyby has allowed models of Uranus' interior to be constructed. The best models have three layers: a small rocky core, a shell with a mixture of gaseous, icy, and rocky components, and a gaseous envelope which goes over to the atmosphere's visible layers (troposphere and above). The magnetic field discovered and mapped by *Voyager 2* implies a field generating region in Uranus' interior which extends out to 0.7 of Uranus radius from the center, and that part of Uranus' interior is a fluid and has a high internal temperature.

Further research

Although the *Voyager 2* flyby of Uranus in 1986 vastly increased our knowledge about the Uranus system, it left many questions unanswered, and has raised even more questions than it has answered. Although the rings and some of the 10 recently discovered satellites can be studied from Earth orbit, especially by using the Hubble Space Telescope, many questions about Uranus can only be answered by observations made by spacecraft sent to Uranus.

See also Jupiter; Neptune; Planetary atmospheres; Satellite; Saturn; Solar system; Space probe.

Further Reading:
Beatty, J.K. "Voyager 2's Triumph." *Sky and Telescope.* 72, No. 4 (October 1986): 336–342.
Bergstrahlh, Jay T., Ellis D. Miner, and Mildred S. Matthews, eds. *Uranus.* Tucson: University of Arizona Press, 1991.
Cuzzi, Jeffrey and Larry Esposito. "The Rings of Uranus." *Scientific American* (July 1987): 52–66.
Dowling, T. "Big Blue: Twin Worlds of Uranus and Neptune." *Astronomy* 18, No. 10 (October 1990): 42–53.
Elliot, James and Richard Kerr. *Rings.* Cambridge, MA: MIT Press, 1984.

Frederick R. West

Urea

Urea is a white, crystalline solid also known as carbamide. It is highly soluble in water and is the major molecule used by mammals and amphibians as a means of excreting nitrogenous waste (which generally comes from proteins). It is used in making fertilizers (where it serves as source of nitrogen) and in cattle feed, where it also raises the nitrogen levels. Urea is also used in the manufacturing of barbiturates and in manufacturing some plastics such as urethanes. Urea melts at 271°F (133°C). Solutions of urea in water are slightly basic. The formula of urea is shown in Figure 1.

The NH_2 groups are derived from nitrogen containing portions of proteins. Urea was first isolated from urine in 1773 by Hillaire-Malin Rouelle. In 1828 urea became the first organic (carbon based) molecule to be synthesized from inorganic components. This was accomplished by Freidrich Wolher by heating ammonium cyanate, forming urea. This synthesis began the decline of a "vital force" theory which held that only living things could make organic compounds.

Urea and metabolism

Urea is the final product of the metabolism of amino acids (the building blocks of proteins) in mammals, amphibians, and turtles. In the liver, ammonia reacts with carbon dioxide and through a series of seven steps that are controlled by enzymes (protein catalysts that speed up specific reactions) urea is produced. Each molecule of urea is "built" from two ammonia molecules (NH_3) and one carbon dioxide (CO_2) molecule. Ammonia itself is toxic so many animals have developed metabolic steps that take the ammonia formed and

Figure 1. Structural formula of urea.

convert it into less toxic and easily dealt with molecules. The extremely high solubility of urea in water (1,000 grams of urea dissolve in a liter of water) make it ideal for eliminating nitrogen–based waste products. The concentration of urea rises in many kidney diseases and blood urea concentration is often used to monitor kidney function. The urea produced by the body is excreted in urine. A healthy adult will excrete about 25 grams of urea per day. Upon standing the urea in urine will decompose to carbon dioxide and ammonia, accounting for the "ammonia" smell of old urine. In many animals and in some vegetarians, cloudy urine is common. This is the result of a precipitate (insoluble compound) formed from urea and calcium or magnesium ions. Medically urea is used as a diuretic, or substance that promotes water loss through urination. Urea–containing creams are used on wounds.

Urea and industry

Industrially, urea is used in the manufacturing of fertilizers (as a source of nitrogen) and in the synthesis of some barbiturates and in the petroleum industry to help separate straight chain and branched hydrocarbons in petroleum. Urea is widely used in the production of many plastics and resins. One of the most common of these is a resin formed by the reaction of urea and formaldehyde. Urea–formaldehyde resins are used in the adhesives industry (urea–formaldehyde resins are used in making laminated woods), in textile finishes, and surface coatings for plastics. These resins are widely used since they accept dyes easily. Over 300,000 kilograms of urea–formaldehyde resins are produced annually in the United States. Urea is also used as a stabilizer for many explosives, allowing greater control over the reactions. Urea is made commercially by reacting ammonia and carbon dioxide under high pressure.

See also Excretory system; Fertilizers.

Further Reading:
Atkins, P.W. *Molecules.* W. H. Freeman, 1987.

Louis Gotlib

KEY TERMS
. . . .

Barbiturates—A group of drugs widely used as tranquilizers and anti–anxiety medications. One of the basic molecules of this class is barbituric acid, which is made directly from urea.

Diuretic—A substance that increases water loss through urination.

Resin—A type of organic polymer. A polymer is a large molecule made of repeating basic units known as monomers.

Urinary system see **Excretory system**

Urology

Urology is the branch of medicine that deals with the urinary tract in females and with the urogenital tract in males. In both sexes, the urinary tract consists of the kidneys, ureters, bladder, and urethra. In males, additional structures such as the prostate gland are included in the urogenital system.

The problems with which a urologist deals tend to fall into three general categories: infection, cancer, and stone formation. Cystitis is any infection of the urinary tract. The condition often appears to be centered in the urinary bladder, but is usually associated with infections of other parts of the urinary system. Cystitis is accompanied by frequent and painful urination. It is treated relatively effectively with antibiotics, although other urinary tract problems with which it is associated may require other treatments.

Enlargement of the prostate gland is now one of the most common disorders among males, especially older males. In some cases, the condition is benign and is primarily a matter of inconvenience for men who find that urination becomes more difficult and more frequent. Non–cancerous enlargement of the prostate is known as benign prostatic hyperplasia (BPH). BPH can be treated surgically by the removal of excess fatty tissue although a number of urologists now recommend the use of a newly approved drug known as Proscar as a way of shrinking the enlarged gland.

Cancer of the prostate has become one of the leading causes of death among older males in the United States and other parts of the developed world. Some physicians hypothesize that carcinogenic substances in the environment accumulate in the prostate, one of the fattiest organs in the body, and induce tumors. Prostate cancer can be treated with the same surgical techniques used with BPH, although the complete removal of the testicles may be recommended if the cancer has metastasized.

Kidney stones form when certain chemicals that normally dissolve in urine begin to precipitate out and form stones ranging from microscopic particles to marble–size structures. In the majority of cases, the stones are expelled from the urinary system without incident. In some cases, however, they may become lodged in various parts of the system: along the ureter, in the bladder, or in the prostate, for example. When this happens, the stone may cut into tissue and cause extreme pain.

Stones can be removed in a number of ways: surgically, with drugs that dissolve the stony material, or with ultrasound therapy. In the last of these treatments, high frequency sound waves are used to break apart a stone, allowing the smaller fragments to be carried away in urine.

See also Surgery.

Uterus see **Reproductive system**

Vaccine

A vaccine is a substance used to confer immunity from infectious disease. Vaccines use a variety of different substances to defend the body against potentially harmful microorganisms, ranging from dead microorganisms to genetically–engineered antigens. Effective vaccines change the immune system so it acts as if it has already developed a disease. The vaccine primes the immune system and its antibodies to react quickly and effectively when threatened by disease in the future. Contemporary researchers seek new vaccinations against Acquired Immune Deficiency Syndrome (AIDS), cancer, and other diseases. The development of vaccines against diseases ranging from polio to smallpox is considered among the great accomplishments of medical science.

"Buying the smallpox"

Even in prehistoric times, physicians observed that individuals who were exposed to an infectious disease and survived were somehow protected against the disease in the future. But prior to the invention of vaccines, infectious diseases swept through towns, villages, and cities with a horrifying vengeance.

The first effective vaccine was developed against smallpox, an international peril which killed many of its victims and left others permanently disfigured. The disease was so common in ancient China that newborns were not named until they survived the disease. The development of the vaccine in the late 1700s followed centuries of innovative efforts to fight smallpox.

The ancient Chinese were the first to develop an effective measure against smallpox. A snuff made from powdered smallpox scabs was blown up the nostrils of uninfected individuals. Some individuals died from the therapy. But in most cases, the mild infection produced offered protection from later, more serious infection.

By the late 1600s, some European peasants employed a similar method of immunizing themselves against smallpox. In a practice referred to as "buying the smallpox," peasants in Poland, Scotland, and Denmark reportedly injected the smallpox virus into the skin to obtain immunity. At the time, conventional medical doctors in Europe relied solely on isolation and quarantine of people with the disease.

This changed in part through the vigorous effort of Lady Mary Wortley Montague, the wife of the British ambassador to Turkey in the early 1700s. Montague had already battled smallpox prior to her travels to Turkey and her face was "badly pockmarked" from the illness.

After observing the success of the Turkish process of "ingrafting" in Constantinople, Lady Montague wrote a friend in 1717 of the technique. "The smallpox, so fatal, and so general amongst us, is here entirely harmless," she wrote to the friend, who herself later died of smallpox. Montague said the Turks injected a preparation of small pox scabs into the veins of susceptible individuals. Those injected generally developed a mild case of smallpox from which they recovered rapidly, Montague wrote.

Upon her return to Great Britain, Montague helped convince King George I to allow trials of the technique on inmates in Newgate Prison. Success of the trials cleared the way for variolation, or the direct injection of smallpox, to become accepted medical practice in England until a vaccination was developed later in the century. Variolation also was credited with protecting U.S. soldiers from smallpox during the Revolutionary War.

Still, doubts remained about the practice. Individuals were known to die after receiving the smallpox injections. There were also questions about whether inoculation interfered with God's will.

The next leap in the battle against smallpox occurred when Edward Jenner (1749–1823) acted on a hunch. Jenner, a country physician and an orphan since the age of five, observed that people who were in contact with cows did not develop smallpox. Instead, they developed cowpox, an illness which caused pox, like small pox, but was not a threat to human life.

In 1796, Jenner decided to test his hypothesis that cowpox could be used to protect humans against smallpox. Jenner injected a healthy eight–year–old boy with cowpox obtained from a milkmaid's sore. The boy was moderately ill and recovered. Jenner then injected the boy twice with the smallpox virus, and the boy did not get sick.

Jenner's discovery launched a new era in medicine, one in which the intricacies of the immune system would be increasingly important. Contemporary knowledge suggests that cowpox was similar enough to smallpox that the antigen included in the vaccine stimulated an immune response to smallpox lead by antibodies specific to the disease. Exposure to cowpox antigen transformed the boy's immune system, generating cells that would remember the original antigen. The smallpox vaccine, like the many others that would follow, carved a protective pattern in the immune system, one that conditioned the immune system to move faster and more efficiently against smallpox in the future.

The term vaccination, taken from the Latin for cow (vacca) was developed by Louis Pasteur (1822–1895) to define Jenner's discovery nearly a century later. The term also drew from the word vaccinia, the virus drawn from cowpox and developed in the laboratory for use in the smallpox vaccine. In spite of Jenner's successful report, critics questioned the wisdom of using the vaccine, with some worrying that people injected with cow pox would develop animal characteristics, such as women growing animal hair. Nonetheless, the vaccine gained popularity, and replaced the more risky direct inoculation with smallpox. In 1979, world health authorities declared the eradication of smallpox, the only infectious disease to be completely eliminated.

From Louis Pasteur to Jonas Salk

The concerns expressed by Jenner's contemporaries about the side affects of vaccines would continue to follow the pioneers of vaccine development. Virtually all vaccinations continue to have side affects, with some of these affects due to the inherent nature of the vaccine, some due to the potential for impurities in a manufactured product, and some due to the potential for human error in administering the vaccine.

Virtually all vaccines would also continue to attract intense public interest. This was demonstrated in 1885, when Louis Pasteur saved the life of Joseph Meister, a nine year old who had been pushed to the ground and

attacked by a rabid dog while walking to school. Pasteur's use of a series of experimental rabies vaccinations on the boy proved the effectiveness of the new vaccine.

Until development of the rabies vaccine, Pasteur had been criticized by the public, though his great discoveries included the development of the food preservation process called pasteurization. With the discovery of a rabies vaccine, Pasteur was finally celebrated, his birthday declared a national holiday and, streets renamed after him.

Pasteur's rabies vaccine, the first human vaccine created in a laboratory, was made of an extract gathered from the spinal cords of rabies–infected rabbits. The live virus was weakened by drying over potash. The new vaccination was far from perfect, causing occasional fatalities and temporary paralysis. Individuals had to be injected 14 to 21 times.

The rabies vaccine was refined many times, with the goal of making each later vaccine more powerful and safe. In the 1950s, a vaccine grown in duck embryos had replaced the use of the weakened live virus, and in 1980, a rabies vaccine developed in cultured human cells was produced.

The story of the development of the most celebrated vaccine in modern times, the polio vaccine, also is a story of discovery and revision. While the viruses that cause polio appear to have been present for centuries, the disease emerged with a vengeance in the early 1900s. At the peak of the epidemic, in 1952, polio killed 3,000 Americans, and 58,000 new cases of polio were reported. The disease caused an epidemic of fear and illness, as Americans searched for an explanation of how the disease worked and how to protect their families.

The creation of a vaccine for poliomyelitis by Jonas Salk (1914–) in 1955 concluded decades of a national drive to find a cure for the disease. When the vaccine was declared safe after massive testing with schoolchildren, the vaccine and its creator were celebrated. The Salk vaccine, a killed virus type, contained the three types of polio virus which had been identified in the 1940s.

In 1955, the first year the vaccine was distributed to the public, disaster struck. Dozens of cases of polio were reported in individuals who had received the vaccine or had contact with individuals who had been vaccinated. The culprit was an impure batch of vaccine which had not been completely inactivated. By the end of the incident, more than 200 cases of polio had developed, and 11 people had died.

Production problems with the Salk vaccine were overcome following the 1955 disaster. Then in 1961, an oral polio vaccine developed by Sabin was licensed in the United States. The continuing controversy over the virtues of the Sabin and Salk vaccines is a reminder of the many complexities in evaluating the risks versus the benefits of vaccines.

The Sabin vaccine, which used weakened, live polio virus, quickly overtook the Salk vaccine in popularity in the United States, and is currently administered to all healthy children. Because it is taken orally, the Sabin vaccine is more convenient and less expensive to administer than the Salk vaccine.

Advocates of the Salk vaccine, which is still used extensively in Canada and many other countries, contend that it is safer than the Sabin oral vaccine. No individuals have developed polio from the Salk vaccine since the 1955 problem with impure vaccine. In contrast, the Sabin vaccine has a very small but significant rate of complications, including the development of polio. The rate of individuals developing polio in the United States is currently approximately four per million. Though polio has not disappeared completely, it has been transformed from an everyday scourge to a rarity.

Contemporary vaccines

Effective vaccines have limited many of the life–threatening infectious diseases. In the United States, children starting kindergarten are required to be immunized against polio, diphtheria, tetanus, and several other diseases. Other vaccinations are used only by populations at risk, individuals exposed to disease, or when exposure to a disease is likely to occur due to travel to an area where the disease is common. These include vaccinations for influenza, yellow fever, typhoid, cholera, and Hepatitis A.

The influenza vaccine, a killed virus vaccine, is one of the more problematic of contemporary vaccines. This is due primarily to the difficulty of immunizing for viruses which are constantly in a state of change. Because influenza viruses change so much, the influenza vaccine must be administered annually. Typically, older people and those considered "at risk" are advised to have the influenza vaccine.

Experts grapple with the difficulty of predicting the particular influenza viruses which will predominate in a given year. When researchers accurately predict the influenza virus, the influenza vaccine is highly effective in reducing the incidence of flu and flu–related complications. When they do not make accurate predictions, the vaccine is less effective.

The classic methods for producing vaccines use biological products obtained directly from a virus or a bacteria. Depending on the vaccination, the virus or bacteria is either used in a weakened form, as in the Sabin oral polio vaccine; killed, as in the Salk polio vaccine; or taken apart so that a piece of the microorganism can be used. For example, the vaccine for Streptococcus pneumoniae uses bacterial polysaccharides, carbohydrates found in bacteria which contain large numbers of monosaccharides, a simple sugar.

These classical methods vary in safety and efficiency. In general, vaccines that use live bacterial or viral products are extremely effective when they work, but carry a greater risk of causing disease. This is most threatening to individuals whose immune systems are weakened, such as individuals with leukemia. Children with leukemia are advised not to take the oral polio vaccine because they are at greater risk of developing polio from the live polio virus vaccine than from one which includes killed virus. Vaccines which do not include a live virus or bacteria tend to be safer, but the protection they provide may not be as great as protection derived from a live product vaccine.

The classical types of vaccines are all limited in their dependence on biological products, which often must be kept cold, may have a limited life, and can be difficult to produce. The development of recombinant vaccines has generated hope for a new generation of man–made vaccines. The hepatitis B vaccine, one of the first recombinant vaccines to be approved for human use, is made using recombinant yeast cells. These cells are engineered to include the gene coding for the Hepatitis B antigen. Because the vaccine contains the antigen, it is capable of stimulating antibody production against hepatitis B. Yet it does not carry the risk that a live hepatitis B vaccine would carry of introducing the virus into the blood stream.

Vaccines of the future

As medical knowledge has increased, researchers have set their sights on a wealth of possible new vaccines, including vaccinations for cancer, AIDS, and numerous other diseases.

The emergence of AIDS in the early 1980s lead to a worldwide search for a vaccine against the disease. Researchers seeking a vaccine against HIV, the virus that causes AIDS, have taken various approaches. Some have focused on the idea of a therapeutic AIDS vaccine, one which attempts to help individuals infected with HIV to fend off further illness. Efforts by these researchers have focused on stimulating components of the immune system. Several researchers have genetically engineered a protein on the surface of HIV, in an effort to prompt the immune system to fight against the virus. Clinical tests on humans of vaccines of this type have been conducted.

Other researchers have attempted to create a vaccine to protect uninfected individuals. The challenges in developing a protective vaccine include the fact that HIV appears to have multiple viral strains and mutates quickly. Other challenges include the difficulty of testing such a vaccine on healthy individuals.

Stimulating the immune system is also considered key by many researchers seeking a vaccine for cancer. Currently numerous clinical trials of cancer vaccines are in progress, with researchers developing experimental vaccines against cancer of the breast, colon, and lung, among other areas. Efforts focus on finding ways to stimulate specific immune reactions against cancer cells.

One of the many experimental vaccines uses the tumor cells of cancer patients to create a genetically–engineered vaccine. The vaccine contains genes for the immune–system messengers interleuken–2 or interferon. Both substances are capable of increasing the immune response in certain settings. Another cancer vaccine under development uses a man–made antibody that resembles an antigen linked to melanoma. The goal is to boost antibody production.

Other experimental techniques attempt to penetrate the body in ways that could stimulate more profound immune responses. These include using bacteria or viruses, both known to be efficient travelers in the body, as carriers of vaccine antigens. Such bacteria or viruses would be treated or engineered to make them incapable of causing illness.

Another technique involves the use of so–called 'naked DNA' in a vaccine. This method uses the direct injection of genetic material taken from influenza or some other illness. An immune response against the illness is stimulated when the genetic material enters cells and begins production of the protein of the microbe. Researchers have reported success using this method in laboratory trials against influenza and malaria.

Current research also focuses on developing better vaccines. The Children's Vaccine Initiative, supported by the World Health Organization, the U.N. Children's Fund, and other organizations, intends to make vaccines easier to distribute in developing countries. A key goal of the effort is to develop a single vaccine that could be administered only once, and provide protection from a wealth of illnesses.

Continuing challenges

The measles epidemic of 1989 was a graphic display of the failure of many Americans to be properly immunized. A total of 18,000 people were infected, including 41 children who died after developing measles, an infectious, viral illness whose complications include pneumonia and encephalitis. The epidemic was particularly troubling because an effective, safe vaccine against measles has been widely distributed in the United States since the late 1960s. By 1991, the number of new measles cases had started to decrease, but health officials warned that measles remained a threat.

The outbreak of measles reflected the limited reach of vaccination programs. Only 15% of the children between the ages of 16 and 59 months (just short of five years old) who developed measles between 1989 and 1991 had received the recommended measles vaccination.

Nearly all children are immunized properly by the time they start school. However, very young children are far less likely to receive the proper vaccinations. For example, only 37% of two–year–olds had been vaccinated properly in 1993.

Problems behind the lack of immunization range from the limited health care received by many Americans to the increasing cost of vaccinations. A series of childhood vaccines increased from about $25 to about $240 between the early 1980s and the early 1990s. Health experts also contend that keeping up with a vaccine schedule, which requires repeated visits, may be too challenging for Americans who do not have a regular doctor or health provider.

Internationally, the challenge of vaccinating large numbers of people has also proven to be immense. Great progress has been made in providing vaccinations to the world's residents. A total of 80% of the world's children had been inoculated for six of the primary infectious diseases in 1990, according to the World Health Organization. These diseases include polio, whooping cough, measles, tetanus, diphtheria, and tuberculosis.

Many children continue to die from infectious disease. Each year, more than two million children die of infectious diseases who have not received any vaccinations. Even polio has continued to be a threat in some parts of the world. As many as 120,000 cases are reported around the world each year, with most occurring in developing regions.

The reluctance of some parents to vaccinate their children due to potential side affects has also limited

KEY TERMS

....

Antibody—A molecule in the immune system which acts only with the antigen that induced its creation, or with antigens closely resembling that one.

Antigen—A substance capable of inducing a particular immune response.

Cultured Cells—Cells grown in a special material that encourages their growth.

Encephalitis—Inflammation of brain cells.

Inactivated Virus—A virus made inactive using heat, chemicals, or other methods.

Recombinant Technology—Methods that involve altering genetic material to create new products.

Vaccinia—The cowpox virus.

Variolation—The practice of direct injection of smallpox.

vaccination use. Parents in the United States and several European countries have balked at vaccinating their children with the pertussis vaccine due to the development of neurological complications in a small number of children given the vaccine. As a result of incomplete immunization, whooping cough remains common in the United States, with 30,000 cases and about 25 deaths due to complications annually. One response to such concerns has been testing in the U.S. of a new pertussis vaccine which has fewer side effects.

Great progress in the development of vaccines has been the rule rather than the exception in the 20th century. However, many more challenges await. Experts bemoan the imperfection of the influenza vaccine, and the lack of vaccines for numerous other infectious diseases. While some researchers seek new vaccines, others continue to look for ways to distribute existing vaccines to those in desperate need. While the flourishing of vaccines since the 18th century has saved lives in every city, every town, and every family, it has raised questions which continue to perplex society.

See also AIDS; Childhood diseases; Cholera; Diptheria; Hepatitis; Influenza; Poliomyelitis ; Rabies; Smallpox; Tetanus; Tuberculosis; Typhoid fever; Whooping cough; Yellow fever.

Further Reading:

Bishop, Jerry E. "A 'Naked' DNA Vaccine Shows Promise in Combating Malaria in Mice Tests." *The Wall Street Journal* Oct 11, 1994.

Cohen, Jon. "Cancer Vaccines Get a Shot in the Arm." *Science*. Nov. 5, 1993.

Hopkins, Donald R. *Princes and Peasants, Smallpox in History*. Chicago: The University of Chicago Press, 1983.

Lakhani, S. "Early Clinical Pathologists. Edward Jenner." *Journal of Clinical Pathology*. Vol. 45 (1992): 756–758.

Plotkin, Stanley A. "Vaccination in the 21st Century." *The Journal of Infectious Diseases*. Vol. 168 (1993): 29–37.

"Public–Sector Vaccination in Response to Measles." *Journal of the American Medical Association*. Vol. 268, No. 8 (August. 26, 1992): 963964.

Sell, Stewart. *Immunology, Immunopathology and Immunity*. Fourth Edition. New York: Elsevier, 1987.

Smith, Jane S. *Patenting the Sun*. New York: William Morrow and Company, Inc., 1990.

Virella, Gabriel. *Introduction to Medical Immunology*. New York: Marcel Dekker, Inc., 1993.

Patricia Braus

Vacuoles see **Cell**

Vacuum

Vacuum is a term that describes conditions where the pressure is lower than that of the atmosphere. A sealed container is said to be "under vacuum" in this case whereas it is "pressurized" when the pressure is higher than atmosphere. In a vacuum, it becomes necessary to define pressure microscopically. This means that the pressure, or force per unit area, is determined by the number of collisions between the atoms or molecules present and the walls of the container.

The first experiments involving vacuum date back to 1644 when Evangelista Torricelli worked with columns of mercury, leading to the first barometer (a device for measuring pressure). The famous experiment of Otto von Guericke in 1654 demonstrated the astounding force of vacuum when he evacuated the volume formed by a pair of joined hemispheres and attached each end to a team of horses that were unable to pull the hemispheres apart.

In order to create a vacuum, some kind of pump is needed. Simple mechanical pumps create a pressure difference, or suction force, which can be sufficient to pump water, for example. The most common use of vacuum, the vacuum cleaner, is simply a chamber and hose which are continuously evacuated by a fan. More sophisticated vacuum pumps must be sealed to prevent air from leaking back into the pumping volume too quickly. These pumps increase in complexity as better vacuum is needed. Pumps can generally be grouped into two categories: dynamic pumps, using mechanical or turbo–molecular action, and static pumps, using electrical ionization or low temperature (cryogenic) condensation.

Vacuum is important for research and industry, especially for manufacturing. Many industrial processes require vacuum either to be efficient or to be possible at all. Vacuum can be used for the prevention of chemical reactions, such as clotting in blood plasma or the removal of water in the process of freeze drying. Vacuum is also necessary for the prevention of particle collisions with background gas, in a television picture tube for example. For the fabrication of integrated electronics, it is very important to avoid impurities on a microscopic scale. It is only with excellent vacuum that such conditions can be obtained.

See also Atmospheric pressure; Vacuum tube.

Vacuum tube

A is a hollow glass cylinder containing a positive electrode and a negative electrode between which is conducted in a full or partial vacuum. A grid between these electrodes controls the flow of electricity.

The hollow cylinder of a vacuum tube contains a filament, typically tungsten coated with another metal. When the filament is sufficiently heated by an electric current, it emits electrons. This filament, or electrode, which emits electrons is known as a cathode and has a negative charge. Because it has a negative charge, it attracts electrons, thus nullifying the process. Therefore, free electrons must be supplied to the cathode. This is usually done by connecting the cathode to the negative terminal of a generator or battery. The other electrode, known as an anode, has a positive charge. The electrons move from the cathode to the anode, resulting in a one–way current within the tube.

History

In 1884, Thomas Edison, while working on his incandescent light bulb, inserted a metal plate between glowing filaments. He observed that electricity would flow from the positive side of the filament to the plate, but not from the negative. He didn't understand why this was so and treated this effect (now known as the Edison effect) as a curiosity. Unwittingly, he had created the first diode.

Later, John Ambrose Fleming of England, one of Edison's former assistants, became involved in designing a radio transmitter for Guglielmo Marconi. In 1904 Fleming realized that the diode had the ability to convert alternating current (AC) into direct current (DC), and incorporated it into his very efficient radio wave detector. Fleming called his device the thermionic valve because it used heat to control the flow of electricity just as a valve controls the flow of water. In the United States the invention became known as a vacuum tube.

In Germany, Arthur Wehnelt, who also worked with thermionic emission, had applied for a patent in January 1904 for a tube that converted AC into DC. However, he neglected to mention the use of the device in radio wave detection and was unable to sell his invention for that purpose after Fleming applied for his own patent.

Lee de Forest (1873–1961) improved on Fleming's valve by adding a third element in 1906, thus inventing the triode. This made an even better radio wave detector but, like Edison, he didn't realize the full potential of his invention; his device, called an audion, created an electrical current that could be amplified considerably.

In 1912 Edwin Howard Armstrong realized what de Fest had wrought. He used the triode to invent a regenerative circuit that not only received radio signals, it amplified them to such a degree they could be sent to a loudspeaker and heard without the use of headphones.

Diodes were usually made of two concentric cylinders, one inside the other. The cathode emitted electrons and the anode collected them. Fleming's thermionic valve operated at a temperature of 2500°C (4500°F), generating a considerable amount of heat. Deforest placed a grid between the cathode and anode. The electrons passed through the triode's grid, inducing a larger current to flow.

These early vacuum tubes were called soft valves. The vacuum was not the best and some air remained within the tube, shortening its lifespan. Langmuir devised a more efficient vacuum pump in 1915; with a better vacuum, the tubes lasted longer and were more stable. The improved tubes were called hard valves and their operating temperature dropped to 3600°F (2000°C). In 1922 the temperature was reduced yet again, to 1800°F (1000°C), with the introduction of new elements. Indirect heating improved tube efficiency.

Triodes were limited to low frequencies of less than one megahertz. In 1927 American physicist Albert Wallace Hull (1880–1966) invented the tetrode to elim-

KEY TERMS

. . . .

Amplitude—The farthest an object can get from its resting point, as in the highest position a pendulum reaches in its swing.

Filament—A fine wire heated to a high temperature and, thus, emitting electrons.

Kinetic energy—The energy possessed by an object due to the object's movement; for example, the energy in a baseball when it flies through the sky after being struck by a bat.

Semiconductor—A substance which is neither a good conductor nor a good insulator.

Tungsten—A metal which makes a good conductor and has a high melting point.

inate high–frequency oscillations and improve the frequency range. A year later the pentode, which improved performance at low voltage, was developed and became the most commonly used valve.

Over the course of years, a variety of vacuum tubes came into use. Low–voltage/low–power tubes were used in radio receivers as well as early digital computers. Photo tubes were used in sound equipment, making it possible to record and retrieve audio from motion picture film. The cathode–ray tube focused an electron beam, leading to the invention of oscilloscopes, televisions, and cameras. Microwave tubes were used in radar, early space communication, and microwave ovens. Storage tubes, which could store and retrieve data, were essential in the advancement of computers.

Despite its numerous advantages, the vacuum tube had many drawbacks. It was extremely fragile, had a limited life, was fairly large, and required a lot of power to operate its heating element. The successor to the vacuum tube, the transistor, invented by Walter Houser Brattain, John Bardeen, and William Shockley in 1948, had none of these drawbacks. After 1960 the small, lightweight, low–voltage transistors became commercially available and replaced vacuum tubes in most applications, but with the creation of microscopic vacuum tubes (microtubes) in the 1990s, vacuum tubes are again being used in electronic devices.

See also Cathode ray tube; Diode; Transistor.

Further Reading:

"Cold Cathodes: Vacuum microelectronics enter the flat–display race." *Scientific American* 263 (October 1990): 127–128.

Collins, A. Frederick. "Vacuum Tubes." *The Radio Amateur's Handbook*. revised by Robert Herzberg. New York: Harper & Row, 1983.

Goodman, Billy. "Return of the Vacuum Tube." *Discover* 11 (March 1990): 55–57.

Morgan, Alfred. "Electron Tubes–Their Purposes–How they were developed–How they Function." *The Boys' Third Book of Radio and Electronics*. New York: Charles Scribner's Sons, 1962.

Moyer, James A. and John F. Wostrel. *Radio Receiving and Television Tubes: Including Applications for Distant Control of Industrial Processes and Precision Measurements*. New York: McGraw–Hill, 1936.

Oldfield, R. L. "Electron Tubes." *Radio–Television & Basic Electronics*. Chicago: American Technical Society. 1960.

Stollberg, Robert, and Faith Fitch Hill. "Electrons in a Vacuum." *Physics Fundamentals and Frontiers*. rev. ed. Boston: Houghton Mifflin Co, 1980.

Vagina see **Reproductive system**

Vaginal diaphragm see **Contraception**

Valence

The term valence refers to the combining power or strength of an element. It has its origin in the Latin word for strength. The valence of an element can often be deduced by using a few simple patterns based on the element's location on the periodic table.

All atoms have electrons which are located in different energy levels. The electrons in the highest energy level are called valence electrons, and atoms will gain, lose, or share valence electrons in an effort to obtain eight of them (sometimes called an octet), an arrangement which is particularly stable.

In ionic compounds (formed between charged atoms or groups of atoms called ions) the valence of an atom is the number of electrons that atom will gain or lose to reach an octet. In group one of the periodic table, elements have a valence of 1, in group two, 2, in group 17, negative 1 (–1), and in group 18, 0. This means that a group one element will generally react to lose one electron, a group two element will react to lose 2 electrons, and a group 17 element will react to gain one electron. These patterns are general guidelines and many exceptions exist. Group 18 elements (sometimes known as noble gases or inert gases) have a valence of zero, since they rarely combine with other elements, as they already have a stable arrangement of electrons. The term valence can also refer to the "charge" or oxidation number on an atom. In a Magnesium atom, Mg^{+2}, the valence is +2. At atom or ion with a charge of +2 is said to be divalent.

In covalent compounds, which are formed between nonmetals, the valence of an atom may be less obvious. In this case it is the number of bonds formed (whether the bonds are single, double, or triple). A carbon atom with two single bonds and one double bond would have a valence of 4. In water, H_2O, the valence of oxygen is 2 and the valence of hydrogen is 1, as this gives an indication of the number of bonds each atom forms.

See also Chemical bond, Electron; Periodic table.

Van Allen belts

Radiation belts are enormous populations of energetic, electrically charged particles—principally protons and electrons—trapped in the external magnetic field of a planet. Durable radiation belts exist at the planets Earth, Jupiter, Saturn, Uranus, and Neptune but not at Mercury, Venus, or Mars.

Discovery of the radiation belts of Earth

The first successfully launched American satellite of Earth was Explorer I. It was propelled into orbit from Cape Canaveral, Florida, on January 31, 1958, by a four–stage combination of rockets developed by the United States Army Ballistic Missile Agency and the Jet Propulsion Laboratory (JPL). The principal scientific instrument within the payload was a Geiger tube radiation detector developed by Professor James A. Van Allen and graduate student George H. Ludwig of the University of Iowa. The instrument's intended purpose was a comprehensive survey of cosmic ray intensity above Earth's atmosphere.

The launch of an improved version of the radiation instrument was attempted on March 5 on Explorer II, but an orbit was not achieved because the fourth stage rocket failed to ignite. On March 26, the launch of the improved instrument on Explorer III, including the first magnetic tape recorder ever flown in space, was successful.

The in–flight data from the radiation detectors on Explorers I and III revealed that there are enormous numbers of energetic,electrically charged particles trapped in the external magnetic field of Earth. This discovery was promptly confirmed and extended later in

1958 with additional space flights by the Iowa group and others, including Soviet investigators on Sputnik III. In subsequent years the continuing study of this phenomenon has included the efforts of over 1000 scientists in at least 20 different countries.

Description

The populations of energetic particles trapped in Earth's magnetic field have come to be known as radiation belts because the doughnut–shaped regions within which they are confined encircle Earth like huge belts. There are two distinct belts: an inner one whose lower boundary is at an altitude of about 250 miles (402.25 km) and whose less–well defined outer boundary is at a radial distance of about 10,000 miles (16,090 km) and an outer one which extends outward from 10,000 miles (16,090 km) to over 50,000 miles (80,450 km). Both belts encircle Earth in longitude and have the greatest concentration of trapped particles at its magnetic equatorial plane. The concentration diminishes with increasing latitude north and south of the magnetic equator and falls to nearly zero over the north and south polar caps at latitudes greater than about 67°. Each trapped particle spirals around a magnetic line of force, oscillates between magnetic "mirror" points in northern and southern hemispheres, and drifts slowly in longitude. This defines a doughnut–shaped region.

The principal source of particles in the outer belt is solar wind, a hot ionized gas that flows outward from the Sun through interplanetary space. Some of the electrons, protons, and other ions in the impinging solar wind are injected into Earth's external magnetic field. These electrons, protons, and ions subsequently diffuse inward and are accelerated to greater energies by natural fluctuations of electrical and magnetic fields induced by the varying solar wind. The solar wind also sweeps back the outer portion of Earth's magnetic field to produce a long wake called the *magnetotail* extending on the night side of Earth to a distance of about 4,000,000 miles (6,454,000 km) far beyond the orbit of the Moon. In the heart of the outer belt, typical intensities of electrons with energies greater than 1,000,000 electron volts (1.0 MeV) (the most penetrating component there) are 2,000,000 particles per square inch per second. The numbers of particles of lesser energy and lesser penetration are much greater. The outer belt exhibits marked variations on time scales of hours, weeks, and months.

In the heart of the relatively stable inner belt, typical intensities of protons of energy exceeding 30,000,000 electron volts (30 MeV) are 120,000 particles per square inch per second. The residence times of

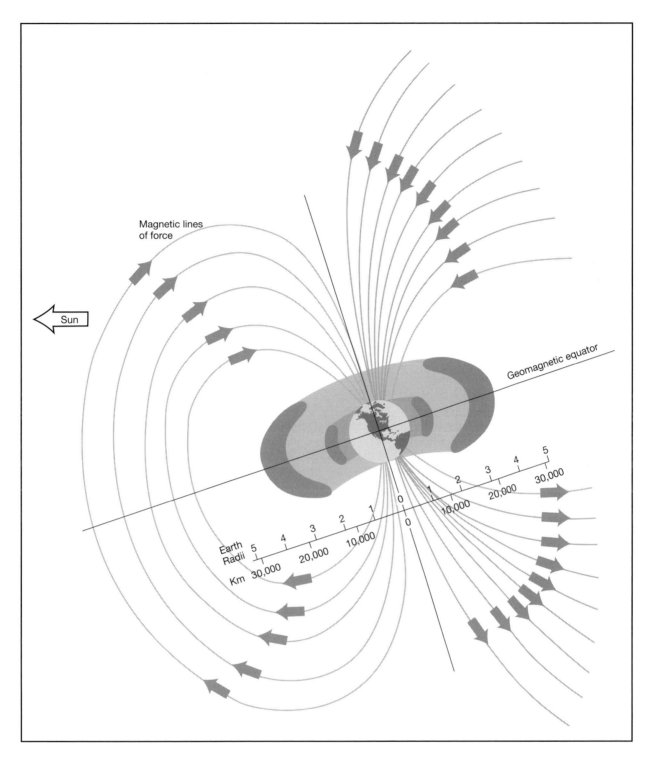

The Van Allen belts.

such protons are many years. Penetrating particles in the inner belt are attributable to neutrons from reactions of cosmic rays in the gas of the upper atmosphere. A small fraction of such (uncharged) neutrons decay into protons, electrons, and neutrons as they move outward. At the points of decay the electrically charged protons and electrons are injected into trapped orbits. A radiation belt of this type would be created around a magnetized planet by cosmic rays even in the absence of the solar wind, though no such example has been found.

The fate of trapped particles is loss into the atmosphere or outward into space. A quasi–equilibrium population of any specified species of trapped particle is achieved when losses are equal to sources.

Radiation belts are part of a more complex system called the *magnetosphere* which also contains large populations of relatively low energy ionized gas (plasma). This gas plays a central role in the overall physical dynamics of the system.

Artificial radiation belts

Nine artificial radiation belts of Earth were produced during the period 1958–62 by the injection of electrons from radioactive nuclei produced by U.S. and U.S.S.R. nuclear bomb bursts at high altitudes. These experiments made important contributions to understanding the natural belts. Since 1962 such high altitude bursts have been prohibited by international treaty.

Related geophysical effects

The aurorae, in both northern and southern latitudes (northern and southern lights) at typical but widely fluctuating magnetic latitudes of about 67°, are one of the visible, widely observed manifestations of magnetospheric phenomena. Aurorae are not a direct product of the outer radiation belt but share the solar wind as the primary agent for their creation. Magnetic storms detected by the fluctuations of sensitive magnetic compasses are attributable to electrical currents in the outer radiation belt.

Limitations on space flight

The inner radiation belt imposes an altitude ceiling on the region around Earth within which orbital flights of humans and animals can be conducted without exposing the occupants to excessive or fatal radiation exposures. Prolonged flights of human crews above an altitude of about 250 miles (402.25 km) are unsafe though rapid traversals of the radiation belts requiring only a few hours (as in the Apollo missions to the Moon) result in moderate exposures.

Two common misperceptions

Contrary to some common statements, trapped particles are *not* radioactive. Rather they are mainly ordinary electrons and protons such as those accelerated in high energy physics laboratories. Radiation belts do *not* shield Earth's surface, though the magnetic field deflects some cosmic rays away from Earth. The atmosphere acts as an effective shield against many solar and other radiations that impinge on it.

Radiation belts of other planets

In 1958–59 radio astronomers discovered that the planet Jupiter has an enormous radiation belt of high energy electrons. This discovery provided a powerful impetus for the investigation of Jupiter and the other planets by scientifically instrumented spacecraft.

Beginning in 1962 in situ investigations of the planets have been conducted by American, Soviet, and European spacecraft. The radiation belt of Jupiter has been explored in detail. Enormous radiation belts of Saturn, Uranus, and Neptune also have been discovered and investigated. It has been found that Venus, Mars, and Mercury have no durable radiation belts, but there are significant magnetospheric effects at these planets because of the obstacles that they present to the flow of the solar wind. Such effects have also been observed at the Moon and at three comets.

A durable radiation belt at a planet can only exist if that planet is strongly magnetized so that energetic electrically charged particles can be trapped durably in its external magnetic field. Earth, Jupiter, Saturn, Uranus, and Neptune meet this condition by virtue of electrical currents circulating in their interiors to produce huge electromagnets.

Venus, Mars, Mercury, the Moon, comets, and asteroids are insufficiently magnetized to retain radiation belts. It is likely that the planet Pluto is also in this group.

Pulsars and other distant astrophysical objects have radiation belts.

See also Magnetosphere; Radiation; Solar wind.

Further Reading:
Van Allen, James A. "Radiation Belts Around the Earth." *Scientific American* 200 (March 1958): 39–47.
Van Allen, James A. *Origins of Magnetospheric Physics.* Washington, D.C.: Smithsonian Institution Press, 1983.
Van Allen, James A. "Magnetospheres, Cosmic Rays, and the Interplanetary Medium" in *The New Solar System,* 3rd ed. Cambridge: Sky Publishing Corporation and Cambridge University Press, 1990.

James A. Van Allen

Van der Waals forces

Van der Waals forces are weak attractive forces between electrically neutral atoms or molecules. They are much weaker than the electrostatic forces which bind charged atoms or molecules (ions) of opposite sign or the covalent forces that bond neighboring atoms by sharing electrons. These forces develop because the rapid shifting of electrons within molecules causes some parts of the molecule to become momentarily charged, either positively or negatively. For this reason, weak, transient forces of attraction can develop between particles that are actually neutral. The magnitude of the forces is dependent on the distance between neighboring molecules. Van der Walls forces cause gas molecules to condense first to a liquid and finally to a solid as the gas is cooled.

The forces are named for the Dutch physicist, Johannes Diederik van der Waals (1837–1930). The discovery of these forces evolved from van der Waals' research on the mathematical equations describing the gaseous and liquid states of matter. These equations are generally known as gas laws and relate the temperature, pressure and volume of gases. Originally derived for an idealized gas, these equations assumed that gas molecules had zero volume and that there were no attractive forces between them. In 1881, van der Waals proposed an empirical gas law which included two parameters to account for molecular size and attraction. This more accurate model was the first serious attempt to formulate gas laws for real gases, and it earned van der Waals the Nobel Prize for physics in 1910.

See also chemical bond; Gases, properties of.

Van de Graaff accelerator see **Accelerators**

Vanadium see **Element, chemical**

Vanilla see **Orchid family**

Vapor pressure

Definition

Vapor pressure is a force exerted by the gaseous phase of a two phase—gas/liquid or gas/solid system.

All liquids and solids have vapor pressure at all temperatures except at absolute zero 523° F (–273° C). The pressure of the vapor that is formed above its liquid or solid is called the vapor pressure. If a substance is in an enclosed place the two phase system will arrive to an equilibrium state. This equilibrium state is a dynamic, balanced condition with no change of either phase. The pressure of the vapor measured at equilibrium state is the equilibrium vapor pressure. This pressure is a fraction of the total pressure, which is equal to 760 mm Hg at sea level. For a given substance, vapor pressure is constant under isothermal and isobarometric conditions, but its value depends on the temperature, pressure, and on the nature of the substance. As temperature increases so does the vapor pressure. At a constant temperature and pressure existing inter–molecular forces of the substance are the determining factors of the vapor pressure. The molecules of polar liquids and solids are held together with relatively large inter–molecular forces (e.g., dipole–dipole forces and hydrogen bounding). Polar compounds such as water, acetic acid and ethyl alcohol have low vapor pressure at a given temperature. Non–polar liquids like ether, hexane and benzene or solids like naphthalene have relatively small intermolecular forces (no hydrogen bounding or dipole–dipole forces). These substances have relatively high vapor pressure and are known as volatile substances. However, it should be noted that substances of high molecular weight evaporate more slowly than similar substances of low molecular weight.

The atmosphere has considerable water vapor in it; noted in the weather report as relative humidity. This relative humidity can be calculated by the equation below.

$$\% \text{ Relative Humidity} = \frac{\text{Actual partial pressure of water vapor}}{\text{Equilibrium vapor pressure of water at existing temperature}} \times 100$$

The water vapor present in the air is temperature, geography, and weather dependent. Many living systems, including humans, are effected by humidity. On a cold, wintry day the air is dry due to the very low water vapor pressure (as low as 4 mm Hg) in the air. On a hot, humid summer day the humidity can be above 40 mm Hg which is close to the equilibrium vapor pressure resulting ~ 90% relative humidity. People use devices like humidifiers and dehumidifiers to compensate for such extreme conditions and keep the relative humidity level around 55 – 60%.

TABLE 1. EQUILIBRIUM VAPOR PRESSURE OF WATER			
TEMPERATURE °C	WATER VAPOR PRESSURE mm Hg	TEMPERATURE °C	WATER VAPOR PRESSURE mm Hg
0	4.6	60	149
10	9.2	70	237
20	17.5	80	355
30	31.8	90	526
40	55	100	760
50	93		

The equilibrium vapor pressure of water at different temperatures is given in Table 1.

Jeanette Vass

Variable

A variable is a mathematical symbol which is used to represent a member of a given set and is typically denoted by a letter such as x, y, or z. The idea of a variable, invented during the late sixteenth century, is characteristic of modern mathematics and was not widely used in ancient times. Since a variable reflects a quantity which can take on different values, its use has become a critical part of nearly all disciplines which use mathematical models to represent the real world.

The idea of using letters to represent variables was first suggested by the sixteenth century mathematician François Viète (1540 – 1603) in his work, *In artem analyticam isagoge* (1591). Although his notations barely resemble our modern day symbolism, they were an important step in the development of the concept of using a letter to represent a changing value in a mathematical equation. His ideas were further developed in the decades that followed. Rene Descartes (1596–1650) is generally credited for making standard, the use of the letters x, y, and z for variables.

Characteristics of a variable

A variable is often denoted by a letter in an algebraic expression and represents a value which can be changed or varied. For example, in the expression x + 2, the letter x is a real variable and can take on the value of any real number. If x is 4 then the expression has a value of 6 because 4 + 2 = 6. Similarly, if x is 10 the expression has a value of 12. The number 2 in this expression is known as a constant because it never changes. Generally, a constant can be any number or letter in an equation whose value does not change.

In an equation, the value of a variable is often not given and is therefore called an unknown. In the equation y + 7 = 12, the letter y is an unknown variable and it represents some number. The value of the unknown which makes the equation true is called the solution or root of the equation. In this example, the solution of the equation is y = 5 because 5 + 7 = 12. Often, there is more than one solution to an equation so the unknown variable is equal to all of these values. The solution to the equation $x^2 = 4$ is both 2 and –2 because each of these values make the equation true.

Variables in a function

Some algebraic equations, known as functions, represent relationships between two variables. In these functions, the value of one variable is said to depend on the value of the other. For instance, the sales tax on a pair of gym shoes depends on the price of the shoes. The distance a car travels in a given time depends on its speed. In these examples, the sales tax and the distance travelled are called dependent variables because their

KEY TERMS

. . . .

Algebraic expression—A symbollic representation of a mathematical statement made up of numbers, letters and operations.

Constant—A part of an algebraic expression which does not change, such as a number.

Dependent variable—A variable in a function whose value depends on the value of another variable in the function.

Function—A mathematical relationship between two or more variables.

Independent variable—A variable in a function whose value determines the value of the dependent variable.

Rhetorical algebra—A method of communicating mathematical ideas by using words to express relationships between values.

Solution of the equation—The value of a variable that makes an equation true.

Unknown—A term used to describe a variable whose value is not evident.

value depends on the value of the other variable in the function. This variable, known as the independent variable, is represented by the price of the gym shoes and the speed of the car.

Using variables to represent unknowns was an important part of the development of algebra. Variables have distinct advantages over the rhetorical (written out) algebra of the ancient Greeks. They allow mathematical ideas to be communicated clearly and briefly. The equation $2x^2 + y = 6$ is much clearer than the equivalent phrase "two times some number times itself, plus some other number is equal to six." Variables also make mathematics more generally applicable. For instance, the area of a certain square with sides of 2 cm is 4 cm². The area of another square with 3 cm sides is 9 cm². By representing the side of any square with the variable s, the area of any square can be represented by s^2.

Although any letter or character can represent any variable, over time, mathematicians and scientists have used certain letters to represent certain values. The letters x, y, and z are the most commonly used variables to represent unknown values in polynomial equations. The letter r is often used to represent the radius of a circle and the character θ is used to signify an unknown angle.

Other commonly used variables include t to represent time, s to represent speed, and p to represent pressure.

See also Algebra; Function; Solution of equation.

Further Reading:

Paulos, John Allen. *Beyond Numeracy*. New York: Alfred A. Knopf, Inc., 1991.

Marcucci, Robert & Harold Schoen. *Beginning Algebra*. Boston: Houghton Mifflin Company, 1990.

Saxon, John. *Algebra I : An Incremental Development*. Norman: Grassdale Publishers Inc., 1981.

Perry Romanowski

Variable stars

Most people regard the stars as constant and unchanging. A character in one of Shakespeare's plays refers to a friend "as constant as the Pole Star." While Shakespeare was probably referring to the constant position of the Pole Star, he did not know about the precession of the equinoxes. Or, if he was referring to the constant light of the Pole Star (Polaris), he was in error there also. Astronomers now know that the light from Polaris varies, visible only with a telescope. Polaris is an example of what astronomers call a variable star. Originally, the term was used only for stars that vary a great deal in brightness, but now it is used to cover a wide range of stars. In fact, all stars probably vary in one way or another. The Sun, for example, has very slight variations in its energy output during the life of one of its sunspot cycles. Here, we will restrict ourselves to stars that are much more variable than the Sun.

Most people today do not observe the stars closely enough to note any of their brightness changes. Ancient people with darker skies did observe some stars changing in brightness. The Arabs noted that a bright star in the constellation Perseus dropped to about half its normal brightness for two hours every three days. They named this star Algol meaning the demon star. We know today that Algol is an example of an eclipsing binary star system. The change in brightness results when a dimmer companion star moves in front of the brighter star, blocking part of the light of the brighter star.

But the change in brightness of most variable stars is due to changes taking place within a single star. These stars are known as intrinsic variable stars. Astronomers have identified several classes of intrinsic variable stars. Some variable stars are classed as periodic, meaning that they go through regular changes in brightness every few hours or within a few days or weeks. This group includes such stars as the cepheid variables and RR Lyrae variables. Other stars are only roughly periodic or non–periodic in their brightness changes and are known as semiregular and irregular variables, respectively. The variable stars that are most apt to capture the attention of the public are called nova and supernova stars. While these are not often seen, they sometimes become bright enough so that they are easy to observe without the use of a telescope.

Cepheid variables are so named because one of the first of this class studied is found in the constellation Cepheus. These stars are all supergiant stars and are many times larger than the Sun. These stars vary because of pulsations within the stars themselves. They go through a cycle of expansion (brightening) and contraction (dimming). Over a period of many weeks the brighter cepheids may vary by a factor of 300% in their energy output. Polaris is an example of a dimmer cepheid and it varies only about 7% over a period of four days. A general pattern of brightness variations of cepheid variables was discovered by a Harvard astronomer, Henrietta Leavitt, early in the twentieth century. She discovered that the brighter cepheids had longer periods of brightness variation and the shorter period cepheids were generally dimmer. This period–luminosity relationship later made it possible for Edwin Hubble to demonstrate that there are galaxies other than our own Milky Way Galaxy.

They are called the RR Lyrae stars because, when studying this class, one of the first stars was found in the constellation Lyra. These stars have very short periods of light variation (usually less than one day) and they are dimmer than the cepheids. They are usually found in large spherical collections of stars called globular clusters. We now know that globular clusters uniformly surround our galaxy. In the 1920s, Harlow Shapley used RR Lyrae variables to map the distribution of globular clusters and concluded that the Sun was not in the center of our galaxy as was generally believed at the time. He found that our Sun and Solar System are located about 30,000 light years from our galactic center.

Some stars vary because they have large spots on their surface. The amount of area covered by these spots changes with time and this effects the output of energy from their surfaces. The Sun is one example of a spotted star. The study of how other spotted stars change their energy output has lead another Harvard astronomer, Sallie Baliunas, to suggest that there may be a link between the number of spots on the sun and the climate patterns on the Earth. Records suggest that when the spots are at a minimum for a long period of time, as they were in the late 1600s, there was a significant change in our climate.

Ancient astronomers noted that once in awhile stars would appear where they had not been seen before. These were called nova stars from the Latin word for "new." Later it was noted that some of these stars were much brighter than other nova and the name supernova was coined. Nova are usually noticed only by astronomers but historical records indicate that some of the supernova were so bright that they could be seen by ordinary people.

Astronomers now believe that nova always occur in double–star systems. Over a long period of time, one of the members of the pair evolves and becomes a white dwarf star. Later, the other member of the pair evolves to become a giant star and a portion of its outer layer is drawn onto the surface of the white dwarf. A temporary nuclear explosion, similar to a hydrogen bomb, takes place.

A supernova, on the other hand, usually results when a single, massive star evolves until it has used up most of its hydrogen fuel. The star then collapses on itself with a tremendous explosion leaving behind small but massive remnants that become either a neutron star or a black hole. If an observer is located in the right orientation, the neutron star may be observed as a object called a pulsar. These objects are some of the most unusual variable stars. They are thought to be highly magnetic, rotating objects only a few miles in diameter. Pulsars release their electromagnetic energy in regular bursts as frequently as a fraction of a second up to 5 seconds.

In a few seconds a supernova can produce as much energy as ten billion Suns. It becomes a brilliant star and even can be seen in the daytime. In our own galaxy we have seen only a few in all of recorded history. The Chinese reported the appearance of supernovas in 1006, 1054 and 1181 A.D. The July 4, 1054 supernova was so spectacular that there are rock carvings recording the event done by Native Americans of the American Southwest. Later, in 1572 and 1604, two other supernova were observed and recorded in Europe, and these are the last seen in our galaxy. Most astronomers believe that we are overdue for a supernova in our own galaxy. Life on any planet near a supernova would be instantly vaporized, but we should not worry. The Sun is not massive enough to become a supernova. The closest likely candidate for a supernova is the supergiant star Betalguese in Orion and it is located nearly 500 light years away. At this distance, there would likely not

KEY TERMS

· ·

Black hole—A hypothetical stellar object from which light cannot escape.

Cepheid variable star—Stars that belong to a class of supergiant pulsating stars.

Eclipsing binary star system—A double star system in which the plane of their mutual orbit is nearly parallel to our line of sight. As one star passes in front of the other star it periodically dims the other.

Intrinsic variable star—Any star that changes its energy output because of changes within the star or on the surface of the star.

Light year—A light year is equal to the distance that light would travel in one year and equals about 6 trillion miles or 9 trillion kilometers.

Neutron star—The result of the collapse of a supernova star. It is believed that they are almost completely composed of neutrons, hence their high densities.

Nova—A start that has a temporary increase in energy output on the order of a thousand times its normal energy output.

Period–luminosity relationship—An empirical relationship exhibited by cepheid variables between the variation in their energy output and the time period for this variation.

Pulsars—Small, dense, rapidly rotating neutron stars whose magnetic fields direct their energy output in much the same way as a light house been that sweeps over the observer.

RR Lyrae variable stars—A class of giant pulsating stars who have periods of about a day.

Sunspot—Cooler and darker areas on the surface of the sun. They appear dark only because they are cooler than the surrounding surface. Sunspots appear and disappear in cycles of approximately 11 years.

Supernova—The final collapse stage of a supergiant star.

Variable star—Any star that has a variation in energy output.

White dwarf star—A highly evolved star about as massive as the sun but with a diameter about that of the Earth.

be any terrestrial effects if the star did become a supernova.

See also Binary star; Star; Stellar evolution; Supernova.

Further Reading:

Abell, George, David Morrison and Sydney Wolff, *Exploration of the Universe* (6th edition). Philadelphia, PA: Saunders College Publishing, 1993.

Berendzen, Richard, Richard Hart and Daniel Seeley, *Man Discovers the Galaxies.* New York, NY: Science History Publications, 1976.

Hartman, William *The Cosmic Voyage.* Belmont, CA: Wadsworth Publishing, 1992.

Hoff, Darrel, Linda Kelsey and John Neff, *Activities in Astronomy.* (Fourth Edition), Dubuque, IA: Kendall/ Hunt Publishers, 1995.

Pasachoff, Jay Astronomy: From the Earth to the Universe (Fourth Edition), Philadelphia, PA: Saunders College Publishing, 1991.

Wheeler, J. and K. Nomoto, "How Stars Explode." *American Scientist* 73 (1985): 240.

Zeilik, Michael *Astronomy: The Evolving Universe* (6th edition). New York, NY: John Wiley & Sons, Inc., 1991.

Darrel B. Hoff

Variance

Variance is a mathematical expression of how data points are spread across a data set. Such expressions are known as measures of dispersion since they indicate how values are dispersed throughout a population. The variance is the average or mean of the squares of the distance each data point in a set is from the mean of all the data points in the set. Mathematically, variance is represented as δ^2, according to the equation: $\delta^2 = [(x_1-\mu)^2+(x_2-\mu)^2+(x_3-\mu)^2+...(x_n-\mu)^2]/n$; where $x_{1,2,3,.....n}$ are the values of specific variables; μ is the mean, or average, of all the values; and n is the total number of values. Variance is commonly replaced in applications by its square root, which is known as the standard deviation or δ.

Variance is one of several measures of dispersion which are used to evaluate the spread of a distribution of numbers. Such measures are important because they provide ways of obtaining information about data sets without considering all of the elements of the data individually.

To understand variance, one must first understand something about other measures of dispersion. One measure of dispersion is the "average of deviations."

This value is equal to the average, for a set of numbers, of the differences between each number and the set's mean. The mean (also known as the average) is simply the sum of the numbers in a given set divided by the number of entries in the set.For the set of eight test scores: 7+25+36+44+59+71+85+97, the mean is 530. The deviation from the mean for any given value is that value minus the value of the mean. For example, the first number in the set, 7, has a deviation from the mean of –46; the second number, 25, has a deviation from the mean of –28; and so on. However, the sum of these deviations across the entire data set will be equal to 0 (since by definition the mean is the "middle" value with all other values being above or below it.) A measure that will show how much deviation is involved without having these deviations add up to zero would be more useful in evaluating data. Such a nonzero sum can be obtained by adding the absolute values of the deviations. This average is the absolute mean deviation. However, for reasons that will not be dealt with here, even this expression has limited application.

A still more informative measure of dispersion can be obtained by squaring the deviations from the mean, adding them, and dividing by the number of scores; this value is known as the average squared deviation or "variance." For example, in the series of test scores cited above, the variance can be calculated as follows:

$$\delta^2 = [(x_1 - \mu)^2 + (x_2 - \mu)^2 + (x_3 - \mu)^2 + ... (x_n - \mu)^2]/n$$

$$\delta^2 = [(7 - 53)^2 + (25 - 53)^2 + (36 - 53)^2 + (44 - 53)^2 + (59 - 53)^2 + (71 - 53)^2 + (85 - 53)^2 + (97 - 53)^2]/8$$

$$\delta^2 = [(-46)^2 + (-28)^2 + (-17)^2 + (-9)^2 + (7)^2 + (18)^2 + (32)^2 + (44)^2]/8$$

$$\delta^2 = [2116 + 784 + 289 + 81 + 49 + 324 + 1024 + 1936]/8$$

$$\delta^2 = 6603/8 \quad \delta^2 = 825.38$$

Theoretically, the value of δ^2 should relate valuable information regarding the spread of data. However, in order for this concept to be applied in practical situations (we cannot talk about squared test scores) we may elect to use the square root of the variance. This value is called the standard deviation of the scores. For this series of test scores the standard deviation is the square root of 825.38 or 28.73. In general, a small standard deviation indicates the data are clustered closely around the mean; a large standard deviation shows the data are more spread apart.

While modern computerization reduces the need for laborious statistical calculations, it is still necessary to understand and interpret the concept of variance and its daughter, standard deviation, in order to digest the statistical significance of data. For example, teachers must be thoroughly familiar with these statistical tools in order to properly interpret test data.

KEY TERMS

Absolute deviation from the mean—The sum of the absolute values of the deviations from the mean.

Average deviation from the mean—For a set of numbers, the average of the differences between each number and the set's mean value.

Measure of dispersion—A mathematical expression which provides information about how data points are spread across a data set without having to consider all of the points individually.

Standard deviation—The square root of the variance.

See also Mean; Set theory; Statistics.

Further Reading:
Dunham, William. *Journey Through Genius*. New York: John Wiley & Sons Inc., 1990.
Facade, Harold P., Cummins, Kenneth B. *The Teaching of Mathematics from Counting to Calculus*. Columbus, OH: Charles E. Merrill Publishing Co., 1970.
Kline, Morris. *Mathematics for the Nonmathematician*. New York: Dover Publications, 1967.
Lloyd, G.E.R. *Early Greek Science: Thales to Aristotle*. New York: W.W. Norton and Company, 1970.

Randy Schueller

Vas deferens see **Reproductive system**

Vasectomy see **Contraception**

Veery see **Thrushes**

Vegetables

The word vegetable is not scientifically defined by botanists. Rather, the plants and plant parts that are considered to be vegetables have been specified by a broad consensus among farmers, grocers, and consumers.

In general, vegetables are plant tissues that are eaten as a substantial part of the main course of a meal. In contrast, fruits have a culinary definition as relatively sweet, often uncooked plant parts that are eaten as deserts or snacks.

Many vegetables are above–ground, leafy tissues or stems of herbaceous plants, for example: cabbage, lettuce, and celery. However, the common understanding of vegetables also includes certain plant parts that are botanical fruits but are normally cooked before being eaten, such as the tomato, bell pepper, cucumber, and squash. Certain below–ground plant parts are also considered to be vegetables; for example: onions, garlic, and carrots, even though other below–ground tissues such as potatoes and yams are not.

Globally, the production of the most important types of vegetables are as follows: tomatoes, 45 million tons; various types of cabbage, 30 million tons; onions and garlic, 20 million tons; cucumber and squashes, 15 million tons; bell and chili peppers, six million tons; peas and beans, eight million tons; and carrots, eight million tons.

Vegetables derived from stems, petioles, or foliage

The cabbage is a species of mustard, originally native to Eurasia. Various agricultural varieties of the cabbage (*Brassica oleracea*) have been developed and are eaten cooked or sometimes raw. The familiar head and savoy cabbages are modifications of the leafy, pre–flowering rosette of the original mustard and can be green or a rich–red color. These cabbages are sometimes served raw, for example, finely chopped and dressed with oil and mayonnaise as cole slaw. Alternatively, these cabbages may be cooked and perhaps used as wrappers of cabbage rolls. Cabbage may also be slightly fermented and pickled, a food known as sauerkraut. Brussels sprouts are small, leafy rosettes that develop abundantly on an upright stem of another variety of cabbage and are served cooked.

Lettuce (*Lactuca sativa*) is another head–forming, leafy vegetable, native to southern Europe and usually served raw in salads. Endive (*Cichorium endivia*) is a similar related species that is also served raw as a salad green.

The celery (*Apium graveolens*) develops thick, fleshy, light–green petioles which are eaten raw or cooked. Rhubarb (*Rheum rhaponticum*) also develops tart, nutritious petioles which are cooked, sweetened with sugar or fruit, and eaten. The leaves of this species are poisonous.

The dark–green leaves of spinach (*Spinacea oleracea*) are an iron–rich vegetable, served steamed or raw.

The young shoots of the asparagus (*Asparagus officinalis*) are collected in the early springtime and are cooked as a tasty vegetable.

The ostrich fern (*Matteucia struthiopteris*) is a species of North America. This plant is not normally cultivated, but it can develop prolific stands in moist bottomlands where its young shoots, known as "fiddleheads," are collected in the early springtime. These are served as a steamed vegetable.

The leafy stem of the leek (*Allium porrum*) is served as a cooked vegetable. The foliage of chives (*A. schoenoprasum*) is usually served raw in salads or as a garnish to other cooked vegetables.

Vegetables derived from fruits or flowers

The cauliflower and broccoli are additional varieties of the cabbage that are derived from modified versions of the inflorescence and are nutritious vegetables. The edible part of the globe artichoke (*Cynara scolymus*) is the pre–flowering inflorescence of the plant which is prepared by boiling or steaming. The fleshy bracts are eaten by drawing them between the teeth to remove the starchy tissues, or the bractless "heart" is served as an unusual vegetable.

The fruits of many species in the pea family are served as cooked vegetables, sometimes intact in their pod. Some of the more common species are the French bean (*Phaseolus vulgaris*), the broad bean (*Vicia faba*), the scarlet runner bean (*Phaseolus multiflorus*), the garden pea (*Pisum sativum*), and the lentil (*Lens esculenta*).

Several species in the tomato family develop fleshy fruits that are used as vegetables. The red, plump fruits of the tomato (*Lycopersicum esculentum*), originally native to South America, are served raw or cooked. The larger fruits of the closely related eggplant or aubergine (*Solanum melongena*) are served cooked. The fruits of the red pepper, bell pepper, capsicum, or chili (*Capsicum annuum*) occur in diverse, domesticated varieties and are served cooked or raw. In Hungary, a red powder called paprika is made from dried capsicum fruits.

The elongate, fleshy fruits of several species in the cucumber family are also served as vegetables. The cucumber (*Cucumis sativus*) is usually served pickled in vinegar, raw, or cooked. The pumpkin, squash, or vegetable marrow (*Cucurbita pepo*) are usually served cooked, or their seeds may be extracted, roasted, and eaten.

Vegetables derived from below–ground tissues

The carrot (*Daucus carota*) is a biennial plant native to Eurasia. The carrot grows a large, starchy, cone–shaped tap–root during its first year of growth. As in many biennials, the large root is intended to support the great metabolic demands of the development of the flowering structure during the second and final year of the life of the plant. In carrots, the root develops a rich, orange color because of the presence of large concentrations of the pigment carotene, a precursor of Vitamin A when eaten and metabolized by animals. Carrots are eaten raw or cooked. In North America and elsewhere, Queen Anne's lace is a weedy variety of carrots that has escaped from cultivation and is a common plant of disturbed places.

The parsnip (*Pastinaca sativa*) is another biennial plant, native to Europe. This plant is also cultivated for its conical tap–root which is usually eaten cooked.

The beet (*Beta vulgaris*) is another biennial plant that is grown for its large root. The beet root develops an intensely red–purple color due to the presence of large concentrations of anthocyanin pigments. Beet root is served cooked or is pickled in vinegar. The foliage of this plant is sometimes served as a steamed, leafy vegetable.

The radish (*Raphanus sativus*) is an annual plant that develops a large, below–ground storage organ which is anatomically a hypocotyl (the tissue between the true stem and the root). Radishes are red–colored on the outside and white inside. A biennial cultivar of the radish develops a large root which can be red, white, or brown colored. Radishes have a pungent flavor due to the presence of mustard oils and are usually served raw.

The Jerusalem artichoke (*Helianthus tuberosus*) is a perennial relative of the sunflower, native to North America. This plant produces tubers on its below–ground stems which are cooked and eaten.

The onion (*Allium cepa*) is a member of the lily family. The below–ground bulbs of this plant are served cooked or raw in salads. The garlic (*A. sativum*) also develops a strong–tasting bulb which is served raw or cooked and is mostly used as a flavoring.

Eat your vegetables

Most vegetables are highly nutritious foods, very rich in carbohydrate energy as well as vitamins, minerals, fiber, and to a lesser degree, protein. A balanced diversity of vegetables is an important component of any healthy diet, and these plant products should be eaten regularly. Our mothers had good reason to demand that we eat our vegetables.

See also Carrot family; Composite family; Gourd family; Legumes; Lily family; Mustard family; Nightshade; Rhubarb; Spinach; Sweet potato; Tuber.

KEY TERMS

Cultivar—A distinct variety of a plant that has been bred for particular agricultural or culinary attributes. Cultivars are not sufficiently distinct in the genetic sense to be considered to be subspecies.

Further Reading:

Hvass, E. *Plants That Serve and Feed Us.* New York: Hippocrene Books, 1975.
Klein, R.M. *The Green World. An Introduction to Plants and People.* New York: Harper and Row, 1987.

Bill Freedman

Veins see **Circulatory system**

Velocity

Velocity is the time rate of change of the position of a body. Mathematically, velocity is a vector quantity having direction as well as magnitude. Speed, on the other hand, is a scalar quantity which has only magnitude. The magnitude of velocity is expressed in units such as miles per hour or meters per second when describing motion along a straight or curved path. A body which is rotating about an axis has angular velocity. Angular velocity is also a vector quantity and is expressed as units of angular rotation per unit of time such as revolutions per minute or radians per second.

See also Scalar; Vector.

Vena cava see **Heart**

Ventricle see **Heart**

Venus

Basic properties

Venus orbits the Sun on a near circular orbit at mean distance of 0.723 Astronomical Units (AU). At aphelion the planet is at a maximum distance of 0.728

The surface of Venus is obscured by a dense layer of clouds composed of sulfuric acid droplets. The cloud cover creates a greenhouse effect that results in surface temperatures over 860° F (460° C), higher than that of Mercury.

AU from the Sun, while at perihelion Venus it is 0.718 AU away. Coming as near as 0.272 AU, no other planet can approach the Earth as close as Venus does.

Since it circles the Sun in an orbit smaller than that of Earth's, Venus is never very far away from the Sun for terrestrial viewers. The greatest angular distance between the Sun and Venus, as seen from the Earth, is 47 degrees. This means that even under the most favorable of conditions Venus will set at most 3 hours after the Sun, or rise no earlier than 3 hours before the Sun. Observed since the most ancient of times, Venus is often called the "morning star," if it rises before dawn, or the "evening star" if it sets after the Sun. The Greek philosopher Homer referred to Venus in his *Illiad* as "the most beautiful star set in the sky."

Next to the Sun and Moon, Venus can be the brightest object in the sky. At its most brilliant, Venus is sixteen times brighter than Sirius (α Canis Majoris), the brightest star in the night sky. The extreme brilliance of Venus is partly due to its occasional closeness to the Earth, and partly due to it having a highly reflective atmosphere.

The time required for Venus to complete one orbit about the Sun, its sidereal period, is 224.701 days, whereas the time for Venus to repeat alignments with respect to the Sun and Earth is 584 days. The best times for viewing Venus is when it is near greatest eastern, or greatest western elongation. Greatest western elongation follows about 5 months after greatest eastern elongation, and greatest eastern elongation's repeat about every 19 months.

As it circles the Sun, Venus shows phases just like the Moon, and the planet Mercury. The phase changes of Venus were first recorded by Galileo Galilei in 1610. Galileo's observations of Venusian phase changes were important since they strengthened his belief in the heliocentric model of the Solar System which had been proposed by Copernicus in his now famous book, *De Revolutionibus*, published in 1543. Galileo reasoned that if Venus circled the Earth, as the then accepted geocentric model of the Universe decreed, it would not show the full range of phases that were observed. Likewise, the correlation between angular size and phase would also be different to that observed if Venus orbited the Earth.

An artist's impression of one of the three continent-sized highland regions of Venus, Beta Regio, which consists of two huge shield volcanoes rising above the plains. Both are about 2.5 miles (4 km) high, and appear to be on a north-south fault line connecting them with other possibly volcanic features in the south. They have smooth surfaces and are shaped like Hawiian volcanoes. The Russian spacecrafts Veneras 9 and 10 landed directly east of Beta Regio and determined that the surface rock was volcanic basalt.

Transits of Venus across the disk of the Sun, as seen from Earth, are not common. If a transit is to occur, however, it will take place in either June or December, when the Earth is at the line along which Venus's orbit cuts the ecliptic – the line of nodes for Venus. A very precise geometrical alignment of the Earth, Venus and Sun is required for a Venusian transit to take place. The last Venusian transit occurred on December 6th, 1882. The next transit will take place on June 8th, 2004. In general, Venusian transits are seen in pairs. Each of the transits in a pair are 8 years apart, and the pair–cycle repeats on an alternating cycle of 121.5 and 105.5 years.

The rotation rate of Venus

The Venusian atmosphere is both optically thick and highly reflective. The upper cloud deck has an albedo of 0.76, meaning that it reflects 76% of the sunlight that falls on it. In addition, the low–lying Venusian clouds are so dense that they completely obscure any optical view of the planet's surface. Not being able to see, or monitor variations in surface detail has meant that astronomers have only recently discovered the true rotation rate of Venus.

While the Venusian atmosphere presents an un–penetrable shroud against optical observations, it is transparent to radio and microwave radiation. Using the giant radio telescope at the Arecibo Observatory in Puerto Rico, astronomers were able to bounce microwave signals off of the surface of Venus. By analyzing the Doppler shift in the returned signals the astronomers were then able to determine the planets rotation rate. The results were a complete surprise.

The microwave measurement of Venus's rotation rate showed that the planet was spinning on its axis in the opposite sense to which it orbits the Sun. If one could stand on the surface of Venus, sunrise would be in the west and sunset would be in the east, the exact opposite to that seen on Earth. When viewed from above, all the planets in the solar system orbit the Sun in a counter clockwise direction. Most of the planets also rotate about their spin axes in a counter clockwise sense. The only exceptions to this rule are the planets Venus, Uranus and Pluto. When a planet spins on its axis in the opposite sense to its orbital motion, the rotation is said to be retrograde.

Venus takes 243.01 days to spin once on its axis. With this slow rotation rate it actually takes 18.3 days longer for Venus to spin once on its axis than it takes for the planet to orbit the Sun. The Venusian day, that is the time from one noon to the next, is 116.8 terrestrial days long. A curious relationship exists between the length of the Venusian day, and the planet's synodic period. The synodic period of Venus, that is, the time for the planet to repeat the same alignment with respect to the Earth and Sun, is 584 days, and this is 5 times the Venusian day (584 = 5 x 116.8). It is not known if this result is just a coincidence, or the action of some subtle orbital interaction. The practical consequence of the relationship is that, should a terrestrial observer make two observations of Venus that are 584 days apart then they will "see" the same side of the planet turned towards the Earth.

Venusian surface detail

At is closest approach the planet Venus can have an angular diameter just slightly larger than 1/60 th of a degree. This angular size translates to a physical diameter of 12,104 km, making the planet about 95% the size of Earth. Given the near similar sizes of the Earth and Venus, it might be expected that the surface of Venus has been shaped by the same geological processes that operate on Earth. This expectation is only partly true.

While radar maps of the surface of Venus were constructed during the 1970s, the most detailed topographic maps obtained to date are those from the *Magellan* spacecraft mission. The *Magellan* spacecraft was placed into Venusian orbit by NASA in 1990, and a powerful on–board imaging radar system was used to map the entire Venusian surface to a resolution of a few hundred meters.

The *Magellan* radar data showed that Venus is remarkably flat, and that some 80% of the planets surface is covered by smooth volcanic plains, the result of many lava out–flows. The altitude map constructed from *Magellan* data has revealed the existence of two large continent–like features on Venus. These features are known as Ishtar Terra (named after the Babylonian Goddess of love), and Aphrodite Terra (named after the Greek Goddess of love). Ishtar terra, which measures some 621 mi (1,000 km) by 931 mi (1,500 km), lies in Venus's northern hemisphere, and has the form of a high plateau ringed with mountains. The largest mountain in the region, Maxwell Montes, rises to a height of 7 mi (11 km). Aphrodite Terra is situated just to the south of the Venusian equator and is some 9,936 mi (16,000 km) long by 1,242 mi (2,000 km) wide. It is a region dominated by mountainous highlands and several large volcanoes.

Given the similarity in size of Venus and Earth, geologists had speculated on the possibility that plate tectonics, which is the primary agent for re–shaping the Earth's surface, might operate on Venus. The *Magellan* probe found no evidence, however, for large scale tectonic activity on Venus. The reasons underlying the absence of any large–scale tectonic activity on Venus are presently unclear, but it may be indicative that the planet has a thinner and weaker lithosphere than Earth.. The ridges and folds that cover many of the plain regions of Venus is indicative, however, of a certain amount of local tectonic activity on the planet.

The *Magellan* maps revealed many large craters on the Venusian surface. There is an apparent cut–off for craters with diameters less than a few kilometers. This is a selection effect imposed by the dense Venusian atmosphere. The atmosphere is in fact such a good filter of incoming meteoroids, that only those objects larger than a few kilometers in diameter survive their passage through the atmosphere, with sufficient mass, to produce a crater at the Venusian surface.

The relative age of different regions on a planet's surface can be gauged by counting the number of craters that appear per unit area. This method of crater counting has proved very useful for dating the various regions on our Moon. The essential idea being exploited in crater count dating is that, assuming the cratering rate is the same over the whole planet, if one region has fewer craters per unit area than another, it implies that some re–surfacing, e.g., by a lava flow, has taken place in the region with fewer craters. The re–surfacing has in effect erased the older craters and re–set the cratering clock.

The number of craters in the Venusian plains is typically about 15% of the crater counts for the lunar maria. This observation indicates that the Venusian plains have an age roughly equivalent to 15% the age of the lunar maria. From the lunar rock samples that were returned from the Apollo Moon landing missions we know that the lunar maria are about 3.2 billion years old, and consequently the likely age of the Venusian plains is about 500 million years.

The main agent for re–surfacing the Venusian plains is believed to be aperiodic but widespread volcanism. Certainly, many (apparently) extinct volcano's were mapped by *Magellan* during its five year survey. Some lava flow regions observed by *Magellan* are believed to be no more than ten millions years old, and they may be much younger.

Some of the more remarkable surface features discovered by *Magellan* were the pancake–shaped volcanoes. These flat–topped, circular volcanoes are unique to Venus, and it is thought that they are probably formed through the surface extrusion of a very thick and viscous lave.

In recognition of Venus being named in honor of the Greek Goddess Aphrodites, whom the Romans called Venus, the International Astronomical Union assigns only female names to the planet's surface features. Craters, for example, can be named after any famous women; linear features are named after Goddesses of War, while plains are named in honor of mythological heroines.

Venusian internal structure

Venus has no natural satellites and consequently its mass has only been determined through the gravitational effect that the planet has on passing space probes. A mass equivalent to 82% that of the Earth's, or 4.9×10^{24} kg, has been found for Venus. The bulk density of Venus is 5240 kg/m^3, slightly smaller than that of Earth's.

The similarity between the mass, radius and bulk density of Venus and Earth suggests that the two planets have similar internal structure. Venus most probably has, therefore, a thin rocky crust, a large silicate mantle and an inner nickel–iron alloy core.

One Venusian anomaly that defies present–day theory relates to the planet's magnetic field, or more correctly to the complete lack of any detectable magnetic field. It is believed that the Earth's magnetic field is created by a dynamo effect that operates in its hot, liquid nickel–iron alloy core. If, as has been previously argued, Venus has an internal structure similar to that of

Earth, why does it not have a similar magnetic field? The answer may lie with the slow Venusian rotation rate. One of the key ingredients of the dynamo theory is that the conducting, liquid core is rotating. Since Venus rotates much more slowly than Earth, by a multiplicative factor of 1/243, it may be that the dynamo effect cannot operate in the planet's core.

The Venusian atmosphere

While Venus is often referred to as the Earth's twin on the basis that the two planets having similar physical characteristics (radius, mass, density, composition, etc), it is far from being the Earth's twin when atmospheric characteristics are compared.

The many spacecraft that have flown past, or landed on the Venusian surface have found that the uppermost cloud tops which obscure the Earth–based observers view of the planet, are about 40 mi (65 km) above the surface. For comparison, on the Earth, the highest clouds are about 10 mi (16 km high). Observations taken at ultraviolet wavelengths reveal that the upper Venusian clouds follow a jet stream–like pattern and circle the planet once every four days, or so. The circulation velocity of the upper cloud deck is much greater than the rotation rate of the planet, and it is believed that this is the result of extensive atmospheric convection driven by solar heating.

The upper cloud deck is about 3 mi (5 km) thick. At about 31 mi (50 km) altitude there is a second much more dense cloud deck. Below about 18 mi (30 km) in altitude the Venusian atmosphere is clear of clouds. The upper cloud deck has been found to contain substantial amounts of sulfur, which give the clouds their dark yellow to yellow–orange color. The lower cloud deck has been found to contain large concentrations of sulfur dioxide, hydrogen sulfide compounds and droplets of sulfuric acid. It has been suggested that the presence of atmospheric sulfides is indicative of very recent volcanic activity on the planet's surface.

The greenhouse effect

Astronomers began to suspect that the surface of Venus was a decidedly inhospitable place when radio telescope measurements, made in the 1950s, indicated surface temperatures as high as 750 K (477° C). It is believed that a greenhouse effect is responsible for maintaining the high surface temperature on Venus.

A green house effect occurs whenever incoming sunlight warms the planetary surface, but the atmospheric gases do not allow the infrared radiation emitted by the heated surface to escape back into space. The net

KEY TERMS

· ·

Albedo—The ratio of reflected to incoming light. Full reflection corresponds to an albedo of unity, while complete absorption corresponds to an albedo of zero.

Doppler effect—The apparent change in the wavelength of a signal due to the relative motion of the source and the observer.

Dynamo effect—A model for the generation of planetary magnetic fields: the circulation of conducting fluids within a planet's hot, liquid inner–core results in the generation of a magnetic field.

Greenhouse effect—A process leading to an increased surface temperature by the trapping of infrared radiation in a planets atmosphere

Lithosphere—The solid outer layer, or crust of a planets mantle.

Mantle—The major portion of a terrestrial planets interior, made of plastic rock.

Retrograde rotation—Axial spin that is directed in the opposite sense to that of the orbital motion.

Tectonic activity—The theory of crustal motion.

result of the atmospheric trapping of infrared radiation is that the atmosphere heats up, and the surface temperature continues to rise.

That a strong greenhouse effect can operate at Venus is not surprising given that its primary atmospheric component is carbon dioxide. This gas has long been recognized as a problematic 'greenhouse' gas on Earth.

Building a spacecraft to land on the Venusian surface has proved to be a major engineering challenge. Not only must a lander be able to operate at temperatures that exceed the melting point of lead, but it must also withstand an atmospheric pressure some 90 times greater than that experienced at sea level on Earth. The pressure exerted by the Venusian atmosphere, at the planets surface, is equivalent to that exerted by a 1 km column of water in the Earth's oceans. The first of only four spacecraft to soft–land, and successfully transmit images of the surface of Venus back to Earth, was the former Soviet Union built spacecraft *Venera 7*. The lander, which set–down on August 17th, 1970 managed to transmit data for 23 minutes.

See also Planet; Planetary atmospheres; Solar system.

Further Reading:

Goldman, Stuart. "Venus Unveiled." *Sky and Telescope* 83 (March 1992).

Luhmann, Janet., Pollack, J., and Lawrence C. "The Pioneer Mission to Venus." *Scientific American*, April 1994.

Paul, Jeffrey. "Venus in 3–D." *Sky and Telescope*, 86, August 1993.

Saunders, Stephen. "The Surface of Venus." *Scientific American*, December 1990.

Martin Beech

Venus fly trap see **Carnivorous plants**

Venus shells see **Bivalves**

Verbena family (Verbenaceae)

The verbena or vervain family (Verbenaceae) is a diverse group of about 3,000 species of plants, most of which occur in the tropics.

Plants in this family can be herbs, shrubs, trees, or lianas (tropical vines). The leaves are usually simple, arranged alternately on the stem, which if often square–sided. The flowers are small, but often occur in attractive inflorescences.

Some species of trees in the verbena family are extremely valuable for the production of lumber.

Tropical hardwoods in the verbena family

Teak (*Tectona grandis*) is one of the world's most prized species of tropical hardwood. Teak is a large tree of mature, tropical forests of South and Southeast Asia, and can grow as tall as 131 ft(40 m). Teak lumber can vary in color from light to brownish yellow, or a deep chocolate–brown. Lumber made from teak is heavy, strong, durable, resistant to splitting and cracking, and highly resistant to damages associated with immersion in water. Teak wood contains an aromatic, resinous oil that makes the wood feel slightly greasy to the touch, and helps to make it almost invulnerable to termites and highly resistant to wood–rotting fungi. Teak is valued for the manufacture of durable decking and trim on boats, and for making flooring, panelling, and fine furniture.

Teak is harvested from tropical forests wherever it occurs in Asia. Typically, teak trees are girdled and stripped of their lower bark, and then left standing for two years prior to felling. This allows the trees to dry somewhat before they are cut down, so the logs will be lighter and can be more easily dragged out of the forest. After the teak trees are felled they are sectioned into manageable–sized logs. These are then transported out of the forest using elephants or mechanical skidders, often to a river, on which the logs are floated to the coast for processing into lumber or veneer.

Unfortunately, teak occurring in natural forests is rarely harvested on a sustainable basis, and the resources of this extremely valuable tropical hardwood are being rapidly mined. Today and more so into the future, much of the teak available in commerce must be grown in plantations established for the production of this precious wood.

Other tropical species of tree in the Verbena family are also valuable as sources of hardwood lumber. These include species of *Petitea*, *Premna*, and *Vitex celebica*. Zither wood is a specialized material derived from *Citharexylum* spp. of Central and South America, and used to manufacture musical instruments.

The tropical trees *Lippia citriodora* and *Vitex agnus–castus* are useful as a source of natural oils, known as oil of verbena.

Ornamental species

Some species in the Verbena family are cultivated for their showy flowers. The most common garden verbenas in North American gardens are *Verbena hortensis* and *V. hybrida*, both frequently used as bedding plants. Two native species with showy flowers, the large–flowered verbena (*Verbena canadensis*) and small–flowered verbena (*V. bipinnatifida*), are commonly grown in gardens, and are often crossed with other verbenas to develop new varieties for horticulture. Purple mulberry (*Callicarpa purpurea*) is an attractive Asian shrub that is sometimes cultivated in North America.

Several vines and shrubs in the genus *Clerodendrum* are sometimes grown as ornamentals in temperate areas, including the bleeding–heart (*C. thomsoniae*) and the pagoda flower (*C. paniculatum*). The shrub known as the lilac chaste tree (*Vitex agnus–castus*) is sometimes cultivated for its attractive, blue or white flowers. The beauty–berry (*Callicarpa americana*) is sometimes grown for its ornamental fruits.

Attractive species of *Lantana* are often cultivated as greenhouse and bedding plants. Unfortunately, some species of *Lantana* have escaped from gardens in the

KEY TERMS

Inflorescence—A grouping or arrangement of flowers into a composite structure.

Tropical hardwood—Generic term for a wide variety of species of tropical, angiosperm trees with a heavy, dense wood that is valuable for the manufacturing of lumber and composite materials such as plywood. Teak and mahogany are among the most prized of the tropical hardwoods.

Veneer—A composite wood product, in which a thin outer covering of a valuable wood is glued onto an interior of less expensive wood.

Weed—Any plant that is growing abundantly in a place where humans do not want it to be.

tropics, and in many places these have become serious weeds of pastures because livestock can be poisoned by eating this plant. Some horticultural species in the verbena family have also become naturalized as weeds in North America.

North American Species

A number of species of wildflowers in the verbena family occur naturally in North America, or have been introduced from elsewhere and have spread to natural habitats.

One of the more familiar native species of verbenas in North America is the blue vervain or wild hyssop (*Verbena hastata*), a common plant of moist, temperate habitats. The French or Bermuda mulberry (*Callicarpa americana*) is a native shrub of moist thickets in southern parts of North America.

The European vervain or berbine (*Verbena officinalis*) is a common, introduced species in North America, and is sometimes an important weed.

Further Reading:

Hartmann, H.T., A.M. Kofranek, V.E. Rubatzky, and W.J. Flocker. *Plant Science. Growth, Development, and Utilization of Cultivated Plants.* Englewood Cliffs, NJ: Prentice–Hall, 1988.
Woodland, D.W. *Contemporary Plant Heigh Systematics.* Englewood Cliffs, NJ: Prentice–Hall, 1991.

Bill Freedman

Vertebrates

Vertebrates are animals classified in the subphylum Vertebrata, phylum Chordata. Vertebrates share a number of features. They all have an internal skeleton of bone and/or cartilage, which includes a bony cranium surrounding the brain and a bony vertebral column enclosing the spinal cord. Vertebrates are all covered by a skin composed of dermal and superficial epidermal layers of scales, feathers or fur, a ventral heart, formed red and white blood cells, a liver, pancreas, kidney, and a number of other internal organs. The most advanced vertebrates also have jaws, teeth, limbs or fins, and an internal skeletal structure with pelvic and pectoral girdles, and thoracic lungs.

Eight classes of vertebrates are recognized. These are listed below, in the order of their first appearance in the fossil record:

(1) The class Agnatha, is a group of jawless, fish–like animals with poorly developed fins, which first appeared more than 500 million years ago, during the late Cambrian. The 75 surviving species include the jawless lampreys and hagfishes.

(2) The class Placodermi, is an extinct group of bony–plated aquatic animals. The placoderms were primitive, jawless, fish–like creatures, whose head was heavily armored by an external shield of bony plates. These creatures were most abundant during the Devonian period, some 413–365 million years ago.

(3) The class Chondrichthyes, includes about 800 living species of sharks, rays, and rat fishes, all of which have a cartilaginous skeleton, true jaws, and a number of other distinctive characters.

(4) The class Osteichthyes, includes some 20,000 species of true fishes, with a bony skeleton, a sutured skull, teeth fused to the jaws, lobed or rayed fins, and a number of other distinguishing features.

(5) The class Amphibia, includes some 3,500 living species of frogs, toads, salamanders, newts, and caecilians, all of which have four limbs (making them tetrapods), a moist glandular skin, external fertilization, and a complex life cycle.

(6) The class Reptilia, are four–legged, tailed animals, with dermal scales, internal fertilization, amniotic eggs, and direct development. Living reptiles include about 6,200 species of crocodiles, turtles, lizards, snakes, and tuataras. Important extinct groups of reptiles include the dinosaurs, hadrosaurs, ichthyosaurs, pterosaurs, and plesiosaurs.

(7) The class Aves, the birds, is a diverse group of about 8,800 species of warm–blooded (or homoiothermic) tetrapods whose forelimbs are specialized for flight (although some species are secondarily flightless). Birds have a characteristic covering of feathers, a beak which lacks teeth, and reproduce by laying eggs.

(8) The class Mammalia, includes more than 4,000 species of homoiothermic tetrapods, with epidermal hair and female mammary glands for suckling the young. All give birth to young, although a very few, primitive species reproduce by laying eggs.

Vertebrates are the most complex of Earth's animal life forms. The earliest vertebrates were marine, jawless, fish–like creatures that probably fed on algae, small animals, and decaying organic matter. The evolution of jaws allowed a more complex exploitation of ecological opportunities, including the pursuit of a predatory life style. The evolution of limbs and the complex life cycle of amphibians allowed the adults to exploit moist terrestrial habitats as well as aquatic habits. The subsequent evolution of internal fertilization and the self–contained, amniotic eggs of reptiles, birds, and mammals allowed reproduction on land, and led to fully terrestrial forms. Birds and mammals further advanced vertebrate adaptations to terrestrial environments through their complex anatomical, physiological, and behavioral adaptations, and this has allowed them to extensively exploit all of Earth's habitable environments.

See also Amphibians; Birds: Bony fishes; Cartilaginous fish; Chordates; Fish; Hagfishes; Invertebrates; Lampreys; Mammals; Reptiles.

Bill Freedman

Vestibule see **Ear**

Vicuna see **Camels**

Video recording

The term video recording refers to storing the video signals on a magnetic recording device such as tape. The term also refers to storage on other devices such as magneto–optical devices and video disks. Video signals have much larger bands with 5 MHZ or so and thus have involved recording technology.

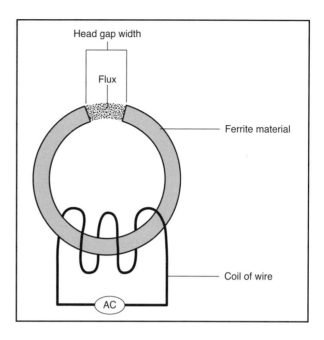

Figure 1. A schematic diagram of a recording head.

Basic principles of video recording

The standard method for storing video signals is magnetic recording technology. In magnetic recording, some type of material is magnetized according to an electrical signal variation. The material is often a flexible tape coated with some type of ferrous oxide. The video signal is first converted into electrical energy (often alternating current, AC) and then passed to a recording head, which consists of a coil of wire wound around a core made of ferrite material (Figure 1). When the AC signal is passed through the recording head, the core of which has two ends close together, magnetic flux extends across the gap. As the AC signal goes through its cycle, the polarity of the two ends of the core changes, resulting in a reversal of the direction of the magnetic flux. The intensity of the AC current determines the strength of the magnetic flux. This flux produces a magnetized area on the flexible tape, which passes over the recording head. These magnetized areas are the recording of the video signal.

In order for the video signal to be recorded properly, the tape has to move at a constant and sufficient speed across the end gap of the head. This leads to magnetization of the discrete areas according to the signal content at each step in time.

Video signal frequency and tape speed

Frequencies of the video signals lie somewhere between 10 Hz and 5 MHz. For a given bandwidth,

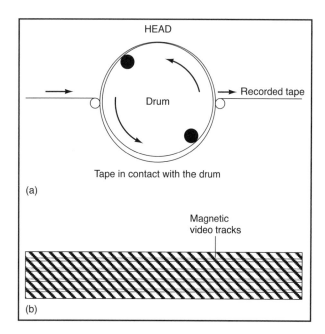

HEAD

Drum

Recorded tape

Tape in contact with the drum

(a)

Magnetic
video tracks

(b)

Figure 2. (A) A schematic representation of the rotating drum and moving tape. (B) A schematic diagram of a magnetic tape which has recorded signals.

assuming a linear motion of the tape over the stationary recording head, the speed of the tape can be obtained from a simple expression given below:

Speed of tape (meters per second) = Width of Gap (meters) x 2 x Frequency (Hertz).

For a 5MHz bandwidth and gap with of 10^{-6} meters, the speed of the tape required is 10 m per second. Thus to record a video program for an hour, the tape length required would be 36,000 meters. This is a huge length of tape for such a small amount of the video signal. However, in practice the linear tape speed for recording video signals is often 24 mm per second.

Recording techniques

Recording of video signals of such high bandwidth requires efficient techniques for the practical use of the recording devices. Some of the techniques used in the past and others currently in use are discussed in the following sections.

Transverse recording

The transverse recording technique is based upon the concept of rotation of the head as well as the transverse movement of the tape over the head. The head rotates at a speed of 14,400 rpm, which gives an efficient writing speed of 38 meters per second. In this

method, a single field image is divided into 16 segments. All these segments are then recorded linearly onto the magnetic tape. This requires a great deal of horizontal synchronization while reproducing the video signal.

Helical recording

Helical recording enables the linear speed of the tape itself to be reduced, while increasing the writing speed. Instead of a single recording head, two heads are set diametrically into a small rotating drum. The magnetic tape wraps around the drum as it moves forward, thus both the head and the tape are moving in the same direction. This drum is tilted at an angle, which causes the heads to traverse the magnetic tape in slanted tracks (Figure 2).

For maximum utilization of the magnetic tape, at least two heads are essential. The two heads are set in the drum so that their gaps are at an angle of 6° plus or minus from the 'zero' position. The 'zero' position is defined as the right angle to the direction of the rotation. This angle is called the azimuthal angle, and this type of recording is also referred to as azimuth recording. The plus and minus sign in the angles ensure that the two heads identify their own tracks while reproducing the video signals. Unlike transverse recording, the picture field is divided into two segments and each segment is recorded by each head. Thus in one rotation of the drum one picture field is written completely.

The width of these magnetic tracks is 0.049 mm. The total width of the tape is 12.65 mm. In addition to the video tracks, the tape has two other tracks—one corresponds to the associated sound track and the other is the control track for synchronizing tape speeds. The later two tracks are stored in a linear fashion.

Frequency modulation

The wide bandwidth of a video signal poses a problem, due to the way that the inductive impedance of the recording head rises with the increase in the frequency. For normal recording a thousand times more head voltage will be required for 5 MHZ signal than for 30 Hz signal. To avoid this problem, the wide width luminance signal is not recorded directly, but is instead recorded using a process called frequency modulation (FM), where a high frequency carrier signal is used. This effectively increases the ratio of the lowest and highest frequencies but does not reduce the band width. FM signals give a better signal–to–noise performance and are less sensitive to unwanted interference.

Video systems

Video systems are dependent on the format of the television signals broadcast. In various parts of the world electrical standards are different for the power supply. Two of the most common power frequencies are 50 Hz and 60 Hz. In order to match the frequency of the power supply, the television signals had to adapt to those standards. In countries like the United States, Canada, and Japan with 60 Hz frequency, 30 frames per second of the video signals are transmitted, while in countries like Australia, India and some European countries with 50 Hz frequency, 25 frames per second are transmitted. The picture to be transmitted is reconstructed as a series of dots. For a black and white picture the dots are black, grey, and white. In color pictures, these dots are usually red, green, and blue. These dots are usually very small and almost invisible to the human eye; hence, a series of these dots are synchronized in the form of horizontal lines and vertical lines. These horizontal lines also determine the bandwidth of the television signal. The number of horizontal lines varies along with the number of frames for transmission. Countries with 60 Hz use 525 horizontal lines while others use 625 lines. There is no world standard yet for these horizontal lines and the number of frames for transmission. This led to the various video recording systems. There are three major types of video recording: NTSC (National Television System Committee); PAL (phase alternation line); and SECAM (sequential color and memory). The major differences in the three systems are:

Horizontal lines	525	625	625
Fields per second	60	50	50
Frames per second	30	25	25

Besides these major differences there are variations in their sub carrier frequency, luminance, and chrominance bandwidths. There are subsystems for these video systems, the differences being mainly in the frequency modulation bandwidths.

Video formats

The video signal is recorded using the helical scanning technique. Use of different azimuthal angles for recording leads to different video formats.

VHS format

This is one of the most commonly used video formats. The azimuthal angle is +6 or –6 degrees. The writing speed is usually 4.85 m per second, while the linear speed of the tape is 23.99 mm per second. The video track width is 0.049 mm and the actual tape width is 12.65 mm.

Betamax format

The azimuthal angle for this format is +7 and –7 degrees. The linear speed of the tapes is 18.7 mm per second slower than the VHS tape speed, although the writing speed is 5.83 m per second. The video track width is 0.0328 mm on a tape 12.7 mm wide.

Video–8 format

This format uses azimuthal angles of +10 and –10 degrees. The standard video tracks are 0.0344 mm wide on a tape that is 8 mm wide. The writing speed is 3.12 m per second with a linear tape speed of 20.051 mm per second. The drum size used in this format is smaller than those used in VHS or Betamax format.

VHS–C format

VHS–C stands for VHS compact. This format is widely used in video recording cameras and is fully compatible with the standard VHS format. The tape width is same as in VHS, but the drum is 41.33 mm instead of 62 mm in VHS. The other difference is that VHS–C uses four–head helical scanning in order to produce the same magnetic pattern in VHS.

Digital recording

Most of the current video recording devices are analog recorders. The video signal is recorded using frequency modulation, and the information is converted to differences in distance between the zero–crossing points of the FM signal. This type of recording has limitations on the picture quality, etc. In order to obtain higher picture quality, digital recording is used. Digital recording is achieved by means of pulse–code modulation (PCM). In PCM, the distance between the zero–crossing points is a discrete value which is an integer times the bit period. Here the analog signal is spliced into segments of fixed width and amplitude and the discrete values are then recorded on the magnetic device using binary digits.

Digital recording currently has a drawback since it requires high density recording technology due to the large range of frequency, but it has many advantages over analog recording including greater reliability, low cost, improved picture quality, and automatic adjustment.

KEY TERMS

Alternating current (AC)—The electrical current which changes in polarity.

Chrominance—The color transmission signal.

Luminance—The basic monochrome signal.

Monochrome—Single color.

Video disk recording

Current video recording is done on longitudinal wound tapes, which are efficient in terms of the amount of the information they can store. However, tape recording has several drawbacks including the length of time required for retrieving the data and the inability to instantly and repetitively replay selected signals. These difficulties can be overcome by use of video disk recording technology. In video disk recording two plated rigid disks with four recording surfaces and four heads are utilized. These four heads are used in a technique called record–move–erase. A complete signal field is recorded in a concentric circle. This enables the reproduction instantly and repetitively of any video signal, as the head moves in the circle with desired segments of the picture. Recording in concentric circles requires high recording density. Work towards cheaper and smaller size video recording disks is in progress by making use of flexible disks, magnetic powders, etc. See also.

Further Reading:

Mee, C. Denis, and Eric D. Daniel. *Magnetic Recording.* Vol. III. New York: McGraw–Hill, 1988.

Bhusan, Bharat. *Tribology and Mechanics of Magnetic Storage Devices.* New York: Springer–Verlag, 1990.

Satyam Priyadarshy

Violet family (Violaceae)

The violet family (Violaceae) includes about 900 species of plants. Species in this family occur in all parts of the world, but are mostly in the temperate zones, and at high altitude in the tropics. The largest group in the family is the genus containing violets and pansies (*Viola* spp.), with about 500 species.

Most species in this family are annual or perennial herbs. The leaves are simple, commonly heart–shaped, and are alternately arranged on the stem, or arise from a basal rhizome. In most species the flowers are irregular, that is, they are composed of two complimentary halfs. The flowers of most species have both female (pistillate) and male (staminate) organs. Most species flower in the spring and early summer and have relatively large and showy flowers, sometimes grouped into an inflorescence. They typically produce fragrance and nectar to attract insect pollinators. Later in the growing season, some species also develop self–fertilized flowers that do not fully open, an unusual trait known as cleistogamy. The fruit is a many–seeded berry or capsule.

The major commercial value of species in the violet family is horticultural. One species is important in perfumery, and a few are used as medicinals.

Species native to North America

Most species of violets native to North America are wildflowers of the spring and early summer. Blue–colored violets are relatively common, with some of the more widespread species including the wooly blue violet (*Viola sororia*), northern blue violet (*V. septentrionalis*), New England blue violet (*V. novae–angliae*), western blue violet (*V. retusa*), prairie or larkspur violet (*V. pedatifida*), and marsh violet (*V. palustris*).

Some of the more common white–colored violets include the large–leaved white violet (*Viola incognita*), kidney–leaved violet (*V. renifolia*), sweet white violet (*V. blanda*), and northern white violet (*V. pallens*).

Yellow–colored violets include the hairy yellow violet (*Viola pubescens*), smoothish yellow violet (*V. eriocarpa*), and round–leaved yellow violet (*V. rotundifolia*).

The green violet (*Hybanthus concolor*) is a species found in moist forests of eastern North America.

Ornamental violets

Many species of violets and pansies and their diverse hybrids are grown in gardens as ornamentals, particularly as bedding plants. Most commonly cultivated are the so–called garden pansies (*Viola x wittrockiana*), a hybrid complex that is largely based on the European pansy (*V. tricolor*). Ornamental pansies are now available in diverse floral colors, including solid and mixed hues of blue, purple, red, yellow, and white. Some pansy varieties develop quite large flowers.

The English or sweet violet (*Viola odorata*) is also commonly cultivated as an ornamental plant, and it sometimes escapes from cultivation to become a minor weed of North American lawns. Less commonly culti-

KEY TERMS

Chrominance—The color transmission signal.

Cleistogamy—This refers to flowers that do not open, but are self–fertilizing and set viable seed. Various species of *Viola* are cleistogamous.

Emetic—A substance that induces vomiting.

Inflorescence—Any grouping of individual flowers into a cluster.

Luminance—The basic monochrome signal.

Monochrome—Single color.

Weed—Any plant that is growing abundantly in a place where humans do not want it to be.

vated species include the horned violet (*V. cornuta*) and the alpine violet (*V. labradorica*).

Other uses of violets

The sweet violet has been cultivated in large quantities in southern France for the production of a fragrant oil from its flowers, known as oil–of–violets. This oil is used in the mixing of perfumes and other scents. The yield of one tonne of fresh flowers is only 28–43 grams (.98–1.51 ounces) of oil–of–violets. Interestingly, this light–green oil only has a faint scent when in its concentrated, distilled state, but when diluted to about 1:5000 its odor becomes very strong. The scent of violets can now been synthesized by chemists, so natural oil–of–violets is now rare.

Sometimes the flowers of pansies are served as an attractive, edible garnish to well–presented, epicurean foods. Pansies are also sometimes candied as an exotic confectionary.

Some minor organic medicines are prepared from several species in the Violaceae, mostly for use as emetics. These medicinal plants include *Anchietea salutaris*, *Corynostylis hybanthus*, and *Hybanthus ipecacuanha*.

Further Reading:

Conger, R.H.M. and G.D. Hill. *Agricultural Plants*, 2nd ed. Cambridge, UK: Cambridge University Press, 1991.

Hartmann, H.T., A.M. Kofranek, V.E. Rubatzky, and W.J. Flocker. *Plant Science: Growth, Development, and Utilization of Cultivated Plants*. Englewood Cliffs, NJ: Prentice–Hall, 1988.

Woodland, D.W. *Contemporary Plant Systematics*. Englewood Heights, New Jersey: Prentice–Hall, 1991.

Bill Freedman

Vipers

Vipers are snakes in the family Viperidae, a group of short–tailed, (usually) stout–bodied snakes with long fangs at the front of the mouth, sited on a short jawbone that can be rotated to bring the fangs from their resting position parallel with the palate to an erect position for striking.

This efficient venom delivery system allows vipers to eat large (and sometimes dangerous) animals without a struggle that might expose them to harm. Vipers make a swift strike in which the long hollow (hypodermic needle–like) fangs inject a strong venom deep into the prey's body. The snakes then wait until the animal dies, tracking it down if necessary, and then calmly swallowing it. The venom also has the effect of initiating digestion even before the prey is swallowed. Many vipers do not find it necessary to eat more than once a month. The venoms of these snakes are diverse, being adapted to quickly kill the preferred prey animals of each species.

Vipers are an old and diverse group. They are generally divided into the Old World "true" vipers (Viperinae) and the pit vipers (Crotalinae), which are found in Asia and the Americas. One strange viper, (*Azemiops*) from southern China and northern Myanmar (Burma) of unknown relationships, is placed in its own subfamily, Azemiopinae.

Old World vipers

True vipers, (family Viperidae) are found in the Old World and lack facial pits; this distinguishes them from the pit vipers of the Americas. Africa is the home of 30 of the 45 species of Old World vipers. Among the African vipers are the Gaboon viper (*Bitis gabonicus*) and the rhinoceros viper (*B. nasicornis*) that attain lengths of almost 6 ft (2 meters) and have fangs that may be 2 in (5 cm) in length. There are green tree–vipers (*Atheris*), desert–dwelling sandvipers (*Cerastes*), and even a little–known worm–eating, burrowing viper (*Adorhinos*).

The deserts of north Africa and south Asia are home to a number of sandvipers, one of which is the notorious carpet viper (*Echis carinatus*). Although an adult of this snake may be little more than 1 ft (30 cm) in length, its bite is highly toxic and is responsible for many deaths, particularly in the desert regions of Pakistan and western India.

The small European viper or adder (*Vipera berus*), by contrast, is not dangerous to humans. Its bite has been described as "little worse than a bee–sting," and the few reported deaths are apparently due to

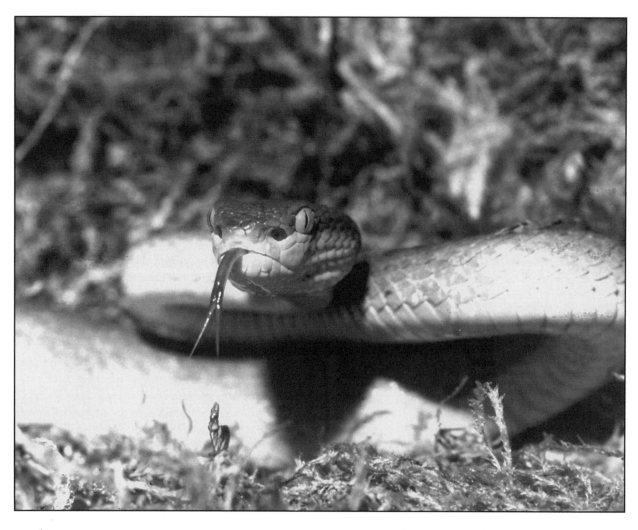

A Pope's pit viper.

over–treatment. This viper is notable in that it is one of very few snakes that ranges above the Arctic Circle in Sweden and Norway.

Some large vipers of the genus *Vipera* range from the eastern Mediterranean eastward through southern Asia. The ill–tempered and highly venomous Russell's viper *(Vipera russelii)* follows the rats into the rice fields when the fields are drained for harvesting. It is the major cause of fatal snake bites (killing perhaps 10,000 people annually) in Burma (Myanmar) and Thailand.

Pitvipers

The pitvipers are easily identified by the loreal pit, a heat–sensitive receptor that lies between the nostril and the eye on either side of the face. With this receptor the snakes can detect and accurately strike a warm–blooded prey animal in absolute darkness, guided by the infra–red (heat) rays that the prey animal produces. The Viperinae lack this heat–sensitive pit.

The pitvipers range from eastern Europe to the East Indies and Japan, and from Canada to Argentina in the Americas. Although the 145 species of New World pit vipers are much more diverse than the Old World vipers, most are terrestrial, with a few (usually green) arboreal species. The best–known pit vipers are the rattlesnakes (*Crotalus* and *Sistrurus*) which are found only in the Americas and whose modified tail skin vibrates to produce a rattling, warning sound. Most rattlesnakes are North American, ranging from southern Canada to Panama, with the greatest number inhabiting the dry regions of the southwestern United States and northern Mexico. However, a small tropical group (*Crotalus durissus* and its relatives) ranges as far as southern Brazil.

KEY TERMS

. . . .

Loreal pit—A sensitive heat receptor found in pitvipers.

Venomous—Having a toxic substance used to subdue prey and in defence.

There are about 60 species of tropical pitvipers (*Bothrops* and relatives) that range from coastal Mexico southward to the Patagonian plains of Argentina. Most of these are relatives of the large terrestrial South American "fer–de–lance" *Bothrops atrox,* but Central America has a more diverse assemblage composed of several genera, some of which are treevipers.

The largest of all vipers is the bushmaster (*Lachesis muta*) of northern South America and Panama, which attains a reported length of 12 ft (4 m). Like the large African vipers, it has very long fangs (2 in/5 cm or more) and a large supply of venom. Very few people are bitten by these snakes, however, because bushmasters live in forested areas and are active only at night.

Asia has a large contingent of pitvipers (including green, arboreal species) similar to the American *Bothrops,* that are placed in the genus *Trimeresurus.* Some of its members are so similar to some of the American species that there is some doubt that they should be in different genera.

The water moccasins (genus *Agkistrodon*) are found both in North America and in Asia. The copperhead (*Agkistrodon contortrix*) is common in the forests of the eastern United States, and is responsible for most of the venomous snakebites in that region. Fortunately, its venom is not highly toxic to humans, and almost no one dies from these bites.

See also Reptiles; Snakes.

Further Reading:

Campbell, J. A., and E. D. Brodie, Jr., eds. *Biology of the Pitvipers.* Tyler, Texas: Selva, 1992.

Campbell, J. A., and W. W. Lamar. *The Venomous Reptiles of Latin America.* Ithaca: Comstock Publ., 1989.

Klauber, L. M. *Rattlesnakes: Their Habits, Life Histories, and Influences on Mankind.* Berkeley: Univ. of Calif. Press, 1982.

Minton, S. A., Jr., and M. R. Minton. *Venomous Reptiles.* New York: Scribner's, 1969.

Russell, F. E. *Snake Venom Poisoning.* Philadelphia: Lippincott, 1980.

Herndon G. Dowling

Vireos

Vireos are 44 species of small arboreal birds that comprise the family Vireonidae, in the order Passeriformes. As it is considered here, the Vireonidae is an assembly of three sub–families: the true vireos or Vireoninae, the shrike vireos or Vireolaniinae, and the pepper shrikes or Cyclarhinae. It should be pointed out, however, that some taxonomic treatments consider these to be separate families.

The vireos only occur in the Americas. Species of vireos range from the temperate forests of Canada, through the rest of North America, Central America, and south to northern Argentina. The northern, temperate species are all migratory, breeding in the northern parts of their biological range, but spending the non-breeding season in tropical and subtropical forests. Vireos occur in all types of tropical and temperate forests, and in shrubby habitats as well.

Vireos are small birds, ranging in body length from 3.9–7.1 in (10–18 cm). The bill is relatively heavy for a small bird, and the upper mandible has a hook at the tip. Depending on the species, the wings are either long and pointed, or short and rounded, while the legs and feet are short but strong. The plumage of vireos is plain, generally olive–green or gray on the back and wings, and lighter colored on the throat and belly. Species may have eye rings, eye stripes, wing bars, and other diagnostically useful markings.

Vireos glean foliage and branches for their food of insects and spiders, and they may also eat small fruits. Compared with other types of foliage–gleaning birds, vireos are rather sluggish and deliberate in their movements. Vireos generally occur as solitary birds, or in family groups. They are aggressively territorial during the breeding season. The territory is demarcated and defended by loud, melodious songs, consisting of multi-syllabic, persistently repeated phrases.

The nest is cuplike, or is an open, pendulous, baglike structure woven of plant fibers, usually located in a horizontal fork of a branch. The clutch size is 2–5. The male helps with incubation, and both sexes cooperate in rearing the young birds.

North American species of vireos

A total of 12 species of vireos breed regularly in the United States or Canada. All of these are in the genus *Vireo,* and all are migratory, spending their non-breeding season in Mexico or further south in Central America, or in the case of the red–eyed vireos, in Amazonia.

A red-eyed vireo (*Vireo olivaceous*).

The red–eyed vireo (*Vireo olivaceous*) is a widespread species, occurring in deciduous forests over much of the continent, except for parts of the southwestern United States. The red–eyed vireo is an abundant species, and is one of the most commonly netted birds at mist–netting sites in eastern North America, where bird migration is studied.

The warbling vireo (*Vireo gilvus*) breeds in much of temperate North America and south into Mexico. The warbling vireo is a secretive bird, and males can be so confident in their camouflage that they will sing from the nest while incubating their clutch.

The solitary or blue–headed vireo (*Vireo solitarius*) breeds in mixed hardwood–conifer forests through much of north temperate North America. This is one of the only species of vireo whose wintering range commonly includes the southern United States.

The white–eyed vireo (*Vireo griseus*) is an abundant species of moist deciduous forests and forest edges in the eastern United States. The yellow–throated vireo (*Vireo flavifrons*) has a bright yellow throat and breast, and is perhaps the most attractive of the North American species. This relatively uncommon species breeds in deciduous forests throughout the eastern United States.

Vireos elsewhere

Most species of true vireos occur in subtropical, tropical, and montane forests of Central and South America, but these species are too numerous and diverse to deal with here in any detail. One representative is the ashy–headed greenlet (*Hylophilus pectoralis*), a species found in the tropical forests of Guyana, Surinam, Brazil, and Bolivia.

KEY TERMS

Nest parasite—A species that lays its eggs in the nests of other species. The host raises the parasitic egg, and usually does not raise any of its own babies.

The shrike vireos are relatively stout, tropical birds with a heavy, hooked bill. The chestnut–sided shrike vireo (*Vireolanius melitophrys*) occurs in tropical rainforests of Mexico and Guatemala.

The pepper shrikes also are more stout than the true vireos, and have a laterally compressed, hooked bill. The rufous–browed pepper shrike (*Cyclarhis gujanensis*) occurs in open forests from Mexico to Argentina.

Vireos and people

In spite of their small size, vireos are economically important. Sightings of these birds are avidly sought by birdwatchers. Birding is a nonconsumptive field sport, and is increasing rapidly in popularity. Birding and related activities such as bird feeding have large economic impacts, and give great aesthetic pleasure to many people.

Unfortunately, the populations of many species of birds that are the targets of these activities, including vireos, are declining greatly because of human activities. This is especially true of many species native to North America.

Vireos and other birds that share their habitat are at risk from changes occurring in both their breeding and wintering ranges. There have been tremendous decreases in the areas of mature forests that most vireos require for breeding in North America. The vireos are affected directly by these losses of area of their essential habitat, as well as by indirect effects associated with the fragmentation of much of the remaining habitat into small woodlots.

Small, isolated, habitat "islands" are highly influenced by their proximity to edges with younger habitat. This circumstance exposes vireos and other birds of the forest–interior to a greater intensity of predation, and to the disastrous effects of nest–parasitism by the brown–headed cowbird (*Molothrus ater*). Many ornithologists believe that these factors are causing large declines in the populations of numerous species of migratory forest birds, including many of the vireos.

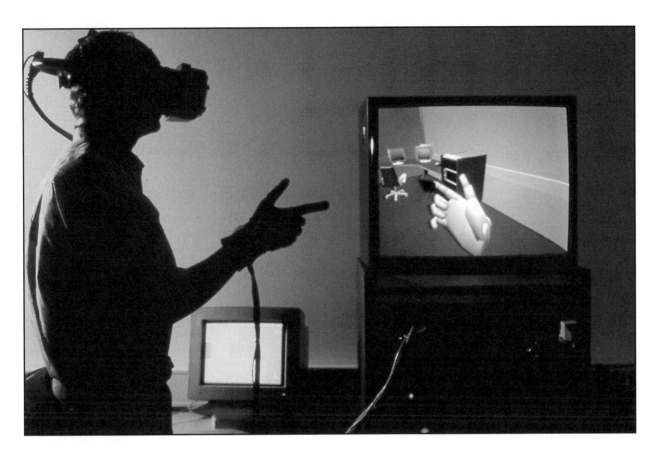

A virtual reality system.

Further Reading:

Ehrlich, P., D. Dobkin, and D. Wheye. *The Birders Handbook.* New York: Simon and Schuster, 1989.

Farrand, J., ed. *The Audubon Society Master Guide to Birding.* New York: Knopf, 1983.

Harrison, C. J. O., ed. *Bird Families of the World.* New York: Abrams, 1978.

Bill Freedman

Virtual reality

Virtual reality combines state–of–the–art imaging with computer technology to allow users to experience a three–dimensional simulated environment called cyberspace (a term coined by science–fiction writer William Gibson). This interactive medium incorporates powerful computers with video displays, sensors, electronic headsets, and gloves. With these tools, users can both see and manipulate a phantom environment that appears real. Virtual reality tools under development include a whole body suit, which, like diving into water, would totally immerse the user in a virtual world. Although virtual reality has been popularized as a new form of entertainment, it has applications in business, industry, and medicine.

History

The concept of virtual reality dates back to World War II and the use of flight simulators to train pilots, but the computerized version of this phenomenal technology can be traced to the mid–1960s. In 1966, Ivan Sutherland conducted experiments with the first head–mounted three–dimensional displays at the Massachusetts Institute of Technology's Lincoln Laboratory. Although the headset was extremely cumbersome, the user was able to view a computer–generated three–dimensional cube floating in space and, by moving his or her head, inspect various aspects of the cube and determine its dimensions. Sutherland moved to the University of Utah, where he built the first fully functional head–mounted display unit in 1970.

Myron Krueger also worked on the infant science of virtual reality, first at the University of Utah and later at the University of Connecticut. His "artificial realities" used both computers and video systems. VIDEO-PLACE was first exhibited in 1975 at the Milwaukee Art Center. Using video displays, computer graphics, and position–sensing technologies, Kreuger was able to create a virtual environment in darkened rooms containing large video screens. People in the room could see their own computer–generated silhouettes and follow their movements in the virtual world projected onto the screen. In addition, people in two different rooms could see each others' silhouettes and interact in the same virtual world.

Much of the initial development of virtual reality was funded by the military. By 1972, the General Electric Corporation had built one of the first computerized flight simulators, using three screens surrounding the training cockpit to provide a 180–degree field of view that simulated flying conditions. In 1979, virtual reality technology was incorporated into a head–mounted display developed by the McDonnell–Douglas Corporation. Three years later, Thomas Furness III, who had created visual displays for the military since 1966, developed the prototype Visually Coupled Airborne Systems Simulator. Donning a specialized oversized helmet, pilots were presented for the first time with an abstract view of flying conditions instead of a reality–based image. Since they were unable to see anything but the computerized cockpit's field of view, pilots became totally immersed in the graphic representation.

While scientists like Sutherland and Furness concentrated on the visual components of virtual reality, Frederick Brooks began experimenting with tactile feedback, or the sense of touch, in the early 1970s at the University of North Carolina. However, it was not until 1986 that the computer industry developed the tools to simulate tactile experience. Brooks was able to develop his GROPE–III system, which used a specialized remote manipulator based on a device that mimicked arm motions to handle radioactive substances. Specifically, the GROPE–III system generated stereoscopic images of molecules and protein structures that could be felt and manipulated as though they existed in the physical world.

Components

In its most basic rendering, virtual reality systems consist of the computer and software—known as the reality engine—and input and output sensors. In standard computer technology, input devices are the familiar keyboard, mouse, knobs, and joysticks; output devices include the printer and video display. Virtual reality input/output devices include head– and ear–mounted equipment for hearing and seeing, and gloves for controlling the virtual world. The fourth "component" is the user, who both directs and reacts to the chosen environment.

The reality engine

The reality engine employs both computer hardware and software to create the virtual world. Reality engines are based largely on the same components that make up a personal computer (PC), although much more computing power is required for the reality engine than what is available in a standard PC.

One key to virtual reality is creating a world that appears real. The images created by the computer and software are extremely complex compared to the relatively simple line–based graphics associated with computer games. Virtual reality images are made with pixels, also known as picture elements, which use hundreds of thousands of dots to make up the images. The more pixels there are per inch, the better or more realistic the image will be. Creating realistic images that can be manipulated is known as "realization." These images can be either opaque, in which all the viewer sees is the virtual world, or see–through, in which the virtual image is projected or superimposed onto the outer world.

Sound enriches the virtual world. The experience of soaring through the air in a simulated cockpit is more realistic if the user hears the roar of the engines. Sound also enhances participation in the virtual world by providing the user with audio cues. For example, the user may be directed to look for the virtual airplane flying overhead.

To incorporate the total experience, the reality engine may use haptic enhancement, which engages the participant's other senses of touch and pressure into the virtual world. Haptic cues however, are complex and expensive and have been used primarily for military and research applications.

Headsets

Head–mounted display (HMD) units use a small screen or screens (one for each eye) that are worn in a helmet or a pair glasses. Unlike a movie, where the director controls what the viewer sees, including the angle and field of view, the HMD allows viewers to look at an image from various angles or change their field of view by simply moving their heads.

HMD units usually employ cathode–ray–tube (CRT) or liquid–crystal–display (LCD) technology. CRTs incorporate optic systems that reflect an image onto the viewer's eye. Although more bulky and heavy than LCD displays, CRT systems create images that have extremely high resolutions. In addition, CRT images can be semi–reflective, allowing the viewer to see the outside world as well. Such units have practical applications since the user can operate a machine or other device while viewing the virtual world.

Although LCD technology has lagged behind CRT in picture quality, LCD systems are slimmer, lighter, and less expensive, making them better suited for home use. These units use liquid crystal monitors to display two slightly different images that the brain processes into a single three–dimensional view. Initial efforts to market this technology to home users failed because of poor LCD image quality. But rapid advances in LCD technology have improved the images, and higher quality LCD–based units have become available for home use.

Audio units

Sound effects in virtual reality rely on a prerecorded sound set that is difficult to alter once the reality engine begins to generate audio. The audio portion of virtual reality is transmitted through small speakers placed over each ear. Audio cues may include voices, singing, the sound of bubbling water, thud–like noises of colliding objects—in short, any sound that can be recorded.

Three–dimensional, or omnidirectional, sound further enhances the virtual reality experience. Sound that seems to come from above, below, or either side provides audio cues that mimic how sounds, like footsteps approaching or a plane flying overhead, are heard in the real world. Three–dimensional sound is achieved through the use of highly complex filtering devices. This technology must take into account factors like interaural time difference (which ear hears the sound first) and interaural amplitude difference (which ear hears the sound louder). The most complex human hearing dynamic is called head–related transfer functions (HRTF). HRTF accounts for how the ear drum and inner ear process sound waves, taking into consideration the various frequencies at which these waves travel as well as how waves are absorbed and reflected by other objects. HRTF audio processing enables the listener not only to locate a sound source but also to focus in on a specific sound out of a multitude of sounds, like distinguishing the call of a peanut vendor out of a crowd at a baseball game.

Gloves

Gloves in virtual reality allow the user to interact with the virtual world; for example, the user may pick up a virtual block, turn it over in the virtual hand, and set it on a virtual table. Wired with thin fiber–optic cables, some gloves use light–emitting diodes (LEDs) to detect the amount of light passing through the cable in relation to the movement of the hand or joint. The computer then analyzes the corresponding information and projects this moving hand into the virtual reality. Magnetic tracking systems are also used to determine where the hand is in space in relation to the virtual scene.

Some gloves use haptic enhancement to provide a sense of touch and feel. In haptic enhancement, the reality engine outputs the tactile experience, which may include force, heat, and texture. Tactile experiences are created by remeasuring a pattern of forces, which is programmed into the reality engine and then relayed back to the user when the appropriate object is touched. Virtual reality gloves may use either air pressure (such as strategically placed, inflated air pockets in the glove) or vibrating transducers placed next to the skin (such as a voice coil from a stereo speaker or alloys which change shape through the conduction of electrical currents) to simulate tactile experience.

Tools under development

Many other virtual reality tools are in the phases of research and development. Remote control robotic or manipulator haptic devices are being tested for industry and medicine. Special wands with sensors, joysticks, and finger sensors such as picks and rings will eventually be as common to virtual reality technology as microwaves are to cooking. The technology to control the virtual world through voice commands is also rapidly advancing.

Perhaps the most impressive technology under development is the whole body suit. These suits would function similarly to the gloves, creating a virtual body that could take a stroll through a virtual world and feel a virtual windstorm.

Applications

The potential for virtual reality as an entertainment medium is apparent. Instead of manipulating computerized images of two boxers or a car race, the virtual playground allows the user to experience the event. Disney World's Epcot Center houses a virtual reality system that propels the user on a magic carpet ride like the one featured in the popular animated feature movie *Aladdin*. Although most entertainment applications are primarily visually based, virtual reality players of the future may also experience a variety of tactile events. For example, in a simulated boxing match, virtual reality users would bob and weave, throw and land punches, and—unless they were very adept—take a few punches themselves.

Virtual reality also has practical applications in the realms of business, manufacturing, and medicine. NASA has developed a virtual wind tunnel to test aerodynamics shape. Virtual reality holds promise for discovering the most efficient manufacturing conditions by allowing planners to evaluate the actual physical motions and strength needed to complete a job. The McDonnell–Douglas Corporation is using virtual reality to explore the use of different materials and tools in building the F–18 E/F aircraft. The study of people in relation to their environments, also known as ergonomics, may also be revolutionized by trials in cyberspace. Engineers at the Volvo car company use virtual reality to test various designs for the dashboard configuration from the perspective of the user. In medicine, virtual reality systems are being developed to help surgeons plan and practice delicate surgical procedures. Philip Green, a researcher at SRI International, is developing a telemanipulator, a special remote–controlled robot, to be used in surgery. Using instruments connected to a computer, doctors will be able to perform the operation in cyberspace, while the computer sends signals to direct the telemanipulator. Virtual reality may even have applications in psychiatry; for example, someone with acrophobia (a fear of heights) may be treated by having the patient stand atop virtual skyscrapers or soar through the air like a bird.

Future generations

Considering the rapid advances in computer technology, virtual reality machines of one decade will be viewed as a crude devices by the next decade. For example, technology is being developed to use the retina of the eye as a screen for images that could be transmitted directly to the brain through the optic nerve. Developing the technology to facilitate the remote operation of aircraft and other machines as though the user were actually in the machine is also under way. Traveling to France or Greece, including the experience of climbing the Eiffel Tower or basking on a sun–drenched beach, may be as easy as donning a headset and body suit and plugging in.

Like most technological advances, virtual reality has social and psychological ramifications. Critics argue that virtual reality could cause some people to forego emotions and interpersonal relationships for the safe, controllable virtual world. But proponents say advances from the proper applications of this technology—both as a means of interacting with the real world

KEY TERMS

Haptic—Pertains to physical sensations such as hearing and the sense of touch.

Pixel—A word used for picture elements, or dots, that make up a computerized image.

Three–dimensional—A visual representation in terms of height, width, and *depth* as opposed to a "flat" image that represents only height and width.

Virtual—Something that is representative or the essence of a thing but not the actual thing.

and as an end of facilitating training and entertainment—far outweigh the potential for antisocial abuse.

See also Cathode ray tube; LCD; LED.

Further Reading:

Larijani, L. Casey. *The Virtual Reality Primer.* New York: McGraw–Hill, 1994.

Pimentel, Ken and Teixeira Kevin. *Virtual Reality: Through the new looking glass.* New York: Intel/Windcrest®/ McGraw–Hill, 1993.

Rheingold, Howard. *Virtual Reality.* New York: Summit Books, 1991.

Rheingold, Howard. "Travels in Virtual Reality." *Whole Earth Review* (Summer 1990): 80.

Stevens, Tim. "Virtual Reality: Is It Really Real?" *Industry Week.* (May 1993): 32–37.

David Petechuk

Virus

A virus is a small, infectious agent that consists of a core of genetic material (either deoxyribonucleic acid [DNA] or ribonucleic acid [RNA]) surrounded by a shell of protein. Viruses cause disease by infecting a host cell and commandeering the host cell's synthetic capabilities to produce more viruses. The newly made viruses then leave the host cell, sometimes killing it in the process, and proceed to infect other cells within the host. Because viruses invade cells, no drug therapy has yet been designed to kill viruses. The human immune system is the only defense against a viral disease.

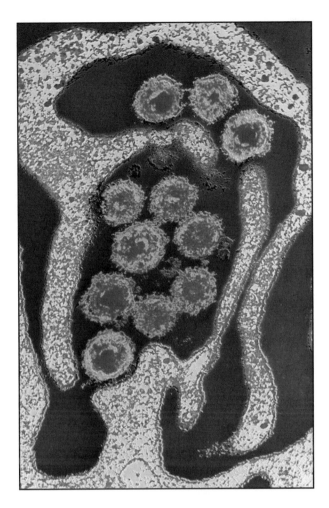

A transmission electron micrograph (TEM) of *Human Herpes Virus type 6 (HHV6)* infecting a human cell. This cell was isolated from an AIDS patient suffering a secondary infection with the virus. *HHV6* is now known to be the cause of the childhood disease *roseola infantum* which produces sudden fever, irritability, and a skin rash.

Viruses can infect both plants, bacteria, and animals. The tobacco mosaic virus, one of the most studied of all viruses, infects tobacco plants. Bacterial viruses, called bacteriophages, infect a variety of bacteria, such as *Escherichia coli,* a bacteria commonly found in the human digestive tract. Animal viruses cause a variety of fatal diseases. Acquired Immune Deficiency Syndrome (AIDS) is caused by the Human Immunodeficiency Virus (HIV); hepatitis and rabies are viral diseases; and the so–called hemorrhagic fevers, which are characterized by severe internal bleeding, are caused by filoviruses. Other animal viruses cause some of the most common human diseases. Often, these diseases strike in childhood. Measles, mumps, and chickenpox are viral diseases. The common cold and influenza are also caused by viruses. Finally, some viruses can cause

cancer and tumors. One such virus, Human T–cell Leukemia Virus (HTLV) was only recently discovered and its role in the development of a special kind of leukemia is still being elucidated.

Although viral structure varies considerably between the different types of viruses, all viruses share some common characteristics. All viruses contain either RNA or DNA surrounded by a protective protein shell called a capsid. Some viruses have a double strand of DNA, others a single strand of DNA. Other viruses have a double strand of RNA or a single strand of RNA. The size of the genetic material of viruses is often quite small. Compared to the 100,000 genes that exist within human DNA, viral genes number from 10 to about 200 genes.

Viruses contain such small amounts of genetic material because the only activity that they perform independently of a host cell is the synthesis of the protein capsid. In order to reproduce, a virus must infect a host cell and take over the host cell's synthetic machinery. This aspect of viruses—that the virus does not appear to be "alive" until it infects a host cell—has led to controversy in describing the nature of viruses. Are they living or non–living? When viruses are not inside a host cell, they do not appear to carry out many of the functions ascribed to living things, such as reproduction, metabolism, and movement. When they infect a host cell, they acquire these capabilities. Thus, viruses are both living and non–living. It was once acceptable to describe viruses as agents that exist on the boundary between living and non–living; however, a more accurate description of viruses is that they are either active or inactive, a description that leaves the question of life behind altogether.

The origin of viruses is also controversial. Some viruses, such as the poxviruses, are so complex that they appear to have been derived from some kind of living eukaryote or prokaryote. The origin of the poxvirus could therefore resemble that of mitochondria and chloroplasts, organelles within eukaryotic cells which are thought to have once been independent organisms. On the other hand, some viruses are extremely simple in structure, leading to the conclusion that these viruses are derived from cellular genetic material that somehow acquired the capacity to exist independently. This possibility is much more likely for most viruses; however, scientists still believe that the poxvirus is the exception to this scenario.

Structure of viruses

All viruses consist of genetic material surrounded by a capsid, but within the broad range of virus types, variations exist within this basic structure (Figure 1).

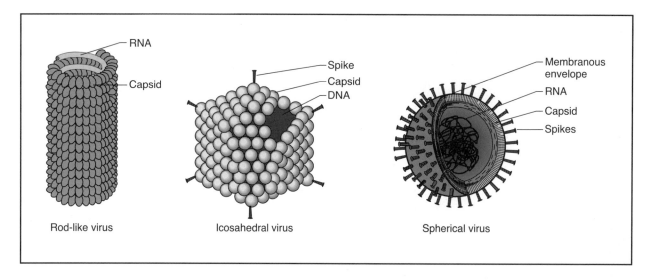

Figure 1. In addition to the capsid, some viruses are surrounded by an envelope, consisting of protein and lipid, which is acquired as the virus exits the host cell. Viruses that have an envelope exit host cells by exocytosis, in which they "bud out" from the host cell. As they bud out, they take pieces of the host cell's plasma membrane with them and use these pieces as the protective envelope.

Studding the envelope of these viruses are protein "spikes." These spikes are clearly visible on some viruses, such as the influenza viruses; on other enveloped viruses, the spikes are extremely difficult to see. The spikes help the virus invade host cells. The influenza virus, for instance, has two types of spikes. One type, composed of hemagglutinin protein (HA), fuses with the host cell membrane, allowing the virus particle to enter the cell. The other type of spike, composed of the protein neuraminidase (NA), helps the newly formed virus particles to bud out from the host cell membrane.

The capsid of viruses is relatively simple in structure, owing to the few genes that the virus contains to encode the capsid. Most viral capsids consist of a few repeating protein subunits. The capsid serves two functions: it protects the viral genetic material and it helps the virus introduce itself into the host cell. Many viruses are extremely specific, targeting only certain cells within the plant or animal body. HIV, for instance, targets a specific immune cell, the T helper cell. The cold virus targets respiratory cells, leaving the other cells in the body alone. How does a virus "know" which cells to target? The viral capsid has special receptors that match receptors on their targeted host cells. When the virus encounters the correct receptors on a host cell, it "docks" with this host cell and begins the process of infection and replication.

Most viruses are rod– or roughly sphere–shaped. Rod–shaped viruses include tobacco mosaic virus and the filoviruses. Although they look like rods under a microscope, these viral capsids are actually composed of protein molecules arranged in a helix. Other viruses are shaped somewhat like spheres, although many viruses are not actual spheres. The capsid of the adenovirus, which infects the respiratory tract of animals, consists of 20 triangular faces. This shape is called a icosahedron. HIV is a true sphere, as is the influenza virus.

Some viruses are neither rod– or sphere–shaped. The poxviruses are rectangular, looking somewhat like bricks. Parapoxviruses are ovoid. Bacteriophages are the most unusually shaped of all viruses. A bacteriophage consists of a head region attached to a sheath. Protruding from the sheath are tail fibers that dock with the host bacterium. The bacteriophage's structure is eminently suited to the way it infects cells. Instead of the entire virus entering the bacterium, the bacteriophage injects its genetic material into the cell, leaving an empty capsid on the surface of the bacterium.

Viral infection

Viruses are obligate intracellular parasites, meaning that in order to replicate, they need to be inside a host cell. Viruses lack the machinery and enzymes necessary to reproduce; the only synthetic activity they perform on their own is to synthesize their capsids.

The infection cycle of most viruses follows a basic pattern (Figure 2).

Bacteriophages are unusual in that they can infect a bacterium in two ways (although other viruses may replicate in these two ways as well). In the lytic cycle of

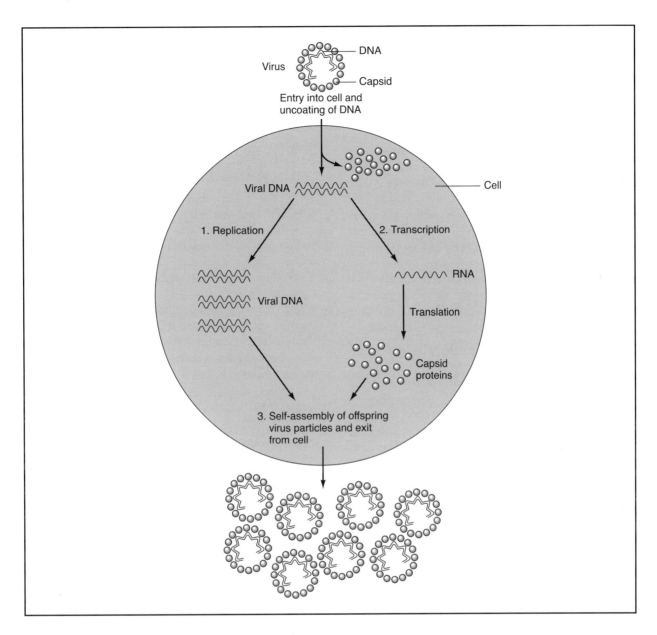

Figure 2. First, the virus docks with the host cell. The genetic material of the virus then enters the host cell and the virus loses its capsid. Once inside the host cell, the viral RNA or DNA takes over the cellular machinery to make more viruses. Viral subunits are produced, which are then assembled to make whole viruses. Finally, the new viruses leave the host cell, either by exocytosis or by destroying the host cell.

replication, the bacteriophage destroys the bacterium it infects. In the lysogenic cycle, however, the bacteriophage coexists with its bacterial host, and remains inside the bacterium throughout its life, reproducing only when the bacterium itself reproduces.

An example of a bacteriophage that undergoes lytic replication inside a bacterial host is the T4 bacteriophage which infects *E. coli*. T4 begins the infection cycle by docking with an *E. coli* bacterium. The tail

fibers of the bacteriophage make contact with the cell wall of the bacterium, and the bacteriophage then injects its genetic material into the bacterium. Inside the bacterium, the viral genes are transcribed. One of the first products produced from the viral genes is an enzyme that destroys the bacterium's own genetic material. Now the virus can proceed in its replication unhampered by the bacterial genes. Parts of new bacteriophages are produced and assembled. The bacterium then bursts, and the new bacteriophages are freed to infect other bacteria. This entire process takes only 20–30 minutes.

In the lysogenic cycle, the bacteriophage reproduces its genetic material but does not destroy the host's genetic material. The bacteriophage called lambda, another *E. coli*–infecting virus, is an example of a bacteriophage that undergoes lysogenic replication within a bacterial host. After the viral DNA has been injected into the bacterial host, it assumes a circular shape. At this point, the replication cycle can either become lytic or lysogenic. In a lysogenic cycle, the circular DNA attaches to the host cell genome at a specific place. This combination host–viral genome is called a prophage. Most of the viral genes within the prophage are repressed by a special repressor protein, so they do not encode the production of new bacteriophages. However, each time the bacterium divides, the viral genes are replicated along with the host genes. The bacterial progeny are thus lysogenically infected with viral genes.

Interestingly, bacteria that contain prophages can be destroyed when the viral DNA is suddenly triggered to undergo lytic replication. Radiation and chemicals are often the triggers that initiate lytic replication. Another interesting aspect of prophages is the role they play in human diseases. The bacteria that cause diphtheria and botulism both harbor viruses. The viral genes encode powerful toxins that have devastating effects on the human body. Without the infecting viruses, these bacteria may well be innocuous. It is the presence of viruses that makes these bacterial diseases so lethal.

Types of viruses

Scientists have classified viruses according to the type of genetic material they contain. Broad categories of viruses include double–stranded DNA viruses, single–stranded DNA viruses, double stranded RNA viruses, and single stranded RNA viruses. For the description of virus types that follows, however, these categories are not used. Rather, viruses are described by the type of disease they cause.

Poxviruses

Poxviruses are the most complex kind of viruses known. They have large amounts of genetic material and fibrils anchored to the outside of the viral capsid that assist in attachment to the host cell. Poxviruses contain a double strand of DNA.

Viruses cause a variety of human diseases, including smallpox and cowpox. Because of worldwide vaccination efforts, smallpox has virtually disappeared from the world, with the last known case appearing in Somalia in 1977. The only places on Earth where smallpox virus currently exists are two labs: the Centers for Disease Control in Atlanta and the Research Institute for Viral Preparation in Moscow. Prior to the eradication efforts begun by the World Health Organization in 1966, smallpox was one of the most devastating of human diseases. In 1707, for instance, an outbreak of smallpox killed 18,000 of Iceland's 50,000 residents. In Boston in 1721, smallpox struck 5,889 of the city's 12,000 inhabitants, killing 15% of those infected.

Edward Jenner (1749–1823) is credited with developing the first successful vaccine against a viral disease, and that disease was smallpox. A vaccine works by eliciting an immune response. During this immune response, specific immune cells, called memory cells, are produced that remain in the body long after the foreign microbe present in a vaccine has been destroyed. When the body again encounters the same kind of microbe, the memory cells quickly destroy the microbe. Vaccines contain either a live, altered version of a virus or bacteria, or they contain only parts of a virus or bacteria, enough to elicit an immune response.

In 1797, Jenner developed his smallpox vaccine by taking pus from a cowpox lesion on the hand of a milkmaid. Cowpox was a common disease of the era, transmitted through contact with an infected cow. Unlike smallpox, however, cowpox is a much milder disease. Using the cowpox pus, he inoculated an 8–year–old boy. Jenner continued his vaccination efforts through his lifetime. Until 1976, children were vaccinated with the smallpox vaccine, called vaccinia. Reactions to the introduction of the vaccine ranged from a mild fever to severe complications, including (although very rarely) death. In 1976, with the eradication of smallpox complete, vaccinia vaccinations for children were discontinued, although vaccinia continues to be used as a carrier for recombinant DNA techniques. In these techniques, foreign DNA is inserted in cells. Efforts to produce a vaccine for HIV, for instance, have used vaccinia as the vehicle that carries specific parts of HIV.

Herpesviruses

Herpesviruses are enveloped, double–stranded DNA viruses. Of the more than 50 herpesviruses that exist, only eight cause disease in humans. These include the human herpes virus types 1 and 2 that cause cold sores and genital herpes; human herpes virus 3, or varicella–zoster virus (VZV), that causes chicken pox and shingles; cytomegalovirus (CMV), a virus that in some individuals attacks the cells of the eye and leads to blindness; human herpes virus 4, or Epstein–Barr virus (EBV), which has been implicated in a cancer called Burkitt's lymphoma; and human herpes virus types 6 and 7, newly discovered viruses that infect white blood cells. In addition, herpes B virus is a virus that infects monkeys and can be transmitted to humans by handling infected monkeys.

Adenoviruses

Adenoviruses are viruses that attack respiratory, intestinal, and eye cells in animals. More than 40 kinds of human adenoviruses have been identified. Adenoviruses contain double–stranded DNA within a 20–faceted capsid.

Adenoviruses that target respiratory cells cause bronchitis, pneumonia, and tonsillitis. Gastrointestinal illnesses caused by adenoviruses are usually characterized by diarrhea and are often accompanied by respiratory symptoms. Some forms of appendicitis are also caused by adenoviruses. Eye illnesses caused by adenoviruses include conjunctivitis, an infection of the eye tissues, as well as a disease called pharyngoconjunctival fever, a disease in which the virus is transmitted in poorly chlorinated swimming pools.

Papoviruses

Human papoviruses include two groups: the papilloma viruses and the polyomaviruses. Human papilloma viruses (HPV) are the smallest double–stranded DNA viruses. They replicate within cells through both the lytic and the lysogenic replication cycles. Because of their lysogenic capabilities, HPV–containing cells can be produced through the replication of those cells that HPV initially infects. In this way, HPV infects epithelial cells, such as the cells of the skin. HPVs cause several kinds of benign (non–cancerous) warts, including plantar warts (those that form on the soles of the feet) and genital warts. However, HPVs have also been implicated in a form of cervical cancer that accounts for 7% of all female cancers.

HPV is believed to contain oncogenes, or genes that encode for growth factors that initiate the uncontrolled growth of cells. This uncontrolled proliferation of cells is called cancer. When the HPV oncogenes within an epithelial cell are activated, they cause the epithelial cell to proliferate. In the cervix (the opening of the uterus), the cell proliferation manifests first as a condition called cervical neoplasia. In this condition, the cervical cells proliferate and begin to crowd together. Eventually, cervical neoplasia can lead to full–blown cancer.

Polyomaviruses are somewhat mysterious viruses. Studies of blood have revealed that 80% of children aged 5–9 years have antibodies to these viruses, indicating that they have at some point been exposed to poly-omaviruses. However, it is not clear what disease this virus causes. Some evidence exists that a mild respiratory illness is present when the first antibodies to the virus are evident. The only disease that is certainly caused by polyomavirses is called progressive multifocal leukoencephalopathy (PML), a disease in which the virus infects specific brain cells called the oligodendrocytes. PML is a debilitating disease that is usually fatal, and is marked by progressive neurological degeneration. It usually occurs in people with suppressed immune systems, such as cancer patients and people with AIDS.

Hepadnaviruses

The hepadnaviruses cause several diseases, including hepatitis B. Hepatitis B is a chronic, debilitating disease of the liver and immune system. The disease is much more serious than hepatitis A for several reasons: it is chronic and long–lasting; it can cause cirrhosis and cancer of the liver; and many people who contract the disease become carriers of the virus, able to transmit the virus through body fluids such as blood, semen, and vaginal secretions.

The hepatitis B virus (HBV) infects liver cells and has one of the smallest viral genomes. A double–stranded DNA virus, HBV is able to integrate its genome into the host cell's genome. When this integration occurs, the viral genome is replicated each time the cell divides. Individuals who have integrated HBV into their cells become carriers of the disease. Recently, a vaccine against HBV was developed. The vaccine is especially recommended for health care workers who through exposure to patient's body fluids are at high risk for infection.

Parvoviruses

Parvoviruses are icosahedral, single–stranded DNA viruses that infect a wide variety of mammals. Each type of parvovirus has its own host. For instance, one type of parvovirus causes disease in humans; another type causes disease in cats; while still another type causes disease in dogs. The disease caused by parvovirus in humans is called erythremia infectiosum, a disease of the red blood cells that is relatively rare except for individuals who have the inherited disorder sickle cell anemia. Canine and feline parvovirus infections are fatal, but a vaccine against parvovirus is available for dogs and cats.

Orthomyxoviruses

Orthomyxoviruses cause influenza ("flu"). This highly contagious viral infection can quickly assume epidemic proportions, given the right environmental conditions. An influenza outbreak is considered an epidemic when more than 10% of the population is infected. In 1918, the influenza virus infected 25 million Americans and killed 22 million people worldwide in 18 months. Most people who require hospitalization due to influenza or who die from the infection are elderly individuals, especially those with a pre–existing chronic lung or heart condition. The most common complication of influenza is pneumonia.

Influenza viruses are spherical, single–stranded RNA viruses, with visible protein spikes that protrude from the capsid. Three strains of influenza virus—strains A, B, and C—cause illness in humans. Strain C causes a relatively mild illness that usually does not balloon into an epidemic. Strains A and B cause more debilitating illnesses and are the frequent cause of epidemics. These strains undergo frequent genetic mutation, so that antibodies that are made in the body against prior strains are ineffective against mutated strains. Strain A is the most common influenza virus; strain B emerges only once every 2–4 years.

A vaccine against the current strain of influenza is prepared each year. This vaccination should be performed during the fall months, so that antibodies against the virus reach optimum numbers by the winter flu season. For reasons that are not clear, flu vaccinations are only 50–60% effective in children, while in the elderly, they can be 70–90% effective. Therefore, most experts recommend that the elderly, who are most at risk for developing serious complications from flu, receive a flu vaccination every year.

Enteroviruses

The enteroviruses are icosahedral, enveloped, single stranded RNA viruses. Five types of enteroviruses cause diseases in humans, including the polioviruses (which cause polio) and echoviruses (which cause viral meningitis). Enteroviruses have an unusual replication cycle. They first enter the body through the upper respiratory tract and replicate within respiratory cells. Once the virus particles have been replicated, they are shed back into the oral secretions and are then swallowed. In the gastrointestinal tract, more replication takes place, and the viruses then enter the bloodstream. From the bloodstream, the viruses are carried to all parts of the body. However, further replication takes place only in cells for which the virus has an affinity. For example, polioviruses enter the nerve cells in the brain. There, viruses undergo further replication, and symptoms begin to appear.

Polio, the disease caused by polioviruses, is now controlled in the United States and other developed countries by the polio vaccine. However, before the introduction of this vaccine in the late 1950s, polio was one of the most feared human diseases. It causes a widespread paralysis of the muscles, sometimes including those of the respiratory system. Prolonged breathing assistance is needed for those individuals in which the respiratory muscles are paralyzed.

Echoviruses, another kind of enterovirus, cause viral meningitis, an inflammation of the nervous system. This disease is not as serious as the meningitis caused by bacteria, called bacterial meningitis.

Rhinoviruses

Rhinoviruses (from the Latin word meaning "nose") cause the common cold. They come from the same family as the enteroviruses, described above, and thus contain a single strand of RNA enclosed within an enveloped, 20–sided capsid. Interestingly, 113 types of rhinoviruses have been classified. These 113 types differ slightly in the composition of their capsids, so antibodies that are made against one type of rhinovirus are often ineffective against other types of viruses. For this reason, most people are susceptible to colds from season to season.

Paramyxoviruses

These helical, enveloped, single–stranded RNA viruses cause pneumonia, croup, measles, and mumps in children. A vaccine against measles and mumps has greatly reduced the incidence of these diseases in the United States. In addition, a paramyxovirus called respiratory syncytial virus (RSV) causes bronchiolitis (an infection of the bronchioles) and pneumonia.

Flaviviruses

Flaviviruses (from the Latin word meaning "yellow") cause insect–carried diseases including yellow fever, an often fatal disease characterized by high fever and internal bleeding. Flaviviruses are single–stranded RNA viruses.

Filoviruses

The two filoviruses, Ebola virus and Marburg virus, are perhaps the most lethal of all human viruses. Both cause severe fevers accompanied by internal bleeding, which eventually kills the victim. The fatality rate of Marburg is about 60%, while the fatality rate of Ebola virus is about 90%. Both are transmitted through contact with body fluids. Marburg and Ebola also infect primates.

KEY TERMS

· ·

Bacteriophage—A virus that infects bacteria.

Capsid—The outer protein coat of a virus.

Deoxyribonucleic acid (DNA)—The genetic material of all cells; in the nucleus, DNA transcribes RNA for the synthesis of proteins.

Envelope—The outermost covering of some viruses; it is composed of lipid and protein acquired from the host cell's plasma membrane as the virus buds out from the cell.

Eukaryote—A type of cell that contains a true nucleus.

Exocytosis—The process by which a virus "buds out" from the host cell.

Genome—The complete genetic sequence of genes within a cell or virus.

Host cell—The specific cell that a virus targets and infects.

Icosahedron—A 20-sided shape.

Lysogenic cycle—A viral replication cycle in which he virus does not destroy the host cell but co-exists within it.

Lytic cycle—A viral replication cycle in which the virus destroys the host cell.

Obligate intracellular parasite—An organism or agent, such as a virus, that cannot reproduce unless it is inside a cell.

Oncogene—A gene that encodes for growth factors; oncogenes are believed to cause the cancerous growth of cells.

Prokaryote—A type of cell without a true nucleus, such as a bacterium.

Retrovirus—A type of virus that contains double-stranded RNA and reverse transcriptase.

Reverse transcriptase—The enzyme that allows a retrovirus to transcribe DNA from RNA.

Ribonucleic acid (RNA)—Nucleic acid that is transcribed from DNA in the nucleus of cells; RNA functions in the synthesis of proteins in cells; it is also the genetic material of many viruses.

Rhabdoviruses

Rhabdoviruses are bullet-shaped, single-stranded RNA viruses. They are responsible for rabies, a disease that affects dogs, rodents, and humans.

Retroviruses

Retroviruses are unique viruses. They are double-stranded RNA viruses that contain an enzyme called reverse transcriptase. Within the host cell, the virus uses reverse transcriptase to make a DNA copy from its RNA genome. In all other organisms, RNA is synthesized from DNA. Cells infected with retroviruses are the only living things that reverse this process.

The first retroviruses discovered were viruses that infect chickens. The Rous sarcoma virus, discovered in the 1950s by Peyton Rous (1879–1970), was also the first virus that was linked to cancer. But it was not until 1980 that the first human retrovirus was discovered. Called Human T–cell Leukemia Virus (HTLV), this virus causes a form of leukemia called adult T–cell leukemia. In 1983–4, another human retrovirus, Human Immunodefiency Virus, the virus responsible for AIDS, was discovered independently by two researchers. Both HIV and HTLV are transmitted in body fluids.

See also AIDS; Bacteriophage; Botulism; Bronchitis; Cancer; Childhood diseases; Cold, common; Diphtheria; Ebola virus; Epstein–Barr virus; Hantavirus; Hepatitis; Immune system; Influenza; Meningitis; Poliomyelitis; Pneumonia; Rabies; Retrovirus; Smallpox; Tonsillitis; Vaccine; Yellow fever.

Further Reading:

Appleton, Hazel. "Foodborne Viruses." *The Lancet* 336 (December 1990): 1362.

Berns, Kenneth I., and Michael R. Linden. "The Cryptic Life Style of Adeno–associated Virus." *BioEssays* 17 (March 1995): 237.

Bloch, Alan B., et al. "Recovery of Hepatitis A Virus from a Water Supply Responsible for a Common Source Outbreak of Hepatitis A." *American Journal of Public Health* 80 (April 1990): 428.

Doerfler, Walter, and Petra Bohm, eds. *Virus Strategies: Molecular Biology and Pathenogenesis*. New York: VCH, 1993.

Fettner, Ann Giudici. *Viruses: Agents of Change*. New York: McGraw Hill, 1990.

Ganem, Don. "Oncogenic Viruses: Of Marmots and Men." *Nature* 347 (20 September 1990): 230.

Kurstak, Edouard, ed. *Control of Virus Diseases*. New York: Marcel Dekker, 1993.

Slater, P. E., et al. "Poliomyelitis Outbreak in Israel in 1988: A Report with Two Commentaries." *The Lancet*: 335 (19 May 1992): 1192.

Thomas, D. Brian. *Viruses and the Cellular Immune Response*. New York: Marcel Dekker, 1993.

Zur Hausen, Harald. "Viruses in Human Cancer." *Science* 254 (22 November 1991): 1167.

Kathleen Scogna

Viscosity

The viscosity of a fluid is a measure of its resistance to continuous deformation caused by sliding or shearing forces. Imagine a fluid between two flat plates; one plate is stationary and the other is being moved by a force at a constant velocity parallel to the first plate. The applied force per unit area of the plate is called the shear stress. The applied shear stress keeps the plate in motion and, when the plate velocity is steady, this shear stress is in equilibrium with the frictional and drag forces within the fluid. The shear stress is proportional to the speed of the plate and inversely proportional to the distance between the plates. The proportionality factor between the shear stress and the velocity difference between the plates is defined as the coefficient of viscosity or simply the viscosity of the fluid. Thick fluids such as tar or honey have a high viscosity; thin fluids such as water or alcohol have a low viscosity.

In general, viscosity is a function of temperature and pressure; however, in some fluids viscosity is dependent on the rate of shear and time. When brushed on (sheared) quickly, fluids such as paint have a low viscosity and flow easily. After paint is applied, only the slow and steady pull of its weight causes it to flow; at this slow shear rate the viscosity of paint is high and its resists the tendency to flow or sag. Fluids that behave in this manner are called non–Newtonian fluids. Other examples are liquid plastics and mud. For gases and non–polymeric liquids like water, viscosity is independent of the fluid's shear stress and history. These are called Newtonian fluids. In the case of gases, the viscosity increases with temperature because of the increased molecular activity at higher temperatures. Liquids, conversely, generally show decreasing viscosity with increasing temperature.

The flow of liquids in pipes, the performance of oil–lubricated bearings in engines or oil–filled automotive shock absorbers, and the air resistance on a moving car or airplane are all dependent on the viscosity of the fluids involved.

Vision

Vision is sight, the act of seeing with the eyes. In humans, sight conveys more information to the brain than either hearing, touch, taste, or smell, and contributes enormously to memory and other requirements for our normal, everyday functioning. Because we see

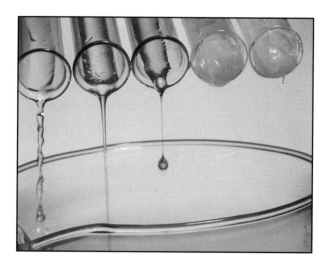

Liquids of different viscosities.

objects with two eyes at the same time, human vision is binocular, and therefore *stereoscopic*. Vision begins when light enters the eye, stimulating photoreceptor cells in the retina called rods and cones. The retina forms the inner lining of each eye and functions in many ways like film in a camera. The photoreceptor cells produce electrical impulses which they transmit to adjoining nerve cells (neurons), which converge at the optic nerve at the back of the retina. The visual information coded as electrical impulses travels along nerve tracts to reach each visual cortex in the posterior of the brain's left and right hemispheres. Each eye conveys a slightly different, two–dimensional (flat) image to the brain, which has the amazing ability to decode and interpret these images into a clear, colorful, three–dimensional view of the world.

Our 3–D view of the world

Because our eyes are separated by about 2.6 in (6.5 cm), each eye has a slightly different horizontal view. This phenomenon is called "binocular displacement." The visual images reaching the retina of each eye is a two–dimensional flat image. In normal binocular vision, the blending of these two images into one single image is called *stereopsis*, which produces a three–dimensional view (one with a sense of depth), and allows the brain to accurately judge an object's depth and distance in space in relation to ourselves and other objects.

Depth and distance perception is also available without binocular displacement and is called *monocular stereopsis*. Even with one eye closed, a car close to us will appear much larger than the same sized car a mile

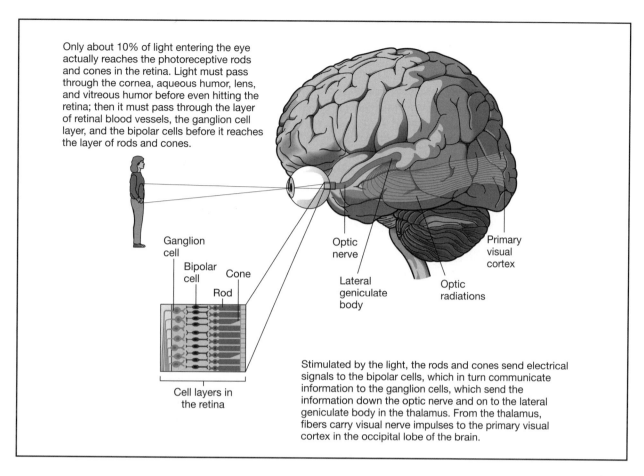

Only about 10% of light entering the eye actually reaches the photoreceptive rods and cones in the retina. Light must pass through the cornea, aqueous humor, lens, and vitreous humor before even hitting the retina; then it must pass through the layer of retinal blood vessels, the ganglion cell layer, and the bipolar cells before it reaches the layer of rods and cones.

Ganglion cell
Bipolar cell
Cone
Rod

Cell layers in the retina

Optic nerve
Lateral geniculate body
Optic radiations
Primary visual cortex

Stimulated by the light, the rods and cones send electrical signals to the bipolar cells, which in turn communicate information to the ganglion cells, which send the information down the optic nerve and on to the lateral geniculate body in the thalamus. From the thalamus, fibers carry visual nerve impulses to the primary visual cortex in the occipital lobe of the brain.

Figure 1.

down the road, or two rails of a railway line appear to draw closer together the further they run off into the distance. The ability to unconsciously and instantaneously assess depth and distance enables us to move about in space without continually bumping into objects or stumbling over steps.

Ocular dominance

Studies strongly indicate there is a *critical period* during which normal development of the visual system takes place—a period when environmental information is permanently encoded within the brain. Although the exact time frame of the critical period is not clear, it is believed that by age six or seven years, visual maturation is complete. Animal studies show that if one eye is completely covered during the entire critical period, neurons in the visual pathway and brain connected to the covered eye do not develop normally. When that eye is finally uncovered, only neurons relating to the eye that was not covered function in the visual process. This

is an example of "ocular dominance," when cells activated by one eye dominate over the cells of the other.

Memory

Just as vision plays an important role in memory, memory plays an important role in vision. The brain accurately stores an incredible amount of visual data which it draws upon every time the eyes look at something. For example, imagine fishing in a quiet stream and the cork on your line begins to bob up and down in the water. Although you cannot see under the water, your brain—from previous knowledge—remembers that a fish tugging at the worm on the hook will cause the floater to bob and tells you to pull the line in.

Electrochemical messengers

The entire visual pathway—from the retina to the visual cortex—is paved with millions of neurons. From the time light enters the eye until the brain forms a visual image, vision relies upon the process of electrochemical communication between neurons. Each neuron has a cell body with branching fibers called dendrites and a single long, cylindrical fiber called an axon. When a neuron is stimulated it sends chemicals called neurotransmitters which causes the release electrical impulses along the axon. The point where information passes from one cell passes to the next is a gap called a synapse and neurotransmitters effect the transmission of electrical impulses on to an adjacent cell. This synaptic transmission of impulses is repeated until the message reaches the appropriate location in the brain.

In the retina, approximately 125 million rods and cones transmit information to approximately one million ganglion cells. This means that many rods and cones must converge onto one single cell. At the same time, however, information from each single rod and cone "diverges" on to more than one ganglion cell. This complicated phenomenon of convergence and divergence occurs along the entire optic pathway. The brain must transform all this stimulation into useful information and respond to it by sending messages back to the eye and other parts of the brain before we can see.

Our eyes adapt to an incredible range of light intensities—from the glare of sunlight on glistening snow to the glow of moonlight on rippling water. Although the pupil regulates to some degree the amount of light entering the eye, it is the rods and cones which allow our vision to adapt to such extremes. Rod vision begins in dim light at the level of darkness and responds for up to five orders of intensity. Cones function in bright light and are responsible for color vision and visual activity.

When light hits the surface of an object, it is either absorbed, reflected, or passes through—as it does through clear glass. The amount of pigment in an object helps us determine its color. The amount of light absorbed by an object is determined by the amount of pigment, or color, contained in that object. The more heavily pigmented the object, the darker it appears because it absorbs more light. A sparsely pigmented object, which absorbs very little light and reflects a lot back, appears lighter.

Color vision

Human color perception is dependent on three conditions. First, whether we have normal color vision; second, whether an object reflects or absorbs light; and third, whether the source of light transmits wavelengths within the visible spectrum. Rods contain only one pigment which is sensitive to very dim light, and which facilitates night vision but not color. Cones are activated by bright light and allow us to see colors and fine detail. There are three types of cones that contain different pigments which absorbs wavelengths in the short (S), middle (M), or long (L) ranges. Cones are often labelled blue, green, and red, because they detect wavelengths in those color spectrums. The peak wavelength absorption of the S (blue) cone is approximately (430 nm; the M (green) cone 530 nm; and the L (red) cone 560 nm.

The range of detectible wavelengths for all three types of cones overlap, and two of them—the L and M cones—respond to all wavelengths in the visible spectrum. Most of the light we see consists of a mixture of all visible wavelengths which results in "white" light, like that of sunshine. However, cone overlap and the amount of stimulation they receive from varying wavelengths, produces a fabulous range of vivid colors and gentle hues present in normal color vision. Approximately eight percent of all human males experience abnormal color vision, or color blindness.

Actually, we do not "see" colors at all. A leaf, for example, appears green because it absorbs long– and short–wavelengths but reflects those in the middle (green) range, stimulating the M cones to transmit electrochemical messages to the brain which interprets the signals as the color green.

Optic pathway

Only about 10% of the light which enters the eye actually reaches the photoreceptors in the retina. This is because light must pass first through the cornea, pupil, lens, aqueous and vitreous humors (the liquid and gel–like fluids inside the eye) then through the blood vessels of the lining of the eye and then through two layers of nerve cells (ganglion and bipolar cells in the retina).

Visual field

The entire scene projected onto the retinas of both eyes is called the "visual field."

Optic chiasma

Synaptic transmission of impulses from retinal cells follows the optic nerve to the *optic chiasma*, an x–shaped junction in the brain where half the fibers from each eye cross to the other side of the brain. This means that some visual information from the right half of each retina (from the left visual field) travels to the right visual cortex, and visual information from the left half of each retina (from the right visual field) travels to the left visual cortex. Information from the right half of our environment is processed in the left hemisphere of the brain, and vice versa. Damage to the optic pathway or visual cortex in the left brain—perhaps from a stroke—

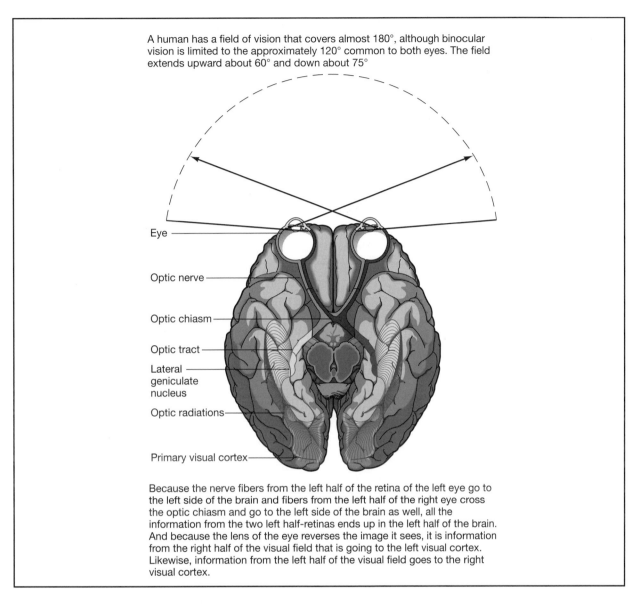

A human has a field of vision that covers almost 180°, although binocular vision is limited to the approximately 120° common to both eyes. The field extends upward about 60° and down about 75°

Eye

Optic nerve

Optic chiasm

Optic tract

Lateral geniculate nucleus

Optic radiations

Primary visual cortex

Because the nerve fibers from the left half of the retina of the left eye go to the left side of the brain and fibers from the left half of the right eye cross the optic chiasm and go to the left side of the brain as well, all the information from the two left half-retinas ends up in the left half of the brain. And because the lens of the eye reverses the image it sees, it is information from the right half of the visual field that is going to the left visual cortex. Likewise, information from the left half of the visual field goes to the right visual cortex.

Figure 2. If you were to draw a line down the center of this scene, what you observe left of that line is your "left visual field," and to the right is your "right visual field." Images from the left visual field project to the right half of each retina, and images from the right visual field project to the left half of each retina.

can cause complete loss of the right visual field. This means only information entering the eye from the left side of our environment is processed, even though information still enters the eye from both visual fields.

Visual cortex

Each visual cortex is about two inches (5 cm) square and contains about 200 million nerve cells which respond to very elaborate stimuli. In primates, there are about 20 different visual areas in the visual cortex, the largest being the primary, or *striate* cortex. The striate cortex sends information to an adjacent area which in turn transmits to at least three other areas about the size of postage stamps. Each of these areas then relays the information to several other remote areas called *accessory optic nuclei*. It is thought that the accessory optic nuclei plays a role in coordinating movement between the head and eyes so images remain focuses on the retina when the head moves.

Visual acuity

Visual acuity, keenness of sight and the ability to distinguish small objects, develops rapidly in infants between the age of three and six months and decreases rapidly as people approach middle age. Good visual acuity is often called 20/20 vision. Optometrists test visual acuity when we have our eyes examined, and poor acuity is often correctable with glasses or contact lenses. As with every other aspect of vision, visual acuity is highly complex, and is influenced by many factors.

Retinal eccentricity

The area of the retina on which light is focused influences visual acuity, which is sharpest when the object is projected directly onto the central *fovea*—a tiny indentation at the back of the retina comprised entirely of cones. Acuity decreases rapidly toward the retina's periphery. It was initially believed this was because cones decrease in number moving out from the retina, disappearing altogether at the retina's periphery where only rods exist. However, recent studies indicate it may result from the decreasing density of ganglion cells toward the retina's periphery.

Luminance

Luminance is the intensity of light reflecting off an object, and influences visual acuity. Dim light activates only rods, and visual acuity is poor. As luminance increases, more cones become active and acuity levels rise sharply. Pupil size also effects acuity. When the pupil expands, it allows more light into the eye. However, because light is then projected onto a wider area of the retina, optical irregularities can occur. A very narrow pupil can reduce acuity because it greatly reduces retinal luminance. Optimal acuity seems to occur with an intermediate pupil size, but the optimum size varies depending on the degree of external luminance. The difference in luminance reflected by each object in an image produces varying degrees of light, dark, or color. Contrast between a white page and black letters enables us to read. The greater the contrast, the more acute the visual image.

Accommodation

Accommodation is the eye's ability to adjust its focus to bring about clear, sharp images of both far and near objects. Accommodation begins to decline around age 20 and is so diminished by the mid–fifties that sharp close–up vision is seldom possible without corrective lenses. This condition, called *presbyopia*, is the most common vision problem in the world.

Common visual problems

Strabismus

Strabismus is seeing two images of a single object. Strabismus results from a lack of parallelism of the visual axes of the eyes. In one form (cross–eyes) one or both eyes turn inward toward the nose. In another form, wall–eyes, one or both eyes turn outward. A person with strabismus does not usually see a double image—particularly if onset was at a young age and remained untreated. This is because the brain suppresses the image from the weaker eye, and neurons associated with the dominant eye (ocular dominance) take over.

While the causes of strabismus are not fully understood, it appears to be hereditary, often obvious soon after birth. In many cases, strabismus is correctable. However, the critical period (probably to age six or seven years) involved in normal neuronal development of vision makes it necessary that the problem be detected and treated as early as possible.

Amblyopia

Amblyopia, or lazy eye, is the most common visual problem associated with strabismus. Amblyopia involves severely impaired visual acuity, and is the result of suppression and ocular dominance; it affects an estimated four million people in the United States alone. One study suggests it causes blindness in more people under 45 years of age than any other ocular disease and injury combined.

Other common visual problems

Slight irregularities in the shape or structure of the eyeball, lens, or cornea cause imperfectly focused images on the retina. Resulting visual distortions include *presbyopia* (far–sightedness, or the inability to focus on close objects), *myopia* (near–sightedness, in which distant objects appear out of focus), and *astigmatism* (which causes distorted visual images). All of these distortions can usually be rectified with corrective lenses.

Valuable vision

Our memory and mental processes rely heavily on sight. There are more neurons in the nervous system dedicated to vision to any other of the five senses, indicating vision's importance in our lives. The almost immediate interaction between the eye and the brain in producing vision makes even the most intricate computer program pale in comparison. Although we seldom pause to imagine life without sight, vision is the most

KEY TERMS

. . . .

Accommodation—The eye's ability to focus clearly on both near and far objects.

Cones—Photoreceptors for daylight, color vision, are found in three types, each type detecting visible wavelengths in either the short, medium, or long, (blue, green, or red) spectrum.

Ganglion cells—Neurons in the retina whose axons form the optic nerves.

Ocular dominance—Cells in the striate cortex which respond more to input from one eye than from the other.

Optic pathway—The neuronal pathway leading from the eye to the visual cortex. It includes the eye, optic nerve, optic chiasm, optic tract, geniculate nucleus, optic radiations, and striate cortex.

Rods—Photoreceptors which allow vision in dim light but do not facilitate color.

Stereopsis—The blending of two different images into one single image, resulting in a three–dimensional image.

Suppression—A "blocking out" by the brain of unwanted images from one or both eyes. Prolonged, abnormal suppression will result in underdevelopment of neurons in the visual pathway.

Synapse—Junction between cells where the exchange of electrical or chemical information takes place.

Visual acuity—Keenness of sight and the ability to focus sharply on small objects.

Visual field—The entire image seen with both eyes, divided into the left and right visual fields being what is seen respectively left and right of an imaginary line drawn down the center of each scene.

precious of all our senses. Without it, our relationship to the world about us, and our ability to interact with our environment, would diminish immeasurably.

See also Brain; Color; Depth perception; Eye; Nervous system; Perception; Vision disorders.

Further Reading:

Hart, William M., Jr., ed. *Adler's Physiology of the Eye.* St. Louis, Baltimore, Boston, Chicago, London, Philadelphia, Sydney, Toronto: Mosby Year Book, 1992.

Hubel, David H. *Eye, Brain, and Vision.* New York: Scientific American Library, 1988.

Leibovic, K.N., ed. *Science of Vision.* New York, Berlin, Heidelberg, London, Paris, Tokyo, Hong Kong: Springer–Verlag, 1990.

Lent, Roberto, ed. *The Visual System—From Genesis to Maturity.* Boston, Basel, Berlin: Birkhauser, 1992.

von Noorden, Gunter K., *Binocular Vision and Ocular Motility—Theory and Management of Strabismus.* St. Louis, Baltimore, Philadelphia, Toronto: The C.V. Mosby Company, 1990.

Marie L. Thompson

Vision disorders

Vision disorders are irregularities or abnormalities either of the eye, visual pathway, or brain, which affect one's ability to see. In healthy vision, visual acuity—often referred to as "20/20 vision"—develops rapidly by three to six months of age and generally decreases rapidly as people approach 45. Poor visual acuity is often correctable with glasses or contact lenses. However, many other factors affect human's ability to see—some preventable or correctable and others not. Vision disorders may manifest from refractive errors, defective eye muscles, cataracts, lens displacement, glaucoma, fundus conditions, color vision deficits, eyelid conditions, orbital diseases, eye injuries, and optic nerve and visual pathway damage.

Refractive errors

When parallel rays of light enter the eye they are refracted (bent) by the crystalline lens and projected into the eye. The healthy eye adjusts for distance, focusing each image perfectly on a minute hollow in the retina at the back of the eye called the fovea. In refractive errors, the image either falls short of the fovea or lands behind it. This causes blurred vision as a result of inadequate adjustment of the eye, irregular axial length (distance from the front to the back of the eyeball), or incorrect curvature of the cornea. These problems can usually be fixed with corrective lenses or surgery, which adjusts the shape of the cornea.

Hyperopia/Presbyopia

When the eye's axial length is shorter than normal, close objects appear blurry. This is called hyperopia or presbyopia, commonly termed long–sightedness. It may be latent—meaning the eye can compensate through accommodation, the ability to adjust; or it may be absolute—in which case correction requires convex or positive lenses. Around middle–age, the eye's ability to accommodate deteriorates, which is why almost all people over 45 or 50 years of age require glasses for close–up vision. Irregular curvature of the cornea or lens will produce the same deficit.

Myopia

When the axial length is longer than normal, distant objects appear blurry. This error is called myopia, or short–sightedness. Myopia can also be caused by irregular curvature of the cornea or lens, and is correctable with concave or negative lenses.

Astigmatism

Astigmatism, irregular curvature of the cornea, causes blurred vision of objects both near and far. It may be regular, which means light rays fall on the retina in two different areas, or irregular, resulting from corneal damage which projects light onto many different points on the retina. The former is correctable with lenses, the latter is not. Sometimes the faulty component is the crystalline lens and in these instances the error is called lenticular astigmatism.

Other refractive errors

While the above refractive errors may be congenital (originating at birth) or occur gradually, fast changes in the eyes' focusing ability should be investigated immediately by an ophthalmologist. Some causes may be senile cataracts (described below); diabetes mellitus—in which fluctuating blood sugar levels cause corresponding fluctuations in focus; external pressure from lumps or cysts on the eyelids distorting the shape of the cornea; subluxation (partial dislocation) of the crystalline lens causing hyperopia when it moves backward and myopia when it moves forward; and keratoconus, the thinning of the cornea allowing irregular curvature of the eyeball.

Strabismus

Strabismus comes from the Greek *strabismos* meaning twisted, and results from a lack of parallelism of the visual axes of the eyes. Often, the cause of strabismus is not known, but it appears to be hereditary and is usually obvious soon after birth. Cosmetically, strabismus causes a squint—convergence or divergence of one or both eyes from the parallel line. Sometimes the term "cross–eyed" is used to describe one or both eyes turning toward the nose, and "wall–eyed" when one or

both eyes turn outward. It may be concomitant (nonparalytic), in which the divergence or convergence remains the same no matter what way the eyes turn; or noncomitant (paralytic), which means the deviation is more noticeable when the eyes look in one direction than in another. Strabismus is often correctable if treated before the age of four or five years.

Nonparalytic strabismus

Nonparalytic strabismus is thought to be due to underdeveloped binocular reflexes within the brain resulting in diplopia, the projection of a double image of a single object to the brain. The brain does not see both images, however—particularly if onset is at a young age and remains untreated—because the visual system develops an adaptive sensory mechanisms to deal with the confusion. This mechanism is called suppression, in which the brain suppresses the image from the weaker eye and neurons associated with the dominant eye take over.

The most common problem associated with suppression is strabismic amblyopia, or lazy eye, which affects more than four million people in the United States and causes blindness in more people under 45 years of age than any other ocular disease and injury combined. If it is present at birth or occurs within the first few months, vision never develops in the affected eye. This is called amblyopia of arrest. When the problem appears during the first two or three years, it is termed suppression amblyopia.

Paralytic strabismus

Paralytic strabismus is caused by some form of interference in the transmission of motor impulses from the brain to the eye muscles. This paralysis results in limited eye movement, particularly when the eyes turn in the direction of the paralyzed muscle. When it occurs a year or more after birth, it is usually the result of diseases such as meningitis, encephalitis, and multiple sclerosis and is termed acquired paralytic strabismus. Some congenital forms are evident at birth, perhaps caused by developmental abnormalities in the neural pathway or head injury during birth.

Cataracts

A cataract is the clouding or opacity of the crystalline lens which alters the amount of light entering the eye. Developmental cataracts are relatively minor and harmless, primarily present at birth or developing in early childhood, but which can occur later in life. No reduction of in vision is noticeable with this type, which are thought to be hereditary. Congenital cataracts are present at birth and may appear as a white or grey pupil; they create a squint like that apparent in strabismus and cause visual impairment. In most instances, the cause is unknown; however, diseases and disorders contracted by the child's mother during pregnancy—such as rubella, syphilis, diabetes mellitus, or birth defects as a result of Down's syndrome, are thought to be causative. Systemic disease–associated cataracts develop as a result of such disorders as diabetes, high doses of steroids over long periods, and a dysfunctioning thyroid. Some cataracts develop secondary to ocular diseases like keratitis (inflammation of the cornea), iritis (inflammation of the iris), radiation (either from radiation therapy or the sun), or from trauma, such as intraocular surgery or penetration of the eye.

The most common cataracts are senile cataracts, a phenomenon of aging that occurs in almost all people over 65 years of age. Sometimes they develop in younger people whose nutrition is poor and are then termed pre–senile cataracts. Both types are probably caused by changes in or loss of enzyme production, which synthesizes nutrients that in turn feed the layer of cells on the lens surface. Senile cataracts grow slowly over months or years, cause no pain, usually affect both eyes, and gradually reduce visual acuity. Symptoms include two or more images from one eye, dark spots in the center of vision, extreme sensitivity to the glare of bright lights or sunshine, and reduced color vision. If not removed surgically, they eventually cause blindness.

Lens displacement

In a normal eye, the crystalline lens fits snugly behind the iris. Either complete (dislocated) or partial (subluxated) lens displacement causes the iris to wobble as the lens is not longer supporting it, or the edge of the lens may be visible through the pupil. If the lens moves forward into the anterior (frontal) chamber or backward into the posterior (rear) chamber, interrupted flow of fluid may cause glaucoma. Immediate rectification is necessary to prevent blindness in the affected eye. Posterior subluxation will also cause cataracts, and—because the lens moves about—the patient experiences rapid and frequent changes in visual acuity.

Glaucoma

Glaucoma is a serious condition which, left undiagnosed and treated, will cause permanent blindness. Glaucoma is the unrelieved increase of intraocular pressure which acts like air in a tire. In a normal eye, pressure is maintained by the continuous production of aqueous humor, its movement through the pupil into the anterior chamber, and its drainage out of the chamber.

When drainage is decreased or prevented, pressure inside the chamber increases.

Chronic simple glaucoma

Because this type occurs gradually and there is no pain or evident loss of visual acuity in the early stages, it causes more blindness word–wide than any other disease. It affects perhaps as many as 2% of the population over the age of 40 years, with the highest incidence after 60 years. This disease is inherited by approximately 10% of all children whose parents are known to be affected. Symptoms are gradual loss of close–up vision but occurring more quickly than presbyopia, and partial loss of visual field, noticeable because the patient frequently bumps into objects.

Acute glaucoma

Acute glaucoma may happen in a matter of hours and causes very fast vision loss, severe pain, and a bloodshot and watery eye. Colored haloes around lights may be visible prior to onset. It primarily affects one eye at a time, usually begins in the evening, and often after a physical or emotional trauma. It is most common in people over the age of 40 years, particularly in the 60–70 year age group. Immediate medical intervention is imperative to prevent damage to the optic nerve and subsequent blindness.

Secondary glaucomas

These are complications commonly caused by other eye diseases such as iritis, injury, blockage to the retinal vein, or long–term use of steroid eye drops for other disorders.

Fundus disorders

The fundus is the lining inside the eye which includes the retina and its blood vessels, the macula, and the optic disc. Viewed through an ophthalmoscope—a special instrument for examining the interior of the eye—the fundus appears a reddish–brown in color, the macula in the center of the retina appears as a darker red spot, and the optic disc located toward the nose side of center a lighter red. Many general health and vision–related abnormalities can be detected by examining the fundus. Congenital myopia appears as a pale crescent moon in the vicinity of the optic disc, while cloudy nerve fibers—which should be the same color as the retina—appear as a whitish patch. Both these conditions are harmless. Others, however, are not.

Vascular conditions

Blood vessels in the fundus affected by hypertension (high blood pressure) are narrow and appear quite bright. Rapid–onset or severe hypertension, which can cause strokes, may first be diagnosed when a patient seeks an eye exam for blurred vision caused by the disorder. Arteriosclerosis (hardening of the arteries) is a normal process of aging and poses no danger to vision. Central retinal artery occlusion and central retinal vein occlusion can cause sudden loss of vision in the affected eye when the blood supply to the retina is obstructed for longer than two hours, or if hemorrhaging occurs within the retina. Vision is then severely limited to light only and damage is virtually irreversible. Causes include hypertension, diabetes mellitus, narrowing of a carotid artery (the primary arteries supplying blood to the head), and blood disorders such as anemia, leukemia, and sickle–cell anemia.

Degeneration of the macula

This is primarily an age–related disorder resulting in deterioration and often distortion of vision. It is one of the leading causes of blindness in developed countries. There is no treatment; however, if detected early, laser treatment may prevent further degeneration.

Detached retina

This condition manifests with the sudden appearance of bright, floating specks and flashes of light in the affected eye with a "shadow" or "curtain" appearing later which may gradually cover the entire visual field. It occurs when part of the retina falls away from the outer layer of cells to which it is normally attached. Breaks or tears in the retina also cause similar symptoms. Although most common in people over 50 years of age, especially those with a high degree of myopia, detachment can also occur in younger people, particularly following trauma. Surgery is the only form of treatment for detachment but laser surgery for a tear or break will sometimes prevent full detachment.

Fundus inflammation and tumors

The choroid is the layer of cells over which the retina lies. Inflammation of this layer is visible through the retina and manifests as rapid onset of blurred vision—usually only in one eye—and haziness and spots over the entire field of vision. It may be caused by a parasitic protozoan infection in the bloodstream; larvae of dog tapeworms (the eggs of which may be accidentally ingested through contact with dog feces); a seriously compromised immune system—from AIDS, for example; a fungus infection called Histoplasmosis; or syphilis passed on to unborn babies.

Benign and malignant tumors

Benign melanomas produce no symptoms and usually cause no loss of vision. Malignant melanomas of the choroid occur primarily around middle–age, producing symptoms similar to those caused by a detached retina—which can occur secondary to the tumor itself—and may result in spread of cancer to the bloodstream. When localized treatment with radiation therapy is not effective, the removal of the entire eye is recommended. Retinoblastoma usually affects children within the first two years of life, is closely related to astrocytoma—a tumor of the brain—and is the only primary tumor which occurs on the retina. It manifests as a "white pupil" or squint and if treatments with radiation therapy are ineffective, the affected eye is removed.

Retinal dystrophies

Retinitis pigmentosa and macular dystrophy are degenerative disorders which appear to be hereditary, generally affect young children and adolescents, and cause night blindness, tunnel vision, slow deterioration of central vision, and increasing loss of sight. As yet, effective treatment has not been found.

Other causes

Many people, especially males, experience color blindness, varying degrees of which range from inability to differentiate between red and green to total inability to see one or more colors. Damage to any area in the visual pathway—including the optic nerve, optic tract, optic chiasm, optic radiations, or visual cortex—will cause vision deficits or loss. Although not vision disorders themselves, diseases, disorders, and damage of the eye lid, eye, and bony orbit (eye socket) may—if severe and left untreated—result in reduced, impaired, or lost vision.

See also Color blindness; Eye; Radial keratotomy; Vision.

Further Reading:

Bankes, James L. Kennerley. *Clinical Ophthalmology—A Text and Colour Atlas.* Edinburgh/London/Madrid/Melbourne/New York/Tokyo: Churchill Livingstone, 1994.

Chawla, Hector Bryson. *Ophthalmology.* Edinburgh/London/Madrid/Melbourne/New York/Tokyo: Churchill Livingstone, 1993.

Stein, Harold A., Bernard J. Slatt and Raymond M. Stein. *Ophthalmic Terminology—Speller and Vocabulary Builder.* St. Louis: Mosby, 1987.

Marie L. Thompson

KEY TERMS

Astigmatism—Irregular curvature of the cornea causing distorted images.

Cataract—Clouding of the crystalline lens.

Diplopia—Double image.

Dystrophy—Atrophy, deterioration.

Fundus—Layers lining the inside of the eye.

Glaucoma—Elevated intraocular pressure.

Hypertroia/presbyoia—Far–sighted; close objects out of focus.

Keratoconus—Thinning of the cornea.

Moypia—Near–sighted; distant objects out of focus.

Stabismus—Non–parallel eye axes.

Vitamin

Vitamins are organic substances found in food; people and animals need them in order to maintain life functions or prevent disease. About 15 different vitamin groups are necessary for the nutritional needs of humans. Only minute amounts are required to achieve their purpose, yet without them, life cannot be maintained. Some vitamins, including vitamins A, D, E, and K, are fat soluble, and are found in the fatty parts of food and body tissue. As such they can be stored in the body. Others, the most notable of which are vitamin C and all the B–complex vitamins, are water soluble. These are found in the watery parts of food and body tissue and cannot be stored by the body. They are excreted in urine and must be consumed on a daily basis.

History

Although vitamins were discovered early in the 20th century, it was common knowledge long before that time that substances in certain foods were necessary for good health. Information about which foods were necessary developed by trial and error, with no understanding of why they promoted health. Scurvy, for example, had long been a dreaded disease of sailors. They often spent months at sea and, due to limited ways of preserving food without refrigeration, their diet consisted of dried foods and salted meats. In 1746, the English naval captain and surgeon James Lind observed that 80 out of his 350 seamen came down with scurvy during a 10 week cruise. He demonstrated that this disease could be prevented by eating fresh fruits and vegetables during these long periods at sea. Because they lasted a long time, limes became the fruit of choice. In 1795, lemon juice was officially ordered as part of the seaman's diet. The vitamin C found in both limes and lemons prevented scurvy in sailors.

In 1897, Dutch physician Christian Eijkman found that something in the hulls of rice not present in the polished grains prevented the disease beriberi. Soon after, British biochemist Sir Frederick G. Hopkins fed a synthetic diet of fats, carbohydrates, proteins, and minerals (but no vitamins) to experimental rats. The rats showed poor growth and became ill, leading Hopkins to conclude that there were some "accessory food factors" necessary in the diet. Eijkman and Hopkins shared the 1929 Nobel Prize in physiology and medicine for their important work on vitamins.

Finally, in 1912 Polish American biochemist Casimir Funk published a paper on vitamin–deficiency diseases. He coined the word *vitamine* from the Latin *vita,* for life, and *amine,* because he thought that all these substances belonged to a group of chemicals known as amines. The *e* was later dropped when it was found that not all vitamins contained an amine group. Funk identified four vitamins (B_1 or thiamine, B_2, C, and D) as substances necessary for good health and the prevention of disease.

Since that time additional vitamins have been isolated from foods, and their relationship to specific diseases have been identified. All of these "accessory food factors" have been successfully synthesized in the laboratory. There is no difference in the chemical nature of the natural vitamins and those that are man–made even though advertisements sometimes try to promote natural sources (such as vitamin C from rose hips) as having special properties not present in the synthesized form.

Nature of vitamins

Vitamins belong to a group of organic compounds required in the diets of man and animals in order to maintain good health—normal growth, sustenance, reproduction, and disease prevention. In spite of their importance to life, they are only necessary in very small quantities (the total vitamins required for one day weigh about one–fifth of a gram). Vitamins have no caloric value and are not a source of energy.

Vitamins cannot be synthesized by the cells of an organism but are vital for normal cell function. Certain plants manufacture these substances, and they are passed on when the plants are eaten as food. Not all vitamins are required in the diets of all animals. For example, vitamin C is necessary for man, monkeys, and guinea pigs, but not for animals able to produce it in their cells from other chemical substances. Nevertheless, all higher animals require vitamin C, and its function within organisms is always the same.

Vitamins were originally classified into two broad categories according to their solubilities in water or in fat. As more were discovered, they were named after letters of the alphabet. Some substances once thought to be vitamins were later removed from the category when it was found that they were unnecessary or that they could be produced by the organism. Four of the better known vitamins, A, D, E, and K, are fat soluble. Other vitamins such as vitamin C and the B complex vitamins are water soluble.

This difference in solubility is extremely important to the way the vitamins function within an organism and in the way they are consumed. Fat–soluble vitamins lodge in the fatty tissues of the body and can be stored there. It is, therefore, not necessary to include them in the diet every day. Because these vitamins can be stored, it is also possible, when consumed in excess, for them to build up to dangerous levels in the tissues and cause poisoning.

The Food and Drug Administration publishes a set of nutritional recommendations called the United States Recommended Dietary Allowances (USRDA) based on the needs of the average adult. These are based on the best information available, but are less than perfect because most of the experimental work is done on animals. Because the amounts of vitamins required are so small, precise work is very difficult.

A person who eats a balanced diet with plenty of fresh fruits and vegetables should receive adequate amounts of all the vitamins. Many vitamins, however, are very sensitive to heat, pressure cooking, cold, and other aspects of food preparation and storage and can be inactivated or destroyed.

There is controversy about vitamins among experts, some of whom believe higher doses are necessary to fight off some common diseases. According to these experts, the USRDA are really minimum requirements, and higher doses will keep a person healthier. Thus, many people worldwide take vitamin supplements as insurance that they are getting all they need. Overdosage on vitamins, especially the fat–soluble ones, can cause serious side effects, and in some cases they even interfere with the proper function of other nutrients.

Vitamin A

Two very similar chemical forms of vitamin A exist: $retinol_1$ (the predominant form) and $retinol_2$. Vitamin A is present in animal tissue, mainly in liver, fish oil, egg yolks, butter, and cheese. Plants do not contain vitamin A, but they do contain beta carotene (in dark green leafy vegetables and in yellow fruits and vegetables, such as carrots, sweet potatoes, cantaloupe, corn, and peaches). Beta carotene is converted to vitamin A in the intestine and then absorbed by the body. The bodies of healthy adults who have an adequate diet can store several years' supply of this vitamin, but young children, who have not had time to build up such a large reserve, suffer from deprivation much quicker if they do not consume enough.

Vitamin A is necessary for proper growth of bones and teeth, for the maintenance and functioning of skin and mucous membranes, and for the ability to see in dim light. There is some evidence that it can help prevent cataracts and cardiovascular disease and, when taken at the onset of a cold, can ward it off and fight its symptoms. One of the first signs of a deficiency of this vitamin is "night blindness," in which the rods of the eye (necessary for night vision) fail to function normally. Extreme cases of vitamin A deficiency can lead to total blindness. Other symptoms include dry and scaly skin, problems with the mucous linings of the digestive tract and urinary system, and abnormal growth of teeth and bones.

Vitamin A is stored in the fatty tissues of the body, and is toxic in high doses. As early as 1596, Arctic explorers experienced vitamin A poisoning. In this region of extreme conditions, the polar bear was a major source of their food supply, and a quarter pound of polar bear liver contains about 450 times the recommended daily dose of vitamin A. Excessive amounts of vitamin A cause chronic liver disease, peeling of the skin of the entire body, bone thickening, and painful joints. It is nearly impossible to ingest beta carotene in toxic amounts, since the body will not convert excess amounts to toxic levels of vitamin A.

Vitamin D

Although several chemical compounds provide vitamin D activity, only two of these substances are commonly found in the diet of animals: vitamin D_2, or calciferol, and vitamin D_3. (There is no vitamin D_1 since the substance originally given this name turned out to be a mixture of compounds, one of which was calciferol.) Vitamin D_2 is produced in animal tissues when a substance called ergosterol (present in yeast and other molds) is activated by sunlight. Vitamin D_3 is produced from a similar substance called 7–dehydrocholesterol which can be obtained from the liver of various fish. It too must be activated by sunlight in order to be effective. Since 7–dehydrocholesterol is present in the skin in large quantities and only needs sunlight to be activated, vitamin D is often called the "sunshine vitamin." It is hard to suffer a deficiency if one gets enough sunshine. Irradiated ergosterol is often added to milk as an additive. Storage and food preparation do not seem to affect this vitamin.

Vitamin D lets the body utilize calcium and phosphorus in bone and tooth formation. Deficiency of this vitamin causes a bone disease called rickets. This disease is characterized by bone deformities (such as bow legs, pigeon breast, and knobby bone growths on the ribs where they join the breastbone) and tooth abnormalities. In adults, bones become soft and porous as calcium is lost.

Excessive amounts of vitamin D cause nausea, diarrhea, weight loss, and pain in the bones and joints. Damage to the kidneys and blood vessels can occur as calcium deposits build up in these tissues.

Vitamin E

Vitamin E is composed of a group of at least seven similar chemicals called the tocopherols. It is present in green leafy vegetables, wheat germ and other plant oils, egg yolks, and meat. The main function of this vitamin is to act as an antioxidant, particularly for fats. When oxidized, fats form a very reactive substance called peroxide, often very damaging to cells. Vitamin E is more reactive than the fatty acid molecule and, therefore, reacts instead of it. Because cell membranes are partially composed of fat molecules, vitamin E is vitally important in maintaining the nervous, circulatory, and reproductive systems and in protecting the kidneys, lungs, and liver.

All of the symptoms of vitamin E deficiency are believed to be due to the loss of the antioxidant protection it offers to cells. This protective effect also keeps vitamin A from oxidizing to an inactive form, and when vitamin E is lacking, vitamin A deficiency also frequently occurs. However, because vitamin E is so prevalent in foods, it is very difficult to suffer from a deficiency of this vitamin unless no fats are consumed in the diet. When it does occur, the symptoms include cramping in the legs, muscular dystrophy, and fibrocystic breast disease.

According to some current theories, many of the effects of aging are caused by the oxidation of fat molecules in cells. If this is true, then consuming extra vitamin E might counteract these effects because of its antioxidant properties.

Vitamin K

Vitamin K was identified in 1934 by Danish biochemist Henrik Dam. Later, in 1943, the Nobel Prize in physiology and medicine was awarded jointly to Henrik Dam and American biochemist Edward Doisey for their work on this vitamin.

Vitamin K is composed of two groups of compounds, vitamins K_1 and K_2. Both can be derived from a synthetic compound called menadione (sometimes referred to as vitamin K_3), which has all the properties of vitamin K. The K vitamins are found in many plants (especially green leafy ones like spinach), in liver, and in the bacteria of the intestine. Nearly all higher animals must obtain these through their diets. Although the exact method by which vitamin K works in the body is not understood, it is known that vitamin K is vital to the formation in the liver of prothrombin—one of the chemicals necessary for blood clotting.

When vitamin K deficiency develops, it is rarely due to an incomplete diet; instead, it results from liver damage and the blood's inability to the vitamin. The deficiency is characterized by the inability of the blood to clot, and manifests in unusual bleeding or large bruises under the skin or in the muscles. Drugs such as warfarin, used to treat blood clots, act by blocking the action of vitamin K and as such are double–edged swords. Newborn infants sometimes suffer from brain hemorrhage due to a deficiency of vitamin K.

Vitamin B

What was once thought to be vitamin B was later found to be only one of many B vitamins. Today, more than a dozen are known, and they are frequently referred to as vitamin B complex. Thiamine was the first of these vitamins to be identified, and it was called. All of the B vitamins are water soluble.

Each of the B vitamins acts by combining with another molecule to form coenzymes. These coenzymes then work with enzymes to perform vital activities within the cell. Their functions within the cell vary, but all are somehow related to the release of energy. The most common members of this group of vitamins include vitamin B_1 (thiamine), vitamin B_2 (riboflavin), vitamin B_6 (pyridoxine), vitamin B_{12} (cobalamin), biotin, folate (also folacin or folic acid), niacin, and pantothenic acid.

Vitamin B₁ is present in whole grains, nuts, legumes, pork, and liver. It helps the body release energy from carbohydrates. Over 4,000 years ago the Chinese described a disease we know today as beriberi, which is caused by a deficiency of thiamine. It affects the nervous and gastrointestinal system and causes nausea, fatigue, and mental confusion. Thiamine is found in the husks or bran of rice and grains. Once the grain is milled and the husks removed, rice is no longer a source of this vitamin. Manufacturers today produce "enriched" rice, flour, etc. by adding thiamine back into the milled products.

Vitamin B₂ helps the body release energy from fats, proteins, and carbohydrates. It can be obtained from whole grains, organ meats, and green leafy vegetables. Lack of this vitamin causes severe skin problems. Vitamin B₆ is important in the building of body tissue as well as in protein metabolism and the synthesis of hemoglobin. A deficiency can cause depression, nausea, and vomiting. Vitamin B₁₂ is necessary for the proper functioning of the nervous system and in the formation of red blood cells. It can be obtained from meat, fish, and dairy products. Anemia, nervousness, fatigue, and even brain degeneration can result from vitamin B₁₂ deficiency.

Niacin is required to release energy from glucose. It is present in whole grains (but not corn), meat, fish, and dairy products. Inadequate amounts of this vitamin cause a disease called pellagra, which is characterized by skin disorders, weak muscles, diarrhea, and loss of appetite. Pellagra was once common in Spain, Mexico, and the southeastern United States, where a large component of the diet consisted of corn and corn products, since niacin exists in corn as part of a large, fibrous molecule that cannot be absorbed by the blood or used by the body. However, after it was discovered that treating corn with an alkaline solution (such as lime water) releases the niacin from the larger molecule and makes it available for the body to use, pellagra became much less common.

Pantothenic acid helps release energy from fats and carbohydrates and is found in large quantities in egg yolk, liver, eggs, nuts, and whole grains. Deficiency of this vitamin causes anemia. Biotin is involved in the release of energy from carbohydrates and in the formation of fatty acids. It is widely available from grains, legumes, and liver. A lack of biotin causes dermatitis.

Vitamin C

Because of its association with the common cold, vitamin C, also known as ascorbic acid, is probably the best known of all the vitamins. Most animals can synthesize this vitamin in the liver, where glucose is converted to ascorbic acid. Humans, monkeys, guinea pigs, and the Indian fruit bat are exceptions and must obtain it from the diet. It is easily oxidized, and food storage or food processing and preparation frequently destroy its activity. Soaking fruits and vegetables in water for long periods also removes most of the vitamin C. Citrus fruits, berries, and some vegetables like tomatoes and peppers are good sources of vitamin C. The exact function of it in the body is still not well understood, but it is believed to be necessary for the formation of collagen, an important protein in skin, cartilage, ligaments, tendons, and bone. It also plays a role in the body's absorption, use, and storage of iron. It is an antioxidant and is therefore believed to offer protection to cells much as vitamin E does. There is increasing evidence that large amounts of vitamin C in the diet lessens the risk of heart disease and cancer.

A deficiency of vitamin C causes a disease called scurvy. Scurvy weakens the connective tissue in bones and muscles, causing bones to become very porous and brittle and muscles to weaken. As the walls of the circulatory system become affected, sore and bleeding gums and bruises result from internal bleeding. Anemia can occur because iron, which is critical to the transport of oxygen in the blood, cannot be utilized. Vitamin C is metabolized very slowly by the body, and deficiency diseases do not usually manifest themselves for several months.

Linus Pauling, the winner of two Nobel Prizes (one for chemistry and one for peace), believed that massive doses of vitamin C can ward off the common cold and offer protection against some forms of cancer. While scientific studies have been unable to prove this theory, they do suggest that vitamin C can at least reduce the severity of the symptoms of a cold. Some studies also suggest that vitamin C can lessen the incidence of heart disease and cancer. If this is true, it could be that the antioxidant properties of the vitamin help protect cells from weakening and breaking down much as vitamin E does. In fact, vitamins A, C, and E all play similar roles in the body, and it is difficult to distinguish among their effects.

See also Malnutrition; Nutrients; Nutrition.

Further Reading:

Cameron, Ewan, and Linus Pauling. *Cancer and Vitamin C.* Philadelphia: Camino Books, 1993.
Cooper, Kenneth H. *Antioxidant Revolution.* Nashville: Thomas Nelson Publishers, 1994.
Dan Eades, Mary. *The Doctor's Complete Guide to Vitamins and Minerals.* New York: Dell, 1994.

KEY TERMS

....

Antioxidant—A substance, such as vitamin E, that can counteract the effects of oxidation.

Beriberi—A disease caused by a deficiency of the vitamin thiamine, and characterized by nerve and gastrointestinal disorders.

Deficiency diseases—Diseases caused by inadequate amounts in the diet of some substance necessary for good health and the prevention of disease.

Fat soluble vitamins—Vitamins such as A, D, E, and K that are soluble in the fatty parts of plants and animals.

Pellagra—A disease caused by a deficiency of the vitamin niacin, and characterized by severe skin problems and diarrhea.

Scurvy—A disease caused by a deficiency of vitamin C which causes a weakening of connective tissue in bone and muscle.

Toxicity—A measure of the degree of the poisonous effect of a substance.

Water soluble vitamins—Vitamins such as C and the B complex vitamins that are soluble in the watery parts of plant and animal tissues.

Health Media of America and Elizabeth Somer. *The Essential Guide to Vitamins and Minerals.* New York: Harper Perennial, 1992.

Lieberman, Shari, and Nancy Bruning. *The Real Vitamin and Mineral Book.* Garden City Park, N.Y.: Avery Publishing Group, 1990.

Lowe, Carl. *The Complete Vitamin Book.* New York: Berkeley Books, 1994.

Leona B. Bronstein

Viticulture see **Horticulture**

Vitiglio see **Albinism**

Viviparity

Viviparity is a form of reproduction found in most mammals and in several other species. Viviparous animals give birth to living young that have been nour-ished in close contact with their mothers' bodies. Humans, dogs, and cats are viviparous animals. Viviparous animals differ from egg–laying animals, such as birds and most reptiles. Egg–laying, or oviparous, animals obtain all nourishment as they develop from the yolk and the protein–rich albumen, or "white," in the egg itself, not from direct contact with the mother, as is the case with viviparous young.

The offspring of both viviparous and oviparous animals develop from fertilized eggs, but the eggs of viviparous animals lack a hard outer covering or shell like the chicken egg. Viviparous young grow in the adult female until they are able to survive on their own outside her body. In many cases, the developing fetuses of viviparous animals are connected to a placenta in the mother's body. The placenta is a special membranous organ with a rich blood supply that lines the uterus in pregnant mammals. It provides nourishment to the fetus through a supply line called an umbilical cord. The time between fertilization and birth of viviparous animals is called the gestation period.

All mammals except the platypus and the echidnas are viviparous. Only these two unusual mammals, called montremes, lay eggs. Some snakes, such as the Garter snake, are viviparous. So are some lizards and even a few insects. Ocean Perch, some sharks, and a few popular aquarium fish, guppies, and mollies are also viviparous.

Although certain snakes give birth to live young, they are not viviparous. These snakes hatch from eggs which never leave the body of the parent snake. Because these young snakes hatch from eggs, and do not receive nourishment directly from the mother's body, this type of reproduction is called ovoviviparity. It is considered a more primitive form of reproduction than viviparity.

Even some plants, such as the mangrove and the tiger lily, are described as viviparous because they produce seeds that germinate, or sprout, before they become detached from the parent plant.

See also Birth; Embryo and embryonic development.

Vivisection

Vivisection originally meant the dissection of a live animal, usually for the purpose of teaching or research. Historically, the word came also to mean the use of a live animal in any experiment. Vivisection, especially in its broader meaning, is a time–tested tool that has helped humans understand how the bodies of animals function, how disease alters that function, and how such diseases can be treated. However, changing attitudes toward animals and a more cynical outlook toward the biomedical enterprise have caused some people to question the continued usefulness and morality of using animals for this purpose.

An ancient history

The practice of true vivisection dates back to ancient times. Around 500 BC, one of the earliest known vivisectionists, Akmaeon of Croton, discovered that the optic nerve is necessary for vision by cutting it in living animals. One of the most well known—and controversial—early vivisectionists was Galen of Pergamon, physician to Roman Emperor Marcus Aurelius. Galen, who lived in the second century AD, is remembered today for his pioneering use of vivisection of animals to understand health and disease in the human body. But Galen was also a poor scientist, failing to identify such major bodily functions as the circulation of the blood. An unquestioning adherence to Galen's false beliefs in succeeding generations of physicians was undoubtedly a major hindrance to medical progress in Europe.

Real progress in medical knowledge began again with the experiments of the Italian physicians Andreas Vesalius and his student, Realdo Colombo, in the sixteenth century. They pioneered the use of vivisection to correct and expand, rather than merely to confirm, Galen's science. In the early seventeenth century, English physician William Harvey used vivisection to discover the circulation of the blood and to debunk many of Galen's other beliefs.

But this century also saw the beginnings of an antivivisectionist movement. Physician Jean Riolan Jr. in France and Irish physician Edmund O'Meara both argued that the painful and violent deaths suffered by vivisected animals—remember, there was no anesthesia yet—were putting the animals into an unnatural state that could lead to faulty assumptions about the functioning of a healthy animal.

Also in this century, vivisection received an important philosophical boost from the French philosopher René Descartes. Descartes believed that the mind and the body are separate entities, and that animals differ from humans in that they have bodies but no true minds. As such, animals were morally no different from machines, and so vivisection was not morally wrong. Descartes even went so far as to say that animals did not feel real pain (a belief that is sometimes still repeated today, although few believe it to be true), although he stressed that vivisection was primarily defensible because it helped humans, not because hurting animals was right. Unfortunately, some of Descartes' later followers lost this fine distinction, and were known for their gratuitous cruelty to animals.

Battle lines are drawn

Around the turn of the eighteenth century, both vivisectionists and their critics gained momentum. English physicist Robert Boyle's experiments with animals in a vacuum chamber were hailed at the time for their contribution to the understanding of breathing and the function of the lungs. But also in England, the literary figures Joseph Addison, Alexander Pope, and Samuel Johnson all condemned the practice of vivisection and live animal experiments as cruel. Johnson suggested that medical students who learned to become insensitive to the suffering of animals in experiments would also become insensitive to human pain—an argument that continues to this day.

But it was the nineteenth century that saw many of today's attitudes forming. The medical advances of this era, derived at least in part from animal experiments, were profound, including widespread use of vaccination (first discovered at the end of the eighteenth century); the understanding of microorganisms as a cause of disease; the use of sterile procedures in surgery; the discovery of the diphtheria antitoxin, which could be used to save patients with that often fatal disease; and the discovery of anesthesia.

This last discovery, however, did not have as great an effect on the vivisection debate as might have been expected. For one thing, antivivisectionists argued that researchers were not using anesthesia as often as they should; they also began to argue that anesthesia was only being given at low levels, to prevent the animal from struggling, rather than the higher levels necessary to control pain. Again, these arguments are repeated today.

A major confrontation between pro–vivisection physicians and antivivisectionists came to a head in turn of the century America. This conflict was sometimes bitter, calling to mind more recent events in the debate. Antivivisectionists were accused of using out of date and misleading pictures of animals in experimental devices to garner sympathy for their cause; they also planted spies in laboratories to expose vivisectionist practices. The fight came to a head at the U.S. Senate hearings of 1896 and 1900, where testimony by some of the world's greatest medical researchers led to the defeat of a bill to regulate vivisection in the District of Columbia.

The debate today

Today the biomedical establishment and antivivisectionists are again locked in a struggle over the appropriateness of animal experimentation. The biomedical research enterprise has become a huge endeavor in the last century; in addition, the pharmaceutical, agricultural, and cosmetics industries use many animals each year to test new products and procedures. A new wrinkle in the debate is scientists' ability to genetically engineer animals—especially mice—to either lack or to contain genes related to human disease.

Present United States law does not require detailed regulation or recording of experiments involving animals except for dogs, cats, and primates, so it is difficult to estimate how many animals are involved in total. In 1991, 108,000 dogs and 35,000 cats were used in biomedical experiments in the United States. By comparison, in England, where detailed records are kept of all animal experiments, the total number of animals used in 1990 was about 3.2 million, with roughly 16,000 being dogs and cats; so we know that the total number of animals used in experiments in the United States must be very large.

Sometimes the debate today may seem a contest between scientists who oppose all regulation and animal extremists who would deny that animal research has helped human beings at all. In 1975 animal rights activist Peter Singer's book *Animal Liberation* suggested that animal research is wrong not merely because it is cruel, but because animals have the same rights as humans not to suffer. This book fueled a movement that has sometimes been violent, including groups such as the Animal Liberation Front that have threatened researchers' lives and broken into and vandalized laboratories. On the other side, occasionally one may hear a scientist voicing the Cartesian opinion that animals can't feel pain, and that the goal of medical knowledge justifies any treatment of animals.

But others have voiced more moderate views that may represent a more realistic goal for the future. Animal welfare activists seek to institute safeguards against cruelty in laboratories without banning animal research. The famous English primatologist Jane Goodall, while recognizing the importance of primate research for human health, has argued that our growing understanding of animal intelligence demands more humane con-

KEY TERMS

. . . .

Animal rights—The philosophy that animals have rights no less compelling than human rights; more extreme animal liberationists believe that no human use of animals is justified.

Animal welfare—The philosophy that humans have a moral obligation to treat animals humanely while using them for human purposes.

Animal welfare committee—A committee at an academic institution that reviews and approves research at that institution with animals.

Antivivisectionist—Someone who believes in the abolition of vivisection, and often other types of animal research as well.

Vivisectionist—A scientist who carries out vivisections or other animal experiments.

ditions in laboratories—especially for highly intelligent animals such as chimpanzees.

Both scientists and laypeople have played an important role in minimizing animal pain in research by serving on the now-required animal welfare committees at institutions engaging in government-funded research—although the political power of such committees has been claimed to vary between different institutions. And the growing use of computer simulations, tissues grown in the laboratory, and other alternatives to animal use is being hailed for its ethical as well as scientific value.

But in the end, it seems unlikely that animal research will either be abolished or will continue without further regulation. Research alternatives, while helpful, must be compared to the real thing in order to be validated: for instance, the safe testing of drugs will continue to require large numbers of animals, even when alternatives are also used. On the other hand, many animal welfare activists note that instances of cruelty and broken regulations continue to be discovered at some laboratories, and that vast numbers of animal experiments in the cosmetics and agricultural industries are hardly regulated at all.

In the end, the question may be as enduring as human beings' ability to view the same event in very different ways. The value of animal experimentation to human health and knowledge is not seriously in doubt. But past "scientific" beliefs—such as that animals cannot feel pain; that an animal rendered motionless by anesthesia cannot feel pain; and that higher animals such as dogs and primates cannot feel anxiety and fear—have been overturned by increased scientific understanding. Perhaps a dose of humility may be appropriate regarding animal research, as we cannot be certain of how our descendants will view our beliefs of today.

Further Reading:

Goodall, Jane. "A Plea for the Chimps." *The New York Times Magazine* (17 May 1987): 108–120.

Orlans, F. Barbara. *In the Name of Science: Issues in Responsible Animal Experimentation.* Oxford: Oxford University Press, 1993.

Paton, William. *Man and Mouse: Animals in Medical Research.* Oxford: Oxford University Press, 1993.

Rupke, Nicolaas A., ed. *Vivisection in Historical Perspective.* Kent, England: Croom Helm Ltd., 1987.

"The New Research Environment." [video recording] Washington, DC: The Foundation for Biomedical Research, in cooperation with the Association of American Medical Colleges and Johns Hopkins University School of Medicine, 1987.

Kenneth B. Chiacchia

Volatility

Volatility is the ease with which a substance is converted to the gaseous, or vapor, state. The term is usually used to describe the speed with which a liquid evaporates, but it can also apply to the process of a solid changing to a gas, known as sublimation. Liquids that boil at low temperatures, such as gasoline, are volatile liquids, while liquids that boil at higher temperatures, such as water, are less volatile or nonvolatile. Extremely volatile substances have such low boiling points that they exist as gases at room temperature, such as oxygen gas.

Several factors affect the volatility of a liquid. In general, larger molecules are less volatile than smaller ones among molecules that share similar composition and construction. For example, ethyl alcohol is more volatile and evaporates more readily than a larger alcohol such as decanol. Almost every chemical is more volatile at higher temperatures than at lower ones. Water, which evaporates faster on a hot day than on a cold one, is a good example of this. Volatility is also affected by atmospheric pressure. Liquids are more volatile at higher altitudes, where atmospheric pressure is less. Some substances that are liquids at sea level will evaporate very quickly on top of a high mountain, assuming no change in other factors such as temperature.

Some compounds, such as water, are extremely nonvolatile; often this is because of strong chemical bonds between the molecules—the most common of which are hydrogen bonds—that resist the tendencies of individual molecules to enter the gaseous state.

See also

Volcanic arc see **Plate tectonics**

Volcanic island see **Plate tectonics**

Volcano

A volcano is a hole in the earth's surface through which molten rock, hot gases, and rocks escape from deep in the earth. Around the holes, or vents, piles of new rock sometimes create mountains tens of thousands of feet high. They are the chimneys of Earth's interior.

Volcanic action played a large part in the forming of the earth's atmosphere, oceans, and continents. When the earth was new, the superheated gases within it streamed out through countless volcanoes to form the original atmosphere and oceans.

If a volcano is known to have erupted within recorded history, or is presently erupting, it is called "active." If a volcano is not known to have erupted within recorded history, it is called "dormant" if geologists think it might erupt again, and "extinct" if they think it will never erupt again.

How volcanoes happen

The plate tectonics of Earth's surface are the visible evidence of a planet–sized heat engine churning beneath the continents. Heating food in a pot of water over a flame causes convection currents. Convection currents carry heat from the bottom of the pot into cooler water near the surface, where some of the heat leaves the water. The cooled water sinks to be heated again, causing what is called a "rolling boil."

The consistency of Earth's mantle below a certain depth resembles thick, moldable rubber (rather than a pot of food). Materials with this consistency are said to be "plastic." Unstoppable convection currents of plastic rock in the mantle carry heat from deep inside the earth (where it is very hot), to cooler levels of the mantle at shallow depths just under the earth's crust. There the

The July 22, 1980 eruption of Mount St. Helens in southern Washington.

heat melts buried slabs of the crust that were once on the surface, and some of the uppermost rocks of the mantle. This melted rock is called magma (or lava if it is at Earth's surface), and when it moves upward and erupts into the open air or ocean, a volcano is born. A volcano, then, is like a chimney that spews heat from out of the planetary furnace.

As magma rises in the mantle and crust, it goes through a process called fractional cystallization (not the same thing as distillation, but it is also one liquid being altered to become another liquid). Because different minerals crystallize at different temperatures, certain minerals form from magma earlier than others. This leaves behind a magma with a slight different composition than when the minerals first began to crystallize because some elements are now depleted. Therefore, the minerals that crystallize later, and the rocks that they form, will be of a different composition than those that form earlier. Fractional crystallization is believed to be a very important way to produce rocks of different compositions from the same magma.

Some magma comes from partial melting of buried pieces of the crust. This process is similar to what happens to a big piece of cheese when it is overcooked in a microwave oven. If you imagine the cheese is a buried slab of earth's crust, then magma is melted out of the slab of crust just the same as butterfat is melted out of cheese solids. A buried piece of the crust is heated by the friction of two continents colliding with each other, and the minerals in it that melt more easily become magma.

This recycled–crust magma moves up toward the earth's surface in a rising blob. Erupted rocks made out of re–melted continental crust appear red, brown, or gray in color. These are called felsic rocks because they are rich in the minerals feldspar and quartz (which is composed of silica). Rhyolite is one of these rocks.

Other magmas emerge on the surface rich in iron and magnesium minerals, blacker and hotter than continental magmas. These are called mafic magmas, and they come from the mantle, barely changed in composition by fractional crystallization. Basalt is a rock formed from mafic magma.

Most volcanoes are formed at one of two locations. Most of the visible volcanoes on earth form wherever there is impact and friction between the plates that make up Earth's crust, that is, along subduction zones. However, thousands of submarine volcanoes occur where new plate is being created at this very moment — along the mid–oceanic ridges.

Mid–oceanic ridges are chains of volcanoes and smaller volcanic vents located at submarine spreading centers. New ocean crust is being formed at these ridges, forcing the two sides of the existing crust or plate to be pushed apart as new crust forms. Where the rate of plate formation is rapid, older crust is quickly pushed out of the way, and only small volcanic vents form. Where the spreading rate is slower, volcanic eruptions may form volcanoes. The mid–oceanic ridges form continuous, winding "seams" that completely encircle Earth. Obviously, as Earth is not increasing in girth, this new plate must be matched by destruction of older plate elsewhere. "Elsewhere" is along subduction zones at the plate margins.

Around the Pacific plate, which is being overrun by the plates surrounding it, are a great number of volcanoes known as the Ring of Fire. This overrunning, or subduction, causes partial melting by forcing the oceanic crust downward into the very hot, super–dense, plastic interior of the Earth. Subduction zones are therefore sources of the magma that spews from many of the world's volcanoes. The volcanoes of the western coast of North and South America, Indonesia, the Philippines, Japan, Kamchatka, and the Aleutians all sit atop subduction zones. In addition to volcanoes, subduction zones are a phenomenon attended by earthquakes, the uplift of mountains and plateaus, and the concentration of mineral deposits essential to industrial civilization.

A few volcanoes are also formed at hot spots. A hot spot is an upwelling of heat from beneath the earth's crust, possibly caused by a disturbance at the boundary between the solid mantle and the liquid outer core of Earth's interior. Hot spots appear on the surface in only one place at any one time, so they are a different phenomenon than the long, sinuous mid–oceanic ridges. But just because hot spots don't look like mid–ocean ridges does not prove that their causes are unrelated. Some

A volcanic cinder cone and lava flow in northern Arizona.

famous hot spots are: Hawaii, Yellowstone National Park (U.S.), Iceland, Samoa, and Bermuda.

Hot spots give us some of our best evidence for global plate tectonic motion, because they clearly show that the continents have been moving, and show the directions in which they moved. Plate motion shows itself in this way: when heat from a hot spot rises out of the mantle and burns the underside of a continent, it burns a hole in it just like a cigar would burn right through a newspaper and typically raises a volcano on the surface. If tectonic forces move the continent while the hot spot is active, the surface evidence of the hot spot will move away with the continent. The hot spot, which doesn't move, will begin to burn through a fresh piece of continent near the first burned–through spot. In this way, the hot spot makes a volcanic "record" of the continent's movement. The Hawaiian Islands mark the track of a hot spot, over which the Pacific Plate has been pushed and dragged in a northwesterly direction, toward Japan. The Snake River Plain traces the progress of the Yellowstone hot spot as it moved under Idaho, scorching holes in it and erupting the lava that makes the Snake River Plain a fertile farmland.

Different kinds of eruptions

Volcanoes are classified by the material they usually erupt. But different eruptive products often come out of the same volcano. Lavas, pyroclastics, and volatile substances are all produced in volcanic eruptions.

Lava flows are fluid streams of hot liquid rock spilled out onto Earth's surface by a volcano or fissure. Two common types of lava have been distinguished in the Hawaiian language. The Hawaiian words adopted into English to describe these different lava rocks are aa (pronounced AH–ah), also called "blocky" lava, and pahoehoe (pronounced pa–HOY–hoy) or "ropy" lava. Aa forms from thicker, more slow moving lava than pahoehoe. This helps explain the more irregular, jagged appearance of aa as compared to the smooth, wavy surface of pahoehoe. Aa lava solidifies into brittle, irregular or "chunky" blocks on the top of the lava flow: blocks move forward by the fluid motion of the flow and fall off the front; these blocks then form a "driveway" over which the flow stiffly rolls, much like a bulldozer's treads. Pahoehoe (or pillow lava, deep under the sea) solidifies into smooth shapes, looking like rope or toothpaste. When it is forming deep under water under enough pressure that boiling cannot occur, the lava emerges in the form of blobs called pillow lava.

Pyroclastia ("firey fragment") deposits are formed from volcanic debris during explosive eruptions. Explosive eruptions happen when magma containing water or gases (or magma that has been in contact with ground water) rises near enough to the surface that the pressure of the rock above it can no longer keep the volatile content of the magma from boiling. Once the volatile stuff starts to boil, nothing can keep it from emerging violently into the atmosphere——and tearing everything between it and the surface into pieces. These pieces are called pyroclastics, and they are the form most commonly taken by erupting felsic magma. Tephra is the term used to describe any kind of pyroclastic material. Several kinds of pyroclastic deposits are:

An ash fall is a rain of pumice and glass dust (volcanic ash) from a cloud of ash, which covers the ground surface evenly, like snow. Ash falls sometimes cover large portions of continents with ash, thinning with distance from the volcano.

A pyroclastic flow is a dense wave of ash, superheated gases and rock that moves as a fluid from an erupting volcano, crossing the landscape and filling valleys with the fluid mixture. This material deflates as it cools. The rock formation that results is called an ignimbrite, and the rock is called tuff. Ignimbrites can cover hundreds of square kilometers of landscape, such as the Mitchell Mesa Tuff of West Texas . The pyroclastic flows from the prehistoric eruption of Taupo, in New Zealand, produced deposits that washed over the tops of hills hundreds of meters tall. A pyroclastic surge is a variety of pyroclastic flow that results from magma encountering ground water close enough to the surface to boil. Also called nuee ardente, a French word meaning "glowing cloud," this was the kind of eruption that destroyed the city of St. Pierre, on Martinique, in 1902. The volcano that is formed by this kind of eruption is called a maar or tuff ring—a very shallow volcano, shaped by small, powerful steam blasts.

Volatile substances are gaseous elements or compounds that are able to escape from the earth's interior during eruptions. The Latin root word for volatile means "winged," and the hydrogen sulfide, water, fluorine, carbon dioxide, radon, and other gases in the magma quickly fly into the atmosphere upon eruption. Large amounts of volatiles in the magma can cause violent explosive eruptions.

Different kinds of volcanic structures

As new rock forms around a volcano's vent, it takes a shape according to the kind of erupted material.

A shield volcano is a broad and rounded volcano made of stacks of runny basaltic lava, which usually forms in the middle of oceanic plates or on continental rifts. These volcanoes resemble the round shields that warriors of ancient times used to protect themselves in battle. The tallest individual mountain on Earth — the island of Hawaii — is a shield volcano. This volcanic island slopes gently down from the 13,796 ft (4205 m) summit of Mauna Kea to the ocean abyss more than 30,000 ft (9,144 m) below. Kenya's Mt. Kilimanjaro, the tallest mountain in Africa, is a shield volcano, as is Olympus Mons, the tallest mountain on the planet Mars. Mountains very much like shield volcanoes have been mapped on the planet Venus by the Magellan spacecraft's radar mapping expedition. Shield volcanoes are known for extruding immense amounts of lava and burying huge areas, but not for violent explosive eruptions.

A stratovolcano, or composite volcano, is a steep–sided volcano made of alternating sequences of lava and tuff, usually found on plate boundaries. Japan's Mt. Fuji is a stratovolcano, as are the Cascade mountains of the American west coast, Mt. Ararat in the Caucasus, and Popocatepetl, near Mexico City. Stratovolcanoes build up over a few million years, and then often collapse in a cataclysmic event, forming a gigantic boiling hot crater — a caldera.

A cinder (or scoria) cone is a steep–sided volcano made of pyroclastic material, a huge pile of rocks that are not melted together. The rocks are blown out of the ground as an incandescent liquid, and cool into cinders in the air, falling in a heap. Landslides sculpt the sides of the still–hot heap of rocks, forming such cinder cones as Mexico's Paricutin, New Mexico's Mt. Capulin, and Arizona's Sunset Crater.

A diatreme is an unusual volcano shaped like an ice cream cone stuck in the ground, a diatreme erupts magma from depths as deep as 200 mi (322 km), where diamonds exist as the normal form of carbon. Because a diatreme may sit on top of a feeder pipe of solidified magma with diamonds in it, diatremes attract the attention of prospectors around the world. The most famous diatreme is the Kimberley Diamond Pipe in the Republic of South Africa. No active diatremes exist today.

Fissure and flood eruptions often have so much magma rise to the surface at once that it pours out of huge cracks in the ground called fissures. Instead of building a mountain in one place, the fissure floods broad areas with basalt lava. This volcanic feature is called a flood basalt. A fissure eruption happened in Iceland in 1783, and the resulting environmental catastrophe wiped out one–fifth of its population. Fissure eruptions have:

- Filled the Rio Grande Rift with hundreds of feet at Taos, New Mexico.

- Built the huge Columbia River Plateau in Washington and Oregon.

- Covered southern India with approximately one million cubic kilometers of basalt to form the Deccan Traps 65 million years ago.

- Formed the Siberian Flood Basalt plateau in northern Russia 250 million years ago, the largest flood basalt in the world.

Some of these catastrophic eruptions happened at the same time great extinctions occurred. No conclusive evidence has been found for a connection between fissure eruptions and global extinction, but there is no doubt that the vast amount of gases and heat released would affect environmental conditions for the worse all over the planet's surface. No amount of pollution produced by humans today could be compared to the amount of natural poisons and pollution released in a large fissure eruption.

Calderas

The most violent, large volcanic eruption is the collapse of a stratovolcano. This local apocalypse normally happens on the active margins of tectonic plates, that is, at subduction zones or along a continental rift valley (where a continent is breaking apart). The process involved in the destruction of a stratovolcanos starts with a mass of molten rock, several miles wide and under high pressure, that rises in the earth's crust and forces its way through cracks all the way to the surface. A stratovolcano is born in clouds of ash and supersonic steam explosions filling the air with hot rock, ash, gases, and noise.

After a series of eruptions, perhaps over millions of years, the volcano has formed a pile of lava and pyroclastic material as much as 2–3 mi (3–4 km) high.

Eventually, there is one more eruption of ash and pyroclastic flows. The stiff, gooey magma begins to boil. The bubbles expand the magma to many times its original volume, and it explodes upward. As it boils, lava is thrown out of the volcano's "exhaust pipe," the vent. Now the boiling and exploding process moves deeper and deeper through the magma in the vent. In a short time, the magma far below the mountain begins to boil explosively and rush furiously out of the vent, the liquid rock floating in superhot gases. The magma

chamber, itself the size of a huge mountain, is rapidly emptied onto the landscape above.

Emptying the magma chamber removes all the hydraulic pressure from it. That hydraulic pressure supported the mountain, allowing it to sit above the magma chamber for millions of years. The monstrous underground room is now unsupported. Cracks open all around the broad base of the mountain as its last structural supports give way. The whole mountain begins to fall into the magma chamber. The result is a caldera, a mountain–sized hole in the ground alive with boiling, exploding ash and superhot gases, into which a tall, scenic volcano has been dropped. Each piece of the mountain that falls into the caldera sends great waves of pyroclastic flows surging out of the caldera, covering and burning the surrounding landscape. Entire local biological communities can be wiped out, and the old landscape they lived in is buried and altered. Ash in the upper atmosphere will circle the globe, causing weather effects worldwide.

Volcanic catastrophes and volcanic benefits

When Mt. St. Helens erupted in 1980, it flattened a forest and killed 57 people, and countless animals and trees. Numerous volcanoes erupt around the world every century, usually in sparsely populated areas. Even so, volcanoes have threatened human civilization throughout history, and will do so as long as people live on the earth's often–violent surface. As the runaway world population tries to find more places to live, more and more people will find themselves living under a volcano.

Today, volcanologists can warn civil authorities to prepare to move a population out of danger. Mt. Pinatubo, a stratovolcano in the Philippine Islands, erupted explosively in 1991. The successful evacuation of the people who had lived under it proved the worth of volcanology as a practical branch of geological science. But those who study it have a huge task before them, because volcanoes threaten humans in a great variety of ways—as these examples show from ancient and modern history.

Mt. Mazama, formerly in southern Oregon, and Mt. Shasta, in California, erupted simultaneously nearly 7000 years ago, culminating in the collapse of Mazama to form Crater Lake. The story of the eruption evolved into a myth, The Battle of Llao and Skell, and was passed from one generation to the next. In 1865, the myth was translated to English, and, in the twentieth century, geologists found the myth to be an accurate description of the collapse of a stratovolcano—nearly 250 generations ago.

The island of Santorini in the Aegean Sea erupted around 1500 BC, leaving a huge caldera. Archaeologists speculate that this natural catastrophe, along with earthquakes, may have been partially responsible for the collapse of Aegean civilization at that time. Tidal waves would have crushed entire coastal towns throughout the region, much as was the fate of coastal settlements around Krakatau's caldera eruption in 1883.

An ash fall from Mt. Vesuvius buried the Roman city of Pompeii in 79 AD. The volcano struck down the people where they lived, and preserved the shapes of their bodies where they fell in the ash. Pompeii is a remarkable volcanic disaster because we can see what the people looked like, and because much of the city was preserved, along with the names, portraits, writings, and even jokes of those who lived there. Plaster casts were made of them as the city was excavated in the late 1700's. The realistic casts of human bodies evoke more empathy from people than lists of tens of thousands of victims of other eruptions—of whom nothing remains. The nearby city of Herculaneum was covered by a pyroclastic flow that destroyed it in seconds.

Kuwae, in Melanesia, erupted in 1453. A legendary chieftain hastily assembled the population, evacuating them to safety in a last–minute evacuation very much like Dunkirk in World War II. The eruption destroyed all remaining life on the previously inhabited island, and tore the island into several pieces. Decades after the caldera eruption, the people returned to the new archipelago of which Epi and Tongoa are the principal islands. Eruptions of this size affect weather and climate worldwide, and cause peculiar optical effects in the atmosphere. Ash in the stratosphere causes the sky to appear strangely colored, and sunlight to be dimmed. Some geologists speculate that the eruption's optical effects in 1453 may have filled the defenders of Constantinople with superstitious dread, hastening the city's doom. Constantinople's siege and overthrow by the Turks that year hastened the age of commercial exploration by Portugal, Spain, Holland, France, and England—and the discovery of America.

The Laki fissure eruption of 1783 produced huge volumes of fluorine gas which poisoned the grass that fed Icelanders' flocks. Approximately 229,000 animals died of fluoridosis, and 10,000 Icelanders starved to death, reducing the population by one–fifth. Benjamin Franklin observed the blue haze that covered Europe, and deduced that the pollution from the eruption must have caused the abnormally cold winter that year.

Tambora, an Indonesian stratovolcano, erupted and collapsed in 1815, chilling the world for the next year in the "year without a summer." This is because the explosion shattered 25 mi (40 cubic km) of rock—enough rock to make a cube–shaped mountain, on each of whose sides four Districts of Columbia could be pasted—and filled the stratosphere with it. Tambora's collapse killed 10,000 people, and another 80,000 starved to death as a result of environmental damage to cropland.

Krakatau, another Indonesian stratovolcano, erupted and collapsed in 1883, causing worldwide cooling similar to Tambora. The collapse was heard by people 2,484 mi (4000 km) away. Tidal waves killed 36,000 people in coastal Java and Sumatra. Spectacularly weird sky phenomena from this eruption included brilliant green sunrises and moonrises in the equatorial latitudes, followed by blue sunlight all day long—and bright green sunsets.

There have been larger caldera eruptions in the geologic past than in this list, which might cause much greater climatic changes than anything the human race has ever experienced. There are many volcanoes likely to erupt catastrophically in the near future. Some of them are located in the world's most populous areas: Seattle, Washington; Guadalajara, Mexico; the Bay of Naples, Italy; and Rabaul, Papua–New Guinea.

Volcanic benefits

The eruption of volcanoes through geologic time built the continents we live on. Some of the world's richest farmland soil draws its fertility from minerals provided by nearby volcanoes. The heat of magma boils water into steam that spins the turbines of geothermal power stations. Geothermal stations now light electric power grids in Iceland, Italy, New Zealand and a few other places. Enough heat flows from the world's volcanic regions and mid–oceanic ridges to power industrial civilization for several hundred million years. This power source awaits only the development of feasible geothermal technology.

Volcanoes, particularly collapsed calderas, develop hydrothermal systems when groundwater or rainwater seep into the volcano. Cold water seeps into the volcano, and quickly heats up. Far underground, water does not boil into steam as it does on the surface due to the higher pressure. Liquid water can be heated so hot that metallic minerals dissolve in it. As the hot water rises through the volcano, through faults and shattered zones, it cools to a temperature where metallic minerals no longer remain dissolved. Crystallizing like rock candy, the minerals accumulate in the passages through which the cooling water flows, clogging the passage like an arteriosclerotic blood vessel. These passages often fill with minerals, and become veins in the rock.

KEY TERMS

Aa—A blocky or chunky lava flow that moves like a bulldozer's treads.

Ash fall—A layer of pumice and pulverized pumice (volcanic ash) that falls out of a cloud of ash and evenly coats the ground surface.

Cinder cone—Also called scoria cone. A steep–sided volcano made of pyroclastic material, a cinder cone (or scoria cone) is a huge pile of rocks that are not melted together, as is lava. The rocks are blown out of the ground as an glowing–hot liquid, and cool into cinders in the air, falling in a heap.

Convection current—The motion of a fluid that rises as it is heated and sinks as it cools, moving in a circular path.

Diatreme—An unusual volcano, shaped like an ice cream cone stuck in the ground; a diatreme erupts magma from depths as deep as 200 mi (322 km) and may contain diamonds.

Fissure—A crack that pours out a tremendous amount of lava in a very brief time, usually forming a flood basalt.

Hot spot—An upwelling of heat from beneath the earth's crust, possibly caused by a disturbance at the boundary between the solid mantle and the liquid outer core, that is not related to the heat currents associated with the mid–oceanic ridge. Lava flows—Fluid streams of hot liquid rock (magma) spilled out onto the Earth's surface by a volcano or fissure.

Lava—Hot liquid rock at the Earth's surface. This is the same material as magma, except for its location.

Magma—Hot liquid rock beneath the Earth's surface, originating in the continental crust and/or the mantle.

Pahoehoe—A lava that solidifies into smooth shapes, looking like rope or toothpaste. When it is forming under enough water pressure that boiling cannot occur, the lava emerges in the form of heaps of blobs called pillow lava.

Pyroclastic—Said of material erupted from a volcano which is made up of lots of pieces: pumice, ash, blobs of molten rock called bombs, and solid boulders.

Pyroclastic flow—A dense wave of superheated air and rock that moves as a fluid from an erupting volcano, sometimes crossing thousands of square kilometers of landscape, and filling valleys with the fluid mixture.

Pyroclastic surge—Also called nuee ardente, or glowing cloud. A variety of pyroclastic flow that results from magma encountering ground water close enough to the surface to boil.

Ring of Fire—The regions that surround the Pacific Ocean and are overriding the Pacific plate, which experience frequent earthquakes and volcanoes.

Mid–oceanic ridge/rift system—A long (40,000 mi; 64,000 km) crack in the earth's crust where new crust is continuously made, causing ocean basins to grow wider.

Shield volcano—A broad and rounded volcano made of stacks of runny basaltic lava, usually formed in the middle of oceanic plates or on continental rifts.

Stratovolcano—A steep–sided volcano made of alternating sequences of lava and tuff, usually found on plate boundaries. Sometimes called composite volcanoes.

Subduction zone—Boundaries between plates of the earth's crust where one of the plates gets forced downwards into a long trench, drawn into the earth by its own weight, as a less dense plate runs over it, a phenomenon attended by earthquakes, volcanoes, and the uplift of mountains and plateaus.

Tephra—A term used to describe any material produced in an explosive volcanic eruption.

Tuff—The rock of a volcanic ash deposit.

In this way, economically valuable minerals such as the ores of molybdenum, silver, and gold concentrate at easily accessible depths in the earth's crust.

See also Plate tectonics; Igneous rocks; Island; Magma; Tectonics.

Further Reading:

Coffin, M. and Eldholm, O. "Large Igneous Provinces." *Scientific American* 269 (1993): 42–49.
Decker, Robert, and Decker, Barbara. *Volcanoes*. New York: W. H. Freeman and Co., 1989.

Grove, N. "Crucibles of Creation." *National Geographic* 182 (1992): 2–41.

Harris, Stephen. *Fire Mountains of the West.* Missoula: Mountain Press Publishing Co., 1988.

Kerr, R. "Volcanologists Ponder a Spate of Deaths in the Line of Duty." *Science* 260 (1993): 289–290.

Wood, D. "Waiting for Another Big Blast." *Canadian Geographic* 113 (1993): 22–34.

Clinton Crowley

Voles

Voles are small mouselike mammals in the family Cricetidae, order Rodentia. Other members of this family include the gerbils, hamsters, lemmings, and the American rats and mice (but not the Old–World mice and rats, which are in the family Muridae). Voles occur in a wide range of open, often grassy habitats, such as alpine and arctic tundra, prairies, savannahs, and pastures and other types of agricultural fields.

Voles have a body length of about 3–5 in (8–12 cm), and typically weigh 1.1–1.8 oz (30–50 g), with mature males being slightly larger than females. Voles have a stout, plump body, a small head, blunt nose, small eyes, short ears, a short neck, and a short, stubby tail. Their pelage is dense, and is typically colored brownish or greyish.

Voles are herbivores, eating a wide range of plant tissues, especially the shoots and rhizomes of grasses and sedges. Voles typically live in tunnels and runways that they dig in the ground and surface litter, equipped with numerous resting dens and food–storage areas. These tunnels are often lived in by communal groups of voles. The runways are kept free of obstructions, and the voles are intimately familiar with the twists and turns of these paths. Consequently, voles can move along their runways much faster than they can run along the ground surface. This is an important advantage when these small animals are attempting to flee from a predator.

Voles remain active throughout the year. During the winter, voles develop tunnels beneath the snow at the snow–ground interface, and they feed on rhizomes and food that they have stored from the previous autumn.

Populations of voles often irrupt in a cyclic fashion, with regularly occurring years of great abundance punctuated by longer periods of time during which these small animals may be rather scarce. Some species of voles have enormous potential for population growth because of their intrinsic fertility. For example, females of the common vole (*Microtus arvalis*) of Europe can become sexually mature before they are two weeks old, and while they are still suckling on their mother's milk! Potentially, a female vole can give birth to her first litter of four to seven young when she is only five weeks old. One captive common vole bore 33 litters, and had a total of 127 young. Because these animals breed more or less continuously during the growing season, and sometimes even in the winter, their population growth rates are potentially enormous.

What prevents an unmitigated growth of voles is mortality associated with predation, coupled with unfavorable environmental conditions, such as the availability of adequate food. In most cases, it appears that the most important ecological factors that allow rapid population growth in voles is the availability of an abundance of food, associated perhaps with relatively favorable growing conditions for one or several years.

Voles are always an important prey item for many species of predators. However, when voles are abundant, they are avidly hunted by virtually all small predators, including weasels, foxes, owls, and hawks, and even some larger animals such as wolves and bears.

Voles are sometimes considered to be pests, because they can cause serious damages to crops growing in fields, and to stored grains and other foods. These damages are caused by the actual eating of foods, as well as by the contamination of stored grains with vole feces, which can render the crops unsalable.

North American voles

There are about 50 species of voles. Most voles are included in the genus *Microtus*. The meadow vole (*M. pennsylvanicus*) is the most common and widespread species of vole in North America, occurring through most of Canada south of the high arctic tundra, and in most of the northern United States. The meadow vole is a familiar species of fields, wet meadows, and disturbed forests. Because of its wide distribution and periodic irruptions of abundance, the meadow vole is both ecologically important as a component of ecological food webs, and economically important as an occasional pest.

The tundra vole (*Microtus oeconomus*) is another widespread species, occurring in arctic tundra and open boreal forests of Alaska, Yukon, and Eurasia. The woodland vole (*M. pinetorum*) is widespread in forests of southeastern North America. The montane vole (*M.*

KEY TERMS

. . . .

Herbivore—An animal that only eats plant tissues.

Irruption—A term in population ecology, used to refer to an event of great abundance of a species.

montanus) occurs in alpine grasslands and tundras of the mountains of the western United States. The prairie vole (*M. ochrogaster*) occurs in the grasslands of the interior of the continent, while the rock vole (*M. chrotorrhinus*) occurs in boulder slopes and other rocky places in northeastern North America. The chestnut-cheeked vole (*M. xanthognathus*) occurs in local populations in the boreal forest of northwestern North America. The long–tailed vole (*M. longicaudus*), singing vole (*M. miurus*), Townsend's vole (*M. townsendii*), Richardson's vole (*M. richardsoni*), and California vole (*M. californicus*) are all species of coniferous forests of western North America.

The heather vole (*Phenacomys intermedius*) occurs widely in boreal and northern temperate forests of Canada and the northwestern United States. This species is very similar in appearance to the meadow vole, and was overlooked as a distinct species by most field biologists until the 1950s, when reliable, diagnostic characters were discovered (these involve the shape of the cheek teeth).

The northern red–backed vole (*Clethrionomys rutilus*) occurs in tundra and open boreal forests of northwestern Canada and Alaska, and also in Siberia and eastern Scandinavia. There is also a disjunct population in coniferous rain–forests of Oregon and Washington. Gapper's red–backed vole (*C. gapperi*) occurs more widely throughout temperate North America, reaching as far south as the mountains of Arizona.

The sagebrush vole (*Lagurus curtatus*) occurs in high altitude sagebrush steppes and semi–deserts of southwestern North America. Richardson's water vole (*Arvicola richarsoni*) is a species of alpine meadows and streams of the Rocky Mountains.

See also Rodents.

Further Reading:

Banfield, A.W.F. *The Mammals of Canada*. Toronto, Ont.: University of Toronto Press, 1974.
Paradiso, J.L. (ed.). *Mammals of the World*, 2nd ed. Baltimore: John Hopkins Press, 1968.
Wilson, D.E. and D. Reeder (comp.). *Mammal Species of the World*. Washington, D.C.: Smithsonian Institution Press, 1993.

Bill Freedman

Volt see **Units and standards**

Voltage see **Electric circuit**

Volume

Volume is the amount of space occupied by an object or a material. Volume is said to be a derived unit, since the volume of an object can be known from other measurements. In order to find the volume of a rectangular box, for example, one only needs to know the length, width, and depth of the box. Then the volume can be calculated from the formula, $V = l \times w \times d$.

Volume of most physical objects is a function of two other factors, temperature and pressure. In general, the volume of an object increases with an increase in temperature and decreases with an increase in pressure. Some exceptions exist to this general rule. For example, when water is heated from a temperature of 0°C to 4°C, it decreases in volume. Above 4°C, however, further heating of water results in an increase in volume that is more characteristic of matter.

Units of volume

The term unit volume refers to the volume of one something: one quart, one milliliter, or one cubic inch, for example. Every measuring system that exists defines a unit volume for that system. Then, when one speaks about the volume of an object in that system, what he or she means is how many times that unit volume is contained within the object. If the volume of a glass of water is said to be 35.6 cubic inches, for example, what is meant is that 35.6 cubic inch unit volumes could be placed into that glass.

Mathematically, volume would seem to be a simple extension of the concept of area, but it is actually more complicated. The volume of simple figures with integral sides is found by determining the number of unit cubes that fit into the figure. When this idea is extended to include all possible positive real numbers, however, paradoxes of volume occur. It theoretically is possible to take a solid figure apart into a few pieces and reassemble it so that it has a different volume.

The units in which volume is measured depend on a variety of factors, such as the system of measurement being used and the type of material being measured. For example, volume in the British system of measurement may be measured in barrels, bushels, drams, gills, pecks, teaspoons, or other units. Each of these units may have more than one meaning, depending on the material being measured. For example, the precise size of a "barrel" ranges anywhere from 31 to 42 gallons, depending on federal and state statutes. The more standard units used in the British system, however, are the cubic inch or cubic foot and the gallon.

Variability in the basic units also exists. For example, the "quart" differs in size depending on whether it is being used to measure a liquid or dry volume and whether it is a measurement made in the British or customary U.S. system. As an example, 1 customary liquid quart is equivalent to 57.75 cubic inches, while 1 customary dry quart is equivalent to 67.201 cubic inches. In contrast, 1 British quart is equivalent to 69.354 cubic inches.

The basic unit of volume in the international system (often called the metric system) is the liter (abbreviated as L), although the cubic centimeter (cc or cm^3) and milliliter (mL) are also widely used as units for measuring volume. The fundamental relationship between units in the two systems is given by the fact that 1 U.S. liquid quart is equivalent to 0.946 L or, conversely, 1 liter is equivalent to 1.057 customary liquid quarts.

The volume of solids

The volume of solids is relatively less affected by pressure and temperature changes than is that of liquids or gases. For example, heating a liter of iron from 0°C to 100°C causes an increase in volume of less than 1%, and heating a liter of water through the same temperature range causes an increase in volume of less than 5%. But heating a liter of air from 0°C to 100°C causes an increase in volume of nearly 140%.

The volume of a solid object can be determined in one of two general ways, depending on whether or not a mathematical formula can be written for the object. For example, the volume of a cube can be determined if one knows the length of one side. In such a case, $V = s^3$, or the volume of the cube is equal to the cube of the length of any one side (all sides being equal in length). The volume of a cylinder, on the other hand, is equal to the product of the area of the base multiplied by the altitude of the cylinder. For a right circular cylinder, the volume

is equal to the product of the radius of the circular base (r) squared multiplied by the height (h) of the cone and by pi (π), or $V = \pi r^2 h$.

Many solid objects have irregular shapes for which no mathematical formula exists. One way to find the volume of such objects is to sub–divide them into recognizable shapes for which formulas do exist (such as many small cubes) and then approximate the total volume by summing the volumes of individual sub–divisions. This method of approximation can become exact by using calculus. Another way is to calculate the volume by water displacement, or the displacement of some other liquid.

Suppose, for example, that one wishes to calculate the volume of an irregularly shaped piece of rock. One way to determine that volume is first to add water to some volume–measuring instrument, such as a graduated cylinder. The exact volume of water added to the cylinder is recorded. Then, the object whose volume is to be determined is also added to the cylinder. The water in the cylinder will rise by an amount equivalent to the volume of the object. Thus, the final volume read on the cylinder less the original volume is equal to the volume of the submerged object.

This method is applicable, of course, only if the object is insoluble in water. If the object is soluble in water, then another liquid, such as alcohol or cyclohexane, can be substituted for the water.

The volume of liquids and solids

Measuring the volume of a liquid is relatively straight forward. Since liquids take the shape of the container in which they are placed, a liquid whose volume is to be found can simply be poured into a graduated container, that is, a container on which some scale has been etched. Graduated cylinders of various sizes, ranging from 10 mL to 1 L are commonly available in science laboratories for measuring the volumes of liquids. Other devices, such as pipettes and burettes, are available for measuring exact volumes, especially small volumes.

The volume of a liquid is only moderately affected by pressure, but it is often quite sensitive to changes in temperature. For this reason, volume measurements made at temperatures other than ambient temperature are generally so indicated when they are reported, as V = 35.89 mL (35°C).

The volume of gases is very much influenced by temperature and pressure. Thus, any attempt to measure or report the volume of the gas must always include an indication of the pressure and temperature under which

KEY TERMS
. . . .

British (customary) system—A system of measurement long used in many parts of the world, but now used commonly only in the United States among the major nations of the world.

Displacement method—A method for determining the volume of an irregularly shaped solid object by placing it in a measured amount of water or other liquid.

International (metric) system—A system of measurement used by all scientists and in common practice by almost every nation of the world.

Unit volume—The basic size of an object against which all other volumes are measured in a system.

that volume was measured. Indeed, since gases expand to fill any container into which they are placed, the term volume has meaning for a gas *only* when temperature and pressure are indicated.

David E. Newton

Vulcanization

Vulcanization is the process by which rubber molecules (polymers or macromolecules made of repeating units or monomers called isoprene) are cross–linked with each other by heating the liquid rubber with sulfur. Cross–linking increases the elasticity and the strength of rubber by about ten–fold, but the amount of cross–linking must be controlled to avoid creating a brittle and inelastic substance. The process of vulcanization was discovered accidentally in 1839 by the American inventor Charles Goodyear (1800–1860) when he dropped some rubber containing sulfur onto a hot stove. Goodyear followed up on this discovery and subsequently developed the process of vulcanization. In 1844, Goodyear was issued United States Patent #3644.

Rubber as a natural product

Natural rubber comes from the rubber tree (*Hevea brasiliensis*) and is a white, milky liquid called *latex*. Most rubber comes from Malaysia and other nations in East Asia. Latex can also be seen as the white fluid in

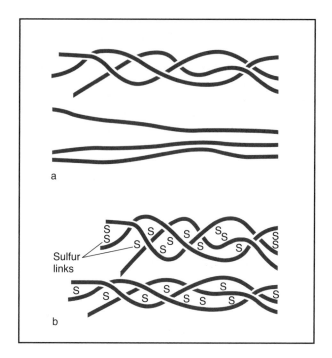

Figure 1. The process of vulcanization.

dandelion stalks. The latex from the tree is actually a suspension of rubber particles in water. Rubber is a polymer (long chain made of repeating units) of isoprene. Natural rubber is relatively reactive, and is especially vulnerable to oxidation.

Vulcanization and properties of vulcanized rubber

In the process of vulcanization, the added sulfur allows some C–H bonds to be broken and replaced by C–S bonds. The process of vulcanization cross–links the chains or polyisoprene to each other. The cross–linked molecules created a three–dimensional network of rubber. Each cross–link is a chain of about 8 sulfur atoms between two long chains of polyisoprene.

Vulcanized rubber is about ten times stronger than natural rubber and is also about ten times more rigid. However, it is still very elastic, which means that is can be stretched reversibly. Polymers that are elastic are sometimes called elastomers. The optimum amount of sulfur to be added to the rubber is about 10% by weight. Adding an excess of sulfur produces a very brittle and inelastic substance called ebonite. Man–made or synthetic rubber can also be vulcanized, and the process is similar.

Figure 1 shows what happens to rubber when the long chains of polyisoprene are cross–linked. In part a,

KEY TERMS

....

Elastomers—Polymers with elastic (reversible stretching) properties.

the macromolecules are bent and randomly arranged. In part b, the chains are cross–linked but still randomly arranged. The molecules become aligned when the rubber is stretched. If the individual chains were not cross–linked, each chain could slide freely past each other.

See also Polymer.

Further Reading:

"Feeling Bad–Latex Sensitivity." *The Economist* 32 (14 November 1992): 105.

Smith, Emily, T. "Rubber That's So Tough it Goes the Extra Mile." *Business Week* (11 February 1991): 80.

Walker, Jearly. "Why are the First Few Puffs the Hardest When You Blow up a Balloon?" *Scientific American* (December 1989): 136.

Louis Gotlib

Vultures

Vultures are large birds of prey that are specialized to scavenge the bodies of dead animals. Species of vultures are assigned to two families in the order Falconiformes. The vultures of the Americas include seven species in the family Cathartidae. The vultures of Eurasia and Africa, numbering 14 species, are specialized members of the Accipitridae, a family that also includes hawks and eagles. The Cathartidae and the Accipitridae are not closely related.

Biology of vultures

Although the vultures of the Cathartidae and Accipitridae have evolved from different ancestral stock, the two groups occupy broadly similar ecological niches. As a result, the vultures in these families are highly convergent in many aspects of their biology and ecology. All vultures have very broad wings with marginated primary feathers at the tips that allow them to soar at great heights and position themselves in thermals, thus flying for hours with little effort. This is a very useful ability for animals with excellent eyesight,

because they can scan for carrion over great expanses of terrain. Once most vultures become airborne, it is unusual to see them flap their wings. In fact, most species are rather weak at active flying, and they sometimes appear to be straining their capabilities when they are taking flight from the ground.

All vultures have a hooked beak. The neck muscles and beak of vultures are too weak to tear the tough skin of recently dead, large animals, but they are able to deal with carcasses that have had some time to decompose. Until this happens, only the eyes of the dead animal, apparently a delicacy among vultures, can be eaten. Vultures have long, clawed toes, but their feet cannot grasp with much strength. Because of their relatively weak beaks and feet, these birds survive almost entirely by scavenging dead animals, and increasingly in many areas, the refuse of human towns and habitations.

Vultures rarely kill anything. They are rather timid when confronted by a living adult animal, even if the creature is obviously unwell, and therefore a potential meal. In such a situation, vultures will typically wait patiently nearby until the animal dies before they begin to eat. However, vultures have been known to attack relatively helpless, recently born, young animals.

Vultures are binge eaters of the first order. Their prey of dead animals is not always plentiful, and these birds sometimes must pass a rather long time between meals. However, when a large corpse is available, vultures will avail themselves of it to the fullest possible degree. Under such conditions, vultures can sometimes become so engorged with ingested carrion that they are unable to fly. If they are disturbed when thus grounded, vultures must lighten their load so that they can become airborne. They do this by regurgitating their food, representing a case of reluctant avian bulimia.

The vultures of the Cathartidae and Accipitridae are significantly different in several respects. One of the obvious distinctions of the American vultures is their perforate nasal septum, which means that when one is looking at a sideways profile of the head of these birds, daylight can be clearly seen through their paired nostrils. Vultures of Eurasia and Africa do not have this trait, and they are generally heavier billed. The Old World vultures have an ancient evolutionary lineage, extending to at least 30 million years, whereas it appears that the American vultures evolved much more recently than this.

It appears that at least some of the American vultures have an excellent sense of smell, a very rare and unusual trait among birds. The turkey vulture (*Cathartes*

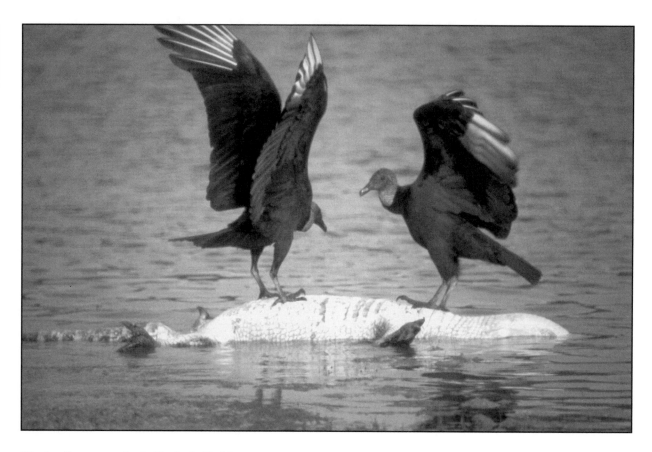

Black vultures on a dead alligator in Florida.

aura), for example, has the largest olfactory system of any bird. There is also a great deal of behavioral evidence that a sense of smell is a significant aid to vultures in finding their food of dead animals. This ability is especially useful for vultures that find some of their fragrant food of carrion in relatively closed–canopied ecosystems, such as shrublands and forests.

Most species of vultures have a featherless, naked head. This is likely an adaptation that facilitates sanitation, because these birds often have to reach far into a decomposing carcass in order to feed. Most species with naked heads have brightly colored and patterned, warty skin on their neck and head, which is important in species recognition and in courting and aggressive interactions. The male Andean condor (*Vultur gryphus*) has a large, fleshy structure known as a caruncle on the top of its naked head, seemingly bizarre to humans, but undoubtedly most alluring to females of the species.

The courtship rituals of American vultures generally involve open–winged strutting on the ground, followed by impressive displays of aerial soaring and gliding. Vultures are monogamous, and both sexes brood the eggs and care for the young. Vulture chicks mature

slowly, taking up to six months to leave the nest, in the case of the Andean condor.

Some old–world vultures have evolved unusual behaviors that help them with aspects of their feeding. The lammergeier or bearded vulture (*Gypaetus barbatus*) of Eurasia and Africa is known to drop large bones onto rocks, in order to break them open so that the nutritious, internal marrow can be eaten. The Egyptian vulture (*Neophron percnopterus*) is known to pick up stones in its beak, and throw them at ostrich eggs to break them, so that the contents can be eaten.

Species of vultures

The most widespread vulture in the Americas is the turkey vulture (*Cathartes aura*), which ranges from southern Canada to South America. This species is migratory in the northern part of its range, often travelling in flocks of several hundred birds. The black vulture (*Coragyps atratus*) is another common species that breeds from southern North America to South America. The only other species of vulture in North America is the California condor (*Gymnogyps californianus*), an endangered species on the edge of extinction.

Other vultures occur in South America. The largest species is the increasingly rare Andean condor, which has a wingspread of three meters, the largest of any living bird. This species, which can weigh more than 14 lb (6.5 kg), is also the heaviest flying bird.

A now–extinct American vulture was the very impressive *Terratornis mirabilis*, which had an enormous wing span of at least 16 ft (5 m). This species is known from fossils collected at the Rancho La Brea tar pits of southern California. *Terratornis mirabilis* may have still been around as recently as the end of the most recent glacial epoch, about 10,000 to 15,000 years ago. This enormous vulture may have become extinct as an indirect consequence of the disappearance at that time of many large species of mammals, an event that was likely due to the first colonization of the Americas by very effective human hunters.

Vultures and humans

As scavengers of dead animals, vultures provide an important ecological service. This has long been recognized by some human societies, which have viewed vultures as useful birds because they contribute to cleaning up some types of unpleasant refuse around habitations. However, in some places these views have recently changed and the presence of these scavengers is no longer encouraged. This has happened, for example, in parts of the Andes, where vulture dropping has been shown to contribute to the contamination of open reservoirs of drinking water with microbial pathogens.

Species of vultures have had great cultural significance to various groups of people. The Maya of Central America commonly used a hieroglyphic associated with the king vulture (*Sarcoramphus papa*) to signify the thirteenth day of each month, and this species also appears to have been a religious symbol. The Andean condor was also culturally important to indigenous peoples over large parts of its range. In regions of India, vultures are given access to human corpses within secluded, walled facilities. This custom is a cultural acknowledgement of the continuity of life and death, and of the relationships of humans with other species and ecosystems.

Unfortunately, because of their feeding habits vultures are regarded with great distaste in some other human cultures. Until rather recently, vultures were erroneously thought to be responsible for spreading some important, contagious diseases of livestock, because they fed on the bodies of animals that had died of those maladies. Vultures have sometimes been shot or poisoned in large numbers for this reason. One American farmer claimed to have shot 3,500 black vultures during a single winter, in an attempt to relieve himself and his ranch of this harmless bird, which he perceived as a pest. Fortunately, vultures are rarely treated this way in North America any more, although they are still persecuted in some other areas, usually by a few misguided people.

The California condor is a critically endangered species of vulture. This species was formerly widespread in North America, especially in the west. However, this slowly reproducing species has declined enormously in abundance because of hunting and poisoning, and until recently it only survived in a critically endangered population of a few birds in the San Joachin Valley of southern California. In 1984, only 15 birds survived, and by 1986 there were only three adult male California condors. The few surviving wild condors are still under threat from shooting, from lead poisoning following ingestion of lead bullets in scavenged carrion, from poisons set to kill agricultural pests such as coyotes, and from habitat degradation.

In 1987, no California condors remained in the wild. The handful of surviving wild condors were caught for use in a captive–breeding program, with the hope that enough birds could be produced to allow the eventual re–introduction of this endangered species into the wild. At that time the total population of the species was only 27 individuals, all in captivity. These last California condors are being used in a program of captive breeding supported by the United States Fish and Wildlife Service, and located at the San Diego Wild Animal Park and the Los Angeles Zoo. Fortunately, this breeding program is showing encouraging signs of success, and in 1991 the first, careful releases of California condors were made to a large ecological reserve created and managed for their benefit in southern California.

The California condor remains a critically endangered species, but there is now guarded optimism for its longer–term prospects of avoiding extinction.

See also Birds of prey; Condors.

Further Reading:

Ehrlich, P.R., D.S. Dobkin, and D. Wheye. *Birds in Jeopardy.* Stanford, CA: Stanford University Press, 1992.
Freedman, B. *Environmental Ecology.* 2nd ed. San Diego: Academic Press, 1994.
Harrison, C. J. O., ed. *Bird Families of the World.* New York: H.N. Abrams, 1978.

Bill Freedman

Vulva see **Reproductive system**

W

Waders see **Shore birds**

Wagtails and pipits

Wagtails and pipits are 48 species of terrestrial birds that make up the family Motacillidae. Species in this group occur on all of the continents but Antarctica. The usual habitat of these birds is deserts and semi–deserts, prairies, tundras, shores, and cultivated fields. Many species are migratory, with northern species travelling to the tropics to spend their non-breeding season, and alpine species moving to lower–altitude valleys and lowlands.

Wagtails and pipits are slender birds, with a body length of 5.1–86.7 in (13–22 cm). They have pointed wings, a long tail, long, slim legs, rather long toes and claws, and a thin, short, straight beak.

Pipits are typically colored in streaked or mottled browns, and the sexes are similar. Wagtails are brighter colored, with bold patterns of yellow, black, and white, and males being brighter than females. The tail of both types is commonly edged with white feathers, and it is wagged frequently as the bird walks, particularly by the well–named wagtails. The flight of these birds is undulating.

These birds hunt on the ground, by walking and searching for their food of small insects, other invertebrates, and seeds, especially during the winter.

Courtship in wagtails and pipits includes song–flights, which feature the male making a rapid ascent, and then undertaking a slower, fluttering, tinkling descent. Wagtails and pipits nest on the ground in a small cupshaped nest woven of plant fibers. The clutch size can range from two to seven, with high–latitude species having a larger number of eggs, and tropical species fewer. Both sexes of wagtails incubate the eggs, but in the pipits only the females do. Both sexes of pipits and wagtails cooperate in feeding the young.

The most widespread species in North America is the water pipit (*Anthus spinoletta*). This bird nests in alpine and arctic tundras. It spends its nonbreeding season in prairies and agricultural fields of the southern United States and Central America, generally occurring as seed–eating flocks of various size. The water pipit also breeds in arctic and alpine tundras of Eurasia.

The Sprague's pipit (*A. spragueii*) breeds in the mixed–grass and short–grass prairies of central North America, and winters in Arizona, Texas, and Louisiana, and as far south as southwestern Mexico.

The yellow wagtail (*Motacilla flava*) breeds in western Alaska and the northern Yukon, and much more widely in northern Eurasia. This species has a number of well–defined subspecies, and these have created some confusion among taxonomists, who in the past have treated certain of these subspecies as full species. The type occurring in Alaska is a subspecies of northeastern Siberia and the Beringean region, known as *Motacilla flava tschutschensis*. The white wagtail (*M. alba*) is another species that breeds widely in northern Eurasia, while also breeding in Greenland and western, coastal Alaska.

Bill Freedman

Wahoo *see* **Tuna**

Walkingsticks

Walkingsticks are insects with a long, thin body, lengthy delicate legs and a brown–green color which

A female walking stick.

gives them a striking resemblance to a twig. Walking-sticks are in the family Phasmidae in the order Orthoptera, which also includes the grasshoppers and crickets. There are almost 2,500 species of walking-sticks (phasmids), ranging in size from 1 in (2.5 cm) to one foot (30 cm), the largest species occurring in the tropics. Some phasmids resemble leaves (rather than twigs) and are called leaf insects.

All species of phasmids are herbivorous and are found on or near vegetation. Often, a phasmid will look like the plant on which it is feeding, an adaptation known as protective resemblance, which blends these insects with their surroundings and protects them from predation. Walkingsticks not only resemble twigs, they also walk with an odd, rocking motion which makes them appear to be a stick being blown in the wind. If phasmids are attacked by a predator then delicate legs

break off so the insect can escape. Some species of phasmids when attacked spray a foul–smelling fluid from glands on their thorax. In large numbers, phasmids can cause extensive defoliation damage to trees, but these insects are otherwise harmless.

After copulation, female phasmids simply lay their eggs while feeding, scattering them on the ground. Some species project their eggs with a flick of the abdomen while others place their eggs in a protected crack or crevice. The eggs usually hatch within two years. Thus, the majority of walkingsticks are usually found every second year. Young phasmids (nymphs) resemble adult insects, and grow in a series of stages (instors) to the adult stage, a type of development known as incomplete metamorphosis.

Wallabies *see* **Kangaroos and wallabies**

Walnut family

The walnut family contains about 60 species of trees in the family Juglandaceae, divided among seven genera. North American representatives are the walnuts (*Juglans* spp.) and hickories (*Carya* spp.). All of these species produce edible nuts and useful wood, and some are cultivated in orchards for the production of these crops.

Biology of walnuts

Species in the walnut family are woody plants that develop as trees, and mostly grow in angiosperm–dominated forests in temperate and subtropical climates. The range of most species is the Northern Hemisphere, although a few species penetrate to the Andes of South America and the southwest Pacific.

The wood of trees in the walnut family is strong and resilient and is highly prized as lumber. The twigs have a chambered pith which is visible in a longitudinal cross–section.

Species in the walnut family have prominent, hairy buds and seasonally deciduous, compound leaves which are shed in the autumn. The flowers are small and greenish. The staminate flowers occur in catkins, while pistillate flowers occur individually. The ripe fruit of the hickories and walnuts is properly termed a drupe in which their large, hard–coated seed is encased in a leathery case. The fruits of walnuts and hickories are edible.

An interesting characteristic of the black walnut and some related species is their ability to apparently poison the soil in their immediate vicinity. Few plants are able to grow beneath a large walnut tree, an observation attributed to the presence of a toxic alkaloid known as juglone. Even walnut seedlings cannot normally grow beneath a parent tree. The production of phytotoxic chemicals by plants for use in a type of chemical warfare with other competing plants is known as allelopathy. Black walnut is often cited by ecologists as an archetypal, allelopathic species.

Species of walnuts

Six species of walnuts occur in North America. The black walnut (*Juglans nigra*) and butternut (*J. cinerea*) are widespread in eastern North America. The little walnut (*J. microcarpa*) and Arizona walnut (*J. major*) range into Texas and Arizona and south into Mexico. The California walnut (*J. californica*) and Hinds walnut (*J. hindsii*) have relatively localized dis-

Pecans growing on a tree (above). Ripened pecans showing nut meat (below).

tributions in southern California. The English walnut (*J. regia*) is native to Europe and Asia but has been widely planted in North America.

Twelve native species of hickories occur in North America. The most famous species is the pecan (*Carya illinoensis*). This species occurs naturally throughout the central United States and south through eastern Mexico, but is now cultivated more widely throughout the eastern United States. Other species that are widespread in southeastern North America are the shagbark hickory (*C. ovata*), mockernut hickory (*C. tomentosa*), pignut hickory (*C. glabra*), and bitternut hickory (*C. cordiformis*).

Economic importance

Various species of walnuts and hickories are economically important trees for both their wood and their edible fruits which may be gathered in the wild but are now mostly grown in plantations.

KEY TERMS

. . . .

Compound leaf—A leaf in which there are several or many leaflets, independently attached to the leaf axis, or rachis.

Drupe—A fleshy fruit, containing a single, hard seed. A cherry is a typical example, but the fruit of a walnut is also a drupe.

Nut—A generic term for a dry, one–seeded fruit with a hard coat which is usually quite difficult to open.

Pith—A large–celled tissue that is found inside of the roots or stems of certain species. Members of the walnut family have a chambered pith in which the tissue is separated into discrete zones of solid tissue and air chambers.

The wood of Black, English, and other walnuts is close–grained, dark–brown colored, and very strong. Walnut wood is used to manufacture lumber and veneers for fine furnitures and cabinets, and it is sometimes carved into components for artisanal furniture. A well–formed tree of black walnut with a good grain and solid core can be worth more than $12,000 as raw material for fine lumber or veneer. Because of this enormous per–tree value, walnut trees are sometimes illegally "rustled" from private or public property to be sold in a black market.

Hickories also provide an excellent hard wood, used to manufacture fine furniture and wooden baseball bats.

The best–known edible fruits harvested from species in the walnut family are those of the European or English walnut (*Juglans regia*), the Black walnut (*J. nigra*), the Pecan (*Carya illinoensis*), and the Hickory (*Carya ovata*). The first three of these species are commonly grown in plantations established for the production of their fruits. When they reach a large size, the walnuts may be harvested from the plantations for their extremely valuable wood. However, this is not done for pecans because their wood does not have qualities that are as desirable as those of large walnut trees.

The most important use of the fruits of walnuts and hickories is directly for eating. However, fresh walnut seeds contain about 50% of their weight as oil, which can be expressed from these fruits and used as an edible oil or to manufacture soap, perfume, cosmetics, or paint.

Walnuts have sometimes been used as minor folk medicines. The inner bark of the black walnut can be used as a laxative, while the fruit rind has been used to treat intestinal parasites, ulcers, and syphilis. An infusion of boiled leaves has been used to get rid of bedbugs.

The doctrine of signatures was a medicinal theory that developed in Europe during the Middle Ages (about 500 to 1,500 years ago), but also occurred independently in some other cultures. This theory held that the potential usefulness of plants for medical purposes was revealed through the growth form of the plant or its parts. For example, a similarity between the form of the plant or its parts and some component of the human anatomy was commonly thought to reveal a signature of usefulness. When the hard, outer shell of a walnut is removed, the seed looks superficially like a human brain, viewed from above with the top of the skull removed. Consequently, it was believed that walnuts were somehow useful for the treatments of insanity and headaches.

Further Reading:

Brockman, C.F. *Trees of North America* New York: Golden Press, 1968.

Klein, R.M. *The Green World. An Introduction to Plants and People*. New York: Harper and Row, 1987.

Woodland, D.W. *Contemporary Plant Systematics*. New York: Prentice–Hall, 1991.

Bill Freedman

Walruses

The walrus (*Odobenus rosmarus*) is one of the largest members of the seal family, order Pinnipedia. Although similar in many respects to other seals, particularly the eared seals, the walrus is sufficiently different to merit being placed in its own family, Odobenidae. It is the sole member of that family, with only a few subspecies. The genus name is derived from the Greek words for "tooth" and "I walk"—thus, "tooth walker," which refers to the walrus's use of its tusks to haul out on ice floes. The species name is derived from the Scandinavian word for walrus.

Walruses are found along the coast of the Arctic Ocean, where they spend most of their time on the seasonal pack ice. (If ice is unavailable, they will gather on land.) They are often found as far south as Nova Scotia, the Aleutians, and the White Sea, and stray individuals have been recorded in more temperate waters, including coastal Massachusetts, Ireland, southern England, France, and even northern Spain.

Walruses (*Odobenus rosmarus*) on Round Island, Alaska.

Among the seals, the walrus is second in size only to the elephant seal. They vary in size according to location; the smallest walruses are found in Hudson Bay, the largest in the Bering and Chukchi seas. Hudson Bay males average 9.5 ft (2.9 m) in length and weigh about 1,753 lbs (795 kg), and the females are about 8.2 ft (2.5 m) long and weigh an average of 1,246 lbs (565 kg). In the Bering Sea population, the adult males are about 10.5 ft (3.2 m) long and weigh in at 2,668 lbs (1,210 kg) and the females are 8.9 ft (2.7 m) long and 1,830 lbs (830 kg).

It is impossible to mistake a walrus for anything but a walrus. First are its distinctive tusks, present in both sexes. Tusk length, like body size, varies among populations, but can exceed 39 in (100 cm) in males and 32 ft (80 cm) in females. The tusks—actually the walrus's canine teeth—grow throughout life. The tusk is almost purely dentine (ivory), which has made the walrus a target of human beings. Although fearsome weapons, the tusks are mostly used as ice axes, for when the animal hauls itself out of the water onto ice floes, and as social signals, much like deer's antlers. The size and shape of tusks differs between males and

females, so it is likely that walruses use these clues to determine sex and age.

Its body is massive. The head, which appears to be set directly on the animal's trunk, is round and the skull is very thick, and the walrus often uses it as a battering ram to break through ice up to 8 in (20 cm) thick. The deeply folded skin is 1.2–1.6 in (3–4 cm) thick, and underlain by a 4 in (10 cm) layer of blubber. In females and young males, the skin is covered with coarse hair of about 0.4 in (1 cm) long, which gives them a soft, velvety look. Older males are nearly hairless, and their thick, folded skin is bare on their necks and shoulders. When an old male hauls himself out of the Arctic water, he may be nearly white; as the sun warms him, though, his skin will turn a rosy shade of pink. The skin is particularly thick on the male's neck, where it can be up to 2.4 in (6 cm). Males also have a pair of pouches extending off the pharynx. When inflated, these pouches produce a distinctive bell–like sound, and help the male float.

The walrus has four flippers, each with five digits. The flippers are thick and cartilaginous. All the flippers have bare, warty soles that provide good traction on ice. Like the eared seals, the walrus can rotate these flippers forward and use them to walk. In the water, however, the walrus propels itself almost entirely with its hind flippers, using the foreflippers only to steer. They swim at an average speed of about 4.3 mi/h (7 km/h), and can reach 21.7 mi/h (35 km/h). However, they are generally not great migrators, and seem to prefer to hitch rides on ice floes that drift with the currents. Dives last about two to ten minutes; the average depth is 32–164 ft (10–50 m), and the deepest known dive was to 262 ft (80 m).

The walrus's eyes are small, and its external ears are mere folds of skin. While these senses may not be particularly good, it is the sense of touch the walrus gets from its distinctive moustache that it depends on most to find food. The moustache, found in both sexes, is composed of about 450 sensitive whiskers.

The whiskers help the walrus detect the bottom–dwelling organisms on which it feeds. Bivalve mollusks such as clams comprise the bulk of the typical walrus's diet. Once the walrus noses the mollusk out of the mud (it is an old wives' tale the walrus uses its tusks to dig up mollusks), it sucks the creature out and spits the shell back into the mud. Thousands of mollusks may make up a meal. The diet also includes crabs, octopus, sea cucumbers, polychaete worms, tunicates, fish, and occasionally, birds. Some individuals have been known to hunt other seals and even whales.

Walruses are gregarious. They seem to enjoy nothing more than sunbathing in great agglomerations called haul–outs. These haul–outs are generally all male or all female during the nonbreeding season, and within them several thousand walruses will lie close together. Within a haul–out there is a hierarchy with the largest animals with the largest tusks at the top. A dominant animal need just show its tusks to a subordinate and the latter will generally move along; sometimes there is violence, but generally there is no lasting injury.

Mating occurs during January and February, in the water, and the female can delay implantation of the fertilized egg until July. The calf is born 10 or 11 months later, about 138.9 lbs (63 kg) in weight, 44.5 in (113 cm) in length, and tuskless. Mothers and calves share a strong bond, and the mother is very protective. Unlike in the eared seals, walrus mothers do not leave their calves for long periods. However, females will "babysit" each other's young, and even adopt orphans. Calves remain with their mothers for 2 years. Females are sexually mature between ages 6 and 7; males mature later, at around 8 to 10, but they generally cannot compete for females until they reach their full

growth at around age 15. Females are full grown between 10 and 12. Walruses can live about 40 years.

Walruses have been hunted for thousands of years by native Arctic peoples, who used all parts of the animal—skin, fat, flesh, bones–for clothing, fuel, food, tools, and boats. Then Europeans realized the walrus was an easy–to–kill source of oil, ivory and skins. By the mid–1800s, Atlantic subspecies (*O. r. rosmarus*) had vanished at many locations they had traditionally visited. This subspecies has never fully recovered from this onslaught; about 30,000 North Atlantic walruses remain. During the 19th century, Western hunters turned their attention to the Pacific subspecies (*O. r. divergens*), and thousands of animals were killed. On the Pribilof Islands alone hunters took 35,280 lbs (16,000 kg) of walrus ivory. *O. r. laptevi,* the walrus of the Laptev Sea, is considered rare, as it numbers only between 4,000 and 5,000 animals.

Although both the United States and Russia have prohibited hunting except by native peoples, some conservationists contend that this "sustenance" hunting is now primarily commercial. Poaching has increased since the international moratorium on elephant ivory. Between poaching and the legal killing of 10,000 to 15,000 walruses each year, the population of all walruses could be cut in half during the 1990s.

Other than human beings, walruses have few natural enemies; they include polar bears, but walruses are quite good at fending them off.

F. C. Nicholson

Wandering jew *see* **Spiderwort family**

W and Z bosons *see* **Subatomic particles**

Warblers

Warblers are small, perching song birds with a large number of species distributed throughout the world. There are two familes of warblers, one in the New World and one in the Old World. The New World warblers (family Parulidae) comprise 113 species that occur throughout the Americas. The Old World warblers (family Silviidae) occur in Eurasia, Africa, and Australia, and include some 325 species. Although the warblers in these two families are not closely related, having evolved from different ancestral stock, many of the species in both families are accomplished and melo-

A male black-throated green warbler (*Dendroica virens*) at Metropolitan Beach Metropark, Michigan. Usually found high in trees, this warbler was in the grass feeding on grounded insects after a cold snap.

dious singers, and this is the main reason for their shared common name.

In addition, birds in both families of warblers are very active hunters of insects, spiders, and other small invertebrates. Most species of warblers are tropical or subtropical. However, many migratory species of warblers breed in forested and shrubby habitats at higher latitudes, and spend the non–breeding season in warmer latitudes. These migratory warblers can be regarded as essentially tropical birds that breed and raise their young in the forests of higher latitudes in order to take advantage of the seasonal abundance of arthropods.

The Old World and American warblers bear a superficial resemblance to each other. This is largely because of convergent evolutionary influences, resulting from the fact that these unrelated birds occupy rather similar niches in their ecosystems—that of small, arthropod–eating birds. One difference between the families is the occurrence of ten primary wing feathers in the Silviidae, compared with nine in the Parulidae. The American warblers, particularly male birds, tend to be much more brightly colored than the Old World warblers.

American warblers

The American warblers are small, brightly colored, insectivorous birds. Most species of American warblers are resident in tropical forests, but some species migrate to northern ecosystems to breed.

At least 52 species of American warblers breed north of Mexico. Some of these species have very wide ranges, occurring over much of the United States and Canada. The yellow warbler (*Dendroica petechia*), for example, is a common species found in shrubby habitats from the northern low arctic through all but the southernmost deciduous forests and western deserts. The common yellowthroat (*Geothlypis trichas*) is similarly widespread in marshes and shrubby habitats, from the subarctic through the southern states and into Mexico. The yellow–breasted chat (*Icteria virens*) is the largest species of warbler in North America, with a body length of 15 in (38 cm). This species also ranges widely, from southern Canada through most of the United States. The yellow–rumped warbler (*Dendroica coronata*) is one of the most familiar species of American forests, because it breeds in many types of conifer forests, and it winters throughout much of the southern United States and down into Mexico and elsewhere in Central America.

Male birds of these and many of the other North American warblers are very colorful. The prothonotary or golden swamp warbler (*Protonotaria citrea*) occurs in hardwood swamps and riparian forests, and has a brilliant yellow plumage, offset by its grey–blue wings. The northern parula (*Parula americana*) occurs in eastern hardwood forests, and has a bright blue back, and a yellow breast with a black–and–red band running across. The male blackburnian warbler (*Dendroica fusca*) of eastern spruce–fir forests has an orange throat framed by black and white markings. The red–faced warbler (*Cardellina rubrifrons*) of southern Arizona and Mexico has a crimson face and throat. The American redstart (*Setophaga ruticilla*) is a widespread forest species with a black body and bright, orange patches on its flanks and tail.

American warblers are a diverse component of the community of birds breeding in most forests of the Americas. In some places in North America, ten or more species may breed in the same stand. Although all of these birds feed on small arthropods, they segregate ecologically by feeding in different parts of the tree canopy, on the surface of tree bark, or on the forest floor.

Old–World warblers

About one–half of the Old World warblers are resident or short–distance migrants that breed in tropical and sub–tropical ecosystems of Africa. Africa is also the wintering ground for most of the other species of old–world warblers, which migrate to more northern latitudes to breed. Various species in this family are widespread throughout Eurasia, breeding as far as the northern tundra, but wintering in the tropics of Africa or Asia. Other migratory species breed in more temperate habitats.

Only a few species of Silviid warblers breed in North America. The ruby–crowned kinglet (*Regulus calendula*) and golden–crowned kinglet (*R. satrapa*) are widespread and common birds of northern conifer forests. The blue–gray gnatcatcher (*Polioptila caerula*) is more southern in distribution, and prefers broad–leaf forests. The black–tailed gnatcatcher (*P. melanura*) occurs in desert scrub. These are all small, very active, insect– and spider–hunting birds. The gnatcatcher was named after it habit of catching small insects while hovering, or through brief, aerial pursuits.

Like other songbirds, male warblers sing to proclaim their breeding territories, and to advertise their availability as a mate to females. Some of the Silviid warblers of Eurasia are very difficult to tell apart on the basis of plumage, but they have different habitat preferences and distinctive songs.

Conservation of warblers

Warblers are small, often colorful birds, and there are many species of both the Parulid and Silviid warblers. As a result, these birds are among the most avidly sought–after sightings by bird–watchers. Birding is a non–consumptive field sport that is rapidly increasing in popularity. Birding, in conjunction with related activities such as bird–feeding, has a very large economic impact, and gives great aesthetic enjoyment to many people. Unfortunately, populations of many of the small birds that are the object of these activities, including warblers, are becoming increasingly at risk from a number of human activities.

In spite of their small size, migrating Old World warblers are commonly hunted as food in the Mediterranean region. These days, they are mostly captured with nets or using sticky perches from which the birds cannot extricate themselves. Large numbers of migrating warblers are caught in these ways, and are eaten locally or are offered for sale as a delicacy at markets. Some of the catch, generally pickled, is even traded internationally. The use of warblers in this way is a quite uncontrolled, free–for–all exploitation, and represents a significant risk to the populations of these tiny birds.

One species of North American warbler apparently became extinct around the 1950s or 1960s. The Bachman's warbler (*Vermivora bachmanii*) used to breed in mature broad–leaf forests of the southeastern United States. This species has not been seen for decades even though there still seems to be sufficient breeding habitat, including intact stands where Bachman's warbler used to successfully breed. The extinction of this species was probably caused by the conversion of its

KEY TERMS

Convergence—An evolutionary pattern by which unrelated species that fill similar ecological niches tend to develop similar morphologies and behavior. Convergence occurs in response to similar selection pressures.

Nest parasite—A bird that lays its eggs in the nests of other species. The host raises the parasitic egg, and often fails to successfully raise any of its own babies.

wintering habitat on the island of Cuba to agriculture. Once the surviving numbers of Bachman's warbler decreased to below a critical threshold of abundance, potential mates were probably unable to locate each other in their relatively large breeding range, and the population collapsed to extinction.

Many other species of North American warblers are at risk from decreases in the area of their wintering and/or breeding habitat. This concern is especially acute for those warblers whose habitat is mature forest. Net losses of natural habitat directly decrease the populations of birds that can be sustained on the landscape. In addition much of the remaining breeding habitat is fragmented into small woodlots. This means that much of the remaining forest habitat is ecologically influenced by proximity to an edge with younger habitat. This factor appears to expose warblers and other forest birds to more intense predation, and to the debilitating effects of nest–parasitism by the brown–headed cowbird (*Molothrus ater*). Many North American ornithologists feel that these factors are causing large declines in the populations of numerous species of migratory, forest birds, including many species of warblers. The same environmental problem, along with hunting, is affecting populations of warblers and other small birds in Europe and elsewhere.

When patience and birding skills allow their close observation, warblers can be wonderfully charismatic. Unfortunately, like so many other creatures native to North America and other parts of the rapidly changing world, many species of warblers are at great risk from the environmental changes being caused by humans and their activities.

See also Wren-warblers.

Further Reading:

Ehrlich, P.R., D.S. Dobkin, D. Wheye. *Birds in Jeopardy.* Stanford, California: Stanford University Press, 1992.

Harrison, C.J.O. (ed.). *Bird Families of the World.* New York: H.N. Abrams Pubs., 1978.

Bill Freedman

Warblers, Australasian *see* **Wrens**

Warthog *see* **Pigs**

Washing soda *see* **Sodium carbonate**

Wasps

Wasps are slim-waisted, stinging insects in the order Hymenoptera. There are two main groups of wasps: the solitary wasps are relatively small parasites of other arthropods, while the social wasps are larger and live in colonies. Some other groups of tinier hymenopterans are also commonly known as wasps.

Wasps are familiar insects to most people, and they are good insects to know about because wasps can deliver a very painful sting when they feel threatened or are agitated. It is less well known that many of the tinier species of wasps provide a very valuable service to humans because these parasites and predators can be quite effective at reducing populations of injurious species of insects.

Biology of wasps

Wasps have a complete metamorphosis with four stages in their life history: egg, larva, pupa, and adult.

Adult wasps have four sparsely veined, membranous wings, and most species have their abdomen joined to the thorax across a very narrow waist. Wasps have chewing mouth parts, useful for masticating their food and for pulping wood to manufacture the paper that wasps often use to build the cell–like walls of their nests. The ovipositor of female wasps is modified into a stinger, located at the end of their abdomen. This organ can deliver a dose of venom to kill or paralyze other insects which may be eaten or used as a living provision for young wasps. The social wasps will also aggressively sting large animals if they feel that their nest is threatened.

There are males and females of most species of wasps. However, as with most species in the order Hymenoptera, males are normally produced from non-fertilized eggs in a developmental process known as parthenogenesis. Female wasps develop from fertilized eggs and are usually much more abundant than males. In some species, male wasps are not even known to occur.

Solitary wasps are relatively small insects that build their nests in burrows in the ground or out of mud on an exposed surface. The nest is then provisioned with a insect or spider that has been paralyzed by stinging and upon which one or more eggs are laid. The prey serves as a living but immobile food for the developing larvae of the wasp. Although quite small, parasitic wasps can be rather abundant, and they can exert a substantial measure of control over the populations of their prey species.

In contrast, the social wasps are relatively large insects that live in colonies of various size. Vespid wasps develop colonies with three castes: queens, drones, and workers. The drones are relatively short–lived males and serve only to fertilize the queens. The queens are long–lived wasps, and their major function is to initiate a colony and then spend their life laying eggs. Once a colony is established, the eggs and young are tended by workers which are nonfertile female wasps that can be very numerous in large colonies. Social wasps cooperatively feed their developing young on a continuous basis, often with chewed–up insects and other animal–derived foods.

Important groups of North American wasps

The most familiar wasps to most people are the relatively large social species, such as hornets, yellow jackets, and potter wasps, all in the family Vespidae. These wasps are brightly colored, have yellow–and–black or white–and–black stripes on their abdomen, and buzz audibly when flying. Adults of these species catch insects as prey, and they also feed on nectar and soft fruits. Vespid wasps build nests out of paper, made from the cellulose fibers of well–chewed wood. These wasps sometimes attack people who have stepped on their nests or are too close for the wasps' comfort. The stings of these large wasps, often delivered in multiple doses, can be very painful and often cause a substantial swelling of the surrounding tissue. Some people develop allergies to the stings of wasps (and bees), and fatalities can be caused if these hypersensitive individuals are stung.

The name yellow jacket is applied to various ground–nesting species in the genus *Vespula*, including *V. pennsylvanica* in western North America and *V. maculifrons* in the east. The closely related bald–faced hornet (*V. maculata*) is a widespread and abundant species

Swan, L. A. and C. S. Papp. *The Common Insects of North America.* New York: Harper & Row, 1975.

Wilson, E. O. *The Insect Societies.* Cambridge, Mass.: Harvard University Press, 1976.

Bill Freedman

KEY TERMS

. . . .

Biological control—The use of a nonpesticidal biological method to control the abundance of a pest. Parasitic and predatory wasps are sometimes used to achieve a measure of biological control of some pest insects.

Parthenogenesis–Reproduction by the development of an unfertilized gamete. In wasps, unfertilized eggs develop into males.

in the United States and Canada. The polistes wasp (*Polistes fuscatus*) builds paper nests that are suspended from tree limbs or the eaves of roofs. The potter or mud–dauber wasp (*Eumenes fraterna*) makes clay nests suspended from branches of trees and shrubs.

The spider wasps (family Pompilidae) build their nests in the ground and provision them with paralyzed spiders. One of the better–known species is the tarantula wasp (*Pepsis mildei*) which is famous for its skills at hunting and subduing tarantula spiders which are much larger than the wasp. Virtually all tarantulas that are located by a tarantula wasp become living pantries for the young of these efficient predators.

Chalcid wasps are various, minute–bodied species of parasitic wasps in the superfamily Chalcidoidea made up of several families. Adult chalcid wasps feed on nectar, plant juices, or honeydew, a sweet secretion of aphids. The young wasps, however, are reared in the bodies of arthropods, usually eventually killing the host. Some species of chalcid wasps are bred in captivity in enormous numbers and are then released into fields or orchards in an attempt to achieve a measure of biological control over important insect pests. For example, the trichogramma wasp (*Trichogramma minutum*), only 0.1 in (2.5 mm) long, will parasitize more than two hundred species of insects. This useful wasp has been captive–reared and released to reduce populations of bollworms of cotton, corn earworms, and spruce budworms in conifer forests.

Further Reading:

Arnett, R. H. *American Insects: A Handbook of the Insects of America North of Mexico.* Gainesville, Fla.: Sandhill Crane, 1993.

Borror, D. J., C.J. Triplehorn, and N. Johnson. *An Introduction to the Study of Insects.* New York: Saunders, 1989.

Ito, Y. *Behaviour and Social Evolution of Wasps.* Oxford, England: Oxford University Press, 1993.

Ross, K. G., and R .W. Matthews (eds.). *The Social Biology of Wasps.* Ithaca, N.Y.: Cornell University Press, 1991.

Waste management

Waste management is the handling of discarded materials. Recycling and composting, which transform waste into useful products, are forms of waste management. The management of waste also includes disposal, such as landfilling.

Waste can be almost anything. It can be food, leaves, newspapers, bottles, construction debris, chemicals from a factory, candy wrappers, disposable diapers or radioactive materials. Civilization has always produced waste. But as industry and technology have evolved and the world's population has grown, waste management has become increasingly complex.

A primary objective of waste management today is to protect the public and the environment from potential harmful effects of waste. Some waste materials are normally safe but can be hazardous if not managed properly. One gallon (3.75 l) of used motor oil, for example, can contaminate a million gallons (3,790,000 l) of water.

Who manages waste? Every individual, business or organization must make decisions and take some responsibility regarding their own waste. On a larger scale, government agencies at the local, state, and federal levels enact and enforce waste management regulations. These agencies also educate the public about proper waste management. In addition, local government agencies may provide disposal or recycling services themselves, or they may hire private companies to perform those functions.

History of waste management

Throughout history there have been four basic methods for managing waste: dumping it; burning it; finding another use for it (recycling); and not creating the waste in the first place (waste prevention). How those four methods are utilized depends on the wastes being managed. Municipal solid waste is much different than industrial, agricultural, or mining waste. Hazardous waste is a category that should be handled sepa-

A household hazardous waste disposal day sponsored by the city of Livonia, Michigan. Residents are asked to bring toxic materials, such as paint, petroleum products, insecticides, and antifreeze, to a central location where they are combined and placed in barrels for disposal.

rately, although it sometimes is generated with the other types.

One recent historical trend has had an enormous impact on all forms of waste management: the increase in government regulation over the past 25 years. This has been especially true in the United States, but has occurred in many other countries as well.

Municipal solid waste

Municipal solid waste is what most people think of as garbage, refuse, or trash. It is generated by households; businesses (other than heavy industry); and institutions, such as schools and hospitals. This does not include bodily wastes or other liquid wastes from these sources, which are commonly handled through public sewage treatment systems.

The first humans did not worry much about waste management. They simply left their garbage where it dropped. But as permanent communities developed, people began to place their waste in designated dumping areas. The use of such "open dumps" for garbage is

still common in some parts of the world. But open dumps have major disadvantages, especially in heavily populated areas. Toxic chemicals can filter down through a dump and contaminate groundwater. The liquid that filters through a dump or landfill is called leachate. Dumps may also generate methane, an explosive gas produced when organic wastes decompose under certain conditions.

The landfill, also known as the "sanitary landfill," was apparently invented in England in the 1920s. At a landfill, the garbage is covered at the end of every day with several inches of soil. Landfilling became common in the U.S. in the 1940s. By the late 1950s, it was the dominant solid waste disposal method in the nation.

Early landfills had significant leachate and methane problems, but those have largely been resolved at landfills built in the past 20 years. Today's landfills are lined with several feet of clay and with thick plastic sheets. Leachate is collected at the bottom, drained through pipes, and processed. Methane gas is also safely piped out of the landfill.

The dumping of waste does not just take place on land. Ocean dumping, in which barges carry the garbage out to sea, was once used as a disposal method by some U.S. coastal cities and is still practiced by some nations. Sewage sludge, or processed sewage, was dumped at sea in huge quantities by New York City as recently as 1992. Also called biosolids, sewage sludge is not generally considered solid waste, but is sometimes composted with organic municipal solid waste.

Burning has a long history in municipal solid waste management. Some American cities began to burn their garbage in the late 19th Century in devices called cremators. These were not very efficient, however, and cities went back to dumping or other methods. In the 1930s and 1940s, many cities built new types of garbage burners known as incinerators. These were gradually shut down, primarily due to air pollution concerns, beginning in the 1950s.

Waste burning enjoyed yet another revival in the 1970s and 1980s. These new incinerators, many of which are still in operation, are called "resource recovery" or "waste–to–energy" plants. In addition to burning garbage, they produce heat or electricity that is used in nearby buildings or residences, or sold to a utility. Many local governments became interested in waste–to–energy plants following the U.S. energy crisis in 1973. But by the mid–1980s, it had become difficult to find locations to build these facilities, once again mainly because of air quality issues.

Another problem with incineration is that it generates ash, which must be landfilled. Incinerators usually reduce the volume of garbage by 70% to 90%. The rest comes out as ash that often contains high concentrations of toxic substances.

Municipal solid waste will likely always be landfilled or burned to some extent. In the past 25 years, however, non–disposal methods such as waste prevention and recycling have flourished. Because of public concerns and the high costs of landfilling and burning (especially to build new facilities), local governments want to reduce the amount of waste that must be disposed of.

Even the earliest civilizations recycled some items before they became garbage. Broken pottery was often ground up and used to make new pottery, for example. Recycling has taken many forms. One unusual type of recycling, called reduction, was common in large U.S. cities from about 1900 to 1930. In reduction plants, wet garbage, dead horses and other dead animals were cooked in large vats to produce grease and fertilizer. A more familiar, and certainly more appealing, type of recycling took place during World War II, when scrap metal was fervently collected to help the war effort. Modern–day recycling has had two recent "booms," from about 1969 to 1974 and from the late 1980s until today.

Reuse and repair are the earliest forms of waste prevention, which is also known as waste reduction. When tools, clothes and other necessities were scarce, people naturally repaired them again and again. When they were beyond repair, people found other uses for them.

Refillable soft drink bottles are another example of reuse. These are still the norm in many countries, but have become increasingly rare in the U.S. One form of waste prevention, called source reduction, is a reduction in the quantity or the toxicity of the material used for a product or packaging.

Agricultural, mining and industrial waste

When it comes to overall waste, municipal solid waste is a drop in the bucket, or the recycling bin. More than 95% of the total 4.5 billion tons of solid waste generated in the U.S. each year is agricultural, mining or industrial waste.

These wastes do not receive nearly as much attention as municipal solid waste because most Americans do not have direct experience with them. Also, agricultural and mining wastes — which make up 88% of the overall total of solid waste — are largely handled at the same places they are generated, at remote mining sites or in the fields.

Mining nearly always generates substantial waste, whether the material being mined is coal, clay, sand, gravel, building stone, or metallic ore. Early mining concentrated on the richest lodes of minerals. Because modern methods of mining are more efficient, they can extract the desired minerals from veins that are less rich. However, much more waste is produced in the process.

Many of the plant and animal wastes generated by agriculture remain in the fields or rangelands. These wastes can be beneficial because they return nutrients to the soil. But modern techniques of raising large numbers of animals in small areas generate great volumes of animal waste, or manure. Waste in such quantities must be managed carefully, or it can contaminate groundwater or surface water.

Industrial wastes that are not hazardous have traditionally been sent to landfills or incinerators. The rising cost of disposal has prompted many companies to seek alternative methods for handling these wastes, such as waste prevention and recycling. Often a manufacturing plant can reclaim certain waste materials by feeding them back into the production process.

Hazardous waste

Hazardous wastes are materials considered harmful or potentially harmful to human health or the environment. Wastes may be deemed hazardous because they are poisonous, flammable, or corrosive, or because they react with other substances in a dangerous way.

Industrial operations have produced large quantities of hazardous waste for hundreds of years. Some hazardous wastes, such as mercury and dioxins, may be released as gases. Many hazardous industrial wastes are in liquid form. One of the greatest risks is that these wastes will contaminate water supplies.

An estimated 60% of all hazardous industrial waste in the U.S. is disposed of with a method called deep well injection. With this technique, liquid wastes are injected down into a well located in a type of impervious rock formation that keeps the waste isolated from groundwater and surface water. Other underground burial methods are also used for hazardous industrial waste and other types of dangerous waste.

Hazardous wastes are also disposed of at specially–designed landfills and incinerators. A 1993 report listed 12 different technologies, some of them still experimental, for incinerating hazardous waste. A controversial issue in international relations is the export of hazardous waste, usually from industrial countries to developing nations. This export often takes place with the stated intent of recycling, but some of the wastes end up being dumped.

Pesticides used in farming may contaminate agricultural waste. Because of the enormous volumes of pesticides used in agriculture, the proper handling of unused or waste pesticides is a daunting challenge for modern waste management. Certain mining techniques also utilize toxic chemicals. Piles of mining waste, known as tailings, may contain hazardous substances. Because of a reaction with the oxygen in the air, toxic acids may form on tailings even if chemicals were not used in the mining.

Hazardous wastes come from the home as well. Many common household products contain toxic chemicals. Examples include drain cleaner, pesticides, glue, paint, paint thinner, air freshener and nail polish. Twenty years ago, most people dumped these products in the garbage, even if the containers were not empty. But local governments do not want them in the garbage. They also do not want residents to pour leftover household chemicals down the drain, since munic-

ipal sewage treatment plants are not well–equipped to remove them.

The trend in the 1980s and 1990s has been for local governments to open centers where residents can take these household hazardous wastes, or to sponsor special collection events for these materials. City and county governments conduct more than 800 of these events each year in the United States.

Modern techniques

Three main inter–related factors influence the way wastes are handled today: Government regulation; cost; and public attitudes. Both industry and local governments must comply with increasingly strict federal and state regulations for landfills and incinerators. Partly because those regulations have driven up the costs of disposal, it has become critical for local governments, industry and businesses of all sizes to find the lowest–cost waste management options.

Public attitudes also play a pivotal role in waste management decisions. Virtually every proposed new landfill or waste–to–energy plant is opposed by people who live near the site. Public officials refer to this reaction as NIMBY, which stands for "Not in My Backyard." If an opposition group becomes vocal enough or powerful enough, a city or county council is not likely to approve the project. The public also wields considerable clout with businesses. Recycling and waste prevention enjoy strong public support.

According to 1994 estimates for U.S. municipal solid waste, 19% is recycled or composted, 10% is incinerated and 71% is landfilled. The recycling rate is expected to rise to 25% by the year 2000.

Waste prevention

Preventing or reducing waste is typically the least expensive method to manage waste. Waste prevention may also reduce the amount of resources needed for a product or packaging.

For example, most roll–on deodorants used to come in a plastic bottle, which was inside a box. Beginning about 1992, deodorant manufacturers eliminated the box from their packaging. In some cases, the companies redesigned the plastic bottle so it would be more stable, and not tip over easily on the store shelf. This is the type of waste prevention called source reduction. It can save businesses money, as well as reducing waste.

Waste prevention includes many different practices that result in using less materials or products, or using materials that are less toxic. A chain of clothing stores ships its products to its stores in reusable garment bags instead of disposable plastic bags. Manufacturers of household batteries have reduced the amount of mercury in their batteries. In an office, employees copy documents on both sides of a sheet of paper, instead of just one side. A family uses cloth napkins instead of paper napkins.

Handling grass clippings and leaves at home, rather than having them picked up for disposal or composting, is another form of waste prevention. A resident can leave grass clippings on the lawn after mowing (known as grasscycling), or can compost leaves and grass in a backyard composting bin, or use them as mulch in the garden.

Waste prevention is preferable over recycling or municipal composting programs because it does not require transportation, processing and administration. But waste prevention does have limitations. It will never eliminate waste; it just reduces the amount that has to be recycled or disposed of. Waste prevention also is very difficult for a government to measure, since waste that was prevented never really existed in the first place. The lack of solid data makes it hard for governments to justify spending money on waste prevention education programs.

Even though waste prevention is less expensive than other forms of waste management in the long run, local governments and businesses may need to spend substantial amounts over the short term, to provide education about waste prevention or to make changes in operating procedures so that less waste is produced.

Waste prevention can also be a valuable tool for managing industrial and hazardous wastes, since disposal of those materials is particularly expensive and heavily regulated.

Farmers can use natural or alternative methods of pest control to replace their use of pesticides, which in turn reduces the amounts of hazardous wastes produced. Many government agencies strongly encourage this. A program started by the province of Ontario, Canada, aims to reduce agricultural pesticide use by 50%.

Recycling and composting

Recycling is a simple concept: Using waste material to make a new product. But in practice, in the 1990s, it's far from simple. Recycling consists of three essential elements: Collection of the waste materials, also known as secondary materials or recyclables; processing those materials and manufacturing them into new products; and the marketing and sale of those new products. Dozens of different materials are recycled, including glass bottles, aluminum cans, steel cans, plastic bottles, many types of paper, used motor oil, car batteries and scrap metal. For each material, the collection, processing and marketing needs can be quite different.

When the current recycling boom began in the late 1980s, markets were virtually ignored. The result: Some materials were collected in large quantities but could not be sold, and some ended up going to landfills. Today, the development of recycling markets is a high priority. "Close the loop," a catch–phrase in recycling education, means that true recycling (the recycling loop) has not taken place until the new product is purchased and used.

To boost recycling markets, many local and state governments now require that their own agencies use products made from recycled materials. In a major step forward for recycling, President Clinton in 1993 issued an executive order requiring the federal government to use more recycled products.

Many managers of government recycling programs feel that manufacturers should take more responsibility for the disposal of their products and packaging, rather than letting municipalities bear the brunt of the disposal costs. An innovative and controversial law in Germany requires manufacturers to set up collection and recycling programs for packaging of their products.

The high cost of government–created recycling programs is often criticized. Recycling supporters argue it is still less expensive than landfilling or incineration, when all costs are considered. Another concern about recycling is that the recycling process itself frequently generates hazardous wastes that must then be treated and disposed of. Air and water pollution may result from recycling processing.

Recycling of construction and demolition (C & D) debris is one of the growth areas for recycling. Although C & D debris is not normally considered a type of municipal solid waste, millions of tons of it have gone to municipal landfills over the years. If this material is separated at the construction or demolition site into piles such as concrete, wood and steel, it can usually be recycled.

Composting is considered either a form of recycling, or a close relative. Composting occurs when organic waste, such as yard waste, food waste and paper, is broken down by microscopic organisms called microbes. The resulting material, compost, looks like rich dirt. Landscapers and gardeners buy compost and add it to yards or gardens to improve the soil.

Yard waste—primarily grass clippings and leaves—makes up about one fifth of municipal solid waste, by weight. Some states do not allow it to be disposed.

These yard waste bans have resulted in rapid growth for municipal composting programs. In these programs, yard waste is collected by trucks (separately from garbage and recyclables) and taken to a composting plant where it is chopped up and regularly turned until it becomes compost.

Waste from food processing plants and produce trimmings from grocery stores are composted in some parts of the country. Residential food waste is the next frontier for composting. The city of Seattle collected food waste from households in a 1994 pilot project. For more details on recycling and composting, see the entries on those topics.

Biological treatment, a technique for handling hazardous wastes, could be called a high–tech form of composting. Like composting, biological treatment employs microbes to break down wastes through a string of chemical reactions. Substances that are toxic, carcinogenic (cancer–causing) or undesirable in the environment for other reasons can be rendered harmless through this method. The new substances that are created can be reused or recycled.

Extensive research on biological treatment is in progress. Genetic engineering — a controversial branch of biology dealing with the modification of genetic codes — is closely linked with biological treatment, and could produce significant advances in this field.

New developments in disposal

Waste management is an expensive proposition in the 1990s, especially for disposal. Waste managers constantly seek innovations that will improve efficiency and reduce costs. Two new ideas in landfilling involve reclamation of resources.

Some landfill operators today, instead of just burning off or releasing the methane gas that is generated within the landfill, collect this methane, purify it and then use it to produce power locally or sell it as fuel. At a few landfills, adventurous managers have experimented with a bold but relatively untested concept known as landfill mining. This involves digging up an existing landfill to recover recyclable materials, and sometimes to re–bury the garbage in the landfill more efficiently. Landfill mining has been criticized as costly and impractical, but some landfill operators believe it can save money under certain circumstances.

In the high–tech world of incineration, new designs and concepts are constantly being tried. One waste–to–energy technology for solid waste being introduced to the U.S. is called fluidized–bed incineration. About 40% of Japan's incinerators use this tech-

nology, which is designed to have lower emissions of some air pollutants than conventional incinerators.

A 1994 U.S. Supreme Court ruling could increase the cost of incineration significantly. The Court ruled that some ash produced by municipal solid waste incinerators must be treated as a hazardous waste, because of high levels of substances such as lead and cadmium. This means ash now has to be tested, and part or all of an incinerator's ash may have to go to a hazardous waste landfill rather than a standard landfill.

A much smaller type of incinerator is used at many hospitals to burn medical wastes, such as blood, surgical waste, syringes and laboratory waste. The safety of these medical waste incinerators has become a major issue in some communities. A three–year U.S. Environmental Protection Agency study released in 1994 said medical waste incinerators were the leading sources of dioxin emissions into the air. The same study warned that dioxins, which can be formed by the burning of certain chemical compounds, pose a high risk of causing cancer and other health hazards in humans.

Trends for the twenty–first century

Even with the tremendous increase in the regulation of waste over the past 25 years, problems still occur with hazardous wastes and other wastes. Citizens often express their concerns. But governments have a very limited amount of money to spend on environmental protection. As the twenty–first century begins, governments and industry will continue to improve the efficiency of recycling and disposal. Governments in the U.S. and elsewhere will also rely more on waste prevention strategies, because of their lower cost.

The greatest impetus for waste prevention will likely come from the public. More and more citizens will come to understand that pesticides, excessive packaging, and the use of disposable rather than durable items have an environmental cost. Through the growth of the information society, knowledge of the environment will increase. This should result in a continuing evolution towards more efficient and environmentally–sensitive waste management.

See also Composting; Emission; Landfill; Recycling; Pollution; Hazardous wastes; Sewage treatment.

Further Reading:

Hirschhorn, Joel and Oldenburg, Kirsten. *Prosperity Without Pollution: The Prevention Strategy for Industry and Consumers.* New York: Van Nostrand Reinhold, 1991.
The League of Women Voters Education Fund. *The Garbage Primer.* New York: Lyons & Burford, 1993.

KEY TERMS

. . . .

Composting—The process by which organic waste, such as yard waste, food waste, and paper, is broken down by microscopic organisms and turned into a useful product for improving soil.

Hazardous wastes—Wastes that are poisonous, flammable, or corrosive, or that react with other substances in a dangerous way.

Incineration—The burning of solid waste as a disposal method.

Landfilling—A land disposal method for solid waste, in which the garbage is covered every day with several inches of soil.

Recycling—The use of waste materials, also known as secondary materials or recyclables, to produce new products.

Source reduction—Reduction in the quantity or the toxicity of material used for a product or packaging; a form of waste prevention.

Waste prevention—A waste management method that involves preventing waste from being created, or reducing waste.

Miller, E. Willard and Miller, Ruby. *Environmental Hazards: Toxic Waste and Hazardous Material: A Reference Handbook.* Santa Barbara, Calif.: ABC–CLIO, 1991.
Rathje, William and Murphy, Cullen. *Rubbish!: The Archaeology of Garbage.* New York: HarperCollins Publishers, 1992.

Tom Watson

Water

Water is the most abundant liquid on Earth. It covers more than 70 percent of the Earth's surface. Including the clouds (which are, of course, also water), it makes our entire planet look blue and white from space.

The Earth's supply of water is constantly being recycled. It is evaporated from the oceans by the sun and is given off by the forests. The vapor condenses into clouds, which rain out onto the land. The land water runs off into the lakes and rivers, which then run back to the seas, and the cycle is complete. The total amount of water on Earth, in the form of oceans, lakes, rivers, clouds, polar ice and chicken soup, is 1.5×10^{18} (one–and–a–half billion billion) tons, occupying a total volume of 8.7 million cubic miles.

It is impossible to overstate the importance of water to almost every process on Earth, from the life processes of the lowest bacteria to the shaping of continents. Water is the most familiar of all chemical compounds known to humans. It is essential to all living things, plant and animal. We drink it, we wash with it, we play in it and we cook in it. In fact, we ourselves are more than half water. A typical 150 lb (68 kg) male is about 60 percent water; females average closer to 50 percent, and fatter people are lower. Babies are as high as 85 percent water.

We never see absolutely pure water because it dissolves so many substances. If we want pure water we have to prepare it laboriously by such means as distillation, ion exchange and reverse osmosis. Moving water even dissolves rock slightly, to form caves and to wear away mountains. All of the water on Earth, therefore, is in the form of solutions. The dissolved substances change the properties of water from what they would be in absolutely pure water. They affect its freezing point and its boiling point, among many other physical and chemical properties. The dissolved or suspended substances in water can be in the form of ions, molecules, or larger particles. The table shows the range of materials that are found in natural water and that must be removed to purify it. For drinking water, bacteria must also be killed.

What water is

Water is an odorless, tasteless, transparent liquid that appears colorless but is actually very pale blue. The color is obvious in large quantities of water such as lakes and oceans, but it can even be seen in a full bathtub. It is a single chemical compound whose molecules consist of two hydrogen atoms attached to one oxygen atom. The chemical formula of this compound is therefore H_2O. The two hydrogen atoms are attached to the oxygen atom in such a way as to make an angle–shaped molecule.

The angle isn't 90°, however, but 104.5°—close to a right angle, but a little wider.

The formula H_2O means that no matter how much water we're talking about, it always contains exactly twice as many hydrogen atoms as oxygen atoms. Considering that a hydrogen atom weighs only about one–sixteenth as much as an oxygen atom, most of the weight in water is due to oxygen: 88.8 percent of the

The structure of ice.

weight is oxygen and 11.2 percent is hydrogen. That goes for everything from a single molecule to a lake full.

Water can be made (synthesized) from hydrogen and oxygen, both of which are gases. When these two gases are mixed, however, they don't react unless the reaction is started with a flame or spark. Then they react with explosive violence. The tremendous energy that is released is a signal that hydrogen and oxygen are very eager to become water. Another way of saying that is that water is an extremely stable compound, compared with loose molecules of hydrogen and oxygen. It is hard to break water molecules apart into its components.

Not only that, but water molecules are stuck quite tightly to each other—at least when compared with similar compounds. The molecule–to–molecule stickiness is caused mainly by the fact that the water molecule is a dipole, because the oxygen atom pulls electrons away from the hydrogen atoms, giving the oxygen corner of the molecule a slight negative charge and the two hydrogen ends a slight positive charge. The negative part of one water molecule then attracts the positive parts of others like a magnet, although they can still slide around over each other as molecules do in any liquid. Water molecules stick to each other also by hydrogen bonds.

An unusual liquid

The strong attractions that water molecules have for each other are responsible for many of water's highly unusual properties, as compared with other liquids of about the same molecular weight. Among these are:

1. Its unusually high boiling point (if it were similar to the other liquids, it would be a gas at room temperature.

2. Its high heat of vaporization (the amount of heat it takes to change the liquid to a gas.

3. Its high heat of fusion (the amount of heat it takes to melt solid ice).

4. Its high heat capacity (the amount of heat it takes to raise its temperature by a certain amount).

5. Its world–champion rank among liquids as a solvent (it has been called the universal solvent because it dissolves so many different substances).

6. The low density (the lightness) of ice, which makes it float on the surface of liquid water. As water is cooled to make ice, it gets slightly denser, like all liquids. But at 39.2° F (4°C) it reaches its maximum density; when cooled below that temperature, it gets less dense until it reaches 32°F (0°C), at which time it freezes and suddenly decreases to 91.7 percent of the density of the water. Being less dense than the water, the ice floats.

The normal boiling point of water is 212°F (100°C), and its freezing point is 32°F (0°C). In fact, zero and 100 degrees on the Celsius scale are defined as the freezing and boiling points of water. Water is also the standard by which many other quantities are measured. For example, the density of a material is often expressed as its specific gravity or specific weight: how many times denser it is than water.

In pure water, one out of every 555 million molecules is broken down—dissociated—into a hydrogen ion and a hydroxide ion:

$$H_2O \longleftrightarrow H^+ + OH^-$$

These ions are enough to make water a slight conductor of electricity. That's why water is dangerous when there is electricity around. The slight dissociation of water is responsible for the acid and base balances of all of the chemical reactions that take place in water, and that includes almost all the chemical reactions that take place anywhere, including those in the human body. Acid–base balance is probably the most important single factor that affects chemical reactions.

See also Groundwater; Hydrologic cycle; Hydrology; Irrigation; Precipitation; States of matter; Water conservation; Water pollution.

Further Reading:

Brady, James E. and Holum, John R., *Fundamentals of Chemistry*, New York: Wiley, 1988.

Ebbing, Darrell D., *General Chemistry*, Boston: Houghton Mifflin, 1990.

Umland, Jean B., *General Chemistry*, Minneapolis: West Publishing, 1993.

Walton, Alan J., *The Three Phases of Matter*, Oxford University Press.

Robert L. Wolke

as parthenogenesis which does not require sex. There are 4–12 post–hatching developmental stages, each beginning with a molt of the cuticle.

Water bears are interesting little creatures which have fascinated zoologists ever since the discovery of microscopy first made these animals visible several centuries ago.

Bill Freedman

Water boatmen *see* **True bugs**

Water bears

Water bears or tartigrades are about 500 species of tiny aquatic invertebrate animals in the phylum Tartigrada, including about 90 species in North America. Water bears have a very widespread distribution, occurring in moist habitats from the Arctic to the Antarctic and on mountains as high as 6,564 mi (6,000 m).

Water bears have roughly cylindrical dark–colored bodies with four body segments and four pairs of stumpy legs each tipped with tiny claws. The awkward, pawing locomotion of these animals was thought to vaguely resemble that of slow–moving bears and hence the common name of these creatures which was given in the 19th century. The mouthparts of water bears are adapted for piercing, and they have a muscular pharynx for sucking the juices of mosses, liverworts, and algae. Water bears do not have active circulatory or respiratory systems; materials move about within their tiny body by simple processes such as diffusion, while respiratory gases diffuse across the surface of the body.

Water bears are typically found in moist films on mosses, lichens, angiosperm plants with a rosette growth form, and plant litter. Water bears can utilize this micro–aquatic habitat because they are only 0.002–0.05 in (0.05–1.2 mm) long. Water bears are highly tolerant of the desiccation that frequently afflicts these sorts of habitats because they have an ability to encapsulate into a shrivelled, spherical state until moist conditions again return. Water bears may also be collected from debris or mud in more typical shallow–water habitats, but they are seldom abundant in ponds or lakes. Some species occur in sandy and pebbly marine habitats above the zone of most vigorous wave action.

Water bears have separate sexes, but males are quite uncommon. Usually males are only relatively abundant during the winter and spring. Some species only produce females, reproducing by a process known

Waterbuck

Waterbucks belong to the large family of bovids, plant–eating hooved animals with horns and four–chambered stomach extracting nutrients from a diet of grass or foliage. These ruminants regurgitate food that is rechewed (chewing the cud). Domestic cattle, also of the bovid family, chew their cud.

Description

Waterbuck belong to a subfamily of bovids called *Reduncinae*, which also includes Kobs, reedbuck, and lechwe. Waterbuck are the largest animals in this subfamily, with males weighing more than 500 lb (250 mg) and standing more than four ft (1.3 m) at the shoulders. Female waterbuck are slightly smaller. Only male waterbuck have horns, which are V–shaped, tapered, ridged, and curve backward, then slightly forward at the tips.

The most familiar of the two subspecies of waterbuck are the common waterbuck *Kobus ellipsiprymnus ellipsiprymaus* and the defassa waterbuck *K.e. defassa*. One distinguishing marking between the two is their coloration. Defassa waterbuck are silvery–gray or reddish to dark brown with a streak of white on their rump. Common waterbuck have a distinctive white ring around the rump, the lower half of the legs are black, and they have white markings at the throat, an eyebrow line, and a white snout. Males tend to darken with age.

Waterbuck lack scent glands, but possess a greasy coat with skin glands that secrete a smelly, musk odor that can be detected as far away as 1600 ft (600 m) away. The greasy, shaggy coat serves to protect waterbuck from the damp habitats. Waterbuck do not run rapidly, moving mostly at a trot.

Habitat and population

Waterbuck have even less tolerance to dehydration than cattle. Therefore, they are usually found close to water in regions with ample rainfall.

Waterbuck prefer to eat the protein–rich grasses, herbs, and foliage found in valleys and areas where rain water drains. Waterbuck are found in the central and south–central African countries of Kenya, Tanzania, Rwanda, Uganda, Zambia, Zimbabwe, and northern parts of South Africa.

In areas where the different subspecies of waterbuck overlap, many *hybrid specimens* have been seen. In a national park in Kenya the population density of waterbuck has been observed to reach as many as 250 animals per sq km while the average is thirty per sq km. These numbers are much higher than their typical density outside the refuge where they average about four animals per sq km. In areas where there is a good water supply, waterbucks tend to live in more dense populations.

Social relationships

The importance of proximity to water plays an important role in the social behavior of waterbuck. Not only do they need the water for drinking, but they also use water to fend off predators, for they are good swimmers. Competition to be near water is reflected among male relationships. Male waterbuck are territorial, but they will tolerate several other males within their territory. These so–called satellite bulls are submissive to the dominant male and will help him defend their territory from other males.

Females have loose, come–and–go relationships, congregating in female herds with as many as seventy animals, including dependent young waterbucks. Female herds may have a home range as large as 1500 acres, while bachelor groups have a range of 250 acres. Young males form bachelor herds of five to forty young bulls and there is evidence of a hierarchy among them. These are also loose social groups with members coming and going. Young males join these groups at the age of nine months until they are six years old, their age of maturity.

Female waterbuck conceive after the age of three, reproducing about once a year after an eight–month gestation period. The mother stays with her calf at night, but during the day wanders away from her young. The calf is nursed three times a day for the first two to four weeks and the calf is weaned at six to eight months. Mothers with young offspring tend to remain in woodland areas as a protection from predators.

KEY TERMS

Coloration—The overall color of an animal, plus distinctive color markings on various parts of the body.

Family—A large group of animals classified together because they share common characteristics of physical structure and consequent behavior.

Herbivores—Animals that only eat plants or parts of plants.

Hybrid animals—Animals that are crosses between species or subspecies that have already been classified.

Regurgitation—The casting up of food that has only been partly digested in a stomach chamber of cud–chewing animals.

Satellite bulls—Submissive bulls that the dominant bull tolerates within his territory and that help defend it from other intruders.

Water dependent—Animals that need to drink water to survive.

See also Antelopes and gazelles; Cattle family.

Further Reading:
Estes, Richard D. *Behavior Guide to African Mammals.* Berkeley: University of California, 1991.
Estes, Richard D. *The Safari Companion.* Post Mills, Vermont: Chelsea Green, 1993.
Grmzimek, Bernhard. *Encyclopedia of Mammals.* New York: McGraw–Hill, 1990.
Haltenorth, T. and Diller, H. *A Field Guide to the Mammals of Africa.* London: Collins, 1992.
Macdonald, David, ed. *The Encyclopedia of Mammals.* New York: Facts on File, 1987.
Nowak, Ronald M. *Walker's Encyclopedia of Mammals.* Baltimore, John Hopkins, 1991.

Vita Richman

Water conservation

Seventy–one percent of Earth's surface is covered by water—an area called the hydrosphere, which makes up all of the oceans and seas of the world. Only 3% of Earth's entire water is freshwater. This includes Arctic and Antarctic ice, groundwater, and all the rivers and freshwater lakes. The amount of usable freshwater is only about 0.003% of the total. To put this small percentage in perspective, if the total water supply is equal to one gallon, the volume of the usable freshwater supply would be less than one drop. This relatively small amount of freshwater is recycled and purified by the hydrologic cycle, which includes evaporation, condensation, precipitation, runoff, and percolation. Since most of life on earth depends on the availability of freshwater, one can say water is life. Worldwide, agricultural irrigation uses about 80% of all freshwater. Cooling water for electrical power plants, domestic, and other industry use the remaining 20%. This figure varies widely from place to place. For example, China uses 87% of its available water for agriculture. The United States uses 40% for agriculture, 40% for electrical cooling, 10% for domestic consumption, and 10% for industrial use.

Water conservation may be accomplished by improving crop water utilization efficiency and by decreasing the use of high water demanding crops and industrial products. The following shows the amount of water, in pounds, required to produce one pound of selected crops and industrial products (one gallon = 7.8 pounds):

1 lb. cotton	16,000
1 lb. beef	6,400
1 lb. rice	4,400
1 lb. loaf of bread	1,200
1 automobile	800,000
1 lb. aluminum	8,000
1 lb. paper	800
1 gallon gasoline	80

Freshwater sources are either surface water (rivers and lakes) or groundwater. Water that flows on the surface of the land is called surface runoff. The relationship between surface runoff, precipitation, evaporation, and percolation is shown in the following equation:

Surface runoff = precipitation – (evaporation + percolation)

When surface runoff resulting from rainfall or snow melt is confined to a well–defined channel it is called a river or stream runoff.

Groundwater is surface water that has permeated through the soil particles and is trapped among porous soils and rock particles such as sandstone or shale. The upper zone of saturation, where all pores are filled with water, is the water table. It is estimated that the groundwater is equal to forty times the volume of all earths freshwater including all the rivers and freshwater lakes of the world.

The movement of groundwater depends on the porosity of the material that holds the water. Most groundwater is held within sedimentary aquifers. Aquifers are underground layers of rock and soil that hold and produce an appreciable amount of water and can be pumped economically.

Water utilization efficiency is measured by water withdrawal and water consumption. Water withdrawal is water that is pumped from rivers, reservoirs, or groundwater wells, and is transported elsewhere for use. Water consumption is water that is withdrawn and returned to its source due to evaporation or transpiration.

Water consumption varies greatly throughout the world. A conservative figure for municipal use in the United States is around 150 gal (568 l) per person per day. This includes home use for bathing, waste disposal, and landscape in addition to commercial and industrial use. The total water demand per person is around 4,500 gal (17,033 l) per person per day when one accounts for the production of food, fiber, and fuel. The consumptive use world wide is considerably less than that for the United States.

According to the United Nations World Health Organization (WHO) five gal (20 l) per person per day is considered a minimum water requirement. The majority of the people in the undeveloped world are unable to obtain the five gallon per day minimum requirement. The WHO estimates that nearly two billion people in the world risk consuming contaminated water. Water–born diseases such as polio, typhoid, dysentery, and cholera kill nearly 25 million people per year. In order to meet this demand for freshwater, conservation is an obvious necessity.

Since irrigation consumes 80% of the worlds usable water, improvements in agricultural use is the logical first step in water conservation. This can be accomplished by lining water delivery systems with concrete or other impervious materials to minimize deep percolation or by using drip irrigation systems to minimize evaporation losses. Drip irrigation systems have been successfully used on fruit trees, shrubs, and landscape plants.

Subsurface irrigation is an emerging technology with extremely high water utilization efficiency. Subsurface irrigation uses a special drip irrigation tubing that is buried 6–8 in (15–20 cm) underground with 12–24 in (26–50 cm) between lines. The tubing contains emitters, or drip outlets, that deliver water and dissolved nutrients at the plants root zone at a desired rate. In addition to water conservation, subsurface irrigation has several advantages that overhead sprinklers do not: no overwatering, no disease or aeration problems, no runoff or erosion, no weeds, and no vandalism. Subsurface irrigation in California has been used on trees, field crops, and lawns with up to 50% water savings.

Xeriscape, the use of low water consuming plants, is a most suitable landscape to conserve water, especially in dry, hot urban regions such as the Southwestern United States, where approximately 50% of the domestic water consumption is used by lawns and non-drought tolerant landscape. Plants such as cacti and succulents, ceanothus, arctostaphylos, which is related to foothill manzanita, trailing rosemary *Rosemarinus officinale*, and white rock rose *Cistus cobariensis* adapt well to hot, dry climate and help conserve water.

In addition to improving irrigation techniques, water conservation can be accomplished by improving domestic use of water. Such a conservation practice is the installation of the ultra–low–flush (ULF) toilets in homes and commercial buildings. A standard toilet uses five to seven gallons of water per flush, while the ultra–low–flush toilet uses 1.5 gal (5.7 l). Research in Santa Monica, California, shows that replacing a standard toilet with an ULF saves 30–40 gal (114–151 l) of water per day, which is equivalent to 10,000–16,000 gal (37,850–60,560 l) per year.

Another way to conserve the freshwater supply is to extract freshwater from sea water by desalinization. Desalinization, the removal of soluble salts and other impurities from sea water by distillation or reverse osmosis (RO), is becoming an increasingly acceptable method to provide high quality pure water for drinking, cooking, and other home uses. It is estimated that the 1993 world production of desalinated water is about 3.5 billion gallons per day (13 billion liters). Most desalinated water is produced in Saudi Arabia, Persian Gulf Nations, and, more recently, in California. The cost of desalinated water depends upon the cost of energy. In the United States, it is about three dollars per thousand gallons, which is four to five times the cost paid by urban consumers and over a hundred times the cost paid by farmers for irrigation water. The idea of using desalinated water for irrigation is, currently, cost prohibitive.

Water has played a vital role in the rise and fall of human cultures throughout history. The availability of usable water has always been a limiting factor for a regions ecological carrying capacity. It is important that humans learn to live within the limit of available natural resources. Conservation of water alone will not extend the natural carrying capacity for an indefinite period of time. Since the supply of available and usable water is finite, the consumption per person must be reduced. A permanent solution to the water shortage problem can be accomplished by living within the ecosystem carrying capacity or by reducing the number of consumers through effective control of population growth.

See also Desalination; Groundwater; Hydrologic cycle; Irrigation; Water pollution.

Further Reading:

Buzzelli, B. *How to Get Water Smart: Products and Practices for Saving Water in the Nineties.* Santa Barbara, CA: Terra Firma Publishing, 1991.

Clarke, R. Water: *The International Crisis.* Cambridge: MIT Press, 1993.

Postel, S. "Plug the Leak, Save the City." *International Wildlife.* 23 (January–February 1993): 38–41.

Yudelman. M., et al. *New Vegetative Approaches to Soil and Water Conservation.* Washington, DC: World Wildlife Fund, 1990.

Water cycle *see* **Hydrologic cycle**

Water hogs *see* **Capybaras**

Water hyacinth *see* **Spiderwort family**

Waterlilies

The water lily, yellow water lily, lotus, and several other aquatic plants are about sixty species of aquatic herbs that make up the family *Nymphaeaceae*. These plants occur in shallow, fresh waterbodies from the boreal to the tropical zones. The usual habitats of these plants are ponds and shallow water around lake edges, as well as slowly–flowing pools and stagnant backwaters in streams and rivers.

Water lilies are perennial, herbaceous plants. Their green foliage dies back each year at the end of the growing season, but the plant perennates itself by issuing new growth from a long–lived rhizome occurring in the surface sediment. The foliage of most species in the family is comprised of simple, glossy, dark–green leaves, which float on the water surface. The solitary, perfect (or bisexual) flowers are held just above the water surface, and are large and showy, with numerous petals and a strong fragrance, making them highly attractive to pollinating insects. In most species, the flowers open at dawn, and close at dusk for the night.

On breezy days, the leaves and flowers of water lilies appear to dance lightly on the water surface. This superficial aesthetic led to the choosing of the family name of these plants (*Nymphaeaceae*) by the famous

White water lilies on a lake in Wisconsin.

Swedish naturalist, Carolus Linnaeus (1707–1778), who likened the water lilies to frolicking nymphs.

Species of waterlilies

Species of water lilies are prominent in many shallow–water habitats, from the boreal zones to the tropics. The genera are described below, with particular reference to species occurring in North America.

There are about forty species of water lily (*Nymphaea* spp.). The water lily, white water lilies, (*Nymphaea odorata* and *Nymphaea tuberosa*) are widespread in North America, and have large, roundish leaves with a triangular cleft at one end, at the point of which the petiole attaches. The large flowers are colored white, or rarely pink. The water lily, blue (*Nymphaea elegans*) occurs in the southern United States and down south into Latin America, and has bluish or pale violet flowers.

The are about ten species of yellow water lily or spatterdock (*Nuphar* spp.), including the widely dispersed North American species species, *Nuphar microphyllum*, *N. variegatum*, and *N. advena*. The floating leaves of these plants are rather oblong in shape, with a basal cleft, at the apex of which the petiole attaches. The flowers are greenish on the outside, and are bright–yellow or sometimes reddish on the inside.

The water–shield (*Brasenia schreberi*) occurs widely in ponds and shallow waters along lake and pond shores in North America, Central and northern South America, and Eurasia. The petiole joins the oblong, floating leaves at their center, a morphology known as peltate. The flowers are relatively small, and are colored a dull red.

There are about seven species of fanwort or water–shield, including *C. caroliniana*, a widespread

species of pools and quiet streams over much of North America. This species has dense, oppositely arranged, finely dissected, submersed foliage, as well as small, alternately arranged, floating leaves. The six–petalled flowers are relatively small, and are colored white or lavender.

The lotus lily or water chinquapin (*Nelumbo lutea*) occurs in scattered populations in North America. The roundish leaves float on the water surface, or are held slightly above, and the petiole is attached at the middle. The flowers are pale–yellow in color. The Oriental sacred lotus (*N. nucifera*) and sacred lotus (*N. nelumbo*) are native species in Asia, and are widely cultivated ornamentals there, and sometimes in North America and Europe.

The largest–leaved species in the Nymphaeaceae is the royal water lily (*Victoria amazonica*) of tropical South America, whose floating leaves can be larger than one–meter across, and can support the weight of a child.

Ecological and economic importance

Species in the water lily family are important components of the plant communities of most freshwater lakes, ponds, and other shallow–water habitats. They provide food for many types of herbivorous animals, and a habitat substrate for others, such as the long–toed birds known as "lily–trotters" or jacanas (family Jacanidae, including *Jacana spinosa* of Central and South America).

Species of water lilies provide a beautiful aesthetic to aquatic habitats, which is greatly appreciated by many people. The sacred lotuses (*Nelumbo nucifera* and *N. nelumbo*) are especially important in this regard in a number of cultures. This is particularly true in India, China, Japan, and elsewhere in Asia, where sacred lotuses are featured prominently in horticultural plantings in many gardens and parks, in paintings and other visual arts, in architectural motifs and decorations, and as symbolism in literature.

KEY TERMS
. . . .

Hydrophyte—A perennial plant that is adapted to growing in permanently aquatic habitats.

Perfect—In the botanical sense, this refers to flowers that are bisexual, containing both male and female reproductive parts.

Several other species in the water lily family are of minor economic importance as horticultural plants, because of the pleasing aesthetics of their floating leaves, as well as their attractive flowers. Various species of water lilies and spatterdocks are commonly planted in gardens which have shallow ponds incorporated into their design. A water lily native to North America, *Nymphaea odorata*, is commercially available in rose–hued flowers, as well as the wild–type color of white.

Another minor use of some species is in the production of food for fishes grown in tropical aquaculture. Water lilies growing in commercial fish ponds are eaten as a food by certain herbivorous fish, and thereby contribute to the productivity of the agricultural ecosystem.

Some people eat the seeds of *Nymphaea*, *Nelumbo*, and *Victoria*, but this is a relatively minor use of the plants.

Further Reading:

Hochkiss, N. *Common Marsh, Underwater, and Floating–leaved Plants of the United States and Canada*. New York: Dover Publications, 1972.

Klein, R.M. *The Green World. An Introduction to Plants and People*. New York: Harper and Row, 1987.

Woodland, D.W. *Contemporary Plant Systematics*. New Jersey: Prentice–Hall, 1991.

Bill Freedman

Watermelon *see* **Gourd family**

Water moccasin *see* **Snakes**

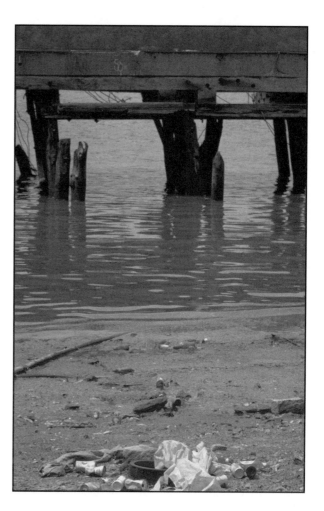

Garbage washed up on the shore of the Hudson river.

Water pollution

Water pollution is judged to occur when environmental stresses associated with chemicals or heat are intense enough to cause ecological damages. Water pollution is most often associated with the effects of sewage dumping, inputs of nutrients, acidification, toxic chemicals, or discharges of industrial hot water. The resulting ecological damages commonly include toxicity caused to organisms, changes in the species composition and trophic structure of communities, and changes in processes such as productivity and decomposition.

Some types of water pollution occur in response to natural stressors, while others are caused by the activities of humans. Acidification, for example, can be associated with natural drainage from peat bogs, or it can be caused by acid rain, acid–mine drainage, and other human influences. Similarly, thermal pollution can be associated with hot–water vents in the deep ocean or with emissions of heated waste waters from nuclear or coal–fired generating stations.

Eutrophication

The productivity of aquatic ecosystems is usually limited by the availability of nutrients. In general, marine ecosystems are limited by the availability of nitrate and freshwater systems by phosphate.

Eutrophication is a type of pollution that occurs when nutrient additions cause a large increase in the productivity of waterbodies, especially that of algae and larger aquatic plants. Eutrophication is most important in fresh waters and shallow marine waters that receive nutrient loading through the dumping of sewage from human or animal wastes or the runoff of agricultural fertilizers. When it is severe, eutrophication is an important environmental problem, largely because of low–oxygen conditions that develop in deeper water when the biomass of algae and other plants sinks and decays. The anoxic conditions result in foul smells and tastes and ruin the quality of the habitat for many species of aquatic animals.

Freshwater lakes that have an aqueous phosphate concentration of less than about 10 mg/l (or 10 parts per billion, ppb) are highly unproductive and are known as oligotrophic lakes. When phosphate is added to these sorts of lakes, the plant life responds vigorously through an increase in productivity because this nutrient is the primary factor limiting their growth. Lakes become eutrophic, or highly productive, when the phosphate concentration in their water exceeds about 35–100 mg/l. Even larger concentrations of phosphate can cause lakes to become extremely productive, known as a hypertrophic condition. These very eutrophic lakes develop a distinct, sometimes intensely green color of their water because of the large biomass of phytoplankton that can be attained.

Eventually, phosphate additions to lakes satiate the requirement of plants for this nutrient. Once this has happened, it is common for nitrogen in the form of nitrate and ammonium to become the primary limiting nutrient to plant productivity. If these forms of nitrogen nutrition are supplied along with phosphate, lakes can become especially eutrophic.

Larger vascular plants known as "macrophytes" account for much of the plant productivity and biomass of shallow waters such as marshes and the fringes of lakes. Microscopic algae, or phytoplankton, are important in deeper waters. When they are extremely abundant, the phytoplankton develop "blooms," which can turn the water a deep green and can sometimes give the water a foul taste and smell.

The increased growths of macrophytes and algae during eutrophication result in changes in the animal community, ranging from the small zooplankton that graze upon phytoplankton to insects and crustaceans that live in the surface sediment to fish and aquatic birds. Small increases in plant productivity may actually benefit these animals by providing them with a richer food base. However, extreme eutrophication represents a severe degradation of the habitat for most aquatic animals.

Sometimes the symptoms of eutrophication can be managed by manipulating the ecological community. For example, a herbivorous fish known as the grass carp (*Ctenopharyngodon idella*, a native of Indonesia)

has been introduced to some shallow eutrophic lakes to reduce the abundance of macrophytic plants which are sometimes considered to be a nuisance. The zebra mussel (*Dreissena polymorpha*) was not deliberately introduced to the Great Lakes of North America (it is a native of Eurasia). However, its enormous populations since the late 1980s have resulted in an increased transparency of the water in some of the more productive regions of those lakes because this mollusk feeds by filtering phytoplankton out of the water. This is somewhat of a benefit of the presence of the invasive zebra mussel, although its overall environmental effect is negative, because of damages caused to native species and the clogging of industrial and municipal water pipes.

These two examples suggest that substantial benefits can sometimes be achieved by bio–manipulating eutrophic ecosystems. Usually, however, the best way to deal with eutrophication is by treating its causes and not its symptoms. Because the primary cause of eutrophication of fresh waters is almost always fertilization with phosphorus, this environmental problem is commonly managed by undertaking efforts to reduce the inputs of this nutrient to waterbodies.

During the 1960s typical domestic detergents contained 12–16% phosphorus. As a result, an important way of rapidly achieving reductions of phosphorus inputs to lake and rivers was by reducing its concentrations in detergents. The use of detergents containing little or no phosphate is now required in many regions.

A more expensive way of reducing phosphorus inputs to waterbodies is by collecting sewage and treating it to remove this nutrient. Treatment of human sewage to remove phosphorus is now fairly common in North American municipalities that border important lakes and rivers such as the Great Lakes. However, many coastal cities do not treat their sewage in part because eutrophication tends to be less of a problem in oceanic waters than in lakes and rivers. In addition, the sewage wastes of agricultural animals are rarely treated nor are those of most low–density residential populations of humans. Sewage from these latter sources may be important in the input of nutrients to inland waters. However, these are relatively diffuse sources of sewage, so the material is difficult to collect and treatment is considered to be too expensive in most cases.

Other effects of sewage

Sewage can also cause pollution directly, and not just as a result of its phosphorus content. Sewage is an organic–rich material, so large quantities of oxygen are required to sustain the decomposition of these wastes. As a result, waterbodies that receive large amounts of sewage are often subject to deoxygenation of their deeper waters. This condition causes great stress to the ecosystem and results in mortality of many animals, including fish. However, some species of invertebrates can tolerate the anoxic conditions that are generally associated with sewage inputs. For example, freshwaters receiving large amounts of sewage often develop a benthic community dominated by various species of red–colored midges and tubificid worms.

Waters receiving untreated sewage are also polluted by large numbers of pathogenic viruses and bacteria and by parasitic nematodes and other worrisome invertebrates. The presence of human pathogens is often assayed through the occurrence and abundance of the gut bacterium known as *Escherichia coli*, a species that is relatively easily isolated and cultured and is therefore useful for monitoring purposes. If a water sample shows a contamination by *E. coli*, this is considered indicative of a general contamination by feces of humans, dogs, or other animals. Depending on the abundance of *E. coli*, the water may be considered unfit for drinking or for swimming. Even cities that carefully treat the domestic sewage of their human populations often have problems with contamination of their lakeside or seaside waters with *E. coli*. This happens because storm waters are not usually treated, and these can become badly contaminated with the feces of domestic dogs and cats when they run off from streets and lawns and then directly into surface waters.

Untreated sewage also causes aesthetic pollution. Many cities do not treat their sewage, dumping it raw or only partially treated into the nearest river, lake, or ocean. The waterfronts of such cities are usually grossly polluted by bad smells and by unsightly floating sewage debris.

Acidification

Fresh water ecosystems can be acidified by a number of processes including drainage from bogs, the deposition of acidifying substances from the atmosphere, acid–mine drainage, and exposures of acid–sulfate soils.

The drainage from bogs is usually acidic, commonly in the range of pH 4–5. This is a natural phenomenon caused by the chemical influence of the dominant group of plants in bogs, mosses known as peat moss, or various species of *Sphagnum*. These plants are capable of very efficiently taking up calcium, magnesium, and other positively charged ions from the nutrient–poor water of bogs. This uptake is accomplished by exchanging hydrogen ions for these nutrient cations, causing an acidification of the water. The drainage

from peat bogs is commonly brown colored because of the presence of large concentrations of dissolved organic acids, and the water is also quite acidic. As a result, lakes and rivers that receive significant inputs of water from this type of wetland are acidified and are often tea–colored because of the organic acids.

Changes in the character of the terrestrial vegetation in the watershed of lakes and rivers can also cause an acidification of those surface waters. For example, a conversion of the forest community from one dominated by angiosperm species of trees to conifers such as pines or spruces can lead to acidification of the soil and of streams draining from the forest.

The deposition of acidifying substances from the atmosphere can also cause an extensive acidification of surface waters. Especially important in this respect are acidic precipitation (including acid rain) and the dry deposition of sulfur dioxide which causes acidification when this gas is oxidized to sulfate within the aquatic ecosystem. Acidification caused by atmospheric depositions is often characterized by marked seasonal variations in water chemistry. This is especially important in regions where there is an accumulation of a snowpack during the winter. The meltwaters in the springtime can be quite acidic and cannot be effectively neutralized by flowing through the soils which are saturated or frozen at that time of year. This leads to the occurrence of so–called "acid shock" events in streams and lakes.

Lakes and streams that are vulnerable to this sort of acidification have little capability for neutralizing inputs of acidity. The natural buffering system in these surface waters is mainly associated with bicarbonate alkalinity. The concentration of bicarbonate in the water is most strongly influenced by the amounts of calcium–rich minerals in the soils of the watershed such as limestone and dolomite. If these kinds of minerals are not present and soils and bedrock of the watershed are dominated by hard calcium–poor minerals such as granite and quartzite, then the surface water will have little acid–neutralizing capacity, and acidification can be easily caused.

The deposition of acidifying substances from the atmosphere has caused a widespread acidification of surface waters in the northeastern United States, eastern Canada, Scandinavia, and in other places. Surface waters acidified by atmospheric depositions commonly develop pHs of about 4.5 to 5.5. Tens of thousands of lakes have been polluted in this way.

Surface waters can also become acidified as a result of a phenomenon called acid–mine drainage. In this type of pollution, large quantities of acidity are generated when sulfide minerals associated with coal or other minerals become exposed to the atmosphere. This can happen as a result of mining activities or sometimes because of construction. Under these conditions, certain bacteria in the genus *Thiobacillus* can metabolically oxidize the sulfide to sulfate, tapping the energy released during this reaction to drive their own autotrophic productivity. These chemoautotrophic bacteria can also oxidize chemically reduced metals such as ferrous iron, a process that generates ferric ion and additional acidity. Surface waters that are affected by acid–mine drainage can become intensely acidic, often developing pHs less than 3 and sometimes less than 2.

Pollution by acidification has many biological consequences including toxicity caused to many species of plants and animals. The toxicity is mostly caused by indirect effects of hydrogen ions. Especially important is the tendency for metals to become soluble in toxic ionic forms under acidic conditions. Other metabolic disruptions include upsets of ionic relations, interference with calcium metabolism, and disruption of the integrity of cellular membranes. Fish are especially vulnerable to the effects of acidification of their aquatic habitat, but many other species of animals and plants are affected.

Pollution by metals

Many industries emit metals to the environment, and in some cases these can pollute fresh and marine waters. For example, lakes in the vicinity of large smelters near Sudbury, Ontario, have been significantly polluted by the fallout of particulates containing copper, nickel, and other metals. The particulates were emitted from the smokestacks of these large facilities. The metals are present in sufficiently large concentrations in some of these waterbodies to cause toxicity to many species of aquatic plants and animals.

Many industrial sources emit metals directly into the aquatic environment as discharges through a pipe into a waterbody. These emitted metals are particular to the type of industry. For example, a metal plating factory may discharge chromium, nickel, and other specific metals into a nearby lake or harbor. In contrast discharges associated with the manufacturing of photographic films would be heavily contaminated by silver. All of these metals can be toxic to aquatic organisms and can cause pollution.

As was noted previously, toxicity associated with metals is a common problem in acidic waters. In this case, the metals may be naturally present in soil, but they normally occur in insoluble forms that are not toxic to organisms. However, under acidic conditions some of the metals become solubilized as ions which can be extremely toxic even in small concentrations. For example, aluminum is commonly present in soils in concentrations of 5–10%, but occurring in insoluble mineral forms. However, some of the aluminum can be solubilized by acidic waters as positively charged ions that can be toxic to fish in concentrations smaller than one milligram per liter (mg/l, or ppm). In non–acidic waters, ionic aluminum occurs in concentrations smaller than 0.01 mg/l (ppm), but in highly acidic waters its concentrations are much larger. At a pH of less than 2, which can be caused by acid–mine drainage, concentrations of aluminum ions can reach hundreds of mg/l, a toxic stress that few species can tolerate. In fact, most of the toxicity of acidic waters is associated with aluminum ions.

Fish are significantly contaminated by mercury in many aquatic environments. In the oceans, this phenomenon can be demonstrated in almost all large fish and sharks. These animals progressively accumulate mercury throughout their lives, and they commonly develop mercury concentrations in their flesh that exceed 0.5 ppm, which is the criterion set by the World Health Organization (WHO) for the maximum concentration in fish intended for human consumption. In this case, it is likely that the oceanic mercury is natural in origin and not associated with human activities.

Severe mercury pollution has also been caused in the vicinity of industrial emissions from certain types of factories such as chlor–alkali plants and pulp mills. The most famous example of mercury–caused pollution occurred at Minamata, Japan where industrial discharges directly into a marine harbor led to the pollution of aquatic life and resulted in the poisoning of fish–eating animals and people. The damages to humans were mostly associated with neurological poisoning and developmental abnormalities, and the toxic syndrome has been named Minamata disease.

Trace toxics

Some chemicals can occur in trace concentrations in water and still result in important environmental damages such as toxicity to aquatic biota. The best known of these so–called trace toxics are the many compounds within the class of chemicals known as chlorinated hydrocarbons. Examples of chlorinated hydrocarbons are the insecticides DDT, DDD, and dieldrin, the class of dielectric fluids known as PCBs, and the chlorinated dioxin TCDD.

These chemicals are extremely insoluble in water but are highly soluble in lipids, that is, fats and oils. In the environment, most lipids occur in the bodies of organisms. As a result, chlorinated hydrocarbons have a very strong tendency to bioaccumulate, that is, to preferentially occur in organisms rather than in the non–living environment. Most chlorinated hydrocarbons are also persistent in the environment because they are not easily degraded by ultraviolet radiation or metabolized by free–living microorganisms or higher plants and animals that have absorbed these chemicals from their surroundings. As a consequence of the tendencies of most chlorinated hydrocarbons to bioaccumulate and also be highly persistent, these chemicals tend to food–web accumulate, occuring in their largest concentrations in top predators at the apex of ecological food webs.

Fish–eating birds are the best–known examples of top predators that have been poisoned by chlorinated hydrocarbons in the aquatic environment. Examples of North American species that have been affected in this way include the bald eagle (*Haliaeetus leucocephalus*), osprey (*Pandion haliaetus*), brown pelican (*Pelecanus occidentalis*), double-crested cormorant (*Phalacrocorax auritus*), western grebe (*Aechmophorus occidentalis*), and herring gull (*Larus argentatus*). The concentrations of chlorinated hydrocarbons in the water of the aquatic habitat of these birds is generally less than 1 µg/l (part per billion, or ppb) and less than 1 ng/l (parts per trillion, or ppt) in the case of TCDD. However, some chlorinated hydrocarbons can food-web accumulate to concentrations of thousands of mg/kg (ppm) in the fatty tissues of fish-eating birds. The resulting toxicity can be severe, characterized by failures to reproduce successfully and sometimes the death of adult birds, both of which can lead to collapses of populations.

Some other trace toxics can also cause ecological damages in surface waters. For example, although it is only moderately persistent in the aquatic environment, the insecticide carbofuran can accumulate in standing water in recently sprayed fields. If geese, ducks, and other aquatic birds utilize those temporary aquatic habitats during their migrations, they can be killed by their exposure to carbofuran. Each year, thousands of waterfowl are killed this way in North America.

Petroleum

Water pollution can also be caused by the presence of hydrocarbons in large concentrations, especially after spills of crude oil or refined products. The most spectacular examples of oil pollution involve accidental spills of petroleum from wrecked tankers, offshore drilling platforms, and broken pipelines, along with spills during warfare as occurred during the massive spills during the Gulf War of 1991. However, smaller discharges associated with tankers disposing oily bilge waters, and chronic releases from oil refineries and urban runoff, are also important sources of oil pollution.

The typical naturally–occurring concentration of hydrocarbons in seawater is about 1 mg/l, mostly resulting from the occurrence of hydrocarbons synthesized by oceanic phytoplankton and bacteria. However, beneath a surface slick of petroleum spilled at sea the concentration of dissolved hydrocarbons can be greater than several mg/l, sufficient to be toxic to some organisms. This soluble concentration does not include pollution by finely suspended droplets of petroleum which become suspended in the water column as a result of wave action. This emulsion of oil in water is highly damaging to organisms that become coated with this substance.

The most obvious form of oil pollution after an accidental spill occurs as surface slicks and relatively thick floating emulsions of oil and water known as "mousse" because of its superficial resemblance to the whipped chocolate desert. Surface slicks and mousse are highly damaging to organisms that become coated with these materials, and these pollutants also cause severe aesthetic damages when they foul beaches and harbors.

Thermal pollution

Thermal pollution occurs when inputs of heated water cause local ecological damages. Naturally thermal waters occur at submarine hot–water vents, often as mineral–rich phenomena known as "black smokers." These vents commonly develop a very unusual, local ecosystem that is energetically based on the productivity of bacteria that oxidize reduced sulfur and iron compounds as a way of gaining energy to sustain their chemoautotrophic productivity.

Thermal pollution can also be caused by human activities, mostly by point–source discharges of heated water from coal–fired and nuclear electrical utilities and from various types of factories. The discharge of heated waste water forms a distinctive plume in the receiving body of water which eventually dissipates to the ambient temperature regime. However, within the heated plume there is a marked gradient of water temperature, and there can be significant thermal stress for many of the naturally occurring species that are normally present in the ecosystem.

Other species may be relatively tolerant of the thermal stress, and they may form distinctive ecological communities in the vicinity of hot–water discharges. Depending on how much the water temperature is increased, some species may be more productive

KEY TERMS

Anthropogenic—Associated with the activities of humans.

Bioaccumulation—The tendency of organisms to accumulate certain chemicals to concentrations larger than those in their non–living environment such as in soil or water, or in the case of animals, larger than in their food.

Chemoautotrophic bacteria—These are bacteria that harness some of the energy content of inorganic chemicals to fix simple chemicals such as carbon dioxide and water into organic molecules through the process of chemosynthesis.

Eutrophication—The process by which productivity of an aquatic ecosystem increases in response to an increase in the rate of nutrient input.

Feed–web accumulation—The tendency of certain persistent, fat–soluble chemicals to occur in their largest concentrations in predators at the top of the ecological food web. As such, chemicals such as DDT, PCBs, and mercury in the aquatic environment have their largest concentrations in predators, in comparison with the non–living environment and with plants and herbivores.

Pollution—The occurrence of chemicals or heat in the environment in a quantity that is greater than particular species or ecosystems can tolerate without undergoing measurable degradation.

Surface waters—Fresh water occurring freely exposed to the atmosphere, as in lakes, ponds, rivers, and streams, and wetlands such as marshes, swamps, and bogs.

in warmed waters. In addition, during the winter in northern regions water will not freeze in the vicinity in a thermal discharge. Sometimes diving ducks spend the winter in that microhabitat, feeding on invertebrates in the sediment beneath the ice–free patch.

Heated industrial waters are occasionally utilized in aquaculture or to heat buildings. This usage prevents some of the ecological damages that would otherwise be caused if the waste heat was directly emitted into the natural environment.

See also Acid rain; Biomagnification; DDT; Dioxin; Eutrophication; Lake; Ocean; Oil spills; Rivers; Sewage treatment; Sulfur cycle; Trophic levels.

Further Reading:

Freedman, B. *Environmental Ecology*, 2nd ed. San Diego: Academic Press, 1994.

Harper, D. *Eutrophication of Freshwaters: Principles, Problems, and Restoration.* New York: Chapman & Hall, 1992.

Hemond, H.F. and E.J. Fechner. *Chemical Fate and Transport in the Environment.* San Diego, CA: Academic Press, 1994.

Manahan, S. *Environmental Chemistry*, 6th ed. Boca Raton, FL.: Lewis Publishers, 1994.

Miller, G.T. *Environmental Science.* Belmont, CA.: Wadsworth Publishing Co, 1991.

Bill Freedman

Water scorpions *see* **True bugs**

Watershed

A catchment or drainage basin which is the total area of land that drains into a water body. It is usually a topographically delineated area that is drained by a stream system. River basins are large watersheds that contribute to water flow in a river. The watershed of a lake is the total land area that drains into the lake. In addition to being hydrologic units, watersheds are useful units of land for planning and managing multiple natural resources. By using the watershed as a planning unit, management activities and their effects can be determined for the land area that is directly affected by management. The hydrologic effects of land management downstream can be evaluated as well. Sometimes land use and management can alter the quantity and quality of water that flows to downstream communities. By considering a watershed, many of these environmental effects can be taken into consideration.

See also Basin; Hydrologic cycle.

Water striders *see* **True bugs**
Water table *see* **Groundwater**

Waterwheel

The waterwheel is considered the first rotor mechanism in which an outside force creates power to spin a shaft. The Greeks are said to have first developed the waterwheel, using it to raise water from rivers. Polls or

The waterwheel of an old mill at Stone Mountain Park, Georgia.

pots were attached around the circumference of a large wheel; then oxen would walk in a circle round a vertical shaft connected through a simple gear to the horizontal shaft of the waterwheel. When possible, the current of a fast–flowing river would do the work of the oxen. By Roman times, ancient engineers realized that the spinning shaft could be used as a power source to turn millstones. However, few were built for this purpose due to the abundance of slaves to grind grain into flour.

After the fall of the Roman Empire, waterwheels spread throughout Medieval Europe largely through the efforts of monks who introduced the technology to landowners, many of whom had lost workers to disease and war. The first factories—textile mills—were powered by water. Other early uses of waterwheels included sawmills for sawing lumber and gristmills for grinding grain. Many large cities owe their existence to power drawn from nearby rivers, but this power source

was not very dependable due to floods and droughts that changed the amount of water flowing in the river.

Several types of waterwheels evolved over the centuries. The two most used were the overshot wheel, which involved water falling on the paddles from above, and the undershot wheel, which was placed directly in the water and worked especially well in swift streams. A more unusual and less frequently used type was the reaction wheel in which water was dropped into a hollow tube from a great height. The tube had hollow spouts attached to it, and the water would spray out the spouts, causing the tube to rotate much like today's lawn sprinklers. The tidal wheel required an enclosed pond with a gate. As the tide rose, water flowed into the pond until the gate was closed, effectively trapping the water. Later, the gate was opened, allowing water to flow out and turn a wheel for power.

By the late eighteenth century, more efficient and powerful steam engines began to replace waterwheels as Europe's primary source of power. However, the principle of the waterwheel lives on in today's water turbines.

Watt *see* **Units and standards**

Wave motion

A wave is nothing more than a disturbance that moves from place to place in some medium, carrying energy with it. Since the behavior of waves is so closely related to the concept of oscillations, that is a good place to start.

There are many examples of simple oscillations, but a very good one is that of an object attached to the end of a spring. We will assume that the other end is held fixed, perhaps by a clamp. Suppose we let the spring hang vertically and slowly lower the object until it becomes stationary. The spring is now stretched enough for its upward pull to balance the weight of the object, which at that location is in equilibrium. Now we disturb the object by lifting it a short distance above that point and letting go. The object then begins to oscillate vertically as it first falls, until the spring stops it and pulls it back upward to the original position, then it falls again, etc. The energy in the oscillating motion came from the original disturbance, which in this case moved the object to a position above the equilibrium point. At that instance, the object was at its maximum displacement whose size is the amplitude. The larger the amplitude, the greater the energy in the motion.

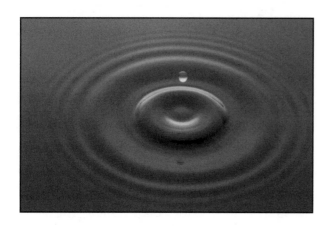

Transverse waves produced by a water droplet penetrating the surface of a body of liquid.

Now, let's try a different experiment. First, let's see what happens if we hang a duplicate object and spring side–by–side with the first one, but without the two being in contact in any way. If we disturb the first object, it oscillates just as before and the second object remains stationary at its equilibrium position. However, the situation becomes different if we connect the two objects with a rubber band and then disturb only the first object. We see that it begins to oscillate as before, but soon the second object starts to oscillate also. The rubber band allows energy to transfer to the second object, which will move with the same frequency as the first oscillation. We can make the experiment more complicated if we use a large number of springs hanging in a row, with each object connected to the one before and after it with rubber bands. If only the first object is disturbed, the oscillation will pass its energy through all the springs. After the energy has been transferred to the next few springs, the first spring will become still with its object back at its equilibrium point. This demonstrates exactly how a disturbance can move as a wave through a medium. In this example, the medium is composed of the objects on springs, which act as coupled oscillators.

The way that a disturbance is transferred from one part of a medium to another in the spring model is very similar to the way that waves move in water, air or a guitar string. We can think of the water, perhaps in a bathtub, as being composed of a great number of H_2O molecules lying very close side–by–side. If the water has been undisturbed for a long time, its surface will be calm and the molecules will be relatively stationary (of course, they are not completely stationary, but their motion is microscopic). Now suppose we disturb the water by tapping it with a finger. This produces a dis-

turbance as many molecules are forced downward, the opposite of what happened in our spring example. We have all seen a wave move on the surface of the water away from the position of our tap, and this is simply the disturbance being transferred from one molecule to another. Just as before, the larger the original displacement, the greater the energy in the disturbance and the bigger the energy that the wave carries. You might ask how the transfer of energy takes place. Actually, the molecules of water all exert some force on their neighbors which are quite close. This holds them together and provides the same effect as the rubber bands.

The wave we just made is an example of a traveling wave since the disturbance moves from place to place in the medium. It can also be classified as a transverse wave because the direction of the disturbance (vertical in this case) is perpendicular to the direction that the wave travels (horizontally). There are also longitudinal waves, like those which carry the energy of sound in air, in which the direction of the disturbance is the same as that of the wave motion. This is easy to visualize if you have ever seen a speaker move when the volume is turned up very loud. The sudden movements of the speaker compress the nearby air and that disturbance moves in the same direction toward you and your ears.

A repeated pattern of individual waves, a wave train, often occurs. A wave train can be produced in water by tapping the surface with a specific rhythm, or frequency. A complementary characteristic of a wave train is the wavelength. Suppose a friend taps the water with a specific frequency and you take a picture of the resulting waves. In effect, this lets you "freeze" the wave train in time and examine it. You will notice that there is a constant distance between the individual waves; this is the wavelength. The frequency tells how often the wave train repeats itself in time and the inverse of the wavelength tells how often the wave train repeats itself in space. Multiplying the numerical values of the frequency and the wavelength gives the speed at which the waves move.

Waves have many interesting properties. They can reflect from surfaces and refract, or change their direction, when they pass from one medium into another. If these properties seem familiar, that is because we are accustomed to light behaving in exactly this way. Obviously light reflects, and an example of refraction is the bending of light when it passes from water into air. For this reason, when you look into water, objects appear to be at different locations than their real positions. Light is therefore considered in these instances to behave as though it was a wave produced by moving disturbances of electric and magnetic fields.

KEY TERMS

Frequency—The number of cycles, or repetitions, of an oscillating motion which occur per second.

Medium—A material in which a disturbance (oscillation) at one location can transfer its energy to nearby locations, for example from one molecule of water to another.

Wave train—A repeated pattern of individual waves which are produced with a specific rhythm, or frequency.

Waves can also combine, or interfere. For example, two waves can reach a particular point at just the right time for both to disturb the medium in the same way (such as if two water waves both try to lift the surface at the same time). This is constructive interference. Likewise, destructive interference happens when the disturbances of different waves cancel. Interference can also lead to standing waves which appear to be stationary—the medium is still disturbed, but the disturbances are oscillating in place. This can only occur within confined regions, like a bathtub or a guitar string (fixed at both ends). For just the right wavelengths, traveling wave trains and their reflections off the boundaries can interfere to produce a wave that appears stationary.

See also Acoustics; Fluid dynamics; Interference; Light; Oscillations.

Further Reading:

Clark, J.O.E. *Matter and Energy: Physics in Action*, New York: Oxford University Press, 1994.

Epstein, L.C. *Thinking Physics: Practical Lessons in Critical Thinking, Second Edition*, San Francisco, CA: Insight Press, 1994.

Ehrlich, R. *Turning the World Inside Out, and 174 Other Simple Physics Demonstrations,* Princeton, NJ: Princeton University Press, 1990.

James J. Carroll

Waxbills

Waxbills are 107 species of finch-like birds that make up the family Estrilidae. Species of waxbills occur in the tropics of Africa, South and Southeast Asia, New Guinea, Australia, and many islands of the South Pacific. Their usual habitats are grasslands, marshes, savannas, forest edges, and disturbed forests. Waxbills are sedentary, nonmigratory birds.

Waxbills are small birds, ranging in body length from 3.2–5.9 in (8–15 cm). The bill is short, stout, conical–shaped, and pointed, and adapted to eating seeds. The plumage of male birds is generally brightly colored, with contrasting patterns that can include hues of red, blue, purple, green, yellow, black, or white. Female birds have a much more inconspicuous coloration.

Waxbills forage on the ground for seeds, fruits, and small invertebrates. Species that occur in open, seasonally dry habitats are gregarious during the drier times of the year, while species occurring in more closed moist habitats defend their territories throughout the year.

All waxbills are territorial during their breeding season, which for many species typically begins immediately after the seasonal rains begin. Their songs are weak hisses, buzzes, and chatterings. Waxbills construct bulky, domed nests of grassy fibers, often lined with feathers on the inside. Waxbills lay 4–10 eggs, which are incubated by both sexes, who also share duties in caring for the young.

Several species of waxbills have been domesticated, and are kept in captivity as cagebirds. These include the zebra finch (*Taeniopygia guttata*) of Australia, the striated finch or white–rumped munia (*Lonchura striata*) of South and Southeast Asia, and the Java finch (*Padda oryzivora*), native to Java and Bali in Indonesia, but widely introduced elsewhere in Indochina and Southeast Asia.

The Gouldian or rainbow finch (*Peophila gouldiae*) is a particularly gaudy bird of northern Australia, which has a yellow bill, black face, purple breast, yellow belly, and green back. The white–crowned mannikin (*Lonchura nevermanni*) is a white–headed, two–toned brown–bodied species that lives within grassy savannahs in southern New Guinea. The red–headed parrot finch (*Erythrura cyaneovirens*) has a red head, blue breast, green belly and back, and burgundy tail. The orange–eyed pytilia or red–faced waxbill (*Pytilia afra*) is a red–faced, grey–bodied species of East Africa.

Some species of waxbills are regarded as serious pests of agriculture. For example, the Java finch is a pest in parts of Southeast Asia, because of the quantities of ripened rice that this flock consumes.

See also Finches.

Bill Freedman

Waxwings

Waxwings are medium–sized, fruit–eating, perching birds found in northern Eurasia and North America, that are included in the family Bombycillidae. Waxwings have a crest on the top of their head, and have soft, sleek, often shiny plumage. The secondary feathers often have a soft, wax–like appendage at the tip, from which the common name of these birds was derived.

Waxwings are largely fruit–eating birds, although they also eat insects, especially during the breeding season. These birds usually catch their insect prey by flycatching, which involves aerial sallies from an observation perch to catch insects on the wing.

The waxwing family includes eight species worldwide. Three species in this family are familiar to North Americans.

The cedar waxwing (*Bombycilla cedrorum*) breeds in a wide range of habitats throughout the range of northern coniferous and broad leaf forests of Canada and the northern United States. The cedar waxwing winters in the southern United States and Central America.

The bohemian waxwing (*B. garrulus*) breeds in coniferous and mixedwood forests and muskegs of northwestern North America, as well as in northern Eurasia, where it is known simply as the waxwing. However, during the non–breeding season the bohemian waxwing aggregates into flocks, which forage widely for berries far to the south of the breeding range, and as far east as the Atlantic coast.

The phainopepla

(*Phainopepla nitens*) is a red–eyed, glossy–black bird that occurs in the southwestern United States and central Mexico. The *phainopepla* is found in semi–arid scrub, and is rather more insectivorous than the waxwings. The *phainopepla* also travels in small flocks during the non–breeding season.

The waxwings are rather irregular in both their breeding and wintering abundances. Waxwings sometimes occur in unusually large numbers outside of their usual range in some winters, probably as a result of poor berry crops in their normal wintering habitat. During such irruptive events of abundance, waxwings often occur in large flocks in cities, avidly feeding on berry–laden, urban trees and shrubs such as junipers and mountain–ash. These winter occurrences of flocks of bohemian and cedar waxwings are unpredictable pleasures that are relished by bird watchers.

Weak acid *see* **Acids and bases**

Weak base *see* **Acids and bases**

Weak electrolyte *see* **Electrolyte**

Weasels

Weasels, ermines, and stoats are various species of small carnivores in the family Mustelidae, which also includes the otters, badgers, martens, minks, skunks, and wolverine. Species of weasels occur in North America, northern South America, northern Africa, Europe, Asia, and Southeast Asia.

Weasels have a long, lithe, almost serpentine body, and short legs. This body shape is highly adaptive for pursuing their prey of small mammals through small holes and along narrow passages. Weasels are very active, inquisitive animals, and they can run remarkably quickly and nimbly when they are chasing their prey.

Weasels have a very soft and dense fur, and although these animals are quite small, they are commonly trapped as furbearers. Northern species of weasels develop a thick, white coat in the wintertime, and these especially valuable furs are known as ermine. Ermine is mostly used as a fine trim for coats and robes, or to make neck–pieces and stoles.

All of the weasels are terrestrial animals, occurring in a wide range of habitats, including tundra, various types of forests, and grasslands. Weasels are voracious carnivores, and they are capable of subduing animals substantially larger than themselves. They will often climb trees to hunt squirrels.

When they are faced with a super–abundance of food, weasels sometimes go on a lustful killing spree. A weasel in a chicken–house, for example, will kill a much larger number of birds than it could ever hope to eat. However, in more natural circumstances, these animals will attempt to cache their excess food. Weasels that learn how to kill chickens can be quite a problem, but they can be selectively killed. There is no need to kill weasels indiscriminately as perceived pests, especially considering the large numbers of small rodents that they kill, thereby providing a valuable service to farmers.

Weasels are generally solitary animals. However, the young stay with their mother until they learn to hunt for themselves. Young weasels engage in rough–and–tumble play, important in learning some of the physical skills that are necessary in hunting.

A long-tailed weasel (*Mustela frenata*).

Weasels are usually most active at night, although they often hunt during the day as well.

Species of weasels

The ermine or stoat (*Mustela erminea*) is a circum-boreal species, occurring widely in conifer–dominated boreal forests and tundras in northern North America, Europe, and Asia. The ermine is a ferocious predator. Although only some are 11.8 in (30 cm) long and weigh no more than 3.5 oz (100 g) (this is the weight of an adult male; females are about half as heavy), this carnivore can hunt and subdue animals as large as rabbits and hares weighing several kilograms. The winter coat of northern populations of this weasel is a well–camouflaged white, except for the black–tipped tail, while the summer pelage is tawny brown above, and yellow–white beneath.

The ermine has delayed implantation. This is characterized by mating in the summer, but the fertilized embryos remaining dormant in the uterus after they are fertilized, and not implanting and developing as embryos until 3–4 weeks prior to birth, which occurs the following spring or early summer. In this species the total post–fertilization gestation period is 200–340 days.

The long–tailed weasel (*Mustela frenata*) occurs from the southern half of North America to northern South America. Like the ermine, the long–tailed weasel has a white coat in winter, and delayed implantation.

The least, dwarf, or pygmy weasel (*Mustela rixosa*) of North America is the smallest of any of the predatory mammals (that is, order Carnivora). This species only attains a length (body plus tail) of 4.9 in (12.5 cm), and a weight of 1.47 oz (42 g). Because of its diminutive size, this species feeds mostly on mice, voles, and other small mammals. Also because of the small size of the least weasel, it must feed voraciously in order to maintain its weight and body temperature. This is because very small animals have a large ratio of body surface to mass, and they therefore lose heat quickly. In fact, the least weasel must eat an amount of small mammals equal to more than one–half of its own body weight each day. Like many other species of weasel, the dwarf weasel has a white coat in winter, and a brown coat in summer.

KEY TERMS

....

Carnivore—An animal that only feeds on other animals.

Circumboreal—A biogeographic distribution that includes the conifer–dominated boreal forests of both North America and Eurasia.

The common or Old World weasel (*Mustela nivalis*) is closely related to the least weasel, and these are sometimes considered to be geographic variants of the same species. The Old World weasel is a diminutive species that occurs in forests of Europe, northern and central Asia, and northern Africa. This species does not display delayed implantation. The Old World weasel has been introduced to New Zealand in a misguided attempt to control introduced rats and mice, but it has caused great damages through its depredations on native species of birds.

The alpine weasel (*M. altaica*) occurs in montane forests and alpine tundra of mountains in Asia. The yellow–bellied weasel (*M. kathiah*) and Siberian weasel (*M. sibirica*) are additional Asian species. The Java weasel (*M. lutreolina*) and bare–footed weasel (*M. nudipes*) are tropical–forest species of Southeast Asia.

Other species in the genus *Mustela* are relatively large in comparison with the true weasels. These include the rare and endangered black–footed ferret (*M. nigripes*) of the shortgrass prairies of western North America, the polecat or ferret (*M. putorius*) of northern Africa and Eurasia, the mink (*M. vison*) of North America, the Eurasian mink (*M. lutreola*) of Europe and Asia, and a tropical weasel (*M. africana*) of northern South America.

Further Reading:

Grzimek, B. (ed.). 1990. *Grzimek's Encyclopedia of Mammals.* London: McGraw Hill.

King, C. 1989. *The Natural History of Weasels and Stoats.* London: Academic Press.

Paradiso, J.L. (ed.). 1968. *Mammals of the World,* 2nd ed. Baltimore: John Hopkins Press.

Wilson, D.E. and D. Reeder (comp.). 1993. *Mammal Species of the World.* Washington, D.C.: Smithsonian Institution Press.

Bill Freedman

Weather

Weather can be defined as the condition of the atmosphere at any given time and place. Weather conditions are determined by six major factors: air temperature, air pressure, humidity of the air, amount and kind of cloud cover, amount and kind of precipitation, and speed and direction of the wind. Weather condition patterns for any one region or for the whole planet can be charted on a weather map containing information about all six of these factors. This information often can be used to produce a weather forecast, a prediction of weather conditions at some future time for some given region.

The study of weather is known as meteorology. No exact date can be given for the beginnings of this science since humans have studied weather conditions for many centuries. Indeed the word meteorology itself goes back to *Meterologica*, a book written by the Greek natural philosopher Aristotle in about 340 B.C. Many scholars date the rise of modern meteorology to the work of a Norwegian father and son team, Vilhelm and Jakob Bjerknes. The Bjerknes' first developed the concept of masses of air moving across Earth's surface affecting weather conditions as they moved. They also created the first widespread system for measuring weather conditions throughout their native Norway.

The six factors determining weather conditions can be regarded as a result of the interaction of four basic physical elements: the Sun, Earth's atmosphere, Earth itself, and natural landforms occur on Earth.

Solar energy

The driving force behind all meteorological changes taking place on Earth is solar energy. Each minute the outer portions of Earth's atmosphere receive an average of 2 calories/sq cm. This value is known as the solar constant. Although the solar constant changes over very long periods of time it does not vary enough to affect the general nature of Earth's weather over short periods of time.

Solar energy reaching the outer atmosphere may experience a variety of fates. About a quarter (25%) reaches Earth's surface directly and another quarter (26%) eventually reaches the surface after being scattered by gases in the atmosphere. Thirty percent of all solar energy is lost to space by means of scattering and by reflection off clouds and Earth's surface. Another 19% is absorbed by gases in the atmosphere and by clouds.

An important factor in determining the fate of solar radiation is its wavelength. Shorter wavelengths tend to be absorbed by gases in the atmosphere (especially oxygen and ozone) while radiation of longer wavelengths tends to be transmitted to Earth's surface.

Solar radiation that reaches Earth's surface is absorbed to a varying degree depending on the kind of material on which it falls. Since darker colors and rougher surfaces absorb radiation better than lighter colors and smoother surfaces soil tends to absorb solar radiation well, and water, not as well.

Solar energy at Earth's surface is then re–radiated to the atmosphere. The re–radiated energy differs from the incoming energy in one important way: it tends to consist of longer wavelengths. This re–radiated energy is likely to be absorbed by other gases in the atmosphere such as carbon dioxide and nitrous oxide. This absorption process, the greenhouse effect, is responsible for maintaining the planet's annual average temperature.

Humidity, clouds, and precipitation

The absorption of solar energy by Earth's surface and its atmosphere is directly responsible for most of the major factors making up weather patterns. For example when water (in oceans, lakes, rivers, streams, and other bodies of water) is warmed it tends to evaporate and move upward into the atmosphere. The amount of moisture found in the air at any one time and place is called the humidity. Humans are very aware of this characteristic of weather.

Water that has evaporated from Earth's surface (or escaped from plants through the process of transpiration) rises to an altitude in the atmosphere at which the air around it is cold enough to cause condensation. When moisture condenses into tiny water droplets or tiny ice crystals clouds are formed.

Clouds are an important factor in the development of weather patterns. They tend to reflect sunlight back into space. Thus an accumulation of cloud cover may contribute to a decrease in heat retained in the atmosphere.

Clouds are also the breeding grounds for various types of precipitation. As water droplets or ice crystals collide with each other, coalesce, and form larger particles, they eventually become large enough to overcome upward drafts in the air and fall to Earth as precipitation. The form of precipitation that occurs (rain, snow, sleet, hail, etc.) depends on the atmospheric conditions through which the water or ice falls.

Atmospheric pressure and winds

Solar energy also is directly responsible for the development of differing atmospheric pressures at various locations on the planet's surface and the winds that result from these differences. Since Earth's surface is different in color and texture from place to place some locations will be heated more strongly by solar radiation than others. Warm places tend to heat the air above them setting convection currents into movement that carry masses of air upward into the upper atmosphere. Those same convection currents then carry other masses of air downward from the upper atmosphere toward Earth's surface.

In regions where warm air moves upward the atmospheric pressure tends to be low; downward air movements are associated with higher atmospheric pressures. These higher or lower atmospheric pressures can be measured by a barometer which provides information not only about current pressures but also about possible future weather patterns.

The existence of areas with different atmospheric pressures accounts for the movement of air (that is, of winds). Wind is simply the movement of air from a region of high pressure to one of lower pressure.

Terrestrial characteristics

If the Sun provides the energy by which weather patterns can develop certain features of Earth itself determine the precise forms in which those patterns may be exhibited. One example has already been provided above. Earth's surface is highly variable ranging from oceans to deserts to cultivated land to urbanized areas. The way solar energy is absorbed and reflected from each of these regions is different, accounting for variations in local weather patterns.

Other characteristics of the planet account for more significant variations in weather patterns. These characteristics include such features as the tilt of its axis to its plane of revolution and variations in Earth's distance from the Sun.

The fact that Earth's axis is tilted at an angle of 23 1/2° to the plane of its orbit means that the planet is heated unevenly by the Sun. During the summer sunlight reaching the Northern Hemisphere strikes more nearly at right angles than it does in the Southern Hemisphere. In the winter, the situation is reversed.

The elliptical shape of Earth's orbit around the Sun also affects weather conditions. At certain times of the year the planet is closer to the Sun than at others. This variation means that the amount of solar energy reaching the outer atmosphere will vary from month to month depending on Earth's location in its path around the Sun.

Even Earth's rotation on its own axis influences weather patterns. If Earth did not rotate, air movements on the planet would probably be relatively simple. Air heated along the equator would rise into the upper atmosphere, travel northward toward the poles, be cooled, and then return to Earth's surface at the poles.

Earth's rotation causes the deflection of these theoretically simple air movements. Instead of a single overall equator–to–poles air movement global winds are broken up into smaller cells. In one cell warm air rises above the equator, moves northward in upper altitudes, is cooled, and returns to Earth in the regions around 30° north and south latitude. A second cell consists of air that moves upward in the regions around 60° north and south latitude, across the upper atmosphere, and then downward at about 30° north and south latitude. The final cell contains winds traveling upward at 60° north and south latitude and then downward again at the poles.

Topographic factors

Irregularities on Earth's surface also affect weather. A mountain range can dramatically affect the movement of air masses that approach them. Suppose that a mass of warm moisture–full air is forced to ascend one side of a mountain range. As the air is pushed upward it cools off and moisture begins to condense out first in the form of clouds then as precipitation. This side of the mountain range will experience high rates of precipitation.

As the air mass continues over the top of the mountain range it does so without its moisture. The winds that sweep down the far side of the range will tend to be warm and dry. The term orographic is used to describe changes in weather patterns like these induced by mountain ranges.

Weather and climate

The terms weather and climate often are used in conjunction with each other but they refer to quite different phenomena. Weather involves atmospheric conditions that currently prevail or that exist over a relatively short period of time. Climate refers to the average weather pattern for a region (or for the whole planet) over a much longer period of time (at least three decades according to some authorities).

Changes in weather patterns are easily observed. It may rain today and be clear tomorrow. Changes in climatic patterns are much more difficult to detect. If the summer of 1997 is unusually hot there is no way of knowing if that fact is part of a general trend towards

KEY TERMS
. . . .
Humidity—The amount of water vapor contained in the air.

Meteorology—The study of Earth's atmosphere and the changes that take place within it.

Orographic—A term referring to effects produced when air moves across a mountain range.

Solar constant—The rate at which solar energy is received at the top of the atmosphere.

Solar energy—Any form of electromagnetic radiation that is emitted by the Sun.

Topography—The detailed surface features of an area.

warmer weather or a single variation that will not appear again for some time.

See also Atmospheric pressure; Atmospheric temperature; Clouds; Precipitation; Seasons; Weather forecasting; Weather mapping; Wind.

Further Reading:

Bramwell, Martyn. *Weather*. New York: Franklin Watts, 1994.
Lutgens, Frederick K., and Edward J. Tarbuck. *The Atmosphere: An Introduction to Meteorology*, 4th ed. Englewood Cliffs: Prentice–Hall, 1989.
Lynott, Robert E. *How Weather Works and Why*. Gadfly Press, 1994.
Thompson, Philip D., Robert O'Brien, and the Editors of Life. *Weather*. New York: Time Inc., 1965.
Watts, Alan. *The Weather Handbook*. Dobbs Ferry: Sheridan House, 1994.

David E. Newton

Weather forecasting

Weather forecasting is the attempt by meteorologists to predict the state of the atmosphere at some future time and the weather conditions that may be expected. Weather forecasting is the single most important practical reason for the existence of meteorology as a science. It is obvious that knowing the future of the weather can be important for individuals and organizations. Accurate weather forecasts can tell a farmer when the best time to plant is; an airport control tower what information to send to planes that are landing and taking off; and residents of a coastal region when a hurricane might strike.

Humans have been looking for ways to forecast the weather for centuries. The Greek natural philosopher Theophrastus wrote a book, *Book of Signs*, in about 300 B.C. listing more than 200 ways of knowing when to expect rain, wind, fair conditions, and other kinds of weather.

Any form of scientific forecasting was not possible until meteorologists were able to collect data about current weather conditions from a relatively widespread system of observing stations in a timely fashion. The invention of the telegraph by Samuel F. B. Morse in the 1830s and the development of a weather station network by Vilhelm and Jacob Bjerknes in the 1920s satisfied these conditions and the age of scientific forecasting was under way.

The National Weather Service

In the United States weather forecasting is the responsibility of the National Weather Service (NWS) a division of the National Oceanic and Atmospheric Administration of the Department of Commerce. NWS maintains more than 400 field offices and observatories in all 50 states and overseas. The future modernized structure of the NWS will include 116 weather forecast offices (WFO) and 13 river forecast centers, all collocated with WFO's. WFO also collects data from ships at sea all over the world and from meteorological satellites circling Earth. The Service annually collects nearly four million pieces of information about atmospheric conditions from these sources.

The forecasting work of NWS is carried out at three major and two smaller centers. The primary center for short– and long–term forecasts is the National Meteorological Center in Camp Springs, Maryland. Severe weather systems such as thunderstorms and hurricanes are monitored at the National Severed Storms Forecast Center in Kansas City, Missouri. Hurricane watches and warnings are issued by the National Hurricane Center in Miami (serving the Atlantic, Caribbean, Gulf of Mexico, and eastern Pacific Ocean) and by the Forecast Office in and Honolulu (serving the central Pacific).

Global weather data are collected at more than 1,000 observation points around the world and then sent to central stations maintained by the World Meteorological Organization a division of the United Nations.

Global data also is sent to NWS's National Meteorological Center for analysis and publication.

Types of weather forecasts

The less one knows about the way the atmosphere works the simpler weather forecasting appears to be. For example if clouds appear in the sky and a light rain begins to fall one might predict that rain will continue throughout the day. This type of weather forecast is known as a persistent forecast. A persistent forecast assumes the weather over a particular geographic area simply will continue into the future.

Persistent forecasting's validity lasts for a few hours but not much longer because weather conditions result from a complex interaction of many factors that still are not well understood and change very rapidly.

A somewhat more reliable approach to weather forecasting is known as the steady–state or trend method. This method is based on the knowledge that weather conditions are strongly influenced by the movement of air masses which often can be charted quite accurately. A weather map might show that a cold front is moving across the great plains of the United States from west to east with an average speed of 10 mph (16 kph). It might be reasonable to predict that the front would reach a place 100 mi (1,609 km) to the east in a matter of 10 hours. Since characteristic types of weather often are associated with cold fronts it then might be reasonable to predict the weather at locations east of the front with some degree of confidence.

A similar approach to forecasting is called the analogue method because it uses analogies between existing weather maps and similar maps from the past. For example suppose a weather map for December 10, 1996, is found to be almost identical with a weather map for January 8, 1993. Since the weather for the earlier date is already known it might be reasonable to predict similar weather patterns for the later date.

Yet another form of weather forecasting makes use of statistical probability. In some locations on Earth's surface one can safely predict the weather because a consistent pattern has already been established. In parts of Peru it rains no more than a few inches per century. A weather forecaster in this region might feel confident that he or she could predict clear skies for tomorrow with a 99.9% chance of being correct.

Long–range forecasting

The complexity of atmosphere conditions is reflected in the fact that none of the forecasting methods outlined above is dependable for more than a few days at best. This reality does not prevent meteorologists from attempting to make long–term forecasts. These forecasts might predict the weather a few weeks, a few months, or even a year in advance. One of the best known (although not necessarily the most accurate) of long–term forecasts is found in the annual edition of the *Farmer's Almanac*.

The basis for long–range forecasting is a statistical analysis of weather conditions over an area in the past. For example a forecaster might determine that the average snow fall in December in Grand Rapids, Michigan, over the past 30 years had been 15.8 in (40.1 cm). A reasonable way to try estimating next year's snowfall in Grand Rapids would be to assume that it might be close to 15.8 inches (40.1 cm).

Today this kind of statistical data is augmented by studies of global conditions such as winds in the upper atmosphere and ocean temperatures. If a forecaster knows that the jet stream over Canada has been diverted southward from its normal flow for a period of months that change might alter precipitation patterns over Grand Rapids over the next few months.

Numerical weather prediction

The term numerical weather prediction is something of a misnomer since all forms of forecasting make use of numerical data like temperature, atmospheric pressure, and humidity. More precisely numerical weather prediction refers to forecasts that are obtained by using complex mathematical calculations carried out with high–speed computers.

Numerical weather prediction is based on mathematical models of the atmosphere. A mathematical model is a system of equations that attempt to describe the properties of the atmosphere and changes that may take place within it. These equations can be written because the gases which comprise the atmosphere obey the same physical and chemical laws that gases on Earth's surface follow. For example Charles' Law says that when a gas is heated it tends to expand. This law applies to gases in the atmosphere as it does to gases in a laboratory.

The technical problem that meteorologists face is that atmospheric gases are influenced by many different physical and chemical factors at the same time. A gas that expands according to Charles' Law may also be decomposing because of chemical forces acting on it. How can anyone make use of all the different chemical and physical laws operating in the atmosphere to come up with a forecast of future atmospheric conditions?

The role of computers in weather forecasting

The answer is that no human can solve such a problem. The mathematics involved are too complex. The task is not too much for computer. Computers can perform a series of calculations in a few hours that would take a meteorologist his or her whole lifetime to finish.

In numerical weather predicting meteorologists select a group of equations that describe the conditions of the atmosphere as completely as possible for any one location at any one time. This set of equations can never be complete because even a computer is limited as to the number of calculations it can complete in a reasonable time. Thus meteorologists pick out the factors they think are most important in influencing the development of atmospheric conditions. These equations are fed into the computer. After a certain period of time the computer will print out the changes that might be expected if atmospheric gases behave according to the scientific laws to which they are subject. From this printout a meteorologist can make a forecast of the weather in an area in the future.

The accuracy of numerical weather predictions depend primarily on two factors. First the more data that is available to a computer the more accurate its results. Second the faster the speed of the computer the more calculations it can perform and the more accurate its report will be. In the period from 1955 (when computers were first used in weather forecasting) to the current time, the percent skill of forecasts has improved from about 30% to more than 60%. The percent skill measure was invented to describe the likelihood that a weather forecast will be better than pure chance.

Accuracy of weather forecasts

Weather forecasters have long been the subject of jokes probably as much today as they were in Theophrastus' time. One reason for this is that there is no standard measure of a "correct" weather forecast. Suppose that a forecaster predicts heavy rain for your area tomorrow. Does a rainfall of 1 in (2.5 cm) prove that prediction correct? Or a rainfall of 1.5 in (1 cm)? Or a rainfall of 5 in (13 cm)?

Forecast accuracy also is difficult to judge since the average person's expectations probably have increased as the percent skill of forecasts also has increased. A hundred years ago few people would have expected to have much idea as to what the weather would be likely 24 hours in the future. Today a good forecast often is possible over this period but it still may not be good enough for the people who live in that area.

KEY TERMS

. . . .

Analogue method of forecasting—A prediction of future weather conditions based on the assumption that current conditions will produce weather patterns similar to those observed in the past.

Hurricane warning—A notice issued when a hurricane has been observed either visually or on a radar screen.

Hurricane watch—A notice to the general public that explains conditions are such that a hurricane may be expected within a particular area.

Long–term forecast—A prediction of weather conditions over a matter of weeks, months, or a year.

Mathematical model—A system of equations that attempts to describe the properties of the atmosphere and changes that may take place within it.

Numerical forecast—A prediction of future weather patterns obtained by using high–speed computers to carry out complex mathematical calculations derived from mathematical models of the atmosphere.

Percent skill—The likelihood that a weather forecast will be better than a pure chance prediction.

Persistent forecast—A prediction of weather conditions based on the assumption that the weather over a particular geographic area will remain constant over the near future.

Short–term forecast—A prediction for weather conditions over a matter of hours or days.

Statistical probability forecast—A prediction of future weather conditions based on an analysis of the likelihood of various conditions having occurred in the past.

Steady–state forecast, Trend method—A prediction of weather conditions based on the movement of air masses over a given geographical area at about the same direction and approximately the same speed as they have been moving.

In general it is probably safe to say that the shorter the time period and the more limited the geographic area involved the more accurate a forecast is likely to be. For periods of less than a day a forecast covering an area of 100 sq mi (259 sq km) is likely to be quite dependable. Predictions about weather patterns six months from now for the state of California are likely to be much less reliable.

See also Air masses and fronts; Atmospheric circulation; Atmosphere observation; Atmospheric pressure; Atmospheric temperature; Global climate; Weather; Weather mapping.

Further Reading:

Battan, Louis J. *Fundamentals of Meteorology*. Englewood Cliffs: Prentice–Hall, 1979.

Lutgens, Frederick K., and Edward J. Tarbuck. *The Atmosphere: An Introduction to Meteorology*, 4th ed. Englewood Cliffs: Prentice–Hall, 1989.

Lynott, Robert E. *How Weather Works and Why*. Gadfly Press, 1994.

Moran, Joseph M., and Michael D. Morgan. *Meteorology: The Atmosphere and the Science of Weather*. New York: Macmillan, 1994.

David E. Newton

Weathering

Weathering is the process by which rocks and minerals are broken down into simpler materials by means of physical (mechanical), chemical, and biological processes. Weathering is an extremely important phenomenon for the human species since it is the mechanism by which one of the planet's most important natural resources—soil—is formed.

The exact way in which weathering occurs in any particular situation depends primarily on two factors: the type of rock and the environmental conditions to which the rock is exposed. For example, rocky formations along a seacoast are likely to be exposed to the mechanical action of waves and tides. But rocks buried underground are more likely to be attacked by chemical reactions made possible by water that runs through them.

Physical (mechanical) weathering

During physical weathering, a large piece of rock is broken down into smaller and smaller pieces. This process can come about as the result of a number of natural processes. For example, the force of gravity may cause a large boulder to break loose from the top of a mountain and fall. When the boulder hits solid ground, it may break apart into many smaller pieces.

Ground movements can also result in physical weathering. As overlying rocks and soils are removed by natural or human–caused forces, underlying rocks may work their way to Earth's surface. As pressure on these rocks is relieved, they may begin to expand outward, often forming an flaky appearance known as exfoliation.

Abrasion can also cause physical weathering. Imagine a wind storm blowing across a broad expanse of sandy desert. Tiny particles of sand are carried along by the wind, a current of air that acts like sandpaper on rocks that stand in its pathway. The wind–sandpaper scours off pieces of grit and sand from these rocks, contributing to their physical weathering.

Temperature and moisture

In many locations, changes in temperature and moisture content of the environment cause significant physical weathering. When rock is warmed, it expands; when it cools, it contracts. In some regions, rocks are heated to relatively high temperatures during the day and then cooled to much lower temperatures during the night. The constant expansion and contraction of the rocks may result in pieces being broken off.

This effect is likely to be more pronounced if water is present. Suppose that water fills the cracks in a rock during the day. At night, if the temperature drops far enough, that water will freeze and form veins of ice in the rock. But water expands as it freezes. Therefore, the veins of ice are likely to break apart pieces of the rock, a process that is repeated day after day and night after night when temperatures follow the pattern described above.

Chemical weathering

Chemical weathering is the process by which changes take place in the very chemical structure of rocks themselves. Chemical weathering represents a second stage of rock disintegration in which small pieces of rock produced by physical weathering are then further broken apart by chemical processes.

Three chemical reactions in particular are effective in bringing about the weathering of a rock: acid reactions, hydrolysis, and oxidation. Acids form readily in the soil. One of the most common such reactions occurs when carbon dioxide in the air reacts with water to form a weak acid, carbonic acid. Carbonic acid has the ability to attack many kinds of rocks, changing them into other forms. For example, when carbonic acid reacts with limestone, it produces calcium bicarbonate, which is partially soluble in water. Caves are formed when underground water containing carbonic acid travels through blocks of limestone, dissolves out the limestone, and leaves empty pockets (caves) behind.

KEY TERMS

Abrasion—The mechanism by which one material rubs against another material, sometimes producing weather in the process.

Chemical reaction—Any change that takes place in which one substance is changed into one or more new substances.

Exfoliation—The process by which skin–like layers form on the outer surface of a rock and, in some cases, eventually peel off.

Oxidation—The chemical reaction by which a substance reacts with oxygen.

Acids produced by human activities can also produce chemical weathering. For example, the conversion of metallic ores to the pure metals often results in the formation of sulfur dioxide. When sulfur dioxide combines with water, it forms the weak acid sulfurous acid and, eventually, the stronger acid sulfuric acid. Both of these acids are capable of attacking certain kinds of rocks in much the way that carbonic acid does.

Hydrolysis is a chemical reaction by which a compound reacts with water to form one or more new substances. A number of rock–forming minerals readily undergo hydrolysis, especially in acidic conditions. For example, the common mineral feldspar will undergo hydrolysis to produce a clay–type mineral known as kaolinite and silicic acid. Both of these new compounds are much more soluble in water than is feldspar. Hydrolysis of the mineral results, therefore, in the degradation of any rocks in which it may occur.

Oxidation occurs when the metallic part of a mineral reacts with oxygen in the air (or from some other source) to produce a new substance that is different in structure or more soluble than the original mineral. The spectacular red, orange, and yellow color of certain natural rock formations—such as those in Utah's Bryce Canyon—are an indication that an oxide of iron has been produced during the chemical weathering of the rock formations.

Biological weathering

The presence of living organisms can also cause weathering. Imagine that a seed falls into a small crevice in a rock and begins to germinate. As the plant continues to grow and send down roots, it will work its way into the rock and eventually make the crevice grow in size. Eventually the plant's roots may actually tear the rock apart.

Rates of weathering

The rate at which rocks disintegrate depends both on the type of rock involved and the external forces to which the rock is exposed. As an example, sandstone tends to weather rather easily, while granite is quite resistant to weathering. The presence of moisture, high temperatures, large temperature variations, and air movement also tend to increase the rate at which weathering takes place. Human activities can also affect the rate of weathering. For example, large quantities of gaseous oxides are produced by electrical power generating plants. When these oxides react with water vapor in the air, they form "acid rain." When acid rain falls to the Earth's surface, it may attack rocky materials in much the same way that natural acids like carbonic acid do.

See also Minerals; Rocks; Soil.

Further Reading:

Jenny, Hans. *Factors of Soil Formation*. New York: McGraw–Hill, 1941.
Larson, Edwin E., and Peter W. Birkeland. *Putnam's Geology*. 4th ed. New York: Oxford University Press, 1982.

David E. Newton

Weather mapping

Weather mapping is the process of representing existing weather patterns and their future development and movement on a map. The process is only possible if two conditions are met. First, current weather conditions must be available at a number of relatively widely distributed stations. Second, reports of those conditions must be transmitted to a central collecting station within a short time period.

History

Weather maps first came in use in the last third of the nineteenth century when the invention of the telegraph made the transmission of weather data from far–flung observing points possible. In 1870 the newly created National Weather Service produced weather maps for limited regions of the United States.

In Norway Vilhelm and Jakob Bjerknes developed one of the most successful early weather mapping systems. The Bjerknes convinced the Norwegian government to set up weather stations in strategically important areas throughout their country. The telegraph–collected data from these stations was assembled in Bergen and used to produce some of the most complete weather maps available at the time.

Data collection and transmission

Today data on weather conditions around the world are collected by more than 10,000 individuals stations, hundreds of ships at sea, and a variety of instruments traveling through Earth's atmosphere. These data are transmitted regularly four times a day: usually at 0:00 hours, 6:00 hours, 12:00 hours, and 18:00 hours (Greenwich Mean Time). The data are used by national weather services to develop weather maps and forecasts for their own regions. Overseeing these individuals forecasts is the World Meteorological Organization (WMO) an international organization consisting of more than 130 nations. WMO is responsible for ensuring that all stations follow standard collection and transmission procedures and for the exchange of weather information among member nations.

The data sent from an observation station to the central collecting point are transmitted by a standard code consisting of number blocks. Meteorologists understand the significance of each block of numbers and translate them into specific weather conditions such as barometric pressure, temperature, and wind speed.

Constructing the weather map

Many different kinds of weather maps exist. Some are complex and contain a great deal of detailed information. Others are simpler and provide only general patterns and trends. Maps can be sub–divided into those that summarize weather close to Earth's surface (surface charts) and those that describe weather at upper altitudes.

One very detailed type of map makes use of the station model. The reporting station is indicated with a small circle and the data received from that station is arranged around the circle in a predetermined pattern. Among the kinds of data plotted in the station model are cloud cover, wind direction, visibility in miles, present weather, barometric pressure, current air temperature, cloud types, dew point, and precipitation.

Most of these variables can be represented by numbers. Visibility might be indicated as 1/2 for 0.5 mi (0.8 km) and current temperature as 22 for 22°C (71°F).

KEY TERMS

. . . .

Barometric pressure—Air pressure; the force exerted by a column of air at any given point.

Cloud cover—The portion of the sky that is covered by clouds at any given time and place.

Dew point—The temperature to which air must be cooled for it to become saturated.

Isobar—A line on a weather map connecting points of equal pressure.

Surface chart—A map that shows weather conditions at and just above Earth's surface.

Visibility—The distance to which an observer can see at any given location.

Other data are represented by standard symbols. Wind direction and speed are indicated by a one–edged arrow. The number of feathers on the arrow indicate the wind speed and the orientation of the arrow indicates the wind direction. A single full feather represents a wind speed of 8–12 knots; a double feather, a speed of 18–22 knots; and so on. A variety of symbols represent current weather conditions, such as * for intermittent snow fall and ' for intermittent drizzle.

The daily weather map

The weather map that appears in daily newspapers can be used to predict with some degree of accuracy conditions in the next few days. It usually does not include as much station information as the more detailed maps described above. Instead the major features of the daily weather map include isobars and high and low pressure areas.

Isobars connect locations with the same barometric pressure. The pressure described by each isobar is often indicated at one end, the other, or both, in inches, millibars, or other unit. Isobars often enclose regions of high or low pressure indicated on the map as H or L.

The outer edge of a concentric series of isobars marks a front. The nature of the front is indicated by means of solid triangles, solid half-circles , or a combination of the two. An isobar with solid triangles attached represents a cold front; one with solid half-circles, a warm front; one with triangles and half-circles on opposite sides, a stationary front; and one with triangles and half–circles on the same side, an occluded front. The daily weather map may also include simpli-

fied symbols that indicate weather at a station as a T enclosed in a circle for thunderstorms, F enclosed in a circle for fog, and Z in a circle for freezing rain.

See also Air masses and fronts; Atmospheric circulation; Atmosphere observation; Atmospheric pressure; Atmospheric temperature; Clouds; Precipitation; Weather; Weather forecasting.

Further Reading:

Ahrens, C. Donald. *Meteorology Today*, 2nd ed. St. Paul: West Publishing Company, 1985.

Lutgens, Frederick K., and Edward J. Tarbuck. *The Atmosphere: An Introduction to Meteorology*, 4th ed. Englewood Cliffs: Prentice Hall, 1989.

McNeill, Robert C. *Understanding the Weather*. Las Vegas: Arbor Publishers, 1991.

Moran, Joseph M., and Michael D. Morgan. *Meteorology: The Atmosphere and the Science of Weather*. New York: Macmillan, 1994.

David E. Newton

Weather modification

The term weather modification refers to any deliberate effort on the part of humans to influence weather patterns for some desirable purpose. Probably the most familiar example of weather modification is the seeding of clouds, most often done in order to increase the amount of precipitation during periods of drought.

The earliest scientific programs on weather modification date to the 1940s when Vincent J. Schaefer carried out experiments on cloud seeding. A half century later, the science of weather modification is still in its infancy with many questions surrounding the most effective way of bringing about the changes desired in any particular setting. The major types of weather modification that are currently in use or under study include cloud seeding, frost prevention, fog and cloud dispersal, hurricane modification, hail suppression, and lighting suppression.

Cloud seeding

A cloud is a large mass of water droplets and ice crystals. Precipitation normally occurs in a cloud only when ice crystals grow large enough to fall to Earth as rain, snow, hail, or some other form of precipitation. When conditions do not favor the growth of ice crystals, moisture remains suspended in the clouds, and precipitation does not occur.

The general goal of cloud seeding is to find some way of converting the supercooled droplets of liquid water in a cloud to ice crystals. Supercooled water is water that remains in a liquid state even below its freezing point. The two substances most commonly used to transform water droplets to ice crystals are dry ice (solid carbon dioxide) and silver iodide.

The ability of dry ice to trigger the condensation of supercooled water droplets was discovered accidentally in 1946 by Schaefer. He had planned to use a block of dry ice to cool a container of moist air, but discovered that the dry ice actually initiated the formation of ice crystals in the container. Shortly after Schaefer's research, the ability of silver iodide to produce similar results was also discovered.

Methods of cloud seeding

Any technique of cloud seeding depends on the release of millions of tiny particles of dry ice or silver iodide into a cloud. One way of accomplishing that goal is to ignite solid silver iodide in burners on the ground. The smoke thus formed consists of many tiny particles of the compound which are then carried upward into a cloud.

A more efficient way of seeding a cloud is to drop the seeding agent from an airplane onto the top of the cloud. If silver iodide is used, it can be released from flares attached to the wing tips of the aircraft. If dry ice is used, it is first pulverized into a fine powder and then sprayed onto the cloud.

Effectiveness of cloud seeding

A number of large experiments have been conducted to determine the effectiveness of cloud seeding as a way of increasing precipitation. The Atmospheric Water Resources Program of the Bureau of Reclamation, for example, has supported about a dozen research projects on cloud seeding. In one of these projects, the Colorado River Basin Project, cloud seeding was thought to have produced an increase of about 30 percent in the amount of snow falling in Colorado's San Juan Mountains. Experts estimated the value of this additional water for farmers and other consumers at about $100 million.

Other agencies at federal, state, and county level have also supported cloud research projects. A group of counties in Kansas, for example, annually join together to support cloud seeding experiments during periods of unusually low precipitation.

A great deal has been learned in the last 50 years about the conditions under which cloud seeding is most likely to be effective. Scientists have discovered, for example, that the optimal rate for seeding with dry ice is 0.17 oz (5 g) for each 0.62 mi (1 km) of cloud surface and 0.89 oz (25 g) per 0.62 mi (1 km) for silver iodide. Still, precise evaluations of the effectiveness of various forms of cloud seeding are often difficult because of the inherent uncertainty about most weather patterns such as cloud formation and dissipation and precipitation rates.

Fog and cloud dispersal

The techniques of cloud seeding can also be used for a second purpose, the removal of clouds and fog. This goal is desirable, as an example, in regions around an airport where prolonged fog can bring air travel to a halt, at great economic cost. The use of dry ice as a seeding agent can cause water droplets in fog to condense on ice crystals, after which they precipitate out of the air. In the process, fog banks and clouds may disappear.

Some dramatic results have been achieved with commercial fog dispersion at airports. In some cases, areas of a few square kilometers have been cleared in a matter of hours by seeding with dry ice.

Hail and lighting suppression

The federal government has been interested to a greater or less extent in programs of hail and lighting suppression for more than two decades. Hail suppression is of interest because of the devastating effects that this form of precipitation can have on crops, while lighting suppression is of importance because of the many forest fires it causes.

The principle underlying most hail suppression research is that hail can be prevented if the atmosphere is flooded with nuclei on which moisture can condense and freeze. The more nuclei present, the argument goes, the less likely large pieces of ice (hail) are to form. Results of research on hail suppression thus far have not been especially encouraging.

Research on lighting suppression, while of considerable economic value, has so far not received a great deal of attention. One suggestion has been to seed thunderheads with very small aluminum fibers in an attempt to dissipate electrical charges in a cloud. Early research in the late 1960s and early 1970s produced some promising results, but relatively little work is now being done in the field.

KEY TERMS
. . . .

Cloud—A large mass of condensed moisture consisting of water droplets and/or ice crystals.

Cloud seeding—The introduction of particles of (usually) dry ice or silver iodide with the hope of increasing precipitation from the cloud.

Dry ice—Solid carbon dioxide.

Fog—A cloud whose base lies at or near the Earth's surface.

Hail—A form of precipitation consisting or relatively large masses of ice.

Precipitation—Any form of solid or liquid water that reaches the ground from the atmosphere.

Supercooled water—Water that is cooled below its normal freezing point without having actually frozen.

Hurricane modification

The control of hurricanes would be another area with very significant economic and human benefit. Some researchers have suggested that cloud seeding techniques might be a way of dissipating the energy stored in a hurricane. Proposals have been made for the seeding of both the hurricane center (its "eye") and the high velocity winds that surround it.

Project Stormfury is an on–again, off–again project of the federal government to test theories of weather modification. The project seeded Hurricane Ester in 1961, Hurricane Beulah in 1963, and Hurricane Debbie in 1969, among others. At its most effective, the seeding process appears to have reduced hurricane winds by as much as 30 percent. Hurricane modification research continues in the early 1990s, but at a relatively modest level.

Frost prevention

The most promising field of weather modification may well be in the prevention of frost. Frost is such a devastating event for grape growers, citrus farmers, and other fields of agriculture that extensive efforts have been made to develop fog prevention systems. The two general principles that underlie most of these systems have been to increase the temperature of air near the ground, where frost forms, and to reduce the amount of heat lost at night, when frost formation usually occurs.

Some of the specific techniques used to accomplish these goals include heaters (to warm air), wind machines (to insure mixing of air), sprinkling systems (to provide water which will release heat when it freezes), and smudge pots (to release heat).

Wartime applications

Some defense experts have suggested the use of weather modification techniques as a military weapon. The claim has been made, for example, that the United States used cloud seeding during the Vietnam war. The hope was that increased rainfall would make the movement of personnel and material along the Ho Chi Minh trail more difficult.

Social and ethical issues

The use of weather modification techniques is often surrounded by controversy. An increase of precipitation over an area might be of benefit to some individuals in the area, but a disadvantage to others. For example, suppose that the owner of a private ski resort wants to have clouds seeded in order to increase snowfall over his or her property. If that effort is successful, the ski area benefits, economically. But other individuals and businesses in the area might suffer from this change in the weather. As an example, the county or state might have to pay more to keep roads and highways clear of the additional snow.

See also Clouds; Precipitation; Tropical cyclone.

Further Reading:

Ahrens, C. Donald. *Meteorology Today.* 2nd ed. St. Paul, Minn.: West Publishing Company, 1985.

Eagleman, Joe R. *Meteorology: The Atmosphere in Action.* 2nd ed. Belmont, Cal.: Wadsworth Publishing Company, 1985.

Fleagle, R. G., et al. *Weather Modification in the Public Interest.* Seattle: University of Washington Press, 1974.

Lutgens, Frederick K., and Edward J. Tarbuck. *The Atmosphere: An Introduction to Meteorology.* 4th ed. Englewood Cliffs, N.J.: Prentice Hall, 1989.

Newton, David E. *Science and Social Issues.* Portland, Maine: J. Weston Walch, Publishers, 1992.

David E. Newton

Weaver finches

Weaver finches are a relatively large family of 156 species of perching birds, comprising the family Ploceidae. Weaver finches are native to Africa, Madagascar, Eurasia, and Malaysia. This group is richest in species in Africa. However, some species have been widely introduced outside of their natural range.

Species of weaver finches occur in a wide range of terrestrial habitats, including semi–deserts, grasslands, savannahs, and various types of forests. Weaver finches do not migrate, although during times of drought and food shortage, they may undertake wanderings covering hundreds of kilometers.

Weaver finches are relatively small birds, most with a body length of 3.9–9.8 in (10–25 cm)—not including the very long tail of some African species. Weaver finches are rather stout–bodied, and they have a short, pointed, conical, seed–eating bill. The coloration and patterns of their plumage are highly variable among species, and are quite attractive in some cases.

Weaver finches mostly eat seeds, but they also eat other small fruits, succulent foliage, and insects.

Most species of weaver finches are gregarious, occurring in flocks during the nonbreeding season, and often nesting in colonial groups. Their calls are harsh and repeated chirps, buzzes, and chatterings, and not very musical.

Nesting and breeding systems are extremely variable among the weaver finches. Nesting strategies range from large, woven colonial nests to individually woven nests. Some species are polygynous, in which a male breeds with as many females as possible, and helps little with the incubation of eggs or care of the young birds. One species, the cuckoo weaver (*Anomalospiza imberbis*), is a parasitic breeder, laying its eggs in the nests of other species, which then raise the parasitic baby. In most species, however, a one–family domed nest is constructed, the clutch size is 2–8, the female or both sexes incubate the eggs, and both parents care for the young.

Species of weaver finches

The typical weaver finches are in the genus *Passer*, including two species that commonly nest in cities and around farms in many regions — the house sparrow (*Passer domesticus*) and the Eurasian tree sparrow (*P. montanum*). Both of these species have been introduced far beyond their original, natural ranges. This includes North America, where the house sparrow in particular is a common bird in cities. In fact, the house sparrow is now one of the world's most widely distributed species of land birds.

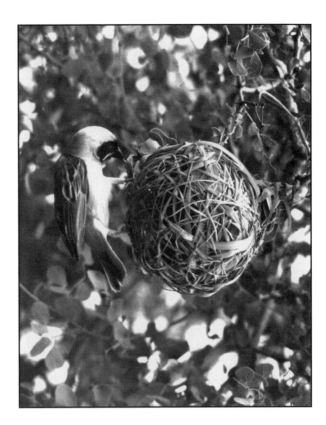

A masked weaver.

The village weaver (*Ploceus cucullatus*) of African savannahs is a colonial nester, with many pairs of birds building individual, pendulous nests from the same tree. The social weaver (*Philetarus socius*) is also a colonial nester. However, this species builds an aggregate, apartmentlike nest, comprised of large numbers of arboreal hanging nests constructed immediately adjacent to each other, so that the finished mass looks rather like a haystack. The entrance holes to the individual compartments are on the underside of the mass, so that entry requires a brief hover.

The snow finch (*Montifringilla nivalis*) is a species existing in alpine tundra in Europe and Asia.

One of the most spectacular weaver finches is the paradise widowbird or whydah (*Steganura paradisea*), which breeds in savannahs of tropical Africa. Males of this polygynous species achieve a length of 13.4 in (34 cm), of which about 3/4 is due to their fabulously long tail, comprised of 3–4 over–developed, black feathers. This attractive bird also has a black face and back, a chestnut breast, a yellow nape, and a whitish belly. Female paradise widowbirds are relatively drab, brownish–and–whitish birds.

Perrins, C. M., ed. *The Birds of the Western Palaearctic. Vol. VIII. Crows to Finches.* Oxford, England: Oxford University Press, 1994.

Bill Freedman

Web-spinners *see* **Embiids**

KEY TERMS

Polygyny—A breeding system in which a male attempts to breed with as many females as possible. In avian polygyny, the female usually incubates the eggs and raises the babies.

Sexual selection—A specialized type of natural selection in which anatomical or behavioral traits are favored because they confer an advantage in courtship or another aspect of breeding.

Field studies have shown that paradise widowbird males with the longest tail are more successful in attracting females. In part, this was demonstrated by clipping the tail of some individuals. These truncated fellows were then considerably less fortunate in their love life than males who had not been tampered with, or had their tail cut, and then glued back on. This is an example of sexual selection, in which traits that may be detrimental in some respects, for example, in foraging or escaping from predators, may nevertheless be selected for because they enhance reproductive success. In this case, the extraordinarily long tail of male paradise weaverbirds is favored by sexual selection, because a long tail has an irresistible appeal to females.

Some other weaver finches also have long tails, for example, the queen whydah (*Vidua regia*), and the pin–tailed weaverbird (*Vidua macroura*), both of tropical Africa.

Conflicts with humans

Some species of weaver finches occur in large numbers in urban and agricultural areas, where for various reasons they may be regarded as pests. The house sparrow and the Eurasian tree sparrow are most important in this respect.

The world's most important avian pest is probably the quelea (*Quelea quelea*) of Africa, which eats large quantities of ripe grains in places where it is abundant. This bird roosts communally in huge numbers, where it is sometimes sprayed with an organophosphate pesticide. It has been estimated that as many as one billion of these weaver finches are killed in this way each year.

See also Finches.

Further Reading:

Harrison, C. J. O., ed. *Bird Families of the World.* H. N. Abrams, 1978.

Weevils

Weevils (Curculionidae) comprise a very large group of insects that are closely related to beetles (order Coleoptera); more than 40,000 species are recognized worldwide, ranging in size from 0.2–2 in (0.5–5 cm). A weevil is easily distinguished from a beetle by its extended head, which forms a rostrum, and long, segmented antennae that are clubbed at the end and are usually bent in an elbow fashion near the base. Most species have a dull colouration—commonly brown, gray, or buff—but others are more brilliantly decorated with tinges of reddish–brown, pale green, and blue. The body of most weevils is covered with a mass of tiny scales that give these insects an iridescent color. Adults usually have two pairs of wings, although several species are wingless and the elytra (wing cases) are fused together. Males are often smaller than females.

All weevils are herbivorous and feed off a wide range of plants. The small mouth is located at the tip of the rostrum. The chewing mouth parts, or mandibles, move in a horizontal manner in most species. In some, the rostrum is used as a boring tool, primarily to create a tiny hole for egg laying, or to reach the inner tissues of a plant stem. Adult weevils lay their eggs either directly on or inserted within their food plants. The larvae do not possess legs, and most feed within roots, stems, or seeds of a wide range of plants. Here they receive some degree of protection from predators such as birds, small mammals, and parasitic insects. When the larvae are fully grown they develop a cocoon and pupate; some root–living species pupate in the soil, but the majority appear to remain within the plant itself.

In view of their life history, weevils are of considerable economic importance, particularly in relation to agriculture. No part of a plant, from the roots to the seeds, is safe from the attacks of one or more species of weevil. Although it is mainly the larval stages that cause the most damage, the adults too can be quite destructive. Some species, such as the grain weevil (*Sitophilus granarius*), are serious pests of stored grains. Others, such as the cotton boll weevils

(*Anthonomus barbirostris*), are responsible for wide-scale destruction of stored cotton in the United States, into which it was introduced in the 1890s from Latin America.

Welding

Welding is a group of processes used to join nonmetallic and metallic materials, by applying heat, pressure, or a combination of both. Most welding procedures require heat, although some procedures require only extreme pressure (cold welding). The welding process chosen to join materials together depends upon the mechanical, physical, and chemical properties of the materials to be joined, and the use for which the product is intended. The welding processes most commonly used today are resistance welding, gas welding, and arc welding. Special welding processes used include electrogas, electroslag, plasma arc, submerged arc welding, underwater, electron beam, laser beam, ultrasonic, friction welding, thermit, brazing, and soldering.

In industry, welding usually refers to joining metals, although materials such as plastics or ceramics are welded. Thermoplastics, such as polyvinylchloride, polyethylene, polypropylene, and acrylics can be welded. Like metal, plastics are welded with localized heat. New welding processes have been developed as new metals, alloys, plastics, and ceramics have been created. Welding is a means of construction, and a method for maintenance and repair. Various welding processes are used in numerous industries, such as aircraft, automotive, mining, nuclear, railroad, shipping, building construction, tool–making, and farm equipment. Welding by robots is one of the more common—and spectacular—applications of robots in industry.

When welding, wearing protective clothing is necessary to avoid injury from sparks, metal fragments, flames, and ultraviolet and infrared rays. Different welding processes require specific clothing. Clothing should be flame resistant, hair and skin should be covered, and special goggles must be worn. Sometimes leather clothing and helmets are recommended, as are steel toed boots. The work area should be properly ventilated; some welding procedures are required to be done in specially vented areas or booths to avoid toxic fumes.

Tests have been devised to inspect welds for flaws and defects. There are two types of testing, nondestructive and destructive. Often, a visual inspection is all that is needed but to test for internal or extremely small defects, other methods are necessary. Some nondestructive methods include air pressure leak tests, and ultrasonic, X ray, magnetic particle, and liquid penetrant inspections. Nondestructive tests do not damage the weld. Destructive tests are used to test the physical properties of the weld. Usually a test piece is removed from the weld, or a sample weld is made and then tested, completely destroying the weld. Some examples of destructive tests are tensile, hardness, bend, impact, pressure, and fillet testing.

Evolution of welding

The oldest type of welding is forge welding, a process that dates to 2,000 B.C. Forge welding is a pressure–heat procedure used by blacksmiths and artisans to form metal into specific shapes, and to join metals such as copper and bronze together. Toward the beginning of the twentieth century, several new welding techniques were developed. The discovery of acetylene gas in 1836 by Edmund Davy led to oxyacetylene welding. Resistance welding was invented in 1877 by the British–born American electrical engineer Elihu Thomson (1853–1937). The electric arc, discovered by Sir Humphrey Davy, was first used for welding by Auguste de Meritens in 1881. In the United States, C. L. Coffin received a patent for a bare metal electrode arc welding process in 1892. As the arc metal welding process was developed and improved, welding replaced riveted joints as a method of joining pieces of metal. In 1918, the first all–welded ship was launched, and in 1920 the first all welded building was constructed. Electric arc processes were used extensively during the post–World War I period. During World War II, inert gas welding was developed, and the gas shielded welding process was developed in 1948. Today, there are around 40 welding processes in use. Some newer welding processes include electron beam welding, laser beam welding, and solid state procedures such as friction and ultrasonic welding.

Welding methods

A weld is defined as a blend or coalescence of two or metals (or nonmetals) by heating them until they reach a critical temperature and flow together. Upon cooling, the metal becomes hard. The piece of metal to be welded is called the base metal, workpiece, or work. The edges of the base metal are often specially prepared for welding by, for example, machining, shearing, or gouging. There are five basic weld joints: butt, lap, corner, "T," and edge. The American Welding Society has developed a system of symbols that are added to mechanical drawings, to convey precisely how a welding site should be prepared, what type of weld should be made, and any other considerations.

Fusion welding, a heat process that sometimes requires the use of a filler metal, uses either electricity (arc welding) or gas (gas welding) as its source of heat energy. Solid state processes, such as friction welding and ultrasonic welding, weld metals at a temperature below their melting points, without the addition of a filler metal. Pressure is always used to achieve a weld with this method. When most metals are heated, a reaction takes place between the base metal and the surrounding atmosphere. For example, some metals oxidize when melted, which can interfere with the quality of the weld. Other common atmospheric contaminants are nitrogen and hydrogen. To control this problem, fluxes and inert gases are used to rid the welding area of impurities, and to protect the area from the atmospheric gases by displacing the surrounding air from the weld site. Welding is done mechanically or manually with welding guns or torches, and can also be performed by robots.

Arc welding

The electric arc used in welding processes, is created between a covered or bare metal electrode and the base metal or workpiece. With shielded metal arc welding (SMAC), an electric circuit is set up between the welding machine (AC or DC continuous power source), the workpiece, the electrical cables, the electrode holder, electrode, and ground wire. To strike an arc, the electrode must be touching the base metal; this is usually done by scratching or pecking the base metal with the electrode. As the electricity begins flowing, the electrode is held away from base metal, creating a gap. The electrical current flows across the gap, resulting in an arc. The intense heat from the arc melts the workpiece and the electrode, which contains metal powder that, when melted, becomes the filler metal. The covering or coating on the metal electrode is a flux material that melts, which removes impurities from the weld and sometimes creates a gas that shields the area from atmospheric contamination. Essentially, the electrode and its shielding control the mechanical, chemical, and electrical characteristics of the weld. The heat—6,000–9,000°F (3,315–4,982°C)—of the electric arc brings the base metal and the consumable electrode to molten state, within a matter of seconds.

Gas metal arc welding (GMAW or MIG) is similar to SMAW. A direct current (DC) is always used with this process and there is a gas supply apparatus. A consumable electrode is housed within a nozzle that supplies an inert shielding gas such as helium or argon.

GMAW has several advantages over SMAW. With GMAW, welding speed is faster, no slag is produced, there is deeper penetration, and the electrode wires are continuously fed so that longer welds can be made. A type of arc welding that does not use a consumable electrode is gas tungsten arc welding (GTAW or TIG). An arc is produced between the base metal and a tungsten electrode, a shielding gas is used, and there must be a water supply to cool off the torch. Instead of a consumable electrode, a metal rod or welding rod is used to provide filler metal, if required. This type of welding is also called heliarc welding.

Gas welding

Gas welding, also called oxyfuel gas welding (OFW), refers to a group of welding processes that use gas as the source of heat energy. Oxyacetylene and oxyhydrogen are two types of fuel gases used. Acetylene is commonly used for welding because, when combined with oxygen, the flame temperature can reach 5,600°F (3,093°C), the highest temperature produced by any fuel gas–oxygen combination. A filler metal rod may or may not be used with this type of welding process. The fuel gas and oxygen are contained in separate pressurized tanks or cylinders. Specially designed hoses run from the gas cylinders and connect to the welding torch. The welding torch has valves that control the amount of incoming gases, and a mixing chamber where the gases are mixed. The blended gases flow to the tip of the torch where the flame is ignited by a torch lighter, usually a flint and steel sparklighter. After the flame is lit, it must be adjusted until the correct balance of gases is achieved (a neutral flame). Oxyfuel gas welding was the primary welding process during the first part of the twentieth century. As newer methods of welding and new materials were developed, other, more suitable, welding processes replaced the oxyfuel gas process. Currently, the oxyacetylene process is used for braze welding, brazing, and soldering.

Resistance welding

Resistance, or spot welding (RW) is a process where two or more layers or pieces of metal, stacked together, are welded together by a combination of pressure and heat. An electrical current, along with an appropriate amount of pressure, is applied to the area or spot of the desired weld. When the electricity flows through the metal, it heats up, due to the metal's resistance to the flow of electricity. When two or more metals are touching, the heat flows through from one piece to the next. The greatest amount of heat is generated at the spot where the two metals are touching. As the temperature reaches the critical point where the metals

KEY TERMS

· ·

Acetylene—Colorless fuel gas. When burned with oxygen, acetylene produces one of the highest flame temperatures.

Arc—A stream of bright light or sparks formed as a strong electric current jumps from one conductor to another. In welding, an arc is formed when an electrode connected to a power supply touches the base metal.

Base metal—Metal to be welded or joined. It is also called workpiece or work.

Brazing—Process of welding in which two base metals are joined with a filler metal heated to above 800°F (430°C), but below the melting point of the base metals. The piecework is grooved, the brazing rod is melted, and the molten filler metal flows into the grooves via "capillary action."

Chemical properties—The way in which a material reacts in a given environment. Some examples are oxidation resistance and corrosion resistance.

Electrode—Terminal point to which electricity is brought to produce the arc for welding. Some electrodes are melted and become part of the weld.

Electron beam welding—Process in which a focused beam of electrons heats and fuses the material being welded.

Filler metal—Metal or alloy added to the base metal to make welded, brazed, or soldered joints.

Flux—A material to facilitate melting and the removal of unwanted contaminants.

Laser beam welding—Welding process that uses the energy of a laser beam to fuse materials.

Mechanical properties—The way a material reacts under loads or forces, such as hardness, brittleness, ductility, and toughness.

Physical properties—The characteristics used to describe or identify a metal, such as color, melting temperature, or density.

Resistance—The property of a material to oppose the passage of an electric current. In welding, metal "resists" the electrical current and heats up.

Shielding gas—A gas that is used to guard the weld from surrounding air contamination.

Soldering—A group of welding processes that join materials by heating a filler metal or solder to around 800°F (426°C), which is below the melting point of the base metal.

melt, a weld is created. Pressure is applied through air pressure, hydraulic pressure, or mechanical leverage. Electrodes used for spot welding are not consumable, and can be manufactured into specific shapes. Some electrodes are shaped like wheels for seam welding.

See also Metallurgy; Solder and soldering iron.

Further Reading:

Althouse, Andrew D., et al. *Modern Welding.* South Holland, IL: Goodheart–Willcox, 1988.
Bowditch, W., and K. Bowditch. *Welding Technology Fundamentals.* South Holland, IL: Goodheart–Willcox, 1992.
Jeffus, L., and H. Johnson. *Welding, Principles and Applications.* 2nd ed. Albany, NY: Delmar, 1988.
Sacks, Raymond. *Essentials of Welding.* N.p. [IL]: Bennett, 1984.

Christine Miner Minderovic

Wels *see* **Catfish**

Wetlands

Wetlands are low–lying, depressional ecosystems that are permanently or periodically saturated with water at or close to the surface. The vegetation of wetlands must be adapted to the physical and chemical stresses associated with flooded substrates. The most common types of wetlands are swamps, marshes, shallow open waters, and mires, the latter consisting of peat–accumulating fens and bogs. Wetlands vary greatly in their productivity, mostly because of intrinsic differences in the rates of supply of nutrients. Wetlands provide important habitat for a wide variety of plants and animals. However, wetlands are rapidly disappearing because they are being drained and infilled for agricultural, urbanization, and industrial purposes. Wetlands are also being degraded by nutrient loading, which causes eutrophication, and by pollution associated with inputs of toxic chemicals and organic materials. Losses of wetlands and the biodiversity that they support are a very important aspect of the environmental crisis.

Types of wetlands

Wetlands can be characterized on the basis of their hydrology, morphology, water chemistry, and vegetation. All of these factors can vary regionally and locally, depending on climate, character of the surrounding watershed, and the species that are present (that is, the biogeographic region). The major types of

Sunset on a wetland near Lake Erie in Crane Creek State Park. During low water periods, mud flats are exposed providing nesting platforms for waterfowl like the Canada goose in the photo.

wetlands are described below, with an emphasis on North American types.

Swamps

Swamps are forested or shrub–dominated wetlands, usually associated with low–lying, periodically or permanently flooded areas around streams and rivers. Water flows through swamps, although the movement can sometimes be imperceptible. In southeastern North America, alluvial and floodplain swamp forests are sometimes extensive, and are typically dominated by such tree species as bald cypress (*Taxodium distichum*), water tupelo (*Nyssa sylvatica*), swamp tupelo (*N. sylvatica*), and eastern white cedar (*Chamaecyparis thyoides*). More northern temperate swamps are usually dominated by red maple (*Acer rubrum*), silver maple (*Acer saccharinum*), American elm (*Ulmus americana*), and green or swamp ash, (*Fraxinus pennsylvanica*). Freshwater tropical swamps can support much–more diverse species of angiosperm trees, while tropical mangrove swamps support a relatively small number of tree species that are tolerant of the brackish water.

Swamps provide habitat for numerous species of animals, many of which have a specific requirement for this type of habitat. For example, swamps of bald cypress in southeastern North America used to support the now–extinct American ivory–billed woodpecker (*Campephilus principalis principalis*), and they still provide habitat for the pileated woodpecker (*Dryocopus pileatus*), red–shouldered hawk (*Buteo lineatus*), prothonotary warbler (*Protonotaria citrea*), Carolina wren (*Thryothorus ludovicianus*), and many other small birds. These swamps also provide nesting habitat for wood duck (*Aix sponsa*) and for colonies of wading birds such as herons and egrets (e.g., great blue heron, *Ardea herodias*, and common egret, *Casmerodius albus*) and wood stork (*Mycteria americana*). Cypress swamps also support mammals, including swamp rabbit (*Sylvilagus aquaticus*), white–tailed deer (*Odocoileus virginianus*), and panther (*Felis concolor*), along with many species of amphibians and reptiles, including the American alligator (*Alligator mississippiensis*).

Marshes

Marshes are a relatively productive wetland in which the vegetation is dominated by tall, emergent, graminoid (that is, grass–like) plants. Typical plants of North American marshes include cattails (e.g., *Typha latifolia*), reeds (e.g., *Phragmites communis*), bulrushes (e.g., *Scirpus validus*), and saw–grass (*Cladium jamaicense*). Marshes dominated by these plants are relatively productive, because they have access to nutrients dissolved in their slowly flowing water. Wet meadows are less productive types of marshes, dominated by shorter graminoid plants such as sedges (*Carex* spp.) or a grass known as blue–joint (e.g., *Calamagrostis canadensis*). Salt marshes are brackish because they are periodically inundated by oceanic water. Temperate salt marshes are dominated by species of cordgrass (e.g., *Spartina alterniflora*).

Because they are rather productive, marshes can support relatively large populations of certain mammals, such as muskrat (*Ondatra zibethicus*). Birds can also be abundant in marshes. This is true of large, extensive marshes, and also of relatively small, fringing marshes around bodies of open water, such as lakes and ponds. For example, small ponds are common in the prairies of North America, where they are called "potholes." The marshy borders of potholes have historically provided important breeding habitat for most of that continent's surface–feeding ducks (these are known as "dabbling" ducks), such as mallard (*Anas platyrhynchos*), pintail (*Anas acuta*), and blue–winged teal (*Anas discors*). Unfortunately, most prairie potholes have been drained or filled to provide land for agriculture. This ecological conversion has increased the importance of the remaining potholes as habitat for declining populations of ducks, other animals, and native plants. Consequently, further losses of this habitat type are vigorously resisted by the conservation community, even though agricultural interests continue to encourage the drainage of these important wetlands.

Farther to the north, extensive salt marshes and, to a lesser degree, freshwater fringing marshes in boreal and sub–arctic regions provide important breeding habitat for geese, especially snow goose (*Chen caerulescens*) and Canada goose (*Branta canadensis*). Historically, these migratory waterfowl wintered in extensive temperate marshes farther to the south, but now many of these birds spend much of the cold months foraging for unharvested grain in agricultural fields.

Shallow open water

This is a heterogenous wetland type, transitional from deeper open–water habitats such as lakes, and more completely vegetated wetlands such as marshes. Shallow, open–water wetlands are known locally by names such as ponds, sloughs, and potholes, all of which are small bodies of surface water, less than about 7 ft (2 m) in depth, and free of emergent plants, but often having floating–leaved vegetation. These wetlands and their fringing marshes can support relatively large populations of waterfowl, amphibians, and other animals. For example, the open–water portions of prairie potholes provide habitat for populations of various diving ducks, such as lesser scaup (*Aythya affinis*), canvasback (*Aythya valisneria*), and redhead (*Aythya americana*), along with coot (*Fulica americana*), western grebe (*Aechmorphorus occidentalis*), and other species of birds. Beaver (*Castor canadensis*) can also be abundant in shallow, open–water wetlands, and in fact they often create such habitat by damming streams.

Fens

Fens are a type of mire, or a peat–accumulating wetland, most commonly found in boreal and sub–arctic regions. Because surface waters percolate slowly through fens (that is, they are minerotrophic), they are relatively well supplied with nutrients and alkalinity, and are only slightly acidic. Consequently, fens are relatively productive, and they are non–acidic or only slightly acidic. Fens have a plant community dominated by short–statured graminoids, especially sedges and rushes, some shrubs, and species of peatmoss (*Sphagnum* spp.) that do not prefer acidic habitats. Because they are not very productive, fens support relatively small populations of animals, although their associated open–water habitat may be used by breeding ducks, geese, and cranes.

Bogs

Bogs are another type of peat–accumulating wetland, but they only receive very small inputs of nutrients and alkalinity, entirely from atmospheric depositions associated with rain, snow, and particulates (that is, bogs are ombrotrophic, or "fed from the clouds"). As a result of their nutrient–poor status, bogs are highly unproductive and acidic, with a pH less than about 4.5 and as low as 3.5. The surface of the most ombrotrophic bogs is often raised above the level of the surrounding terrain, occurring as blankets or raised bogs, which can have peat depths of more than 32.8–49.2 in (10–15 m). The vegetation of bogs is typically dominated by acid–loving species of peatmoss (these are known as acidophilous species, and they are different *Sphagnum* spp. than the ones found in fens), along with various shrub species in the heath family

(Ericaceae). Because they are so acidic and unproductive, not many animals breed in bogs or their associated, brown–water pools.

Wetland ecology

Wetlands are dynamic ecosystems, transitional between terrestrial and aquatic habitats. Over time, most wetlands gradually infill because of the cumulative deposition of sediment and peat. Consequently, wetlands are most numerous in places where geological forces, such as glaciation or the migration of oxbow rivers, periodically create conditions that are favorable to their formation.

The ecological conditions of wetlands are, of course, dominated by the influences of permanent or temporary waterlogging. Clearly, availability of water to sustain plant growth is not a problem in wetlands, as it is in many terrestrial ecosystems. However, waterlogged soils or sediment are usually lacking in oxygen, a factor that inhibits respiration by plant roots. To cope with this stressful environmental condition, some plants have evolved specific adaptations to supply oxygen to their roots. Many herbaceous plants, such as cattails and rushes, have spongy, air–filled stem and root tissues, called aerenchyma, which helps to facilitate the transport of oxygen to underwater tissues. Some trees, such as bald cypress and black mangrove (*Avicennia nitida*), have specialized woody structures called pneumatophores, that extend from roots into the air, and have extensive intercellular spaces that are useful in supplying oxygen to below–water tissues.

The anaerobic nature of wetland substrates also causes other chemical changes that can pose important problems for plants, by affecting their nutrition and exposing roots to toxic chemicals. For example, access to certain nutrients can be difficult under anaerobic conditions, because they may not be present in a chemical form that is easy for roots to assimilate, or because roots cannot sustain the oxygen–demanding respiratory demands required for the active uptake of nutrient ions. Anaerobic conditions also encourage the solubilization of certain potentially toxic metals, such as manganese. In addition, anaerobic metabolism within root tissues can lead to excessive accumulations of alcohols, possibly causing toxicity. In general, wetland plants are adapted to these conditions, although they may nevertheless be physiologically stressed if these factors are severe enough.

Wetland hydrology is, of course, a highly variable character. Some wetlands are permanently flooded, while others are only waterlogged some of the time, usually seasonally. These dynamics are highly influential on the types of plants that can occur in particular wetlands, and on the communities that they develop. Tolerance of permanent or very frequent flooding, as occurs, for example, in saltmarshes, mangroves, some swamps, and other wetlands, requires highly adapted species of plants. In comparison, wetlands that are only occasionally flooded are, in some respects, a more ephemeral transitional between truly aquatic and terrestrial environments. In these situations, plants must only be tolerant of the stresses of sporadic events of flooding, while growing relatively freely when the water recedes and soils are drier.

Another highly influential environmental factor in wetlands is the supply of plant nutrients. In general, wetlands that are well supplied with phosphorus (in the form of phosphate), and to a lesser degree nitrogen (as nitrate or ammonium), sustain relatively large rates of plant productivity, and consequently large populations of animals. This is commonly the case for marshes, which are among the most productive natural ecosystems on Earth. In contrast, wetlands with restricted supplies of nutrients, such as ombrotrophic bogs, sustain only small productivities of plants and animals.

Losses of wetlands

All wetlands have great intrinsic value as natural ecosystems, and they all support species of plants and animals that occur nowhere else. Consequently, wetlands have great value in terms of biodiversity.

Sometimes, the biodiversity–related importance of particular types of wetlands is a matter of their relative abundance, in the regional context. For example, although bogs and fens can be very abundant in boreal and sub–arctic regions of northern North America, these types of wetlands are uncommon farther south, where they usually occur as relict, post–glacial ecosystems. In these southern regions, the few bogs and fens that occur have great conservation value as scarce and unusual ecological communities, and because most of their species of plants and arthropods are locally or regionally rare and endangered. As such, any proposals to "develop" these wetlands into agricultural or urbanized lands are highly controversial, because these conversions would cause an irretrievable loss of natural values.

Wetlands also provide essential habitat for species of birds and mammals that are hunted, and this gives them economic value. Waterfowl such as ducks and geese occurr primarily in marshes and swamps. During the past century the populations of these hunted waterfowl have greatly decreased, as a combined effect of overhunting and loss of natural habitats. Consequently, there are now substantial efforts to regulate hunting, and to preserve or enhance the marshes and swamps that are required as habitat by these birds.

Wetlands are also important because they offer other ecological goods and services, in addition to those previously described. For example, wetlands maintain some control over hydrology, helping to prevent extremes of water flow. This service moderates the risks of flooding caused by heavy rains or the spring flush of snowmelt in northern regions, and helps to extend supplies of water for drinking or irrigation longer into the drier seasons of the year. Wetlands also provide important services by cleansing the water that flows through them of pollutants, including both nutrients and toxic chemicals, such as metals and certain pesticides. Wetlands are useful in protecting shorelines from erosion, controlling sedimentation, and providing essential habitat for fish, birds, and other wildlife. Wetlands have good aesthetics, and this also contributes to their value as an ecological resource.

Unfortunately, in most of the world wetlands are being lost rapidly. The most important causes of the destruction of wetlands are drainage and infilling to provide dry land for agriculture, urbanization, and industrialization, and their use as convenient places for the disposal of mine tailings, municipal solid wastes, and sewage. In some cases, wetlands are degraded or lost because economically useful products can be mined from them, especially peat from bogs, and wood from forested swamps. Wetlands are also degraded if they are subjected to large inputs of nutrients through the runoff of agriculture fertilizers or by sewage dumping. These nutrient inputs can cause eutrophication, with a consequent loss of the initial ecological values of the wetland.

All of these disturbances, stresses, and ecological conversions result in net losses of wetlands. The ecological consequences include endangerment of natural wetland ecosystems, endangerment of their species of plants and animals, and loss of the many important services that wetlands can provide. The loss of wetlands is an important environmental issue, which can only be resolved by protection of those wetlands that still survive, and in some areas where the losses have been especially severe, by the active restoration of wetlands.

The protection and conservation of wetlands is an important activity of many governments and private organizations. In the United States and Canada, wetlands are among the highest priority natural habitats for protection by governments at all levels (national, state or provincial, and local). In addition, non–governmental organizations such as the World Wildlife Fund, The Nature Conservancy, the Nature Conservancy of

KEY TERMS

Alkalinity—Amount of alkali in a solution. In fresh water, alkalinity is mainly associated with bicarbonates, carbonates, and hydroxides, and it is generally measured by titration with acid to a fixed end point.

Anaerobic—Environments in which oxygen is not present, or only present in a very small concentration.

Eutrophication—Aquatic ecosystem process by which increased productivity results from an increase in the rate of nutrient input. Excessive eutrophication and its symptoms are regarded as a type of ecological degradation.

Graminoid—A generic term for plants with a grass–like growth form, such as grasses (*Poaceae*), sedges (*Cyperaceae*), rushes (*Juncaceae*), and cattails (*Typhaceae*).

Hydrology—Distribution, movement, and properties of water in Earth's atmosphere, on the surface, and in the near–surface ground.

Minerotrophic—Wetland that receives much of its nutrient supply as substances dissolved in water draining from a part of the watershed that is higher in altitude.

Ombrotrophic—Wetland with no input of nutrients from ground water or surface water, so that all of the nutrient supply arrives from the atmosphere with precipitation and dusts.

Watershed—The expanse of terrain from which water flows into wetland, waterbody, or stream.

Canada, and Ducks Unlimited have made the conservation and protection of wetlands a high priority in their activities. Internationally, the *Convention on Wetlands of International Importance, Especially as Waterfowl Habitat* (also known as the Ramsar Convention, after the city in Iran where it was negotiated), is an intergovernmental treaty that provides a framework for worldwide cooperation in the conservation of wetlands. The activities of all of these agencies are important and useful, but much more needs to be done to give wetlands and their species the degree of protection that they require.

See also Alluvial systems; Anaerobic; Biodiversity; Brackish; Eutrophication; Flooding; Hydrology; Water pollution.

Further Reading:

Barbour, M.G. and W.D. Billings. *North American Terrestrial Vegetation.* Cambridge: Cambridge University Press, 1988.

Barbour, M.G., J.H. Burk, and W.D. Pitts. *Terrestrial Plant Ecology, 2nd ed.* Ontario: Benjamin/Cummings Pub. Co., Don Mills, 1987.

Finlayson, M. and M. Moser. *Wetlands.* New York: Facts on File, 1991.

Bill Freedman

Whales *see* **Cetaceans**

Wheat in southeastern Wisconsin.

Wheat

Wheat is one of the oldest and most important cereal crops. Wheat is grown for its grain, which is ground into flour used to make breads and pastas. Wheat consists of approximately 20 species in the genus *Triticum* of the grass family (Poaceae). The most important wheats are: *Triticum aestivum*, used to make bread, *T. durum*, used to make pasta, and *T. compactum*, used to make softer cakes, crackers, cookies, and pastries.

Wheat plants have slender leaves and, in most varieties long, hollow stems. Each stem is topped by a single head or spike, which is an aggregation of 20–100 individual flower clusters called *spikelets.* Each flower cluster may contain up to six flowers, and each fertilized flower produces a single, edible grain.

About 13% of the mass of the ripe grain is formed by the fused layers of the fruit wall, seed coat, and aleurone. These layers, known as the bran, are nutritionally important because they contain fiber, some protein, and the vitamins thiamine, riboflavin, niacin, and vitamin A. About 84% of the grain is endosperm, a food–storage tissue which consists mainly of starch. The embryo, or germ, represents only 2.5% of the grain and contains most of the oil and protein. Because wheat provides a balance of several vitamins, starch, proteins, and oils, it is an excellent source of nutrition. Furthermore, because of its small water content, generally about 12%, wheat grains are easily transported and stored, and are resistant to microbial spoilage.

Wheat was one of the first plants to be domesticated. Along with barley (*Hordeum vulgare*), wheat provided the agronomic basis for development of the earliest civilizations in Mesopotamia, and has been found at archaeological sites in the region dating back to 7000 BC. The cultivation of wheat gradually spread by trade from Mesopotamia to other parts of the world, becoming established in India by 3000 B.C., and in Europe by 2000 B.C. Wheat did not occur in the New World until brought there by the Spanish in 1520. Wheat was introduced by settlers to the United States in the early 1600s. Nowadays, wheat is grown on every arable continent, and it is the most important food for people living in the temperate regions of the world (it is replaced by rice in the tropics).

By far the most important wheat is the common bread wheat (*Triticum aestivum*). This species evolved by a series of natural hybridizations followed by chromosome doubling (polyploidy) about 6,000 years ago in the Middle East, where its wild relatives still occur. The first hybridization is believed to have been between a primitive einkorn wheat (*Triticum urartu*) and an unknown species of wild goat grass (related to *Triticum speltoides*), each with 14 chromosomes. The resulting hybrid doubled its chromosome number and became fertile, producing emmer wheat (*Triticum turgidum*) with 28 chromosomes. Emmer wheat then hybridized with another wild species of goat grass (*Triticum tauschii*), which had 14 chromosomes, and the hybrid doubled its chromosome number to produce bread wheat with 42 chromosomes. Some of this hybridization and chromosome doubling has been duplicated experimentally in modern times, to yield an "artificial" wheat that resembles certain cultivars of bread wheat.

Winter wheats are planted in the fall and germinate before winter. The seedlings can survive cold winter temperatures—in fact, the low temperatures are needed for proper growth and development of the grain. The seedlings start growing again in the spring as soon as the frost is out of the ground, and by late spring the mature plants are ready for harvest. In contrast, spring wheats are planted in the spring and harvested in the fall.

For thousands of years, wheat was laboriously harvested using a sickle, and then *threshed*, or beaten, to separate the grains from the heads and flower parts (*chaff*). In the first half of the 1800s, the reaper was developed, which mechanized cutting and greatly reduced the amount of labor that was required. Nowadays, cutting the standing plants, threshing the heads, separating the grain from the chaff, cleaning the grain, and discharging it into bags, are all combined in a large, self–propelled machine called a *combine*.

About 25% of the world's farmland is devoted to wheat cultivation. This is more than is used for any other crop. About 566 million acres (229 million hectares) are sown to produce 478 million U.S. tons (527 million metric tons) of wheat. The world's greatest wheat producing countries are: the United States, China, Ukraine, India, Canada, Australia, Turkey, and Pakistan. The major wheat–exporting countries are the United States, Australia, Canada, and Argentina. Nearly all wheat–growing countries have breeding programs to improve the races of wheat adapted to local conditions. These programs strive to enhance qualities such as yield, disease and insect resistance, and nutrient content of the grain.

If wheat grains are eaten whole or ground whole by traditional stone grinding, all of the nutrients are retained. Modern milling methods, however, remove the germ and bran, thereby eliminating most of the proteins, oils, and nearly all vitamins. The resulting white flour stores longer and tastes good but is nutritionally impoverished. For this reason, wheat flour is often artificially enriched with vitamins to improve its nutritional value.

Wheat flour is primarily used to bake bread. Wheat flour is especially suited for this purpose because it contains two proteins, glutenin and gliadin (collectively known as gluten), that make a sticky, elastic dough. During baking, the dough traps bubbles of carbon dioxide produced by yeast or by chemical leaveners such as baking powder or baking soda. The trapped bubbles cause the bread to rise. (The holes you see in sliced bread were formed by the trapped gas bubbles.) Other cereal grains, such as rice, barley, corn, and oats, do not contain glutenin and gliadin and therefore are not suitable for making leavened bread.

Durum wheat (*Triticum durum*) does not rise as well as bread wheat because of the different protein composition of its grain. Therefore, durum wheat is used for making spaghetti, macaroni, and other kinds of pasta. Other products made from wheat include bulgur,

---

KEY TERMS

Aleurone—The protein–rich, outer layer of the endosperm in cereal grains.

Endosperm—The food–storage tissue of a flowering–plant seed. It consists mostly of starch.

Bran—The fused fruit wall, seed coat, and aleurone layer of a cereal grain. It is usually removed during the milling process.

Cereal—A member of the grass family with edible grains, such as oats, barley, rye, maize, and wheat.

Combine—A self–propelled tractor–like machine that combines the separate functions of cutting, threshing, cleaning, and bagging grains.

Germ—The embryo of a grain.

Grain—The dry, one–seeded fruit of a grass, differing from other one seeded fruits (such as nuts and achenes) by having the fruit wall fused to the seed. Known botanically as a *caryopsis*.

Leavened bread—Wheat bread that has been made to raise by the action of its dough trapping carbon dioxide gas produced by yeast, baking soda, or baking powder.

Wheat flour—The powder that results from grinding grains of wheat.

White flour—Wheat flour made from grains having the bran and embryo removed.

Whole–wheat flour—Flour made from milling the whole grain; that is, grain with the endosperm, bran, and embryo left intact.

---

which is prepared by cooking, dehydrating, and peeling wheat. Wheat germ, which is removed in the milling process, has a large vitamin E and protein content, and is often added to or sprinkled on other food as a nutritional supplement. Entire wheat grains, either rolled or puffed, are often used in breakfast cereals. In addition, starch and gluten are extracted from wheat grains. The starch is used in laundering and in making a sweet syrup. The gluten is used in making monosodium glutamate (MSG), a flavor enhancer of cooked foods, especially commonly used in oriental cooking. Wheat is the most important grain fed to poultry. However, wheat is not generally fed to livestock, because it is more expensive than other suitable grains such as maize, barley, or oats.

See also Crops; Grasses; Hybrid.

Further Reading:
Klippart, John H. *The Wheat Plant.* 1985.
Stoskopf, Neil. *Cereal Grain Crops.* 1985.

Robbin C. Moran

Wheatear *see* **Thrushes**

Whelk *see* **Snails**

Whimbrel *see* **Curlews; Sandpipers; Shore birds**

Whip-poor-will *see* **Caprimulgids; Goatsuckers**

Whisk fern

The whisk fern (*Psilotum* spp., family Psilotaceae) splays its leafless, whisk–like branches upward, and is a living fossil from the time before the dinosaurs. It can grow as an epiphyte in moist climates or as a terrestrial plant in drier areas. Found in the tropics from around the world, the whisk fern is descended from the first vascular land plants, the Rhyniophytes, which appeared about 400 million years ago. It is not a true fern, unlike the popular Boston fern, but both the whisk fern and true ferns are ancient plants when compared to the flowering plants or angiosperms.

The leaved genus *Tmesipteis* (family Tmesipteridaceae) and *Psilotum* are the only representatives of the division Psilophyta (order Psilopsida). The principal usefulness of *Psilotum* to humans lies in their limited decorative use, and in scientific study as a living example of a very ancient land plant.

The primitive nature of the whisk fern is underscored by its having flagellated sperm, unlike the more advanced flowering plants, the angiosperms. The simple branched stems of *Psilotum* recalls the structure of the rhyniophytes, and the whisk fern is unique among living vascular plants in its lack of roots and leaves.

In place of roots the whisk fern has rhizomes, that is, modified underground stems. In *Psilotum nudum* the rhizome occurs with a mutualistic fungus in a type of mycorrhiza useful for obtaining necessary nutrients. Because *Psilotum* is without leaves, the interior parts of the stem conduct food and water, known as the vascular cylinder. In *Psilotum* the vascular cylinder lacks a central part made of large, open–looking cells, called pith. The lack of these cells defines the type of vascular cylinder known as a protostele.

The lack of seeds in the reproductive cycle of the whisk fern is another example of its ancient evolutionary origins. In place of the pollen and ovule of angiosperms, *Psilotum* has multicellular male and female gametophytes, and the whisk fern has spores which give rise to the gametophytes.

The gametophyte is the stage of the plant life cycle which has a haploid complement of chromosomes (1n). The gametophytes of flowering plants are extremely reduced in size. The pollen grain and the seven–celled ovule are hidden within the unpollinated ovary. However, in ancient plants such as the whisk fern, the gametophyte is relatively large. The gametophyte of *Psilotum* even has vascular tissue and a distinct area of food–and water–conducting tissues, unlike the gametophytes of more ancient plants, such as moss and liverworts. The cigar–shaped gametophytes also grow underground, unlike the gametophytes of many other plants, where they are nourished by an endophytic fungus. Scientists have now learned how to germinate the spores of some species of *Psilotum* in the laboratory, allowing for a more complete study of their gametophytes.

White-crowned mannikin *see* **Waxbills**

White dwarf

During the first quarter of this century astronomers found that the brightest star in the sky, Sirius, was orbited by a much fainter companion. Analysis of the orbit yielded a mass for the companion similar to that of the sun while an analysis of its light suggested that its size was approximately the same as Earth's. Further observation revealed that these small massive stars are reasonably common but had gone undetected because they are so faint. The stars of this unique class are called white dwarfs. They range in mass from perhaps a third to just under one and a half times the mass of the Sun. We now know that these stars have exhausted their supply of nuclear fuel, which would enable them to shine like the Sun and other ordinary stars. Under the weight of their own matter, they have collapsed to roughly a hundredth the size of the Sun. A fundamental law of quantum mechanics (i.e. the Pauli Exclusion Principle) limits the ability of the crushing gravity to pack electrons into an ever decreasing volume. The pressure of these highly packed electrons balances the weight of the overlying stellar material, stopping any further collapse. Since the electron pressure results from a simple packing of the electrons in a particular volume, there is no need for them to be heated by nuclear fusion, as is the case in normal stars (the nuclear fusion produces the pressure to balance the weight of overlying material). We call such densely packed matter electron–degenerate. A teaspoon of such matter would weigh 40 tons (36.3 tonnes) on Earth. Thus, white dwarfs are stable stars which slowly cool off, becoming dark stellar cinders.

Since two thirds of all stars occur in binary star systems where the components orbit one another, it is not surprising that many white dwarfs are found in binary systems. As the companion of the white dwarf ages it will expand and begin to lose matter to the gravitational pull of the white dwarf. This results in the injection of hydrogen–rich matter from the normal companion into the outer layers of the white dwarf. After a certain amount of this matter accumulates, it will undergo a nuclear fusion explosion which will blow off the outer ten–thousandth of the white dwarf. The energy released during this explosion will cause the system to brighten perhaps a million times or more, forming what we call a nova. The extent of the explosion critically depends on aspects of the donor star as well as the white dwarf. Smaller explosions may be called dwarf novae. This material will be blown clear of the system and the expanding shell will become visible to later observers.

There is a limit in mass to which the white dwarf can grow because there is a limit to the extent that electrons can resist the increased gravitational forces. Depending on the chemical composition of the white dwarf, this limit occurs when it reaches between 1.2 and 1.4 times the mass of the Sun. In binary systems where donated mass from the companion forces the white dwarf beyond this limit, the white dwarf will collapse by a factor of one thousand to become a neutron star. The circumstances of the collapse may be so violent as to result in an explosion called a Type I Supernova. Such an explosion is far more violent than a nova and may result in the disruption of the binary system.

See also Nova; Stellar evolution; Supernova.

White–eyes

White–eyes are 85 species of small, perching songbirds that constitute the family Zosteropidae. White–eyes occur in sub–Saharan Africa, South Asia, Japan, Southeast Asia, New Guinea, Australia, New Zealand, and many other islands in the Pacific and Indian Oceans.

White–eyes are arboreal birds, occurring in a wide range of forest types, including mangroves, lowland forests, and montane forests. They also occur in brushy habitats, especially at higher altitude on mountains.

White–eyes are small birds, ranging in body length from 2.8–5.5 in (7–14 cm). They have a slender, pointed bill, with the upper mandible slightly downward curved. The wings are rounded, and the tail square backed. The plumage is subdued in coloration, similar among the various species, and is most commonly brown, olive–green, grey, or yellow, the latter usually occurring on the throat or belly. Most species have a white–feathered eye–ring, from which these birds are given their common name. The sexes are similar in plumage.

White–eyes forage actively in trees and shrubs for insects and spiders. White–eyes also feed on fruits, nectar, and pollen. Some species poke holes into soft, larger fruits, and feed on the pulp and juice using specialized, brushlike structures at the end of their tongue.

White–eyes commonly occur in flocks, which can be quite large during the nonbreeding season. They may also be part of mixed–species foraging flocks with other insectivorous birds.

White–eyes are territorial during the breeding season, when they declare their territories with soft, warbling songs. They build a deep, cup–shaped nest of woven fibers and spider webs, located in a horizontal fork of a branch. The clutch size is 1–5. The eggs are incubated by both parents, who also share the feeding and care of the nestlings.

The genus Zosterops accounts for 62 of the 85 species in the family Zosteropidae. The oriental white–eye (Z. palpebrosa) occurs from Afghanistan to south China, and south into Indonesia. The black–capped white–eye (Z. atricapilla) occurs in the tropical forests of Sumatra, Borneo, peninsular Malaya, and Thailand in Southeast Asia.

The cinnamon white–eye (Hypocryptadius cinnamomeus) is a brown–backed species, with a dark eye but lacking in a white eye–ring, that breeds in the Philippines.

Bill Freedman

White-faced ant-catcher see **Antbirds and gnat-eaters**

White matter see **Brain**

Whole number see **Integers**

Whooping cough

Whooping cough is a highly contagious disease caused by the bacteria *Bordatella pertussis*. It is characterized by classic paroxysms (spasms) of uncontrollable coughing, followed by a sharp intake of air which creates the characteristic "whoop" of the disease name.

B. pertussis is uniquely a human pathogen, meaning that it neither causes disease in other animals, nor survives in humans without resulting in disease. It exists worldwide as a disease–causing agent, and causes epidemics cyclically in all locations.

B. pertussis causes its most severe symptoms by attacking specifically those cells in the respiratory tract which have cilia. Cilia are small, hair–like projections which beat constantly, and serve to constantly sweep the respiratory tract clean of such debris as mucus, bacteria, viruses, and dead cells. When *B. pertussis* interferes with this normal, janitorial function, mucus and cellular debris accumulate and cause constant irritation to the respiratory tract, triggering the cough reflex and increasing further mucus production.

Children under the age of two, particularly infants, are most at risk for serious infection, although the disease can occur at any age. However, once an individual has been exposed to *B. pertussis*, subsequent exposures result in mild illness similar to the common cold, and thus usually not identifiable as resulting from *B. pertussis*.

Symptoms and progression of whooping cough

Whooping cough has four somewhat overlapping stages: incubation, catarrhal stage, paroxysmal stage, and convalescent stage.

An individual usually acquires *B. pertussis* by inhaling droplets infected with the bacteria, coughed into the air by an individual already suffering from whooping cough symptoms. Incubation is the period of 7–14 days after exposure to *B. pertussis*, and during which the bacteria penetrate the lining tissues of the entire respiratory tract.

The catarrhal stage is often mistaken for an exceedingly heavy cold. The patient has teary eyes, sneezing, fatigue, poor appetite, and a very runny nose. This stage lasts about 10–14 days.

The paroxysmal stage, lasting two to four weeks, is heralded by the development of the characteristic whooping cough. Spasms of uncontrollable coughing, the "whooping" sound of the sharp inspiration of air,

and vomiting are hallmarks of this stage. The whoop is believed to occur due to inflammation and mucous which narrow the breathing tubes, causing the patient to struggle to get air in, and resulting in intense exhaustion. The paroxysms can be caused by overactivity, feeding, crying, or even overhearing someone else cough.

The mucus which is produced during the paroxysmal stage is thicker and more difficult to clear than the waterier mucus of the catarrhal stage, and the patient becomes increasingly exhausted while attempting to cough clear the respiratory tract. Severely ill children may have great difficulty maintaining the normal level of oxygen in their systems, and may appear somewhat blue after a paroxysm of coughing due to the low oxygen content of their blood. Such children may also suffer from encephalopathy, a swelling and degeneration of the brain which is believed to be caused both by lack of oxygen to the brain during paroxysms, and also by bleeding into the brain caused by increased pressure during coughing. Seizures may result from decreased oxygen to the brain. Some children have such greatly increased abdominal pressure during coughing, that hernias result (hernias are the abnormal protrusion of a loop of intestine through a weaker area of muscle). Another complicating factor during this phase is the development of pneumonia from infection with another bacterial agent, which takes hold due to the patient's weakened condition.

If the patient survives the paroxysmal stage, recovery occurs gradually during the convalescent stage, and takes about three to four weeks. Spasms of coughing may continue to occur over a period of months, especially when a patient contracts a cold or any other respiratory infection.

Children who die of pertussis infection usually have one or more of three conditions present: 1) severe pneumonia, perhaps with accompanying encephalopathy; 2) extreme weight loss, weakness, and metabolic abnormalities due to persistent vomiting during paroxysms of coughing; 3) other pre–existing conditions, so that the patient is already in a relatively weak, vulnerable state (such conditions may include low birth weight, poor nutrition, infection with the measles virus, presence of other respiratory or gastrointestinal infections or diseases).

Diagnosis

Diagnosis based just on symptomatology is not particularly accurate, as the catarrhal stage may appear to be a heavy cold, a case of the flu, or bronchitis. Other viruses and tuberculosis infections cause symp-

KEY TERMS

Cilia—Tiny, hair–like projections from a cell. In the respiratory tract, cilia beat constantly in order to move mucus and debris up and out of the respiratory tree, in order to protect the lung from infection or irritation by foreign bodies.

Encephalopathy—A swelling and degeneration of the brain.

Pathogen—A disease causing agent, such as a bacteria, virus, fungus, etc.

toms similar to those found during the paroxysmal stage. The presence of a pertussis–like cough along with an increase of certain specific white blood cells (lymphocytes) is suggestive of *B. pertussis* infection, although it could occur with other pertussis–like viruses. The most accurate method of diagnosis is to culture (grow on a laboratory plate) the organisms obtained from swabbing mucus out of the nasopharynx (the breathing tube continuous with the nose). *B. pertussis* can then be identified during microscopic examination of the culture.

Treatment

Treatment with the antibiotic erythromycin is helpful only at very early stages of whooping cough: during incubation and early in the catarrhal stage. After the cilia, and the cells bearing those cilia, are damaged, the process cannot be reversed. Such a patient will experience the full progression of whooping cough symptoms, which will only abate when the old, damaged lining cells of the respiratory tract are replaced over time with new, healthy, cilia–bearing cells. However, treatment with erythromycin is still recommended to decrease the likelihood of *B. pertussis* spreading. In fact, all members of the household in which a patient with whooping cough lives should be treated with erythromycin to prevent spread of *B. pertussis* throughout the community.

Other treatment is supportive, and includes careful monitoring of fluids, rest in a quiet, dark room to decrease paroxysms, and suctioning of mucus.

Prevention

The mainstay of prevention lies in the mass immunization program which begins in the United States when an infant is two months old. The pertussis vac-

cine, most often given as one immunization together with diphtheria and tetanus, has greatly reduced the incidence of whooping cough. Unfortunately, there has been some concern about serious neurologic side effects from the vaccine itself. This concern led huge numbers of parents in England, Japan, and Sweden to avoid immunizing their children, which in turn led to major epidemics of disease in those countries. Multiple carefully constructed research studies, however, have disproved pertussis vaccine as the cause of neurologic damage.

See also Childhood diseases; Respiratory diseases; Respiratory system; Vaccine.

Further Reading:

Berkow, Robert, and Andrew J. Fletcher. *The Merck Manual of Diagnosis and Therapy*. Rahway, NJ: Merck Research Laboratories, 1992.

Krugman, Saul, et al. *Infectious Diseases of Children*. St. Louis: Mosby–Year Book, Inc., 1992.

Sherris, John C., et al. *Medical Microbiology*. Norwalk, CT: Appleton & Lange, 1994.

Rosalyn Carson–DeWitt

Whydah *see* **Weaver finches**

Widgeons *see* **Ducks**

Wild canary *see* **Finches**

Wildebeest *see* **Hartebeestes**

Wildfire

Wildfire is a periodic ecological disturbance, associated with the rapid combustion of much of the biomass of an ecosystem. Once ignited by lightning or by humans, the biomass oxidizes as an uncontrolled blaze, until the fire either runs out of fuel or is quenched. Wildfire is best known as a force affecting forests, although savannah, chaparral, prairie, and tundra also burn. A large wildfire can kill mature trees over an extensive area, after which a process of ecological recovery ensures, called secondary succession. Fire can be an important factor affecting the nature of ecological communities. In the absence of wildfire or other catastrophic disturbances, relatively stable, climax communities tend to develop on the landscape, the nature of which is determined by climate, soil, and the participating biota. However, intervening wildfires can arrest this process, so that the climax or other late–successional

Mature trees

Climax forest

1.

Species from other sites invading

3.

Buried seeds sprouting   Roots regenerating

Ash layer

Buried seeds

Deposition of minerals

2.

Recovered forest

4.

A climax forest (1) destroyed by wildfire (2) and its recovery (3,4).

process, so that the climax or other late–successional communities are not reached.

The nature of wildfire

Wildfire is especially frequent in ecosystems that are seasonally droughty, for example, boreal forests, temperate pine forests, tall–grass prairie, chaparral, and savannah. Wildfires can be very extensive, and in aggregate they affect tremendous areas of landscape each year. For example, an average of about three million hectares of forest burns each year in Canada. Most of those fires are started by humans, although most of the actual burned area is ignited naturally by lightning. The natural fires predominantly affect northern, non–commercial forests, where most fires are not actively quenched by humans, so that individual burns can exceed one million ha in area. However, even vigorously fought fires can be enormous, as was the case of the famous Yellowstone fires of 1988, which burned more than 500,000 ha (1,235,500 acres), including 45% of Yellowstone National Park. Even moist tropical rainforest will occasionally burn, as happened over more than 3,000,000 ha (7,413,000 acres) of Borneo during relatively dry conditions in 1982–1983.

Fire causes a number of changes in soil quality. Depending on the intensity of the burn, much of the organic matter and litter of the forest floor may be consumed, and mineral soil may be exposed. The combustion of organic matter results in a large emission of carbon dioxide to the atmosphere, along with gaseous oxides of nitrogen derived from the oxidation of organic nitrogen, and sooty particulates. The layer of ash that deposits onto the soil surface is of a basic quality, so soil acidity is temporarily decreased after a fire. The ash also supplies large quantities of certain nutrients, especially calcium, magnesium, potassium, and phosphorus, some of which leaches from the site. Often, post–fire soils are relatively fertile for several years as a net effect of these physical and chemical changes, and plant growth can be rather lush until the intensity of competition increases when the canopy closes again.

Post-fire succession

When an ecosystem is disrupted by a wildfire, it can quickly suffer an intensive mortality of its dominant species, along with disruptions of its physical ecological structure and other damages. However, except in the case of rare, extremely intense fires, some plants survive the disturbance, and these can contribute to the post–fire regeneration that immediately begins.

Plant species vary greatly in the strategies that they have evolved to survive wildfire, and to regenerate afterwards. Often, the below–ground tissues of certain plants can survive the fire even though the above–ground biomass was killed by combustion or scorching, and the regeneration may then occur through stump– or root–sprouting. In North America, trembling aspen (*Populus tremuloides*), other woody plants, and many understory herbs commonly display this sort of survival and regeneration strategy.

Other plants may survive the fire as long–lived seeds that are buried in the forest floor, and are stimulated to germinate by post–fire environmental conditions. Species such as pin cherry (*Prunus pensylvanica*) and red raspberry (*Rubus strigosus*) can regenerate vigorously from this so–called buried seedbank. A few conifers maintain their seedbank in persistent, aerial cones, which are stimulated to open by the heat of the burn, so that seeds are released to the fire–prepared seedbed immediately afterwards. These fire–adapted tree species often form even–aged stands after fire, as is the case of knobcone pine (*Pinus attenuata*) in the southwestern United States, and jack pine (*Pinus banksiana*) farther to the north.

In other cases, species may invade the burned site, by dispersing from unburned communities nearby. Species with light, windblown seeds are especially efficient at colonizing burned sites, as is the case for white birch (*Betula papyrifera*), fireweed (*Epilobium angustifolium*), and various species in the aster family, such as goldenrod (e.g., *Solidago rugosa*).

The post–fire ecological recovery that is manifest in the regenerating vegetation is a type of secondary succession. In the absence of another wildfire, or some other catastrophic disturbance of the stand, the post–fire secondary succession often restores an ecosystem similar to the one that was present prior to the fire.

If the return frequency of natural wildfire is shorter than the time required for a climax ecosystem to develop, then disturbance by fire may be important in maintaining the land in an earlier successional stage. For example, most of the region of North America that supported a tall–grass prairie was climatically suitable for the development of an oak (*Quercus* spp.) dominated forest. It was only the periodic burning of the prairie that prevented the encroachment of shrubs and trees, and maintained the natural prairie. Today, tall–grass prairie is an endangered ecosystem, because most of its original area has been converted to agricultural purposes. To maintain the ecological integrity of the few, small remnants of tall–grass prairie that remain

KEY TERMS

Succession—An ecological process occurring after disturbance, and involving the progressive replacement of earlier biotic communities with others over time. In the absence of further disturbance, succession culminates in a stable climax community.

Secondary succession—A succession that follows any disturbance that is not so intense as to eliminate the regenerative capabilities of the biota. Secondary succession occurs on soils that have been modified biologically, and on sites where plants survived the disturbance. In contrast, primary succession occurs on a bare substrate that has not previously been influenced by organisms.

in ecological reserves, these areas must be deliberately burned to prevent them from successively turning into forest.

Even stands of the giant sequoia (*Sequoiadendron giganteum*) appear to require periodic ground fires of a particular intensity if that community type is to be sustained over the longer term. Fire helps to maintain stands of this species, by reducing fuel loads and thereby preventing catastrophic fires that could kill mature trees, by optimizing recruitment of seedlings, and for other reasons.

Management of fires

Sometimes, to achieve particular ecological objectives, fire may be used as a tool in ecosystem management. The use of prescribed burns to maintain prairie was previously described, but similar practices have also been used to manage other ecological communities, and even some species. For example, prescribed burning is an essential component of the management strategy used to maintain an appropriate habitat of jack pine required by Kirtland's warbler (*Dendroica kirtlandii*), an endangered bird that only nests in northern Michigan. Prescribed burning is also used in forestry in some regions, to reduce the quantities of slash left after logging operations, to prepare a suitable seedbed for particular species of trees, or to prevent large build–ups of fuel that could lead to a more catastrophic wildfire.

To protect stands of timber that are important commercially or for other reasons, many agencies actively engage in fire protection activities. Fire protection is usually achieved by attempting to prevent humans from starting uncontrolled blazes, by using prescribed burns to prevent dangerous accumulations of large quantities of fuel, and by quenching fires that are accidentally or deliberately ignited. However, fire is a natural, ecological force, and even the greatest efforts of humans are not always capable of preventing or quenching large fires. This fact is occasionally brought to our attention when uncontrollable conflagrations destroy homes, commercial timber, or protected areas such as parks.

See also Disturbance, ecological.

Further Reading

Barbour, M.G., et. al. *Terrestrial Plant Ecology*, 2nd ed. Don Mills, Ont.: Benjamin/Cummings Pub. Co, 1987.
Christensen, N.L., et. al. "Interpreting the Yellowstone Fires of 1988." *BioScience*, 39 (1989): 678–685.

Bill Freedman

Willets *see* **Shore birds**

Willow family

Willows are a diverse group of about 300 species of woody angiosperm plants in the genus *Salix*, family Salicaceae. Willows are widely dispersed and occur on all continents except Antarctica, but they are most diverse in cooler regions of the Northern Hemisphere.

All willows are woody plants, but the species vary greatly in size. Some species of willows are trees that can grow taller than 49 ft (15 m), while others are dwarf shrubs of the tundra that never get any taller than a few centimeters.

Biology of willows

Willows have simple, slender leaves, alternately arranged on the twigs, and with toothed or entire margins. The foliage of willows is seasonally deciduous, being shed in the autumn. Willow plants are dioecious, meaning that particular individuals bear either male or female flowers but not both. Both types of flowers usually produce nectar so that pollination is by insects. The flowers of willows are arranged in elongate inflorescences, known as catkins. The fruits are a capsule, containing tiny seeds with tufted hairs that make them aerodynamically buoyant so that they can be dispersed widely by the wind.

Willows are rather fast growing woody plants, but they are relatively short lived. Some species of willows

Willow in bloom.

sprout prolifically, and they may form dense thickets in moist, recently disturbed habitats. Most willows are relatively easy to cultivate from stem cuttings.

The usual habitat of willows is moist places, often beside streams, rivers, lakes, and other surface waters.

Species of willows

More than 100 species of willows are native to North America. Most of these are shrubs or dwarf shrubs, but about forty species reach tree size. Willow species commonly hybridize with each other and this, along with their relatively great richness of species, can make some of the willows difficult to identify.

Some of the more common species of willow that can attain the size of trees include the following: the black willow (*Salix nigra*) is a widespread tree in low–lying and riparian habitats in the eastern United States and southern Ontario; the peachleaf willow (*S. amygdaloides*) is also widespread in central North America; the Pacific willow (*S. lasiandra*) is another tree–sized species, occurring widely from southern California to central Alaska.

Shrub–sized species of willows are richer in species and include the following: The sandbar willow (*S. interior*) occurs widely in eastern and central North America and through the boreal forest to central Alaska. This species often forms thickets in flat, moist, alluvial habitats. The arroyo willow (*S. lasiolepis*) occurs in moist canyons and along streams in the western United States. The Mackenzie willow (*S. mackenzieana*) is a northwestern species. The coastal plain willow (*S. carolineana*) is widespread in the southeastern United States. The Bebb willow (*S. bebbiana*) is a common shrub of boreal and cool–temperate regions. The feltleaf willow (*S. alaxensis*) is widespread in the northeastern boreal forest.

Many species of willows are dwarf shrubs, occurring in alpine and arctic tundra. The stems of these tiny willows grow horizontally along the ground, and in some cases they never rise any higher than several centimeters above the ground surface. The most widespread of the dwarf willows is the arctic willow (*S. arctica*). This species occurs throughout much of the tundra of North America, Greenland, and Eurasia, as far north as the limits of land. Another arctic species is the reticulated willow (*S. reticulata*).

Economic and ecological importance of willows

Many species of willows are important ecologically. Willows are often species of early succession, and they are important in the early and middle stages of successional recovery after disturbance. Willows are commonly an important browse of mammals such as deer, moose, rabbits, hares, and other species, especially during the winter when herbaceous forage is not very available.

Tree–sized willows are sometimes used for lumber. The black willow is the only species used much for this purpose in North America. Because its wood is not very strong, it is generally used to manufacture boxes and similar goods.

Because willows can be so productive, there has been research into the cultivation of tree–sized willows in plantations for use as a biomass fuel. This use of willows as a source of renewable energy may prove to be important in the future. The willow biomass can be burned directly, or it can be chemically converted into more easily portable liquid fuels such as alcohol or a synthetic, petroleum–like mixture which can be manufactured under heat and pressure.

Because willows grow quickly and are so easy to propagate using stem cuttings, they are often used to vegetate stream banks to help prevent erosion and sometimes to re–vegetate other types of disturbed lands.

Willows have long had some use in folk medicine. Many cultures are known to have chewed willow twigs to relieve pain and fever. The original source from which salicylic acid was extracted was the bark of the white willow (*S. alba*) of Europe. This chemical is used to manufacture acetylsalicylic acid or ASA (sometimes known as aspirin), an economically important analgesic useful for treating pain, fever, and inflammation.

Willows may be an important source of nectar for bees in the early spring, a time when few other species of insect–pollinated plants are flowering. Willow honey may be a locally significant product in some areas.

Willow twigs are rather flexible and have been used to weave baskets, for caning, and to make woven fences and other lattices.

Some species of willows have good aesthetics and are utilized in horticulture. One of the best known species for this purpose is the weeping willow (*Salix babylonica*), a beautiful, pendulous tree. This species is

KEY TERMS

Browse—The twigs, foliage, and flowers of woody plants that are eaten by mammalian herbivores such as rabbits and deer, especially during the winter when more succulent herbage is not available.

Catkin—A type of spike–like inflorescence, or grouping of flowers, containing either female or male flowers, but not both. Catkins are the floral type of the willow family.

Dioecious—Refers to the occurrence of separate staminate (or male) and pistillate (or female) plants.

native to northern China. However, the weeping willow was considered to be so beautiful by the famous Swedish botanist Carl von Linnaeus, who gave the species its scientific name, that he decided that it must have been present in the biblical Garden of Babylon; hence, the origin of the geographically inaccurate, scientific binomial of the weeping willow.

The weeping willow has been widely introduced to North America as an ornamental tree. Other non–native species that are commonly used in horticulture include the crack willow (*S. fragilis*) of Eurasia and the white willow (*S. alba*) and basket willow (*S. viminalis*) of Europe. Some of these species have escaped from cultivation and have become locally invasive in natural habitats.

Wild willows also have pleasant aesthetics. Most famous in this sense are the several species known as "pussy willows," especially the pussy willow (*Salix discolor*). These species produce large, attractive catkins in the early springtime. In fact, stems of these species can be collected in the late winter before they have bloomed and placed in water in a vase. In a short time, the pussy–willow stems will bloom indoors to pleasantly herald the arrival of spring.

Further Reading:

Brockman, C.F. 1968. *Trees of North America* New York: Golden Press.
Klein, R.M. 1987. *The Green World. An Introduction to Plants and People*. New York: Harper and Row.
Woodland, D.W. 1991. *Contemporary Plant Systematics*. New York: Prentice–Hall.

Bill Freedman

Willy willies *see* **Tropical cyclone**

Wind

The term wind refers to any flow of air relative to the Earth's surface in a roughly horizontal direction. Breezes that blow back and forth from a body of water to adjacent land areas—on–shore and off–shore breezes—are examples of wind.

The ultimate cause of Earth's winds is solar energy. When sunlight strikes Earth's surface, it heats that surface differently. Newly turned soil, for example, absorbs more heat than does snow.

Uneven heating of Earth's surface, in turn, causes differences in air pressure at various locations. On a weather map, these pressure differences can be found by locating isobars, lines that connect points of equal pressure. The pressure at two points on two different isobars will be different. A pressure gradient is said to exist between these two points. It is this pressure gradient that provides the force that drives air from one point to the other, that is, that is responsible for winds blowing from one point to the other. The magnitude of the winds blowing between any two points is determined by the pressure gradient between those two points.

The Coriolis effect and wind direction

In an ideal situation, one could draw the direction of winds blowing over an area simply by looking at the isobars on a weather map. But the Earth is not an ideal situation. At least two important factors affect the direction in which winds actually blow: the Coriolis effect and friction. The Coriolis effect is a force that appears to be operating on any moving object situated on a rotating body, such as a stream of air traveling on the surface of the rotating planet. The effect of the Coriolis force is to deflect winds from the straight–forward direction that we might expect them to take simply from an examination of isobars. In the Northern Hemisphere, the Coriolis effect tends to deflect winds to the right and in the Southern Hemisphere, it tends to drive winds to the left.

Imagine how the Coriolis effect will determine the movement of winds in the Northern Hemisphere. Suppose that air initially begins to move from west to east as a result of pressure gradient forces. At once, the Coriolis effect will begin to drive the stream of air to the right, that is, to the south. The actual path followed by the wind, then, is a compromise between the pres-

sure gradient force and the Coriolis force. Since each of these forces can range widely in value, the precise movement of wind in any one case is also variable.

At some point, the two forces driving the wind are likely to come into balance. At that point, the wind begins to move in a straight line that is perpendicular to the direction of the two forces. Such a wind is known as a geostrophic wind.

Friction and wind movement

The picture described above applies to winds that blow in the upper atmosphere. At distances of more than a kilometer or so above the ground, pressure gradient and Coriolis forces are the only factors affecting the movement of winds. Thus, air movements eventually reach an equilibrium point between pressure gradient forces and the Coriolis force, and geostrophic winds blow parallel to the isobars on a weather map.

Such is not the case near ground level, however. An additional factor affecting air movements near the Earth's surface is friction. As winds pass over the Earth's surface, they encounter surface irregularities and slow down. The decrease in wind speed means that the Coriolis effect acting on the winds also decreases. Since the pressure gradient force remains constant, the wind direction is driven more strongly toward the lower air pressure. Instead of developing into geostrophic winds, as is the case in the upper atmosphere, the winds tend to curve inward towards the center of a low pressure area or to spiral outward away from the center of a high pressure area.

Friction effects vary significantly with the nature of the terrain over which the wind is blowing. On very hilly land, winds may be deflected by 30 degrees or more, while on flat lands, the effects may be nearly negligible.

Local winds

In many locations, wind patterns exist that are not easily explained by the general principles outlined above. In most cases, unusual topographic or geographic features are responsible for such winds, known as local winds. Land and sea breezes are typical of such winds. Because water heats up and cools down more slowly than does dry land, the air along a shoreline is alternately warmer over the water and cooler over the land, and vice versa. These differences account for the fact that winds tend to blow offshore during the evening and on–shore during the day.

KEY TERMS

· ·

Coriolis effect—An apparent force experienced by any object that is moving across the face of a rotating body.

Geostrophic wind—A movement of air that results from the balance of pressure gradient and Coriolis forces and that travels across isobars.

Isobar—A line on a weather map connecting points of equal atmospheric pressure.

Further Reading:

Ahrens, C. Donald. *Meteorology Today*, 2nd ed. St. Paul, MN: West Publishing Company, 1985.

Battan, Louis J. *Fundamentals of Meteorology.* Englewood Cliffs, NJ: Prentice–Hall, Inc., 1979.

Holton, James R. *An Introduction to Dynamic Meteorology*, 2nd ed. New York: Academic Press, 1979.

Lutgens, Frederick K., and Edward J. Tarbuck. *The Atmosphere: An Introduction to Meteorology*, 4th ed. Englewood Cliffs, NJ: Prentice Hall, 1989.

David E. Newton

The presence of mountains and valleys also produces specialized types of local winds. For example, Southern Californians are familiar with the warm, dry Santa Ana winds that regularly sweep down out of the San Gabriel and San Bernadino Mountains, through the San Fernando Valley, and into the Los Angeles Basin, often bringing with them widespread and devastating wildfires.

See also Atmospheric circulation; Atmospheric pressure.

Wind chill

Wind chill is the temperature felt by humans as a result of air blowing over exposed skin. The temperature that humans actually feel, called the *sensible temperature*, can be quite different from the temperature measured in the same location with a thermometer. The reason for such differences is that the human body constantly gives off and absorbs heat in a variety of ways.

WIND CHILL EQUIVALENT TEMPERATURE TABLE
DRY BULB TEMPERATURE (°F)

WIND VELOCITY (MPH)	45	40	35	30	25	20	15	10	5	0	−5	−10	−15	−20	−25	−30	−35	−40	−45	WIND VELOCITY (MPH)
4	45	40	35	30	25	20	15	10	5	0	−5	−10	−15	−20	−25	−30	−35	−40	−45	4
5	43	37	32	27	22	16	11	6	0	−5	−10	−15	−21	−26	−31	−36	−42	−47	−52	5
10	34	28	22	16	10	3	−3	−9	−15	−22	−27	−34	−40	−46	−52	−58	−64	−71	−77	10
15	29	23	16	9	2	−5	−11	−18	−25	−31	−38	−45	−51	−58	−65	−72	−78	−85	−92	15
20	26	19	12	4	−3	−10	−17	−24	−31	−39	−46	−53	−60	−67	−74	−81	−88	−95	−103	20
25	23	16	8	1	−7	−15	−22	−29	−36	−44	−51	−59	−66	−74	−81	−88	−96	−103	−110	25
30	21	13	6	−2	−10	−18	−25	−33	−41	−49	−56	−64	−71	−79	−86	−93	−107	−109	−116	30
35	20	12	4	−4	−12	−20	−27	−35	−43	−52	−58	−67	−74	−82	−89	−97	−105	−113	−120	35
40	19	11	3	−5	−13	−21	−29	−37	−45	−53	−60	−68	−76	−84	−92	−100	−107	−115	−123	40
45	18	10	2	−6	−14	−22	−30	−38	−46	−54	−62	−70	−78	−85	−93	−102	−109	−117	−125	45

VERY COLD

BITTER COLD

EXTREME COLD

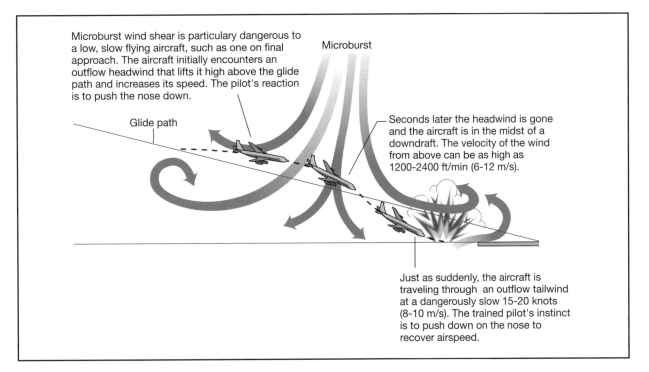

Microburst wind shear is particulary dangerous to a low, slow flying aircraft, such as one on final approach. The aircraft initially encounters an outflow headwind that lifts it high above the glide path and increases its speed. The pilot's reaction is to push the nose down.

Microburst

Glide path

Seconds later the headwind is gone and the aircraft is in the midst of a downdraft. The velocity of the wind from above can be as high as 1200-2400 ft/min (6-12 m/s).

Just as suddenly, the aircraft is traveling through an outflow tailwind at a dangerously slow 15-20 knots (8-10 m/s). The trained pilot's instinct is to push down on the nose to recover airspeed.

A typical microburst wind shear scenario involving a descending aircraft.

For example, when a person perspires, evaporation of moisture from the skin removes heat from the body, and one feels cooler than the true temperature would indicate.

In still air, skin is normally covered with a thin layer of warm molecules that insulates the body and produces a sensible temperature somewhat higher than the air around it. When the wind begins to blow, that layer of molecules is swept away, and body heat is lost to the surrounding atmosphere. An individual begins to feel colder than would be expected from a thermometer reading at the same location. The faster the wind blows, the more rapidly heat is lost and the colder the temperature appears to be.

The National Weather Service has published a wind chill chart that shows the relationship among actual temperature, wind speed, and wind chill factor, or the temperature felt by a person at the given wind speed. According to this chart, a wind speed of 4 mi/h (6 km/h) or less results in no observable change in temperature sensed. At a wind speed of 17 mi/h (30 km/h) and a temperature of 32°F (0°C), however, the perceived temperature is 7°F (–14°C).

The colder the temperature, the more strongly the wind chill factor is felt. At a wind speed of 31 mi/h (50 km/h), for example, the perceived temperature at 32°F

(0°C) is 7°F (–18°C), but at –40°F (–40°C), the perceived temperature is –112°F (–80°C).

Wind energy *see* **Alternative energy sources**

Windpipe *see* **Respiratory system**

Wind shear

Wind shear is the difference in speed or direction between two layers of air in the atmosphere. Wind shear may occur in either a vertical or horizontal orientation. An example of the former situation is the case in which one layer of air in the atmosphere is traveling from the west at a speed of 31 mph (50 km per hour) while a second layer above it is traveling in the same direction at a speed of 6.2 mph (10 km per hour). The friction that occurs at the boundary of these two air currents is a manifestation of wind shear.

An example of horizontal wind shear occurs in the jet stream where one section of air moves more rapidly than other sections on either side of it. In this case, the wind shear line lies at the same altitude as various currents in the jet stream, but at different horizontal distances from the jet stream's center.

Wind shear is a crucial factor in the development of other atmospheric phenomena. For example, as the difference between adjacent wind currents increases, the wind shear also increases. At some point, the boundary between currents may break apart and for eddies that can develop into clear air turbulence or, in more drastic circumstances, tornadoes and other violent storms.

Wind shear has been implicated in a number of disasters resulting in property damage and/or loss of human life. The phenomenon is known as a microburst, a strong localization down draft (down burst) which, when it when reaches the ground, continues as an expanding outflow. For example, it is associated with the movement of two streams of air at high rates of speed in opposite directions. An airplane that attempts to fly through a microburst passes through the wind shear at the boundary of these two air streams. The plane feels, in rapid succession, an additional lift from headwinds and then a sudden loss of lift from tailwinds. In such a case, a pilot may not be able to maintain control of the aircraft in time to prevent a crash.

See also Atmospheric circulation; Wind.

Wintergreen

Wintergreen is the common name for an evergreen shrub belonging to the genus *Gaultheria* and heath family, Ericaceae. *Gaultheria procumbens* is native to eastern North America and grows wild in sandy, wooded areas or shady clearings. This shrub grows 4–6 in (10–15 cm) high with creeping stems. Stalks grow from the stems and have elliptical, shiny green leaves and leathery leaves. During mid–summer, white, drooping, bell–shaped flowers grow; in the fall, wintergreen has bright red edible berries. The berries, called deerberries or checkerberries, contain several seeds and remain on the plants into the winter season.

Some plants of the genus *Chimaphila*, related to *Gaultheria*, are also called wintergreens. One plant of interest is pipsissewa (*C. umbelata*), which comes from the Cree word pipisisikweu, meaning "[the juice] breaks it into small pieces." It has been speculated that the Cree used this type of wintergreen as a remedy for kidney stones.

Wintergreen is also called teaberry or checkerberry. The whole plant, particularly the leaves, is a source of

the volatile oil that has made wintergreen's spicy, sweet taste very popular. Wintergreen oil is used to flavor gum, candy, toothpaste, mouthwash, and birch beer (a carbonated soft drink). The oil is also used in topical antiseptics and liniments. The active element of wintergreen is methyl salicylate, which is a derivative of salicylic acid (an important ingredient of aspirin). American Indians of the eastern woodlands made poultices from wintergreen leaves as a remedy for muscle and joint aches, inflammations, and toothaches. The Indians also taught early settlers how to make wintergreen tea for sore throats, nausea, and fevers.

During the early colonization days of North America, large amounts of wintergreen were gathered, dried, and transported to distilleries where the oil was extracted from the leaves. Today chemical factories make synthetic oil of wintergreen in the form of methyl salicylate. The leaves of natural wintergreen can be chewed; at first they will taste sweet, but the taste turns bitter very quickly. One should be careful when using pure wintergreen oil, as it can be irritating to the skin and poisonous if ingested internally. Many drugstores no longer sell pure wintergreen oil, as it is illegal to sell it in many local jurisdictions.

Christine Miner Minderovic

Wire chamber *see* **Particle detectors**

Wolverine

The wolverine (*Gulo gulo*) is an uncommonly large member of the weasel family (Mustelidae) that occurs in the subarctic and boreal forests of North America and northern Eurasia. The wolverine is famous for its aggressive, combative nature and its remarkable strength. Although the wolverine is only a medium–sized animal, it can dominate much larger animals during an aggressive encounter at a food source. For example, wolverines are capable of driving away a bear, or a group of wolves, from an animal carcass. If the movement of a moose or deer is hampered by snow, it can be killed by a single, much smaller wolverine.

Wolverines typically have a body length of 5.5–8.5 ft (2–2.5 m) plus a tail of about 8–12 in (20–30 cm). Adult animals weigh 30–60 lb (14–28 kg). Female wolverines are typically smaller than males. Wolverines have a long, dense, rather lustrous fur, usually dark

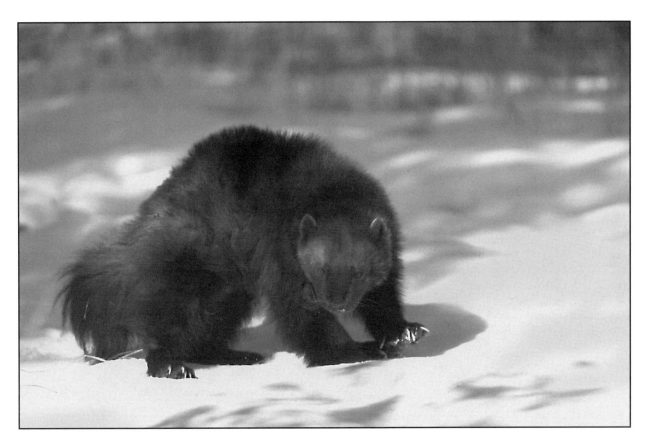

A wolverine on the snow.

brown or black. They generally have lighter brown–colored bands on each side of the body, extending from the shoulders to the rump.

Wolverines are rather omnivorous in their feeding habits. They are primarily eaters of carrion, that is, animals that have died of natural causes, or have been killed by other species of predators. The wolverine has powerful jaws and teeth, and it can crush the bones of dead animals to extract the nutritious marrow. Their food of carrion is mostly located by smell, as wolverines have rather poor vision. Wolverines sometimes kill their own prey. However, this only happens opportunistically, because these animals are rather slow moving and often cannot run down a healthy prey animal. Wolverines will also eat bird eggs, insect larvae, and berries when these foods are abundant. Wolverines are famous for their avaricious appetite, as is reflected in some of their alternative common names, such as glutton.

Adult wolverines are solitary animals, and they are active throughout the year. The territories of male wolverines can be very large, as much as thousands of square kilometers in extent, but shared with several res-

ident females. Wolverines move over their territories with a persistent, loping gait, but they are also adept at climbing trees in pursuit of prey.

The fur of the wolverine is very highly regarded by northern peoples for use in the ruff around the hood of parkas. Wolverine fur is relatively effective at repelling the moisture emitted during breathing, so it does not frost up to the degree of other furs.

Wolverines are indicators of wilderness and of ecosystems that are relatively unaffected by humans. Unfortunately, trapping has eliminated wolverines from much of their natural range, and they are becoming increasingly rare in those ranges where they still manage to hang on. It is critical that this special animal of wild landscapes be allowed to survive in its remaining territory, and perhaps be reintroduced to parts of its former range where an extensive area of suitable habitat still remains.

Wolves *see* **Canines**

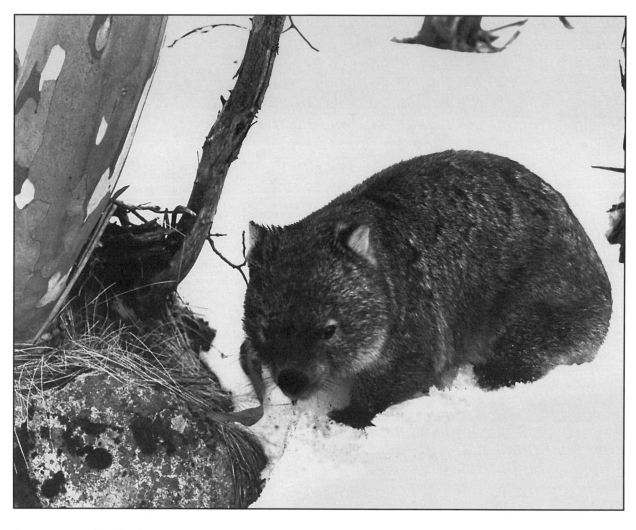

A common wombat (*Vombatus ursinus*) in mid-winter at Mount Buller, Victoria, Australia.

Wombats

Wombats are thickset, bearlike Australian marsupials (order Marsupalial) about the size of small dogs that dig burrows, and have perpetually growing teeth like rodents. Wombats are members of the family Vombatidae, which includes three species, one of which is endangered. The Queensland or northern hairy–nosed wombat *(Lasiorhinus krefftii)* is limited to a small region of Queensland national park, where the remaining animals (as few as 40 individuals) live in burrows in an old riverbed. The southern hairy–nosed wombat *(L. latifrons)* lives in dry grasslands of southern Australia, such as the Nullabor Plain, along the Great Australia Bight. These hairy–nosed wombats have fine white hairs on a fairly large nose, while the nose of the common wombat *(Vombatus ursinus)* is leathery and

bare. The common wombat lives in forests on mountainsides, and is characterized by rounded ears.

Wombats can weigh more than 80 lb (40 kg) and can be 3 ft (1 m) long. They are gray or brownish–gray, and are darker on the back than on the belly. The fur of the common wombat is coarse, while that of the hairy–nosed wombats is soft and silky. The feet of wombats have bare, leathery pads that withstand the energetic digging by their broad, flat, shovel–like claws (five on the front feet, four on the back).

In Australia and nearby islands, wombats occupy the ecological niche of a burrow–living plant–eater which is occupied in North America by the woodchuck. Wombats have chisel–like teeth which grow continuously and are eroded by constant chewing on coarse grasses and roots like those of rodents (such as the woodchuck). Wombats are quick and efficient at digging, which they do by lying on their sides and using their heavy–clawed front feet to dig and their hind feet to push the soil backward. Wombats usually lie near the entrance to their burrow and bask in the sun, feeding at night.

Hairy–nosed wombats dig systems of interconnecting tunnels, while the common wombat is likely to inhabit a limited system of only two or three tunnels. Common wombats establish territories of up to 60 acres (25 hectares) but don't demand exclusivity, for this often overlaps with that of another wombat. Common wombats may even share the same burrow, though they occupy it at different times of day.

Wombats have a poorly developed cooling system, and if they get too hot they can die. They usually avoid high temperatures by retreating to their burrows, which provide cooler places in the summer and a warmer spot in winter. The hairy–nosed wombats rarely drink, getting all their water from the plants that they eat. Their food is digested very slowly in order to get the most nourishment from it.

Wombats are solitary animals, except during the mating season, and then only if there is sufficient food available. Males fight for mating rights and females fight off males during courtship, so the pair that mate are often bloody and scarred. After a gestation of only three or four weeks, a single offspring is born, which is carried in a rear–facing pouch, similar to the koala's. The wombat's pouch is held closed by a strong muscle. As the tiny wombat grows and begins to move around, this pouch muscle relaxes, and the infant wombat may be seen peering out from between its mother's hind legs. It takes at least five months for the eyes to open and the fur to grow in. The young wombat does not leave the pouch until it is about a year old. Wombats make amiable pets and have lived in captivity for over 25 years.

See also Marsupials.

Further Reading:

Lavine, Sigmund A. *Wonders of Marsupials.* New York: Dodd, Mead & Co., 1978.
Lyne, Gordon. *Marsupials and Monotremes of Australia.* New York: Taplinger Publishing, 1967.
Triggs, Barbara. *Wombats.* Boston: Houghton Mifflin, 1991.

Jean F. Blashfield

Wood

Wood, also known as *secondary xylem*, is a composite of tissues found in trees. Secondary xylem is composed primarily of cells, called vessel elements in angiosperms, or of slightly different cells in gymnosperms called *tracheids*. These cells of secondary xylem, along with specialized cells of a type called *parenchyma*, are made by a meristematic tissue called the *vascular cambium*. As the vascular cambium generates new cells, secondary xylem accumulates on its inside, and the tree increases in diameter.

Newly made vessel elements and tracheids are water conduits from the roots of plants to their leaves. When first made, vessel elements and tracheids are alive but once they mature and become functional, they die. The functional vessel elements or tracheids occur in a few cell layers behind the vascular cambium, in a water–conducting section of the secondary xylem known as *sapwood*.

The parenchyma are made by the vascular cambium along with the vessels or tracheids, and are located at certain points along the perimeter of the vascular cambium. As the tree expands through growth, these narrow columns of parenchyma cells, called xylem rays, become longer, and ultimately extend from the vascular cambium to very near the center of the tree trunk. The function of xylem rays is to transfer aqueous material horizontally along the diameter of the tree, at a right angle to the flow of water in vessel elements and tracheids. The parenchyma cells of the xylem rays are alive in their mature, functional state.

As newer vessel elements or tracheids are made, older ones become buried under successive layers of more recently formed xylem. As the tree gets progressively larger in diameter, older secondary xylem tissues no longer conduct water. After this happens, these non–conducting cells are used to store waste products, such as resins. The xylem rays function to conduct wastes from actively functioning cells near the vascular cambium, to the non–functioning xylem cells. This waste–filled secondary xylem, is called *heartwood*. By the time that a tree is larger than about 4–8 in (10–20 cm) in diameter, most of its biomass is composed of heartwood. New sapwood is created during each growing season but, within 2–3 years these cells become part of the heartwood. It is the heartwood of trees that is harvested to manufacture the lumber and paper used by people.

Wood of different species varies in density and strength, due to the size and density of the vessel elements or tracheids in the secondary xylem. For example, heartwood of the Brazilian ironwood (*Caesalpinia ferrea*) has very tiny vessel elements and is extremely dense. At the opposite extreme, the heartwood of balsa (*Ochroma pyramidale*) has very large vessel elements,

KEY TERMS

. . . .

Meristem—A cluster of similar, undifferentiated dendrochronology plant cells that produce cells which do differentiate, and become mature tissues.

Parenchyma—A non–vascular tissue composed of large, thin–walled cells that may differ in size, shape, and structure of cell wall.

Tracheids—Thick walled, lignified elements of xylem which have no perforations on the cross-walls of adjoining cells. Instead, water is transferred among tracheid cells through holes in the side of the cell walls known as bordered pits.

Vascular cambium—A lateral meristem that only gives rise to secondary tissues, such as secondary xylem and secondary phloem.

Vessel elements—Thick–walled, lignified elements of xylem which have perforated or missing end walls. The relatively large openings in the crosswalls between adjoining cells allow a continuous, vertical transport of water.

Xylem—The tissue that is primarily responsible for conducting water and water soluble minerals in woody vascular plants. The primary components of xylem are vessel elements or tracheids.

drochronologists can determine past periods of drought, flood, and unseasonal cold or heat, by studying variations in the width of growth rings.

Vessel elements and tracheids differ in length between angiosperms and gymnosperms. Although the length of individual cells makes little difference in the ability of trees to conduct water, the length of cells is of great importance to the paper industry. The length of these cells corresponds to the fiber length of pulp that is to turned into paper, and influences the quality of paper that can be produced. Short fibers make fine grade papers, while longer fibers make coarser grade papers.

See also Paper; Tree.

Further Reading:
Bell, P. R. *Green Plants, Their Origin and Diversity.* Portland, OR: Dioscorides Press, 1992.
Fahn, A. *Plant Anatomy,* 5th ed. New York: Pergamon Press, 1990.
Lewington, A. *Plants for People.* New York: Oxford University Press, 1990.

Stephen R. Johnson

Woodchuck *see* **Groundhog**
Woodcocks *see* **Shore birds**

and is correspondingly light in density. The wood of typical gymnosperms is generally soft and light in density, because tracheids do not fit together as closely as the vessel elements in the xylem of most angiosperms.

The size of tracheids and vessel elements also varies within a single tree, according to the season of the year that they were laid down during growth. In spring, when air temperatures are cool and soil moisture is typically plentiful, the vascular cambium of trees makes large diameter xylem cells. As the moisture wanes and temperatures increase in the summer, the vascular cambium makes smaller diameter cells. In the winter, no new cells are made, because of the cold temperatures. This cycle repeats itself every year and makes visible growth rings in the tree (except in the tropics). These rings are evident because spring wood, with larger diameter cells, is relatively dark in appearance, while summer wood is lighter in color. This annual repetition of differing cell sizes in growth rings is useful in ecological studies through *dendrochronology*. Because the size of vessel elements or tracheids is dependent on both air temperature and water, den-

Woodpeckers

Woodpeckers are birds in the family Picidae, which includes about 200 species of true woodpeckers, wrynecks, as well as the diminutive piculets. Woodpeckers are widespread in the world's forested areas, occurring everywhere but Australia, New Zealand, New Guinea, Madagascar, and Antarctica. Birds in the woodpecker family range in size from the relatively enormous imperial woodpecker (*Campephilus imperialis*) of Mexico, with a body length of 21.7 in (55 cm) and weight of 1.1 lb. (550 g), to tropical piculets only 3.2 in (8 cm) long.

Instinctive behavior

Woodpeckers spend a great deal of their time pecking wood and chiseling bark off trees. They do this for several reasons—to search for their principal food of wood–boring arthropods, to excavate their nesting and roosting cavities, and to proclaim their territory and impress potential mates by loud drumming. Woodpeckers accomplish these tasks by hammering vigorously at

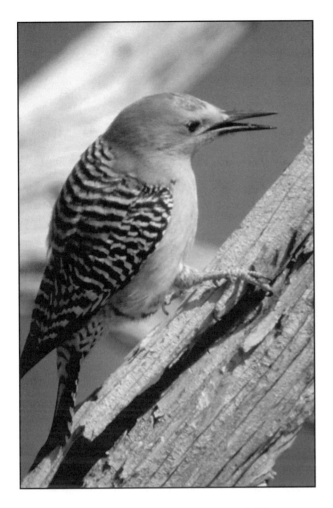

A male Gila woodpecker (*Melanerpes uropygialis*).

the woodpecker is long, barbed, and sticky to help extract insects from crevices, and the organ is supported by an extended hyoid bone and its muscles. The bill of woodpeckers is stout and pointed, and it grows continuously because of the wear to which it is subjected. As an adaptation for gripping vertical bark surfaces, woodpeckers have feet in which two toes point forward and two backward. The stiff, downward–propping tail feathers of woodpeckers also provide mechanical support while they are pecking.

Most woodpeckers live in forests eating arthropods in or on trees, but a few species occur in more open habitats, where they often forage on the ground for arthropods. Some species are at least partly herbivorous, seasonally eating soft fruits and nuts. Many species of woodpeckers are migratory, while others are resident throughout the year in or near their territories. All of the true woodpeckers nest in cavities that they excavate in the soft, rotted interior of living or dead trees. However, some birds in the family use natural cavities or are secondary users of the abandoned excavations of other birds.

Woodpeckers in North America

About 21 species of woodpeckers regularly breed in North America. The largest species is the 18 in (46 cm) American ivory–billed woodpecker (*Campephilus principalis*) of the southeastern United States, although this species is rare and may even be extinct.

The pileated woodpecker (*Dryocopus pileatus*) is another large species, with a body length of 15 in (38 cm). This species is still widespread, although uncommon throughout its range.

The northern flicker (*Colaptes auratus*) occurs very widely across North America. The yellow–shafted flicker is a subspecies (*C. a. borealis*) with bright yellow underwing feathers and is predominant in the eastern and northern range, while the red–shafted flicker (*C. a. cafer*) is southwestern in distribution. Flickers often feed on the ground eating ants and other insects.

The yellow–bellied sapsucker (*Sphyrapicus varius*) drills a horizontal series of holes in trees, which then ooze sugary sap that attracts and ensnares insects. They are later eaten by the sapsucker, as is some of the sap. The acorn woodpecker (*Melanerpes formicivorus*) occurs in oak forests of the southwestern United States. This species collects and caches acorns for future consumption, storing them in small holes that it excavates in tree bark. The acorn woodpecker lives in social groups of 4–10 closely related individuals. These cooperating birds engage in communal defense of a breed-

softer, fungal–rotted parts of living and dead trees, using their chisel shaped bill. In their territorial drumming, however, woodpeckers tend to choose more resonant, unrotted trees. Some woodpeckers habitually use telephone poles and tin roofs as their sonorous drumming posts. Both males and females engage in drumming displays, which may be supplemented by loud, raucous, laughing calls. Woodpeckers use their cavities for both nesting and roosting. Although both sexes participate in brooding the eggs and young, only the male bird spends the night in the nesting cavity.

Physical Adaptions

Woodpeckers have a number of adaptations which permit the vigorous hammering of wood without damaging the bird. Their skull is thick walled and the brain is cushioned by absorbent tissue which helps withstand the physical shocks of their head blows. The tongue of ing territory, and they collect and store their acorns together.

The hairy and downy woodpeckers (*Picoides villosus* and *D. pubescens*) are the most widespread species in North America, occurring in almost every forest. The downy woodpecker is more abundant and familiar, often occurring in suburban environments. Both species will feed on suet and peanut butter at feeders.

Woodpeckers and humans

Woodpeckers have sometimes been regarded as pests. Sapsuckers occasionally cause damage when their horizontal rows of drillings girdle trees and prevent the free flow of sap and water. Pileated woodpeckers can damage wooden utility poles, sometimes requiring their premature replacement. Overall, woodpeckers provide more benefit than detriment to humans because they feed on injurious insects, provide nesting cavities for a wide range of other species of wildlife, and have positive aesthetics for birdwatchers and other people who enjoy sightings of these interesting and personable birds.

The populations of some species of woodpeckers have decreased greatly as a result of human activities. The American ivory–billed woodpecker may never have been very abundant in the North American part of its range, and it quickly declined when its preferred habitat of bottom land forests of angiosperm trees and swamps of cypress were cleared for agriculture or harvested for lumber. This species has not been seen in North America since the 1940s, and it is probably extirpated. The subspecies known as the Cuban ivory–billed woodpecker (*Campephilus principalis bairdii*) is also critically endangered, as is the closely related Imperial woodpecker of Mexico.

The red–cockaded woodpecker (*Picoides borealis*) occurs in old–growth pine forests in the southeastern United States. This species breeds colonially, and has a relatively complex social system, involving clan–helpers that aid in the rearing of broods. There have been large reductions in the pine forests that satisfy the relatively stringent habitat requirements of the red–cockaded woodpecker, because these ecosystems have been converted to agricultural uses, plantation forests, and residential developments. The diminished populations of red–cockaded woodpeckers are now extremely vulnerable to further losses of their habitat through human activities or because of natural disturbances such as wildfire and hurricanes, and the species is listed as endangered. To prevent the extinction of this species, it is necessary to protect suitable habitat, and to manage these protected areas sustainably. In other areas

---

KEY TERMS

Cavity nester—A bird that builds its nest in a hollow in a tree. Woodpeckers excavate their own cavities, but other species of birds and some mammals use natural cavities, or excavations created and abandoned by other species, especially woodpeckers.

Integrated management—A management system that focuses on more than a single economic resource. In forestry, integrated management might be designed to enhance the resource of lumber and pulpwood, as well as the needs of hunted animals such as deer, non–hunted animals such as song birds and woodpeckers, the aesthetics of landscapes, and other values (see entry on forestry).

Snag—An erect but dead tree.

---

of suitable habitat which lack protection, it is necessary to greatly restrict the types of forestry that are permitted in the vicinity of known colonies of this endangered species.

Beyond the specific case of the endangered red–cockaded woodpecker, intensive forest management poses a more general risk to woodpeckers. This happens because the birds require a forest habitat that contains standing dead trees (snags), in which they can excavate cavities, feed, and display. Forestry tends to greatly reduce the numbers of snags in the forest, because dead trees can pose a tree–fall hazard to workers, and because they take up space without contributing to the economically productive forest resource. This is especially true of forestry plantations, where large snags may not be present at all, therefore depriving woodpeckers of an opportunity to utilize these industrial forests. One of the sensible accommodations that will have to be made by foresters to encourage woodpeckers (and the many other species of birds and mammals that utilize dead wood in forests) will be the provision of snags in managed forests to allow the native animals to sustain breeding populations. This would mean the integrated management of the land for both forest products and for woodpeckers and other species of wildlife.

See also Wrynecks.

Further Reading:
Bent, A.C. *Life History of North American Woodpeckers (Deluxe Edition).* Indiana University Press, 1992.

Brooke, M. and T. Birkhead. *The Cambridge Encyclopedia of Ornithology.* Cambridge, U.K.: Cambridge University Press,1991.

Godfrey, W.E. *The Birds of Canada.* Toronto: University of Toronto Press, 1986.

Harrison, C.J.O. (ed.). 1978. *Bird Families of the World.* New York: H.N. Abrams Pubs.

Koenig, W.D. and R.L. Mumme. 1987. *Population Ecology of the Cooperatively Breeding Acorn Woodpecker.* Princeton University Press.

Bill Freedman

Wood shrew *see* **Hedgehogs**

Work

Who is doing more work, a weight lifter holding up, but not moving, a 200 lb (908 kg) barbell, or an office worker lifting a pen? The weight lifter is certainly exerting more effort, and many people would say doing more work. To a physicist, however, the office worker is doing more work as long as the weight lifter does not actually move the barbell. The weight lifter does a considerable amount of work lifting the barbell in the first place, but not in holding it up.

The term work has a very specific meaning in physics that is different from the everyday use of the term. In physics, the amount of work is the distance an object is moved times the amount of force applied in the direction of the motion. If the force is not parallel to the direction of motion, the force must be multiplied by the cosine of the angle between the force and the direction of motion to get the component of the force parallel to the motion.

If the force applied in the direction of motion is zero, then the work done is zero regardless of the amount of motion. Likewise, if the distance moved is zero, then the work done is zero regardless of the force applied. Any number multiplied by zero is still zero. In the above example, the weight lifter is exerting a large force, but as long as he doesn't actually move the weight he is doing zero work, just exerting a lot of effort. The office worker does not need to exert much force to lift the pen, but the force is not zero. So lifting and moving the pen is more work than supporting but not moving the weight. Now think about the weight lifter actually lifting the weight. There is a large force required to lift the weight, and it moves several feet. The weight lifter is now doing quite a bit of work. To

do work you must actually move something. Just exerting a force, no matter how large, is not enough.

See also Energy.

Wreck fish *see* **Bass**

Wrens

Wrens are 63 species of small, restless perching birds in the family Troglodytidae. Species of wrens are most diverse in North America and South America, although one species, the winter wren, breeds widely in Europe, Asia, and North Africa. Wrens occur in a wide range of habitats, including semidesert, prairie, savanna, forests, and wetlands. Species of wrens breed from the boreal zone to the humid tropics.

Wrens are small, stout birds, ranging in body length from 3.9–8.7 in (10 to 22 cm). They have short, rounded wings, and long, strong legs, feet, and claws, and they hold their tail cocked upwards. Their bill is rather long, slender, pointed, and downward curved. Wrens are relatively dull colored, commonly in grey, brown, or rufous hues, patterned with white or black bars, mottles, or spots, and often a white belly. The sexes do not differ in coloration, and juveniles are similar to adults.

Wrens are active birds, often chattering and flitting about in dense undergrowth or shrubbery in search of their food of insects and other invertebrates. However, wrens are furtive animals and do not often emerge from dense cover, so that in spite of their bustling activity, they are not frequently seen. Wrens roost in concealed nestlike structures at night. During cold weather, wrens may roost together in huddled social groups.

Wrens are territorial. Males proclaim and defend their breeding territory using a rapidly phrased, melodious song. The nest may be placed in a hollow cavity, or it may be constructed as a dome–shaped structure of plant fibers and twigs, usually placed on or close to the ground. The clutch size ranges from 2 to 11, with larger numbers of eggs being laid by birds of temperate ecosystems, and smaller clutches by wrens breeding in tropical habitats. The female incubates the eggs, but males help with raising the brood. Some species of wrens breeding in boreal and temperate habitats are commonly polygynous, particularly in situations where the territory of the male is of high quality.

A marsh wren (*Cistothorus palustris*) perched in cattail stalks at Stoney Point, Ontario, Canada.

KEY TERMS
. . . .

Polygynous—A breeding system in which a male will attempt to breed with as many females as possible. In birds, the female of a polygynous species usually incubates the eggs and raises the babies.

Species of wrens

Ten species of wrens breed regularly in North America.

The winter wren (*Troglodytes troglodytes*) breeds in moist, conifer–dominated forests, and winters in the eastern United States and western coastal forests. This species is the widest–ranging of the wrens, breeding extensively in North America, and also in Eurasia and North Africa, where it is known as the common wren. The winter wren breeds in a wide range of habitats, from boreal, conifer forests on offshore islands, to densely shrubby suburban gardens and parks.

The house wren (*Troglodytes aedon*) is a widespread and familiar species, breeding through much of southern Canada and extensively through the United States, except for parts of the southeast. The house wren winters as far south as southern Mexico and the Gulf Coast of the southern states. This species will often accept a nest box located in a shrubby habitat, and in this way can be lured to breed in suburban gardens.

Bewick's wren (*Thryomanes bewickii*) is a relatively common breeder in the western United States and south to Mexico, and is less abundant in the eastern states.

The Carolina wren (*Thryothorus ludovicianus*) is a relatively abundant breeding species in southern Ontario and most of the eastern United States. This species is partial to thick, brushy habitats in open forests, along forest edges, and in parks and gardens.

The long–billed marsh wren (*Cistothorus palustris*) breeds abundantly in its habitat of tall marshes with bulrushes, cattails, and reeds across much of central and southern North America. This species

winters in the southern United States and Central America. The sedge wren or short–billed marsh wren (*Cistothorus platensis*) is a less common species in its range in central–eastern North America, and breeds in shorter wet meadows and fens dominated by sedges. This species winters in coastal marshes of the southern Atlantic states and Gulf of Mexico.

The rock wren (*Salpinctes obsoletus*) breeds in semiarid rocky habitats through the western United States to Costa Rica in Central America.

The cactus wren (*Campylorhynchus brunneicapillus*) is the largest of the North American wrens, achieving a length of almost 6.7 in (17 cm). This species breeds in deserts with thorny shrubs and large cactus plants, especially saguaro, from the southwestern United States through Central America.

Wrens and humans

Some species of wrens in North America have suffered greatly from habitat losses associated with human activity. Other stressors have also been important, including the use of pesticides in agriculture, forestry, and in the shrubby parks and gardens in which some wrens breed.

The San Clemente Bewick's wren (*Thryomanes bewickii leucophrys*) was a resident breeder on San Clemente Island off southern California. This subspecies of the Bewick's wren became extinct through severe habitat damages that were caused by introduced populations of goats and sheep. These are generalized herbivores that essentially devoured the limited habitat of the San Clemente Bewick's wren, and that of other native local species of plants and animals.

Other populations of wrens have also declined in many places in North America. The leading causes of these changes are habitat losses associated with the conversion of natural ecosystems into land–uses associated with agriculture and housing, and to a lesser degree, with forestry. Pesticide use is also important in some cases.

Further Reading:

Ehrlich, P. R., D. S. Dobkin, and D. Wheye. *Birds in Jeopardy.* Stanford, Cal.: Stanford University Press, 1992.

Farrand, J. (ed.). *The Audubon Society Master Guide to Birding.* New York: Alfred A. Knopf, 1983.

Harrison, C. J. O. (ed.). *Bird Families of the World.* New York: H. N. Abrams Pubs., 1978.

Bill Freedman

Wrentit *see* **Babblers**

Wren–warblers

The wren–warblers or Australian warblers are 83 species of birds that constitute the family Maluridae. These are nonmigratory birds, occurring in New Guinea, Australia, New Zealand, and nearby islands. Their usual habitat is forests, shrublands, and heaths.

Wren–warblers are small birds, with a body length of 3.9–7.9 in (10 to 20 cm), including the long, cocked tail that many species have. Their wings are short and rounded, and the bill is small and weak. The males of most species are brightly colored in contrasting patterns of blue, red, brown, black, or white. Other species, however, are more drab in coloration, and the sexes do not differ.

Wren–warblers are gregarious, and they hunt in small flocks for their prey of insects and other small invertebrates in canopy foliage. Some species also eat seeds.

Wren–warblers are loosely territorial during their breeding season. The males of most species are good singers, and they defend their individual territories in this way. However, the fairy wrens (*Malurus* spp.) often breed in a social group, in which one male is dominant, and is the most handsomely colored. One or more other males assist with his breeding effort, and if anything happens to the dominant individual, another will quickly moult to a brighter plumage and assume the central role.

The nest of wren–warblers is a dome–shaped structure with a side entrance. The clutch size is 2–5 eggs, which are incubated by the female. Both sexes rear the young birds.

The fairy wrens (*Malurus* spp.) are especially lovely. The variegated wren (*Malurus lamberti*) occurs in southeastern Australia, and has a sky blue cap and tail, a violet throat, and chestnut–and–black wings. The superb blue wren (*M. cyaneus*) has a similar range, and a violet throat and tail, light blue cap and face, and a brown back.

The emu wren (*Stipiturus malachurus*) breeds in southern Australia and Tasmania. This species has a chestnut cap, a bright blue throat, and a light brown body.

See also Warblers; Wrens.

Bill Freedman

Wrynecks

Wrynecks are two species of small, woodpecker-like birds. Wrynecks are in the family Picidae, which also includes the woodpeckers and piculets. However, the distinctively different wrynecks are in their own subfamily, the Junginae. Wrynecks received their common name from their habit of twisting their head and neck when disturbed.

The plumage of wrynecks is a mottled and cryptic brown, grey, and black. Wrynecks are somewhat less specialized feeders than the true woodpeckers. They lack the stiff propping tail feathers of the woodpeckers, do not climb vertical tree–trunks, and do not drill holes in bark and wood. Wrynecks do, however, nest in cavities in trees, although they do not excavate these for themselves.

Wrynecks forage on the ground for their food of ants and other small invertebrates. Their usual habitat is angiosperm–dominated forests.

The wryneck (*Jynx torquilla*) breeds widely in forests of Eurasia and north Africa, and migrates to sub–Saharan Africa and tropical Asia. The African wryneck (*J. ruficollis*) occurs in forests in Africa.

Bill Freedman

Xenon *see* **Rare gases**

X rays

X rays are electromagnetic waves with wavelengths covering a fairly broad range from about 3×10^{-8} ft (10^{-8} m) to 3×10^{-11} ft (10^{-11} m). There is no sharp boundary between x rays and ultraviolet light on the long wavelength side of this range. Similarly, on the short wavelength side, x rays blend into that portion of the electromagnetic spectrum called gamma rays which have even shorter wavelengths. X rays have wavelengths much shorter than visible light, which occurs between 1.2×10^{-6} and 2.1×10^{-6} ft (4×10^{-7} and 7×10^{-7} m), and they also behave quite differently. They are invisible, are able to penetrate substantial thicknesses of matter, and can ionize matter. Since the time of their discovery in 1895 they have been an extremely important tool in the physical and biological sciences and the fields of medicine and engineering.

History

X rays were discovered in Germany in 1895 by William Roentgen (1845–1923) quite by accident while he was studying the conduction of electricity through gases at low pressure. The discovery was made when these mysterious "X" rays were observed to light up a fluorescent screen a few meters from the source. Roentgen soon found that these rays were quite penetrating and was actually able to insert his hand between the source and the screen and see on the screen the faint shadow of the bones in his hand. This indicated that more dense materials such as bone absorbed more x rays than less dense material such as human flesh. He soon found that photographic plates were sensitive to x rays and was able to make the first crude x-ray photographs.

Roentgen had been experimenting with what was called a cathode ray discharge tube, i.e., a partially evacuated glass tube with metal electrodes at each end. When a high electrical voltage was applied between the electrodes a discharge took place in the tube. One effect of the discharge was to produce electrons which acquired high velocities as they were attracted to the positive electrode. When they hit this metal electrode the x rays were produced. It was not until 1913 in the United States that W. D. Coolidge (1873–1975) invented the x–ray tube similar to those still used today. Coolidge removed as much air from the tube as possible and used a hot tungsten filament as the source of electrons. This permitted more careful experiments in which the high voltage applied to the tube and the rate at which electrons hit the target could be varied independently.

Mechanisms for x–ray production

The intensity of x rays from an x–ray tube varies with wavelength. A diagram of the wavelength spectrum from an x–ray tube shows several sharp peaks superimposed on what appears to be a continuous distribution. The peaks and the continuous region are produced by two quite different mechanisms. The continuous spectrum is produced by the incident electrons as they strike and enter the metal target. They are attracted by the positively charged nuclei of the atoms in the target and are suddenly deflected. Electromagnetic theory tells us that when electric charges are accelerated they radiate. Similarly, in the antenna of a radio or TV transmitter, electrons are made to oscillate rapidly back and forth, but in that case the accelerations are not as large and the wavelengths are much larger being measured in meters or centimeters.

A completely different mechanism produces the sharp peaks in the x–ray spectrum. These peaks are at very specific wavelengths and occur at different wavelengths for different targets. This radiation is produced

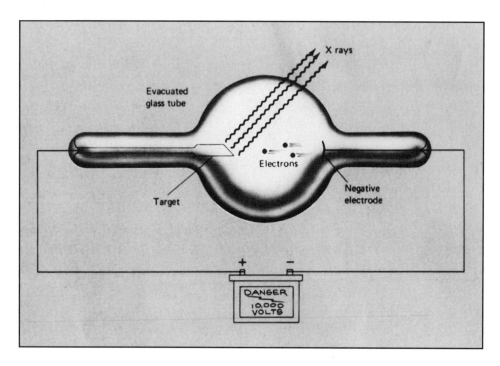

An X-ray tube.

when an incident electron knocks an electron out of one of the inner or low energy levels of the atom. An electron in a higher energy level falls into the vacant level and in the process an x ray is given off. The energy of this x ray is equal to the difference in energy between these two levels. Characteristic x rays have wavelengths ranging from about 10^{-11} m for uranium to 2.5×10^{-8} m for lithium.

Measuring x–ray wavelengths

Development of the x–ray tube greatly speeded up the detailed study of x rays, the origin and nature of which had finally been discovered by 1912, with the help of the suggestion by the German scientist Max von Laue (1879–1960) that x rays could be diffracted by three–dimensional crystals and thus must be electromagnetic radiation similar to visible light. This new approach was necessary because the wavelengths of x rays are so small that the diffraction gratings used for visible light will not work because the lines on the grating cannot be made with small enough spacings. A "natural" three–dimensional grating in the form of a single crystal of a material such as sodium chloride (salt) or calcite works very well since the spacing of the atoms in the crystal is roughly the same as the x–ray wavelengths of interest. Intrigued by von Laue's discovery of x–ray diffraction, English physicist W. L. Bragg (1890–1971), working with his father W. H.

Bragg (1862–1942), began a series of experiments that culminated in the invention of the x–ray spectrometer in 1913. This device allowed the Braggs to examine the structure of certain crystals, laying the foundation for the science of x–ray crystallography. Ultimately, the development of the x–ray spectrometer led to important advances in atomic physics and an improved understanding of the periodic table.

In 1913, the English physicist H. G. J. Moseley (1887–1915) used a Bragg–type spectrometer to look at the characteristic x rays from many of the elements. Taking advantage of the regular decrease in wavelength of characteristic x rays as one looks at successively heavier elements, he discovered that it was possible to tell one element from another by looking at the characteristic x rays. He found that elements should be listed in the periodic table in terms of their atomic number, not the atomic weight as had previously been done. He determined, for example, that cobalt should come before nickel even though cobalt had a larger atomic weight. He was also able to predict the existence of several elements, such as scandium and promethium, which were then unknown but later discovered.

Detection of x rays

In order for the Bragg spectrometer to be useful, the reflected rays must be detected. The detection of x rays is always based on their ability to eject electrons from atoms i.e. to ionize matter. Thus the detector in the first Bragg spectrometer was an ionization chamber which collected the electric charge produced by x rays as they impacted a gas filled chamber. This ionization chamber was soon replaced by the familiar Geiger counter, developed in the study of radioactivity which was discovered at about the same time as x rays.

Applications of x rays

The uses of x rays in the fields of medicine and dentistry have been extremely important. X–ray photographs utilize the fact that portions of the body such as bones and teeth with higher density are less transparent to x rays than other parts of the human body. X rays are widely used for diagnostic purposes in these fields. Examples might include the observation of the broken bones and torn ligaments of football players, the detection of breast cancer in women, or the discovery of cavities and impacted wisdom teeth.

Since x rays can be produced with energies sufficient to ionize the atoms making up human tissue, it is not surprising that x rays can be used to kill these cells. This is just what is done in some types of cancer therapy in which the radiation is directed against the malignancy in the hope of destroying it while doing minimal damage to nearby normal tissue. Unfortunately, too much exposure of normal tissue to x rays can cause the development of cancer, a fact that was learned too late for many of the early workers in this field. For this reason, great care is taken by physicians and dentists when taking x rays of any type to be sure that the exposure to the rest of the body is kept at an absolute minimum.

A relatively new technique for using x rays in the field of medicine is called computerized axial tomography, producing what are called CAT scans. These scans produce a cross–sectional picture of a part of the body which is much sharper than a normal x ray. This is because a normal x ray, taken through the body, often shows organs and body parts superimposed on one another. To produce a CAT scan, a narrow beam of x rays is sent through the region of interest from many different angles and a computer is used to reconstruct the cross–sectional picture of that region.

Moseley found that various natural elements can be identified by measuring the energy of their characteristic x rays. This fact makes a useful form of elemental analysis possible. If x rays of sufficient energy impact a sample of unknown composition, electrons will be knocked out of the atoms of the various elements in the sample and characteristic x rays will be given off by these atoms. Measurement of the energy of

these x rays permits a determination of the elements present in the sample. This technique is known as x–ray fluorescence analysis. It is often used by chemists to perform a nondestructive elemental analysis and by law enforcement agencies when it is necessary to know what elements are present in a sample of hair or blood or some other material being used as evidence in a criminal investigation.

X rays are used in business and industry in many other ways. For example, they are sufficiently penetrating; x–ray pictures of whole engines or engine parts can be taken to look for defects in a nondestructive manner. Similarly, sections of pipe lines for oil or natural gas can be examined for cracks or defective welds. Airlines also use x–ray detectors to check the baggage of passengers for guns or other illegal objects.

In recent years an interesting new source of x rays has been developed called synchrotron radiation. Many particle accelerators accelerate charged particles such as electrons or protons by giving them repeated small increases in energy as they move in a circular path in the accelerator. A circular ring of magnets keeps the particles in this circular path. Any object moving in a circular path experiences an acceleration toward the center of the circle, so the charged particles moving in these paths must radiate and therefore lose energy. Many years ago, the builders of accelerators for research in nuclear physics considered this energy loss a nuisance, but gradually scientists realized that accelerators could be built to take advantage of the fact that this radiation could be made very intense. Electrons turn out to be the best particle for use in these machines, called electron synchrotrons, and now accelerators are built for the sole purpose of producing this radiation which can be adjusted to produce radiation anywhere from the visible region up to the x ray region. This synchrotron radiation, from which very intense beams at nearly one wavelength can be produced, is extremely useful in learning about the arrangement of atoms in various compounds of interest to biologists, chemists, and physicists.

One of the more important commercial applications of synchrotron radiation is in the field of x–ray lithography, used in the electronics industry in the manufacture of high density integrated circuits. The integrated circuit chips are made by etching successive layers of electric circuitry into a wafer of semiconducting material such as silicon. The details of the circuitry are defined by coating the wafer with a light sensitive substance called a photoresist and shining light on the coated surface through a stencil like mask. The pattern of the electric circuits is cut into the mask and the exposed photoresist can easily be washed away leaving

KEY TERMS

Bragg x-ray spectrometer—A device using a single crystal with regularly spaced atoms to measure the wavelengths of x rays.

Continuous x-ray spectrum—The x rays produced by the electrons in an x-ray tube as they strike the target and are suddenly deflected. A broad range of wavelengths is produced.

Synchrotron radiation—Electromagnetic radiation from electron accelerators called synchrotrons that can range from the visible region to the x-ray region.

X-ray fluorescence analysis—A method of detecting the presence of various elements in an unknown sample by observing the characteristic x rays given off by the sample when excited by sufficiently energetic x rays.

X-ray tube—Evacuated tube in which electrons moving at high velocities are made to hit a metal target producing x rays.

the circuit outlines in the remaining photoresist. The size of the circuit elements is limited by the wavelength of the light—the shorter the wavelength the smaller the circuit elements. If x rays are used instead of light, the circuits on the wafer can be made much smaller and many more elements can be put on a wafer of a given size, permitting the manufacture of smaller electronic devices such as computers.

See also Accelerators; Computerized axial tomography; Diffraction grating; Electromagnetic spectrum.

Further Reading:

Dyson, Norman A. *X Rays in Atomic and Nuclear Physics.* White Plains, NY: Longman, 1973.
March, Robert. *Physics for Poets.* New York: McGraw Hill, 1970.
Hewitt, Paul. *Conceptual Physics.* New York: HarperCollins, 1993.
Young, Hugh. *University Physics.* Reading, MA: Addison–Wesley, 1992.

Robert L. Stearns

X-ray astronomy

At the high-energy end of the electromagnetic spectrum, x rays provide a unique window on some of the hottest and most violent objects in the universe. Since the discovery of extra-solar x-ray sources in 1962, scientists have investigated a large number of phenomena which emit x rays. With each new space mission, more sources and more details of the structure of the x-ray universe have been gleaned.

Background

Although they are among the most energetic of the electromagnetic spectrum, and thus provide a window on some of the most violent processes in the universe, x rays are not able to penetrate Earth's atmosphere; they are absorbed at about 100 kilometers above the surface. Thus, only with the advent of rocket and satellite astronomy were astronomers able to study the wide-ranging phenomena which produce x rays. The highest energy x rays have also been studied by balloons high in Earth's atmosphere, but there are far fewer photons at these energies than at the lower energies that can be observed above the atmosphere.

X rays are also difficult to bring to a focus, since their energies are so high. Therefore, an important breakthrough in x-ray astronomy was the advent of imaging telescopes, replacing instruments which could only crudely tell in which direction an x-ray source was located. The telescopes with which we are most familiar, consisting of lenses or mirrors, won't work in the x-ray region of the spectrum, since the x rays pass through or are absorbed by the optics. Instead, grazing incidence telescopes are used, in which the light from the source strikes mirrors at angles of only a few degrees, rather than perpendicular to the surface. By combining two mirrors, the energy can be focused onto a detector in order to provide a sharp image of the source.

History

Although the temperature of the sun's surface is only about 6000 K, by the 1930s there was evidence that the outer regions of the solar atmosphere were much hotter, meaning that they could be a source of x rays. At that time there was no way to verify this prediction, however. After World War II, when captured V–2 rockets allowed scientists to place instruments outside the protective atmosphere for the first time, a number of experiments were able to show that the Sun did indeed produce x rays. The strongest early evidence came in 1948, when x-ray detectors showed that x rays were coming from the direction of the Sun. Further investigations showed that the total x-ray output of the Sun was only a tiny fraction of the total energy generated by the Sun. Because the total x-ray output was so small, many believed that no other sources would be found, since the Sun is much closer than the next closest star.

In 1962, a rocket looking for x rays from the Moon (which was theorized to generate x rays due to solar wind bombardment), discovered the first nonsolar astronomical source of x rays, in the constellation Scorpio, along with a diffuse background coming from all directions; no emission was seen from the Moon. The source was called Scorpius X–1.

Since that time, a large number of rocket and earth–orbiting satellites have discovered tens of thousands of x–ray sources in the sky, many of which are many orders of magnitude brighter than the Sun. The Crab Nebula, for instance, produces approximately 2000 times more energy in the x–ray region of the spectrum than the Sun does over all wavelengths. Thus we now know that the Sun is relatively quiet as far as x–ray sources go.

Among the largest and most productive x–ray missions were Uhuru (1970), which catalogued 339 x–ray sources; Einstein (also known as HEAO–2, 1978–1981); and EXOSAT (1983–1986). In addition, there have been many smaller–scale observations.

The more recent missions, such as the German ROSAT (Röntgensatellit), launched in 1990, and the planned Advanced X–ray Astrophysics Facility (AXAF), contain very sophisticated instrumentation, including detectors and grazing incidence telescopes, which can pinpoint the location of an x–ray source to very high accuracy, and take x–ray pictures to show the shape and distribution of the source. This is an important improvement over early missions, which often were not able to determine the exact location of the x–ray sources, making it difficult to correlate the source with an object that could be detected in another wavelength region. Recent missions have also been able to measure the x–ray spectrum, or strength of the radiation in different energy bands. This allows the identification of particular elements in the source. ROSAT identified more than 50,000 x–ray sources during its survey phase, when it scanned the sky for six months. It also finally succeeded in detecting x rays from the Moon, nearly 30 years after the first attempt to do so.

The x–ray universe

A wide variety of x–ray sources have been seen since the first extrasolar identification in 1962. A few of the most interesting types of sources are:

The Sun—A number of x–ray satellites have monitored the Sun. Solar flares produce enhancements in its x–ray output.

KEY TERMS

Grazing incidence telescope—A telescope design in which the incoming radiation strikes the mirrors at very small angles.

Spectrum—A display of the intensity of radiation versus wavelength.

Stars—Many stars, particularly those with coronae or rapid stellar winds, emit x–rays from their outer layers.

Groups of galaxies in hot clouds—Bright x–radiation is seen emanating from clusters of galaxies, which, due to their enormous gravitational pull, trap gas in the region. This gas is very hot, and there is a large amount of it. It thus glows in the x–ray region.

X–ray Background—The sky is not dark in the x–ray region of the sky like it is in the visible. The diffuse background which was detected in the rocket flight described above is still not understood, although some believe it may be the result of many individual, unresolved sources.

X–ray binaries—These are close binary stars in which gas from one star falls onto its companion, heats up and gives off x–rays. This is especially bright when the companion is a compact stellar remnant such as a neutron star or black hole, because the enormous gravitational field compresses and heats the incoming gas, causing it to glow at x–ray wavelengths.

Supernova Remnants—Explosions of stars, or supernovae, show traces of the heavy elements that are formed there when their x–ray spectra are examined.

Quasars and active galactic nuclei—These are among the most energetic objects in the universe, and they emit enormous quantities of radiation at x–ray wavelengths. It is thought that the ultimate source of this energy is a supermassive black hole, surrounded by an accretion disk of in–falling gas that is heated to many millions of degrees.

See also Telescope; X rays.

Further Reading:
Beatty, J. Kelly. "ROSAT and the X-ray Universe," *Sky & Telescope*. August, 1990, p. 128.
Margon, Bruce. "Exploring the High–Energy Universe," *Sky & Telescope*. December 1991, p. 607.
Tucker, Wallace and Giacconi, Riccardo. *The X–ray Universe*. Cambridge: Harvard University Press, 1985.

Van den Heuvel, Edward P. J. and van Paradijs, Jan. "X–ray Binaries," *Scientific American*. November 1993, p. 64.

David Sahnow

X-ray stars *see* **X-ray astronomy**

Xylem *see* **Plant**

Yak

The yaks are members of the family Bovidae (oxen), order Artiodactyla, which also includes the domestic cattle and existing wild cattle species such as the aurochs, the gaur or seladang, and the koupray. The generally accepted species name for yak is *Bos grunniens*, and it seems to have an affinity to bisons, which belong to the same genus *Bos*.

Like some other *Bos* species the yak is a large, massive animal with stout limbs and a long tail, usually tufted at the tip. Wild yak males measure 10.5 ft (3.25 m) in head and body. The shoulder height is over 6.5 ft (2 m), and they weigh 1,800–2,200 lb (820–1,000 kg). Females are smaller, and weigh about one third as much.

Both sexes bear horns which are black and positioned quite far apart on each extremity of the top of the skull. In the male, they are larger, curving up and then down. They are approximately oval in cross–section. There are no suborbital, inguinal, or interdigital glands in yaks. The body is covered with long hair, blackish brown in color; it hangs down almost to the ground like a fringe around the lower part of the shoulders, the sides, the flanks, and the thighs. Wild yaks live on the Tibetan plateau where temperatures in winter may drop to –40°F (–40°C). The long, thick coat protects the yak from these frigid temperatures.

Domesticated yaks are smaller, have weaker horns, and may vary greatly in color: red, mottled brown, or black.

Wild yaks inhabit desolate steppes at up to 20,000 ft (6,100 m) above sea level. They are expert climbers, sure–footed and sturdy. During the relatively warmer months of August and September, wild yaks remain in high areas with permanent snow, but spend the rest of the year at lower elevations. They feed chiefly on grass, herbs, and lichens.

The females with young congregate in large herds up to 1,000 animals. The males live alone most of the year, or in groups of not more than 12. The bulls join the herd and fight for the females when mating season begins in September. Only during that time do wild yaks make a strange grunting sound, which domesticated yaks emit all year round. After a gestation period of nine months, a single calf is born, usually in June, with births occurring every other year. The newborn becomes independent after a year, and reaches full size at six to eight years of age. Maximum life span for the wild yak is estimated at 25 years. Domesticated yaks may give birth every year. Wild yaks are classified as endangered by IUCN—The World Conservation Union. They are officially protected in China, but their numbers have declined due to uncontrolled hunting.

Yaks were probably domesticated during the first millennium B.C., and now they are found in association with people in the high plateaus and mountains of Central Asia. They are docile and powerful, and they are surely the most useful of domesticated animals at elevation above 6,500 ft (2,000 m). The serve as mounts, beasts of burden, for milk and meat, and are also sheared for their wool. There are about 12 million domesticated yaks, but perhaps no more than a few hundred wild ones.

Yam

Yams are any of the ten economically important species of *Dioscorea*, a genus in the monocotyledonous family Dioscoriaceae. These species, all tropical in their origin, are cultivated for their edible tubers (enlarged, fleshy, usually underground storage stems). In the United States, the name *yam* is often misapplied to the sweet potato (*Ipomea batatas*).

Yams are herbaceous plants whose stems twine up and around bushes, trees, or poles. Depending on the species of yam, stems twine either clockwise or

A yak in Langtang Valley, Nepal.

counter–clockwise. The stems bear stalked, palmately veined leaves that are simple and entire, altthough a few species have three–lobed leaves. All yams have a dioecious lifestyle, which means that the staminate and pistillate flowers are borne on separate plants. The flowers are inconspicuous, being only 1/8 in (2–4 mm) long and whitish or greenish. The fruits produced from the flowers are three–angled and contain winged seeds. Some cultivars of yam, however, rarely flower or set seed.

In commonly cultivated yams, the tubers lie underground and are one (rarely two or three) per plant. These tubers resemble huge, elongated potatoes, typically growing 2–6 ft long (0.6–2 m) and weighing 11–33 lbs (5–15 kg). A thin skin protects their outer surface, and on the inside they are filled with starch which can be white or yellow depending on the species. One cultivated yam (*Dioscorea bulbifera*) bears small tubers along the aerial stems in the leaf axils (the angle between the stem and leaf stalk).

There are two centers of yam cultivation worldwide. The first is the high rainfall region of western Africa, from the Ivory Coast to Cameroon. Here the most important species are the white yam (*Dioscorea rotundata*) and the yellow yam (*D. cayenensis*), named for the color of their tuber's flesh. The second center is Vietnam, Cambodia, Laos, and neighboring regions where the most commonly cultivated species is the Asiatic yam (*D. alata*). Secondary areas of yam cultivation are the West Indies, Pacific islands, and southeastern United States (from Louisiana to Georgia). Most yam species originated in Asia and Africa; only one, the cush–cush yam (*D. trifida*), is native to the New World.

The world production of yams amounts to about 22 million tons (20 million metric tons) per year, of which two–thirds comes from tropical West Africa. Yams are to tropical West Africans what wheaten bread is to North Americans and Europeans. In tropical west–Africa, many social and religious festivals are associated with planting and harvesting yams.

Yams are propagated from cuttings of the tuber. Because the plants climb, they are provided with poles or trellises for support. It generally takes 7 to 10 months before the tubers can be harvested, and this must be done by hand because mechanical harvesters tend to damage the tubers. Yams store better than most tropical tuber crops and this is one reason why they are widely grown. Before eating, yams are usually peeled and then either boiled, roasted, or fried. In Africa yams are usually prepared as *fufu* or *four–fou*, made from peeling, cutting, and boiling the tuber, and then pounding it into a gelatinous dough. It is served with soups or stews or cooked raw in palm oil. Nutritionally, the yams are equivalent to the common potato, containing 80–90% carbohydrates, 5–8% protein, and about 3.5% minerals. Yam production is now declining because cassava (*Manihot utilissima*) and sweet potatoes (*Ipomea batatas*)–sources of starch that are easier to cultivate–are increasingly being used. Yams are not fed to livestock because they are more expensive than other kinds of animal feed.

Yams are a source of steroids and alkaloids–chemicals that are extremely active physiologically in vertebrate animals. The most important yam steroid is diosgenin used in the production of birth–control pills. Alkaloids from yams have been used to kill fish and to poison darts and arrows for hunting. Some yams are poisonous to humans because of their high alkaloid content, and their tubers must be boiled before eating to remove the toxins.

Yeast

Yeasts are single celled fungi, belonging mainly to the Ascomycetes, that serve as nutrient recyclers in nature, but are also important in industry, biotechnology, and as the agents of disease in humans. The term yeast is generically used in reference to many species of single–celled, budding fungi, including *Saccharomyces*—used in baking and brewing, and *Candida*—an infectious yeast common in people with compromised immune systems, such as AIDS victims.

Life cycle

Yeasts secrete enzymes that break down carbohydrates (through fermentation) to yield carbon dioxide

Yeast (*Anthrocobia muelleri*).

and alcohol. The source of carbohydrates are either living hosts or non–living hosts such as rotting vegetation, or the moist body cavities of animals. Yeasts are considered by some scientists to be closely related to the algae, lacking only in photosynthetic capability—perhaps as a result of an evolutionary trend toward a lifestyle dependent upon host nutrition. Ecologically yeasts are decomposers that secrete enzymes which dismantle the complex carbon compounds of plant cell walls and animal tissues, which they convert to sugars for their own growth and sustenance. Yeast reproduction may involve sexual spore production or asexual budding, dependent upon surrounding conditions. Though yeasts are highly tolerant of environmental variations in temperature and acidity, they thrive in warm and moist places high in oxygen and low in carbon dioxide. Whether or not they reproduce through asexual budding depends on the favorability of surrounding conditions: when times are good, yeast clones are produced by budding. In times of environmental stress, yeasts produce spores which are capable of withstanding periods of environmental hardship—perhaps even to lie dormant, until conditions improve and the mingling of genes can take place with the spore of another yeast. This rare version of yeast reproduction provides for genetic variation when conditions demand it, though budding is the predominant mode of yeast reproduction.

The importance of yeast for humans

People have been using yeast in bread baking for centuries, but suffering from its scourges for much longer. The biochemical by–products of yeast sugar metabolism—carbon dioxide and alcohol, are essential in baking and brewing. Bakers yeast (*Saccharomyces cerevisiae*), when added to baker's dough, produces

KEY TERMS

Candidiasis—Infection of the yeast *Candida albicans* which may take many forms depending upon the site of infection—from inflammation of the heart (endocarditis) to throat and lung infections.

Eukaryotes—The cells of animals, plants and fungi, characterized by a complex internal organization, including, organelles (some bound by membranes), and a distinct nucleus containing DNA.

Human genome—The entire human gene library, consisting of an estimated 100,000 genes encoded in the tightly woven DNA of 23 chromosomes.

Microbial flora—Benign, naturally–occurring of bacteria and fungi found on, and in, the human body including the intestinal tract, the mucous membranes, and the skin.

carbon dioxide pockets that make bread rise. Brewer's yeast, another strain of *Saccharomyces*, takes advantage of the yeasts characteristic of switching to anaerobic fermentation when deprived of oxygen to produce alcohol as a by–product of incomplete sugar breakdown. Yeasts that occur naturally on the skins of grapes also play a vital role in fermentation—converting the sugars of grapes into alcohol for wine production.

Yeasts also comprise some of the natural microbial flora residing in and upon animals, including humans. The yeast species *Candida albicans* is perhaps the most notorious of the yeast inhabitants of the human body, responsible for the affliction Candidiasis, which may take many forms. Through normal health and hygiene, *Candida* is held in check by the populous and benign bacterial residents of our skin and mucous membranes. But in instances of compromised health, *Candida albicans* can result in skin sores (such as Thrush), urogenital tract infections (such as vaginitis), and internally, endocarditis (heart muscle infection), inflammation of the spleen, liver, kidneys and lungs. Victims of AIDS are particularly susceptible to Candidiasis.

Biotechnology and yeast

Yeasts are rising stars in the toolbox of biotechnologists. Early in the development of biotechnology, which used cells as recipients of transplanted genes, bacteria were the organism of choice. However, limitations involving differences between bacterial cells and our own have relegated bacteria to a second place behind yeasts. Both yeast cells and human cells are eukaryotic—possessing a nucleus and membrane–bound organelles such as ribosomes and mitochondria. As biotechnology techniques have progressed over the last decade, yeasts have come to the fore as host cells for human gene implantation and as potential surrogate cells for housing human chromosomes. Yeasts have also been subjected to the alteration of their own genes, as biotechnologists attempt to develop strains of yeast more efficient in the metabolism of sugars for food and industrial applications.

By studying yeast genetics, scientists hope to gain insight into how the genes of all eukaryotic cells, including our own, function. In 1993 the first yeast chromosome was completely mapped, and the function of each of the 182 genes has yielded insight into such vital genetic processes as mutation repair, enzyme production, and cellular division regulation. These findings may yield insights into such fundamental human health issues as cancer and the aging process. Yeasts have also been transfomed through genetic engineering to produce the first genetically engineered vaccine for hepatitis B. Insulin and hemoglobin are also being commercially manufactured by yeast cells which have been re–coded by inserted human genes. Yeasts are a hopeful host cell for housing the entire human genome in an international effort to decipher the gene library of human cells.

See also Biotechnology; Brewing; Fermentation.

Further Reading:

Davis, Joel. *Mapping the Code: The Human Genome Project and the Choices of Modern Science.* Wiley, 1990.

Gross, Cynthia S. *The New Biotechnology: Putting Microbes to Work.* Lerner, 1988.

Hanlin, Richard, and Miguel Ulloa. *Atlas of Introductory Mycology,* 2nd Ed. H. W. Wilson Co., 1988.

Hoffman, M. "Yeast Biology Enters a Surprising New Phase." *Science* (20 March 1992): 1210–1511.

Sagan, Dorion. *Garden of Microbial Delights: A Practical Guide to the Subvisible World.* Harcourt Brace Jovanovich, 1988.

Stephens, R. B., ed. *Mycology Guidebook*, Mycology Guidebook Committee, Mycological Society of America, University of Washington Press, 1981.

Jeffrey Weld

Yellow-bellied sapsucker *see* **Woodpeckers**

Yellow-breasted chat *see* **Warblers**

Yellow fever

Yellow fever is a severe illness that causes outbreaks of epidemic proportions throughout Africa and tropical America. The first written evidence of such an epidemic dates back to a 1648 outbreak in the Yucatan Peninsula in Mexico. Since that time, much has been learned about the interesting transmission patterns of this devastating illness.

How yellow fever is spread

Many of the common illnesses in the United States, including the common cold, diarrhea, and influenza or flu, are spread via direct passage of the causative virus between human beings. Yellow fever, however, cannot be passed from one human being to another. Rather, the virus responsible for yellow fever is transmitted through an intermediate vector—a mosquito—which carries the virus from one host to another. The hosts of yellow fever include both humans and monkeys. The cycle begins when an infected monkey is bitten by a tree–hole breeding mosquito. This mosquito acquires the virus, and can pass the virus to any number of other monkeys which it may bite. When a human is bitten by such a mosquito, the human may acquire the virus. In the case of South American yellow fever, the infected human may return to the city, where an urban mosquito (*Aedes aegypti*) serves as a viral vector, spreading the infection between humans.

The host–vector–host cycle of yellow fever was first described by Walter Reed (1851–1902), the military surgeon for whom the Walter Reed Medical Center in Washington, D.C. is named. Reed was commissioned by the United States government to study yellow fever transmission. Reed's discovery of the mosquito as an intermediate vector led to improved control over the spread of the disease, ultimately allowing the building of the Panama Canal in an area prone to yellow fever epidemics.

Clinical course of yellow fever

Once a mosquito has transmitted the yellow fever virus to a human, the likelihood of symptomatic disease development is about 5–20%. Some infections may be warded off by the host's immune system; others may be subclinical, meaning they lack the severity of symptoms that would usually result in the identification of infection.

After a human host has received the yellow fever virus, there are five distinct stages through which a classic yellow fever infection evolves. These have been termed the periods of incubation, invasion, remission, intoxication, and convalescence.

The incubation period is the amount of time between the introduction of the virus into the host and the development of symptoms. For yellow fever this period is three to six days. During this time there are generally no symptoms identifiable to the host.

The period of invasion lasts two to five days; it begins with an abrupt onset of symptoms, consisting of fever and chills, intense headache, lower backache, muscle aches, nausea, and extreme exhaustion. The patient's tongue shows a characteristic white furry coating in the center, surrounded by beefy red margins. While most other infections that cause an elevation in temperature also cause an increase in heart rate, yellow fever produces an unusual symptom, called Faget's sign—the simultaneous occurrence of a high fever with a slowed heart rate. Throughout the period of invasion, there are still viruses circulating in the patient's blood stream, so continued viral transmission through mosquito vectors is possible.

The next phase is called the period of remission. The fever falls, and symptoms decrease in severity for a period of several hours to several days. In some patients, this signals the end of the disease; in other patients, this proves to be only the calm before the storm.

The period of intoxication is the most severe and potentially fatal phase of the illness. During this time, lasting three to nine days, a type of degeneration, or tissue breakdown, of the internal organs—specifically the kidneys, liver, and heart—occurs. This fatty degeneration results in what is considered the classic triad of yellow fever symptoms: jaundice, black vomit, and the release of protein into the urine. Jaundice causes the skin and the whites of the patient's eyes to take on a distinctive yellow tint. This yellow color is due to liver damage, resulting in the accumulation of bilirubin normally processed by a healthy liver. The liver damage also results in a tendency toward bleeding; the patient's vomit appears black due to the presence of blood. Protein, which is normally kept out of the urine by healthy and intact kidneys, appears in the urine due to disruption of the kidneys' composition by fatty degeneration.

Patients who survive the period of intoxication enter into a relatively short period of convalescence, and recover with no long term deficits related to the yellow fever infection. Further, infection with the yellow fever virus results in lifelong immunity against repeated infection with the virus.

Five to ten percent of all diagnosed cases of yellow fever are fatal. The occurrence of jaundice during a yel-

KEY TERMS
. . . .

Degeneration—Breakdown of tissue.

Faget's sign—The simultaneous occurrence of a high fever with a slowed heart rate.

Host—The organism, such as a monkey or human, in which another organism, such as a virus or bacteria, is living.

Vector—A carrier organism, such as a fly or mosquito, that serves to deliver a virus or other agent of infection to a host.

low fever infection is an extremely grave predictor, with 20–50% of these patients dying from their infection. Death may occur due to hemorrhaging (massive bleeding), often following a lapse into a comatose state.

Diagnosis

The diagnosis of yellow fever is made through examining the blood using various techniques in order to demonstrate the presence of either yellow fever viral antigens—the part of the virus that initiates the patient's immune response—or specific antibodies—the cells produced by the patient's immune system that are specifically directed against the yellow fever virus. Yellow fever is strongly suspected when Faget's sign is present, or when the classic triad of symptoms is noted.

Treatment

Medical management of yellow fever infection is directed toward relief of symptomatology. No active anti–viral treatment currently exists. Fevers and pain should be relieved with acetaminophen; neither aspirin nor ibuprofen should be used, because either one could exacerbate the bleeding tendency already present. Dehydration, due to fluid loss both from fever and bleeding, must be carefully avoided. The risk of bleeding into the stomach can be decreased through the administration of antacids and other medications. Hemorrhages may require blood transfusions, and kidney failure may require dialysis, a process that allows the work of the kidneys in clearing the blood of potentially toxic substances to be taken over by a machine that is outside of the body.

Prevention

A very safe, highly effective yellow fever vaccine exists, with about 95% of vaccine recipients acquiring long–term immunity to the yellow fever flavivirus. Careful measures to decrease mosquito populations in both urban areas and jungle areas in which humans are working, along with programs to vaccinate all people living in such areas, are necessary to avoid massive yellow fever outbreaks.

See also Mosquitoes; Vaccine.

Further Reading:

Andreoli, Thomas E., et al. *Cecil Essentials of Medicine*. Philadelphia: W. B. Saunders, 1993.

Berkow, Robert, and Andrew J. Fletcher. *The Merck Manual of Diagnosis and Therapy*. Rahway, NJ: Merck Research Laboratories, 1992.

Isselbacher, Kurt J., et al. *Harrison's Principles of Internal Medicine*. New York: McGraw Hill, 1994.

Mandell, Douglas, et al. *Principles and Practice of Infectious Diseases*. New York: Churchill Livingstone, 1995.

Sherris, John C., et al. *Medical Microbiology*. Norwalk, CT: Appleton & Lange, 1994.

Rosalyn Carson–DeWitt

Yellow figbird *see* **Orioles**

Yellow jacket *see* **Wasps**

Yellowthroat *see* **Orioles**

Yew

Yews are various species of tree– or shrub–sized, woody plants that comprise the conifer family, Taxaceae. All yews are in the genus *Taxus*, and about seven species are known, occurring in moist, temperate forest habitats in North America, Europe, Asia, and Africa.

Biology of yews

Yews have dark–green colored, rather soft, evergreen, needle–like leaves. Yews usually have separate male and female plants, although sometimes these flowers will develop on separate branches of the same plant. The male flowers are small and inconspicuous, and develop as globular bodies in leaf axils. The female flowers of yews develop in the springtime, and they occur singly and naked in the axis of a leaf. The fruit is a relatively large, hard seed, encased in a bright–red or scarlet, fleshy, cup–like structure known as an aril. The arils are sought by birds as food, which eat and disperse the seeds. The seeds of yews are poisonous to people and other mammals, although the fleshy arils are not.

The symptoms of poisoning by yew seeds or foliage are dilation of the pupils, pain, and vomiting, leading to coma and death if the dose is large enough.

The wood of yews is dense, strong, flexible, and resistant to decay. The bark is thin, fibrous, scaly, and dark colored. The young twigs of yews are generally greenish in color.

Yews are slow growing and highly tolerant of shading. As a result, yews can survive in the shade beneath a closed forest canopy. This can be especially true beneath angiosperm trees, which allow the yews to grow relatively freely during the spring and autumn when the trees are in a leafless condition. However, yews also do well beneath conifer trees, as long as occasional gaps in the canopy allow exposure to light as brief sunflecks during the day.

Yews have a dense foliage and so cast a rather deep shade. As a result of this shade, as well as a toxic quality of the yew's leaf litter, few plants will grow beneath a closed canopy of yew tree or shrubs.

Species of yew

Three species of yew grow naturally in North America. The Pacific or western yew (*Taxus brevifolia*) is the only species that reaches the size of a small tree, typically 19–39 ft (6–12 m) tall, but as tall as 75 ft (23 m). The western yew is a species of the sub–canopy of conifer rain forests of the Pacific coast, ranging from central California to southern Alaska. The species also occurs on the relatively moist, western slopes of the Rocky Mountains in Washington and southern British Columbia. The western yew is relatively widespread in mature, conifer–dominated rain forests, but it is rarely abundant.

The Florida yew (*T. floridana*) is a rare, small tree that occurs in northern Florida. The Canadian yew (*T. canadensis*), also known as ground hemlock or poison hemlock, is relatively widely distributed in coniferous and mixed–wood forests of cool–temperate regions of eastern North America. The European or English yew (*T. baccata*) of Europe and Asia is a relatively tall species, which can grow to almost 65 ft (20 m) in height.

Economic and ecological importance of yews

Yew wood is very tough and elastic, a consequence of the structural qualities of its elongated, water–conducting cells known as tracheids. The wood of yews is of minor commercial importance. However, it is prized for certain uses in which strength and flexibility are required. During medieval times in western Europe, the wood of European yew trees was favored for the manufacture of bows. Today, bows are mostly made of synthetic materials, but some traditional archers still like to use bows made from yew. Canoe paddles are also sometimes carved from yew wood.

Yews are very popular shrubs in horticulture, probably being used more commonly than any other types of conifers. Various species are cultivated, but the European yew is the most common, and it is available in a number of cultivated varieties, or cultivars. It is quite easy to propagate desired cultivars of yews because these plants will root from stem cuttings, a relatively unusual trait for a conifer.

Yews are commonly used to accent the lines of buildings, or to create interesting entrances around doors. Very attractive hedges can also be developed using dense plantings of yews, which may be sheared to achieve a desired shape.

Sometimes, the dense foliage of taller yews is sheared in interesting ways, to create a special visual effect. For example, yews can be trimmed to develop globular or cubed shapes, or to look like animals of various sorts. Yews are best sheared in the late summer.

Other yews that are commonly used in horticulture are the Japanese yew (*T. cuspidata*), and the columnar shaped *T. hicksi* and *T. hilli*, all originally from Asia. These and some other species of yews have been widely introduced into North America and elsewhere as attractive species in horticulture. However, there is no indication that any of these non–native yews have escaped from cultivation and become invasive pests of natural habitats.

Medicinal uses of yews

Yews have widely been recognized as toxic to livestock and humans. In smaller doses, yew has been used as a minor folk medicine in some parts of its range. Example of the medicinal uses of yews include the induction of menstruation, and the treatment of arthritis, kidney disease, scurvy, tuberculosis, and other ailments. However, in recent years, yews have become famous for their use in the treatment of several deadly cancers.

In particular, the dark–brown or purple bark of western yew has been found to contain relatively large concentrations of an alkaloid known as taxol. Taxol has been demonstrated as being an effective treatment against advanced cases of ovarian and breast cancer, two deadly diseases. The use of taxol for these purposes is now approved by the U.S. Food and Drug Administration and by regulatory agencies in other

KEY TERMS
. . . .

Aril—A fleshy, often brightly colored covering that partially encases a seed. The aril is edible and is intended to encourage an animal to eat the fruit and thereby disperse the seed.

Cultivar—A cultivated variety of a plant used in agriculture or horticulture. The distinct qualities of the cultivar are genetically based, but are not sufficient to render it a different species or subspecies. However, economically successful cultivars are given common names and marketed as distinct entities.

Part per million (ppm)—A unit of concentration, equivalent to 0.0001 percent, or one milligram in a kilogram, or one milliliter in a liter.

Sunfleck—A transient patch of sunlight that travels over the forest floor as the sun arcs overhead during the day.

Taxol—An alkaloid chemical that can be extracted from the bark and other tissues of yews and is active in the treatment of human ovarian and breast cancers.

countries. This recently developed use of western yew has led to an essentially insatiable demand for its bark.

The concentrations of taxol in bark are variable, ranging from only one part per million (ppm) to 690 ppm. The concentration of taxol in foliage of western yew is generally smaller, ranging from 12 to 80 ppm. At the present time, taxol is most efficiently extracted from yew bark. Unfortunately, it takes about fourteen kilograms of yew bark to yield only one gram of taxol, equivalent to 3 to 12 yew trees per cancer patient treated. Clearly, very large amounts of yew bark must be collected in order to have sufficient material to satisfy the medical and research demands.

Yew is not a commercial species in forestry, and up until about 1989 the species was routinely trashed and usually burned after logging. Today, however, the bark of western yew is routinely stripped from the survivors of the logging aftermath. In addition, the bark is now widely stripped from living western yews in unlogged

forests, including old–growth rainforests of the Pacific coast, where this species tends to be most abundant. Sometimes, this process is rather inefficient, and in some cases of poaching, the bark has only been taken from the lower part of taller yew trees, where it can be easily reached. Unfortunately, the removal of its bark usually kills the yews by destroying its vascular system, so bark stripping is a rather wasteful use of the plant. A system has been designed and implemented to regulate the harvest of yew bark, but it is difficult to enforce over extensive areas, and a great deal of poaching occurs.

The enthusiastic collection of western yew bark, while contributing to the successful treatment of some cancer cases, threatens to exhaust the very resource upon which this treatment depends, as it is extremely wasteful and does not aim to conserve the species for future use. This dilemma may be resolved if pharmaceutical biochemists develop a economical method of synthesizing taxol in the laboratory, making the extraction of the alkaloid from western yew bark unnecessary. Alternatively, means could be found to economically extract the taxol found in relatively small concentrations in other parts of the yew, especially the foliage. Another possibility is to establish managed plantations of western yew for the specific purpose of obtaining taxol. This is actually being done, but the western yew is slow growing, and it will take some years before the plantations can be economically harvested.

So far, these relatively sustainable approaches have not been developed to the point where pressure on wild western yews can be relieved, and this plant is being rapidly mined from its natural habitats. Because the western yew is not naturally abundant, its populations will rapidly become depleted, and the species will become endangered in the wild.

Further Reading:
Brockman, C. F. *Trees of North America*. Golden Press, New York: 1968.
Daly, D. "Tree of Life." *Audubon* 70 (1992): 76–85.
Joyce, C. "Taxol: Search for a Cancer Drug." *BioScience* 43 (1993): 133–36.

Bill Freedman

Ytterbium *see* **Lanthanides**
Yttrium *see* **Element, chemical**

Z

Zebras

Zebras are members of the horse family (Equidae) that inhabit tropical grasslands (savannas) in much of sub–Saharan Africa. Three of the seven species of equids are zebras. Zebras are herd–living social ungulates (hoofed mammals) recognized by a black–and–white (or cream or yellowish) striped coat, short erect mane, and a tail averaging about 18 in (0.5 m) long. The body length of a zebra is about 6–8.5 feet (2–2.6 m) long, and body weight can reach 770 lb (350 kg), with males slightly bigger than females.

There are three species and several subspecies of zebra. The common, Burchell's, or plains zebra *(E. burchelli)* lives throughout much of eastern and southern Africa, and is the best–studied species. Grévy's zebra *(Equus grevyi)* is found in Somalia, Kenya, and Ethiopia, and is the largest of the wild horses, characterized by large ears, narrow stripes, and a thick neck. The third species is the mountain zebra *(E. zebra)* found in the hill country of Angola, Namibia, and western South Africa.

The adaptive value of the stripes of the zebra camouflaging the animal in the waving grasses of the African grasslands, especially at dusk and dawn. Zebras rest in herds in open ground where they can see predators approaching, rather than lying down in the grass. When a herd of zebras is being chased by predators such as lions or hyenas, their stripes make it difficult for predators to visually latch on to a specific animal to attack. Other suggestions are that the stripes identify individual zebras as part of a group and also initiates mating behavior.

The common zebra

The common or Burchell's zebra stands about 50–52 in (1.3 m) tall at the shoulder. It has the widest stripes of all zebras, and the stripes continue down to the belly of the animal. The stripes of Burchell's zebra become fainter and almost disappear in southern populations.

There are several subspecies of the common zebra, distinguishable by the pattern of stripes on the rump. Grant's zebra (*E. burchelli granti*) has wide rump stripes, the Chapmann's or Damaraland zebra has tan shadow stripes between the black stripes, and Selous's zebra has only faint shadow stripes between the black stripes. A subspecies known as the "true" Burchelli's zebra had reddish–brown stripes, and became extinct in the early 1900s.

Herds of common plains zebras are actually a collection of family groups. Each family group is headed by a dominant male stallion and one female is dominant over the other seven or eight females and their young.

When the group is feeding or drinking, one animal stands guard. If a predator approaches, such as a troop of wild dogs or lions, the stallion zebra moves to the back of the fleeing herd and ensures that no single animal falls behind or gets separated and becomes vulnerable to attack. Zebras that become isolated call attention to their plight by making a harsh sound like a combination bark and bray, which draws the other zebras back to protect it.

The zebra's large, rounded ears turn in every direction and are able to pick up the slightest sound. The zebra's primary defense is running, which it can do at speeds approaching 40 mph (64 kph), though for only a short time. Given the chance, a zebra fights primarily by kicking with its hind hooves. However, an attacking predator is likely to grasp the animal's neck with one quick leap that prevents the zebra from acting.

After a young mare mates for the first time, she will stay with the same family group for the rest of her life. Males that have not yet developed herds—or that have been ousted from their herds by other males—live in male–only bands (bachelor herds), which they leave

Grevy's zebras (*Equus grevyi*).

KEY TERMS

Dewlap—A fold of extra skin that hangs from the neck.

Equid—Any member of family Equidae, including horses, zebras, and asses.

Gestation—Pregnancy.

to find mates at about six years old. If stallions try to take mares from an existing family group, they will have to fight that group's stallion.

Gestation lasts approximately one year, with only one offspring produced. The young are born with disproportionately long legs and are ready to run with the herd within a few minutes. The brown–striped coat of a new foal gradually changes to the familiar black and white.

Mountain zebras

There are two subspecies of mountain zebras in South Africa which live on rough, rocky highlands, but once also occurred in large numbers in the grassy lowland plains. The Cape mountain zebra of South Africa is the smallest zebra, standing about 4 ft (1.2 m) at the shoulder and weighing about 600 lb (272 kg). The stripes of the Cape mountain zebra are slightly wider and shorter than those of the other subspecies, Hartmann's mountain zebra of Namibia. The Cape mountain zebra has a dewlap under the lower jaw, which other zebras do not have.

Herds of the common zebra readily mix with herds of wildebeest, but Cape mountain zebras tend to keep apart from other animals. Hartmann's zebras have the ability to locate water in apparently dry valleys.

Grévy's zebra

Grévy's zebra is quite different in both appearance and behavior from the common zebra. It stands close to 5 ft (1.5 m) tall at the shoulder and weighs about 850 lb (400 kg). Its stripes are very narrow, do not cross over the lower back as they do in the Cape mountain zebra.

Grévy's zebras live in semidesert country and do not form herds. Instead, only the mother foals remain together, while the males and the young females drift off. Individual stallions have remarkably large breeding territories, and any female found within the territory belongs to the male. A stallion will tolerate other males in his territory only if they do not try to mate with the mares. The gestation period of the Grévy's zebra is 12 1/2 months, one month longer than other species of zebra.

The recently extinct zebralike quagga (*E. quagga*) looked like a combination wild ass and zebra and had a reddish coat and stripes only on the head, neck, and shoulders. The name quagga is derived from the odd bray of this species, which was described as "kwa–ha." The quagga lived throughout South Africa but was killed by 19th–century settlers for its meat and hides. The last quagga died in an Amsterdam zoo in 1883.

The populations of the common zebra are high, especially in the Serengeti Plains of Tanzania and Kenya, where zebras run with the huge wildebeest herds on their annual migrations.

Grévy's zebra and the Cape mountain zebra are both endangered. There are probably fewer than 15,000 Grévy's zebras in Ethiopia, Somalia, and Kenya, in three separate populations. A major herd of Grévy's zebra is protected in a game reserve in Kenya. There are less than 200 Cape mountain zebras which live in Mountain Zebra National Park in South Africa, and this small number makes the long–term survival of this species doubtful.

Further Reading:

Arnold, Caroline. *Zebra.* New York: William Morrow & Co., 1987.

Duncan, P., ed. *Zebras, Horses and Asses: An Action Plan for the Conservation of Wild Equids.* Island Press, 1992.

Scuro, Vincent. *Wonders of Zebras.* New York: Dodd, Mead And Co., 1983.

Special Publications Division. *National Geographic Book of Mammals.* Vol. 1 & 2. Washington, D.C.: National Geographic Society, 1981.

Stidworthy, John. *Mammals: The Large Plant–Eaters.* Encyclopedia of the Animal World. New York: Facts On File, 1988.

Willis, Terri. *Serengeti Plain.* Wonders of the World series. Austin, Tex.: Raintree Steck–Vaughan Publishers, 1994.

Zebras. Zoobooks. San Diego: Wildlife Education, Ltd., 1989.

Zero

Zero is often equated with "nothing," but that is not a good analogy. Zero can be the absence of a quality, but it can also be a starting point, such as 0° on a temperature scale. In a mathematical system, zero is the *additive identity*. It is a number which can be added to any given number to yield a sum equal to the given number. Symbolically, it is a number 0, such that a + 0 = a for any number a.

In the Hindi–Arabic numeration system, zero is used as a placeholder as well as a number. The number 205 is distinguished from 25 by having a 0 in the tens place. This can be interpreted as no tens, but the early use of 0 in this way was more to show that 2 was in the hundreds place than to show no tens.

Zero is used in some ways that take it beyond ordinary addition and multiplication. One use is as an exponent. In an exponential function such as $y = 10^x$ the exponent is not limited to the counting numbers. One of its possible values is 0. If 10^0 is to obey the rule for exponents — $10^m = 10^{m+0} = 10^m \times 10^0$ — 10^0 must equal 1. This is true not only for 10^0 but for any a^0, where a is any positive number. That is, $a^0 = 1$.

Another curious use of zero is the expression 0!. Ordinarily n! is the product $1 \cdot 2 \cdot 3 \cdot \ldots \cdot n$, of all the integers from 1 to n. In a formula such as n!/r!(n − r)!, which represents the number of different combinations of things which can be chosen from n things r at a time, 0! can occur. If 0! is assigned the value 1, the formula works. This happens in other instances as well.

The symbol for zero does not appear before about 800 A. D., when it appears in connection with Hindu–Arabic base–10 numerals. In these numerals it functions as a place holder. The Mayans also used a zero in writing their base–20 numerals. It was a symbol which looked something like an eye, and it acted as a place holder.

The reason that the symbol appeared so late in history is that the number systems used by the Greeks, Romans, Chinese, Egyptians, and others didn't need it. For example, one can write the Roman numeral for 1056 as MLVI. No zero as a place holder is needed. The Babylonians did have a place–value system with their base–60 numerals, and a symbol for zero would have eliminated some of the ambiguity that shows up in their clay tablets, but was probably overlooked because, within each place, the numbers from 1 to 59 were represented with wedge–shaped tallies. In a tally system all that is required to represent zero is the absence of a tally. Sometimes Babylonians did use a dot or a space as a placeholder, but failed to see that this could be a number of its own.

The word zero appears to be a much metamorphosed translation of the Hindu word "sunya," meaning void or empty.

Zero also has the property a x 0 = 0 for any number a. This property is a consequence of zero's additive property.

In ordinary arithmetic the statement ab = 0 implies that a, b, or both are equal to 0; that is, the only way for a product to equal zero is for one or more of its factors to equal zero. This property is used when one solves equations such as (x − 2)(x + 3) = 0 by setting each factor equal to zero.

The multiplicative property of zero is also used in the argument for not allowing zero to be used as a divisor or a denominator. The law which defines a/b is (a/b)b = a. If one substitutes 0 for b, the result is (a/0)0 = a, which forces a to be 0. But even when a is 0, the law allows 0/0 to be any number, which is intolerable.

Zero sometimes appears in disguise. In even–and–odd arithmetic we have "even plus odd equals odd," "odd times odd equals odd," and so on. The various combinations can be listed in the tables

+	even	odd		x	even	odd
even	even	odd		even	even	even
odd	odd	even		odd	even	odd

Is there a zero? Is there an element 0 such that 0 + a = a for either of the possible values of a? The top line in the addition table says that there is. "Even" is such an element. Does 0 • a = 0 for both values of a? The top line of the multiplication table says that it does. Does ab = 0 imply that one or both of the factors is 0? Only if both factors are odd, is product is odd; so, yes, it does.

Thus this miniature arithmetic has a zero, and it is "even."

Another arithmetic is clock arithmetic. In this arithmetic 3 is three hours past twelve; 3 + 7 is ten hours past twelve; and 3 + 12 is fifteen hours past twelve. But on a clock, every twelve hours the hands

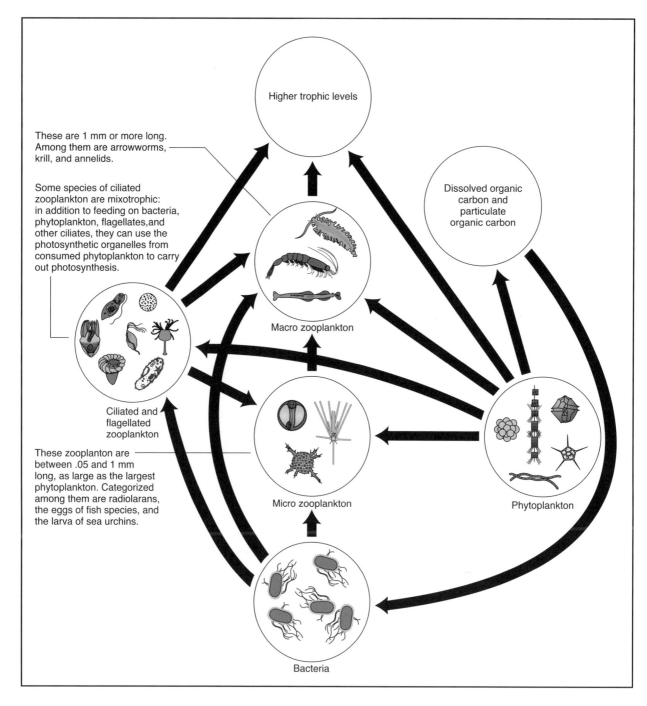

These are 1 mm or more long.
Among them are arrowworms,
krill, and annelids.

Some species of ciliated
zooplankton are mixotrophic:
in addition to feeding on bacteria,
phytoplankton, flagellates,and
other ciliates, they can use the
photosynthetic organelles from
consumed phytoplankton to carry
out photosynthesis.

Higher trophic levels

Dissolved organic
carbon and
particulate
organic carbon

Macro zooplankton

Ciliated and
flagellated
zooplankton

These zooplanton are
between .05 and 1 mm
long, as large as the largest
phytoplankton. Categorized
among them are radiolarans,
the eggs of fish species, and
the larva of sea urchins.

Micro zooplankton

Phytoplankton

Bacteria

The planktonic ecosystem; arrows show the movement of biomass through the food chain.

return to their original position; so fifteen hours past twelve is the same as three hours past twelve. For any a, a + 12 = a. [In number–theory symbolism this would be written a + 12 ∫ a (mod 12).] So in clock arithmetic, 12 behaves like 0 in ordinary arithmetic.

It also multiplies like 0. Twelve 3–hour periods equal 36 hours, which the hands show as 12. Twelve periods of a hours each leave the hands at 12 for any a (a is limited to whole numbers in clock arithmetic), so 12 x a = 12.

Thus, in clock arithmetic 12 doesn't look like zero, but it behaves like zero. It could be called 0, and on a digital 24–hour clock, where the number 24 behaves like 0, 24 is called 0. The next number after 23:59:59 is 0:0:0.

In this arithmetic, unlike ordinary arithmetic, the law "ab = 12 if and only if a, b, or both equal 12" does not hold. The "if" part does, but not the "only if." Six times 2 is 12, but neither 6 nor 2 is 12. Three times 8 is 12 (the hands go around twice, passing 12 once and ending at 12), but neither 3 nor 8 is 12. Thus in clock arithmetic there can be two numbers, neither of them zero, whose product is zero. Such numbers are called divisors of zero. This happens because we use 12–hour (or 24–hour) clocks. If we used 11–hour clocks, it would not.

See also Numeration systems.

Further Reading:

Eves, Howard. *An Introduction to the History of Mathematics*. New York: Holt, Rinehart and Winston, 1976.

J. Paul Moulton

Zero-tillage systems *see* **Herbicides**

Zinc *see* **Element, chemical**

Zirconium *see* **Element, chemical**

Zooplankton

Zooplankton are small animals that occur in the water column of either marine and freshwater ecosystems. Zooplankton are a diverse group defined on the basis of their size and function, rather than on their taxonomic affinities.

Most species in the zooplankton community fall into three major groups–Crustacea, Rotifers, and Protozoas. Crustaceans are generally the most abundant, especially those in the order Cladocera (waterfleas), and the class Copepoda (the copepods), particularly the orders Calanoida and Cyclopoida. Cladocerans are typically most abundant in fresh water, with common genera including *Daphnia* and *Bosmina*. Commonly observed genera of marine calanoid copepods include *Calanus*, *Pseudocalanus*, and *Diaptomus*, while abundant cyclopoid copepods include *Cyclops* and *Mesocyclops*. Other crustaceans in the zooplankton include species of opossum shrimps (order Mysidacea), amphipods (order Amphipoda), and fairy shrimp (order Anostraca). Rotifers (phylum Rotifera) are also found in the zooplankton, as are protozoans (kingdom Protista). Insects may also be important, especially in fresh waters close to the shoreline.

Most zooplankton are secondary consumers, that is, they are herbivores that graze on phytoplankton, or on unicellular or colonial algae suspended in the water column. The productivity of the zooplankton community is ultimately limited by the productivity of the small algae upon which they feed. There are times when the biomass of the zooplankton at any given time may be similar, to or even exceed, that of the phytoplankton. This occurs because the animals of the zooplankton are relatively long–lived compared with the algal cells upon which they feed, so the turnover of their biomass is much less rapid. Some members of the zooplankton are detritivores, feeding on suspended organic detritus. Some species of zooplankton are predators, feeding on other species of zooplankton, and some spend part of their lives as parasites of larger animals, such as fish.

Zooplankton are very important in the food webs of open–water ecosystems, in both marine and fresh waters. Zooplankton are eaten by relatively small fish (called planktivorous fish), which are then eaten by larger fish. Zooplankton are an important link in the transfer of energy from the algae (the primary producers) to the ecologically and economically important fish community (the consumers).

Species of zooplankton vary in their susceptibility to environmental stressors, such as exposure to toxic chemicals, acidification of the water, eutrophication and oxygen depletion, or changes in temperature. As a result, the species assemblages (or communities) of the zooplankton are indicators of environmental quality and ecological change.

See also Crustacea; Copepods; Protozoa; Shrimp.

Index

Benzodiazapine   405, 3699

Benzoic acid   454-455, 3343

Berberis canadensis, see American barberry

Berberis thunbergii, see Japanese barberry

Berberis vulgaris, see Common barberry

Berg, Paul   1618

Bergamot   830, 2346

Berger, Hans   3315

Bergy bits   1886

Beriberi   2195, 2574, 3861

Berkeley, George   3217

Berkelium   1309

Bernard, Claude   667, 676

Bernoulli, Daniel   455, 996, 1503

Bernoulli effect   88

Bernoulli, Jakob   2866, 3430

Bernoulli, Johann   3724

Bernoulli's principle   1503

Berthellot, C. L.   167, 3350

Berthelot, Pierre Eugäne   641

Berthemot, D.   623

Berthier, P.   149

Berthold, A. A.   1347

Berthollet, Claude Louis   913

Bertillon, Alphonse   1523

Bertillon system   1523

Berylliosis   3120

Beryllium   127

Berzelius, J. J.   137, 349, 355, 704, 914, 1300, 3579

Bessel, Friedrich   889, 1778, 2689

Bessemer converter   1977, 2652

Bessemer, Henry   1977, 2284, 3480

Bessemer process   3697

Best, Charles   1121, 1935

Beta-blockers   455, 457-458, 1765

Beta decay   2494

Beta-hemolytic streptococcus bacteria   3209

Beta maritima, see Wild beet

Beta rays   3036

Beta turn   2954

Beta vulgaris crassa, see Sugar beet

Beta vulgaris escuelenta, see Agricultural beet

Beta vulgaris, see Beet

Beta-carboline   1732

Beta-carotene   2577

Betalguese   3822

Betamax video   3835

Betel leaf   2721

Betel palm   2677

Bethe, Hans   1305, 2544

Bettong   2009

Bettongia lesueur, see Boodie

Bettongia penicillata, see Bettong

Bettongia tropica, see Northern rat-kangaroo

Betula alleghaniensis, see Yellow birch

Betula papyrifera, see White birch

Betula papyrifera, see Paper birch

Bewick's wren   3958

Bib blue stem   1681

Bicarbonate   673

Bickford, William   1427

Bidens frondosa, see Beggar ticks

Bidentate ligands   762

Big bang theory   458-461, 986, 1063, 2995, 3382, 3492

Big blue-stem   1681

Big skate   3302

Bigcone pine   2800

Bighead carp   539, 2339

Bighorn sheep   3288

Bigleaf maple   2208

Bigmouth buffalo fish   3535

Bigollo, Leonardo Pisano   1469

Bilateral symmetry   2668

Bile   798, 1992

Bilirubin   1992

Billis perennis, see Daisy

Binapacryl   1574

Binary operations   311, 548

Binary satellite   3193

Binary star   461-464

Binary system   11, 2570, 3496

Binary system (mathematics)   927

Binder   1187

Binford, Lewis   1398

Binocular   3852

Binocular cues   1102

Binocular vision   2723

Binomial   123, 464

Binomial coefficients   883, 2707

Binomial theorem   464-465

Binomial triangle, see Pascal's triangle

Binswanger's disease   1081

Bioaccumulation   465, 485, 952, 1068, 1514, 1733, 2741, 2880

Bioaerosols   1908

Bioassays   466-467

Biocentrism   221

Biochemical changes   3509

Biochemical oxygen demand   467-468

Biochemicals   1357, 2663, 2863

Biochemistry   465, 469, 670, 740, 1373, 1867, 2632

Biodegradable   2879

Biodegradable waste   2042, 3069

Biodigester   2043

Biodiversity   469-473, 1078, 1235, 1341, 1346, 1432, 1528, 1533, 1883, 3049, 3128

Bioenergy   473-476

Bioengineering   475
Biofeedback   143, 184, 476-477
Biogas   474
Biogenesis   1643, 3437
Biogenic amines   1165, 2490
Biogeochemical cycles   1241
Biogeography   1346, 1500
Biolistics   2824
Biological assay   465
Biological clock   68, 497, 562
Biological community   477-480
Biological determinism   1837
Biological diversity   1229
Biological macromolecules   2358
Biological rhythms   497-499, 761
Biological warfare   480-483
Biology   483-484, 1034, 2588
Bioluminescence   484-485, 2145
Biomagnification   485-489, 1514
Biomass   142, 640, 1021, 1237, 1239, 1357, 1363,
    1527, 1531, 1733, 1791, 1842, 2013, 2392, 3049,
    3054, 3211
Biome   478, 489-495, 1239, 1500, 2200, 3048
Biomedical research   2159, 3135
Biomolecules   1292
Biomphalaria snails   3740
Bionics   2947
Biopolymers   3016
Biopsy   651, 1123, 1809, 3044
Bioremediation   495-497, 1749, 3069
Biosolids   3266, 3894
Biosorbents, see Bioremediation
Biosphere   499-501, 1239-1240, 1357, 2889
Biosyntheses, see Anabolism
Biotechnology   495, 501-503, 1091
Biotic communities   831, 979, 1372
Biotin   3863
Bipedal locomotion   1836
Bipolar disorder   2117, 2202, 2204, 2967, 3699
Bipolar-junction transistor   3704
Birches   504-505, 1532, 2438, 3532, 3943
Birchleaf buckthorn   586
Bird watching   3840
Bird-of-paradise plant   400
Birds-foot trefoil   2082
Birdseye, Charles   1520
Birds'-eye primrose   2927
Bird's-nest soup   3575
Bird's-nest plant   691
Birth   509-513
Birth control   960
Birth defects   65, 513-517, 1460, 1510, 2628
Birth weight   1461, 1872
Bishop's cap   3205

Bismuth   3036
Bismuth subsalicylate   3784
Bison   517-519, 2900
Bison bison athabascae, see Wood bison
Bison bison bison, see Plains bison
Bison bison, see American bison
Bison bonasus, see European bison
Bissell, George H.   2594, 2747
Biston betularia, see Peppered moth
Biting midge   3749
Bitis gabonicus, see Gaboon viper
Bitis nasicornis, see Rhinoceros viper
Bitter apple   1674
Bitter cassava   3442
Bitter orange   829
Bitterns   519-521
Bitternut hickory   3885
Bivalves   521-522
Bjerknes, Jacob   92, 1324, 3916, 3919, 3923
Bjerknes, Vilhelm   92, 3916, 3919, 3923
Bjerrum, N.   23
BL Lacertae object   529-530, 2995
Black body radiation   3415
Black brant   1598
Black bulbul   597
Black bullhead   706
Black caiman   1017
Black colobus monkey   869
Black ducks   1179
Black eagle   1194
Black flies   3749
Black gibbon   1646
Black hole   11, 524-527, 991, 1063, 1579, 2013, 2325,
    2994, 3092, 3382, 3455, 3489, 3822
Black huckleberry   1770
Black hunter thrips   3663
Black, Joseph   627, 641, 673
Black lemur   2087
Black locust   2081
Black lung disease   3120
Black mamba   1247
Black mangrove   1531, 2200, 3934
Black maple   2208
Black marlin   2213
Black mustard   2431
Black oystercatcher   2654
Black pepper   2720
Black rat   3061
Black sea bass   419
Black smokers   1868
Black snake-root   691
Black spotted cuscus   2751
Black spruce   3440
Black swift   3575

Bristly black currant   3205
Brittle star   571-572
Broad bean   2523, 3825
Broad fish tapeworm   1487
Broad-footed mole   2368
Broad-headed skink   3309
Broad-leaf forest   3719
Broad-band width   180
Broad-billed roller   3164
Broad-faced binturong   830
Broad-footed marsupial mice   2223
Broad-nosed gentle lemur   2087
Broad-shouldered hawk   1744
Broad-tailed hummingbird   1842
Broad-winged hawk   614, 1745
Broadbill swordfish   2213
Broca, Pierre Paul   3418, 3431
Broca's area   252
Broccoli   2431
Broglie, Louis de   344
Brome-grass   1686
Bromeliads   573-574, 3049
Bromides   404
Bromine   1733-1734
Bromus tectorum, see Downy brome-grass
Bronchi   313, 3123
Bronchial tubes   3118
Bronchioles   313, 1336, 3118
Bronchitis   574-575, 1335, 3118, 3849
Bronchodilators   314, 3119
Bronsted-Lowry definition   2492
Brontosaurus   1143
Bronze   972
Bronze Age   137, 973
Brook stickleback   3498
Brook trout   539
Brookesia stumpfi, see Stump-tailed chameleons
Brookesia superciliaris, see Stump-tailed chameleons
Brookesia tuberculata, see Stump-tailed chameleons
Brooks, Frederick   3842
Brotogeris versicolorus, see Canary-winged parakeet
Brotulid   722
Broussonetia payrifera, see Paper mulberry
Brown algae   118-119
Brown anole   209
Brown bears   430
Brown bullhead   706
Brown butterflies   607
Brown dwarf   575-576, 729, 1063
Brown fat   1803
Brown howler monkey   2507
Brown hyena   1870
Brown kiwi   1496
Brown lemming   2084

Brown lemur   2087
Brown lesser mouselemur   2085
Brown, Louise   1963
Brown pelican   2713
Brown, R. Hanbury   1949
Brown, Robert   1501
Brown thrasher   2354, 3375
Brown towhee   3400
Brown tree snake   1344
Brown trout   539
Brown-banded cockroach   855
Brown-headed cowbird   523, 3840
Brown-headed nuthatch   2573
Brown-headed spider monkey   2507
Brownian motion   576-577, 868
Brucella abortis, see Brucellosis
Brucella melitensis, see Brucellosis
Brucella suis, see Brucellosis
Brucellosis   481, 577-578
Brunhes, Bernard   2665
Brush rabbit   2032
Brush-tailed porcupines   2894
Brush-tailed tuans   2223
Brush-tailed marsupial mice   2223
Brush-tailed rat-kangaroo   2009
Brushtail possum   1434, 2750
Brussel sprouts   2431
Bryde's whale   753
Bryophyte   578-582
Bryozoa   556, 2757
Bubalus bubalis, see Water buffalo
Bubalus depressicornis, see Lowland anoa
Bubalus mindorensis, see Tamaraw
Bubalus quartesi, see Mountain anoa
Bubble chamber   2705
Bubo bubo, see Eagle owl
Bubo virginianus, see Great horned owl
Bubonic plague   582-584, 1368, 1490, 2307, 3060,
   3163
Bubulcus ibis, see Cattle egret
Buccinum undatum, see Whelk
Bucephala clangula, see Common goldeneye
Buceros bicornis, see Great hornbill
Buceros rhinoceros, see Rhinoceros hornbill
Buchla, Don   3585
Buchner, Eduard   1374, 1452
Buckeyes   1825, 1826
Buckland, William   1629
Buckminsterfullerene   584-586
Buckthorn   586
Buckwheat   586-587
Bud   587-588
Budding   300, 587-588, 1675, 1846
Budgerigar   2697-2698

C

Cabbage 296, 904, 2431, 3825
Cabbage lettuce 904
Cable television 3627
Cacajao calvus, see White uakari
Cacajao melanocephalus, see Black-headed uakari
Cacajao rubicundus, see Red uakar
Cacatua galerita, see Sulfur-crested cockatoo
Cacatua leadbeateri, see Pink cockatoo
Cacatua roseicapilla, see Galah
Cacatua sanguinea, see Little corella
Cackling Canada goose 1599
Cacomistle 3002
Cacti 617-620, 1790, 3443
Cactoblastis cactorum, see South American cactus
   moth
Cactus wren 619, 3958
Cadaverine 161
Caddisflies 621
Cade, John 2117
Cadtomea sakua, see Sweet chestnut tree
Caecilians 623
Caesalpina brasiliensis, see Brazilwood
Caesalpina sappan, see Sappanwood
Caesalpinia ferrea, see Brazilian ironwood
Caesar, Augustus 636
Caffeine 131, 176, 623-624, 3119
Cailletet, Louis Paul 675, 1030, 1588
Caiman crocodilus, see Spectacled caiman
Caimans 1014, 1017
Cairina moschata, see Muscovy duck
Caisson 624-625
Cajal, Santiago Ramon y 561, 3328
Cajanus cajun, see Pigeon pea
Cakile edentula, see Sea rocket
Calamagostis canadensis, see Blue-joint grass
Calamian stink badger 395
Calamondin 830
Calamospiza melanocorys, see Lark bunting
Calamovilfa longifolia, see Sand-reed
Calanoids 970
Calcareous stone 3501
Calcarius lapponicus, see Lapland longspur
Calcarius mccownii, see McCown's longspur
Calcarius ornatus, see Chestnut-collared longspur
Calceolaria purpurea, see Purple calceolarias
Calcite 627, 721
Calcium 626, 1139, 1741, 1821, 2637
Calcium carbonate 626-627, 1942, 2010, 2636
Calcium cyanamide 167
Calcium fluoride 626
Calcium oxide 626-627
Calcium propionate 628

Calcium silicate 1977
Calcium sulfate 626, 628
Calculations 12
Calculator 628-632, 918, 3052
Calculus 632-635, 1568, 1925, 1937, 1959, 2237
Calderas 2035, 3872
Caledonides Mountains 1406
Calendar 261-262, 636-638
Calibration 639
Calico crab 1004
Calidris alba, see Sanderling
Calidris canutus, see Red knot
Calidris pusilla, see Semipalmated sandpipers
California buckeye 1826
California buckthorn 586
California condor 933, 1451, 2525, 3880
California flying fish 1511
California gull 1717
California killifish 2016
California laurel 1770, 2062
California newt 2503
California poppy 2822, 2888
California quail 2982
California red fir 1480
California red scale 3207
California squirrel 3449
California sycamore 2803
California thrasher 2354
California tree poppy 2888
California vole 3876
California walnut 3885
Caliper 639-640
Callendar, G. S. 674
Callicarpa american, see French mulberry
Callicarpa americana, see Beauty-berry
Callicarpa purpurea, see Purple mulberry
Callicebus moloch, see Dusky titi
Callicebus personatus, see Masked titi
Callicebus torquatus, see White-handed titi
Callimico goeldii, see Goeldi's marmoset
Callinectes sapidus, see Common blue crab
Callipepla squamata, see Scaled quail
Callisto 2001
Callithrix argentata, see Silvery marmoset
Callithrix humeralifer, Tassel-ear marmoset
Callithrix jacchus, see White-headed marmoset
Callitroga hominivorax, see Screw-worm fly
Calluna vulgaris, see Scotch heather
Calmette, Albert 3755
Calomel 2266
Calomyscus bailwardi, see Mouselike hamster
Calopogon pulchellus, see Grass-pink orchid
Caloprymnus campestris, see Desert rat-kangaroo
Calopterix maculata, see Black-winged damselfly

Chernozem soil   3353
Cherry   2466, 3251, 3252, 3532, 3943
Chervil   691
Chestnut-backed mousebird   2411
Chestnut-bellied starling   3462
Chestnut blight   898
Chestnut blight   438
Chestnut-collared longspur   3400
Chestnut-mandibled toucan   3688
Chestnut-cheeked vole   3876
Chestnut-crowned ant-pipit   246
Chestnut-sided shrike vireo   3840
Chestnuts   437, 438, 898, 1826, 2572
Chevreul, Michel Eugene   3338
Chi square test   3470
Chick pea   2082, 2820
Chickadees   3375, 3676
Chickaree   3448
Chicken louse   2095
Chicken mite   2349
Chicken pox   775-777, 3145, 3290, 3848
Chickens   1023, 2127
Chicle   3191
Chicory   904
Chicxulub crater   2344
Chiggers   2349
Chilbea bracteata, see Drongo
Childhood diseases   777-781
Children's Vaccine Initiative   3812
Chilean flamingo   1484
Chilean tinamou   3675
Chili pepper   2511
Chilicote   1675
Chimaeras   206, 781-782
Chimaphila maculata, see Spotted wintergreen
Chimaphila umbellata, see Pipsissewa
Chimney swift   3575
Chimpanzees   250, 251, 782-786, 1671, 1836
Chimphila umbelata, see Pipsissewa
Chinaberry   2190
Chinch bug   3744
Chinchilla brevicaudata, see Short-tailed chinchilla
Chinchilla laniger, see Long-tailed chinchilla
Chinchillas   786-787
Chinese alligator   1017
Chinese buckthorn   586
Chinese ferret badger   395
Chinese lilac   2105
Chinese little bittern   520
Chinese pangolin   2682
Chinese wax scale   3207
Chinese wisteria   2084
Chinkapin   438
Chinook   3185

Chipmunks   787-788
Chipping sparrow   3399
Chiron   2342
Chiropotes satanas, see Black-bearded saki
Chiropractic medicine   143
Chitin   1942
Chitons   788
Chives   2107, 3825
Chlamydia   3276
Chlamydia psittaci, see Pneumonia
Chlamydia trachomatis, see Chlamydia
Chlamydotis undulata, see Houbara
Chlidonias niger, see Black tern
Chloracne   65
Chloralkali process   1277
Chloramphenicol   3778
Chlorates   791
Chlordane   789
Chlorella   118
Chlorinated hydrocarbons   1068, 1905, 1941, 2741
Chlorine   330, 677, 738, 769, 789-791, 1733, 1855,
   1861, 2878, 2880, 3350
Chloroaliphatics   1788
Chloroceryle americana, see Green kingfisher
Chlorodibenzodioxins   65
Chlorofluorocarbons   99, 330, 773, 791-794, 1359,
   1725, 1733, 1851, 1855, 2651, 2656, 2658, 3081
Chloroform   181, 794
Chloromycetin   740
Chlorophenoxy acids   1788
Chlorophyll   667, 674, 793, 795, 2391, 2439, 2623,
   2776, 2815, 2828
Chloroplasts   732, 737, 795-796, 2778
Chloroquine   2191, 3584, 3738
Chlorosis   790
Chloroxybacteria   2780
Chlorpromazine   242, 2967
Chlortetracycline   225
Choeropsos liberiensis, see Pygmy hippopotamus
Cholera   387, 796-797, 1379, 3740
Cholesterol   240, 276, 457, 798-799, 1765, 2076,
   2116
Choline   2073
Cholodny-Went Theory of Tropic Curvature   2782
Choloepus hoffmanni, see Hoffman's two-toed sloth
Chondestes grammacus, see Lark sparrow
Chondroblasts   2636
Chondropython viridis, see Green tree python
Chondrus crispus, see Irish moss
Chordates   799-800, 2670
Chordeiles acutipennis, see Lesser nighthawk
Chordeiles minor, see Nighthawk
Chorea   1080, 3136
Chorion   800, 1329

Chorionic gonadotropin   1329

Chorionic villi   800

Chorionic villus sampling   173, 800-801, 935, 1331, 2918

Choristoneura fumiferana, see Spruce budworm

Choroid   1438, 1854, 3860

Chorus frogs   1558

Christenson, J. H.   2694

Christmas cactus   619

Christy, James   2854

Chromatin   735, 801-802, 812, 2350

Chromatography   802, 803-805, 2230, 2985

Chromatophores   757

Chrominance signal   3626

Chromium dioxide   2181

Chromolyn sodium   315

Chromomeres   802

Chromophores   1188

Chromosomal abnormalities   805-810

Chromosomes   203, 800, 802, 805-814, 935, 1460, 1602, 1608, 1613, 1620, 2258, 2349, 2391, 2562

Chromosphere   3453, 3545

Chronic carrier state   1783

Chronic diseases   1377

Chronic fatigue   3700

Chronic obstructive pulmonary disease   575, 3430

Chryaanthemum maximum, see Shasta daisy

Chrysanthemum cinerariaefolium, see Chrysanthemums

Chrysanthemum coccinium, see Chrysanthemums

Chrysanthemum coronarium, see Summer chrysanthemum

Chrysanthemum lace bug   3744

Chrysanthemum leucanthemum, see Ox-eye daisy

Chrysanthemum roseum, see Chrysanthemums

Chrysanthemums   903, 904

Chrysochromulina polylepis, see Planktonic algae

Chrysocyon jubatus, see Maned wolf

Chrysolophus amherstiae, see Lady amherst's pheasant

Chrysolophus pictus, see Golden pheasant

Chrysoperta carnea, see Lacewings

Chu, C. W.   3552

Chub mackerel   2172

Chubb, Jeremiah   2133

Chuck-will's-widow   661, 1668

Chuckwallas   1889

Chukar   2706

Churchill, Winston   1069

Chyme   1136

Chytrids   1569

Cicadas   814-816

Cicer arietinum, see Chick pea

Cichorium endivia, see Endive

Cichorium intybus, see Chicory

Ciconia ciconia, see White stork

Cicuta bulbifera, see Bulb-bearing water hemlock

Cicuta maculata, see Cowbane

Cigar-box cedar   2190

Cigarette smoke   816-819

Cigarettes   816, 3027, 3120, 3784

Cimex lectularius, see Common bed bug

Cinchona   146

Cinchona calisaya, see Cinchona tree

Cinchona ledgeriana, see Bolivian chinchona tree

Cinchona tree   129, 408

Cinchonism   2997

Cingulectomy   2970

Cinnabar   2266

Cinnamon camphora, see Camphor tree

Cinnamon tree   2062

Cinnamon white-eye   3939

Cinnamonum zeylanicum, see Cinnamon tree

Circadian rhythms   3314, 3319

Circaetus gallicus, see Short-toed eagle

Circle   260, 819, 834, 1634

Circle graph   3469

Circuit breakers   1262, 2593

Circulation patterns   1200, 1201

Circulatory system   191, 530, 820-824, 1340, 1421, 1562, 1757, 1762, 3121, 3692

Circulifer tenellus, see Beet leafhopper

Circumference   260, 819

Circumscribed   824

Circumstellar matter   2497

Circus cyaneus, see Hen hawk

Cirrhosis   113, 824-825, 1137, 1784

Cirsium arvense, see Field thistle

Cirsium arvense, see Canada thistle

Cirsium eriophorum, see Woolly thistle

Cirsium vulgare, see Bull thistle

Cistothorus palustris, see Long-billed marsh wren

Cistothorus platensis, see Sedge wren

Cistus cobariensis, see White rock rose

Citellus beecheyi, see California squirrel

Citellus lateralis, see Golden-mantled ground squirrel

Citellus richardsonii, see Richardson's ground squirrel

Citellus townsendi, see Townsend ground squirrel

Citellus tridecemlineatus, see Thirteen-lined ground squirrel

Citellus undulatus, see Arctic ground squirrel

Citellus variegatus, see Rock squirrel

Citral   115

Citrate   2025

Citrate synthetase   2025

Citric acid   826, 828

Citric acid cycle   183, 826, 2024, 3113

Citron   829

Citronella grass   1685

Citrullus colocynthis, see Bitter apple
Citrullus lanatus, see Watermelon
Citrullus vulgaris, see Watermelon
Citrus aurantifolia, see Lime
Citrus aurantium, see Sour orange
Citrus bergamia, see Bergamot
Citrus limon, see Lemon
Citrus maxima, see Shaddock
Citrus mealybug 3207
Citrus media, see Bitter orange
Citrus medica, see Citron
Citrus mitis, see Calamondin
Citrus paradisi, see Grapefruit
Citrus reticulata, see Mandarin
Citrus sinensis, see Sweet orange
Citrus trees 826-830
Citrus trifoliata, see Wild orange
Civet oil 830
Civets 830-831, 1625
Civilization 1398
Clades 2786
Cladina alpestris, see Reindeer lichen
Cladistics 2668, 2786, 3602
Cladium jamaicensis, see Sawgrass
Cladophora, see Green algae
Cladorhynchus leucocephalus, see Banded stilt
Cladrastis lutea, see Yellow-wood
Clams 2369
Clangula hyemalis, see Oldsquaws
Clapper rail 3048
Clarias 539
Clarius batrachus, see Walking catfish
Clark, Barney 291
Clary 2345
Classical conditioning 3086
Classification systems 3218
Clausius, Rudolph 3653
Clavaria vermicularis, see White worm coral
Claviceps purpurea, see Ergot
Clavicle 3305
Clavius 637
Clay 565, 748, 3501
Clay-colored sparrow 3400
Cleaning compounds 3338
Clearcutting 1414, 1529
Cleavers 1738
Cleft palate 935
Clements, Frederic 831
Clephane, James O. 2929
Clerodendrum paniculatum, see Pagoda flower
Clerodendrum thomsoniae, see Bleeding-heart
Clethrionomys gapperi, see Gapper's red-backed vole
Clethrionomys rutilus, see Northern red-backed vole
Cliff swallow 3568

Climate 1659, 1883, 2309, 2665, 2870, 3235, 3352, 3356, 3918
Climate change, global 64, 636, 673, 887, 1078, 1234, 1359, 1369, 1407, 1533, 1699, 1856, 1885, 1905, 2515, 3313
Climatology 1112, 1209, 1539
Climax 831, 3533
Climax community 3053
Climax ecosystem 2599
Climbing mouse 2305
Clinical trials 2802
Clitoris 3105
Clivia 157
Cloaca 1826, 2380, 2850, 3291, 3774
Clock arithmetic 3977
Clocks 3673
Clonal selection 1899
Clones 299 ,832-833, 1786, 2823
Clonic seizures 1381
Cloquet, Hippolyte 3328
Closed curve 834-836
Clostridium botulinum, see Botulism
Clostridium perfringens, see Gas gangrene
Clostridium tetani, see Tetanus
Closure 1705
Closure property 268, 836
Clotting factor 536
Cloud chamber 2539, 2704
Cloud condensation nuclei 2909
Cloud cover 1359
Cloud seeding 3924
Clouded leopard 710
Clouds 93, 329, 335, 836-838, 2806
Clover 1960, 2080, 2082
Cloves 2444
Club mosses 839-840, 1454
Clupea sprattus, see Brisling
Cluster designation 484
Clytoceyx rex, see Shoe-billed kingfisher
Cnicus benedictus, see Holy thistle
Cnidarians 977
Cnidocytes 1846
Coadaptation 39
Coagulation 56, 1780
Coal 63, 840-843, 1914, 1977, 3159, 3331, 3480, 3541
Coalescence 3666
Coast 843-846
Coast mole 2368
Coast redwood 3570
Coastal currents 3797
Coastal plain willow 3945
Coatis 846-847
Coaxial cable 3628

Decongestants 136, 3118

Decyl aldehyde 115

Deep well injection 3895

Deepwater sculpin 3222

Deer 1072-1075, 3793

Deerberry 1770

Deer fly 3749

Deere, John 72

Deer mouse 1075-1076, 2305

Defassa waterbuck 3900

Defense mechanism 866, 1925

Defoliation 769, 1530, 2740

Deforestation 94, 226, 693, 1076-1078, 1345, 1434, 1532, 1668, 1701, 1824, 1866, 1883, 2611, 2645, 2793, 2892, 3311, 3772

Degeneration, neurological 3604

Degree 200, 1078, 3630

Dehydration 768, 3710

Dehydroepiandrosterone (DHEA) 50

Deicer 12

Deinonychus 1145

Deisenhofer, Johann 2777

Delaroche, Paul 2772

Del Chinchón, Anna 2996

Delesse, Achilles 2665

Deliquescent solid 626

Delirium tremens 113

Delisle, Jean Baptiste Louis Romé 1034

Delonix gilliesii, see Paradise poinciana

Delonix regia, see Royal poinciana

Delta 140, 3525

Delta hepatitis 3278

Delusions 242, 1097, 2967, 3213

Dementia 153, 1011, 1078-1082, 2967

Dementia praecox, see Schizophrenia

Democritus 341, 348, 3328

Demographics 1835, 1915, 2891

Demoiselle crane 1008

Demolition, military 1428

DeMoyleyns, Frederick 1901

Dempster, A. J. 2230

Demyelination 1713

Dendragapus obscurus, see Blue grouse

Dendrimers 1609, 3682

Dendrite 153, 730, 2152, 2478, 2485, 3854, see also Neuron

Dendroapsis polylepis, see Black mamba

Dendrochronology 1066, 1177, 2800, 3954

Dendrocygna bicolor, see Fulvous tree duck

Dendrohyrax arboreus, see Tree hyraxes

Dendrohyrax dorsalis, see Hyraxes

Dendroica coronata, see Yellow-rumped warbler

Dendroica fusca, see Blackburnian warbler

Dendroica kirtlandii, see Kirtland's warbler

Dendroica petechia, see Yellow warbler

Dendrology 3717

Dengue fever 1082-1083, 1219

Denis, Jean-Baptiste 536

Denisyuk, Yuri 1812

Denitrification 1083-1084, 2515, 2521

Denominator 3057-58

Density 1084, 2983

Density, mean 1198

Dentistry 1084-1090

Deoxyribonucleic acid (DNA) 47, 69, 159, 183, 204, 251, 385, 502, 732, 802, 805, 810, 833, 1034, 1090-1095, 1117, 1293, 1328, 1602, 1604, 1608, 1612, 1614, 1618, 1621, 1836, 2061, 2349, 2561, 2563, 2624, 2700, 2818, 2822, 2953, 3131, 3142

Dephenylmethanes 3701

Depo-Medroxyprogesterone Acetate (DMPA) 964

Deposit 1095-1096

Deposition 17, 1390, 2045

Deposition, mechanical 1096

Depression 234, 250, 1080, 1097-1102, 1165, 2202, 2204, 3699

Depth perception 1102-1105, 2723, 2925

Derivative 1105-1107, 1937, 2241

Dermal papillae 1944

Dermanyssus gallinae, see Chicken mite

Dermatemys mawii, see Central American river turtles

Dermatitis 701, 3864

Dermis 867, 1943

Derrick 1006

Derrick, Godfrey 1006

Derris 2083

Desalination 1107-1108, 1124

Desalting 1107

Desargues, Gerard 2940

Descartes, Rene 187, 693, 931, 1033, 1349, 1566, 1679, 3430, 3866

Deschampsia Antarctica 213

Descriptive statistics 3467

Desensitization 2755

Desert 302, 492, 1108-1111, 1533, 3054, 3353

Desert cottontail rabbit 2032

Desert iguana 1889

Desert jerboas 1994

Desert pupfish 2017

Desert rat-kangaroo 2009

Desert sparrow 3400

Desert tortoises 3777

Desertification 59, 63, 1111-1113

DeSilva, Ashanthi 37

Desipramine 234

Desktop publishing 2930

Desmana moschata, see Desman

Desmodium canadense, see Tick-trefoil

Dimetrodon   1144

Dimictic   2037

Dimorphism   800, 1879

Dinarides mountains   1409

Dingo   3596

Dinitroanilines   1788

Dinitrogen   1083, 2519

Dinocap   1574

Dinoflagellates   117, 121

Dinornis maximus, see Giant moa

Dinosaurs   472, 953, 1141-1148, 1431, 2672

Diode   1148, 1726, 1938, 3814

Diodora cayenensis, see Key-hole limpet

Dionaea muscipula, see Venus flytrap

Dione   3198

Dioscorea alata, see Asiatic yam

Dioscorea batatas, see Yam

Dioscorea bulbifera, see Yam

Dioscorea cayenensis, see Yellow yam

Dioscorea rotundata, see White yam

Dioscorea trifida, see Cush-cush yam

Dioscorides   550, 1500

Diospyros mespiliformis, see Jackal's berry

Diospyrus crassiflora, see African ebony

Diospyrus macassar, see Macassar ebony

Diospyrus virginiana, see American persimmon

Dioxin   65, 681, 1148-1150, 1749

Diphtheria   386, 1150-1151, 3811

Diphyllobothrium latum, see Broad fish tapeworm

Diplodactylus williamsi, see Australian spiny-tailed gecko

Diplodocus   1146

Dipole   115-152, 1151-1152, 1281, 3899

Diprotic acid   22

Dipus sagitta, see Hairy-footed jerboa

Dirac, Paul Adrain Maurice   241, 1290, 3518

Direct variation   1152-1153

Directly Observed Therapy (DOT)   3756

Directrix   2686

Disaccharides   667

Disarmament   772

Disassociative identity disorder, see Multiple personality disorder

Discrete variables   3467

Discriminant   1962

Discs   3690

Disease   181, 390, 1122, 1153-1154, 1316, 1401, 1431, 1642, 1738, 2738, 3438

Disease, sexually transmitted   961, 1919

Disease transmission   1379, 1641, 1918, 1930, 3754, 3779

Dish   2316

Dish-rag gourd   1674

Disinfectant   1862, 3350, 3541

Disjunction logic   3581

Dislocation   2628

Dispersants   2597, 3407

Dispersion, measures of   3823

Displacement   376, 598, 3912

Displacement phenomena   334

Dissection   3865

Dissociation   1154-1155

Dissolution, chemical   2045

Distance   1155-1157

Distillation   109, 1108, 1157-1159, 2651, 3466

Distribution, frequency   3468

Distributive law   2416, 3057

Distributive law (mathematics)   900

Distributive property   1159

Disturbance, ecological   1159-1160

Dithiocarbonate   1574

Diuretics   1242

Diurnal inequality   3670

Divergence   2055

Divergent sequence   3257

Diving ducks   1180

Diving petrel   2744

Division   268, 1160-1162, 1414, 1916

Divisors of zero   3979

DNA, see Deoxyribonucleic acid

DNA testing   1090, 1525, 2985

Dîbereiner, Johann   704

Dobson unit (DU)   2656

Dobsonflies   1162

Dobzhansky, Theodosius   1417

Dodds, Edward   1128

Dodecahedron   2849

Dodo   1014, 1430, 3309

Doell, Richard   1214

Dog, domesticated   654, 1961, 2999

Dog flea   1489

Dog, wild   653

Dog-biting louse   2095

Dog-sucking louse   2095

Dog-tooth violet   2106

Dogwood tree   1162-1163

Doisey, Edward   3863

Doldrums, atmospheric   325

Dolichonyx oryzivorous, see Bobolink

Dollarbird   3164

Dolomite   128, 1741, 2010

Domagk, Gerhard   162

Domain   1163-1164, 1566, 2206, 3089

Dome   1061

Domestic bactrian camel   643

Domestic guinea pig   1715

Domestic Guinea fowl   1715, 3773

Domestic rabbit   2127

Dutch elm disease   1323, 1571
Dutch Mordant   1366
Dutrochet, H.   2632
Dwarf antelopes   1185-1186
Dwarf bushbaby   2142
Dwarf Caiman   1017
Dwarf cornel   1163
Dwarf fan-palm   2676
Dwarf galago   2144
Dwarf galaxies   2325
Dwarf guenon   1712
Dwarf hamster   1737
Dwarf huckleberry   1770
Dwarf lemurs   2085
Dwarf novae   3939
Dwarf olive ibis   1882
Dwarf siamang   1646
Dwarfism   1351, 1710
Dye   874, 1187-1188, 1783, 2082, 2097
Dynamic random access memories (DRAMs)   3554
Dynamite   1426
Dynamo effect   2271
Dynorphins   858
Dysarthria   3418
Dysentery   1188-1189
Dyslexia   1189-1191
Dysphonia   3418
Dysphotic zone   2590
Dysplasia   1192
Dyssomnia   3318
Dysthymia   1097

E

E (number)   1193
Eagle owl   2644
Eagle rays   3063
Eagles   1193-1195
Ear   29, 1195-11981752, 1754
Eardrum, see Tympanic membrane
Eared grebe   1697
Eared seal   3229, 3232
Early saxifrage,   3205
Earth   635, 674, 723, 1061, 1198-1215, 1629, 1918, 2307, 2407, 3154, 3797, 3918
Earth beads, see Abacus
Earth Day   1369
Earth hares   1994
Earth science   1209-1210
Earthquakes   303, 1202-1209, 1408, 1834, 2587, 2845, 3254, 3524, 3608, 3751
Earth's crust   2120, 2407, 2844, 3341
Earth's interior   1210-1214

Earth's magnetic field   1214
Earth's rotation   1214
Earthstars   1572
Earthworm   1960, 3121, 3253
Earwigs   1215-1216
East African oryx   2630
East African rift   59
East Caucasian tur   1666
East coast hard-shelled ticks   2149
East Coast lobster   2130
East Indian woodcock   3190
Easter Island   3380
Easter lily   2106
Eastern american mole, see Common American mole
Eastern Australian native cat   2222
Eastern bluebird   3461
Eastern box turtle   3775
Eastern chipmunk   787
Eastern coral snake   1247
Eastern coralbean   2081
Eastern cottontail rabbit   2032
Eastern fox squirrel   3447
Eastern gopher   1670
Eastern gray kangaroo   2006
Eastern grey squirrel   3447
Eastern hemlock   2872
Eastern hemlock   2872
Eastern hop hornbeam   504, 505
Eastern kingbird   3782
Eastern lowland gorilla   1671
Eastern newt   3182
Eastern phoebe   3782
Eastern red cedar   1998
Eastern white cedar   3932
Eastern white pelican   2714
Eastern white pine   2800
Eastern wood peewee   3782
Eastman, George   2883
Eating disorders   1216-1218
Ebbinghaus, Hermann   931, 2250
Ebola virus   1218-1219, 1379, 3850
Ebony   1219-1221, 3051
Ebony leaf monkey   2049
Eccentricity   2267, 2686
Ecdysone   2294
Echidna   218, 2380
Echidna zebra, see Zebra moray
Echinocactus asterias, see Star cactus
Echinocactus polycephalus, see Barrel cactus
Echinocactus texensis, see Horse crippler cactus
Echinocereus triglochidiatus, see Red-flowered hedgehog cactus
Echinochloa colona, see Shama millet
Echinochloa crusgalli, see Barnyard millet

Eucalyptus tree   1024

Eucalyptus viminalis, see Manna gum tree

Euclid   948, 1633, 2102, 2527, 2803, 2926, 2978, 3059, 3649, 3708

Eudocimus albus, see White ibis

Eudoxus   319, 3059

Eudromia elegans, see Crested tinamou

Eugenics   1613

Euglena   2958

Euglenoids   117

Euglenophyta   117

Eukaryotes   730, 742, 813, 1401, 1482, 2561-62, 2623, 2814, 3279, 3578

Euler, Leonhard   159, 455, 882, 1566, 2564, 2727, 3702, 3724

Eulipoa wallacei, see Moluccan megapode

Eumeces fasciatus, see Five-lined skink

Eumeces laticeps, see Broad-headed skink

Eumeces obsoletus, see Great plains skink

Eumeces tetragrammus, see Four-lined skink

Eumenes fraterna, see Mud-dauber wasp

Eumetopias jubatus, see Stellar sea lion

Eunectes murinus, see Green anaconda

Eunuchoidism   2972

Euoticus slegantulus, see Needle-nailed galagos

Eupalinus   257

Eupatorium purpureum, see Hemp agrimony

Euphagus carolinus, see Rusty blackbird

Euphonia musica, see Blue-hooded euphonia

Euphorbia cyparissa, see Cypress spurge, Graveyard spurge

Euphorbia esula, see Leafy spurge, Wolf's-milk spurge

Euphorbia ingens, see Naboom

Euphorbia maculata, see Spotted spurge

Euphorbia polygonifolia, see Beach spurge

Euphorbia pulcherrima, see Poinsettia

Euphorbia splendens, see Crown-of-thorns euphorbia

Euphorbia tirucalli, see Pencil cactus

Euphotic zone   2036, 2590, 2760

Eupoda montana, see Mountain plover

Eurasian badger   394

Eurasian beaver   434

Eurasian bittern   520

Eurasian brown bear   431

Eurasian cuckoo   1040

Eurasian hazel   1750

Eurasian hydrangea   3205

Eurasian mink   2339, 3916

Eurasian mistletoe   2347

Eurasian pitcher plant   688

Eurasian red deer   2127

Eurasian river otter   2639

Eurasian supercontinent   1402

Eurasian tree sparrow   3927

Eurasian woodcock   3190

Europe   954, 1401-1410

European ant   247

European bison   517, 717

European blackbird   3665

European buckthorn   586

European chameleon   759

European common toad   3677

European corn borer   2396

European cowslip   2927

European earwig   1215

European echiurans   1221

European eel   3745, 3746

European Federation of Biotechnology   501

European fritallaria   2107

European goosefish   202

European hare   2031

European hedgehog   1773

European honey bee   440

European linden   420

European lobster   539, 2130

European mole   2368

European monkey   2375

European nightcrawler   1960

European pansy   3836

European plaice   1485

European polecat   1458

European rabbit   2031

European ragwort   1941

European robin   3150

European roller   3164

European salamander   3181

European skate   3303

European sole   1485

European song thrush, see Thrushes

European Space Agency   3384, 3394

European spring crocus   1975

European starling   3461

European swallow   3568

European sweet chestnut   438

European white fir   1480

European white pelican   2714

European wild cat   712

European wine grape   1676

European yew   3973

Euros   2008

Euryhaline   558

Eurystomus orientalis, see Broad-billed roller, Dollarbird

Eusociality   2366

Eustachian tube   1197, 3123, 3680

Eutamias amonoeus, see Yellow pine chipmunk

Eutamias minimus, see Least chipmunk

Euthynnus pelamis, see Skipjack tuna

F

Forster's tern   3639

Forsythia viridissima, see Golden bell forsythia

Fortran (computer program language)   926

Fossa   1537-1538

Fossey, Dian   1672

Fossil Fuel Age, see Geologic time scale

Fossil fuels   56, 100, 340, 473, 640, 671, 840, 863, 957, 1233, 1396, 1408, 1885, 2593, 2665, 2870, 3098, 3525

Fossil kangaroo   2008

Fossil, living   1807, 3753

Fossilization   1538-1544, 3590

Fossils   60, 178, 767, 952, 957, 977, 1538-1544, 1629, 1633, 1836, 2223, 2404, 2624, 2664, 2668, 2871, 3161

Fostiropoulos, K.   584

Foucault, Jean   2104

Foucault, Leon   1215

Foucault's pendulum   1215

Four-dimensional space-time   3382

Four-lined plant bug   3743

Four-lined skink   3309

Four-fou   3969

Four-horned antelope   715

Fourdrinier, Henry   2684

Fourdrinier, Sealy   2684

Fourier analysis   3585

Fourneau, Ernest   162

Fourneyron, Benoit   3767

Fourth dimension   3094

Fovea   2723, 3857

Fowl, domesticated   1715

Fowler, William   1306

Fox   3000

Fox sparrow   3399

Fox-grape   1677-1678

Foxglove   1763, 3338

Foxtail millet   1684

Fracastorius, Heironymous   243

Fracastoro, Girolamo   3274

Fractal   1545-1546, 1962

Fraction, common   45, 1161, 1547-1550, 1924, 1979, 2073, 2416, 3057-3058, 3702

Fracture   2332, 2628, 2637, 2587

Fragaria vesca, see Strawberry

Fragaria virginiana, see Strawberry

Fragipan   1819

Fragrant sumac   703

Frank, I. M.   752

Franklin, Benjamin   1250, 1262, 1287, 1294

Franklin convention current   1264

Franklin's gull   1717

Frasch process   2336, 3537

Fraser fir   1480

Fraunhofer diffraction   1130

Fraunhofer, Joseph   1550

Fraunhofer lines   1550

Fraxinus americana, see White ash

Fraxinus anomala, see Ash

Free radicals   240, 1516, 1974, 3015, 3028

Free ribosomes   734

Free-space wave   220

Freeman, Walter J.   2969

Freeway   1551-1553

Freeze-drying   1520

Freezing point   3464, 3630

Fregata andrewsi, see Christmas Island frigate bird

Fregata aquila, see Ascension frigate bird

Fregata magnificens, see Common seabird

Fregata minor, see Lesser frigate bird

Frege, F. L. G.   2895

French bean   3825

French mulberry   3832

Freons   791

Frequency   27, 1263, 1553-1554, 1742, 1928, 2316, 2631, 2775, 3020, 3046, 3053, 3110, 3405, 3413, 3468, 3834, 3912

Freshwater   1554-1555, 3902

Freshwater bass   418

Freshwater cave fish   722

Freshwater eels   3745

Fresnel, Augustin Jean   2104

Fresnel diffraction   1130

Freud, Sigmund   144, 249, 851, 1190, 2250, 2414, 2755, 2959-2960, 3215

Fricke, Hans   859

Friction   1555-1556, 2499, 3396, 3947

Fried chicken mushroom   2426

Friedmann, Alexander   460, 991

Friend, Richard   2077

Friendly fantail   2370

Frigate birds   1556-1557

Frigate mackerel   2173

Fringe pattern   1946

Fringe shift   2308

Fringed antbeetle   444

Fringing reefs   973

Frisch, Otto   2558

Frisius, Gemma   3564

Fritallaria aurea, see Turkish fritallaria

Fritallaria meleagris, see European fritallaria

Fritallarias   2107

Frith, Francis   2772

Fritts, Charles   2768

Frogmouths   660

Frogs   1557-1561, 3123

Frog's-bit family   1561-1562

Frontal bone   3304

H

Halite   3186, 3527

Halitosis, see Bad breath

Hall, Asaph   3195

Hall, Charles Martin   149, 1277, 2289

Hall, E. H.   1726

Hall effect   1726-1727

Hall probe   2185

Hall-Héroult process   149

Halley, Edmond   320, 889, 990, 1727

Halley's comet   320, 889, 1727-1729

Hallucinations   242, 1097, 1729, 2724, 2967, 3213

Hallucinogens   1729-1733, 2425, 2440

Halobacteria   2781

Haloes   335

Halogenated hydrocarbons   1733, 1851

Halogens   1300, 1724, 1733-1736, 2281

Halophiles   387

Halophosphates   1508

Halosaurs   1736-1737

Halothane   195

Halteres   1490, 2389, 3747

Halticus bractatus, see Garden fleahopper

Hamadryas baboon   381

Hammer   1197

Hammer, Adam   1763

Hammond, William   851

Hamsters   1737-1738, 3163

Hand-foot syndrome   3296

Handaxe   1738

Hand tools   1738-1740

Hanging parrots   2698

Hanging scorpion fly   3221

Hanging valley   2045

Hansen's disease, see Leprosy

Hantavirus   1219, 1740-1741

Hantavirus pulmonary syndrome (HPS)   1740

Hapalemur griseus, see Gray gentle lemur

Hapalemur simus, see Broad-nosed gentle lemur

Haploid   1328, 1460

Haplothrips mali, see Black hunter thrip

Harbor seals   3232

Hard water   1741

Hard-shelled European ticks   2149

Hard-shelled exan ticks   2149

Hard-shelled ticks   2149

Hardness   2332

Hares   2031-2033

Hargreaves, James   1914

Harlan's hawk   615

Harlequin bug   3744

Harmonics   27, 1741-1742

Harp seal   3232

Harpactes erythrocephalus, see Red-headed trogon

Harpacticoids   971

Harpagomantis discolor, see South African flower-dwelling mantis

Harpephyllum caffrum, see Kaffir plum

Harpia harpyja, see Harpy eagle

Harpy eagle   1194

Harpyopsis novaguineae, see New Guinea harpy eagle

Harriers   1744

Harrington, Joseph   621

Harris, Rollin   918

Harrison, Ed   990

Harrison, James   3081

Harrison, Michael R.   2916

Harris' hawk   615

Hartebeestes   1742-1743

Hartley Bandwidth Rule   3625

Hartmann's mountain zebra   3976

Harvestmen   259

Harvey, William   483, 1642, 1759, 1762, 1876, 3559, 3866

Haustoria   1569

Hauy, R. J.   128

Hawaiian archipelago   1343

Hawaiian boxfish   556

Hawaiian crow   1027

Hawaiian honeycreeper   1817

Hawaiian stilt   3499

Hawk moths   2396

Hawkesbee, Francis   1294

Hawking, Stephen   526, 3092

Hawkins, Gerald   1225

Hawkins, Richard   2195, 2574

Hawks   1743-1745

Hawksbill turtle   3776

Hay fever   134, 3118

Hazardous waste   1903, 2041, 2493, 3266

Hazardous waste stabilization   1749

Hazardous wastes   1745-1750, 1903, 2041, 2493, 3895

Hazel   504, 1750

HCFC, see Hydrocholorfluorocarbons

HCG, see Human chorionic gonadotropin

HDPE, see High-density polyethylene

Head injuries   3115

Head louse   2095

Headaches   2663, 3700

Headwater systems   1864

Heal-all   2346

Hearing   1751-1754, 2525

Hearing aid   1756

Hearing disorders   1754-1757

Heart   239, 1757-1761, 1794

Heart attacks   273, 1167, 1326, 1763

Heart defects   1173

Heart diseases   821, 1761-1766, 1927, 2262, 3662

Jerboas   1994-1995
Jerusalem artichoke   904, 3826
Jervis, John B.   3696
Jesuit bark   2996
Jet airplane   90
Jet engine   90, 1995-1997, 3769
Jet lag   498, 3315, 3319
Jet stream   326, 1054, 2382, 3920
Jetties   845
Jewitt, David   1728
Jib-crane   1006
Jig boring machines   2164
Jimson weed   130, 2513
Jird   1640
Job's tears   1685, 3252
Johannsen, Wilhelm   1602
Johansen, Donald   1837
John dory   1169
Johnson, H. L.   3490
Johnson, Samuel   3866
Joints   2046, 3303-3306
Jorgenson, Christine   3271
Josephson, Brian   3551
Josephson junctions   3552
Joubert, Jules Francois   223
Joule   1354, 1357, 1768
Joule, James Prescott   641, 1031, 1354, 3653
Joule-Thompson effect   1031
Jovian planets   2468
Juan Fernandez fur seal   1343
Juglans californica, see California walnut
Juglans cinerea, see Butternut
Juglans hindsii, see Hinds walnut
Juglans major, see Arizona walnut
Juglans microcarpa, see Little walnut
Juglans nigra, see Black walnut
Juglans regia, see English walnut
Juglone (soil poison)   3885
Julian calendar   636
Jumping bristletails   571
Junco hyemalis, see Dark-eyed junco
Junction diode   3705
Juncus articulatus, see Rushes
Juncus balticus, see Baltic rush
Juncus bufonius, see Toad rush
Juncus effusus, see Soft rush
Juncus militaris, see Rushes
Juncus squarrosus, see Wicker rush
Juncus tenuis, see Path rush
Junegrass   1682
Jungles   305
Junin grebe   1697
Juniper   1997-1998, 2438
Juniperus communis, see Common juniper

Juniperus excelsa, see Mediterranean juniper
Juniperus thuridera, see Mediterranean juniper
Juniperus virginianus, see Virginia juniper
Juno   2341
Jupiter   1998-2003, 2341-2342
Jura Mountains   1409
Jurassic period, see also Geologic time scale   58,
   1142, 1557, 2535, 2671, 3445, 3773
Just-in-time production   2229
Justification   2929
Jynx ruficollis, see African wryneck
Jynx torquilla, see Wryneck

K

Köppen, Wladimir   1658
Kühne, Willy   705
Kaffir plum   702
Kaibab squirrel   3447
Kaka   2698
Kakapo   2698
Kala Azar   3739
Kalahari Desert   63
Kalmia angustifolia, see Sheep laurel
Kalmia latifolia, see Mountain laurel
Kamchatkan marmot   2218
Kames   2045
Kanamycin   225
Kangaroo Island   360
Kangaroo mice   2005
Kangaroo rats   2005-2006
Kangaroos and wallabies   2006-2009
Kant, Immanuel   1778
Kantrowitz, Adrian   290
Kaolin   148
Kaolinite   3922
Kaon   2694, 3518
Kapok tree   2453, 3301
Kaposi's sarcoma   82, 1951
Karakoram   306
Karelian Mountains   1404
Karst topography   2009-2011, 3524
Karyotype   800, 805, 811
Kashmir markhor   1666
Katabatic winds   213
Katydids   1012
Kay, John   1913
Kea   2697-2698
Keating, R. E.   3096
Keck telescope   3623
Keeled sternum   3675
Keen, W. W.   2487
Keewenaw rift   2536

L

Latin American centipede 746
Latitude 1918, 3272
Latitude hook 3272
Lattice 2076
Laughing gas, see Nitrous oxide
Laughing gull 1717
Laughing hyena 1870
Laughing kookaburra 2018
Laurasia 954
Laurel family 2061-2063
Laurus nobilis, see Sweet bay
Laurussia 1406
Lauryl aldehyde 115
Lava 720, 2046, 2846, 3160, 3870
Lavandula officinalis, see Lavender
Lavender 2345
Laver 120
Laveran, Alphonse 2191
Lavoisier, Antoine-Laurent 342, 348, 667, 673, 886, 1300, 1857, 2646, 2650, 2777
Law of superposition 983
Lawrence, Ernest Orlando 9, 1055, 1310
Lawrence, Florence 2399
Lawrencium 1310
Laws of motion 2063-2064, 3155
Laws of stellar structure 3452
Lawson confinement parameter 2546
Lawsonia intermis, see Henna
Laxatives 1217
Laysan albatross 104
LCD (Liquid Crystal Display) 2064-2065
LD50 2862
LDPE, see Low-density polyethelene
Le Châtelier, Henry 1387
Le Châtelier's Principle 1387
Le Système International d'Unités, see International System of Units
Leach field 3268
Leaching 2065-2066, 2620, 3893
Lead, see also Periodic table of elements 2066-2069
Leadtrees 2081
Leaf 2069-2072
Leaf monkeys 868, 2049-2051
Leaf-toed gecko 1597
Leafcutter ant 247
Leafcutting bee 440
Leafhoppers 2072-2073
Leafy spurge 3443
Leakey, Louis 785, 1837
Leakey, Mary 1837
Leap year 638
Learned behavior, see Behavior
Learning 3088
Learning disabilities 1189

Least bittern 520, 1796
Least chipmunk 3449
Least common denominator 2073
Least flycatcher 3782
Least grebe 1696
Leather crocodile 1018
Leavitt, Henrietta Swan 459, 1576, 3822
Lebistes reticulatus, see Guppy
Leblanc, Nicholas 3338, 3346
LeBlon, J. C. 875
Lecithin 2073-2076
LeConte's sparrow 3400
LeConte's thrasher 2354
LED (Light-Emitting Diode) 2076-2078
Ledger, Charles 2996
Ledum groenlandicum, see Labrador-tea
Lee, Tsung Dao 2693
Leeches 3254
Leeks 2107, 3825
Leeuwenhoek, Antoni van 384, 648, 1327, 1642, 2311, 2690, 3437
Left ventricular assist device 289
Lefteye flounder 1485
Legionella pneumophila, see Legionnaire's disease
Legionnaire's disease 1909, 2078-2080
Legumes 2080-2084, 2521, 2523, 3577
Leibniz, Gottfried Wilhelm 464, 630, 632, 1105, 1566, 2112, 3681
Leiolopisma laterale, see Ground skink
Leishmaniasis 3739
Leistes militaris, see Red-breasted blackbird
Leith, E. N. 1812
Lek 2901, 3642
Lemaireocereus weberi, see Cadebobe cactus
LeMaître, Georges-Henri 460, 991
Lemmings 2084-2085, 3163
Lemmon, Mark 3199
Lemmus lemmus, see Norway lemming
Lemmus sibiricus, see Brown lemming
Lemna minor, see Duckweed
Lemon 829, 1676
Lemon grass 1685
Lemur catta, see Ring-tailed lemur
Lemur fulvus, see Brown lemur
Lemur macaco, see Black lemur
Lemur mongoz, see Mongoose lemur
Lemurs 2085-2089, 2946
Length 2301
Lens 1438, 2089-2092, 3857
Lens esculenta, see Lentil
Lenti virus 84
Lentil 2082, 3251, 3825
Lenz's Law 1284
Leonov, A. A. 3385

Lowell Observatory 2219
Lowell, Percival 726, 2219, 2854
Lowland anoa 718
Lowry, Thomas 23, 2492
Loxodonta africana africana, see African bush elephant
Loxodonta africana cyclotis, see African forest elephant
Loxodonta africana, see African elephant
Loxops parva, see Anianiau
LSD, see Lysergic acid diethylamide
Lubrication 377, 1556
Lucania parva, see Rainwater killifish
Luciferase 484
Luciferin 484
Ludwig, George H. 3816
Luffa cylindrica, see Loofah
Lugworm 3253
Lumbar puncture 1794
Lumber 438, 505, 1528, 1826, 2189, 2208, 2443, 2800, 3051, 3300, 3441, 3570
Lumber, plastic 2884
Lumbricus terrestris, see Earthworms
Lumiere, Auguste 2399
Lumiere, Louis 2399
Luminance signal 3626
Luminescence 2144-2146, 2758, 2764, 3445
Luminiferous ether 2307
Luminosity 1577, 3453
Lunar calendar year 636
Lunar day 3670
Lunar eclipse 2384
Lunar module 3386
Lunar roving vehicle (LRV) 3386
Lunar shadow 1223
Lunar tidal bulges 3669
Lung cancer 1380, 3120
Lung disease 313, 816, 1057, 2856, 3662
Lung inflammation 2858
Lungfish 545, 2146-2149
Lungs 1336, 1762, 1794, 2146, 3112, 3121, 3430, 3714
Lupines 2080-2081
Lupinus perennis, see Lupines
Luster 2332
Luteal phase 2973
Luteinizing hormone (LH) 1348, 2972
Lutra canadensis, see North American river otter
Lutra lutra, see Eurasian river otter
Lutra perspicillata, see Smooth otter
Lutra provocax, see Southern river otter
Lycaenid butterfly 39
Lycippus 2464
Lycoperdon pyriforme, see Pear puffball
Lycopersicum esculentum, see Tomato

Lycopodium clavatum, see Common club moss
Lycopsides 3719
Lycopus europaeus, see Water horehound
Lye 3349
Lyell, Charles 2460, 3794
Lyerly, J. G. 2969
Lygaeus kalmii, see Small milkweed bug
Lygidea mendax, see Apple red bug
Lygus lineolaris, see Tarnished plant bug
Lyman, Henry 3317
Lymantria dispar, see Gypsy moth
Lyme disease 2149-2151
Lymphadenopathy 83
Lymphatic diseases 1316, 2153
Lymphatic filariasis 1316
Lymphatic system 823, 1808, 1892, 2151-2154, 3123
Lymphedema 2153
Lymphocytes 37, 134, 823, 1808, 1899, 2151
Lymphoid tissue 3679
Lymphomas 1808, 2153
Lynx 712, 2033
Lynx canadensis, see Canada lynx
Lynx lynx, see Lynx
Lynx rufus, see Bobcat
Lyon, M. F. 802
Lyonization 802
Lyophyllum decastes, see Fried chicken mushroom
Lyrebirds 2154-2155
Lysergic acid amide 1732
Lysergic acid diethylamide (LSD) 1729
Lysiloma bahamensis, see Bahama lysiloma
Lysosomes 734, 1401
Lythrum salicaria, see Purple loosestrife
Lyttleton, Raymond 889

M

M-discontinuity 1210
M87 33, 3042
Maar 3871
Macaca mulatta, see Rhesus monkeys
Macaca sylvanus, see Babary ape
Macadamia nut 2952
Macaques 2157-2159
MacArthur Basin 363
MacArthur, R. H. 1985
Macassar ebony 1220
Macaws 2696, 2698
Mach, Ernst 2170, 2725
Mach number 53, 2170-2172
Machine tools 2162-2168, 2227
Machine vision 2168-2170
Machines, simple 2159-2162

Machining   751, 2162

Mackenzie, James   1763

Mackenzie willow   3945

Mackerel   2172-2173

Macleod, Colin M.   1602

Maclura pomifera, see Osage-orange

Macmillan, E. M.   2735

Macroalgae   494

Macrobrachium rosenbergii, see Giant prawn

Macrocephalon maleo, see Maleo

Macrocheira kaempferi, see Giant Japanese crab

Macrochelys temminckii, see Alligator snapper

Macroclimate   2309

Macrolides   223, 1394

Macromolecules   1037, 2359, 2884

Macronucleus   2958

Macronutrients   75, 2578

Macrophages, see also Immune system   534, 1895

Macrophytes   1410, 3906

Macropus eugenii, see Tammar wallaby

Macropus fuliginiosus, see Western gray kangaroo

Macropus giganteus, see Eastern gray kangaroo

Macropus parma, see Parma wallaby

Macropus parryi, see Whiptail wallaby

Macropus robustus, see Euros

Macrotis lagotis, see Greater bilby

Macular degeneration   3860

Macular dystrophy   3860

Mad cow disease, see Bovine spongiform encephalitis

Madagascan boa   542

Madagascar jacana   1991

Madagascar orchid   2873

Madagascaran cockroach   854

Madogna, see Dik-diks

Madonna lily   2106

Madras tree shrew   3722

Madreporite   3457

Madrone   1771

Magalini, Sergio I.   3583

Magellanic Clouds   2977, 3492, 3556

Magic square   2173-2174

Magicicada septendecum, see Periodical cicada

MAGLEV   2174-2176, 2178-2180, 3698

Magma   312, 1203, 1403, 1834, 1888, 2046, 2176-2177, 2290, 2585, 2587, 2844, 3160, 3797, 3869

Magnesite   128

Magnesium   127, 1741, 2177, 2288

Magnesium carbonate   2177

Magnesium oxide   127, 750

Magnesium sulfate   2177

Magnet   1214, 1447, 3554

Magnetic declination   1214

Magnetic field   708, 1201, 1214, 1256, 1267, 1282, 1356, 1447, 1726, 1917, 2178, 2183, 2230, 2312,

2470, 2496, 2665, 3357, 3360, 3460, 3527, 3542, 3703, 3802, 3816, 3829

Magnetic flux   1282

Magnetic force   1280, 2321

Magnetic levitation   2174-2176, 2178-2180

Magnetic maps   3528

Magnetic minerals   2666

Magnetic moment   2185

Magnetic poles   2178, 2666

Magnetic recording   2180-2183, 2756, 3833

Magnetic resonance imaging (MRI)   495, 562, 651, 1011, 2488, 2985, 3044, 3411

Magnetic reversals   2845

Magnetic separation   2284

Magnetic storms   3547

Magnetic surveys   2594, 2845

Magnetism   1287, 1290, 1294, 2180, 2183-2187, 2789

Magnetite   1976, 2183

Magnetization   2666

Magnetoencephalography   562

Magnetohydrodynamics   142

Magnetometer   2185, 2666, 3528

Magnetopause, see Magnetosphere

Magnetosheath, see Magnetosphere

Magnetosphere   2187-2188, 2271, 2470, 3802, 3818

Magnetostriction   3786

Magnetotail   3816

Magnification   1962, 3618, 3619

Magnitude, absolute   3490

Magnitude, apparent   3489

Magnitudes, modern   3490

Magnolia   2188-2189

Magnus, Albertus   3437

Magnus Huss   112

Mahogany   1024, 2189-2190

Mahonia aquifolium, see Oregon grape

Maianthemum canadense, see Lily-of-the-valley

Maidenhair fern   2190-2191

Maidenhair tree   1051, 1649, 1720

Maiman, Theodore   1812, 2055, 2059, 2314

Main Asteroid Belt   726

Main sequence stars   3493

Maize   1683, 1959, 3251, 3578

Major histocompatibility complex, see Immune system

Makaira indica, see Black marlin

Makaira nigricans, see Blue marlin

Malachite-crested kingfisher   2018

Malaclemmys terrapin, see American salt-water terrapin

Malacology   3334

Malagasy broad-striped mongoose   2372

Malagasy narrow-striped mongoose   2371

Malania anjouanae, see Coelacanth

Malapterurus electicus, see Electric catfish

Maya   261-262
Mayflies   2243-2245
Maypole bowers   553
Maypop   2709
Mayr, Ernst   1418, 3401, 3599
McCandless II, Bruce   3395
McCarty, Maclyn   1602
McCormick, Cyrus H.   73
McCormick, Katherine   963
McCown's longspur   3400
McCrae, John   2889
McDermott, Jeanne   482
McKay, Frederick   1509
McKay's bunting   3400
McKee, Alexander   2465
McMillan, E. M.   1308
Meadow   2898
Meadow buttercup   606
Meadow fox-tail   1685
Meadow saffron   2107
Meadow vole   3875
Meadowgrass   1685
Meadowlarks   523
Mealies   1683
Mealybugs   3207
Mean   2245, 3469
Mean Solar Time   638
Measles   3741, 3850
Measurement   200, 1045, 2301
Measurement error   2141
Mechanical advantage   2160
Mechanical systems   3152
Mechanical vibarations   3373
Mechanics   2789, 3260
Mecke, Reinhardt   3375
Medawar, Peter   3712
Median   2245-2246, 3469
Median basins   416
Median eye   3753
Median nerve   689
Median valley   2587
Mediator particles   344, 3516
Medicago sativa, see Alfalfa
Medical waste   1905
Medician stars   2001
Medicinal esters   1394
Medicinal skink   3189
Medicinal violet   3837
Medicine, Chinese   3180
Meditation   3700
Mediterranean forest   3719
Mediterranean fruit fly   3748
Mediterranean juniper   1998
Mediterranean pine   2800

Mediterranean tortoises   3775
Medium   26
Medulla   858, 2477, 3125
Medulla oblongata   560, 2152, 2477
Medusa   1868, 1933
Meerkats   2371
Mefloquine   2193
Megacephalon, see Scrubfowl
Megaceryle alcyon, see Belted kingfisher
Megaleia rufa, see Red kangaroo
Megaloblastic anemia, see Anemia
Megaloceros gigantus, see Irish elk
Megalops atlanticus, see Tarpons
Megalops cyprinoides, see Tarpons
Megalosaurus   1143
Megaphylls   1454, 2072
Megapodes   2403-2404
Megapodius eremita, see Melanesian megapode
Megapodius pritchardii, see Polynesian megapode
Megaptera novaeangliae, see Humpback whale
Megaspores   3439
Meiosis   802, 805, 811, 1603, 1621, 2246-2248, 2391, 3279
Meiospores   3439
Meissner corpuscles   1944, 3689
Meissner effect   3550
Meissner, Georg   3596
Meissner, W.   3550
Meister, Joseph   3810
Meitner, Lise   2539, 2558
Melaleuca quinquinerva, see Bottlebrush tree
Melanerpes erythrocephalus, see Red-headed woodpecker
Melanerpes formicivorus, see Acorn woodpecker
Melanesian megapode   2404
Melanin   106, 191, 1943
Melanitta perspicillata, see Surf scoters
Melanogrammus aeglefinus, see Haddock
Melanoma   3860
Melanorrhoea usitata, see Burmese lacquer tree
Melanosuchus niger, see Black caiman
Melatonin   498, 1349
Meleagris gallopavo, see Turkey
Meles meles, see Eurasian badger
Melia azedarach, see Chinaberry
Melies, Georges   2399
Melilotus alba, see Sweet clovers
Melilotus officinalis, see Sweet clovers
Melissa officinalis, see Balm
Melliovora capensis, see Honey badger
Mellisuga helenae, see Bee hummingbird
Melogale moschata, see Chinese ferret badger
Melogale orientalis, see Bornean ferret badger
Melogale personata, see Indian ferret badger

O

Oncology   648

Oncopeltus fasciatus, see Milkweeds

Ondatra zibethicus, see Muskrat

One-edged arrow   3924

One-flowered wintergreen   1770

One-humped Arabian camel   643

One-humped camel   2127

One-to-one correspondence   2603

One-to-one function   2603-2605

Onion   2106, 3826

Onnes, Heike Kamerlingh   1031, 1588, 2266, 3550

Onopordum acanthium, see Scotch thistle

Onopordum arabicum, see Scotch thistle

Ontogeny   1118

Onza   710

Oogenesis   3103

Oort cloud   888, 3360

Oort, Jan   890

Opacity   872

Opah   2605

Oparin, Aleksandr Ivanovich   767, 2625

Operant conditioning   3086

Operating systems (computer)   927

Opercula   815, 3121

Ophiolite   1210

Ophiophagus hannah, see King cobra

Ophiopluteus   572

Ophioroids   571

Ophiostoma ulmi, see Ascomycete fungus

Ophis   571

Ophrys apifera, see Bee orchid

Ophthalmic surgery   2059

Ophthalmology   130

Opiates   185, 1729, 2450

Opioid analgesics   857

Opioid antagonists   2450

Opioids   818, 2450, 2490

Opisthocomus hoazin, see Hoatzin

Opium   2388, 2889

Opium poppy   130, 2388, 2888

Opossums   1451, 2605-2606

Oppenheimer, J. Robert   2541, 2558, 2976

Opportunistic species   684, 2606-2607

Opposite   2467

Optic chiasma   3854

Optic lobe   2477

Optic nerve   1438, 3857

Optical axis   2089

Optical cavity   2055

Optical character recognition   3209

Optical coupling   2078

Optical data processing   3625

Optical data storage   2607-2609

Optical disk, magneto (MO)   2607

Optical disk, write once, read many times (WORM)   2607

Optical disks, read only memory (ROM)   2607

Optical microscope, see Microscopy

Optical radiation detector   3010

Optical telescope   3618

Optical terrain matching navigation   1917

Optics   2789

Opuntia compressa, see Beaver-tail cactus

Opuntia ficus-indica, see Prickly-pear cactus

Oral cavity   1084

Oral contraceptives   963

Orang-utans   250, 2609-2611

Orange   1676, 3252

Orange lily   2106

Orange-winged sittella   2573

Orbit   1727, 1728, 2011, 2611-2613, 2852

Orbit, Earth's   638, 3917

Orbit, hyperbolic   2612

Orbital   353, 1420

Orbital activities   3395

Orbital diseases   3857

Orbital distance   3670

Orbital Maneuvering System (OMS) Engines   3395

Orbital maneuvers   3395

Orbital module   3385

Orbital plane   1224

Orbiter   3394

Orbiting object   3193

Orchid family   2439, 2613-2615, 3049

Orchis   2614

Orchis rotundifolia, see Round-leaved orchis

Orchis spectabilis, see Showy orchis

Orcinus orca, see Killer whales

Order   3402

Ordered pairs   900, 3088

Ordered set   1915

Ordinate   187, 694

Ordovician Era   62, 362, 1829, 2670

Ore   2616-2619

Ore deposits   1096, 1408, 2617

Ore deposits, hydrothermal   2617, 2914

Ore dressing   3481

Oreanmnos americanus, see Mountain goat

Oregon grape   402

Oreophasis   757

Oreortyx pictus, see Mountain quail

Oreoscoptes montanus, see Sage thrasher

Oreotragus oreotragus, see Klipspringer

Ores   972, 2067, 2616, 2617

Organ   2619-2620

Organ donation   3716

Organ of Corti   1198, 1752

Organ transplants   535, 1878, 3714, 3716

Outer planets 2804

Ova 1029, 1581, 1, 1963

Oval window 1197, 1752

Ovalipes ocellatus, see Crabs

Ovaries 1347, 1350, 1964, 2263, 2971, 3103

Ovenbirds 2641-2642

Overfishing 857, 3286

Overhunting 1600, 2427, 2793

Overshot wheel 3911

Overtones 1742

Ovibos moschatus, see Muskoxen

Oviducts 1460

Oviraptor 1145

Ovis aries, see Sheep

Ovoviviparity 179, 2642

Ovoviviparous 2642-2643

Ovulation 962, 1720, 3104

Ovules 2873

Ovum 1720

Owen, Robert 1370

Owens, Michael J. 1657

Owens, Richard 2700

Owen's chameleon 759

Owen's Valley pupfish 2018

Owlet frogmouth 661

Owlet nightjar 661

Owls 2643-2645

Ox warble fly 3749

Ox-eye daisy 903

Ox-peckers 1652

Oxalic acid 2645

Oxaloacetate 2025

Oxalosuccinate 2025

Oxidant 2654

Oxidation 32, 611,734, 886, 1665, 1842, 1908, 1978, 2068, 2279, 2283, 2514, 2597, 2650, 2880, 3121, 3350, 3481, 3922

Oxidation numbers 2646, 2650, 3815

Oxidation reaction 208

Oxidation-reduction 738,2025, 2645-2650

Oxidative phosphorylation 183, 2279

Oxides 913

Oxidizing agent 56

Oxidizing smogs 2529

Oxpeckers 3462

Oxyfuel gas welding 3930

Oxygen 114, 150, 327, 355, 388, 467, 531, 535, 667, 671, 673, 677, 704, 886, 1575, 1878, 2646, 2650-2653, 2898, 3062, 3112, 3121

Oxygen deficiency 1410

Oxygen therapy 2652

Oxygen-deficient waters 1410

Oxyhemoglobin 468, 676

Oxyhydrogen torch 1858

Oxyporhamphus micropterus, see Smallwing flying fish

Oxytocin 509, 1351

Oxytropis, see Locoweeds

Oxyura jamaicensis, see Ruddy duck

Oxyuranus scutellatus, see Taipan

Oxyurinae, see Stiff-tailed duck

Oyctolagus cuniculus, see Domestic rabbit

Oystercatchers 2654, 3290

Oysters 539, 2369

Oyza sativa, see Rice

Ozone 328, 1359, 1397, 1735, 1855, 2651, 2654-2655, 2878, 3016, 3238, 3332

Ozone depletion 330, 1084, 1235, 2655-2659

Ozone layer 768, 1855

Ozone pollution 2655, 2658

P

P waves 1212

P-aminobenzoic acid 162

P-waves 1205

Pacas 70

Pacemaker 1760, 1764, 2661-2662

Pacific barracuda 412

Pacific boas 542

Pacific dogwood 1163

Pacific halibut 1485

Pacific mackerel 2172

Pacific Ocean 1323, 3733

Pacific salmon 539, 1960, 3184

Pacific sardine 1798, 3192

Pacific silver fir 1480

Pacific walrus 3888

Pacific willow 3945

Pacific yew 408, 2599, 3973

Pacinian corpuscles 1944, 3689

Padda oryzivora, see Java finch

Pademelons 2009

Paeonia brownii 2720

Paeonia californica 2720

Paeonia lutes 2720

Paeophyta, see Brown algae

Paganini, Nicolo 159

Paget, Stephen 1764

Pagoda flower 3831

Pagophila eburnea, see Ivory gull

Pahoehoe 3870

Pain 35, 2662-2664, 3689

Pain receptors 2663

Pain relief 144, 858, 857

Painted buckeye 1826

Paints 2068

Pak-choi   2432
Pakaraima Mountains   3382
Pakistan   306
Palawan, see Calamian stink badger
Palawan tree shrew   3721
Paleobotany   452, 1051, 2644-2665
Paleocene Epoch   2674
Paleolithic Period   1398
Paleomagnetism   1214, 2665-2668, 2845
Paleontologists   1541
Paleontology   1142, 1541, 2668-2675
Paleoplacers   2913
Paleosuchus palpebrosus, see Dwarf caiman
Paleosuchus trigonatus, see Smooth-fronted caiman
Paleozoic Era   62, 364, 557, 1408
Paley, William   38
Palisade mesophile   2070
Palitzch, Johann   1728
Pallas   2341
Pallas' cat   712
Palm cockatoo   853
Palmer, Daniel David   145
Palmer, Nathaniel   215
Palmeria dolei, see Crested honeycreeper
Palmitic acid   1448
Palms   2675-2678
Palometa   1992
Palpation   1123
Palps   1687
Palynology   264, 2665, 2870
Pampas   1689, 3380
Pampas grass   1685
Pan   3198
Pan paniscus, see Pygmy chimpanzees
Pan troglodytes, see Common chimpanzee
Pan-African event   1404
Panama Canal   2132
Panama orange   830
Panax ginseng, see Oriental ginseng
Panax quinquifolium, see American ginseng
Panax, see Ginseng
Panax trifolium, see Dwarf ginseng
Pancaking   1206
Pancreas   1057, 1120, 1137, 1347, 1349, 1656, 1935
Pancreatic disorders   1993
Pandaka pygmaea, see Philippine goby
Pandanus odoratissimus, see Breadfruit pardanus
Pandanus tictorius, see Thatch screwpine
Pandanus vetchii, see Screwpine
Pandas   429, 2678-2681
Pandion haliaetus, see Osprey
Pandora   3197
Pangaea (Pangea)   63, 952, 1406, 2844
Pangenesis   1416

Pangolins   2681-2682
Panic attacks   3699
Panic grass   1681
Panicum capillare, see Tumble panic-grass
Panicum miliaceum, see Proso millet
Panicum virgatum, see Panic grass
Panspermia   2627
Panthalassa   954
Panther   3932
Panthera leo atrox, see American lion
Panthera leo, see Lion
Panthera onca, see Jaguar
Panthera pardus, see Leopard
Panthera tigris, see Tiger
Pantothenic acid   3863
Panulirus argus, see Caribbean spiny lobster
Panulirus interruptus, see West coast spiny lobster
Pap test   1721
Papain   2683
Papanicolaou, George   1721
Papaver aculeatum, see Poppy
Papaver dubium, see Common poppy
Papaver nudicaule, see Iceland poppy
Papaver orientale, see Oriental poppy
 Papaver rhoeas, see Corn poppy
Papaver, see True poppy
Papaver somniferum, see Opium poppy
Papaver Somniferum, see Poppy
Papaya   2682-2683
Paper   1528, 1782, 2683-2686, 3051
Paper birch   504
Paper mulberry   2412
Paper rush   3241
Paperbark   2445
Papilloma virus   3278, 3849
Papin, Denis   886, 3475
Papio cynocephalus, see Common savanna baboon
Papio hamadryas, see Hamadryas baboon
Papio papio, see Guinea baboon
Papoviruses   3849
Pappus of Alexandria   3687
Papuan frogmouth   660
Papuan mynah   2442
Papule   2149
Papyrus   696,3240, 3241
Para-aminobenzoic acid   239
Para-xylene   453
Parabola   188, 395, 836, 888, 1046, 1320, 2686-2688
Parabolic reflectors   2688
Parabolic spiral   3430
Paracelsus   108, 1300, 1858, 2862, 3690
Paracortex   2152
Paradigm   3218
Paradise flycatchers   2370

Phantom limb 2663

Phantom midge 3749

Pharaoh's ant 247

Pharmaceuticals 1338, 1650

Pharomachrus mocino, see Resplendent quetzal

Pharyngeal bones 688

Pharyngeal pouches 3887

Pharynx 3123

Phascogale, see Brush-tailed marsupial mice

Phascolarctos cinereus, see Koala

Phaseolus aureus, see Mung bean

Phaseolus lunatus, see Lima bean

Phaseolus multiflorus, see Scarlet runner

Phasianus colchicus, see Ring-necked pheasant

Phasianus colchicus, see Ring-necked pheasant

Phasianus versicolor, see Japanese pheasant

Phasmids, see Walkingsticks

Phasotrons 10

Pheasant pigeon 2791

Pheasant-tailed jacana 1991

Pheasants 2751-2753

Phenacomys intermedius, see Heather vole

Phenelzine 235

Phenethylamine 176

Phenetics 3602

Phenlyalanine 163

Phenobarbital 1381

Phenolic resins 454

Phenolphthalein 1906

Phenols 13, 245, 454, 2741

Phenotype 203, 1614

Phenyl 2879

Phenyl group 453, 2753-2755

Phenylformic acid 454

Phenylketonuria (PKU) 1615, 2274

Phenytoin 233

Pheochromocytoma 50

Pheromones 1002, 3173, 3330

Philacte canagica, see Emperor goose

Philemon yorki, see Helmeted friar bird

Philetarus socius, see Social weaver

Philippine colugo 877

Philippine goby 545

Philippine gymnure 1774

Philippine monkey-eating eagle 1194

Philippine tarsier 3594

Philippine tree shrew 3721

Philodendron 296

Philodendron scandens, see Philodendron

Philohela minor, see American woodcock

Philohela minor, see Woodcocks

Philomachus pugnax, see Ruff

Philosophy 108, 864, 1369

Phlebitis 3664

Phlegm 3117

Phlegmariurus dichotomus, see Hanging fir moss

Phleum pratense, see Timothy

Phloem 407, 2817, 3166, 3718

Phlogiston 2777

Phlogiston theory 886

Phlox divaricata, see Wild blue phlox

Phlox drummondii, see Drummond's pink

Phlox maculata, see Sweet-william

Phlox paniculata, see Garden phlox

Phlox pilosa, see Downy phlox

Phlox subulata, see Moss pink phlox

Phloxes 2755

Phobias 917, 2584, 2755-2756

Phoca hispida 432

Phocomelia 3648

Phodopus roborovskii, see Dwarf hamster

Phodopus sungorus, see Dwarf hamster

Phoebe 3198

Phoeniconaias minor, see Lesser flamingo

Phoenicoparrus andinus, see Andean flamingo

Phoenicoparrus jamesi, see James's flamingo

Phoenicopteridae, see Flamingos

Phoenicopterus chilensis, see Chilean flamingo

Phoenicopterus ruber, see Common flamingo

Phoenix dactylifera 2677

Phoenix theophrasti, see Cretan palm

Phonograph 2182, 2756-2757

Phonophobia 2318

Phoradendron flavescens, see American mistletoe

Phoresy, see Commensalism

Phoronids 2757

Phosphate 469, 1821, 1912, 2073, 2759

Phosphatidylcholine, see Lecithin

Phospholipids 732-733, 2073, 3478

Phosphor 708

Phosphorescence 1506, 2145, 2333, 2591, 2758

Phosphoric acid 2758-2759

Phosphorus 1410, 2110, 2759, 2878, 3166

Phosphorus removal 2759-2760

Phosphorylation 704, 743

Photic zone 2760-2762

Photoautotrophs 379, 388, 1236

Photoautrophism 2514

Photocell 2769

Photochemical reactions 793, 2654, 2656

Photochemistry 2762-2765

Photoconducting surface 2765

Photoconductive effect 2769

Photoconductivity 1254

Photocopying 2765-2767, 3208

Photodissociation 2656, 2764

Photoelectric cell 2767-2768, 3153

Photoelectric effect 916, 2104, 2768-2769, 2775

GENERAL INDEX

Protonotaria citrea, see Golden swamp warbler; Prothonotary warbler

Protons   341, 347, 351, 355, 1264, 1289, 1296, 1974, 2226, 2281, 2562, 2730, 2957, 3036, 3516, 3543

Protoplasm   174, 2309

Protopterus, see Lungfish

Protostars   3460

Protostele   3938

Prototype   1365

Protozoa   299, 480, 2632, 2814, 3438, 2690, 2958-2959, 3321

Protozoan diseases   2191

Protractor   949

Proust, Joseph-Louis   342, 913

Proxima Centauri   3453

Prozac, see fluoxetine

Prunus avium, see Sweet cherry

Prunus pensylvanica, see Pin cherry

Prunus triflora, see Japanese plum

Prusiner, Stanley B.   2026, 2932

Pryor, Richard   852

Przewalski's horse   1827

Psallus seriatus, see Cotton fleahopper

Pseudocalanus, see Copepods

Pseudococcus longispinus, see Greenhouse mealybug

Pseudodementia   1080

Pseudoephedrine   176

Pseudohermaphrodism   1792

Pseudomyrmex ferruginea, see Tropical ant

Pseudopleuronectes americnus, see Winter flounder

Pseudopodia   2958

Pseudopods   174

Pseudorca crassidens, see False killer whale

Pseudotriton ruber, see Red salamander

Pseudotsuga menziesii, see Douglas fir; Lichens

Psidium littorale, see Strawberry guava

Psilocybin   1731, 2425

Psilotum nudum, see Whisk fern

Psittacids   2697

Psittaculirostria diophthalma, see Double-eyed fig-parrot

Psittacus erithacus, see African grey parrot

Psittirostra kona, see Grosbeak finch

Psoroptes ovis, see Sheep scab mite

Psychedelic drugs   1729

Psychiatry   2959-2960

Psychoanalysis   2250, 2960-2962

Psychogenic amnesia   171

Psychology   864, 2962-2964

Psychometry   2964-2966

Psychosis   242, 2966-2968, 3212

Psychosomatic   2802

Psychosurgery   2968-2971

Psychotherapy   2203, 2959, 3215, 3510

Psychotic disorders   3212

Psychrophiles   387

Ptarmigans   1707

Ptelea trifoliata, see Three-leaved hop tree

Pteridospermales, see Seed ferns

Pterocnemia pennata, see Darwin's rhea

Pteroglossus viridis, see Green aracari

Pteronura brasiliensis, see Giant otter

Pterosaurs   472, 1146, 1431, 2673

Pterospora andromeda, see Pine-drops

Pterygotus rhenanus, see Giant sea scorpion

Ptilocercus lowi, see Pen-tailed tree shew

Ptolemy, Claudius   696, 1626, 1775, 2527, 3059, 3218, 3724

Ptychodera, see Worms, acorn

Ptychodiscus, see Dinoflagellates

Pubarche   2972

Puberty   1710, 2265, 2971-2974

Public works   1551

Puccinia graminis tritici, see Wheat rust

Puck   3804

Pueblans   261

Pueraria lobata, see Kudzu-vine

Puerto Rican nightjar   1668

Puffballs   1572, 2425

Puffbirds   2975

Puffer fish   2603, 2975-2976

Puffing billy   3695

Pug mill   566

Pulex irritans, see Human flea

Pull-apart basins   417

Pulley   1006, 2159

Pulmonary alveoil   1336

Pulmonary artery   1759

Pulmonary circulation   822

Pulmonary fibrosis   3120

Pulmonary semilunar valve   1759

Pulmonary veins   1760

Pulmonary ventilation   3121

Pulp   2683, 2684

Pulpwood   1479

Pulque   158

Pulsar   729, 1436, 1583, 2496, 2976, 3042, 3092

Pulsations   3822

Pulse, acoustic   3373

Pulse-code modulation   3835

Puma concolor, see Cougar

Puma, see Cougar

Pumping unit   1982

Pumpkin   1673, 3252, 3825

Pungitius pungitius, see Ninespine stickleback

Pupa   2294

Pupil   1438, 3006

Purine base adenine   46

Q

R

Rabbit fish   781
Rabbits   2031, 2032, 3932
Rabi, I. I.   2548
Rabies   2999-3001, 3002, 3851
Raccoons   3001-3003
Rachischisis   3423
Racquet-tailed roller   3164
Rad unit   3013
Radar   91, 1257, 1286, 1887, 1917, 2688, 2866, 3003-3006, 3100
Radar platform   103
Radial keratotomy   3006-3008
Radial velocity   318
Radian   201
Radiation   652, 986, 988, 1066, 1772, 2068, 2809, 3008-3009, 3010, 3016, 3359, 3408, 3450, 3460, 3493, 3632, 3635, 3758, 3963
Radiation, acoustic   3012
Radiation belts   3816, 3818
Radiation, coherent   1812
Radiation, cosmic background   991
Radiation detectors   3009-3012, 3816
Radiation, electromagnetic   1505, 1928, 1972, 2662, 2983, 3008, 3012, 3045
Radiation exposure   3012-3015
Radiation, gamma   1287-1288, 3029
Radiation, heat   1878
Radiation, infrared   327, 338, 1359, 2806, 2985, 3013, 3097, 3414
Radiation, ionizing   651, 1515, 1973, 2433, 3008, 3012, 3032, 3044
Radiation, microwave   991
Radiation, particulate   3008
Radiation, synchrotron   11
Radiation therapy   2495
Radiation, ultraviolet   57, 99, 106, 328, 339, 792, 1231, 1357, 1725, 1733, 1855, 1864, 1885, 1943, 1973, 2059, 2656, 2763,2806, 3013, 3082, 3099, 3414, 3762, 3789
Radiation, x-ray   3013
Radiative core, central   3486
Radiative transport   3493
Radiatively active gases   1701
Radical (chemical)   3015-3017
Radical (mathematical)   3017-3020
Radicand   3017
Radicle   1639, 1641
Radii of curvature   2089
Radio   1286, 3020-3024, 3045, 3046, 3414, 3612, 3789
Radio astronomy   3039-3042
Radio frequency waves   2969

Radio galaxies   3041
Radio pulse   2140
Radio star   2976
Radio telescope   3039, 3624
Radio transmitters   3021
Radio waves   318, 330, 1579, 2324, 2730, 2976, 2994, 3020, 3039, 3045-3047, 3612
Radioactive decay   1631, 1708, 1724, 3025
Radioactive fallout   2560, 3013, 3024-3025
Radioactive isotopes   3026
Radioactive materials   2495, 3009
Radioactive pollution   3026-3029
Radioactive tracers   2550, 3029-3032
Radioactive transformation   1308
Radioactive waste   1724, 2553, 3013, 3032-3034
Radioactivity   31-32, 350, 356, 1296, 1724, 1988, 2333, 2496, 2559, 2735, 2957, 3024, 3026, 3029, 3034-3039
Radiocarbon dating   985, 1066, 2871, 3289
Radioisotopes   1724, 1989, 2406, 3032, 3034, 3044
Radiolocation navigation systems   1917
Radiology   407, 3042-3045
Radiometric dating   985, 1142, 1631
Radionuclides   2549, 3030, 3044
Radiopaque substances   3043
Radiopharmaceuticals   2550, 3030
Radiosonde   331
Radiotherapy   1810
Radish   2431, 3826
Radium   127, 3012, 3035, 3799
Radius   819, 3306
Radius vector   3429
Radon   681, 1908, 3013, 3036, 3055, 3799
Radon-222   3027
Ragi millet   1684
Ragweed   905, 2871
Ragwort   904, 1961
Rails   3047-3048
Rain forest   305, 470, 492, 572, 671, 1324, 1346, 1434, 1531, 1653, 3048-3051, 3379, 3719
Rainbow finch   3913
Rainbow lorikeet   2698, 2699
Rainbow runner   1992
Rainbow trout   539, 1023, 3185
Rainbow-bird   439
Rainbows   334
Rainwater killifish   2016
Raising   3646
Raja batis, see European skate
Raja binoculata, see Big skate
Raja erinacea, see Little skate
Rallus elegans, see King rail
Rallus limicola, see Virginia rail
Rallus longirostris, see Clapper rail

Respiratory therapy   1337
Resplendent quetzal   3730
Restless leg syndrome   3319
Restoration ecology   3126-3130
Restricted three-body problem   728
Restriction enzymes   386, 1607
Resurrection fern   1455
Reticular formation   560
Reticular tissue   943
Reticulated giraffe
Reticulated willow   3946
Reticulistics   3603
Reticulum   3174
Retina   873, 1103, 1438, 2059, 2722, 3006, 3852
Retina, detached   3860
Retinitis pigmentosa   3860
Retinoblastoma   3860
Retinoic acid   3635
Retinol 1   3862
Retinol 2   3862
Retrograde amnesia   171
Retrograde motion   2469, 3130-3131, 3361, 3828
Retroviruses   84, 651, 680, 1094, 1608, 3130-3131,
    33613851
Reverse fault   1204
Reverse osmosis   1108, 2634
Reverse transcriptase   84, 3131
Reversible reaction   1384, 1386
Revolution   200, 1198
Reye, Ralph D.   3134
Reye's syndrome   14, 1340, 3134
Reynolds number   52, 1503, 3770
Reynolds, Osborne   1503, 3770
Reynolds, Richard   3694
Rh disease   3138
Rh factor   3138-3140
Rh immune globulin   3138
Rhabda, Nicolaus   629
Rhabdoviruses   3851
Rhagoletis pomonella, see Apple maggot
Rhamnus betulaefolia, see Birchleaf buckthorn
Rhamnus californica, see California buckthorn
Rhamnus caroliniana, see Carolina buckthorn
Rhamnus cathartica, see European buckthorn
Rhamnus frangula, see Alder buckthorn
Rhamnus globosus, see Chinese buckthorn
Rhamnus purshiana, see Cascara buckthorn; Western
    buckthorn
Rhamnus utilis, see Chinese buckthorn
Rhazes   790
Rhea   1495, 3198
Rhea americana, see Common rhea
Rhebok, see Grazing antelopes
Rheobatrachus silus, see Australian frog;

Gastric-brooding frog
Rhesus disease   230
Rhesus monkeys   2157, 3134-3135
Rheum officinale, see Medicinal rhubarb
Rheum rhaponticum, see Rhubarb
Rheumatic fever   3136
Rheumatoid arthritis   277
Rhinitis, allergic   134
Rhinoceros   3140-3141, 3793
Rhinoceros auklet, see Auks
Rhinoceros hornbill   1824
Rhinoceros sondaicus, see Javan rhinoceros
Rhinoceros unicornis, see Great Indian rhinoceros
Rhinoceros viper   3837
Rhinophrynus dorsalis, see Burrowing frog
Rhinoplax vigil, see Helmeted hornbill
Rhinoptilus africanus, see Double-banded courser
Rhinoptilus cinctus, see Three-banded courser
Rhinoviruses   865, 3850
Rhipidura albolimbata, see Friendly fantail
Rhizobium   2081
Rhizoids   578, 2122
Rhizome   156, 272, 686, 1648, 3141, 3938
Rhizophora apiculata, see Mangrove
Rhizophora mangle, see Red mangrove
Rhodesian ebony, see Jackal's berry
Rhododendron calendulaceum, see Flame azalea
Rhododendron californicum, see California mountain
    laurel
Rhododendron canadense, see Rhodora
Rhododendron catawbiense, see Red laurel
Rhododendron indicum, see Asian azalea
Rhododendron maximum, see Great laurel; White laurel
Rhododendron nudiflorum, see Pinksterflower
Rhododendron roseum, see Mountain azalea
Rhododendron sinense, see Garden azalea
Rhododendron viscosum, see Swamp azalea
Rhododendrons   1769
Rhodophyta, see Red algae
Rhodopseudomonas viridis, see Anaerobic
    photosynthetic bacteria
Rhodora   1770
Rhodostethia rosea, see Ross's gull
Rhodymenia palmata, see Sea kale
Rhombus, see parallelogram
Rhubarb   4141-3142, 3825
Rhus aromatica, see Fragrant sumac
Rhus copallina, see Mountain sumac
Rhus coriaria, see Sicilian sumac
Rhus glabra, see Scarlet sumac
Rhus radicans, see Poison ivy
Rhus trilobata, see Skunkbush
Rhus typhina, see Staghorn sumac
Rhus verniciflua, see Lacquer tree

Ruderals   899

Rufescent tinamou   3675

Ruff   3190

Ruffed grouse   1706

Ruffed lemur   2087

Ruffini endings   3689

Ruffled grouse   1533

Rufous hummingbird   1842

Rufous-sided towhee   3400

Rufous-browed pepper shrike   3840

Rufous-fronted ovenbird   2642

Rumen, see Rumination

Ruminants   643, 716, 1073, 1185, 2386, 3287

Rumination   518, 2942, 3174, 3900

Runnels   3146

Runner, scarlet   2082

Runoff   1459, 1864

Rupicola rupicola, see Guianan cock-of-the-rock

Rushes   3174-3176, 3241

Russell, Henry Norris   1799

Russell's viper   3838

Russian pigweed   3757

Rust   1978, 2648, 2653

Rusts   1455, 1569, 1572, 1574, 3176-3177

Rusty blackbird   523

Rutherford, Daniel   2516

Rutherford, Ernest   343, 350, 2562, 2702, 3035, 3516, 3764

Ruwenzori otter shrew   2640-2641

Rye   1681, 1684-85

S

S waves   1205, 1212

Sabatier, Paul   675

Sabertooth cat   1432, 3793

Sabin, Albert   2867, 3811

Sabine's gull   1717

Sable   2224

Saccharin   1052

Saccharomyces cerevisiae, see Baker's yeast

Saccharomyces ellipsoides   1678

Saccharum officinarum, see Sugar cane

Saccheri, Girolamo   2527

Sacramento sucker   3535

Sacred ibis   1882

Sacred lotus   3904

Saddle-bill stork   3505

Saddleback tamarin   2216

Sadler, Windham   398

Sadomasochism   2662

Safflower   903

Sag ponds   2046

Sage grouse   1707

Sage sparrow   3400

Sage thrasher   2354

Sagebrush vole   3876

Sages   2345

Sagnac, Georges   1947

Sagnac interferometer, see Cyclic interferometer

Sago palm   2677

Saguaro cactus   618

Saguinus bicolor, see Pied tamarin

Saguinus fuscicollis, see Saddleback tamarin

Saguinus imperator, see Emperor tarmarin

Saguinus oedipus geoffroyi, see Geoffroy's tamarin

Saguinus oedipus, see Pinche tamarin

Sahara Desert   59

Sahel   63

Saiga antelope   3179-3180, 3793

Saiga tatarica, see Saiga antelope

Sailplane   87

Saimiri oerstedii, see Central American squirrel monkey

Saimiri sciureus, see Squirrel monkey

Salam, Abdus   2184

Salamanders   3180-3183

Salicin   13

Salicylic acid   185

Salicylic acid acetate   1394

Salinity   557, 2034

Saliva   1135

Salivary glands   1656

Salix alaxensis, see Feltleaf willow

Salix alba, see White willow

Salix amygdaloides, see Peachleaf willow

Salix arctica, see Arctic willow

Salix babylonica, see Weeping willow

Salix bebiana, see Bebb willow

Salix carolineana, see Coastal plain willow

Salix discolor, see Pussy willow

Salix fragilis, see Crack willow

Salix interior, see Sandbar willow

Salix lasiandra, see Pacific willow

Salix lasiolepis, see Arroyo willow

Salix mackenzieana, see Mackenzie willow

Salix nigra, see Black willow

Salix reticulata, see Reticulated willow

Salix viminalis, see Basket willow

Salk, Jonas   1153, 2867, 3810

Salmeterol   314

Salmo gairdneri, see Rainbow trout

Salmo salar, see Atlantic salmon

Salmo trutta, see Brown trout

Salmon   2321, 3183-3185

Salmonella   466, 2307, 2433

Salmonella typhe, see Bacteria

Salmonella typhi, see Typhoid fever
Salmonflies, see stoneflies
Salpinctes obsoletus, see rock wren
Salps 3236-3237
Salt 129, 769, 1155, 1520, 1554, 1862, 2492, 3185-3187, 3248, 3347, 3350
Salt domes 3527
Salt lakes 3186
Salt-marsh crocodile 1017
Saltpeter, see Potassium nitrate
Saltwater 3186, 3284
Saltwater bass 418
Saltwater intrusions 3187
Salvage excavations 265
Salvarsan 3274
Salvelinus fontinalis, see Brook trout
Salvelinus namaycush, see Lake trout
Salvia officinalis, see Common sage
Salvia sclarea, see Clary
Salvia splendens, see Garden sage
Salyut 3386
Sammelweiss, Ignaz 244
Sample 3187-3188, 3467
Sample, random 3187
Sample space 2936
Sampling 3585
San Clemente Bewick's wren 3958
San Clemente sage sparrow 3401
San Jose scale 3207
Sanatoriums 3119
Sand 1183, 3298
Sand cat 712
Sand dollar 3188
Sand dunes 302, 414, 2045
Sand geysers 1206
Sand martin 3568
Sand skink 3309
Sand-reed 1682
Sandbar willow 3945
Sandboas 541
Sanderling 3190
Sandfish 3189
Sandhill crane 1006
Sandpipers 3189-3190, 3290-3291
Sandroller 3742
Sandstone 3160, 3501
Sandworm 3253
Sanforizing 3646
Sanger, Frederick 1935
Sanger, Margaret 962
Sanitation 1783, 2867, 3784
Santos-Dumont, Alberto 101
Sap 1719
Sapodilla tree 3191

Saponification 679, 1448, 3338
Sappanwood 2083
Saprophytes 1802
Sapwood 3718, 3953
Saracophilus harrisii, see Tasmanian devil
Sarcoplasmic reticulum 2423
Sarcoramphus papa, see King vulture
Sarcoscypha coccinea, see Scarlet elf cup
Sardina pilchardus, see Sardines
Sardines 3191-3192
Sardinops sagax, see Pacific sardine
Sarracenia purpurea, see Pitcher plant
Sarus crane 1008
Sassafras 2062
Sassafras albidum, see Sassafras
Satanellus albopunctatus, see Northern native cat
Satanellus hallucatus, see Northern native cat
Satellite imagery 697, 3098
Satellites 1215, 1929, 2316, 2589, 2612, 3045, 3097, 3192-3193, 3394, 3528, 3564
Saturated fatty acid 1448
Saturation 873
Satureja hortensis, see Summer savory
Saturn 2813, 3193-3199
Satyr tragopan 3693
Saurischians 1144
Sauromalus, see Chuckwallas
Sauropods 1142, 1145
Saussure, Horace Bénédict de 331
Savanna 491, 1883, 3199-3202, 3719
Savanna baboon 381
Savannah sparrow 3399
Savants 3202-3204
Savery, Thomas 371, 886, 3475
Savoy cabbage 2431
Sawfish 3204
Sawgrass 3240, 3933
Sawing machines 2166
Sawmill 3911
Sawyer, James 3317
Sawyer, William 1901
Saxifraga aizodes, see Golden saxifrage
Saxifraga cernua, see Bulblet saxifrage
Saxifraga flagellaris, see Spider-plant
Saxifraga nivalis, see Snow saxifrage
Saxifraga oppositifolia, see Purple mountain saxifrage
Saxifraga pensylvanica, see Swamp saxifrage
Saxifraga tricuspidata, see Prickly saxifrage
Saxifraga virginiensis, see Early saxifrage
Saxifrage 3204-3206
Saxitoxin 481, 952, 2603, 3075
Sayornis phoebe, see Eastern phoebe
Scabies 2349, 2692
Scads, see Jacks

T

Tympanuchus cupido, see Greater prairie chicken
Tympanuchus pallidicinctus, see Lesser prairie chicken
Tyndall effect   868
Tyndall, John   1468
Typesetting   2928
Typhoid fever   391, 1368, 3777-3779
Typhoons   3732
Typhus   1490, 2307, 3779-3780
Typical owls   2643
Tyrannosaurus rex   1144, 3106
Tyrannus tyrannus, see Eastern kingbird
Tyrannus verticalis, see Western kingbird
Tyrant flycatcher   3781-3782
Tyrocidine   224
Tyrosine   106, 2490
Tyrothricin   224

U

U-boats   3523
UBV system   3490
Uhuru sattelite   1695
Ukrainian shield   1404
Ulcers   1138, 3783-3785
Ulex europaeus, see Gorse
Ulmus americana, see American elm
Ultracentrifuge   495, 748, 3785
Ultrasaurus   1146
Ultrasonic beams   2970
Ultrasonics   3785-3789
Ultrasonography   1327
Ultrasound   172, 800, 935, 1921, 1965, 2788, 3043, 3785
Ultrasound probe   3007
Ultraviolet astronomy   3789-3791
Ultraviolet photoelectron spectroscopy   1973
Ultraviolet radiation   99, 768, 2432, 2782, 2878, 3542
Ultraviolet telescope   3789
Ultraviolet-visible spectroscopy   3412
Ulva lactuca, see Sea lettuce
Umbilical cord   1330
Umbilical ring   1794
Umbra   3548
Umbrella-bird   993
Umbriel   2473, 3800
Uncia uncia, see Snow leopard
Unconformity   3508, 3791-3793
Underground deposits   3537
Undershot wheel   3911
Underwoodisaurus milii, see Australian barking gecko
Ungulates   1879, 3793
Uniaxial pressing   751
Unicornfish   1011

Uniformitarianism   705, 3793-3794
Union   2936
Uniparental embryos   206
Unique tangent line   1925
Unit volume   3876
United States Recommended Dietary Allowances (USRDA)   3862
Units and standards   3794-3797
Units of solubility   3368
UNIVAC   920
Universal gas constant   3656
Universal set   548
Universal Time (U.T.)   638
Universe   986
Universe, creation of   458, 991, 3093, 3471- 3473
Unmanned instrumented spacecraft   3390
Unmanned spacecraft   1437
Unsaturated fatty acid   1448, 2602
Unstable atmosphere   3666
Unterseeboot   3523
Upatnieks, J.   1812
Updrafts   3666
Uplift   2407, 3797
Upper cretaceous period   452, 840
Upper devonian period   3719
Upper jurassic period   3180
Upper mantle   2120
Upper respiratory infection   865
Upupa epops, see Hoopoe   1818
Upwelling   493, 1324, 2761, 3797-3798
Uracil   3143
Uranium   32, 63, 626, 1307, 3012, 3035, 3798-3799
Uranium ores   3799
Uranium series dating   1066
Uranium-233   2554
Uranium-235   2542, 2554
Uranium-238   2542, 3799
Uranium-239   2542, 2557
Uranus   3799-3806
Urban archaeology   264
Urban mosquito   3971
Urban planning   593, 1498
Urea   160, 3806
Urea-formaldehyde resins   3806
Urediniospores   3176
Ureter   1422
Urey, Harold   768, 1116, 1202, 1858
Urginea maritima, see Squill
Uric acid   1421
Urinalysis   1423
Urinary bladder   1422
Urinary system   191, 1421-1423, 2918, 3807
Urogale everetti, see Philippine tree shrew
Urography   1423

Von Weizsacker, C.F.   1305
Von Wroblewski, S.F.   1030
Von Zeppelin, Ferdinand   87, 102
Voskhod   3385
Vostok   3384
Voyager spacecraft   2740, 3801, 3194
Vredefort Ring   316
Vulcanization   1913, 3878-3879
Vultur gryphus, see Andean condor
Vultures   3879-3881
Vulturine guinea fowl   1715

W

Wühler, Friedrich   670
Wühler, H.   149
Waals, Johannes Diederik van der   3819
Waders   3290
Wagner, Rudolf   3596
Wagner, W. H.   3603
Wagtails and pipits   3883
Wahl, A.   1308
Wahoo   3759
Wake-robins   2106
Waksman, Selman   224
Waldeyer's ring   3679
Waldrapp ibis   1882
Walker, Gilbert   1324
Walking catfish   706
Walkingsticks   3883-3884
Wall gecko   1597
Wallabies   2006
Wallace, Alfred Russell   1416, 2460, 2625
Wallace's Line   1451
Wallaroos   2008
Walleye   2726
Walnut   1532, 3251, 3885
 Walnut family   3885-3886
Walnut wood   3886
Walpole, Horace   103
Walruses   3886-3888
Wapiti   2127, 3793
Warble fly   3749
Warblers   3888-3891
Warbling vireo   3840
Warburg, Otto   2780
Warfarin   231
Warm front   3924
Warp   3645
Warren, J. C.   1398
Warships   3522
Warthog   2795
Warts   3849

Warty angler   202
Washington, George   143
Washingtonia filifera   2678
Wasps   1930, 2294, 3891-3892
Wassermann test   229
Waste heat   862, 2876
Waste incinerators   3067
Waste, industrial   3894
Waste management   2553, 1903, 3892-3898
Waste prevention   3892, 3895
Waste-to-energy   142, 1904, 3894
Wastewater   2759, 2878
Wastewater treatment   1453
Water   836, 929, 1154, 1359, 1554, 1741, 1769, 1866,
     1957, 2492, 3465, 3630, 3898-3900, 3907-3098
Water bears   3900
Water boatman   3744
Water buffalo   1023, 2127, 3793
Water chestnut   981, 3241
Water column   3979
Water conduits   3953
Water conservation   257, 2878, 3901-3903
Water crowfoot   606
Water cycle   1863
Water density   1044
Water diversion   1499, 1979
Water expansion   3651
Water frame   1914
Water gas   676, 1858
Water glass   3342
Water hemlock   691
Water hogs   666
Water horehound   1961
Water mite   2348
Water moccasins   3839
Water molds   1569
Water pipit   3883
Water pollution   757, 1561, 1585, 1867, 2041, 2244,
     2759, 2878, 3185, 3540, 3905-3910
Water purification   151, 789, 1475, 1783, 1978, 2652
Water quality   2529
Water scorpion   3744
Water softening   762, 1741
Water strider   3745
Water supply   256, 1178
Water table   1414
Water tupelo   3932
Water turbine   3911
Water vapor   328
Water velocity   257
Water-crowfoot, yellow   606
Water-flag iris   1974
Water-shield   3904
Waterbucks   1742, 3900-3901

Z